THE NATIONAL UNDERWRITER COMPANY

a division of ALM Media, LLC

THE TOOLS & TECHNIQUES OF LIFE INSURANCE PLANNING
7TH EDITION

Stephan R. Leimberg and Keith A. Buck

Life insurance remains one of the cornerstones of financial planning. If you provide life insurance planning to clients, or are looking to expand your business in this key area, this book is a must-have.

The expert authors of The Tools & Techniques of Life Insurance Planning, 7th Edition, deliver:

- Detailed information about the entire range of life insurance products that can be used by estate and financial planners in a wide variety of circumstances

- Planning techniques for retirement income needs, estate and gift tax avoidance, estate liquidity needs, and long-term care planning

- Plain-language descriptions of the tax consequences of various life insurance products and strategies that plans can use to minimize tax liabilities

- Planning techniques for individuals and businesses, including key personnel policies and buy-sell agreements

The 7th edition covers:

- Completely updated tax and accounting information

- Expanded coverage of 1035 exchange rules, including partially tax-deferred exchanges

- Improved planning techniques for pension maximization and buy-sell agreements

- Detailed discussion of annuity types and tax consequences

- Newly revised comparisons of permanent life insurance features, including joint life, single premium, and limited pay options

- In-depth analysis of life insurance riders

- Planning techniques for using life insurance in qualified and nonqualified plans

And, as with all the resources in the highly acclaimed Leimberg Library, every area covered in this book is accompanied by the tools, techniques, practice tips, and examples you can use to help your clients successfully navigate the complex course of life insurance planning and confidently meet their needs.

Whether you're a newcomer to this area or a seasoned planning professional, this is the one resource that leads you quickly to the life insurance planning answers you need.

Related Titles Also Available:

- The Tools & Techniques of Trust Planning

- The Tools & Techniques of Estate Planning

- The Tools & Techniques of Estate Planning for Modern Families

- The Tools & Techniques of Financial Planning

- The Tools & Techniques of Income Tax Planning

- The Tools & Techniques of Charitable Planning

- Tax Facts on Insurance & Employee Benefits

- Tax Facts on Individuals & Small Business

- Field Guide: Estate & Retirement Planning, Business Planning & Employee Benefits

- The Advisor's Guide to Annuities

For customer service questions or to place additional orders, please call 1-800-543-0874.

7TH EDITION

The Tools & Techniques of
Life Insurance Planning

LEIMBERG LIBRARY

Stephan R. Leimberg

Keith A. Buck

Library of Congress Control Number: 2017948338

ISBN: 978-1-945424-48-9

Circular 230 Notice – The content in this publication is not intended or written to be used, and it cannot be used, for the purposes of avoiding U.S. tax penalties.

THE NATIONAL UNDERWRITER COMPANY

Copyright © 1993, 1999, 2004, 2007, 2013, 2015, 2017

The National Underwriter Company
A division of ALM Media, LLC
4157 Olympic Blvd., Suite 225
Erlanger, KY 41018

Seventh Edition

Printed in the United States of America

ABOUT THE NATIONAL UNDERWRITER COMPANY
a division of ALM Media, LLC

For over 110 years, The National Underwriter Company, *a division of ALM Media, LLC* has been the first in line with the targeted tax, insurance, and financial planning information you need to make critical business decisions. Boasting nearly a century of expert experience, our reputable Editors are dedicated to putting accurate and relevant information right at your fingertips. With *Tax Facts, Tools & Techniques, National Underwriter Advanced Markets, Field Guide, FC&S®, FC&S Legal* and other resources available in print, eBook, CD, and online, you can be assured that as the industry evolves National Underwriter will be at the forefront with the thorough and easy-to-use resources you rely on for success.

Update Service Notification

This National Underwriter Company publication is regularly updated to include coverage of developments and changes that affect the content. If you did not purchase this publication directly from The National Underwriter Company, *a division of ALM Media, LLC* and you want to receive these important updates sent on a 30-day review basis and billed separately, please contact us at (800) 543-0874. Or you can mail your request with your name, company, address, and the title of the book to:

The National Underwriter Company
a division of ALM Media, LLC
4157 Olympic Boulevard
Suite 225
Erlanger, KY 41018

If you purchased this publication from The National Underwriter Company, *a division of ALM Media, LLC*, directly, you have already been registered for the update service.

Contact Information

To order any National Underwriter Company title, please

- call 1-800-543-0874, 8-6 ET Monday – Thursday and 8 to 5 ET Friday

- online bookstore at www.nationalunderwriter.com, or

- mail to Orders Department, The National Underwriter Company, *a division of ALM Media, LLC*, 4157 Olympic Blvd., Ste. 225, Erlanger, KY 41018

FOREWORD

Once upon a time (it seems so long ago), the father of a boy I played marbles with down the street fell off a roof and died. I was very young, far too young to know much of how the world worked. So I really didn't understand why—just a few months later—his mother and sister and he had to move out of their house and out of our neighborhood. The words "can't afford" didn't mean anything to me at the time; I just knew I missed my friend.

That was my first introduction to life insurance—or rather the effect on people of the absence of life insurance. Since that day, I've written many books, taught many classes, and given many lectures throughout the country on the subject to fellow attorneys, CPAs, insurance agents, and other professionals. And, early on in my adult career, long before I went to law school, I sold life insurance.

All of that intellectual and practical knowledge has merely added to the more important truth I already knew as a child; without adequate amounts of properly arranged life insurance, totally unexpectedly and frighteningly suddenly a family's dignity can turn into despair!

No less a loss can occur in a business setting. The day an owner or key employee dies, because of inadequate amounts of the capital and income that could have been provided with life insurance, the business often dies with that person—and the financial security of not only the owner's family—but also the employees of the business—is in great jeopardy—if not totally lost.

In this book, you'll find voluminous facts, valuable information, and the benefit of our years of experience that will help you learn how life insurance works, how best to use and arrange it, and its legal, tax, and economic aspects. You'll also find—from time to time—our opinion on certain ways life insurance should—or should not—be used.

You'll have to add the ethics. You'll have to take the wealth of knowledge in this book and match the products with the problems to be solved. You'll have to consider the viable alternatives/and or supplements to life insurance and their pros and cons. You'll have to apply what you've learned as objectively and honestly, openly, and as clearly as possible. Because you will be the authority, the "high priest," and it will be up to you to convey to your clients the most important— and the most difficult message of all when it comes to life insurance, i.e. the urgency and significance of action!

Steve Leimberg

PREFACE TO THE SEVENTH EDITION

Life insurance is an essential tool in good financial, estate, and business planning. Anyone who has people dependent upon them, or for whom death would create an economic loss, needs some form of life insurance as part of their complete financial and estate plan. Life insurance ensures that a family is protected even when an important physical and financial presence passes away.

The seventh edition of *The Tools & Techniques of Life Insurance Planning* is written to help planners and advisors understand the tools needed to use life insurance as a part of a successful financial, business, or estate plan, and to how to use these tools in the most effective ways.

We had one major goal in mind when writing this book:

"To create the single best source of up-to-date, pragmatic, and transferable information on the topics you need to help others."

With the growing labyrinth of highly technical and interrelated tax and other laws that have an impact upon clients and their plans, our task—and yours—has become exceedingly difficult. We believe *The Tools & Techniques of Life Insurance Planning* will be of significant help in this regard. Throughout the chapters of this book, you'll find unique charts, checklists, graphs, examples, and references to assist you in absorbing these highly complex concepts and product nuances. In turn you will be able to convey these to clients in a clear and simple manner.

As experts working in this field, we have provided our opinions as to what should be done about problems your estate and business planning clients will face with respect to life insurance decisions. These will help you quickly identify problems, determine appropriate solutions, decide upon the most efficient and effective course to take, and convey to your clients the urgency and significance of action.

Although it is not designed as an exhaustive treatise on the laws regarding life insurance, it will be highly useful to students, CPAs, attorneys, trust officers, and others whose professional task is to advise others. Because it carefully defines each new term, it also will be of immense use to the layperson searching for a reliable objective source of information and to the professional searching for perspective.

It has been our goal to provide a timely, invaluable learning tool, reference manual, and practical guide for helping others make major life insurance decisions and for those who must make those decisions for themselves.

We hope to provide you with the most useful tool available, as such; we invite you to provide us with your feedback so that we may make future editions as useful as possible.

Stephan R. Leimberg
Keith A. Buck

ABOUT THE AUTHORS

Stephan R. Leimberg

Stephan R. Leimberg is CEO of LISI, Leimberg Information Services, Inc., at leimbergservices.com, a provider of e-mail/internet news and commentary for professionals on recent cases, rulings, and legislation; CEO of Leimberg and LeClair, Inc., an estate and financial planning software company; and President of Leimberg Associates, Inc., a publishing and software company in Bryn Mawr, Pennsylvania at leimberg.com.

Leimberg is the author of numerous books on estate, financial, and employee benefit and retirement planning and a nationally known speaker. Leimberg is the creator and/or principal author of the entire nine book *Tools & Techniques* series including *The Tools & Techniques of Estate Planning, The Tools & Techniques of Financial Planning, The Tools & Techniques of Employee Benefit and Retirement Planning, The Tools & Techniques of Life Insurance Planning, The Tools & Techniques of Charitable Planning, The Tools & Techniques of Income Tax Planning, The Tools & Techniques of Investment Planning, The Tools & Techniques of Risk Management, and The Tools & Techniques of Practice Management*. Leimberg is co-author, with noted attorney Howard Zaritsky, of *Tax Planning with Life Insurance, The Book of Trusts* with attorneys Charles K. Plotnick and Daniel Evans, and *How to Settle an Estate* with Charles K. Plotnick, and *The Buy-Sell Handbook*.

Leimberg is creator or co-creator of many software packages for the financial services professional including *NumberCruncher* (estate planning), *IRS Factors Calculator* (actuarial computations), *Financial Analyzer II,*

Estate Planning Quickview (Estate Planning Flow Charts), *Toward a Zero Estate Tax* (PowerPoint Estate Planning Client Seminar), *Gifts That Give, Gifts That Give Back* (Powerpoint Client Charitable Planning Seminar), and Long-Term Care (Powerpoint Client Seminar).

A nationally known speaker, Leimberg has addressed the Miami (Heckerling) Estate Planning Institute, the NYU Tax Institute, the Notre Dame Law School and Duke University Law School's Estate Planning Conference, The American Bar Association Planning Techniques for Large Estate and Sophisticated Planning Techniques courses of study, the National Association of Estate Planners and Councils, and the AICPA's National Estate Planning Forum. Leimberg has also spoken to the Federal Bureau of Investigation, and the National Aeronautics and Space Administration.

Leimberg, a 2004 recipient of the National Association of Estate Planners and Councils Distinguished Accredited Estate Planner award, was named 1998 Edward N. Polisher Lecturer of the Dickinson School of Law, and was awarded the Excellence in Writing Award of the American Bar Association's Probate and Property Section. He has been honored as Estate Planner of the Year by the Montgomery County Estate Planning Council and as Distinguished Estate Planner by the Philadelphia Estate Planning Council. He is also recipient of the President's Cup of the Philadelphia Life Underwriters, a three time Boris Todorovitch Lecturer, and the first Ben Feldman Lecturer.

Keith A. Buck

Keith A. Buck, J.D., LLM, CLU, FLMI, is an Assistant Vice President with Pacific Life's Advanced Designs Unit. He has over twenty-three years of experience working in the life insurance industry as an estate and business planning attorney. As part of his role at Pacific Life, Keith provides support to life insurance producers and professional advisors on a variety of estate, business, and retirement planning issues. He also travels extensively where he gives presentations to life insurance producers and professional advisors. He has spoken at several national industry conferences

such as the MDRT Top of the Table Conference, LIMRA Advanced Sales Conference, and the AALU Annual Meeting. He has also had several articles published in various publications, including Best's Review, Journal of Financial Service Professionals, Estate Planning Journal, and Steve Leimberg's LISI newsletter.

Keith obtained his law degree from Drake Law School in Des Moines, Iowa. While at Drake, Keith was the Projects Editor of the Drake Law Review and, ultimately, graduated Order of the Coif. He subsequently went on to receive his Master of Laws (LL.M.) in taxation from Boston University Law School. He also holds the Chartered Life Underwriter (CLU) and the Fellow, Life Management Institute (FLMI) designations.

Keith resides in Laguna Niguel, California with his wife, Sharon, and their five boys.

ABOUT THE PUBLISHER

Kelly B. Maheu, J.D., is Vice President in charge of the Practical Insights Division of ALM Media, which produces National Underwriter's professional publications. Kelly has been with National Underwriter since 2006, and has served as the Managing Director of National Underwriter's Professional Publishing Division as well as performing editorial, content acquisition, and product development roles.

Prior to joining The National Underwriter Company, Kelly worked in the legal and insurance fields for LexisNexis®, Progressive Insurance, and a Cincinnati insurance defense litigation firm.

Kelly has edited and contributed to numerous books and publications including the *Personal Auto Insurance Policy Coverage Guide, Cyberliability and Insurance, The National Underwriter Sales Essentials Series*, and *The Tools & Techniques of Risk Management for Financial Planners*.

Kelly earned her law degree from The University of Cincinnati College of Law and holds a BA from Miami University, Ohio, with a double major in English/Journalism and Psychology.

ABOUT THE MANAGING EDITOR

Richard H. Cline, J.D., is the Manager, Tax and Insurance Content for the Practical Insights Division at The National Underwriter Company. He is responsible for both the print and online versions of Tax Facts as well as developing new tax products for our customers.

Richard joined the company in 2013 but has over twenty-five years of tax editing and publishing

experience. Prior to joining our team, Richard worked for Lexis-Nexis, CCH, Inc., and PricewaterhouseCoopers.

He has a B.S. degree from Franklin and Marshall College in Lancaster, Pennsylvania, and earned his law degree from Tulane University in New Orleans, Louisiana.

ABOUT THE EDITOR

Jason Gilbert, J.D., M.A., is an assistant editor with the Practical Insights Division of The National Underwriter Company, a division of ALM Media, LLC. He edits and develops publications related to tax and insurance products, including titles in the *Advisor's Guide* and the *Tools & Techniques* series of investment and planning products. He also develops content for National Underwriter's other financial services publications and online products. He has worked on insurance and tax publications for more than nine years.

Jason has been a practicing attorney for more than a dozen years in the areas of criminal defense, products liability, and regulatory enforcement actions. Prior to joining National Underwriter, his experience in the insurance and tax fields has included work as a Westlaw contributor for Thomson Reuters and a tax advisor and social media contributor for Intuit. He is an honors graduate from Wright State University and holds a J.D. from the University Of Cincinnati College Of Law as well as a master's degree in Economics from Miami University in Ohio.

EDITORIAL SERVICES

Connie L. Jump, Senior Manager, Editorial Operations.

Emily Brunner, Editorial Assistant.

GUIDELINES FOR THE PROFESSIONAL

Life insurance is the only certain way to create "instant" capital. That capital, in turn, can be used by clients to solve a multiplicity of personal and business problems.

To understand how life insurance can, and should, be used (the planners' imagination, creativity, and ethical perspectives are the only major boundaries limiting the scope of life insurance's uses), you must first focus on the problems. Then, the planning team must

MATCH THE PRODUCTS WITH THE PROBLEMS TO BE SOLVED IN THE PRIORITY ORDER THE CLIENT ASSIGNS TO THOSE PROBLEMS

Here are the major problems the client's family will face:

1. **Lack of liquidity**: Not enough cash to pay death taxes, administrative costs, attorneys' fees, appraisal fees, and other death-generated expenses as they fall due. (This is one of the major and most obvious reasons for life insurance.)

2. **Improper disposition of assets**: The wrong thing goes to the wrong person at the wrong time in the wrong manner. Many times the awesome responsibility of safeguarding, investing, and distributing the income from complex property or the task of running a business interest is thrust upon persons who are unable or unwilling to handle it. (Life insurance is often used as a substitute for such property, i.e., life insurance can be paid to or owned by a trust for the benefit of a beneficiary who cannot or should not manage a complex portfolio or run a business while the more competent, capable, and willing beneficiaries can be left securities or a business interest.)

3. **Inadequate amounts of income or capital at the client's death, disability, retirement, or for special needs**: College costs continue to climb. This in turn exhausts funds that might otherwise have been used for retirement and leaves many facing retirement with debt rather than assets. Clients are living longer, and having greater medical expenses during retirement and surprisingly higher (rather than as expected lower) standards of living and consequent maintenance

costs. In many cases they have more leisure time to travel, try new hobbies, and spend money than they did before they retired and less of their expenses are paid for after retirement by their companies. (Cash value life and disability insurance are obvious answers to part of these problems if the protection is coordinated with other investment planning.)

4. **The value of the client's assets** (particularly real estate portfolios or business interests) **has not been stabilized or maximized**: When all or the bulk of an estate consists of real estate, the cash required to pay taxes often far outstrips the cash available to pay those taxes. The result is often a forced sale of the real estate at the worst possible time. Likewise, a business which loses a key employee through death (or disability) often loses value needlessly. Without a "buy-sell" agreement, the client's family will seldom obtain a full and fair price for a business interest. The result of the absence of a buy-sell agreement between business owners is a total lack of a market for the business interest or at best a forced sale at pennies on the dollar (a "fire sale"). (Life and disability income insurance have been the traditional means of "shock absorbers" to stabilize a business at a key employee's death or to buy-out and bail out the heirs of a shareholder-employee.)

5. **Excessive transfer costs**: The cost of transferring wealth from one generation to another continues to increase because of increasing federal and state taxes, probate costs, attorneys' fees, and other "slippage." When property is owned in more than one state, "ancillary administration" (multiple probates) results in unexpected aggravation, delay, and expense. In many cases the ownership of property is set up in a manner that aggravates rather than minimizes the tax burden and other costs. (Life insurance can be set up in a manner that avoids all of these problems.)

6. **Special needs**: Successful clients often express a strong desire to "give back" to their schools, churches, synagogues, communities, or other charitable organizations. Many clients have spouses or children with certain gifts or handicaps which require larger than usual amounts

of both capital and income—or who have asset management needs that would not be served by an outright disposition of property to them. (Life insurance is often the most effective means—and sometimes the only way—of raising large amounts of cash to create financial security for an organization or an individual.)

Only when the planner has started with and identified the need(s) and the client has expressed preference as to the order of needs should the planner attempt to formulate a strategy. Few clients can solve all their financially-oriented problems simultaneously. Resources must therefore be allocated to the tools or techniques which are most cost effective in solving these problems.

EXAMINE THE PROS AND CONS OF THE VIABLE ALTERNATIVES

Life insurance is a unique product in that a small premium payment can generate a vastly disproportionate amount of capital and guarantee the availability of that capital almost instantly. Death, the event which creates the need for large amounts of capital, creates the capital to satisfy that need through life insurance.

Clearly, life insurance is one of the most important of all the wealth creation and wealth transfer tools. Yet, the planner should never choose ANY tool or use ANY technique without asking:

"What are the no-cost or less costly alternatives to this product or device that could also solve the client's problem—and what are their pros and cons?"

Once the advantages and disadvantages of the viable alternatives are examined, the planner can objectively ask and ascertain:

"Which course(s) of action will result in the highest present value of capital and income for the family unit as a whole and which course(s) of action will result in the lowest present value in terms of financial and other costs?"

In many cases life insurance will be the indicated tool. How that life insurance is arranged makes a considerable difference in the tax implications and ultimate cost effectiveness. One last question that the planner and every member of the client's advisory team—and the client—must ask is:

"What if I (we) do nothing?" "What happens—or doesn't happen?"

Decisions in financial, estate, business and employee benefit planning with respect to life insurance (or any other tool or technique) must not be made in a vacuum. *A planner will be held accountable—not only for what is said and done—but also for the advice which is not given that should have been.*

LIFE INSURANCE AS A PROBLEM SOLVING TOOL

Only when the thought process described above has been employed should the planner arrive at a particular tool or technique—and the process should continue even after that selection.

Assuming life insurance has been chosen as the best vehicle for the job of solving one or more of these client problems and it has been ascertained that it can be used in a cost-efficient manner, the question then becomes, "what specific life insurance ownership and beneficiary strategy would best meet the client's objectives?"

Planners must continue to ask and answer many additional questions such as:

"What is the right type of life insurance for this client and how much is needed?"

"What specific life insurance ownership and beneficiary strategy would best meet the client's objectives?"

"What company (or combination of companies) could answer the identified product needs best?"

Use *The Tools and Techniques of Life Insurance Planning* as a complementary text to the other *Tools and Techniques* books to round out your ability to ask and answer questions such as these.

The Tools and Techniques of Life Insurance Planning will focus on life insurance as a problem solver and:

(a) define each tool or technique;

(b) explain when the tool or technique is indicated and should be considered;

(c) illustrate through an example how the tool or technique is implemented;

(d) cover the tax ramifications of the strategy; and

(e) cover various questions regarding the practical application of the strategy.

TABLE OF CONTENTS

PART I: TOOLS

PART II: TECHNIQUES

APPENDICES

For substantive updates to this product please visit: pro.nuco.com/booksupplements.

INTRODUCTION TO LIFE INSURANCE

CHAPTER 1

INTRODUCTION

Life insurance is a complex amalgamation of legal, tax, and economic elements. Basically, it is a unique wealth creation tool that assures the accumulation of a desired amount of liquid capital at death. Depending on the plan of insurance, it may also create more or less capital for lifetime needs.

Through its unique capital creation feature and tax advantages, life insurance can help people solve a host of personal and business problems. However, insurers offer a wide variety of life insurance policies that are suited to a broad host of financial planning problems. Once an insurance adviser identifies a client's problems, the adviser must match the appropriate life insurance products to the problems. To do so, the planner must first fully understand the legal, tax, and economic elements of life insurance and the particular features of each type of policy.

This chapter will provide an overview of, as well as an introduction to, the multifaceted aspects of life insurance. Use this chapter to gain and maintain perspective and balance. Because life insurance is not really one product but a multiplicity of products, above all, learn to "MATCH THE PRODUCT WITH THE PROBLEM!"

PRINCIPAL USES OF LIFE INSURANCE

Broadly stated, life insurance is indicated only when there is a NEED.

The following is a checklist of common *estate building* and *estate conservation* needs that life insurance can satisfy the following:

- Provide for income needs of surviving dependent family members

- Pay federal and state death taxes and other estate settlement costs

- Pay debts

- Provide for children's education

- Shift wealth from one generation to another in the most cost effective manner possible

- Meet "special" financial demands of physically or mentally handicapped or learning-disabled children or parents or other dependents with physical or mental limitations

- Benefit a charity

- Relieve survivors of financial management burdens by providing an inexhaustible lifetime annuity

- Create an "instant estate"

The following is a checklist of *business insurance* needs that life insurance can satisfy:

- Fund a buy-sell agreement

- Finance nonqualified deferred compensation arrangements

- Finance Death Benefit Only (DBO) plans

- Provide a basic level of financial security for families of all employees

- Recruit, retain, retire, and reward key employees

The operative word is NEED. Planners should recommend life insurance only if, and to the extent, a need exists. Thus, financial services professionals must first identify the need and then match the type and amount of the product to that need.

ADVANTAGES

The advantages offered by life insurance vary with the type of policy and the problem to which the policy is applied. These advantages are highlighted in subsequent chapters that describe the particular types of policies and the applications to which they are most suited. However, all types of life insurance policies provide certain favorable features, which are listed below.

1. Life insurance provides a guarantee of large amounts of cash payable immediately at the death of the insured. The amount of the death benefit payable is usually significantly greater than the premiums paid for the policy.

2. Life insurance proceeds are not part of the probate estate. The only way life insurance benefits become part of probate is when they are paid to or for the benefit of the estate of the insured. Therefore, the insurance company can pay death proceeds to the beneficiary without the delay caused by administration of the estate.

3. There will be no public record of the death benefit amount or to whom it is payable.

4. Life insurance policies generally have some protection against creditors of both the policyowner and of the beneficiary. The amount of protection varies from state to state.

5. Life insurance cash values provide instant availability to cash through policy loans. The interest rate (or interest-rate formula) for policy loans is known in advance and is usually lower than the rate applicable to loans from other sources.

6. The death benefit proceeds from a life insurance policy generally are not subject to federal income taxes.

7. The increases in the cash value of a life insurance policy enjoy federal income tax deferral. Interest earned on policy cash values generally is not taxable unless or until the policyowner surrenders the policy for cash.

8. Life insurance proceeds often are exempt from state inheritance taxes.

9. Despite some highly publicized life insurance company insolvencies, the life insurance industry remains unparalleled in safety among the financial intermediaries such as the savings and loan, banking, and mutual fund industries. It is commonly noted that not a single dollar of death claim has been lost or denied because of a life insurance company insolvency or failure.

DISADVANTAGES

1. Life insurance is not available to persons in extremely poor health (although almost all individuals in poor health can obtain insurance).

2. Life insurance is an extremely complex product that is hard to evaluate and compare. The time required to gather policy information, decipher it, and compare it with other policies discourages purchasers from engaging in comparison shopping.

3. The cost of coverage reduces the amount of funds available for current consumption or investment.

LEGAL ASPECTS OF LIFE INSURANCE

Legally, life insurance is a contract, governed principally by state law. A life insurance contract promises to pay a specified amount of money to a designated beneficiary when the insured person dies. The contract is between the insurance company and the policyowner, who pays premiums in exchange for the promised death (and other) benefits. Frequently the policyowner is the person insured, but someone other than the insured may own the policy.

In return for its promise to pay death and other benefits under the contract, the insurance company charges a premium to provide adequate funds to pay death benefits when they come due and to cover insurance company expenses and profits. (Ultimately, though, the death benefit paid by the insurer on any given policy may significantly exceed the total of the premium(s) paid by the policyowner.)

Although state laws vary, life insurance contracts are issued with a number of standard provisions. In the typical policy, these provisions:

1. spell out who the parties to the contract are;

2. explain the need for an insurable interest by the policyowner in the life of the insured;

3. describe the legal form and contents of the contract;

4. describe the insured's rights to name and change the beneficiary;

5. limit the insurer's right to contest or challenge the validity of the contract after (usually) two years, even if the policyowner made a material or fraudulent misrepresentation in acquiring the policy;

6. provide a one-month grace period for the payment of premiums;

7. limit the insurer's obligation to pay death benefits if the insured commits suicide within (usually) two years of policy issue;

8. provide for an adjustment in the death benefit in the event the insured's age is misstated;

9. describe how the policyowner may apply or use dividends, if the policy is participating;

10. assure minimum cash values in the event of lapse or termination of the policy and provide certain standard options as to how the policyowner may receive these "nonforfeiture" values;

11. explain the policyowner's right to reinstate and the procedures for reinstating the policy in the event of lapse;

12. provide a number of alternative settlement options that beneficiaries may elect when receiving death proceeds from the insurer;

13. explain the policyowner's right to borrow cash values, and spell out the conditions and terms of such loans, including the method of determining the interest rate;

14. give the policyowner the right to automatically have policy loans pay premiums if premiums are not paid by the end of the grace period; and

15. explain the policyowner's right to assign the policy to another person or entity.

Each of these legal provisions is discussed in detail in Chapter 5, "Legal Aspects of Life Insurance".

Additionally, in order for a contract to qualify as life insurance for income and other tax purposes it must exhibit risk-shifting and risk-sharing and it must meet the Internal Revenue Code's definition of life insurance, as provided in Code Section 7702. Code Section 7702 limits the amount of cash value relative to the face amount of coverage.

If the cash value were allowed to be too high relative to the face amount of coverage, there would be: first, insufficient risk shifting and second, an incentive to shelter otherwise taxable investment income in life insurance products. Increases in the cash values inside a contract that fails to meet the standards of Code Section 7702 are taxable to the policyowner as earned, rather than being tax deferred, as in qualifying life insurance contracts.

TAX ASPECTS OF LIFE INSURANCE

1. In general, the tax law does not permit policyowners to deduct premium payments on life insurance policies. Notable exceptions are for premium payments for group life insurance provided by an employer for employees and for "bonus" payments to employees for payment of premiums under Code Section 162 plans.

2. Dividends received by the policyowner generally are not subject to federal income taxation. Dividends are not usually taxable income until the aggregate of dividends paid exceeds the aggregate of premiums paid by the policyowner.

3. Cash value increases in a life insurance policy, attributable to investment income, are not usually taxable income as long as the policy remains in force. Cash value buildup in a life insurance policy generally enjoys an indefinite deferral from taxation while it remains in force and an exemption from taxation if the policy terminates in a death claim. However, if the policy is surrendered for cash, gain on the policy is subject to federal income taxation. Gain on a surrendered policy is the amount by which the net cash value payable plus any policy loan forgiven

exceed the owner's basis in the policy. Basis in the policy equals the premiums actually paid in cash less policyowner dividends and withdrawals recovered tax free, if any.

4. Withdrawals of cash values, when permitted, usually are taxed on a First-In, First-Out (FIFO) basis, or under what is called the cost-recovery rule. Specifically, a withdrawal is considered to be a nontaxable recovery of cost basis or premiums until the policyowner's entire cost basis has been withdrawn. Only then are additional withdrawals treated as taxable distributions of interest or gain in the policy.

5. A withdrawal of cash values within the first fifteen policy years may be taxed on a Last-In, First-Out basis (LIFO), or under what is called the interest-first rule, if a reduction in the face amount of coverage accompanies the withdrawal. Specifically, in these cases a withdrawal will be taxable to the extent of gain in the policy. The excess is then treated as a nontaxable recovery of basis in the policy.

6. Distributions or withdrawals under the contract at any time before death from policies that are classified as Modified Endowment Contracts (MECs) are taxed under the interest-first rule, even if they are not accompanied by a reduction in the face amount of coverage. In addition, if such distributions are received before age 59½, the taxable portion may be subject to an additional 10 percent penalty tax. (For the definition of a modified endowment contract, see Chapter 22).

7. Policy loans, except from modified endowment contracts, generally are not treated as taxable distributions, even if the loan exceeds the policyowner's cost basis in the policy.

8. Any interest paid or accrued on debt with respect to corporate-owned life insurance or annuity or endowment contracts generally is not deductible. This rule bars the deduction for interest even if the deduction would not be disallowed under any other rule (e.g., the four-out-of-seven rule). (See Chapter 24 for a further discussion of deductibility of policy loan interest.)

For policies purchased before June 21, 1986, the limitation on the deduction does not apply. However, the IRS has privately held that interest on contracts governed by prior law had to be valid

interest to be deductible; that is, paid for the use or forbearance of money for a valid underlying debt obligation. According to the IRS, policies with a high premium structure together with loading dividend and partial withdrawal mechanisms served no economic purpose and did not produce debt for tax purposes.

Generally, even if a policy qualifies under the exception described above, the interest paid on loans secured by a key employee life insurance policy is not deductible unless one or more of the following exceptions are met:

a. *"Four out of seven" exception* – At least four of the first seven annual premiums are paid without recourse to policy loans.

b. *"$100 a year" exception* – If the interest does not exceed $100 for any taxable year, the interest deductions will not be disallowed even if there is a systematic plan of borrowing.

c. *"Unforeseen event" exception* – If the debt was incurred because of an unforeseen substantial loss of income or substantial increase in obligations, the deduction will not be disallowed even though the policy loan was used to pay premiums.

d. *"Trade or business" exception* – If the debt is incurred in connection with the client's trade or business, the interest deduction will not be disallowed. Generally, the amounts to finance key employee coverage will not be considered to fall within this exception.

9. Personal interest, including interest on policy loans used for personal purposes, is no longer deductible. In general, if a policyowner uses policy loans to pay premiums on the policy or for any other personal purpose other than to finance an investment or for business use, the interest is subject to the personal interest limitations.

10. Interest paid on policy loans used for investment purposes is subject to different deductibility limits. In general, the interest on all the taxpayer's loans, including life insurance policy loans, used to finance investments is deductible each year but only to the extent it does not exceed the taxable investment

income from all investments. If interest expense exceeds investment income in one year, the taxpayer carries the excess forward and may deduct the excess interest in future years when the taxpayer has adequate investment income.

11. In general, life insurance death proceeds are not subject to federal income taxation. However, life insurance policies that have been sold from one policyowner to another may be subject to the transfer for value rule. Under this rule, the portion of the death proceeds in excess of the sum of the purchase price and any premiums paid after the transfer is subject to taxation as income. In other words, if an existing life insurance policy or an interest in an existing policy is transferred for any type of valuable consideration in money or money's worth, all or a significant portion of the proceeds may lose its income-tax-free status when the insured dies. However, certain transfers are exempt from the transfer for value rule. Policyowners can safely transfer policies to: (1) the insured; (2) a partner of the insured; (3) a partnership in which the insured is a partner; or (4) a corporation in which the insured is a shareholder or officer, without subjecting the policy proceeds to income tax under the transfer for value rule.

12. Proceeds from corporate-owned life insurance policies paid to the corporation may generate an Alternative Minimum Tax (AMT). Under a worst case scenario, this tax could amount to roughly 15 percent of the total policy proceeds paid to a corporate beneficiary. The AMT is basically an alternative tax calculation that assures a corporation pays at least a minimum amount of tax if certain "preferred" types of income that are excludable for regular tax purposes or special deductions reduce the regular income tax "too much."

13. The estate of the insured will include the proceeds of a life insurance policy for federal estate tax purposes if the insured held "incidents of ownership" at any time during the three years prior to death or if the proceeds from the policy were payable to or for the benefit of the estate of the insured. Incidents of ownership include such things as the right to: (a) change the beneficiary; (b) take out a policy loan; or (c) surrender the policy for cash.

14. Death benefits paid to someone other than the owner-insured or the owner-insured's estate are not treated as gifts for gift tax purposes.

15. Premium payments by an owner-insured on a policy that names someone other than the insured or the insured's estate as beneficiary generally are not considered gifts for gift tax purposes. However, gift tax law does treat premium payments by anyone on a policy owned by someone other than the person paying the premiums as gifts and may subject the premium payments to gift tax if the annual premiums exceed the annual exclusion ($14,000 in 2015 as indexed for inflation). Such premiums generally qualify for the annual exclusion.

Later chapters discuss the income, estate, gift, and generation-skipping transfer taxation of life insurance in more detail. Also, any special tax considerations with respect to particular types of policies and their use in various particular applications are discussed where appropriate in the chapters describing the policies or in the "techniques" section of the book.

ECONOMIC ASPECTS OF LIFE INSURANCE

Life Insurance as a Savings and Investment Vehicle

Life insurance can be a superb savings and investment vehicle. All conventional investment vehicles serve the same purpose, but the unique feature of life insurance is that it assures a desired accumulation at a specific, but uncertain time; namely at the time of the insured's death. No other savings or investment tool makes such a guarantee.

If the time of death were certain, life insurance would be unnecessary. A person could accumulate any desired target amount by investing in a traditional investment vehicle and employing a systematic plan of saving, or what is called a "sinking fund." For example, if a person's objective is to accumulate $1,000 in five years and he or she could be assured of surviving that long, this person could simply invest a specific lump-sum amount today in a traditional investment vehicle that with interest would grow to $1,000 in five years.

Example. If $620.92 is invested today at 10 percent interest, the fund will grow to $1,000 in five years. Alternatively, if this person does not have $620.92 to invest today, he or she could finance the accumulation over time, for instance, by investing $148.91 at the beginning of each year for the next five years. However, if this person died any time before the end of the five-year period, the amount accumulated at the time of death would be less than the desired $1,000.

Most discussions of life insurance describe it as a combination of "pure death protection" that decreases, and "savings" or "investment" that increases over a person's lifetime. This perspective can be useful for some discussions of the nature of life insurance, but it also can be confusing and misleading. Life insurance, when viewed in its entirety, is also a special type of investment or accumulation vehicle that uniquely matures at death.

The bifurcation of a life insurance policy into its "death protection" and "savings" elements can be useful, if it is understood for what it really is. The savings component is the noncontingent part of the overall investment accumulation that is available not just at death, but also during life, similar to any conventional investment or savings instrument.

The relative size of these two components depends on the life product and how the life insurance is financed. At one extreme is annually renewable term insurance, which is essentially 100 percent pure death protection and 0 percent savings. At the other extreme are deferred annuities during the accumulation phase (and other conventional investments), which are essentially 0 percent pure death protection and 100 percent savings.[1] The other life insurance products fall somewhere between these extremes.

Making the distinction between the "pure death protection" and "savings" components actually ignores half the spectrum of "life" products. In a manner analogous to life insurance, annuities may be described as a combination of "pure *life* protection" and "savings" elements after the annuity starting date. The savings component of annuities is the noncontingent part of the overall investment that is available regardless of whether one lives or dies, similar to any conventional investment or savings instrument. In other words, the savings component is the guaranteed or refund amount provided by some annuities that is payable even if the annuitant dies. The pure life protection component is a contingent investment that matures or is available only if the annuitant lives. At one end of this spectrum is full-refund or term-certain annuities (or conventional investments) that are essentially 100 percent savings and 0 percent pure life protection. At the other end of the spectrum are no-refund life annuities that are 0 percent savings (theoretically) and 100 percent pure life protection.[2]

Figure 1.1 shows how various "life" products from term insurance to annuities fall within the pure death/life protection and savings element spectra. But keep in mind that both components make up the total investment. Any assessment that evaluates the "investment" potential of a life product by looking only at the savings element (the amounts that are available regardless of whether a person lives or dies) ignores the fact that the pure death/life protection component is properly viewed as a type of contingent investment that matures or is available only when the death or life contingency occurs.

Simplified Life Insurance Financial Mathematics

The following simplified example illustrates the basic operation of life insurance as a capital accumulation

Figure 1.1

Table A DEATH PROTECTION, LIFE PROTECTION, AND SAVINGS ELEMENTS OF LIFE PRODUCTS									
← Death Protection ===				Increasing			=== Life Protection →		
Annually Renewable Term	Level Premium N-Year Term	Modified and Graded Premium Whole Life	Level Premium Whole Life	Limited-Pay Whole Life	Single-Premium Whole Life (Endowments)	Deferred Annuity During Accumulation Phase (Conventional Investments)	Full Refund and Term-Certain Annuity	Life Annuity with Period Certain or Partial Refund	Pure Life Annuity with No Period Certain or Refund
Increasing Savings Component									

vehicle with both death protection and savings components. Suppose five people form a capital accumulation lottery pool or syndicate with the objective that each of them will receive $1,000 from the pool over a five-year period. Each person will contribute the same amount to the pool in each year that he or she still participates. However, at the end of each year, one of them, selected by lot, will be paid his or her $1,000 payout and will drop out of the pool. Only those persons remaining continue to make whatever contributions are necessary to fund for the $1,000 distributions in subsequent years. The expected or average number of years until any given participant in this pool will receive his or her payout is three years.[3] Assuming a 10 percent rate of return, the amount any one of them would have to save at the beginning of each year for three years to accumulate $1,000 is $274.65.

Figure 1.2 shows how much each participant would have to contribute each year to assure the necessary funds to pay $1,000 out of the pool each year to the person selected by lot using various funding or financing arrangements that are similar to typical insurance premium payment plans.

For example, in the "level-annual payment" section of Figure 1.2 each participant is assumed to contribute a level $284.99 at the beginning of each year that he or she is still a participant in the pool. With these contributions the pool will be adequately funded throughout the five-year period. Specifically, each of the five participants pays $284.99 the first year for a total of $1,424.96. With interest credited at 10 percent, the end of year balance before distribution of the first $1,000 lottery payout is $1,567.46. The lucky winner is selected and paid $1,000, leaving $567.46 in the pool to help fund later distributions. This works out to $141.87 for each person who remains in the pool. In the second year, each of the remaining four participants again contributes $284.99, totaling $1,139.97. This amount, together with the carryover balance from the prior year, $567.46, will grow at 10 percent to $1,878.17 by the end of the second year when the second payout occurs. After paying $1,000 to the lucky winner, $878.17, or $292.72 per remaining participant, is left in the pool. The aggregate amount in the pool first increases and then declines as participants receive their $1,000 payouts and drop out. However, the balance or "reserve" per participant continues to increase each year until the last year when the remaining balance plus the last year contribution and interest earnings thereon equal the final required payout of $1,000.

This lottery pool arrangement is a simplified description of how a level-premium life insurance plan works.

If this were a level-premium life insurance plan, the probabilities used would represent the chance of any given person dying each year rather than the chance of winning the lottery.[4] The "premium" each participant would pay ($284.99) is very close to the amount he or she would have to save each year ($274.65) to accumulate $1,000 by the end of his or her "life expectancy," which, in this simplified case is three years. However, just like in real life, although each participant can expect to live a certain period of additional years, in this case three years, some will die sooner and some will die later. The pooling arrangement is a risk sharing mechanism that assures each participant that he or she will receive $1,000 regardless of when he or she dies, just as if he or she were certain to live to life expectancy and saved virtually the same amount as the premium each year.

Those participants who die sooner may be losers in the "game of life," but they are compensated by winning the lottery. They obviously receive more from the pool than they could have accumulated outside the pool arrangement by the time they die. For comparison, column (L) in Figure 1.2 shows how much any given participant would have accumulated by the end of each year if contributions had been invested outside the pool at the same 10 percent rate of return. For example, in the level-payment plan, the person who dies the first year and receives $1,000 would have accumulated only $313.49—or $686.51 less if the "premium" had been invested outside the plan.

The participants who die late are winners in the "game of life," but losers in the lottery. They actually receive less than they would have accumulated outside the pool by the time they die. For example, once again looking at the level-payment plan, the person who dies in year five, receiving $1,000, would have accumulated almost twice as much, $1,913.88, if premiums had been invested outside the plan.[5] However, because nobody knows who will die sooner and who will die later, all participants are "winners" if their mutual objective is to assure that they will receive no less than $1,000 regardless of when they die. For essentially the same annual payment as it would take to accumulate the desired sum if they each lived to life expectancy, they eliminate the risk of under-accumulating if they should die early. And, if they happen to be one of the longer-lived participants, they are still assured they will accumulate at least the minimum desired amount of $1,000.

As is characteristic of level-premium and other cash-value life insurance, the pool builds up reserves or cash values that are necessary to cover shortfalls that arise when there are fewer participants remaining who pay into the pool in later years. These values are shown in column (K). Although the aggregate reserves or cash value balances in the pool decline in the later years [columns (E) and (G)], they continue to increase throughout the five-year payout period on a per-participant basis, which is analogous to how level-premium life plans work. This per-person reserve or cash balance is the "savings" element of the arrangement and is the source for policy loans, cash surrender values, and other "living" benefits in cash-value insurance plans. If a person dropped out of the pool before dying, he or she could take his or her individual cash balance without jeopardizing the cash accumulation necessary to ultimately pay $1,000 to the remaining participants.

The second section of Figure 1.2 shows a "pay-as-you-go" lottery pool that is analogous to an annually renewable term insurance plan. Similar to the level-annual payment lottery pool described above, the pool pays $1,000 at the end of each year to one participant determined by lot. Each remaining participant's contribution each year is equal to the amount that, when aggregated and invested at 10 percent interest, is just sufficient to pay $1,000 out of the pool at the end of the year with nothing left over. In contrast with the level-annual payment lottery pool and level-premium life insurance plans, there is no accumulated reserve or cash balance, which is analogous to an annually renewable term insurance plan. As this example clearly demonstrates, the pay-as-you-go annually renewable term plan starts with lower required premium payments than the level-premium plan, but they quickly increase and exceed the level-premium payments by the third year. The annually renewable term plan creates bigger economic "winners" and bigger economic "losers" than the level-premium plan. Those who die sooner, get a much greater effective return on their "investment" because their total payments into the pool are much less. Those who die later, get a much lower (negative) return on their investment, because they must make much greater total payments to the pool. However, once again, all participants are "winners" under this arrangement relative to a savings plan outside the pool if their principal objective is sharing the risk to assure they each accumulate at least $1,000 regardless of when they die.

The last two sections of Figure 1.2 use the lottery analogy to show how single-premium life and limited-pay life compare to level-premium life and annually renewable term plans in this simplified example. When the paying period is shortened relative to the payout period, the total contributions necessary to fund later payouts

are accelerated and the annual amounts paid in must necessarily increase. However, the per-person reserves or cash balances also increase: the savings component of each participant's total investment increases while the pure death protection component decreases. Furthermore, the total amount any given participant must pay, even the longest surviving participant, declines. In other words, from an economic standpoint there is a smaller difference in the total cost of the program between the "winners" who die early and the "losers" who die late because the contingent or pure death protection component of the total investment has decreased.

Elements of Life Insurance Premium Pricing and Cash Value Calculations

Risk Shifting and Risk Sharing

A common misconception about life insurance is that the risk of premature death is transferred to the insurance company. Although insurance companies must have a certain amount of surplus or paid-in capital to cover potential excess losses, they price their products to maintain or even increase the surplus and paid-in capital over time. Therefore, risk is shifted to or shared among all insureds in the insurance pool. Those policyowners who live a long time carry the economic burden for those who do not. However, there is less risk sharing with premium-payment plans that generate a greater "savings" component, such as single-premium life insurance, than with those that have a greater "pure death protection" component, such as annually renewable term. One can view the savings component of life insurance, similar to other investments, as a form of self-insurance, because it is available regardless of whether the insured lives or dies. If the self-insurance component is greater, the amount of risk that all participants in the pool must share among themselves is obviously less.

Premiums and Costs

Another common misconception is that higher premiums mean higher cost. The various payment plans in Figure 1.2 demonstrate the fallacy of that conception. By design, each of the premium payment plans in Figure 1.2 is actuarially equivalent. In each case, the expected value of each participant's payments is exactly equal to his or her expected return, $1,000. In principle, life insurance companies determine premiums in the same way. From an actuarial standpoint, there are no differences between one premium-payment plan and another for a given level and term of coverage because

Figure 1.2

	(A)	(B)	(C)	(D)	(E)	(F)	(G)	(H)	(I)	(J)	(K)	(L)
							Table B					
					LOTTERY ANALOGY TO THE OPERATION OF LIFE INSURANCE							
Year	BOP Balance	# In BOP	Pmt Per Person	Total Pmts (BxC)	Balance Before Interest (A+D)	Interest (at 10%) (Ex10%)	Balance After Interest (E+F)	EOP Payout	Balance After Payout (G-H)	# In EOP (B-1)	Balance Per Person (I÷J)	Amt Outside Each Person
Level-Annual Payment (Level Premium Whole Life)												
1	$0.00	5	$284.99	$1,424.96	$1,424.96	$142.50	$1,567.46	($1,000)	$567.46	4	$141.87	$313.49
2	567.46	4	284.99	1,139.97	1,707.43	170.74	1,878.17	(1,000)	878.17	3	292.72	658.33
3	878.17	3	284.99	854.98	1,733.15	173.32	1,906.47	(1,000)	906.47	2	453.23	1,037.65
4	906.47	2	284.99	569.99	1,476.45	147.65	1,624.10	(1,000)	624.10	1	624.10	1,454.90
5	624.10	1	284.99	284.99	909.09	90.91	1,000.00	(1,000)	0.00	0	0.00	1,913.88
Pay-As-You-Go (Annually Renewable Term)												
1	$0.00	5	$181.82	$909.09	$909.09	$90.91	$1,000.00	($1,000)	$0.00	4	$0.00	$200.00
2	0.00	4	227.27	909.09	909.09	90.91	1,000.00	(1,000)	0.00	3	0.00	470.00
3	0.00	3	303.03	909.09	909.09	90.91	1,000.00	(1,000)	0.00	2	0.00	850.33
4	0.00	2	454.55	909.09	909.09	90.91	1,000.00	(1,000)	0.00	1	0.00	1,435.37
5	0.00	1	909.09	909.09	909.09	90.91	1,000.00	(1,000)	0.00	0	0.00	2,578.91
One-Time Payment (Single-Premium Life)												
1	$0.00	5	$758.16	$3,790.79	$3,790.79	$379.08	$4,169.87	($1,000)	$3,169.87	4	$792.47	$833.98
2	3,169.87	4	0.00	0.00	3,169.87	316.99	3,486.85	(1,000)	2,486.85	3	828.95	917.37
3	2,486.85	3	0.00	0.00	2,486.85	248.69	2,735.54	(1,000)	1,735.54	2	867.77	1,009.11
4	1,735.54	2	0.00	0.00	1,735.54	173.55	1,909.09	(1,000)	909.09	1	909.09	1,110.02
5	909.09	1	0.00	0.00	909.09	90.91	1,000.00	(1,000)	0.00	0	0.00	1,221.02
3-Period Payment (Limited-Pay Life)												
1	$0.00	5	$341.03	$1,705.15	$1,705.15	$170.51	$1,875.66	($1,000)	$875.66	4	$218.92	$375.13
2	875.66	4	341.03	1,364.12	2,239.78	223.98	2,463.76	(1,000)	1,463.76	3	487.92	787.78
3	1,463.76	3	341.03	1,023.09	2,486.85	248.69	2,735.54	(1,000)	1,735.54	2	867.77	1,241.69
4	1,735.54	2	0.00	0.00	1,735.54	173.55	1,909.09	(1,000)	909.09	1	909.09	1,365.86
5	909.09	1	0.00	0.00	909.09	90.91	1,000.00	(1,000)	0.00	0	0.00	1,502.45

they are all priced to be equivalent on a present value or prospective basis.

The actual after-the-fact cost to the insured may vary substantially from one premium payment plan to another, as is also clearly demonstrated by the illustrated values in Figure 1.2. If a person dies soon, the pay-as-you-go term insurance plan is relatively the best economic deal. But it is also the worst deal for a person who lives a long time. Conversely, the single-premium plan is relatively the best deal if a person lives a long time, but the worst deal if death comes early. Clearly, all else being equal (which it is not because of the unique income and estate tax features as well as other characteristics of life insurance), if a person could be sure that he or she would live longer than average for his or her age, the best deal would be to invest outside of life insurance in conventional investments. But nobody can ever have that assurance.

Interest Rates

The required contribution levels (premiums) under the various payment plans in the Figure 1.2 illustrations were computed using an interest assumption of 10 percent and highly simplified mortality factors. Similarly, insurance companies must make assumptions about the interest they will earn on assets and the mortality experience of their pool of insureds to compute the required premiums. If the insurance company assumes that it can invest the reserves (the "savings" component) to earn high interest rates, the required premiums will be lower. If the company assumes a lower interest rate, premiums will be higher. For most life insurance policies, life insurance companies guarantee that they will credit an interest rate to the policyowners' "savings" components that will equal or exceed a certain minimum rate, ranging from 4 to 6 percent (except on variable life products). The maximum interest rate that an insurer may assume when computing required premiums and reserves is limited by statute.

Mortality and Morbidity and the Law of Large Numbers

Mortality refers to the number of deaths within a given time or a given community. Generally, it is expressed as a rate reflecting the proportion of deaths to population, or to a specific number of the population such as per 1,000, 10,000, or 100,000 lives. Actuaries compute mortality for various large groups of people based upon demographic factors such as sex, age, race, and country or area or residence, and other factors such as occupation, educational level, income level, and habits or hobbies (e.g., smoker versus nonsmoker). They create tables of mortality exhibiting the average relative number of persons who survive, or who have died, at the end of each year of life, out of a given number supposed to have been born at the same time.

The term morbidity is sometimes used in the same sense as mortality, but it is actually a more general term relating to the incidence of disease within a community, including both fatal and nonfatal cases.

Insurance companies base their mortality assumptions on the experience of large groups of people. By the law of large numbers, actuaries can estimate the proportion of a large group of people with similar characteristics of a given age who will die within a given year with remarkable accuracy. Technically, the law of large numbers says that in repeated, independent trials with the same probability "p" of success in each trial, the chance that the percentage of successes differs from the probability "p" by more than a fixed positive amount "e > 0" converges to zero as the number of trials "n" goes to infinity, for every positive "e." In other words, as the number of people of the same age and with similar characteristics increases, the rate of actual deaths experienced by the group will get closer and closer to the expected rate of deaths for the group at any given age.[6]

Adverse Selection and Moral Hazard

Adverse selection is one of two main sorts of market failure often associated with insurance. The other is moral hazard. Adverse selection can be a problem when there is asymmetric information between the seller of insurance and the buyer. What this means is that insurance may not be profitable when buyers have better information about their risk of claiming than does the insurer. Ideally, insurance premiums should be set according to the risk of a randomly selected person in the insured slice of the population (fifty-five-year-old male smokers, for instance). In practice, this means pricing based upon the average risk of that group. However, people who know they have a higher risk of claiming than the average of the group will tend to find the price attractive and buy the insurance, whereas those who have a below-average risk may tend to feel it is too expensive to be worth buying. In this case, premiums set according to the average risk will not be sufficient to cover the claims that eventually arise because, among the people who have bought the policy, more will have above-average risk than below-average risk. In general, raising the premium will not solve this problem, for as the premium rises the insurance policy will become unattractive to more of the people who know they have a lower risk of claiming.

The concept of moral hazard is related to the fact that people with insurance may take greater risks than they would tend to take without the insurance because they know they are protected. Consequently, the insurer may get more or earlier claims, on average, than expected. Insurers try to avoid these problems by requiring prospective insureds to take physical exams and by employing comprehensive underwriting procedures. They also negotiate with employers, associations, and other groups, to provide group coverage where essentially every member of the group is covered, so there is relatively little opportunity for adverse selection.

Underwriting Process

Through their underwriting process, insurance companies classify or rate insureds by their risk characteristics. Health, occupation, avocations, gender, and habits (e.g., whether or not the insured smokes or drinks) are the types of factors considered when rating insureds. Depending on the rating, premiums may be based on "standard" or "preferred" mortality charges or multiples of up to five or even more times the standard mortality charges. Many insurers specialize in substandard risks. They will insure people with certain high-risk health characteristics, such as heart conditions, diabetes, or other diseases or debilitating conditions, or who are employed in high-risk occupations or practice high-risk avocations. Except for people in extremely poor health, almost anyone can acquire insurance, but perhaps only at very high rates. Insurers guarantee that mortality charges will not exceed certain maximums. But similar to interest rates, mortality rates insurers may use when computing required premiums and reserves must exceed certain statutory minimums by age and classification of insured.

Expenses and Risk Loadings

Although interest and mortality are the two principle factors in premium calculations, in reality insurance companies must include other factors. When insurers set premiums, they include various expenses as well as risk loadings. One major expense is agent sales commissions, which for a level-premium whole life insurance policy typically run about 55 percent or more of the annual premium in the first year and about equal to one to two annual premium in total over the life of the contract. Although this may seem high, it is not out of line with commissions and sales fees on other types of investments such as stocks, bonds, and mutual funds over the same period as a whole life insurance policy would typically be in force. For instance, in the case where the total commission is equal to one annual premium, the total commission expense would be equal to 4 percent of the total premiums a forty-year-old would pay to age sixty-five. The sales fees or commissions on stocks and bonds and other types of investments are lower as a percent of the amount invested, but they are typically incurred both when buying and selling. If instead of

paying premiums, this same person bought and held stocks and paid only a 2 percent commission on each purchase, he or she would have paid total commissions equal to only 2 percent of total investments by age sixty-five. But this person would still have to pay 2 percent of the accumulated balance when selling the stocks. Because the accumulated balance would presumably be much greater than the total amount invested as a result of the growth in the value of the stock, the selling commissions would be considerably greater than another 2 percent of the total amount invested over the years.

The total "round trip" commissions on the stocks would almost certainly be greater than the total commissions paid for the insurance. Furthermore, it would be a rare individual indeed who never had any turnover (sales and repurchases) of his or her investments in the intervening years. Sell/buy transactions in the intervening years would further increase the commissions paid on the stock investment relative to the life insurance purchase. Compared with other types of investments, the sales commissions paid on life insurance look more and more favorable the longer the policy is expected to remain in force.

In addition to the expenses described above, the insurance company also must recover other typical business expenses for home office salaries and administrative costs, advertising and promotion, research and product development costs, underwriting, investment management fees, rent, and other operating and overhead expenses. These expenses together with agent sales commissions are typically recovered through some combination of front- and/or back-end charges and annual policy fees that the insurer must recover from premiums or from the "savings" component of the policy.

Finally, the insurance company must charge loadings for various risks in addition to mortality risk. Because the bulk of the expenses associated with a policy is incurred when the policy is first issued, (but the majority of these expenses are not recovered through expense charges for several years) policies that are lapsed or terminated within the first few years are a drain on the company's surplus. Therefore, the company must estimate lapse rates when setting premiums. It also adds a risk charge or load to cover the risk that the actual lapse rate will exceed projected rates. Also, because the insurance company bears a risk that it will not actually earn the guaranteed minimum rate on its investments, it must include a risk loading to the premium to cover this contingency. Similarly, although the insurer can predict with remarkable accuracy the number of people who will die each year out of a large group of people with similar characteristics and of the same age, the insurer still faces a residual risk that the company's actual mortality experience will be worse than was anticipated. Because a life insurance company guarantees that mortality charges will not exceed certain maximums, it adds a risk loading when setting premiums to help cover the risk that its actual mortality experience is worse than projected.

Similar to the lottery illustrated in Figure 1.2, insurance companies combine their interest, mortality, lapse and expense assumptions, and loading factors to determine the premium that is necessary for any given premium payment plan to equate the present value of the expected future benefit payouts and expenses with the present value of the expected premium pay-ins from the group of similar policies. If the premium payment plan is other than a pay-as-you-go annually-renewable term plan, per-policy reserves (the savings component) will build up and serve as the basis for cash values that are available for policy loans or as surrender values if a policy is terminated. Based on statutorily mandated conservative assumptions, the insurance company can guarantee a minimum schedule of cash values. In the initial years, the cash value available to the policyowner is usually less than the reserve, because either front- or back-end charges are imposed to recover the high initial policy issue costs. However, as the years pass and issue costs are fully recovered, the cash value that is available to policyowners grows ever closer to the entire reserve.

Participating and Nonparticipating Policies

Because insurance companies must guarantee death benefits and a minimum schedule of cash values in most policies (except variable life policies), they must be conservative when estimating the values of the various premium pricing factors (interest, mortality, expenses, lapse rates, and risk loading factors) used to compute the required premiums under any particular premium payment plan of insurance.

In the case of *nonparticipating* policies, all elements—premiums, death benefits, and the schedule of cash values—are guaranteed and fixed. If a company's experience is more favorable than assumed with respect to any or all of the pricing factors, the premiums in excess of the amount needed to pay the company's obligations add to the company's profit or surplus. However,

competitive pressures within the industry as well as from alternative investments have made such entirely guaranteed but nonparticipating policies unattractive in the marketplace. Now most policies issued are participating in one way or another, meaning that they share the benefits of the company's favorable mortality, investment, expense, or lapse experience with the policyowners.

In what are called *traditional participating* life insurance products (typically, but not exclusively issued by mutual rather than stock insurance companies[7]), policyowners participate in the favorable experience of the company through dividends. Life insurance dividends are not like stock dividends, which represent a return *on* investment. Instead, they are more like a return *of* investment and are generally treated for tax and other purposes as a nontaxable return of prior overpayment of premiums.

Insurers typically give policyowners of participating policies a number of options as to how they may use dividends, such as to reduce current premiums, to buy paid-up additional insurance, to buy additional one-year term insurance, to repay policy loans, to increase policy cash values and to shorten the premium paying period, or to accumulate at interest. In any case, dividends reduce the overall cost of insurance and make participating life insurance policies more attractive and competitive with alternative investments.

Purchasers of participating policies are presented with a schedule of projected dividends when they buy the policy. Basically, the projected dividends generally reflect the company's best estimate of the values of the various pricing factors as compared with the conservative assumptions built into their premium calculations. But in contrast with quoted premiums, death benefits, and cash value schedules, dividends are *not* guaranteed. Insurers cannot guarantee dividends because the dividends depend on the insurers' actual experience relative to their conservative pricing assumptions. The insurers cannot know their performance until the experience actually unfolds.

In relatively recent years, a new type of participating life insurance, generically called current-assumption life insurance, has become popular.[8] In contrast with traditional participating policies, these types of policies do not pay dividends. Rather, if the company's experience is more favorable than assumed in its premium pricing computations, the favorable experience is reflected directly in the amounts credited to the policy's cash values. In other words, if the company's experience is favorable, cash values grow larger and more quickly than shown on the schedule of guaranteed minimum cash values.

Depending on the type of policy, the policyowner may have several options as to how they may use these additional cash value increases. In some cases, policyowners may withdraw the additional cash value without otherwise affecting their death benefits, premium payments, and minimum guaranteed cash values; the insurer may permit policyowners to reduce the level of future premium payments while maintaining the same face amount of coverage; the insurer may allow policyowners to increase the face amount of coverage while maintaining the same premium level; policyowners may keep the face amount and the premium payment level the same but shorten the required premium-payment period; or they may choose some combination or variation of these options.

Purchasers of current-assumption policies are presented with an illustration of projected premiums, cash values, and death benefits that use the company's current assumptions regarding the various premium pricing factors as well as an illustration showing the minimum guaranteed values based on the current premium and the statutorily mandated conservative pricing assumptions. Similar to projected dividends with traditional participating policies, the projected cash values and any projected death benefit increases above those shown using the required conservative pricing assumptions are *not* guaranteed. In many cases, even the premiums and the term of the policy are not guaranteed. If the company's experience turns out less favorably than currently assumed, the policyowner may have to pay premiums for a longer period than anticipated or pay increased premiums in order to maintain the face amount of coverage. Alternatively, the policyowner may have to accept a reduction in the face amount of coverage or a shortened term of coverage.

Variable life policies are the ultimate in participating policies, at least with respect to investment performance. The policyowner bears (almost) all the investment risk and reaps all the investment rewards from the underlying investments; the insurer provides no minimum interest guarantee with respect to cash values. In most cases the policyowner may choose to invest premium dollars among a number of mutual fund type investments. As in other types of policies, the insurer guarantees that mortality charges will not exceed certain maximums and that the death benefit will not fall below

a certain minimum, regardless of the investment performance of the underlying assets. However, the insurer makes no assurances regarding cash values. Depending on the type of variable life policy, favorable investment performance may increase the face amount of coverage or the insurer may give policyowners a number of flexible options similar to those described above for certain current-assumption policies.

SUMMARY COMPARISON OF POLICIES

Figure 1.3 summarizes and compares the characteristics, markets, advantages and disadvantages, and other features of various types of life contracts. More complete information is provided in separate chapters on the various products.

WHERE CAN I FIND OUT MORE?

1. B. Baldwin, *The Complete Book of Insurance: The Consumer's Guide to Insuring Your Life, Health, Property and Income, Revised Edition* (Chicago, IL: Irwin Professional Publishing, 1996).

2. B. Baldwin, *New Life Insurance Investment Advisor: Achieving Financial Security for You and Your Family Through Today's Insurance Products*, 2nd ed. (Hightstown, NJ: McGraw-Hill Trade, 2001).

3. J. Belth, *Life Insurance: A Consumer's Handbook*, 2nd ed. (Bloomington, IN: Indiana University Press, 1985).

4. K. Black, Jr. and H. Skipper, Jr., *Life and Health Insurance*, 13th ed. (Old Tappan, NJ: Prentice Hall Inc., 1999).

5. *Journal of Financial Service Professionals* (Bimonthly), (Newton Square, PA: The Society of Financial Service Professionals, at www.financialpro.org).

6. *Best's Review — Life/Health Edition* (Monthly), (Oldwick, NJ: A. M. Best Company).

7. H. Zaritsky and S. Leimberg, *Tax Planning with Life Insurance*, 2nd edition. (Boston, MA: Warren, Gorham & Lamont, updated yearly).

8. E. Graves, Editor, *McGill's Life Insurance*, 5th ed. (Bryn Mawr, PA: The American College, 2009).

Figure 1.3

	Table C					
LIFE INSURANCE POLICY COMPARISON CHART						
PRODUCT	CHARACTERISTICS	MARKET	DEATH BENEFIT	PREMIUM	CASH VALUE (CV)	CV AND/OR DIVIDENDS USE CURRENT INTEREST?
Term Life	"Pure" life insurance with no cash value element; initially, the highest death benefit for the lowest premium.	Short to intermediate term need; need max. death benefit for min. initial premium.	Fixed, level.	Fixed, increasing.	No cash value.	N/A
Whole Life	Most common and easily understood form of lifetime coverage; known max. cost and min. death benefit levels; dividends may reduce premiums, pay-up policy, buy paid-up additions, accum. at interest, be paid in cash.	Anybody who needs lifetime coverage.	Fixed, level.	Fixed, level.	Fixed with min. guaranteed interest rate; excess through dividends.	Yes.
Current Assumption Whole Life	Mixes characteristics of universal life and traditional ordinary life; future premiums, face amount, and/or cash value based on interest, expense, mortality experience.	Upper and middle income prospects.	Fixed, level.	May change based on insurer's experience; Max. guaranteed but insurer may charge less.	May change based on insurer's experience; guaranteed min.; Min. guaranteed interest; excess lowers premium or increases CV.	Yes.
Variable Life	Whole life contract with assets supporting policy held in separate account; choice of investment assets; death benefits depend on investment results.	Upper and middle income prospects with investment acumen.	Guaranteed min; can increase based on investment performance.	Fixed, level.	Based on investment performance; not guaranteed.	N/A.
Adjustable Life	May select death benefit and, within limits, choose premiums; face amount and premiums are fixed between adjustment periods; usual features of whole life.	Young families starting insurance program; need for flexibility with guarantees.	Adjustable.	Adjustable at option of policyowner.	Varies depending on premium/death benefit mix; fixed with min. guaranteed interest; excess through dividends.	Yes.
Universal Life	Flexible premium current-assumption adjustable death benefit policy; policy elements unbundled; two death benefit options.	Middle and upper income looking for ultimate in flexibility.	Adjustable; Option A like Ord. Life; Option B like Ord. Life plus term rider equal to cash value.	Flexible at option of policyowner.	Varies depending on face amount and premium; min. guaranteed interest excess interest increases cash value.	Yes.
Universal Life III — Universal Variable Life	Combines features of universal and variable life.	Middle and upper income with investment acumen looking for ultimate in flexibility.	Adjustable.	Flexible at option of policyowner.	Varies depending on face amount, premium, and investment performance; not guaranteed.	N/A
Annuities	Combine tax advantages, investment choice, flexibility and guarantees with various lifetime payout options that cannot be outlived.	Middle and upper income; qualified (IRA) and non-qualified retirement arrangements.	Accumulation period: max. of premiums or cash value; payout period: depends on option.	Fixed or flexible.	Varies depending on investment performance; min. guaranteed interest rate unless variable annuity.	Yes.

Figure 1.3 (cont'd)

Table C
LIFE INSURANCE POLICY COMPARISON CHART

PARTIAL SURRENDERS PERMITTED?	POLICY ELEMENTS	DIRECT BORROWING RECOGNITION	ADVANTAGES TO BUYER	DISADVANTAGES TO BUYER	RISKS TO BUYER
N/A	Bundled.	N/A	Low outlay for large face amounts; develop outside investment program.	Increasing outlay; buyer may not invest difference or may realize lower return.	Increasing premium. Failure to earn more aftertax on investments than insurer.
Yes, but through paid up additions only.	Bundled.	Yes, with many policies.	Familiar product; predictable; helps buyer discipline; share in favorable interest, mortality and expense experience.	Costly if lapsed early.	Failure to meet premium commitment.
Yes.	Unbundled.	Yes.	Take advantage of high current interest rates and improved mortality.	Premiums can be higher or cash value lower than projected; policy can lose paid-up status.	If assumptions change adversely, premiums can be higher or cash value can be lower than with traditional products.
No.	Bundled, but to some degree shown in prospectus.	No.	Take advantage of growth in economy.	Must decide on underlying investments and monitor them for change; few guarantees.	Investment risk is great. Typically higher expenses than traditional products.
Yes.	Bundled.	Yes.	Flexibility to adjust to changing needs; only one policy needed.	If needs are known and not likely to change, other products may be less costly per unit of protection.	Changes made by buyer to satisfy short-term needs may have an impact on the satisfaction of long-term goals.
Yes.	Unbundled.	Yes.	Greater transparency and more flexibility than Adj. Life.	Flexibility places greater responsibility on buyer; buyer assumes greater investment and mortality risks.	Adverse change in assumptions can affect satisfaction of long-term goals and drop cash value below that of ordinary life.
Yes.	Unbundled.	No.	Epitome of flexibility in all respects.	Equity performance unpredictable; relatively high expenses; few guarantees.	Combined risks of universal and variable life products.
Yes.	Partially unbundled.	Yes, if permitted.	Cannot outlive benefits if life option elected.	Expenses can be higher than alternative investments.	Under life options, payouts cease at death: if death occurs early, total benefits less than with alternative investments.

CHAPTER ENDNOTES

1. The life insurance product "closest" to a 0 percent pure death protection and 100 percent savings combination is a single-premium endowment policy. An endowment policy is essentially a whole life policy that will mature or "endow," that is, pay the face amount of coverage, if the insured is still alive at a specified age, such as age sixty-five. Similar to other life insurance products, it also pays the face amount if the insured dies before the policy endows. By analogy, traditional whole life policies are really endowment policies that endow at age ninety-five or 100. Since policies that endow before age ninety-five or 100 build substantial cash values relative to the face amount of coverage, they usually will be classified as modified endowment contracts (MECs) for tax purposes or will fail the Code Section 7702 definition of life insurance altogether. In either case, the adverse tax consequences of such classification have made endowment policies unpopular. (MECs and the Code Section 7702 definition of life insurance are covered in Chapter 19 and 21, respectively.)

    Although some endowment policies that meet the Code Section 7702 definition of life insurance (but are generally classified as MECs) are offered by some insurance companies, in general consumers have turned to deferred annuities to accomplish the same basic tax-advantaged accumulation objective. Deferred annuities enjoy the same tax-deferred accumulation as endowments and other cash-value life insurance products without the risk and adverse tax consequences of failing the Code Section 7702 definition of life insurance.

    In reality, most deferred annuities provide a slight measure of pure death protection during the accumulation period before payout. In general, if the insured-annuitant dies before the time when payouts are scheduled to begin, the insurance company guarantees that the gross amount payable will not be less than the total premiums paid, even if the investment performance is such that the accumulated value would otherwise be less than the total premiums paid.

2. Even "pure" no-refund life annuities may be considered to have some "savings" component or provide some element of recovery even in the event of death since (1) they may sometimes be exchanged for annuities with refund or guaranteed features, (2) companies may permit the annuitant to "surrender" all or a part of the annuity for its commuted value, or (3) in very limited circumstances and in limited amounts, the annuitant may be permitted to take loans.

3. The expected or average number of years until payout may be determined by summing the number of years all participants must wait in total until each receives a payout and dividing that total by the number of participants. In this simple example, one participant must wait one year, another two years, another three years, another four years, and the last participant, five years. The sum is fifteen years. Therefore, the expected or average number of years each participant must wait is three years.

    The expected or average number of years until payout is analogous to the concept of life expectancy when dealing with probabilities of death and should not be confused with the number of years until there is a 50 percent chance that a given participant will receive a payout or the number of years until half the participants will have received a payout. The initial probability that any particular participant will receive the payout in any given year, given that he or she is still a participant at the beginning of the year is 20 percent for each year. This probability is determined by multiplying the probability of "winning" the lottery in any particular year, given the number of participants remaining in the pool, by the probability of being one of the remaining participants going into that year. Specifically, in the first year, the probability of winning the lottery is 1/5, since all five participants are in the pool in the first year. The probability of winning the lottery in the second year, given that a person is still in the pool, is 1/4, since there will then be only four participants remaining. The probability of being one of the four participants remaining in the pool is 4/5. Therefore, the initial probability of winning the lottery in the second year is also 20 percent (1/4 × 4/5). Similarly, the initial probability of winning the lottery in the third, fourth, or fifth years is 20 percent [(1/3 × 3/5), (1/2 × 2/5), (1 × 1/5), respectively].

    The probability of winning the lottery on or before a given year is determined by summing the probabilities up to and including that year. Specifically, for any given participant, there is a 20 percent chance of winning the lottery in the first year, a 40 percent chance of winning the lottery within the first two years, a 60 percent chance of winning within three years, and 80 percent chance of winning within four years, and a certainty (probability of one) of receiving the payout within five years. Since there is a 40 percent chance of receiving the payout within two years and a 60 percent chance of receiving the payout within three years, the expected or average number of years until half the participants receive a payout (that is, there is a 50 percent chance of receiving the payout) is 2.5 years (although this number is purely theoretical in this case since payments are never made in the middle of the year and, furthermore, half the number of participants is 2.5). (If the pool had been set up for six years, rather than five, and with six participants, rather than five, the number of years until half the participants (3) received payouts—the number of years until any given participant had a 50 percent chance of winning the lottery—would be exactly three years. However, the expected or average number of years until any given participant could expect a payout in this case would still be greater, 3.5 years.)

    It is a common misconception with respect to the use of life expectancy tables that the life expectancy for a given age represents the additional number of years until half the people that age can be expected to die, or alternatively, beyond which half the people can be expected to live. Depending on the "force of mortality" over the relevant range of years, the life expectancy may be longer or shorter than the number of years until half the people of a given age can be expected to die. For virtually any age for most of the commonly used life expectancy tables, life expectancy is less than the number of years until half the people that age can be expected to die.

4. The probabilities used in Figure 1.2 are unlike real mortality probabilities since the number of people assumed to die each period is known with certainty; the only uncertainty is which of the participants is the unlucky one. By the law of large numbers, the proportion of a population of people of the same age and characteristics that will die each year can be predicted with greater and greater accuracy as the number of people in the population increases. However, there is always some residual risk that more or less than the predicted number will die in any given year. The only certainty with a group of real lives is that, ultimately, they will all die.

5. The comparison of the amount that could be accumulated "outside" with the amount accumulated inside the plan assumes all else is equal, which is unrealistic. Life insurance has tax and other favorable features other than the payment of death benefits that would be difficult if not impossible to reproduce outside the life

insurance vehicle. However, regardless of the specifics of how one should best compare investments outside the life insurance plan with the total investment aspects of a life insurance plan, the general principle remains true. Life insurance is a risk-sharing pool where, by necessity, some people (those who die early) will receive more than they could ever have accumulated without life insurance and others (those who die later) may receive less than they could have accumulated without life insurance. The various tax advantages and other advantageous features of life insurance help to increase the number of economic "winners" relative to "losers." But for every pool of insureds there will always be some—those who live the longest, if they could have only known beforehand—who might have done better by investing their premium dollars in something other than insurance.

6. Note two things: The difference between the number of successes and the number of trials times the chance of success in each trial (the expected number of successes) tends to grow as the number of trials increases. (In fact, this difference tends to grow like the square root of the number of trials.) Although the chance of a large difference between the percentage of successes and the chance of success gets smaller and smaller as n grows, nothing prevents the difference from being large in some sequences of trials. The assumption that this difference always tends to zero, as opposed to this difference having a large probability of being arbitrarily close to zero, is the difference between the Law of Large Numbers, which is a mathematical theorem, and the Empirical Law of Averages, which is an assumption about how the world works that lies at the base of the Frequency Theory of probability.

7. Stock insurance companies are, like regular corporations, owned by stockholders who put up the required capital with the objective of earning profits on the difference between the premiums paid for policies and the various death and living benefits paid out. Mutual insurance companies are in principle owned by the policyowners rather than stockholders. "Profits," as such, do not exist. Premiums paid in excess of the amount necessary for the company to pay benefits increase the company's surplus (similar to a stock company's capital account or owner's equity account). A certain amount of surplus is required as a reserve to assure payment of all of the company's obligations under their life insurance contracts and to finance the company's growth, but any excess, called divisible surplus, may be shared with and distributed to policyowners.

8. Originally, current-assumption policies were developed and sold by stock insurance companies to compete with the participating policies offered by mutual insurers. Today, current-assumption types of policies are the bread-and-butter of stock companies, but they are also offered in various forms by many mutual insurers.

HOW TO ESTIMATE THE INSURANCE NEED

CHAPTER 2

INTRODUCTION

Financial planning professionals apply diversified techniques to determine the life insurance needs of a family. Life insurance planning involves essentially three principal, but often overlapping needs areas:

- Income replacement and family needs analysis

- Business insurance needs analysis

- Estate preservation and liquidity needs analysis

A comprehensive study of the client's financial needs and concerns generally is the best way to conduct life insurance planning. The process of life insurance planning must begin and end with the objectives and goals of the client being paramount, even if such objectives and goals do not conform to what the adviser considers proper or appropriate values or concerns. This is not to suggest that the adviser does not have a responsibility to educate the client about the potential uses and abuses of insurance, issues normally considered when assessing life insurance needs, ownership issues, tax effects, and the like. However, ethics and prudence require that the insurance plan satisfy the client's objectives; clients simply will not implement a plan, however well-conceived and however appropriate, if they are not satisfied that it meets their objectives.

INCOME REPLACEMENT AND FAMILY NEEDS ANALYSIS

Any method of determining a family's insurance needs will be an estimate. Future circumstances will change in unexpected ways and basic assumptions about earnings, interest rates, inflation, and similar factors will never replicate actual experience. Consequently, every insurance program must be monitored and periodically updated to assure that the client's needs are still being met.

Personal computers have made it possible to perform increasingly comprehensive and sophisticated analyses of insurance needs. The problem with this trend is that, as the analyses become more comprehensive and sophisticated, what is already an inherently confusing subject becomes even more so, often further reducing the client's ability to understand and accept the insurance plan. There is frequently an unfortunate, but necessary, trade-off between comprehensiveness and comprehension.

Insurance advisers basically use three approaches to estimate family life insurance needs:

- Rules of thumb

- Income replacement approach

- Needs approach

Rules of Thumb

The simplest methods to understand, and the least reliable, are various rules of thumb that planners frequently use to roughly estimate either the amount of insurance that clients need or the amount of premium clients should be spending on insurance.

One rough guide planners use to estimate the amount of insurance required is six to eight times annual gross income. For instance, based on this rough guide, a parent earning $50,000 per year should have between

$300,000 and $400,000 of life insurance. A similar rule that takes immediate cash needs at death into account is five times gross income, plus mortgage, debts, final expenses, and any other special funding need (e.g., college fund).

Example. Your client, a parent earns $50,000 per year but also that the mortgage is $60,000, other personal debts are $10,000, final expenses are expected to be $15,000, and that the parent needs $35,000 for the children's college expenses. Using this rule, the parent would need insurance coverage of about $250,000 (5 × $50,000) plus $120,000 ($60,000 + $10,000 + $15,000 + $35,000), or $370,000 total.

Another rule is that the family should spend about 6 percent of the breadwinner's gross income plus another 1 percent for each dependent on premiums for life insurance. Under this rule, a person with a nonworking spouse and three children should be spending about 10 percent of gross income on premiums for life insurance. In some cases, the rule may express the amount of premium as a percent, ranging from 5 to 15 percent, of after-tax take-home pay.

Clients may find such rules of thumb useful as a very rough starting point. They can give clients a broad sense of the scope of the problem in terms they can quickly understand. However, these rules are, at best, very limited. Individual needs vary widely and the rules of thumb do not take such variations into account. They do not consider the insured's age, the dependents' ages, or whether the family is a one- or two-income household. Stating the objective in terms of required premium outlays is even more limited, because premiums will vary greatly for the same amount of coverage depending on the insured's age and plan of insurance.

Multiples-of-Salary Method

A somewhat more precise rule-of-thumb method is the use of multiples-of-salary charts such as presented below. This approach is actually a hybrid method combining the simpler rule-of-thumb methods with elements of the income replacement and needs analysis approaches discussed later. The chart is based on the assumption that the average family can live adequately and maintain its standard of living on 75 percent of the wage earner's after-tax income and that the insured

is the only breadwinner in the family. If income were to drop below 60 percent, the family's living standard would suffer. The chart also assumes social security coverage and that insurance proceeds are invested at a net annual rate of 5 percent.[1]

To use this chart:

1. Find the column showing the spouse's current age.

2. Locate the point in the column at which the client's earnings intersect the spouse's age (the 75 percent column is recommended).

3. Multiply the client's salary by the appropriate factor.

MULTIPLES-OF-SALARY CHART

Your Client's Present Gross Earnings	Present Age of Your Client's Spouse							
	25 Years		35 Years		45 Years		55 Years	
	75%	60%	75%	60%	75%	60%	75%	60%
$7,500	4.0	3.0	5.5	4.0	7.5	5.5	6.5	4.5
9,000	4.0	3.0	5.5	4.0	7.5	5.5	6.5	4.5
15,000	4.5	3.0	6.5	4.5	8.0	6.0	7.0	5.5
23,500	6.5	4.5	8.0	5.5	8.5	6.5	7.5	5.5
30,000	7.5	5.0	8.0	6.0	8.5	6.5	7.0	5.5
40,000	7.5	5.0	8.0	6.0	8.0	6.0	7.0	5.0
65,000	7.5	5.5	7.5	6.0	7.5	6.0	6.5	5.0

Source: Cady, *Field Guide to Estate Planning, Business Planning & Employee Benefits*, (National Underwriter Company, 2012).

If the age or earnings differ from those shown in the chart, interpolate using the nearest salaries and ages.

Example. A client has a $35,000 salary and a forty-year-old spouse. Since $35,000 is halfway between the $30,000 and $40,000 earnings rows and also halfway between the age thirty-five and age forty-five columns shown in the chart, one would find the multiplier by averaging the four factors shown in these row/column combinations ($30,000 row and age thirty-five column: 8.0; $30,000 row and age forty-five column: 8.5; $40,000 row and age thirty-five column: 8.0; $40,000 row and age forty-five column: 8.0). Therefore, the multiplier is 8.1 [(8.0 + 8.0 + 8.0 + 8.5) ÷ 4]. According to this rule, the estimated amount the family needs to meet its income requirements is $283,500 ($35,000 × 8.1).

In general, one would increase this amount to account for immediate capital or cash needs at death. Such capital needs would commonly include funds to pay funeral and other final expenses, to pay off debts, such as mortgages or personal loans, to fund special projects, such as children's educations, and to set up an emergency reserve.

Example. If your client has a $50,000 mortgage and estimated final expenses of $20,000, wanted $40,000 to fund the children's educations, and felt that the equivalent of one year's salary ($35,000) should be set aside for emergencies; the total capital needs would be $145,000. Adding the $145,000 required to fund capital needs to the $283,500 required to fund income needs would result in a total need of $428,500.

Finally, one can determine the amount of additional insurance one needs by subtracting any insurance already in force and the value of other assets that are available for this purpose from the total calculated need.

Example. Assume the client already has $150,000 of group insurance provided through his or her employer and has otherwise saved $30,000. One would compute the amount of additional insurance needed by subtracting $180,000 from the estimated total need of $428,500 to derive the final result, $248,500.

The multiples-of-salary chart method still suffers from many of the limitations associated with the simple rules of thumb. It does not take account of the age of the insured, premium costs, or the number of dependents who must be protected. Although it does adjust for the spouse's age (and implicitly, the number of years for which the surviving spouse needs support), it does not adjust for the ages of children. In addition, it is not a suitable method in the increasingly common case where both spouses work. Similar to the simpler rules of thumb, it does not take into account differences in tax rates or investment rates of return that may apply in different family situations.

However, if these limitations are kept in mind, this method can provide reasonable first approximations of the insurance need in simple situations.

The Income Replacement Approach

The human life value concept is the basis for a second approach that advisers use to estimate life insurance needs. The human life value concept has often been applied in wrongful death litigation and basically holds that the measure of the economic value of a life to those who depend on that person is the present value of the future earnings potential of that person. The income replacement approach to life insurance needs analysis is based on the premise that the fundamental objective of life insurance is to replace some or all of the earnings lost if an income-producing family member should die. In other words, the insurance coverage should equal the value of that person's future earnings potential to the surviving family members.

Although one may question the basic premise—because it ignores other equally valid reasons why people may purchase life insurance—the method does allow one to estimate a theoretical maximum consistent with the idea that a person should never be worth more economically to beneficiaries dead than alive. This method may provide a more accurate starting point than simple rules of thumb, while still being relatively easy conceptually—if not computationally—to understand.

Human Life Value

A person's human life value depends on numerous factors including future income levels, taxes, education, training, promotions, and various normal decremental factors such as the possibility of illness, disability, periods of unemployment, and the like. However, one usually can compute reasonable estimates of the present value of future earnings using four key inputs or assumptions:

1. Current annual after-tax earnings (C)

2. The projected rate of growth of earnings (g)

3. The future working lifetime (n)

4. An after-tax discount rate (r)

Given these four factors, one computes the present value of future earnings using the present value of an annuity formula, equation 2.1, as follows:[2]

Equation 2.1

$$\text{PV Future Earnings} = C \times \left[\frac{1-(1+i)^{-n}}{i}\right] \times \left[\frac{1+i}{1+(r \div 2)}\right]$$

where $i = \dfrac{r-g}{1+g}$, the growth-adjusted discount rate, and $r \neq g$.

If $r = g$, the present value is simply equal to $n \times C$.

The formula assumes earnings are paid annually in the middle of the year, which is a reasonable approximation to monthly or other periodic payments throughout the year.

Example. A thirty-five-year-old client's after-tax income is currently $50,000 per year, and she estimates that it will grow at an average annual rate of 5 percent and that she will work until age sixty-five. Assume an appropriate after-tax discount rate of 6 percent. The present value of her future earnings is about $1,275,000, computed as follows:

PV Future Earnings

$$= \$50,000 \times \left(\frac{1-(1.009524)^{-30}}{0.009524} \right) \times \left(\frac{1.009524}{1+(0.06 \div 2)} \right)$$

$$= \$50,000 \times \left(\frac{1-1.75249}{0.009524} \right) \times \left(\frac{1.009524}{1.03} \right)$$

$$= \$50,000 \times 25.988062 \times 0.98012$$

$$= \$1,273,575 \approx \$1.275 \text{ million}$$

The value of $1,275,000 is the amount that, if invested today at a 6 percent after-tax rate of return, could provide an after-tax income stream payable in the middle of each year for the next thirty years, with the initial after-tax amount starting at $50,000 and each subsequent payment growing by 5 percent. After thirty years, the entire $1,275,000 would be used up.

Basic Assumptions

The present value of future earnings is very sensitive to changes in the underlying earnings growth and discount rate assumptions.

Example. Using the facts from the example above, if the client estimates that earnings will grow at 2 percent rather than 5 percent and the discount rate remains at 6 percent, the present value is $881,000, or almost 1/3 less. If instead, one assumes as before that earnings will grow at 5 percent, but the discount rate is only 3 percent, the present value is just over $1,980,000, or more than half again greater.

What are reasonable assumptions for the earnings growth and discount rates?

Earnings growth rate – The earnings growth rate usually will depend on inflation rates and tax rates, as well as career opportunities. As a guideline, keep in mind that the average annual compound U.S. growth rate of inflation-adjusted disposable (after-tax) income has been just over 2 percent over the long run. In other words, on average, after-tax incomes have increased by about 2 percent more than inflation each year. Year to year, the rate has varied widely, but for estimation purposes, long-term trends are most appropriate.

Inflation itself has averaged slightly more than 4 percent per year over the period 1977 to 2006, but it too varies widely from year to year or from subperiod to subperiod. For the period from 1977 to 1986, inflation averaged 10.68 percent per year. This is considerably higher than the 3.65 percent average for the period from 1997 to 2006. The recent trend of inflation rates has been down. However, there have been long periods where inflation rates remain quite high.

The 2 percent U.S. average growth in inflation-adjusted disposable earnings is an average across all industries and occupations and all age groups. But it is not necessarily a good estimate of real average annual earnings growth for any particular individual. First, every individual is unique and may advance faster or slower than others within his or her occupation. Second, earnings growth rates vary among industries and occupations. Some occupations or occupations within certain industries experience greater than average earnings increases as computed across all occupations while other occupations are experiencing less than average increases.[3] So estimates of earnings growth rates must take close account of the particular talents and potential of the client and the character of the lifetime earnings profile of his or her chosen occupation.

As a practical matter, estimates of future real inflation-adjusted earnings growth rates are unnecessary in many cases. Many family breadwinners desire to provide a standard of living comparable to that the family currently enjoys if they should die. However, they do not feel quite the same responsibility to insure the increasing standard of living the family might enjoy while they live. If the objective is to maintain the family's current standard of living, it is only necessary to estimate future inflation rates, not also earnings growth rates in excess of inflation. In these cases, an estimate of the average future inflation rate would be substituted for the earnings growth rate in equation 2-1. The value so calculated is the amount that if invested today at the assumed after-tax rate of return could replace the wage earner's current level of real inflation-adjusted after-tax income each year for the rest of what would be the wage earner's remaining working lifetime.

After-tax discount rates – Estimating reasonable after-tax discount rates can be just as problematic. The basic question is: At what after-tax rate of return could the life insurance proceeds be invested over the long run? That depends on the risk one is willing to assume, tax rates, and inflation rates. As a guideline, Figure 2.1 presents average nominal and real (inflation-adjusted) compound returns for principal categories of marketable assets and inflation for the World War II period 1946 to 2011.

Using the post World War II period 1946 to 2011 as a basis for estimating returns, an investment in long-term high-quality corporate bonds could be expected to return about 10.59 percent before tax compounded annually. A 50/50 mix of high quality corporate bonds and common stocks—which is about as aggressive as one would want to assume the assets would be invested—could be expected to return about 8.30 percent. As Figure 2.1 shows, the real annual inflation-adjusted compound return for corporate bonds over this period was just 2.03 percent after adjusting

for inflation (which averaged 3.89 percent); for a 50/50 bond/stock mix, about 4.24 percent. Chances are that returns for all asset classes will tend toward the long run average over time, but there is no assurance of when or even if that will actually happen.

Because the present values one computes will vary substantially depending on the assumed rate of return, it is best to discuss alternative assumptions with clients and let them be the guide—within informed reason—on selecting the appropriate discount rate. Because present values vary inversely with the assumed discount rate, the conservative and prudent practice is to err on the side of lower, rather than higher, assumed rates.

To determine the appropriate discount rate, one must adjust whatever estimate of return one starts with for taxes. The tendency is to overstate tax rates because appropriate adjustments for standard deductions and personal exemptions, as well as the tax-free recovery of investment, are neglected. The effect of the standard deduction and personal exemptions may be to reduce the appropriate tax rate for use in equation 2.1 to about 20 percent to 80 percent of the marginal tax bracket rate for a comparable level of adjusted gross income. The effect of the exclusion of amounts treated as a recovery of the initial investment may further reduce the effective average tax rate by 1/3 or more. In general, it is suitable to apply tax rates ranging from about 4 percent to about 10 percent when determining after-tax discount rates to use in equation 2-1.

Family Support Ratio

Under the income replacement approach, insurance value is always less than human life value. The portion of after-tax income spent for self-maintenance is not

Figure 2.1

AVERAGE ANNUAL NOMINAL AND REAL COMPOUND RETURNS (1946-2011)		
	Nominal	Real
Large Stocks (S&P 500)	10.59%	6.45%
Corporate Bonds (Moody's AAA)	6.00%	2.03%
Government Bonds (10 Year)	6.03%	2.06%
Treasury Bills (3 Month)	4.35%	0.44%
Inflation (Consumer Price Index)	3.89%	NA
Source: Ibbotson SBBI 2012 Classic Yearbook, Morningstar, Inc., Chicago, IL		

available for the family, so only the remaining portion is what is devoted to or spent in support of the family. Advisers often assume that breadwinners spend about 25 percent of after-tax income for self-maintenance and the remaining 75 percent for family support. However, this ratio may vary widely from family to family. In general, the proportion spent in support of the family is somewhat less at higher incomes than at lower incomes and is higher the greater is the number of children. In addition, under the basic premise of this method, one of the important elements of family support is the cost of the insurance itself. Because the amount spent for insurance is not otherwise available to support the family's standard of living, this cost should further reduce the proportion of income that is insured to support the surviving family members' standard of living.

Therefore, once one estimates the breadwinner's human life value, one should multiply that amount by the family support ratio. For example, if the calculations determine that the present value of future earnings is $1 million and one also assumes that the family needs 70 percent of the breadwinner's after-tax income to support the surviving family members' standard of living, then the amount needed to maintain the family in the event of the breadwinner's death is $700,000.

Other Adjustments

The amount so determined is not necessarily the amount of additional insurance required. Planners should further reduce this amount by the amount of any assets that are currently available to fund the survivor's income needs and by any life insurance currently in force. Among the assets that planners should count are marketable securities, savings account balances, and the like, as well as current vested account or benefit balances in employer-sponsored pension and profit-sharing plans, Code section 403(a) or (b) tax-deferred annuity plans, Individual Retirement Arrangements (IRAs) and Roth IRAs, Simplified Employee Pensions (SEPs), Keogh plans, and SIMPLE IRAs.

Many advisers feel that the family should also increase the support ratio to account for contributions or credits that the breadwinner would make to employer-sponsored retirement plans (qualified and nonqualified) while the breadwinner lives.

Example. Assume the employer sponsors a 401(k) plan that will match 50 percent of employee contributions up to 6 percent of pay. If the employee has 6 percent of pay deducted for the 401(k), the reported after-tax salary is reduced by about 6 percent. However, the 401(k) plan increases by 9 percent of pay. Assuming, for simplicity, that the employee is in the 33 percent tax bracket, this is effectively equivalent to an offsetting 6 percent increase in the employee's after-tax income. Therefore, planners should compute the family support ratio based upon the reported after-tax income increased by the effective after-tax value of the 401(k) contributions. If one otherwise assumes the family support ratio is 70 percent, one should increase it to 74.2 percent to account for the equivalent after-tax value of the employer-sponsored plan (70 percent × 6 percent = 4.2 percent).

In addition, many advisers strongly suggest that the family should increase the amount by any outstanding debts, such as personal loans and the home mortgage, and by anticipated final death expenses. Although it violates the general premise of the income replacement method (which is to provide a fund sufficient, but no larger than that necessary, to replace what the breadwinner would provide to the family if and while he or she lives), in some cases advisers further recommend that family breadwinners acquire additional insurance to fund special objectives, such as college education funds for the children. In general, many families consider such funding objectives part of their normal support obligation and implicitly include such objectives when selecting the family support ratio.

Adjustment for Social Security Survivor Benefits

Most workers are covered by Social Security or some other government program that provides survivor benefits to surviving spouses with dependent children and surviving spouses alone after age sixty. This is a form of income-replacement insurance and should reduce the present value of the family support obligation accordingly. The amount paid to a surviving spouse with at least one eligible child (under age sixteen or disabled before age twenty-two) is 75 percent of the deceased spouse's Primary Insurance Amount (PIA) at the date of death. For each eligible child, an additional 75 percent of the PIA is payable. Children are eligible for a child's benefit until age eighteen, or until age nineteen if in high school, or as long as they are disabled if disability occurs before age twenty-two. A spouse alone is eligible for reduced benefits equal to 71.5 percent of the PIA starting at age sixty, or if receipt of benefits is delayed, up to 100 percent of the PIA starting at normal retirement age.[4] A disabled spouse is eligible for 71.5 percent of the PIA starting at age fifty. The total amount payable to the family is subject to a limit, called the maximum family benefit, which can range from 150 percent to about 187.5 percent of the PIA.

The PIA depends on both the level of pay and the number of years in covered employment. An annual Social Security Statement is sent to most participants within three months of their birthdays. This statement provides information regarding a person's current insurance status in the Social Security program, earnings history, current PIA, and estimates of benefits. Any participant who does not receive the automatic Statement by one month before her month of birth or who needs a Statement sooner than she is scheduled to receive it may request a statement at any time. A person may process the request online or by mailing Form SSA-7004-PC to the Social Security Administration.[5]

Figure 2.2 can be used to estimate survivor benefits. The figures are for 2012 and are based on the assumption that the worker has been employed steadily and received 5 percent pay raises throughout his or her working career. In the case of the $110,100 wages, wages are assumed to be equal to or greater than the maximum OASDI wage base for all years. Normal retirement age depends on when a person was born. Like other Social Security benefits, survivor benefits are increased each year to reflect changes in the cost of living. Therefore, readers may use the table to estimate benefits in 2012 and later years by scaling the appropriate figures up by the rate of increase in the CPI since 2012.

Example. Your client, Mike Fox, is married and is currently earning $60,000 in FICA wages, is age forty-five. His wife, Mary, is also age forty-five and they have two children, ages nine and five. According to Figure 2.2, Mary and each of Mike's two children are eligible for survivor benefits of $1,304 per month, or $3,912 total in 2012 dollars. However, the maximum monthly family benefit is $3,088 in 2012 dollars. The annual benefit of $37,056 (12 × $3,088) would be payable for nine years until Mike's nine-year-old turns age eighteen (or nineteen if the child is still in high school). (All benefits would increase each year for inflation.) After that, $31,296 (12 × $1,304 × 2: the maximum family benefit limit is higher

at this point and no longer applies) would be payable for two years until Mike's second child reaches age sixteen. At this point, Mary's benefit payments would cease until she reaches age sixty. Mike's second child would continue to receive a child's benefit of $15,648 (12 × $1,304 × 1) for two more years until age eighteen (or nineteen if a full time high school student).

When Mary reaches age sixty, she will be eligible for $1,244 per month (in 2012 dollars) for life, or if she waits until age sixty-seven (her normal retirement age) to begin receiving payments, $1,739 (in 2012 dollars). Of course, Mary's benefits must also be adjusted for anticipated increases due to inflation until benefits begin. The mechanics of this adjustment are explained in the following section.

Converting Social Security Survivor Benefits to Present Values

To account for these Social Security benefits when determining the amount of insurance required, one must convert the Social Security benefits into a present value using equation 2.1. Using the prior example to demonstrate the procedure, the benefits payable during the children's eligibility period are best viewed in three components:[6]

1. a stream of $15,648 (12 × $1,304 in 2012 dollars) annual payments for thirteen years (the youngest child's benefit until reaching age eighteen); and

2. a stream of $15,648 (12 × $1,304 in 2012 dollars) payable for eleven years (Mary's benefit until the youngest child reaches age sixteen); and

3. a stream of $5,760 ($37,056 Maximum Family Benefit - $31,296 [$15,648 × 2: Mary's and youngest child's benefits] in 2012 dollars) payable for nine years (the incremental benefit payable to the oldest child as limited by the maximum family benefit).

Assuming benefits continue to inflate at a 3 percent rate each year and that 6 percent is a reasonable interest rate assumption, equation 2-1 would be used to determine the present values as follows:

$$i = \frac{0.06 - 0.03}{1.03} = 0.02913$$

Figure 2.2

APPROXIMATE MONTHLY SURVIVORS' BENEFITS FOR YOUR FAMILY ASSUMING STEADY EARNINGS AND DEATH IN 2012								
		Earnings in 2012						
Age[7]	Family	$30,000[1]	$45,000[1]	$60,000[1]	$75,000[1]	$90,000[1]	$105,000[1]	$110,100 or More[2]
35	Your spouse and one child[3]	$1,742	$2,280	$2,816	$3,104	$3,358	3,608	3,876
	Your spouse and two children[4]	1,964	2,794	3,288	3,624	3,918	4,212	4,523
	One child only	871	1,140	1,408	1,552	1,679	1,804	1,938
	Your spouse at NRA[5]	1,161	1,520	1,878	2,070	2,238	2,406	2,584
	Your spouse at age 60[6]	830	1,087	1,343	1,480	1,600	1,720	1,848
45	Your spouse and one child[3]	1,636	2,122	2,608	2,984	3,212	3,438	3,814
	Your spouse and two children[4]	1,774	2,654	3,088	3,482	3,748	4,013	4,451
	One child only	818	1,061	1,304	1,492	1,606	1,719	1,907
	Your spouse at NRA[5]	1,091	1,415	1,739	1,989	2,141	2,293	2,542
	Your spouse at age 60[6]	780	1,012	1,244	1,422	1,531	1,639	1,818
55	Your spouse and one child[3]	1,554	1,998	2,444	2,886	3,096	3,302	3,776
	Your spouse and two children[4]	1,625	2,430	2,941	3,369	3,613	3,855	4,407
	One child only	777	999	1,222	1,443	1,548	1,651	1,888
	Your spouse at NRA[5]	1,037	1,333	1,629	1,924	2,064	2,202	2,517
	Your spouse at age 60[6]	741	953	1,165	1,376	1,476	1,574	1,800

1. Assumes earnings increased at 5 percent annual growth rate from age 22 through 2012.
2. Assumes earnings equal to or greater than the OASDI wage base from age 22 through 2012.
3. Amounts shown also equal to the benefits paid to two children, if no parent survives or surviving parent has substantial earnings.
4. Equals the maximum family benefit.
5. Normal retirement age (66 to 67) depends on year of birth. Amounts payable in 2012. Spouses reaching NRA in the future would receive higher benefits.
6. Amounts payable in 2012. Spouses turning 60 in the future would receive higher benefits.
7. Spouse is assumed to be the same age as the insured.

Note: The accuracy of these estimates depends on actual earnings, which may vary significantly from those shown here.

PV Benefit Stream (1)

$$= \$15{,}648 \times \left(\frac{1-(1.02913)^{-13}}{0.02913} \right) \times \left(\frac{1.02913}{1+(0.06 \div 2)} \right)$$

$$= \$15{,}648 \times 10.69437 \times 0.999155 = \underline{\$167{,}204}$$

PV Benefit Stream (2)

$$= \$15{,}648 \times \left(\frac{1-(1.02913)^{-11}}{0.02913} \right) \times \left(\frac{1.02913}{1+(0.06 \div 2)} \right)$$

$$= \$15{,}648 \times 9.29737 \times 0.999155 = \underline{\$145{,}362}$$

PV Benefit Stream (3)

$$= \$5{,}760 \times \left(\frac{1-(1.02913)^{-9}}{0.02913} \right) \times \left(\frac{1.02913}{1+(0.06 \div 2)} \right)$$

$$= \$5{,}760 \times 7.81779 \times 0.999155 = \underline{\$44{,}992}$$

PV Benefit Stream (1) + (2) + (3)

$$= \$167{,}204 + \$145{,}362 + \$44{,}992 = \underline{\$357{,}558}$$

The present value of Social Security benefits payable to the spouse, Mary in this case, is determined in a similar manner, except that the present value must be adjusted for the fact benefits will not be paid until Mary reaches at least age sixty.[7] This can be accomplished in several ways, but the easiest method is to use a two-step procedure where one first calculates the present value as if the payments were to begin today and then discounts this value at the assumed inflation-adjusted rate of return for the number of years until payments would actually begin. The formula for finding the present value of a future lump sum value of the spouse's benefits is:

Equation 2.2

Present Value of Future Lump Sum (FLS) =

$$\text{FLS} \times \left(\frac{1}{1+i}\right)^n$$

where i is computed using the assumed before-tax discount rate. The before-tax discount rate is used because Social Security benefits generally are paid free of income tax.[8]

Equation 2-1 can be used in the first-step calculation to determine the lump sum value of the benefit stream payable to Mary, assuming that Mary were currently age sixty (or at normal retirement age, depending on which age benefits are assumed to start). The term of the payment period should be Mary's life expectancy at the age payments are assumed to begin. Based on IRS Table V (see Figure 2.3),[9] life expectancy for a sixty-year-old is 24.2 years. Of course, adjustments should probably be made for any known health problems, the family history of longevity, and the fact that females still tend to live longer than males, although the gap is narrowing slightly.[10] Assuming payments will begin at Mary's age sixty, her monthly payments will be $1,244, or $14,928 annually. If the appropriate life expectancy is 24.2 years, the discount rate is 6 percent, and the inflation rate is 3 percent (that is, i = 0.02913), the future lump sum value of Mary's benefit stream when she is age sixty using 2012 dollars is:

Future Lump Sum Value Spouse's Benefit Age 60

$$= \$14,928 \times \left(\frac{1-(1.02913)^{-24.2}}{0.02913}\right) \times \left(\frac{1.02913}{1+0.06 \div 2}\right)$$

Future Lump Sum Value Spouse's Benefit Age 60
$$= \$14,928 \times 17.19404 \times 0.999155 = \$256,456$$

Equation 2-2 is now applied to complete the second step of the calculation. In this case, Mary is currently

age forty-five, so the future Social Security benefits will begin in fifteen years at age sixty. The present value of the future lump sum value of Mary's benefits is computed as follows:

Present Value of Future Lump Sum (FLS)

$$= \$256,456 \times \left(\frac{1}{1.02913}\right)^{15}$$

$$= \$256,456 \times 0.65005 = \underline{\$166,709}$$

The present values of all Social Security benefits to the family are summed to determine the current insurance value of the Social Security benefits. In this case, the present value of the Social Security benefits payable to Mary and the children while the children are young is approximately $360,000, and payable to Mary upon reaching age sixty is approximately $167,000, for a total of about $527,000. The present value of the family support obligation otherwise determined should then be reduced by this amount in deriving the required amount of insurance.

Income Replacement Approach – Step by Step

Figure 2.4 presents a work sheet that summarizes the nine basic steps in using the income replacement approach to determine insurance need.

For example, in the case of the Mike Fox family, the analysis would proceed as follows. Assume Mike's after-income-and-FICA tax take-home pay is $50,000. Assume also that Mike expects his income to grow at 4 percent [about 1 percent more than the rate of inflation, which is assumed to be 3 percent (to be consistent with assumptions regarding Social Security benefits)]. Also assume, that a 2 percent after-tax return in excess of inflation is reasonable, or about 5 percent. In this case, then, the earnings-adjusted discount rate for computing the present value of Mike's future earnings is about 1 percent (5 percent less 4 percent). Further assume Mike's employer provides an insurance benefit equal to one and one-half times Mike's gross pay of $60,000, or $90,000 and that he has $30,000 in marketable assets and cash available to help fund the family's income need. Assume further that Mike's current mortgage balance is $110,000, which he would like paid off in the event of his death and that final death expenses are expected to be about $15,000. Finally, assume about 75 percent of Mike's after-tax income would be necessary to support the family's current standard of living should he die.

Figure 2.3

TABLE V
ONE LIFE-EXPECTED RETURN MULTIPLES

Age	Multiples (Life Expectancy)	Age	Multiples (Life Expectancy)	Age	Multiples (Life Expectancy)
5	76.6	42	40.6	79	10.0
6	75.6	43	39.6	80	9.5
7	74.7	44	38.7	81	8.9
8	73.7	45	37.7	82	8.4
9	72.7	46	36.8	83	7.9
10	71.7	47	35.9	84	7.4
11	70.7	48	34.9	85	6.9
12	69.7	49	34.0	86	6.5
13	68.8	50	33.1	87	6.1
14	67.8	51	32.2	88	5.7
15	66.8	52	31.3	89	5.3
16	65.8	53	30.4	90	5.0
17	64.8	54	29.5	91	4.7
18	63.9	55	28.6	92	4.4
19	62.9	56	27.7	93	4.1
20	61.9	57	26.8	94	3.9
21	60.9	58	25.9	95	3.7
22	59.9	59	25.0	96	3.4
23	59.0	60	24.2	97	3.2
24	58.0	61	23.3	98	3.0
25	57.0	62	22.5	99	2.8
26	56.0	63	21.6	100	2.7
27	55.1	64	20.8	101	2.5
28	54.1	65	20.0	102	2.3
29	53.1	66	19.2	103	2.1
30	52.2	67	18.4	104	1.9
31	51.2	68	17.6	105	1.8
32	50.2	69	16.8	106	1.6
33	49.3	70	16.0	107	1.4
34	48.3	71	15.6	108	1.3
35	47.3	72	14.6	109	1.1
36	46.4	73	13.9	110	1.0
37	45.4	74	13.2	111	.9
38	44.4	75	12.5	112	.8
39	43.5	76	11.9	113	.7
40	42.5	77	11.2	114	.6
41	41.5	78	10.6	115	.5

Figure 2.4

INCOME REPLACEMENT APPROACH WORK SHEET			
Step	Description	Values	
1	PV of future after-tax earnings stream [Equation 2.1]		————
2	Family support ratio		————
3	PV of family support obligation (1 × 2)		————
4	PV of Social Security benefits	————	
5	Other decremental adjustments[1]	————	
6	Total decrements (4 + 5)	————	
7	Net family support obligation (3 – 6)		————
8	Special adjustments[2]	————	
9	Insurance Required (7 – 8)		════

1. Includes insurance already in place on insured plus marketable assets, cash, and other assets such as vested retirement benefits.
2. Such as final expenses, debt repayment, college education funds.

Based on these assumptions and using equation 2-1, the present value of Mike's twenty years of future after-tax earnings is about $892,186, which is entered in Step 1 of the work sheet (see Figure 2.5). Multiplying this present value by the 75 percent family support ratio determines the present value of the family support obligation, which is $669,140. As described above, the present value of the survivorship benefits under Social Security is $527,000. This amount, together with the $90,000 of employer-provided life insurance and $30,000 of available assets, reduces the present value of the family support obligation by $647,000 to just $22,140. When the special funding needs totaling $125,000 are added, the amount of insurance required is determined to be about $147,140. This amount represents just about 2.5 times Mike's current gross income of $60,000.

Needs Analysis

In contrast with the income replacement approach, which is founded on the premise that the insurance need should be based on the income that would be lost if the insured dies, the needs approach estimates the insured's family income needs directly. The typical needs of a family can be divided into two categories.

The first category of needs consists of lump sum cash needs at death, typically including:

- administrative/final expenses;

- estate settlement costs;

- debt liquidation;

- tax liabilities;

- an education fund;

- an emergency fund; and

- any other special funding needs.

The second category of needs consists of multi-period income needs and is comprised of:

- an adjustment period income;

- the surviving spouse's income needs;

- the children's income needs; and

- the spouse's retirement needs.

Figure 2.5

Step	Description	Values	
	INCOME REPLACEMENT APPROACH WORK SHEET: THE MIKE FOX CASE		
1	PV of future after-tax earnings stream [Equation 2.1]		$892.186
2	Family support ratio		0.75
3	PV of family support obligation (1 × 2)		$669,140
4	PV of Social Security benefits	$527,000	
5	Other decremental adjustments[1]	120,000	
6	Total decrements (4 + 5)		(647,000)
7	Net family support obligation (3 – 6)		$22,140
8	Special adjustments[2]		125,000
9	Insurance Required (7 – 8)		$147,140

1. Includes insurance already in place on insured plus marketable assets, cash, and other assets such as vested retirement benefits.
2. Such as final expenses, debt repayment, college education funds.

Four common special needs and the types of policies used to fund those needs are as follows:

- *Mortgage-repayment policy* – Here, all that is needed is the current amount at risk and how long that risk or need will need to be covered.

- *Other major-debt-repayment policies* – These could be for cars or any other type of nonmortgage long-term debt.

- *Education-fund-accumulation policy* – This would be a policy to pay projected education costs for family members, if death occurred prematurely.

- *Estate-tax-liability policy* – On estates below $2,000,000 (in 2007, with living spouse: $4,000,000) there would be little or no estate tax liability. Above these amounts, an estate tax may be due. The purchase of life insurance could obviate the necessity of the surviving spouse selling off assets to pay estate taxes.

The income needs are met from various sources including Social Security (survivor's income), spouse's earnings, annuity payments, employer-provided pension survivor benefits, and investment income. The excess of income needs over the expected income from these sources must be covered by income from reinvesting a lump sum life insurance death benefit or by taking an annuity settlement from the insurance company.

The lump sum required to generate a predetermined monthly income depends on whether or not the capital will be depleted or preserved. Essentially, the decision to preserve some or all of the capital can be viewed as a third category of need or objective—the desire to leave something to heirs, or perhaps to a favorite charity, after the surviving spouse dies.

As a practical matter, the capital necessary to fund the spouse's income needs is often calculated in two ways that provide an upper and lower boundary on the required capital. First, the more conservative approach is to plan to preserve capital. The required capital is then the amount that is sufficient to pay the required cash income from interest on the capital alone. This approach assures income to the surviving spouse regardless of how long the spouse may live and provides an extra margin of security. However, the cost of insurance may exceed the amount that the insured feels is affordable.

The second approach is to assume that both income and capital will provide the required cash income and capital will be entirely consumed over a specified period. In general, the payout period is set equal to or slightly greater than the spouse's remaining life expectancy. If the spouse's remaining life expectancy is long and the assumed interest rate sufficiently high, the difference between the amount necessary if capital is preserved and the amount necessary if capital is depleted is relatively small.

Insurance Needs Analysis Work Sheet

The "Insurance Needs Analysis Work Sheet" shown in Figure 2.6 summarizes the steps in applying this approach. First, current cash needs are estimated and totaled. Then the capital necessary to fund the lifetime income needs of the spouse and children is estimated. Finally, the total value of assets currently available is subtracted from the sum of the current cash needs and the capital necessary to fund the income needs to determine the current surplus or deficit. Additional insurance is required if there is a deficit.

The work sheet calculates the capital necessary to fund the spouse's income needs, both if capital is preserved and if it is consumed over a period equal to or greater than the spouse's remaining life expectancy. Given the prevalence of two-income families, the capital necessary to fund the spouse's income needs should be reduced by the present value of her estimated lifetime earnings, if any.

The interest rate assumption is critical. As discussed earlier in regard to the income replacement approach, the assumed interest rate should be an after-tax interest rate. Also, if the objective is to maintain the family's real inflation-adjusted standard of living, the assumed interest rate should be an inflation-adjusted after-tax interest rate. For example, if inflation is expected to average 4 percent per year and the after-tax rate of return is expected to average 7 percent per year, about a 3 percent interest rate should be used in the work sheet to estimate the required capital.

Because the income needs of the children usually terminate when they leave the home, typically after they complete school, begin their own careers, and start their own families, the capital necessary to fund their income needs is computed assuming that it is depleted, rather than preserved. The children's Social Security benefits may be accounted for either by reducing their required monthly income on the work sheet by their estimated monthly Social Security survivor benefits or by including the present value of their benefits in the section of the work sheet listing the capital assets that are currently available. If there is an objective to provide children with a nest egg or hope chest to start their independent careers, the present value of the desired amount may be included in the current cash needs. Alternatively, the number of years of income funding may be extended beyond the time when the children would normally be expected to leave the home. The work sheet aggregates the income needs of all children into one calculation, but it can be modified to calculate the capital required for each child separately.

Most insurance advisers also recommend funding for an adjustment period income for one to two years. The adjustment period income helps to defray costs that continue until the family is able to adjust to its new situation. For example, the family may be locked into certain obligations of the insured, such as car leases, rents, or health club memberships, which may not terminate until sometime after the insured's death. Also, the confusion and disorientation that often follows the death of a loved one frequently may affect the family's ability to manage its financial affairs. The adjustment income provides an extra income cushion until they can adapt.

Insurance Needs Analysis Case Study

Figure 2.7 shows the work sheet filled out for the Sam Sample family. If Sam were to die today, it is estimated that final expenses would be $20,000, $100,000 would be required to pay off the mortgage, and $24,000 would be required to pay off other debts and taxes ($10,000 + $4,000 + $10,000). It is also assumed, based on the current cost for a private college, that $75,000 would be required today to fund Sam's twelve-year-old son's college education starting in six years. Finally, Sam would also like to set up an emergency fund of $25,000 in the event he dies. Therefore, a total cash need in the event of Sam's death is $244,000.

Based on his family's current lifestyle, Sam estimates that his wife would need $3,500 per month after tax in current dollars to maintain her standard of living if Sam died. Assuming available assets could be invested at an average annual after-tax return (6 percent) that is 3 percent greater than inflation (3 percent), the capital required to provide this level of real inflation-adjusted income indefinitely (that is, by preserving the real purchasing power of the capital) is about $1,403,500. Sam's wife, who is age forty, has a life expectancy of 42.5 years, according to Table V. The capital required to

Figure 2.6

INSURANCE NEEDS ANALYSIS WORK SHEET

Current cash needs:

Final expenses... $_____
Emergency fund .... $_____
Mortgage fund.. $_____
Notes & loans payable.. $_____
Taxes payable .... $_____
Education expenses (NPV) .... $_____
Other .... $_____

Total cash need .... _____

Plus capital needs:	Preserving Capital	Liquidating Capital

For spouse's income:
_____ per month forever at
_____ % annual interest (r) with
_____ % annual growth rate (g) ....$_____ †
_____ years only (n) .... $_____ ‡

Less spouse's wages:
_____ per month with
_____ % annual growth rate for
_____ years till retire .... ($_____)‡

For children's income:
_____ per month for
_____ % annual growth rate for
_____ years .... $_____ ‡

For adjustment period income:
_____ per month for
_____ % annual growth rate for
_____ year(s) .... $_____

Total capital needs.. $_____ $_____

Total needs... $_____ $_____

Less capital assets:

Life insurance .... $_____
Cash, savings, etc. .... $_____
Investment assets .... $_____
Social Security (NPV) .... $_____
Pension benefits.. $_____
Other .... $_____

Total capital assets.. $_____

Surplus or (deficit) .... $_____ $_____

† This value is determined by adding one month's income to the quotient of the monthly income divided by 1/12th of the annual growth-adjusted interest rate or, equivalently: Monthly Income × [1 + (12 ÷ i)]. If I <= 0, there is no solution.
‡ Apply equation 2.1 using 12 times the monthly income as the annual income replacement amount.

Figure 2.7

INSURANCE NEEDS ANALYSIS WORK SHEET

Current cash needs:

Final expenses..	$20,000
Emergency fund	$25,000
Mortgage fund..	$100,000
Notes & loans payable..	$10,000
Taxes payable...	$4,000
Education expenses (NPV)	$75,000
Other	$10,000

Total cash need $244,000

Plus capital needs:	**Preserving Capital**	**Liquidating Capital**

For spouse's income:

$3,500.00	per month forever at		
6.09%	annual interest (r) with		
3.00%	annual growth rate (g)................................	$1,403,500‡	
45	years only (n)		$1,029,336‡

Less spouse's wages:

$1,200.00	per month with	
3.00%	annual growth rate for	
25	years till retire	($250,640)‡

For children's income:

$1,000.00	per month with	
3.00%	annual growth rate for	
12	years	$119,396‡

For adjustment period income:

$1,000.00	per month with	
3.00%	annual growth rate for	
2	year(s)...	$22,952

Total capital needs..	$1,295,208	$921,044

Total needs..	$1,539,208	$1,165,044

Less capital assets:

Life insurance	$200,000
Cash, savings, etc.	$25,000
Investment assets	$200,000
Social Security (NPV)	$100,000
Pension benefits..	$50,000
Other	$25,000

Total capital assets.. $600,000

Surplus or (deficit)	($939,208)	($565,044)

† This value is determined by adding one month's income to the quotient of the monthly income divided by 1/12th of the annual growth-adjusted interest rate or, equivalently: Monthly Income × [1 + (12 ÷ i)]. If I <= 0, there is no solution.

‡ Apply equation 2.1 using 12 times the monthly income as the annual income replacement amount.

provide Sam's wife with an inflation-adjusted after-tax monthly income equivalent to $3,500 in current dollars for forty-five years is less, at about $1,029,000.

Sam's wife works and earns about $1,200 per month after-tax. Assuming that she would continue to work until age sixty-five (for twenty-five years) and her earnings would increase at the rate of inflation, the present value of her income stream is about $250,650. This amount reduces the amount of capital required to fund Sam's wife's income needs. The amount of income currently required to maintain Sam's son's standard of living is about $1,000 per month. Sam wants to provide for his son until he graduates from college, which should occur in twelve years. The capital required to fund this need, once again adjusted for inflation, is about $119,400.

Finally, Sam would like to provide an additional income of about $1,000 per month (adjusted for inflation) for two years to help the family through the adjustment period in the event he dies. He needs about $23,000 to provide this income.

The total capital required to fund the family's income needs is about $1,295,000 if the capital required to fund Sam's wife's income is to be preserved, or $921,000, if it is to be depleted over forty-five years. The difference, $374,000, is significant. The difference in the two approaches is especially striking if it is couched in future value terms. If the capital is liquidated, in forty-five years no capital will remain. If the capital is preserved, and inflation averages 3 percent per year, in forty-five years the capital value will exceed $5.3 million.[11]

The assets available to fund the current cash and income needs total $600,000. Therefore, the insurance need is somewhere between $565,000 and $940,000 depending on whether or not the capital required to fund Sam's wife's income needs is preserved or liquidated. By selecting an intermediate amount, Sam can assure adequate income at least until his wife reaches age eighty-five with a reserve in case she lives longer or an inheritance for Sam's son if she does not survive beyond age eighty-five. The choice will usually depend on the insured's overall objectives and ability to pay insurance premiums.

Static versus Dynamic Analysis

Each of the approaches discussed above is a static analysis that bases the estimate of the required insurance on the needs that must be funded if the insured were to die immediately. But in most cases, the insured will not die immediately. A dynamic analysis looks at how the insurance need is expected to change over time based on current expectations if the insured lives. How the insurance need is expected to change over time may have a strong effect on the most appropriate insurance plan and the selection of the most suitable policies.

The first impression is usually that the insurance need should decline as the insured ages, since the period of the family's income need should be shorter. However, first impressions can be mistaken. For example, Figure 2.8 shows an analysis of Sam's insurance need in six years. All of the cash needs are assumed to grow at about the rate of inflation, 3 percent, except the mortgage fund, notes payable, the education expenses, and the taxes payable. The mortgage is assumed to be paid down from $100,000 to $80,000. The notes payable are assumed to remain the same. The taxes payable are assumed to have been entirely repaid. The education fund that is necessary to fund college expenses immediately is estimated to be $120,000, not $75,000, since it must be increased both for inflation plus the interest that was implicitly assumed would be earned on the education fund had Sam died six years earlier. Therefore, current cash needs increase by $31,670, from $244,000 to $275,670.

The income needs for Sam's wife and son and the adjustment period income are each increased by the assumed 3 percent rate of inflation from $3,500, $1,000, and $1,000, to $4,179, $1,194, and $1,194, respectively. Similarly, Sam's wife's wages are also expected to increase with the rate of inflation from $1,200 to $1,433. In six years, at age 46, Sam's wife's life expectancy will be 36.8 years (from Table V). Adding the 2.5 year margin that was included in the original analysis, the liquidation period is down from forty-five years to 38.3 years. Also, Sam's wife's remaining working career is reduced by six years from twenty-five years to nineteen years. Similarly, the income payout period for Sam's son is reduced by six years from twelve years to six years.

Finally, all of the capital assets available to fund the family's needs are assumed to grow by about 10 percent except the insurance amount and the Social Security benefits. The life insurance is the same on the assumption that Sam had not purchased additional insurance six years earlier. The Social Security benefits are $60,000, or $40,000 less, since the period when Sam's son would receive survivor benefits has been eliminated. The only amount remaining is the present value of Sam's wife's survivor benefit which will not be payable for another

Figure 2.8

INSURANCE NEEDS ANALYSIS WORK SHEET

Current cash needs:

Final expenses... $23,880
Emergency fund $29,850
Mortgage fund.. $80,000
Notes & loans payable.. $10,000
Taxes payable... $0
Education expenses (NPV) $120,000
Other $11,940

Total cash need $275,670

Plus capital needs:	**Preserving Capital**	**Liquidating Capital**

For spouse's income:

$4,179   per month at
6.09%   annual interest (r) with
3.00%   annual growth rate (g)...........................$1,675,779‡
38.3   years only (n) ....$1,132,257‡

Less Spouse's Wages:

$1,433   per month for
19   years till retire..($264,204)‡

For Children's Income:

$1,194   per month for
6   years..$77,584‡

For Adjustment Period Income:
$1,194   per month for
2   year(s)...$27,404

Total Capital Needs..$1,534,563..$991,041

Total Needs   ....$1,810,233..$1,266,311

Less capital assets:
Life Insurance $200,000
Cash, Savings, Etc. $44,300
Investment Assets $354,400
Social Security (NPV) $60,000
Pension Benefits $88,600
Other $44,300

Total capital assets.. $791,500

Surplus or (deficit) ....($1,018,633)...($475,111)

† This value is determined by adding one month's income to the quotient of the monthly income divided by 1/12th of the annual growth-adjusted interest rate or, equivalently: Monthly Income × [1 + (12 ÷i)]. If I <= 0, there is no solution.
‡ Apply equation 2.1 using 12 times the monthly income as the annual income replacement amount.

nineteen years. Therefore, the total assets available to fund the family's needs increases by $191,600, from $600,000 to $791,600.

Based on these quite reasonable assumptions, the required insurance has increased by about $80,000, from approximately $939,000 to $1,019,000, if the objective is to fund Sam's wife's income needs without liquidating capital. However, if the capital liquidation approach is used, the insurance need declines slightly, from approximately $565,000 to about $475,000, or by about $90,000.

As this example demonstrates, it is important to look beyond an immediate snapshot of the insurance need to future needs based upon reasonable assumptions. Beyond this, it is critical to periodically update and review insurance plans, since the future virtually never unfolds exactly as projected. The greater the uncertainty of future events, the more important it is to build flexibility into the insurance plan to handle all eventualities.

BUSINESS INSURANCE NEEDS ANALYSIS

Life insurance is used in business applications to insure key employees, fund buy-sell agreements, and in various compensation arrangements, such as in death-benefit only plans, Section 162 plans, split dollar arrangements, and in qualified pension and nonqualified deferred compensation plans. The insurance need in most of these cases depends on circumstances peculiar to each case, and is beyond the scope of the current discussion. However, the insurance need in most key employee situations is amenable to a systematic and generic type of analysis, which is presented in the following paragraphs.

Key Employee Insurance

In most businesses, especially in smaller firms, one or a few key employees are responsible for a significant portion of the firm's earning capacity. The premature death or disability, or an untimely resignation, of these employees can have a severe impact on the firm's profitability, and may even cause the firm to fail. Noncompete clauses in employment/severance agreements, crosstraining among key employees, and a management philosophy and practice of mentoring subordinates, along with attractive and properly-designed compensation packages, can help to prevent or minimize the

risk of early resignation. Life and disability insurance on key employees is the logical choice to help the firm weather the financial loss of a premature death or serious disability. But the critical question remains—how do you determine the insurable value of the key employee to the firm?

A commonly held maxim of management is that no one is irreplaceable. That is generally true, but it does not mean that replacement is costless and that full value can always be recouped. In any event, the loss of a key employee will generally cause business and management disruptions and will entail a period of adjustment before a new replacement is up to speed and the company can adapt to the new arrangements. A properly designed insurance plan can provide the funds necessary to finance the transition period. Since most companies, and especially smaller firms, do not have unlimited cash resources for insurance premiums, it is critical to have enough, but not too much insurance.

Critique of Ad Hoc Rules of Thumb and Common Key Employee Valuation Approaches

Various ad hoc rules of thumb and approaches have been used to estimate the value of a key employee. These rules, although simple to apply, are conceptually limited. For example, estimating an employee's value as some multiple of salary is entirely arbitrary. What multiple is appropriate? In addition, it takes no account of the timing of cash losses. The effect, in many cases, may not actually appear in revenues until future periods.

Alternatively, a key employee's value is sometimes estimated by capitalizing the corporate earnings attributable to the employee's efforts, skills, knowledge, talents, contacts, sales results, or other attributes. A similar approach is to estimate the percentage reduction in the firm's going concern value that would result from loss of the key employee and to multiply that percentage by the firm's going concern value. One problem with these approaches is that they implicitly or explicitly require a valuation of the firm in order to value key employees. Although key employees are an important component contributing to a firm's value, the relationship is not often clear or direct. And although up-to-date and continuous knowledge of a firm's going-concern value would always be welcome for a host of reasons, it is usually neither easy nor inexpensive to perform such valuations, especially in small closely held businesses.

A second and more basic problem with these approaches is that they implicitly assume the key employee is irreplaceable, and his or her loss is a dead weight and irrecoverable loss to the firm. These approaches tend to overestimate the loss to the firm. In virtually all cases, if there is adequate liquidity to cover the transition period, a replacement can ultimately be found who can fulfill many, if not all, of the functions of the lost key employee and the company's management practices can be adapted over time to compensate for the loss.

Basic Principles of Key Employee Valuation

A conceptually sound approach to key employee valuation should:

- measure the financial loss based on what the employee would have contributed to the future success of the firm;

- adjust the financial consequences for the timing of those lost contributions;

- account for trends in the employee's contributions;

- realize that, in every case, a key employee's contribution to the firm will terminate at some point, either through death, disability, resignation, or retirement; and

- recognize that most, if not all, of the value of the key employee's contribution to the firm can and will be recovered over time, either by hiring and training a replacement, adapting or changing the management practices and functions of other key employees, or some combination.

Although an employee's past contributions are often a major component in determining the employee's present compensation, the cost to the firm of the employee's loss depends on the *future*—on what the employee could be expected to contribute in subsequent years. In this regard, both the timing and trend of these future contributions are critical. The loss of an employee who is essential to the successful close of a major deal is much more costly if the deal is expected to close within the next few months than if it is not expected to close for a year or two. Similarly, the trend is important. It is much more costly to lose a relatively new "rainmaker," who

is still in the process of bringing new accounts within the firm, than to lose the same employee later, after many of those accounts have been acquired and become accustomed to and comfortable with the firm.

One mistake frequently encountered in key employee valuations is the failure to account for the fact that every key employee, sooner or later, for one reason or another, will *terminate* employment with the firm. It is not a question of if the key employee is lost, but when. This is a simple fact of life that every firm must face. And while it is true that without proper planning the loss of a key employee could, in some circumstances, sound the death knell for a firm, it is usually entirely avoidable. If a firm can anticipate and survive a key employee's retirement, it should also be able to plan for and survive the loss as a result of death, disability, or resignation.

Any valuation based on the presumption of a permanent and irrecoverable loss will usually be invalid and overstated. The impact of the loss of a key employee's contributions to the firm will virtually always diminish over time as the firm adjusts its practices and reallocates or replaces lost resources. And although a replacement may not be able to exactly replicate the contributions of the lost employee, over time much of the lost contributions can be recovered through training and experience. In addition, the replacement will frequently bring her own unique talents to the job, adding dimensions that the key employee may have lacked. Therefore, ultimately no permanent or ongoing loss to the firm should result.[12]

Key Employee Valuation Method

Figure 2.9 presents a key employee valuation work sheet that incorporates the principal elements of a complete and systematic method of valuation.[13] The method estimates the difference between the key employee's and a replacement employee's contributions to the firm each year over a transition training period. The present value of the differences is an estimate of the amount of insurance required to carry the firm through the transition period.

The following factors are required inputs:

1. The number of years that would be necessary to locate, hire, train, and develop a replacement for the key employee until the replacement could be expected to match the contributions expected from the key employee. In general,

Figure 2.9

		Year 1	Year 2	Year 3	Year 4	Year 5
	KEY EMPLOYEE VALUATION WORK SHEET					
1	Estimated Total Revenues (I)					
2	% of (1) Attributed to KE (I)					
3	Total of (1) Due to KE (1×2)					
4	KE's Total Compensation (I)					
5	KE's Net Contribution (3-4)					
6	Relative Value of RE (I)					
7	Revenue from RE (3×6)					
8	Total Cost of RE (I)					
9	RE's Net Contribution (7-8)					
10	Loss in Net Contribution (5-9)					
11	Present Value Factor (I)†					
12	PV of Loss (10×11)					
13	Cumulative PV of Loss (Year1 + Year2 +…+ Year5)					

Key:
KE	Key Employee
RE	Replacement Employee
(I)	Input cell
(x#y)	Indicates calculation:
x, y	Row of values
#	Mathematical operator

†Discount Rate: _____ = r

$1/(1+r)^n$

$n = 1,2,3,4,5$

for each year.

this would be expected to take five years or less, but the worksheet could be expanded beyond five years, if necessary.

2. The firm's estimated gross revenues for each year of the transition period assuming the key employee were still with the firm. (Line 1)

3. An estimate of the percentage of gross revenues attributable to activities of the key employee. (Line 2)

    This percentage may be assumed to be equal each year, or it may be varied, depending on the firm's development plans and the key employee's role in those developments.

4. The expected total compensation to the key employee each year over the transition period. (Line 4)

    This may be determined as a percentage of revenues or sales, as might often be the case

with a key salesperson, or as some anticipated combination of salary and bonus, as might often be the case with key executives. This amount should include all compensation, including various employee benefits, such as medical benefits and pension contributions, as well as Social Security payments.

5. The total direct (and indirect) costs of locating, recruiting, hiring, installing, compensating, and training a replacement for each year of the transition period. (Line 8)

    Direct costs, especially in the first year, would include payments for the services of a professional recruiter; advertising; reimbursement of travel, meals, lodging, and local transportation expenses for replacement candidates; moving expenses and the like for the new hire; office outfitting and other possible expenses, such as the cost for a salesperson's automobile; and the similar costs of recruitment for necessary new support positions, such as an administrative assistant to the replacement key employee; as well as the legal fees often associated with negotiating employment contracts with high-level executives and top salespersons. Indirect costs that should not be overlooked are the opportunity cost of management time spent in the recruitment effort as well as the additional burdens placed on remaining key employees and management, both to cover the lost key employee's duties until the replacement employee can fully shoulder the burden and to help train or acclimate the new employee.

6.   An estimate of the contribution the replacement employee could be expected to make each year to the revenues of the firm relative to the contributions projected for the key employee (as a percent). (Line 6)

Virtually nobody can be expected to step in and immediately match the performance of a true key employee. (If it were easy, the employee would not be considered a key or vital contributor to the firm's success.) The transition period generally depends on the qualifications and experience of the specific person hired, which is difficult to estimate before the fact. However, there is usually a tradeoff between the time it takes for the replacement employee to develop her full contributory potential and the initial compensation level of the replacement employee. Trying to attract a person who is extremely well qualified and a better immediate match for the key employee will usually require a premium compensation package and may take more search time, sometimes a year or longer for specialized positions. Thus, it may be more an issue of management preference, than total cost, which route is taken to replace the key employee. If management plans to go the premium replacement route, higher compensation levels (generally even higher than that paid to the key employee) and recruitment expenses should be entered in line 8. Also, correspondingly higher relative performance percentages should be entered in line 6, but perhaps deferred for a year or so to reflect the longer expected time to find the premium replacement. The work sheet can be used to help evaluate the relative benefit or cost of each replacement strategy.

7.   The discount rate for calculating present values. (Bottom of Work Sheet)

The discount rate should reflect the firm's cost of capital or borrowing rate. The rate should be adjusted for the firm's tax rate. Although death benefits will (usually[14]) be tax free, the returns on investment will be subject to tax.

The rest of the work sheet operates as follows. Line 3 computes the total projected revenues attributable to the key employee. Line 5 shows the key employee's net projected contribution to the firm based on the difference between the key employee's compensation and contribution to the firm. The replacement employee's contribution to the firm relative to the contribution of the current key employee is calculated in line 7. The replacement employee's net contribution (plus or minus) is computed in line 9. Line 10 computes the difference between the net contribution of the current key employee and the replacement employee. The discount factors for computing present values should be entered in line 11. The formula for computing each year's discount factor is shown at the bottom of the work sheet. Line 12 computes the present value of each year's loss in net contribution. Finally, line 13 shows the cumulative present value of the loss in net contributions to the firm each year. The value in the last year of the transition period is the present value of the total loss and represents the amount that should be insured.

Figure 2.10 illustrates the use of the key employee valuation method described here. In this case, the firm's plans are such that the key employee's relative contribution is expected to decline somewhat (as indicated by the percentages in line 2) as the firm moves into some new operations. However, as indicated in line 3, the key employee's contribution is still expected to be substantial and growing. It is assumed the relative contribution of a replacement employee will start at only 50 percent of the key employee's contribution, but grow to 100 percent in five years. Although the replacement employee's compensation is expected to be less than the key employee's, the first year expenses of recruitment and placement, together with compensation, are expected to exceed the key employee's compensation. In subsequent years, the replacement employee's compensation is expected to be less than the key employee's, but the replacement employee's net contribution will still remain lower than what the key employee would have contributed. Based on the projected figures, the insurable value of the key employee is about $482,000.

Figure 2.10

		Year 1	Year 2	Year 3	Year 4	Year 5
\multicolumn{7}{c}{**KEY EMPLOYEE VALUATION WORK SHEET**}						
\multicolumn{7}{c}{**(Values expressed in \$1,000s)**}						
1	Estimated Total Revenues (I)	2,200	2,420	2,700	3,100	3,500
2	% of (1) Attributed to KE (I)	0.20	0.19	0.18	0.16	0.15
3	Total of (1) Due to KE (1 × 2)	440.00	459.80	486.00	496.00	525.00
4	KE's Total Compensation (I)	120.00	130.00	140.00	145.00	150.00
5	KE's Net Contribution (3 – 4)	320.00	329.80	346.00	351.00	375.00
6	Relative Value of RE (I)	0.50	0.60	0.70	0.85	1.00
7	Revenue from RE (3 × 6)	220.00	275.88	340.20	421.60	525.00
8	Total Cost of RE (I)	150.00	100.00	110.00	130.0	150.00
9	RE's Net Contribution (7 – 8)	70.00	175.88	230.20	291.60	375.00
10	Loss in Net Contribution (5 – 9)	250.00	153.92	115.80	59.40	0.00
11	Present Value Factor (I)†	0.909091	0.826446	0.751315	0.683013	0.620921
12	PV of Loss (10 × 11)	227.27	127.21	87.00	40.57	0.00
13	Cumulative PV of Loss	227.27	354.48	441.48	482.05	**482.05**
	(Year1 + Year2 +…+ Year5)					

Key:	KE	Key Employee	† Discount Rate: 0.10 = r
	RE	Replacement Employee	
	(I)	Input cell	$1/(1+r)^n$
	(x#y)	Indicates calculation:	
	x, y	Row of values	n = 1,2,3,4,5
	#	Mathematical operator	for each year.

The work sheet may be a useful tool in justifying the desired amount of key employee coverage and convincing the insurer that there is sufficient insurable interest to issue the policy. In addition, it may be helpful in supporting the accumulation of contingency funds in excess of what may otherwise be allowed under the excess accumulated earnings provisions if challenged by the IRS.[15]

ESTATE PRESERVATION AND LIQUIDITY NEEDS ANALYSIS

For large estates, planning to minimize estate taxes and to assure adequate liquidity to pay estate taxes that cannot be avoided is of paramount importance. Planning should consider a host of techniques, including lifetime gifts, optimal use of the marital deduction, various marital and family trust arrangements, and charitable gifts, as well as life insurance. Estate and gift tax planning is beyond the scope of this chapter, but see Chapters 27, 28, and 29 for discussions of federal estate, gift, and generation-skipping tax issues and planning.

CHAPTER ENDNOTES

1. The table was developed by the staff of First National Bank (Citibank).

2. The first part of equation 2-1 is the standard formula for the present value of an annuity with payments at the end of each period (year). The second part of the equation is an adjustment factor to move the payments to the middle of each period (year) rather than the end. The value can be computed easily using a financial calculator.

3. National or industry occupational averages may be misleading when trying to estimate earnings growth for a particular occupation for another reason. In many occupations, especially in the professions and in executive or managerial positions, the normal lifetime profile of any average individual's earnings growth may show greater real growth than the average increase for that occupation as a whole.

4. The amount a spouse will get is a percentage of the deceased's basic Social Security benefit. The percentage depends on age and the type of benefit. Normal Retirement Age (NRA), the age at which full Social Security retirement benefits are generally available, had been sixty-five for many years. However, beginning with people born in 1938 or later, NRA gradually increases until it reaches sixty-seven for people born after 1962. The following chart shows the steps in which the NRA will increase. For more information on widow(er)s benefits, see http://www.ssa.gov/pubs/10084.html.

Year of Birth*	Normal Retirement Age	Age 60 Reduction Months	Monthly % Reduction**
1939 or earlier	65	60	.475
1940	65 and 2 months	62	.460
1941	65 and 4 months	64	.445
1942	65 and 6 months	66	.432
1943	65 and 8 months	68	.419
1944	65 and 10 months	70	.407
1945–1956	66	72	.396
1957	66 and 2 months	74	.385
1958	66 and 4 months	76	.375
1959	66 and 6 months	78	.365
1960	66 and 8 months	80	.356
1961	66 and 10 months	82	.348
1962 and later	67	84	.339

* Persons born on January 1 of any year should refer to the previous year.
** Monthly reduction percentages are approximate due to rounding. The total % reduction for anyone who receives benefits at age sixty is always 28.50.

5. One can download Form SSA-7004 at www.ssa.gov/online/ssa-7004.pdf and file the completed form by mailing it to:

    Social Security Administration
    Wilkes Barre Data Operations Center
    P.O. Box 7004
    Wilkes Barre, PA 18767-7004

    An excellent and concise source of information on Social Security benefits is *Social Security & Medicare Facts*, The National Underwriter Company, published annually.

6. Where the maximum family benefit applies, individual social security benefits are generally reduced proportionately. The three categories here are not shown proportionately in order to facilitate calculation of the present value of the total benefits.

7. The question of whether a surviving spouse should begin taking Social Security benefits at age sixty or later depends on a number of factors. There is a trade-off. Although if payments are started at age sixty, they will be paid longer, the amount is reduced. In general, it is optimal for a normal healthy surviving spouse to begin taking benefits at age sixty, rather than delaying the start to normal retirement age, even though payments are lower, if the appropriate inflation-adjusted discount rate for those future payments is above 3 percent. If the discount rate is below 3 percent, the spouse will be better off waiting to take payments. For a comprehensive discussion of the factors involved in this decision, see "When to Take Early Social Security Benefits,"

Robert J. Doyle, Jr., *The Journal of the American Society of CLU & ChFC*, Vol. XLIV, No. 1 (January, 1990), pp. 30-37.

8. Up to 85 percent of Social Security benefits are taxable under current law if modified taxable income—defined basically as normal taxable income plus tax-exempt bond interest income plus 50 percent of Social Security income—exceeds $34,000 for single taxpayers or $44,000 for married taxpayers.

9. Table V is the unisex annuity life expectancy table described in Treas. Reg. §1.72-9.

10. Based on Table 90CM, the IRS table used for valuing annuities, life estates, and remainders for income, gift, and estate tax purposes, the unisex life expectancy at age sixty is 20.9 years. These values represent a more conservative estimate of life expectancy and, as a result, produce a smaller present value for surviving spouse Social Security benefits. The effect is to increase the amount of insurance needed, all else being equal.

11. In order to provide a level real inflation-adjusted income from interest only, that is, a nominal income that increases at the rate of inflation, the capital value must increase each year by the rate of inflation. By using a 3 percent inflation-adjusted interest rate to compute the required capital, the work sheet implicitly assumes the capital value grows at the rate of inflation. If inflation averages 3 percent per year, the capital value will grow by 3 percent per year. At a 3 percent annual growth rate, a dollar invested today will increase 3.7816 times in forty-five years ($1.03^{45} = 3.7816$). Therefore, after subtracting the first month's interest, which is assumed to be paid in advance, the remaining $1,400,000 should grow to $5.3 million in forty-five years. Of course, the required monthly income will also grow correspondingly to $13,236 ($3,500 × 3.7816), or to $158,827 per year.

    If the after tax inflation-adjusted interest is assumed to be 3 percent and inflation is 3 percent, the after tax rate of return must be 6.09 percent [which is determined by solving for x in the equation for the inflation-adjusted interest rate: $0.03 = (x - 0.03) ÷ (1.03)$]. For example, if $100 is invested to earn an after tax rate of return of 6.09 percent, the total income and principal at the end of the year would be $106.09. If inflation is 3 percent, the real inflation-adjusted end-of-period value is $103 ($106.09 ÷ 1.03). Therefore, the real inflation-adjusted return is 3 percent. If the objective is to provide $3 of real income and inflation is 3 percent, $3.09 must be distributed at the end of the year ($3 × 1.03). After paying the $3.09, the remaining balance is $103. Since inflation is assumed to be 3 percent, the real inflation-adjusted value of the capital remains intact. In other words, since the capital value increases by the rate of inflation each year, the fund is able to distribute 3 percent in real terms each year indefinitely.

12. In those relatively rare cases where the key employee is the firm, for all practical purposes, his or her death would constitute a permanent and irreplaceable loss. In these cases, insurable value could be determined using a human life value income replacement approach as described earlier in this chapter.

13. This work sheet is adapted from one developed by Robert Crowe as presented in *The Financial Services Professional's Guide to the State of the Art*, Chapter 8, (The American College, 1989).

14. Insurance proceeds may be subject to regular income tax if the policy was acquired in a transaction subject to the transfer for value rule, which should generally be avoided, if possible. (See Chapter 25.) Otherwise, life insurance proceeds will generally be

received by the corporation tax free if it has a legitimate insurable interest in the insured. However, corporate-owned life insurance proceeds are an item of tax preference and may be subject to an effective maximum alternative minimum tax rate of 15 percent. See Chapter 24 and Chapter 35 for further discussion of the tax issues with respect to corporate-owned life insurance in general and key employee insurance in particular.

15. Suggested references for further information on the subject of key employee valuation include:

Black, Jr. and Black III, "Insurable Interest and Key Man Life Insurance Benefits," *The CPA Journal*, August 1987, p. 46.

Robert M. Crowe, Time and Money: Using the Time Value Analysis in Financial Planning (Dow Jones-Irwin, 1987).

HOW TO DETERMINE THE RIGHT COMPANY

CHAPTER 3

INTRODUCTION

Until the 1980s and 1990s, most consumers rarely seriously questioned the financial strength of most life insurance companies. Financial strength was usually only a cursory consideration when selecting life, annuity, and health insurance policies. However, the collapses of the junk bond and real estate markets in the 1980's had an unprecedented impact on the financial stability of many insurance companies. Thirty-four life and health insurers with total assets of $1 billion went bust over an eighteen-month period in 1990-91, compared with a mere five with total assets of $41 million in 1981. Others started facing serious financial or solvency problems. Since 1988, TheStreet.com ratings[1] reports that 258 life and health insurance companies have failed.

The number of failures may seem enormous and disturbing, but it is not quite as large or as serious as it might first seem. First, most of these failures have been among small and inadequately capitalized companies that were (correctly) rated very poorly by the rating agencies. Second, the definition of "failed company" deems any company a failure "if at any time it was either (sic): (1) under supervision of an insurance regulatory authority; (2) in the process of rehabilitation; (3) in the process of liquidation; or (4) voluntarily dissolved after disciplinary or other regulatory action by an insurance regulatory authority." Finally, the intercession of the various state regulatory agencies together with the industry-sponsored procedures for guaranteeing solvency and bailouts, when necessary, have continued to prevent any of these failures from leading to any instances where any policyowner or beneficiary failed to receive death benefits.

Selecting the best insurance company involves more than evaluating its financial stability and operations,

although that should be the paramount consideration. Additional factors include product availability and reputation for service and fairness to policyholders.

Because policy illustrations are only as good as the underlying mortality, expense, and investment assumptions, the first and most important step in selecting a life insurance policy is to assess the financial strength of the insurance company. Once one selects a group of strong companies, then one can compare the pricing, illustrations, contracts, and service of the strongest companies.

LIFE INSURANCE COMPANY DUE CARE[2]

To serve the best interests of their clients, as well as to protect themselves from potential malpractice claims, planners should research insurance companies using an analytical methodology similar to the due diligence process required for limited partnership and similar investments. This process should include essentially three steps:

1. An assessment of the company's rating by the major rating services

2. An evaluation of the general characteristics and financial information of the company

3. A review of recent trends for various "indicative" tests of profitability, leverage, and liquidity

In the past, a rating of A+ or A from A.M. Best or a similar rating from one of the other rating agencies was usually considered satisfactory evidence of a company's financial strength. However, because many companies are not rated by these agencies and recent history has shown that even A rated ("Excellent") companies have faced financial difficulties, relying on the company's rating alone is insufficient.[3]

Company Rating Services

For some years, the A.M. Best Company was the only player in the life insurance company rating business. Four other major financial rating companies now provide a similar service—Moody's, Standard & Poor's, Fitch, and Weiss Ratings. Each of these companies provide extensive reports on company operations and related statistics as well as letter rating classifications. In addition, the National Association of Insurance Commissioners (NAIC) has developed the Insurance Regulatory Information System (IRIS) to assist state insurance departments in overseeing the financial condition of insurance companies.

A.M. Best

The A.M. Best Company has been rating life insurance companies for over one hundred years and provides full ratings for the largest number of insurance companies among the rating agencies. It charges a relatively low fee for a company to be included in its rating service. Perhaps the most important of Best's publications for assessing the financial soundness of an insurance company is *Best's Insurance Reports – Life/Health*, which provides detailed statistical reports on the financial position, history, and operating results of life insurance companies. The *Best Insurance Reports* are now available online via *BestLink* The 2012 Life/Health Edition of the *Best Insurance Reports* contains approximately 2,300 insurance companies, representing virtually all active insurers operating in the United States. The 2012 Edition contains Canadian life companies and reports on United States, European, and Canadian Branches.

Best's Insurance Reports provides one-year assessments of each company's financial situation and Best's letter credit ratings. The objective of Best's rating system is to provide an opinion concerning a company's relative financial strength as well as the company's ability to meet its contractual obligations by reviewing factors that can impact the company's performance. The letter ratings are intended to categorize each company with respect to its claims-paying ability. The letter ratings range from A++ to F. Some companies are not rated

because of their relative newness in the market. A listing of the rating categories is presented in Figure 3.1.

In addition, A.M. Best uses several rating modifiers, including:

- (g) – group rating

- (p) – pooled rating

- (r) – reinsured rating

- (u) – under review

Companies that are not assigned ratings by Best are given one of five "Not Rated" (NR) designations:

- NR-1 – insufficient data

- NR-2 – insufficient size or operating experience

- NR-3 – rating procedure is inapplicable

- NR-4 – company request

- NR-5 – not formally followed

As a first level of review, planners should favor companies that have received at least an A+ rating for a number of years (e.g., ten years). Traditionally, many commentators have recommended avoiding companies with a ranking lower than A.

Best also ranks companies according to financial size categories (FSC) from I through XV. This designation is based on the company's size as determined by capital, surplus, and conditional reserve funds ranging from under $1 million to $2,000 million and above. Although the larger companies do not necessarily have the best products, they may be more capable of weathering adverse mortality experience, market changes, and other financial or economic fluctuations than smaller companies.

Moody's

Moody's Investors Service assigns "financial strength ratings" to life insurance companies that range from Aaa (the highest) to C (the lowest). A listing of Moody's rating categories is included in Figure 3.1. In rating life insurers on a stand-alone basis, Moody's focuses on both qualitative and quantitative characteristics in the following areas:

Business Profile	Financial Profile
Factor 1: Market Position and Brand Factor	Factor 4: Asset Quality
	Factor 5: Capital Adequacy
Factor 2: Distribution Factor	Factor 6: Profitability
Factor 3: Product Focus and Diversification Factor	Factor 7: Liquidity and ALM
	Factor 8: Financial Flexibility

The fee Moody's charges a company to be included in its rating service can be substantial. As a result of the relatively high rating fees, Moody's rates a limited, self-selected universe of companies that would probably not choose to be rated if they did not expect high ratings. Consequently, almost no companies are rated lower than Ba2. Differences in the numerical ranking order of Best's and Moody's (e.g., the highest ranking from one company versus the third highest ranking from another) should be a red flag indicating that the company's financials should be given especially close scrutiny.

Fitch Ratings

In 2006, Fitch Ratings introduced a new rating methodology supporting the new insurance capital model they call Prism. "Fitch believes that the knowledge it has gained in developing the Prism model gives it an advantage in interpreting insurers' own capital models, which will allow the agency to better incorporate in-house models into its rating conclusions, alongside Prism."[4]

Fitch's Insurer Financial Strength (IFS) Rating provides an assessment of the financial strength of an insurance organization. The IFS Rating is assigned to the insurance company's policyholder obligations, including assumed reinsurance obligations and contract holder obligations, such as guaranteed investment contracts. The IFS Rating reflects both the ability of the insurer to meet these obligations on a timely basis, and expected recoveries received by claimants in the event the insurer stops making payments or payments are interrupted, due to either the failure of the insurer or some form of regulatory intervention. In the context of the IFS Rating, the timeliness of payments is considered relative to both contract and/or policy terms but also recognizes the possibility of reasonable delays caused by circumstances common to the insurance industry, including claims reviews, fraud investigations and coverage disputes.

The IFS Rating does not encompass policyholder obligations residing in separate accounts, unit-linked products or segregated funds, for which the policyholder bears investment or other risks. However, any guarantees provided to the policyholder with respect to such obligations are included in the IFS Rating.

Expected recoveries are based on the agency's assessments of the sufficiency of an insurance company's assets to fund policyholder obligations, in a scenario in which payments have ceased or been interrupted. Accordingly, expected recoveries exclude the impact of recoveries obtained from any government sponsored guaranty or policyholder protection funds. Expected recoveries also exclude the impact of collateralization or security, such as letters of credit or trusteed assets, supporting select reinsurance obligations.

The IFS Rating does not address the quality of an insurer's claims handling services or the relative value of products sold.

Fitch historically categorizes companies from AAA (the highest rating) to D (the lowest rating). Figure 3.1 lists their rating categories. Similar to Moody's, Fitch charges insurance companies substantial fees to be included in their rating service. But if a relative ranking differs from the ranking provided by Best's or Moody's, it is an indication that the planner should look more closely at other indicators of the company's financial condition.

Standard & Poor's

As of May 2007, Standard and Poor's Corporation updated the way it assesses the capital adequacy of insurance companies worldwide. With all the charges having been reviewed and updated there has been some impact to the model results on capital adequacy. The materiality of these changes depend on the risk profile of the company in question and how well it seeks to manage its risks relative to its capital.

Similar to Moody's and Fitch, S&P charges companies substantial fees to be included in their claims-paying ability rating service. S&P rates companies from AAA (highest) to R (lowest). Figure 3.1 lists S&P's rating categories.

As with both Moody's and Fitch's ratings, it appears that basically only the better companies are willing to pay the substantial fee to be included in S&P's rating

Figure 3.1

RATING CATEGORIES USED BY BEST, S&P, MOODY'S, D&P, AND WEISS

Ratings				
Best	**S&P**	**Moody's**	**Fitch**	**Weiss**
A++	AAA	Aaa	AAA	A+
A+	AA+	Aa1	AA+	A
A	AA	Aa2	AA	A-
A-	AA-	Aa3	AA-	B+
B++	A+	A1	A+	B
B+	A	A2	A	B-
B	A-	A3	A-	C+
B-	BBB+	Baa1	BBB+	C
C++	BBB	Baa2	BBB	C-
C+	BBB-	Baa3	BBB-	D+
C	BB+	Ba1	BB+	D
C-	BB	Ba2	BB	D-
D	BB-	Ba3	BB-	E+
E	B+	B1	B+	E
F	B	B2	B	E-
S	B-	B3	B-	F
	CCC+	Caa1	CCC+	
	CCC	Caa2	CCC	
	CCC-	Caa3	CCC-	
	CC	Ca	CC	
	C	C	C	
	D		DDD	
			DD	
			D	

listings. The relatively high ratings may also reflect the fact that companies are permitted to withdraw from the S&P listing if they find S&P's rating unacceptable.

In addition, S&P provides a system of "qualified solvency ratings," its "pi (for "public information") ratings for insurance companies. In contrast with the claims paying ability rating service that requires the cooperation of the insurance company's management and access to proprietary company information, the "pi" rating is a mechanical rating system based solely on public information from financial statements filed with state regulators. Qualified solvency ratings are issued for each company that is in the NAIC data base of public filings for insurance companies and that does not have an S&P claims paying ability rating.

The qualified solvency rating system was developed in order to provide some financial stability rankings to the public for companies that do not choose to pay to be listed in the claims-paying ability rating service. Companies are assigned to one of three broad categories:

- BBBq – Above average

- BBq – Average

- Bq – Below average

Although S&P admits that their assessments are limited by the lack of the "inside" information they use to make their claims paying ability ratings, they consider insurers rated BBBq to be candidates for claims-paying ability ratings in the secure range. Some insurers rated BBq may qualify for secure claims-paying ability ratings while insurers rated Bq are unlikely to be viewed as secure.

Weiss Ratings[5]

Weiss Ratings has its own proprietary rating system that tracks the financial safety of approximately 875 U.S. life and annuity insurance companies (about 1700, including health insurers) each and every quarter, which, in contrast with the other services, is almost exclusively dependent on publicly available information collected by the National Association of Insurance Commissioners (NAIC), and supplemented by data Weiss collects from the insurance companies themselves.

Weiss Ratings are assigned for life, health, and annuity insurance companies based on a complex analysis of hundreds of factors that are synthesized into a series of indexes: capitalization, investment safety, profitability, liquidity, and stability. These indexes are then used to arrive at a letter grade rating. A good rating requires consistency across all indexes. A weak score on any one index can result in a low rating, as insolvency can be caused by any one of a number of factors, such as inadequate capital, unpredictable claims experience, poor liquidity, speculative investments, inadequate reserving, or consistent operating losses.

The primary components of the Weiss Financial Strength Rating are as follows:

- **Capitalization Index** gauges capital adequacy in terms of each insurer's ability to handle a variety of business and economic scenarios as they may impact investment performance, claims experience, persistency, and market position. The index combines two Risk-Adjusted Capital ratios as well as a leverage test that examines pricing risk.

- **Investment Safety Index** measures the exposure of the company's investment portfolio to loss of principal and/or income due to default and market risks. Each investment area is rated by a factor that takes into consideration both quality and liquidity. This factor is measured as a separate index only for life, health, and annuity insurers.

- **Profitability Index** measures the soundness of the company's operations and the contribution of profits to the company's financial strength. The profitability index is a composite of five subfactors: 1) gain or loss on operations; 2) consistency of operating results; 3) impact of operating results on surplus; 4) adequacy of investment income as compared to the needs of policy reserves (L&H companies only); and 5) expenses in relation to industry norms for the types of policies that the company offers.

- **Liquidity Index** values a company's ability to raise the necessary cash to settle claims and honor cash withdrawal obligations. We model various cash flow scenarios, applying liquidity tests to determine how the company might fare in the event of an unexpected spike in claims and/or a run on policy surrenders.

- **Stability Index** integrates a number of subfactors that affect consistency (or lack thereof) in maintaining financial strength over time. These subfactors will vary depending on the type of insurance company being evaluated but may include such things as: 1) risk diversification in terms of company size, group size, number of policies in force, types of policies written, and use of reinsurance; 2) deterioration of operations as reported in critical asset, liability, income and expense items, such as surrender rates and premium volume; 3) years in operation; 4) former problem areas where, despite recent improvement, the company has yet to establish a record of stable performance over a suitable period of time; 5) a substantial shift in the company's operations; 6) potential instabilities such as reinsurance quality, asset/

liability matching, and sources of capital; and 7) relationships with holding companies and affiliates.

Unique to Weiss's statistical analysis is a measure of how well each insurer would fare, given their financial position today, in "average" and "severe" recessions. Companies with considerable liquidity and low-risk investments are rated higher than companies with less liquidity or less secure investments that might have to drop a weak product line or upgrade the quality of financial assets to weather a financial crisis. Figure 3.1 lists Weiss' rating categories.

In general, the Weiss ratings have been much more severe than those of the other rating services. They have tended to rate insurers lower, sometimes much more so, than their competitors. Weiss ratings tend to look like a typical academic bell curve. Only a small portion earns an A or B rating, reflecting "excellent" or "good" financial health. The largest portion of the companies rated fall into the C (average/fair) range. Unlike the same grade from the other rating services, a C from Weiss may not be that bad a grade. The last portion of companies rated get D (weak), E (very weak), or F (failed) grades. The companies that get a B+ or better grade earn a spot on Weiss' list of companies that are recommended for safety.

Given Weiss's much more conservative ratings compared to the ratings given by the other rating services, it would seem that companies with high ratings from Weiss are the most secure companies. However, Weiss uses less information in making its rankings than the other services. In addition, it does not consider the quality and history of management to avoid financial crisis when overall economic conditions turn sour.

Reliability of Ratings

Critics have questioned the reliability and predictive power of insurance company ratings. Since company obligations are long-term, the question naturally arises, do insurance company ratings predict solvency or indicate relative financial strength over the long-term horizons that most policyowners and annuitants are concerned with? Since policy surrenders within the first few years of ownership may be costly (especially for annuity contracts), and surrenders and access to cash values and loans may be severely restricted if a company becomes insolvent or is placed under state supervision, insurance consumers are not likely to view ratings that downgrade a company one or two years before failure as an adequate warning.

Dr. Lee Slavutin did a study assessing the likelihood of an insurer's failure in five, ten, or fifteen years, given its A.M. Best rating.[6] The study is based on an historical analysis of company failures and Best ratings since 1978. According to Moody's, their corporate bond ratings and insurance financial strength ratings are intended to be comparable. Consequently, as a basis for comparison, Dr. Slavutin's study contrasts the predictive power of Best's insurance ratings with the predictive power of comparable bond ratings issued by Moody's and S&P. The highlights of Slavutin's study follow.

Company Failure Rates in Relation to A.M. Best's Ratings Classifications

Figure 3.2 presents the proportions of all companies rated by A.M. Best in categories A+ through C in the years 1978 through 1981 that have failed within five to thirteen years of receiving the indicated rating.

The figure shows virtually no correlation between insurers' failure rates and Best's ratings for failures that occur within five years of Best's rating. In other words, Best's ratings have had little value in predicting which companies may fail within five years of receiving the rating. However, the overall insurer failure rate within five years of rating for all rated insurers was quite low, less than 2 percent for every rating category and less than 1 percent for all rating categories combined. In addition, the five-year failure rate for companies rated A+ was only about three per thousand.

The correlation is significant between Best's ratings and insurer failures within ten years and even more so for failures within thirteen years. Failure rates progressively increased for each lower rating category. In other words, Best's ratings have had predictive power in identifying the companies with a higher risk of failure over longer periods. However, insurance consumers may consider failure rates of 1.3 percent within ten years and 3.3 percent within thirteen years as unacceptably high for insurers who received Best's highest rating at that time (A+). The substantial increase in the

Figure 3.2

	5-yr. failure rate (%)		10-yr. failure rate (%)		13-yr. failure rate[2] (%)	
Best's Rating	**by class[3]**	**cumulative[4]**	**by class[3]**	**cumulative[4]**	**by class[3]**	**cumulative[4]**
A+	0.3	0.3	1.3	1.3	3.3	3.3
A	1.4	0.9	3.0	2.2	3.7	3.5
B+	0.4	0.8	3.4	2.5	6.0	4.2
B	1.1	0.8	6.4	3.0	10.5	4.9
C+	1.9	0.9	8.9	3.5	11.3	5.5
C	1.0	0.9	19.6	3.9	23.1	6.0

A.M. BEST RATINGS AND COMPANY FAILURE RATES[1] FOR COMPANIES RATED IN 1978-1981

1. The average percentages of rated companies that failed.
2. The 13-yr. failure rate columns include only companies rated in 1978.
3. The "by class" columns show failure rates for each rating category. For example, 3.0 percent of the companies rated A in 1978 through 1981 failed within 10 years.
4. The "cumulative" columns show that aggregate or cumulative failure rates for all companies in the indicated rating category and all higher-rated categories. For example, 2.5 percent of all companies rated B+ or better in 1978 through 1981 failed within 10 years.

The "cumulative" columns show that aggregate or cumulative failure rates for all companies in the indicated rating category and all higher-rated categories. For example, 2.5 percent of all companies rated B+ or better in 1978 through 1981 failed within 10 years.

thirteen-year failure rates over the ten-year failures is largely attributable to the recent upswing in the number of failing companies. Although the difference in failure rates within ten years between A+ (1.3 percent) and A (3.0 percent) rated companies was significant, the difference diminished considerably for failure rates within thirteen years (3.3 percent and 3.5 percent for A+ and A, respectively).

A.M. Best's Insurance Ratings Compared with Moody's and S&P's Bond Ratings:

In the absence of sufficient data to evaluate Moody's and S&P's insurance ratings, Slavutin compared insurer failure rates for each of Best's rating categories with bond default rates for comparable bond rating categories for Moody's and S&P. The rationale for this procedure was that "both Moody's and S&P's ratings have been shown to discriminate between 'investment-grade' and 'speculative' bonds and therefore serve as a model of a 'successful' rating system."[7] In addition, according to Moody's, they intend that their corporate bond and insurer ratings should be comparable. Figure 3.3 shows the results of this comparison of insurer failures

and bond defaults within ten years of receiving their respective ratings.

This figure shows that the ten-year insurer failure rate for insurers with Best's highest A+ rating (1.3 percent at ten years) is comparable to the default rate of bonds with Moody's highest bond rating of Aaa (1.1 percent at ten years), but higher than the S&P's AAA default rate of 0 percent. The A ("Excellent") and B+ ("Very Good") Best's ratings show significantly higher failure rates for insurers than the default rates on bonds rated comparably by Moody's and S&P. For example, 3 percent of the companies A.M. Best rated as "A" failed within ten years, but only 1 percent of the bonds rated comparably by Moody's defaulted. This suggests that the A rating is actually weaker than Best claims it to be.

Lack of Discrimination in Ratings for Large Insurer:

Slavutin also showed that Best may award the A+ rating to insurers more easily than S&P, Moody's, and Duff & Phelps (now Fitch). He used a weighting scheme to rank the ratings for the major GIC issuers. The weighting scheme gives a progressively higher

Figure 3.3

	Best's	Moody's		S&P
Class[1]	By Class[2]	Average[3]	Aggregate[4]	Aggregate 1971-1986[5]
1	1.3	1.1	1.0	0.0
2	3.0	1.0	1.4	0.2
3	3.4	2.0	1.8	0.3
4	6.4	4.7	4.4	2.5
5	8.9	17.2	16.1	6.3
6	19.6	27.8	31.6	32.2

10-YEAR INSURER FAILURE RATES AND 10-YEAR CORPORATE BOND DEFAULTS

1. Classes 1-6 correspond, each respectively to Best's ratings A+, A, B+, B, C+, C; Moody's ratings Aaa, Aa, A, Baa, Ba, B; S&P's ratings AAA, AA, A, BBB, BB, B.
2. From Figure 3.3.
3. Average cumulative 10-year default rates [for bonds rated by Moody's] in 1978, 1979, 1980, and 1981.
4. Average cumulative default rates [for bonds rated by Moody's] in the years 1971 through 1990.
5. Adjusted cumulative mortality rates by original S&P bond rating covering issues from 1971-1986.

Source: Based on tables found in Slavutin, "Life Insurance Company Ratings – How Reliable is A.M. Best?", *Financial and Estate Planning*, CCH, Inc., August, 1991, at p. 24,997.

numerical score for each lower rating. The weighted-average ratings were as follows:

Rater	Weighted Score	Average Rating
Best's	1.07	A+
S&P	2.27	AA+
D&P	2.67	AA
Moody's	3.38	Aa2

In other words, for this group of insurance companies, the average rating given by Best was its top rating whereas the average rating given by Moody's was its third highest rating. This suggests that Moody's ratings are more conservative. Slavutin similarly compared the rating services based on ratings of 59 life insurance companies published in the April 1991 issue of *The Insurance Forum*.[8] The scores were as follows:

Rater	Weighted Score
Best's	1.41
S&P	2.66
Moody's	3.32

Once again, both S&P and Moody's appear to rate companies more conservatively than Best, with Moody's being the most conservative of all.

Recommendations

Based on his analysis, Slavutin makes the following recommendations for selecting a strong insurance company:[9]

1. The A.M. Best rating system should be used in conjunction with the other major rating agencies.

2. Look only at insurers whose A. M. Best rating is A+ for at least ten consecutive years—and to be even safer, for every year since the letter ratings began in 1976—together with the strongest policyholder recommendation ("most favorable" operating results and "most substantial" margins for contingencies) in 1975.

3. Avoid insurers rated A+ (contingent), A, or lower by A.M. Best.

4. The insurer should be rated by A.M. Best and at least two out of three of the other major rating agencies.

5. Look for a rating of AAA or AA with S&P and/or Fitch.

6. Look for a rating of Aaa or Aa with Moody's.

7. Avoid companies on the NAIC watchlist with four or more IRIS ratios outside the "usual" ranges.

8. Use multiple insurers when buying large amounts of insurance to diversify and spread risk.

LIFE INSURANCE COMPANY DUE CARE CHECKLIST

Figure 3.4 presents a checklist that planners may use to perform the life insurance company due diligence process.[10] The form begins with basic information regarding the name, address, and phone number of the company, its ratings by the various rating services, its size, and age. Clearly, if a company does not have sufficiently high ratings, the process is complete. What follows is a discussion of some key items on the checklist.

Company Size and Age

The size and age of the company may be important if a history of growth and survival are indications of a company's likelihood of surviving the future decades over which policies purchased today must be secured. While there is no direct relationship between size and stability, large, well established companies are likely to weather adverse trends more successfully than smaller and newer, less well established companies.

Part 1: Company Financial Information

Beyond the ratings, company size, and age, the financial issues raised on the checklist should help planners to focus on other important financial variables.

Percent of Premium That Is Individual Life Premium

The percentage of the company's total premium that is individual life premium may be important for several reasons. First, if life insurance is not the largest segment

Figure 3.4

LIFE INSURANCE COMPANY DUE CARE CHECKLIST

COMPANY: ADDRESS: TELEPHONE	RATING: COMPANY SIZE: COMPANY AGE:	Best S&P Fitch Moody

PART 1: FINANCIAL INFORMATION

1. Percent of total premium which is individual life premium:
2. Investments (percent of total assets with comments)
   - (a) Bonds:
   - (b) Stocks:
   - (c) Mortgages:
   - (d) Real estate:
   - (e) Short term (cash):
   - (f) Policy loans:
   - (g) Other:
3. Investment yield comments:
4. Separate account comments (if applicable):
5. Company history (stability, growth, unusual comments):
6. Management and operations
   - (a) Mutual/Stock:
   - (b) Management experience:
   - (c) Participating/Nonparticipating/Both:
7. Operating ratios
   - (a) Lapse ratio and trend
   - (b) Average policy size issued:
   - (c) Average ordinary premium/thousand:
   - (d) Renewal expense ratios   Trends:
8. Operating comments
   - (a) Net yield:
   - (b) Reserves:
   - (c) Expenses: Comments:
   - (d) Mortality:
   - (e) Lapses:
   - (f) Policy loans:
   - (g) Dividends:
9. Business trends
   - (a) New business issued:
   - (b) Insurance in force:
   - (c) Company development:

	Increasing	Level	Decreasing

PART 2: TRENDS

FROM: TO: TESTS	TREND ADJUSTMENTS	MIN.	NORM.	MAX.

1. Profitability
   (a) Return on equity:
   (b) Change in capital and surplus:
2. Leverage
   (a) Change in net premiums written:
   (b) Net premiums written to capital and surplus:
   (c) Surplus relief:
   (d) Insurance exposure to capital and surplus:
3. Liquidity
   (a) Current liquidity:
   (b) Affiliated investments to capital and surplus:				

of the company's business, the company may become distracted and place more emphasis on its other lines, such as health insurance, to the detriment of life insurance policyholders.

Average Policy Size

Another factor is the average policy size issued by the company. Statistics show that larger policies, which are purchased by more affluent people as part of estate or business continuation planning, lapse less frequently than smaller policies. Since the first year commission and the cost of putting a policy on the books are a large portion of the total expenses associated with a policy, companies with longer persistency tend to have lower average expenses than companies with shorter persistency. Keep in mind that average policy size and company size are not related. For example, the two largest insurers, Prudential and Metropolitan, have the lowest average policy sizes among the ten largest insurers.

Quality of Investment Assets

The quality and composition of the underlying assets is the key to the potential long-run performance and financial stability of the company. The most critical categories of assets are bonds, mortgages, real estate, and policy loans. Many insurers that have faced financial difficulties have had a large portion of their portfolio invested in junk (below investment grade) bonds and/or have had large portions invested in nonperforming real estate or mortgages that are in arrears. Each of the rating services lists company assets by category and investment grade. Avoid companies whose portfolio is heavily invested in junk bonds.

Also, companies with a shorter weighted average bond maturity are more liquid than those with longer bond maturities. All else being equal, shorter average maturities are considered less risky than longer maturities.

Assessing the quality of a company's real estate and mortgage investments is difficult; planners should be wary of insurers whose real estate and mortgage holdings exceed industry averages.

Policy loans are typically relatively low yielding investments, especially if a large portion of the loans

are attributable to older policies with fixed loan rates of 5 percent to 8 percent. Therefore, if policy loans represent a relatively large proportion of the company's portfolio, the overall performance of the portfolio may suffer. Also, because policy loan interest is generally no longer tax deductible, this may tend to increase the lapse ratio and overall expenses.

The following table showing the asset distribution of U.S. life insurers in 2010 may serve as a helpful guideline when evaluating an individual company's investment asset mix.

Distribution of Life Insurer Assets, by Account Type All U.S. Insurers (2015)

Asset	Percentage of Portfolio		
	General Account	Separate Accounts	Combined
Corporate Bonds	48.4	7.9	33.2
Government Bonds	10.6	2.8	7.7
Mortgage-Backed Bonds	11.1	4.4	8.6
Mortgages	10.3	0.9	6.7
Stocks	2.2	78.4	30.9
Real Estate	0.6	0.8	0.7
Policy Loans	3.2	0.2	2.1
Short-Term Investments	1.5	0.8	1.2
Cash	1.5	0.8	0.9
Misc. Other (excl. cash)	10.9	3.2	8.0

Source: The American Council of Life Insurance, *Life Insurance Fact Book* (2016), Chapter 2: Assets, Table 2.1, p. 11.

Investment Yield

The return on an insurer's general portfolio is the principal source of funds supporting its dividends on participating policies and the basis for interest credited to interest sensitive and Universal Life (UL) policies. Planners should compare the portfolio yield to the interest rate assumed in the dividend projections on participating policies or the quoted current interest rate for UL policies. If the rate assumed for dividend scales for par policies or the current interest rate for UL policies exceeds the portfolio rate, the probability that the company can support the projected dividends for par policies or actually credit interest on UL policies at the current rate in future years is questionable.

As a standard for comparison, the following table shows the net rate of investment income for United States life insurance companies (before federal income taxes) for recent years.

Net Rate of Return for U.S. Life Insurance Companies (Before Federal Income Tax)

Percentage Return

Year	Total Assets	General Account Only
1985	9.63	9.87
1986	9.35	9.64
1987	9.10	9.39
1988	9.03	9.41
1989	9.10	9.47
1990	8.89	9.31
1991	8.63	9.09
1992	8.08	8.58
1993	7.52	8.04
1994	7.14	7.63
1995	7.41	7.90
1996	7.25	7.75
1997	7.35	7.86
1998	6.95	7.58
1999	6.71	7.49
2000	7.05	7.40
2001	6.31	7.13
2002	5.38	6.64
2003‡	5.03	6.17
2004‡	4.80	5.93
2005‡	4.90	5.88
2006‡	5.35	5.95
2007‡	5.71	6.01
2008‡	5.70	5.63
2009‡	4.60	5.25
2010‡	4.33	5.37
2011‡	4.35	5.29
2012‡	4.25	5.07
2013‡	4.20	5.09
2014‡	4.61	5.91
2015‡	4.81	4.91

Source: The American Council of Life Insurance, *Life Insurance Fact Book* (2016), Chapter 4: Income, Table 4.13, p. 45.
‡ Includes fraternal benefit societies.

Separate Accounts

The separate account item only applies if a variable life, variable annuity, or variable universal life product is being evaluated. By law, variable products must be kept in separate accounts. Planners should inspect several key items. The percentage of the company's total assets in separate accounts indicates how important this type of product is within the company's overall product offerings. The breakdown between stocks, bonds, real estate, and other assets will indicate the overall risk level of the separate account portfolio and whether or not it meets the potential policyowner's investment objectives. Planners should assess the quality of investment assets of the separate account in the same way they would when evaluating a company's general portfolio when considering nonvariable policies. The liabilities and payments to surplus accounts indicate the level of charges applied against the funds. The account's net investment income for the current and recent years should be compared with net investment income on separate accounts from competing companies. Also, disbursements for management fees, changes in reserves, and credited income to contract holders should be compared with similar types of disbursements from other companies' separate accounts.

Company history, management and operations – These sections of the checklist can be used to document and compare various items related to company history and management. When was the company founded? Is it a stock or mutual company; has it changed its status, and if so why? Is it a subsidiary of another company? Have there been recent changes in management and, if so, why? Has it shown better than average growth and stability of growth? How does its size compare industry wide? How are its products distributed, and what is the size of its agent/broker field force? In which states is the company licensed to do business? If it is not admitted to do business in New York, is it to avoid the generally stricter regulatory requirements of that state? What are the company's most important product lines and the proportion of its business in each line?

Operating Ratios

The lapse ratio tells how many ordinary policies are lapsing annually. As a general rule of thumb, planners should look for companies with lapse ratios less than 11 percent and renewal persistencies greater than 87 percent.

Greater than average lapse ratios will usually mean higher than average expenses and may mean less than average service to policyowners. In extreme cases, it may suggest that policyowners are being "churned," that is, being systematically encouraged by agents to surrender policies in force for new policies (on which, the agent receives new, high first-year commissions). The trend in lapses should be decreasing if interest rates are declining since it should be difficult for the company's policyowners to find higher rates with new policies. The trend in lapses relative to the industry in general may offer a clue to policyowners' satisfaction and the overall quality of the company's book of business.

As discussed above, the expense of issuing policies generally decreases as the policy size increases and larger policies have tended to experience lower lapse rates than smaller policies. Therefore, all else being equal, it is generally considered better to buy policies with companies with larger average policies.

The average ordinary premium per thousand dollars of coverage generally should have declined in recent years. If premiums have risen, it probably means the company has issued more substandard or rated policies or has had adverse mortality experience.

Renewal expenses have been declining as a percentage of premiums on an industry-wide basis. If a company's renewal expense ratio is not declining in a similar manner it may indicate poor management of expenses or other cost control problems.

Operating Comments

Planners should compare the company's net yield with the industry-wide average and look for suitable reasons why the company's net yield may be higher or lower than the norm. Higher than average net yield may be attributable to better than average investment management and control of investment expenses; it could also mean higher than average risk in the company's portfolio. Analogously, lower than average net yields may indicate poor investment management and control of investment expenses. It could also mean the company has invested its portfolio more conservatively, and safely, than the industry average.

Reserves represent the security, or set-aside, required to pay the benefits promised from the company's policies. Surrender values are related to reserves in that the reserves represent the claim against the assets by policyowners who discontinue their policies. Most simply, but somewhat incompletely stated, the statutory reserve is the amount that, together with future net premiums and interest, will be sufficient, according to certain valuation assumptions, to pay future claims.

Companies may use one of several valuation methods to compute reserves. The net level premium method is generally considered the strongest valuation method,

but companies have significant latitude in the interest rates and mortality tables they use for valuation. In addition, companies that are growing swiftly (which may be an indication of strength), may have a "capacity" problem (since new policies require increases in reserves in excess of the premiums received). Consequently, these companies may use alternative reserve valuation methods that are less restrictive than the net level premium method. A full assessment of a company's reserve method requires technical knowledge that is beyond the scope of this discussion.[11]

Overall, expenses vary greatly from company to company. Clearly, companies with lower expenses are presumably better managed than those with higher expenses and should be preferred. Commonly used measures of expenses include:

- the ratio of total expenses to the total amount of insurance in force;

- the ratio of total expenses to premiums received; and

- the ratio of total expenses to total income.

These ratios should be used carefully when comparing companies, since they can be misleading, unless applied to similar companies. The first ratio is more appropriate for comparing insurers who are almost exclusively life insurers with little or no annuity, health, disability, or accidental death business. It gives no weight to annuities, supplementary contracts, health insurance, disability and accidental death benefits, and miscellaneous company operations and, therefore, would tend to be biased against companies that offer these other products by skewing the ratio upward.

In addition, it makes no allowance for the difference between first-year and renewal year expenses and would, therefore, tend to be biased against faster growing companies. The first ratio also makes no distinction between expenses on ordinary, group, credit, and industrial business and is, therefore, difficult to use when comparing companies with different mixes between these product lines. It also makes no allowance for differences in the companies' books of business by age, sex, and plan or type of insurance, which would tend to bias the measure against those companies that may place more of their book of business in the higher expense areas.

The second ratio gives some weight to annuities, health insurance, and disability and accidental death benefits (but not necessarily the proper weight), but it gives no weight to supplementary contracts. Therefore, the second ratio would be more appropriate than the first ratio for comparing companies with this broader book of business. It otherwise still has the same limitations described for the first ratio.

The third ratio is the broadest overall measure, including weighting for supplementary contracts. However, it still suffers from most of the criticisms of the other two ratios related to variations in companies' books of business, age distribution of policies, differences in ages, sex, and types of plans, etc. Consequently, each of these ratios may provide some relative indication of a company's ability to manage its expenses, but each ratio should be used with the cited limitations clearly in mind.

Mortality experience also varies widely among companies. Companies with better mortality experience typically have higher underwriting standards and better "risks" among their policyowners. All else being equal, it is preferable to acquire a policy from a company with tough standards, if one can qualify because future mortality experience—and, therefore, the amounts potentially available to pay dividends or to credit to cash values—is more likely to be favorable. In addition, lapse rates and expenses tend to be lower in policies from companies with tougher underwriting standards.

Dividends

How a company has performed in relation to its promises is indicated by the actual history of dividend payments and interest rates in comparison with the dividend scales and interest rates shown on whole life, universal life, and interest sensitive policy illustrations. Planners should also compare dividends paid with the net operating gain before dividend payments. Surplus will be depleted if dividends exceed net operating gain.

Business Trends

This area of the checklist is used to report on trends in new business issued, management plans for new lines of business, changes in the amount of insurance in force, and other company developments. Clearly, the best companies are those with the best trends. For companies that are introducing, or have introduced, new lines of business or new types of policies, expenses can be expected to be higher than average. Look for trends of declining expenses and evidence of success in any new offerings.

Trends

This section of the checklist is used to summarize trends in profitability and liquidity.

Profitability

Return on equity: Look for companies with a history of increasing earnings and better than average returns on equity.

Change in capital and surplus: The change in net capital and surplus is essentially a measure of net worth. Capital and surplus represent the excess of assets over liabilities. The greater a company's surplus, the less risk of insolvency—all else being equal. Experts often compare companies using the ratio of surplus plus Mandatory Securities Valuation Reserve (MSVR) to total assets. The MSVR is a reserve for losses on securities held in the company's general portfolio. Higher values should be preferred and planners should look for growth in surplus.

Leverage

Change in net premiums written: The leverage tests measure whether a company's obligations are growing at a rate that may exceed its ability to handle them. The change in net premiums written should be positive, but not excessive. As discussed above (in regard to reserves), putting new policies on the books is a drain on surplus since reserves initially must increase faster than the premium income.

Net premiums written to capital and surplus: The ratio of net premiums written to capital and surplus is often considered a more useful measure for comparing companies with respect to excess growth. Companies with lower ratios should generally be preferred.

Surplus relief: The surplus relief ratio is the ratio of net commissions and expense allowances on reinsurance to capital and surplus. Virtually all insurance companies reinsure a portion of their business. That is, they cede or pass on to another insurer some of the risk of their policies and pay the other company a premium to assume the risk. Similarly, many companies of the companies who reinsure a portion of their own business also serve as reinsurers for other companies. In this way, large risks are shared among many insurance companies. For insurers whose commissions on reinsurance assumed exceed the commissions on reinsurance ceded, this ratio will be negative. Large positive values for this ratio may indicate that the company's management believes the surplus is inadequate. Extreme negative values may indicate that the additional reserves required for the reinsurance assumed is beginning to strain capital and surplus or that excessive commissions and expenses are being incurred by the company acquiring that business.

Insurance exposure to capital and surplus: This ratio, sometimes expressed inversely as the ratio of capital and surplus per $1,000 of insurance in force, is a measure of mortality exposure or mortality leverage. It is a relative measure of how much adverse mortality the company can handle. A lower ratio of insurance exposure to capital and surplus or a higher ratio of capital and surplus per $1,000 of insurance is preferred.

Liquidity

Current liquidity: Liquidity tests measure whether a company can meet its current and future obligations. The current liquidity test is the most important since it measures whether the company could pay all net obligations if they came due in thirty days. The value should be as high as possible.

Affiliated investments to capital and surplus: This test applies when a company is part of an affiliated group of companies. It consolidates the investments of all affiliated companies and compares it to the consolidated capital and surplus. Once again, a higher ratio is preferred.

MUTUAL COMPANIES VERSUS STOCK COMPANIES

Most life insurance companies are either stock or mutual companies. Fraternal benefit societies provide a small fraction of life insurance coverage, and the Department of Veterans Affairs also provides coverage for veterans under six different insurance programs and it oversees three other life insurance programs for members of the uniformed services. Among mutual and stock companies, the vast majority are stock companies—1,076, or 92 percent of the industry, in 2002.[12]

A mutual company is a corporation that has no shareholders.[13] The policyholders are the members of the corporation and they have membership rights. These rights derive from the insurance contract, the corporation's bylaws and charter or articles of incorporation, state laws, and case law. These membership rights are similar to stock owners' rights in a regular corporation and include:

- the right to contractual benefits, including dividends declared by the board of directors;

- the right to participate in corporate governance, usually by electing directors to oversee the operation of the company;

- the right to receive any remaining value if the corporation is liquidated or demutualized (i.e., converted to a stock company);

- the right to expect that the corporation will be run primarily for the benefit of the members;

- the right to bring legal action against the directors and officers for violating their fiduciary duties.

Individual members cannot sell their rights to someone else and these membership rights terminate when a member cancels the policy or dies.

Stock life insurance companies are corporations that have shareholders, who may or may not be policyholders. In contrast with mutual policyholders, shareholders may generally sell their ownership interest in a stock company. The corporation is run primarily for the benefit of the shareholders, although its relationship with its customers must respect commercial laws and the need to compete in the marketplace.

Advantages and Disadvantages

Because a mutual company has no shareholders, there is no conflict of interest between shareholders and policyholders. This makes it possible to fulfill the company's primary mission: to provide insurance at its cost. However, mutual companies still must make profits to remain afloat. Mutual companies need profits to maintain financial strength and to support future growth. In contrast with stock companies that can issue new shares of common stock to raise capital and expand their growth, mutual companies generally raise capital by retaining a portion of the premiums they receive in excess of the amount they expect to pay out to cover expenses and benefit payments. In general, however, mutual companies have a lower profit goal than stock companies, because they do not have to satisfy the demands of outside investors. Management can also tend to take a long-term view in running the business, because they do not have to pay attention to daily fluctuations of a stock price. As a result, it is probably true that the net return on cash values has been somewhat higher and the net cost of insurance somewhat lower to mutual policyholders than to stock company policyholders, although this is not unquestionably so in all cases.

These advantages are offset by several disadvantages.

- Mutual companies have limited flexibility to raise capital and to merge with or acquire other companies, because they cannot issue stock.

- Financial reporting is less flexible because all transactions are reflected on the parent's books.

- Noninsurance subsidiaries may receive a valuation penalty for being associated with a heavily regulated parent.

- A mutual company's identification as a life insurance company may hinder efforts to provide other comprehensive financial services (as compared to a stock company with subsidiaries in various financial services).

- Management performance is not subject to the same level of scrutiny as it is at stock companies, because there are no outside investors. In most cases, unhappy policyholders find it almost impossible to replace directors who are not fulfilling their duties. Policyholders have to rely on rating agencies to place constraints on management actions.

- Mutual companies may also have a higher tax burden than stock companies, although this has been a subject of debate.

From the insurance buyer's point of view, the major distinction between mutual and stock companies originally was in the types of policies they issued. Stock companies originally issued "nonparticipating"

policies where premiums, cash values, benefit levels, and dividends, if any, were guaranteed, but fixed. Any investment performance above that assumed in setting the guaranteed cash values and dividends (if any) and any savings in expenses, mortality rates, and any of the other assumptions involved in pricing the policy (such as lapse rates and the like), went to the companies' shareholders, not the policyholders.

In contrast, mutual companies issued "participating" policies where premiums, cash values, and benefit levels were also guaranteed at some level. However, if the company had favorable investment results or better than anticipated expense or mortality experience, or better experience with respect to the other factors involved in policy pricing, the benefits would be passed on to the policyholders through higher than projected dividends. Of course, if results were unfavorable, the dividends could fall below the projected dividend level, since dividends are not guaranteed.

So in general, policyholders in stock companies had a fixed and guaranteed and, therefore, known cost for the insurance. In contrast, mutual companies tended to charge somewhat higher premiums, all else being equal, but gave the policyholders the opportunity to participate in the favorable experience of the company through higher than projected future dividend payments. As a result, the real cost over time to policyholders in mutual companies tended to be less than that for policyholders in stock companies.

Competition and innovation over time tended to blur the distinction between policies offered by mutual and stock companies. To compete, stock companies first started to offer interest-sensitive policies that paid higher dividends or, more frequently, credited higher cash value accumulations (rather than pay dividends) over time if the investment performance of the insurer's general fund earned rates of return in excess of those rates assumed when setting the premiums. These types of policies evolved over time into the current-assumption policies where favorable experience with respect to virtually all variables used in the premium pricing decision (expenses, mortality rates, lapse rates, etc.) would be passed through to policyholders, generally in the form of higher credits to the accumulating cash value.

Similarly, mutual companies expanded their product offerings and began to offer current-assumption type policies similar to those offered by stock companies. Consequently, today, potential insurance buyers have a whole assortment of policies ranging from the traditional "nonpar" (infrequently offered) to traditional dividend-paying "par" policies, "interest-sensitive" policies, "current-assumption" policies, and to "flexible-premium current-assumption" (universal life) policies offered by both stock and mutual companies.

REINSURANCE

Reinsurance refers to situations where insurance companies insure against losses they may incur. Insurance companies have a limited amount of capital and to protect this capital they will often cap the losses they may incur by purchasing reinsurance. Typically, the smaller the insurer the more reinsurance they will buy. Reinsurance also can reduce the risk facing a company when policies are issued with a high probability of lapse or surrender, as in policies whose premiums rise sharply from one year to the next. Similarly, reinsurance may limit the investment risk inherent in high concentrations from single products—especially annuities.

A second reason for reinsurance is to obtain the reinsurer's underwriting assistance and expertise. The risk pool from which reinsurers develop and provide underwriting knowledge is generally much larger and wider than that of a single primary insurer.

A third reason companies reinsure is to help them either enter or exit given lines of business or product lines. A company associated with a given product line that wants to discontinue that line can reinsure most or all of the risk on that product. Alternatively, a company desiring to offer a new product line can obtain the help of reinsurers to develop and underwrite the product until the company develops its own expertise in the underwriting of that particular line of business. In some cases, the reinsurance agreement (or treaty, as the reinsurance agreement is typically called) has provisions that permit the ceding company to take back some of the risk the reinsurer had assumed as the ceding company's ability to assume the risk grows over time.

Another reason for the use of reinsurance is to help a company manage its financial position. A reinsurer can provide allowances based upon its anticipation of future profits. This may increase the ceding company's statutory earnings and surplus during the year paid. By ceding business, the reinsurer sets up reserves on its books and lessens the amount the ceding company has to set up in reserves. If a company is growing quickly, this is especially advantageous since initial costs (expenses plus reserves) are higher than premiums received.

Sixty-nine percent of life insurers ceded life premiums from some of their policies as reinsurance in 2002.

In traditional reinsurance, or indemnity reinsurance, the company transferring the risk (the ceding company) retains its financial relationship with, and legal obligation to, the policyholders. In most cases, the policyholders are not even aware that part of the risk on their policies is covered by a reinsurer (the assuming company).

Types of Reinsurance

A number of different types of reinsurance are available. The two main types are proportional reinsurance and nonproportional reinsurance.

Proportional Reinsurance

Proportional reinsurance is an arrangement where the reinsurer takes a share of each loss the insurer incurs. This is also sometimes referred to as *quota share* reinsurance—the risk is allocated by a specified percentage that the ceding company and reinsurer will assume. The capital held by the insurer might only allow it to accept a risk with a value of $1 million but purchasing proportional reinsurance might allow it to, for example, double or triple its acceptance limit.

Four main categories of reinsurance arrangements are considered proportionate reinsurance:

1. *Yearly Renewable Term (YRT) reinsurance* – YRT reinsurance permits the ceding company to transfer mortality risk, but leaves the ceding company entirely responsible for establishing reserves. The premium the ceding company pays to transfer the risk to the reinsurer varies each year with the net amount at risk and the ages of the insureds.

2. *Coinsurance* V – The ceding company transfers a proportionate share of all the policy risks and cash flows except the policy fee. Therefore, the reinsurer receives its proportionate share of premiums, pays its share of benefits, sets up its share of reserves, and pays an allowance to the ceding company. In contrast with YRT

reinsurance, coinsurance helps to relieve the strain on the ceding company's surplus because it is not entirely responsible for setting up the reserve.

3. *Coinsurance with funds withheld* – The ceding company keeps the premiums normally paid to the reinsurer and the reinsurer keeps the allowances normally paid to the ceding company, thereby limiting the cash flow between the companies.

4. *Modified coinsurance* – The reinsurer transfers its share of reserves back to the ceding company while the risk remains with the reinsurer. In return, the ceding company must pay interest to the reinsurer to compensate for what the reinsurer would have earned had it retained the reserves.

Both coinsurance with funds withheld and modified coinsurance permit a ceding company to take statutory credit for reserves in certain circumstances, reduce its credit risk, secure credit, and retain control over investments.

Nonproportional Reinsurance

Nonproportional reinsurance only pays if the loss suffered by the insurer exceeds a certain amount. This type of arrangement, sometimes, called *excess of retention* reinsurance, allocates risk by amount. The ceding company sets a dollar amount on the level of risk it is willing to retain and cedes the excess to the reinsurer, up to what is called the reinsurer's "retention limit." The retention limit is the maximum amount the reinsurer is willing to assume. In many cases, the reinsurer will itself reinsure risks above its retention limit, thereby permitting the original ceding company to transfer all risks over the level it is willing to assume to the reinsurer who then handles the problem of reinsuring risks even beyond its retention level.

Nonproportionate plans include several different arrangements:

1. *Stop loss* – The reinsurer covers some or all of a ceding company's aggregate claims above a predetermined dollar amount or above a percentage of premium during a specified period.

2. *Catastrophe* – The reinsurer covers losses exceeding a specified amount or number of insureds

due to a single event resulting in more than one loss, such as from an airplane crash, train wreck, or natural disaster.

3. *Excess of loss* – In this form of reinsurance, the insurer is prepared to accept a loss of, say, $1 million for any loss that may occur and purchases a layer of reinsurance of, say, $5 million in excess of $1 million. If a loss of $3 million occurs, the insurer pays $1 million themselves and recovers $2 million from the reinsurer. In this example, the insurer will incur for their own account any loss exceeding $6 million unless they have purchased a further layer of reinsurance.

Companies often reinsure with reinsurance syndicates or groups, rather than with single company reinsurers. The reinsurer who sets the terms (premium and policy conditions) for the reinsurance program is called the *lead* reinsurer; the other companies subscribing to the program are called *follow* reinsurers.

The life, health, property reinsurance market is dominated by a small number of very large companies such as Munich Re, Swiss Re, and Berkshire Hathaway, who own several reinsurers including General Re and Faraday in London. However, there is a wide range of smaller reinsurers who may lead reinsurance programs less frequently but who may often participate as a follow market. Most of the above reinsurance programs or treaties cover every risk accepted by the insurer of the type described in the reinsurance policy. However, companies may purchase reinsurance on a per risk basis, in which case it is known as *facultative* reinsurance. The range of companies accepting facultative reinsurance is far wider than those underwriting treaty programs.

Reinsurance companies themselves also purchase reinsurance and this is typically known as retrocessional coverage.

LAWS AND REGULATIONS

Insurance companies are entrusted with huge amounts of money—in the $50 billion to $200 billion range in the case of the largest life insurance companies (e.g., Prudential, Metropolitan Life, and New York Life). The insurance business thus is regulated in an effort to ensure that the public and its funds are dealt with honestly, and to prevent the insurers from taking unwarranted risks with the money they are holding.

The primary purposes of insurance regulation historically have been (1) to maintain the insurers' financial solvency and soundness so they can carry out their long-term obligations to policyholders and pay claims; and (2) to guarantee the fair treatment of current and prospective policyholders and beneficiaries by both insurers and the people who sell their policies.

State Regulation

Insurance companies in the United States are primarily regulated by the individual states. There is no one federal regulatory agency that specifically oversees insurance companies (such as the Securities and Exchange Commission that has a central role in regulating the securities industry, or the Comptroller of the Currency who oversees national banks). The name of the state insurance regulatory agency typically is the "Insurance Department," "Division of Insurance," "Insurance Bureau," or something similar. A state government official—usually called the "Commissioner of Insurance," "Superintendent of Insurance," "Director of Insurance" or something similar—heads these state agencies. The governor of the state appoints the head of the insurance regulatory agency in most states. However, in some states the insurance commissioner is an elected office.

Each state assumes primary responsibility for overseeing the financial operations and management of insurance companies that are incorporated in that state. For example, Prudential is incorporated in New Jersey, so that state has a primary role in its regulation. Metropolitan is incorporated in New York, which has the primary regulatory role for that company. (Companies have their statutory home office in the state where they are incorporated.) Each state also regulates the local operations of insurance companies it has licensed to do business with in the state, particularly as they relate to policy forms, rates, sales agents, and their practices.

The National Association of Insurance Commissioners (NAIC)

The National Association of Insurance Commissioners (NAIC), made up of the states' insurance regulators, is a group that coordinates the regulatory processes for each of the fifty states and the District of Columbia, Puerto Rico, and the U.S. Virgin Islands. This organization discusses current issues and works to cooperate (more or less) in developing a common form for financial statements. In addition, it suggests model laws that the states' legislatures then sometimes enact and it promulgates model regulations that the state regulators sometimes adopt.

Most states have laws regulating the conduct of insurance business to ensure fairness in the way companies deal with applicants for insurance and policyholders. One of the functions of a department of insurance is to enforce these so called "unfair trade practices" and "unfair claims practices" laws by investigating complaints by consumers and taking action, when appropriate, to get companies to stop conduct that violates the laws and impose penalties for violations. Other duties of a department of insurance include reviewing and approving the policy forms used by insurance companies and approving rates charged for various types of insurance to assure compliance with state laws that regulate insurance rates.

UNDERWRITING

Life insurance companies each have their own extensive policy and procedure manuals they are supposed to follow in determining whether or not to issue an individual life insurance policy, and in pricing that policy. The insurer's underwriters typically use a combination of factors that experience shows equates with the risk of death (and premature death).

They include the applicant's answers to a series of questions such as:

1. age;

2. sex (except in several states that require "unisex" rates, even though actuarial data shows women live longer than men);

3. height and weight;

4. health history (and often family health history—parents and siblings);

5. the purpose of the insurance (such as for estate planning or business or family protection);

6. marital status and number of children;

7. the amount of insurance the applicant already has, and any additional insurance the applicant proposes to buy (as people with far more life insurance than they need tend to be poor insurance risks);

8. occupation (some are hazardous and increase the risk of death);

9. income (to help determine suitability);

10. credit history (relates to character and responsibility);

11. smoking or tobacco use (this is an important factor, as smokers have shorter lives);

12. alcohol (excessive drinking seriously hurts life expectancy);

13. certain hobbies (such as race car driving, hang-gliding, or piloting noncommercial aircraft); and

14. prevalence or frequency of foreign travel (certain foreign travel is risky).

Most life insurers require the applicant to undergo a physical examination by a doctor, nurse, or a paramedical technician on large policies. At that time, the examiner typically takes samples of the applicant's blood and urine. The insurer usually will also request the applicant's medical records from his or her physicians, and have the underwriters review them. In addition, the underwriters check the applicant's health history with the Medical Information Bureau, the driving record, credit records, and do other investigations that seem warranted. The greater the amount of insurance sought by the applicant, the greater the extent of the investigation into the applicant's medical, financial, and personal history.

After the application and medical information is completely gathered, the underwriters make their underwriting decisions. First—if the policy has underwriting requirements—they decide whether the applicant qualifies for insurance at all. For example if someone had cancer within the past year, or has AIDS, the applicant might not be unable to buy underwritten life insurance at any price or only at a very high cost from a company that specializes in issuing policies to those who have the applicant's high-risk profile.

Second, underwriters classify the risk, which affects the price of the coverage. Most applicants receive either a "preferred" classification (intended for those who are above average risks) or a "standard" classification. If a person has a history or characteristics that suggest the applicant is riskier than average (perhaps because the applicant is fifty pounds heavier than average for his or her age and height, has high cholesterol, or had heart bypass surgery five years ago) the policy would be "rated," and offered at a higher price based on that rating, given the applicant's age.

Each insurer may evaluate an applicant differently, so that a person one company would regard as "preferred" would be "standard" at another company, and perhaps even "rated" at yet another company. Also, some companies rate up to 70 percent of all applicants as "preferred" (to make applicants and agent feel good about themselves and the company) but charge more than other companies would charge for a "standard" rating.

COMPANY SERVICE AND FAIRNESS TO POLICYHOLDERS

The quality of a company's service is difficult to quantify, but nonetheless an important criterion in company selection. Look for evidence regarding the company's turnaround time for requests for information, policy loans, initial underwriting and application processing, and processing of death claims as well as other administrative matters. The company may provide statistics on such matters, if requested. Also, it is wise to inquire among life insurance professionals who are familiar with the service provided by various companies.

The level of services provided by agents varies greatly from company to company. Some companies spend considerably more than others on training and efforts to keep their agents informed about legal, tax, and planning issues that affect their ability to provide on-going service to policyowners. In general, if a large proportion of the company's agent force has professional designations—such as the CLU (Chartered Life Underwriter), ChFC (Chartered Financial Consultant), or CFP® (CERTIFIED FINANCIAL PLANNER™)—or other credentials certifying their competence in a specialty area, it is evidence of strong support for and encouragement of education and training of their agency force. In addition, since these professional designations generally take some years to earn, it suggests the company appeals to long-term and committed life insurance professionals. Presumably, these professionals prefer to work for companies that provide the highest standards of service to the field force and their clients.

Whether a company has a history of fairness to its policyowners is also difficult to quantify but of considerable importance when selecting a company. A key fairness issue is whether policyowners share equitably in the company's favorable performance. Are distributions to owners of participating or interest sensitive types of policies equitable relative to the total distributable surplus? Similarly, are existing policyowners (or blocks of policies) treated equitably with respect to new policyowners (or new blocks of policies)? Do policyowners of one type or class of policies receive their equitable share of distributable surplus relative to other types or classes of policies? Each of these questions is difficult to answer but some evidence may be gained by inspecting company financial statements regarding distribution of surplus. Further clues may be unearthed by comparing a company's past dividend illustrations with the amounts of dividends actually paid.[14] Many companies have a history of paying higher dividends than they originally illustrated, quite often by design, so a careful analysis may require comparisons among a number of different classes or types of policies and with differing issue dates to uncover any systematic "unfairness" by class or age of policy. If actual dividend payments are frozen or below the amounts shown in illustrations, it should arouse suspicions. However, under the current competitive and financially uncertain environment, we are likely to see far more policies than in the past that are not paying dividends or crediting interest at the rate originally illustrated.

PROTECTIONS FOR POLICYHOLDERS

So far, no one has lost any death benefit from life insurance. In general, policyowners are protected in two ways. First, smaller insolvent companies are taken over by larger, more secure companies that assume the obligations of the smaller company to its policyowners.

Second, in the event an insurer fails (and its obligations are not assumed by another company), policyowners have one primary source of protection, the state "guaranty fund." To help protect policyowners in the event of insolvency, most states maintain guaranty funds for life and health insurers.

When necessary, the guaranty fund intervenes to pay insurance claims, settle policy surrenders, etc. Most state guaranty funds set an upper limit of $100,000 for life insurance cash values or annuities and $300,000 for death benefits. (The state insurance department of an individual state can provide information about the terms of the state's guaranty fund.) These limits are quite generous when compared to the banking and savings and loan industries' deposit insurance programs.

However, the state guaranty system is not without its problems. Some states' guaranty funds are unfunded, relying essentially on current contributions from other insurers in the state to pay claims as they arise. If several large companies experience difficulties at the same time, it could, at worst, overtax the remaining insurers and force the guaranty fund to leave some claims unpaid or, at best, force the guaranty fund to defer the payment of claims, perhaps for years.

Switching Insurers

A policy holder who is insured by a financially troubled insurer may consider switching insurers. Whether this is a good idea depends on many factors, including the type of policy and the method of switching. In most cases, surrendering an ordinary cash value life insurance policy with the intention of investing cash values more safely elsewhere and acquiring a new policy from a more financially stable company is inadvisable. A policyowner who hangs onto the policy may earn a lower rate of dividend interest and may be inconvenienced if the company fails, but the death benefit is generally safe up to the limit of the state's guaranty fund.

Switching might even be expensive. For example, a whole life policyowner switching policies (i.e., surrendering the old policy and purchasing a new one) will enter the new policy at a higher age and higher premium. In addition, the policyowner will pay a new commission, probably have to take a new medical exam, and, if the old policy has been in force for a number of years, may have to pay tax on the excess of the cash surrender value over the amount of premiums paid. However, if the company becomes insolvent, the policyowner may not be able to borrow against cash values. Therefore, it may be advisable to borrow cash values and invest them somewhere else. The cost of assuring this liquidity is essentially the difference between the borrowing rate in the policy and the rate earned on the invested proceeds (also, some companies will reduce the amount earned on cash values by about 2 percent).

For similar reasons, it is probably inadvisable to surrender universal life or interest sensitive policies in financially troubled companies. The principal risks of keeping a policy are that the interest credited to cash values may be reduced to the guaranteed rate (typically 4 percent) if the insurer becomes insolvent and, in the case of universal life policies, mortality and expense charges may be increased to their maximums. In general, it may be wise to put universal life policies into term mode and use accumulated cash values to continue premiums or to pay only the minimum amount necessary to maintain the face amount of coverage. The amount that would otherwise be paid in premiums may be invested elsewhere.

As with whole life and universal life policies, death benefits on variable life policies are generally secure to the level set by the state guaranty fund. Since the cash values are secured by the specific assets of the separate account, rather than the company's general portfolio, variable life policyowners may always cash their policies in at market value. A possible risk of keeping the policy with a financially troubled company is that borrowing against the policy may be restricted during a period of reorganization if the company becomes insolvent.

Using a Section 1035 Exchange

Although surrenders of cash value policies held by financially troubled companies with the intent of purchasing policies in more financially secure companies do not seem advisable, Section 1035 exchanges should be seriously considered. Such an exchange may avoid taxation of gain, if any, and avoid some, but generally not all, of the expenses associated with the purchase of a new policy. (See Chapter 20.)

In addition, it may be advisable to consider the reduced paid-up insurance option or the extended term option for existing policies together with the purchase of new policies with more financially secure companies to cover the difference.

In the case of term policies held by financially troubled insurers, death benefits are generally secure to the level set by the state's guaranty fund. The principal risk is that the company will raise renewal premiums to the maximum permitted under the policy, which may be considerably higher than premiums charged by more financially secure competitors. Also, if the policyowner is in poor health and the company becomes insolvent, another company can refuse to pick up the coverage. Therefore, if the policyowner is healthy and can qualify for coverage from a more financially secure company, it is advisable to switch.

Annuity contracts present more difficult problems. If a financially troubled company becomes insolvent during the accumulation phase, the new guarantor may pay interest at a lower rate than the original insurer. Annuity owners who surrender an annuity contract within the first seven years will usually pay a surrender charge ranging from about 7 percent in the first year to 1 percent in year seven. In addition, annuity owners must pay income tax on gains and a 10 percent tax penalty on the taxable portion of the distribution if it is received before age 59½ (and none of the other exceptions to the premature distribution penalty applies). These tax disadvantages can be avoided if the contract is properly exchanged for another one under Code section 1035.

SELECTED REFERENCES AND SOURCES

1. A. M. Best Company, Ambest Road, Oldwick, NJ 08858.

    *   *Best's Insurance Reports, Life/Health*

    *   *Best's Insurance Management Reports, Life/Health*

    *   *Best's Key Rating Guide, Life/Health*

    *   *Best's Review, Life/Health*

    *   *Best's Agent's Guide*

    *   *Best's Advanced Rating Reporting Service*

2. Standard and Poor's Insurance Rating Services, 25 Broadway, New York, NY 10004.

    *   *S&P's Insurer Solvency Review, Life/Health*

3. Moody's Investor Services, 99 Church Street, New York, NY 10007.

    *   *Moody's Insurance Credit Report Service*

    *   *Moody's Investor Service Life Insurance Handbook*

4. Joseph M. Belth, P.O. Box 245, Ellettsville, IN 47429.

    *   *The Insurance Forum*

5. American Bar Association, Section of Real Property, Probate and Trust Law, 750 N. Lake Shore Drive, Chicago, IL 60611.

    *   *The Life Insurance Counselor, Vol. I, Life Insurance Products, Illustrations and Due Diligence*

6. The Townsend and Schupp Company, 100 Wells Street, Suite 802, Hartford, CT 06103.

    *   *Life Insurance Business Risk Analysis*

7. Fitch Ratings, One State Street Plaza, New York, NY 10004.

   • *Fitch Ratings Delivery Service*

8. Prentice Hall, Englewood Cliffs, New Jersey 07632.

   • K. Black, Jr. and H. Skipper, Jr., *Life Insurance* (12th ed. 1994)

9. Weiss Research, Inc., 15430 Endeavour Dr., Jupiter, FL 33478.

   • *Weiss Ratings' Guide to Life, Health and Annuity Insurers*

FREQUENTLY ASKED QUESTIONS

Question – What is the best way to locate the home office of a life insurance company?

Answer – There are many situations where it is necessary to locate the home office of an insurer. One place to start is a local phone book and the number of the company's local office. This office, in turn, can often refer callers to the address of their home office. Here is a list of some alternatives:

1. Many company websites have the company's contact information, including the location of the home office. These websites can usually be found by using common internet search engines, such as Google.

2. Call the office of the state insurance commissioner. Detailed records of insurance companies licensed to do business in the state will be available here. State insurance commissioner offices will also track the mergers, acquisitions, and liquidations of insurance companies.

3. Visit the web site of the National Association of Insurance Commissioners (NAIC) at: www.naic.org. The NAIC is an organization of insurance regulators from the fifty states, the District of Columbia, and four United States territories. From this web site there is a direct link to most state insurance departments.

4. Visit the web site of the A.M. Best Company at: www.ambest.com/resource/insdir.html. This is the location of A.M. Best's searchable database of nearly 7,000 insurance companies.

5. Review About.com's "Big List" of insurance company home pages at: www.insurance.about.com/blbiglist.htm.

CHAPTER ENDNOTES

1. http://www.weissratings.com/FailedCompanies.asp?ind=ins&type=LH.

2. The following discussion draws heavily upon Slavutin and Kaplan, "Life Insurance Companies and Products: Evaluation and Due Diligence—Part One," *Financial and Estate Planning*, Commerce Clearing House, Inc., June 1990, p. 24,777.

3. The principal point is not that A M. Best's rating was incorrect or that A M. Best should have detected the problem sooner, but rather than relying on ratings alone may be inadequate.

4. Fitch Ratings, Insurance, Criteria Report Exposure Draft: Insurance Capital Assessment Methodology and Model (Prism)—Executive Summary, June 2006.

5. In 2006, the Weiss Group, LLC, parent of Weiss Ratings, sold Weiss Ratings to TheStreet.com. In 2010, TheStreet.com sold the insurance and bank ratings back to the Weiss Group and made an agreement between the two firms that Weiss would also distribute TheStreet.com's stock, mutual fund, and ETF ratings.

6. See Slavutin, "Life Insurance Company Ratings – How Reliable is A.M. Best?" *Financial and Estate Planning*, Commerce Clearing House, Inc., August, 1991, p. 24,991.

7. See Slavutin, "Life Insurance Company Ratings – How Reliable is A.M. Best?" *Financial and Estate Planning*, Commerce Clearing House, Inc., August, 1991, p. 24,993.

8. See "Ratings of Life-Health Insurance Companies by A M. Best, Standard & Poor's, Moody's, and Duff & Phelps," 18 *The Insurance Forum* 199 (April 1991).

9. See Slavutin, "Life Insurance Company Ratings – How Reliable is A.M. Best?" *Financial and Estate Planning*, Commerce Clearing House, Inc., August, 1991, p. 24,995.

10. This checklist is based on the one discussed in Bevington, "Covered Assets," 18 *Financial Planning* 31, 34 (January 1989).

11. See K. Black, Jr. and H. Skipper, Jr., *Life Insurance* (Prentice Hall Inc., 12th ed. 1994), pp. 559-571.

12. The American Council of Life Insurance, *Life Insurance Fact Book* (2003), p. 1.

13. Portions of the following discussion are adapted from "Mutual Life Insurance Company Reorganizations: An Overview," by Glenn S. Daily, at www.glenndaily.com.

14. For example, see *Best's Review*, Life/Health edition, (published monthly).

HOW TO DETERMINE THE RIGHT POLICY

CHAPTER 4

INTRODUCTION

Attorneys, accountants, life insurance agents, and other financial services professionals constantly are required to provide an opinion as to the efficacy of a policy for the particular client and to assist in selecting between competing policies. This discussion will focus on the factors that professionals must consider in determining the right policy. The material provides rule of thumb guidelines that should speed up the decision-making process and help professionals determine if the factors they are considering follow generally accepted life insurance planning principles. Once professionals determine the proper amount of coverage or insurance need (see Chapter 2, "How to Estimate the Insurance Need"), they have a responsibility to perform analyses in the following four areas:

1. selecting the type of insurance product (or product mix) that is appropriate for the client;

2. deciphering life insurance policy illustrations;

3. reviewing policy comparison measurements; and

4. studying company comparison measurements.

Although the life insurance industry as a whole has an incredibly good record for safety, performance, and service, the past insolvencies of a few major life insurance companies make it more important than ever to select the insurance company carefully. Given such importance and timeliness, a separate chapter (Chapter 3, "How to Determine the Right Company") discusses the criteria for comparing and evaluating the financial strength of insurance companies.

SELECTING THE TYPE OF PRODUCT

Above all, the planner must always "MATCH THE PRODUCT TO THE PROBLEM." The particular type of life insurance coverage appropriate for a given client is a function of four factors:

1. the client's personal preferences, prejudices, and priorities;

2. the amount of insurance needed;

3. the client's ability and willingness to pay a given level of premiums (cash flow considerations); and

4. holding period probabilities (duration of need considerations).

Preferences, Prejudices, and Priorities

The selection of a particular type of life insurance policy or policy mix is to a great extent a very personal decision. Just as some individuals prefer, by psychological nature, to lease an automobile or rent an apartment, others prefer to make their purchases with a minimum down payment and stretch out the length of payments as long as possible, while others prefer to make a relatively large down payment and to pay off the loan or mortgage as quickly as possible. For many clients there is emotional comfort in "owning," while others feel that owning ties them down and restricts their freedom of choice and flexibility.

Similar comparisons can be made to life insurance policies. Some clients do not want to "pay, pay, pay...

and have nothing to show for it at the end of the term," while others have been told all their lives to "buy term and invest the difference." In reality, both positions are correct, and not correct. Even the advice of knowledgeable planners has been tainted by their own prejudices. For most clients, the right course of action usually lies where they are most comfortable—because peace of mind is really the impetus for the purchase of life insurance in the first place.

Another useful analogy is the purchase of technology tools by professionals. Some tend to purchase the highest quality, most expensive tools that they can afford so that the tools will serve them well over a lifetime (or at least the reasonably expected lifetime of the tools). They do not tend to purchase lower priced, lower quality tools that will have to be replaced by other tools because they wear out, were inadequate to begin with, or break. But others cannot afford to (or will choose not to) purchase top quality tools. They may have other priorities. They may prefer to have the money to invest or to spend on current consumption. They may end up spending more over the length of their careers on tools and may be inconvenienced in the process of continually replacing the original tools.

Although this "preference/priority"-based decision making is not necessarily the most logical, it is a strong and important process that requires the planner to take into consideration the client's psychological makeup. The rules of thumb here are as follows:

1. Buy term if the client has a high risk-taking propensity.

2. Buy term if the client has a "lease rather than own" preference.

3. Buy some type of whole life insurance if the client has an "own rather than loan" type personality.

4. Buy some type of whole life insurance if the client wants something to show for his money at any given point. The more important it is for the client to have cash values and dividends at any given point, the more whole life type coverage is indicated.

5. Buy a mix of term and whole life if the client is—like most clients—not solidly on one end of the spectrum or the other.

Amount of Insurance Needed

When the amount of insurance needed is so great (as it often is for families with young children or for couples with high living standards relative to their incomes) that only term insurance or a term/whole life combination is feasible, the need for death protection should be given first priority. This results in simple rules of thumb:

1. Buy term insurance when there is no way to satisfy the death need without it. The term insurance can be converted to another form of protection at a later date, if and when appropriate.

2. Buy a combination of term and permanent insurance when the client can cover the entire death need and is able and willing to allocate additional dollars to appropriate permanent coverage.

Keep in mind, however, that buying term insurance means paying ever-increasing premiums for a constant amount of coverage. People with little prospect of increasing their income sufficiently to pay ever-increasing term premiums face a difficult trade-off. They can buy term insurance for the amount of coverage they think they currently need, and face the prospect of being unable to afford that coverage in the future. Or they can purchase as much permanent insurance (e.g., level-premium whole life) as they can afford and be relatively assured that they can maintain the coverage for the long term, but have less coverage than they think they need.

Cash Flow Considerations

There are a large number of premium payment configurations that provide considerable flexibility for policyowners. Some clients will prefer to fully prepay for their coverage and take advantage of the tax-deferred internal buildup of investment return. This limits the total amount of premium that they will pay, even if the insureds live well beyond life expectancy. Other clients will be more comfortable with the payment of premiums at regular intervals for a fixed period or for the life of the insured (or for the working life of the insured). This "installment" purchase of life insurance is most beneficial to the policyowners who die shortly after they purchase the policies, because they would pay a much lower total premium before their deaths.

Conceptually, the insurance company itself is indifferent to the premium payment method selected; all of these patterns of payment, if applied to the same level of death benefit and continued for the same duration of time, will have the same actuarial value. So clients' abilities to pay and their preferences are the major factors in the decision. The rules of thumb are as follows:

1. Prepay coverage (buy vanishing premium or limited payment whole life permanent insurance) if the client expects to live longer than average.

2. Pay on the installment basis (purchase term or low outlay whole life coverage) if the client thinks he or she faces a greater than average mortality risk.

3. Purchase Yearly Renewable Term (YRT) or shorter term insurance (e.g., five-year term) if the client wants or needs to pay absolutely minimal initial premiums, but is willing to pay increasingly larger premiums each consecutive year (or at each renewal date) to keep the same level of coverage in force.

Duration of Need

In many cases, the planner's decision must be dictated at least in part by how long the need is expected to last. Some rules of thumb here are:

1. buy term insurance if the need will probably last for ten years or less;

2. buy term and/or whole life if the need will probably last for ten to fifteen years;

3. buy some type of whole life coverage if the need will probably last for fifteen years or longer;

4. buy some type of whole life coverage if the policy will probably be continued up to or beyond age fifty-five;

5. buy some type of whole life coverage if the policy is purchased to solve a buy-sell need;

6. buy some type of whole life coverage if the policy is designed to pay death taxes, or to transfer capital efficiently from one generation to another, or to replace capital given to charity or otherwise diverted from the client's intended beneficiaries.

USING POLICY ILLUSTRATIONS AND LEDGER STATEMENTS

The policy illustration or ledger statement is the principal source of financial information regarding a new-issue policy. The separate chapters on the various types of policies provide ledger statement illustrations and describe in considerable detail what to look for in these statements. Here, we present a general overview. Understanding these ledger statements is important, because the information they provide serves as the basis for the various policy comparison measures that are discussed below.

The first step in understanding a policy illustration is to identify the columns that state the following:

- Yearly premium payments

- Year-end policy cash values

- Projected policy dividends

- Cumulative cash value at given policy durations

- The death benefit from the basic policy

- The death benefit provided by any dividends

The critical questions are:

1. What does the client pay, year by year—compared to what he gets if he lives and what his family receives if he dies?

2. What portion of those amounts does the insurer guarantee—and what portion of those amounts are just insurer projections?

3. What interest or other assumptions do insurers build into these figures?

Financial services professionals should examine a policy illustration with particular emphasis on the following:

- Surrender charges

- Cash value projections

- Policy loans

- Dividends

Surrender Charges

Determine what the company charges if the client surrenders the policy in a given year by looking at the cash value columns. Where there are two columns for cash values—one that reflects the net surrender value of the contract and the other, the year-end cash value for the policy—the difference between these two amounts is the surrender charge for the given year.

Cash Value Projections

Ascertain the "premium level safety" by looking at the cash value projections on universal life and interest-sensitive life products. It is common under these two types of policies to show future cash values based on:

1. the guaranteed interest rate; and

2. one or more higher interest rates related to either:

   a. current portfolio earnings; or

   b. whatever earnings level the agent has selected for the illustration.

Question the long term reasonableness of the assumptions. Are they unrealistic? Does the cash value associated with the guaranteed interest rate drop to zero after some years of duration? This indicates that the premium being charged for the contract will at that point become inadequate to support the coverage in force if the insurer is only able to credit cash values with the guaranteed interest rate. The client will be forced to pay higher premiums unless the contract earns interest higher than the guaranteed rate. If the illustration shows positive cash values at all policy durations, the premium will be adequate to carry the policy indefinitely.

Policy Loans

The notes to the ledger statement should explain what interest rate the insurer charges on policy loans and if the rate is fixed or variable. If the rate is variable, is the rate being used for illustration reasonable over the period shown?

Check the illustration to see if loans are part of a systematic plan of borrowing to pay premiums. This is called a "minimum deposit" plan. Although no longer a popular approach to financing insurance premium payments, this is evidenced by a regular pattern of increasing outstanding loan balances where the increases are tied closely to the interest rate applicable to the previous outstanding balance and the premium payment due under the contract.

Dividends

Remember that dividends are not guaranteed. Many insurance companies have recently, and significantly, reduced dividends below their original projections. If the ledger statement shows policy loans, the notes to the ledger statement should explain whether dividends are reduced when loans are outstanding. Check to see whether the projected dividends reflect reductions attributable to any projected policy loans. Also, determine what interest rate the company assumes it must earn to pay the projected dividends. If the assumed interest rate seems too high or too optimistic over a period of time, run another ledger with projected dividends based on a more supportable long-run interest assumption. Also, check the interest rate that the insurer will pay on any dividend left with it to earn interest. (The interest is currently taxable, even though the dividend itself will not be taxable to the policyowner.)

The ledger statement should reflect how the dividends will be used. For example, if the client desires additional insurance to build up at net (no commission or overhead) cost, dividends could be used to purchase "paid-up additional insurance" ("paid-up ads") or to purchase one-year term insurance (also a very cost-effective purchase). Alternatively, policyowners could use the dividends to reduce premiums or as additional premiums ("vanishing premium" option) or to repay any projected policy loans. Obtain a ledger statement with dividends used in whatever manner is planned.

Here are some questions to ask the insurer/agent:

1. Is the illustration from the home office or is it printed on the agent's (or some other source's) computer? Demand a ledger printout from the insurance company's home office to compare one policy with another.

2. Is the interest rate used reasonable over a long period of time?

3. Are dividends "puffed"? (Does a comparison of the company's past projected dividends with its past actual dividends—or with the records of other companies' products you are examining—suggest that the company has been overly optimistic?) This can have a significant impact upon when, or if, premiums will "vanish" or when they will unexpectedly reappear.

4. Are cash flow amounts in one illustration comparable with those in another? Cash flow amounts will be similar only if death benefit amounts and premium payments, as well as any projected policy loans or withdrawals, are for similar amounts for each policy's duration. The more the values of these variables differ from one illustration to another, the less meaningful are differences in cash values, death benefits, or dividends levels.

5. In comparing universal life products, demand to know what variables are incorporated in the illustration and then insist that all competitive illustrations use the same (reasonable) assumptions.

HOW TO COMPARE POLICIES

At best, life insurance is a very complicated product that is extremely difficult to evaluate and compare. Life insurance policies are complex amalgams of varying legal, financial, and probabilistic elements that cannot really be reduced to an all-encompassing unitary measure for comparison purposes. However, there are a number of commonly used measures or methods for policy comparison that can be of aid in evaluating purchase alternatives. Keep in mind that none of these methods does, or could, take into account all of the factors that should be considered when making the purchase decision. But, if planners use several methods and they keep in mind the strengths and weaknesses of each during the comparison process, these methods will be quite helpful in at least eliminating policies that should not be considered. The following are commonly used policy comparison techniques:

*   The "traditional net cost" method

*   The "interest-adjusted net surrender cost" method

*   The "interest-adjusted net payment cost" method

*   The "equal outlay" method

*   The "cash accumulation" method

*   The "Linton yield" method

*   The "Belth yearly yield" method

*   The "Belth yearly price of protection" method

*   The "Baldwin" method

Traditional Net Cost Method

The traditional net cost method works like this:

1. Add up the premiums on the ledger sheet over a stated period of time such as ten, fifteen, or twenty years.

2. Add up the dividends projected on the ledger sheet over the same period of time.

3. Subtract the total dividends from the total premiums to find the total net premiums paid over the period being measured.

4. Add the cash value and any "terminal dividends" shown on the ledger statement as of the end of such period (and minus any surrender charge) to find the net cash value.

5. Subtract the net cash value from the total net premiums to arrive at the total net cost of the policy over the selected period.

6. Divide the total net cost by the face amount of the policy (in thousands) and again by the number of years in the selected period to arrive at the net cost of insurance per thousand dollars of coverage per year. (In Figure 4.1, numbers were calculated per $1,000 of coverage from the start.)

Figure 4.1

TRADITIONAL NET COST METHOD $25,000 POLICY FOR A MALE AGE 35 (per $1,000 of coverage)					
Year	Premium	Dividends	Cash Value	Terminal Dividends	Surrender Charges
1	$22.24	$0.00	$0.00	$0.00	$0.00
2	22.24	3.40	16.00	0.00	1.75
3	22.24	4.00	33.00	0.00	1.50
4	22.24	4.70	51.00	0.00	1.00
5	22.24	5.50	69.00	0.00	0.50
6	22.24	6.00	84.00	1.05	0.00
7	22.24	6.75	104.00	2.35	0.00
8	22.24	7.50	122.00	3.25	0.00
9	22.24	8.25	141.00	4.25	0.00
10	22.24	9.00	160.00	5.25	0.00
TOTALS	$222.40	$55.10			

(1)	Total premiums		$222.40
(2)	Minus total dividends		− 55.10
(3)	Equals total net premiums		$167.30
(4)	Cash value in year 10		$160.00
	Plus terminal dividend		+ 5.25
	Minus surrender charge		− 0.00
	Equals net cash value		$165.25
	Total net premiums		$167.30
	Minus net cash value		−165.25
(5)	Equals total net cost		$ 2.05
	Total net cost		$2.05
(6)	Divided by number of years		÷ 10
	Equals traditional net cost per $1,000 per year		**$0.205**

This is the easiest method to understand and use, but its simplicity is its weakness. This measure ignores the time value of money, which makes it possible to manipulate policy illustrations by shifting cash flows. Even without intentional manipulation, the traditional net cost method grossly understates the cost of insurance coverage and, in many cases, implies that the average annual cost of coverage is zero or negative. The result could be misleadingly low measures of policy costs. Few states sanction this method for comparing policy costs, although it can be used by the planner, together with the other methods described below, to make a quick and rough first-level relative comparison of policies.

Interest-Adjusted Cost Methods

The interest-adjusted methods of comparing the cost of life insurance policies consider the fact that policyowners could have invested the money spent on premium dollars elsewhere earning some minimum after-tax return (5 percent is usually assumed.) Because a policy may terminate, either when the policyowner surrenders the policy or when the insured dies, there are two different interest-adjusted indexes to measure the cost: (1) the net surrender cost index; and (2) the net payment cost index. The indexes do not necessarily define the true cost of policies, but they are useful in comparing the relative costs of similar policies. All other things being equal, a low index represents a better value than a high index. Note, however, that the interest-adjusted indexes are only indexes and nothing more. The true cost of a life insurance policy, if it can actually be measured prospectively, depends on when and how a policy terminates.

Interest-Adjusted Net Surrender Cost Index

This index is a relative measure of the cost of a policy assuming the policy is surrendered. It works like this:

1. Accumulate each year's premium at some specified rate of interest. (Most policy illustrations use a 5 percent rate.) Perform the calculation over a selected period of time such as ten, fifteen, or twenty years.

2. Accumulate each year's dividends projected on the ledger sheet at the same assumed rate of interest over the same period of time.

3. Subtract the total dividends (plus interest) from total premiums (plus interest) to find the future value of the total net premiums paid over the period being measured.

4. Add the cash value and any "terminal dividends" shown on the ledger statement as of the end of such period (and minus any surrender charge) to find the net cash value.

5. Subtract the net cash value from the future value of the net premiums to arrive at the future value of the total net cost of the policy over the selected period.

6. Divide the result by the future value of the annuity due factor for the rate assumed and the period selected. The result is the level annual cost for the policy.

Future value of the annuity due factors (5% interest)

Years	Factor
5	5.8019
10	13.2068
15	22.6575
20	34.7193
25	50.1135
30	69.7608

7. Divide the level annual cost for the policy by the number of thousands in the face amount of coverage. The result is the interest-adjusted net annual cost per thousand dollars of coverage using the surrender cost index. (In Figure 4.2, numbers were calculated per $1,000 of coverage from the start.)

Interest-Adjusted Net Payment Cost Index

This index is a relative measure of the cost of a policy assuming the insured dies while the policy is in force. It works like this:

1. Accumulate each year's premium at some specified rate of interest. (Most policy illustrations use a 5 percent rate.) Perform the calculation over a selected period of time such as ten, fifteen, or twenty years.

2. Accumulate each year's dividends projected on the ledger sheet at the same assumed rate of interest over the same period of time.

3. Subtract the total dividends (plus interest) from the total premiums (plus interest) to find the future value of the total net premiums paid over the period you are measuring.

4. Divide the result by the future value of the annuity due factor for the rate assumed and the period selected. (Use the same factors that were used in the Net Surrender Cost Index, above.) The result is the level annual cost for the policy.

5. Divide the level annual cost for the policy by the number of thousands in the face amount of coverage. The result is the interest-adjusted net annual cost per thousand dollars of coverage using the payment cost index. (In Figure 4.2, numbers were calculated per $1,000 of coverage from the start.)

Planners usually will not have to do these computations because most ledger sheets will contain these

Figure 4.2

INTEREST-ADJUSTED COST METHOD
$25,000 POLICY FOR A MALE AGE 35
(per $1,000 of coverage)

Year	Premiums				Dividends	
	Per Year	Accum. at 5.00%	Per Year	Accum. at 5.00%	Cash Value	Terminal Dividends
1	$22.24	$23.35	$0.00	$0.00	$0.00	$0.00
2	22.24	47.87	3.40	3.57	16.00	0.00
3	22.24	73.62	4.00	7.95	33.00	0.00
4	22.24	100.65	4.70	13.28	51.00	0.00
5	22.24	129.03	5.50	19.72	69.00	0.00
6	22.24	158.84	6.00	27.01	184.00	1.05
7	22.24	190.13	6.75	35.44	104.00	2.35
8	22.24	222.99	7.50	45.09	122.00	3.25
9	22.24	257.49	8.25	56.01	141.00	4.25
10	22.24	293.72	9.00	68.26	160.00	5.25
TOTALS	$222.40		$55.10			

Surrender Cost Index			Payment Cost Index	
(1)	Premiums compounded at 5.00 percent	$293.72	(1) Premiums compounded at 5.00 percent	$293.72
(2)	Minus dividends compounded at 5.00 percent	−68.26	(2) Minus dividend's compounded at 5.00 percent	− 68.26
(3)	Equals future value of net premiums	$225.46	(3) Future Value of net premiums	$225.46
(4)	Cash value	$160.00		
	Plus terminal dividends	+ 5.25		
	Minus surrender charge	− 0.00		
	Equals net cash value	$165.25		
	Future value of net premiums	$225.46		
	Minus net cash value	165.25		
(5)	Equals future value of net cost	$60.21		
	Future value of net cost	$60.21	Future Value of net premiums	$225.46
(6)	Divided by annuity due factor	÷13.2068	Divided by annuity due factor	÷ 13.2068
	Equals surrender cost index (per $1,000 of coverage)	**$4.56**	**Equals payment cost index (per $1,000 of coverage)**	**$17.07**

indexes at the bottom of the front page of the ledger statement. However, the ledger statement usually shows the indexes only for ten and twenty years, and sometimes for the insured's age sixty-five.

Most states require that insurers/agents provide prospective policyowners with a policy's interest-adjusted indexes. Planners should therefore understand how this measure works, understand its limitations, and be able to explain it to sophisticated clients. Among the weaknesses of the interest-adjusted methods are these:

1. If the policies being compared are not quite similar, the index results may be misleading. For instance, if the outlays differ significantly, the planner should establish a hypothetical side fund to accumulate the differences in the annual outlays at the assumed rate of interest to properly adjust for the differences. This will be the case where an existing policy is compared with a potential replacement. There will almost always be a material difference in the projected cash flows. This makes the interest-adjusted methods unsuitable (unless adjusted) for "replacement" comparisons.

2. The interest-adjusted methods are subject to manipulation (although to a lesser extent than the traditional net cost method) and in the commonly used measuring periods, such as ten or twenty years, insurers/agents can design them to provide more favorable estimates of cost than for other selected periods.

3. The interest-adjusted methods are valid only to the extent that the projections of cash flows materialize as assumed. Therefore, the calculations cannot consider the impact of an overly optimistic dividend scale.

4. It is possible in the comparison between two policies for each policy to be superior when ranked on one of the two indexes and inferior when ranked on the other index. However, relative rankings on each index tend to be highly correlated. That is, a policy that is ranked higher than others using one index tends to also rank similarly using the other index.

The Equal Outlay Method

The equal outlay method works like this: The client is assumed to outlay (pay out) the same premium for each of the policies to be compared. Likewise, the client is assumed to purchase, in each policy under comparison, essentially equal amounts of death benefits year by year.

The equal outlay method is easiest to employ when comparing flexible premium type policies (e.g. universal life) because it is easy for the insurer/agent to generate the illustration with equal annual contributions.

Planners should demand that:

- the illustration projects cash values using the guaranteed rates for the policy;

- the insurer/agent run separate illustrations showing a selected intermediate interest rate assumption; and

- the insurer/agent run separate illustrations showing the current interest rate the company credits to policies.

An inspection of the projected cash values in future years should make it possible to identify the policy with the highest cash values and, therefore, to determine which is the best purchase. The procedure will be more complicated where the equal outlay method is used to compare a fixed premium contract with one or more flexible premium polices. Here, the net premium level (adjusted for any dividends) and the death benefit of the flexible premium policies must be made to match the corresponding values for the fixed premium contract for all years over the period of comparison. This makes it possible to compare future cash values in the same manner as when comparing two flexible premium policies.

As shown in Figure 4.3, planners also can use the equal outlay method to compare two or more fixed-premium policies, or to compare a term policy to a whole life policy, in the following manner: Hypothetically, "invest" the differences in net annual outlay in a side fund at some reasonable after-tax rate of return that essentially keeps the two alternatives equal in annual outlay. Compare cash values and total death benefits (including side fund amounts for both).

Note, quite often the result of this computation will show that term insurance (or a lower-outlay whole life policy) with a side fund will outperform a permanent type whole life plan during a period of perhaps the first seven to ten years but then lose that edge when the projection is carried to a longer duration.

There are a number of disadvantages to the equal outlay method:

1. When comparing a fixed to a flexible premium contract, the underlying assumptions of the

Figure 4.3

EQUAL OUTLAY METHOD Ordinary Life (OL) versus Yearly Renewable Term (YRT) $100,000 face value for age 35 male nonsmoker							
Year	OL Prem.	YRT Prem.	Diff. in Prem.	Diff. Accum. at 6%	OL Surrend. Values	YRT Plus Side Fund	OL with Paid-up Ads
1	$1,445	$145	$1,300	$1,378	$0	$101,378	$100,010
2	1,445	148	1,297	2,836	175	102,836	100,111
3	1,445	154	1,291	4,375	1,670	104,375	100,309
4	1,445	162	1,283	5,997	3,324	105,997	100,848
5	1,445	172	1,273	7,706	5,167	107,706	101,817
6	1,445	185	1,260	9,504	7,189	109,504	103,231
7	1,445	200	1,245	11,394	9,435	111,394	105,105
8	1,445	219	1,226	13,377	11,986	113,377	107,458
9	1,445	242	1,203	15,455	14,768	115,455	110,316
10	1,445	268	1,177	17,630	17,898	117,630	113,678
11	1,445	299	1,146	19,903	21,243	119,903	117,611
12	1,445	333	1,112	22,276	25,007	122,276	122,056
13	1,445	373	1,072	24,749	29,147	124,749	127,057
14	1,445	417	1,028	27,324	33,634	127,324	132,669
15	1,445	466	979	30,001	38,579	130,001	138,903
16	1,445	521	924	32,780	44,126	132,780	145,821
17	1,445	581	864	35,663	50,167	135,663	153,454
18	1,445	646	799	38,650	56,913	138,650	161,813
19	1,445	716	729	41,741	64,238	141,741	171,062
20	1,445	791	654	44,939	72,295	144,939	181,159

* This table assumes that dividends are used to purchase paid-up additions.

In this case, the yearly renewable term option is superior if the policy is surrendered before about year ten or if the policy is maintained and death occurs before about year thirteen. By the end of the tenth year, the surrender cash value of the whole life policy exceeds the side fund accumulated with the yearly renewable term option. However, the whole life policy's death benefit, assuming dividends are used to buy paid-up additions, does not exceed the total death benefit (term insurance plus side fund) of the YRT option until after year twelve. This example demonstrates that term policies will often be a better choice when insurance needs are short term. But term policies are generally increasingly less attractive the longer the duration of the insurance need.

contracts are not the same and, therefore, the analysis cannot fairly compare them. For instance, many universal life cash value projections are based on "new money assumptions," while ordinary life policy dividends are usually based on the "current portfolio rate" of the insurer (a rate that often varies significantly from the new money rate). Because the portfolio of the insurance company includes investments made in prior years that will not mature for several years, the portfolio rate tends to lag behind new money rates. If new money rates are relatively high, the portfolio rate will generally be less than new money rates. However if new money rates are trending down, portfolio rates will generally be higher than new money rates.

This difference in the rate used to make illustrations can be misleading. For example, if new money rates are greater than the portfolio rate and the trend of high new money rates continues for some time, cash values in universal life contracts are more likely to materialize as projected. But if these economic conditions hold true, then it is likely that the portfolio rate will also rise. This means dividends paid would increase relative to those projected based on the current portfolio rate. The equal outlay method does not take into consideration either the fluctuations in rates or the differences in how they are computed.

2. The required adjustments in most comparisons can quickly become burdensome. In many cases, it is quite difficult to equate death benefits under the comparison policies while maintaining equal outlays.

3. When comparing an existing policy with a potential replacement policy, the analysis must consider any cash value in the existing policy at the time of the comparison. Generally, it is easiest to assume that the cash value will be paid into the new policy. Otherwise, the analysis should probably account for the time value of that cash value and should, as closely as possible, equate total death benefits including any side fund.

4. The results, even after many adjustments have been made, may be ambiguous. Quite often the results can be interpreted as favoring one policy for certain durations, favoring another policy for certain durations, and favoring even another policy for other durations.

Cash Accumulation Method

The cash accumulation method works like this:

1. Equate outlays (much in the same manner as the equal outlay method) for the policies being compared.

2. Change the face amount of the lower premium policy so that the sum of the side fund plus the face amount equals the face amount of the higher premium policy. Note that this would yield the same result as where it is possible to set both death benefits and premium payments exactly equal—in flexible premium policies.

3. Accumulate any differences in premiums at an assumed rate of interest.

4. Compare the cash value/side fund differences over given periods of time to see which policy is preferable to the other.

The cash accumulation method is ideal for comparing term with permanent insurance. But planners must use this analysis with caution; the use of the appropriate interest rate is critical because, as is the case with any time-value measurement, a higher assumed interest rate will generally favor a lower premium policy/side fund combination relative to a higher premium policy.

We suggest a two-part approach:

1. If planners perform this comparison without regard to a specific clients and merely to determine the relative ranking of the polices, the planners should assume a relatively conservative risk-free, after-tax rate comparable to the rate that one would expect to earn on the cash values of the higher premium policy. This will more closely equate the combination of the lower premium/side fund with the risk-return characteristics of the higher premium policy.

2. Alternatively, if the comparison is being conducted for a specific client, the planner should use that individual's long-run after-tax opportunity cost rate of return, which may be considerably higher than the rate of return anticipated on the cash value of the higher premium policy.

A full and fair comparison is made more difficult because of the impact of death taxes, probate costs, and creditor laws. This is because the cash accumulation method uses a hypothetical side fund to make the comparison. But money in a side fund—if in fact it were accumulated—would not be eligible for the exemptions or special rate reductions afforded to the death proceeds of life insurance. Therefore, each dollar from that side fund would be subjected to a level of transfer tax that life insurance dollars would not. Likewise, the side fund would be subjected to the normal probate fees and attorney's costs to which cash or other property is subject. Furthermore, this method does not consider the value of state law creditor protection afforded to the death benefits in a life insurance policy, but not to amounts held in most other types of investments.

The bottom line is that the side fund money may appear to have more value than it actually would have in the hands of those for whom it was intended. It is therefore apparent that, while the cash accumulation method has strengths that overcome many of the weaknesses of other comparison methods, it also has weaknesses that prevent it from being the single best answer to the financial planner's policy comparison problem.

Figure 4.4

CASH ACCUMULATION METHOD							
Ordinary Life (OL) versus Yearly Renewable Term (YRT)							
$100,000 face value for age 35 male nonsmoker							

Year	OL Prem.	YRT Prem.	Diff. in Prem.	Side Fund at 6.00%	OL Surrender Value	YRT Face Amount	YRT Plus Side Fund	OL with Paid-up Ads
1	$1,445	$143	$1,302	$1,380	$0	$98,630	$100,010	$100,010
2	1,445	144	1,301	2,842	175	97,269	100,111	100,111
3	1,445	148	1,297	4,388	1,670	95,921	100,309	100,309
4	1,445	154	1,291	6,020	3,324	94,828	100,848	100,848
5	1,445	162	1,283	7,741	5,167	94,076	101,817	101,817
6	1,445	173	1,272	9,554	7,189	93,677	103,231	103,231
7	1,445	187	1,258	11,460	9,435	93,645	105,105	105,105
8	1,445	206	1,239	13,461	11,986	93,997	107,458	107,458
9	1,445	229	1,216	15,557	14,768	94,759	110,316	110,316
10	1,445	257	1,188	17,750	17,898	95,928	113,678	113,678
11	1,445	292	1,153	20,037	21,243	.97,574	117,611	117,611
12	1,445	332	1,113	22,420	25,007	99,636	122,056	122,056
13	1,445	381	1,064	24,893	29,147	102,164	127,057	127,057
14	1,445	439	1,006	27,453	33,634	105,216	132,669	132,669
15	1,445	507	938	30,094	38,579	108,809	138,903	138,903
16	1,445	589	856	32,807	44,126	113,014	145,821	145,821
17	1,445	685	760	35,582	50,167	117,872	153,454	153,454
18	1,445	797	648	38,403	56,913	123,410	161,813	161,813
19	1,445	929	516	41,254	64,238	129,808	171,062	171,062
20	1,445	1,084	361	44,112	72,295	137,047	181,159	181,159

* This table assumes that dividends are used to purchase paid-up additions.

The whole life policy and the term rates used in this example are the same as those used in the equal outlay example (see Figure 4.3). The cash accumulation example differs from the equal outlay example chiefly in that it keeps the total death benefits equal each year under each option by adjusting the face amount of the term coverage. This method unambiguously identifies the whole life policy as the superior strategy for years ten and beyond.

Linton Yield Method

The Linton yield method works like this: The planner computes the rate of return that the policyowner must earn on a hypothetical (or real) side fund assuming death benefits and outlays are held equal for every year over the period being studied. The policy that should be selected according to this method is the one that has the highest Linton yield, that is, the policy that—given an assumed schedule of costs (term rates)—has the highest rate of return.

In essence, this method is just the reverse of the interest-adjusted surrender cost method, which holds the assumed interest rate level and solves for cost; the Linton method holds cost level and solves for interest. It should therefore be an excellent way to check the interest-adjusted method results because the two methods should rank policies virtually identically.

As demonstrated in Figure 4.5, planners can compare dissimilar policies through the Linton yield method. Note, however, that planners must use the same term

Figure 4.5

20-YEAR LINTON YIELD Ordinary Life (OL) versus Yearly Renewable Term (YRT) $100,000 face value for age 35 male nonsmoker								
Year	OL Prem.	YRT Prem.	Diff. in Prem.	Side Fund at 9.696%	OL Surrend. Value	YRT Face Amount	YRT Plus Side Fund	OL with Paid-up Ads
1	$1,445	$143	$1,302	$1,428	$3	$98,582	$100,010	$100,010
2	1,445	144	1,301	2,994	175	97,117	100,111	100,111
3	1,445	147	1,298	4,708	1,670	95,601	100,309	100,309
4	1,445	153	1,292	6,582	3,324	94,266	100,848	100,848
5	1,445	160	1,285	8,630	5,167	93,187	101,817	101,817
6	1,445	171	1,274	10,864	7,189	92,367	103,231	103,231
7	1,445	184	1,261	13,301	9,435	91,804	105,105	105,105
8	1,445	200	1,245	15,956	11,986	91,502	107,458	107,458
9	1,445	221	1,224	18,846	14,768	91,470	110,316	110,316
10	1,445	246	1,199	21,988	17,898	91,690	113,678	113,678
11	1,445	276	1,169	25,403	21,243	92,208	117,611	117,611
12	1,445	310	1,135	29,112	25,007	92,944	122,056	122,056
13	1,445	350	1,095	33,135	29,147	93,922	127,057	127,057
14	1,445	397	1,048	37,498	33,634	95,171	132,669	132,669
15	1,445	451	994	42,225	38,579	96,678	138,903	138,903
16	1,445	513	932	47,341	44,126	98,480	145,821	145,821
17	1,445	584	861	52,875	50,167	100,579	153,454	153,454
18	1,445	665	780	58,857	56,913	102,956	161,813	161,813
19	1,445	757	688	65,319	64,238	105,743	171,062	171,062
20	1,445	861	584	72,293	72,295	108,866	181,159	181,159

* This table assumes that dividends are used to purchase paid-up additions.

The difference between the OL premiums and the YRT premiums is invested at 9.696 percent in the side fund. The side fund virtually equals the cash value in year twenty.

rates for each policy that the planners are evaluating or the results will be misleading. The higher the term rate that the planners use, the higher is the Linton yield that the analysis will produce—and, of course, the reverse is also true. This emphasizes the importance of using this method only for a relative comparison of policies and not to measure the "true rate of return" actually credited to the cash value of a give policy.

Computationally, the Linton yield method is a variation on the cash accumulation method. Using the cash accumulation methodology described above, the Linton yield is the rate of return that equates the side fund with the cash surrender value for a specified period of years. For example, in the cash accumulation method example above (see Figure 4.4) the side fund was just about equal to the cash surrender value in year ten when the side fund was invested at 6 percent. Therefore, the Linton yield for the whole life policy (assuming the YRT rates are competitive) is about 6 percent for ten years. The example in Figure 4.5 shows that the twenty-year Linton yield for this policy is 9.696 percent.

Belth Method

Joseph M. Belth, Ph.D., Professor Emeritus of Insurance at Indiana University has been a leading researcher, constructive critic, and writer on life insurance policy comparison methods and other life insurance issues. He devised two comparison methods that give comparable ranking results:

- The yearly rate of return method

- The yearly price of protection method

The reason he developed two methods follows from what has already been said (implicitly, if not explicitly) about comparison methods: If you prefer to compare policies based on a measure of the price of protection, you must specify or assume the cost of protection. In contrast with the methods discussed earlier, which essentially reduce comparisons to a relative measure of one rate of one cost index for each policy being compared for a specified term, the Belth methods compute the rates of return or the prices of protection for all years, or any subset of years, that the policies may be in force. One of the more attractive features of Belth's methods is that they are easier to use (with caveats) than the other methods when trying to decide whether to replace an existing policy with a new policy.

Belth Yearly Rate of Return Method

The Belth yearly rate of return method works like this:

1. Compute "benefits" from the policy for the year, which is the sum of:

   (a) the cash value at the end of the year;

   (b) the dividends paid during the year; and

   (c) the net death benefit for the policy year.

2. Compute the "investment" in the policy for the year. The investment is defined as the sum of:

   (a) the premium paid for the year; plus

   (b) the cash value at the beginning of the year.

3. Divide the benefits for the year by the investment for the year and subtract one from the result. Stated as a formula, the computation is:

$$\text{Yearly Rate of Return} = \frac{\text{Benefits}}{\text{Investment}} - 1$$

4. Repeat the calculations for each year over the desired duration or planning period.

This yearly rate of return method is especially useful in comparing policies over many different durations. The policy with the highest yearly rates in the greatest number of years is generally the best choice.

As is the case with the comparison methods described above, this system has its weaknesses and potential flaws:

1. The calculated yearly rates of return may be misleading where cash values are small.

2. The results can be manipulated or unintentionally affected by the term rate assumed. The planner must specify an assumed yearly cost for insurance in order to calculate the benefits for the policy year. In other words, planners must use one-year term rates. But if the term rates used are neither competitive nor realistic, the results would not accurately portray how well a "buy term and invest the difference" plan performs in comparison to a "buy whole life and build the cash values" plan.

3. Typically, no one policy will be better than another year after year. This means the "best policy" may not be easy to select. One policy may provide the higher yearly rates of return in early years, but not in later years.

Belth Yearly Price of Protection Method

The Belth yearly price of protection method works like this:

1. Accumulate the "investment" in the policy for one year at an assumed rate of interest. The investment is the sum of:

   (a) the cash surrender value at the end of the previous year; plus

   (b) the current premium.

2. Compute the year-end policy surrender value. The year-end policy surrender value is the sum of:

   (a) the year end cash surrender value; plus

   (b) any dividend.

3. Subtract the year-end policy surrender value from the year's accumulated investment.

4. Divide the result of (3) by the year's net amount at risk (face amount minus current year's cash surrender value) in thousands to derive the cost of protection (per thousand dollars of coverage) for the year. Stated as a formula, the computation is:

$$\text{Cost per } \$1000 = \frac{(P + CVP) \times (1 + i) - (CSV + D)}{(F - CSV) \times (0.001)}$$

Where
P = **P**remium
CVP = **C**ash surrender **V**alue **P**revious year
i = net aftertax **i**nterest rate
CSV = **C**ash **S**urrender **V**alue current year
D = **D**ividend current year
F = **F**ace amount of coverage

The result is an estimate of the cost in any given year of the net death benefit (death benefit minus cash value). The policy with the lowest yearly price of protection in

the most years is generally the contract that should be selected under this method.

As a complement to the yearly price of protection method, Belth has developed: (1) benchmark costs per thousand dollars of term insurance for various age ranges, see table below; and (2) rules of thumb for using this method in replacement situations. He describes the benchmark rates (see below) as follows:

The benchmarks were derived from certain United States population death rates. The benchmark figure for each five-year age bracket is slightly above the death rate per $1,000 at the highest age in the bracket. What we are saying is that if the price of your life insurance protection per $1,000 is in the vicinity of the 'raw material cost' (that is the amount needed just to pay death claims based on population death rates), your life insurance protection is reasonably priced.[1]

JOSEPH BELTH'S BENCHMARK PRICE OF INSURANCE

Age	Price
Under Age 30	$1.50
30-34	2.00
35-39	3.00
40-44	4.00
45-49	6.50
50-54	10.00
55-59	15.00
60-64	25.00
65-69	35.00
70-74	50.00
75-79	80.00
80-84	125.00

Belth suggests the following rules of thumb for applying the benchmarks in replacement situations:

1. If the policy price per thousand is less than the benchmark for the insured's age, replacement would probably be inadvisable.

2. If the price per thousand is between one and two times the benchmark, probably no change is indicated.

3. If the price is greater than two times the benchmark, consider replacing the policy.

Figure 4.6

BELTH YEARLY RATE OF RETURN (YROR) AND YEARLY PRICE OF PROTECTION METHODS (YPOP)
Ordinary Life (OL) policy of $100,000 face value for age 35 male nonsmoker, assuming certain Yearly Renewable Term (YRT) rates per $1,000 of coverage

Year	OL Prem.	Dividends	OL Cash Value	YRT Rate Per $1000	Yearly Benefits	Yearly Invest.	YROR	YPOP at 9.00%
1	$1,445	$3	$0	$1.45	$148	$1,445	−89.779%	$15.72
2	1,445	26	122	1.48	296	1,445	−79.494%	14.28
3	1,445	53	1,352	1.54	1,557	1,567	−0.640%	3.07
4	1,445	149	2,618	1.62	2,925	2,797	4.569%	2.89
5	1,445	278	3,919	1.72	4,363	4,063	7.377%	2.41
6	1,445	418	5,252	1.85	5,845	5,364	8.961%	1.87
7	1,445	572	6,619	2.00	7,378	6,697	10.168%	1.16
8	1,445	742	8,020	2.19	8,963	8,064	11.146%	0.31
9	1,445	928	9,455	2.42	10,602	9,465	12.011%	(0.73)
10	1,445	1,133	10,923	2.68	12,294	10,900	12.797%	(1.97)
11	1,445	1,355	12,423	2.99	14,039	12,368	13.516%	(3.39)
12	1,445	1,584	13,960	3.33	15,830	13,868	14.150%	(4.97)
13	1,445	1,837	15,527	3.73	17,679	15,405	14.764%	(6.78)
14	1,445	2,116	17,127	4.17	19,588	16,972	15.415%	(8.97)
15	1,445	2,424	18,757	4.66	21,559	18,572	16.087%	(11.54)
16	1,445	2,766	20,418	5.21	23,598	20,202	16.811%	(14.62)
17	1,445	3,140	22,105	5.81	25,698	21,863	17.541%	(18.16)
18	1,445	3,552	23,823	6.46	27,867	23,550	18.332%	(22.39)
19	1,445	4,011	25,570	7.16	30,114	25,268	19.178%	(27.39)
20	1,445	4,514	27,345	7.91	32,434	27,015	20.059%	(33.21)

* Dividends are not used to buy paid-up additions.

Yearly benefit = cash value + dividend + net death protection benefit
Net death protection benefit = YRT rate × ($100,000 – cash value) × .001
Yearly investment = premium + prior year's cash value
YROR = (yearly benefit ÷ yearly investment) – 1
YPOP = [(premium + cash value prior year) × (1 + interest rate) - (cash value + dividend)] ÷ ($100,000 – cash value) × .001

The flaws and potential weaknesses of this method are:

1. The yearly prices of protection may have no relation to the actual mortality costs charged against the policy in any given year. To compare the calculated yearly "prices" (which have been critically affected by the rate of return assumed by the planner) with term insurance rates may be misleading. But, if the same assumed rate of interest is used when computing the yearly prices for all policies under consideration, the yearly rates for each policy should provide a good indication of where various polices stand in relation to others. Planners should use an

assumed rate as close as possible to the rate actually used by the insurance company in its cash value and dividend illustrations. This will enable a fair comparison of the yearly prices of protection from the policy to yearly renewable term insurance.

2. Where the net amount at risk for the year is relatively small, the yearly prices of protection will tend to fluctuate widely and have little meaning.

3. As is the case with previous methods, in some years one policy may look better, while in other years another policy will appear more favorable. This method may not always lead to an unambiguous choice.

4. Like other methods, this method does not take policy loans into consideration. Since policy loans do affect the amount of investment in the contract, the rate of return and the price of protection may be miscalculated if loans are ignored. Also, policy loans will generally affect (usually reduce) dividend payments.

Baldwin Method[2]

The Baldwin method is a somewhat more complete variation of the Belth yearly rate of return method that seeks to cure some of the inadequacies of the previously discussed comparison methods. Perhaps its most notable feature is that it combines both rate of return with the value of the insurance actually received into one measure. It also adjusts for policy loans and for the opportunity cost of funds and incorporates tax considerations. Despite this relative comprehensiveness, it is basically a user friendly system. It works like this:

1. Determine how much life insurance is provided by the policy in any given year. This is computed by subtracting the total current asset value (what you would get if you cashed the policy in today) from the total death benefit to determine the "net amount at risk."

2. Determine what has been paid to maintain the life insurance in force for the year. This is computed by adding the premium, the net after-tax loan interest cost (if any), and the net after-tax (opportunity) cost of cash left in the policy. The opportunity cost of the cash left in

the policy is the cost of not borrowing from the policy if you could have invested policy loans at a greater after-tax return than the after-tax cost of borrowing from the policy.

3. Determine the cash benefits received as a result of maintaining the policy in force for the year. This is computed by adding the current year's divided (if any) to the current year's increase in cash value, account value, or asset value.

4. Determine the investment in the contract. This is computed by subtracting any loans outstanding (plus any unpaid interest) from the total asset or cash value.

5. Determine the dollar amount of return (net gain or loss) earned in the current policy year. To derive this amount, subtract the costs derived in (2) from the benefits derived in (3).

6. Determine the cash-on-cash return for the year. This is computed by dividing the net gain or loss [from (5)] by the amount invested [from (4)].

7. Determine the equivalent taxable return. To derive the before-tax rate of return that is necessary to provide an after-tax return that is equal to the currently tax-free return in the policy, divide the rate of return in (6) by (one minus the combined tax rate).

Example. If the combined local, state, and federal tax rate is 40 percent and the rate of return in the policy is 5.4, you would need to earn 9 percent in taxable investments to have 5.4 percent left after tax [$5.4\% \div (1-40\%) = 9\%$].

---

8. Determine the value of the life insurance protection received for the year. This is the truly new element added by Baldwin's method. It recognizes that the value of life insurance protection can vary from person to person and is at least partly subjective. Some people have no need for insurance protection and place no value on the life insurance protection provided by the policy. For these people, the equivalent taxable rate of return in the policy [see (7)] is the total measure of the value of the policy.

However, most people will place at least some value on the insurance protection. In general, if protection is desired, its value should be equal to at least the absolute minimum term insurance cost for an equivalent amount of protection available to the insured. That is, the most accurate cost per thousand dollars of coverage would be the figure you could obtain as a result of applying to an insurance company for an equivalent amount of term insurance, submitting to medical examination, and receiving an offer for term insurance at a contractually guaranteed rate. Once the equivalent retail value of term insurance is determined, it is multiplied by the amount of life insurance (in thousands) provided by the contract [from (1)] to determine the value of the insurance in the contract.

9.   Determine the total value received (total benefits) as a result of continuing the life insurance contract. The total value is equal to the year's net gain or loss [from (5)] plus the life insurance value [from (8)].

10.   Determine the percentage return on the total benefits. This is computed by dividing the total benefits [from (9)] by the amount invested [from (4)].

11.   Determine the equivalent after-tax return that matches the tax-deferred/tax-free return from the life insurance contract. Divide the percentage rate of return [from (10)] by (one minus the combined tax rate).

The Baldwin method overcomes some of the problems associated with the other comparison methods, but still depends on the values shown on the ledger statement, which must be closely scrutinized for accuracy and the reasonableness of the underlying assumptions. Also, like the Belth methods, it provides a series of annual rate of return figures for as many policy years as you wish to measure. It is quite possible for each of two policies to show superior performance for some years and inferior performance for others relative to each other. Therefore, rankings of policies may be ambiguous.

Policy Comparison Measures Summary

The Summary of Policy Comparison Measures in Figure 4.7 should prove helpful in reviewing these methods and in deciding which should be used or how to properly overcome their flaws. Other considerations in using these techniques are listed below.

1.   Remember that a policy comparison based on policy illustrations created by a source other than an insurance company's home office may not be officially sanctioned, accurate, or complete. Demand computer printouts from the insurer's home office for comparative purchasing purposes.

2.   Policy dividends are not guarantees—a point the consumer often does not hear or understand (or sometimes does not want to hear or understand). The financial advisor should not only emphasize this in comparing policies but also in making presentations to clients.

3.   The longer the period into the future, in which values are projected or illustrated, the less likely they are to be accurate.

4.   The method used to decide rates credited to cash values and to allocate the amount of dividends to policyowners and then apportion them among policyowners will significantly affect policy comparisons. Check to see if the company is using the "portfolio" method or the "investment year" method (sometimes called the "new money" method). Most companies now use the investment year method.

Under the investment year method, the assets acquired with the premiums paid during a particular year are treated as a separate cell of the insurance company's general asset account. The investment returns earned by the assets in each calendar-year cell are credited to the cell. Each year as the composition of the cell changes due to maturities, repayments, sales, and other transactions, the changing investment performance of the cell is allocated to the policies that paid the premiums to acquire the assets in the cell. This method promotes equity, since policyholders receive the investment results that are directly attributable to their premium contributions.

If the portfolio method is used, all policies are credited with the rate earned on the company's overall portfolio, despite the fact that earnings on premium dollars received in some years may actually be earning higher or lower returns than the portfolio rate. For instance, in periods of declining interest rates, the premium dollars received on new policies will probably be invested by the company at rates that are lower than the company earns on its existing portfolio. Also, when using the portfolio method, these new policyholders will benefit at the expense of the prior policyholders, because they will be credited with higher returns than their premium dollars are actually earning. Conversely, if interest rates are increasing, use of the portfolio method will be disadvantageous for new policyholders, but beneficial to existing policyholders. Make sure all the illustrations are based on the same method, if possible.

5. Supplementary benefits and riders impact upon policy comparisons. For example, the total premium for a policy with waiver of premium should be adjusted to take into account the extra charge.

6. In deciding whether to purchase whole life insurance or to "buy term and invest the difference," be sure to consider the value of:

   a. protection from creditors;

   b. probate savings;

   c. federal gift/estate tax savings implications;

   d. state gift/death tax savings implications;

   e. dividend options (such as one year term);

   f. loan/collateral uses; and

   g. settlement (annuity) options.

POLICY REPLACEMENT

The previous discussions of the various policy comparison methods and the summary table of the common policy comparison methods suggest which of these methods is potentially suitable for evaluating replacement policies. As those discussions indicate, some of the comparison methods are not suitable for comparisons between existing and new policies, and planners may need to adjust or modify a method when applying it in certain circumstances. Even those methods planners can use to compare existing to new policies may give ambiguous results. In addition, there are broader implications and considerations that insureds and planners should address when evaluating whether to replace an existing policy with a new policy.

When evaluating whether to replace an existing policy, insureds and planners should return to the original admonition: "MATCH THE PRODUCT TO THE PROBLEM." Often when an insured's objectives change and an existing policy is not entirely suitable for the revised objectives, it may be best to keep the existing policy in place and to purchase additional coverage with the flexibility and features one needs. Sometimes it may be wise to keep an existing policy in place and to use borrowing from the cash value to pay premiums on new supplemental coverage, rather than to exchange the old policy for a new policy.

In almost all replacement cases where the old policy is just not suitable and must be replaced (or where replacement is being considered because of the financial weakness of the company that issued the old policy), the insured should consider using the provisions of Internal Revenue Code section 1035 to assure that the exchange is treated as a nontaxable event. If the insured surrenders the old policy and uses the cash surrender value to help finance the new policy, two adverse tax consequences could ensue.

First, to the extent of gain in the policy (that the cash value exceeds the net premiums paid), the surrender value will be subject to income tax at the policy owner's ordinary tax rate.

Second, if a large after-tax surrender value is placed in the new policy, the new policy could be treated as a Modified Endowment Contract (MEC) with very adverse tax consequences with respect to any lifetime withdrawals or loans.[3] Even if the policy is not treated as a MEC, the insured may be subject to the fifteen-year rule with respect to withdrawals, where amounts withdrawn within the first fifteen years may be taxed on the interest-first rule rather than the cost-first rule.[4]

Finally, whenever an old policy is exchanged for a new policy, the insured surrenders certain rights. For example, the new policy generally is issued with a new suicide period and a new incontestable period, even if the old policy had long surpassed the reach of those provisions. In addition, the insured may forfeit more favorable guarantees as to minimum rates credited to the cash values, and more favorable provisions and rates for policy loans.

The insured and the planner should compare the relative merit of all the provisions of the existing policy as compared to the provisions and promises of the new policy.

Figure 4.7

SUMMARY OF KEY POINTS OF COMMON POLICY COMPARISON METHODS

	Traditional Net Cost	Interest Adjusted Net Cost	Interest Adjusted Payments Index	Equal Outlay	Cash Accumulation	Linton Yield	Belth Yield	Belth Price	Baldwin Method
Technique	Net premiums less cash value and dividends; ignores interest	Net premiums at interest less dividends at interest and cash value, divided by annuity due factor	Average time value adjusted difference between net premiums at interest and dividends at interest	Accumulate premium differences at interest	Accumulate premium differences at interest while holding death benefits constant	Accumulate premium differences at interest rate that causes equal future values and equal death benefits	Ratio of "benefits" to "investment"	Policy "investment" less "benefits"	Rate of cash and life insurance "benefits" to "investment"
Solves for	"Net cost"	Average net cost	Average net cost	Surrender value and death benefit differences	Surrender value differences	Average rate of return that causes equality	Yearly rate of return	Yearly price of protection	Yearly rate of return
Assumptions needed	Money has no time value	Rate of return	Rate of return	1 Rate of return 2 Equal outlay 3 Equal death benefits	1 Rate of return 2 Equal outlay	1 YRT rates 2 Equal outlay 3 Equal death benefits	YRT rates	Rate of return	YRT rates
Compares similar policies?	No	Yes	Yes	Yes, but results often ambiguous	Yes	Yes, if common YRT rates used	Yes, if common YRT rates used	Yes	Yes, if Common YRT rates Used
Compares dissimilar policies?	No	No	No	Yes, but results often ambiguous	Yes	Yes	Yes	Yes	Yes
Good for Replacement evaluation?	No	No	No	Yes, with modification	Yes, with modification	Yes, with modification	Yes, but results often ambiguous	Yes, but results often ambiguous	Yes, but results may be ambiguous

WHERE TO FIND POLICY RATING INFORMATION

The most authoritative independent sources of information on premiums, cash values, dividends, interest adjusted indexes, dividend histories, settlement option values, and other essential data for policy comparison are:

1. *Best's Flitcraft Compend*, available from the A.M. Best Company in Oldwick, New Jersey, (and Amazon) is an excellent, but dated, source of information on the historical performance of various policies offered by many insurance companies (discontinued in 1994). It includes a historical policy performance section showing projected and actual dividend and interest histories and projected and actual interest-adjusted net payments and surrender cost indices for various issue ages for many of the policies that had been offered in the market in the '80s and '90s.

2. *Life Rates & Data*, published by the National Underwriter Company in Cincinnati, Ohio. While last published in 1989 and no longer available from the publisher, it remains an excellent source for historical comparisons.

3. *Best's Review*, a monthly magazine, runs policy comparisons and each year compares dividend histories of different companies. This magazine is also a valuable source of information about new products.

4. *Consumer Reports* does some evaluations for nonprofessionals but is unfortunately limited in the number of companies and policies reviewed.

CHAPTER ENDNOTES

1. *The Insurance Forum* 168 (June 1982).

2. This discussion of the Baldwin method is adapted from B. Baldwin and W. Droms, *Life Insurance Investment Advisor: A Guide to Understanding and Selecting Today's Insurance Products (Probus Publishing Company,* 1988), pp. 145-155.

3. See Chapter 23, "Section 1035 Exchanges," for a complete discussion of the operation of the Section 1035 provisions.

4. See Chapter 24, "Taxation of Benefits," under "Policy Withdrawals" for a discussion of the potential tax implications.

LEGAL ASPECTS OF LIFE INSURANCE

CHAPTER 5

INTRODUCTION

This chapter will provide an overview of some of the general principles governing life insurance as a legally enforceable contract and examine the terms and conditions under which life insurance is sold.[1] This chapter is not meant to be a legal treatise and will only provide a basic survey of general life insurance principles. Each state's law may (and often does) differ from another state's law. And, each courts' interpretations of a general principle may vary (from slightly to radically) when compared with the conclusions of courts in another state. This chapter will not cover life insurance contract formation because the legal aspects of the contract will depend on the insurer's policies and contract terminology in addition to state law.

While reading this chapter, planners should consider the documentation necessary to create a "paper trail" of evidence as to what happened, who said and who did what, and when and how each step of the contractual process occurred. Careful record keeping can prove invaluable for tax purposes as well as in the event of a dispute among the parties.

A more thorough understanding of the legal safeguards and peculiarities of the life insurance contract with respect to the few duties it imposes on the policyowner or his or her beneficiaries, as well as the multitude of privileges, powers, and rights it bestows will enhance the planner's appreciation for this unique and incredibly useful product.

Topics in this chapter include:

1. parties to the contract;

2. requirement of insurable interest;

3. legal form and contents of the contract;

4. one-month grace period for premium payments;

5. incontestable clause;

6. suicide clause;

7. misstatement of age adjustment clause;

8. dividend clause;

9. nonforfeiture provisions (cash surrender, extended term and paid up insurance);

10. policy lapse and reinstatement clause;

11. naming and changing the beneficiary;

12. modes of settlement;

13. policy loans;

14. assignments of a life insurance policy; and

15. waiver and estoppel.

PARTIES TO THE CONTRACT

A life insurance policy is a legally enforceable contract issued by the insurer in consideration of the application and the payment of premiums. The essence of that contract is that:

If the insured dies while this policy is in force, we will pay the Sum Insured to the Beneficiary, when we receive at our Home Office due proof of the Insured's death, subject to the provisions of this policy.

There are four parties to the life insurance contract:

1. the insurer;

2. the insured;

3. the applicant-policyowner; and

4. the beneficiary.[2]

The *insurer* is the first party to a life insurance contract. The insurer almost always operates in corporate form and must be licensed in each state in which it does business.

The *insured* is the second party to the contract.[3] Almost any natural person can be an insured.[4]

The *applicant-policyowner* is the third party, and is often (but not always) the same as the insured. This is the party who applies for and owns the contract that has been made with the insurer. Again, generally, almost any natural person and most entities such as trusts, corporations, partnerships, limited liability companies, or sole proprietorships can apply for and own life insurance on one or more person's lives.[5] Some state laws give those with "limited contractual capacity" (e.g., a minor) a statutory right to enter into a contract of life insurance and then to void that contract and regain the premiums paid.[6]

The *beneficiary* is the fourth (or third, if the insured and the policyowner are the same) party to the contract. Although the beneficiary does not sign the application for insurance and may not even be aware of the existence of the insurance, because the contract is for that party's direct benefit, that party can sue the insurer after the insured's death to collect the policy proceeds. So in a very real sense, at the instant the policy matures through the insured's death, a life insurance policy is a contract for the benefit of the third party beneficiary.

INSURABLE INTEREST

Insurable interest is a key principle in life insurance law. It is the requirement imposed by law (and by insurers) to prevent a "gaming" or "wagering" by one party on the life of another through insurance. Simply put, to insure the life of an individual, the applicant must have an insurable interest, i.e., a greater concern in the insured's living than dying. Courts (and insurers) look for "a reasonable ground … to expect some benefit or

advantage from the continuance of the [insured]."[7] Stated in another manner, the public has an interest in preventing the contract of insurance where the applicant has no interest in the continuation of the insured's life other than the prospect of profiting from the insured's early demise.

Virtually everyone accepts that a person has an unquestionable insurable interest in his or her own life. "The mere fact that a man of his own motion insures his life for the benefit of either himself or of another is sufficient evidence of good faith to validate the contract."[8] Most applicant-insureds will face no insurable interest issue in obtaining life insurance. Nor will their naming of someone other than their estates as beneficiary usually pose a problem because it is generally assumed that the insured will not name as beneficiary someone who wished him harm or who would wager on his life.[9] Of course, if the policy was obtained expressly for the purpose of wagering or if the policy was really purchased by and soon after issue assigned to the third party beneficiary, the courts will declare such a contract void.[10] Public policy will not allow one to accomplish by fraudulent indirection what the law clearly prohibits one from doing directly.

State Law Issues

Every state has either statutory law or case law on insurable interest and all require that either the beneficiary or applicant hold such interest at the inception of the contract. Most states do not require that either the beneficiary or assignee of a policy have an insurable interest. The majority of states hold that there is nothing conclusively illegal about an assignment to one who holds no insurable interest—even where the insured is paid value for the assignment.[11] But some states do require that the assignee have an insurable interest—even though some of the same states allow the insured to name a beneficiary who does not have an insurable interest.

Because each state is free to create its own laws on insurable interest and because different state courts have come to different conclusions on the issue, it is impossible to develop rules that apply without question in every state. Most state laws do not question the insured's insurable interest in his own life nor the interest of close relatives related by blood or law and bonded through natural love and affection with the insured. With respect to others, statutes favor persons who stand to profit by the insured's continued life, suffer economic loss at the insured's death, and who have more to gain by the insured's continued life than death.

Types of Insurable Interests

Insurable interests are based on the relationship between the policyholder and the insured. These types of relationships fall into three broad categories: blood relatives, marriage, and business relationships.

Blood Relatives

The following blood relationships will generally give rise to an insurable interest:

- A parent usually is deemed to have an insurable interest in his or her child's life.

- A child usually is deemed to have an insurable interest in his or her parent's life. (But once the child becomes a financially independent adult, it is not certain that all courts would hold that the blood relationship alone would be sufficient to meet insurable interest tests).

- A grandchild usually is deemed to have an insurable interest in the life of a grandparent.

- A grandparent usually is deemed to have an insurable interest in the life of a grandchild.

- Siblings usually are deemed to have an insurable interest in the life or lives of brothers and sisters.

- Other relatives, such as an aunt, uncle, niece, nephew, or cousin, generally are not deemed to have an insurable interest merely by virtue of their blood relationship (but may have an insurable interest arising out of a business or financial transaction or out of financial dependency on the insured).

Marriage

Spouses have an insurable interest on each other's lives,[12] and a few courts have held that a person engaged to another has an insurable interest in the other's life.[13]

Other individuals related to the insured by marriage are usually deemed not to have an insurable interest based solely on a marriage relationship (but may have an insurable interest based on financial dependency). In-laws, for example, or step-sons or daughters, or foster children have no per se insurable interest based on family relationships but can obtain insurable interest because of dependency.

Business Relationships

Any legal entity (which may include natural persons and businesses, whether incorporated or not) that would suffer a financial loss at the insured's death will usually be deemed to have an insurable interest, though the amount of coverage must bears a reasonable relationship to the loss that would be suffered at the death of the insured.[14] Business relationships which are commonly insured include:

- an employer insuring an employee;

- an employee insuring an employer;

- a partner insuring a partner;

- a partnership insuring its partners;

- a surety insuring the life of his principal;

- a member of a commercial enterprise insuring an individual whose death would adversely affect the financial stability or profits of the .

Although a business generally has an insurable interest in the lives of officers, directors, and managers, or others on whose continued life or lives the business' success may depend upon, a corporation may not have insurable interest in the life of a shareholder who has no working or other financial relationship with the business. The point is that it is not the mere legal relationship that creates the insurable interest, but rather the "existence of circumstances which arise out of or by reason of" the entity.

Where business associates have insured each other to fund a purchase of the business interest at the insured's death or the business itself has insured an owner to fund a purchase of that person's interest at death, usually there will be an insurable interest.

Creditors have been allowed to purchase policies on debtors as long as the relationship between the amount of insurance and the debt were proportionate.

But at the point where the transaction was more of a wager than an effort to secure a debt (decided on a case by case basis), the policy is void as lacking insurable interest.[15] So the closer the insurance amount is to the debt owed, the more likely insurable interest will not be an issue.[16] (However, once the policy has been issued to a creditor, the creditor typically is allowed to keep the entire amount of the proceeds even if the amount exceeds the debt.)

When Must the Insurable Interest Be Present?

Most states require that an insurable interest be present only at the time when the life insurance contract is entered into (i.e., at the inception of the policy) and need not be present at the insured's death.[17] Therefore, a wife who is married at the time the insurance is purchased on her husband's life but divorced from him at his death is not barred from collecting.[18] Likewise, if a corporation purchases insurance on the life of a key employee, by definition there is an insurable interest at that time. If the employee later leaves the firm, the corporation can still collect the proceeds of the policy on his life.[19]

Even if the insurable interest tests are met by a third party applicant, state law will void the contract if the insured is not informed and the insured's consent is not obtained.[20] Even a spouse cannot lawfully purchase a policy on the other spouse's life in most states without that person's knowledge and consent.[21] However, there is a practical exception to this general rule: a parent can, without the child's consent, purchase relatively small amounts of life insurance on the life of a minor child since the child does not have the legal capacity to consent and so such consent would be meaningless.

Passing of the contestable period will not bar an insurer from asserting a lack of insurable interest since the strength and validity of the incontestable clause is predicated on the existence of a valid contract. Absent insurable interest, there never was a valid contract.

An insurer has a legal duty to use reasonable care in ascertaining the existence of insurable interest and in assuring that the insured did in fact consent to the coverage. If the insurer does not use reasonable care in both duties, it may be liable for the harm that occurs to the insured and/or beneficiaries.[22] For this (and sound underwriting economic) reason(s), insurance companies are often more stringent than state law requires.

Financial Underwriting and Insurable Interest

The principle of insurable interest is of great philosophical and moral significance but would be of little practical value without some means to measure it. The process of financial underwriting is the means by which the theoretical concept of insurable interest is applied in real-world situations.

The basic purpose of financial underwriting is to determine if the insurance need can justify the amount of insurance. If the amount applied for is in excess of the amount of the potential economic loss, then poor persistency or adverse selection may occur; it suggests potential moral hazard. The term "moral hazard" refers to the intention of the proposer. If the insurance proposal is made with an intention to seek undue advantage from the policy, then there is some moral hazard.

Underwriters have to judge the existence of moral hazard through secondary factors such as lifestyles, income as compared to premium payable, reputation for integrity, present financial condition, etc. If they suspect moral hazard, then the insurer usually will decline the proposal. One of the indicators of moral hazard is the amount of the insurance proposed compared to the income of the applicant. The extent of insurable interest of a person in his own life is usually assumed to be unlimited. Generally, the level of coverage is not necessarily limited to his current levels of income, because the insurer gives applicant-insureds the benefit of the doubt and assumes that these levels of income can go up some reasonable degree in the near future.

However, although dreams may become reality in the turn of a day (a pauper may go on to win a million dollar lottery, and a struggling actor may become an overnight sensation) such projections may not be valid while making an application for a life insurance policy. This is because the applicant will have to pay insurance premiums out of present income, and a person's worth is calculated by his present income; and not by what he thinks he may earn a decade later.

Therefore, underwriters need to check the source of income. If the applicant is not paying (or does not have adequate resources to pay) the premiums and someone else pays or will have to be paying on his behalf, then there could be issues of insurable interest and wager (betting). Even if the underwriters can reasonably rule out moral hazard, other factors enter into an insurer's decision to accept an application, for insurance. If the premium paid is large compared to the income, the possibility of lapse is very high. Other possibilities include higher claims, money laundering and fraud.

Making a judgment on all these factors is what the insurance industry calls financial underwriting. When all is said and done, the question financial underwriters need to answer is: *"Does the proposal make sense?"*

In summary, financial underwriting is that area of underwriting which aims to determine, first, if the applicant has a legitimate insurable interest in the life being insured and, second, whether the amount being applied for is consistent with that insurable interest, the level of the applicant's insurance need, and the financial capacity of the applicant to pay required premiums. In this process, the financial underwriters are trying to ensure that there is no question of over-insurance, or speculation or possibility of fraud arising out of pure monetary considerations. If there is evidence of over-insurance or fraud, there exists moral hazard, and there is only one decision in such cases; to decline the proposal.

FORM AND CONTENTS OF THE CONTRACT

The life insurance policy is highly consumer protection oriented and unique in the law of contracts. In legal parlance, it is an "aleatory, unilateral contract of adhesion."

Aleatory means that the insurer's promise to pay the policy proceeds is conditioned upon an uncertain event (i.e., the insured's death within the term of the contract).

Unilateral describes the fact that the insurance company is the only party to the contract which makes a legally enforceable promise. (The policyowner's payment of premiums is technically a "condition precedent" to the insurer's liability.) The insurer promises to pay a specific dollar amount if the insured dies while the policy is in force. Note that the policyowner makes no promise to continue paying premiums and there is no way the insurer can require the policyowner to continue paying premiums.

Adhesion is a legal recognition that the policyowner was not in a position to negotiate with the insurer on the terms of the contract and the resulting document is not evidence of the normal "give and take" negotiation and bargaining found in a standard contract. The insured may adhere to the terms of the policy but

cannot change them. Furthermore, the legal terms of the life insurance contract and underlying mathematical assumptions make it difficult for the policyowner to understand. For these reasons, courts will not insist that the policyowner meet the same degree of strict compliance to the terms of the life insurance contract as it might in the case of the typical agreement. Because the insurance contract is a "take it or leave it" agreement in which the insurer selects all wording and there is no negotiation of the terms, ambiguities are typically interpreted in the policyowner's (and beneficiary's) favor and against the insurer.[23]

For these reasons, many courts have adopted one or more theories that have made it possible to construe insurance policy language strictly against the insurer.[24] But because the life insurance contract is one requiring a great deal of reliance on the statements of the insured and/or applicant-owner, honesty—rather than reliance on the leniency of the courts—should be the watchword in the contractual process.

The "Face Page"

Almost all life insurance contracts have a similar format; there will be a "face page" and both required and optional provisions on succeeding pages. Most contracts also have a page that contains the definitions of terms used in the contract.

The face page contains: the basic promise of the insurer to pay a stated amount upon the insured's death; a statement as to the type of policy that is issued (e.g., term or whole life), the length of time premiums are payable (most provide premiums that are payable for a stated period or until the insured's death) and whether or not dividends are payable; a table of contents guide to the other provisions of the policy; and a statement regarding any additional benefits. It must contain the signatures (facsimile is sufficient) of the president and secretary of the insurer.

Certain provisions are required by state law to safeguard the interests of the policyowner and the beneficiary. These almost universally required provisions[25] include:

1. one-month grace period for premium payments;

2. incontestable clause;

3. suicide clause;

4. misstatement of age adjustment clause;

5. dividend clause;

6. extended term and paid-up insurance clause; and

7. policy lapse and reinstatement clause.

Some states prohibit the insurer from inserting certain types of provisions for the same reasons. There are prohibitions in various states against such provisions which:

1. limit (to less than the period fixed by that state's general statute of limitations) the time in which a suit may be brought against the insurer;

2. permit backdating the policy more than a specified period of time (usually six months);

3. allow a forfeiture of the policy for failure to repay a policy loan;

4. make the insurer's agent the client's agent; and

5. cut back the insurance ostensibly provided on the face page.

Almost all states forbid the use of the term "warranty" (a statement guaranteed true in every respect) and now hold that a statement by an applicant or by the insured is a "representation" (a statement that must be true only as to facts material to the risk). The distinction is crucial to the protection of the policyowner and his or her beneficiaries. A warranty is part of the contract but a representation is not. Therefore, the breach of a warranty makes the contract rescindable by the insurer but in the event the insurer proves misrepresentation by the applicant and/or insured, the insurer cannot rescind the contract—unless the fact misrepresented is material to acceptance of the risk. Almost every state requires that the policy itself must provide that—*in the absence of fraud*—all statements by or for the insured are deemed to be representations and not warranties.

Each policy contains an entire contract provision stating that the policy—together with the copy of the application that is attached and is legally a part of the policy—is the entire contract. The insurer agrees in this provision not to fight a lawsuit on the basis of any statement unless that statement is made in the application and a copy of the application was attached to the policy when it was issued.[26] The insured and/or policyowner is then put on notice that no one (including the agent, the insured, or the policyowner) has the authority to waive or change a provision in the policy.

Many states allow (and some require) an insurer to insert a provision on the face page of the policy that provides a free look—a trial examination period to examine and decline the policy within a given period of time (usually ten days, but in some cases as long as twenty days). If declined, the contract would be deemed void from inception and the insurer would be obligated to return the policyowner's money (typically without interest).

GRACE PERIOD

The policyowner's payment of the premium is a "condition precedent" to the insurer's duty to pay a death claim. So nonpayment of premiums will cause a life insurance policy to lapse.[27] Even an insured in a coma or a person legally adjudicated mentally incompetent must pay premiums in a timely manner or the coverage will end. The insured's rights under the contract end if the specified premium is not paid at the dates specified in the contract.[28]

Most states' laws require that the contract of life insurance contain a grace period provision. A grace period gives the policyowner an additional period of time after the due date of the premium during which the policy remains in full force. So if the insured dies during that period of grace, (typically thirty-one days from the due date[29]) the insurer will pay the full death benefit (less the premium that should have been paid but was not[30]). If the premium is not paid by the last day of the grace period and the insured is still alive, the policy owner does not owe the insurer for the unpaid premium, but of course, the policy lapses.

INCONTESTABLE CLAUSE

The incontestable clause typically is stated as follows:

We will not contest the validity of this Policy, except for nonpayment of premiums, after it has been in force during the Insured's lifetime for two years from the policy date. This Provision does not apply to any rider providing disability or accidental death benefits.

So after the specified period of time (usually two years[31]) starting on the policy date[32] and running for such period of time during the insured's lifetime,[33] the insurance company is barred from challenging the validity[34] of the contract. Stated in a more legalistic manner, the insurer is "estopped from contesting even a material or fraudulent misrepresentation in the policy."

The incontestable clause provides a balance between the legitimate interests of the parties:

Insurer – The incontestable clause allows a reasonable time for the insurer to discover and resist fraud by the insured and/or applicant-policyowner and deny liability, repudiate the policy, and return the policyowner's premiums.

Policyowner and beneficiaries – The incontestable clause avoids the necessity of a long, expensive, and uncertain litigation to prove the truth of statements made in the application for the policy while the insured was alive and to obtain the policy proceeds after the insured's death.[35]

In other words, the incontestable clause can be considered a statute of limitations on the insurer to investigate statements made in the application, for insurance, and deny coverage on the basis of that inquiry. Once the contestable period expires, even fraud will not vitiate the contract.

Planners should note that the typical incontestable clause will carve out certain exceptions. For instance, the insurer is not barred from resisting a claim if premiums are not paid. Many clauses also except from the protection of the incontestable clause any accidental death or disability payable under a policy rider or exclude from the incontestable clause's scope "war hazards" (where the insured is killed as the result of military service).[36] Some policies will provide within the incontestable clause a statement that if the insured's age is misstated, the amount payable will be appropriately adjusted.

There are also other reasons why payment under a life insurance contract may be legally refused in spite of the incontestable clause. If these are proved by the insurer, the policy will be void (i.e., there never was a valid contract with the proposed insured).

1. *Fraudulent impersonation*[37] (i.e., someone, claiming to be the insured, signs the application and/or takes the physical examination using the insured's name) – Either there never was a valid contract or if the contract was valid, it was with someone other than the insured.

So the incontestable clause does not bar the insurer from contesting the policy even after the expiration of the contestable period.

2. *Lack of insurable interest*[38] – If there is no reasonable expectation of benefit or advantage from the continued life of the proposed insured, the life insurance contract becomes a form of wagering or gaming. To prevent profiting on the lives of others, all states void a contract in which there was no insurable interest at the inception of the contract regardless of the contestable period expiring.

3. *Procurement of the policy with intent to murder* – Public policy will not allow a contract to come into existence where it was entered into with the express purpose of murdering the insured. "Where the contract falls, it brings with it all of its constituent parts" and so the incontestable clause, being "no more a part of the contract than any of its provisions" must fall with the contract.[39]

SUICIDE CLAUSE

Suicide is the intentional killing of oneself. A typical policy will provide that:

If the insured commits suicide, while sane or insane, within two years from the Policy Date, our liability will be limited to the amount of the premiums paid, less any debt and partial surrenders, and less the costs of any riders.

If the insured commits suicide, while sane or insane, within two years from the effective date(s) of any increase in insurance or any reinstatement, our total liability shall be the cost of the increase or reinstatement.

The insurer is stating that the promised death benefit will not be paid if the insured dies as the result of a suicide within the specified period of (usually) two years.[40]

Like the incontestable provision, the suicide clause provides a legitimate balance between the interests of the parties:

Insurer – The insurer is responsible to other policyowners (in a mutual company) or to shareholders (in a stock company) for matching premium charges with risk. If individuals contemplating suicide were allowed to purchase life insurance without restriction, the insurer's increased and accelerated liability would be reflected in higher costs that eventually would be passed on to policyowners (or shareholders). The mere knowledge that suicide within two years would not accomplish the intended goal of enriching beneficiaries at the insurer's expense is thought to discourage those who would take a policy out with the specific intent of committing suicide. The imposition of what amounts to a relatively short waiting period for full coverage substantially reduces the threat of unfair additional costs levied upon other policyowners.

Policyowner and beneficiaries – The policyowner and his or her beneficiaries need the insurance regardless of the cause of the insured's death and should not have to bear the expense, aggravation, and uncertainty of litigation if suicide—no matter how long after the contract was purchased—would cause a loss of the proceeds the contract was designed to furnish. Regardless of whether the insured was sane or insane, once the suicide period expires, the insurer is liable at the death of the insured.[41]

Most cases dealing with the suicide clause are concerned with one (or both) of two issues:

1. Was the cause of death suicide or some outside force? (Was the insured murdered?)

2. Assuming the insured killed himself, did he or did he not intend to do so? (Was the death accidental rather than intentional?)

The presumption is that the insured did not commit suicide and the insurer must prove that the facts reasonably demonstrate death did not occur by accident. This burden of proof shifts, however, in the case of accidental death riders. There, the beneficiary must prove that the insured died accidentally and not by self destruction.

Absent a suicide provision, if the insured dies as a result of suicide, in most cases the insurer will be required to pay no matter how soon death occurs after the policy is issued—unless the insurer can prove that the insured purchased the policy with the deliberate intent of killing himself and enriching his beneficiaries at the expense of the insurer by that fraud (the implicit agreement that when a policy is purchased the insured is not intending to do himself in).[42]

Because a suicide is by definition a deliberate act, it will mean the insurer is not liable to pay any accidental death benefits. "A suicide is not an accidental death."[43]

When the clock starts to tick on the (typically two year) suicide exclusion time period varies depending upon the following:

Policy backdated to "save age" – Most courts will start the time at the "issue date" if it is clearly stated in the policy.[44] But, if the terms of the contract are ambiguous, the time may start at the back date rather than the issue date.

Conversion of term to permanent – Assuming the new policy is obtained through an individual term or group option to convert, many courts will treat the transaction as a continuance of the original contract. This means if the original individual term or group term life was covered by a suicide clause, it continues (and the clock ticks) from the original date. If there was no suicide clause in the original, the new policy would not carry one.

After the suicide period has expired, the insurer is liable for paying the death proceeds regardless of the cause of death.

MISSTATEMENT OF AGE ADJUSTMENT CLAUSE

Yet another protection for the policyowner of an individual contract and policy beneficiaries is the "misstatement of age" clause[45] that is required by law in most states and will typically read similarly to this:

This policy is issued at the age shown on page ___, which should be the age attained by the insured on the last birthday before the Policy Date. If the Policy Date falls on the Insured's birthday, the age should be the Insured's attained age on the Policy Date.

If the insured's age is incorrectly shown on page ___, the proceeds payable under this policy will be adjusted to the proceeds that would have been purchased at the correct age based upon our rates in effect when this policy was issued.

Mortality can vary considerably with age. So obviously, age is a crucial factor in the calculation of the proper life insurance premium for a given class of risk. If the wrong age is stated on the application (regardless of whether by deliberate misstatement or because the insured just did not know his date of birth), the insurer cannot charge the appropriate premium and the policyowner may pay much more or much less than what should have been paid. The insurance company trusts the applicant to be truthful and as a matter of convenience to both parties (and as a good marketing practice) does not require a birth certificate or other proof of age at the time of purchase. In fact, it is not until the insured dies and the death certificate accompanies the claim for payment that the insurer has documentation as to when the insured was born. So it is not until then that the insurer can compare the ages, meet its burden of proving that the age in the application was incorrect,[46] and make the appropriate adjustment.

The misstatement of age provision provides a legitimate balance between the interests of the parties:

Insurer – The insurer pays neither more nor less than is appropriate for the proper age of the insured at issue and avoids expensive litigation and loss of public goodwill inherent in defenses of claims on the grounds of improper age. This serves as a cost effective escape valve for handling innocent mistakes.[47]

Policyowner and beneficiaries – Even if a misstatement of age (a material misrepresentation) is found after the death of the insured,[48] there is assurance that the proper amount of proceeds will be paid, uncertainty will be avoided, and litigation to obtain the rightful amount from the insurer will not be necessary.

An insurer that finds it charged premiums based on an incorrect age can make the adjustment of benefits even if the discovery is made after the policy became incontestable on the grounds that the insurer is not denying the liability to make payments but is merely adjusting an error in how much should be paid.

DIVIDEND CLAUSE

Owners of participating life insurance contracts are entitled to dividends if the insurer has sufficient earned surplus. The term participating means that the policyowner can participate in that surplus—if there is one. Confusion may result for the following reasons:

1. Both mutual insurance companies (owned solely by policyowners) and stock companies (owned solely by outside shareholders) can legally issue participating (par) policies (although stock companies traditionally have issued nonparticipating (nonpar) contracts).

2. Both types of companies can write checks called dividends.

Profits enjoyed by a stock company are not typically shared with the policyowners; they usually go only to investors (shareholders) in the company's stock and are taxed in the same manner dividends from General Motors or IBM would be.

But the distributed surplus paid to owners of participating policies is very different than the profits paid out to owners of a stock company even though both distributions may be called dividends. A dividend paid to an owner of a participating contract is actually deemed to be a return of "excess premium" due to the generous margins built into the premium calculation assumptions.[49] In other words, the premium in a participating contract is set high enough to provide not only the amount the insurer expects to need to pay its bills and meet its obligations but also an extra amount to provide a margin of safety. Planners should note that policyholders of participating insurance cannot be surcharged by the insurer. Although dividends may not be as favorable as projected, the policyowner will not have to pay more than the set premium regardless of how poorly the insurer does financially.

Three factors—actually, the insurer's experience in three areas—influence *if* (dividends are projections only and NOT guaranteed) and *how* much the insurer will pay in dividends:

1. mortality;

2. interest; and

3. loading.[50]

Mortality represents the insurer's ability to match risk with premiums—that is, how carefully the insurer underwrites policies and how closely the experience (rate of deaths) that actually occurs parallels what was projected by the insurer in setting its rates. If more deaths occur in a given period than expected, dividends will be adversely affected. If fewer deaths occur than projected, dividends will be positively affected.

Interest really represents the insurer's investment success with net after-cost premium dollars. If assets earn less than projected, dividends will be adversely affected. If earnings and growth are greater than projected, dividends will be positively affected.

Loading is a term that encompasses all the insurer's business expenses in marketing, issuing, administering, and paying claims on policies. If the insurer's cost of doing business is greater than projected, dividends will be adversely affected. If the insurer is able to contain costs and keep them below the projected amounts, dividends will be positively affected.

The interplay between all three of these factors, and the level of additional financial safety the insurer's officers deem necessary determines (as stated above) whether the company will be able to refund the excess amounts of premium the policyowner paid in and the extent of that refund. Once this refund is decided upon, it must be "fair." This does not mean that every class of policyowners must be treated equally. For instance, policies purchased twenty-one years ago may be entitled to higher dividends than those issued five years ago (perhaps because the premiums charged to policyowners twenty-one years ago were higher than those charged to policyowners five years ago). Likewise, preferred risk policies (i.e., those requiring the purchase of larger amounts and/or more stringent underwriting) may be awarded higher dividends than standard policies. But fairness does imply that distributions among the policyowners in any class must be equal.

Dividends are payable to and legally the property of the policyowner and, therefore, policyowners may have assigned them with or separately from the policy itself.[51] At the policyowner's death, dividends that were held by the insurer to earn interest technically should pass to the policyowner's estate unless previously assigned or disposed of in another manner in the policy.

Most participating policies provide five ways a policyowner can choose to accept dividends:

1. take dividends in cash;

2. have the insurer automatically use the dividend to reduce the next premium;

3. have the insurer automatically use the amount of the dividend to purchase "paid-up" additional insurance ("paid up" adds) in the same type as the basic policy;[52]

4. have the insurer automatically hold the dividends in an account for the policyowner and pay interest on that account; or

5. have the insurer automatically purchase units of one-year term insurance equal in amount to the cash value of the policy at the date the term insurance is purchased. This is the "fifth dividend option" that policyowners often use in split dollar arrangements but also can use to considerably increase insurance coverage on a very cost effective net rate basis for other reasons, such as the repayment of a policy loan.

Policyowners also commonly use policy dividends to help pay up the policy more quickly than otherwise expected. If policyowners continue to pay premiums and add the dividends to the premium payments, the policy will become fully paid up sooner than if they use the dividends in some other way.

If policyowners elect to use dividends to pay premiums, a policy cannot lapse if their insurer holds a sufficient amount of the policyowners' dividends to pay a full premium. If policyowners select any of the other four options, the insurer will not apply dividends to pay premiums even if the policy will lapse.

High levels of dividends have been used to help create the appearance that premiums would become suspended, or seem to vanish. Essentially, once dividend levels rise high enough, if policyowners use dividends to pay premiums, dividends will be sufficient to pay all the premiums. Of course, the premiums do not really "vanish." This marketing presentation of dividends depends on dividends being paid at the (sometimes optimistic) level projected by the insurer and, in difficult economic times, the suspension of premium payments may not occur when scheduled. It is also possible (if the insurer's performance is very poor), but highly unlikely, that policyowners, whose dividends had risen to the level where they were sufficient to entirely pay periodic premiums, would later have to begin to pay some premiums because dividend levels had fallen.

Policyowners can prospectively change dividend options. Policyowners can also mix and match these options. For example, a policyowner might choose to use dividends to purchase one-year term insurance to the extent allowable and have the balance of the dividend—if any—to reduce premiums, purchase paid up additions, or take the remainder in cash.

If policyowners do not select a dividend option and the contract itself is silent on the default use of dividends, state laws direct the disposition of that money. However, state laws do allow insurers to specify in the policy a default rule that will apply when policyowners do not select a dividend option. For instance, the contract might state that if the policyowner has not selected an option (or if there is excess money from a dividend after another option is selected), the insurer will use the dividend (or any excess) to purchase paid up additional insurance. This is called the "automatic dividend option."

NONFORFEITURE PROVISIONS

State laws and policy provisions combine to provide a number of protective options for the policyowner who stops paying premiums (for whatever reason) after the policy has been in force for a number of years.[53] The policyowners do not lose the equity in their policies (assuming the type of policies in which the premiums exceed the current cost of carrying term insurance), but can use it advantageously in several ways. In other words, in level-premium contracts where policies require that a reserve be established in early years to meet higher insurance costs as the insured grows older and the probability of death grows greater, the insurer releases that reserve to the policyowner when the insurer is no longer obligated under the contract. The policyowner will receive an equitable portion of the total values his or her premiums have helped to accumulate.

How much the policyowner will receive is a function of: (1) a statutory formula; and (2) the insurer's internal policies (the insurer can promise to pay more than the statutory minimum). The values the insurer will pay are printed in the policy. Generally, at least twenty years' (or the term of the policy, if less) of values are shown.

The policyowner usually has three nonforfeiture options:

1. *Cash surrender* – Cashing in (technically called a cash surrender of) a policy is the simplest nonforfeiture option.[54] The policyowner physically surrenders the contract to the insurer and the insurer issues a check to the policyowner for the policy's cash value. The cash value (also called "cash surrender value") is the amount shown in the policy itself (sometimes "per thousand dollars" of face amount) as the cash available at the end of specified policy years (reduced by any loans against the policy).[55] The contract will contain a table showing year by year the amount that is available if the policyowner cashes in the policy and will make certain other statements in compliance with state law nonforfeiture rules. Although most states allow the insurer to defer the payment of this cash surrender value for up to six months after the policyowner tenders to contract to the insurer (to insulate insurers from a run on its cash reserves and the consequent self-generating economic crisis such a drain could precipitate), payments are almost always made within days or weeks of the policyowner's surrender of the policy.

2. *Extended term option* – If the policyowner elects to use the cash in the policy to create extended term, the face amount of the coverage is undiminished. The same death benefit payable under the original contract remains payable after the option becomes operative (less any outstanding loan). In essence, the insurer takes the policyowner's cash value in the policy and purchases term insurance for the policyowner (without the payment of commissions or charging of other expenses against the policy). Because the death benefit for the extended term policy is the same as for the original policy, only the term of time for which coverage will last changes. If the insured dies during the term, the insurer must pay. If the insured dies after the term, the insurer has no liability. Once the term expires, the policyowner cannot continue the coverage—except by formal reinstatement according to the provisions of the contract (see below). The extended term option would be a good choice where the insured had a shortened life expectancy because of an accident or illness. Once policyowners elect the extended term nonforfeiture option, they can no longer take policy loans, because extended term coverage makes no provision for policy loan values.

3. *Reduced paid up insurance option* – As its name implies, an insurer takes the cash values of the policyowner's contract and uses that money to pay up the contract for the life of the insured. Unlike extended term where the face amount is unchanged but the term is shortened, with the reduced paid up option the insurer reduces the face amount to what a net single premium in the amount of the policy's cash value will

purchase at the attained age of the insured. The same type of insurance continues at that reduced amount for the insured's life no matter how long he lives (up until the maturity date of the policy). The amount of paid up coverage is listed in the contract itself. The amount of coverage purchased is a function of the insured's age at the date the policyowner elects as well as the type of coverage being purchased and the level of cash values available. The insurer reduces the death benefit by the value of any loans against the policy (and increase the death benefit by any dividend accumulations). Reduced paid-up insurance, unlike extended term, has both cash and loan values and is, therefore, more flexible than extended term. The reduced paid up option would be a good choice where the insured is in average or superior health but, for whatever reason, the policyowner stopped paying premiums.

State law requires that the policy state an "automatic nonforfeiture benefit" if the policyowner has not selected a forfeiture option upon (or within sixty days of) the lapse of a policy. In the case of a rated (premiums adjusted to reflect a higher than standard mortality risk) policy, the automatic nonforfeiture benefit is reduced paid-up insurance. With respect to all other policies, the automatic nonforfeiture benefit is extended-term insurance.

Where an insured dies after selecting a nonforfeiture option but before receiving any benefits from it, the general rule is that, even if the insured dies before the insurer has completed its obligation under the nonforfeiture option, the option and not the death benefit is payable.[56]

POLICY LAPSE AND REINSTATEMENT CLAUSE

A policy lapses when the policyowner does not pay premiums by the end of the grace period.[57] (A policy expires when it has run past its grace period with premiums unpaid and has exhausted any benefits available under the nonforfeiture option or when the policyowner has allowed the policy to lapse by not paying the next premium due and then decides to cash in the policy.)

However, policyowners can resuscitate a lapsed policy if the insured meets certain tests and the policyholder puts the insurer back to the financial position it would have been in had the policyowner never allowed the policy to lapse. Almost all states require that life insurance contracts contain a clause allowing reinstatement—a restoration and, according to most courts, a continuation of the original contract.[58]

Such a clause might read as follows:

This policy may be reinstated at any time by a request, in writing and submitted to the Company's Home Office within five years from the date of default in premium payments, unless the policyowner has surrendered the policy for its cash value, if the policyowner:

1. *applies for reinstatement;*

2. *provides evidence of insurability satisfactory to the insurer;*

3. *pays all overdue premiums with interest at a rate not exceeding 6 percent per year compounded annually; and*

4. *pays or reinstates any policy indebtedness with interest at a rate not in excess of the applicable policy loan rate or rates determined in accordance with the policy's provisions.*

There are many reasons why this reinstatement provision can be quite valuable.[59] When compared to newly-issued policies at the insured's attained age, the original policy may have more favorable:

1. annuity purchase rates (as applied to payouts under the settlement options or nonforfeiture options);

2. policy loan rates;

3. mortality or interest assumptions; and

4. lower premium payments.

In addition:

5. A new policy would take a considerable amount of time to start to build up cash values and dividends.

6. The process of reinstatement is often quicker and simpler than applying for a new contract.

7. Typically, the suicide clause does not run anew from the date of reinstatement but instead starts

to run from the original date of the contract.[60] (This assumes the reinstatement was not procured with the intention of committing suicide and also assumes the reinstatement clause itself did not start another suicide period to run.)

8. On a new contract, the incontestable and suicide clauses start anew.

Of course, reinstatement may always not be the appropriate course of action for a particular client. Reasons for applying for a new policy rather than reinstating an older one include:[61]

1. Insurers now may have a type of policy that was not available when the policyowner applied for the original coverage and the new coverage may be more appropriate than the old.

2. Reinstatement often requires a large outlay because the policyowner must not only pay all unpaid premiums but also interest for the period of time that has elapsed since the past premiums were due.

3. Rates for new insurance may be lower than the rates charged per thousand of death benefit on the original coverage.

Insurers are usually more liberal than state law requires them to be with respect to policy reinstatement.[62] But to prevent those who are ill or at greater risk from selecting against the insurer (this is called adverse selection), state statutes and policy provisions uniformly require that the insured must be insurable—to the insurer's satisfaction[63]—at the date of reinstatement. Were it not for such a provision, former insureds who have become uninsurable would uniformly seek to become insureds again and by doing so adversely affect the mortality experience of the insurer.

Merely completing the application for reinstatement is not sufficient to restore the policy's benefits. The insured and policyowner must meet all the conditions of reinstatement before the insurer becomes liable to pay anything other than any nonforfeiture benefits that already existed before the application for reinstatement. So if the proposed re-insured dies after signing the reinstatement form but before satisfying all the requisite tests, the insurer is not liable to pay the policy death benefit.

However, once all of these conditions precedent to the insurer's liability are met (such as full compliance with all the contractual terms including insurability and payment of back premiums and interest), if the insured then dies from a cause such as an accident unrelated to insurability before the reinstatement is approved, most courts will hold that the reinstatement holds and dates back to the time the application and back premiums were tendered to the insurer.[64] An unreasonable delay on the insurer's part may be held to bar the insurer from declining coverage.[65]

Can a reinstated policy be contested? Most courts have held that for other purposes the reinstated contract should be considered the exercise of a contractual right under the original policy, i.e., a continuation of the original. This follows the ordinary meaning of the term "reinstatement," that is "to restore to the former state or position." But for purposes of contestability, a new period applies—but solely to statements made in the reinstatement application.[66] In other words, the incontestable clause runs anew as to fraud or misrepresentations in the application for reinstatement. Generally, the same contestable period that applied to the original contract applies to the reinstatement.[67]

NAMING AND CHANGING THE BENEFICIARY

A beneficiary is a person (or entity) named (or designated such as by a check off) by the policyowner to receive the death benefits under a life insurance policy at the death of the insured.[68] A revocable beneficiary is one whose potential receipt of the proceeds can be cut off, or revoked, at any time by the policyowner. An irrevocable beneficiary is one whose interest in the contract cannot be changed or reduced by the policyowner without his consent of the beneficiary. Such a beneficiary has a vested right to the death benefit as soon as he or she is named irrevocably.

Within reasonable limits, the policyowners can change the beneficiaries as often during lifetime as they want—and name anyone else they want as beneficiaries—subject to the procedures specified in the policy[69] and the following limitations:

1. Some states require that the beneficiary have an insurable interest in the insured's life where the policyowner is someone other than the insured.

2. Community property residents are during their marriages, unable to freely dispose of community assets without the written consent

of their spouses. This is because (aside from gifts and inheritances received before or during the marriage) each spouse is deemed to own a one-half, undivided interest in property acquired during the marriage while living in a community property state. If either spouse uses community funds to pay premiums, each spouse has an interest in the policy. So neither spouse can name someone else as beneficiary of the entire proceeds—even a child—without the other spouse's consent (but can name anyone he or she wants with respect to the policyowner's one-half interest).

3. State laws frequently limit the class of beneficiaries that policyowners can name where a minor is the insured. Typically, such statutes allow the naming of the insured's parent, spouse, sibling, or grandparent. A minor, upon reaching the age of legal competency, can change the beneficiary designation at that time.

4. Many states bar an insured under group term life coverage from naming the employer as beneficiary.

5. If the policyowner has named an irrevocable beneficiary, the policyowner cannot change the beneficiary without that party's written consent. An irrevocable beneficiary has a vested right to receive the proceeds of the policy—but contingent on surviving the insured. If the irrevocable beneficiary predeceases the insured, his or her beneficiary rights terminate.

6. Divorce does not, per se, affect the policyowner's right to change the beneficiary nor does it effect a change of beneficiary in most states. However, in some states, there is automatic termination of a spouse's interest after divorce while in others the policyowner can change the beneficiary even if it was irrevocable before the divorce. Furthermore, the right to change the beneficiary may be restricted by the divorce decree or property settlement agreement. On the other hand, sometimes at the remarriage of a spouse or upon the legal majority of the children, the policyowner regains the right to change the beneficiary.

7. A legally adjudicated incompetent cannot make or change a policy beneficiary nor can one who is mentally incompetent though not legally declared so. However, the test in the latter case is essentially the same as the test for competency to make a will: Does the policyowner have sufficient capacity to understand the extent of the property (i.e., the amount of the proceeds), the nature of the disposition, and the people who were the natural objects of his bounty? Usually, there is a presumption of competency. The burden of proof of incompetency is placed on the party that alleges the policyowner is incompetent (typically the person who would have been the beneficiary had it not been changed).

8. A beneficiary can collect the proceeds of a life insurance policy if he or she kills the insured in an accident (even though it may involve gross carelessness or manslaughter) or in self defense. But every state bars an intentional and wrongful killer from enrichment because of that act.[70] Typically, once such a person is disqualified, a secondary beneficiary or the insured's estate will receive the proceeds. (In most situations the issue is not whether the insurer is liable to pay but rather who is the payee. However, if the beneficiary was also the applicant-policyowner and purchased the policy with the express intent of killing the insured, it is likely that the contract is void and the insurer will not be liable to anyone.[71]) Also, the insurer may have no legal liability to make payment to anyone where the insured is legally executed[72], but in a number of states unless the insurer has specifically excluded death by legal execution, the insurer is liable to pay (particularly if the contestable period has passed).

9. A policyowner can, of course, name children as beneficiaries of life insurance but, except for very small amounts, insurers generally will not make settlements directly to minors. This means a guardian would have to be appointed (and suggests to the planner the use of a trust for the benefit of the child (children) to receive the death benefits).

Multiple Beneficiaries

A policyowner can and should name more than one beneficiary. A planner is derelict in duty if the policyowner is not told of the privilege and advantages of naming both a primary beneficiary (which can be more than one person or entity) and one or more contingent or secondary beneficiaries. Throughout this book are numerous examples of tax savings and creditor protection available through properly arranged life insurance. The authors have found few instances where allowing the policyowner's estate to dispose of insurance proceeds (by default in not naming a contingent beneficiary) is advantageous in comparison to shifting wealth directly through the insurance contract.

The primary beneficiary is the first person (or class of persons) in line to receive the proceeds when the insured dies. But to be entitled to the proceeds, the primary beneficiary must be living on the date the insured dies. Otherwise, the insurer pays the proceeds to the class of beneficiary whose interest is contingent upon surviving both the insured and the primary beneficiary. This class is appropriately called the contingent beneficiary.

The policyowner may name more than one individual, entity, or combination of individuals and entities in each beneficiary class. For example, a policyholder may name his spouse if living and otherwise his two children. Where more than one beneficiary is in a given class, they typically share the proceeds equally unless the policyowner specifies otherwise in the beneficiary designation.

Policyowners can (and in the opinion of the authors, should) even name a third level of beneficiaries or final beneficiaries in case all beneficiaries in a higher class have predeceased the insured. Often, parents, nieces, nephews, cousins, or a charity such as a church, synagogue, or university are named at this level. Alternatively, the policyowner can designate the estate of the insured and the proceeds will become part of the probate assets where the insured's will (or, if no will exists, the state's intestate laws) determines the disposition.

Usually, a lower class' rights are extinguished if the policy makes payments to members of a higher class. For instance, a contingent beneficiary will receive nothing if the primary beneficiary is alive when the insured dies. Likewise, the final beneficiary has no expectancy of a share of the proceeds if the contingent beneficiary survives the insured and the primary beneficiary predeceased the insured. Even if proceeds are taken in installments, once they are payable to a higher class of beneficiaries, any remainder payable at the death of a member of that higher class will be payable to the decedent's estate (or contingent payee) rather than to the next class of beneficiary.

Even where it seems inherently unfair, the insurer is almost always held by the courts to be bound to pay the proceeds to the named beneficiary. There are numerous cases where the proceeds were payable to a spouse long divorced by the insured because the policyowner had forgotten to designate a new beneficiary.

Specificity is essential. The beneficiary designation should describe the person with sufficient clarity and certainty so that the insurer can easily identify the proper person, make payment, and obtain a valid release.

Common Disasters

Where the beneficiary and the insured die in a common disaster, the disposition of the proceeds is generally governed by the Uniform Simultaneous Death Act (USDA) that has now been enacted in some form in almost every state. The general rule is as follows:

> Where the insured and the beneficiary die and there is no sufficient evidence that they have died in a manner other than simultaneously, the proceeds of the policy shall be distributed as if the insured survived the beneficiary.

The USDA does, however, specifically allow the policyowner to override that result in the policy's beneficiary form by making a presumption of a reverse simultaneous death (as if the insured was survived by his or her beneficiary). Planners should note that policyowners may use such a clause to reduce federal estate taxes by fully utilizing the surviving spouse's unified credit.[73]

The USDA will not apply if:

1. there is evidence that the insured and beneficiary died other than simultaneously; or

2. one of the parties did in fact survive the other for any length of time no matter how short.[74]

The problem here is that if the named beneficiary survives for even one minute the proceeds are paid to his or her estate and pass under the deceased beneficiary's will (if a valid will exists, otherwise by intestate law) and not necessarily to the person the policyowner-insured wanted to benefit.

One solution is a time (or "delay") clause. This requires the beneficiary to survive the insured by a given period of time, such as thirty or sixty days, before he or she will be entitled to the proceeds. Beware, however, of a time delay clause lasting for more than 180 days as this may cause the loss of the federal estate tax marital deduction.[75] A simple and practical solution is for the policyowner to elect a settlement option and name contingent payees to receive any proceeds not payable to the primary payee at his or her death. The insurance contract itself will provide the mechanism for payments to continue with almost no delay or cost at the death of the primary payee.

Special Situations

Planners should therefore take special care in the following beneficiary situations:

1. *The policyowner's spouse is specifically named* – Courts look to the person's name rather than description as husband or wife or fiancée. So even if that person is no longer a husband, wife, or fiancée when the insured dies, absent specific state law to the contrary, the proceeds will still be payable to the named person.[76] Courts do not pass on the morality of its citizens and recognize the right of the policyowner to make any beneficiary designation he or she pleases.

2. *The policyowner merely says, "To my husband" or "To my wife" but does not name the person* – Here, proceeds are payable to the person who, at the time of the insured's death, meets that description.[77]

3. *The policyowner names each child individually and describes the relationship* – This is the clearest and safest approach. But a child born after the beneficiary form is signed may be excluded.

4. *The policyowner names his children as a class rather than naming them individually* – The insurer may have difficulty in verifying who is included in the class—especially if name changes have occurred. The term "my children" may also cause legal problems and in many cases will include illegitimate, legally adopted, and children from a prior marriage as well as children born after the beneficiary form is signed and even those born after the insured's death.[78] The term "lawful children" will disqualify illegitimate children.

5. *The policyowner names "My Issue and Heirs"* – "Issue" is a term far broader than children and includes any lineal descendant no matter how far down the line. So grandchildren and even great grandchildren would be included. Heirs means those who would inherit under state intestacy laws (i.e., in the absence of a valid will). This designation is not generally recommended.

6. *The policyowner names a class of beneficiaries per capita or per stirpes* – A per capita (by the heads) distribution means that the proceeds will be split according to the number of beneficiaries in the class. If there are three children, each takes one-third. If there are only two out of the three that survive the insured, each takes one-half. A per stirpes (by the branches) distribution means that the distribution is first divided among the class—including a share for any predeceased member that is then split among that member's children. If two out of three children survive, the proceeds are split three ways with the deceased child's children equally splitting the share the deceased child would have had.[79] The choice between per capita and per stirpes is personal but often causes confusion. The authors recommend the policyowner's intent be specified with an example.

7. *The policyowner names a minor as beneficiary* – Few states would allow payment of policy proceeds to a minor and few companies would agree to do so even if not forbidden by law because minors cannot give a valid release to the insurer. For this reason, policyowners should name a trustee as beneficiary in most cases involving minors.[80]

8. *The policyowner names a trust as beneficiary* – This designation provides the ultimate in flexibility, by assuring that the trustee will survive the insured and spouse, and increasing the chances of proper investment management and higher returns.[81]

9. *The policyowner names a corporation, partnership, limited liability company, or charity* – It is essential that the full legal name of the entity be specified.

10. *The policyholder names himself* – This is common and proper practice where one party owns life insurance on the life of another. In fact, there

are almost always income or gift tax problems where one party owns insurance on the life of another but makes a third party the beneficiary. We call this the "Unholy Trinity."

11. *The policyowner has failed to name a beneficiary* – Some smaller policies and group term life contracts provide a facility of payment clause that enables the insurer to pay a limited amount directly to the providers of the insured's last illness and burial expenses. Insurers will pay most larger amounts according to the policy provisions that specify the recipient when no beneficiary has been designated (or where all primary and contingent beneficiaries predecease the insured). Selecting a beneficiary by default is obviously not the preferable manner for disposing of policy proceeds.

Reviewing Beneficiaries

Planners have an obligation to suggest to clients that they review the beneficiary designations made under life insurance policies (as well as employee benefit and retirement contracts) at least every two to three years or upon the occurrence of circumstances marking changes in marital status (the client's or the beneficiaries'), the beneficiaries' needs or abilities to handle money, or tax law. It is also important that life insurance beneficiary designations be coordinated with the entire estate plan.

Planners should note that a designation in a will typically does not result in a change of life insurance beneficiary (especially if the method of beneficiary change in the policy is exclusive which it almost always is) nor, as stated previously, does divorce make a change effective in most states.[82]

MODES OF SETTLEMENT

Beneficiaries can choose to settle with the insurer in a number of ways aside from the obvious and common method of a lump sum payment.[83] These optional modes of settlement include the following:

1. leave the proceeds with the insurer and receive annual interest payments;

2. accept the proceeds in installments for a specified period of time (fixed years installments);

3. accept the proceeds in installments of a specified amount (fixed amount option); and

4. accept the proceeds as a life annuity (systematic liquidation of principal and interest) for the life of one or more persons.

Interest Option

Here, the insurer guarantees to pay at least a specified minimum interest rate which the insurer may increase by paying excess interest (also called a dividend extra interest or surplus interest) to keep the insurer competitive with alternative investments. The insurer and beneficiary agree upon payment intervals such as annually, semiannually, quarterly, or monthly, (unless the policyowner preselects the intervals). The insurer can give the payee the right to change to another settlement option and either a limited or unlimited right to take all or any portion of the principal. In some cases, the policyowner may select an interest beneficiary payout option that gives the income beneficiary no right to make a withdrawal of capital. In such cases, any benefit balance upon the income beneficiary's death will pass to the payee's estate or to a third party depending on the terms of the agreement. Generally, at the option of the beneficiary, someone other than the interest recipient may receive the principal. The policyowner or the beneficiary should always name a successor-payee to receive any amount remaining payable at the primary payee's death.

Planners utilize this option as a temporary investment repository to give beneficiaries time to make a rational and studied decision on how to invest the proceeds. The interest-only option is also convenient if the beneficiary does not currently need income under one of the other options but is planning to utilize one of them at a later date.

Installments over a Fixed Period of Years Option

Under this option, the insurer makes payments in equal amounts over a specified period selected by the beneficiary. If the primary payee does not survive to the end of the payment period, the insurer will pay the balance of the payments to the contingent payee. The contract contains a table that shows the amount of the individual payments (usually per $1,000 of death benefits) that the insurer can make over various periods of time ranging from one to thirty years. Any extra interest the insurer pays will increase the amount of income it pays (rather than extend the period). This option is indicated where the beneficiary needs the largest possible guaranteed income over a relatively short and fixed period of time.

Fixed Amount Option

Payments under this fixed amount option are paid to the beneficiary (and to the beneficiary's successor-payee after the original beneficiary's death) for as long as the proceeds (compounded at a guaranteed interest rate) last. If the insurer pays excess interest, the period over which the insurer will make payments will increase accordingly (while the amount of each payment remains the same). Planners use this easy to explain option to augment Social Security benefits and other income.

After payments commence, beneficiaries generally can ask the insurer to commute any remaining unpaid installments under either the fixed years or fixed amount option (i.e., the beneficiary can choose to take the present value of the future stream of income in an immediately payable lump sum) or have the commuted value of the remaining unpaid installments applied under another option.

Life Income Option

Under this option, the insurer makes periodic payments over the lifetime of the beneficiary. The insurer essentially uses the proceeds to purchase (the insurer charges no commissions or other acquisition costs) a single-premium life annuity for the designated payee. That annuity then pays out to the named payee an income of a guaranteed amount for the payee's lifetime. Beneficiaries can choose for the annuity to have a period certain guarantee—a guarantee that payments will continue for a selected period of years, regardless of whether the payee is alive or dead. The period-certain guarantees commonly run for ten-, fifteen-, or twenty-years, and sometimes longer.

The life income option can take one of four basic forms:

1. *Straight life (annuity) income* – Payments will last for as long as the payee lives and stop at the payee's death. This provides the highest annual income of the four forms of life income because it stops when the payee dies.

2. *Life income with period certain* – The insurer makes payments for a period selected by the beneficiary. The insurer will continue payments to a contingent payee for the balance of the period if the primary payee dies before the period ends.[84]

3. *Life refund annuity* – The insurer makes payments to the payee (and/or contingent payee) until the insurer pays an amount at least equal to the proceeds paid at the insured's death.

4. *Joint and survivor annuity* – The insurer makes payments to two individuals as long as both are alive and then continues the same or a lesser amount for the life of the survivor. Beneficiaries may elect to take payments of a smaller amount that continue at the same level for both lives (until the second death) or to take payments of a larger amount that continue until the first of the two payees dies and then a lower amount to the survivor until the survivor's death.

Planners should consider settlement options where the amount of insurance is relatively small and the cost of establishing a trust is relatively high. Some consider a settlement option the "poor man's trust." These optional modes of settlement do have a number of advantages including:

1. the insurer makes no separate or special charges;

2. no other commercial institution can pay a life income; and

3. the insurer guarantees both principal and a minimum rate of interest.

But planners should also consider the following downside costs and disadvantages:

1. they may be able to get higher earnings from alternative investments;

2. a trust may prove more flexible; and

3. a trust may be more responsive to the beneficiaries' needs and circumstances.

Figure 5.1

	A COMPARISON OF SETTLEMENT OPTIONS TO TRUSTS	
	SETTLEMENT OPTIONS	**TRUSTS**
Discretion	Must be administered strictly in accordance with policy provisions and terms of the settlement agreement.	Trustee can exercise considerable discretion if the grantor directs the trustee to do so.
Flexibility	Although some flexibility can be provided, variations must be specified in advance.	Generally, trusts are more flexible than settlement agreements; amounts payable to the beneficiary can be changed frequently.
Guarantees	Safety of proceeds is guaranteed; minimum rate of interest is guaranteed; a share of any excess interest earned by the insurer is guaranteed.	No guarantees whatsoever are offered, either as to principal or income.
Return on Investments	Investment possibilities open to an insurer are, by law, limited and conservative.	The prospects for gain (and loss) may be enhanced if a grantor chooses to free the trustee from investment restrictions typically imposed on trusts.
Life Income	Proceeds under a life income option can be guaranteed when left with the insurer.	Income for life can be specified but neither the amount nor the duration can be guaranteed.
Expense	Available from insurers at no additional cost.	A corporate trustee charges a fee to administer a trust.
Counseling	Insurers will not function as personal counselors.	A trustee can act as personal counselor to the trust beneficiary.
Title	The insurer and the payee have a debtor-creditor relationship.	A trustee has legal title to the proceeds, and a trust beneficiary has equitable title.
Segregation of Funds	Insurance proceeds retained by a life insurer are commingled for investment purposes with the insurer's other funds.	The property of an individual trust is generally kept separate from the property of other trusts.

Figure 5.1 compares settlement options to trusts.

POLICY LOANS

The ability to use the contract as a source of emergency or opportunity cash is one of the most valuable attributes of permanent life insurance. Virtually all cash-value policies include a policy loan provision.[85] As property, the policy can also serve as collateral for a loan from a bank or other lender but more often the insurer will provide the cash under the more favorable terms of the policy's loan provisions.[86]

When a policyowner borrows money directly from the insurer what is actually occurring is something other than a loan in common parlance. The difference is this: In a true loan the borrower must agree to repay the money. A policy loan does not require repayment. It is more like an advance of the money the insurer will eventually pay out under the contract.[87] The policyholder is receiving an advance—of his own money.

Even though federal tax law treats a policy loan as a classic loan, it is not. A debt, per se, never exists and the policyowner and insurer do not have a traditional debtor-creditor relationship. During the insured's lifetime, the insurer is always 100 percent secured against loss because the amount that the policyowner can borrow can never exceed the amount the insurer would have to pay the policyholder if he chose to surrender the policy. In fact, during lifetime, the loan can never exceed that amount (less the interest payable on it). Furthermore, the insurer can (and will) deduct the loan value, plus interest from the proceeds otherwise payable if policyowner has not repaid the loan before the death of the insured.

Once the insurer advances money to the policyowner, that person or entity can use the money for any purpose.

Policyowners who wish to take policy loans generally do not require the permission of a revocable beneficiary because that party has a mere expectancy in the net (face amount less indebtedness) proceeds. Even an irrevocable beneficiary has no right to demand consent to a policy loan—if the policy states clearly that such consent is not required.[88] However, once policyowners make an absolute assignment (i.e., a total and irrevocable transfer of all interests in their policy) to third party beneficiaries, even if the former policyowners are the insureds, they may take no further loans from the policy.[89]

The amount of the loan is limited essentially to the policy's cash value (less a holdback for interest). Technically, the policy might state something to the effect of:

The loan value is the amount which, with interest at a daily loan interest rate of ___ percent,[90] will equal the policy's cash value.[91] Interest on the loan will be payable on each policy anniversary but if not paid when due it will be added to the loan.

Every year the amount that the insurer can advance to the policyowner increases as the cash value grows. But once the total of principal and accumulated unpaid interest equals or exceeds the policy's cash surrender value, the policy will (after a one month's notice) terminate and the insurer will cancel all benefits.[92]

Why does the insurer charge interest on an advance of money that will someday be paid to the policyowner? Because the insurer's statement of what policy values will be year after year is based on the assumption that the insurer will have a reserve (i.e., an amount in excess of that needed to pay for the current year's costs) to invest and earn interest so that the insurer can keep its future contractual promises. If premiums unused for costs in early years are not on hand, the insurer cannot invest that money and pay the amounts promised in the future. The charge made to policyowners who accept these advances puts the insurer back where it would have been had it been able to invest the money. (In fact the interest rate may be somewhat higher than the amount assumed by the insurer in calculating policy loan values because the insurer needs to pay for administrative costs in making, keeping track of, and repaying these loans and, to some extent, to create a disincentive to borrowing.)

Policyowners may repay a policy loan at any time while the insured is alive (subject to a minimum payment for administrative aggravation and cost purposes). Once the insured has died (or the policy has been placed on extended term status), typically the insurer will not accept repayment of a loan.[93] If the policyowner does not repay the advance, the insurer will reduce either the cash value of the policy available to the policyowner or the death proceeds paid to beneficiaries.

Automatic Premium Loan (APL) Provision

"Premium loans are advances of policy cash values that the insurer makes to the policyowner for the purpose of paying the premium. Automatic premium loans are advances the insurer makes under a policy clause providing that, if the policyowner fails to pay a premium by the end of the grace period, the insurer will automatically advance the amount of the premium if the policy has a sufficient net cash value."[94] Usually, the insurer notifies the policyowner of this action.

If the loan value of the policy is insufficient to pay an annual premium, the insurer will typically pay a semi-annual, quarterly, or monthly premium[95] although it is not required to do so.[96] When the loan value is so small that it will not even cover a monthly premium, nonforfeiture benefit options will apply.

In most states, the payment of premiums by APL has the same result as paying premiums with cash, so the death benefit continues (decreased by the policy loan) and cash values continue to increase. Most states do not require an insurer to notify a policyowner that there is insufficient cash value to make a policy loan through APL or to tell a policyowner how long the loan will keep the policy in force.

A device that pays premiums at the end of a grace period by automatic loan from policy values is an incredibly valuable safety device to keep insurance protection in full force.[97] But the automatic premium loan is effective to prevent a policy lapse only if it is requested by the policy-applicant (or at some later date by the policyowner at a time when no premium is unpaid beyond the policy's grace period). The authors suggest that this provision is extremely valuable and should be considered in every case—especially because the policyowner may cancel the applicability of the automatic premium loan provision at any time.

There are downsides to the automatic premium loan when abused. First, "the automatic premium loan provision makes it too easy for the insured to avoid the payment of premium in cash."[98] Second, to the extent interest is still deductible, it is not deductible in the case of an automatic premium loan because the policyowner borrows the interest from the insurer rather than paying it in cash.[99] A third potential disadvantage is that the contract may last longer if placed on extended term rather than allowing the policy to exhaust itself through automatic premium payments. But planners should keep in mind what this provision is really intended to do: prevent an accidental lapse.

ASSIGNMENTS OF A LIFE INSURANCE POLICY

As property,[100] policyowners can transfer their life insurance contracts to other persons or entities. A policyowner can transfer either all or only some of the "bundle of rights" that comprises a life insurance policy to almost any person or entity.[101]

The two basic ways of making a lifetime transfer[102] of a policy are: (1) the absolute assignment; and (2) the collateral assignment. An absolute assignment, as its name implies, transfers all the policyowner's rights irrevocably. A collateral assignment, again as its name implies, assigns so much of the death benefit as necessary for as long as necessary to secure a lender's rights. But no more of the proceeds will go to the lender than the amount of debt owed.

Requirements

The assignment does not have to be of any particular form (absent specific provision in state law or the contract to the contrary). Because life insurance is treated as personal property, policyowner may transfer ownership rights, not only by many different types of documents[103], but also by many different actions. For example, if a person sells a business and the business owns a life insurance policy, the sale of all the assets of the business carries with it the personal property the business owned—including the life insurance.

Likewise, a property settlement in connection with a divorce may have the effect of transferring the ownership of life insurance on the life of one or the other (or both) spouse(s) even though no one ever uses the word "assignment" with regard to these transfers. But this type of transfer (where a clause in the divorce decree disposes of life insurance) is both very dangerous and very awkward. If a policyowner names his new spouse as beneficiary of the insurance proceeds and the insurer has no notice or knowledge of the divorce decree's change, both spouses are likely to claim the proceeds.[104] Furthermore, if the decree requires the policyowner spouse to maintain the policy for the benefit of his or her ex-spouse, the policyowner cannot obtain a policy loan-even to keep the policy in force through a premium loan.

Before either the absolute or collateral type of assignment or any other instance of a policy ownership transfer is valid, the policyowner must notify the insurer (and, where required by the terms of the contract, the insurer must consent to the assignment). Once notified in writing at the insurer's home office, the insurer must honor the policyowner's transfer—unless the terms of the contract itself forbid assignments. So if the insurer then disregards (by intention or neglect) the assignee's rights and makes payment to someone else, the courts may force the insurer to make a second payment to the assignee. If the policyowner gives no notice to the insurer, it will be protected in a transaction initiated by a former owner. For instance, if the former owner applies for a policy loan and he has not given the insurer proper notice that he had assigned the policy, the insurer is protected in making that loan.[105]

The insurer does not, however, have to verify the bona fides of the transaction between the policyowner and the transferee nor the validity of the transaction. In other words, the insurer is not accountable for the mental or legal capacity of the policyowner to make the assignment (unless it had knowledge that the policyowner was not legally competent to make it or there were irregularities in the assignment form).

Absolute Assignments

Policyowners use an absolute assignment in life insurance planning when the policyowner wants to sell or give away all of his or her rights under the contract. The goal might be to obtain valuable consideration, to save estate taxes, avoid creditors, or purely for love and affection and to assure the transferee of financial security. There are many common examples of sales and gifts:

- A client might sell a policy on his life to his business.

- A business might sell a policy on an employee's life to the employee or to the employee's spouse or child or trust (or to a pension plan).

- A shareholder might sell a policy on his life to a new business associate.

- A client might give a policy on her life to her spouse.

- A client might give a policy on his life to his children or to a family trust.

Tax Implications

Both sales and gift transactions have important and sometimes unexpectedly expensive tax implications. Planners should thoroughly read Chapter 25 before allowing any sale of a life insurance policy. Chapter 28 should be considered before allowing a client to make a gift of a policy. A valid gift requires that the donor have contractual capacity and intent to make a voluntary gratuitous transfer and the gift must be delivered to and accepted by the donee (assignee).

Nontax Implications

Planners must be aware of the nontax implications of an absolute assignment in order to avoid them and/or alert the client to their potential effect. Some of these are:

- Although an absolute assignment itself may not per se change the interest of a revocable beneficiary, as a practical matter the new owner can immediately change the beneficiary and often makes that change almost simultaneously with the assignment. Some absolute assignment forms state that the new owner is automatically the primary policy beneficiary until the new owner makes a change to the beneficiary designation.[106]

- If the policyowner made an irrevocable beneficiary designation before making an absolute assignment of the policy, in most states the assignment will not defeat that designation (without the written consent of the beneficiary) and the transferee should be apprised of this fact.

- Absolute assignments may put the policy and its proceeds beyond the claims of the policyowner's creditors, but planners should inform policyowner that—like diamonds— an absolute assignment is forever. There is a loss of both control and flexibility from the transferor's viewpoint.

Collateral Assignments

Policyowners use a collateral assignment (as the creditor's interest may appear) form of transfer almost exclusively as a secondary source of payment when they pledge a policy on a temporary basis as collateral for a loan.[107] The term "collateral" implies that the policyowner-debtor is primarily liable for the loan and only if he or she defaults will the lender call upon policy values to back up that obligation. The cash values in the policy serve as protection to the lender as long as the insured lives and the death benefit protects the lender if the insured dies. Once the debtor/policyowner repays the loans, all rights in the policy automatically revert to the policyowner.

Policy rights transferred when policyowners use the collateral assignment form of transfer generally include the right to:

1. receive the death benefit (but the lender must transfer the excess over the debt unpaid at the insured's death to the beneficiary specified by the policyowner);[108]

2. cash in the policy in the event the policyowner defaults on a loan or fails to pay premiums[109] (but the lender must give reasonable notice and transfer the excess over the debt unpaid at that time to the policyowner);

3. exercise nonforfeiture options; and

4. receive policy dividends.

The major right virtually always retained by the policyowner is the right to change the beneficiary.

After the debtor/policyowner repays the debt, the transferee must reassign all policy rights back to the policyowner. Again, the lender/assignee must inform the insurer in writing at its home office before it will allow the policyowner to resume exercising all policy rights.

WAIVER AND ESTOPPEL

Waiver

Waiver, the intentional and voluntary surrender of a "known right,"[110] is an act which the insurer may (or may not) have committed in many situations.[111] A waiver occurs if the insurer knew it had the right to do or demand some action but acted with the deliberate intention of giving up that right.[112] For example, an insurer who gives a policyowner extra time after the grace period has expired to pay premiums and agrees to keep the policy in force during that time may have waived its right to deny a claim in that time period for nonpayment of premiums.

Planners should be conscious of potential waiver (and estoppel) situations in the following situations:

- *Taking and submission of an application* – The agent or medical examiner writes false answers on the application or the insurer fails to follow up on an incomplete answer.

- *Premium payment process* – The insurer routinely lets the policyowner slide with respect to the prompt payment of premiums or customarily accepts an overdue premium or accepts a late payment after it has knowledge that the insured has died or fails to send premium notices as required by state law.

- *Submission of claims under a life insurance contract* – The insurer does not promptly send proof of loss forms upon request by the beneficiary or fails to notify a beneficiary that it intends to dispute a claim or the insurer receives what it feels is a defective proof of loss but does not request additional documentation or the insurer promises to pay a claim it has grounds to resist.

Insurers cannot waive, abrogate, or contract away three types of rights:[113]

1. *Rights designed to protect not only a party to the contract but also the public.* An example would be the right of an insurer to demand that an applicant have an insurable interest in the life of the insured. Other examples would include the right of the policyowner to be notified of premiums due or the right to take policy values under nonforfeiture options. "The public policy involved overrides the freedom of contract of the parties."[114]

2. *Rights that would create coverage where none previously existed.* Waivers cannot create risk (legal exposure) if that risk was not already encompassed in the contract nor can coverage be established by waiver where the contract specifically excluded it. In short, insurers cannot invoke the doctrine of waiver to create liability for benefits for which the insured never contracted.[115] For instance, if the contract provided benefits for 10 years from the date of issue, the insurer's acceptance of a premium beyond the tenth year would not create a right in the policyowner to continue coverage into the eleventh year. The insurer would have the right to refund any premium for coverage beyond the tenth year even if the insured died while the insurer held the excess premium and could not waive the expiration of insurance.

3. *Rights to receive a sum of money cannot be waived.* An agent, for example, cannot waive the insurer's right to receive premiums. A person can, of course, sign a "release" to an insurer stating that the claim of legal liability is satisfied. But a person or entity can only give a release in return for consideration. For instance, when a beneficiary signs the check for the policy death proceeds, he or she is acknowledging that the insurer is released from its obligation in return for that money.

People make waivers. In the case of an insurer those people are its authorized agents (used here in a broader sense than sales force). So the term authorized agent may encompass sales personnel, officers, medical examiners, underwriters, and "others whose actions affect the insurer's contractual relationships."[116] In many cases, the central issue is whether the party making the waiver was in fact authorized by the insurer to do so. If the agent has no power to make a waiver, it will be ineffective assuming the applicant-policyowner knows (or has reasonable notice that) the agent lacks such authority. Notice to the applicant-policyowner on limitations of an agent's authority is usually spelled out in both the application and the life insurance contract itself in a nonwaiver clause similar to the one that follows:

No agent is authorized to make or modify contracts, to waive any of the Company's rights or requirements, or to bind the Company by making or receiving any promise, representation, or information, unless it is: (1) in writing; (2) submitted to the Company; and (3) made part of the contract.[117]

Quite often, the contract will contain a further statement to the effect that:

Only the President of the Company, our Executive Vice President, or our Secretary has the authority to waive or modify any policy provision. Such waiver must be made in writing. No agent or any other person has the authority to change or waive any provision of this policy.

Because the statement appears in the contract and many states hold the applicant-policyowner responsible for reading the contract, he or she will be bound by a limitation-of-right-to-make-a-waiver clause appearing in both the application and policy. This, of course, does not typically bind a beneficiary (who has no reasonable notice of the existence or contents of the nonwaiver clause) to conditions that must be met after a loss occurs. Therefore, an agent of the insurer could waive such policy provisions as those regarding notice to the insurer or the documents required for proof of the insured's death regardless of the nonwaiver clause.

Three types of waivers occur in life insurance situations: express waivers, implied waivers, and waivers by silence.

1. *Express waivers* – The surrender of a legal right expressly declared by written or oral words of an agent empowered to act for the insurance company are called express waivers. An insurer might deliberately waive a right, despite a breach of condition by the policyowner or beneficiary, in order to "keep the business on the books" or to maintain or obtain good public relations.

2. *Implied waivers* – Here, the conduct of the waiving party clearly infers the intention to forego a legal right—even though that surrender is not stated in writing or even orally. For instance, if an insurer time after time accepted premiums tendered by the policyowner well after the grace period expires, a court is likely to conclude that by its repeated inaction (not lapsing the policy) and pattern of actions (acceptance of the premiums beyond the grace period), the insurer, with full knowledge of its rights to lapse the policy, knowingly and voluntarily failed to assert that right. So if the insured died after the grace period but within the time the insurer had customarily accepted late premiums, the insurer would be liable to pay the death benefit.[118] It had waived its right to deny the claim.

3. *Waivers by silence* – Where an insurer has the legal duty to speak but fails to do so, the rights of the policyowner or beneficiary that would be lost by the inaction are instead protected.[119]

Waiver by silence could occur, for instance, where the insurer gains knowledge of some material misrepresentation but deliberately (or negligently) withholds its knowledge more than a reasonable period of time and the insured dies within the contestable period. Most courts would hold the insurer waived its rights by lulling the policyowner or beneficiary into a false sense of security when it should have taken action in sufficient time for the policyowner to redress the situation with the insurer or obtain alternative coverage elsewhere.

Once a people make waivers, they cannot then retroactively revoke them. For instance, assume a policyowner breached a condition of the contract (such as payment of premiums) but the insurer notified the policyowner that it would allow the contract to continue for a specified period of time (say one month) after the grace period in spite of the breach. If the insured died during the extra allotted time, the insurer would be liable. It could not revoke its waiver. But if the insurer notified the policyowner within a reasonable time that with respect to future nonpayment's, the grace period limitation on coverage would be strictly enforced, the former waiver would not protect the policyowner in the future.

Estoppel

Estoppel is a legal way of arriving at a fair and just result when one party (typically the insurer) has through words or conduct either directly or through its agent mislead the policyowner or beneficiary into an action or inaction that results in that party's loss. The key elements of estoppel are therefore that the policyholder or beneficiary suffers a detriment by acting to his prejudice in reliance upon a belief engendered by the insurer through its agent's words or actions.[120] Words and actions of the insurer must have lead the policyowner to act (or not act) so that the policyowner was harmed, the policyowner must not know the true facts, and because of a good faith belief in the insurer's (or insurer's agent's) words or actions acted (or failed to act).

For instance, if an insurance agent (the insurer's agent) tells an applicant that:

"You can ignore that one time you fainted. The insurance company is only concerned with a long history of fainting or blackouts."

If the insurer denies the death claim on the grounds that the fainting was not admitted by the applicant, the policy beneficiary can ask the court to estop the insurer from using misrepresentations as grounds for denial. Even though there was in fact misrepresentation, the insurer, through its agent's statement that one blackout does not count induced the applicant into taking action based on that misstatement and is therefore estopped (forbidden) from using the misstatement to deny liability (even if it can be proven that there was in fact a material misrepresentation).

There has been (and continues to be) confusion between the concepts of waiver and estoppel with some courts separating and distinguishing between the two while others treat them as essentially synonymous (and others seem to blend the two). What is important to the planner is (in the opinion of the authors) this: The law will generally try by whatever means necessary, and available, to balance the interests of the parties and the public. It will insist on a meeting of the responsibilities of the relationships between them by using one or the other doctrine to prevent the insurer from taking an unfair advantage of the policyowner and his or her beneficiaries (and vice versa).[121]

CHAPTER ENDNOTES

1. The following two texts will prove invaluable in reviewing the essential elements of contract law and researching the nontax oriented legal aspects of life insurance: M. Crawford, *Law and the Life Insurance Contract*, 7th ed. (Burr Ridge, IL: Irwin Professional Publishing, 1994); B. Anderson, *Anderson on Life Insurance* (Boston, MA: Little, Brown and Company, 1991).

2. Although technically, a beneficiary is not a party to the contract, if a contract is for the direct benefit of a third person who is not a party to the contract, that person can sue for damages incurred as the result of a breach of contract. For this reason, the authors have included the beneficiary among the parties to the contract.

3. It is the insurability of the insured that is the linchpin of the agreement between the insurer and the policyowner. It is the termination of the insured's life that marks the liability of the insurer to pay the face amount of the policy at death, and it is the insured's life that determines the date of the policy's lifetime maturity. Although the insured may not be viewed by some authorities as a party to the contract, it is the authors' opinion that this position is less than complete. Without the insured's consent to the issuance of the policy, there is no legally binding contract.

4. State law may bar a legally adjudicated insane or mentally infirm person from being an insured. Generally, other legal incompetents such as minors are not prohibited from being an insured.

5. Life insurance contracts between enemy aliens or citizens of a country at war with the United States will be void. A corporation's capacity to purchase a life insurance contract depends on the provisions in its charter, by-laws, and the laws of the state where it is domiciled. A corporation can purchase a life insurance policy even if that power is not expressly granted in its charter or the state laws under which it was created if that action is necessary to exercise its express powers. Most corporations and other business entities can therefore purchase life insurance. However, the corporation's board of directors should formally endorse such an action and document its approval in the corporation's minutes.

6. Many states allow a minor fifteen years old or over to purchase a life insurance contract on his or her own life but upon reaching the age of majority, he or she can void the contract. The insurer is bound by a life insurance contract made with a minor unless and until the minor disaffirms it. A child generally may disaffirm (void the contract) at any time while the child is a minor under state law or within a reasonable amount of time after reaching legal majority. Once the policy is void, the former minor is entitled to a return of whatever premiums he or she has paid but must return any dividends or other money received from the policy.

    Note that many of these statutes allow the minor to make benefits payable only to close family members such as parents or siblings or the minor's estate. Some, but not all states, limit the insured to the minor himself. Others allow the minor to insure the life of a child or spouse.

7. *Black's Law Dictionary*, 5th ed. (West Publishing Company 1979), p. 720.

8. See Anderson, note 1 above, p. 360.

9. See, e.g., *Continental Ca. Co. v. Brightman*, 437 F.2d 67 (10 Cir. 1971). A few states do require that a party cannot be named as beneficiary unless that party has an insurable interest in the life of the insured.

10. If, as part of a scheme to avoid the insurable interest rule and pursuant to a plan with a third party, the insured-applicant purchases a policy on his own life and then transfers the policy to that third party (who never had an insurable interest), the court will probably declare the policy void. See *Lakin v. Postal Life & Cas. Ins. Co.*, 316 S.W.2d 542 (Mo. 1958). See also, 17 *Couch on Insurance* 63A:23 (Lawyers Co-Operative Publishing Co. 1983).

11. Beware, however, the transfer for value rule discussed in Chapter 25.

    In the past few years, certain life insurance arrangements referred to as "stranger-owned life insurance" (STOLI) or "investor-owned life insurance (IOLI) have generated considerable debate. For a description of a typical transaction and the potential risks involved, see Stephan R. Leimberg, "Stranger-Owned Life Insurance: Killing the Goose That Lays Golden Eggs!" *Estate Planning Journal*, January 2005, Vol. 32, No. 1, p. 43 (reprinted in Tax Analysts *Insurance Tax Review*, Vol. 28, No. 5, May 2005). See also Stephan R. Leimberg, "The Many Troublesome Facts of STOLI: An Update on Recent Developments," *Keeping Current*, June 2007.

12. See, e.g., *Mutual Life Ins. Co. v. Allen*, 138 Mass. 24 (1884).

13. In an era where many couples live together without the benefit of marriage, it would seem that an applicant-beneficiary cohabiting with the insured could claim to be a dependent and as such show an insurable interest. But see the (in the authors' opinion relatively ancient) case of *Mikesell v. Mikesell*, 40 Pa. Super. 392 (1909).

14. The opposite is also true: if the applicant has no valid relationship with the insured other than merely as a business associate, this

relationship will not per se be sufficient to generate an insurable interest. The courts (and the insurer) are likely to ask:

(a) Did the insured contribute capital or make some other financial contribution to the business that would be lost or jeopardized at his or her death?

(b) Does the insured have any particular skill, technical knowledge, or ability as a worker or manager that would be lost by the enterprise at his or her death?

(c) Is there anything special (such as experience or business contacts) that the insured brings to the firm that would die when he or she dies?

COLI Death Proceeds: Note that under the recently modified rules governing employer-owned life insurance, employers must now satisfy certain notice and consent requirements in order for the death proceeds to be received tax-free. The insured employee must be notified in writing that the employer intends to insure the employee's life, and the maximum face amount the employee's life could be insured for at the time the contract is issued. The notice must also state that the policy owner will be the beneficiary of the death proceeds of the policy. And the insured employee must also give written consent to coverage continuing after the insured employee terminates employment. Under another set of requirements, the insured employee must have been an employee at any time during the twelve-month period before his death (or at the time the contract was issued, the insured was a director or highly compensated individual). See IRS Sections 101(j) and 6039I, as amended by the Pension Protection Act of 2006 (PPA 2006).

15. See, e.g., *Nuuanu Mem. Park v. Briggs*, 434 P.2d 750 (Haw. 1967).

16. See, e.g., *Equitable Life Ins. Co. v. Hazlewood*, 12 S.W. 621 (Tex. 1889), where no more would be collected by the creditor than would be necessary to discharge the debt.

17. Almost all states adhere to this principle including Texas which up until 1981 required the beneficiary to have an insurable interest when the proceeds were payable. See Tex. Rev. Civ. Stat. Ann. art.3.49-1 (Vernon 1981). See also, "Insurable Interest in Life," 18 *Col. L. Rev.* 381, 394 (1921).

18. However, be aware that some states have passed statutes that automatically terminate the insurable interest upon divorce unless the policy in question is specifically referenced in the divorce decree. See, e.g., Ohio Rev. Code §5815.33.

19. See, e.g., *Secor v. Pioneer Foundry Co.*, 173 N.W.2d 780 (Mich. 1969).

20. See, e.g., *Metropolitan Life Ins. Co. v. Manahon*, 42 S.W. 924 (Ky. 1897).

21. See, e.g., *Ramey v. Carolina Life Ins. Co.*, 135 S.E.2d 362 (S.C. 1964).

22. For instance, say a relative other than a parent insured the life of a niece or nephew and then murdered the child. If it can be shown that the applicant-policyowner-beneficiary never obtained the consent of the child's parent, a court is likely to hold that the insurer failed to exercise due care. In this instance, such negligence could easily result in contributing to the insured's murder. See *Liberty National Life Ins. Co. v. Weldon*, 100 So.2d 696 (Ala. 1957).

23. This is why constraints are imposed on the form and content of a contract. More and more states are insisting that—to the degree possible—a life insurance contract be written in language that is simple and understandable by the typical client. There is a "Life and Health Insurance Policy Language Simplification Model Act" adopted by the National Association of Insurance Commissioners (NAIC) in 1977. This act forbids fine print, encourages short sentences, requires an index or table of contents for most contracts, and suggests a physical format that lends itself to a balanced emphasis throughout the policy.

If a provision required by law is omitted from the contract, it will be construed as though the clause were included. The adhesion concept is also why statutes require certain provisions while forbidding others.

24. Two such theories are the "doctrine of reasonable expectation" and the "doctrine of constructive ambiguity." The first of these suggests an open disregard of policy language (i.e., that the courts should honor the objectively reasonable expectations of applicants and beneficiaries regarding policy terms even though a careful study of the policy terms or language might negate those expectations). See R. Keeton, *Insurance Law—Basic Text* (West Publishing Company 1971), p. 351. See also *Keene Corp. v. Ins. Co. of North America*, 667 F.2d 1034 (D.C. Cir. 1981), *cert. denied*, 455 U.S. 1007 (1982). The latter doctrine holds that ambiguities in contract language should be resolved against the party who drafted the contract. See Keeton, above. Others describe constructive ambiguity as courts disregarding clear policy language and finding ambiguity where none reasonably exists in order to come to the "right" result. See Anderson, note 1 above, at p. 187.

As Anderson in the text cited above properly points out, "The function of the insurer is to distribute the risk and in fairness to individual policy holders to fix a premium rate commensurate with its estimate of the risk. This is difficult enough when a court indulges in what other courts refer to as 'constructive ambiguity', meaning ambiguity is found where none reasonably exists, but when a court in the absence of legislative authority completely disregards clear policy language, the insurer's task is almost impossible."

25. Many states pattern their statutes on these required provisions on the New York standard policy provision law. Most provide that the actual wording in the policy does not have to be exactly the same as long as it conveys the same substance. In most cases, these laws allow the insurer to insert more favorable terms (from the consumer's viewpoint). There is usually an exemption allowing omission of the required provisions if they would be inappropriate for the type of policy in question. For instance, no dividend statement would be necessary in a nonparticipating contract.

26. Thus, the policyowner must be provided with a copy of the application that both eliminates uncertainties as to what is contained on it and also assures the policyowner that the policy in his or her hands contains every relevant document. The insured and/or policyowner is given a chance to be sure that his or her responses to the agent's (and/or medical examiner's) questions were properly recorded and request changes if they were not.

However, the entire contract provision works both ways. The policyowner cannot claim ignorance of the statements made in the application. This serves as notification of all the terms and conditions and imposes a responsibility on the insured (and/or policyowner) to read and, if appropriate, to apprise the insurer of errors.

As a practical matter, then, the insurance agent should review the copy of the application attached to the policy with the client and the terms of the policy when it is delivered. Of course, the problems discussed above generally will not be of concern if the insured has survived the period after which the policy becomes incontestable by the insurer.

27. Under common usage, a lapse is what occurs after the policy has run out of steam. Legalistically, however, a lapse is defined as "a default in premiums before a policy has a nonforfeiture value." L. Davids, *Dictionary of Insurance*, p. 173. According to this definition, a policy could lapse except as to its nonforfeiture benefits or lapse and then be cashed in for its surrender value. Then it would be said to expire.

In certain situations during war when timely payment was impossible, or where some action or inaction by the insurer prevented timely payment, some courts have held that the insurer could not lapse the policy for lack of premium payments.

28. Many states require that the insurance company must notify the policyowner not more than forty-five days or less than fifteen days before the due date of the premium. That notice must specify the amount payable, when it is due (the due date), and where it is payable. Some of these statutes penalize the insurer who does not give timely notice by extending the life of the contract for some period of time (e.g., six months to a year) after the due date. But these laws (to prevent fraud on the part of the policyowner) allow the insurance company's mail department to testify that notice was mailed. Once that occurs, the burden often shifts to the policyowner to prove that it was not mailed. Even if this presumption is successfully rebutted, the policyowner must also have brought suit within the statutory limit after the due date.

29. Some insurers make what is known as a late remittance offer. This gives the policyowner an additional period of time after the grace period expires during which a lapsed policy can be reinstated without the requirement that the insured prove insurability. The insured must, however, be alive on the date payment is tendered to the insurer. This late remittance offer does not extend the grace period.

30. Some statutes also allow the insurer to add interest on the unpaid and overdue premium but, for public relations purposes, many insurers will waive the interest charge even if they have the legal right to collect it.

31. Some companies substitute a one-year period of time rather than the customary two-year limit on contests. This is done for marketing and public relations reasons and obviously is a consideration that should be added to the checklist of a planner deciding upon which policy is best for a client.

32. Usually the contestable period runs from the date of issue which is typically the same as the policy date. But the policy date is not necessarily the date of issue. For instance, if an applicant wants to "backdate" the policy to save age (i.e., obtain a lower premium by paying a premium for which no insurance was in force in return for a continuing lower premium), the policy date could be as much as six months earlier than the actual issue date. The contestable period starts at the earlier policy date rather than the issue date in this case. (Most states limit dating back a policy to a six-month period starting at the date of the application.) Backdating is one way to provide incontestability to the policyowner and beneficiary at the earliest possible time.

33. The phrase "during the insured's lifetime" makes it clear that if the insured dies before the end of the contestable period, the policy never becomes incontestable since it was not in force for two years during the lifetime of the insured.

34. "Void" means no contract exists. "Void ab initio" means no contract ever existed. From the beginning, there was never any legally enforceable contract. A voidable contract is one which is legally enforceable and valid—unless and until a party who has

the right to do so disaffirms (avoids) the obligations and benefits of the contract. A minor, for example, can upon reaching legal majority, void a contract. Lack of capacity, mutual mistake, and material misrepresentation can all make a contract voidable.

35. See the statement of Justice Holmes in *Northwestern Mutual Life Ins. Co. v. Johnson*, 254 U.S. 96, 101 (1920), that says, "The object of the clause is plain and laudable – to create an absolute assurance of the benefit, as free as may be from any dispute of fact except the fact of death ..."

36. There are conflicts in various state courts as to the effect of adding to the incontestable clause an exclusion for certain items but not others. Some say that if the insurer specifies one or more items to be excluded, although those are exempted from the incontestable clause protection, any exclusion clause not mentioned is automatically meant to be ineffective after the incontestable period. (i.e., "the insurer could not contest its obligation to pay except for a reason plainly reserved in the wording of the incontestable clause itself." *Bernier v. Pacific Mutual Life Ins. Co.*, 139 So. 629 (La. 1932). But most courts now hold that an insurer is free to specify risks it is unwilling to assume throughout the life of the contract (even though—after two years—the validity of the contract itself has become incontestable). See, e.g., *Metropolitan Life Ins. Co. v. Conway*, 169 N.E. 642 (N.Y. 1930). So the incontestable clause in most jurisdictions is not "a mandate as to coverage." It implies only—within the limits of the coverage the contract intended—that after the contestable period has expired, the company cannot protest that the policy was invalid in its inception or became invalid because a condition of coverage was broken.

37. See, e.g., *Obartuch v. Security Mutual Life Ins. Co.*, 114 F.2d 873 (7th Cir. 1940), *cert. denied*, 312 U.S. 696 (1941).

38. See, e.g., *Aetna Life Ins. Co. v. Hooker*, 62 F.2d 805 (6th Cir. 1933), *cert. denied*, 289 U.S. 748 (1933).

39. *Henderson v. Life Ins. Co. of Va.*, 179 S.E. 680 (S.C. 1935).

40. A few states impose a one-year limit. Some insurers for competitive and public relations purposes use only a one year period even though state law permits a two-year period. Planners should consider this factor when deciding upon the appropriate policy for a client.

41. See, e.g., *John Hancock Mutual Life Ins. Co. v. Moore*, 34 Mich. 46 (1876); *Connecticut Mutual Life Ins. Co. v. Akens*, 150 U.S. 468 (1893).

42. Self destruction of the insured, even though deliberately done while sane, is one of the risks assumed by the insurer unless it is by express terms excepted. *Grand Lodge Independent Order of Mut. Aid v. Wieting*, 48 N.E. 59 (Ill. 1897).

43. See Crawford, note 1 above, at p. 430.

44. See, e.g., *New York Life Ins. Co. v. Noonan*, 215 F.2d 905 (9th Cir. 1954).

45. Many insurers are now calling this clause an "Incorrect Age or Sex" clause and adjusting the proceeds if sex is incorrectly shown in the same manner as if age had been incorrectly stated.

46. The presumption is that the age stated by the applicant-insured is correct. See, e.g., *Southern Ins. Co. v. Wilson*, 108 So. 5 (Ala. 1926).

47. This provision is not intended to shield fraud or collusion. The insurer can deny payment of the proceeds if it can prove the parties intended to cheat the insurer. See, e.g., *Lucas v. American Bankers' Ins. Co.*, 141 So. 394 (La. Ct. App. 1932).

48. If the error as to age is discovered by the insurer prior to the insured's death, either premiums or coverage can be adjusted.

Usually, if the insured's age was higher than stated in the application, the insurer will allow the policyowner to pay the difference in premiums (with interest) and keep the original policy or it may issue a new policy with a lower death benefit with the original premium level. If the insured was younger than stated in the application, the insurer will almost always refund the excess premiums (often with interest).

49. When a stock company issues a contract which is nonpar, the company usually fixes the premium at a lower amount than a mutual company issuing a similar par policy. This nonpar policy's lower premium, of course, is initially appealing from a consumer's viewpoint. However, the buyer has no hope of sharing in the financial success of the company (unless he or she also buys stock in the insurer). From the insurer's perspective, the marketing advantage gained by a lower premium is offset to some extent by lower-per-thousand of insurance investable revenue, the fact that premiums once set cannot be changed even if the company experiences financial difficulties, and the lack of any cushion in the premium to take up the slack in that event.

50. State law is also a factor in how much is paid and under what conditions. Most states specify what the term "participate" means in terms of legal rights. Almost always, state laws will specify how soon the policy will share in the insurer's surplus (typically not later than the end of the second or third policy year), how the dividend may be applied, and what the insurer must state in the contract about those rights.

51. This ownership exposes dividends and the interest they earn to the claims of the policyowner's creditors to the extent state law does not exempt or otherwise protect them.

52. This is the most frequently selected dividend choice for the automatic option. One reason is that an insured who is insurable only at a higher-than-standard rate or even one who has become uninsurable can purchase additional coverage at net (no commissions or other acquisition charges are added to the cost of this coverage) rates. Paid up additions may be cashed in separately from the underlying policy which adds to the policyowner's flexibility.

53. During the first year or two of a contract, the insurer's costs to put the contract in force and provide current coverage far exceed the amount paid in by the policyowner. So no benefit is required to be provided under state law until the policy has been in force for two (or, in some states, three) years.

54. If the beneficiary of the policy is revocable, no consent is needed for the policyowner to exercise any of the nonforfeiture provisions. If the beneficiary is irrevocable, consent of the irrevocable beneficiary is required to cash in the policy (unless the policy specifies consent is not required) but no consent is usually required to select extended term or reduced paid up insurance.

55. Actually, the amounts shown in the policy assume premiums are paid to the end of the year. Since surrenders rarely occur exactly on that date, the insurer will interpolate and calculate for the policyowner the exact amount due on any given date.

56. The rationale is that the right to exercise a nonforfeiture option is a continuing irrevocable offer made by the insurer to the policyowner. That offer becomes binding on both parties as soon as it is accepted by the policyowner.

57. Technically, once a policy develops a nonforfeiture value, if the policy lapses, it lapses "except as to the nonforfeiture benefits."

58. See *Trapp v. Metropolitan Life Ins. Co.*, 70 F.2d 976 (8th Cir. 1934). Although a few courts have held that reinstatement is actually the start of a new contract, most follow the rule in *Trapp*.

The distinction is important for many reasons. For instance, the continuation theory bars an insurer from imposing new contractual restrictions or burdens on the policyowner at the time of reinstatement. This means the insurer cannot add an exclusion (e.g., for death while in military service) that was not in the original policy. See *Schiel v. New York Life Ins. Co.*, 178 F.2d 729 (9th Cir. 1949), *cert. denied*, 339 U.S. 931 (1950). So no new conditions or restrictions can be imposed at the time of or as a condition of reinstatement. See Smith, "What Conditions May an Insurer Impose Upon Reinstatement of a Life Policy?" *Legal Proceedings* (American Life Convention 1948), p. 130.

59. Crawford, note 1 above, at p. 358.

60. See, e.g., *Tatum v. Guardian Life Ins. Co.*, 75 F.2d 476 (2nd Cir. 1935).

61. Crawford, note 1 above, at p. 359.

62. For instance, some insurers provide for reinstatement in term insurance contracts even when there is no state law requirement that they do so. Likewise, although state law does not generally require insurers to allow reinstatement when extended term insurance runs out, quite often the insurer will not deny a policyowner's application.

63. In most states, the insurer may consider the same factors as if underwriting the contract for the first time when considering insurability. These factors include not only the insured's physical, mental, and emotional health, but also his or her habits, finances, occupation, and avocations. See, e.g., *Volis v. Puritan Life Ins. Co.*, 548 F.2d 895 (10th Cir. 1977).

Of course, most courts will not allow an insurer to act arbitrarily and capriciously in determining if the proposed re-insured should be insured again according to its standards and will hold the insurer to a reasonable position based on industry practices. See, e.g., *Sunset Life Ins. Co. v. Crosby*, 380 P.2d 9 (Idaho 1963).

64. See, e.g., *Bowie v. Bankers Life*, 105 F.2d 806 (10th Cir. 1936).

65. See, e.g., *Gressler v. New York Life Ins. Co.*, 163 P.2d 324 (Utah 1945).

66. See, e.g., *Sellwood v. Equitable Life Ins. Co. of Iowa*, 42 N.W.2d 346 (Minn. 1950).

67. See, e.g., *Johnson v. Great Northern Life Ins. Co.*, 17 N.W.2d 337 (N.D. 1945).

68. Crawford, note 1 above, at p. 241. Crawford points out that there are two types of beneficiaries: intended and incidental.

Intended beneficiaries are the only type with standing (i.e., a legal position that bestows the right) to sue the insurer to enforce their rights under the contract. As its name implies, an intended beneficiary is one who the parties to the contract expected would benefit from its performance. Such parties include those who were named without consideration (so called "donee beneficiaries") and those named in satisfaction of a debt (so called "creditor beneficiaries").

An incidental beneficiary is one who only incidentally benefits because of the existence of the insurance. For instance, if a policy were payable to the policyowner's estate, a creditor of the policyowner could satisfy that debt by informing the estate's executor. All or a portion of the proceeds might incidentally be used for payment. But an incidental beneficiary never acquires rights under the life insurance policy and so cannot sue the insurer. The policy was not taken out for that party's benefit. Crawford, note 1 above, at p. 245-46.

69. To name a new beneficiary, the policyowner must meet the terms of the policy. Commonly, it will require the policyowner to file a written request (usually on the insurer's form) with the insurer. The policy itself is not filed. A copy of the change is sent

to the policyowner. Usually, that change becomes retroactively effective to the date the policyowner signed the insurer's change of beneficiary request form (but must first be recorded at the insurer's home office).

Under the doctrine of substantial compliance, once the policyowner has done everything reasonably possible to comply with the insurer's procedure, the change will not fail if circumstances beyond the policyowner's control make it impossible to meet every condition. See, e.g., *Dooley v. James Dooley Assocs.*, 442 N.E.2d 222 (Ill. 1982).

On the other hand, anything less than substantial compliance will be inadequate to make an effective change in benefit. Mere intent without positive action is insufficient. The policyowner must have taken every reasonable step in his power to effect a change of beneficiary. This rule is to protect the interests of the prior beneficiary. See, e.g., *O'Connell v. Brady*, 72 A.2d 493 (Conn. 1950).

70. Neither the killer nor anyone claiming under or through the killer (such as an assignee) can benefit from the life insurance. See McGovern, "Homicide and Succession to Property," 64 *Mich. L. Rev.* 65, 78 (1969) and Statler, "The Wrongful Killing of the Insured by the Beneficiary," *XXII Proceedings* (Association of Life Insurance Counsel 1971), p. 521. Note that intent to kill must be present before the beneficiary will be denied the policy proceeds.

71. See, e.g., *New York Life Ins. Co. v. Henriksen*, 415 N.E.2d 146 (Ind. Ct. App. 1981).

72. See, e.g., *Northwestern Mutual Life Ins. Co. v. McCue*, 223 U.S. 234 (1912). National Service Life Insurance will not pay if death is inflicted as lawful punishment for crime or for military or naval offense (unless inflicted by an enemy of the U.S.). Only the cash value must be paid to the designated beneficiary. 38 U.S.C. 1911. This provision also applies to Servicemen's Group Life Insurance. 38 U.S.C. 1973.

73. To utilize the marital deduction at the first spouse's death, he or she must be survived by a U.S. citizen spouse.

What is the value of a life insurance policy where the owner and beneficiary was the spouse of the insured and both died in a common accident? Since the insured is deemed to have survived, the value the instant before the deaths (rather than the face amount) was held to be the proper figure. See *Estate of Wien v. Comm'r.*, 441 F.2d 32 (5th Cir. 1971); *Chown v. Comm'r.*, 428 F.2d 1395 (9th Cir. 1970); *Old Kent Bank and Trust Co. v. U.S.*, 430 F.2d 392 (6th Cir. 1970).

74. The burden of proof is on the party trying to prove the deaths were not simultaneous where the deaths occur in a common disaster.

75. See Chapter 27.

76. The name is controlling even if the relationship no longer applies. See, e.g., *Outling v. Young*, 398 So. 2d 256 (Ala. 1981). Even if the description is not correct, where the insured's intention is clear, courts will carry out that desire. See, e.g., *Burkett v. Mott*, 733 P.2d 673 (Ariz. Ct. App. 1986).

77. There are both advantages and disadvantages to this designation. Obviously, if the policyowner changes marital status, a new wife would be benefited under a "to my wife" designation. This is probably the result desired. On the other hand, the ambiguity and therefore litigation potential is significantly enhanced. The best course of action is to properly name and describe each beneficiary, back up each beneficiary with a contingent beneficiary, and quickly change beneficiary designations when marital status changes.

78. Stepchildren are not generally included. Planners should suggest that clients specify which children are not to be included—especially if children from a prior marriage are to be excluded. See, e.g., *Pape v. Pape*, 119 N.E. 11 (Ind. Ct. App. 1918).

79. If the deceased child had left no children, the surviving two children would split the entire amount of the proceeds. It is best when making a per stirpes distribution to specify what is meant since different jurisdictions have varying interpretations of the per stirpes rule. For example, the insured might say something to the effect of:

"I leave the proceeds of this policy in equal shares to my children who survive me but if any predecease me and leave issue who survive me, that deceased child's share is to pass to his or her issue in equal shares, per stirpes."

80. Naming a guardian can cause problems because:

(a) it is not certain that the guardian will survive the insured and the insured's spouse;

(b) the court may not appoint the same individual as the policyowner selected; and

(c) the children may be legally competent by the time the insured dies. Crawford, note 1 above, p. 251.

Some states, such as Pennsylvania, provide for what is sometimes called a naked or informal guardian. This is a perhaps misnamed but highly useful creature of statutory law that allows a policyowner to invoke that statute in the beneficiary designation without the trouble and expense of setting up a formal trust during lifetime by appointing a guardian in a life insurance policy. Pennsylvania's statute provides that a person may appoint a guardian of a minor or otherwise incompetent on the insurer's beneficiary form. Payment by an insurance company to the guardian discharges the insurer to the same extent as if it made payment to an otherwise duly appointed and qualified guardian. This type of procedure is a good compromise when the total proceeds do not warrant the creation of a formal trust.

81. When naming a trustee as policy beneficiary, it is good practice to name a backup beneficiary in case the trust is terminated (or for some reason never comes into existence or is for any reason found to be defective). Consider providing that if the trustee cannot accept the proceeds within a specified number of days (such as ninety) after the insured's death, the insurer may make settlement to the insured's estate. This prevents an indefinite delay and benefits both insurer and beneficiaries. Usually, if a bank is trustee or co-trustee a provision should be inserted in the beneficiary designation exonerating the insurer from liability once it pays the proceeds to the trustee.

82. See, e.g., *United Benefit Life Ins. Co. v. Cody*, 286 F. Supp. 552 (W.D. Wash. 1968); *Cook v. Cook*, 111 P.2d 322 (Cal. 1941).

83. Settlement options are sometimes forbidden to assignees, trustees, and corporations who are restricted to lump sum cash payments (or are allowed to choose options only with the consent of the insurer). This is because some insurers do not wish to provide settlement options (which are expensive) for no charge to entities who are in the business of providing similar services at a charge to the consumer.

84. Planners should carefully compare this option with the interest option. Payees may actually be better off taking interest only. Female payees will not receive as much each year under this option as males because their life expectancies are so much longer. At older ages, the "straight life annuity" might have a significant payout advantage over an annuity with period certain.

85. Extended term does not have loan values so no loans are available from it but loans can be made from a policy placed on reduced paid up status. When there is a loan outstanding at the time a policy is placed on reduced paid up status (or extended term or cash surrendered), the amount available is reduced by the amount of that loan.

86. Mechanically, a policy loan is typically made through loan forms and insurers can but do not require the policyowner to send in a contract for a stamped endorsement (notice) stating that there is a loan against the contract. The policy loan agreement usually requires the policyowner to certify that the policy has not already been pledged as collateral for a loan.

87. See, e.g., *Board of Assessors v. New York Life Ins. Co.*, 216 U.S. 517 (1910). Typically, the beneficiary of a life insurance policy subject to a loan is entitled only to the net proceeds, i.e., the proceeds remaining after the loan is deducted from the amount otherwise payable. Compare this with the beneficiary of a policy pledged as collateral for a loan; such a beneficiary is generally entitled to have the loan paid from the assets of the estate and may be entitled to the full face amount of the policy. See, e.g., *Chaplin v. Merchants National Bank of Aurora*, 186 F.Supp. 273 (N.D. Ill. 1959).

88. See, e.g., *Mallon v. Prudential Ins. Co.*, 5 F.Supp. 290 (W.D. Mo. 1934).

89. See, e.g., *State Mutual Life Assur. Co. v. Webster*, 148 F.2d 315 (9th Cir. 1945).

90. Most companies now use a variable policy loan interest rate (such as Moody's Monthly Corporate Bond Yield Average) to prevent "disintermediation" (i.e., a strong flow of cash out of the insurer's hands when interest rates that can be earned outside the life insurance contract are far higher than the fixed interest rates charged by the insurer a policy loan). Variable loan rates presently incorporated in newly-issued policies are not retroactive to older contracts. The older contracts may provide fixed rates as low as 5 percent. Planners should keep this potential advantage in mind in analyzing the value of older as compared to newer policies (but some insurers have lowered dividends payable on policies with 5 and 6 percent loan rates).

91. Interest is typically computed to the following premium date (or if the policy is paid up or single premium to the next policy anniversary). For this reason, the later in the year the loan is made, the more money can be advanced to the policyowner—because less interest need be charged.

92. See, e.g., *Keeley v. Mutual Life Ins. Co.*, 113 F.2d 633 (7th Cir. 1940); *Protective Life Ins. Co. v. Thomas*, 134 So. 488 (Ala. 1931); *Cory v. Mass. Mutual Life Ins. Co.*, 170 A. 494 (R.I. 1934).

93. Some insurers will waive this so that total proceeds can be distributed under a settlement option.

94. Crawford, note 1 above, at p. 325.

95. The terms of the automatic premium loan provision usually give the insurer the right to change the frequency of premium payments.

96. See, e.g., *First Nat'l Bank v. Lincoln Nat'l Life Ins. Co.*, 824 F.2d 277 (3rd Cir. 1987).

97. It is deemed so valuable that the insurer is allowed to continue using policy cash values to pay premiums even if the policyowner is declared legally bankrupt. 11 U.S.C. 542(d).

98. Anderson, note 1 above, at p. 296.

99. See Chapter 24.

100. Personal property has been defined as any property which is not land or attached to land. The Supreme Court in *Grigsby v. Russell*, 222 U.S. 149, 156 (1911), held that life insurance is personal property. Writing for the Court, Justice Holmes said:

    "[L]ife insurance has become in our days one of the best recognized forms of investment and self-compelled saving. So far as reasonable safety permits, it is desirable to give to life policies the ordinary characteristics of property... To deny the right to sell ... is to diminish appreciably the value of the contract in the owner's hands."

101. Among the sticks in the bundle of rights are the right to obtain a policy loan, the right to withdraw or direct the application of dividends, and the right to surrender the policy for its cash value.

    The policyowner should be free to give away or sell his rights under a life insurance policy for his own advantage according to *Mutual Life Ins. Co. v. Allen*, 138 Mass. 24 (1884). (But that well-seasoned case assumed the insured and the policyholder would be the same and therefore ignored the potential for the gaming element in a sale). Even if the assignee has no insurable interest (defined above), the assignment will be valid in almost every state—unless it is shown that there was a lack of good faith and intent to sidestep the insurable interest rule. See, e.g., *Butterworth v. Mississippi Valley Trust Co.*, 240 S.W.2d 676 (Mo. 1951). See also, note 10 above.

102. If the policyowner owns a policy on the life of another, at the policyowner's death prior to the death of the insured or the lifetime maturity of the contract, the policy (absent specific provision in the contract regarding successive ownership) will pass into the policyowner's estate and therefore be disposed of according to his or her will or, if there is no valid will, according to the intestate law (i.e., the statutory provisions that direct the disposition of assets of a decedent who dies without a valid will) of the state of domicile.

103. It is best and most convenient to use the insurer's forms where available.

104. If the insurer discovered the first spouse's claim prior to paying the proceeds, the insurer would pay the proceeds into a court in a process called "interpleader" in which the court would decide the proper payee. It is the process used when two or more parties claim property held by a third party who does not claim to own the property but cannot determine who the legal owner is. The court decides the identity of the proper owner. This is, of course, an expensive process.

105. Keep in mind that this presumes the policy is usually not required to be submitted in conjunction with a policy loan. See, e.g., *Elledge v. Aetna Life Ins. Co.*, 406 S.W.2d 374 (Ark. 1966).

106. Planners should beware of "unholy trinity" situations where the policy on the life of the insured is owned by a second party and made payable to a third party. This almost invariably leads to adverse income or gift tax results (and potentially a malpractice suit against the planners who failed to spot the issue).

107. The American Bankers Association Collateral Assignment Form No. 10 is the most commonly used collateral assignment form.

108. In order to avoid litigation, the collateral assignment form will typically require the signature of the policyowner's beneficiary. This puts the beneficiary on notice that there has been a collateral assignment and that he or she may not be receiving the entire death benefit. It also makes it more convenient for the lender to exercise any policy rights while the insured is still alive. Most importantly, because the beneficiary is consenting

to the collateral assignment when he or she signs the form, he or she cannot later object if the proceeds must be used to pay off the loan.

109. A collateral assignment does not bind the transferee lender to pay life insurance premiums even if the policyowner defaults. If the lender does so, the amount of those premiums can be added to the total debt owed to the lender.

110. An insurer is typically presumed to know the rights it holds under the life insurance contract. However, if pertinent (i.e., material) facts are unknown or deliberately withheld from the insurer, the insurer's actions in ignorance of these facts will not constitute a waiver of its rights. So if a premium payment were accepted on a policy applied for on a nonsmoking basis, the insurer's right to deny a claim would not be forfeited if the insured was in fact a heavy and long term smoker. The insurer did not have knowledge of this material fact.

Harsh as it may sometimes seem, most courts hold that "an applicant is responsible for the truth of statements in an application he or she signs"—even if the agent (or medical examiner) knew of a misstatement and filled in an answer accidentally—or on purpose—falsely. In other words, the knowledge of the agent is not universally imputed to the insurer. Nor will knowledge of the agent be imputed to the client—even in those courts which do not hold the applicant responsible for reading the contract and the copy of the attached application—if the client colluded with the agent to defraud the insurer. See, e.g. *Aetna Life Ins. Co. v. Routon*, 179 S.W.2d 862 (Ark. 1944). Since the insurer has neither actual nor imputed knowledge, it cannot "knowingly" waive its rights to cancel the policy.

Most courts hold the insured responsible for reading the application—before signing it! That also binds the policyowner's beneficiaries. Obviously, this rule would not be applied if the agent lied on the application in order to make a sale and ripped out the copy before giving the policy to the policyowner. See, *Hart v. Prudential Ins. Co.*, 117 P.2d 930 (Cal. 1941).

111. Any party to the life insurance contract can waive a right or be estopped from asserting a right. For simplicity, the authors will explain these two terms using the insurer as the violator and the policyowner or beneficiary as the injured party even though in many cases the reverse is true.

112. Crawford, note 1 above, p. 116.

113. These forbidden waivers also apply to the doctrine of estoppel.

114. See, e.g., *Fayman v. Franklin Life Ins. Co.*, 386 S.W.2d 52, 58 (Mo. 1965).

115. See, e.g., *Pierce v. Homesteaders Life Ins. Assoc.*, 272 N.W. 543 (Iowa 1937).

116. Crawford, note 1 above, at p. 123.

117. Here the term "agent" is used in the more narrow sense of a soliciting agent only. Decisions as to whether to allow a waiver would be submitted in writing by the soliciting agent to the appropriate home office agent.

118. See, e.g., *Hoffman v. Aetna Life Ins. Co.*, 22 N.E.2d 88 (Ohio Ct. App. 1938).

119. Silence will not generally operate to change a legal relationship unless particular circumstances impose a duty to speak (i.e., when remaining silent would prove inequitable to the other party).

Anderson, note 1 above, at p. 413, states general rules which have evolved in this area:

(a) Mere nonaction is not enough to bar an insurer from declaring a policy is lapsed where the cause is nonpayment of premiums—unless the insurer had habitually kept the policy in force after the policyholder's default or unless the insurer failed to give adequate notice that premiums were due.

(b) The insurer must notify the insured within a reasonable time when it learns of a ground of forfeiture (other than nonpayment of premiums) or lose the right.

(c) Where the insured dies before the insurer learns of a ground for forfeiture, the insurer by its silence after the loss is not considered to have waived its rights since the policyowner or beneficiaries are not prejudiced by the insurer's silence.

120. Crawford, note 1 above, p. 116, states that estoppel (technically equitable estoppel) can only be raised as a defense if three elements are present:

(a) words or conduct of one party (typically the insurer) mislead the other party (usually the policyowner or beneficiary) into believing that facts which were untrue were true;

(b) the injured party had no knowledge of the true facts; and

(c) the party requesting that the other be "estopped" was reasonable in relying on the untrue words or conduct and was consequently injured.

121. But see Anderson, note 1 above, at p. 402, who disagrees with the opinion of the authors and states, "cases frequently arise in which the distinction between the two concepts is vital to the sound disposition of the cause [sic]."

SPECIAL POLICY PROVISIONS AND RIDERS

CHAPTER 6

INTRODUCTION

In addition to the many required legal provisions of a life insurance contract (as described in Chapter 5), many life insurance contracts include special provisions, permit special endorsements, and/or allow special riders to be attached to the basic contract. The purpose of these provisions and riders often is to enhance the flexibility and fit of the policy to the policyowner's needs. However, in some cases, they serve to restrict the policyowner's options and to limit the insurer's exposure. Also, some of the standard policy provisions, such as the dividend provision, the nonforfeiture provision, the policy-loan provisions, and the settlement provisions, usually include default options that policyowners may request the insurer to replace with other options. However, the options are not uniform among contracts; some companies offer a more restrictive list of choices than others or include other limiting features or provisions.

To select the policy or insurance package with the most favorable combination of features one must know not only the options available, but also something about how those options may differ among companies and contracts.

The policy provisions and riders discussed in this chapter include:

1. term riders;

2. limitation riders;

3. cost-of-living riders;

4. accidental death benefit riders;

5. disability waiver of premium riders;

6. disability waiver of policy charges riders;

7. disability income riders;

8. additional purchase options (guaranteed insurability riders);

9. accelerated death benefit riders;

10. catastrophic illness riders;

11. long-term care riders;

12. extension of benefits riders;

13. high early cash value riders;

14. automatic premium loan provisions;

15. policy loan interest rate;

16. dividend options;

17. bailout provisions;

18. change of plan provisions;

19. change of insured provisions;

20. additional insured riders;

21. common accident provision (survivorship clause); and

22. settlement options.

TERM RIDERS

The most common and familiar rider is the term insurance rider. When purchasing insurance, buyers may add virtually any form of term insurance—increasing, decreasing, or level—to a base permanent policy. The principal advantage to the insured of using a term rider is that the insurer issues the additional insurance on a net cost basis, without some of the fees typical of new issues. Policyowners frequently use such riders when they have a temporary need above their long-term base need or when the policyowners cannot afford to pay the premiums for a permanent policy for the full amount of insurance they need, but still wish to assure coverage for the full amount of their need.

Term riders normally provide that the policyowner can change the rider to a separate policy or convert it into a permanent form of coverage within a specified period or before a specified age without evidence of insurability. Companies differ with respect to the length of the period of coverage they will permit under the term rider. For instance, some companies limit both the coverage period and the conversion period to the insured's age sixty-five or younger; others will permit coverage and conversion to later ages, such as age seventy-five or older.

Two of the critical elements people seeking insurance should investigate are the current term rates charged by the prospective companies as well as these companies' maximum guaranteed term rates. Some companies guarantee that their current term rates will never increase. However, their current term rates may be higher than those of companies who reserve the right to increase term rates, subject to a maximum, if their experience so dictates. Also, if prospective insureds anticipate that they may wish to convert term riders in the future, they should check the companies' conversion charges, which may vary widely.

LIMITATION RIDERS

Insurance companies may add certain riders or endorsements to the base contract to limit their liability under the base policy. The most common forms of limitations are the war rider, the aviation rider, the hazardous occupation or hazardous avocation rider, and the limited-benefit-period rider.

War Rider

The war rider provides that insurance will not pay a death benefit in the event of death due to war or acts of war. As a result of the Korean and Vietnam conflicts, insurers generally have broadened this rider to cover what are now described as military police actions as well.

Aviation Rider

The aviation rider excludes payment of death benefits in the event of death as a result of an airplane crash unless the insured is on a regularly scheduled commercial airline flight. This limitation is less frequently encountered today, because aviation is much safer and the hazards more predictable than in the past. In most cases now, companies will charge an additional premium, which varies according to the experience of the pilot, the type of aircraft, and other factors such as the general nature of the flights, common destinations, and types of cargo. Most commercial pilots qualify for standard rates and can acquire standard insurance. Some insurers specialize in offering policies to noncommercial pilots. These insurers may underwrite some nonpilots—such as business executives—similarly to noncommercial pilots if they frequently use noncommercial flights to conduct business and travel to what the insurers consider hazardous landing facilities, such as small foreign landing fields. In some cases, the rider may exclude coverage for death in an airplane accident that occurs in a foreign country.

Hazardous Occupation or Avocation Rider

Many companies either will not issue policies on persons in hazardous occupations or who practice hazardous avocations or will exclude death benefits if death occurs as a direct result of practicing the occupation or engaging in the avocation. The hazardous occupation classification varies by company and may cover dozens of jobs from astronaut to lumberjack to skyscraper window cleaner. High risk avocations normally include such things as skydiving, scuba diving, hang-gliding, mountain climbing, spelunking, race car driving, motocross racing and similar high-risk activities. However, for almost any hazardous occupation or avocation there is an insurer who specializes in writing insurance on such risks.

Limited Benefit Period Rider

Policies with limited benefit period riders are a form of modified death benefit policy. Generally, this rider limits death benefits to a return of premiums if death occurs within a specified period after policy issue, typically two years. After the limitation period, the face amount either jumps up to a higher permanent level or increases gradually over a specified period of time. Insurers often issue policies with this rider when the insureds have a pre-existing health condition that would otherwise make them uninsurable. For example, someone who recently underwent cancer surgery might not otherwise qualify for coverage. However, if the person survives for a certain period of time after surgery, the probability of long-term survival increases. Consequently, after a certain limited benefit period, the insurer can be relatively assured that the risk of imminent death has decreased and can increase the face amount of coverage. In general, these policies are still highly rated with much higher than standard premiums relative to the face amount of coverage.

Similar to the case with hazardous occupations and avocations, some companies specialize in writing coverage on various forms of substandard health or unusual diseases.

COST OF LIVING (COL) RIDERS

The COL rider typically is a term insurance rider providing automatically increasing coverage each year, or every few years, equal to the increase in the cost of living as measured, normally, by the Consumer Price Index (CPI). The insurer bills policyowners for the additional coverage with the regular notice for the base policy. The insurers require no evidence of insurability; however, if policyowners reject the additional coverage at any time by nonpayment of the additional premium, they usually will have to provide evidence of insurability in order to receive future COL adjustments. Once the insurer increases coverage, the new level of coverage remains in effect, even if the owner later rejects increases or the CPI declines.

Some companies guarantee the term rates for the COL additions, while others do not.

In the case of adjustable life products, the COL increases typically are part of the readjusted base policy, rather than term additions, and insurers adjust the premiums accordingly. In universal life policies, insurers may increase the face amount of coverage for COL adjustments without the need for the policyowner to pay additional premiums if the policy has sufficient cash value to support the higher death benefit at the current premium level.

ACCIDENTAL DEATH BENEFIT (ADB) RIDERS

Many insurers offer an accidental death, or double indemnity, rider that—for a small additional premium—provides some multiple of the base face amount (typically double) if death is accidental. Most experts feel there is little use for this coverage, because the insurance need is rarely tied to the means of death. In fact, a *nonaccidental* death rider, if it were available, would be a better option, because death benefit needs are likely to be higher if death occurs after a prolonged and expensive illness than if it occurs suddenly as a result of an accident.

If policyowners purchase such a rider, they must take care to determine what the policy means by using the term "accidental" death. Insurers use two different clauses: the "accidental means" and the "accidental death" type clauses. Most companies now use the accidental death clause which provides that when death occurs as a result of accidental bodily injury, the insurer pays the accidental death benefit.

If the contract uses the accidental means clause, both cause and result must have been accidental. The insurer will not pay the ADB if death is accidental but did not occur as a result of an accidental means or cause. For instance, if a person dies as a result of falling down his stairs, it is an accidental death, but it might not qualify for the ADB if the means were not also accidental (he intended to go down the stairs). Only if the fall resulted from an accidental means (he tripped on his child's roller skate), would the insurer pay the ADB.

Whatever merit an ADB rider may have, it is virtually useless if the insurer uses the accidental means clause to determine when they will pay the ADB. A person probably would be better off taking a chance spending the additional premium amount on the lottery.

Companies differ with respect to the minimum and maximum ages of coverage under the ADB rider. Some companies do not specify either minimum or maximum ages.

Those that do, set age one or five as the minimum age and most set age seventy as the maximum age, although some set earlier maximum ages, such as age sixty-five or sixty. Companies also differ with respect to the period of time after an accident during which death must occur for the insured to be paid the ADB. Most companies limit the period of time to ninety days, but some set the period at 120 or 180 days or one year. A few companies allow payment as long as the rider is in force.

Finally, some companies offer a curious limited ADB rider that pays a multiple benefit if death occurs on a common carrier, such as an airline, bus, taxi, or train. Some contracts include school buses and private passenger automobiles and/or will pay the ADB if death occurs as a result of being struck while a pedestrian. Once again, unless one has a gambling nature and spends a lot of time on common carriers in high-risk areas, the policyowner would be better off using the premium dollars spent on such an ADB rider buying additional coverage that will pay off regardless of the cause or means of death.

DISABILITY WAIVER OF PREMIUM RIDER

The waiver-of-premium rider is a form of disability insurance that provides that the basic policy (and often other riders) will continue in force if the insured becomes disabled and incapable of paying premiums. However, if policyowners have taken loans against their policy cash values, interest is still due on the loans. If interest on the policy loans is drawn from policy cash values (rather than paid in cash by the policyowner) and loan balances and interest charges are large relative to the net cash value, the policy could still lapse if the interest charges deplete the net cash value to close to zero.

Waiver of premium riders differ among companies and polices with respect to the period of coverage, the waiting period needed to qualify, and the definition of total disability.

Period of Coverage

In the event of disability, the insurer essentially pays the premiums for the policyowner/insured for a specified period of time that varies from company to company. If disability occurs before age sixty, most companies will waive premiums for as long as the

disability continues or until the policy would otherwise terminate or endow. Some policies become paid up at age sixty-five. If the waiver of premium rider is in effect at the time a policy becomes paid up, the insurer would not require the insured to resume premium payments even if he should overcome his disability.

If the insured becomes disabled after age sixty, about half the companies' provisions provide no waiver of premium benefit. Of those companies that do provide a waiver of premium benefit for disabilities occurring after age sixty, most will waive premiums only to age sixty-five, although some specify a period equal to the longer of a specified minimum number of years or to age sixty-five or seventy. For example, the rider may specify that if disability occurs after age sixty, premiums will be waived for two years or until the insured is age sixty-five, whichever is longer.

Most companies use a waiting period of six months before insureds qualify for disability waiver of premium benefits. However, some companies use a shorter period of four months or less.

Definition of Total Disability

The definition of total disability varies widely and may be more or less liberal. It is therefore critical when shopping for a policy to determine which definition insurers are using in the policies one is considering.

A majority of the insurers use what advisers generally consider the most liberal definition:

Inability to perform one's own job for two years, then any job for which reasonably suited by education, training, and experience.

A sizable minority of insurers use a somewhat less liberal definition:

Inability to perform any job for which reasonably suited by education, training, and experience.

A few insurers use a very limiting definition of total disability:

Inability to perform any job for pay or profit.

Many insurers use a duration-varying definition of disability where, for instance, they will use the most liberal "own job" definition for the first two to five years of disability and then switch to the somewhat less liberal "job for which reasonably suited" definition. Some insurers may even switch again at a later date to the "inability to perform any job" standard. Given the many possibilities or combinations of disability definitions and time frames when the insurers use the various definitions, persons seeking to buy insurance with a waiver of premium rider should review the specifics of the rider carefully.

Most insurers' definitions also include conditions that are presumptive of total disability. Typically insurers presume the "loss of use of" or less liberally, the "loss of" two body members such as an arm and a leg, or of sight, to constitute total disability qualifying for waiver of premium. Some companies even include total loss of hearing as a presumptive condition. A minority of insurers include no presumptive conditions in their definition of total disability.

DISABILITY WAIVER OF POLICY CHARGES RIDER

The disability waiver of policy charges rider (also called a disability waiver of deductions rider) essentially serves the same purpose as the disability waiver of premium rider, except that it applies with respect to universal life policies and other flexible-premium policies. UL and other flexible-premium policies generally do not set required periodic premium payment levels and policyowners usually are free to vary their premium payments over time. Thus, instead of stating the benefit in terms of waiving required premium payments, the rider states the benefit in terms of waiving virtually all monthly deductions such as mortality charges, expenses, and other fees and loads generally including charges for any special provisions and riders. However, also similar to disability waiver of premium riders, a disability waiver of policy charges rider will help policyowners to avoid lapses of their policies in the event of their becoming disabled and being unable to pay premiums. However, lapses could still occur if the policyowners have taken large loans from their policies relative to the cash values. If their net cash values are insufficient to pay ongoing interest on these loans until the policyowners are again able to pay amounts at least large enough to cover the interest charges, their policies will lapse.

Similar to disability waiver of premium riders (described above), disability waiver of policy charges riders for UL policies and other flexible-premium

policies differ with respect to the period of coverage, the waiting period needed to qualify, and the definition of total disability. However, the differences from company to company and policy to policy are of the same types and ranges of differences as were described above in the discussion of disability waiver of premium riders.

DISABILITY INCOME RIDER (DIR)

The disability income rider provides both a waiver of premium (or a waiver of policy charges) and a supplementary income if the insured becomes totally disabled. The definition of total disability is the same as that used for purposes of the waiver-of-premium or waiver of policy charges riders. Customarily, the policies express the disability income benefit as a specified percentage of the face amount payable monthly. The common percentage is 1 percent. For example, if the face amount of the policy is $50,000, the DIR will pay $500 per month in the event the insured becomes totally disabled.

As with regular disability income insurance policies, insurers generally place maximum limits on the amount of disability income they will issue to some stated figure, such as $1,000 per month. Also, through coordination of benefits provisions, they may further limit the amount of disability income they will issue and pay based on the total amount of income payable on all other disability income policies on the insured. As a general rule, insurers are reluctant to issue disability income policies when aggregate disability income payments may exceed 65 to 80 percent of the insured's net earned income.

Commonly, disability must continue for a six-month waiting or elimination period before benefit payments commence, although a few companies use a four-month waiting period. As with the waiver of premium or waiver of policy charges riders, if the insured overcomes the disability, disability income payments cease and the insured must commence paying premiums on the life insurance policy once again. However, in those cases where the disability ceases after age sixty-five and when the waiver of premium or policy charges provision pays-up the policy at age sixty-five, insurers require no further premium payments.

The additional premium companies charge for a given disability income benefit varies among companies, but generally will be higher for policies issued by the companies that use the most liberal definition of total disability (as described above for the waiver of premium) and lower for those that use the most restrictive definition. Regardless of the definition used, the DIR generally will only pay if the insured is totally disabled and the disability is presumed to be permanent. Therefore, advisers generally do not consider the DIR to be the most suitable form of disability income insurance. For insureds who need disability income protection, insurers generally will tailor comprehensive disability income policies (independent of their life insurance policies) to fit their needs better and more cost effectively.

ADDITIONAL PURCHASE OPTIONS (GUARANTEED INSURABILITY RIDERS)

Most commonly, insurers sell permanent policies with attached Additional Purchase Options (APOs) or Guaranteed Insurability Options (GIOs) on the lives of younger insureds. The APO gives the younger insureds who cannot afford the premiums for large face amounts the option to purchase additional insurance without evidence of insurability at specified times in the future or upon the occurrence of certain life events. The traditional pattern provides regular options every three years usually beginning with age twenty-five and ending at age forty. However, some companies start options earlier and/or may continue the options at regular or specified intervals to age sixty-five.

Most companies also provide alternate purchase options and dates based on the occurrence of certain critical life events that would normally warrant additional life insurance coverage. Most companies allow exercise of the option in case of marriage or birth, with multiples for multiple births. Some companies also will allow exercise if and when the insured adopts a child. In most cases, the exercise of an alternate purchase option will preempt exercise of the next regularly-scheduled purchase option.

The option amounts generally are scheduled on the specifications page of the contract and usually are equal to or less than the original face amount of coverage. In some cases, companies also specify a minimum purchase amount, such as $5,000 or $10,000.

A sizable minority of insurers automatically include a disability waiver of premium (or policy charges if a UL policy) in their new policies if the original policy included it. Many other insurers will include the disability waiver of premium (or policy charges), if requested. However, there is a great diversity in the conditions for the disability waiver of premium (or policy charges) benefit in new policies issued under an APO. The waiver may be automatic, but only if the original policy is whole life or premiums are payable to an advanced age, such as age ninety-five. In other cases, the insurer will include the waiver if the policyowner requests it but then only if the premium on the new policy is equal to or less than that of the whole life policy. In some cases, the disability waiver of premium (or policy charges) benefit is available only if the insured is not already totally disabled at the time the insurer issues the new policy. In other cases the insurer will include the waiver if the policyowner requests it and the company consents.

In virtually all cases, insurers require the new policy to be a type of whole life or endowment policy. However, a few companies permit the insured to purchase term insurance.

In addition to the traditional APO for young insureds, some companies now offer special APOs or GIOs in other circumstances. For example, some companies offer a GIO for the survivor to a joint life contract. Also, some companies offer GIOs or APOs with policies issued to fund business buy/sell agreements. This permits the policyowners to increase necessary coverage as business values increase.

ACCELERATED DEATH BENEFIT (ADB) RIDERS[1]

Accelerated death benefit riders, also called living benefit or advanced death benefit riders, are a relatively recent innovation with many variations. In general—for policies with this rider—insurers will pay part or all of the policy face amount of coverage in advance on the diagnosis of certain dread diseases or in the event of circumstances significantly affecting the insured's longevity and quality of life, such as a major organ transplant or entering a nursing home.

The amount that companies may pay in advance varies by company and circumstance. The percentage of the face amount of coverage that policies may pay out in advance ranges from 25 to 100 percent. In those policies with high percentage-of-face payouts, the limits may depend on the reason for payout. For example, policies may make 70 to 85 percent of the death benefit available under the nursing home option and 90 to 98 percent under the terminal illness option. The insurers reduce the advanced death benefit amount by actuarial computation to reflect the earlier and determinable payout.

Among the factors that affect the actual amount available are the face amount of death coverage, the insured's actual future mortality, outstanding policy loans, current interest rates, future scheduled premiums, and administrative charges.

In most cases, once insureds meet the conditions necessary to trigger accelerated payments, they can elect to receive benefits in a single lump sum or as a series of installment payments. However, paid under the option, the amount of money insureds may receive generally is more than they would realize by surrendering the policy for cash or by taking a policy loan. Insureds usually do not have to use amounts they receive under the option to pay medical or nursing home expenses. Rather, they generally may use these amounts in any manner they desire.

The policyowner may make the ADB election with respect to less than the total available insurance, provided the minimum election is for at least a specified amount, typically $25,000, and at least a specified amount of death benefit, such as $25,000, remains in force. When policyowners elect to receive an advanced payment of only a portion of the total benefit, the insurer reduces the life policy proportionately as to death benefit, premium, and value.

ADB Trigger Events

Some policies permit early payout more liberally than others. The most restrictive policies limit advance payments to cases where doctors diagnose life expectancy to be six months or less. Other policies are somewhat less restrictive. For instance, some companies will permit early payouts to commence if the insured is confined to a long-term care facility for a certain period of time, such as six months, and the expectation is that such care is permanent. The broadest options permit payouts not only for diagnosis of a terminal illness or confinement to a nursing home, but also for life-threatening conditions—even if death is not virtually imminent. These conditions may include heart attack, heart surgery, cancer, stroke, major organ transplant, kidney failure, paraplegia, blindness, serious injury, or inability to perform two or three normal activities of daily living, such as general care, feeding, and bathing.

Closely related to the triggering events is the company's policy with respect to pre-existing conditions. Some companies place no restrictions based on pre-existing conditions. Others institute what is the equivalent of a waiting period of from one to six months before they will pay advance benefits. They may also limit the number of times insureds may collect a benefit. For example, some companies may permit advance payments only once for illness but more than once for successive internments in a nursing home facility.

Policies to Which Insurers May Attach ADB Riders

Virtually any type of policy may include an ADB rider. However, companies vary widely with respect to the age limit on purchase of the ADB option. The maximum age ranges from fifty to eighty. They also vary widely with respect to the premium charge. Some companies offer the rider with no charge to any new insured who requests it. Others charge a level premium, while still others charge an increasing premium over time. Those companies that charge an additional premium for the ADB rider may or may not provide a waiver-of-premium benefit with respect to the ADB rider. Often insurers waive the premium during any period in which the insured qualifies for waiver-of-premium under the base policy.

Income Taxation of ADB Payments

Insureds who are terminally ill or chronically ill and who receive amounts under a life insurance contract may exclude such amounts from their gross income as amounts paid by reason of the death of an insured.[2] A similar exclusion applies to amounts received for the sale or assignment of any portion of a death benefit under a life insurance contract to a viatical settlement provider.[3] However, the exclusion applies only if the insured under the life insurance contract is either terminally ill or chronically ill.[4] Further, excludable amounts paid to a chronically ill individual are subject to a per diem limitation that changes annually, as indexed for inflation. (See Chapter 30.)

A person is terminally ill if that person has been certified by a physician as having an illness or physical condition that the physician reasonably can expect to result in death within twenty-four months of the date of certification.[5] A person is a chronically ill individual if a licensed health care practitioner has certified within the previous twelve months that the person has met one of three qualifying criteria. These criteria include:

1. being unable to perform without substantial assistance at least two activities of daily living

(e.g., eating, toileting) for at least ninety days due to a loss of functional capacity;

2. having a similar level of disability; or

3. requiring substantial supervision to protect him from threats to health and safety due to severe cognitive impairment.[6]

The term chronically ill individual does not include a terminally ill individual.

In the case of chronically ill individuals, the income-tax exclusion applies only if the case meets detailed requirements. For example, the payee must use payments for costs incurred by the payee (not compensated for by insurance or otherwise) for qualified long-term care services provided for the insured for that period. Under the terms of the contract, the payment must not be a payment or reimbursement of expenses reimbursable under Medicare (except where Medicare is a secondary payor, or the arrangement provides for per diem or other periodic payments without regard to expenses for qualified long-term care services).[7]

The income-tax exclusion may not apply to amounts paid to a taxpayer other than the insured in certain circumstances. The exclusion is denied if the noninsured payee has an insurable interest in the insured's life because the insured is a director, officer or employee of the payee, or because the insured is financially interested in any trade or business carried on by the payee.[8]

ADB Riders versus Viatical Settlements

Qualifying insureds with an accelerated benefit rider usually may request an accelerated payment of all or part of their benefits payable under the option. When policyowners receive only a partial advancement of benefits from their insurers, the policyowners remain the owners of the policies, but now with proportionately reduced death benefits. They still retain all the rights of ownership, including the right to name and change beneficiaries. Therefore, the people who the policyowner has named as beneficiaries still will receive some remaining percentage of the face amount of coverage as tax-free death benefits when the insured dies.

In contrast, viatical settlement companies generally buy the life insurance policy outright from the policyowner by paying the policyowner a percentage (less than 100 percent) of the death benefit upfront.

Viatical settlements as a rule, do only full—not partial—advances of death benefits. Thus, in return for making the full advance payment to the policyowner, the policyowner assigns the policy to the viatical settlement company. The viatical settlement company then assumes payment of all the remaining premiums and, as owners and sole beneficiary of the policy, receives the full death benefit when the insured dies.

Although the total amounts paid in either case may be (or may not be) close to equal either way, the ADB rider typically gives the policyowner more flexibility with respect to the amount and timing of payments as well as more control over who, ultimately, will get benefits. In addition, if the insured needs only partial acceleration of benefits, the beneficiaries named in the policy receive the remaining amounts as death benefits when the insured dies. Under current tax rules, these death benefit payments are virtually always received tax free. In contrast, if the full payment of benefits in a viatical settlement exceeds qualifying amounts, a part of the settlement may be subject to tax. This is an amount that, almost certainly, would not be subject to tax if the insured took a partial payment under an ADB rider and the remainder ultimately was paid as life insurance death benefits.

For more information, see Chapter 30, "Viatical and Life Settlements."

CATASTROPHIC ILLNESS RIDER

A benefit sometimes included with an ADB rider, but which insurers also offer separately, is the catastrophic illness rider. When buyers add a catastrophic illness rider to a life insurance policy (usually requiring them to pay an additional premium), a portion (usually 25 to 50 percent) of the face amount is payable upon diagnosis of specified illnesses. The named illnesses differ among insurers but typically include organ transplantation.

As insurers pay benefits under either a catastrophic or terminal illness rider, they reduce the face amount of the basic policy an equal amount. Also, an interest charge applies in some policies. Insurers reduce cash values either in proportion to the death benefit reduction or on a dollar-for-dollar basis.

LONG-TERM CARE RIDER (LTC)

Some life insurance issuers offer life insurance with a long-term care rider available for an additional charge.

Essentially, an LTC rider is a variation of the accelerated death benefits rider. Persons who buy a policy with this rider can pay the premium in a single lump sum or by making periodic payments. In any case, the policies with the LTC rider provide policyowners with a death benefit that they can also use to pay for long-term care related expenses, should they incur them.

The insurer bases the amount of death benefit and the long-term care allowance on the insured's age, gender, and health at the time the policyowner buys the policy. The appeal of this combination policy lies in the fact that either policyowners will use the policy to pay for long-term care expenses or their beneficiaries will receive the insurance proceeds at the insureds' death. In either case, someone will benefit from the premiums policyowners pay.

Insurers add the long-term care benefit to the life insurance policy by either an accelerated benefits rider or an extension of benefits rider.

Accelerated benefits rider – An accelerated benefits rider makes it possible for policyowners to access the death benefit to pay for expenses related to long-term care. The insurer reduces the death benefit by the amount used for long-term care expenses, plus a service charge. If policyowners need long-term care for a lengthy period of time, they will eventually deplete their death benefit. Policyowners also can use this same rider if they have a terminal illness that may require payment of large medical bills. Because (as described above under the accelerated death benefits rider) accelerating the death benefit can have unfavorable tax consequences, one generally should not exercise this option before consulting a tax professional.

Example. Policyowner pays a single premium of $50,000 for a universal life insurance policy with a long-term care accelerated benefits rider. The policy immediately provides approximately $87,000 in long-term care benefits or $87,000 as a death benefit. If the insured incurs long-term care expenses, the accelerated benefits rider allows the insured to access a portion, such as 3 percent ($2,610), of the death benefit amount ($87,000) each month to reimburse some or all of the long-term care expenses. The insurer will continue payments until total payments exhaust the total death benefit amount of $87,000 in about 33.3 months. Whatever the policyowner does not use for long-term care will be left to heirs as a

death benefit. (The hypothetical example is for illustration purposes only and does not reflect actual insurance products or performance. Guarantees are subject to the claims-paying ability of the issuer.)

Typically, qualifying for payments under a long-term care rider is similar to the qualifying for payments under most stand-alone long-term care policies. Insureds must be unable to perform usually two or three of the activities of daily living (bathing, dressing, eating, getting in or out of a bed or chair, toilet use, or maintaining continence) or suffer from a severe cognitive impairment.

An elimination period may also apply: policyowners pay for the initial cost of long-term care out-of-pocket for a specific number of days (usually thirty to ninety, but sometimes longer) before they can apply for payments under the policy. As with all life and long-term care insurance, the insurance company will require prospective insureds to answer some health-related questions and to submit to a physical examination before they issue a combination policy.

Deciding whether a combination policy is the right choice depends on a number of factors. First, a combination policy is almost never a good choice if the prospective insured does not need both life insurance and long-term care coverage.

Second, one should ask how much life and long-term care one needs and whether no one combination policy can adequately satisfy these needs. A long-term care rider may not provide as many features as a stand-alone long-term care policy. For example, the combination policy may not cover assisted living or home health aides. It also may not provide an inflation adjustment, an important feature considering the rising cost of long-term care. Given the greater flexibility of tailoring two distinct policies to meet the needs and also the inherently greater range of choices and flexibility with stand-alone long-term care policies, more often than not, a two-policy approach will better fit one's needs.

Third, when it comes to long-term care, nobody can ever be sure how long he or she might need long-term care coverage. The critical question is: will the long-term care part of a combination policy provide sufficient coverage even if one adds an EOB rider?

Fourth, keep in mind that accelerated death benefits that the insurer pays for whatever reason deplete the face amount of the life insurance. The combination policy may be a risky proposition if one wants to maintain the level of the death benefit payable to heirs with a reasonably high probability.

Finally, the tax benefits offered by a qualified long-term care policy may not apply to the long-term care portion of combination policies, which could result in taxation of long-term care benefits received from the policy.

EXTENSION OF BENFITS RIDER (EOB)

Policyowners can add extension of benefits riders to their policies with accelerated death benefit (ADB) riders to increase their coverage beyond their policies' death benefits under the various forms of the ADB riders including benefits covering terminal, chronic, or critical illnesses and long-term care expenses. This rider differs from company to company as to its specific application.

Depending on the issuer, the extension of benefits rider either increases the total benefit amount available for terminal, chronic, or critical illnesses or for long-term care expenses (while the death benefit remains the same) or lengthens the number of months over which the insurer will pay benefits. In either case, benefit payments will reduce the available death benefit of the policy. However, some companies still pay a minimum death benefit even if the total of all accelerated benefit payments exceeds the policy's death benefit amount.

Continuing from the example above under the "Long-Term Care Rider" section, if a policy's extension of benefits rider increases the long-term care benefit (the death benefit—$87,000—remains the same) to three times the death benefit ($261,000), the monthly amount available for long-term care increases to $7,830. On the other hand, if the extension of benefits rider extends the length of time the monthly long-term care benefit is available, then the monthly payments ($2,610) are extended for an additional twenty-four to thirty-six months beyond the initial number of months (33.3) available.

HIGH EARLY CASH VALUE RIDER

The early cash value rider is an optional rider providing for higher cash values in the early years of a policy in the event of a full surrender for cash. It effectively waives the surrender charges and premium load associated with a life insurance policy, or returns all or part of the cumulative paid premiums, whichever provides the greater benefit. In exchange for the early high cash value, the cash value in the later years of the policy will be lower than it would have been without the rider.

Insurers have designed the early cash value rider primarily for the business market. Businesses can use it in a nonqualified supplemental retirement plan when a company wants to reward a key employee. Additionally, business may add the early cash value rider when using life insurance in qualified plans, for premium financing and other instances where having high early-year cash values are important.

AUTOMATIC PREMIUM LOAN PROVISION

Many companies provide an automatic premium loan provision, but the policyowner must in some states actively elect to make the feature operative. When operative, if a premium is unpaid at the end of the grace period and there is sufficient cash value, the policy automatically will advance a loan to pay the premium and prevent lapse. Most companies place no restrictions or limitations on the use of the automatic policy loan provision. However, some companies permit policyowners to use the provision to pay premiums only a limited number of consecutive times before the policy will lapse, even if the cash value is sufficient to continue using loans to pay premiums.

POLICY LOAN INTEREST RATE

Despite the fact that companies may use a variable policy loan interest rate, the majority of companies still use a fixed rate, which is commonly 8 percent, although it varies by company and from one policy type to another. This suggests that many consumers prefer the certainty of a fixed rate. Companies that use a variable rate usually determine that rate using the *greater* of: (1) Moody's corporate bond yield for the month ending two months before; *or* (2) 1 percent plus the rate being credited to cash values. The impression seems to be widely held that the variable rate cannot exceed 8 percent or Moody's composite yield. However, this is in fact not generally true. There is no absolute limit in most cases except that which may be specifically imposed under state law.

Another apparently widely held misconception is that most companies using variable policy loan rates also generally permit policyowners to elect to use a fixed rate.

Only a subset of the companies using variable rates permit policyowners to elect to use a fixed rate instead.

When market interest rates exceed 8 percent, most policyowners feel that fixed rates are more attractive than variable rates. However, companies that use a fixed rate typically also use an offset provision that credits cash values backing policy loans with a lower rate than they currently credit to other cash values. In the case of dividend-paying policies, the dividend-allocation formula typically will take account of loan balances and credit lower dividends to policies with higher loan balances. Consequently, it is not at all clear that the fixed policy loan rate is more economically beneficial than a variable rate.

Given the misconceptions and misunderstandings regarding policy loan rates, offset provisions, and the availability of an election between fixed and variable loan rates, it is important to closely inspect the policy loan interest rate provisions of all policies under consideration.

DIVIDEND OPTIONS

Although most companies provide the basic four dividend options:

1. cash;

2. reduced premiums;

3. dividend accumulations at interest; and

4. additional paid-up insurance.

Some do not provide all these options. In fact, one large New York company provides no options: the company uses dividends exclusively to reduce premiums. Many other companies, but certainly not most companies, also permit the policyowner to use dividends to buy one-year term insurance. In most cases, the insurer limits the term amount to either the cash value or the total of premiums paid to date. However, some companies are more liberal and will permit the policyowner to use dividends to buy as much term insurance as the dividends will purchase. Also, many companies permit the policyowner to apply dividends as additional premium to more quickly pay-up the policy and to accelerate the period until the premiums vanish.

Most state laws require insurance policies to clearly indicate which option is the default option if the policyowner does not make an election at the time the insurer issues the policy. The paid-up option is used most frequently as the default option, but some states mandate the cash option, reduction-of-premium option, or the accumulation option. Although policyowners often take dividend options for granted, to assure maximum flexibility it is wise to carefully inspect the dividend options provided in any participating policy being considered and to actively select the desired option when the insurer issues the policy.

BAILOUT PROVISIONS

Most current assumption and universal life policies use surrender charges rather than front-end loads to recover issuing expenses if the owner terminates the policy in the early years. Some of these policies provide a bailout provision that reduces or eliminates the surrender charge for early termination if the current rate credited to cash values falls below specified levels. This is an extremely attractive feature because it provides some assurance that the company is not using inflated current rates to encourage policy sales, only to lower the rates once they issue the policy.

CHANGE OF PLAN PROVISION

Many policies provide a change of plan provision that gives the policyowner the privilege of exchanging the policy for some other contract issued by the company. In essence, this feature is an in-house Code section 1035 exchange provision. In term contracts this generally is the conversion option that allows the policyowner to exchange a term contract for some form of permanent cash-value contract. In permanent cash value contracts, the privilege normally is to change to some other form of cash-value contract. In general, the insurer permits the exchange without evidence of insurability if the new plan is a higher-premium, higher cash value type of policy. Also, the new policy generally must have the same policy date and the same underwriting class and issue age as the original policy.

Despite these commonalities, the companies' change of plan provisions operate in diverse ways. In some contracts, the insurers allow certain types of exchanges only with the approval of the company. In a few other companies' contracts, policyowners may exchange virtually any type of policy for any other type, including permanent for term, with evidence of insurability but otherwise without the need for approval by the company. In many contracts, the change of plan clause states that the new policy may not have any riders attached, even if the old policy included certain riders, unless the company agrees. Although in most cases companies permit existing riders to continue in the new policy, some companies' change of plan clauses specifically state that riders may continue in the new policy without the need for special approval by the company.

Policy exchange fees also vary widely. In some contracts, the insurers treat the new policy as a new issue with new issue charges and commissions. In other cases, the insurers issue the new policy at net cost, that is, without new issue fees and commissions. These companies levy only a minimal charge to cover the administrative and clerical costs of handling the paperwork.

CHANGE OF INSURED PROVISION OR RIDER

The change of insured provision or rider is an attractive option in business insurance applications such as key person insurance or buy/sell funding. It is a special form of change of plan provision that essentially permits the policyowner to exchange a policy on one life for a similar policy on another life with evidence of insurability. The key attraction is that this type of policy exchange is less expensive than terminating the old policy and acquiring a new policy. It avoids surrender charges or fees on termination of the old policy and generally avoids most of the new issue charges and commissions that the policyowner would otherwise pay on the new policy. Insurers base the premium for the new policy on the age and underwriting class of the new insured for the same death benefit as in the old policy. In general, the new policy will continue the change of insured rider and other riders may from the old policy. The company usually will charge an additional premium for the change of insured rider, but if the probability of changing insureds is relatively high, the premium cost usually is much lower than the cost of terminating old policies and acquiring new policies when changing insureds.

ADDITIONAL INSURED RIDERS

Additional insured riders generally are term insurance riders on insureds other than the insured named in the base policy. One of the most common uses of the additional insured rider is in what is called the family policy. The family policy insures all or selected members of the family in one contract. Typically the base policy is some form of permanent cash value policy on the principal breadwinner with term riders on the spouse and children. Although variations exist, the usual plan calls for a specified percentage of coverage for the spouse and children for each unit of coverage on the principal breadwinner. For example, for each $10,000 of coverage on the husband, the plan provides $3,000 of term coverage for the wife and $2,000 of term coverage for each child under a specified age, generally age eighteen. All children living with the family are covered, even if born or adopted after the insurer issued the policy.

Additional insured riders also are commonly used in first-to-die plans, often in business applications, such as to fund buy/sell agreements. The principal advantages in either case are the economies of one policy issue and administration and the flexibility to structure the plan to meet specific planning needs.

COMMON ACCIDENT PROVISION (SURVIVORSHIP CLAUSE)

Only about one in three contracts issued specifically includes a common accident provision, or what is sometimes called a survivorship clause or common disaster clause. Insurers have designed the clause to avoid inclusion of death benefits in the beneficiary's estate if he or she dies within a designated period after the insured. Where found, the provisions provide that the principal beneficiary must survive the insured by anywhere from seven to thirty days to receive the policy death benefits. If the principal beneficiary does not survive for the designated period, the policy pays death benefits to the contingent beneficiary. At least one company permits the policyowner, if other than the insured, to change the beneficiary for up to sixty days following the death of the insured.

SETTLEMENT OPTIONS

The commonly offered and state mandated settlement options include payments made as follows:

1. in cash;

2. in a fixed amount over some period of time;

3. for a fixed period of time in some amount; or

4. any of the common annuity options.

The critical element to examine is not the options, per se, but whether or not the insurer makes age or time adjustments to the settlement options. A relatively small number of companies have provisions that are apparently intended to make an adjustment for anticipated increases in longevity so as to decrease the present value of future benefits for persons who are expected to begin receiving life annuity benefits well into the future. In other words, the annuity rates for annuity settlement options specified in the contract become less favorable the farther in the future one expects the insurer to pay the annuity. Although these reductions may be warranted if life expectancies increase as these companies apparently believe they will, the longevity improvements may not materialize as anticipated. Regardless, companies that have not made adjustments to the future annuity settlement rates in their policies are clearly more attractive than those that have made adjustments.

CHAPTER ENDNOTES

1. See Chapter 30 for a more complete discussion of the features, operations, and planning implications of ADB riders and viatical settlements.

2. I.R.C. §101(g)(1).

3. A viatical settlement provider is an entity that regularly buys or takes assignments of life insurance contracts on the lives of the terminally ill and that meets detailed standards.

4. I.R.C. §101(g)(2)(A).

5. I.R.C. §101(g)(4)(A).

6. I.R.C. §§101(g)(4)(B) and 7702B(c)(2).

7. I.R.C. §101(g)(3).

8. I.R.C. §101(g)(5).

ADJUSTABLE LIFE

CHAPTER 7

INTRODUCTION

Adjustable Life (AL) is a "flexible premium" "adjustable death benefit" type of permanent cash value insurance. It is essentially a hybrid combination of Universal Life (UL) and ordinary level premium participating life insurance.

AL Has Features of Universal Life

In contrast with ordinary level premium, level death benefit policies and similar to UL, AL gives the policyowner the flexibility to change the plan of insurance. That is, within limits, the policyowner may change the premium and/or the level of death benefit. Note that when policyowners make changes to an AL contract, the guarantee period will also change. In general, the policyowner may:

- increase or decrease the premium;

- increase or decrease the face amount;

- lengthen or shorten the guaranteed protection period; and/or

- lengthen or shorten the premium payment period.

Increases in the face amount usually require evidence of insurability. Also, an increase in premiums requiring an increase in the face amount to stay within the definition of life insurance guidelines of Code section 7702 usually will require evidence of insurability.

Despite its similarities, do not confuse AL with universal life (UL), which is often called flexible premium adjustable life. Direct-recognition, current assumption policies, such as UL, "unbundle" the policy elements and explicitly show mortality and expense charges and interest credits. In addition, they credit interest directly to cash values.

In contrast, most AL policies' elements are bundled. Like traditional participating policies, the pure protection and savings components are not segregated or stated separately. However, policyowners may make partial surrenders, up to the sum of premiums they have paid, without surrendering the entire policy, or paying income tax (assuming the policy is not treated as a modified endowment contract).

Like many participating policies in the market today, most AL policies are "indirect recognition interest sensitive" or "indirect recognition current assumption" policies. The insurance company's favorable investment, mortality, and expense experience are indirectly reflected in the level of dividends that the company actually pays, or directly reflected as additional credits to cash values.

AL Has Features of Ordinary Level Premium Whole Life Insurance

In addition to the bundled nature of its policy elements, AL has all the usual features of ordinary level premium whole life insurance including:

- a minimum interest guarantee;

- guaranteed maximum mortality charges;

- cash values;

- nonforfeiture values;

- a policy loan provision;

- dividend options;

- a reinstatement period; and

- settlement options.

Similar to other traditional forms of insurance, various options or riders are available including:

- waiver of premium;

- guaranteed purchase or insurability;

- accidental death benefits; and

- cost of living adjustments.

Although the policyowner has flexibility in selecting the plan of insurance, changes are generally permitted only at specified intervals and with advance notice to the insurer. Between adjustment periods, the policy is a level premium, level death benefit policy. Depending on the particular premium and death benefit levels chosen, the policy can assume the form of almost any traditional term or whole life policy from low-premium term through ordinary whole life to high premium, limited pay whole life.

Policyowners generally may ask to set premiums to zero without the policy lapsing (or without invoking the automatic policy loan provision), although this virtually always requires notice to the insurer. The minimum annual premium is typically equivalent to the premium for a five-year term policy. In contrast with UL and similar to ordinary level premium policies, once a policyowner has selected a given plan of insurance, the policyowner must pay premiums as scheduled unless the policyowner notifies the insurer of his or her desire to change the plan of insurance. The plan of insurance defines the length of the guarantee at any point in time. The insurance company computes the schedule of cash values based on the current program of premium payments, the face value, and the term or duration of coverage. The insurance company recomputes the cash value schedule each time the policyowner opts to change the plan of insurance.

WHEN IS THE USE OF THIS DEVICE INDICATED?

Insurance shoppers can consider AL for almost any life insurance need. Initially, the policyowner can have the insurance company configure an AL policy's death benefit and premium level to resemble virtually any type of life insurance policy from five-year term insurance to single premium whole life. However, because of policy costs, AL is generally best suited for longer-term coverage needs. For short-term coverage needs where future insurability is not a factor, a nonrenewable term policy generally would be more cost effective.

1. AL is indicated whenever insureds need or desire greater flexibility over time in life insurance coverage, need or want guaranteed protection, and prefer the forced savings feature of ordinary level premium whole life insurance. Policyowners whose circumstances change can later reconfigure the policy by changing the schedule of premium payments and/or the face amount or duration of coverage.

2. The insurance industry has marketed AL as the only policy a person will ever need. The flexibility makes it very useful in the family market. For example, a young parent with a growing family and modest income can acquire an AL policy that is initially configured with low premiums and a high death benefit to resemble a traditional term policy. As the parent's income grows, they can increase the scheduled premiums to build up tax-sheltered cash within the policy. At later times when they need cash, such as to pay for children's educations, they can reduce the scheduled premiums. The policyowner can use partial surrenders or policy loans to help pay the school expenses. After a time, the policyowner can increase scheduled premiums, once again, to build cash values that policyowner and spouse can use for their retirement. Similarly, if the amount of death protection that is needed changes, the policyowner may increase or decrease the death benefit or reduce or extend the term of coverage. Keep in mind, increases in death benefits usually will require evidence of insurability. Each time the policyowner requests a change, the insurance company recalculates the guarantee period.

3. The flexibility of AL also makes it suitable for many business life insurance needs. AL offers a conservative and guaranteed vehicle for all sorts of business applications where the policyowner may frequently require adjustments in death benefits and/or cash accumulations, including split-dollar plans, nonqualified deferred compensation plans, death benefit

only plans, key person insurance, buy/sell agreements, retiree benefits funding, and in qualified retirement plans that use insurance.

Advantages

1. Policyowners have discretion or flexibility in selecting the schedule of premiums that they will pay until they next request a change in the plan of insurance.

2. Similar to ordinary level premium whole life policies, once a policyowner has chosen a premium payment plan, the policy has an element of forced saving until the policyowner requests a change in the premium payment plan. Many people who lack the discipline to continue a regular savings program will find this feature attractive.

3. The policyowner may change the face amount of coverage or the term of coverage. The insurance company will permit decreases in the face amount of coverage at virtually any time. Policyowners who reduce death benefits within the first seven years of issue should do so only with the advice and counsel of their insurance advisers because such death benefit reductions may subject them to adverse tax consequences under the Modified Endowment Contract (MEC) rules. Insurance companies generally permit increases in face amounts, subject to evidence of insurability. Increases in the death benefit may also subject the policy to a new test period under the MEC rules. (See discussion under "Tax Implications" below).

4. Most AL policies offer a cost of living agreement that automatically increases the face amount in response to increases in the CPI without evidence of insurability. Commonly, the premium is also correspondingly adjusted upwards.

5. Cash value interest or earnings may accumulate tax-free or tax-deferred, depending on whether gains are distributed at death or during lifetime.

6. The cash values are not subject to the fluctuations in market value characteristic of longer-term municipal bonds and other longer-term fixed income investments when market rates change.

7. Policyowners can borrow policy cash values at a low net cost. Although policyowners must pay interest on policy loans, cash values continue to grow and are credited with at least the minimum guaranteed rate in the policy. Consequently, the actual net borrowing rate is less than the stated policy loan rate.

Disadvantages

1. Some AL policies, similar to many ordinary whole life policies, use what is called the direct recognition method to determine how favorable investment, mortality, and expense experience is allocated to dividends on policies with policy loans. Under this method, the insurance company reduces the amount of dividends allocated to policies with policy loans to account for the generally lower yield the company earns on policy loans relative to other investments in their general portfolio. Companies most commonly use the direct recognition method in policies with fixed policy-loan rates. Typically, policies with variable-loan rates, and some others with fixed-loan rates, do not employ the direct recognition method and instead allocate dividends without regard to loans. There are also some AL policies that do not have dividends, but credit current mortality and interest to cash values, similar to UL.

2. Lifetime distributions or withdrawals of cash values are subject to income tax to the extent attributable to gain in the policy.

3. Surrender of the policy within the first five to ten years may result in considerable loss because cash surrender values reflect the insurance company's recovery of sales commissions and initial policy expenses.

4. Interest paid on policy loans generally is nondeductible.

5. The flexibility with respect to premium payments and death benefits permits policyowners to change the policy in such a way that it may inadvertently become a modified endowment contract (MEC) with adverse tax consequences.

TAX IMPLICATIONS

The tax rules for AL policies are generally the same as the tax rules for other types of life insurance policies. Death benefit payments are usually free of any federal income tax. AL policies also are subject to the same estate, gift, and generation-skipping transfer taxation rules as all other types of life insurance policies. See Chapters 22 through 29 for a complete discussion of the taxation of life insurance.

Similarly, the tax rules for living benefits from AL policies are also the same as the tax rules for living benefits from other types of life insurance policies. The annuity cost recovery rules of Code section 72 govern annuity-type distributions. These rules state that policyowners recover their investment in the contract (generally, total premiums paid less prior nontaxable distributions) ratably over the expected payout period.

Generally, the cost recovery rule governs the taxation of all types of nonannuity living benefits. The cost recovery rule, which is sometimes called the FIFO (First-In-First-Out) rule, treats amounts received by the policyowner as a nontaxable recovery of the policyowner's investment in the contract. Only after the policyowner fully recovers the investment in the contract are additional amounts received treated as taxable interest or gain in the policy. Included in this category of living benefits are policy dividends, lump-sum cash settlements of cash surrender values, cash withdrawals, and amounts received on partial surrender. The policyowner includes such amounts in gross income only to the extent they exceed the investment in the contract (as reduced by any prior excludable distributions received from the contract). In other words, policyowners generally treat nonannuity distributions during life first as a return of the policyowner's investment in the contract, and then as taxable interest or gain. If the insurer holds any living benefits under an agreement to pay interest, the policyowner must report and pay taxes each year on all the interest the insurer pays on or credits to the living benefits.

Exception to the Cost Recovery Rule

The general cost recovery rule has an important exception for withdrawals within the first fifteen years after the policy issue date that also are coupled with reductions in death benefits. In general, insurance companies do not permit withdrawals from AL policies without a complete or partial surrender of the policy. In other words, to the extent permitted, withdrawals typically will entail reductions in the amount or term of death benefits. Reductions of the face amount or term of coverage could force out some of the cash value under the rules of Code section 7702. If such withdrawals or distributions occur within the first fifteen contract years, the policyowner generally will have to report and pay income tax on the amount withdrawn or distributed to the extent attributable to gain in the policy.

Such withdrawals or distributions are taxed in whole or in part as ordinary income to the extent forced out of the policy as a result of the reduction in the death benefits. The taxable amount depends on when the policyowner makes the withdrawal:

- *Within the first five years* – If the distribution takes place within the first five years after policy issue, a very stringent and complex set of tests apply.[1] Potentially, a larger portion, or perhaps all, of any withdrawal within the first five years will be taxable if there is gain in the policy.

- *Fifth to fifteenth years* – For distributions between the end of the fifth year and the end of the fifteenth year from the issue date, a mathematical test applies. Essentially, the policyowner is taxed on an income-first basis to the extent the cash value before the withdrawal exceeds the maximum allowable cash value under the cash value corridor test for the reduced death benefit after the withdrawal.[2] Frequently, only a portion or none of the withdrawal will be taxable in these cases.

Caveat: Potential Taxation under the MEC Rules

The flexibility inherent in AL policies with respect to changes in premiums and face amounts raises the possibility that the policy could become a modified endowment contract (MEC).[3] The penalty for classification as a MEC relates to distributions. If a policy is classified as a MEC, distributions under the contract are taxed under the interest-first rule rather than the cost recovery rule. In addition, to the extent taxable, these distributions are subject to a 10 percent penalty if they occur before the policyowner reaches age 59½, dies, or becomes disabled. So MEC classification of an AL contract means both faster taxation of investment gains and a possible penalty tax for early receipt of that growth.

Distributions under the contract include living benefits (as described above), partial surrenders, policy loans, loans secured by the policy, loans used to pay premiums, and dividends taken in cash. Distributions under the contract generally do *not* include dividends used to pay premiums, dividends used to purchase paid-up additions, dividends used to purchase one-year term insurance, or the surrender of paid-up additions to pay premiums.

Changes in premiums or death benefits may inadvertently cause an AL policy to run afoul of the MEC rules in basically three ways:

1. An increase in premium payments during the first seven contract years may push the cumulative premiums above the amount permitted under the seven-pay test.[4]

2. A reduction in the death benefit during the first seven contract years triggers a recomputation of the seven-pay test. The seven-pay test is applied retroactively as of the original issue date as if the policy had been issued at the reduced death benefit.

3. A material increase of the death benefit at any time triggers a new seven-pay test which is applied prospectively as of the date of the material change.

When issued, AL policy illustrations show the maximum amount (the seven-pay guideline annual premium limit) that the policyowner may pay within the first seven years without having the policy classified as a MEC. When a policyowner inadvertently exceeds that maximum, the policyowner can avoid MEC status if the insurer returns excess premiums to the policyowner with interest within sixty days after the end of the contract year in which the excess occurs. The policyowner typically will have to report and pay tax on this interest.[5]

A policy will fail the seven-pay test if, in any year, the cumulative premiums paid to that year exceed the sum of the seven-pay guideline annual premiums to that year.

Example. Assume the guideline annual premium is $10,000 based on the original death benefit. The policyowner pays $9,000 each year for the first six years. In year seven, the policyowner reduces the face amount which forces out $18,000 of the cash value. The recomputed guideline premium is $8,000. The policy now fails the seven-pay test and is a MEC because cumulative premiums paid in just the first year, $9,000, (and through year six as well) exceed the sum of the recomputed guideline annual premiums of $8,000. The policyowner will pay tax on the $18,000 to the extent of any gain in the policy. In addition, unless the policyowner

is over age 59½ or disabled, the tax law imposes an additional 10 percent penalty on the taxable portion of the distribution.

Any reduction in death benefits attributable to the nonpayment of premiums due under the contract will not trigger a recomputation of the seven-pay test if the policyowner (and insurer) reinstate the prior benefit level within ninety days after being reduced.[6]

The term "material" change is not defined in the statute. However, the statute states that it "includes any increase in death benefit under the contract,"[7] but not increases attributable to dividends (for paid-up additions), interest credited to the policy's cash surrender value, increases necessary to maintain the corridor between the death benefit and the cash surrender value required by the definition of life insurance,[8] or cost-of-living adjustments. The rules generally consider increases in death benefits that require evidence of insurability as material changes that invoke a new seven-pay test. (See Chapter 22 for more information.)

ALTERNATIVES

Universal Life (UL)

Universal life is the principal alternative to adjustable life. When the insurance industry introduced AL, the industry promoted it as the perfect policy for virtually everyone. It could be adjusted to meet anyone's changing insurance needs throughout life. However, with the introduction of universal life, the popularity of adjustable life has waned for several reasons:

1. *AL provides somewhat less flexibility to adjust premiums and death benefits than UL policies.* Generally, UL policyowners may vary their premiums at will or skip premium payments altogether if the policy has sufficient cash values to cover mortality and expense charges. In contrast, unless an AL policyowner officially requests a change in the premium payment plan, skipping premium payments will either cause the policy to lapse or trigger policy loans under the automatic premium loan provision. In addition to the inconvenience of having to make requests in advance regarding a change in the premium payment plan or face amount or duration of coverage, the insurance company may limit or restrict such requests to specific dates or intervals.

2. *AL policy elements are bundled whereas UL policy elements are unbundled.* The annual statements for UL policies report mortality and expense charges and interest credits to cash values separately. This allows policyowners to easily monitor actual versus projected performance. The insurance company also issues new cash value schedules and schedules of projected dividends for AL policies when the policyowner requests a change in the plan of insurance, but there is no regular and separate accounting for mortality and expense charges and interest credits. (Note, however, that some AL policies are unbundled.) Although higher than projected dividend payments or lower current mortality and interest charges may reflect favorable company experience, most companies do not regularly report how dividends actually paid compare with those projected. This makes it more difficult for policyowners to monitor actual versus projected performance as compared to unbundled UL policies.

3. *AL has more restrictive withdrawal rules than UL.* In general, insurance companies permit withdrawals from AL policies only when accompanied by reductions in the face amount of coverage. Many UL policies permit withdrawals of up to 10 percent of the cash value, and sometimes more, without reductions in the face amount of coverage.

4. *UL offers two death benefit options: option I – level total death benefit, and option II – level insurance benefit plus cash value) whereas AL offers only the traditional level total death benefit.* Note, however, that a policyowner can reconfigure an AL to resemble the UL option II program with the purchase of a term rider or by using dividends to purchase paid-up additions. With over a dozen dividend options, this type of AL policy can return benefits to a client by reducing premiums, strengthening the plan of insurance or growing cash value.

Despite these relative disadvantages, some people may prefer AL to UL for several reasons:

1. *AL offers more certainty regarding cash value accumulations than UL.* Like ordinary level premium whole life policies, the insurance company guarantees an AL policy's cash value schedule for as long as the policyowner maintains the selected plan of insurance. When a policyowner

arranges a new premium payment plan or a new face amount, the insurer produces a new guaranteed cash value schedule. In contrast, illustrations of UL policy cash values are just that—projected nonguaranteed illustrations.

2. *AL dividends give the policyowner more options as to how to use or apply the favorable investment experience of the company than UL policies.* UL policies reflect favorable investment performance directly in the amounts credited to cash values. In virtually all AL policies, the level of dividends the insurer pays reflects the insurer's favorable investment performance. The policyowner may use these dividends in several ways. Policyowners can have the insurer pay the dividends in cash, use them to reduce premiums, accumulate them at interest, use them to purchase additional term insurance (with a rider), or add them to policy cash values.

3. *The requirement to pay scheduled premiums under the selected plan of insurance with AL provides a forced saving feature that is absent with UL.* AL policyowners have a strong incentive to continue scheduled premiums because failure to do so will often have adverse consequences. If an AL policyowner fails to pay scheduled premiums under the selected plan of insurance without requesting a change in the plan, the policy may lapse and be put on either the extended term or the paid-up nonforfeiture option, depending on the default option under the contract. AL policies typically have very liberal reinstatement provisions, but they do normally require evidence of insurability. Policyowners can avoid lapses with the automatic premium loan provision, but then each failure to pay premiums will incur a loan against the policy.

Preprogrammed Combinations of Differing Life Insurance Policies

To the extent a person can anticipate future life insurance needs and premium paying ability, a program combining various cash value and term insurance products may meet an insured's needs. However, most people cannot anticipate all the ways their insurance needs may change over time. Therefore, they must rely on the possibility of buying new insurance and their rights to lapse, change, or surrender old policies, to keep their programs up-to-date. The Code section 1035 exchange provisions provide some flexibility to change the plan of insurance. Also, some companies include change provisions that permit limited changes to the face amount of coverage. To some extent policyowners can assure the right to buy additional insurance with guaranteed purchase options, but the amounts guaranteed may turn out to be insufficient. Policy loan provisions, the dividend options on participating policies, and the renewable and convertible features of term insurance all give policyowners some flexibility in their overall plan of insurance. Although these features and provisions are useful for limited adjustments in the plan of insurance, insureds may find it difficult to arrange major changes within these somewhat constrained options.

FEES AND ACQUISITION COSTS

Life insurance companies are free to set their premiums according to their own marketing strategies. Almost all states have statutes prohibiting any form of rebating (sharing the commission with the purchaser) by the agent. The premium includes a loading to cover such things as commissions to agents, premium taxes payable to the state government, operating expenses of the insurance company such as rent or mortgage payments and salaries, and any other applicable expenses.

A few companies offer no-load or low-load life insurance policies. These policies are not really no-load, because certain expenses are unavoidable (e.g., the premium tax), but rather pay either no sales commission or a very low sales commission. Consequently, the cash value buildup tends to be larger in the early years. Although commissions are lower, these companies typically must spend somewhat more money on alternative methods of marketing and, therefore, may incur generally higher expenses in this area than companies that pay commissions to agents.

The bulk of an insurance company's expenses for a policy are incurred when the policy is issued. It may take the company five to nine years or longer to recover all its front-end costs. The state premium tax is an ongoing expense that averages about 2 percent of each premium payment. Many companies pay 55 percent first year commissions when the plan of insurance is similar to an ordinary whole life policy. They will typically pay somewhat lower rates on low premium and high premium plans. Under most plans, the aggregate commissions paid to the selling agent over the years is approximately equal to the first year premium on the policy configured as an ordinary whole life policy. Commissions are typically paid on a renewal basis over

a period of three to nine years. When a new plan of insurance requires additional premiums, the change is usually treated as a new sale for commission purposes as it would be with other policies.

Most adjustable life policies have no explicit surrender charges. However, many will pay a terminal dividend when the policy is surrendered. The terminal dividend is typically higher the longer the policy has remained in force. In essence, this is a form of surrender charge since the company is essentially holding back dividends it could otherwise pay currently and rewarding those policyholders who maintain their policy longer with a greater terminal dividend.

The costs of administration, recordkeeping, and service generally are somewhat higher with adjustable policies than with traditional fixed premium, fixed benefit policies. In addition, the company faces greater risk of adverse selection. Policyowners are more likely to exercise their rights to increase face amounts within the limits not requiring evidence of insurability and/or to reduce premium payments without reducing the face amount if the insured's health declines. Consequently, expense charges and mortality charges tend to be somewhat higher in these policies than in otherwise comparable fixed premium, fixed benefit policies.

SELECTING THE BEST OF ITS TYPE

Although policyowners may change the plan of insurance, AL is essentially a traditional fixed premium, fixed benefit policy at any given point in time. Some of the key considerations are: the policy loan provisions; the policy loan interest rate; whether or not the company uses a direct recognition method to determine the dividend paid on policies with policy loans; the dividend interest rate (the rate that must be earned on the company's investments to justify the projected dividends); the current crediting rate; the method used to determine the amount of investment income allocable to the policy (portfolio method, new money method, or some weighted average); and, of course, the financial stability and strength of the company. Each of these items is discussed, where appropriate, in Chapter 14 "Ordinary Level-Premium Whole Life Insurance," Chapter 13, "Limited-Pay Life Insurance" and Chapter 15, "Single Premium Life Insurance." What to look for in a policy illustration or ledger statement is similar to that discussed in Chapter 13, "Limited-Pay Life Insurance."

The items of special importance when evaluating AL policies are the adjustment provisions and the commonly offered guaranteed insurability options. Look for policies with more liberal adjustment provisions. All else being equal, prospective insureds probably should favor policies that permit more frequent changes in the plan of insurance and that permit them sooner after the policy issue date. Similarly, they should prefer policies that permit larger and more frequent face amount increases without evidence of insurability. However, all else is never quite equal. More liberal adjustment provisions may involve higher expense charges. More liberal guaranteed insurability provisions generally will require higher premium charges.

Another key consideration is the quality of service. Changes in the plan of insurance require recomputation of the premium payment plan, cash value schedules, and projected dividend schedules and may involve a new underwriting evaluation if the company requires evidence of insurability. This service generally comes from a combination of the insurer and the agent. If either the agent or the insurer is slow to perform his or its part, desired changes may not take effect for months.

FREQUENTLY ASKED QUESTIONS

Question – How does the adjustments provision of AL differ from the change provision often found in ordinary whole life insurance policies?

Answer – Adjustments in AL policies are made prospectively only, affecting the future but in no way amending the past. The change provisions in traditional policies typically require payment of back premiums and/or other retroactive adjustments that may affect cash values. Such changes typically become increasingly and prohibitively expensive the longer the policy has been in force.

Question – Do AL policies offer dividend options that are not available with ordinary whole life policies?

Answer – AL policies offer the conventional dividend options—cash, premium reduction, accumulate at interest, and paid-up additions. Some AL policies offer what is called a policy improvement dividend option. With this option, dividends become a part of the cash value and thereafter lose their separate identity. If the current plan of insurance is equivalent to some form of whole life insurance, this option causes the face amount to increase without an increase in premiums or without changing the premium paying period. The effect is essentially the same as buying paid-up additions, except that the policyowner cannot later surrender these amounts without surrendering the policy as a whole. Generally, policyowners of traditional whole life policies may surrender regular paid-up additions separately. If the current plan of insurance is of a term nature, this option will increase the term of coverage.

Question – Can policyowners make unscheduled additional premium payments on AL policies similar to those permitted for universal life?

Answer – Most AL policies permit unscheduled additional premium payments. Such payments will lengthen the term of coverage or shorten the premium paying period depending on whether the current plan of insurance is in a term mode or a whole life mode. For example, a large enough payment might change a plan from term to age fifty to term to age sixty-five, or from a life paid-up at age seventy-five to a life paid-up at age sixty-five. Some companies restrict the availability of this feature in the first few policy years.

Question – Will a change in the plan of insurance cause an AL policy to become a modified endowment contract (MEC)?

Answer – Generally, a change in the plan of insurance that either lengthens the period of coverage or increases the face amount of coverage is treated as a material change in the policy that triggers a new seven-pay test. However, the reconfigured policy is treated as a MEC only if it fails the seven-pay test in its new configuration. In general, the insurance company will inform the policyowner if the desired change may cause the policy to fail the seven-pay test.

Also, a reduction of the face amount of coverage (or, in the authors' opinion, a shortening of the term of coverage) within the first seven policy years triggers a recomputation of the seven-pay test that is based on the reduced death benefit level and is retroactive to the original policy issue date. The closer earlier premium payments were to the original seven-pay premium limit, the more likely is a reduction of death benefits within the first seven years to trigger reclassification as a MEC.

In the authors' opinion, a change in the premium payment plan that does not change the level of benefits, such as a change from a whole life level premium payment plan to a paid-up at age sixty-five plan, should not be treated as a material change and should not require new seven-pay testing. However, if the change in premiums requires a change in the face amount to meet the requirements of life insurance under Code section 7702, the change should be considered material and require new seven-pay testing. See Chapter 22 for a more complete discussion of the material change rules and the seven-pay test.

Question – If the option to increase the face amount of coverage requires new evidence of insurability, of what benefit is this option if a person becomes uninsurable?

Answer – The companies that offer AL policies realize that the flexibility to increase the face amount is not that significant if increases require evidence of insurability. Consequently, most companies offering AL policies issue them with guaranteed purchase or insurability riders. This provision allows the policyowner to periodically purchase (e.g., every three to five years) a limited amount of additional coverage without proving insurability. In general, a purchase option expires if the policyowner does not exercise it when it matures, but the later options remain open without proof of insurability. Any desired increase in face amount beyond the limits set in the guaranteed insurability option will require evidence of insurability.

Do not confuse the guaranteed insurability option with the Cost-Of-Living Adjustment (COLA) provision that most companies also offer in their AL policies. The companies generally grant the COLAs without proof of insurability. In some cases, the insurer increases the policy face amount automatically each year by the increase in the Consumer Price Index (CPI) unless the policyowner elects otherwise. The insurer also correspondingly adjusts the premium payment plan upwards. In other policies, the insured has the option to periodically (e.g., every three years) increase the face amount by the change in the CPI since the last adjustment period. In contrast with the guaranteed insurability option, if the policyowner declines the additional coverage at any time, the insurer will permit future COLA increases only after the insured proves insurability.

CHAPTER ENDNOTES

1. I.R.C. §§7702(f)(7)(B)-(C).
2. I.R.C. §§7702(f)(7)(B), 7702(f)(7)(D). The cash value corridor test is discussed in Appendix F.
3. In cases where there are extreme reductions in the death benefit or very large premium payments, it is even possible for a policy to fail the tests for life insurance under I.R.C. §7702 with much more disastrous tax consequences. See the discussion of the definition of life insurance in Chapter 21.
4. I.R.C. §7702A(a)(1)(B). Classification as a MEC occurs in the year when the seven-pay test is first violated and for each year thereafter. See Chapter 22 for a more complete discussion of the seven-pay test.
5. I.R.C. §7702A(e)(1).
6. I.R.C. §7702A(c)(2)(B).
7. I.R.C. §7702A(c)(3).
8. I.R.C. §7702. See Chapter 21.

ANNUITIES

CHAPTER 8

INTRODUCTION

Annuities are the only investment vehicles that can guarantee investors that they will not outlive their income, and they do this in a tax-favored manner. In addition, annuities are available with a host of features to meet a wide variety of investor needs. Below is a brief description of the various types of annuities that are available. See "Types of Annuities" below for more details.

Accumulation and Payout Phases

Technically, annuities are contracts providing for the systematic liquidation of principal and interest in the form of a series of payments over time.[1] However, this really refers to the payout phase of an annuity; in point of fact, annuities can (and often do) have an *accumulation phase* that also lasts for a substantial period of time.

An annuity is established when an investor makes a cash payment to an insurance company, which invests the money. This may be a single large cash payment or a series of periodic payments over time. During the accumulation phase the money remains invested with the insurance company and is periodically credited with some growth factor. In return for making the deposit(s) into the annuity, the insurance company ultimately agrees to pay the owner(s) a specified amount of payments periodically, beginning on a specified date. This is the *payout phase* of the annuity.

Immediate vs. Deferred Payouts

If the specified date for payouts to begin is within one year of the date the contract is established (i.e., a single cash payment is made and the insurance company

begins a systematic liquidation of the payment back to the owner within one year), the annuity is called an *immediate annuity*.

If, alternatively, the specified date for payouts to begin is later than one year, the annuity is called a *deferred annuity* because deposits are made now, but the payout is deferred. An immediate annuity only has a payout phase; a deferred annuity has both an accumulation and a payout phase.

Life vs. Fixed-period Payouts

If the payout phase of the annuity is a *life annuity*, the company promises that payouts will continue for as long as the annuitant (or annuitants) lives; the annuitant(s) can never outlive the income stream. (*Note*: technically, although, the owner of the annuity and the annuitant typically are the same person, occasionally the owner and the annuitant *are* different individuals.)

If the payout phase is a *fixed-period annuity* (also called a *term-certain annuity*), the company promises to pay stipulated amounts for a fixed or guaranteed period of time independent of the survival of the annuitant. An annuity payout can also utilize a combination of the life and fixed-period options, such as "for the greater of ten years or the life of the annuitant(s)."

Fixed vs. Variable Annuities

In addition to differentiating between immediate and deferred annuities and fixed-period and term-certain payouts, insurers also categorize annuities as to whether they are fixed or variable. (Be careful not to confuse a fixed annuity with a fixed-period payout.)

Classification as a fixed or variable annuity refers to the underlying investments during the accumulation phase of the annuity:

- A *fixed annuity* is invested in the general fixed account of the insurance company.

- A *variable annuity* is invested in separately managed subaccounts (that function similarly to mutual funds) selected by the annuity owner.

Variable annuities often have additional features to help manage the risk of their underlying investments, such as guaranteed death benefits or newer living benefits that provide company guaranteed payments for owners or beneficiaries even if (or especially if) they would be higher than actual investment performance would provide for.

Newer annuities also may offer a variable option during the payout phase (whether for a fixed or term-certain period). A variable annuitization contract provides payments that may fluctuate up or down depending upon the performance of the underlying subaccount investments. A fixed annuitization contract provides payments that remain the same through the payout phase (or occasionally increase by some set rate to keep pace with inflation. However, this rate is:

- predetermined and contractual;

- still invested in the insurance company's general account; and

- thus, still considered a fixed payout.

Commercial vs. Private Annuities

Annuities purchased from an insurance company are called commercial annuities while those purchased from a person or entity that is not in the business of selling annuities are called private annuities.[2] Technically, the living proceeds received from a life insurance contract are also considered annuities if they consist of periodic payments of both principal and interest.

WHEN IS THE USE OF THIS DEVICE INDICATED?

The risk and return characteristics of fixed and variable annuities are so fundamentally different that each type is more or less suitable for various purposes.

However, some form of annuity would be indicated in the following circumstances:

1. When investors want a retirement income that they can never outlive.

2. When investors (often retired) want a monthly income equal to or higher than could be generated by other conservative investments and are willing (or especially if they *want*) to liquidate principal.

3. When persons would like to avoid probate and pass a large sum of money by contract to heirs to reduce the possibility of a will contest.[3]

4. When investors desire a tax deferred accumulation of interest. The interest earned inside an annuity owned by an individual grows income tax-free and is not taxed until it is withdrawn.[4]

5. When investors want to be free of the responsibility of investing and managing assets (in the case of a fixed annuity or an annuity payout; this is not applicable to a variable deferred annuity, as the owner still retains the burden of making all investment selections).

6. As a supplement to an IRA. With limited opportunity for pretax contributions to IRAs, many clients are seeking opportunities of making regular after-tax contributions to an investment vehicle after reaching the IRA contribution limits. The annuity may be a good choice because contributions are not limited.

7. Fixed annuities, in particular, would be indicated: (a) when safety of principal is a paramount consideration (this can be particularly important in some retirement planning scenarios); (b) when investors want a guarantee that a given level of interest will be credited to their investment for a long period of time; or (c) when investors desire a conservative complement to other investment vehicles.

8. Variable annuities, in particular, would be indicated: (a) when investors want more control over their investment and are willing to bear the risk associated with their investment selections; or (b) when investors are looking to increase their potential retirement income.

9. When investors would like to invest their money in the types of vehicles available in variable subaccounts, but desire some aspect of risk management, such as the guaranteed death benefits or living benefits offered by most insurance companies.

Advantages

1. The guarantees of safety, interest rates, and particularly lifelong income (if selected) give the purchaser peace of mind and psychological security.

2. An annuity protects and builds a person's cash reserve. The insurer guarantees principal and interest (in the case of a fixed annuity; a variable annuity is subject to the performance of the underlying selected subaccounts), and the promise (if purchased) that the annuitant can never outlive the income stream. This makes annuities particularly attractive to those who have retired and desire, or require, fixed monthly income and lifetime guarantees.

3. An annuity allows a client to invest in the market while moderating risk. The insurer may provide guarantees of death proceeds or a certain annuitization amount (if purchased) within a variable annuity, thus providing clients with guarantees that otherwise would be unavailable to those clients who purchased the underlying investments directly. This makes a variable annuity particularly attractive to those clients who have retired or are nearing retirement and need (or want) to hold riskier investments while trying to moderate risk.

4. A client can time the receipt of income and shift it into lower bracket years. This ability to decide when to be taxed allows the annuitant to compound the advantage of deferral.

5. Because the interest on an annuity is tax deferred, an annuity paying the same rate of interest (after expenses) as a taxable investment will result in a higher effective yield.

6. Because of the risk management factors available, especially in variable annuities, clients may be able to take on greater risk in the underlying investment options (e.g., equities, smaller capitalization equities, high yield bonds, etc.) while still maintaining a reasonable overall risk exposure due to the underlying guarantees.

7. Adjusted Gross Income (AGI) may be reduced in years where the annuity is held with no withdrawals (thanks to the tax deferral features of the accumulation phase). In addition, annuitants may recognize less taxable income during the payout phase, due to the partial recovery of basis associated with each payment. A reduced AGI can bring tax savings, as many other income tax rules are calculated based upon AGI and, generally, a lower AGI results in lower taxation (and vice versa). A reduced AGI can create tax savings by lowering the amount of Social Security includable in income, reducing the floor threshold for deduction of medical expenses (10 percent of AGI) or miscellaneous itemized deductions (2 percent of AGI), and avoiding the threshold for phase out of exemptions and itemized deductions.

Disadvantages

1. Receipt of a lump sum (either at retirement, or to a beneficiary at death) could result in a significant tax burden because income averaging is not available (however, planning can moderate this if the proceeds are annuitized).

2. The cash flow stream of a fixed payout may not keep pace with inflation, particularly for longer-term payout phases such as a life annuitization.

3. Annuity owners generally incur a 10 percent penalty tax on withdrawals of accumulated interest during the accumulation phase prior to age 59½, unless the annuity owner is disabled (this may also apply to the annuitization phase if the annuity was not an immediate annuity and the owner selected certain short payout terms).[5]

4. With a few limited exceptions, annuity contracts held by corporations or other entities that are not natural persons, are not treated as annuity contracts for federal income tax purposes. This means that income on the contracts for any taxable year are treated as current taxable ordinary income to the owner of the contract regardless of whether or not the owners make any withdrawals.

5. If the client is forced to liquidate the investment in the early years of an annuity, management and maintenance fees and sales costs could prove expensive. Total management fees and mortality charges can run from 1 percent to 2.5 percent of

the value of the contract (occasionally as high as 3 percent in the case of variable annuities with a number of underlying guarantees). Most insurers charge a back-end surrender charge if the owners terminate contracts within the first few years after purchase to compensate the insurers for the sales charges that they typically do not levy up front.

6. Owners are taxed on investment earnings at the owners' ordinary income tax rates when the owners receive payments, regardless of the source or nature of the returns. Consequently, investment earnings attributable to long-term capital appreciation (typically in variable annuities) do not enjoy the more favorable long-term capital gain tax rate that otherwise generally would apply. This has become even more disadvantageous in recent years with the reduction of the maximum long-term capital gain rate. Furthermore, investment earnings attributable to dividends on stocks that would qualify for the 15 percent maximum tax rate if the stocks were held outside an annuity also are taxed at the owner's ordinary income tax rate (although owners/annuitants will not be taxed on these dividends until they receive payments). Consequently, variable annuities—where the annuity owners, generally, are more inclined to invest in equities under a tax regime of lower capital gains and dividend tax rates—have been much less attractive than previously. (See the "Frequently Asked Questions" below for a discussion of mutual funds versus variable annuities.)

ALTERNATIVES

Municipal Bond Funds

These funds are an attractive option for retirement savings. The income they produce is exempt from federal and in many cases state income tax (although the sale of the bonds may result in taxable capital gains or losses, and some municipal bonds may be subject to the alternative minimum tax).

If a municipal bond fund's average yield is 3 percent, the equivalent taxable yield is almost 4.3 percent if the investor is in the 30 percent personal tax bracket. Investors can withdraw money from a municipal bond fund at any time without a tax penalty. A drawback of municipal bond funds as compared with annuities is the lack of a guaranteed return (bond rates may go down in future years, resulting in a lower yield on reinvestments

of interest and matured bonds), and the potential for capital losses (if interest rates rise and bonds must be sold before maturity).

Single Premium Life Insurance (SPLI)

This type of life insurance offers many of the same advantages of annuities, but incorporates a death benefit at issuance that is higher than the cash deposit (whereas, for annuities that contain a death benefit feature, the guarantee is usually *equal* to the amount of the cash deposit). However, there are important differences between an SPLI policy and other types of life insurance.

Generally, no income tax or penalties are payable until or unless the owner surrenders the policy. However, single premium life insurance policies issued after June 21, 1988 generally are modified endowment contracts (MECs). Distributions from MECs are taxed under essentially the same rules as annuity contracts. This means that owners will be taxed on any policy distributions, including loans, at the time received to the extent that the cash value of the contract immediately before the payment exceeds the investment in the contract. Additionally, a 10 percent penalty tax may apply to certain distributions. In effect, the MEC rules remove the tax-free borrowing possibilities otherwise associated with life insurance policies.

Planners should not direct a client to a product—any product—merely for its tax advantages, because these are at the mercy of a voter-conscious Congress, as demonstrated by the effect of legislation passed in 1988 on SPLI, discussed above (although Congress generally provides some level of grandfathering provisions for most tax law changes, as it did for the new MEC rules in 1988). Certainly, if a client does not need the leverage that life insurance provides, the costs and restrictions make SPLI less attractive once one considers the cost for the death benefit which reduces the capital available for investment growth.

Mutual Funds

During the accumulation period, variable annuities offer investment options that essentially are the same as mutual funds. Mutual funds do not enjoy the tax-deferred accumulation associated with variable annuities. However, under recent tax rules, tax on the capital appreciation of the assets in a mutual fund is deferred until the gains are realized. In addition, the realized gains are taxed as either long- or short-term capital gains, depending on the holding period. In contrast, all gains and income on the assets in the separate accounts of a variable annuity are taxed at ordinary income tax rates when paid. Also, under recent tax rules, mutual funds receive a step-up in basis at death in the hands of the heir. There is no step-up in basis in annuity values in the hands of the beneficiary when the annuity contract owner dies. The as-yet-untaxed income in the policy is treated as income in respect of a decedent and is taxable to the beneficiary as ordinary income when paid.

TYPES OF ANNUITIES

There are number of different types of annuities. They can be classified according to:

- how premiums are paid;

- disposition of proceeds, or what residual values—if any—are paid upon the death of the annuitant;

- when benefit payments begin;

- how many lives are covered;

- what investment options are available to the owner of the annuity contract;

- how benefits are calculated.

It is important to bear in mind that a change in almost any of the above classifications results in an adjustment in the payout the annuity provides to maintain an actuarially equivalent benefit. Figure 8.1 shows how annuities are classified.

Premium Payment Methods

Single premium annuities are often the ideal vehicles for people who have come into large cash sums. A single premium annuity will convert such amounts, for example, from an inheritance, from the sale of a business or a large piece of real estate, or from a qualified

Figure 8.1

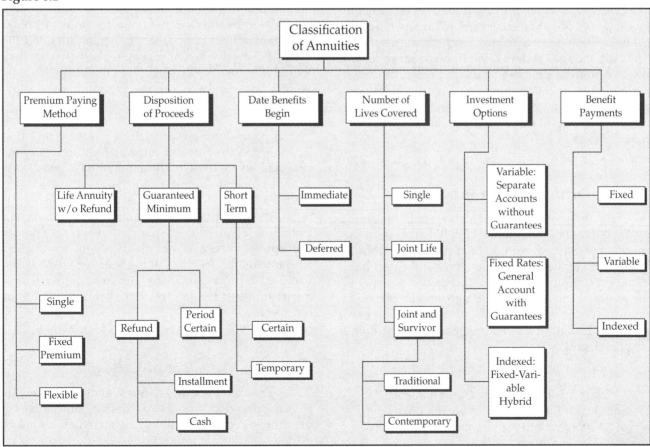

pension or profit-sharing plan lump-sum distribution, into a lifetime or certain fixed-period stream of payments. Immediate annuities are virtually always single-premium annuities (clients with subsequent investment amounts would simply purchase another immediate annuity). Single-premium structures also occur sometimes with deferred fixed annuities that provide for guaranteed interest crediting rates for a specified period (to prevent subsequent investments at these guaranteed rates if general interest rates decline in the future). Single-premium structures are relatively rare amongst deferred variable annuities.

Fixed-premium annuities are favored by investors who do not have large cash sums to invest but who desire a regular investment program with a forced saving feature. Typically, these instruments require purchases to make fixed annual (semiannual, quarterly, monthly or even weekly) premium payments that continue until the desired annuity starting date (the date when payouts begin). Because the periodic premiums are fixed, the total accumulation, and therefore the ultimate annuity payout is very predictable. Fixed-premium annuities today are relatively uncommon, having been replaced instead by flexible-premium annuities.

Flexible-premium annuities allow the contract owner to invest (make premium contributions) at any time and in any amount desired. In rare instances, the insurance company requires certain minimum annual contributions within the first few years, but after this initial period (or from the start in most cases) the insurers generally place no restrictions or requirements on purchasers with regard to the timing or amount of further contributions.

Disposition of Proceeds

A *life annuity* with no refund feature continues annuity payouts only as long as the annuitant (or one of the annuitants) survive, with no final payment or refund at the death of the last annuitant, even if the total paid out of the annuity is less than the amount invested in the contract. This can involve a high amount of risk, as the death of a lone annuitant shortly after contract issuance could result in a forfeiture of virtually the entire original deposit.

Example. Mr. Smith purchases an immediately annuity for $50,000 that provides for payments of $300 per month for life, and dies after only

receiving two payments, his total return out of the contract will be only $600. He will forfeit the remaining $49,400 of his original deposit to the insurance company, which will use the proceeds to help offset the payments due to annuity holders that outlive their life expectancies.

Because many investors are reluctant to forfeit a portion of their investment in the event of the premature death of the annuitant—particularly if they have heirs that will ultimately inherit all assets not consumed by the individual during his/her life, insurance companies also offer annuity contracts with minimum payback guarantees. These guarantees take two forms.

Refund annuities promise to pay the difference between the amount invested in the contract (generally the total of the premiums paid) and the annuity payments actually paid out before the death of the annuitant. This refund takes the form either of a lump-sum cash payment or of installment payouts.

Period-certain annuities promise to make payments for a stipulated period, such as 5, 10, or 20 years, or for the annuitant's life, whichever is longer. However, keep in mind that, due to the time value of money, this guarantee still does not make the annuity holder entirely whole in comparison to having invested the assets in an alternative to begin with (where they would have ostensibly been *growing* during this time period, not merely preserving the original principal amount).

The payout period also may be short-term—that is, for a specified period generally shorter than the expected life (or lives) of the annuitant(s). *Term-certain annuities* operate similarly to the amortization of a loan. Payments continue for a specified term only, regardless of when the annuitant dies. A *temporary annuity* is a variation on the period-certain annuity concept. However, rather than paying a specified amount for the *longer* of the annuitant's life or the specified term, a temporary annuity continues payments only for the *shorter* of the annuitant's life or the specified term.

Date Benefits Begin

An *immediate annuity* begins annuity payments within one year after the purchaser contributes all premiums. People commonly use immediate annuities when they wish to convert a large lump-sum amount, such as a substantial distribution from a qualified pension or profit sharing plan, the settlement proceeds of a lawsuit, or simply a sizeable amount of cash, into an immediate income stream.

In contrast, *deferred annuities*, as the name suggests, delay or defer payments for a period of time (the 'accumulation phase') after the purchaser has completed making premiums or contributions. People frequently use deferred annuities when they have cash to invest before retirement and wish to postpone the beginning of the annuity payments until retirement or later.

Number of Lives Covered

The annuity payout period may depend on one or two lives—or less commonly—more lives. A *single-life annuity* (with no refund feature) makes payments until the single covered life (the sole annuitant) dies. In the case of annuities based on two or more lives, payouts may continue until the last annuitant dies (or more rarely, only until the first annuitant dies, depending upon the exact terms of the contract).

Annuities whose payments continue until the last death of the covered lives are called *joint-and-last-survivor annuities*, or just joint-and-survivor annuities. Those annuities whose payments cease upon the first death are called *joint-life annuities*. Currently, joint-and-survivor annuities are much more common than joint-life annuities.

A joint-and-survivor annuity may pay one amount while both annuitants are alive and the same, or another (lesser) amount, after the first death. The surviving annuitant often receives some specified percentage (called the survivor-benefit ratio) of the amount payable before the first death. Survivor-benefit ratios typically range from 50 to 100 percent, with 50 percent, 66 percent, 75 percent, and 100 percent being the most common ratios.

Example. A joint-and-75-percent-survivor annuity paying a $50,000 annual joint benefit would pay $37,500 per year to the survivor after the first death. The amount of the survivor-benefit ratio generally is selected at the inception of the payout phase (annuitization) of the contract.

The benefit payable to the survivor also may depend on which annuitant dies first. The *traditional joint-and-survivor annuity* has a principal annuitant and a secondary annuitant or beneficiary. The survivor-benefit ratio applies only to the benefit payable to the surviving secondary annuitant after the principal annuitant's death. If the principal annuitant outlives the secondary annuitant, the insurer does not reduce the benefit payments. These types of payment structures are particularly common in joint-and survivor-annuity payments from defined-benefit pension plans (where the former employee is the principal annuitant).

In recent years an alternative form of the joint-and-survivor annuity has become popular. This *contemporary joint-and-survivor annuity* pays the reduced benefit to the survivor regardless of which annuitant dies first. These types of payment structures are most common from commercially available joint-and-survivor annuities. For a given total investment, insurance companies can afford to pay relatively higher joint-and-survivor benefits on these annuities than on traditional joint-and-survivor annuities.

Investment Options

Fixed-rate annuities are similar to universal life policies in that amounts credited to cash values are based on the insurer's current declared rate, subject to a minimum guarantee of 3 to 4.5 percent (varying by annuity contract and insurance company). Insurers may guarantee rates paid on new money (current contributions) for one to five years (or occasionally as long as ten years).

The currently declared rate depends on the performance of the insurer's general investment portfolio or general account, which is largely invested in fixed income investments such as bonds and mortgages. Although interest credits to the annuity depend on market rates on these types of fixed income investments, the cash value itself is not market valued. Similar to a savings account, once the insurer credits interest, the cash value will not decline if the market value of the underlying assets in the insurer's general account declines. (However, some insurers levy a market adjustment to the annuity contract value based upon interest rate changes in the event of early surrender). The insurer bears the market risk.

Variable annuities are similar to variable insurance policies. The annuity owner may choose to invest contributions and cash values in a broad spectrum of investment options or separate accounts, which are similar to mutual funds (although the investor is limited to the selection of investment choices that are offered within the annuity contract).

The investment options usually include diversified stock, bond, and money market funds and frequently include specialized stock funds, foreign stock and bond funds, real estate equity and mortgage funds, and even asset allocation funds (a type of balanced fund where the insurer's investment manager allocates investments among the other funds). In contrast with fixed-rate annuities, cash values depend on the market value of the underlying assets in the selected separate accounts.

Variable annuity owners bear the market risk of investment and forego minimum interest rate guarantees (although some limited guarantees may be available, subject to additional costs and substantial restrictions). However, they have the flexibility to choose their investment portfolio and the potential to earn far greater total returns than they would earn on fixed-rate annuities. See "Variable Annuities" below for more detailed discussion of their various features.

Equity-Index Annuities (EIAs) are a hybrid of fixed and variable annuities. The returns on EIAs are linked to an equity index, such as the S&P 500 index. However, the annuity is not actually invested in the stocks making up the index. Rather, like with fixed annuities, the insurer pays the returns to EIAs from its general account.

However, the insurer bases the amount allocated to the EIA on some percentage, for example, 85 percent, of the appreciation in the reference index (often subject to annual caps and/or interest spreads). If the index declines in value, the insurer credits the EIA with a minimum guaranteed amount (which may be 0 percent, but is generally never negative). In this way, EIAs attempt to provide investors with some of the upside potential of the equity markets with the downside protection of more conservative general-account investments. See "Equity-Index Annuities" below for more detailed discussion of their various features.

Benefit Payments

Annuity benefit payments may be fixed or variable:

- *Fixed-benefit annuities* guarantee a minimum annuity benefit payment per dollar of accumulated value, similar to settlement options under life insurance policies.

- *Variable*-benefit annuities make no guarantees. Variable benefit payments depend on the market value of the assets in the separate accounts.

About 90 percent of all outstanding annuity contracts fall into the fixed-rate category, but variable annuities are becoming increasingly popular (variable annuities are also fairly new compared to the long history of fixed annuities). The investment account in a fixed-rate contract operates much like the cash value account of a universal life policy. The annuity investment earns a fixed rate, which the insurer often guarantees for the first one to five (occasionally as many as ten) years of the contract. After that time, the rate depends on the investment success of the insurer's general portfolio (subject to a guaranteed floor, typically 3 to 4.5 percent). The fixed-rate contract gives the contract owner no choice or say in the underlying investments.

Some fixed-rate contracts have a bailout provision. If the contract return falls below the bailout rate, the contract owner can terminate the contract without cost (i.e., without surrender charges).

In the past two decades variable annuities have become quite popular because, in return for the assumption of greater risk, the contract owner may obtain both greater investment flexibility and a (potentially) higher return. (However, since the bear market of 2007-2009, not surprisingly, variable annuities have been less popular.) The contract owner can select from among a number of separate accounts that are similar to mutual fund investments. The investment options typically include diversified stock, bond, and money market funds. Most insurers also now offer a broad array of alternative funds such as specialized stock funds (sector funds, small capitalization stock funds, index funds), foreign stock and bond funds, junk bond funds, real estate equity and mortgage funds, GNMA-type funds, and asset allocation funds (where the company's investment manager selects portfolio weights allocating investments among the other funds). It is important to note that although there is a great deal of latitude in investment selection, the investor is limited exclusively to the selection of investment choices that are offered within the annuity contract.

Joint-Life and Joint-and-Last-Survivor Annuities

A *joint-life annuity* is a contract that provides a specified amount of income for two or more persons named in the contract. Income ends upon the first death.

A *joint-and-last-survivor* contract is much more popular because payments continue until the last death among the covered lives. Obviously, this form of annuity is more expensive than other forms because, on average, it will pay income for a longer time. This increased cost is reflected in a lower annuity payment than would be paid under a single-life annuity at either of the ages of the two annuitants, or under the joint-life annuity structure.

Clients can purchase the joint-and-survivor annuity on either a pure life basis (ending at the later death) or with a certain number of payments guaranteed. Most insurers offer a form of joint-and-survivor annuity that pays the full amount while both annuitants are alive and then two-thirds or one-half of that income when the first annuitant dies. This is called a joint-and two-thirds or joint-and one-half annuity.

TAX IMPLICATIONS

The taxation of annuities is governed by Internal Revenue Code section 72. Annuities grow tax deferred during the accumulation phase, although withdrawals during this phase are taxed on a Last In, First Out (LIFO) basis—meaning that withdrawals during the accumulation phase are considered to be withdrawals of growth first (fully taxable) and principal second.[6] Payouts during the annuitization phase are split: a portion of each payment is considered principal, and a portion is deemed interest/growth. Insurers determine the proportions of each payment that is principal and interest/growth at the annuity's beginning payment date. They determine these proportions based upon the already accumulated growth, an assumed internal growth factor for the payout period, and the expected length of the payout period. All amounts distributed that are considered interest/growth are taxed as ordinary income, regardless of the phase or timing of the withdrawal. In addition, certain withdrawals before the age of 59½ may be subject to an additional 10 percent tax penalty.

Although investors may find the tax-deferral feature of annuities to be quite advantageous, the primary reason investors should consider purchasing annuities is for their risk management features. Annuities can provide a variety of guarantees, whether protecting against interest rate risk, reinvestment risk, superannuation (living too long, such as outliving one's assets), or certain market volatility risks. Annuities are first and foremost a risk management tool.

Taxation during the Accumulation Period

Income earned by a variable annuity (see Questions and Answers below) is not taxed during the accumulation period. No tax will be payable until the earlier of: (a) the surrender of the contract; (b) a withdrawal from the contract; or (c) the time payments under the annuity begin (annuitization). To obtain annuity treatment, however, the underlying investments of the segregated asset account must be adequately diversified according to IRS regulations.[7]

Payments made as an annuity under a variable annuity are not subject to the same exclusion ratio as is a regular fixed annuity. This is because it is impossible to determine the expected return. Instead, the following formula is used:[8]

$$\frac{\text{Investment in Contract}}{\text{Number of Years of Expected Return}}$$

If there is a period certain or refund guarantee, the investment in the contract is adjusted accordingly. If payments are made for a fixed number of years without regard to life expectancy, the divisor is that fixed number of years. If payments are made for a single life, use IRS Table V. If payments are to be made on a joint and survivor basis, use Table VI. As in the case of a fixed annuitization, the exclusion ratio no longer applies once an annuitant reaches his life expectancy and has fully recovered his investment in the contract.

If payments drop below the excludable amount in any given year, the annuitant can elect to redetermine the excludable amount in the next tax year in which he receives an annuity payment. The loss in exclusions is divided by the number of years remaining (in the case of a fixed period annuity). In the case of a life annuity the loss is divided by the annuitant's life expectancy computed as of the first day of the first period for which an amount is received as an annuity.[9]

Example. Assume a sixty-five-year-old taxpayer purchased an annuity for $20,000. The contract provides variable monthly payments for life. Because his life expectancy is twenty years (Table V), he may exclude $1,000 of each annuity payment from income ($20,000/20). Assume on his seventieth birthday he receives only $200, $800 less than his excludable amount. At age seventy, his life expectancy is sixteen years. He may elect to add $50 ($800/16) to his $1,000 exclusion, a total of $1,050 which he may exclude that year and in subsequent years.

Natural Persons Only

Tax-free buildup within the contract is allowed only to natural persons.[10] If an annuity contract is held by a person who is not a natural person, then the annuity contract is not treated as an annuity and the income on the contract is treated as ordinary income received or accrued by the owner during that taxable year.

Corporations are not natural persons. Neither is the typical trust, although a trust acting as the agent for a natural person would itself be considered a natural person. But if an employer is the agent for its employees, the contract will be considered as if owned by the employer. The employer will therefore be taxed on the inside build up. This means that annuities are no longer appropriate tax advantaged investments for nonqualified deferred compensation agreements. Exceptions from the natural persons rules allow tax-free buildup of the following annuities:[11]

(a) Annuities received by the executor of a decedent at the decedent's death

(b) Annuities held by a qualified retirement plan or IRA

(c) Annuities considered qualifying funding assets (used to provide funding for structured settlements and by property and casualty insurance companies to fund periodic payments for damages)

(d) Annuities purchased by an employer on termination of a qualified plan and held until all amounts under the plan are distributed to the employee or his beneficiary

(e) Annuities which are immediate (i.e., those which have a starting date no more than one year from the date the annuity was purchased and provide for a series of substantially equal periodic payments to be made at least annually over the annuity period)

Withdrawals Prior to the Annuity Starting Date

Owners of annuities often take dividends, make cash withdrawals, or take other amounts out of their annuity contracts before the annuity starting dates. Such amounts are taxable as income to the extent that the policy cash value exceeds the investment in the contract—this results in a Last In, First Out (LIFO) type of treatment where all interest/growth is taxed before any tax-free return of capital payments can occur.[12]

This interest first rule was imposed to discourage the use of annuity contracts as short term investment vehicles. Under this rule, a loan is treated as if it were a cash withdrawal.

Likewise, to the extent the owner uses a contract as collateral for a loan, the owner will be taxed on the amounts borrowed (to the extent that the amount received is less than or equal to the gain inherent in the contract). If the amount received exceeds the built in gain, the excess of what was borrowed over potential gain is considered a tax-free return of the contract owner's investment. With respect to contracts entered into after October 21, 1988, amounts borrowed increase investment in the contract to the extent they are includible in income under these rules.

In applying the interest first rule, all contracts entered into after October 21, 1988 and issued by the same company to the same policyholder during any twelve-month period are treated as one contract.

When an owner makes a partial withdrawal from the contract and takes a reduced annuity for the same term, a portion of the amount withdrawn will be subject to income tax.

When an owner makes a partial withdrawal from the contract (allocable to an investment in the contract made after August 13, 1982) and chooses to take the same payments for a different term, to the extent the cash surrender value of the contract exceeds the investment in the contract, gain will be realized in the form of a taxable withdrawal of interest.

Premature Distributions

Premature distributions (those made before certain dates listed below) are subject not only to the normal tax on ordinary income but also to a penalty tax of 10 percent. The 10 percent penalty applies only to the amount of the distribution that is included in income.

The penalty for premature distributions will not apply to any of the following:[13]

- payments that are part of a series of substantially equal periodic payments made for the life (or life expectancy) of the taxpayer or the joint lives (or joint life expectancies) of the taxpayer and his beneficiary (unless the series of payments is modified under certain circumstances);

- payments made on or after the time the contract owner reaches age 59½;

- payments made on account of the contract owner's disability;

- payments made from qualified retirement plans and IRAs (but these are subject to other similar premature distribution requirements);

- payments made to a beneficiary (or annuitant's estate) on or after the death of an annuitant;

- distributions under an immediate annuity contract;

- an annuity contract purchased on the termination of certain qualified employer retirement plans and held until the employee separates from service;

- payments allocable to investment in the contract before August 14, 1982.

Taxation during the Payout Period

Annuitants' investment in an annuity is returned in equal tax-free (return of capital) amounts during the payout phase. Any additional amount received is taxed at ordinary income rates. This means each payment consists of two parts: the first part is considered return of capital and is therefore nontaxable, while the second part of each payment is considered return on capital (income) and is therefore, taxable at ordinary rates.

The amount of each period's payment that will be considered nontaxable is determined by the

exclusion ratio. The exclusion ratio is expressed as a percentage, applies to each annuity payment equally through the payout phase, and is calculated as follows:[14]

$$\frac{\text{Investment in Contract}}{\text{Expected Return}}$$

"Investment in the contract" is defined as the consideration paid for the contract (i.e., the premium) less any amounts received back from the insurer that were income tax free.[15] Premium cost does not include any premiums paid for waiver of premiums, disability income, or accidental death ("double indemnity").[16]

"Expected return" is defined as the aggregate payments the annuitant can be expected to receive under the annuity contract. In other words, expected return is the sum of the guaranteed payments if (a) payments are for a fixed period, or (b) if payments are of a fixed amount with no life expectancy.[17] If payments are for the life (or lives) of the annuitant(s), then expected return is the sum of one year's annuity payments multiplied by the life expectancy of the live or lives involved.[18]

Example. Assume a seventy-year-old purchases an annuity. He pays (the investment in the contract is) $12,000 for the annuity. Assume his expected return throughout the payout phase is $19,200.

The exclusion ratio is $12,000/$19,200, or 62.5 percent. If the monthly payment he receives is $100, the portion that he can exclude from gross income is $62.50 (62.5 percent of $100). The $37.50 balance of each $100 monthly payment is ordinary income.

The full amount of each annuity payment received would be tax-free if the investment in the contract exceeds the expected return (i.e., when the exclusion ratio would be greater than or equal to 100 percent).[19]

The excludable portion of any annuity payment may not exceed the unrecovered investment in the contract (unless the annuity started before

January 1, 1987).[20] The unrecovered investment in the contract is the policyowner's premium cost, reduced by any dividends received in cash or used to reduce premiums, and by the aggregate amount received under the contract on or after the annuity starting date to the extent it was excludable from income. Thus, the unrecovered investment in the contract is reduced each time an annuity payment is made, by the amount of the payment that is excluded from income by the exclusion ratio. This rule limits the total amount the policyowner can exclude from income to the total amount of his contribution. Once an annuitant has fully recovered his investment in the contract, which generally occurs at the end of the *expected* payout term, 100 percent of each subsequent payment will be taxable. Payments can continue beyond the expected payout term when the annuitant actually lives longer than his or her actuarial (expected) life expectancy.

Some annuities provide a refund if the annuitant dies before recovering his entire cost. The present value of the refund option must be ascertained by government tables and subtracted from the investment in the contract.[21] This would also apply if the annuity payout phase incorporated a combined life expectancy and term certain structure.

The expected return is the total amount that the owner (or owners) should receive given the payments specified (which include an assumed internal growth rate) multiplied by the certain term or life expectancy according to the government's tables (currently Table V for single lives and Table VI for joint and survivor annuities).

Example. Under Table V, a seventy-year-old has a life expectancy of sixteen years. If he (or she, since the life expectancy tables are unisex) receives $100 a month, the expected return would be $19,200 ($1,200 for each of sixteen years).

The taxable portion of annuity payments is considered investment income that may be subject to the 3.8 percent Net Investment Income tax (NIIT) depending on the annuitant's level of income. However, because annuities are often used to defer taxation until later in life when the annuitant's income is otherwise likely to be lower, the NIIT may not be an important factor in annuity planning.

Death of the Annuitant Prior to Contract Maturity

When an annuitant dies before receiving the full amount guaranteed under a refund or period-certain life annuity, the owner or beneficiary receiving the balance of the guaranteed amount will have no taxable income (unless the amount received by the beneficiary plus the amount that had been received tax free by the annuitant exceeds the investment in the contract).

If the refund or commuted (present) value of the remaining installments is applied by the owner or beneficiary to purchase a new annuity, payments received will be taxed under the annuity rules to the beneficiary. The insurer will consider the refund amount to be the beneficiary's investment in the new contract and the insurer will determine a new exclusion ratio. This option often is selected if the guaranteed refund amount will exceed the unrecovered investment in the contract and would otherwise create a partially taxable lump-sum payment.

If the owner was receiving payments under a joint and survivor annuity, the surviving owner excludes from income the same percentage of each payment that was excludable by the first annuitant (assuming that the joint annuitants were joint owners). An income tax deduction may be available to the survivor owner/annuitant to the extent inclusion of the annuity in the estate of the first to die generated an estate tax (under the rules for income in respect of a decedent).

If an annuitant dies before payments received equal cost, the owner can take a loss deduction for the amount of the unrecovered investment, provided the annuity starting date was after July 1, 1986. So if a wife purchases a single premium nonrefundable annuity (whether on her own life, or alternatively on the life of her husband), and the annuitant dies before all costs have been recovered, a loss deduction will be allowed.

The deduction for the unrecovered investment in the contract is an itemized deduction, but not a miscellaneous deduction.[22] Therefore, it is not subject to the 2 percent floor. If the decedent/annuitant is the owner, the loss is taken on the decedent's final return, and will be treated as a business loss, eligible to be carried back if the loss exceeds the income shown on the decedent's final return. Otherwise, if the owner is not the decedent/annuitant, the owner takes the loss on his tax return. In addition, these deductions can ultimately be taken by the estate or any other beneficiary that receives postdeath payments.[23]

The 10 percent premature distribution penalty tax does not apply to required after-death distributions.

Payments to Beneficiaries

Amounts payable under a deferred annuity contract at the death of an annuitant (prior to the contract's maturity) will be partially taxable as ordinary income to the beneficiary. The taxable amount is equal to the excess of: (a) the death benefit (plus aggregate dividends and any other amounts that were received tax free); over (b) total gross premiums.

Beneficiaries can elect to delay reporting of the gain in the year of the annuitant's death if the beneficiary applies the death benefit under a life income or installment option within sixty days of the annuitant's death. The beneficiary will then report income according to an exclusion ratio. The beneficiary's investment in the contract will be the same as the annuitant's investment in the contract. The expected return is based on the income the beneficiary will receive and the beneficiary's life expectancy.[24]

If an annuity owner dies before the starting date of the annuity payments, the cash value of the contract must either be distributed within five years of death or used within one year of death to provide a life annuity or installment payments payable over a period not longer than the beneficiary's life expectancy. However, if the surviving spouse is the beneficiary, the spouse can elect to become the new owner of the contract instead of selecting one of the above options.[25]

Gifted Annuities

If the annuity contract is transferred by gift, the tax deferral on the inside build up—which was allowed to the original contract owner—is terminated. The donor of the gift is treated as having received nonannuity income in an amount equal to the excess of the cash surrender value of the contract over the investment in the contract at the time of the transfer. The recipient of the gift will take a new basis in the contract equal to the donor's investment in the contract, plus the amount of gain recognized on the gift (note that the new basis, the sum of the donor's basis and the donor's investment in the contract, is generally equal to the fair market value of the contract).

PURCHASING ANNUITIES

Almost all life insurance companies offer annuities, and these companies distribute annuities to customers through:

- life insurance agencies;

- many stock brokerage firms;

- independent insurance agents and financial planners;

- independent insurance brokerage firms;

- direct to consumers through the mail and the internet. In addition, many banks now offer annuities (often through internal broker-dealers).

Variable annuities are considered securities under the federal securities laws. Consequently, only agents who are licensed and have passed the applicable securities examinations may offer and sell variable annuities. In addition, prospective buyers must be given a prospectus. The prospectus must describe the product and its features and the company offering the product. The prospectus also must explain and detail expense charges, contract options, investment options, and related information.

Fees and Acquisition Costs

There are five typical fees or charges that investors usually incur when purchasing annuities, particularly variable annuities. These include:

1. *Investment management fees* – These fees are typically anywhere from a 0.25 to 1 percent, but sometimes higher for specialized funds such as foreign stock funds, sector funds, REIT-type funds, and others.

2. *Administration expense and mortality risk charge* – This charge ranges from a low of about 0.5 percent to a high of about 1.3 percent. Additional riders and features can increase this cost to as high as nearly 2.0 percent. However, in recent years a market has grown for low load annuity products sold primarily by fee-only financial planners, with mortality risk charges

155

and loads totaling less than 0.5 percent to as low as 0.2 percent or even lower.

3. *Annual maintenance charge* – This charge typically ranges from $25 to $100. However, often it is waived once total investments exceed a specified amount, such as $25,000.

4. *Charge per fund exchange* – This charge can be up to $10, but most funds will permit a limited number of charge-free exchanges per year. In addition, automatic rebalancing programs usually do not count towards this limit.

5. *Maximum surrender charge* – Surrender charges vary by company and policy and generally phase-out over a number of years. If the charge is lower, the phase-out range tends to be longer. For example, typical charges and phase-out periods are 5 percent of premium decreasing to 0 percent over ten years or 8 percent of premium decreasing to 0 percent over seven years.

The prospectus for a variable annuity must specify items (1) through (4) above. In a fixed annuity, these costs generally are incorporated into the management of the insurance company's general account and are simply netted out of the return credited to annuity holders. Thus, when comparing fixed annuities, cost comparisons (although other noncost aspects are also analyzed) generally are restricted to an evaluation of the comparable crediting rates of the general account and the surrender charges.

How Do I Select the Right Annuity?

1. Compare on a spreadsheet the costs and features of selected annuities. Consider all of the five costs discussed above as well as how much money owners can withdraw from the contract each year without a fee. Be certain to completely read through the *full* details of costs/charges, guarantees, riders, and special features in the prospectus of a variable annuity.

2. Compare the total outlay with the total annual annuity payment in the case of fixed annuities. Be certain to incorporate the time value of money if the payment schedules of the contracts being compared are different.

3. In an analysis of variable annuities, evaluate the total return for the variable annuity subaccounts

over multiple time periods (Lipper Analytical Services, Inc., and Morningstar, Inc., both have information to help assess this).

4. Compare the relative financial strength of the companies through services such as A.M. Best. Insist on a credit rating of A+ (or at the very least, thoroughly discuss with the prospective buyer the risks involved in purchasing from a company with a lesser rating).

VARIABLE ANNUITIES

The variable annuity was the product of a search for a tool that would provide a guaranteed lifetime income that could never be outlived and also provide a relatively stable purchasing power in times of inflation by allowing for returns that may keep pace with (or even exceed) inflation. This can be contrasted with the level payments generally payable from fixed annuities, whose purchasing power will be eroded over time by inflation.

The variable annuity is based on equity investments. Purchasers pay premiums to the insurance company during the accumulation phase. The insurer places that money into one or more separate accounts as directed by the owner. The funds in these accounts are separate from the other assets of the insurer. Each year, the insurer takes some money out of the contract owner's premium (or from the account value) for expenses. The insurer applies the balance to purchase units of credit in the separate accounts.

The number of credits purchased depends on the current valuation of a unit in terms of dollars. For example, if each unit was valued at $10 per unit based on current investment results, a $100 level premium (after expenses) would purchase ten units. If the value of a unit dropped because of investment experience, the premium would purchase more units. If the value of a unit increased, the same premium would buy fewer units. The price of a unit of a separate account is analogous to the NAV price of a share of a mutual fund. This unit purchasing continues until the maturity of the contract.

At the transition to the payout phase (annuitization) of the contract, the insurer credits the value of the contract owner's total accumulation units to a retirement fund. A value of a given number of accumulation units will purchase so many retirement income units (based on actuarial principles). Note that a variable annuitization does not promise to pay a fixed number of dollars each month but rather a fixed number of retirement income units. In other words, the dollar amount of each payment depends on the dollar value of a retirement income unit (also called an annuity unit) when the payment is made. The dollar value of an annuity unit is in turn based on the investment results of the separate accounts. For example, assume an annuitant was entitled to a payment based on ten annuity units each month. If the dollar value of an annuity unit varied from $12.10 to $12.50 to $12.80 over three months, the annuitant would be paid $121, $125, and $128, respectively.

Under a variable annuity, the insurer assumes only the risk of fluctuations due to mortality and expenses (guaranteeing that the annuitant will not outlive his or her income and that internal expense fluctuations will be absorbed). This means the contract owner is assuming the entire investment risk. If the separate accounts are invested poorly or in the wrong investments, the annuitant could receive fewer dollars of income than would have been paid under a fixed annuity.

Assumed Investment Rate (AIR)

Under most variable annuity contracts there is an Assumed Investment Rate (AIR) that the investment portfolio must earn in order for benefit payments to remain level. If the investment performance exceeds the AIR, the level of benefit payments will increase. On the other hand, if the selected investments underperform the AIR, the level of benefit payments will decrease.

———

Example. Assume a variable annuity contract is issued with a 6 percent AIR and a beginning unit value of $20. The contract is issued with a payout of one hundred units per month (providing an initial monthly payment of $2,000 per month). Assume the investment yield during the first month of the contract was 10 percent; during the second month the investment yield was 4 percent. The monthly benefit can be calculated by monitoring the changes in the unit value and by comparing the actual performance with the assumed 6 percent interest rate. During the first month, the 10 percent return on the portfolio exceeds the assumed 6 percent AIR by 4 percent—which leads to a 4 percent increase

in the $20 unit value. The new unit value is now $20.80 ($2,080 per month). During the subsequent month, because the actual return is only 4 percent, which is 2 percent less than the AIR, there will be a 2 percent reduction in the unit value to $20.38 ($2,038 per month). The unit value could actually drop below the beginning $20 value ($2,000 per month) if investment performance remains below the assumed 6 percent level for an extended period of time. However, for an increased cost, some annuities provide a guarantee that the monthly payment will never drop below the initial monthly payment, regardless of adverse investment performance.

———

Selecting an AIR

Under some contracts, the purchaser is able to select the AIR from a narrow range of possible rates (such as 3, 5, or 7 percent). It is much easier to receive an increasing stream of benefit payments by selecting a lower AIR; however, initially this can be more expensive (meaning the starting monthly payment will be reduced). The effect of choosing a different AIR can be demonstrated by returning to the example of the previous question.

If an AIR of 8 percent rather than 6 percent is chosen, the benefit increase in the first month will be 2 percent instead of 4 percent. The unit value changes to $20.40 instead of $20.80. The next month's decrease in benefits is more drastic, a 4 percent reduction rather than the 2 percent reduction. The unit value decreases to $19.58 instead of $20.38 from the lower AIR. Choosing the less costly higher AIR will start with a higher initial benefit (i.e., with an 8 percent AIR, the starting payment in the above example would likely have been higher than $2,000) but will increase the likelihood that benefit payments increase less rapidly and decrease more rapidly.

Keep in mind that although variable annuity contracts are intended to provide a hedge against inflation and protect the purchasing power of the benefits through positive market returns, the increases in market value have not always occurred at exactly the same time that prices increase. Often prices go up significantly before the market provides high returns and increases the level of benefits. These temporary mismatches between price increases and benefit increases are inevitable and can lead to a temporary loss of purchasing power.

Flexible-Premium Deferred Annuity (FPDA)

An FPDA is a Flexible-Premium Deferred Annuity. As the last two words indicate, the contract provides for the accumulation of funds to be applied at some future time designated by the contract owner to provide an income based upon the life of the annuitant(s) (or for a certain term). Premium payments are flexible—they can be paid as frequently or infrequently as the owner desires. They can be paid monthly, annually, or one or more years can be skipped as there is no specified contribution amount or required payment frequency. Most insurers do set a minimum payment level for administrative purposes—typically this runs from $25 to $50 for most companies.

Most FPDA contracts have no front-end load. Annual loads vary but many are under $50 per year. Some companies charge loads based on a percentage of each contribution, as a percentage of the annuity fund balance, or as a percentage of both. The insurer often does charge a back-end load (a surrender charge) when a cash withdrawal in a year exceeds a stipulated percentage of the fund balance—typically the annual free withdrawal amount is 10 percent of the premium deposits or contract value. The surrender charge will typically reduce year by year to 0 percent by the seventh or eighth contract year.

With fixed FPDAs, insurers guarantee minimum interest rates (typically 3 to 4.5 percent) but usually pay much higher rates. The actual rate will depend on the earnings rate of the insurer. Current rates have ranged from 5 to 11 percent in recent years but are subject to rapid change as interest rates trend upward or downward (although the crediting rate is often set on the contract anniversary date and is valid for the entire year). Focus should be placed on the net (after loads and charges) return earned, over the entire expected holding period, when comparing fixed annuities.

Most variable annuities are FPDAs. Fixed annuities are often FPDAs, but some types do not have flexible premiums, or are immediate annuities. Equity-indexed annuities are virtually always deferred annuities, but often do not have flexible premiums.

Single-Premium Deferred Annuity (SPDA)

An SPDA is a Single-Premium Deferred Annuity. It provides, as its name implies, a promise that an annuity will begin at some time in the future in return for a single premium.

For fixed annuities (variable annuities are rarely single premium contracts), a minimum stated rate of interest is guaranteed but most insurers pay competitive market rates. The actual rate paid is a function of: (1) the current investment earnings of the insurer; and (2) how competitive the insurer is determined to be. The rate is subject to change by the insurer.

The SPDA, like the FPDA, is back-end loaded. No front-end charges are imposed. Surrender charges are graded and partial withdrawals are often allowed without charge. Bailout provisions allow the contract owner to withdraw all funds without the imposition of a surrender charge if the interest rate actually credited falls below the bailout rate (typically set at the inception of the contract as 1 percent to 3 percent below the rate being credited at that time). Keep in mind that on any withdrawal both an ordinary income tax and a penalty tax may apply.

EQUITY-INDEXED ANNUITIES (EIAS)

Equity-Indexed Annuities (EIAs) are annuities with a crediting rate (return) that is tied to an index such as the S&P 500 stock index. But they are not the same as a variable annuity that invests directly in the securities of a market index (such as the S&P 500) through the use of subaccounts. Rather, the assets deposited under an EIA are held directly by the insurance company, which invests the funds as necessary to apply a certain unique, formulaic crediting rate. EIAs promise to credit to the annuity-holder some percentage of the amount by which the underlying index has increased, subject to annual caps, if the index goes up, and to cut the investor's losses at zero (or even guarantee a slight positive return), if the index goes down.

The fundamental point is this: if the market goes up, the investor is happy because the value of the annuity will increase by some partial amount of the market increase. If the market goes down, the investor is happy because the annuity still has an underlying guarantee against loss.

However, the gain on the index does not include dividends, if any, earned by the companies making up the index. The loss of dividend income, a cap on market gains, and the possibility that the investor will only receive a percentage (such as 40, 60, or 80 percent) of the market return, can be a major drag on performance.

EIAs issued by one company will differ (possibly quite dramatically) from EIAs issued by another company, but the annual investment returns generally are tied to a percentage (which could easily range from 40 to 80 percent or higher, and may be subject to periodic adjustments) of the S&P 500's gains (or occasionally other indexes such as the NASDAQ 100), not including dividends. The percentage (usually less than 100 percent) of market returns and cap on gains is offset by protection against market losses.

It is not possible to compare historical fixed annuity, variable annuity, and EIA results because EIAs have only been available for several years. But, it is possible to construct a theoretical comparison by using the Vanguard Index Trust 500 portfolio and fixed annuity yields from August 1, 1976, to December 31, 1995. The results are shown in Figure 8.2.

As suggested by the data in Figure 8.2, "does not include dividends" can be a drag on an EIA's performance. Dividends accounted for about 29 percent of the total return for the Vanguard Index Trust 500 (an S&P 500 index fund), over the twenty years from 1976 to 1995. Giving up dividends plus imposing a cap on

Figure 8.2

THE VANGUARD INDEX TRUST RETURNS AND FIXED ANNUITY RATES: 1976-1995				
Vanguard Index Trust 500*				
Year Ended	Capital Return (%)	Income Return (%)	Total Return (%)	Fixed Annuity Rates** (%)
1976	4.1	1.2	5.3	2.1
1977	−11.7	3.7	−8.0	7.0
1978	0.8	5.0	5.8	7.3
1979	12.1	5.9	18.0	7.8
1980	25.5	6.4	31.9	8.4
1981	−9.8	4.6	−5.2	9.5
1982	14.8	6.1	20.9	11.0
1983	16.2	5.1	21.3	11.5
1984	1.5	4.7	6.2	12.0
1985	26.1	5.1	31.2	12.1
1986	14.0	4.0	18.0	11.2
1987	2.3	2.4	4.7	9.8
1988	11.6	4.6	16.2	9.5
1989	26.7	4.6	31.3	9.0
1990	−6.8	3.4	−3.4	8.4
1991	26.3	3.9	30.2	7.8
1992	4.4	3.0	7.4	7.5
1993	7.1	2.7	9.8	6.5
1994	−1.5	2.6	1.1	6.2
1995	34.4	3.0	37.4	6.1

* Vanguard Index Trust 500 portfolio data from its inception August 1, 1976, to December 1995. Includes reinvestment of income dividends and any capital gains distributions and is adjusted for account maintenance fees.
** Representative fixed annuity rates for the period August 1, 1976, to December 1995.

market capital gains can be a severe penalty to pay for protection against periodic market losses, as will be shown below. In many cases, consumers may not even realize that dividends are not included in the index performance measure used by EIAs.

Figure 8.3 simulates the results for a fixed annuity, variable annuity, and indexed annuity, had they been purchased August 1, 1976. The table shows results through the end of 1995, in five-year increments, using the data from Figure 8.2.

Figure 8.4 shows the same simulation, but for the period January 1991 through the end of 1995. Isolating these five years is interesting because fixed annuity rates were much lower, while equity returns were robust,

which are the market results that motivated insurance companies to develop the hybrid EIA.

Please note that Figures 8.3 and 8.4 are not an attempt to predict possible future results for fixed, variable, or indexed annuities. The only purpose of these tables is to show how the EIA formulas affect results relative to fixed and variable annuities.

If these twenty years offer any guidance (as shown in Figures 8.3 and 8.4), EIAs are a poor substitute for a variable annuity invested in the S&P 500 index. The benefit of eliminating periodic market losses is simply overwhelmed by the deficits of giving up reinvested dividend income and placing a limit on the capital gains in figuring the index. When the proper choices

Figure 8.3

Time Period	Variable Annuity Vanguard 500* Projected		Fixed Annuity Projected		Company A Indexed** Projected		Company B Indexed** Projected	
	Value ($)	Return (%)	Value ($)	Return (%)	Value ($)	Return (%)	Value ($)	Return (%)
8/76-12/80	152,340	10.3	136,980	7.6	125,190	5.4	131,050	6.5
8/76-12/85	282,310	11.8	233,073	9.5	181,310	6.6	193,930	7.4
8/76-12/90	491,520	11.8	368,187	9.5	278,980	7.4	273,320	7.4
8/76-12/95	1,005,300	12.7	512,018	8.8	480,320	8.5	396,170	7.4

VARIABLE VS. FIXED VS. INDEXED ANNUITIES: A THEORETICAL HISTORICAL COMPARISON (BASED ON A $100,000 INVESTMENT, AUGUST 1976 - DECEMBER 1995)

* Vanguard Index Trust 500 portfolio total returns reduced by 100 basis points to simulate variable annuity expenses.
** Company A computes the cash value every five years by taking 83 percent of the highest S&P 500 market value, not including dividends, during the five-year period. For example, if the starting investment is $100,000 and the five-year high point is $130,353, the fifth-year cash value is $125,190 – 83 percent of the highest capital gain for the five years. Each five years the equity-indexed annuity-holder can decide to cash it in, convert to a traditional fixed annuity or lock into the equity-indexed annuity for another five years. Company B allows for 85 percent of the S&P 500 market gain (not including dividends), capped at 14 percent in any one year, but treats market losses as zero. For example, if the S&P 500 (without dividends) went up 10 percent in year one, Company B would recognize 8.5 percent; if it went up 20 percent in the second year Company B would recognize 14 percent; and if the index went down 5 percent in year three, Company B would recognize 0 percent.

Figure 8.4

Time Period	Variable Annuity Vanguard 500* Projected		Fixed Annuity Projected		Company A Indexed** Projected		Company B Indexed** Projected	
	Value ($)	Return (%)	Value ($)	Return (%)	Value ($)	Return (%)	Value ($)	Return (%)
1/91-12/95	213,283	16.4	139,065	6.8	172,169	11.5	140,712	7.1

VARIABLE VS. FIXED VS. INDEXED ANNUITIES: THE LAST 5 YEARS (BASED ON A $100,000 INVESTMENT, JANUARY 1991 - DECEMBER 1995)

are identified, most astute investors will conclude that variable annuities are a better choice than EIAs.

However, these conclusions do not mean to imply that EIAs have no use whatsoever. In certain circumstances, investors in their fifties and sixties who are making their final investment push to retirement may wish to consider EIAs because their investment time horizon might be just five to ten years. As they have so little time to earn back any losses caused by market setbacks or investment mistakes, new investments and the repositioning of equity-invested assets might now be considered with an eye on conservation. If fixed income yields are low and expected to remain so, an EIA can be a reasonable investment product for this investor. It will allow for the potential of outperforming fixed income returns while not being fully exposed to market risk.

COMPARING ANNUITIES TO MUTUAL FUNDS

Conceptually, variable annuities are simply mutual funds wrapped in an instrument that permits tax on all income, whether ordinary or capital gain, to be deferred until monies are distributed. If annuitized, distributions are taxed under the rules of Code Section 72, which essentially prorates the recovery of basis over the distribution period. In addition, and *more importantly*, the investor may enjoy any number of a myriad of contractual guarantees in a variable annuity contract (although the details of these guarantees are *highly* variable across various contracts). However, an investor must pay a price for these advantages.

First, the amount of each annuity payment in excess of the amount of basis recovery is taxed at ordinary income tax rates, regardless of whether it is attributable to ordinary investment income (i.e., interest or dividends, including the potentially tax-favored qualifying dividends) or capital appreciation. Because an investor's marginal ordinary income tax rate virtually always equals or exceeds the applicable capital gains rate (depending upon whether the gains are short-term or long-term), he/she will forfeit the favorable lower tax treatment on the portion of payments that is attributable to previously unrecognized capital gains. In addition, the taxpayer will be unable to take advantage of capital losses as they accrued (although capital losses will still offset gains within the contract, ultimately reducing the amount of growth taxed as ordinary income at withdrawal).

Second, variable annuities incur mortality and expense (M&E) charges (for other various riders and guarantees) that range from about 0.5 to 1.25 percent (and occasionally as high as 2.0 percent with additional riders, features, and guarantees) in addition to the usual fund expenses. Fund expenses average anywhere from 0.6 to 1.25 percent on equity funds, and can occasionally be as high as 2.25 percent for small cap equity or international equity funds.

Third, most variable annuities impose surrender charges if owners withdraw money within the first five to nine years. The charge typically declines to zero in steps of 1 percent per year. As a general rule, variable annuities are less attractive than mutual funds if there is any possibility the contract will be surrendered within the first five to seven years. For terms this short, the period of tax deferral generally will be insufficient to overcome the additional fees and surrender charges. It is notable that in recent years, an increasing assortment of variable annuities are being offered to the public that allow for substantially reduced periods of surrender charges (as short as three years, or even one year) or no surrender charges. However, these contracts have increased M&E charges to compensate for the higher risk (to the insurance company) of an early liquidation.

Fourth, and potentially more problematic, is the 10 percent early withdrawal penalty on distributions from annuities before age 59½. Distributions that are not part of a series of substantially equal periodic payments for the life (or joint life) expectancy of the annuitant(s) are in most cases subject to a 10 percent penalty tax on the taxable amount withdrawn from the annuity, in addition to the ordinary income tax due.

Keep in mind that, although equity mutual funds do not enjoy the same degree of tax deferral as variable annuities, they are nonetheless, tax favored investments. Although the tax on ordinary dividend and interest income earned by a fund is paid by the shareholders in the year the income is earned, the tax on capital gains is deferred until the gains are recognized, either through buy and sell transactions within the mutual fund portfolio or when the investor sells his shares in the fund.

Therefore, when trying to decide whether variable annuities or mutual funds are more appropriate for a particular client situation, the results (particularly the analysis of comparable returns) depend on certain critical assumptions regarding the size of the differential in fees and loads, the rate of return, tax rates on ordinary income, qualifying dividends, and long-term capital gains, the turnover rate of the underlying investments, the length of accumulation period, and whether annuity distributions will be subject to a 10 percent penalty. In addition, the relative merit depends on how the variable annuity will be liquidated. Variable annuities are relatively more attractive if proceeds will be annuitized rather than taken in a lump-sum (because longer time periods generally favor the annuity's tax deferral benefits).

In most cases, investors who accumulate substantial sums for retirement, either inside or outside of an annuity, do not take a lump-sum distribution, which would then trigger the immediate recognition and taxation of all deferred income or accumulated gains. Instead, they make periodic withdrawals (and/or outright annuitize the contract) which enables them to continue to enjoy the benefits of tax deferral on the remaining balance over the distribution years. This continuation of tax deferral increases the relative benefit of the variable annuity as compared to the mutual fund.

Assuming a distribution period of twenty years, Figure 8.5 shows the effective annual compound after-tax and after-expense rates of return for the entire accumulation and distribution period and the number of years in the accumulation period (the crossover year) until the variable annuity would outperform (provide greater annual after-tax distributions than) the mutual fund. These crossover years were calculated using the same assumptions as listed above plus the following assumptions with regard to the taxation of distributions during the twenty-year distribution period:

- Distributions from the annuity are assumed to be level and taxed under the rules of Code section 72. Under these rules, basis is recovered in a pro rata fashion over the distribution period. For example, if the basis is $100,000

and the distribution period is twenty years, 1/20 of the basis, or $5,000 of each annual payment is treated as a nontaxable recovery of basis. The remaining portion of each annual payment is taxable as ordinary income. Given the assumptions of a level 35 percent tax rate on ordinary income and level annual distributions, the after-tax payments from the annuity will also be level each year over the distribution period.

- The amount withdrawn in any given year from the mutual fund is the amount necessary to provide equal after-tax annual distributions over the twenty-year distribution period. It is assumed that the after-tax dividend income each year is the first money withdrawn. If, in a given year, the after-tax dividend income is less than the desired after-tax distribution, shares in the mutual fund must be sold to make up the difference. It is assumed that gain is recognized and taxed on the sale of such shares in the same proportion as the ratio of the total accumulated gains within the portfolio to the total value of the portfolio.

Example. If the total value of the portfolio is $100,000 and the built-in gain is $40,000, a sale of $5,000 worth of securities would result in the recognition and taxation of $2,000 of gains. The remaining $3,000 would be tax-free recovery of basis.

The variable annuity becomes relatively more advantageous when the continuing benefits of tax deferral over an extended payout period are also included in the analysis. However, even if funds are to be liquidated

Figure 8.5

MUTUAL FUND VERSUS VARIABLE ANNUITY 20-year Annuitization			
	Effective After-tax ROR		
Total ROR	MF	VA	Crossover Year
12%	8.0920%	8.0920%	13.8
11%	7.3265%	7.3265%	16.5
10%	6.5683%	6.5683%	20.4
9%	5.8156%	5.8156%	26.4
8%	5.0670%	5.0670%	36.3
7%	4.3235%	4.3235%	54.5

over a twenty-year period, the variable annuity becomes the better alternative (under the listed assumptions) only if the accumulation period is still quite long.

Example. An investor expects to invest at a total pre-tax and pre-expense rate of return of about 10 percent (matching the long-term compound average annual rate of return on the S&P 500 index). The investor can expect the variable annuity to outperform a mutual fund only if the investor plans to accumulate money in the variable annuity for about 20.4 years before beginning distributions over a twenty-year payout period. Stated another way, an investor who plans to retire at age sixty-five, for instance, would gain by making contributions to a variable annuity before age forty-five. However, any further investments made after age forty-four would be better invested in the mutual fund outside the variable annuity. The after-tax payments associated with a systematic liquidation of the mutual fund for a twenty-year period starting at age sixty-five for contributions after age forty-four would be greater than for comparable contributions to the variable annuity.

Figure 8.6 through 8.9 show break-even periods assuming the new tax rates for capital gains and qualifying dividend income will continue indefinitely into the future for taxpayers in the 35 percent, 30 percent, 25 percent, and 15 percent tax brackets, respectively.

Because dividend income is taxed differently than interest income, the tables compute break-even periods by assuming that the income component of the return on the underlying mutual fund is composed of equal shares of dividend and interest income. Therefore, the preferential dividend income tax rate applies to half of the fund's income and the taxpayer's ordinary tax rate applies to half of the fund's income.

In addition, given the change in tax rates, it is assumed that variable annuities will have to reduce their mortality charges and expenses to have much chance to compete with mutual fund investments. Consequently, the additional variable annuity mortality charge is assumed to be just 0.75 percent rather than 1 percent as in the analyses above.

Otherwise, the analysis remains essentially the same, except that the new tax rates are used and the crossovers or break-even periods are computed for a number of different capital gain proportions. That is, the break-even periods are shown not just for a mutual fund with

Figure 8.6

MUTUAL FUND VERSUS VARIABLE ANNUITY BREAK-EVEN YEARS FOR TAXPAYER IN 35% BRACKET								
	Assumed Return							
	6%	**7%**	**8%**	**9%**	**10%**	**11%**	**12%**	**13%**
0%	60+	47+	33+	24+	19+	15+	12+	10+
15%	60+	60+	41+	30+	24+	19+	16+	14+
30%	60+	60+	53+	39+	31+	25+	21+	18+
45%	60+	60+	60+	51+	40+	33+	28+	24+
60%	60+	60+	60+	60+	54+	44+	37+	32+
75%	60+	60+	60+	60+	60+	60+	52+	45+
90%	60+	60+	60+	60+	60+	60+	60+	60+
95%	60+	60+	60+	60+	60+	60+	60+	60+

Assumptions: 0.75 percent variable annuity mortality charge; 1.00 percent management and operating expense rate of both mutual fund and VA; 35 percent tax rate on ordinary income; 15 percent tax rate on long-term capital gain; 15 percent tax rate on dividend income; 25.0 percent averaged tax rate on mutual fund dividend and interest income; 20 percent portfolio turnover rate (portion of built-up gain taxed each year as a result of portfolio turnover); 50 percent dividend income portion of mutual fund income; twenty-year payout period.

Capital Gain Portion (left column): the proportion of the fund's total return attributable to capital appreciation.

Figure 8.7

MUTUAL FUND VERSUS VARIABLE ANNUITY BREAK-EVEN YEARS FOR TAXPAYER IN 30% BRACKET							
Assumed Return							
	6%	7%	8%	9%	10%	11%	12%	13%
0%	60+	50+	32+	24+	18+	14+	12+	9+
15%	60+	60+	41+	30+	23+	18+	15+	13+
30%	60+	60+	52+	38+	29+	24+	20+	17+
45%	60+	60+	60+	49+	38+	31+	25+	22+
60%	60+	60+	60+	60+	50+	40+	34+	29+
75%	60+	60+	60+	60+	60+	55+	46+	40+
90%	60+	60+	60+	60+	60+	60+	60+	59+
95%	60+	60+	60+	60+	60+	60+	60+	60+

Key: 0.75 percent: variable annuity mortality charge; 1.00 percent: management and operating expense rate of both mutual fund and VA; 30 percent: tax rate on ordinary income; 15 percent: tax rate on long-term capital gain; 15 percent: tax rate on dividend income; 22.5 percent: averaged tax rate on mutual fund dividend and interest income; 20 percent: portfolio turnover rate (portion of built-up gain taxed each year as a result of portfolio turnover); 50 percent: dividend income portion of mutual fund income; twenty-year payout period.
Capital Gain Portion (left column): the proportion of the fund's total return attributable to capital appreciation..

Figure 8.8

MUTUAL FUND VERSUS VARIABLE ANNUITY BREAK-EVEN YEARS FOR TAXPAYER IN 25% BRACKET							
Assumed Return							
	6%	7%	8%	9%	10%	11%	12%	13%
0%	60+	56+	35+	24+	17+	13+	10+	8+
15%	60+	60+	43+	30+	22+	18+	14+	11+
30%	60+	60+	54+	37+	28+	22+	18+	15+
45%	60+	60+	60+	47+	35+	28+	23+	19+
60%	60+	60+	60+	60+	46+	36+	30+	25+
75%	60+	60+	60+	60+	60+	49+	40+	34+
90%	60+	60+	60+	60+	60+	60+	57+	48+
95%	60+	60+	60+	60+	60+	60+	60+	55+

Key: 0.75 percent: variable annuity mortality charge; 1.00 percent: management and operating expense rate of both mutual fund and VA; 25 percent: tax rate on ordinary income; 15 percent: tax rate on long-term capital gain; 15 percent: tax rate on dividend income; 20 percent: averaged tax rate on mutual fund dividend and interest income; 20 percent: portfolio turnover rate (portion of built-up gain taxed each year as a result of portfolio turnover); 50 percent: dividend income portion of mutual fund income; twenty-year payout period.
Capital Gain Portion (left column): 1.71 the proportion of the fund's total return attributable to capital appreciation.

Figure 8.9

	MUTUAL FUND VERSUS VARIABLE ANNUITY BREAK-EVEN YEARS FOR TAXPAYER IN 15% BRACKET							
	Assumed Return							
	6%	**7%**	**8%**	**9%**	**10%**	**11%**	**12%**	**13%**
0%	60+	60+	60+	60+	60+	60+	44+	33+
15%	60+	60+	60+	60+	60+	60+	60+	49+
30%	60+	60+	60+	60+	60+	60+	60+	60+
45%	60+	60+	60+	60+	60+	60+	60+	60+
60%	60+	60+	60+	60+	60+	60+	60+	60+
75%	60+	60+	60+	60+	60+	60+	60+	60+
90%	60+	60+	60+	60+	60+	60+	60+	60+
95%	60+	60+	60+	60+	60+	60+	60+	60+

Key: 0.75 percent: variable annuity mortality charge; 1.00 percent: management and operating expense rate of both mutual fund and VA; 15 percent: tax rate on ordinary income; 5 percent: tax rate on long-term capital gain; 5 percent: tax rate on dividend income; 10 percent: averaged tax rate on mutual fund dividend and interest income; 20 percent: portfolio turnover rate (portion of built-up gain taxed each year as a result of portfolio turnover); 50 percent: dividend income portion of mutual fund income; twenty-year payout period.
Capital Gain Portion (left column): the proportion of the fund's total return attributable to capital appreciation.

60 percent of the return attributable to capital appreciation but for capital gain proportions ranging from 0 percent to 95 percent of the return. All other assumptions remain the same as those used in computing the values in Figure 8.5. The charts find the number of years that money must be invested in the variable annuity before payouts commence in order for the after-tax payouts from the annuity over the twenty-year payout period to exceed the after-tax payments the investor could obtain from the mutual fund.

Not surprisingly, the crossover or break-even period is longer uniformly than under the previous tax regime. For example, Figure 8.6 assumes the taxpayer is in the 35 percent tax bracket, just as was assumed when computing the values in Figure 8.5. Capital appreciation comprised 60 percent of the return in Figure 8.5. The grayed cells of Figure 8.6 show the corresponding values using the new tax rates for long-term gains and qualifying dividends for a taxpayer in the 35 percent bracket. The crossover or break-even period under the new tax rules until an amount invested in the variable annuity could provide the same after-tax payout over a twenty-year period as the investment in the mutual fund outside the annuity is over sixty years until the rate of return exceeds 9 percent. At a 10 percent rate of return, the crossover occurs after fifty-four years. This is about twenty-four years longer, or more than twice

as long, as the crossover period of 20.4 years under the old tax rules. If the investment earns 12 percent, the crossover occurs under the new rules after thirty-seven years, or about twenty-three years longer than under the previous tax rules.

As Figure 8.9 shows, the crossover point is over sixty years in almost all circumstances for taxpayers in the 15 percent bracket. This is primarily because taxpayers in the 15 percent tax bracket pay long-term capital gains tax rates of only 5 percent (rather than 15 percent in all prior scenarios).

Figures 8.3 through 8.6 also show the crossovers if it is assumed no portion of the return (0 percent) is attributable to capital gains. This could conceivably be the case if the portfolio were invested in preferred stocks and bonds (it would also be applicable in a high turnover portfolio, where all capital gains are taxed as short-term capital gains). Even if a taxpayer in the 35 percent bracket could earn 10 percent on such a portfolio, the crossover still does not occur for nineteen years. For taxpayers in the 30 percent and 25 percent tax brackets, the crossover is only a year shorter for each step down in the tax bracket.

Figure 8.10 presents the results for a taxpayer in the 35 percent tax bracket assuming that the variable

Figure 8.10

MUTUAL FUND VERSUS VARIABLE ANNUITY BREAK-EVEN YEARS FOR TAXPAYER IN 35% BRACKET								
No Variable Annuity Mortality Charge								
	Assumed Return							
	6%	7%	8%	9%	10%	11%	12%	13%
0%	14+	12+	10+	8+	7+	6+	5+	5+
15%	19+	15+	13+	11+	10+	8+	7+	7+
30%	23+	20+	17+	14+	13+	12+	10+	10+
45%	30+	25+	21+	17+	16+	15+	14+	13+
60%	36+	30+	26+	23+	21+	19+	17+	17+
75%	44+	38+	33+	29+	27+	24+	22+	21+
90%	54+	46+	41+	36+	33+	31+	29+	27+
95%	58+	49+	44+	39+	36+	34+	33+	30+

Key: 0.00 percent: variable annuity mortality charge; 1.00 percent: management and operating expense rate of both mutual fund and VA; 35 percent: tax rate on ordinary income; 15 percent: tax rate on long-term capital gain; 15 percent: tax rate on dividend income; 25 percent: averaged tax rate on mutual fund dividend and interest income; 20 percent: portfolio turnover rate (portion of built-up gain taxed each year as a result of portfolio turnover); 50 percent: dividend income portion of mutual fund income; twenty-year payout period.
Capital Gain Portion (left column): the proportion of the fund's total return attributable to capital appreciation.

annuity assesses **no mortality** charge at all. In other words, it assumes the variable annuity and the mutual fund have exactly the same expenses. The table shows that if investors can find annuities with very low mortality charges, and the investors are planning to invest in assets with low appreciation potential, the annuities could be viable alternatives. However, based upon current rates of return for fixed-income investments, a 6 percent return would probably be an aggressive assumption, at least for the first few years of the investment. At 6 percent, investors still need to invest in the annuities for at least fourteen years before they plan to start taking distributions to make the investment profitable compared to investing outside the annuity.

Our entire analysis up to this point has assumed a level annual return. However, in point of fact, we know that annual returns are *not* level. Although the S&P 500 index has had a long-term compound average annual rate of return of approximately 10 percent over the past seventy-five years or so, individual year returns have ranged dramatically, and substantial losses in a particular year are possible. If withdrawals need to be made from the investment, either on account of retirement (or other) spending needs, or because of a death

of the account-holder, the guarantees provided by the annuity may become highly relevant. A severe market downturn shortly before a substantial withdrawal can provide an *immense* savings to the annuity holder as the contractual guarantees are exercised. Over the long run, if the annuity is properly priced, individual fluctuations will average out and will approach the long-term averages (and concomitant long-term-based results) shown in the charts contained herein. However, on an individual basis, the guarantees may be vitally important to an individual client.

In addition, the provision of underlying guarantees may allow an investor to otherwise take a higher level of risk than he/she may otherwise be comfortable with. Consequently, an annuity investor might potentially earn an average rate of return of 10 percent in an S&P 500-like investment, while the mutual fund holder might only earn an average rate of return of 8 percent, due to a more conservative investment in light of the lack of underlying guarantees. The potential for a higher rate of return to an annuity holder in light of higher investment risk taken on (mitigated by reduced total risk due to annuity contractual guarantees) can substantially shorten the break-even period necessary.

Because the appropriate amount of risk can vary tremendously on an individual basis, and risk characteristics can change over time, the primary factor in the decision to select a variable annuity should be its value as a *risk management* tool, not merely as a tax deferral method. Because of the tremendous variety of contractual guarantees, with varying costs, available through commercial variable annuity providers, full analysis of the relevant options, and the client's needs and concerns, is *vital* to the decision to utilize a variable annuity and the appropriate selection of a particular contract.

WHERE CAN I FIND OUT MORE ABOUT IT?

This chapter has still only lightly covered some of the complexities of annuities. The broad range of choices, and the numerous changes in tax law as applied to annuities, necessitates a thorough understanding for anyone wishing to seriously delve into this investment tool. For further reading on annuities, see *The Advisor's Guide to Annuities*, 4th Edition by John Olsen and Michael Kitces (Cincinnati, OH: The National Underwriter Company, 2014).

Information on annuities can also be obtained in newspapers (especially the *Wall Street Journal's* quarterly report on mutual funds and variable annuities) and in three major statistical sources: (1) A.M. Best Co.; (2) Lipper Analytical Services Inc.; and (3) Barron's. One often can obtain substantial comparative information, particularly for fixed annuities, from insurance brokerage firms that deal with multiple annuity product providers.

FREQUENTLY ASKED QUESTIONS

Question – What happens to the money paid to the insurance company when the annuitant dies?

Answer – A pure life annuity is one in which the continuation of payments by the insurer is contingent upon the continuing survival of one or more lives. The remaining consideration (premium) paid for the annuity that has not been distributed (including accrued interest) is fully earned by the insurer immediately upon the death of the annuitant. This is why annuities payable for the life or lives of one or more annuitants frequently include a minimum payment guarantee. In other

words, many annuities include both life and fixed period or refund elements so that if death occurs prematurely, the annuitant and the annuitant's survivors will recover a total of at least some minimum amount. Therefore, each annuity payment where a minimum guarantee has been purchased is composed of: (1) return of principal; (2) interest or earnings on invested funds; and (3) a survivorship element.

If an annuitant dies before having recovered the full amount guaranteed under a refund or period-certain life annuity, the balance of the guaranteed amount is not taxable income to the refund beneficiary—until the total amount received tax-free by the annuitant plus the total amount received tax-free by the beneficiary equals the investment in the contract. From that point on, all additional amounts received are ordinary income.[26]

Question – What is a temporary life annuity?

Answer – A temporary life annuity is one which provides for fixed payments until the earlier of the death of the annuitant(s) or the end of a specified number of years. To compute the annuity exclusion ratio, expected return is found by multiplying one year's annuity payments by a multiple from the appropriate IRS annuity table.[27]

Question – What is the difference between an owner-driven and annuitant-driven contract?

Answer – The differentiation between owner-driven versus annuitant-driven contracts addresses the consequences of the death of an annuitant during the accumulation phase of a deferred annuity.

In the past, almost all contracts were annuitant-driven, but recently some contracts are occasionally owner-driven. It is important to read the details of the annuity contract to determine which type of contract is being evaluated or is in force.

Under the classic model of an annuitant-driven contract, if the annuitant were to pass away during the accumulation phase, the contract would pay the death benefit to the primary beneficiary of the contract. Any special death benefit provisions of the contract apply at the death of the annuitant. In situations where the owner and annuitant of the contract are the same person, this is not consequential. However, this can have substantial impact if the owner and annuitant are different people.

For example, let us assume that John Doe owns an annuitant-driven contract on his wife, Jane Doe. John Doe is the primary beneficiary, and John's son Daniel is the contingent beneficiary. The annuity contract has a current value of $120,000, and the death benefit is $150,000. In the event that Jane dies, the enhanced death benefit of $150,000 will be paid to John. However, it is important to remember that all annuities, whether owner- or annuitant-driven, must pay out at the death of the owner.[28] Therefore, we must contrast this with the result in the event that John Doe dies. If John Doe were to pass away, under an annuitant-driven contract, the enhanced death benefit would not be paid; the current value would be paid out, and Daniel would receive $120,000, *not* $150,000.

Alternatively, the results of an owner-driven contract reverse these results. Under an owner-driven contract, the death of the owner, John Doe, will cause a payout of the enhanced death benefit. A death of the annuitant, Jane Doe, simply creates an annuitant-less contract, and the owner will have the option of assigning a new annuitant.

Because of the radical differences in potential payouts at the death of the owner or annuitant, it is critical to understand whether a contract is owner-driven or annuitant-driven when structuring the setup of owners, annuitants, and beneficiaries.

Question – How does the new DOL fiduciary rule affect the sale or availability of annuities?

Answer – That remains to be seen. In general terms the new fiduciary rule prohibits advisors from receiving compensation that varies based on what products they sell. Given the wide variety in types of annuities described above, it is not surprising that sales commission on annuities have also varied widely. The new rule does include a newly modified Prohibited Transaction Exemption (PTE) 84-24, which allows for the sale of annuities with variable compensation under a limited set of circumstances. However, the new PTE 84-24 is much more restrictive in that it only applies to the sale of fixed rate annuities and mutual funds.

Additionally, the DOL has delayed implementation of the new rules and announced that major provision are under review and may yet be changed. The new rule will almost certainly change how annuities are sold and may well lead to new annuity products (or new ways of pricing and selling old products).

CHAPTER ENDNOTES

1. The term "annuity" encompasses all periodic payments resulting from the systematic liquidation of principal. A payment of interest only would not be an annuity payment. See Treas. Reg. §1.72-1.

2. See Leimberg, Stephan R., et al., *The Tools and Techniques of Estate Planning*, 17th ed. (Cincinnati, OH: The National Underwriter Company, 2015).

3. This only applies to annuities purchased *outside* a retirement plan; investments purchased *inside* a retirement plan already pass by beneficiary designation and are not subject to probate. Annuities provide no additional probate avoidance benefits *inside* a retirement plan that are not already provided by the underlying plan.

4. This only applies to annuities purchased *outside* a retirement plan; investments purchased *inside* a retirement plan are already tax-deferred by virtue of the retirement plan. Annuities provide no additional tax-deferral benefits *inside* a retirement plan, and thus should be purchased for other reasons, such as risk management.

5. Annuitization of a deferred annuity during the accumulation phase will be subject to the pre-59½ penalty unless the I.R.C. §72(q)(2)(D) requirements for substantially equal periodic payments are met.

6. Except for FIFO, for withdrawals from contracts that have not been substantially modified and were entered into prior to August 14, 1982.

7. Rev. Rul. 2003-91, 2003-33 IRB 347.

8. Treas. Reg. §§1.72-2(b)(3), 1.72-4(d)(3).

9. Treas. Reg. §1.72-4(d)(3)(ii).

10. I.R.C. §72(u).

11. I.R.C. §72(u)(3).

12. Different rules apply to contracts purchased on or before August 13, 1982, allowing withdrawal of principal first and interest/growth second. I.R.C. §72(e)(5).

13. I.R.C. §72(q)(2).

14. I.R.C. §72(b)(1). Round the quotient to 3 decimal places. See Treas. Reg. §1.72-4(a)(2).

15. I.R.C. §72(c).

16. Rev. Rul. 55-349, 1955-1 CB 232.

17. I.R.C. §72(c)(3)(B). See also Treas. Reg. §§1.72-5(c-d).

18. I.R.C. §72(c)(3)(A).

19. Treas. Reg. §1.72-4(d)(2).

20. If the "annuity starting date" (first day of first period for which an amount is received as an annuity) is after December 31, 1986, the exclusion ratio applies to all payments received until the annuitant has fully recovered his or her investment in the contract. Once the annuitant's investment is fully recovered, further payments are subject in full to ordinary income tax. I.R.C. §72(b)(2).

But if the annuity starting date was prior to January 1, 1987, the amount tax-free under the annuity exclusion ratio remains income tax-free for as long as the annuitant receives payments, no matter how long he or she lives. I.R.C. §72(b)(4)(A), before amendment by §1704(I)(1), PL 104-188, 8/20/1996.

21. See I.R.C. §72(c)(2).

22. I.R.C. §72(b)(3)(A).

23. I.R.C. §72(b)(3)(B).

24. I.R.C. §72(h).

25. I.R.C. §72(s)(3).

26. I.R.C. §72(e)(2).

27. Table IV or VIII of Treas. Reg. §1.72-9. See also Treas. Reg. §1.72-5(a)(3).

28. I.R.C. §72(s)(1).

CURRENT ASSUMPTION WHOLE LIFE

CHAPTER 9

INTRODUCTION

Current Assumption Whole Life insurance (CAWL) is essentially a hybrid of traditional cash value whole life insurance and Universal Life insurance (UL). At the time of issue, the premium and death benefit levels are fixed, similar to traditional whole life policies. However, like UL, the insurer credits separately identifiable interest and assesses separately identifiable mortality and expense charges to an accumulation account.

As a result of this combination of features of both ordinary whole and universal life, CAWL is sometimes called interest-sensitive whole life or fixed-premium universal life. But neither of these terms is quite accurate.[1] The term "fixed premium" is not apt because premium and death benefit levels generally remain fixed only for a certain period of time, such as five years, based on anticipated interest, mortality, and expenses. At the end of each period, the premium level and sometimes the death benefit level are recalculated taking into account the actual accumulation account value and new experience assumptions. Also, the term "interest sensitive" is not correct because most CAWL policies are "sensitive" not only to interest or investment performance on the underlying assets but also to the mortality and expense experience of the company.

Features of universal life possessed by CAWL include:

1. In contrast with traditional whole life and similar to UL, CAWL policy elements are "unbundled," or separately reported, and the actual cash value accumulation is prospectively indeterminate.

The insurer uses an accumulation account to track cash values. Each year the insurer adds premium less annual expense charges to the preceding year's accumulated account balance. The insurer credits interest to the balance in the cash value accumulation account based on the company's current rate. The policy promises to pay a rate not less than the contract guaranteed rate, which has historically varied from about 4 to 6 percent, but has been lower on more-recently issued policies because of the relatively low market interest rates over the last decade. Finally, the insurer deducts from the account mortality charges, which are based on the net amount at risk (face amount less cash value). The maximum mortality rate the company may charge is also specified in the contract. Because the interest rates that the insurer will credit and the mortality charges that it will debit to the cash accumulation account balance in future years are uncertain, neither the insurer nor the policyowner can know the future accumulation account balance with any certainty.

Some CAWL policies have no explicit expense charges. Instead, the insurer may wrap expense charges into mortality charges or include them as an adjustment to the current rate that the insurer credits to cash values. Also, a few CAWL policies are truly interest-sensitive policies only. Similar to many traditional whole life policies, on these interest-only sensitive policies the insurer fixes and guarantees the mortality charges.

2. Most CAWL policies have very low or no front-end loads and, instead, impose back-end surrender charges.

Typically, the insurer adds the entire first-year premium, less the usual yearly expense charge, to the accumulation account. Therefore, most of the policyowner's premium payment immediately begins to earn interest. The insurer levies the back-end charge when and if the policyowner lapses or surrenders the policy. The insurer usually specifies the surrender charge as a percentage of the premium or cash accumulation account. The surrender charge rate typically declines each year until it reaches zero in nine to fifteen years.

3. Some insurers offer CAWL policies that provide a death benefit similar to UL option II. Thus, the death benefit of these policies equals a level face amount plus the balance in the cash accumulation account.

4. Some CAWL policies link the current interest rate to a specific index, such as the yield on Treasury bills or an index of high-grade corporate or government bonds. This has become more common in recent years because of the historically low interest rates of the past decade.

5. Policyowners usually may withdraw the excess in the cash accumulation account without impairing the base policy, subject to any surrender charges.

Features of traditional level premium life insurance possessed by CAWL include:

- level premiums and a level face amount between each "redetermination period;"

- a minimum interest guarantee;

- guaranteed maximum mortality charges;

- minimum guaranteed cash values;

- nonforfeiture values;

- a policy loan provision;

- a reinstatement period; and

- settlement options.

Contract provisions similar to traditional forms of insurance that policyowners can obtain as options in CAWL include:

- waiver of premium;

- guaranteed purchase of insurability;

- accidental death benefits; and

- cost of living adjustments.

WHEN IS THE USE OF THIS DEVICE INDICATED?

CAWL is indicated when a person wants the fixed premium, "forced savings" feature of traditional whole life and the potential for better investment results than those guaranteed in traditional policies. CAWL has a minimum guaranteed cash value accumulation, but the policyowner bears the risk that the investment performance and mortality experience of the company will be less favorable than originally assumed. The insurer may have to periodically increase required premiums or decrease the face amount of coverage if performance does not meet expectations.

Advantages

1. Premiums are level and fixed between each redetermination period.

2. Cash value interest or earnings accumulate tax-free or tax-deferred, depending on whether gains are distributed at death or during lifetime.

3. CAWL frequently pays a higher effective interest rate on cash values than the rate available with tax-free municipal bonds.

4. Cash values are not subject to the market risk associated with longer term municipal bonds and other longer term fixed income investments.

5. Policyowners can borrow policy cash values at a low net cost. Although policyowners must pay interest on policy loans, cash values continue to grow as the insurer credits cash values with at least the minimum guaranteed rate in the policy. Consequently, the actual net borrowing rate is less than the stated policy loan rate.

6. The policy is "transparent"—that is, policy illustrations and annual reports explain each of the policy elements separately. This "unbundling" allows

the policyowner to specifically identify and track premiums, death benefits, interest credits, mortality charges, expenses, and cash values. Furthermore, the policyowner can compare projections with actual performance over time.

7. Many polices have cost of living riders that, without evidence of insurability, automatically increase the policy death benefit periodically by the increase in the Consumer Price Index (CPI).

8. In contrast with most traditional whole life policies, most CAWL policies use "back-end loads," or surrender charges, rather than "front-end loads." (A load is the charge imposed by an insurer to recover the initial policy expenses. The terms front-end and back-end refer to when the charge is imposed.) Consequently, most of the policyowner's initial premiums go into cash values, subject, of course to regular annual expense and mortality charges. Therefore, cash values build more quickly than with traditional whole life policies.

9. Many CAWL policies permit policyowners to withdraw excess cash value accumulations without impairing the policy or changing the death benefit.

Disadvantages

1. In the early years, the amount of protection is lower relative to the premium spent with CAWL than with term insurance. However, later, as term rates rise while the premium for CAWL remains relatively level, the reverse typically will be true.

2. Surrender of the policy within the first five to ten years may result in considerable loss because surrender values reflect the insurance company's recovery of sales commissions and initial policy expenses. In addition, most CAWL policies levy surrender charges rather than up-front fees or loads. These surrender charges generally decline each year the policyowner holds the policy. After approximately nine to fifteen years, depending on the company and policy, the insurer no longer assesses any surrender charges if the policyowner surrenders the policy.

3. Although traditional participating whole life policies are indirectly "interest-sensitive," mortality and expense charges are guaranteed. In contrast, current assumption policies only guarantee that mortality

charges and expense rates will not exceed certain maximums. Consequently, policyowners bear more of the risk of adverse trends in mortality or expenses than if they owned traditional whole life policies. Conversely, if the trend of mortality costs and expenses improves, CAWL policyowners may participate in the improvement through lower charges.

4. Some CAWL policies, similar to many traditional whole life policies, use what is called the "direct recognition" method to determine amounts the insurer credits to cash values subject to policy loans. Under this method, the insurer credits with the current rate only the portion of the cash value that is not used to secure a loan. The insurer credits amounts backing the loan with the minimum guaranteed rate or a rate usually one to two percentage points lower than the loan rate. Policies that have fixed loan rates most commonly use the direct recognition method. Typically, policies with variable loan rates, (and some with fixed loan rates) do not employ the direct recognition method and instead credit current rates on the entire cash value without regard to loans.

5. A CAWL policy will lapse if the policyowner does not pay the premium. However, some policyowners may view this feature as an advantage because it forces them to pay the premiums regularly. CAWL differs from universal life in this respect because a UL policy will not necessarily lapse if the policyowner misses a premium payment.

TAX IMPLICATIONS

The tax rules for CAWL policies are generally the same as the tax rules for other types of life insurance policies. Death benefit payments are usually free of any federal income tax. CAWL policies are subject to the same estate, gift, and generation-skipping transfer taxation rules as all other types of life insurance policies. See Chapter 22 through 30 for a complete discussion of the taxation of life insurance.

Similarly, the tax rules for living benefits from CAWL policies are also the same as the tax rules for living benefits from other types of life insurance policies. The annuity cost recovery rules of Code section 72 govern annuity-type distributions. These rules state that policyowners recover their investment in the contract (generally, total premiums paid less prior nontaxable distributions) ratably over the expected payout period.

The "cost recovery rule" for taxation generally applies to all other types of living benefits. The cost recovery rule, which is sometimes called the First-In-First-Out (FIFO) rule, treats amounts received by the policyowner as a nontaxable recovery of the policyowner's investment in the contract. Only after the policyowner fully recovers the investment in the contract are additional amounts received treated as taxable interest or gain in the policy. Included in this category of living benefits are policy dividends, lump-sum cash settlements of cash surrender values, cash withdrawals, and amounts received on partial surrender. The policyowner includes such amounts in gross income only to the extent they exceed the investment in the contract (as reduced by any prior excludable distributions received from the contract). In other words, policyowners generally treat nonannuity distributions during life first as a return of the policyowner's investment in the contract, and then as taxable interest or gain. If the insurer holds any living benefits under an agreement to pay interest, the policyowner must report and pay taxes each year on all the interest the insurer pays on or credits to the living benefits.

Exception to the Cost Recovery Rule

The general cost recovery rule has an important exception for withdrawals within the first fifteen years after the policy issue date that are also coupled with reductions in death benefits. Because the insurer generally reduces death benefits in an amount equal to any withdrawal of cash values, policyowners generally will have to report and pay income tax on the amount withdrawn or distributed to the extent attributable to gain in the policy.

Such withdrawals are taxed in whole or in part as ordinary income to the extent that they are "forced out" of the policy as a result of the reduction in the death benefits. The taxable amount depends on when the policyowner makes the withdrawal:

- *Within the first five years* – If the withdrawal takes place within the first five years after policy issue, a very stringent and complex set of tests applies.[2] Potentially, a larger portion, or perhaps all, of any withdrawal within the first five years will be taxable if there is gain in the policy.

- *Fifth to fifteenth years* – For withdrawals between the end of the fifth year and the

end of the fifteenth year from the issue date, a mathematical test applies. Essentially, the policyowner is taxed on an income-first basis to the extent the cash value before the withdrawal exceeds the maximum allowable cash value under the cash value corridor test for the reduced death benefit after the withdrawal.[3] Frequently, only a portion or none of the withdrawal will be taxable in these cases.

ALTERNATIVES

1. *Traditional Participating Whole Life Insurance* – CAWL has many of the features of traditional whole life. Also, many participating whole life policies now offered are essentially a type of current assumption policy, with current mortality and expense experience as well as interest reflected in the level of dividends paid.

2. *Universal Life* – UL and CAWL are both "unbundled" current assumption policies. In most respects, CAWL can be described as a form of fixed premium universal life.

3. *Variable Life (VL)* – If a VL policyowner selects a portfolio of investments within the policy that is similar to the general investment portfolio of the insurance company (mostly long-term bonds and mortgages), the policyowner can expect investment performance and cash value accumulations to be similar to that of CAWL.

4. *A combination of a level-premium deferred annuity and decreasing term insurance* – Cash values accumulate in both annuities and CAWL policies on a tax-deferred basis. Therefore, a combination of a level premium deferred annuity and a decreasing term policy can provide levels of tax-preferred cash accumulation and death benefits similar to a CAWL policy.

Some important differences exist, however. The tax rules treat withdrawals, lifetime distributions, or loans from each arrangement differently. Although most CAWL policies do not permit withdrawals, as such, except to the extent of excess cash values, a policyowner is taxed on amounts withdrawn or partial surrenders under the cost recovery rule. That is, the policyowner includes the amounts in taxable income only to the extent they exceed the investment in the contract. In contrast, the owner of an annuity is taxed on such nonannuity distributions under the interest-first rule. In other words, nonannuity distributions are fully taxable until the annuity owner recovers the entire amount in the contract in excess of the investment in the contract. So, in the case of nonannuity distributions, with the CAWL the policyowner generally recovers all nontaxable basis first, then taxable gain. With the annuity contract, the owner generally recovers all taxable gain in excess of basis first, then nontaxable basis.

In addition, nonannuity distributions from an annuity contract received before age 59½ may be subject to a 10 percent penalty tax. Also, while loans from life insurance policies are not subject to tax, loans from annuities, if permitted, are treated as distributions and taxed under the interest-first rule. That is, loan proceeds are subject to regular income tax and may be subject to the 10 percent penalty tax. Also, loan provisions of deferred annuity contracts generally are more restrictive than those of life insurance policies.

The annuity/term combination will require increasing premiums over the years for the term coverage. In addition, the mortality charges for term insurance coverage typically are higher than the mortality charges in a CAWL policy. Finally, the death proceeds from the insurance policy generally may pass to the beneficiary entirely income and estate tax free—regardless of whom the beneficiary is—if the policyowner has no incidents of ownership in the policy. In contrast, the beneficiary still will have to pay tax on the gains in the annuity contract and only will avoid estate taxation if the beneficiary is the annuitant's spouse and they can take advantage of the estate tax marital deduction.

5. *A combination of investments in tax-free municipal bonds and decreasing term insurance* – This combination can create a cash accumulation and death benefit similar to a level death benefit CAWL policy. Similar to the cash values in a life insurance policy, municipal bonds owners may use the bonds as collateral for loans without any adverse income tax consequences. However, interest paid on debt secured by municipal bonds generally is not tax deductible. Although not the general rule, in some cases, the interest paid on life insurance policy loans may be tax deductible. (See Chapter 24 for a further discussion of policy loans.) The life insurance

policy transfers the death benefits by operation of the contract, which avoids probate. In contrast, municipal bonds are part of the probate estate and pass by will. Once again, if the policyowner has no incidents of ownership, the death proceeds escape estate tax. The municipal bonds will avoid estate tax only if they are left to the spouse who takes advantage of the estate tax marital deduction.

WHERE AND HOW DO I GET IT?

Most life insurance companies in the United States offer some form of current assumption or interest-sensitive whole life policies. Most of these companies are stock rather than mutual life insurance companies.

FEES AND ACQUISITION COSTS

Most CAWL policies have low or no initial charges or front end fees. Rather, the insurer adds most or all the first year premium to the cash accumulation account which begins to earn interest immediately. However, the commission and other start-up costs of issuing new policies are substantial and the insurer must recover these costs somehow. Insurers generally recover these costs through a combination of annual expense charges and surrender charges.

Insurers may set the surrender charge in the first year as high as 100 percent of the first year premium. After the first year, insurers usually compute the surrender charge as a declining percentage of the cash accumulation account. The rate typically will reach zero in nine to fifteen years. As a result of competition in the industry, the trend has been towards shorter surrender charge phase-out periods.

Policyowners can determine the surrender charge explicitly by looking at the policy illustration or ledger statement. This statement shows both a cash value figure and a net cash value figure for each policy year. The cash value is the amount on which the insurer bases interest credits. The net cash value is the amount that the company would pay if the policyowner surrendered the policy. The difference is the surrender charge.

Commissions paid to agents are one of the principal components of the total issue costs. Commissions are commonly 50 percent or more of the first year premium for an ordinary whole life design policy. If the policy is of a limited-pay type, the insurer typically pays a lower effective commission rate ranging anywhere from 3 to 20 percent on the amount of premium in excess of the ordinary whole life premium. Commissions on renewal premiums are lower. Total initial and renewal commissions generally equal about one year's level premium if the original plan of insurance remains the same.

Insurance Companies also must charge for ongoing administrative and state premium tax expenses. Furthermore, they typically include an allowance for contingencies and a margin for contribution to the company's surplus or profit. Premium taxes average about 2.5 percent of the premium paid. The ongoing expenses vary by company but are reflected in their expense charges. Insurers often include allowances for contingencies and profit by grossing-up mortality charges and/or grossing-down the current interest rate from the net rate actually earned on company funds.

Insurers may recoup policy expenses and commissions in a number of ways including a flat policy assessment charge, a percentage of premium charge, a fee based on each $1,000 of face amount, or some combination of each. The trend has been towards lower policy assessment charges and level percentage of premium charges. Many insurers now charge about $25 to $50 per year plus 2.5 to 20 percent of each premium. The percentage of premium insurers charge generally is lower for higher premium, higher death benefit policies than for lower premium, lower death benefit policies.

SELECTING THE BEST OF ITS TYPE

Selecting the best cash value life insurance policy is a difficult task involving a number of complicated concepts and analyses. (See Chapter 4 for further discussion.) However, because the amount insurers credit to cash values on CAWL policies is a critical element of the overall cost of the protection, prospective insureds should put primary focus on how the company determines the amount they credit to the cash accumulation account.

The amount insurers credit to the accumulation account each year depends on four factors:

1. expenses charged against the policy;

2. mortality charges assessed against the policy;

3. net investment yield earned by the insurer on its portfolio of investments; and

4. method used to allocate interest to various blocks of policies.

The cash value at the end of any given year is equal to the cash value from the end of the prior year plus premiums (or less withdrawals) paid during the year, less the insurer's expense and mortality charges and plus the insurer's interest credits. The annual report should usually explicitly show the expense and mortality charges and the amount of interest the insurer credits each year.

Expense Charges

As described above, principally two elements comprise the expense charge: (1) a fixed annual fee, plus (2) a percentage of premiums paid. The company may or may not reveal these fees in its original policy illustration. However, even if it does, the company usually does not guarantee that the expense charges will not change. Actual expense charges may increase or decrease in future years.

Mortality Charges

A CAWL contract explicitly states the maximum mortality rates it will charge for all ages and guarantees that mortality rates will not exceed those maximums. Many companies now use the 2001 Commissioner's Standard Mortality (CSO) table as the basis for their contractually guaranteed maximum rates on newly issued policies, but some companies still use the older 1980 CSO mortality table for their new policies. In addition, all policies issued before about 2002 used the 1980 CSO mortality table or even the 1958 CSO mortality table. All three tables are very conservative—that is, they assume mortality rates that are considerably higher than what is expected—but the 1980 CSO table and, even more so, the 1958 CSO table are more conservative than the 2001 CSO table. Virtually every company currently charges less than the stated maximums, but those using the more conservative 1980 or 1958 CSO tables have even more room to increase mortality charges in future years if their mortality experience is poor.

Although annual statements explicitly show actual mortality charges, many policy illustrations do not. In fact, some illustrations assume very low or no mortality charges, which tend to show projected cash values that are overstated relative to what can actually be expected. Other illustrations include mortality charges based on rates the company is currently assessing, but they may also assume that there will be improvements in mortality experience in future years. If the mortality improvements do not materialize as anticipated, actual cash values are unlikely to match the projected cash values.

Net Investment Yield on Investment Portfolio

Over the long run, insurance companies cannot credit more interest to policy cash values than they earn on their general investment portfolios. To assess a company's long run interest crediting ability, one should evaluate the insurer's current portfolio and its investment philosophy.

As a general rule, insurance companies invest their portfolios predominantly in long-term corporate and government bonds and mortgages. However, the proportions invested in each type of asset as well as the quality, duration, yields, and risk of the particular assets differs by company. In the past, some companies were pushed to insolvency because of overly aggressive investments in high yield and high risk junk bonds and developmental mortgage loans. Therefore, potential insureds' should try to select companies with investment portfolios and investment philosophies that show a reasonable and acceptable combination of risk and return. What is reasonable and acceptable, of course, depends on the level of risk and the certainty of return desired by the policyowner.

Procedures for evaluating the investment portfolios of insurance companies are discussed in Chapter 3, "How to Determine the Right Company."

Interest Crediting Methods

All CAWL policies, just like other types of cash value policies (except variable life), have a guaranteed minimum interest rate. Historically, the guaranteed rates typically ranged from 4 to 6 percent. However, over the last decade of relatively low market interest rates, guaranteed rates on newer policies have declined. The rate insurers actually credit to cash values, called the current rate, is (or has historically been) higher than the guaranteed rate.

Companies use various methods to determine the current rate they credit to cash values. Included in a list of such methods are the:

- linked rates method;

- discretionary method;

- portfolio method;

- new money method;

- blending method;

- modified portfolio method;

- direct recognition method; and

- bonus for persistency method.

Chapters 18 through 21 dealing with various types of Universal Life Insurance, contain extended discussions of these methods.

HOW TO NAVIGATE THROUGH A CAWL LEDGER STATEMENT

The principal source of information regarding a new policy is the policy illustration or ledger. Figure 9.1 shows an annotated policy illustration with the following commentary.[4]

1. Base mandatory premium combined with a rider (similar to a paid-up additions rider for a traditional whole life policy) which accommodates additional money, resulting in an annual payment of $2,001.

2. Insurability classification for this company. Preferred means nonsmoker and not rated extra because of medical and occupational reasons.

3. Gender and issue age—male, age forty-five.

4. This is an end-of-year ledger statement.

5. Base premium of $732.94 that must be paid each and every year that the policy is in force.

6. Rider premium of $1,268.06 in addition to the mandatory base premium of $732.94. In year twenty-one and for every year thereafter,

Figure 9.1

CURRENT ASSUMPTION WHOLE LIFE Annual Premium Save Plus Rider 1 Preferred Classes 2 Male, Age 45 3						
4 Policy Year	**5** Base Premium	**6** Rider Premium	**7** Total Premium	**8** Total Death Benefit	**9** Total Accumulation Account	**10** Total Cash Value
1	$732.94	$1,268.06	$2,001.00	$103,674	$ 2,079	$ 1,298
2	732.94	1,268.06	2,001.00	107,435	4,310	3,282
3	732.94	1,268.06	2,001.00	111,317	6,441	5,359
4	732.94	1,268.06	2,001.00	115,331	8,744	7,700
5	732.94	1,268.06	2,001.00	119,490	11,237	10,300
6	732.94	1,268.06	2,001.00	123,807	13,938	13,119
7	732.94	1,268.06	2,001.00	128,297	16,862	16,078
8	732.94	1,268.06	2,001.00	132,978	20,029	19,279
9	732.94	1,268.06	2,001.00	137,867	23,456	22,740
10	732.94	1,268.06	2,001.00	142,977	27,153	26,470
11	732.94	1,268.06	2,001.00	148,325	31,136	30,522
12	732.94	1,268.06	2,001.00	153,927	35,426	34,880
13	732.94	1,268.06	2,001.00	159,797	40,038	39,561
14	732.94	1,268.06	2,001.00	165,951	44,991	44,582
15	732.94	1,268.06	2,001.00	172,404	50,299	49,958
16	732.94	1,268.06	2,001.00	179,170	55,973	55,700
17	732.94	1,268.06	2,001.00	186,305	62,081	61,877
18	732.94	1,268.06	2,001.00	193,838	68,650	68,514
19	732.94	1,268.06	2,001.00	201,800	76,707	75,639
20	732.94	1,268.06	2,001.00	210,226	83,281	83,282
21	732.94	−732.94	0.00	215,755	89,472	89,472
22	732.94	−732.94	0.00	221,679	96,098	96,098
23	732.94	−732.94	0.00	228,022	103,194	103,195
24	732.94	−732.94	0.00	234,818	110,804	110,804
25	732.94	−732.94	0.00	242,105	118,974	118,974
26	732.94	−732.94	0.00	249,924	127,739	127,740
27	732.94	−732.94	0.00	258,313	137,128	137,128
28	732.94	−732.94	0.00	267,331	147,179	147,180
29 11	732.94	−732.94	0.00	277,039	157,940	157,941
30	732.94	−732.94	0.00	287,491	169,455	169,455

$732.94 is withdrawn [minus sign (–)] from the rider to pay the base premium of $732.94.

7. Total premium is $2,001, consisting of $732.94 base premium and $1,268 paid into the rider. $2,001 is paid each year for twenty years. Starting in year twenty-one and every year thereafter, the premium outlay is zero. Base mandatory premium of $732.94 is paid by withdrawing $732.94 each year from the rider.

8. Total death benefit.

9. Accumulation account money.

10. Total cash value.

11. Life expectancy is twenty-nine years for a forty-five-year-old, or to age seventy-four.

What Ledger Statements Do Not Tell

Insurance companies or their agents should tell purchasers of life insurance, either verbally or in writing, the following additional information:

1. The investment strategy employed by the life insurance company, (e.g., pure portfolio rate, modified portfolio rate, weighted average portfolio rate, old money or new money) in order to warrant the current interest rate assumption. Although not reflected in the ledger statement of Figure 9.1, the current interest rate assumption is 10.25 percent for one year and 9.5 percent thereafter. The guaranteed rate at all times is 5.5 percent.

2. In addition to the explanation of the investment strategy employed, purchasers should receive a definitive explanation of mortality charges as to the ratio of current charges to the maximum charges that the insurer can impose.

3. Another item of importance is the interest rate on any loan against the cash value. More specifically, the company or agent should disclose how much interest the insurance company charges on the loan and how much interest the insurance company pays on the cash value equal to the amount borrowed. For this ledger statement, the rate charged for the loan is 7.41 percent in advance (most companies

charge interest in arrears) and the rate paid on the amount of cash value equal to the loan is 6 percent.

4. Another figure that company or agent should make clear is the total accumulation account value, which is the amount of money that is earning interest based on the current interest rate assumption. This amount is not, generally the amount of money that the policyowner would receive on surrender of the policy. It also is not generally the amount of money that the policyowner can borrow against.

5. In Figure 9.1, note that the total cash value includes the value of the rider plus the guaranteed reserve (cash value) of the policy. This is the amount of money that the policyowner would receive on surrender of the policy and the amount of money that the policyowner can borrow against. For balance sheet purposes, one must use this value, not the total accumulation account value. These respective values become the same in year twenty. They differ before year twenty because this policy is a twenty-year, rear-end loaded contract. Thus, the insurer imposes penalties if the policyowner terminates the policy before twenty years.

6. The insurer should give the rate of return expressed in terms of compound interest on the ledger statement or through the life insurance agent. Ideally, the insurer should provide it for each year.

7. The rate of return upon death for this policy for sequential years is as follows:

Year	Rate of Return
1	5,081.11%
5	98.20
10	34.46
20	14.10
29 (life expectancy)	9.66

8. Once one knows the rate of return upon death, one can then determine what one would have to earn before taxes (it is assumed that the death benefit is considered life insurance proceeds and as such not subject to federal or state income taxes) in other financial services products (e.g., mutual funds, certificates of deposit,

real estate, or commodities) to duplicate the tax-exempt rate of return provided by life insurance. One determines the before-tax rate of return by dividing the life insurance rate of return by the marginal tax bracket subtracted from 100 percent—for 15 percent, the factor is 0.85; for 25 percent, 0.75; for 28 percent, 0.72; for 33 percent, 0.67; and for 35 percent, 0.65. The results are shown in Figure 9.2.

9. The insurer or agent should also provide the rate of return upon surrender. When the rate of return upon surrender is positive, it means that taxes are due. Taxes are due on the difference between the cash surrender value and the premiums paid.

10. In this case, generally, the rate of return upon surrender even before taxes never equals the interest assumption of 10.25 percent for one year and 9.5 percent thereafter.

11. The ledger statement is the official ledger statement produced by the computer service of the life insurance company. It should be "bug-free." In addition, the ledger statement should contain the following information: guaranteed interest rate to be paid on the cash value, the current interest rate, mortality charges statement, interest-adjusted index, guaranteed fixed loan rate charged for loans made against the cash value, and interest paid on borrowed money.

WHERE CAN I FIND OUT MORE?

The following references include authoritative discussions of various types of life insurance including CAWL:

1. B. Baldwin, *New Life Insurance Investment Advisor: Achieving Financial Security for You and Your Family Through Today's Insurance Products*, 2nd ed. (Hightstown, NJ: McGraw-Hill Trade, 2001).

2. J. Belth, Life Insurance: *A Consumer's Handbook*, 2nd ed. (Bloomington, IN: Indiana University Press, 1985).

3. K. Black, Jr. and H. Skipper, Jr., *Life Insurance*, 13th ed. (Old Tappan, NJ: Prentice Hall Inc., 1999).

4. E. Graves, Editor, *McGill's Life Insurance*, 5th ed. (Bryn Mawr, PA: The American College, 2004).

The following references are useful guides for policy and company rating information:

1. *Best Insurance Reports* (Oldwick, NJ: A. M. Best Company, published annually).

2. *Best's Review – Life/Health Edition* (Oldwick, NJ: A. M. Best Company, published monthly).

FREQUENTLY ASKED QUESTIONS

Question – What is meant by the term, "redetermination period?"

Answer – Often insurers initially configure CAWL to resemble a traditional whole life policy with level premiums payable for life or as a limited pay policy where higher level premiums are paid for some specified period, such as ten, fifteen, or twenty years, or until age sixty-five. At the time of issue, the premium and death benefit levels are fixed, just as with traditional whole life policies. However, after a time, called the "redetermination period," the company recalculates the premium and sometimes the face amount using the same or new assumptions as to future interest and/or mortality. The redetermination period is commonly five years, but some companies redetermine premiums every three years or even annually.

Insurers need to do periodic redeterminations due to uncertainty of the value of the cash accumulation account. The insurer determines the new premium such that, together with the current cash accumulation account value, the new premium payment schedule will be able to maintain a level death benefit to the end of life under the current interest and mortality assumptions. The insurer guarantees that the premium will never exceed a certain maximum. The guaranteed maximum premium is the premium computed using the minimum interest guarantee and the maximum mortality charges stated in the contract.

If the redetermined premium is *lower* than before, the policyowner may usually choose one of three options:

Figure 9.2

BEFORE-TAX RATE OF RETURN					
Year	15% taxpayer	25% taxpayer	28% taxpayer	33% taxpayer	35% taxpayer
1	5,977.78%	6,774.81%	7,057.10%	7,583.75%	7,817.09%
5	115.53	130.93	136.39	146.57	151.08
10	40.54	45.95	47.86	51.43	53.02
20	16.59	18.80	19.58	21.04	21.69
29 (life expectancy)	11.36	12.88	13.42	14.42	14.86

1. Continue to pay premiums at the old higher level, maintain the old face amount, and add excess premiums to the cash accumulation account. This option effectively shortens the premium paying period until the policy reaches paid-up status.

2. Pay the new lower premium and maintain the old face amount.

3. Continue to pay premiums at the old higher level and use the excess premiums to pay for an increased death benefit, subject to proof of insurability.

If the redetermined premium is *higher* than before, the policyowner may usually choose one of three options:

1. Continue to pay premiums at the old lower level with the face amount reduced to the level supportable at that premium level.

2. Pay the new higher premium and maintain the old face amount.

3. Continue to pay premiums at the old lower level, maintain the old face amount, and draw down the cash accumulation account to pay the premium deficiency. To elect this option, the cash accumulation account value must exceed certain minimums necessary to sustain the policy until the next readjustment period.

When and if the policy's cash accumulation account exceeds the amount necessary to fully fund the current death benefit for life (that is, it equals or exceeds the net single premium based on current interest and mortality assumptions), the policy is very much like a traditional paid-up policy. However, it is not exactly the same as a traditional paid-up policy. The policyowner may discontinue paying premiums only for as long as the cash accumulation account continues to exceed the net single premium at each redetermination period. If the accumulation account falls below this net single premium amount, the policyowner will have to pay additional premiums to maintain the current face value or accept a reduction in the face amount of coverage. The policyowner may proceed under one of the three options described above when the redetermined premium increases.

CHAPTER ENDNOTES

1. What is otherwise considered a traditional dividend paying whole life policy may also be properly described as a type of current assumption policy if the dividend formula reflects the insurer's current mortality and expense experience as well as its current investment performance. Many participating whole life policies now use current experience for interest, mortality, and expenses in their dividend formulas. However, these policies are not what are currently known generically as current-assumption whole life policies. See Chapter 13, "Limited Pay Life," Chapter 14, "Ordinary Level Premium Whole Life Insurance," and Chapter 15, "Single Premium Life Insurance," for discussions of these traditional, yet often current assumption-type, policies.

2. I.R.C. §§7702(f)(7)(B), 7702(f)(7)(C).

3. I.R.C. §§7702(f)(7)(B), 7702(f)(7)(D). The cash value corridor test is discussed in Chapter 24, "Taxation of Benefits."

4. This analysis is adapted from the excellent discussion on this topic in *The Life Insurance Buyer's Guide*, by William D. Brownlie with Jeffrey L. Seglin, published by McGraw-Hill Publishing Company (1989).

DISABILITY INCOME INSURANCE

CHAPTER 10

INTRODUCTION

Most working Americans' greatest assets are not their homes, nor their pensions, nor even their health and fitness, it is their human capital; their ability to work and produce an income over their lifetimes. When family breadwinners die (prematurely), their families are left to fend for themselves without the breadwinners' financial support, unless of course, the families have life insurance policies on the lives of the breadwinners that will pay death benefits sufficient to replace the lost incomes.

As bad as an early death of a breadwinner may be to a family, it actually can get much worse, at least in financial terms. When breadwinners suffer serious long-term or permanent disabilities, their families not only lose their breadwinners' income streams, but also, in contrast with when the breadwinners' die, they continue to incur the direct and indirect costs of feeding, clothing, housing, and caring for (which often involves additional uninsured medical expense) the disabled breadwinner. Although the problem is less severe, even single workers must worry about how they will support themselves in the event they suffer a serious disability. Basically, disability is double-whammy risk that has led some in the insurance industry to describe such serious long-term or permanent disabilities as a living death.

Disability Income (DI) insurance is living death insurance designed to provide benefit payments (salary replacement) when the insured individual is unable to work due to a disability. Disability may result from either an injury or an illness. DI policies have an elimination period, or waiting period, until benefits commence after the insured becomes disabled. The waiting period is often ninety days, but policyowners usually can elect shorter or longer waiting periods with corresponding changes to premium charges. Insurers usually limit the benefit payments to an amount less than 100 percent of the individual's salary, typically about 60 to 65 percent of income.

Individuals may acquire their disability income benefits through a group insurance plan provided by their employer or they may purchase it as an individual policy. Although disability income policies offered by different insurers have similarities, they also differ in substantial ways from one policy to the next. Disability income policies are contracts and the provisions within may vary. Before purchasing a disability income policy, the potential policyowner should carefully review and understand the policy's provisions.

WHEN IS THE USE OF THIS DEVICE INDICATED?

Virtually all workers, whether self-employed or employed by another person or company, need access to financial resources in the event they become disabled and are unable to work for any substantial period of time. For most workers, providing for this need is one of the most critical, if not *THE* most critical, financial planning issue(s). A small percentage of workers may have access to sufficient financial resources, such as sizeable cash reserves or significant amounts of other marketable investments they can tap into without jeopardizing their own and their families' long-term financial security. Additionally, a small percentage of workers may have well-heeled parents or relatives who will be able to sustain them financially if they should become disabled. In such cases, the need for disability income insurance may not be quite as critical.

For all other workers, however, the possibility of serious long-term disability is the most serious risk they face. The financial consequences are dire and the potential consequences for the workers and their families are more severe than for any other peril they face, including the possibility of their premature deaths. Therefore, assuring disability income coverage—one way or another—is an unquestionably crucial component of every worker's risk and protection analysis. In order to perform such a risk and protection assessment, some understanding of the disability risk workers face is critical.

As most people are aware, nearly all workers with dependents feel it necessary to have life insurance so that their dependents will have sufficient financial resources to carry on in the event of the worker's premature death.

Modern medicine is doing many incredible things. Above all else, it is keeping us alive longer! These medical advances, however, do not mean we will miss fewer days of work.

The reality is quite the contrary. In a recent study of more than 2,000 severely ill patients from five medical centers around the country, the *Journal of the American Medical Association* reported that nearly a third of the families lost most of their life savings as a result of the patient's illness. The study found that although 96 percent of patients had some form of medical insurance, 31 percent still lost their savings.

"Home care and disability costs may now be more devastating to patients and their families than the costs incurred in the hospital," said the study. These expenses include the unreimbursed costs of home care, health aides, special transportation, and related medical costs. In addition, 29 percent of the families studied lost a major source of income, either because the patient no longer could work, or because another family member had to quit a job in order to care for the patient.

Likelihood of Disability

So is it more likely that a worker will die before age sixty-five, or experience a long-term disability before age sixty-five?

Figure 10.1 shows the probability of having a disability lasting at least ninety days versus dying before age sixty-five starting at various ages ranging from age

Figure 10.1

PROBABILITY OF A DISABILITY LASTING AT LEAST 90 DAYS VS. DEATH BEFORE AGE 65

| | % more likely to become disabled than to die | |
Age	Male	Female
25	32.00%	147.00%
30	31.00%	141.00%
35	32.00%	135.00%
40	32.00%	125.00%
45	32.00%	111.00%
50	33.00%	94.00%
55	32.00%	79.00%
60	9.30%	10.60%

Source: Mortality based on 2001 CSO Ultimate table (composite smoking status).

Disability based on 1985 CIDA, ninety-day elimination period, occupation class 1. Statistics vary by occupation.

Occupation Class 1: includes professional, technical and managerial occupations that are generally office duties only.

1985 CIDA is the most current morbidity table for individual disability claim incidence adopted by most State Departments of Insurance.

twenty-five through sixty for both males and females. For males ages twenty-five to fifty-five (over most of their working careers), the risk at each age of having a disability lasting at least ninety days by age sixty-five is about one-third higher than the risk of dying by age sixty-five. Stated another way, throughout most of their normal working careers, approximately four working men will experience a long-term disability by age sixty-five for every three working men who die by age sixty-five.

The risk of long-term disability versus death before age sixty-five is much higher for females than for males, ranging from about 4.5 times higher at age twenty-five to 2.5 times higher at age fifty-five. Above age fifty-five, the risks are almost identical.

The reasons for the differences between men and women are numerous, including that childbirth generally is treated as a disability and complications from childbirth can certainly extend periods out of work, sometimes far beyond ninety days. In addition, women as a whole experience lower mortality rates than men at all ages. In addition, working men, on average, perform work in more dangerous jobs than women. This means, on average, that men are exposed to a greater risk of work-related death than the average working woman. Therefore, because of the higher mortality rates for working men compared to working women, even if the average disability rates at each age were identical for men and women, the percentage of women who are more likely to become disabled versus dying by age sixty-five would be much higher.

So what *ARE* the probabilities of long-term disability for men and women?

Figure 10.2 shows the probability of a disability lasting at least ninety days before age sixty-five for men and women at various working ages ranging from twenty-five through fifty-five. For males, the disability probabilities range from about 20 percent at age twenty-five down to about 13 percent at age fifty-five. For example, an average working man age twenty-five has about a one-in-five chance (20.2 percent) of experiencing a disability lasting at least ninety days before reaching the age sixty-five. At age fifty-five, about one out of eight working men (12.6 percent) will become disabled for at least ninety days before reaching age sixty-five.

For women age twenty-five, the disability probability is about 50 percent greater than for men age twenty-five (29.9 percent vs. 20.2 percent), but this difference declines at older ages until at age fifty-five the women's disability rate is only about 7 percent more than the men's rate (13.5 percent vs. 12.6 percent). Thus, the statistics show that younger working women have significantly greater risk than similarly aged men of experiencing a disability lasting at least ninety days before they reach age sixty-five, but this additional risk tends to dissipate as working women age. By age fifty-five, the disability rates differ by just 0.9 percent.

The reasons for the disability probability differences between men and women, once again, are numerous and not altogether known, but certainly one known factor is child-bearing. As described above, however, on average, men work in environments where the risk of death and disability is higher than for the environments where, on average, women work. Therefore, one would naturally expect that disability rates for women, at least outside the child-bearing years, would be lower than for men. However, that is not what the statistics

Figure 10.2

PROBABILITY OF A DISABILITY LASTING AT LEAST 90 DAYS UP TO AGE 65		
Age	Male	Female
25	20.20%	29.90%
30	19.60%	28.60%
35	19.00%	27.00%
40	18.20%	24.80%
45	17.10%	21.80%
50	15.40%	18.10%
55	12.60%	13.50%

Source: Disability based on 1985 CIDA, ninety-day elimination period, occupation class 1. Statistics vary by occupation.

Occupation Class 1: includes professional, technical and managerial occupations that are generally office duties only.

1985 CIDA is the most current morbidity table for individual disability claim incidence adopted by most State Departments of Insurance.

reveal. Even outside the child-bearing years, women have higher disability rates than men.

The analyses so far have looked at disabilities lasting at least ninety days. Quite frankly, ninety days is on the shorter side of long-term. Most workers can probably manage to self-insure for ninety-day periods or even 180-day periods, if necessary. In fact, the standard disability income policy is designed with an elimination period or waiting period of ninety days of disability before the policy will begin to pay benefits.

The risk that workers must seriously worry about is multiyear or permanent disability. Figure 10.3 shows the probabilities for males and females of remaining disabled for two and five years after satisfying a ninety-day disability waiting period.

Figure 10.2 reveals that 20.2 percent of males (or one-in-five) experience disabilities lasting at least ninety days between ages twenty-five and sixty-five. Figure 10.3 reveals that 5.5 percent of males age twenty-five (or one-in-eighteen) will experience disabilities lasting ninety days plus two years between age twenty-five and sixty-five. Thus, for each male age twenty-five who experiences a disability lasting at

Figure 10.3

PROBABILITY OF REMINING DISABLED AFTER MEETING A 90-DAY ELIMINATION PERIOD				
	Male		Female	
Age when disabled for at least 90 days	% still disabled after 2 years	% still disabled after 5 years	% still disable after 2 years	% still disable after 5 years
25	5.51%	2.34%	7.53%	3.89%
30	6.02%	3.25%	8.07%	4.98%
35	6.61%	4.14%	8.69%	6.02%
40	7.17%	4.97%	9.15%	6.84%
45	7.61%	5.63%	9.16%	7.24%
50	7.65%	5.90%	8.54%	6.99%
55	6.88%	5.42%	7.05%	5.85%

Source: Disability based on 1985 CIDC, ninety-day elimination period, occupation class 1. Statistics vary by occupation.

Occupation Class 1: includes professional, technical and managerial occupations that are generally office duties only.

1985 CIDC is the most current morbidity table for individual disability claim incidence adopted by most State Departments of Insurance.

least ninety days before reaching age sixty-five, more than one-in-four will still be disabled two years later (5.5%/20.2% ≈ 27%).

Figure 10.3 also shows that 2.3 percent of age twenty-five males (or one-in-forty-three) will experience disabilities lasting ninety days plus five years. The 2.3 percent five-year rate is only slightly less than half of the 5.5 percent two-year rate, or about 12 percent of the 20.2 percent ninety-day rate. Thus, about three-in-seven of the males age twenty-five who experience disabilities for ninety days plus two years will still be disabled in three more years (five years and ninety days after the onset of their disabilities).

Figures 10.1 and 10.3 show that disability rates for females are higher than for males at all ages (twenty-five to fifty-five) for all disability periods lasting at least ninety days and up to five years and ninety days. However, Figure 10.3 also shows that the disability rate differentials between females and males diminish for all disability periods up to five years and ninety days at all ages from twenty-five to fifty-five.

Not surprisingly, individual disability income coverage is an especially vital concern for self-employed individuals. In the event of a disability, unless they have disability income coverage in place, self-employed

individuals probably will not receive any income with which to meet living expenses. One study has concluded that almost one-half of bankruptcies are filed due to disabling medical conditions.[1] This combined with the fact that one American in three between the ages of thirty-five and sixty-five will suffer a serious disability highlights the importance of disability income coverage.[2]

But despite this importance, many working individuals do not have disability income coverage. According to one source, only 27 percent of American income earners have disability income insurance.[3] Another source concludes that about 82 percent of American workers either have no long-term disability income insurance or believe that the coverage they do have is not sufficient.[4]

For workers who are employees, their employers may provide coverage. Other self-employed workers and business owners may purchase their own coverage. Those employees who feel that their employers are not providing a sufficient disability income benefit for their perceived needs can purchase supplemental disability income policies directly from insurers up to certain combined limits set by insurers based upon a whole host of underwriting factors such as age, income level, class of work, avocations, other health risks, etc.

Figure 10.4

LEADING CAUSES OF DISABILITY	
Musculoskeletal/Connective tissue disorders	30.1%
Nervous System related	13.9%
Cardiovascular/Circulatory System diseases	12.3%
Cancer	8.9%
Source: 2012 CDA Long Term Disability Claims Review	

So, one interesting conclusion is that the reason Americans are so much more likely to suffer a disability during their working years is exactly because they are so much less likely to die during their working years. Since 1960, the frequency of death from the four leading causes has decreased, while the frequency and durations of disability have increased. For reference, Figure 10.4 shows the leading causes of disability in the United States.

Advantages

The most obvious advantage of disability income insurance is that the policy will provide a benefit payment equal to a certain percentage of the disabled individual's income for the duration of the disability or the length of the policy's benefit period, as explained below. This benefit payment will make it easier for the disabled individual to continue to support his family and meet basic living expenses.

Also, the insured may receive the benefits all or partially tax free, as is explained further in the following section entitled "Tax Implications."

Disadvantages

If an individual does not have the benefit of an employer paying the cost of disability income coverage, the cost or premium needed to buy the coverage could be substantial. This usually will be the case with self-employed persons. Typically, the older individuals become, the less likely they are to be inclined to purchase disability income insurance. According to one study, 75 percent of Americans age eighteen to forty-four were willing to pay for disability coverage but only 56 percent of Americans between the ages of forty-five and sixty-four were willing to pay for the cost of the coverage. But it may be that the viewpoint that this type of coverage is costly is not entirely justified. According to a study conducted by an insurance company, the typical cost for disability income coverage is only about 2 percent of the individual's income.[5]

If individuals do not have the benefit of their employers paying the cost of disability income coverage, the cost or premium needed to buy the coverage could be substantial. This typically will be the case with self-employed persons. Also, disability income insurance generally does not cover any of the medical or rehabilitative costs associated with being disabled. Of course, if the individual has health insurance, this type of coverage generally will pay these costs.

Business Uses

Group disability income insurance coverage is a fairly typical benefit provided to employees by large and medium size employers as part of the benefits package. It is probably accurate to say that this is a benefit employees expect from employers, with the possible exception of smaller businesses. While employees may expect a disability income benefit, the employer does not always pay the full cost of providing this benefit. Some plans require a contribution from the employees to cover the cost of the disability benefit. Or, an employee may have to contribute to the cost in order to receive a greater level of coverage such as disability income benefit payments equal to 60 percent of his salary rather than some lesser percentage paid for by the employer.

Another type of disability insurance is used in conjunction with buy-sell agreements. If a shareholder/employee becomes disabled and, after a certain period of time, it appears that he or she will not recover from the disability sufficiently to be able to return to work, this insurance coverage provides a sum with which the disabled shareholder's interest in the business is bought out. This allows the shareholder/employee to recover the value of his interest in the business and allows the business to hire a replacement for the disabled person and move forward with its business activities.

TAX IMPLICATIONS

Disability income policies offer some income tax advantages. In summary, although individuals who pay premiums for individually-owned disability income policies generally may not deduct the premium payments from income for income tax purposes,[6] disability income benefit payments received from personally-purchased policies are exempt from income taxation.[7]

Disability Income Premium Payments

Generally, premiums paid by an individual for an individually owned disability income policy are not considered premiums paid for medical care and, thus, are not deductible from income for income tax purposes.[8]

In contrast, premiums paid by an employer for disability income policies provided to employees are deductible to the employer in the year paid.[9] This deduction is available for both individual disability income policies and group disability income policies. The reason why the rules permit employers to deduct the premiums they pay for their employees' disability coverage is that these payments are treated as part of the employees' compensation. However, this deduction for disability income premiums is available to the employer only if the benefits are payable to employees or their beneficiaries. It cannot be taken if the disability benefits are payable to the employer.[10]

Disability Income Benefit Payments

Generally, disability income benefits from personally-purchased policies are exempt from income tax. Further, there is no limit on the amount of disability income benefits that insureds can receive tax-free under personally-owned disability income policies.[11]

On the other hand, employee-insureds must fully include in their gross income and pay tax on the disability income payments they receive from disability income policies on which their employers have paid the premiums.[12] If employees receive benefits under a plan for which they have contributed some of the cost, the employees will receive the portion of the disability income attributable to the employees' contributions income-tax free.[13] But if employees choose in advance to reimburse their employers for premiums their employers pay on disability income policies, the employees are entitled to exclude any benefit payments that they receive while disabled from their reportable income.[14]

If the employer and employee share the cost of the disability income insurance, only that portion of the disability income benefits attributable to the employer's

premium payments is includable in the employee's income.

Example. Suppose the employee pays one-third of the premium and his employer pays the remaining two-thirds of the premiums. If the employee becomes disabled, one-third of the benefits received from the policy will be tax-exempt and two-thirds of the disability income benefit will be taxable.[15]

If the employer pays all the premiums but they are not excludable from the employee's gross income in the year the employer pays them, any disability income benefits the employee-insured may receive will be tax-exempt.[16]

Where benefit amounts are determined by other methods, the income taxation of benefit payments may differ. For example, benefits from a plan for injured football players where the benefit amount was determined by the number of seasons played rather than the type and severity of the injury as required were not excludable from income.[17] Furthermore, benefits determined as a percentage of disabled employees' salaries, rather than being based on the nature of their injuries, typically are not excludable from income.[18]

Tax Credit for the Elderly and the Permanently and Totally Disabled

Section 22 of the Internal Revenue Code offers an income tax credit to qualified individuals who were totally disabled when they retired. The amount of the credit is 15 percent of the taxpayer's section 22 amount.[19] Disability income is defined as the taxable amount individuals receive under their employers' plans as wages or payments in place of wages for the period they are absent from work due to disability.[20]

Qualified individuals are those who are age sixty-five or older or who are under age sixty-five, retired on disability, and considered permanently and totally disabled.[21] Permanent and total disability is the inability "to engage in any substantial gainful activity by reason of any medically determinable physical or mental impairment which qualified doctors can expect to result in death or which has lasted or doctors reasonably can expect to last for a continuous period of not less than twelve months."[22]

To determine the amount of the credit, individuals must determine their Section 22 amount for the taxable year. The credit equals 15 percent of that amount; however, because it is a nonrefundable credit, it may not exceed the taxpayer's income tax liability for the taxable year.[23]

The base Section 22 amount is $5,000 for a single taxpayer or married taxpayers filing jointly if only one spouse qualifies for the credit; $7,500 for married taxpayers filing jointly if both qualify; and $3,750 for married taxpayers filing separately.[24] The base figure (or the amount of disability income in the case of individuals under age sixty-five if that is less) is reduced dollar-for-dollar by one-half of adjusted gross income in excess of $7,500 (single taxpayer); $10,000 (joint return); or $5,000 (married filing separately).[25]

Gift, Estate, and Generation-Skipping Transfer Taxation

Basically, disability income premiums or benefit payments are not affected in any special way by the gift tax, the estate tax, and the generation-skipping transfer tax. An individual can make a gift of any amount of cash that the recipient will use to pay disability income premiums. Such a gift would be considered a present interest gift and, as such, would qualify for the gift tax annual exclusion of $14,000 in 2015. Because insurers only pay disability income benefits during the insured's life, after his or her death, nothing remains to be transferred to an heir or beneficiary.

DESIGN FEATURES – STANDARD PROVISIONS

Occupational Definitions and Applications

How the policy defines disability is a critical element of the coverage. Whether an individual policyholder will receive benefit payments is closely linked to this definition. Generally, disability income policies define disability in three ways: total disability, partial disability, and residual disability.

Total disability – The broadest definition of total disability is centered on the concept of the insured's own occupation. This is the best definition of disability from the policyholder's point of view. Under this definition of disability, insured policyholders will qualify for disability income payments if they are unable to perform the major functions of their own regular occupation.[26] In other words, if a surgeon is unable to perform surgery, the insurer will consider her disabled for purposes of this type of definition. As mentioned earlier in this chapter, this inability to perform the duties of one's occupation may arise as the result of either an injury or an illness.

Technically, an insured individual with this definition of disability could become disabled and unable to work in his own occupation, begin collecting disability benefits, return to work in another field, and still continue to collect disability benefits. In response to this possibility, some policies use a modified own-occupation definition of disability. This modified definition generally provides that insureds who become disabled and cannot work in their own occupation will receive benefits unless those individuals decide (and are able) to return to employment in another occupation.

Still other policies use a definition of total disability that changes over time. Basically this approach provides that the insurer will apply the own-occupation rule for the first few policy years that the insureds cannot work in their own occupation. Then, after this relatively short time period (two years or so, typically), the insureds will continue to receive benefits only if they are still unable to work in *any* occupation for which they are suited by education and training. Thus, if the surgeon mentioned above, could work in a research setting or a teaching setting, she might not qualify to continue receiving disability income benefits.

Partial disability – Partial disabilities are those in which the insured individuals cannot perform some of the duties of their own occupation, but can perform other duties of their own occupation. After a period of total disability—when the insureds can return to work and perform some of their duties—their policies will pay a partial disability income benefit such as 50 percent of their total disability benefit payment.

Residual disability – Some disability income policies will pay a benefit for a residual disability. These policies provide benefits based on how much income an individual has lost. Some policies simply require a loss of earnings as the result of a disability caused either by an accident or an illness. Others may require a prior period of total disability.[27]

A second type of residual disability provision comes into play in a situation where individuals are first totally disabled and then recover to the point where they can resume work but not at the same income level as before the disability. The residual disability benefit will pay the difference between the insureds' predisability income and the amount they are able to earn after their disability. This type of benefit is probably most easily understood with an example.

Example. Assume that Mr. Jones earns $8,000 per month before he becomes disabled. After six months, he is able to return to work but earns only $5,000. The residual disability benefit would pay Mr. Jones $3,000 per month, the difference between the $8,000 predisability amount and the current monthly income of $5,000.

A policy may pay residual disability benefits on a pro-rata basis according to the percentage of pre-disability earnings lost, or may pay benefits on a sliding scale based on earnings lost. For example, with a pro-rata policy, individuals with a $3,000 monthly disability benefit who lose 60 percent of their predisability earnings would receive an $1,800 monthly benefit (60 percent of $3,000). With a sliding scale policy, individuals with a loss of earnings between 20 and 50 percent might receive a 50 percent benefit. With a loss of earnings between 50 and 80 percent, they might receive a pro-rata benefit amount. With lost earnings of greater than 80 percent, they might receive 100 percent of the full disability benefit.

Recurrent disability – This definition of disability addresses when insurers deem a period of disability to have ended. Generally, if insured policyholders have been found to be totally disabled and then their condition improves to the point where they are no longer disabled, this provision says that if a new period of disability begins within (typically) six months of the end of the prior period, the insurer will deem the two periods as being one continuous period of disability. When this is the case, the insured policyholders then do not have to satisfy the elimination period again.

Underwriting Standards and Premiums

Disability insurance is priced according to several factors. The price will depend on the length of the elimination period, the maximum benefit period, age, optional riders, premium structure, occupational class, avocations, gender, state, health, level and type of coverage, and benefit amount. As a rule of thumb, individuals considering the purchase of a quality long-term disability income policy can expect to pay 1 to 3 percent of their annual income, but sometimes more, depending on a whole host of underwriting factors.

Very few people can sail through the underwriting process. It is not easy to obtain maximum coverage at competitive rates. Insurance agents specializing in disability insurance will work diligently with the underwriter to provide the best disability coverage available from the insurer. But, having said that, insurance companies will not offer coverage to just anyone because they see some people as being too risky, or as a potential "claim waiting to happen" under the disability insurance contract. Also, even if the insurer is willing to offer a contract, many conditions require the disability insurance company to limit the benefit period, extend the elimination period, add an exclusion rider, or add an additional rated premium onto the policy.

People who are thinking about getting disability insurance need to keep an open mind going into the process. Relatively few people come out of underwriting with a preferred risk discount, even if a life insurer has recently offered them a preferred-risk discount on a life policy. Life insurance and disability insurance underwriting differ in a number of significant ways.

The disability insurance company must assesses the probability of insureds becoming unable to perform the material and substantial duties of their regular occupations or professions, which is much more involved and complex than evaluating the comparably simpler and predictable odds of insureds dying in the next few years. Items such as chiropractic visits, arthritis, back problems, neck pain history, mental or nervous counseling, use of antidepressant medication, and many other conditions play a major role in disability insurance underwriting.

Benefit Period

The benefit period for a disability income policy, as with long-term care insurance, is the period of time over which the insurer will make benefit payments. The insurer will pay disability income benefits for the length of the benefit period that the owner selects when purchasing the policy, assuming the disability continues for this entire time. Generally, the shorter is the benefit period the insured selects, the lower is the premium the insured must pay for the disability income coverage.

Typically insurers offer benefit periods for disability income coverage for a certain length of time, such as one year or five years or until a certain age such as sixty-five or seventy. After this age, the disabled individual likely will be receiving retirement benefits from retirement plans and government programs such as Social Security. At one time it was possible to select a lifetime benefit period under a disability income policy, but this is not widely available today. Of course, it is best to purchase the longest benefit period that the individual can reasonably afford.

Elimination Period

The elimination period (or waiting period) is the period of time after disability begins until the disability income policy begins paying disability benefits. An individual disability income policy typically will offer the purchaser a choice of several elimination periods at the time the policy is purchased. And, as might be expected, the longer is the elimination period that the insured selects, the lower is the premium the insured must pay for the coverage.

The effect of the policy premium is one item to consider in selecting an elimination period. However, individuals should also factor in the amount of assets they have available to meet living expenses during a period of disability. If assets are sufficient to pay living expenses for sixty days but not necessarily ninety days, then sixty days may be the best elimination period to select. While companies may offer elimination periods from thirty days up to as long as two years, the most commonly selected period is ninety days.[28]

Benefit Amount

The benefit amount of a disability income policy is the amount of the benefit that insured individuals will receive each month in the event they become disabled. In arriving at the benefit amount needed, potential purchasers must determine and factor in the other sources of income that they reasonably may expect to have available during a period of disability, as well as the living and health care expenses they would most likely expect to arise. Some sources that may provide income during disability include Social Security disability payments, group disability income provided by an employer, workers' compensation, and income earned by a spouse.

Renewability

The renewability feature of a disability income policy dictates whether and at what premium rate the owner may renew the policy. This policy feature is important because the choice among the renewability provision involves critical cost-benefit tradeoffs. The three principal renewability provisions include: noncancelable; guaranteed renewable; and conditionally renewable.

Noncancelable – A noncancelable renewability provision gives policy owners the right to renew coverage at the same rate, unusually until age sixty-five. In other words, the policy owners will not see an increase in their policy premiums regardless of whether the insured has or has not made any claims under the policy. In effect, a noncancelable policy offers premiums that are guaranteed, at least to age sixty-five. As one might expect, generally insureds will have to pay higher premiums for a noncancelable policy than for a policy that is not noncancelable. Typically, if one can afford the premiums, the best policy is one that is noncancelable.[29]

Guaranteed renewable – This guaranteed renewable provision is similar to the noncancelable provision with the exception that the insurance company can increase the premium that the insured must pay for the policy. However, this feature is somewhat less adverse than it might at first seem. Insurers can increase premiums, but not on individual policies. Rather, if the insurance company wants to raise the premiums at renewals, it must increase the premiums on all policies that fall within a particular category. Consequently, the insurer cannot pick and choose among those policyowners who had had the worst experience within the class to raise the premiums, so they are only likely to increase premiums if the average claim experience throughout the whole class of insureds is poor. Consequently, prospective insureds may find that a disability income policy with the guaranteed renewable provision may prove to be not just more affordable, but also better overall on a cost-benefit basis.

Conditionally renewable – With the conditionally renewable, the insurance company imposes certain conditions that the policyholder must meet in order to be able to renew the policy. One fairly common requirement is that policyholders must be employed full-time in order to renew coverage. Also, unlike the noncancelable provision, the insurance company may raise rates at renewal dates under this type of plan.

Riders

As with life insurance policies, disability income policies may offer additional and optional benefits that owner-insureds can add to their base policies by purchasing riders:

- *Waiver of premium* – The waiver of premium provision or rider allows policyholders to stop paying premiums once they begin to receive disability income benefits. Thus, the policy will continue in force during a period of disability.

- *Automatic benefit increases* – This provision is similar to the inflation protection provision in a long-term care insurance policy. Basically, this provision automatically increases the benefit payable under the policy by a certain percentage each year. The percentage is usually based on the Consumer Price Index (CPI).

- *Partial Disabilities and Residual Riders* – Designed to address the fact that recovering from a disability is a gradual process, these riders pay partial disability benefits during the time that an individual returns to work on a part-time basis.

- *Pension Contributions and Retirement Protection Riders* – These recently-developed types of riders ensure that an individual's retirement plans continue to receive contributions during a period of disability.

OTHER TYPES OF DISABILITY POLICIES

Short-term Disability Insurance

Short-term disability insurance generally is an employer-sponsored group plan. It pays a specified percentage of disabled employees' salaries for a specified amount of time if they become ill or injured and cannot perform the duties of their job. Benefit payments usually commence anywhere from one to fourteen days after employees suffer a condition that leaves them unable to work. Many times, the plan requires employees to use up sick days before short-term disability kicks in, if

they have an illness that keeps them out of work for an extended period of time. This provision is why the plan usually has a different policy for short-term disability caused by sickness versus injury.

Sometimes the employer pays the premiums, sometimes employees pay the premiums, and sometimes the employer and the employees split the cost of premiums for a short-term disability policy. More often, though, short-term disability coverage is employer-paid. Companies do have a choice of having employees pay in whole or in part for coverage, with certain tax implications.

Basically, group coverage for short-term disability can be attained in two ways:

1. contract agreement through an insurer that covers disability;

2. through a self-funded plan set aside by the employer directly.

Employers can create a policy dictating that employees must use up sick days before going on short-term disability for an extended illness. They frequently also require documentation from a doctor to prove an illness or injury.

Different short-term disability plans dictate different terms for qualifications. The main terms are listed below:

- Employees need to work for the employer for a certain amount of time before coverage kicks in.

- Employees need to work full time or near full time, usually thirty hours or more per week.

- The following features are part of what a short-term disability plan benefits package may include:

  - percentage of weekly salary paid out (typically between 50 and 70 percent of weekly salary);

  - duration of short-term disability benefits (typically between ten and twenty-six weeks);

  - maximum amount of time covered under this disability program.

While most states do not require employers to provide short-term disability benefits, some states, such as Hawaii, New Jersey, New York, and Rhode Island mandate that companies above a certain size (in employment) provide short-term disability benefits for up to twenty-six weeks.

Supplemental Disability Income Insurance

Group long-term disability insurance typically covers around 60 percent of base salary to a monthly maximum benefit of $5,000 or $10,000. The actual policy definitions typically are more restrictive than the definitions in an individual disability insurance plan, and if the employees' company is making the premium payments for the employees, then the benefits are taxable during a claim. In many cases, after subtracting taxes, the net benefit might be 45 to 50 percent (60 percent minus taxes) of the disabled employees' incomes, with restrictive provisions and definitions. In addition, such insurance plans usually are not portable—the plan does not permit employees to take their disability income coverage to another employer. For many employees this arrangement is not optimal, either in terms of the amount of coverage or in the flexibility of the plan. This is where supplemental disability insurance can help fill the employees' needs.

A supplemental disability insurance policy can increase the percentage replacement of income up from the actual 45 to 50 percent (60 percent minus taxes during the claim), can guarantee the ability to have portable disability insurance, and can likely one more comprehensive disability coverage.

Many group long-term disability insurance plans have very restrictive definitions that define when an employee gets paid for a disability claim. Typically the policy defines disability in terms of one's own-occupation for only the first two years in a claim, then it changes to a gainful occupation definition of total disability. Usually, group LTD policies also have a limited partial disability benefit and, generally, do not offer any inflation protection as well.

Insurers offer supplemental disability insurance policies that can have a more comprehensive definition of total disability, a significantly better residual disability rider, and can also help protect against inflation with the addition of an optional Cost of Living Adjustment Rider (for extra premiums).

Remember, people sometimes make a huge mistake thinking that they will always be insurable. This type of insurance is not something that is easy for anyone to get. Without even realizing it, many people may be unable to obtain a supplemental disability insurance policy even now. The insurer will review detailed medical records to make sure applicants do not already have a potential disability. Even people who are perfectly healthy now, have no assurance that they will be healthy a year from now. They could develop back problems, diabetes, a heart condition, or some other condition that prevents them from getting a policy or complete coverage. By purchasing a supplemental disability insurance policy people can guarantee themselves they will always have income protection no matter how much money they earn, what company they work for, or what medical condition they develop in the future.

Business Overhead Expense Disability Insurance

Insurers designed business overhead expense disability insurance with the cash-flow needs of (generally small- to medium-sized closely-held) business owners in mind. If business owners should become disabled, business overhead expense disability insurance will help them keep their businesses strong by covering the normal, necessary and customary expenses incurred to run their businesses—including such things as mortgage payments or rent, utilities, salaries, taxes, interest on debt, loan payments and more.

There are several tax advantages of overhead expense disability insurance. First, premium payments are tax-deductible as ordinary and necessary business expenses. Also, overhead expense benefits received during a period of disability are taxable upon receipt: however, they are used to pay business-related expenses that are tax-deductible, so the net tax impact is neutral.

Business overhead expense disability insurance is a complicated product, so business owners should take great care to figure out what expenses they need to have covered. Generally, they should not buy overhead expense insurance for their total monthly overhead. For instance, if the business's monthly overhead is $25,000, the business owner should determine which of these fixed expenses would continue in the event of his disability. Business owners should take time to review their Schedule C's and/or cash-flow statements to find the expenses that would indeed stop or diminish in the event of the business owner's disability. To keep the costs within reason, business owners should make sure they only purchase an amount they truly need during a disability. The selling agents and underwriters typically will make recommendations on monthly benefits during the underwriting process.

ALTERNATIVES

Alternatives to disability income coverage include self-insuring against the possibility of a disability, purchasing a life insurance policy with a waiver of premium benefit or rider, purchasing critical illness insurance, and being able to qualify to receive Social Security disability income payments.

The only real alternative to disability income coverage is to self-insure against the possibility that an individual will become disabled and unable to work. Any financing vehicle that allows individuals to withdraw funds as needed and without significant tax penalties or surrender charges is an appropriate place to put the funds that individuals may use to provide an income in the event of a disability.

Another alternative that may provide some assistance during a period of disability is a life insurance policy with a waiver of premium benefit or rider. In the event of a permanent disability, this benefit will pay the premiums due on the life insurance policy. Not only is this a financial benefit in that the disabled policyholder does not have to pay the premiums, it is also a benefit in that it keeps the policy in force. A disabled policyholder may find that he or she is unable to purchase additional life insurance after becoming disabled.

Another possible alternative to disability income insurance is critical illness insurance. This type of insurance pays a lump sum benefit to the insured individual upon the diagnosis of a covered critical illness. Most policies of this type cover a number of different critical illnesses including strokes, heart attacks, certain cancers, kidney failure, and Alzheimer's disease.

Finally, a disabled individual may qualify to receive disability payments from Social Security. The definition of disability the government uses is a quite conservative one which requires the individual to have a serious and expected long-term or permanent disability to qualify for benefits. Generally, for purposes of receiving social security disability income benefits, the individual must be unable to engage in any substantial gainful activity by reason of a mental or physical disability. The disability must be expected to end in death or to last for a period of at least twelve months. In other words, to receive disability income benefits from Social Security, individuals must be disabled to such a degree that they cannot work at any job, not just be unable to work at their previous job or profession.

WHERE CAN I FIND OUT MORE ABOUT IT?

1. *Tax Facts on Insurance & Employee Benefits* (Cincinnati, OH: The National Underwriter Company, published 2015).

2. Jeff Sadler, *How to Sell Disability Income Insurance* (Cincinnati, OH: The National Underwriter Company, 2005).

3. *Social Security and Medicare Facts* (Cincinnati, OH: The National Underwriter Company, published 2015).

FREQUENTLY ASKED QUESTIONS

Question – What definition of disability does the government use to determine one's eligibility for disability benefits under Social Security?

Answer – Disability for Social Security purposes is defined as the inability to engage in any substantial gainful activity by reason of any medically determinable physical or mental impairment that can be expected to result in death or can be expected to last for a period of at least twelve months or longer. This is a fairly difficult definition to meet because it requires that disabled individuals be so severely disabled that they not only be unable to work at their previous occupations or professions but be unable to engage in any kind of gainful employment at all.

Question – What is the regular care and attendance of a physician requirement?

Answer – Generally, an element of meeting the definition of disability under a disability income policy is that the insured person must be under the care of a qualified physician in order to continue to receive disability income benefit payments.

Question – Are disability income benefit payments subject to FICA and FUTA tax?

Answer – Payments made to disabled employees by either an employer or an insurer are subject to social security tax (FICA) and federal unemployment tax (FUTA) for the first six months after the last month in which the employees worked for their employers. After six months, such payments are exempt from social security and federal unemployment tax.[30] However, if the employees contributed to the plans that pay the benefit payments, the portion of such payments attributable to the employees' contributions is not subject to social security tax.[31]

Question – Are disability income benefit payments subject to income tax withholding?

Answer – While the tax laws generally require employers to withhold income tax from disability income benefit payments, the tax rules do not require withholding on benefit payment amounts that the employees can excluded from their income. Further, if an insurance company or other entity under an accident or health plan makes the disability benefit payments, the tax rules require no withholding of income tax.[32]

Question – How is a disability income benefit received under a life insurance policy treated for income tax purposes?

Answer – When policyowners receive disability income benefits under a disability rider attached to a life insurance policy, the tax rules treat the amounts as separate accident or health benefits and not as proceeds from the life insurance policy. Thus, such benefit payments are excludable from income as "amounts received through accident or health insurance… for personal injury or sickness."[33]

Question – What is disability buy-out insurance?

Answer – Disability buy-out insurance is designed to provide coverage funds to buy out the disabled individual's interest in a business upon the total and permanent disability of a shareholder or partner.

Because of the many factors involved as well as the increased potential for adverse selection and moral hazard, insurers underwrite these policies very tightly and require the businesses and the key employee-owners to meet stringent business, financial, and personal standards before they will permit a business to purchase this type of coverage. For example, insurers typically require a company to have been in business for a certain amount of time, to have consistent profits and revenues, and stable and strong management before they will issue a disability buy-out insurance policy.

Question – Do any insurance companies offer temporary disability insurance?

Answer – The authors are not aware of any companies that offer temporary disability insurance. Upon reflection, at least one reason such insurance plans are rare or nonexistent seems pretty obvious. With health insurance coverage, such as when people are between jobs, or even one-year or other shorter-term life insurance policies (which are typically renewable and convertible into long-term permanent policies), the risks to the insurer can be high, but manageable and predictable, with the potential for temporary buyers to become purchasers of long-term continuing coverage policies.

With a temporary disability plan, the policy would remain in force for only a temporary period, say until the prospective insured's employer establishes a LTD plan in the coming year. So the insured would be planning to keep the policy in force and pay premiums only for a year or so. However, with disability income insurance the risk generally is extremely long term, because a disability occurring during the temporary, premium-paying period while the policy is in force could involve the insurer having to make benefit payments replacing 50 percent, 60 percent, or more of the insured's earnings for many years, until the insured reaches age sixty-five, usually. It would be hard for the insurer to even design a plan with low enough premiums to make a temporary plan feasible.

However, a few insurers (Guardian, for example) offer a slightly different product, called a short-term disability program, in most cases involving group disability insurance sponsored by employers. More insurers also offer what is called supplemental disability insurance which is designed to be an additional tier of coverage on top of a primary disability income policy, which the employer usually provides.

CHAPTER ENDNOTES

1. A Harvard University study referred to in "Crafting Disability Income Plans for the Small Business Market," by Angie Makkyla,

The National Underwriter, Life and Financial Services ed., September 18, 2006.

2. An American Council of Life Insurers study referred to in "Crafting Disability Income Plans for the Small Business Market," by Angie Makkyla, *The National Underwriter*, Life and Financial Services ed., September 18, 2006.

3. Department of Labor statistics referred to in "The Once-Huge Throng of DI Providers has Evaporated," by W. Harold Petersen, *The National Underwriter*, Life and Financial Services ed., March 1, 2004, p. 14.

4. Survey completed by the Consumer Federation of America and the American Council of Life Insurance, cited in "Consumer, Insurer Groups Work to Inform Americans About Disability Income Insurance," *The National Underwriter*, NU Online News Service, April 23, 2001.

5. Allison Bell, "Boomers Shy Away from Paying for Income Protection," The National Underwriter Company, Life and Financial Services ed., November 27, 2006.

6. I.R.C. §213(d)(1).

7. I.R.C. §104(a)(3).

8. I.R.C. §213(d)(1).

9. Treas. Reg. §1.162-10(a).

10. Treas. Reg. §1.162-10(a); Rev. Rul. 58-90, 1958-1 CB 88; Rev. Rul. 56-632, 1956-2 CB 101.

11. I.R.C. §104(a)(3).

12. *Cash v. Comm'r.*, TC Memo 1994-166. See also *Crandall v. Comm'r.*, TC Memo 1996-463.

13. Treas. Reg. §1.105-1(c).

14. See I.R.C. §104(a)(3); *Bouquett v. Comm'r.*, TC Memo 1994-212.

15. I.R.C. §104(a)(3).

16. I.R.C. §104(a)(3).

17. See I.R.C. §105(c)(2); *Beisler v. Comm'r.*, 814 F.2d 1304 (9th Cir. 1987).

18. *Colton v. Comm'r.*, TC Memo 1995-275; *Charles Webster v. Comm'r.*, 94-2 USTC ¶50,586 (M.D. Tenn. 1994).

19. I.R.C. §22(b).

20. I.R.C. §22(c)(2)(B)(iii).

21. I.R.C. §22(b).

22. I.R.C. §22(e).

23. I.R.C. §22(a).

24. I.R.C. §22(c)(2)(A), 22(e)(1).

25. I.R.C. §22(d).

26. Jeff Sadler, *Disability Income: The Sale, The Product, The Market*, 2nd ed. (Cincinnati, OH: The National Underwriter Company, 1995), p. 105.

27. Jeff Sadler, *Disability Income: The Sale, The Product, The Market*, 2nd ed. (Cincinnati, OH: The National Underwriter Company, 1995), p. 106.

28. Jeff Sadler, *Disability Income: The Sale, The Product, The Market*, 2nd ed. (Cincinnati, OH: The National Underwriter Company, 1995), p. 30.

29. Marcia Little, "Replacing Existing DI: What You Should Know," *The National Underwriter*, Life and Financial Services ed., March 1, 2004, p. 19.

30. I.R.C. §§3121(a)(4), 3306(b)(4).

31. See I.R.C. §6051(f)(2)(B); Treas. Reg. §31.6051-3(b)(4).

32. Treas. Reg. §31.3401(a)-1(b)(8); Rev. Rul. 77-89, 1977-1 CB 300.

33. I.R.C. §104(a)(3).

GROUP LIFE INSURANCE

CHAPTER 11

INTRODUCTION

Group life insurance, as its name implies, provides insurance for a group—typically, but not necessarily, ten or more employees—under a master contract between the insurer and the employer. Technically, the insured individuals are not part of that contract. Planners should note that almost 40 percent of all life insurance in force in this country is issued on a group basis.

Group insurance is almost always issued as yearly renewable (one-year) term insurance. This means that the coverage expires at the end of each year but is renewed automatically without a medical examination and without further evidence of insurability. The premium rate per $1,000 of protection increases from year to year. Death benefits are paid upon the insured's death from any cause.

WHEN IS THE USE OF THIS DEVICE INDICATED?

1. When an employer wants a means of acquiring an employee benefit that most employees appreciate, and even expect.

2. When insurance is difficult to obtain at standard rates because a key employee has a health condition or a dangerous avocation.

3. When an employer would like to provide life insurance protection in amounts up to $50,000 in a cost effective manner for shareholder-employees as well as others.

Advantages

1. Helps to satisfy an employer's moral obligation to the dependents of employees.

2. Contributes to employee morale and productivity.

3. Provides a before-tax benefit to employees that they otherwise would have to pay for with personal after-tax dollars.

4. Is expected in most firms as part of the employee benefit package. Its absence would put an employer at a competitive disadvantage in hiring and retaining employees.

5. Costs less for the employee than an individual policy, even though the plan may be contributory. From the employee's perspective, group life insurance (especially with respect to the first $50,000) is a bargain since, in most cases the employer pays all or most of the premium.

6. Provides insurance for those who otherwise might be uninsurable and provides insurance at standard rates for those who might be insurable only at an increased premium.

7. Through the conversion privilege, enables terminated employees to convert to individual policies without submitting evidence of insurability.

8. Forms a base on which an employee can build a personal financial program.

9. Allows an employer to deduct the premiums for group life insurance.

Disadvantages

1. Group life insurance is temporary in nature—it runs out, or is significantly reduced at the very time it is

needed by most clients. This drop-off particularly impacts wealthy clients with high postretirement living standards.

2. The Table I cost (reportable income for tax purposes as discussed below) increases significantly as insured individuals grow older. Ironically, in the postretirement years when medical and other expenses are high but income is low, the reportable income from group term life—and, therefore, the tax payable—is highest.

3. Because group life insurance is a welfare benefit plan, it is subject to certain ERISA (Employee Retirement Income Security Act) limitations and requirements, including certain reporting obligations.

4. The employer must provide group life insurance coverage for a number of employees. This may increase the employer's cost significantly over nondeductible plans that allow the employer to pick and choose who the plan will cover, and on what terms.

5. The employer's out-of-pocket cost can skyrocket if no new employees enter the plan. This is due to the yearly renewable term aspect of group insurance. As the pool of employees grows older, the average age increases and, consequently, premiums also increase. This problem is particularly acute in professional corporations with little employee turnover.

6. A group term life plan cannot cover shareholders who are not employees. Further, the employer flexibility is limited in picking and choosing who the plan will cover, the amount of coverage, or the terms and conditions of coverage. This is because the plan must include certain design features in order to ensure that it meets certain tax law requirements listed in Section 79 of the Internal Revenue Code.

7. Employees have no guarantee that the employer will continue group coverage because a group policy is a contract solely between the employer and the insurer. Therefore, the employer may discontinue or change the plan without employee approval. Furthermore, retired employees may lose postretirement coverage if an employer files for bankruptcy.

8. When an employer terminates an employee or the employee leaves the employer, the employee loses the group insurance protection. Although a conversion option usually is available, relatively few

persons ever execute this privilege because of the high premiums at the attained age. Furthermore, if many employees did, in fact, exercise the right to convert, group insurance would become highly expensive for the employer because the insurance company typically imposes a conversion charge on the employer when an employee chooses to exercise the conversion feature.

9. By design and formula, group protection generally ceases, or is significantly reduced, at retirement.

10. Employees may be lulled into complacency, being under the misconception that the group term provided by their employer provides adequate benefits and, therefore, not utilize the services of a professional insurance agent. Adequacy of coverage does not necessarily equate to the proper arrangement or ownership, nor does group term provide the collateral planning advice found only through competent financial services professionals.

WHAT ARE THE REQUIREMENTS?

ERISA

The Employee Retirement Income Security Act (ERISA) requires that any employee benefit plan (including group life insurance) meet certain requirements.[1] Among these requirements are that the plan must be established and maintained in writing, plan documents must provide for one or more named fiduciaries who administer the plan, and the plan document must provide a procedure for amending the plan and specify the basis on which payments are to be made to and from the plan. Additionally, the plan must provide a claims review procedure.

IRC Section 79

A group term life plan must meet the following requirements under Code section 79. Life insurance can provide permanent protection as well as term and still receive the favorable tax treatment afforded to group term if certain requirements are met. Such insurance has come to be called "Section 79" insurance.

The requirements that must be met are:

- the policy itself, or the employer under a separate document, must state the portion of the death benefit that is group term coverage; and

- the portion of the death benefit generated by the group term life portion of the coverage must not be less than the difference between the total death benefit provided under the policy and the employee's deemed death benefit at the end of the policy year.[2]

A Section 79 plan is one designed to solve some of the problems inherent in any term vehicle and yet retain some of the cost advantages of group coverage. Group term insurance builds no cash values to keep premiums paid after the covered employee retires. Furthermore, there are no paid-up policy values to carry the coverage into the postretirement period. So generally, when the employee retires, the coverage terminates (although some employers provide a reduced amount of coverage).

The Section 79 plan employs a permanent product designed to provide tax-favored, postretirement insurance coverage. Specifically, it is group life insurance that provides a combination of both term and permanent insurance under a master contract, under separate policies, or under a combination of the two. Alternatively, a Section 79 plan may be superimposed on an existing plan of group term life insurance that covers more than ten employees.

Additional requirements include the following:[3]

- The plan must provide a death benefit that meets the definition of a life insurance contract.

- The plan's benefits must be provided to a group of employees as compensation for services.

- Benefits must be provided under a policy carried directly or indirectly by the employer.

- The amount of insurance provided to each employee must be computed under a formula that precludes individual selection.

Nondiscrimination Rules

To satisfy nondiscrimination rules, a group insurance plan must not discriminate in favor of key employees in terms of eligibility to participate; and benefits provided.[4]

To meet *eligibility* nondiscrimination rules, a plan must meet at least one of the following three tests:

1. the plan benefits 70 percent or more of all of the employer's employees; or

2. at least 85 percent of plan participants are not key employees; or

3. the plan benefits employees under an employer-specified classification that is approved by the IRS as nondiscriminatory.

To meet *benefit* nondiscrimination rules, a plan must provide all participants with benefits at least as great as those provided to key employees. It is permissible, under this rule, to base benefits on a uniform percentage of compensation.

If a plan discriminates in favor of key employees, either as to eligibility or with respect to the kind or amount of benefits, the cost of the entire amount of life insurance coverage becomes taxable to key employees. Thus, the exclusion for the cost of the first $50,000 of coverage is lost.[5]

If a plan is discriminatory, key employees (and only key employees) must include as taxable income the higher of: (a) the actual cost; or (b) the Table I cost of all insurance provided on their behalf.

A key employee is defined as a person who, during the plan year or any one of the four preceding plan years, was:

- an officer whose compensation exceeds a certain limitation;[6] or

- an employee owning both more than a ½ percent interest and one of the ten largest interests in the employer; or

- a more-than-5 percent owner of the employer firm; or

- a more-than-1 percent owner of the employer receiving compensation of $150,000 or more.

If a person is a key employee at retirement, that person remains a key employee indefinitely.[7]

HOW IT IS DONE

Master Policy

The only contract issued in a group term life plan is between the employer and the insurer. This is called the master policy and it is the only contract required regardless of how many employees are covered by the plan. The master policy states the contractual relationship between the policyholder (the employer) and the insurance company.

Each employee, the individual insured, is issued a certificate that provides essential information such as who is covered, when the coverage takes effect, how long it lasts, the amount of insurance provided, the claims procedures, etc. Typically, the certificates are included in the announcement booklet distributed to the insureds at the time that a group insurance plan is installed.

The master contract will usually provide that the insurer cannot refuse to renew the contract as long as the employer wishes to continue coverage and pays premiums. (However, it is true that the insurer may increase premium rates to the point where, for all practical purposes, the right to renew is not of any value.) The insurer will also provide that, in the master contract, if the number of employees drops below a specified amount (e.g., ten employees), the plan may be canceled.

Typical clauses found in master contracts also include:

- *Adjustment in premiums clause* – If an employee's age is overstated, the employer will receive a refund. If the age is understated, there is no change in coverage, but the employer must make up the difference in premiums.

- *Incontestability clause* – The policy is incontestable, except for fraud.

- *Grace period* – Coverage continues for thirty-one days after the premium is due.

- *Claims limitation* – The death benefit claim must be made within one year of the last premium paid for a deceased employee.

Coverage

Employees are required to meet certain requirements before their coverage becomes effective. For instance, an employee must be actively at work on the date he or she becomes eligible for initial coverage or for subsequent increases in benefits.

Once the group insurance is in effect, new employees must satisfy a probationary period before they can enroll. This typically runs thirty to ninety days. From the time the probationary period has been satisfied, employees have thirty-one days to enroll. If an employee does not sign up during the enrollment period, generally he must submit evidence of insurability when applying at a later date.

Benefits

A benefit schedule is a predetermined statement of the formula under which benefits will be provided. Benefit schedules generally base coverage amounts on:

1. *Earnings* – Proponents of an earnings basis schedule point out that this type of formula benefits survivors by providing an amount equal to full salary for a limited time after death and because it is tied to salary, will tend to increase with inflation. More productive employees who presumably are paid more are rewarded appropriately and if the plan requires contributions, cost is directly related to the employee's ability to pay.

2. *Occupational classifications* – Uniform amounts of coverage are provided within each classification. The advantage of this type of formula is that it is easy to administer and is somewhat related to the employee's survivors' needs, the employer's assessment of the employee's worth to the business, and the employee's ability to pay in the case of a contributory plan.

3. *Flat benefit* – This type of schedule provides a flat benefit amount for all participants. Giving everyone the same benefit is, of course, the easiest formula to administer and to the extent wage rates within the group are relatively uniform, coverage bears a close relationship to needs and abilities to pay. This is obviously not the correct formula to use in a multilevel business, but would be appropriate for very large multiple-employer groups providing coverage under collective bargaining agreements.

4. *Length of service* – This formula rewards long term employees (some call this rewarding loyalty) and may tend to decrease an employee's incentive to leave the firm. In reality, few employees would stay with a firm merely because of the group coverage or its formula, and the insurance coverage provided to employees under this method bears no relationship to their needs or ability to pay in the case of contributory coverage.

5. *A combination of these factors* – The most common formula bases the amount of insurance on a multiple of the employee's income—from one to three times earnings. Most insurers require a minimum of $5,000 on each covered employee or even $10,000 in the case of smaller groups. Some insurers require a minimum coverage for the entire group. Maximum coverage depends on the total volume of the group and state law ceilings, if any. Most companies will issue up to $500,000 or more on a given life although to protect themselves for ultra large amounts, group insurers use medical examinations, reinsure at least a portion of the coverage, and sometimes establish special reserves.

Disability Coverage

Typically, group master contracts will contain provisions for the protection of disabled employees. Two of these provisions are "waiver of premium" and "maturity value benefit." The waiver of premium provision, as its name implies, relieves the employer of the requirement of paying premiums for any covered employee who becomes totally and continuously disabled prior to a specified age. (Age sixty is common.) The maturity value benefit provides for the payment of the face amount of an employee's group life insurance in a lump sum or in monthly installments when an employee becomes totally and permanently disabled prior to age sixty. This provision is much less commonly used than the waiver of premium feature.

Reduction Formulas

The master contract will often contain a reduction formula. This provision reduces the coverage of those insureds who reach a certain age (age seventy is typical). Age discrimination laws (such as the Age Discrimination in Employment Act—ADEA) have slowed down the reduction so that a common clause might provide that, "Benefits reduce to 65 percent of original amount at age seventy and 50 percent of original amount at age seventy-five."

Beneficiaries

Each covered employee has absolute freedom to name any beneficiary she wants, although some states prohibit the naming of the employer as a beneficiary. Also, the employee may change the beneficiary as often as she wants. If the named beneficiary does not survive the insured, and there is no secondary beneficiary named, the death benefit will be paid to the estate of the covered employee or to a successive beneficiary specified in the master contract. In other words, the master contract may give the insurer the option of paying the proceeds to one or more of the following survivors: spouse; parents; children; brothers and sisters; or the estate's executor.

A facility of payment clause in the master contract allows the insurer to pay part of the proceeds (typically up to $500) to any person who has incurred funeral or last illness expenses for the covered employee (even though the named beneficiary may still be alive). Furthermore, the facility of payment clause may allow the insurer to make payments on behalf of a minor beneficiary or legal incompetent to a relative assumed to have "custody and principal support" of the beneficiary until a guardian is appointed.

The recipient of the proceeds can elect an optional method of settlement in place of a lump sum. (See Chapter 5 for a discussion of settlement options.)

Experience Rating

Insurance companies renew group term life year by year and may adjust premiums up or down at that time or guarantee an upper limit for a specific period of time (e.g., for two or three years). Experience rating means that premiums (and/or dividends) in the future are based at least in part on the number of deaths and administrative costs in administering the specific employer's actual group rather than by the experience of a larger pool of employers. Experience rating should be considered where the group is large, the employees covered in the group are young, and a steady number of young healthy individuals come into the plan, leading to below average claims.

Competition for group sales may have some effect on the size of employer that is experience rated and the amount of the ratings. Group term premiums are recalculated annually and based on the average age of the group, which is then adjusted for the aggregate experience. Usually, experience ratings are based on claims and expense experience of groups of 200 or more employees. Premiums of smaller employers will typically be based on the experience of a large pool of employers covered by similar master contracts. In a pooled rate situation, a uniform rate is applied to all the groups in the pool.

Termination

When an employee is terminated or retires, a legal right (subject to certain conditions) called a conversion privilege comes into play. This conversion privilege allows the employee to convert what was group term life insurance into individual protection through the issuance of a personal contract.

When an employee quits or is fired or the employee continues working but the master contract is terminated, he generally has thirty-one days in which to apply for a converted policy without submitting evidence of insurability. That new individual policy may be any of the insurer's permanent life policies in an amount up to but not exceeding the term coverage. The insurer is not allowed to apply a rating (an extra premium charge for impaired health or avocation), and must issue the policy at its standard premium. The premium will be at the insured's attained-age (nearest birthday) rates for up to a specified maximum face amount.

If an employee is laid off, granted a leave of absence, or is disabled for a short period of time, at the employer's discretion, (but on a nondiscriminatory basis) coverage can be continued for some limited period of time (e.g., six months), but the individual employee will be responsible for payment of the premiums. Coverage will be terminated at the end of that continuation period. At that point, the insured has the right to the extension of benefits as well as the right to convert the term coverage to a permanent individual policy.

EMPLOYEE TAX IMPLICATIONS

An employee does not have to report any income with respect to the first $50,000 of life insurance coverage provided by the group plan. Although term insurance protection provided by an employer to an employee is income tax-free for amounts of insurance up to $50,000, an employee must report and pay income tax on the economic benefit (i.e., the term insurance cost) of coverage in excess of $50,000.[8]

The amount reportable is computed by multiplying the Table I rates shown in Figure 11.1 by the amount of coverage in excess of $50,000. To determine the total annual economic benefit received and reportable by the employee, one must add these monthly rates/amounts together for each month of the year in which the employee is covered.

For purposes of Table I, the age of the employee is the employee's attained age on the last day of the employee's taxable year.

In the case of a contributory plan (i.e., the employee pays a portion of each month's premium), the employee may reduce the reportable amount by the amount the employee has paid.[9]

Figure 11.1

TABLE I. UNIFORM PREMIUMS FOR $1,000 OF GROUP TERM LIFE INSURANCE PROTECTION	
Rates Applicable to Cost of Group Term Life Insurance	
5-Year Age Bracket	Cost per $1,000 of Protection for One-Month Period
Under 25	$0.05
25 to 29	0.06
30 to 34	0.08
35 to 39	0.09
40 to 44	0.10
45 to 49	0.15
50 to 54	0.23
55 to 59	0.43
60 to 64	0.66
65 to 69	1.27
70 and above	2.06

The steps in the computation process are:

1. Find the total amount of group term life insurance coverage in each calendar month of the taxable year. (If the employee was covered with different amounts of group term life during the coverage period, average the amount payable at the beginning and the end of the period to find the proceeds payable.)

2. Subtract $50,000 from each month's coverage.

3. Apply the appropriate rate from Table I.

4. From the sum of the monthly costs, subtract total employee contributions for the year. (The employee's contributions can be allocated entirely to the cost of the excess coverage over $50,000 to reduce or eliminate current tax cost to the employee. However, any unused portion of the employee's contributions may not be carried over into later years.)

Example. Your client is age fifty-six, and her employer provides her with $150,000 of group term life insurance. She makes no contribution to the coverage. The excess amount over $50,000 is $100,000. The monthly rate, $0.43 per $1,000, is multiplied by 100 (000) to arrive at $43 per month. If she was covered for twelve months, the yearly income reportable by her would be $516. Had she made a contribution of $200, her taxable economic benefit would be reduced to $316.

It is obvious that Table I costs will increase dramatically once the client reaches his early sixtiess. Group coverage at retirement, if it is still available, becomes extremely expensive in terms of reportable income. This problem is particularly acute with respect to shareholder-employees with group life insurance significantly in excess of $50,000.

The economic benefit generated by coverage in excess of $50,000 will *not* be taxed to the employee to the extent:

*   the employer is the beneficiary;

*   a qualified charity is the sole beneficiary for the entire period for which the cost otherwise would be taxed to the employee; or

*   the employee has terminated employment with the employer because of disability.[10]

None of the $50,000 exclusion is available for group term insurance provided through a Code section 401(a) qualified retirement plan, such as a pension, profit sharing, stock bonus, or qualified annuity plan.[11] Generally, this means the employer premium for the entire amount of protection afforded with employer contributions is taxable to the covered employee. Table I rates may not be used.

The amounts reportable as income by the employee are also treated as additional salary for purposes of FICA and FUTA.[12] State unemployment and workers' compensation taxes may also apply in some states.

A beneficiary of group life insurance receives the death benefit income tax-free.[13]

Gift and Estate Tax

Proceeds of group term life insurance are includable in the insured's estate if they are payable to or for the benefit of the insured's estate, or if at death the insured holds any incident of ownership regardless of who is named as beneficiary.[14] Incidents of ownership include the right to change the beneficiary and the right to assign the policy or revoke an assignment. The proceeds of group term life may be removed from an employee's estate if certain requirements are met.[15]

A gift is made from the covered employee to the assignee when an absolute assignment is made of the employee's rights under group term insurance.[16] A further series of gifts is made by the covered employee to the third party assignee when the employer makes each additional premium payment.[17] Table I rates are used if the group term plan was nondiscriminatory or if the covered employee was not a key employee. If the plan is discriminatory and the covered employee is a key employee, the actual cost allocable to the employee's entire insurance coverage must be used (unless Table I costs are higher).[18] Depending on the facts and circumstances, those gifts may or may not be present interest gifts qualifying for the gift tax annual exclusion.[19]

Group term life insurance may result in a taxable gift where it passes to someone other than the primary beneficiary and it was not disclaimed in a timely manner.[20]

EMPLOYER TAX IMPLICATIONS

Premiums paid by the employer for group term life insurance are income tax deductible as ordinary and necessary business expenses (unless the employer is directly or indirectly the beneficiary of the coverage).[21] No deduction is allowed for premiums paid for the coverage on partners or sole proprietors because the premiums would be considered in payment of personal coverage. However, premiums paid to cover the partners' or sole proprietor's common law employees are typically deductible. Shareholder-employees of S corporations who own more than 2 percent of the stock of the business are treated in the same way as a partner.

Small Groups

Special tax treatment applies to small groups (i.e., groups insuring under ten lives). In under-ten group term life plans, premiums are tax deductible for the employer and not taxable income up to the $50,000 limit only if the following conditions are met:[22]

1. The employer provides group coverage for either:

    a. all full-time employees; or

    b. all full-time employees who can prove, to the insurer's satisfaction, insurability assuming that evidence of insurability affects eligibility.[23]

2. The amount of insurance is computed:

    a. as a uniform percentage of compensation; or

    b. on the basis of coverage brackets established by the insurer.

3. The plan may provide for a reduction in the amount computed under either method for employees who do not provide satisfactory evidence of insurability.

4. No bracket may exceed two-and-one-half times the next lower bracket.

5. The lowest bracket must be at least 10 percent of the highest bracket.

6. The plan may establish a separate schedule of coverage within similar guidelines for employees who are over age sixty-five.

7. Evidence of insurability, if required, is limited to a medical questionnaire completed by the employee and the plan may not require a physical examination.

Even if all three of these requirements are not met, a group term plan with less than ten lives will still qualify for favorable tax treatment if it meets the following requirements:

1. Coverage is available under a common plan to employees of two or more related employers.

2. Coverage is restricted to, but must be provided for, all employees who belong to an organization (such as a union) that carries on other substantial activities on behalf of the employer.

3. Evidence of insurability is not required, and in no way does that affect the amount of insurance available to individual employees.

TYPES OF POLICIES

Group Universal Life (GUL)

As its name implies, group universal life combines the economy of scale and other advantages of group coverage with the flexibility and potential for gain of a universal life contract. It is a combination of group term life insurance with a cash accumulation feature. The insurer issues a master contract to an employer who in turn makes it available to employees who receive certificates of coverage and who pay the entire premium.

The policy is divided into two separate portions: (1) pure life insurance protection; and (2) the cash values. A part of each premium goes toward mortality costs (i.e., the charge for the term insurance), while the balance of the covered employee's premium is placed (after certain expense charges are subtracted) into the cash value portion of the policy. Premiums are flexible, not fixed. Each insured can, at his discretion, increase or decrease the premium, increase or decrease the benefits, or borrow against the cash value. (All of these flexible options are subject to some limit on frequency to keep administrative costs down.) As is the case with individual policy universal life, an employee's premium payments can be suspended, and coverage will continue as long as the cash value is high enough to meet the insurer's mortality and expense charges.

The typical group universal life contract is held by a large group of 1,000 or more employees. Employees pay the entire premium for the coverage and the employer's only outlay is for indirect costs such as installation and administration.

A GUL contract can be purchased as a standalone employee benefit or it may be combined with group term. An employee may participate in either or both plans. An employee who participates in the GUL plan must pay premiums high enough to build some cash value. An employee who begins in the term insurance plan may later switch to the GUL plan, or vice versa.

Death benefits are usually pegged to some multiple of salary (e.g., one to five times earnings). Some plans of smaller employers limit the salary multiple to some lower amount, such as three times salary, or provide for specific dollar limits such as $25,000 or $50,000. For administrative simplicity, the plan will offer either level or the more popular increasing death benefits, but once the employer makes the decision all employees must use the same option.

GUL plans usually guarantee the initial interest rate on cash value accumulations for one year. The rate is then adjusted every three to six months, subject to some guaranteed minimum. This rate adjustment is made at the sole discretion of the insurer.

Taxation is the same as under an individual universal life policy. Thus, premiums are nondeductible, cash values accumulate tax free, and death proceeds are generally income tax free.

Advantages to GUL are enjoyed by both the employer and employee. Some of these include:

1. The employer's direct costs are limited to the expenses of installation, payroll deductions, and ongoing administration.

2. Although the plan entails no direct employer out-of-pocket cost for premiums, the existence of the plan has the psychological effect of reducing the pressure for employer provided postretirement benefits.

3. Employees who participate in a group universal life plan receive universal life insurance at group rates.

4. Covered employees can continue coverage into retirement.

5. Employees can purchase coverage based on their individual needs.

6. Policy cash values of the plan are available to employees through either a withdrawal or loan.

Withdrawals and Loans

Withdrawals or loans may be made against cash values of a GUL, subject to restrictions on frequency and subject to minimum amounts in order to control costs. As is the case with all universal life contracts, sufficient cash must be left in the cash value portion to pay mortality and expense charges for some specified period.

Loans and withdrawals decrease the death benefit under the increasing death benefit option (but do not reduce the benefit if the employer has selected the level death benefit option). When money is borrowed out of a GUL, a reduced interest rate is credited on the cash value equal to the loan amount.

Termination

When an employee retires or is terminated, she has a number of choices:

1. The coverage may be continued.

2. The policy can be cashed in for its cash value.

3. Policy cash values can be taken under a settlement option.

4. In some cases, the insurance can be continued under a reduced paid-up policy.

Dependent Life

Dependent life is optional coverage for the spouse and/or dependent children of covered employees. Generally, this coverage is limited to no more than 50 percent of the employee's coverage and is almost always further limited by insurers to $5,000 or $10,000. For tax reasons, most coverage for dependents is $2,000, or less. Coverage on the lives of children is usually $1,000 or $2,000. Not all states permit dependent life.

Employer-paid premiums for dependent life are tax deductible by the employer and tax-free to the employee only to the extent the coverage is considered incidental. Incidental is defined as "not exceeding $2,000," so the premiums paid by an employer on $2,000 or less of coverage for a spouse and each dependent child can be totally excluded from a covered employee's gross income.[24] If the coverage exceeds $2,000 per individual dependent, it is not incidental. In that case, the Table I costs of the excess dependent coverage (less any employee contribution) must be included in the gross income of the employee.

Where there are less than ten employees in the group, dependent coverage should be provided to all employees if provided at all. A safe way to determine the amount of benefits would be to provide coverage as a uniform percentage of each employee's compensation or perhaps as a percentage of the coverage provided on the life of each employee.

Group Survivor Income Benefit Insurance

Group survivor income benefit insurance provides a continuing monthly income benefit to qualified family survivors at the death of a covered employee. The benefit is typically a fixed percentage of the covered employee's basic monthly earnings, a flat specified amount applicable to all insureds, or an amount dependent on job classification. Group survivor plans are often designed to supplement group term life, Social Security benefits, and income from other sources. The initial value of these survivor benefits can range from three to ten times an employee's annual salary.

By design, death benefits are made only in the form of monthly payments, paid only when a beneficiary is a qualified member, and only if that family member survives the covered employee. Qualified family members are typically a spouse or an unmarried, dependent child.

Payments made to a surviving spouse stop at the earlier of a specified age (e.g., age sixty-two), or the survivor's death. Some benefits cease at the age at which Social Security retirement payments become available or on remarriage of the surviving spouse. Payments made to surviving children usually end when the youngest unmarried child reaches age nineteen.

For purposes of computing the covered employee's income tax liability under group survivor income benefit insurance, proceeds payable, (i.e., the amount that is multiplied by the Table I rates) is the present value of the named beneficiary's right to receive payments under the employee's certificate. Likewise, the present value of payments to be made at a covered employee's death would be the amount includable in the decedent's estate.

WHERE CAN I FIND OUT MORE?

The discussions of group life insurance contained in the following publications can be helpful:

1. *Introduction to Group Insurance*, 5th ed. (Chicago, IL: Dearborn Financial Publishing, Inc., 2001).

2. *The Advisor's Guide to Group Life and AD&D* (Cincinnati, OH: The National Underwriter Company, 2012).

FREQUENTLY ASKED QUESTIONS

Question – Can group insurance be used to fund a buy-sell agreement?

Answer – The use of group insurance to fund a buy-sell is generally not a sound idea. First, if the buyout price is artificially reduced in return for a corresponding increase in the group term coverage (under the pretext that "This makes your buy-sell partially tax deductible. What's the difference where the family gets the money as long as they get the same number of dollars?"). The difference is that the family is cheated because it does not receive a fair price for the business interest held by the estate plus the group insurance to which it is entitled. Furthermore, since the IRS is likely to claim that the corporation is an indirect beneficiary of the group term insurance (by virtue of the reduction in the buy-sell price) the premium for the additional life insurance may not be deductible.[25] Moreover, the price set in the agreement will not be binding on the IRS or on the courts, and the estate could conceivably pay an estate tax greater than the money it receives for the stock.[26]

Another ploy that will be unsuccessful (and that is dangerous from a tax viewpoint as well) is for two shareholders to sign a cross purchase buy-sell agreement and name each other the beneficiary of the coverage on their respective lives. In return, they lower the price of a decedent's interest in a buy-sell. Under these circumstances, there has been a transfer of an interest in a policy (i.e., when one shareholder named the other as beneficiary), and that transfer of an interest has been made for valuable consideration (i.e., reciprocity of the other's action). This is clearly a "transfer for value" and it will cause the proceeds to be income taxable.[27]

Yet another trick that is periodically suggested is to name one's own family as the beneficiary of an increased amount of group term life, but agree that the increase will in turn be considered payment made to the family of the deceased insured in return for a full or partial payment for his or her stock. Mechanically, it is almost impossible to match insurance needs with the group schedules of benefits because of the nondiscrimination rules. Furthermore, once the family has received the proceeds, but still holds the stock, if they decide not to transfer the shares, how (aside from an expensive and aggravating lawsuit) will the surviving shareholder obtain the stock?

Question – When an employee becomes older, the reportable income tax cost of very large amounts of group term life insurance tends to increase very rapidly. What are the techniques available to solve this problem?

Answer – It is true that a very substantial amount of income can be generated by group term life as the employee ages. For ages sixty-five to sixty-nine, the reportable cost per thousand per month is $1.27, while for ages seventy and over, the reportable cost per thousand per month is $2.06.[28]

One solution is the executive bonus carve-out, a simple arrangement that provides up to $50,000 of coverage for all employees (including retired employees) through the group insurance plan, but carves out selected employees for special treatment.

Specifically, the chosen individuals are provided with amounts of individual term and/or whole life insurance by the employer. Premiums are paid by the employer, but reportable by the employee as income. To make up for the income tax burden, an additional bonus is paid in cash to the employee. This is particularly appealing when the corporation is in a higher bracket than the executive.

Permanent insurance is often preferable in a group carve-out since the goal is to reduce or eliminate the out-of-pocket cost and reportable income of retired executives. This can be accomplished by using a limited-pay policy along with applying dividends to pay premiums so that the policyowner's out-of-pocket premium-payments diminish over time, usually to zero in seven to ten years. Because the shareholder-employees and other key executives generally want substantial and permanent coverage, one solution is the executive bonus carve-out life insurance plan. The characteristics that make this approach appealing include the following:

- The plan is simple and easy to present to corporate officers.

- They can use the corporation as a vehicle to provide individually-owned permanent life insurance for shareholder-employees and key executives.

- The plan avoids the complex and costly nondiscrimination rules for excess coverage.

- The plan is flexible and the company can provide additional insurance amounts through Code Section 162 bonus or split-dollar coverage.

- Leveraging may be possible because the corporate deduction may be greater than the taxable income incurred by the participants in the plan.

See Chapter 40 for a more complete discussion of Section 162 Bonus Plans.

Question – Does the substantial individual insurance benefit available under a Section 162 plan render the Section 79 group term plan obsolete?

Answer – The answer to this question depends on many factors:

1. Does the corporation already have a group insurance plan in place that benefits employees?

2. Does the current plan meet the nondiscrimination rules?

3. Does the corporation wish to continue to provide group term life insurance coverage to nonhighly compensated rank-and-file employees?

Generally the group term life insurance plan is still favorable on a nondiscriminatory basis. The corporation is allowed an ordinary business expense deduction for contributions to the plan.

Employees, including the shareholder-employees and other key executives, receive the first $50,000 of coverage income tax-free.

Therefore, there are many reasons to continue an existing group term plan. The corporation may also want to avoid the adverse morale consequences of terminating a popular fringe benefit plan covering a broad cross-section of employees and replacing it with a highly discriminatory life insurance plan covering only a few key employees.

What is generally recommended is that the shareholder-employees and other key executives who require (and for whom the corporation wishes to provide) more substantial life insurance coverage participate in either a Code Section 162 bonus or split dollar life insurance plan to supplement a Section 79 plan. The group term plan can still provide key employees with the $50,000 of tax-free coverage. Excess coverage can instead be carved out of the group term life insurance plan and provided through a discriminatory arrangement.

Generally, the Section 162 bonus plan makes more sense when the corporation is in a higher bracket than the participant and the plan is limited to shareholder-employees. Under the Section 162 plan, the corporation pays the entire cost as deductible compensation and the participant is taxed on the full amount of the premium bonus. No reimbursement of corporate contributions will be available.

The split dollar approach is favored when the size and permanency of the corporation's outlay is a concern and the corporation is in a lower bracket than the participant. Split dollar becomes more favorable if coverage extends beyond the shareholders. Since the employer's share of the premium is nondeductible, the higher bracket corporation should generally avoid the substantial nondeductible outlays in a split dollar plan and instead provide deductible bonuses through a Section 162 bonus life insurance plan.

Question – Can a group plan include an owner-employee?

Answer – Yes. The employer may be a sole proprietorship, partnership, or close corporation. Employees eligible for coverage may include sole proprietors, partners, and employee-shareholders. (Note, however, that tax rules are different for self-employed individuals

and partners than for common law employees.) Some group contracts also cover employees of an employer's subsidiary. Retired employees may also be included.

Question – Can a trade association offer life insurance to its members?

Answer – Yes. Employers in the same type of business or industry can sponsor voluntary insurance plans for their members. For instance, a national association or state association of teachers, doctors, lawyers, or CPAs might sponsor such a plan. Generally, a trust acts as the master policyholder for trade association plans. Additionally, depending on the nature of the group that is offering the plan, the same ERISA requirements that employers face may apply.

Question – What is group creditor life?

Answer – Banks, finance companies, credit unions, retailers, and others may qualify for group life insurance on the lives of individuals who borrow money from the creditor. Although one purpose of group creditor life is to protect lenders against possible financial loss due to the death of a debtor, these companies are often in the business of selling the insurance and, therefore, profit from the sales directly.

CHAPTER ENDNOTES

1. ERISA §§402, 403, 503.
2. Treas. Reg. §1.79-1(b).
3. Treas. Reg. §1.79-1.
4. Church and synagogue plans are exempt from the nondiscrimination rules per I.R.C. §79(d)(7).
5. I.R.C. §79(d)(1).
6. At most, only fifty employees of an employer can be treated as "officers" for purposes of the key employee test. If the firm employs less than fifty officers, the maximum number is the greater of (a) three employees or (b) 10 percent of all employees.
7. I.R.C. §79(d)(6).
8. I.R.C. §79(a). This $50,000 exemption must be reduced if the applicable state law imposes a lower maximum on group coverage on one life. Treas. Reg. §1.79-1(e). Most states, however, no longer have such limits.
9. I.R.C. §79(a).
10. I.R.C. §79(b).
11. I.R.C. §79(b)(3); Treas. Reg. §1.79-2(d); See also I.R.C. §72(m)(3).
12. See I.R.C. §§3121(a)(2)(C), 3102(d). Only the cost of coverage in excess of $50,000 is generally subject to the Social Security tax.
13. Proceeds of life insurance are generally excludable from income under I.R.C. §101(a).

14.   I.R.C. §2042.

15.   See Rev. Rul. 72-307, 1972-1 CB 307 which modified Rev. Rul. 69-54, 1969-1 CB 221. See also *Estate of Max J. Gorby v. Comm'r.*, 53 TC 80, acq. 1970-1 CB xvi; *Landorf v. U.S.*, 408 F.2nd 461 (1969).

16.   See Rev. Rul. 76-490, 1976-2 CB 300.

17.   See Rev. Rul. 79-47, 1979-1 CB 312.

18.   I.R.C. §79(d)(1).

19.   The employer's premium payments were considered present interest gifts and therefore did qualify for the gift tax annual exclusion in Revenue Ruling 76-490, 1976-2 CB 300, where the assignment was to an irrevocable trust the employee had created and the trust terms fortuitously provided that, immediately upon the insured's death, the entire proceeds were to be distributed to the beneficiary or the beneficiary's estate. Most trust instruments will not provide beneficiaries with immediate distribution of or access to proceeds and are, therefore, not likely to qualify for the annual exclusion. See Rev. Rul. 79-47, 1979-1 CB 312.

20.   See Priv. Ltr. Rul. 8702024.

21.   I.R.C. §§162(a), 264(a). Deductibility assumes that amounts paid are compensation for services actually rendered and that the total compensation paid to the employee is reasonable when viewed with respect to the services actually performed for the employer.

22.   Treas. Reg. §1.79-1(c).

23.   See Treas. Reg. §1.79-1(c)(2)(i). Generally, an employer can exclude employees over a certain age, employees who work less than full-time, and employees who waive their right to participate.

24.   Notice 89-110, 1989-2 CB 447. See also Treas. Reg. §1.61-2(d)(2).

25.   I.R.C. §264(a).

26.   I.R.C. §2703.

27.   I.R.C. §101(a)(2). See Chapter 25, "The Transfer for Value Rule."

28.   Treas. Reg. §1.79-3(d).

JOINT LIFE (FIRST-TO-DIE) INSURANCE

CHAPTER 12

INTRODUCTION

Joint Life (JL) insurance, which is sometimes called multilife insurance, is first-to-die coverage on two or more insureds. Insurers have offered joint life coverage in many forms, including base policies of permanent or term insurance or Additional Insured Riders (AIRs) to single life policies. Typically, planners have used traditional whole life, current assumption life, or universal life when designing permanent plans. In recent years, the demand for joint life base plans funded with permanent insurance has waned with additional insured riders more frequently being employed to serve this particular need. These AIRs are usually, but not exclusively, term riders, depending on the facts, circumstances, and objectives of the application.

However, some insurers still offer permanent joint life policies and the need for permanent plans in certain circumstances stills exists, so the following discussion addresses these planning applications, strategies, and issues.

WHEN IS THE USE OF THIS DEIVCE INDICATED?

1. *In the dual-income family market* – JL may provide a cost effective means of replacing income at the first spouse's death. Advisers often recommend joint life to fund specific goals and objectives that depend on the presence of the second of two incomes because the family frequently needs insurance at the second death even more than at the first death. For example, a family might use a JL policy to pay off a mortgage or fund a child's education in the event one spouse dies. Because the liquidity needs of the family often depend more on when the first death occurs than

on which spouse dies first, JL is often a useful tool in conjunction with Survivorship Life (SL).

The JL/SL combination is often a better plan than two single life policies. For example, assume a husband and wife are each making about the same income and their estate plan calls for maximum use of the marital deduction to defer the bulk of their estate tax until the second death. Assume, as well, that they wish to assure certain benefits for their children, such as funding for education, in the event of either spouse's premature death and regardless of who dies first. Just for illustration, assume they will need about $1 million at the first death and $3 million at the second death, regardless of who dies first. It would be difficult to determine just what amount of single life insurance coverage they would need on each spouse to assure their goals are met, because they do not know who will die first. However, a JL policy with $1 million of coverage and a SL policy with $3 million would exactly meet their needs.

2. *In the key employee business insurance market* – Purchase of separate single life policies on all key employees can be costly and at times unnecessary. The cost of a multilife policy on several key persons will be less than the total cost of separate policies on all insureds. In these cases, the base policy often includes, for additional cost, a guaranteed insurability option that permits all, or selected, remaining key employees to be insured under a new JL policy after the first death without evidence of insurability. Some companies also offer a substitute insured rider that permits the owner of the policy to replace one insured with another, with evidence of insurability. This is an attractive feature if employees in key positions may leave and be replaced by others.[1]

3. *For use in business buy-sell funding* – Perhaps the principal use of JL to date has been to fund buy-sell agreements in closely-held businesses. Because it is the first death among the owners that triggers the need, JL is perfectly designed to meet the need. Similar to key employee cases, guaranteed insurability riders and substitute insured riders frequently are attractive options.

Advantages

1. In the family market, a JL/SL combination may provide a more cost effective match with insurance needs than two separate single life policies on the spouses.

2. In the business insurance market, JL may eliminate the need for redundant coverage when the need is simply to insure the first death among several lives.

Disadvantages

1. Unless the JL policy is coupled with a guaranteed insurability rider, all coverage ceases upon the first death.

2. The cost of a JL policy is greater than the cost of a single life policy with the same face amount because the insurer must pay the benefit at the first death of two insureds. The expected time until the first death of two insureds is less than the expected time to the death of either insured separately.

Example. Assume that the life expectancy of a fifty-five-year-old is 23.8 years. However, the expected time until the first death of two fifty-five-year-olds would be less, approximately 17.6 years. Therefore, all else being equal, an insurance company would have to charge roughly 35 percent more in annual premium for the joint life coverage than for a single life policy with the same death benefit because they expect the insurer will have to pay the joint life death benefit about six years sooner than they would have to pay the single life death benefit, on average. However, if the alternative is to insure *both* lives for the same face amount as the joint life policy, the annual premium cost should be about 20 percent *less* than the combined cost of the two single life policies.

---

3. A number of important ownership issues and tax traps await the unwary. Failure to adhere to certain guidelines can have adverse tax consequences.

TAX IMPLICATIONS

JL is taxed in the same manner as other life insurance for income tax purposes. Death benefits are generally received income tax-free. As long as the policy is not classified as a Modified Endowment Contract (MEC), cash values build without current taxation. Withdrawals or distributions during the "before a death" claim generally are taxed under the "cost recovery" rule. That is, amounts are treated as tax-free recovery of principal or basis (generally, net premiums paid) until the policyowner has fully recovered basis in the policy, and only then as taxable gain on the policy. However, also similar to other types of insurance, withdrawals or distributions within the first fifteen policy years that are coupled with a reduction in the policy's death benefits may trigger recognition of income. Subject to a statutory ceiling, all income or growth in the cash surrender value may be deemed to have been received by the policyowner if such withdrawals or distributions occur within the first fifteen years.[2] See Chapter 22 for more information on MECs.

Income Taxation of Split Dollar Arrangements

In a pure vanilla split dollar arrangement, the economic benefit of a single life policy generally is measured by the cost of the pure insurance element of the policy (the difference between the face amount of coverage and the cash surrender value). This cost generally is based upon the lesser of the Table 2001 rates or the term rates actually used by the company, if clearly identifiable. If the company pays the entire premium, the economic benefit so measured is taxable income to the policyowner. In theory, the economic benefit should be measured in a similar way for JL policies using joint life first-to-die rates rather than single Table 2001 rates or term rates, but the matter has not yet been resolved. For example, is the economic benefit for each insured in a two-life JL policy where each insured is the beneficiary if the other dies first the other insured's single life Table 2001 or term cost? This is not an unreasonable assumption because the insurance company will have to pay the benefit if either or both die within the year. Therefore, the insurer's term cost should be equal to the sum of the individual term costs.

In the case of JL policies with three or more insureds, the argument is that the economic benefit of each insured would be equal to the sum of the term rates for the other insureds times his or her respective share of the pure death benefit.

Estate and Gift Taxation

Similar to other life insurance, issues of ownership are critical in determining how the policy will be treated for estate and gift tax purposes. When companies use JL in a business application, they should take great care to avoid adverse estate and gift tax consequences. This issue is addressed in the question and answer section below.

Corporate Owned Life Insurance (COLI)

Because corporations frequently own JL and they use it for business purposes such as key person insurance or stock redemption buy-sell plans, the corporate alternative minimum tax may be a consideration in its use. For AMT purposes, a corporation must adjust its tax base to take into account certain items. The net death proceeds from a life insurance contract are one such adjustment. The maximum effective alternative minimum tax rate is 15 percent.[3] In some cases where the AMT applies, the strategy is to gross up the amount of insurance to pay the expected AMT. In any event, any payment of AMT becomes a credit available in future years to offset a portion of a corporation's regular tax liability.

Estate Inclusion when Policy Owned by Corporation

If a key employee/controlling stockholder of a corporation dies and the corporation has complete control over the policy, or at least the right to borrow against the policy, the employee/stockholder will be treated as having sufficient incidents of ownership for the policy to be included in his or her estate.[4]

ALTERNATIVES

The principal alternative for a JL policy is separate single life policies on each insured. If the need for insurance terminates at the first death, JL is the more cost effective method of insuring the risk. If the need for insurance on the survivors will continue after the first death, often separate policies on each insured or some combination of JL and survivorship life might be a better alternative. If the need for insurance on the survivors is uncertain or the amount of coverage required on the survivors is uncertain, guaranteed insurability options on JL policies may provide "wait-and-see" flexibility in determining whether to exercise the full option on each insured after the first death.

WHERE AND HOW DO I GET IT?

JL is somewhat more of a "specialty" item than in the past but a number of insurers still offer a variety of forms. A fair number of insurance companies offer some form of term or permanent JL plan insuring two lives. Fewer companies offer JL products insuring three or more lives.

FEES AND ACQUISITION COSTS

Insurers offer JL policies in a number of configurations including annually renewable term, level term, ordinary life, current assumption life, universal life, and as additional insured riders to single life policies. The various policy fees, charges, expenses, and commissions associated with JL policies are similar to those of comparable single life policies relative to the premium. However, because JL policies usually require evidence of insurability for each named insured, the issue expenses associated with underwriting the policy will be proportionally higher than for single life policies with comparable death benefits. Premiums, of course, will also be correspondingly higher, because the insurer must assess yearly mortality charges that are essentially equivalent to single life mortality charges on each insured.

SELECTING THE BEST OF ITS TYPE

As with any type of insurance policy, the insurer's ability to pay as measured by its financial strength and stability is a critical element in the selection process. (See Chapter 3, "How to Determine the Right Company," for a discussion of this issue.)

Otherwise, the best policy is the one that has the combination of features desired at the lowest overall cost. (See Chapter 4, "How to Determine the Right Policy," for a discussion of cost comparison methods.)

The basic plan of insurance will greatly affect the schedule of premiums and the availability, if any, of cash values. Annually renewable term JL will offer the lowest initial premiums, but premiums will escalate rapidly as the named insureds age. Level premium term JL will offer lower annual premiums than permanent plans, but will provide little, if any, cash value accumulations. If the need for insurance is short-term as, for example, may be the case with certain key employees who will retire at a specified age, level premium JL may be the best plan. Permanent types of insurance will require larger premium outlays, but will assure coverage at a known maximum premium outlay for an extended term in the event the insureds live longer than expected. If tax-preferred cash value accumulations are also desirable, some type of permanent plan probably would best serve the need. Permanent plans, and especially universal life plans under option B, offer increasing death benefits if one expects the insurance need to increase over time.

Other policy features and riders also are available. Among the options are:

- *Substitute insured options* – Some insurers offer riders that permit substitution of insureds with evidence of insurability. This is an attractive feature in buy-sell plans or key person plans where there is a potential for change of partners or stockholders or in personnel in key positions.

- *Guaranteed purchase riders* – Some insurers also offer guaranteed purchase riders that permit surviving insureds to buy insurance either on themselves or other surviving insureds without evidence of insurability which may be a critical element in buy-sell arrangements.

- *Joint premium waiver* – Several companies offer a joint disability premium waiver that is designed principally for the family market.

- *Split option* – Some companies permit insureds to split the policy into two separate policies on each insured, each with a face amount of coverage equal to the JL face amount. The insurers usually require evidence of insurability to exercise this option.

- *Graded premium plans* – If resources to pay premiums are initially low but are expected to increase over time, policyowner(s) may find a graded premium plan attractive. A graded premium plan permits policyowners to pay

lower initial premiums comparable to term premiums that increase over time to a level somewhat above what the level premium would be with traditional whole life.

- *Common disaster clause* – Some policies include a provision that if both insureds die in a common disaster, the insurer will pay the face amount on each death. In such cases, it is imperative to name contingent beneficiaries.

BUSINESS USES

Proper planning of ownership and other policy rights is always an important concern with any life insurance policy to insure the most advantageous treatment for income, gift, and estate tax purposes. Ownership issues are generally not problematic in family situations as long as the husband and wife are the insureds and beneficiaries of the other's death benefit. Major ownership concerns arise when three distinct parties are involved as insured, owner, and beneficiary. For example, assume a wife owns a JL policy with herself and her husband as insureds. Their son is named as beneficiary. If the husband dies first, the wife will have made a taxable gift of the death benefit to her son.[5] They could have eliminated this adverse result by having the son own the policy.

The planning is also relatively easy in a typical key person business situation. The key person policy is usually owned by and payable to the company. If the company owns the policy and names itself as beneficiary of all death benefits, no special problems exist when using JL as compared with any other type of insurance to insure key persons. The one potential tax problem with any corporate-owned life insurance is the Alternative Minimum Tax (AMT). Because life insurance death proceeds are an item of corporate tax preference, the proceeds could become subject to AMT. The maximum effective AMT rate is generally 15 percent of any amount so included in AMT income.

Ownership issues become more complicated when JL is used to fund business buy-sell agreements. Stock redemption buy-sell agreements present no special ownership planning problems when a company uses JL as the funding instrument. In fact, JL is uniquely suited to fund stock redemption agreements in small, closely-held businesses because one policy owned by the corporation on many lives is less expensive than many polices on each owner. Plus, the policy matures when the first owner dies, exactly when it is needed. For other reasons, however, entity buyout plans are often considered less favorable than cross-purchase agreements because of AMT, family attribution, and tax basis issues. (See Chapter 31, "Buy-Sell Agreements," for further discussion of life insurance in buy-sell agreements.)

Although cross-purchase buy-sell plans avoid the corporate AMT and provide survivors with an increased basis, they also require, in the absence of some other funding mechanism, that each owner have life insurance on the other. The number of separate single life policies required can add up quickly as the number of owners increase. For example, with five owners, each one would need to acquire four policies covering each of the other owners, a total of twenty policies. If they use JL, they reduce the required number of policies to just five—one owned by each—covering the lives of the remaining four owners. If the buy-sell plan uses a trust, it is feasible that a single JL policy on all owners could fund the buy-sell agreement.

Cross-purchase Buy-sell Agreements

Although joint ownership by both insureds of a JL policy in a case with two business owners might seem to be the natural choice, it would be extremely unwise. As a joint owner of the policy, the death proceeds as well as the deceased's share of the business value would be included in the estate, effectively causing double taxation. Even if the policy is owned by just one of the business owners, there is still a chance the policyowner will die first, with exactly the same double taxation as with joint policy ownership. They can avoid double taxation only if the business owner who does not own the policy dies first. However, if the business owners knew who would die first, a JL policy would not be necessary.

The key is to keep death proceeds out of the deceased's estate through third party ownership of the JL policy. In the case of two business owners, this is traditionally accomplished through a trusteed plan. In the case of three or more owners, the alternatives include:

- a trusteed plan using a single JL policy on all owners;

- ownership by each business owner of a separate JL policy on all the other business owners' lives; or

- a partnership organized to facilitate business continuity.

Trusteed Plans

In a trusteed plan, the company sets up a trust for the benefit of the shareholders. The trust would then apply for and own the JL policy insuring all the owners. Each business owner would have a specific and limited interest in the trust equal to his or her ownership interest less the interest of the decedent. The shareholders would have no other rights to the insurance policy, cash values, or the trust. For example, in a business with five equal owners, each survivor would be entitled to ¼ of any insurance proceeds on the decedent.[6]

If corporate contributions to the trust pay the premiums, they would be taxable either as income or dividends to the shareholders.[7] Alternatively, shareholders could make nondeductible contributions to the trust in proportion to their ownership interests. The trust would actually pay the premiums.

When the first shareholder dies, the death proceeds will pass to the surviving shareholders who can then use the proceeds to purchase their respective portions of the deceased's interest in the corporation.[8]

WHERE CAN I FIND OUT MORE?

Because joint life is somewhat of a "specialty" product, most life insurance texts give it little coverage. Perhaps the best source of information is the insurers' product informational brochures.[9]

FREQUENTLY ASKED QUESTIONS

Question – In a trusteed plan, is there a potential transfer for value problem after the first death?

Answer – The transfer for value rule essentially says that death benefits will be subject to income tax to the extent they exceed the consideration paid for the policy if the policy has been transferred for valuable consideration.[10] The question arises after the first death whether the increase each shareholder now has in the death benefit payable on the next to die (assuming, of course, that the trust exercises options to keep an equivalent JL coverage on the surviving shareholders) is an indirect transfer from the first deceased (upon his or her death) which violates the transfer for value rule. The value in this case would be the consideration on the part of all shareholders for entering into the agreement.[11] If the transfer for value rule applies, the increase in the death benefit after the first death would be subject to tax to the extent it exceeds consideration paid.

Experts are divided on the question, but some have argued that a properly designed trust will avoid the problem. The key, it is argued, is to draft the trust instrument so that the shareholders only have an interest in a trust and not an interest in an insurance policy. With the trust as the owner and beneficiary and with each shareholder's interest in the trust limited to a life interest only, there is nothing transferred at death and, consequently, no transfer for value.[12]

Also, shareholders can avoid the transfer for value problem if each shareholder owns a JL policy insuring the other shareholders. However, after the first death, the face value on the policies owned by each survivor on the lives of the remaining survivors generally would be inadequate to buy out the second-to-die shareholder's ownership interest (which would typically increase after the first death). Also, the value of the policy owned by the first shareholder to die on the other shareholders would be included in the deceased's estate. Because a transfer of the deceased's policy to the surviving shareholders would represent a transfer for value, the recommended plan of action is to transfer the policy to the corporation. The transfer of policies on the lives of shareholders to a corporation is an exception to the transfer for value rule.[13] They could then amend the buy-sell agreement to effect a combination cross-purchase-entity-buyout plan.

Question – Is JL suitable for S corporations and partnerships?

Answer – S corporations and partnerships are flow-through entities. Consequently, unlike regular corporations, no items, such as the AMT or increased basis, favor the cross-purchase plan over the entity buyout plan. As discussed above, JL is especially well suited to stock redemption plans if the participants can avoid transfer for value problems. In general, in these business forms, using JL to fund buy-sell agreements should present no transfer for value problems.

CHAPTER ENDNOTES

1. It should be noted that the exercise of a substitute insured or exchange-of-insured option may bring unanticipated income tax results. In Revenue Ruling 90-109, 1990-2 CB 191, the substitution of one insured for another was treated as a sale rather than a tax-free exchange under Section 1035.

2. I.R.C. §7702(f)(7). See Appendix F for a further discussion of the fifteen-year rules.

3. Over the range of corporate alternative minimum taxable income (AMTI) from $150,000 to $310,000, the maximum effective AMT rate is actually 18.75 percent, because of the phase out of the $40,000 exemption at $0.25 on the dollar. Otherwise, the 20 percent AMT rate applies to 75 percent of the net proceeds, thus the 15 percent maximum rate, if the entire amount is subject to the AMT.

4. Treas. Reg. §20.2042-1(c)(6); Rev. Rul. 82-145, 1982-2 CB 213.

5. *Goodman v. Comm'r.*, 156 F.2d 218 (2nd Cir. 1946).

6. The formula in the trust agreement should state that each shareholder during lifetime is entitled to a portion of the death proceeds paid on account of the death of any shareholder who is party to the agreement.

7. As long as premiums are being paid as part of the owner/ employee's compensation, and compensation is "reasonable" within the guidelines of I.R.C. §162, they should be taxable compensation to the owner/employees and deductible by the company. If an owner is not also an employee or compensation does not fall within "reasonable" limits, the premiums will be treated as nondeductible dividend payments and would be included in each such shareholder's income based on his or her proportionate ownership of the corporation.

8. I.R.C. §101(a), 641(a)(1).

9. See, e.g., *First-To-Die Life Insurance: An Analysis of Ownership Issues* by Keith Staudt, Fidelity Union Life Insurance Company, Dallas, Texas. The discussion in the following questions and answers on the use of JL in business applications is adapted from this treatise.

10. I.R.C. §101(a)(2).

11. *Monroe v. Patterson*, 197 F. Supp. 146 (N.D. Ala. 1961).

12. See "Meet Closely Held Business Buy/Sell Needs with an OPPO Plan," Chasman, *Life Association News*, October 1990. Chapters 25 and 40 also address the transfer for value rule.

13. I.R.C. §101(a)(2)(B).

LIMITED PAY WHOLE LIFE INSURANCE

CHAPTER 13

INTRODUCTION

Whole life insurance, as the name implies, is designed to provide protection over the insured's entire lifetime. Although coverage continues throughout life, insurers offer policies that allow the owner to pay for the coverage over virtually any duration. At one extreme is the ordinary level premium whole life policy where the owner pays level premiums each year for as long as the insured lives (or generally to a maximum age of one hundred). At the other extreme is the single premium life policy where just one large premium payment is sufficient to purchase lifetime coverage. (See Chapter 15 for more on single premium life insurance.)

The principal characteristics of ordinary limited pay whole life are:

1. level or fixed periodic premiums payable for a specified number of years;

2. a level or fixed death benefit; and

3. a fixed schedule of minimum cash surrender values that increase over time.

The policy owner agrees to pay a fixed or level premium at regular intervals for the specified period, or until the insured dies, if sooner. Once the policy owner has paid premiums for the stipulated number of years, the policy is "paid up" for its full face amount. In other words, the owner needs to pay no more premiums past that point to keep the policy in force for as long as the client lives. In return, the insurance company agrees to pay a fixed death benefit when the insured dies even if the death occurs after the premium paying period.

As the length of the premium payment period increases, limited pay policies more closely resemble ordinary level premium whole life policies. However, because limited pay policies require premium payments for a term that is less than the term of the contract, the insurer must charge larger annual premiums than for ordinary level premium whole life. The annual premiums insurers charge become increasingly larger as the specified premium paying period grows shorter. Correspondingly, policy cash values grow more quickly for policies with shorter premium payment periods than for policies with longer payment periods.

Limited pay policies are commonly offered with ten, fifteen, twenty, thirty years, or longer premium payment periods. Most companies also offer policies where the set payment period is based on the insured's age. The most common form is the life-paid-up-at-age-sixty-five (LP65) policy which allows the insured to discontinue premium payments at retirement (age sixty-five) while the policy remains in force for the rest of the insured's life.

In almost all respects other than the premium paying period, limited pay policies have the contract features and characteristics of ordinary level premium whole life insurance policies. All limited pay policies contain the same nonforfeiture, settlement, dividend options, rider availability, loan provisions, mortality, expense, interest guarantees, and other features as ordinary life policies. However, limited pay policies with short premium payment periods (generally seven years, or less) may be classified as Modified Endowment Contracts (MECs). MECs are subject to less favorable tax treatment than ordinary life policies, if they fail the seven-pay test. (See Chapter 22 for a discussion of the MEC rules.)

WHEN IS THE USE OF THIS DEVICE INDICATED?

Prospective insureds may want to consider limited pay policies in any circumstance where they desire whole life coverage and the policy owner has the financial resources to pay the higher premiums necessary for less than the full term of the coverage. Limited pay policies are generally not well suited to persons whose need for coverage is great and whose income is limited. In particular, limited pay policies are often preferred in the following situations:

1. *To acquire insurance protection for juveniles –* Parents often wish to acquire a minimum amount of insurance protection for their children and to pay for the coverage before the children leave the nest, typically at age twenty-one. In the unfortunate event of a child's death, the insurance may provide a fund for funeral and other expenses. In the more common case where the child survives to adulthood, the policy cash values can serve as part of a nest egg to start him or her on his or her way. In addition, if a child should become uninsurable, he or she will have some life insurance protection, even if he or she is not able to pay the premiums.

2. *To assure insurance protection after retirement without the need for additional premium payments –* Many people wish to keep insurance protection in force after they retire to pay estate tax bills, provide estate liquidity, fund charitable bequests, and provide for dependents. A limited pay policy whose premium payment period terminates when an individual retires assures that person that the policy will remain in force even if the individual no longer has the income for ongoing premium payments.

3. *For many business life insurance applications –* Perhaps the most common use of limited pay policies is in business insurance applications. Businesses typically want to know exactly what their financial commitment is to the insurance and want to fund obligations over fixed periods. Businesses frequently use limited pay policies for key employee insurance and for nonqualified deferred compensation funding. For example, businesses often use limited pay policies with payment periods equal to the time until executives are scheduled to retire with nonqualified deferred compensation

arrangements. If an executive participating in the plan dies before retirement, the policy proceeds can be used to pay survivor benefits under the plan. If the executive survives to retirement, cash values can be used to pay part or all of the obligations to the executive under the plan. In the meantime, cash values have grown without any current tax, and life insurance proceeds can ultimately repay the company for earlier premium outlays.

4. *When the client's working lifetime or high income period is limited –* For instance, a professional athlete such as a football player has high income, but for a relatively short period of time. By compressing payments into a relatively short period that coincides with his or her expected high income years, the policy terms are matched to the client's circumstances more appropriately than if the premium payment period were extended beyond the professional's career.

Advantages

In addition to all the advantages attributable to life insurance in general, and whole life insurance in particular (see Chapter 14), limited pay policies have three distinct advantages:

1. Forecasting the total dollar outlay for limited pay policy coverage is easier than for ordinary level premium whole life insurance. Because premiums on ordinary life continue throughout the insured's lifetime, a person who enjoys a longer than average life may pay more in total premiums for the ordinary level premium whole life policy than for a limited pay policy.

2. Limited pay policies build tax-favored cash values more quickly than ordinary life policies. Therefore, policy owners enjoy greater tax-deferred earnings in the policy. This faster growth makes policy cash values available more quickly and in larger amounts in a given year than with a whole life policy of a comparable face amount.

3. Once policyowners have paid all required premiums, their policies will remain in force for the remainder of their lives. Therefore, they face less risk that the policy may lapse for failure to pay premiums if they experience financial difficulties in the future.

Disadvantages

The disadvantages of limited pay policies are similar to those of ordinary level premium whole life policies. Because premium payments are necessarily greater than for level premium policies, these policies are even less affordable for persons of limited income than level premium policies. In addition, because limited pay policies build cash values more quickly than level premium policies, in the early years the amount of protection (the difference between the face amount of coverage and the cash value) is lower relative to the premium spent than with level premium policies or term policies.

TAX IMPLICATIONS

Non-MEC Policies

Limited pay policies that are not classified as Modified Endowment Contracts (MECs) are taxed in the same manner as ordinary level premium whole life insurance. In general, death benefits are subject to the same income, estate, gift, and generation-skipping transfer taxation rules as all other types of life insurance policies. See Chapters 22 through 30 for a complete discussion of the taxation of life insurance.

In summary, life insurance death proceeds are generally paid free of any federal income tax.[1] Living benefits are taxed under the rules of Section 72 of the Internal Revenue Code. Under the section 72 rules, annuity payments are treated as part taxable income or gain and part nontaxable recovery of the investment in the contract until the entire investment in the contract has been recovered. After the investment in the contract has been fully recovered, additional annuity payments are entirely taxable as income.

Payments of interest only are generally taxable in full when paid.[2] Other amounts not received as an annuity, such as dividend payments, lump-sum cash settlements of cash surrender values, cash withdrawals (if permitted), and amounts received on partial surrender are taxed under the cost recovery rule. That is, these amounts are initially treated as nontaxable recovery of investment in the contract, and, only after the entire investment has been recovered, taxable income or gain.[3]

Policy loans are not treated as distributions. If a policy loan is still outstanding when a policy is surrendered, the borrowed amount becomes taxable at the time of surrender to the extent of gain in the contract.[4]

MEC Policies

Policies that fail the seven-pay test will be treated as MECs.[5] In summary, similar to non-MEC policies, death benefits will generally be paid free of federal income taxation[6] and the cash value buildup is not subject to current taxation. However, in contrast with non-MEC policies, distributions, including loans (even if the loan proceeds are retained by the company to pay premiums) and dividends that are either paid in cash or retained by the insurer to pay either interest or principal on a policy loan, generally will be taxed under the interest-first rule rather than the cost recovery rule. That is, amounts received are treated first as taxable income to the extent the cash value exceeds premiums paid, and only then as nontaxable recovery of investment in the contract.[7] In addition, taxable amounts are subject to a 10 percent penalty tax unless the distribution is made after the taxpayer becomes disabled, attains age 59½, or the distribution is part of a series of substantially equal periodic payments made for the taxpayer's life or life expectancy, or the joint lives or life expectancies of the taxpayer and his or her beneficiary.[8] Dividends that are retained by the insurer for the purpose of purchasing paid-up additions are not treated as taxable amounts received under the contract.[9]

ALTERNATIVES

There is no substitute for life insurance of some type if an individual desires to provide an immediate estate upon his or her death. All types of life insurance policies can provide income tax-free cash upon death. The unique features of limited pay life insurance are its predictable total premium outlay and accelerated, tax favored cash buildup. It provides lifetime coverage even though premiums cease at the end of the specified premium-paying period. As a by-product of the limited-premium payment financing, the policy creates a tax-free, or tax deferred, cash buildup.

People who desire a combination of tax preferred cash accumulation and life insurance may want to explore several other alternatives:

1. *A combination of a limited payment premium deferred annuity and decreasing term insurance –* Cash values accumulate in both annuities and limited pay life insurance policies on a tax deferred basis. Therefore, a combination of a limited premium payment deferred annuity and a decreasing term policy can provide

levels of tax preferred cash accumulation and death benefits similar to a level premium policy.

There are some important differences, however. The tax rules treat withdrawals, lifetime distributions, or loans from each arrangement differently. Although most ordinary life policies do not permit withdrawals, as such, if a withdrawal of cash values is permitted or the policy is partially surrendered, the amount distributed is taxed under the "cost recovery rule." That is, the amounts are included in taxable income only to the extent they exceed the investment in the contract. In contrast, distributions from annuities are taxed under the interest-first rule. In other words, the amounts are fully taxable until the policyowner has recovered all of the excess over the investment in the contract. In addition, nonannuity distributions from an annuity contract before age 59½ may be subject to a 10 percent penalty tax. Also, loans from life insurance policies are not subject to tax; loans from annuities, if permitted, are treated as distributions and taxed under the interest-first rule. That is, loan proceeds are subject to the regular income tax and may be subject to the 10 percent penalty tax. Also, loan provisions of deferred annuity contracts are generally more restrictive than those of life insurance policies.

The annuity/decreasing term combination will require some additional and increasing premiums over the years for the term coverage. In addition, the mortality charges for term insurance coverage are typically higher than the mortality charges in a whole life policy. Finally, the death proceeds from the insurance policy generally may pass to the beneficiary entirely income and estate tax-free, regardless of who is the beneficiary, if the policy owner has no incidents of ownership in the policy. The gains on the annuity contract will still be taxable income to the beneficiary and will avoid estate taxation only if the annuitant's spouse is the beneficiary and certain conditions are met.

2. *A combination of investments in tax-free municipal bonds and decreasing term insurance* – This combination can create a cash accumulation and death benefit similar to a limited pay policy. Similar to the cash values in a life insurance policy, bond owners may use municipal bonds as collateral for loans without any adverse income tax consequences. However, interest paid on debt secured by municipal bonds generally is not deductible. Similarly, interest paid on life insurance policy loans is rarely deductible. With the life insurance policy, the death benefits transfer by operation of the contract, thus avoiding probate. Municipal bonds are part of the probate estate and must be distributed by will. Once again, if the policyowner has no incidents of ownership, the life insurance death proceeds are estate tax free. The municipal bonds will escape estate tax only if they are left to the spouse and sheltered by the marital deduction.

3. *A universal life policy configured as a limited pay policy.* A universal life policyowner can initially configure the UL to resemble a limited pay life policy. However, in contrast with "true" limited pay ordinary life policies, charges for mortality and expenses can change in the universal life policy in such a way that the policyowner would have to pay additional premiums in the future to maintain the face value of coverage.

WHERE AND HOW DO I GET IT?

Nearly 2,000 life insurance companies actively market coverage in the United States. Most of these companies offer limited pay whole life policies as well as other permanent forms of life insurance. In addition to commercial insurance companies, some fraternal organizations, savings banks, professional associations, membership organizations, and stock brokerage houses offer limited pay whole life policies. Prospective insureds can purchase policies through many agents representing a licensed insurance company.

FEES AND ACQUISITION COSTS

Life insurance companies are free to set premiums according to their own marketing strategies. The premium includes a "loading" to cover such things as commissions to agents, premium taxes payable to the state government, operating expenses of the insurance company, such as rent or mortgage payments and salaries, and any other expenses.

A few companies offer "no-load" or "low-load" life insurance policies. These policies are not really no-load, because certain expenses are unavoidable (e.g., the premium tax), but rather pay either no sales commission or a very low sales commission. Consequently, the cash value buildup tends to be larger in the early years. Although commissions are lower, these companies typically must spend more money on alternative methods of marketing and may, therefore, incur generally higher expenses in this area than companies that pay commissions to agents.

The bulk of an insurance company's expenses for a policy are incurred when it issues the policy. It may take the company five to nine years or even longer to recover all its front-end costs. The state premium tax is an ongoing expense that averages about 2 percent of each premium payment. With most cash value policies, the aggregate commissions paid to the selling agent are approximately equal to the first year's premium on the policy. About half (often 55 percent) is payable in the year of sale and the other half is paid on a renewal basis over a period of three to nine years.

Most ordinary whole life insurance policies have no explicit surrender charges. However, most participating policies will pay a terminal dividend. The terminal dividend is typically higher the longer the policy has remained in force. In essence, this is a form of surrender charge because the company is essentially holding back dividends it could otherwise pay currently and rewards those policy holders who maintain their policies longer with a greater terminal dividend.

SELECTING THE BEST OF ITS TYPE

Selecting the best cash value life insurance policy is a difficult task involving a number of complicated concepts and analyses. (See Chapters 2 through 4 for a further discussion of the basic principles.) However, because the level of dividend payments on participating ordinary limited pay life insurance is a critical element of the overall cost of the protection, one primary area of focus should be how the company determines the dividends it pays.

Using Ledger Statements of Whole Life Policies Paying Dividends as Declared[10]

The ledger statement or policy illustration in Figure 13.1 is for a traditional, ordinary level premium whole life policy that is configured to operate like a

twenty-pay life policy. This is accomplished by using dividends as projected to buy paid-up additions until the twentieth policy year. After year twenty, dividends are used first to pay the annual premium with any remainder applied to the purchase of paid-up additions. A true twenty-pay life policy would have higher annual premiums that would terminate after twenty years with no need to apply dividends to pay premiums. Each of the numbers in the ledger corresponds to the following notes:

1. The length of time in years that the gross premium is to be paid.

2. The plan of life insurance (in this case, it is twenty-pay whole life paying dividends as declared).

3. The insurability status (e.g., nonsmoker, smoker (would be standard)) or rated (extra charge because of being a higher risk for medical or occupational reasons). For this life insurance company, "preferred" risk means the insured is a nonsmoker and is not rated.

4. The gender is male, and the issue age is forty-five.

5. The gross premium (i.e., the premium charged not taking dividends into consideration) not including any additional benefits provided by any riders (e.g., waiver of premium).

6. The initial amount of life insurance that will be payable to the named beneficiary upon the death of the insured.

7. The beginning-of-the-year ledger statement versus the end-of-the-year ledger statement. Dividends, when paid, are not paid until the end of a specific year. If an end-of-the-year ledger statement is used, it would show dividends paid during the first year, which would be inaccurate.

8. The amount of premium to be paid each year.

9. The cash amount of premium to be paid each year. In this case it is $2,001 for the first twenty years, and $0 thereafter.

10. The cumulative guaranteed amount of reserve (i.e., the guaranteed cash value) that has accumulated for each year.

Figure 13.1

LEDGER STATEMENT FOR WHOLE LIFE PAYING DIVIDENDS AS DECLARED

1   20-PAY LIFE ILLUSTRATION

+Plan: Ordinary Life   **2**

Class: Preferred Standard   **3**

Male Age 45   **4**

5   Basic Annual Premium: $2,001.00

6   Face Amount: $100,000

7 Beg. Pol. Year	**8** Premium Payable*	**9** Cash Premium Pmt.*	**10** Guar. Cash Value	**11** Total Cash Value*	**12** Ann. Incr. in Total Cash Value*	**13** Total Cash Value Incr.(−) Cash Prem.*	**14** Div. Adds Death Benefit*	**15** Total Death Benefit*
1	$ 2,001	$2,001	$ 0	$ 0	$ 0	−$ 2,001	0	$100,000
2	2,001	2,001	1,026	1,058	1,058	−943	113	100,113
3	2,001	2,001	2,938	3,043	1,985	−16	354	100,354
4	2,001	2,001	4,890	5,130	2,087	86	780	100,780
5	2,001	2,001	6,881	7,347	2,217	216	1,460	101,460
6	2,001	2,001	8,909	9,724	2,377	376	2,456	102,456
7	2,001	2,001	10,971	12,289	2,565	564	3,830	103,830
8	2,001	2,001	13,069	15,085	2,796	795	5,646	105,646
9	2,001	2,001	15,202	18,150	3,065	1,064	7,965	107,965
10	2,001	2,001	17,366	21,526	3,376	1,375	10,848	110,848
11	2,001	2,001	19,432	25,135	3,609	1,608	14,362	114,362
12	2,001	2,001	21,520	29,152	4,017	2,016	18,573	118,573
13	2,001	2,001	23,626	33,632	4,480	2,479	23,544	123,544
14	2,001	2,001	25,746	38,531	4,899	2,898	29,109	129,109
15	2,001	2,001	27,878	43,890	5,359	3,358	35,297	135,297
16	2,001	2,001	30,016	49,735	5,845	3,844	42,119	142,467
17	2,001	2,001	32,160	56,220	6,485	4,484	49,829	150,519
18	2,001	2,001	34,304	63,404	7,184	5,183	58,476	159,553
19	2,001	2,001	36,445	71,235	7,831	5,830	67,884	169,393
20	2,001	2,001	38,580	79,762	8,527	6,526	78,085	180,071
21	−3,984	0	40,702	87,033	7,271	7,271	85,431	187,939
22	−4,544	0	42,805	94,954	7,921	7,921	93,586	196,232
23	−5,178	0	44,882	103,597	8,643	8,643	102,638	205,420
24	−5,878	0	46,925	113,028	9,431	9,431	112,655	215,572
25	−6,655	0	48,929	123,322	10,294	10,294	123,723	226,773
26	−7,510	0	50,892	134,563	11,241	11,241	135,923	239,103
27	−8,445	0	52,820	146,848	12,285	12,285	149,336	252,644
28	−9,458	0	54,718	160,272	13,424	13,424	164,033	267,466
29 **16**	−10,551	0	56,596	174,946	14,674	14,674	180,088	283,645
30	−11,723	0	58,458	190,978	16,032	16,032	197,564	301,243
31	−12,993	0	60,303	208,489	17,511	17,511	216,551	320,351
32	−14,389	0	62,124	227,616	19,127	19,127	237,172	341,092
33	−15,963	0	63,912	248,530	20,914	20,914	259,620	363,658
34	−17,699	0	65,651	271,379	22,849	22,849	284,057	388,211
35	−19,613	0	67,331	296,317	24,938	24,938	310,667	414,934

Figure 13.1 (cont'd)

Beg. Pol. Year	Premium Payable*	Cash Premium Pmt.*	Guar. Cash Value	Total Cash Value*	Ann. Incr. in Total Cash Value*	Total Cash Value Incr.(−) Cash Prem.*	Div. Adds Death Benefit*	Total Death Benefit*
36	−21,690	0	68,947	323,488	27,171	27,171	339,605	443,982
37	−23,913	0	70,499	353,028	29,540	29,540	371,007	475,489
38	−26,277	0	71,989	385,977	32,049	32,049	404,998	509,580
39	−28,780	0	73,426	419,802	34,725	34,725	441,699	546,378
40	−31,441	0	74,818	457,379	37,577	37,577	481,251	586,024

17   *Dividends are used to purchase paid-up insurance in years 1 through 20. Thereafter, dividends are used to reduce premiums, and if necessary, a portion of the paid-up insurance is surrendered to pay the balance of the premium.

Summary† Page 18

	19 Guar. Cash Value	20 Total Cash Value*	21 Cash Premium Payments	22 Total Cash Value Less Prem. Payments	23 Guar. Paid-up Insurance	24 Total Paid-up Insurance*
5 Years	$ 6,881	$ 7,696	$10,005	$ 2,309-	$17,453	$ 19,519
10 Years	17,366	23,069	20,010	3,059	37,811	50,228
15 Years	27,878	47,945	30,015	17,930	52,791	90,792
20 Years	38,580	89,420	40,020	49,400	64,503	149,504
Age 65	38,580	89,420	40,020	49,400	64,503	149,504

25   Terminal dividend*
     Interest-adjusted indexes* based on a 5.00% interest rate, for basic policy only:

26   Life insurance net payment cost index   10 years: $16.24   20 years: $ 9.89   Age 65: $ 9.89

    Life insurance surrender cost index   10 years: 3.09   20 years: 1.95-   Age 65:   1.95-

    Equivalent level annual dividend   10 years: 3.77   20 years: 10.12   Age 65:   10.12

27   Premium information: Annual   Semiannual   Quarterly   Pac.
    Ordinary Life $2,001.00 $1,025.70 $520.56 $173.20

Figure 13.1 (cont'd)

20-PAY LIFE ILLUSTRATION
Explanatory Notes

*Includes dividend values. Dividends are not guaranteed. **28**

Illustrated dividends are based on the company's current mortality, expense, and investment experience. Actual dividends may be higher or lower than shown as a result of future changes in the company's experience, especially the interest rates earned on investments. A terminal dividend is payable upon surrender, lapse, or death, after at least 15 policy years, but only if declared by the company at such time, and is included in the total death benefit, in summary values for total cash value and total paid-up insurance, and in the interest-adjusted surrender cost index.

*Illustrated dividends assume no loans on policy. Policy loans will affect dividends. **29**

+The values shown in the ledger assume an annual mode of premium payment and a fixed policy loan interest rate of 8.00% applied in arrears, except in the case of a partial cash premium payment; then, a change to the automatic monthly premium modes has been assumed. The issuance of any policies or riders is subject to the company's regular underwriting practices. The amounts of coverage and premiums for any policies or riders, if issued, may differ from those illustrated. **30**

†Summary values are calculated as of the end of the year. **31**

---

11. The cumulative total amount of reserve (i.e., the guaranteed cash value), including the nonguaranteed cash value of the additional paid-up life insurance purchased each year, starting at the beginning of year two, with the yearly declared paid dividend.

12. The yearly amount of increase in the total reserve (i.e., the guaranteed cash value and the nonguaranteed cash value of the additional paid-up insurance purchased each year).

13. The yearly difference between the gross premium of $2,001 and the yearly guaranteed cash value increase and the yearly increase of the nonguaranteed cash value of the additional paid-up life insurance purchased by the yearly declared paid dividend. A minus sign (–) means the combined yearly increase is less than the gross premium of $2,001. The figures do not reflect the time value of money.

14. The amount of additional paid-up life insurance purchased by the declared paid dividend.

15. The yearly total death benefit including the projected additional paid-up life insurance purchased through the projected dividends. From year sixteen on, the projected terminal dividend is included.

16. The life expectancy of a forty-five-year-old male is 29.1 years (age seventy-four) based on life expectancies for males of all races from *Vital Statistics of the United States*, for the year 1980.

17. A statement indicating that dividends are used to purchase paid-up insurance. The gross premium of $2,001 is paid during the first twenty years. Thereafter, dividends are used to reduce the gross premium of $2,001 and, if necessary, a portion of the paid-up insurance is surrendered to pay the balance of the gross premium. Looking at column 8 in year twenty-one reveals that this is unnecessary. The projected dividend in year twenty-one is $3,984, more than the gross premium of $2,001. A minus sign (–) in this column indicates that the projected dividends exceed the gross premium. Finally, from year twenty-one on, the dividend in excess of the gross premium is used to purchase additional paid-up life insurance. If desired, the death benefit could be frozen at $180,071 (year twenty), and the dividend amount in excess of the gross premium could then be paid in cash.

18. The summary page values for this insurance company's ledger statement are different from the values shown on the nonsummary pages for two reasons. First, the yearly declared dividend is assumed to be paid at the end of the year. Second, the terminal dividend is included.

The insurance company assumes for the summary page that the policy is surrendered for the years shown.

19. The cumulative amount of guaranteed cash value for the years shown.

20. The cumulative amount of total cash value for the years shown including the nonguaranteed cash value of additional paid-up insurance purchased through the dividends.

21. Each figure represents $2,001 times the number of years shown.

22. The difference between columns 21 and 20. Although mathematically correct, it does not take into consideration the time value of money.

23. The amount of paid-up life insurance for the years shown that can be purchased by the guaranteed cash value. Once purchased, no additional premiums are required and the insurance company pays a paid-up dividend per $1,000 of paid-up insurance.

24. The amount of paid-up life insurance for the years shown that can be purchased by the total cash value.

25. The terminal dividend may be payable after the policy has been in force fifteen years or longer.

26. The interest adjusted index.

27. The premium information for various payment options [i.e., annual (once a year), semiannual (twice a year), quarterly (four times a year), and preauthorized monthly payment through checking account (PAC)]. The cost is higher if paid more frequently than annually. This is because of the expenses incurred to send a premium notice more than once a year and the time value of money (the insurance company does not have the use of your money all at once). The company is implicitly charging 10.34 percent interest for semiannual payments, 10.88 percent for quarterly payments, and 8.37 percent for monthly payments of the premiums.

28. A statement that dividends in any form are not guaranteed.

29. A statement that a loan against the reserve (i.e., cash value) will affect dividends.

30. A statement that the guaranteed fixed contractual interest rate charged for loans against the reserve is 8 percent payable in arrears, meaning that interest is due one year from the date of the loan.

31. A statement about the summary page calculations.

Ledger Statements Do Not Tell All

In addition to the ledger statement, the following additional information should be available, either verbally or in writing:

1. The rate of return the insurance company assumes it must earn on premium payments to warrant the dividends it projects. In this case the dividend interest assumption rate is 11.57 percent for the first year, graded up over a twenty-year period to 11.73 percent.

2. The investment strategy employed by the insurance company, which dictates the dividend interest assumption rate. In this case the investment strategy is a *weighted-average portfolio rate*. This means that 40 percent is weighted toward old money and 60 percent is weighted toward new money. The insurance company, as part of its investment strategy, anticipates gains from real estate and common stock investments.

3. The conditions in which dividends will be reduced if a loan is taken against the reserve (i.e., guaranteed cash value) of the policy. As stated in the ledger statement, the fixed guaranteed interest rate charged for loans against the reserve is 8 percent. Because the insurance company assumed that it must earn from 11.57 percent to 11.73 percent on money coming in to pay the projected dividend, the dividend will be reduced if the policy owner borrows money from the policy because the insurance company is earning 3.57 to 3.73 percent less than it assumed.

4. Although not stated on the ledger statement, this particular insurance company gives the option of electing a variable loan rate versus the

fixed loan rate. If the variable loan rate is equal to the dividend interest assumption rate, the dividend should not be reduced. If the variable loan rate exceeds the dividend interest assumption rate, the dividend may be increased. Variable loan rates change with market rates and are often explicitly linked to an index, such as the average yield on government bonds with five years to maturity. The information should also be included on the ledger statement.

5. The rate of return expressed in terms of compound interest should be given either on the ledger statement or by the life insurance agent. Ideally, it should be provided for each year. If the agent does not have the proper financial decisions software, it will be economically impossible to provide yearly rates of return. A financial decisions calculator can be used, however, on an economical basis to provided rates of return for various years (year one, year five, year ten, year twenty, and to life expectancy).

6. The rate of return upon death for this policy for sequential years is as follows:

Year	Rate of Return
1	4,897.50%
5	90.50
10	30.00
20	12.87
29 (life expectancy)	9.77

7. Once the rate of return upon death is known, then it can be determined what would have to be earned before taxes (it is assumed that the death benefit is considered life insurance proceeds and, as such, not subject to federal or state income taxes) in other financial services products (e.g., mutual funds, certificates of deposit, real estate, or commodities) to duplicate the tax-exempt rate of return provided by life insurance. The before-tax rate of return is determined by dividing the life insurance rate of return by the marginal tax bracket subtracted from 100 percent (for 15 percent, the factor is 0.85; for 25 percent, 0.75; for 28 percent, 0.72; for 33 percent, 0.67; and for 35 percent, 0.65). The result is shown in Figure 13.2.

8. The rate of return upon surrender should also be provided. When the rate of return upon surrender is positive, it means that taxes are due. Generally, taxes are due on the difference between the cash surrender value and the premiums paid. The result before taxes is as follows:

Year	Rate of Return
1	−100.00%
5	−8.62
10	2.57
20	7.16
29 (life expectancy)	7.40

9. The ledger statement should be the official ledger statement produced by the computer service of the life insurance company. If it is not "bug-free," the bugs should be revealed.

WHERE CAN I FIND OUT MORE?

See the list of references in Chapter 14, "Ordinary Level Premium Whole Life Insurance."

Figure 13.2

BEFORE TAX RATE OF RETURN					
Year	15% taxpayer	25% taxpayer	28% taxpayer	33% taxpayer	35% Taxpayer
1	5,761.76%	6,530%	6,802.08%	7,309.7%	7,534.62%
5	106.47	120.67	125.69	135.07	139.23
10	35.29	40.00	41.67	44.78	46.15
20	15.14	17.16	17.88	19.21	19.80
29 (life expectancy)	11.49	13.03	13.57	14.58	15.03

FREQUENTLY ASKED QUESTIONS

Question – What is the difference between a "paid-up" policy and a "matured" policy?

Answer – A policy that is "paid-up" requires no further premium payments to keep the policy's full face amount of coverage in force for the remaining term of the contract (generally to age one hundred). This results when premium payments have been sufficiently large to build the reserve necessary to support the policy for the remaining term. However, the reserve, which is closely tied to the cash surrender value of the policy, will always be less than the face value of the policy until the end of the term of the contract. At the time when the reserve equals the face value of the contract, the policy has "matured." In other words, the face value (death benefit) and the cash value of a matured policy are equal (or nearly so). In a paid-up policy, the cash value is less than the face value until the end of the term of the contract when it matures.

Question – Can a limited pay policy with scheduled premium payments for more than seven years still fail the seven-pay test and be treated as a modified endowment contract (MEC)?

Answer – In general, insurance companies are careful to design limited pay policies so that they pass the seven-pay test under the MEC rules. If the policy initially fails the seven-pay test, the policy illustration or ledger statement should clearly say so. However, even if the policy initially satisfies the seven-pay test, it may later fail the test if dividends are applied as additional premiums. It is conceivable that a ten-pay policy, for example, may fail the seven-pay test if the insured continues to pay the full annual premiums and dividends are applied as additional premiums. See Chapter 22 for a full discussion of the MEC rules (including the procedure allowing life insurance companies to correct the payment of excess premiums).

CHAPTER ENDNOTES

1. I.R.C. §101(a).
2. I.R.C. §72(j); Treas. Reg. §1.72-14(a).
3. I.R.C. §72(e).
4. *Id.*
5. I.R.C. §7702A(a).
6. I.R.C. §101(a).
7. I.R.C. §72(e).
8. I.R.C. §72(v).
9. H.R. Conf. Rep. No. 100-1104, (TAMRA '88) *reprinted in* 1988-3 CB 592.
10. This analysis is adapted from the excellent discussion on this topic in *The Life Insurance Buyer's Guide* by William D. Brownlie with Jeffrey L. Seglin published by McGraw-Hill Publishing Company (1989).

ORDINARY LEVEL PREMIUM WHOLE LIFE INSURANCE

CHAPTER 14

INTRODUCTION

Whole life insurance, as the name implies, is a contract designed to provide protection over the insured's entire lifetime. There are many types of whole life policies, but the oldest and still the most common type of whole life policy is ordinary level premium whole life insurance, or simply ordinary life. This form of insurance is also known as "straight life," "traditional whole life," or "continuous premium whole life." If the term "whole life" is used alone, it is generally accepted that the reference is to ordinary level premium whole life as opposed to any other type of lifelong policy.

This type of contract features level or fixed periodic premiums computed on the assumption that the policyowner can retain the policy for the life of the insured. The death benefit remains level throughout the lifetime of the contract. Insurers invented the level premium concept to make the whole life contract affordable for as long as the policyowner decided to keep it.

As an outgrowth and natural byproduct of the fixed and level premium, the whole life contract develops cash values. These values result from the reserve the insurer needs to accumulate in the early years of the policy's life so that they will have sufficient money (together with interest earned on the reserve) in later years to pay the promised death benefit while keeping premiums level. Absent this reserve, the level premium would be insufficient to pay the increasing mortality costs as the insured ages. The policy contains a fixed and guaranteed schedule of the cash values that the policyowner may borrow for any reason (such as an emergency or opportunity) at any time or take upon surrendering the contract.

The policyowner agrees to pay a fixed or level premium at regular intervals for the rest of the insured's life (generally only up to age one hundred, if the insured lives that long, or in some cases, to age ninety-five). In return, the insurance company agrees to pay a fixed death benefit when the insured dies if the policyowner has continued to pay the premiums. Policyowners who discontinue paying premiums and terminate their policies are entitled to the scheduled cash surrender value.

WHEN IS THE USE OF THIS DEVICE INDICATED?

There are nearly 2,000 life insurance companies actively marketing life insurance coverage in the United States. Most of these companies offer level premium whole life policies as well as other permanent forms of life insurance. In addition to commercial insurance companies, some fraternal organizations, savings banks, professional associations, membership organizations, and stockbrokerage houses offer level premium whole life policies. Prospective insureds can purchase policies through many agents representing licensed insurance companies.

In general, some type of life insurance is indicated when a person needs or wants to provide an immediate estate upon his or her death. This need or desire typically stems from one or more of the following reasons.

1. To provide income for dependent family members until they become self-supporting after the head of household dies.

2. To liquidate consumer or business debts or mortgages, or to create a fund that would enable the surviving family members to do so when the head of household dies.

3. To provide large amounts of cash at death for children's college expenses or other capital needs.

4. To provide cash for federal estate and state inheritance taxes, funeral expenses, and administration costs.

5. To provide funds for the continuation of a business through a "buy-sell" agreement.

6. To indemnify a business for the loss of a key employee.

7. To help recruit, retain, retire, or reward one or more key employees through a salary continuation plan and to finance the company's obligations under that plan to the dependents of a deceased key employee.

8. To fund bequests of capital to children, grandchildren, or others without the erosion often caused by probate costs, inheritance taxes, income taxes, federal estate taxes, transfer fees, or the generation-skipping transfer tax.

9. To fund charitable bequests.

10. To preserve confidentiality of financial affairs. Life insurance proceeds payable to someone other than the deceased's estate are not part of the probate estate and are not a matter of public record. It is not unusual for a beneficiary to be a lover, illegitimate child, or to have some other relationship to the insured that the insured may not want to publicly acknowledge. Likewise, the insured may not want the amount payable to the beneficiary to become a matter of public record.

11. To assure nearly instant access to cash for surviving dependents. Insurers generally pay life insurance proceeds to beneficiaries within days of the claim. There is no delay, as might be the case with other types of assets, because of the intervention of state or other governmental bodies due to settlement of tax issues, or because of claims by the decedent's creditors.

12. To direct family assets to family members in a way that minimizes state, local, and federal taxes.

13. Level premium whole life, in particular, is the preferred type of policy when the need is long-term and there is a desire to maintain a relatively fixed annual premium cost. For many families, it is the most "affordable" form of long-term coverage on the principal breadwinners.

14. Level premium whole life may satisfy various business related life insurance needs (e.g., financing vehicles for buy-sell agreements, key person insurance and nonqualified deferred compensation arrangements). It is especially suitable if the objective is also to receive tax sheltered returns and the company has accumulated earnings problems. The cash buildup in life insurance policies held for legitimate business purposes is not counted towards the accumulated earnings limitation.

15. Level premium whole life insurance is often the preferred type of insurance for split dollar arrangements. (See Chapter 41 for a further discussion.)

16. Level premium whole life is a tax-sheltered way to finance post-retirement health insurance for a selected group of executives or key employees by using life insurance policies on their lives. Cash values are available to the corporation to help meet future cash needs for health insurance premium payments for retirees. When the employee dies, the corporation receives the death proceeds free from federal income tax (except for some potential alternative minimum tax liability). The corporation is reimbursed for part or all of its costs for the postretirement health insurance. Corporate Owned Life Insurance (COLI) offers certain advantages over other methods for recovering postretirement health insurance liabilities.

Advantages

1. A fixed and known annual premium. Although, it should be noted that net premiums (fixed premiums minus dividends) for par policies generally will decline over the years.

2. Guaranteed ceiling on mortality and expense charges and guaranteed floor on interest credited to cash values.

3. Cash value interest or earnings accumulate tax-free or tax deferred, depending on whether gains are distributed at death or during lifetime.

4. Ordinary life, through the combination of guaranteed cash values and dividend formulas, frequently pays higher effective interest on cash values than is available from tax-free municipal bonds.

5. Cash values are not subject to the market risk associated with longer term municipal bonds and other longer term fixed income investments.

6. Policyowners can borrow cash values at a low net cost. Although policyowners must pay interest on policy loans, cash values continue to grow and as the insurance company credits at least the minimum guaranteed rate in the policy. Consequently, the actual net borrowing rate is less than the stated policy loan rate.

7. Life insurance proceeds are not part of the probate estate, unless the estate is named as the beneficiary of the policy. Therefore, the beneficiary can receive the proceeds without the expense, delay, or uncertainty caused by administration of the estate.

8. There is no public record of the death benefit amount or to whom it is payable.

9. In most cases, the death benefit proceeds are not subject to federal income taxes.

10. The death benefit proceeds are often fully or partially exempt from state inheritance taxes unless payable to the insured's estate.

11. Policyowners can use life insurance policies as collateral or security for personal loans.

Disadvantages

1. Lifetime distributions of cash values are subject to income tax to the extent attributable to gain in the policy.

2. The premium may be unaffordable for persons of limited financial resources.

3. In the early years, the amount of protection is lower relative to the premium spent than with term insurance. However, later, as term premiums rise while the premiums for ordinary life remain level, the reverse typically will be true.

4. Surrender of the policy within the first five to ten years may result in considerable loss because surrender values reflect the insurance company's recovery of sales commissions and initial policy expenses.

5. Policyowners generally may not deduct interest paid on policy loans on their tax returns.

6. Cash values accumulating in the contract are subject to inflation. Whole life insurance is by definition a long-term purchase and the guaranteed return on this type of policy provides little inflation protection. However, a partial hedge against inflation is provided by the dividends paid on participating policies which reflect the favorable mortality, investment, and business expense results of the insurer.

7. The overall rate of return on the cash values inside traditional whole life contracts has not always been competitive in a before-tax comparison with alternative investments. However, when safety of principal, contractually guaranteed liquidity, and the cost of term insurance if purchased outside the policy are factored into the analysis, whole life often compares favorably to alternative types of policies as well as nonlife insurance investments on an aftertax basis.

USING ORDINARY LIFE AS A SAVINGS VEHICLE

One can view ordinary level premium whole life mathematically (but not legally) as a combination of decreasing term insurance and increasing "savings fund." Although the level premium payment method permits the policyowner to pay the lowest up-front outlay necessary to acquire lifetime coverage, the premiums are still greater than the mortality costs in the early years. Because premiums remain level while mortality costs increase at later ages, the insurer must set premiums in the early years high enough to prefund the excess of mortality costs over premiums in the later years. Consequently, ordinary level premium whole life policies build reserves to pay the future excess mortality costs and to serve as the basis for determining the policyowner's cash surrender values.

The cash value normally increases each year until it reaches the face value at age one hundred. The cash value grows more slowly in the early years and more swiftly in the later years because the company typically recovers the expenses associated with the sale of the policy over the early years.

Policyowners may directly access cash values in ordinary life policies in two ways. First, policies permit policyowners to borrow cash values. As long as the policyowner continues to pay premiums, the policy remains in force, but the death benefit is the face amount reduced by any outstanding policy loans and unpaid interest on the policy loans.

Alternatively, policyowners may terminate or surrender their policies and receive the net cash surrender value shown in the policy as of the date of surrender. The net surrender value is:

- the gross cash value shown in the policy;

- *minus* any identifiable surrender charges, outstanding policy loans, and unpaid interest on policy loans;

- *plus* any prepaid premiums, dividends accumulated at interest, cash values attributable to paid-up additions, and any additional terminal dividends.

In this case, however, the policyowner must give up the insurance protection.

Because policyowners may access virtually the same amount of cash through policy loans as through surrender of the policy, loans are generally the better alternative if the policyowner expects the need for protection to continue.

In some cases, the policies may permit partial surrenders. Some participating policies permit policyowners to surrender paid-up additions without surrendering the base policy. Although it is not a matter of legal right, in practice some companies also will allow partial surrenders of ordinary life policies. In these cases, the insurer reduces the death benefit and premiums in proportion to the reduction in the cash value.

One additional method to access cash values without giving up coverage entirely may be to exchange a policy for another policy with a lower cash value under the exchange rules of Code section 1035. These rules are discussed in Chapter 23.

POLICY FEATURES

Par and Nonpar Policies

The premiums, the death benefit, and the minimum cash surrender value schedule are initially fixed in ordinary level premium whole life policies. However, if the policy is a dividend paying, or "participating" (par) policy, the premiums may effectively decrease and the death benefit and the scheduled cash surrender values may increase. Only if the policy is a "guaranteed-cost, nonparticipating" (nonpar) policy that does not pay dividends will each of these features truly remain fixed for the life of the insured. See Chapter 1, "Introduction to Life Insurance" for a general discussion of the differences between par and nonpar policies.

Use of Dividends

Policyowners have considerable flexibility in choosing how to use dividends paid on par policies. Dividends may be paid to the policyowner in cash, though most policyowners find one of the other options more attractive. In addition, dividends may be applied against policy loans and/or interest on policy loans, or in some cases, treated as additional premium payments.

Beyond these relatively straight-forward options, policyowners may elect to have dividends:

- allocated to pay premiums;

- applied against outstanding policy loans;

- accumulated at interest;

- used to purchase paid-up additional amounts of insurance;

- used to purchase a one-year term insurance policy.

Policyowners may change these options at any time in most policies.

Premium Reduction Option

One of the more frequently used options is to apply dividends against required premium payments. This option is really just an administratively convenient cash option, because, in either case, dividends effectively serve to reduce premiums. In general, the amount of dividends insurers pay on a policy increases over time, ever reducing the policyowner's net premium outlay (premiums less dividend payments), sometimes to zero or less after the policy has been in force for a long period of time. At this point, the policyowner usually must elect another option for the excess dividend payments.

Under the cash option or the premium reduction option, the policyowner's net premiums effectively decline over time (because the dividend level generally increases) while the death benefit remains level and the cash surrender schedule remains fixed. Policyowners may also use the "vanishing premium option" described in the "Frequently Asked Questions" section below.

Policy Loan Repayment Option

Similar to the premium reduction option, this option is really just an administrative convenience variation on the cash option. Rather than having the company pay the dividends in cash to the policyowner and then have the policyowner turn around and write a check to the insurance company to pay policy loans or interest on loans, the policyowner may have the dividends applied directly against the policy loans and/or interest on loans.

Accumulate at Interest Option

Policyowners may elect to leave their dividend payments with the insurance company to accumulate in a fund appended to the policy. In other words, the insurance company will provide a savings-type account for dividends. The interest rate payable on the fund is guaranteed to equal or exceed a specified minimum (historically about 4 to 6 percent, but in the past decade of low market interest rates, considerably lower), but most companies have historically credited rates higher than the guaranteed minimum. Policyowners may withdraw cash from the fund at any time. If the insured dies the policy pays the face value. If the policy is surrendered, it pays the net cash surrender value plus the value of the dividend accumulation account.

Paid-up Additions Option

Under this option, the insurer applies each dividend payment to buy as much paid-up single premium whole life insurance as the dividend will allow at the insured's attained age. Consequently, under this option the premiums payable by the policyowner remain level while the total death benefit and the schedule of total cash values increases over time.

The paid-up additions are available without evidence of insurability. The insurance is purchased at net rates, that is, without any of the commissions and other front-end charges associated with new sales of insurance. Therefore, this is a low cost method of acquiring additional insurance without having to prove insurability.

The paid-up additions usually (but not always) are participating. This means the annual dividends paid on the paid-up additions further escalate overall dividend payments and further supplement the policy's total death benefit and cash values. Similar to cash values under the base policy, the policyowner may borrow against the cash values of the paid-up additions. As described above, some companies will permit policyowners to surrender paid-up additions for the net surrender values while keeping the underlying policy in force.

One-year Term Insurance Option

Under the general form of this option, the insurer applies each year's dividend to purchase as much one-year term insurance as the dividend will allow at the insured's attained age. Similar to the paid-up option, the policyowner acquires the term insurance at net rates and without the need to prove insurability.

Under a second form of this option, the insurer uses the dividend to buy one-year term insurance in an amount up to the cash value of the policy. The policyowner may apply any excess dividends under one of the other options. This form of the option frequently is used with split dollar insurance which is commonly used in key person and other business life insurance applications. (See Chapter 41 for a further discussion of split dollar life insurance arrangements.) With the split dollar arrangement, the premium payer, generally the insured's company, is entitled to the cash value or an amount equal to the cash value from the death proceeds. The net amount at risk (the difference between the face amount and the cash value) generally is payable to whomever the insured so designates, often the spouse or child of the insured. Under this form of the one-year term option, the insured's designated beneficiary can receive a death benefit equal to the full face value of the underlying policy.

Policy Loans

All cash value policies must allow policyowners to borrow cash values from the policy. For many policyowners, the cash values in their life insurance policies represent an important source of emergency funds. The loan provision typically has the following features:

1. In general, policyowners may borrow up to the cash value less interest on the loan as of the subsequent policy anniversary.

2. The interest rate may be fixed or variable, depending on the policy and, sometimes, on the election of the insured.

3. Policyowners generally have no obligation to repay loans and interest on any fixed schedule; they may repay in whole or in part at any time. However, if they terminate their policy or if the insured dies, the cash surrender value or the death benefit is reduced by any outstanding policy loans and unpaid interest. Also, if policy loans equal or exceed the cash value, the policyowner generally must repay the loan in full or in part within thirty-one days of being notified by the company, otherwise the policy will terminate.

4. If the policyowner does not pay interest when due, the company usually automatically charges an additional loan against the policy equal to the unpaid interest.

5. Policy loans require no approval and are confidential.

6. The amount of loan available generally includes the cash value of any paid-up additions.

Interest Rates on Policy Loans

At one time, insurers issued virtually all policies with fixed policy loan rates, often as low as 5 percent or 6 percent. However, when market interest rates were higher than policy loan rates, insurance companies found themselves squeezed by disintermediation—the process whereby policyowners borrow their cash values at low rates and invest outside their policies in higher-yielding market investments. The insurance companies found themselves with an ever-increasing portion of the investment portfolio in low yielding policy loans and their investment performance suffered. As a result, dividends paid on many participating ordinary life policies were not competitive with the interest being credited to current assumption and universal life policies.

The insurance companies took three steps to counter this trend. First, they offered new policies with variable or adjustable loan rates. In these policies, the insurers tied the variable loan rate to an index of corporate bonds and adjusted the rate at least once a year, but, in some cases, as frequently as quarterly. Some insurers still issue policies with fixed rates, but at generally higher rates, ranging from 7 to 10 percent. Many new policies allow policyowners to choose either a fixed or variable loan rate. However, in most cases, insurers offer policyowners potentially higher dividends if they are willing to accept the adjustable loan rate.

Second, insurance companies offered incentives for policyowners of existing policies with low fixed loan rates to either agree to a higher fixed loan rate (usually 8 percent) or to an adjustable loan rate. In return, the company promised to move the policy into a higher dividend rating class. Many companies allow existing policyowners to exchange their existing low loan rate policies for new adjustable loan rate policies with favorable terms or conditions such as enhanced cash value schedules, higher face amounts, a higher dividend classification, and lower than normal upfront exchange fees.

Third, many new policies have "direct recognition" provisions that permit the insurer to adjust dividends within a class of policies based on policy loan activity. Dividends insurers pay on policies with loans outstanding may be lower than those they pay on similar policies without policy loans. This is an important concept because it is essentially an indirect method of increasing the policy loan rate. For example, assume the policy loan rate is fixed at 8 percent. The policyowner would pay $80 interest per year on each $1,000 borrowed from the policy. However, assume that for this class of policies that dividends paid on policies with loans are $10 less for each $1,000 of borrowing than on policies without any loans. The policyowner is actually paying an effective rate of 9 percent on the amount borrowed, not the stated 8 percent policy loan rate. This can have even further implications if, for instance, a policyowner is using dividends to purchase paid-up additions. The additional paid-up face amount and the additional cash value will be less than it otherwise would have been. Also, if the paid-up additions are participating, future dividends will be less than they would otherwise have been as a result of the lower cash values in the paid-up additions, even if the policy loan is later repaid.

Automatic Premium Loans

Most ordinary life policies are issued with an automatic premium loan provision that authorizes the company to automatically pay the premium by borrowing against the cash value if the premium remains unpaid at the end of the thirty-one-day grace period. This provision prevents the policy from lapsing if the policyowner inadvertently misses a premium payment. In most states, the provision is operative unless the policyowner specifically indicates that it should not be operative. In some other states, the provision becomes operative only if the policyowner specifically elects to make it operative.

The automatic premium loan generally is a "no charge" provision that policyowners should look for to avoid unintentional lapses. In most cases, the policy may be reinstated if it inadvertently lapses, but the insured must usually show evidence of insurability.

PREMIUMS

Life insurance companies are free to set premiums according to their own marketing strategies. Almost all states have statutes prohibiting any form of rebating (sharing the commission with the purchaser) by the agent. The premium includes a "loading" to cover such things as commissions to agents, premium taxes payable to the state government, operating expenses of the insurance company such as rent, mortgage payments and salaries, and other company expenses.

A few companies offer "no-load" or "low-load" life insurance policies. These policies are not really no-load, because certain expenses are unavoidable (e.g., the premium tax), but rather pay either no sales commission or a very low sales commission. Consequently, the cash value buildup tends to be larger in the early years. Although commissions are lower, these companies typically must spend somewhat more money on alternative methods of marketing and may therefore incur generally higher expenses in this area than companies that pay commissions to agents.

The bulk of an insurance company's expenses for a policy are incurred when the policy is issued. It may take the company five years or longer to recover all its front-end costs. The state premium tax is an ongoing expense that averages about 2 percent of each premium payment. With most cash value policies the aggregate commission paid to the selling agent is approximately equal to the first year premium on the policy. About half (often 55 percent) is payable in the year of sale and the other half is paid on a renewal basis over a period of three to nine years.

Most ordinary level premium life insurance policies have no explicit surrender charges. However, most participating policies will pay a terminal dividend. The terminal dividend is typically higher the longer the policy has remained in force. In essence, this is a form of surrender charge because the company is essentially holding back dividends it could otherwise pay currently and rewarding those policyholders who maintain their policy longer with a greater terminal dividend.

Frequency of Premiums

Insurance companies usually quote insurance premiums on an annual basis, but the insurer can convert the annual payment to monthly or quarterly payments, if the policyowner desires. When insurers convert annual premiums to monthly or quarterly payments, they typically charge an implicit interest rate on the payments that are deferred until later in the year. In other words, the insurance company essentially is loaning the policyowner a portion of the annual premium that the policyowner then repays over the term of the year with a "borrowing" rate equal to the implicit rate. If the implicit rate is greater than the policyowner's after-tax opportunity cost of funds (the policyowner's potential after-tax investment rate), he or she should pay the premium annually, if possible. Conversely, if the implicit rate is less than the policyowner's potential after-tax investment rate, the policyowner will be better off deferring payments by electing to pay monthly or quarterly.

If, for cash flow reasons, the policyowner cannot pay the premiums annually, the issue is whether the insurance company's implicit rate is greater than or less than the after tax-rate at which the policyowner could otherwise borrow money to pay the annual premium. If the implicit rate is higher than the policyowner's after-tax borrowing rate, he or she should borrow the money elsewhere and pay the premium annually. Conversely, if the implicit rate is lower than the after-tax borrowing rate, the policyowner should elect to pay premiums quarterly or monthly.

The decision as to which payment plan to elect depends on the insurance company's implicit rate. One may determine the implicit rate in the following manner. The ratio of the monthly (or quarterly) premium to the annual premium is called the monthly (or quarterly) conversion factor. Once one knows (or computes) the conversion factor, one can determine the interest rate that the insurance company is implicitly charging for the monthly or quarterly payment plan. For example, if the monthly payment is equal to 1/12 (.083333) of the annual premium, the insurance company is charging 0 percent interest on the premium payment plan.

In virtually all cases, however, the monthly payment is greater than 1/12 (.083333) of the annual premium because of an implicit interest charge. Figure 1 shows the interest rate the insurance company is implicitly charging for various monthly and quarterly conversion factors. For example, assume the premium for a policy is $1,000 if paid annually or $88.75 if paid monthly. The monthly conversion factor is the ratio of the monthly premium to the annual premium, $88.75/$1,000, or 0.08875. According to the table, the

implicit interest rate for this monthly conversion factor is about 14 percent.

TAX IMPLICATIONS

Death benefits are usually free of any federal income tax. In general, death benefits paid under these policies are subject to the same income, estate, gift, and generation-skipping transfer taxation rules as all other types of life insurance policies. See Chapters 22 through 30 for a complete discussion of the taxation of life insurance.

Taxation of Living Proceeds

Section 72 of the Internal Revenue Code governs the taxation of living proceeds from life insurance policies.

Figure 14.1

IMPLICIT INTEREST RATES FOR CONVERTING ANNUAL PREMIUMS TO QUARTERLY OR MONTHLY PREMIUMS		
Quarterly Conversion Factor*	Monthly Conversion Factor*	Implicit Interest Rate
0.25000	0.083333	0%
025094	0.083716	1
0.25187	0.084099	2
0.25281	0.084482	3
0.25374	0.084867	4
0.25468	0.085252	5
0.25561	0.085638	6
0.25654	0.086025	7
0.25747	0.086412	8
0.25840	0.086800	9
0.25933	0.087189	10
0.26119	0.087969	12
0.26304	0.088752	14
0.26397	0.089144	15
0.26489	0.089537	16
0.26674	0.090325	18
0.26858	0.091116	20
0.27317	0.093105	25
0.27774	0.095109	30

*Ratio of monthly or quarterly premium to annual premium.

Living proceeds are generally any amounts received during the insured's lifetime. For tax purposes, payments are separated into three classes: (1) annuity payments; (2) payments of interest only; and (3) amounts not received as an annuity.

Annuity payments – Annuities include all periodic payments received from the contract in a systematic liquidation of the cash value. This includes both life contingent annuities and fixed term or fixed amount annuities. The rules of IRC Section 72 determine what portion of each payment is treated as a tax-free recovery of investment in the contract and what portion is treated as taxable income or gain. To oversimplify, the rules essentially pro rate the recovery of investment in the contract over the expected payout period. Therefore, each payment is treated partially as recovery of investment and partially as taxable interest until the entire investment in the contract has been recovered. Any further payments are treated entirely as taxable income. (See Chapter 8 for a more in depth discussion of the taxation of annuities.)

Payments of interest only – Payments consisting of interest only (i.e., they are not part of the systematic liquidation of a principal sum) are not annuity payments and are not taxed under the annuity rules. In general, if living benefits are held by the insurer under an agreement to pay interest, the interest payments are taxable in full when distributed or simply credited to the account.

Amounts not received as an annuity – In general, all living proceeds except for interest and annuity settlements are taxed under the "cost recovery rule." Included in this category are policy dividends, lump-sum cash settlements of cash surrender values, cash withdrawals, and amounts received on partial surrender. These amounts are included in gross income only to the extent they exceed the investment in the contract (as reduced by any prior excludable distributions received from the contract). In other words, nonannuity distributions during life are first treated as a return of the policyowner's investment in the contract (generally premiums paid less dividends received), and then as taxable interest or gain.

MEC Rules

The exceptions to this rule are generally unlikely to arise with level premium policies. The first exception is with respect to policies that initially fail the seven-pay test under the Modified Endowment Contract (MEC) rules. Because level premium policies are designed to have premiums payable for the life of the insured, they are not likely to fail the seven-pay test. The second exception is with respect to policies that originally satisfied the tests to avoid MEC treatment, but that as a result of certain changes in the benefits of the contract, subsequently fail the tests. Once again, the types of changes that would jeopardize favorable MEC status are unlikely to arise with ordinary level premium whole life policies. Problems are more likely to arise with limited pay policies and universal life policies. If any life insurance contract is treated as a MEC, cash distributions are generally taxed under the interest-first rule. Under this rule, distributions are first attributed to interest or gain in the contract and are fully taxable. Only when the interest or gain is exhausted are distributions treated as a nontaxable recovery of investment in the contract.

Loan Proceeds

Policy loans under non-MEC life insurance policies are not treated as distributions. If a policy loan is still outstanding when a policy is surrendered, the borrowed amount becomes taxable at the time of surrender to the extent the cash value exceeds the policyowner's investment in the contract. Loans are essentially treated as if the borrowed amount was actually received at the time of surrender and used to pay off the loan.

SELECTING THE BEST OF ITS TYPE

Selecting the best cash value life insurance policy is a difficult task involving a number of complicated concepts and analyses. (See Chapter 4, "How to Determine the Right Policy" for a further discussion.) However, because the level of dividend payments on participating ordinary level premium life insurance is a critical element of the overall cost of the protection, one primary area of focus should be how the company determines the dividends it pays.

Evaluating the Dividends Paid on Par Policies

1. Compare the current rate credited to policy cash values and the length of the guarantees. All else being equal, policies with higher current rates and longer guarantee periods will be better than those with lower current rates and shorter guarantees.

2. Check to see how the company will determine the rate credited to policy cash values after the guarantee period. Policies that determine the rate based on a specific money rate or bond index leave the company with little room to manipulate the amount credited in an adverse way.

3. Look at the current mortality and expense factors and compare them with the guaranteed maximum mortality and expense factors. The mortality factors currently used should be competitive. If the difference between the current mortality rates and the maximum rates is small, the company has little room to use higher mortality charges as a means of reducing the effective rate credited to cash values.

4. Look for a bailout provision that reduces or eliminates surrender charges if investment performance does not meet reasonable guidelines.

5. Check the policy loan provision to see if the company uses an "offset" provision to credit borrowed amounts with a lower rate than nonborrowed amounts. If the insured anticipates borrowing from the policy, a company that does not use the offset method is preferable. If borrowing is not anticipated, a company that uses the offset method may be more desirable because the company, in theory, should be able to credit higher interest to policies without borrowing than they otherwise would be able to credit without the offset provision.

6. Check the financial soundness of the company using the criteria in Chapter 3, "How to Determine the Right Company." In the past, some insurance companies attempted to increase their portfolio yield by investing a substantial portion of their assets in relatively high yield but also high risk "junk" bonds. As a result of adverse market conditions and increased defaults on these bonds, some of these companies experienced serious financial stress and reduced portfolio yields.

Using the Ledger Statement of an Ordinary Life Policy

What to look for in the ledger statement of an ordinary level premium policy is similar to the items that one should evaluate in relation to any whole life policy. See Figure 13.1 in Chapter 13, "Limited-Pay Whole Life Insurance" for a discussion of what to look for in whole life policy illustrations.

ALTERNATIVES

There is no substitute for life insurance that provides an immediate estate upon a person's death. All types of life insurance policies can provide tax-free cash upon death. The unique feature of level premium life insurance is its "affordability." It provides lifetime coverage at the lowest level annual cost relative to other types of whole life policies. As a byproduct of level premium financing, the policy creates a tax-free or tax deferred cash buildup. Persons desiring a combination of tax preferred cash accumulation and life insurance may want to explore other alternatives:

1. *A combination of a level premium deferred annuity and decreasing term insurance* – Cash values accumulate in both annuities and level premium life insurance policies on a tax deferred basis. Therefore, a combination of a level premium deferred annuity and a decreasing term policy can provide levels of tax preferred cash accumulation and death benefits similar to a level premium policy.

There are some important differences, however. The tax rules treat withdrawals, lifetime distributions, or loans from each arrangement differently for tax purposes. Although most ordinary life policies do not permit withdrawals, as such, if a withdrawal of cash values is permitted or the policy is partially surrendered, the amount distributed is taxed under the cost recovery rule. That is, the amounts are included in taxable income only to the extent they exceed the investment in the contract. In contrast, distributions from annuities are taxed under the interest-first rule. In other words, the amounts are fully taxable until owner has recovered all of the excess over the investment in the contract. In addition, nonannuity distributions from an annuity contract before age 59½ may be subject to a 10 percent penalty tax. Furthermore, loans from life insurance policies are not subject to tax; loans from annuities, if permitted, are treated as distributions and taxed under the interest-first rule (i.e., loan proceeds are subject to the regular income tax and may be subject to the 10 percent penalty tax). Finally, loan provisions of deferred annuity contracts are generally more restrictive than those of life insurance policies.

The annuity-term combination will require some additional and increasing premiums over the years for the term coverage. In addition, the mortality charges for term insurance coverage are typically higher than the mortality charges in a level premium policy. Finally, the death proceeds from the insurance policy generally may pass to the beneficiary entirely income and estate tax free, regardless of who is the beneficiary, if the insured has no incidents of ownership in the policy. The gains on the annuity contract still will be income taxable to the beneficiary and will avoid estate taxation only if the annuitant's spouse is the beneficiary and is a United States citizen.

2. *A combination of investments in tax-free municipal bonds and decreasing term insurance* – This combination can create a cash accumulation and death benefit similar to a level premium policy. Similar to the cash values in a life insurance policy, bond owners may use municipal bonds as collateral for loans without any adverse income tax consequences. However, interest paid on debt secured by municipal bonds is not deductible. Although not the general rule, in some cases, the interest paid on life insurance policy loans may be tax deductible. The life insurance policy allows the death benefits to be transferred by operation of the contract and avoids probate. Municipal bonds are part of the probate estate and must be distributed by will. Once again, if the policyowner has no incidents of ownership, the death proceeds are paid estate tax free. The municipal bonds will escape estate tax only if they are left to the spouse and sheltered by the marital deduction.

3. *A universal life policy configured as a level premium policy* – A universal life policy can be initially configured to resemble a level premium life policy. However, in contrast with "true" level premium life policies, charges for mortality and expenses can change in the universal life policy in such a way that the policyowner could need to pay additional premiums in the future to maintain the death benefit coverage.

WHERE CAN I FIND OUT MORE?

The following references include authoritative discussions of various types of life insurance including ordinary level premium whole life insurance:

1. B. Baldwin, *New Life Insurance Investment Advisor: Achieving Financial Security for You and Your Family Through Today's Insurance Products*, 2nd ed. (Hightstown, NJ: McGraw-Hill Trade, 2001).

2. J. Belth, *Life Insurance: A Consumer's Handbook*, 2nd ed. (Bloomington, IN: Indiana University Press, 1985).

3. K. Black, Jr. and H. Skipper, Jr., *Life Insurance*, 13th ed. (Old Tappan, NJ: Prentice Hall Inc., 1999).

4. E. Graves, Editor, *McGill's Life Insurance*, 5th ed. (Bryn Mawr, PA: The American College, 2009).

The following references are useful guides for policy and company rating information:

1. *Best Insurance Reports* (Oldwick, NJ: A. M. Best Company, published annually).

2. *Best's Review – Life/Health Edition* (Oldwick, NJ: A. M. Best Company, published monthly).

FREQUENTLY ASKED QUESTIONS

Question – What is meant by the "vanishing premium" option?

Answer – This option is similar to the premium reduction option except that the dividends are applied as additional premiums while the policyowner continues to pay the full annual premium. Under this option, the policyowner is essentially converting what is an ordinary level premium whole life policy into a form of increasing premium limited pay policy. After a number of years, the policy will be entirely paid-up and the policyowner will require no further premiums to keep the full face amount in force for the remainder of the insured's life. In other words, if the assumptions are met the premium "vanishes". (Of course, if the level of dividends projected is not met, it will take longer than anticipated for this to occur.) Once the policy reaches paid-up status, policyowners typically use additional dividends to buy paid-up additions, but they generally may apply the additional dividends under any of the other dividend options.

Although it would be unusual, if a policyowner applies dividends as additional premiums, it is theoretically possible for dividend payments to reach a sufficiently high level soon enough to violate the modified endowment contract (MEC) rules. Because having the policy classified as a MEC would have adverse tax consequences, policyowners and their advisers should take some care when this dividend option is selected to assure that premiums do not exceed the MEC levels. (See Chapter 22 for a further discussion of the MEC rules.)

SINGLE PREMIUM LIFE INSURANCE

CHAPTER 15

INTRODUCTION

Single Premium Life Insurance (SPLI) is permanent cash value whole life insurance that is purchased with a single large premium. As its name implies, it requires no further premiums to keep the coverage in force for the life of the insured.

Single premium life insurance represents one end of the spectrum in terms of the payment schedules policyowners may choose to purchase lifetime coverage. Ordinary level premium whole life insurance represents the other extreme. Limited pay policies (for example, where premiums are paid for ten or twenty years or until the insured reaches age sixty-five) represent the middle ground.

In each case, the premiums charged by the insurance company must be sufficient to pay all anticipated death benefits from the group of similar policies issued by the company over the lives of all the insureds. All other things remaining the same, as the number of payments decreases the annual premium, and consequently, the rate of growth of policy cash values, becomes correspondingly larger. Therefore, single premium life insurance, for those who can afford the premium, provides the maximum allowable tax-free investment buildup permitted in a life insurance policy (or tax deferred buildup, depending on how the proceeds are received).

These policies are designed so that the cash value invested in the policy earns a rate of interest that is competitive with other investments of comparable risk. The initial interest rate is typically guaranteed for one year, although there are some three-year and even five-year guarantees available. These policies also provide a long-term guarantee that the rate credited to cash values in later years will not fall below a certain minimum. Historically, some policies have guaranteed a rate of 6 percent, while others have guaranteed rates ranging up from 4 percent. Over the past decade of quite low market interest rates, insurers have had to lower their guaranteed rates. Over the longer term, insurance companies cannot guarantee to pay rates on their policies that are higher than the rates they can earn on their investments.

Single premium life insurance has existed for many years. However, it increased in popularity after the Tax Reform Act of 1986, which severely limited the tax benefits associated with many other popular tax-sheltered investments. At that time, the tax rules treated single premium life insurance just like any other life insurance contract. Cash values accumulated with no current taxation, death proceeds were paid income tax free, and the policyowner could borrow against the policy cash values without taxation.

Subsequent legislation diminished this special tax shelter-like status for SPLI. In 1988, congress passed the Tax and Miscellaneous Revenue Act (TAMRA) which created a new class of life insurance contracts called Modified Endowment Contracts (MECs)[1]. MECs enjoy fewer tax benefits than other types of life insurance contracts. (See Chapter 22.) Generally, all single premium life insurance contracts issued on or after June 21, 1988 are likely to be MECs. Single premium life insurance contracts issued before June 21, 1988 were grandfathered from the provisions of the new law. However, they can become MECs and lose their favorable tax status under certain circumstances, which are discussed below.

WHEN IS THE USE OF THIS DEVICE INDICATED?

In general, some type of life insurance is indicated when a person needs or wants to provide an immediate estate upon his or her death. This need or desire typically stems from one or more of the reasons discussed in detail in Chapter 14. Single premium life insurance may be appropriate for any of these purposes, but is more appropriate for some and is uniquely suited for other purposes. Single premium life, in contrast with term insurance, which provides the highest possible death benefit for the lowest initial premium outlay, provides the lowest initial death benefit for the level of premium paid. Consequently, the single most important reason for buying a single premium policy is the desire for maximum tax deferred or tax-free investment in conjunction with life insurance. If the investment objective is not present, or at least, not highly important, some other form of insurance typically will be more suitable.

If the need for at least some insurance is not present, typically annuities or other investments are more suitable. However, if both life insurance and tax deferred investment objectives are present, single premium life provides a unique combination of attractive features.

Because all new single premium policies are likely to be MECs, the prospective buyers must fully consider the limitations applying to MECs (discussed below under "Tax Implications") when assessing whether a single premium policy or some other form of life insurance is most appropriate for the intended use.

Single premium life insurance in particular is indicated in the following circumstances:

1. *When the objective is to entirely prefund a specified minimum death benefit for a specific purpose, such as a charitable bequest or a legacy for children* – The single premium policy permits the policyowner to assure the bequest with no further concern about possible lapse due to failure to pay premiums. Further, the premium payment is determined based on competitive tax-free rates of return. In addition, in most cases if the investment and mortality experience of the company is favorable, the face value of coverage will increase in order to continue to satisfy the IRC Section 7702 tests to qualify as life insurance.

2. *As a vehicle for gifts* – For example, a grandparent can give up to $14,000 (the gift tax annual exclusion in 2015, as indexed) a year gift tax free to a child as custodian for a grandchild. The parent can then use the cash to purchase a single premium policy with a $14,000 premium on the life of the grandparent for the grandchild's benefit. The $14,000 is removed from the estate of the grandparent without federal gift tax cost, and can provide an income and estate tax free transfer to the child greatly in excess of the original $14,000.

3. *In exchange for ordinary whole life policies at retirement* – Under the Section 1035 exchange provisions, a policyowner may exchange an existing ordinary whole life policy that has substantial cash values and continuing premium payments for a single premium policy. The exchange would eliminate future premium payments, provide a relatively high tax-free rate of earnings on the underlying cash values, and may provide a higher death benefit. Policyowners should compare such possible exchanges to the reduced amount paid-up nonforfeiture option available with all cash value policies.

4. *As a substitute for tax-free municipal bonds and other investments so as to reduce exposure to income tax on Social Security benefits* – Both single and married persons with adjusted gross incomes exceeding certain levels are subject to income tax on up to 85 percent of their Social Security benefits. Taxable income from certificates of deposit, money market funds, and other taxable investments as well as what is otherwise tax-free municipal bond interest is included in determining the amount of Social Security benefits subject to income tax. The interest earned on cash values of life insurance policies is not included. Therefore, taxpayers could convert investment funds into a single premium policy, thereby reducing taxable income and the taxpayer's tax base, and eliminating the tax on Social Security benefits.

5. *As an emergency fund reserve* – Although proceeds from MEC policy loans are taxable to the extent attributable to earnings in the policy, after age 59½ there is no 10 percent penalty on the taxable income portion of policy loan proceeds.[2] Because interest on investments of comparable risk, such as Treasury bills, is taxable as earned, the total tax deferred return on cash values often exceeds that on such comparable

investments. With the single premium policy, the only portion subject to taxation is the income portion of proceeds actually withdrawn as a loan.

6. *As a safe haven from future potential creditors –* In many cases life insurance cash values are afforded significant protection under state law from the claims of creditors. The amount that is exempt from creditor claims varies from state to state. Because single premium policies permit the highest potential cash values, they also provide the greatest potential safe haven from creditors.

7. *To build a fund for retirement income –* Similar to deferred annuities, cash values in single premium policies accumulate on a tax deferred basis. Also, distributions or loans from single premium policies that are classified as MECs are taxed similarly to distributions from annuities (see Chapters 8 and 22). The nonforfeiture options under a single premium policy are essentially identical to the payout options for annuities. Therefore, policyowners can use a single premium policy to build a tax deferred fund for retirement, similar to a deferred annuity, while also guaranteeing a death benefit in excess of that paid from an annuity if the insured dies before retirement.

8. *As a means of eliminating the tax liabilities on corporate retained earnings –* If used in conjunction with some other bona fide corporate purpose, such as key employee insurance, the company can contribute substantial amounts to single premium policies and reduce exposure to the tax on excess retained earnings. This may still give the company flexibility to use the cash values at some later date for other corporate purposes.

9. *As a vehicle for financing an employer's obligation under nonqualified deferred compensation plans –* Although companies cannot assign cash values in single premium policies to employees without such amounts being currently taxable as compensation to the employees, employees generally feel more secure if promises under a deferred compensation plan are financed with earmarked assets. A single premium policy can provide reasonable tax deferred earnings to pay deferred compensation benefits at retirement and tax-free death proceeds to pay benefits for a deceased employee's family under the agreement.

10. *As an investment vehicle for a net rollover that is not tax free –* Generally, a tax-free rollover to an IRA is the preferred rollover vehicle for distributions from qualified plans that would otherwise be subject to tax. However, participants may not roll over certain nontaxable portions of such distributions, such as amounts attributable to PS 58 costs in insured pension plans to an IRA. They may invest these after-tax portions in a single premium life policy and continue to enjoy tax deferred growth. Also, single premium policies could be suitable investments for other types of large after-tax or tax-free dollar receipts such as after-tax proceeds from the sale of a business, tax-free proceeds from a life insurance policy, or the proceeds from a maturing tax-free bond issue.

Advantages

1. The initial guaranteed rate in a single premium policy generally is quoted "net" of commissions and other fees. Therefore, the policyowner's entire premium goes into the cash value.

2. Cash value interest or earnings accumulate tax-free or tax deferred, depending on whether gains are distributed at death or during lifetime.

3. Single premium current assumption life insurance (and ordinary life, through dividend formulas) frequently pays higher interest on cash values than are available from tax-free municipal bonds.

4. Variable policies give the policyowners wide discretion to direct the investments that back the cash values by selecting among various types of mutual-fund-type investment assets.

5. In current assumption policies and ordinary policies, cash values are not subject to the market risk associated with longer term municipal bonds and other longer term fixed income investments. Although policyowners can expect the interest the insurer credits to cash values to vary with market conditions, the cash value itself will not be subjected to the market value swings associated

with market prices of longer term fixed income investments.

6. Policyowners can borrow cash values at a low or zero net interest rate cost.

7. Policyowners can use life insurance policies as collateral or security for personal loans. Note, however, that because single premium policies issued after June 20, 1988 are likely to be MECs, the tax rules treat loans or amounts received through collateral assignments of these policies as "amounts received under the contract." Therefore, the amounts received generally will be subject to the ordinary income tax and, if received prior to age 59½, subject to an additional 10 percent penalty tax. Income and penalty taxes apply only to the gain in the policy.

8. Policies issued before June 21, 1988 are "grandfathered" from the MEC rules. (See the discussion under "Tax Implications.")

Disadvantages

1. Lifetime distributions or loans of cash values may be subject to income tax and, if received before age 59½, a 10 percent penalty tax.

2. The premium may be unaffordable.

3. The amount of protection is low relative to the premium paid.

4. Surrender of the policy within the first five to ten years may result in substantial surrender charges.

WHERE AND HOW DO I GET IT?

There are nearly 2,000 life insurance companies actively marketing life insurance coverage in the United States. Many of these companies offer single premium life policies as well as other permanent forms of life insurance. In addition to commercial insurance companies, some fraternal organizations, savings banks, professional associations, membership organizations, and stock brokerage houses offer single premium policies. Policies can be purchased through many agents representing licensed insurance companies.

Most insurance companies that offer single premium life insurance will issue policies only up to certain ages, typically age seventy-five or less, although some companies may issue policies to age eighty in special circumstances.

Universal life policies, because of their flexibility, have become more popular than single premium life insurance in recent years. Consequently, agents may be inclined to offer a universal life policy that is configured to resemble a single premium life contract if the insured's objective is to build high cash values in a life insurance policy. However, with the universal life policy the policyowner may have to pay additional premiums to maintain the face amount of coverage in the future if investment, mortality, and/or expense experience is below expectations. In general, therefore, unless the policyowner needs or desires the flexibility inherent in universal life, a single premium policy—where the policy owner is guaranteed that no further premiums will ever be required—may be more suitable.

FEES AND ACQUISITION COSTS

The sales commission is generally about 3 to 10 percent on these products. In addition, the insurance company typically pays a state premium tax of about 2½ percent. However, these fees generally are taken into account when the company quotes the short-term guaranteed net rate that it will credit to the policy in the first or first few years. For example, to help recover up-front costs, most policies might be subject to a surrender charge, say 8 percent, in the first year with the charge typically declining each year thereafter by 1 percent until it reaches 0 percent after the eighth policy year. When companies assess surrender charges, they can afford to apply the entire premium to the cash value.

In current assumption policies, the interest the insurer credits to the policy each year is usually net of mortality charges and expenses. In ordinary life policies, the dividends reflect the mortality, investment, and expense experience and, therefore, the amount of the paid-up additions that the insurer credits to the policy.

SELECTING THE BEST POLICY

Selecting the best cash value life insurance policy is a difficult task involving a number of complicated concepts and analyses. (See Chapter 4 for a further discussion of the basic principles.) However, because the investment element of single premium life insurance is a paramount concern, focus should center on the following factors:

1. Compare the current rate being credited to policy cash values and the length of the guarantees. All else being equal, policies with higher current rates and longer guarantee periods will be better than those with lower current rates and shorter guarantees.

2. Check to see how the company will determine the rate credited to policy cash values after the guarantee period. Policies that determine the rate based on a specific money rate or bond index leave the company with little room to manipulate the amount credited in an adverse way.

3. Look at the current mortality and expense factors and compare them with the guaranteed maximum mortality and expense factors. The mortality factors currently being used should be competitive. If the difference between the current mortality rates and the maximum rates is small, the company has little room to use higher mortality charges as a means of reducing the effective rate credited to cash values.

4. Look for a bailout provision that reduces or eliminates surrender charges if investment performance does not meet reasonable guidelines.

5. Check the policy loan provision to see if the company uses an "offset" provision to credit borrowed amounts with a lower rate than non-borrowed amounts. If the insured anticipates borrowing from the policy, a company that does not use the offset method is preferable. If borrowing is not anticipated, a company that uses the offset method may be more desirable since the company should, in theory, be able to credit higher interest to policies without borrowing than they otherwise would be able to without the offset provision.

6. Check the financial soundness of the company using the criteria in Chapter 3.

TYPES OF SINGLE PREMIUM LIFE INSURANCE POLICIES

There are generally three types of single premium life insurance policies, with many slight variations, that are available:

1. single premium ordinary whole life;

2. single premium current assumption (interest sensitive) whole life; and

3. single premium variable life.

(Chapters 9, 14, and 19 discuss the features of current assumption whole life insurance, ordinary whole life insurance, and variable life insurance, respectively.)

Although insurers and policyowners can configure universal life insurance policies initially to mimic single premium policies, policyowners have no assurance that they will not have to pay additional premiums at a later date to maintain the face value of the coverage. (See Chapters 18 through 21 for a complete discussion of the types and features of universal life insurance.) Therefore, single payment universal life insurance technically is not single premium life insurance.

Single Premium Ordinary Whole Life

When participating ordinary whole life insurance is configured as a single payment policy, the policyowner is guaranteed that:

1. They will never have to pay additional premiums to keep the policy in force.

2. The face value of the policy will never decline.

3. The cash values will grow exactly as shown in the schedule in the contract. The cash value schedule is based on a guaranteed minimum rate of interest (historically, between about 4 percent and 6 percent, but lower in recent years because of relatively lower market rates of interest). The guaranteed rates for single premium policies historically have been generally higher than those guaranteed on policies with continuous premiums.

The policy also generally will show a schedule of projected dividends. The dividend schedule is not guaranteed. If the company's investment and mortality experience is favorable, dividends paid on the policy may be higher than projected; if experience is unfavorable, dividends may fall below projections.

Policyowners typically use dividends paid on participating single premium ordinary whole life policies to buy "paid-up additions," which are essentially just small additional single premium policies. In general, policyowners can expect the total face amount of coverage to increase over time. Also, the paid-up additions build additional cash values that increase the total cash value above that originally projected in the basic policy. In some cases the policyowners can use dividends to buy additional term insurance without evidence of insurability that, over the years, can substantially increase the face amount of coverage.

Because all newly purchased single premium policies are likely to be MECs, dividends paid to the policyowner in cash or retained by the insurer to pay principal or interest on a policy loan are treated as payments received under a contract and may be subject to income tax. (See Chapter 22.)

Although some stock companies have offered nonparticipating single premium policies in the past, these policies are virtually nonexistent today, having been replaced in most instances by single premium current assumption whole life policies.

Single Premium Current-assumption Whole Life

Most single premium policies are "current assumption whole life," which are also (somewhat misleadingly) called "interest sensitive whole life." The interest sensitive label is understandable, however, because insurers market these policies by focusing on the interest rate that they credit to cash values. They generally guarantee a very competitive rate for at least one year after the policy issue date and sometimes for up to five (and even ten) years. After that, the rate generally depends on the company's investment and mortality experience.

Actually, current assumption whole life insurance is a type of participating policy where the company's favorable investment and mortality experience is reflected directly in the interest rate credited to cash values rather than through dividends.

Similar to ordinary whole life policies (and in contrast to universal life policies), current assumption whole life policies usually guarantee that mortality charges will not exceed certain maximums. However, the interest rate the insurer credits to cash values is usually quoted net of mortality and other expenses. In other words, in contrast with universal life policies,

the policy illustrations make no explicit recognition of mortality charges. Specifically, the insurer does not break out and separately state the mortality charges. As a result, policyowners will have difficulty determining whether any reductions in the interest rate credited to cash values are attributable to poor investment performance or excess mortality.

To counter this problem, some policies provide that the rate credited to cash values will never be less than a specified percentage of the rate earned on the investment assets backing the policy or on a specified index, such as the government long-term bond index. But this too presents problems because companies' practices vary with respect to how they determine the return on their assets and how they allocate investment performance to various blocks of policies.

Similar to single premium ordinary life policies, single premium current assumption policies generally guarantee that:

1. the policyowners will never have to pay additional premiums to keep the policy in force;

2. the face value will never decline;

3. the cash values will never fall below a fixed schedule of minimum values based on a guaranteed minimum interest rate (historically, between 4 and 6 percent, but lower in recent years because of lower market rates of interest).

In contrast with single premium ordinary policies, single premium current assumption policies typically specify current and maximum allowable mortality charges. However, this is really a distinction with little practical value because companies will adjust dividends on participating single premium ordinary policies to reflect changing mortality (and expense) experience.

If the investment and mortality experience is favorable, the cash values may grow enough to exceed the amount permissible under the Code section 7702 definition of life insurance for the original face amount of coverage. When this happens, the company automatically increases the face amount to keep the policy in compliance with the requirements. Consequently, similar to single premium ordinary whole life, policyowners generally can expect the total face amount of coverage for single premium current assumption whole life to increase over time.

Single Premium Variable Life

Only a relatively few companies offer single premium variable life policies. This product is very similar to single premium current assumption life, with one important difference. The similarities include guarantees that:

1. the policyowners will never have to pay additional premiums to keep the policy in force;

2. the face value will never fall below the initial face amount of coverage;

3. mortality charges will never exceed specified maximums;

4. the growth of the cash value will depend on the investment performance of the assets backing the policy.

The key distinction is that the single premium variable life policy does not guarantee that the company will credit at least a minimum rate of interest to cash values; in fact, it does not guarantee *any* level of cash value. In other words, policyowners who purchase single premium variable life contracts bear virtually all of the investment risk associated with their policies.

The lack of a minimum interest rate guarantee has several corresponding consequences. First, because the company does not have to earn a minimum rate on the investments backing the policy, the insurers can give the policyowners wide latitude in choosing the types of investments into which they will invest the cash values in their policies.

Policyowners can choose to allocate the premium to a number of mutual fund-type accounts that typically include:

1. diversified common stock accounts;

2. fixed income (bond-type) accounts; or

3. money market accounts.

Some companies offer a wider range of specialized accounts that are invested in such vehicles as zero coupon bonds, mortgage-backed securities, nondiversified (industry sector) common stocks, gold, real estate, and foreign equities or bonds.

Second, generally policyowners are also given considerable flexibility in transferring funds between accounts. Some companies allow virtually unlimited shifts between accounts without charge, but most companies limit free transfers to between two and five times per year. Insurers usually impose a transaction fee for transfers in excess of the specified number per year.

Third, the securities laws treat variable life as a security and, as such, it is subject to regulation by the Securities and Exchange Commission (SEC) as well as by the state insurance regulators. This means that prospective policyowners must be given a current prospectus describing the investment characteristics of the product, similar to that which is given to mutual fund investors. Only persons who have passed a specific securities examination may sell single premium variable life contracts. Also, the SEC requires that policy illustrations include projections based on several specified rates of return. The illustration may include additional projections, but the assumed rate of return may not exceed an upper limit.

The assumed rate of return in policy projections is extremely important so one should keep the assumed rate in perspective. Although market rates of returns on bonds and equities vary and may be extremely high for some relatively short periods of time, projections should be based on realistic long-term trends.

What is a reasonable and realistic long-term rate? The long-term average compound annual rate of return on the S&P 500 stock index (which is considered by many experts as the "best indicator" of the U.S. equity market performance overall) for the forty-year period from 1972 through 2011 was about 9.8 percent. The average for long-term corporate bonds and government bonds was about 8.8 and 9.0 percent, respectively. For intermediate-term government bonds, the return was about 7.8 percent and for Treasury bills was about 5.47 percent. So, depending on the asset mix selected by the policyowner, long-term projections using rates exceeding 10 percent would appear overly aggressive and unrealistic.

Similar to single premium current assumption policies, the company will automatically increase the face value of variable life coverage to remain within the section 7702 definition of life insurance if the investment performance of the policyowner's account(s) exceeds that assumed when the company set the premium. However, if the investment value of the policyowner's account(s) later declines, the face value of coverage also will decline, but never below the initial face amount.

CONTRACT PROVISIONS OF SINGLE PREMIUM LIFE INSURANCE POLICIES

All life insurance policies have certain contract provisions that they may apply somewhat differently depending on the type of policy. (See Chapter 5 for a general discussion of contract provisions.) Those that need special attention when purchasing single premium life insurance include the following.

Loan provision – Many single premium policies allow the policyowner to borrow against the interest accumulated in the policy at what the companies call a "0 percent net cost" (i.e., the interest rate on borrowed funds equals the rate credited to the funds in the policy). The borrowing interest rate for principal amounts (the original premium) is generally 1 to 2 percent higher than the rate credited to policy cash values.

From a quick reading of the paragraph above, it would appear that the cost of borrowing would be offset dollar for dollar with the earnings of the fund; however, this may be misleading. One should check policy loan provisions carefully because the net borrowing rate may be effectively higher than the stated rate in many cases. Frequently, in current assumption policies the company sets aside an amount of the remaining cash value as collateral for the loan. The insurer may credit this "set aside" with interest at the minimum guaranteed rate in the policy (or some higher rate that is still less than that credited to nonborrowed amounts), while they credit nonborrowed cash values that are not subject to the set aside provision with a higher current rate.

For example, assume the insurer is crediting non-borrowed funds with 6 percent interest and the loan rate on interest accumulations is also 6 percent, while the guaranteed rate is 3 percent. If the company sets aside an amount equal to the debt balance and credits it with only 3 percent interest, the effective interest on borrowed funds is 9 percent (6 percent on the loan and 3 percent in foregone interest on the amount set aside).

Similarly, in participating single premium ordinary policies, many companies "adjust" dividends to reflect borrowing activity. In other words, they pay lower dividends on policies with policy loans. Although the loan rate may be equal to (or only slightly higher than) the interest rate credited to the policy, the actual cost of borrowing is equal to the borrowing rate plus any decrease in dividends relative to that which is paid to policies without loans.

Surrender Charges

Most single premium policies charge a "back-end" fee if the owner surrenders the policy within the first five to ten years. The charge usually starts at 7 to 10 percent of the initial premium and declines each year the policy is in force. For example, for a $10,000 single premium policy, the surrender charge might be $700 the first year, $600 the second year, $500 the third year, and so on until the eighth and later years when the insurer charges no surrender fees.

Other policies charge a declining percentage of the cash value. For instance, the charge may be 7 percent of the first year's cash value the first year, 6 percent of the second year's cash value the second year, and so on. Because cash values grow each year, surrender charges will generally be higher on those policies that charge a declining percentage of the cash value than on those that charge a declining dollar fee each year or a declining percentage of the premium.

Bailout Provisions

Some companies have "bailout plans," which are money back guarantees that enable the policyowner to cash in the policy without penalty if interest rates drop a percentage point or two below the initial guaranteed rate. (The insurer waives any surrender charge.) The bailout provision may have a limited duration, such as the first two to seven years, depending on the length of the original interest rate guarantee.

A bailout feature allows policyowners to change their minds after the policy is issued and still obtain a refund of their entire original investment if the specified conditions are met. But keep in mind that the bailout provision applies only to the insurance company surrender charges, not to any income tax or income tax penalties that may be payable on amounts received upon surrender.

Interest Crediting Method

How the insurance company determines the amount of interest to credit to single premium current assumption policies (and indirectly to ordinary life policies through the dividends) is extremely important. Some policies make this very clear by indexing the policy's current interest rate to interest rates on third party money instruments, such as Treasury bills or certain bond indexes. In other cases, insurance companies credit interest to individual policies using one of two distinct methods: (1) "portfolio rates" or (2) "new money" rates.

If the company uses the *portfolio* method, all nonborrowed values within all contracts receive the same rate, regardless of when the company receives the premium. In other words, all policyowners share equally in the company's overall portfolio performance, including both old and new investments.

New money methods, in contrast, credit to new premiums an interest rate that reflects current investment conditions. If current market investment rates are higher than previous rates (and therefore, higher than the overall rate on the company's investment portfolio), cash values attributable to new premiums are credited with higher rates than cash values attributable to previous premiums. Conversely, if market rates are down, new money is credited with a rate that is lower than the company's overall portfolio rate.

Renewal values receive some form of "aged" portfolio rate depending on how the contracts are grouped. Insurers may group contracts by issue year or by contract type. The insurers account for the assets and liabilities for each group or block of policies separately, with each block thus developing its own portfolio rate.

Because single premium policyowners make just one payment, the trend of market rates will determine whether the portfolio method or the new money method is more favorable. If market rates are historically high, the new money method will give the most favorable performance. In contrast, if market rates are historically low, the portfolio method will be most favorable. Over a decade or more, the initial advantage will vanish and the differences will be small, or perhaps even nonexistent.

In the late 1970's and early 1980's, market rates of interest were historically high, and most single premium policies were issued using new money rates and an "aging" formula that gradually shifted to the portfolio method. As interest rates began to fall in the late 1980's and early 1990's, the new money rates were not as high and single premium policies using new money rates became less attractive. As a result, some companies shifted to using the portfolio method for new single premium policies to make them more attractive.

Because variable life policy cash values are invested in separate accounts similar to mutual funds, the issue of how the insurer credits interest to cash values is essentially moot. Investment earnings in separate accounts are allocated to all policyowners essentially in proportion to their ownership of the fund in much the same way as earnings are allocated to mutual fund shareholders.

TAX IMPLICATIONS

Death benefits under single premium life policies usually are paid free of any federal income tax. In general death benefits paid under these policies are subject to the same federal and state income, estate, gift, and generation-skipping transfer taxation rules as all other types of life insurance policies. See Chapters 22 through 30 for a complete discussion of the taxation of life insurance.

Taxation of Lifetime Distributions and the MEC Rules

Taxation of lifetime distributions and loans from single premium policies generally depends on when the policy was acquired. Policies issued after June 20, 1988 are likely to be MECs; polices issued before June 21, 1988 were "grandfathered," and are generally not subject to the MEC rules.

Policies issued after June 20, 1988 – Single premium life policies issued after June 20, 1988 are Modified Endowment Contracts (MECs). Under the MEC rules, amounts received under the policy because of surrender or lapse of the policy or as loans from the policy are subject to income tax, to the extent of "gain" in the policy.[3]

Gain in the policy is determined by subtracting the adjusted premium from the policy cash value. In single premium policies, the adjusted premium is generally simply the initial premium paid. The Last-In First-Out (LIFO) method is used to determine whether amounts distributed are gain or return of principal (premium). This means that amounts received under the contract are treated as first coming from income or gain; only when the gain is exhausted are they treated as a return of principal or premium.

Loans secured by the collateral assignment of a single premium policy as well as interest accrued on policy loans are also generally treated as potentially taxable amounts received under the policy. The policyowner will receive an increase in the basis in the policy to the extent that any loan or pledge is taxable.

Dividends paid in cash, as well as dividends retained by the insurance company as principal or interest on a policy loan, are amounts received under the contract and are potentially taxable. Amounts not treated as received under the contract (and, therefore, not subject to tax) include dividends retained by the insurer to purchase paid-up additions or contractually mandated additional term insurance, to acquire other qualified additional benefits, or which are treated as other consideration for the contract.

Any amounts received under a contract that are taxable are also subject to an additional 10 percent tax *unless*:

1. made on or after a taxpayer attains age 59½;

2. attributable to a taxpayer becoming disabled; or

3. part of a series of substantially equal periodic payments (not less frequently than annually) made for the life (or life expectancy) of the taxpayer or for the joint lives (or joint life expectancies) of the taxpayer and beneficiary.[4]

Generally, contracts owned by "non-natural persons," such as corporations, are not eligible for these penalty exceptions.

Policies issued before June 21, 1988 – Policies issued prior to June 21, 1988 are "grandfathered" and avoid the MEC rules unless there is a "material change" in the policy.[5] In particular, this means that proceeds from policy loans will not be subject to income tax and that other withdrawals or distributions of cash values before age 59½ will not be subject to the additional 10 percent tax.

A material change is any increase in the future benefits under the contract, with the following exceptions:

1. cost-of-living increases that are based on a broad-based index, such as the Consumer Price Index;

2. death benefit increases inherent in the policy design due to the crediting of interest or other earnings; or

3. death benefit increases necessary to keep the relationship between the death benefit and cash values required to maintain the tax code definition of life insurance under Code section 7702.[6]

In general, grandfathered single premium policies should meet the second or third exception. Therefore, policyowners who own grandfathered policies enjoy a special tax privilege allowing them to borrow from their policies without being subject to LIFO-based income taxes. However, they can lose their grandfathered status if a policy is exchanged for a new policy, or if the face value of the policy is increased in such a way that it is treated as a material change.

A warning is in order regarding the future taxation of single premium policies. Congress has been looking at the tax deferred cash accumulation feature of life insurance as a potential source of additional tax revenues. Although many experts believe cash value life insurance will retain its tax deferred accumulation feature, if Congress acts to discontinue or limit this tax deferral feature, it will be single premium and other limited premium payment, high cash value policies that Congress will most likely target. In the event of tax changes in this area, the likelihood of a grandfather provision for existing policies is uncertain. In the authors' opinion, existing policies will have possibly only very limited protection. Amounts already accumulated in these types of policies may be grandfathered if and when reforms are enacted, but future accumulations will probably not be sheltered.

ALTERNATIVES

All life insurance policies can provide tax-free cash upon death. The unique feature of single premium life insurance is its large tax-free or tax deferred cash buildup. If a person desires a combination of high tax-preferred cash accumulation and life insurance coverage, they should consider exploring several others:

1. *The combination of a single premium deferred annuity and decreasing term insurance* – Cash values accumulate in both annuities and single premium life insurance policies on a tax deferred basis. Withdrawals, lifetime distributions, or loans from each are treated similarly for tax purposes (assuming the life insurance policy is treated as a MEC). Therefore, the combination of a single premium deferred annuity and a decreasing term policy can provide levels of tax preferred cash accumulation and death benefits similar to a single premium policy.

    However, there are some important differences. The annuity-term combination will require some additional and increasing premiums over the years for the term coverage. In addition, the mortality charges for term insurance coverage are typically higher than the mortality charges in a single premium policy. Also, loan provisions of deferred annuity contracts are generally more restrictive than those of single premium life policies. Finally, the death proceeds from the single premium policy generally may pass to the beneficiary entirely income and estate tax free, regardless of who is the beneficiary, if the policyowner has no incidents of ownership in the policy. The gains on the annuity contract still will be taxable income to the beneficiary.

2. *A combination of tax-free municipal bonds and decreasing term insurance* – This combination can create a cash accumulation and death benefit similar to a single premium policy. In contrast with the cash values in a single premium policy, bond owners may use the municipal bonds as collateral for loans without any adverse income tax consequences. Similar to life insurance policy loans, the interest paid on the borrowed funds generally is not deductible. Death benefits from a single premium policy transfer by operation of the contract and avoid probate. Municipal bonds are part of the probate estate and must be distributed by will. Once again, if the policyowner has no incidents of ownership, the life insurance death proceeds are paid estate tax free. The municipal bonds will escape estate tax only if they pass to the spouse and, thus, qualify for the estate tax marital deduction.

3. *A single payment universal life policy* – The insurer and policyowner initially can configure a universal life policy to resemble a single premium life policy. However, in contrast with "true" single premium life policies, charges for mortality and expenses can change in the universal life policy in such a way that the policyowner would be required to pay additional premiums in the future to maintain the face value of coverage.

WHERE CAN I FIND OUT MORE?

The following references include authoritative discussions of various types of life insurance including single premium life insurance:

1. B. Baldwin, *New Life Insurance Investment Advisor: Achieving Financial Security for You and Your Family Through Today's Insurance Products*, 2nd ed. (Hightstown, NJ: McGraw-Hill Trade, 2001).

2. J. Belth, *Life Insurance: A Consumer's Handbook*, 2nd ed. (Bloomington, IN: Indiana University Press, 1985).

3. K. Black, Jr. and H. Skipper, Jr., *Life Insurance*, 13th ed. (Old Tappan, NJ: Prentice Hall Inc., 1999).

4. E. Graves, Editor, *McGill's Life Insurance*, 5th ed. (Bryn Mawr, PA: The American College, 2004).

The following references are useful guides for policy and company rating information:

1. *Best Insurance Reports* (Oldwick, NJ: A. M. Best Company, published annually).

2. *Best's Review – Life/Health Edition* (Oldwick, NJ: A. M. Best Company, published monthly).

FREQUENTLY ASKED QUESTIONS

Question – Is single premium whole life a good idea for an individual who does not need death benefit coverage?

Answer – Probably not. A single premium policy does provide a death benefit, which means the client is paying mortality charges. If the client does not need or want life insurance protection, a single premium deferred annuity can provide similar tax sheltered cash buildup benefits without the mortality charges.

Question – How can insurance companies guarantee higher rates of interest on single premium policies than on other life insurance policies?

Answer – The insurance company receives the full premium that will be paid under the policy at the beginning of the contract. This permits it to invest the money in long-term assets with fairly certain or predictable long-term returns. These longer term assets generally pay a higher yield than shorter term investments. In addition, regulations permit the insurance company to base its reserve calculations on rates as high as 6 percent annually for single premium policies. The upper limit on assumed interest rates for reserve calculations is lower for policies with periodic premium payments.

Question – Is a single premium life insurance policy a good short-term investment?

Answer – Not generally. Single premium policies typically have significant surrender charges in the early years. Also, because newly-issued policies are likely to be MECs, if the policyowner terminates the policy before age 59½, he or she may incurs a 10 percent penalty tax in addition to the income tax payable on any taxable gain from the terminated policy.

Question – Do the bailout provisions found in some single premium life insurance policies make them good short-term investments?

Answer – Bailout provisions may eliminate or reduce surrender charges imposed by the insurer, but they cannot waive the penalty tax applicable to persons under age 59½. Generally, better short-term investments are available without the mortality charges and the potential penalty tax.

Question – Does MEC status of a single premium policy affect the taxation of the policy death benefit?

Answer – The MEC rules have essentially no effect on the taxation of death benefits. The death benefits generally are exempt from federal income tax, and federal estate and gift taxes are applied in the same manner as for policies that are not classified as MECs.

Question – Is a single premium policy with an interest rate guarantee that is for a longer period than competing policies necessarily the "best buy" of those available?

Answer – Not necessarily. The long-term performance is most important. Insurers have wide discretion in setting the interest rates they credit to policies after the guarantee period expires. It is possible to promise high rates for the initial guarantee period and then compensate for that early promise by lowering the rates credited after the guarantee period expires.

CHAPTER ENDNOTES

1. I.R.C. §7702A.
2. I.R.C. §72(v).
3. I.R.C. §§72(e), 7702A.
4. I.R.C. §72(v).
5. Section 5012(e)(1) of P.L. 100-647, Technical and Miscellaneous Revenue Act of 1988.
6. I.R.C. §7702A(c)(3)(B).

SURVIVORSHIP LIFE

CHAPTER 16

INTRODUCTION

In its pure form, Survivorship Life (SL), which is also called second-to-die or last-to-die life insurance, is a life insurance policy or, often, a combination of policies and riders that pays a death benefit only when the last of two or more named insureds dies. It is most frequently used to insure two lives, typically a husband and wife, but some companies offer products that will insure three or more lives.

The three-or-more-insureds policies offer some variation on the last-to-die concept. In some policies, the policyowner may choose at the time of issue at what point the insurer will pay death policy proceeds. For example, if the policy covers four lives, the policyowner could elect to have the insurer pay the proceeds after the third death, rather than the last death. In addition, some of the three-or-more-lives policies allow the policyowner to choose to have multiple payouts. For instance, the policyowner might elect to have the insurer pay the face amount when the first and last, but not the second and third, of four named insureds dies.

The basic policy in a survivorship life plan is generally a permanent form of life insurance—traditional whole life, current assumption whole life, or universal life—but some companies offer term survivorship life. As a result of competitive pressures in the industry to keep premium costs down, many survivorship life plans now involve a combination of permanent and term life elements.

WHEN IS THE USE OF THIS DEVICE INDICATED?

1. *To provide estate liquidity at the second death of a married couple* – Couples most often use SL where there is a substantial estate and the couples plan to make heavy use of the marital deduction. Use of the unlimited marital deduction, either outright or in conjunction with some form of marital trust, permits deferral of all or most federal estate taxes until the second death. SL provides liquidity when it is most needed, upon the second death, often at the lowest possible outlay.

2. *To protect two-career families* – If both husband and wife have successful careers, they may be able to tolerate the loss of one income, but the loss of both incomes would leave remaining dependents with no support. SL provides a relatively low cost method of protecting the family against the loss of income of both parents.

3. *To provide key person business insurance* – In many cases, the loss of a single employee in a key area may present some transitional inconvenience, but it is not insurmountable. Often, companies cross-train employees or assign some overlap of responsibility among key executives to minimize the risk of loss of just one key employee. However, the loss of two key employees in a sensitive area may cause serious disruption in a development effort. Similarly, the loss of one key financial backer may be acceptable, but the loss of two could seriously jeopardize a company. In these types of situations, survivorship life may provide the most economical means of protecting the company.

4. *In split dollar plans* – The same rationale justifying the use of a split dollar single life applies to survivorship life. One should calculate the annual taxable cost of insurance by taking into account the probability of both insureds dying in a given year, rather than the costs used for single life insurance

policies. Consequently, the tax cost to the employee is many times lower than what the cost would be on separate policies at the same ages.

5. *To help fund charitable bequests* – Survivorship life can provide the resources necessary to fund charitable bequests after both husband and wife have died. Also, when properly used in combination with contributions of appreciated assets to charitable remainder trusts, couples can replace all or most of the assets passing to a charity with insurance proceeds at a low overall premium cost. In many instances, the combined income and estate tax savings will be more than the total premiums paid on the insurance.

Advantages

1. If used in conjunction with the unlimited marital deduction, proceeds are payable when needed—at the second death.

2. Premiums are lower than for equivalent coverage in two separate policies.

3. A number of alternative term/permanent life combinations are available that provide wide latitude and flexibility in premium payment and death benefit arrangements.

4. A lower taxable "economic benefit" is reportable in split dollar plans.

5. Medical underwriting standards are often eased (at least for one of the two insureds) due to the fact that death benefits are not paid until the last death.

Disadvantages

1. SL provides no death benefits upon the first death. If coverage is desired or needed for the first death, a special rider paying the desired amount can be added to the SL policy. Otherwise, one should consider a combination of SL and joint life (first-to-die) insurance with death benefits associated with each policy appropriate to the need.

2. In term/permanent plans, there is a risk that premiums could escalate prohibitively if dividends are lower than projected and/or term rates increase.

POLICY FEATURES

Competition and special needs have fostered the development of a number of new SL product innovations including:

- *Graduated premiums* – Graduated premium policies that start with lower premiums which increase over time may make an SL plan more affordable for couples who expect to have a greater premium-paying capacity over time. They should exercise care in selecting these policies, however, because they may fail if the policyowner(s) are unable to pay the increasing premiums. Also, if the policy is put in trust, as the premiums increase they may exceed the amount the policyowner(s) can give the beneficiary without adverse gift tax consequences.

- *Substitute insured* – Some companies will permit substitutions of insureds, with evidence of insurability. This feature is attractive when SL is used in business insurance applications such as to fund partnership buy-sell agreements where partners may change and in key person insurance situations.

- *Enhanced death benefit* – Death benefits payable to an irrevocable trust on a policy transferred by the deceased within three years of death are included in the estate. To cover this contingency some companies will increase the death benefit during the policy's first three years to cover the additional estate tax.

- *Guaranteed death benefit* – Universal life SL policies typically do not guarantee the death benefit. Some companies, however, provide death benefit guarantees on their universal life SL policies.

- *First-death rider* – SL policies with this rider provide a specified death benefit to the surviving insured to cover probate, funeral, and other expenses associated with the first death.

- *Survivorship riders* – These riders, which are attached to single life policies on a husband or wife, can be tailored to mimic a SL policy while providing important additional flexibility (see below for more details).

Survivorship Riders

Survivorship riders are a form of guaranteed purchase option. A survivorship rider naming someone other than the insured as the "designated life" is attached to a single life policy. If the designated life dies before the insured, the policyowner has the right to increase coverage on the insured without evidence of insurability. The rider provides "wait-and-see" flexibility because the policyowner may exercise the right to the full amount of additional insurance or any portion thereof.

Survivorship riders with single life policies on a husband and wife can be designed to mimic a SL plan. Each spouse names the other spouse as the designated life. This arrangement is essentially equivalent to a three-policy survivorship life plan where there is a single life policy on each spouse and a SL policy on both spouses. In contrast with many SL plans, the survivorship rider plan will require additional premiums to pay for the added coverage after the first death. However, premium payments will cease (if they have not already ceased under a vanishing premium plan) on the policy of the deceased. Also, depending on how ownership and beneficiary designations are selected, the death proceeds from the single life policy on the first-to-die may be available to pay premiums on the survivor's policy or as a lump-sum payment into the survivor's policy. Similar to SL, an irrevocable life insurance trust may hold the policies. Because the additional coverage is optional, the trustee has the flexibility to select only that amount of additional coverage that is deemed necessary after the first death.

Survivorship riders can also provide great versatility in business insurance planning, such as in cross-purchase buy-sell arrangements.

Example. Assume each of three shareholders (A, B, and C) purchases policies on the other two shareholders equal to one-sixth of the company's value. They also attach survivorship riders to the policies allowing them to purchase additional insurance on the survivors equal to one-third of the business value. In specific dollar terms, if the company is worth $6 million, A would purchase policies on B and C with base amounts of $1 million. The policy on B would name C as the designated life and vice versa. The survivorship riders would permit A to buy an additional $2 million of coverage on B if C died first or on C if B died first. B and C would make analogous arrangements.

Now assume C dies. A and B would receive $1 million each in insurance proceeds, which together is enough to buy out C's $2 million interest in the company. A and B now each own 50 percent of the $6 million company, but the face value on the base policies each owns on the other is only $1 million. However, the survivorship rider permits them to purchase an additional $2 million of coverage on each other for a total of $3 million. They each will then have sufficient insurance in the event of the other's death to buy out the other's $3 million interest in the company.

TAX IMPLICATIONS

SL is treated in the same manner as other types of life insurance for income tax purposes. Death benefits are paid tax free. If the policy is not classified as a Modified Endowment Contract (MEC), nonannuity distributions or withdrawals will be taxed on the "cost recovery" or first-in first-out basis. That is, amounts received will be treated as a tax-free recovery of investment in the contract until the entire cost basis is recovered. Once basis is recovered, any further amounts will be taxed at ordinary rates as gain in the policy. Annuity distributions will be taxed as a combination of tax-free recovery of cost basis and taxable interest or gain as described in Code section 72. Loan proceeds are not taxable and, in general, interest paid on policy loans will be treated as nondeductible consumer interest.[1]

If a SL policy is treated as a MEC, lifetime distributions and loans are essentially taxed under the "interest-first" rules applicable to annuities.[2] Additionally, if the policyowner receives distributions prior to age 59½, a 10 percent penalty is imposed on the taxable portion of the distribution. However, in the typical case where an SL policy is part of an estate plan that makes maximum use of the unlimited marital deduction to defer estate taxes until the second death, MEC status may be almost immaterial. In these cases, one has little incentive to withdraw cash values because it could jeopardize the plan. In cases where it is unlikely policyowners will withdraw cash values prior to the second death, tax treatment of the SL policy as a MEC will be of little consequence.

Consequently, it may be advantageous, if the policyowner has sufficient cash, to pay up the policy as quickly as possible, even if doing so results in the policy being treated as a MEC. However, one should be careful to avoid MEC status if the plan contemplates borrowing from the policy to pay premiums. Also, MEC status could lead to adverse consequences if borrowing becomes necessary to finance premiums because dividends are lower than projected and/or term rates are higher than projected in a plan using a large portion of term insurance.

Income Tax Implications in Split Dollar Plans

SL policies provide a significant income tax advantage while both insureds are alive when an employer uses the policy in a split dollar arrangement. In a basic endorsement split dollar plan with a single life policy, the employee generally is taxed on the term cost of the insurance as measured by the lesser of the P.S. 58 costs or Table 2001 rates (for plans entered into after January 28, 2002) or the actual term rates used.

If the employer uses a SL policy (typically naming the employee and his or her spouse as the insureds), joint and survivor rates based on U.S. Table 38 or the joint and survivor life mortality factors underlying Table 2001 (for plans entered into after January 28, 2002) typically are used to measure the pure term cost. The joint and survivor rates are significantly lower than the single life rates. At younger ages, for a spouse five years younger than the insured, the joint and survivor rates can be 1/200 of the corresponding single life rates. This differential declines at older ages but still may be as much as 1/20 the single life rates at age seventy-five.

After the first death, the single life rates apply with respect to the survivor, not the joint-life rates.

Estate Taxation

SL is treated in the same manner as other types of insurance for estate tax purposes, with certain special consideration, and policy pays death proceeds only upon the second death of two insureds. Estate tax consequences may or may not arise as of the first death depending on who owns the policy. (Throughout the following discussion, please keep in mind that insurance proceeds received by an insured's estate generally are also included in the insured's estate under Code section 2042 even if the insured is not the policyowner.) Basically, the policy may be owned in one of three ways:

1. A third party may own the policy.

2. One or the other insured may own the policy exclusively.

3. Both insureds may jointly own the policy.

Similar to any other insurance policy, if neither insured has any incidents of ownership in the policy and they have not transferred ownership within three years of death, it will not be included in the gross estate of either insured. However, under the three-year rule of Code section 2035, the policy will be included in the estate of the second to die if, and only if, both spouses die within the three-year period after the policy is transferred and the transferor spouse is the last to die.

If both spouses die within the three-year period and the transferor spouse is the first to die, there should be no inclusion of the proceeds under section 2035.[3] If the transferor is the first to die, the policy would not have been included in his or her gross estate under Code section 2042 or any of the other specified code sections had the transfer not been made. Therefore, the policy proceeds do not fall within the scope of section 2035 and should not be included in the gross estate of either insured if the transferor is the first to die within the three-year period following a transfer of the policy.

Under Code section 2033, an insurance policy owned by the decedent on the life of another is included in his or her gross estate at the replacement cost of comparable policies of the issuing company or the interpolated terminal reserve.[4] If both insureds own the policy jointly, the deceased's portion of the policy's value (which is arguably best determined as the actuarial value of his or her probable survivorship benefits estimated as if he or she had not died) is included in his or her gross estate.

If the deceased transfers the policy by will to the surviving insured who is the decedent's spouse, the transfer qualifies for the marital deduction. In this case, there will be no estate tax at the first death. If the surviving insured becomes the owner of the policy when the first insured dies and continues to own the policy until the second insured's death, the proceeds of the policy will be included in the second insured's gross estate. However, if the policyowner who dies first transfers the policy by will to someone other than the surviving insured, the proceeds generally will not be included in the gross estate of the surviving insured when the surviving insured dies. The proceeds would be included only if the three-year rule of section 2035 discussed above applied or if the surviving insured retained an incident of ownership in the policy.

If the second insured dies within six months after the policyowner dies and the policyowner's executor elects to have the assets of the estate valued as of the alternate valuation date, then the proceeds of the policy will be included in the policyowner's estate. The death benefits will not be included in the estate of the second to die (assuming he or she was not the policyowner at any time within three years of his or her death and proceeds are not received by his or her estate).

If the insured who does not have any incidents of ownership in the policy dies first, nothing will be included in his or her estate because the policy proceeds are not payable at his or her death and such insured has no ownership rights in the policy. At the owner-insured's later death, the proceeds will be includable in the owner-insured's gross estate, unless he or she has transferred the policy more than three years before his or her death and has retained no incidents of ownership.

Estate Inclusion When Policy Owned by Corporation

If a key employee/controlling stockholder of a corporation dies and the corporation has complete control over the policy or at least the right to borrow against the policy, the employee/stockholder will be treated as having sufficient incidents of ownership for the policy to be included in his estate.[5]

Gift Taxation

Gift taxation becomes an important planning issue when a married couple wants a very large policy to be owned by a third party so it will not be included in their estates and also wants to make gifts of premiums at minimal gift tax cost. If a son or daughter, for instance, owns the policy outright, the parents may make tax-free joint gifts of up to $28,000 (as indexed for inflation in 2015) each year under the annual gift tax exclusion. If annual gifts in excess of the annual gift tax exclusion amount are necessary, the parents will have to use up part of their unified gift and estate tax credit.

The parents can leverage the amount qualifying for the annual gift tax exclusion by making gifts to multiple beneficiaries, which is most appropriate if the parents have several children. However, as they include

more independent donees in the arrangement, the risk increases that donees may not use the gifts as intended to pay the required premiums. Also, outright ownership of the policy by the parents' children presents other related problems. The parents have no assurance that the children will not raid cash values and essentially undermine their not-so-well-laid-out plans.

One can avoid these problems by using an irrevocable life insurance trust to own the policy. Through proper planning and use of the Crummey withdrawal rights[6], the parents can provide up to $28,000 (as indexed for inflation in 2015) of annual premium gift tax free to the trust for each primary and contingent beneficiary of the trust.[7] In addition, they can put certain restrictions on how trust assets are used for the benefit of the beneficiaries and when principal passes to the beneficiaries.

ALTERNATIVES

Survivorship life is a unique life insurance product for its intended purpose: to provide death benefits only when the last covered insured dies. The closest alternative strategy is to insure each life separately, but that strategy may often be a relatively poor solution.

Typically, after a death, the estate's personal representative has three principal alternatives if estate taxes must be paid: (1) to sell estate assets; (2) to borrow money; or (3) to have cash available.

Selling estate assets may result in an economic loss to the heirs because of adverse economic conditions at the time assets must be sold. Also, forced sales of illiquid assets may in fact become fire sales, where the amount received is only a fraction of the real value.

Borrowing may only delay the day of reckoning, while incurring additional interest expense to further deplete the estate. Cash will be available in the absence of life insurance only if assets were converted to cash before death. Because most people do not know when they will die, this implies they must keep a large portion of their assets in low-yielding liquid instruments at all times.

The opportunity cost of foregoing more lucrative but less liquid investments can be sizable over time. If preservation of wealth for heirs is a major objective, life insurance frequently is the best way to reach this goal. If the goal of the estate plan also is to defer much of the estate tax until the second death, survivorship life frequently is the best choice.

WHERE AND HOW DO I GET IT?

Many U.S. insurers offer survivorship life products. Because the market for survivorship life is dynamic and competitive, with new product innovations, riders, and package plans being introduced at a rapid pace, it is probably wise to consider products from several companies as well as alternative plans offered by the same company.

FEES AND ACQUISITION COSTS

Many different survivorship life plans use the various types of permanent policies as the base policy together with a host of riders and premium payment plans. The fees, charges, and commission rates are similar to those charged for similar types of single life policies with similar riders and premium payment plans, relative, of course, to the generally lower premium level for survivorship life for any given level of coverage. Generally riders or options that are unique to survivorship life, such as the split options available with many plans, involve additional charges.

PREMIUMS

One of the key attractions of SL is that the premium cost for a SL policy is less than the combined premium cost to purchase separate policies on each named insured. This is possible because the premium is based on the probability of paying benefits on someone other than the first to die. To illustrate, based on the IRS' most recent mortality table in nine out of ten cases involving two people of average health who are age fifty-five and fifty-two, at least one will die within 31.3 years. However, the probability that both people will die within 31.3 years is only 46 percent. In other words, an insurer would be almost twice as likely to pay a death claim within 31.3 years if it issued two separate policies rather than a single survivorship life policy.

Premiums normally continue after the first death, and in some plans may increase dramatically. Other plans provide that premiums cease after the first death. The premium schedule depends on how the plan is designed, the relative proportions of permanent and term coverage, as well as other factors. Because the

insurer's reserve requirements are low while both insureds live, even relatively modest premiums (compared to the total payments that would be necessary for two separate policies) may build substantial cash values. However, after the first death, the policy essentially becomes a traditional single life policy. As a result, the company's reserves generally must increase substantially after the first death. If earlier premium payments were not sufficiently high to build the cash value necessary to support the higher required reserve, the policyowner may have to pay higher premiums or suffer a reduction in the face amount of coverage.

SELECTING THE BEST OF ITS TYPE

Survivorship life policies may require more careful scrutiny and analysis than other life insurance products both because of the extended expected period of coverage and because of the many options and policy features. A key consideration when selecting any insurance policy, but especially survivorship life because of the relatively long term of coverage, is the financial strength and stability of the insurance carrier. See Chapter 3, "How to Determine the Right Company," for a discussion of this issue. The following discussion outlines the key issues and questions concerning the selection of a SL policy.

What is the Composition of the Base Policy?

The base policy is typically a permanent type of insurance—traditional whole life, current assumption whole life, or universal life. Whole life generally is preferable in the simpler situation where the plan envisions a vanishing premium that will endow the policy. Universal life usually is more desirable for older insureds who are looking for a low premium and more flexibility. For example, using current (nonguaranteed) assumptions to determine the premium can produce a premium that is as little as half that for a traditional whole life policy. However, the low-premium universal life plan will usually require premium payments each year until the second death. Premium payments under the whole life plan may vanish well before the expected time until the second death. In general, one can expect the present value of the premium payments to be about the same under each policy. Therefore, the critical element is the desire for flexibility versus relative certainty. Although the performance of each type of policy is uncertain, because the insurer guarantees neither projected dividends nor projected interest credits, the whole life plan typically involves more advanced and "forced" funding. Therefore, the policyowner has more assurance the plan will be completed as originally contemplated, even if the premium payment period must be extended beyond that originally planned because actual dividends are lower than were projected.

If the policyowner desires a growing benefit to cover a potentially increasing estate tax liability, a whole life policy without a vanishing premium (and without term insurance blends) where the policyowner uses dividends to buy paid-up additions or a universal life policy under option B (net level death benefit plus cash value) is often the preferred plan of insurance. Assuming premium payments and other elements are similar, in most cases the UL plan will provide a faster growing benefit. However, at longer durations the whole life plan may surpass the benefits provided under the UL plan.

How Much Term Insurance is Included in the Recommended Plan?

Many survivorship life plans involve combinations or blends of permanent and term insurance. Critical questions include what are the proportions of term and permanent insurance and what term cost is built into the sales illustration. What is the difference between the illustrated term cost and the maximum cost the company *may* charge in the future under the contract?

The objective of the term/perm blending technique is to reduce the required premiums. Because term insurance generally builds no cash values and premium costs increase with age, the initial term premium typically is only a fraction of the premium cost of the permanent insurance. In theory, dividends on the permanent insurance should be sufficient to buy paid-up additions that reduce the amount of term insurance required over time before the escalating cost of the term insurance explodes. The death benefit of a term/perm plan will generally remain level until the term insurance is entirely replaced by paid-up additions.

The period until the term insurance is phased-out depends on the proportion of term to permanent insurance, the design of the term rider, the dividend performance of the permanent insurance, and the term rates. Insurers use variations on essentially three types of term riders in their term/perm plans, which involve varying degrees of risk to the policyowner.

1. *Term rider cost paid by dividends* – The riskiest plan, but also, all else being equal, the lowest premium plan, is where policy dividends pay the entire term insurance cost. This plan uses excess dividends to buy paid-up additions that theoretically will ultimately entirely replace the term insurance.

   This type of plan is the riskiest because its performance depends on two variable and non-guaranteed factors: (i) the dividends that will actually be paid on the underlying permanent policy; and (ii) the term rates actually charged for the term coverage. Although term rates may not exceed guaranteed maximums, most illustrations use current term rates that are below the guaranteed maximum. If dividends fall short of projections and/or term rates increase, the dividends available to purchase paid-up additions will fall short of projections. If the paid-up additions grow too slowly, the ever increasing cost of the term at each advancing age may ultimately exceed the dividends available to pay for the term coverage and the policy will "explode." The policyowner is then left with the choice of paying significantly higher premiums or reducing the amount of coverage.

   Most experts suggest that one can minimize the risk of an exploding policy if this type of term insurance does not exceed 50 percent of the total coverage.

2. *Term rider cost paid by additional premium* – The risk of an exploding policy is reduced but not entirely eliminated, depending on the term/perm blend, if an additional premium is charged for the term rider. In the typical additional-premium plan, the additional premium is a level annual amount that vanishes once paid-up additions entirely replace the term coverage. Because the premium is level, it initially exceeds the actual term cost. This plan uses the excess term premium in the early years and policy dividends to buy paid-up additions that grow more quickly than in the dividend-only-pay-term/perm plan. Because the term rates may increase to guaranteed maximums and insurers do no guarantee projected dividends on the permanent insurance, the policyowner still may bear some risk that the policy will explode. However, for term/perm blends of about 50/50 or less, this risk is virtually eliminated. The only

risk is that the premium vanish may take longer than projected.

3. *Convertible term rider* – A convertible term rider is the least risky, but generally the highest premium alternative, all else being equal. This plan uses dividends to buy paid-up additions and to increase the total face amount of coverage, but they otherwise may be applied against premiums to keep the face amount of coverage level while net premiums decline over time. The principal risk with this plan is that the conversion right may expire before the second death. To keep the coverage in place, the policyowner must convert, which will require an increase in premiums. Also, charges often are associated with the conversion.

How is the Policy Affected by the First Death?

Originally, insurers designed survivorship life policies to revert to single life pricing after the first death. As a result, the mortality charges for the pure insurance protection jumped significantly after the first death. However, reserves and cash values also increased substantially after the first death, reducing the pure insurance protection. Depending on when the first death occurred and whether the older or younger insured died first, a sizable increase in the premiums could be required to keep the level of coverage in place. To avoid the possibility of a premium increase after the first death, insurers designed and priced some policies essentially to include a first death element that would provide enough additional cash value to keep premiums level after the first death. Insurers now design most permanent SL policies to avoid a premium increase after the first death. Some companies even offer a rider (what is essentially a joint life—first death—rider) for additional premium that pays up the policy and eliminates the need to pay premiums after the first death.

However, term/perm plans often are still subject to the risk of a premium increase after the first death. Companies use one of two term pricing strategies. Some companies have two schedules of term rates. The rates they use when both insureds are living are the low second-death rates. This keeps premiums to the absolute minimum while both insureds live. However, after the first death, the term rates jump up to the single life mortality rates, which can be a sizable

increase. Other companies use a blended rate both before and after the first death. All else being equal, the required premium for a plan using blended rates will be higher than for a plan using two schedules of rates while both insureds live, but the premium will not increase after the first death.

What Yields or Interest Rates are Assumed?

Are illustrated yield values based on the company's "portfolio rate" or a "new money" rate? Policy illustrations with new money rates will tend to look more favorable than those using portfolio rates when market rates are currently high. Similarly, policies using portfolio rates may look more favorable than those using new money rates when market rates are currently down.

Is the Level of Projected Yields or Interest Rates Reasonable?

If one company's illustration uses higher yields than another, are they justified based on the portfolio compositions of the insurers? If not, one should base comparison on similar yield assumptions. If differences in the insurers' portfolios warrant a higher yield assumption, are the investments of the higher yielding company riskier and is the additional risk justified?

What is the Sensitivity of the Plan to Changes in Yields or Interest Rates?

Typically, plans that employ a greater proportion of term insurance are more sensitive to changes in the interest rate. Survivorship plans that combine participating whole life and term insurance often use dividends to buy paid-up additions to reduce the term component over time. If interest rates fall below the yield assumed with projected dividends, the actual dividend payments will be insufficient to reduce the term component as projected. Because term rates escalate rapidly as age increases, the term cost can explode.

The interest rate sensitivity also is significant if the insurance is designed as a vanishing premium plan. Under a vanishing premium plan, the policyowner is not required to pay premiums after a specified period if interest credits accrue as assumed and cash values reach the equivalent of the paid-up level. However, if interest rates do not maintain the assumed level, the vanishing point will lengthen, perhaps substantially. With some products, a 2 percent decrease in a dividend interest rate may double the number of years needed for premiums to vanish. The premium paying period will tend to lengthen more for a given deficiency in the interest rate for plans that are more heavily weighted with term insurance. Even if the premium vanishes at one point, it may reappear later at a substantially higher rate than the original premium. In some cases, policyowners may face the unpleasant choice of paying substantially increased premiums or reducing the face amount of coverage.

To determine the sensitivity of the plan to changes in interest rates and to avoid unpleasant surprises, one should ask the company or agent to prepare illustrations showing how the plan plays out with the initial premium based on current rates but with future projections based on lower assumed dividend rates or cash value credit rates.

Do the Illustrations Assume Bonus Credits or Terminal Dividends?

Bonus credits, which insurers designed to reward persistency, usually take the form of an extra crediting rate to policies in force for a specified period of years. Often the illustrations will show higher rates being credited to policies after the tenth year, even higher rates after the fifteenth year, and even higher rates after the twentieth year. These bonus credits usually are not guaranteed, so, potentially, insurers could use excessive illustrated bonus credits to enhance the illustrated performance relative to competitive policies that do not project bonus credits.

Insurers similarly use terminal dividends, which are paid at death or when a policyowner surrenders a policy to reward persistency. They are typically greater the longer the policy remains in force. Although many companies provide some form of guarantee with respect to bonus credits (although it generally is a relative guarantee that dividends or cash value credits will be relatively higher on policies that have been in force longer, not an absolute guarantee as to the actual dollar level of credits), they generally do not guarantee terminal dividends.

If bonus credits and terminal dividends are not guaranteed, one should ask insurers to illustrate results in three ways:

1. with the projected bonus credits and terminal dividends;

2. without these credits; and

3. with an intermediate assumption such as at two-thirds the projected rates.

Are Mortality Assumptions Realistic?

Both dividend illustrations on participating policies and the interest credited on "excess" premiums and cash values in current assumption and universal life policies depend on the assumed mortality charges. Lower assumed mortality charges allow an illustration to show favorable results at a lower premium cost. In addition, some companies show illustrations that assume mortality will improve in the future. However, if actual mortality experience is worse than assumed, the long-term cost of the policy will increase either because dividends are lower than projected or because direct charges to cash values are greater than assumed. In either case, net premiums effectively will have to increase from the level projected to maintain benefits as projected.

Care should be exercised in selecting policies with lower than average assumed mortality charges. Is it reasonable to assume a company may be so much more selective in its underwriting that it can maintain lower than average mortality costs even well beyond the ten- to fifteen-year period when the benefit of selective underwriting is usually assumed to completely "wear off"? If a company that has used aggressive mortality assumptions or has projected mortality improvements turns out to be correct, it is also quite likely other companies that have used more conservative assumptions will also experience better than projected mortality. These companies will be able to pass on substantially better results in future years than are currently being illustrated. All else being equal, it may be better to select companies using more conservative mortality assumptions. This may reduce the risk of having to pay additional premiums in the future to maintain the level of benefits when such payments may be most difficult to sustain. The alternative may be a decrease in benefit levels. If mortality experience is better than assumed, few policyowners will complain if their premium costs decline or vanish sooner than projected.

Does the Policy Illustration Use Loans to Finance any Premium Outlays?

Some plans show very quick premium vanishes based on borrowing the required premium from the cash values. These illustrations assume that dividends will be sufficient to pay interest on the loans. If dividends are lower than projected, the policyowner will have to pay more into the policy than projected to pay interest or borrow more each year to cover the shortage. Because loans are netted against the death benefit, this could lead to substantially lower net death benefits than projected.

Are Assumed Lapse Rates Realistic?

Another component of policy pricing and illustrations is the assumed lapse rate for blocks of similar policies. The lapse rate assumption is a two-edged sword that can have adverse effects if it is either over estimated or under estimated. Although most experts expect lapse rates for survivorship policies to be two to four times lower than for single life policies, there has not yet been enough experience to know for sure. If a product is priced for a number of early lapses, the company may have a problem if the lapses do not occur as expected. The company will have to pay higher death benefits than assumed and higher cash values on later lapses. However, if more policies lapse and they lapse sooner than assumed, the company pricing will not include sufficient loadings to recover initial policy issue expenses and commissions. In either case, remaining policyowners ultimately must pay the cost of incorrectly estimating the number and timing of policy lapses.

It is generally not easy to discover what lapse rate assumptions a company uses. One may acquire general information from the state department of insurance or ask the company to provide the assumptions in writing.

What Split Options are Offered?

The SL policy split option is a desirable feature, because it permits the SL policy to be split into two individual policies. The most common occasion for exercising the split option is when a married couple becomes divorced. Some insurers permit the policyowners to split SL policies if the tax law changes in such a way that the survivorship life policy would no longer be an effective estate planning tool, such as if the unlimited marital deduction was repealed. In some cases the policyowners may exercise a split option only if both insureds show evidence of insurability. In general, the split option allows each insured to acquire individual coverage equal to half the face amount of the survivorship policy. However, some companies allow the policyowner to elect unequal splits at the time they issue the survivorship policy. If a couple's assets are not split evenly, as is generally the case, this feature is attractive.

What are the Underwriting Standards?

Most companies will issue policies on highly rated lives if the other life is within the standard rating class or only slightly rated. Some companies will even issue policies if one of the insureds is otherwise uninsurable if the second life is insurable. In these cases, the premium is usually about equal to that for a single life policy on the insurable life alone. Because there is always some probability that the insurable person will die before the highly rated or uninsurable person, a survivorship life policy can be of immense benefit in providing protection where there would otherwise be none.

What is the Death Benefit Internal Rate of Return?

Given the broad array of plan designs and options, comparisons of SL plans for a given case are difficult. A method frequently used to evaluate SL plans is the "death benefit Internal Rate of Return" (IRR). First, one inspects each potential policy's illustration to assure that the assumptions used and the projected premiums are reasonable. Then the IRR method basically answers the question of what rate of return a person would have to earn to equal the benefit payable after the second death if net premiums were invested outside the life insurance policy. Typically, one assumes the second death will occur, for instance, in fifteen, twenty, or thirty years, at the insureds' joint and survivor life expectancy, and five years before and after the insureds' joint and survivor life expectancy. The plan with the highest IRR is the "best" buy.

Although the IRR method ignores intermediate cash values, they are usually irrelevant in the typical survivorship life plan where the principle objective is to assure payments of benefits at the second death. The IRR method puts all policies on a common base, regardless of whether premiums are high or low, whether plans are current assumption or not, whether the insurance plan includes term coverage or not, whether premiums are level or changing, or whether premiums are to be paid until death or are expected to vanish at some specified time.

However, if access to cash values in the intermediate term is an important consideration, the death benefit

IRR method would be a less satisfactory method of plan comparison unless all the plans being considered had similar projected cash value buildups. To overcome this limitation, one can apply the IRR method to cash values at various durations, in addition to death benefits. To compare policies, one would apply a weighting factor to the cash value IRR ranking and the death benefit IRR ranking. For example, if one considers the death benefit IRR three times more important than the cash value IRR, a plan's composite "score" at any specified duration for comparison purposes among policies would be 0.75 multiplied by the death benefit IRR plus 0.25 multiplied by the cash value IRR. Or if one considers the cash value return just as important as the death benefit return, one would compute the score by adding each IRR together and dividing by 2.

ESTATE PLANNING USES

SL is uniquely designed to provide for a married couple's estate planning needs. The demand for this popular product has grown in recent years because of several distinct needs created by the second death of two spouses. First, the number of two-income families has increased which means that significant income will continue to be available to the family after the death of the first spouse to die in a two-income family. The need for death benefits to protect dependents is often greatest at the second death of two income-earning parents. SL exactly matches the maturity of the need with the maturity of the policy should both parents die prematurely with young children still dependent upon the parents' income. In addition, SL is generally a less expensive method to provide this coverage for young two-income parents on a tight budget.

Second, planners typically design estate plans to take advantage of the current tax laws and the unlimited marital deduction to defer most or all estate tax until the surviving spouse dies. The unlimited marital deduction permits most or all of the couple's assets to pass to the surviving spouse without estate tax. As a result, the typical estate plan defers the most significant death taxes until the second death of the two spouses. Once again, the timing of SL's death benefit perfectly matches the timing of the need.

Finally, SL is appropriate for even the most rudimentary estate plan. Many married individuals own much of their property jointly in the form of tenancy by the entireties. This means the surviving spouse automatically has survivorship rights in the property that passes by operation of law when the first spouse dies. This automatic transfer avoids probate costs and qualifies for the unlimited marital deduction from estate taxes. All probate costs and federal estate taxes associated with property held jointly by the spouses will be incurred at the second death—the exact time when SL will provide its cash benefit.

Use in ILITs

A policyowner may transfer a SL policy to an irrevocable life insurance trust and this is often the solution for many estate planning problems. First, if the trustee of an irrevocable life insurance trust owns the SL policy, the estates of the insured spouses (assuming the spouses held no incidents of ownership within three years of death) will not include the death proceeds. The SL trust will pass the substantial death benefits to the heirs of the insured spouses outside of their estate tax base. Therefore, the SL trust will avoid compounding estate settlement costs facing the usual estate. A SL trust will also avoid the risks associated with using the children as individual third party owners. The assets of the SL trust generally will be protected from the creditors of both the insureds and the beneficiaries.

Closely-held Family Businesses

SL can be an effective tool in the estate plan of the family business owner. Often the parents will retain majority ownership of a family business until the death of the second spouse. To avoid estate tax upon the first death, much of the deceased parent's ownership interest will be transferred to the surviving spouse, which qualifies for the marital deduction. As a result, the surviving spouse's estate will include most of the business value for estate tax purposes and death taxes could be significant. Frequently the family business, which is usually highly illiquid, is the major estate asset. In addition, the family heirs often desire to continue the business. If the liquidity needs cannot be met out of other estate assets, the family business may have to be liquidated or sold to outsiders to pay these costs.

SL coverage on the lives of parents who own a family business is designed to provide for these liquidity needs. A SL policy will provide benefits at the exact time they are needed—when the surviving spouse dies. The SL benefits can be used to provide the needed liquidity to the estate and provide distributable cash for family members who will not inherit the business interest. The use of a SL policy in these circumstances will both preserve the business of the family heirs and provide family harmony for the next generation.

Use in Split Dollar Plans

Like single life policies, one can use SL in split dollar plans, permitting business funds to finance the purchase of insurance coverage. This is particularly attractive if the retained corporate dollars used to finance the premium payments are taxed at a corporate rate that is lower than that of the stockholder-employee. Because the premium payments are nondeductible, it will be tax cost effective to use lower-taxed corporate dollars to finance this insurance.

The stockholder-employees share of the split dollar SL proceeds can provide estate liquidity to solve the problems discussed earlier for the family-owned business. The corporation can retain a share of the proceeds through a collateral assignment split dollar arrangement and be repaid fully for its entire contribution. Alternatively, the corporation share can be rolled-out or bonused to the stockholder-employee at a later date.

The design of the split dollar SL plan can serve favorable income and estate tax purposes. The insured stockholders can avoid all estate tax consequences if a SL trust enters into the split dollar agreement with the employer. The insureds should obtain no incidents of ownership in the policy if the SL trust is both the policyowner and applicant. In addition, the corporation should avoid obtaining incidents of ownership (e.g., access to the cash surrender value) if an insured is a majority shareholder. Any incidents of ownership held by the corporation will be attributed to the majority shareholder if the proceeds are not payable to or for the benefit of the corporation.

The design of the plan controls the income tax consequences of the split dollar SL plan. If the employer pays the entire premium, the stockholder-employee is taxed annually on the economic benefit of the coverage.

The SL split dollar plan works the same way as the single life split dollar plan except that very low rates are likely to be used to measure the pure term insurance cost while both insureds under the SL policy are alive. Depending on the age of the insureds, the premium rates may be significantly lower than the single life rates. What this means is that the taxable benefit in the employer-pay-all SL split dollar plan is only a fraction of what it would be if the plan used a single life policy.

DIVORCE

Almost all currently available survivorship contracts allow policy splits between divorced spouses. However, some policies force the husband and wife to prove evidence of insurability at the time of the split, which is a major disadvantage, especially at older ages, when a person is more likely to be rated and it is more difficult to find coverage for substandard risks. In addition, some split-option riders or exchange riders add significant costs to the contract each year the policy is in force or allow the company to charge a split or exchange fee that can further erode cash values. Also, survivorship plans that use term riders often exclude them from the split option.

Usually the insurer offers two new single life policies with premiums based on the insureds' ages when the survivorship life policy was issued. The cash value generally is evenly split into the new policies. A problem may arise if the premium on the new policy and the divisible share of the cash value from the survivorship policy are insufficient to cover the necessary reserves on the new policies. If a policy split occurs many years after issue of the survivorship policy and dividends have been sizable, the probability that this problem will arise is negligible. However, the likelihood of a problem increases if the split occurs soon after issue or if dividends have been low, especially in the male's policy. The insured may have to make a lump-sum payment to cover the shortfall or have the benefit reduced. Some companies offer the option of paying higher premiums to fund the shortfall over time. Other companies avoid this problem by issuing new policies at attained ages. In these cases the premiums are based on higher mortality charges and the policyowners must pay full commissions and other new policy costs once again. If the split occurs at later ages, many insureds may find the premium cost prohibitive.

Other companies issue survivorship policies that allow splits without evidence of insurability and without new policy charges. However premium costs may be somewhat higher on the survivorship policy to compensate the company for these potential costs.

WHERE CAN I FIND OUT MORE?

Although the references cited in the other chapters contain discussions of survivorship life, the dynamic nature of this relatively new product market makes any discussion dated relatively quickly. Perhaps the best and most up-to-date source is the product information brochures prepared by the various insurers. In addition, the following articles may be informative:

1. "Factors to Analyze in Selecting a Second-To-Die Life Insurance Policy," Philip J. Lyons, *Estate Planning*, May/June 1991, pp. 166-171.

2. "Survivor Life Insurance and The Gatewood Endorsement: An Update," Robert P. Gatewood, *Journal of the American Society of CLU & ChFC*, July 1991, pp. 42-46.

3. "Survivorship Riders: Funding Estate and Buy/Sell Plans," Timothy J. Archbold, *Life Insurance Selling*, October 1991, pp. 164-169.

4. "Due Diligence and Product Design Considerations in Purchasing Survivor Life Insurance," Robert D. Stuchner, *CCH Financial and Estate Planning*, Vol. 3, 1991, ¶29,551, pp. 24,945-24,950.

5. "Evaluating A Survivorship Life Insurance Plan for Clients," James Brogan, *Trusts and Estates*, January 1991, pp. 35-38.

6. "Survivorship Life Insurance: Providing The Liquidity to Preserve Family Wealth," Thomas J. Hakala and David S. Dauman, *The Journal of Taxation of Trusts and Estates*, Winter 1990, pp. 47-51.

7. "New Developments Affect Second-To-Die Insurance Policy Products and Planning," Howard Saks, *Estate Planning*, November/December 1990, pp. 372-374.

8. "An Agent's Guide to Last Survivor Plans 1991," *Life Insurance Selling*, October 1991, pp. 90-144.

FREQUENTLY ASKED QUESTIONS

Question – What is the difference between survivorship life and joint life insurance?

Answer – Timing! SL and joint life are at opposite ends of the spectrum. SL is last-to-die insurance and joint life is first-to-die insurance. They are designed to satisfy entirely different estate and financial planning needs. SL provides cash to meet the costs resulting from the last death among the covered insureds and is typically used to provide estate liquidity. Joint life provides cash to meet the costs resulting when the first of the covered insureds dies and is more frequently used in business applications, such as to fund buy-sell agreements.

Question – Should single life insurance be considered as an adjunct to survivorship life?

Answer – Survivorship life, although a useful tool, is not a panacea for all estate planning needs. In many cases complicating factors may make survivorship life alone an insufficient tool to meet estate liquidity needs and asset transfer objectives. Single life insurance is often needed when use of the maximum marital deduction is inconsistent with wealth transfer objectives. For instance, if a significant estate tax liability is anticipated at the first death, it is obviously important to continue to hold individual insurance on the life of each spouse. If one anticipates first death costs to be minor, the cash surrender value on the SL policy may be available to provide liquidity to the surviving spouse to handle these costs. In many SL plans, the cash surrender value under the SL policy increases dramatically at the death of the first spouse. This substantial cash surrender value may alleviate any liquidity problems caused by first death costs.

Advisers also may recommend single life insurance in other circumstances. For example, in some cases one spouse wishes to provide for children from a prior marriage at his or her death without having to wait until the subsequent death of the spouse. In these cases amounts transferred outright to children are included in the deceased's estate. Single life insurance can provide the necessary cash to pay estate taxes without the need to liquidate estate assets, thus preserving the assets for the children.

Advisers also may suggest keeping assets with substantial appreciation potential out of the surviving spouse's estate. In such cases, one could use life insurance on the first-to-die (payable to an irrevocable trust or a family partnership) to purchase the assets. Under current law, the income tax on any unrealized gain at the time of the first death is avoided because the assets receive a step-up in basis. If, as is commonly the case, the insurance proceeds are invested to provide income for the surviving spouse and the appreciation potential of the assets is substantially greater than any accumulated income on the insurance proceeds, the differential in value avoids estate taxation at the second death.

Question – Would not individual policies on each spouse meet their estate planning needs as well as a SL policy?

Answer – Individual policies on the life of each spouse certainly would provide benefits to fund the costs of the death of either spouse. However, if the objective is to provide for the costs of the second death, the SL policy is substantially more cost-effective. As described earlier, the addition of a second life in a SL policy dramatically reduces the cost for a given level of coverage.

In cases where the objective of the estate plan is to defer most or all of the potential estate tax liability to the time of the second death, the use of single life policies on each spouse will provide benefits at the first death, which is earlier than needed. If the deceased has any incidents of ownership in the policy, these benefits will be included in his or her estate and generally *added to* the assets included in the estate of the surviving spouse. Although these benefits will provide liquidity for the costs of settling the second estate, they unnecessarily increase the tax base of that estate. It is easy to demonstrate that SL is the most cost-effective method to provide life insurance benefits to handle the liquidity needs caused by the second death of two spouses.

Question – Why not simply insure the spouse with the longest life expectancy (generally the younger spouse)?

Answer – In some instances, one spouse is much younger than the other. Under these circumstances, the younger spouse is quite likely to be the last-to-die. A single life policy on the younger spouse would provide the necessary liquidity for the second death costs in most cases. This approach, however, has some inherent flaws. First, despite any differences that exist between the age and health of the two spouses, it is never a certainty that one particular spouse will die first. Most people underestimate the probability of the younger spouse predeceasing the older spouse. The probability remains quite significant even for sizable differences in ages.

Example. The probability that a forty-year-old will predecease a sixty-five-year-old is 12

percent, or more than one in ten, based on mortality factors in the IRS Table 2000CMT. If the older spouse should survive, the single life policy on the younger spouse will pay the benefits at an inappropriate time and further increase the settlement costs of the older spouse's eventual estate. Also, as described earlier, an individual policy covering the younger spouse will be more costly than a SL policy covering both spouses. In all events, the addition of this life will cause a decrease in the required premium for a given face amount if all other factors are equal.

Question – But isn't a single life policy on the younger spouse the only option if the older spouse has impaired health or is uninsurable?

Answer – No! Most insurers will issue SL policies even if one of the insureds is highly rated or otherwise uninsurable. The insurance company is never at greater risk on a SL policy where one spouse is highly rated or otherwise uninsurable than they would be on a single life policy issued on the healthy insurable spouse. There is always some probability that the healthy spouse will die first, regardless of the severity of the second spouse's health impairment. Although the premium for the SL policy may be almost as great as the premium for the single life policy on the healthy spouse, it will never be more.

Therefore, prospective insureds can obtain a SL policy that should always cost less than a single life policy and that will provide the necessary coverage for the surviving impaired-health spouse in the event the healthy spouse dies first. In other words, the single life policy will always provide less advantageous coverage for greater cost in these circumstances. A SL policy is an especially attractive plan of insurance in these cases.

CHAPTER ENDNOTES

1. Deductibility of interest on policy loans may depend on how the loan proceeds are used as described in I.R.C. §163. See Chapter 24, *Taxation of Benefits,* for a complete discussion of the taxation of policy loan interest.

2. For a complete discussion of the MEC rules, see Chapter 22, *Modified Endowment Contracts.*

3. This conclusion is based on the language of I.R.C. §2035(a)(2), which provides that transfers made within the three-year period prior to death will be included in the gross estate

of the transferor only if "the value of such property (or an interest therein) would have been included in the decedent's gross estate under sections 2036, 2037, 2038, or 2042 if such transferred interest or relinquished power had been retained by the decedent."

4. The interpolated terminal reserve is essentially the cash value of the policy adjusted for any unearned premiums, earned dividend credits, partial mortality charges, and other expense adjustments.

5. Treas. Reg. §20.2042-1(c)(6); Rev. Rul. 82-145, 1982-2 CB 213.

6. See Chapter 34, *Irrevocable Life Insurance Trusts*, for a thorough discussion of irrevocable life insurance trusts and Crummey powers.

7. The Tax Court's decision in *Est. of Maria Cristofani v. Comm'r.*, 97 TC 74 (1991), acq. in result, 1992-2 CB 1, held that Crummey powers granted to minors who were contingent remainder beneficiaries of a trust created gifts of a present interest qualifying for the annual exclusion. The IRS argued that holders of such Crummey withdrawal powers must have current beneficial interests in the trust for gifts to be present interests qualifying for the annual exclusion.

TERM INSURANCE

CHAPTER 17

INTRODUCTION

The two principal characteristics of term insurance are: (1) the insured must die for any benefits to be paid; and (2) by definition, the contract expires at the end of the term. Stated more specifically, a term life insurance policy promises to pay a death benefit to a beneficiary only if the insured dies during a specified term.

The contract makes no promise to pay anything if the insured lives beyond the specified term. Generally, no cash values are payable under a term life insurance contract. If the insured survives the specified term, the contract expires and provides no payment of any kind to the policyowner.

WHEN IS THE USE OF THIS DEVICE INDICATED?

In general, some type of life insurance is indicated when a person needs or wants to provide an immediate estate upon his or her death. This need or desire typically stems from one or more of the following reasons:

1. Providing income for dependent family members until they become self-supporting after the head of household dies.

2. Liquidating consumer or business debts, or to create a fund, enabling the surviving family members to do the same when the head of household dies.

3. Providing large amounts of cash at death for children's college expenses or other capital needs.

4. Providing cash for federal estate and state inheritance taxes, funeral expenses, and administration costs.

5. Providing funds for the continuation of a business through a buy-sell agreement.

6. Indemnifying a business for the loss of a key employee.

7. Helping recruit, retain, or retire one or more key employees through a salary continuation plan, and finance the company's obligations to the dependents of a deceased key employee under that plan.

8. Funding bequests of capital to children, grandchildren, or others without the erosion often caused by probate costs, inheritance taxes, income taxes, federal estate taxes, transfer fees, or the generation-skipping tax.

9. Funding charitable bequests.

10. Preserving confidentiality of financial affairs. Life insurance proceeds payable to someone other than the deceased's estate are not part of the probate estate and are not a matter of public record. It is not unusual for a beneficiary to be a lover, illegitimate child, faithful domestic servant, or have some other type of relationship with the insured that he or she may not want to be publicly acknowledged.

11. Assuring nearly instant access to cash for surviving dependents. Life insurance proceeds are generally paid to beneficiaries within days of the claim. There is no delay, as might be the case

with other types of assets, because of the intervention of state or other governmental bodies due to settlement of tax issues, or because of claims by the decedent's creditors.

12. Directing family assets to family members in a way that minimizes state, local, and federal taxes.

Generally, term insurance is not the most effective type of life insurance for all of these death benefit needs. However, term insurance may serve the insured's needs in many circumstances. Because term insurance is not just one product, but rather many variations on a general theme different types of term insurance are indicated for different types of needs.

Keep in mind, term insurance, more than any other type of insurance, is pure death protection with little or no ancillary or lifetime benefits. Therefore, the two overriding considerations in the use of term insurance, regardless of the specific application, are: (1) Will death protection alone meet the need?; and (2) Will the coverage last as long as the need? In short, with term—as with any other decision about the appropriate type of coverage—*the product must match the problem.*

With these thoughts in mind, term insurance would be indicated in the following circumstances:

1. *When the need for life insurance is temporary* – For example, assuming a parent has adequate income to pay college expenses on a pay-as-you-go basis and adequate life insurance for other purposes, the parent might use term insurance to assure payment of a child's college education expenses in the event of the parent's death during the child's college years. For this type of need, a five-year nonrenewable term policy might offer the best cost/benefit relationship. Similarly, decreasing term policies are often used to pay off the mortgage on the family's principal residence in the event of the breadwinner's death.

2. *When the need is long-term but cash flow is currently insufficient to buy the needed coverage using higher premium ordinary whole life* – Parents in younger families often have major long-term support obligations for their young children and spouses, have committed expenses that already strain the family's budget and, therefore, simply cannot afford the premiums necessary to buy the amount of coverage they need

to protect their families using ordinary whole life insurance.

Term insurance, especially at the younger ages, provides the greatest possible coverage for the lowest premium outlay. In these circumstances, one-year or five-year renewable and convertible term insurance is generally recommended. As the family breadwinner moves into his or her higher earning years and can afford the higher premium outlay, it is often advisable to convert to ordinary whole life insurance. Upon conversion there will be a one-time premium increase. But premiums will remain level from then on.

3. *When the policyholder has better investment opportunities outside the insurance policy than inside the policy* – If the policyholder has investment opportunities that will pay a higher tax-free or after-tax yield with the same level of safety as the insurance policy, it may be better to buy renewable term insurance and to invest the early years' premium savings outside the insurance contract. However, they should not base this "buy-term-and-invest-the-difference" choice solely on differentials in potential yields inside and outside the policy. The cash value policy may offer many features not available on the outside investment including: (a) creditor protection; (b) a minimum rate guarantee; (c) waiver of premium in the event of disability; (d) loan provisions; and (e) a host of flexible nonforfeiture and settlement options.

4. *To guarantee a savings fund* – Many parents set up a savings program for their children's college educations well before their children start college. A decreasing term policy is often a perfect vehicle to assure the necessary savings fund if the parent dies before completing the funding. One can use term insurance to assure an adequate savings fund in many other similar types of applications.

5. *For liquidity in the event of death* – One major life insurance application is to provide estate liquidity and to pay estate and inheritance taxes. Because of the ages typically involved, term insurance applications for estate planning and estate liquidity purposes are rather limited (and discussed further in Chapter 27, "Estate Taxation of Life Insurance").

However, the need for liquidity may stem from temporary special or extenuating circumstances not directly associated with payment of death taxes. New business startups are a case in point. The cash flow needs of starting a new family business preclude the higher premiums of cash value policies until the business passes a critical break-even point or attains minimum profitability. Similarly, it is not uncommon for a successful small business owner to tie up virtually all of his or her assets in the business. This general lack of liquidity becomes even more severe when the business is expanding and engaging in capital improvement projects, such as building a new warehouse or plant, or starting new projects, such as developing and marketing a new product line. If the business owner should die while the expansion project is in process, it might jeopardize not only the expansion project, but also the entire business.

Although liquidity in the event of death will always be a problem (which might best be solved using a whole life policy), one can often best hedge the temporary added liquidity risk during these expansion periods using a term policy. Similar logic may apply in dealing with any potential liquidity squeeze. Instances would include an executive who has received sizable bonuses of restricted stock in his or her company, an investor who has committed a significant portion of his or her portfolio to a temporarily illiquid position, and a real estate developer who is in the process of subdividing and developing a large tract of land.

6. *For business purposes* – Term insurance may be the most suitable form of insurance for business purposes in many circumstances. For example, one problem of funding buy-sell agreements with a cross-purchase arrangement when the ages of the business owners are disparate is the relatively high premium cost that the younger business owner must pay for coverage on the older owner. Initially, at least, term insurance or some combination of term insurance and ordinary life insurance may provide an affordable alternative.

Similarly, often term insurance may be the most affordable alternative when insuring key employees, especially when these employees are engaged in special projects where their expertise is critical to the successful completion of the particular task or project. (These and other business uses of term insurance and other forms of life insurance are discussed in more detail in Chapter 31, "Buy-Sell Agreements," Chapter 35, "Key Employee Life Insurance," Chapter 37, "Nonqualified Deferred Compensation," and Chapter 41, "Split Dollar Life Insurance".)

7. *When insureds desire additional death benefits in conjunction with other permanent forms of life insurance or packages of policies* – Insurers often package level, increasing, or decreasing term riders with permanent forms of life insurance to create a combination of death benefits and living benefits that fit a person's particular needs and resources. For instance, a person can use a participating whole life policy combined with a decreasing term rider when that person cannot afford the premiums necessary to fully insure using whole life insurance alone. One can design the package so that the policyowner uses dividends on the whole life to buy paid-up additions that replace the term insurance as its face amount declines over time.

Family policies are another example. The family package policy consists generally of some level of ordinary whole life insurance on the principal breadwinner, half that amount in term insurance on the spouse, and about half that amount again of term insurance on each of the children. It is less expensive for the insurance company to cover several persons in one policy than to issue separate policies for each person. The savings help to reduce the overall cost of the coverage to the family.

8. *To assure coverage in the event of unemployment or loss of employer-provided coverage* – Renewable and convertible term insurance provides a relatively low cost method to cover the contingency of continuing protection in the event of unemployment or discontinuation of employer-provided coverage.

Advantages

1. Term insurance allows a person to acquire the greatest death benefit for the lowest premium outlay when the policy is first issued. However, this does

not mean that term insurance is necessarily the least expensive form of insurance over the full duration of needed coverage. Because term premiums increase at each renewal, at the later ages the premium cost will far exceed the level premium that would have been charged for an ordinary whole life policy issued at the same age as the original term policy.

2. Term insurance is the best alternative for temporary life insurance needs. Usually term insurance is the best alternative if protection is needed for less than ten years. Conversely, some form of cash value life insurance will generally be the best alternative if protection must continue for fifteen or more years. If the duration of the needed protection is between ten and fifteen years, the best alternative depends upon the facts and circumstances of the case. As a general rule of thumb, term insurance will tend to be better than cash value insurance at issue ages below age forty-five, and worse at older issue ages if the length of the need for protection is between ten and fifteen years.

3. Younger persons may acquire substantial face amounts of coverage at relatively low immediate cost, perhaps more than their immediate needs, and thereby guarantee that they will have the necessary level of coverage when their needs and family obligations later increase, even if they are then uninsurable.

4. The conversion feature of renewable and convertible term allows policyholders to enjoy higher death protection than they could otherwise afford and later allows them to lock-in their premiums and build cash values when their ability to pay premiums increases.

5. Various types of term insurance—level, decreasing, and increasing—can be combined as riders with other types of permanent insurance to create a package that meets a person's special death protection, savings, and affordability needs.

6. Life insurance proceeds are not part of the probate estate, unless the estate is named as the beneficiary of the policy. Therefore, the proceeds can be paid to the beneficiary without any delay caused by administration of the estate.

7. There is no public record of the death benefit amount or to whom the death benefit is payable (if paid to someone other than the deceased's estate).

8. The death benefit proceeds are generally not subject to federal income taxes.

9. The death benefit proceeds are often exempt from state inheritance taxes.

10. Life insurance policies can be used as collateral or security for personal loans. Although lenders generally prefer permanent types of policies because of the cash values, a term policy is often sufficient if the borrower is a good credit risk and the loan is very likely to be repaid unless he or she dies.

Disadvantages

1. Term insurance has no tax-free, automatic savings feature as permanent coverage does.

2. The premiums increase until payment becomes prohibitive at later ages. This is one of the main reasons for the purchase of whole life insurance because coverage is useless if it cannot be held until the date it is needed most.

3. Term insurance generally has little or no loan values and little or no living benefits.

4. Term insurance only provides coverage for the term of the contract, not for the insured's entire life. In other words the term coverage may expire before the need does. A person may become uninsurable at a later age when the need for insurance still exists.

5. Life insurance of any kind is generally not available to persons in extremely poor health. However, persons in moderately poor health can often obtain insurance at substandard rates (a reference to the insured person's health, not to the quality or strength of the insurance company), which means higher premiums. It is easier to find ordinary whole life policies than term policies for persons who fall into the substandard rating categories.

TAX IMPLICATIONS

Term insurance is subject to the same income, estate, gift, and generation-skipping transfer taxation rules as all other types of insurance policies. See Chapters 22 through 29 for a complete discussion of the taxation of life insurance.

ALTERNATIVES

There are no good alternatives to life insurance for providing tax-free cash upon death. The alternative forms of life insurance discussed in the other chapters of this book may be better than term insurance for many life insurance needs. If an individual is uninsurable and, therefore, cannot obtain life insurance of any kind, the best alternatives are accumulation funds and tax-deferred investments.

The most important thing is to *match the product to the problem!*

WHERE AND HOW DO I GET IT?

There are nearly 2,000 life insurance companies actively marketing coverage in the United States. Many, but not all, of these companies offer term insurance policies as well as other permanent forms of life insurance. In addition to commercial insurance companies, coverage is also available through fraternal organizations, certain savings banks in some states, professional associations, membership organizations, employer group benefit packages, and insurance purchasing groups. Policies can be purchased through many licensed agents representing a licensed insurance company.

For persons having difficulty finding coverage because of health problems, there are agents who specialize in what is called the substandard market. They know which insurance companies are likely to write coverage for people with specific problems.

People who cannot obtain life insurance coverage in traditional life insurance markets can acquire it through credit life insurance. This is a form of group insurance associated with lenders for the purchase of automobiles, furniture and other consumer durables, and even homes. This coverage is generally extremely expensive because it is priced to cover all ages and health conditions for the same premium, but it is available to anyone who qualifies for the loan at the same premium rate.

Some insurance companies offer limited benefit policies that repay all premiums in the event the insured dies within the first few years (usually two) after they issue the policy, but pay no death benefit. If the insured survives the first few years of the policy, the death benefit amount becomes the face amount. These policies often are offered during open-enrollment periods when the insurance company agrees to issue a policy to anyone who applies. Typically, the offer is restricted to persons within specified ages, such as between ages forty and sixty-five. Because the company is accepting any applicants and it knows many of these applicants are not otherwise insurable, the premium rates are extremely high. Insurers often market this type of coverage through television advertisements which emphasize that no one can be rejected for coverage.

FEES AND ACQUISITION COSTS

Life insurance generally is sold on a specified price basis. Life insurance companies are free to set their premiums according to their own marketing strategies and classifications. The premium set by the insurance company includes a loading (a specified part of each premium payment). Typically, loading will cover such things as:

- commission payments to agents;

- premium taxes payable to the state government;

- operating expenses of the insurance company, such as rent or mortgage payments and salaries;

- federal income taxes;

- other applicable expenses, such as claims handling and policy change services.

The bulk of an insurance company's expenses are incurred when they issue the policy. It may take an insurance company five to nine years, or even longer, to recover all of its front-end costs. The state premium tax applicable to all life insurance premium payments is an ongoing expense. The average level of this tax is about 2 percent of each premium payment.

The aggregate commission payable to the selling agent on term insurance policies is generally less than on cash value policies. This is due to two factors. First, initial premiums for term insurance policies are lower than for permanent forms of life insurance. Therefore, even if the commission rates were equal, the amount paid would be lower.

Second, the commission rate on term policies generally is lower than the commission rate on permanent forms of insurance. Whereas the total commission on a permanent policy typically is equal to about one year's premium with about 55 to 80 percent generally being paid in the first year, commission rates on term insurance policies tend to run about 40 to 60 percent of the first year's premium, and about 5 to 8 percent of each successive premium.

Some life insurance companies sell no-load life insurance policies. That is, they do not pay a commission to the selling agent. However, the premiums charged by these companies tend to be as high as those charged by companies that pay commissions to agents. Although there are no commission costs on these no-load policies, these companies apparently tend to incur, in the aggregate, about the same level of direct mail and other marketing costs to sell their policies as other companies pay in commissions to agents to market their policies.

SELECTING THE BEST OF ITS TYPE

In contrast with permanent cash value types of insurance, the term insurance policy with the lowest premium among all identical term insurance policies generally is the least expensive policy. This would seem to indicate that prospective insureds can buy term insurance as a commodity with the lowest price being the indicator of the best policy among insurers of acceptable quality and financial strength.

Term policies are generally issued with one-year or five-year durations or terms. Some companies issue ten-year, twenty-year, or longer term policies, or term to age sixty-five or seventy. The premium charges for longer term contracts are generally level over the life of the policy.

As the term of the policy increases it tends to take on more of the characteristics of permanent or ordinary cash value whole life policies. In fact, level-premium term insurance to age one hundred is, by definition, ordinary whole life insurance. Specifically, because premiums are level over the term of the policy, longer term policies will begin to generate some cash values because the company must overcharge in the early years to build a reserve to cover the undercharge in the later years as mortality costs increase. If a level term policy is surrendered before the end of the term, the owner may be entitled to a return of a portion of the reserve.

Comparing Term Policies

One must check all of the policy provisions to see if the policies provide identical benefits. In most cases, the policies available from different companies will not be identical. Therefore, the one needs to weigh the slight differences in the policy provisions against the differences in the premiums.

Here are some factors to consider:

1. In the case of renewable term policies, check the schedule of future renewal premiums. A policy with the lowest initial premiums may have higher renewal premiums than other policies.

2. Check the age to which coverage may be continued without evidence of insurability. A policy with a lower premium may discontinue the automatic renewal right before other higher premium policies.

3. Check the grace period provision to see if the policy remains in effect for thirty-one days after the expiration of the term of the policy. A policy that does not provide the grace period may leave the client uninsured if he or she happens to be late with a renewal premium.

4. Check the age to which a convertible policy may be converted to ordinary whole life at attained age without evidence of insurability. It may be worth some additional premium dollars to guarantee this conversion right for additional years.

5. Check whether the incontestability and suicide clauses of the conversion policy will be modified to provide that the two-year qualifying periods will run from the issue date of the term policy if the term policy is converted to whole life.

6. Check whether the conversion clause permits the client to convert the policy to an ordinary whole life policy with the waiver of premium rider without evidence of insurability. If it does, check whether there are any limitations due to pre-existing conditions.

The right to include the waiver of premium rider in the converted policy can be an important feature, particularly if the conversion to a policy with a waiver of premium rider can be made even if the insured is already disabled. Also, in those policies that permit conversion to a policy with a waiver of premium rider, check to see if there is a minimum age to convert (such as age fifty-five) if the insured individual is already disabled. In general, it is worth it to pay higher premiums to acquire a policy with more liberal rules regarding conversion to an ordinary whole life policy with the waiver of premium rider.

7. Even if a company offers a very attractive and competitive term policy, it does not mean that the permanent policies into which the policyowner may convert the term policy are equally attractive and competitive compared to other companies' permanent policies. Consequently, if the possibility of conversion is an important consideration in an evaluation of term policies, one must look beyond the features of the term policy alone and into the relative attractiveness and competitiveness of the permanent policies into which the term could be converted as compared to other companies' products.

8. Check the soundness of the company using the criteria in Chapter 3, "How to Determine the Right Company."

TYPES OF TERM POLICIES

In addition to the length of the term, term policies can be categorized by examining the following features:

- Does the policyholder have the contractual right to renew the policy at the end of the term?

- May the policy be exchanged for another type of (permanent) policy at some point during the term?

- Is the death benefit level during the term, or does it increase or decrease?

- Do the premiums change during the term?

These differences are explored below. These factors may be different or inapplicable for group term insurance, which is described in Chapter 11.

Renewable Term Policy

Term policies are either renewable or nonrenewable. This means, for a small additional premium, the policyowner has the contractual right to continue or renew the contract at the end of the term. If a policy is renewable, the policyholder may unconditionally renew the coverage for successive terms at higher premiums (appropriate for the given renewal age) merely by paying the indicated premium. Insureds do not have to sign forms or provide evidence of good health at each renewal period.

If the policy is nonrenewable, at the end of the term of coverage the policyholder has no legal right to continue the insurance. This means the policyowner must reapply for new insurance. If the insured's health has deteriorated, he or she may no longer qualify for coverage, or coverage may be obtainable only at a significantly higher rate.

Although premiums typically are higher for renewable policies than for nonrenewable policies, the added cost is generally worth it if the policyholder expects the need for insurance to continue beyond the initial term of the policy. In many cases what was thought to be a temporary need continues far longer than was originally anticipated.

Some term policies are renewable to age one hundred. However, many policies restrict renewability after certain ages, typically between ages seventy-five and eighty-five. In addition, most insurance companies do not offer renewable term policies to new applicants after a certain age, typically between age sixty and seventy.

Convertible Policy

This is one of the most important options a policyholder should consider in purchasing term insurance. In return for a slightly larger premium (to compensate the insurer for the extra risk it is assuming), most renewable term policies give the policyholder a contractual right to exchange the term policy for some other type of life insurance policy without evidence of insurability. Typically, the conversion privilege gives the policyholder an absolute contractual right to convert the term insurance into some form of permanent insurance that builds cash values, typically ordinary whole life.

The conversion feature is often attractive when a person's circumstances change and there is a need for lifetime coverage. Conversion allows the policyholder to lock-in the premiums, albeit at a higher rate than the current renewal term rates, and avoid the ever increasing term premiums at later ages. For the client who becomes ill or permanently disabled on a long term basis, conversion to a whole life contract will represent the best means of continuing insurance coverage beyond the originally anticipated term.

The conversion privilege often expires after a specified number of years or after the insured reaches a certain age. Typical examples would be one-year renewable term policies that are convertible for twenty years or that the policyowner may convert until the insured reaches age sixty. The upper age limit on conversion is usually lower than the renewability limitation. A policyowner, owning a policy renewable to age sixty, for example, may only be able to convert the policy until age fifty-five or fifty-nine. This limitation helps to prevent extreme cases of adverse selection against the insurance company whereby persons in poor health convert their policies just before the expiration of their rights to renew coverage without evidence of insurability.

All convertible term policies allow what is called attained age conversion. The company issues a new policy based upon the insured's attained age in the year of conversion. In other words, the new policy is issued and the policyholder pays premiums as if the policy were based on an entirely new application, except that there is no need to prove insurability.

Some company's term policies allow the policyholder to elect to convert in another way called "original age conversion." In this case, the new policy is written as if it had been issued as of the issue date of the term policy that is being converted. The premium is based on the insured's age when the term policy was issued, not the insured's attained age. Consequently, when companies use the original age conversion method, the premiums for the converted policy generally will be less than when companies use the attained age method.

However, because the new policy is usually some form of permanent cash value insurance, the insurer must make an adjustment for the fact that the policyholder has not been paying the higher premiums associated with the new permanent form of insurance. Typically, the policyholder must pay the difference in premiums since the issue date of the term policy, along with 5 or 6 percent interest compounded annually

on these differences. Because the adjustment factor becomes quite large and, in most cases, unaffordable, unless the term policy is converted within a few years, this type of conversion is often offered only for a limited period, such as only within five years of the issue date of the term policy.

Level Term Insurance

As its name implies, level term means that the death benefit remains level throughout the selected term of coverage. Insurers may issue term policies with virtually any initial face amount (i.e., the amount payable at death). However, they typically issue policies only in increments of $5,000 or $10,000. Generally, premiums for level term increase each time the policyowner renews the contract even though the face amount remains the same.

Increasing Term Insurance

Insurers typically offer increasing term only as a rider (i.e., a low cost add-on) to another basic policy, such as ordinary whole life, or as part of a package of policies. This type of coverage is commonly called a return-of-premium benefit or a return-of-cash-value benefit. The basic idea is that in the event of the insured's death while the increasing term policy is in effect, the beneficiaries receive the entire face amount on the basic policy plus a return of the premiums paid or the cash value. In essence, it is equivalent to owning a level term policy plus a savings account equal to the cash value of the basic policy. Increasing term riders typically do not extend for a period of more than twenty years.

Decreasing Term Insurance

Decreasing term is a popular form of term coverage that families frequently use to assure the family will have the resources to pay-off a home mortgage and/or other loans in the event the family's primary breadwinner dies. For this reason, it is often called mortgage insurance.

The policyowner selects an amount of initial coverage. Then, over a specified period, the death benefit declines steadily until it reaches zero at the end of the term. This decrease in face value may occur monthly or annually. Premiums typically remain constant and are payable for the duration of coverage or for a shorter term. Because the coverage is decreasing while the premiums remain level, as the insured ages each dollar of outlay buys less insurance.

The coverage may continue for a specified term of years, typically ten, fifteen, twenty, or thirty years, or until the insured reaches a certain age, often age sixty-five. The duration is usually selected to coincide with the time normally required to repay the loan.

Increasing Premium, Level Death Benefit Term Policy to Age Sixty-five

Term policies with level death benefits and annually increasing premiums are simply one-year renewable term policies. An increasing premium, level death benefit term policy to age sixty-five is simply a one-year term policy renewable to age sixty-five. One-year renewable term policies, which are also known as Yearly Renewable Term (YRT) policies or Annually Renewable Term (ART) policies, were originally the most common form of term insurance sold. However, today, other level premium term programs for various durations ranging from five to twenty years, or longer, have become more popular and common.

USING LEDGER STATEMENTS OF YEARLY RENEWABLE TERM[1]

Policy illustrations or ledger statements are typically presented to potential purchasers to describe the financial aspects of the policy being considered under various assumptions regarding credited interest rates, dividend payments, and premium payment plans. Figure 17.1 shows a sample ledger statement for yearly renewable and convertible reissue term. Although the market for yearly renewable and convertible term has diminished in recent years in favor of five-year, ten-year, or longer term policies, the basics of how a policy of any term works is probably best presented by the workings of the foundational original yearly-renewable term policy. Each of the numbers in the ledger corresponds to the following notes:

1. The death benefit is level, in this case, $100,000.

2. The plan of term insurance is yearly renewable to age ninety-five.

3. The gender is male, and the issue age is forty-five.

4. The insurability status (e.g., smoker or non-smoker), or rated (extra charge because the insured is a higher risk for medical or occupational reasons). The preferred risk for this life insurance company refers to a nonsmoker, nonrated policyholder—the company's best insurability category.

5. The face amount of life insurance is $100,000.

6. The ledger statement shows values at the beginning of each year, rather than at the end of each year.

7. The gross premium charged (not taking dividends into consideration) on a nonreissue basis.

8. The projected dividend payable at the end of the prior year (i.e., at the beginning of the following year). In this case, the first projected dividend is to be paid at the beginning of year six.

9. The net annual premium (gross premium charged on a nonreissue basis taking projected dividends into consideration).

10. A column showing premiums on a reissue basis for the first reissue period. Each successive column shows reissue premiums at subsequent reissue dates.

11. At the beginning of year five, the insured may apply for reissue rates. If the insured satisfies the underwriting requirements of the insurance company (just as though applying for new insurance), the premium for year five will be $286, not $568. If underwriting requirements are not met, the net projected premiums in column 9 will apply.

12. At the beginning of year nine, those who qualified for reissue rates at the beginning of year five apply again. If their application is denied, their year nine premium will be $738, and then the nonreissue rates (column 9) apply. If they qualify for reissue rates, their premium in year nine will be $378.

13. The net projected premium in year ten is $902 for those who did not qualify for reissue.

14. The premium is $378 in year nine for those who did qualify for reissue.

Figure 17.1

LEDGER STATEMENT FOR YEARLY RENEWABLE TERM

LEVEL TERM LEDGER STATEMENT 1
⁺Plan: Yearly Renewable Term to Age 95 2   Male: Issue Age 45 3
CLASS: Preferred Standard 4   Face Amount: $100,000 5

6	7	8	9	10	See 14	See 17	See 20
Beg. Pol. Year	Basic Ann. Prem#	Div. End of Prior Year*	Net Ann. Prem*	Reissue Premiums@ 1	Reissue Premiums@ 2	Reissue Premiums@ 3	Reissue Premiums@ 4
1	$ 238	$ 0	$ 238				
2	314	0	314				
3	395	0	395				
4	479	0	479				
5	568	0	568	**11** $286			
6	842	171	671	388			
7	898	178	720	497			
8	984	183	801	614			
9	1,042	189	853	**12** 738	**14** $378		
10	1,126	224	902	**13**	449		
11	1,244	245	999		592		
12	1,319	266	1,053		742		
13	1,421	317	1,104		**15** $900	**17** $498	
14	1,531	377	1,154	**16**		585	
15	1,689	417	1,272			773	
16	1,781	460	1,321			964	
17	1,929	471	1,458			**18** $1,164	**20** $ 700
18	2,097	487	1,610	**19**			902
19	2,287	508	1,779	Reissue Premiums@ 5			1,166
20	2,498	536	1,962				1,418
21	2,830	668	2,162	**23** $1,034			**21** $1,665
22	3,072	733	2,339	**22** 1,405			
23	3,372	860	2,512	1,758	Reissue Premium@ 6		
24	3,665	1,010	2,655	2,083			
25	3,920	1,125	2,795	**24** $2,380	**26** $1,580		
26	4,342	1,293	3,049	**25**	2,231		
27	4,674	1,309	3,365		2,720		
28	5,289	1,486	3,803		3,159		
29	5,692	1,625	4,067	**28**	**27** $3,567		
30	6,035	1,675	4,360				
31	6,480	1,725	4,755				
32	7,110	1,797	5,313				
33	7,867	1,992	5,873				
34	8,775	2,062	6,713				
35	10,280	2,130	8,150				
36	11,116	2,192	8,924				

Dividends used to reduce premiums.*
Dividends are not guaranteed and will vary.

Figure 17.1 (cont'd)

LEVEL TERM LEDGER STATEMENT

Summary and Explanatory Notes

Summary:	29	Total Annual Premiums+		Total Annual Dividends*		Total Net Premiums*		Total Reissue Premiums@
5 years		$ 1,994		$ 171		$ 1,823		$ 1,712
10 years		6,886		1,190		5,696		4,038
15 years		14,090		3,027		11,063		7,228
20 years		24,682	31	5,697	32	18,985	33	12,378
Age 60		14,090		3,027		11,063		7,228
Age 65		24,682		5,697		18,985		12,378
Age 70	30	41,541		10,718		30,823		20,238

Interest-adjusted indexes* based on a 5.00% interest rate, for basic policy only without reissue.

		10 years:	20 years:	Age 65:
34	Net payment cost index	$5.45	$8.36	$8.36
	Surrender cost index	$5.45	$8.36	$8.36
	Equivalent level annual dividend	$1.01	$2.21	$2.21

35 +Plan renews automatically each year on payment of a renewal premium, but not beyond insured's age 95. Convertible to any life or endowment policy with a level face amount prior to the insured's age 90.

36 @If satisfactory evidence of insurability is submitted at the end of each 4-year period, but not beyond age 69, the lower premium rates may apply. Otherwise the original rates apply.

37 *Includes dividend values. The dividend levels in this illustration are based on the company's current experience with respect to mortality, persistency, taxes, expenses, and investments. They are not guaranteed. The dividends actually paid will be determined by the company's future experience in these factors and will likely differ from those illustrated, being either higher or lower.

38 Among these dividend factors, investment earnings are of major significance. The illustrated dividends assume continuation of the company's current investments experience. If all other dividend factors were to remain at current experience levels, future dividends would be higher or lower than those illustrated, depending upon future investment earnings. To demonstrate this, dividend levels resulting from future investments that are 2% higher and 2% lower than the illustrated scale are also available.

39 &Summary values are calculated as of the end of the year and, because of rounding, may differ slightly from values shown on the ledger page.

40 +Issuance of this plan for the values shown is subject to underwriting approval.

---

15. At the beginning of year thirteen, those who qualified for reissue rates at the beginning of year nine apply again. If denied, their premium in year thirteen will be $900, and then the non-reissue rates (column 9) apply. If they qualify for reissue rates, their premium in year thirteen will be $498.

16. The net projected premium is $1,154 in year fourteen for those who do not qualify for reissue.

17. The premium is $498 in year thirteen for those who do qualify for reissue.

18. At the beginning of year seventeen, those who qualified for reissue rates at the beginning of year thirteen apply again. If denied, their year seventeen premium will be $1,164; and then the nonreissue rates (column 9) apply. If they qualify for reissue rates, their premium in year seventeen will be $700.

19. The net projected premium in year eighteen for those who do not qualify for reissue is $1,610.

20. The premium is $700 in year seventeen for those who do qualify for reissue.

21. At the beginning of year twenty-one, those who qualified for reissue rates at the beginning of year seventeen apply again. If they are denied, their year twenty-one premium will be $1,665, and then the nonreissue rates (column 9) apply. If they qualify for reissue rates, their premium in year twenty-one will be $1,034.

22. The net projected premium in year twenty-two for those who do not qualify for reissue is $2,339.

23. The premium is $1,034 in year twenty-one for those who do qualify for reissue.

24. At the beginning of year twenty-five, those who qualified for reissue rates at the beginning of year twenty-one apply again. If they are denied, their year twenty-five premium will be $2,380, and then the nonreissue rates (column 9) apply. If they qualify for reissue rates, their premium in year twenty-five will be $1,580.

25. The net projected premium in year twenty-six for those who do not qualify for reissue is $3,049.

26. The premium is $1,580 in year twenty-five for those who do qualify for reissue.

27. The premium in year twenty-nine for those who do qualify for reissue rates at the beginning of year twenty-five. In year twenty-nine, the insured is beyond age sixty-nine; therefore, reissue rates no longer are available.

28. The net projected premium in year twenty-nine (based on the life expectancy for a forty-five-year-old male) for those who do not qualify for reissue is $4,067. For those still alive after age seventy-four, who want to have their insurance continue in force, the net projected premiums in column 9 will apply.

29. This is a summary page.

30. The total gross nonreissue premiums for the years shown without adjustment for dividends. These sums do not adjust for the time value or opportunity cost of money.

31. The total projected dividends for the years shown. Projected dividends are not guaranteed. These sums do not adjust for the time value or opportunity cost of money.

32. The total net projected premiums on a nonreissue basis (gross premium minus projected dividends) for the years shown. The sums do not adjust for the time value or opportunity cost of money.

33. The total premiums on a reissue basis. These sums do not adjust for the time value or opportunity cost of money.

34. The interest-adjusted indexes for the years are shown on a nonreissue basis.

35. A statement about the renewability as term insurance and convertibility to a nonterm plan.

36. A description of the reissue rules.

37. The dividend statement explaining that dividends are not guaranteed.

38. A statement explaining that dividends are related to the company's investment experience, and that illustrations with higher or lower assumed dividend interest rates are available.

39. A statement about summary values which are based on the end of the year, not the beginning of the year.

40. A statement explaining that the illustrated values are only applicable if the insured meets the company's underwriting standards.

Information the Ledger Statements Do Not Provide

Although ledger statements are the principal source of information about the economic aspects of the policy, they generally do not provide all of the information necessary to properly and fully evaluate and understand the policy. The following additional information should also be provided, preferably in writing:

1. A full explanation of the *reissue* rules. The company will reissue the policy on its terms, which may mean the insured will have to undergo an entirely new medical checkup or provide other evidence of good health. In general, the actual reentry premium will be what the insurance company deems proper at the time. Depending on the company's experience on its block of similar policies, premiums may be higher or lower than the reissue premiums shown on the current ledger statement.

2. The compound rate of return upon death on both a nonreissue basis and a reissue basis. Although it would be best to know rates for each year, it is generally satisfactory to know rates for each five-year period for up to twenty-five years and for the insured's life expectancy.[2]

    The rate of return upon death on a nonreissue basis is:

Year	Rate of Return
1	41,916.81%
5	200.04
10	58.83
20	17.45
29 (life expectancy)	6.85

    The rate of return upon death on a reissue basis is:

Year	Rate of Return
1	41,916.81%
5	200.62
10	61.26
20	20.53
29 (life expectancy)	9.78

3. The rate of return upon death should then be compared with the before-tax rate of return one would have to earn in another noninsurance investment such as mutual funds, bonds, or certificates of deposit to duplicate the tax-exempt rate of return provided by life insurance. The before-tax rate of return may be determined by dividing the life insurance rate of return by the insured's marginal tax bracket subtracted from 100 percent (e.g., for 15 percent, the factor is 0.85; for 25 percent, 0.75; for 28 percent, 0.72; for 33 percent, 0.67; and for 35 percent, 0.65).

    The before-tax rate of return required in another noninsurance investment to duplicate the rate of return upon death on a nonreissue basis is shown in Figure 17.2.

    The before-tax rate of return required in another noninsurance investment to duplicate the rate of return upon death on a reissue basis is shown in Figure 17.3.

4. Because annually renewable term policies generally provide no surrender cash value, the rate of return upon surrender is always 100 percent compound.

Figure 17.2

	BEFORE-TAX RATE OF RETURN TO DUPLICATE TERM INSURANCE RATE OF RETURN ON A NONREISSUE BASIS				
Year	15% taxpayer	25% taxpayer	28% taxpayer	33% taxpayer	35% taxpayer
1	49,313.89%	55,889.08%	58,217.79%	62,562.40%	64,487.40%
5	235.34%	266.72%	277.83%	298.57%	307.75%
10	69.21%	78.44%	81.71%	87.81%	90.51%
20	20.53%	23.27%	24.24%	26.04%	26.85%
29	8.06%	9.13%	9.51%	10.22%	10.54%

Figure 17.3

	BEFORE-TAX RATE OF RETURN TO DUPLICATE TERM INSURANCE RATE OF RETURN ON A REISSUE BASIS				
Year	15% taxpayer	25% taxpayer	28% taxpayer	33% taxpayer	35% taxpayer
1	49,313.89%	55,889.08%	58,217.79%	62,562.40%	64,487.40%
5	236.02%	267.49%	278.64%	299.43%	308.65%
10	72.07%	81.68%	85.08%	91.43%	94.25%
20	24.15%	27.37%	28.51%	30.64%	31.58%
29	11.51%	13.04%	13.58%	14.60%	15.05%

WHERE CAN I FIND OUT MORE?

The following references include authoritative discussions of various types of life insurance including term insurance:

1. B. Baldwin, *New Life Insurance Investment Advisor: Achieving Financial Security for You and Your Family Through Today's Insurance Products*, 2nd ed. (Hightstown, NJ: McGraw-Hill Trade, 2001).

2. J. Belth, *Life Insurance: A Consumer's Handbook*, 2nd ed. (Bloomington, IN: Indiana University Press, 1985).

3. K. Black, Jr. and H. Skipper, Jr., *Life Insurance*, 13th ed. (Old Tappan, NJ: Prentice Hall Inc., 1999).

4. E. Graves, Editor, *McGill's Life Insurance*, 5th ed. (Bryn Mawr, PA: The American College, 2004).

The following references are useful guides for policy and company rating information:

1. *Best Insurance Reports* (Oldwick, NJ: A. M. Best Company, published annually).

2. *Best's Review – Life/Health Edition* (Oldwick, NJ: A. M. Best Company, published monthly).

FREQUENTLY ASKED QUESTIONS

Question – Do term policies carry a waiver of premium provision?

Answer – The waiver of premium rider, which is a common rider to most permanent or ordinary whole life policies, provides that premiums are waived if the insured becomes totally and permanently disabled. This rider is available on many renewable term policies.

Company practice is not uniform with respect to the inclusion of the waiver of premium rider in a new policy obtained by converting a term policy that includes a waiver of premium rider. Some companies do not allow a waiver of premium rider in the converted policy unless the insured shows evidence of insurability. Some companies will permit the converted policy to include a waiver of premium rider without evidence of insurability, but will restrict its operation to disabilities that are the result of injuries sustained or of diseases contracted after the date of conversion.

Question – If a person is in good health, does it pay to apply for new insurance rather than to continue to renew a YRT policy?

Answer – The hassle and inconvenience of applying for new insurance every year while one maintains his or her health is not worth it. However, it may pay to purchase new insurance every ten years or so if the individual is still healthy.

Insurance companies can afford to charge relatively low premiums in the first few years after issue because they have had the opportunity to screen their applicants and select only those who are in good health. Insureds tend to remain in good health for the first few years after the policy is issued. However, over the years, the pattern is for some of the policyholders who are in the best health to drop the coverage and for those with the worst health to continue their coverage. This is known as adverse selection because the worst (most likely to die early) risks remain and the best (the most likely to survive to older ages) risks no longer support the pool of dollars available to pay claims.

Consequently, the insurers must build additional renewal premium charges into the policy in later years to cover the additional mortality costs associated with this adverse selection against the insurance company. If an individual is in good health, he can apply for new insurance by showing evidence of insurability and once again enjoy the lower "select" mortality charges associated with new policy issues.

This process of adverse selection against the insurance companies is what has led many companies to offer reentry term policies, which are also sometimes called select and ultimate term policies. As long as the insured continues to show evidence of insurability at periodic intervals (typically every two, three, or five years) the renewal premiums, which are based on the lower select mortality charges, remain comparable to the premiums for newly-issued policies.

If the insured's health deteriorates, the renewal premiums increase and reflect what is called ultimate mortality charges. In general, if the insured fails to show evidence of satisfactory health, the renewal premiums are higher than the renewal premiums for regular renewable term, which are

based on data from both select and ultimate mortality experience.

Question – What is universal term insurance?

Answer – Universal term is a type of flexible term insurance contract. Similar to, and actually a variation of, universal life insurance, it allows the policyholder to set up a customized pattern of premiums and face amounts. The insurer also may allow changes after issue, within limits.

Question – Is the cost per $1,000 of face value on term policies lower for higher total face amounts?

Answer – Yes, most companies charge a lower rate per $1,000 for greater amounts of coverage. The break points vary by company. Term, like whole life or any other form of permanent coverage, is "cheaper by the dozen."

CHAPTER ENDNOTES

1. Adapted from the excellent book by William D. Brownlie with Jeffrey L. Seglin, *The Life Insurance Buyer's Guide* (McGraw Hill Publishing Company, Inc., 1989).

2. The compound rate of return upon death is an internal rate of return calculation that requires the use of a computer or a financial calculator. The internal rate of return is computed finding the discount rate that equates the present value of the net premium payments with the present value of the death benefits. For simplicity, it is usually assumed that premiums are paid at the beginning of each year and death benefits are paid at the end of the year of death.

UNIVERSAL LIFE

CHAPTER 18

INTRODUCTION

Universal Life (UL) is a "flexible premium" "current assumption" "adjustable death benefit" type of cash value life insurance. The term flexible premium means the policyowner is permitted to select whatever premium he or she wishes to pay—within limits—and later to adjust or change the premium. Policyowners may even skip premium payments as long as the cash value is sufficient to cover policy charges. The term current assumption means that current interest rates, as well as current mortality and expense charges, are used to determine additions to cash values. The term adjustable death benefit means that the policy permits policyowners to raise or lower their policy death benefits. However, increases may require evidence of insurability.

As a result of this tremendous flexibility, UL has captured a major share of the new insurance market since its introduction in the late 1970's. Some insurance companies use the term flexible premium adjustable life to describe their UL policies.

WHEN IS THE USE OF THIS DEVICE INDICATED?

Potential policyowners may consider UL for any life insurance need. Initially, the insurer and policyowner may configure a UL policy's death benefit and target premium level to resemble virtually any type of life insurance policy from annually renewable term insurance to single premium whole life. However, because of policy costs, UL generally is best suited for long-term coverage needs. For short-term (less than five to ten years) needs, a nonrenewable term policy generally will be more cost effective.

1. UL is indicated whenever policyowners desire the ultimate in flexibility in life insurance. Policyowners whose circumstances change can later reconfigure the policy by changing their premium payments and/or the death benefit.

2. UL is extremely popular in the family market. For example, young parents with growing families and modest incomes can acquire UL policies that they initially configure with low premiums and a high death benefits to resemble traditional renewable term policies. As the parent's incomes grow, they can increase premiums to build tax-sheltered cash within the policy. At later times when they need cash, such as to pay for a child's education, they can reduce premium payments or stop them altogether and use the cash values to help pay the school expenses. After a time, they can increase premiums once again to build cash values. Similarly, if the amount of death protection that they need changes, they may decrease or increase the death benefit. However, increases in death benefits usually will require evidence of insurability.

3. UL also has become extremely popular in the business market where flexibility often is essential. UL has become the preferred vehicle in all sorts of business applications including split dollar plans, funding for nonqualified deferred compensation plans, key person insurance, funding vehicles for buy-sell agreements, and even in insured qualified retirement plans.

Advantages

1. The policyowner has wide discretion or flexibility in selecting the premiums that they pay. Provided that the policy has enough cash value to cover mortality charges, the policyowner may even skip premium payments. In contrast with other types of policies, skipping premiums does not result in the creation of policy loans.

2. The policyowner may change the level of death benefits. Insurers permit policyowners to decrease death benefit at virtually any time. However, the tax rules may subject policyowners who reduce death benefits within the first seven years of issue to adverse tax consequences under the Modified Endowment Contract (MEC) rules. Insurers generally permit policyowners to increase the face amount, subject to evidence of insurability. Increases in the death benefit also may subject the policy to a new test period under the MEC rules. (See Chapter 22, "Modified Endowment Contracts.")

3. The policy is transparent. That is, policy illustrations and annual reports break out and report each of the policy elements separately. This unbundling of the policy allows the policyowner to specifically identify and track premiums, death benefits, interest credits, mortality charges, expenses, and cash values and to check projections against actual performance over time.

4. Many companies permit policyowners to attach a cost-of-living rider to UL policies that, without evidence of insurability, automatically increases the policy death benefit each year by the increase in the Consumer Price Index (CPI).

5. In contrast with most traditional whole life policies, many UL policies use back-end loads, rather than front-end loads. (A load is the charge imposed by an insurer to recover the initial policy expenses. The terms front-end and back-end refer to when the charge is imposed.) Consequently, most or all of the policyowner's initial premiums go into cash values—subject of course to regular annual expense and mortality charges. Therefore, cash values build more quickly than with traditional whole life policies.

6. UL, as a current assumption policy, allows policyowners to directly participate in the favorable investment, mortality, and expense experience of the company. Although a traditional participating whole life insurance policy is essentially a type of interest sensitive current assumption policy—as reflected in dividend payments—the connection is indirect and difficult to measure. The annual UL policy statements explicitly show the amount of credited interest and expense and mortality charges for the year.

7. Cash value interest or earnings may accumulate tax-free or tax-deferred, depending on whether gains are distributed at death or during lifetime.

8. UL policies have historically paid a higher effective rate of interest on cash values than have tax-free municipal bonds. Rates credited to UL policies have more closely tracked rates paid on high grade corporate and government bonds and mortgages.

9. Although the interest credited to cash values will vary with market rates, the cash values are not subject to the fluctuations in market value characteristic of longer-term municipal bonds and other longer-term fixed income investments when market rates change.

10. Policyowners can borrow policy cash values at a low net cost. Although insurers charge interest on policy loans, cash values continue to grow as insurers continue to credit these cash values with at least the minimum guaranteed rate in the policy. Consequently, the actual net borrowing rate is less than the stated policy loan rate.

11. In most UL policies, policyowners may withdraw a portion of their cash value without surrendering the policy. However, if policyowners withdraw money, the insurer typically reduces the pure life insurance portion of the death benefit by the amount of the withdrawal. In addition, policyowners may be subject to income tax on part of all of the amounts withdrawn.

Disadvantages

1. The flexibility associated with premium payments can be a disadvantage because policyowners can too easily allow their policies to lapse. There is no forced savings feature, because UL policies do not require premium payments as long as the cash value is sufficient to carry the policy. To reduce the likelihood of lapse, most companies have a voluntary

provision where the policyowner agrees to let the insurer bill for a target premium set by the policyowner. (As is discussed in Chapter 21, "Guaranteed No-Lapse Universal Life," the insurance market has evolved and many insurers now offer UL policies with provisions and guarantees which are designed to ensure that cash values do not fall below levels necessary to keep the policies in force (i.e., do not lapse as a result of paying inadequate premiums).

2. Although traditional participating whole life policies are indirectly interest sensitive, insurers guarantee the mortality and expense charges. In contrast, current assumption policies, including UL, only guarantee that mortality charges and expense rates will not exceed certain maximums. Consequently, policyowners bear more of the risk of adverse trends in mortality or expenses than if they owned traditional whole life policies. The converse is also true. If the trend of mortality costs and expenses improves, UL policyowners may participate in the improvement through lower charges.

3. Although most new UL policies do not use a two-tiered interest crediting approach, some new (and most older) policies do. The two-tiered method credits interest on the first $1,000 or so of cash value at the minimum rate guaranteed in the contract, historically, 4 to 4.5 percent. The insurer credits cash value amounts in excess of $1,000 with the current rate. Consequently, on policies that credit interest in this manner policyowners do not earn the current rate on the entire cash value.

4. Some UL policies, similar to many traditional whole life policies, use what is called the direct recognition method to determine the amounts the insurer will credit to cash values that are subject to policy loans. Under this method, insurers credit the current rate to only that portion of the cash value that is not used to secure a loan. Insurers credit amounts backing loans with the minimum guaranteed rate or a rate usually 1 to 2 percentage points lower than the loan rate. Insurers most commonly use the direct recognition method in policies that have fixed loan rates. Typically, policies with variable loan rates, and some others with fixed loan rates, do not employ the direct recognition method and instead credit current rates on the entire cash value without regard to loans.

5. Surrender of the policy within the first five to ten years may result in considerable loss because

surrender values reflect the insurance company's recovery of sales commissions and initial policy expenses. In addition, most UL policies now assess surrender charges rather than up-front fees or loads. These surrender charges generally decline each year the owner holds the policy. Typically, after about seven to fifteen years insurers assess no explicit charges if the owner surrenders the policy.

6. The flexibility with respect to premium payments and death benefits permits policyowners to change the policy in such a way that it inadvertently may become a Modified Endowment Contract (MEC) with adverse tax consequences.

WHERE AND HOW DO I GET IT?

There are about 2,000 life insurance companies actively marketing coverage in the United States. The majority of these companies offer UL policies as well as other forms of permanent life insurance. In addition to commercial insurance companies, some fraternal organizations, savings banks, professional associations, membership organizations, and stock brokerage houses offer UL policies. A person can purchase a policy through one of many agents that represent a licensed insurance company.

Most companies have minimum death benefit requirements, ranging from $25,000 to $100,000, depending on age and policy form.

FEES AND ACQUISITION COSTS

UL policies charge front-end and/or back-end loads or surrender charges to recoup commissions paid to the selling agent and the expense of issuing the policy. Originally, UL policies were front-end loaded, but now most policies are issued with little or no front-end load. In other words, the insurer credits the policyowner's entire premium to the cash value. In lieu of front-end loads, companies assess a surrender charge that generally declines with longer durations. Surrender charges often start declining yearly after about the fifth policy year or sooner and reach zero in from seven to fifteen years. As a result of competition in the industry the trend has been towards starting the phase out of surrender charges sooner and more quickly.

Policyowners can determine the surrender charge explicitly by looking at the policy illustration or ledger statement. This statement shows both a cash value figure and a net cash value figure for each policy year. The cash value is the amount on which the insurer bases interest credits. The net cash value is the amount that the company would pay if the owner surrendered the policy. The difference is the surrender charge.

Commissions paid to agents depend on the size and timing of premium payments and how the insurer/policyowner initially configure the policy. Commissions typically range from 20 to 55 percent (or higher) of the first-year premium for premium amounts up to the target level premium. The target level premium generally is the level annual premium the policyowner would have to pay if the policy was configured as a level premium whole life policy. The commission on the portion of any premium payment that is in excess of the target level premium is lower, often about 3 to 8 percent. Commissions on subsequent premiums are usually lower. Total initial and renewal commissions generally equal about one year's target level premium if the original plan of insurance remains the same.

Insurers may recoup policy issue expenses and commissions in a number of ways including a flat policy assessment charge, a percentage of premium charge, a fee based on each $1,000 of face amount, or some combination of each. The trend has been towards lower policy assessment charges and level percentage of premium charges. Many insurers now charge about $25 to $50 per year plus 2½ percent to 20 percent of each premium. The percentage of premium charge generally is lower for higher premium, higher death benefit policies than for lower premium, lower death benefit policies.

SELECTING THE BEST OF ITS TYPE

Selecting the best cash value life insurance policy is a difficult task involving a number of complicated concepts. (See Chapter 4, "How to Determine the Right Policy," for a further discussion of the basic principles.) However, because the amount insurers credit to cash values on UL policies is a critical element of the overall cost of the protection, one primary area of focus should be how the company determines the amount it credits to cash values.

The amount insurers credit to cash values each year depends on four factors:

1. The expenses insurers charge against the policy

2. The mortality charges insurers assess against the policy

3. The net investment yield earned by the insurers on their portfolio of investments

4. The method insurers use to allocate interest to various blocks of policies

The cash value at the end of any given year is equal to the cash value from the end of the prior year plus premiums (or less withdrawals) paid during the year less expense and mortality charges and plus interest credited. The annual report usually will explicitly show the expense and mortality charges and the interest credits each year.

Expense Charges

As described above, two elements usually comprise the expense charge, a fixed annual fee plus a percentage of premiums paid. The company may or may not reveal these fees in its original policy illustration. However, even if it does, the company usually makes no guarantee that they will not change the expense charges. Actual expense charges may increase or decrease in future years.

Mortality Charges

Every UL contract explicitly states the maximum mortality rates it will charge for all ages and guarantees that mortality rates will not exceed those maximums. Many companies now use the 2001 Commissioner's Standard Mortality (CSO) table as the basis for their contractually guaranteed maximum rates, but some companies still use the older 1980 CSO mortality table for their new policies. In addition, all policies issued before 2002 used the 1980 CSO mortality table or, possibly, the 1958 CSO mortality table. All three tables are very conservative—that is, they assume mortality rates that are considerably higher than what is actually expected—but the 1980 CSO table and, even more so, the 1958 CSO table are considerably more conservative than the 2001 CSO table. Virtually every company currently charges less than the stated maximums, but those using the more conservative 1980 or 1958 CSO tables have more room to increase mortality charges in future years if their mortality experience is poor.

Although annual statements explicitly show actual mortality charges, many policy illustrations do not. In fact, some illustrations assume very low or no mortality charges, which tend to show projected cash values that are overstated relative to what policyowners can actually expect. Other illustrations include mortality charges based on rates the company is assessing currently, but they also may assume that mortality experience will improve in future years. If the mortality improvements do not materialize as anticipated, actual cash values are unlikely to match the projected cash values.

Net Yield on Investment Portfolio

Over the long run, insurance companies cannot credit more interest to policy cash values than they earn on their general investment portfolios. To assess a company's long-run interest crediting ability, one should evaluate the insurer's current portfolio and its investment philosophy.

As a general rule, insurance companies invest their portfolios predominantly in long-term corporate and government bonds and mortgages. However, there are differences in the proportions invested in each type of asset and in the quality, duration, yields, and risk. In the past, overly aggressive investments in high yield and high risk junk bonds and developmental mortgage loans pushed some companies to insolvency. Therefore, one's objective should be to select companies with investment portfolios and investment philosophies that show a reasonable and acceptable combination of risk and return. What is reasonable and acceptable, of course, depends on the level of risk and the certainty of return desired by the policyowner.

Procedures for evaluating the investment portfolios of insurance companies are discussed in Chapter 3, "How to Determine the Right Company."

Interest-Crediting Methods

All UL policies, just like all other types of cash value policies, have a guaranteed minimum interest rate. The guaranteed rates, historically, have ranged from 4 to 6 percent. In the recent years of historically low market rates of interest, many insurers have lowered the guaranteed rates to 3 percent, 2.5 percent, or even lower. The rate insurers actually credit to cash values, called the current rate, is (or has historically been) higher than the guaranteed rate. Companies use various methods to determine the current rate they credit to cash values:

- *Linked rates* – Some companies link their current rates to some specified external, well-known index of yields, such as one-year T-bill rates or an index of intermediate-term, high-quality corporate or government bond yields. For example, the current rate might be set at ½ of 1 percent less than the yield on the specified index.

- *Discretionary* – Many UL policies provide that the insurance company may use its discretion to determine the current rate. In other words, other than the upper limit set by the investment performance of its general portfolio, the insurance company may credit any rate it wishes. The insurer makes no guaranteed link between the rate earned by the company and the rate credited to policies. However, competitive pressures prevent companies from abusing their discretion and most companies use formulas related to their investment performance to allocate interest to policies.

- *Portfolio* – The formulas used by companies to determine their current rates on nonindexed UL policies may be based on new-money rates, portfolio rates or, more commonly, some weighted average of new-money and portfolio rates. The new-money rate is the rate of return being earned on the new investments the company acquires with current premium dollars. It is essentially the average current market rate of return on the company's new investments. The portfolio rate is the rate of return on the company's general investment portfolio (or the portfolio of investments backing the block of policies). The portfolio rate actually is a blend of the rates earned on new and old money.

- *New money* – Because insurers invest principally in long-term fixed income types of investments, new-money rates are clearly more responsive to changing market interest rates than portfolio rates. This can work for or against the policyowner. If market rates generally are rising, UL cash values credited with new-money rates will grow faster than those credited with portfolio rates. Conversely, if market rates are falling, UL policies credited with portfolio rates will have faster growing cash values.

- *Blending* – Most companies use a weighting scheme to produce a current rate that is a blend of new- and old- money rates somewhere between the portfolio rate and the new-money rate. One method, called the weighted-average portfolio method, computes the current rate by blending new- and old-money rates in a specified proportion. For example, the insurer may set the current rate at 20 percent of the new-money rate and 80 percent of the old-money rate. If the new-money rate is 10 percent and the old-money rate is 8 percent, the insurer would set the current rate at 8.4 percent.

- *Modified portfolio* – Another method, sometimes called the modified-portfolio method, is the weighted-average percentage rollover method. This method credits a specified proportion (the rollover percentage) of the cash value and current premium payments with the new-money rate each year. The insurer continues to credit the rest of the cash value with the old new-money rates that applied in previous years. That is, the insurer rolls over the specified percent of previously invested money plus interest on the cash value over each and every year into a new-money rate.

Example. Ignoring mortality and expense charges, assume the rollover percentage is 20 percent and the annual premium is $1,000.

Year 1: New-money rate = 9 percent. The first-year premium is credited with 9 percent. End of year value, $1,090.

Year 2: New-money rate = 8 percent. The insurer credits the second-year premium, $1,000, plus 20 percent of the first-year premium and interest, $218 (0.2 × $1,090), with 8 percent. The insurer credits the remaining portion of the first-year premium plus interest, $872, with 9 percent. Total end of second-year value is $2,265.92 [($1,218 × 1.08) + ($872 × 1.09)]. End of year second-year money is $1,315.44. End of year remaining first-year money is $950.48.

Year 3: New money rate = 10 percent. The insurer credits the third-year premium, $1,000, plus 20 percent of remaining first year's money plus interest, $190.10 (0.2 × $950.48), plus 20 percent of second year's money plus interest, $263.09 (0.2 × $1,315.44), which totals $1,453.19, with 10 percent interest. The remaining first-year money plus interest, $760.38 (0.8 × $950.48), continues to get 9 percent. The insurer credits the remaining second-year money plus interest, $1,052.35 (0.8 × $1,315.44), with 8 percent. Total end of third-year value is $3,563.86 [($1,453.19 × 1.10) + ($1,052.35 × 1.08) + ($760.38 × 1.09)]. End of year third-year money is $1,598.51. End of year remaining second-year money is $1,136.54. End of year remaining first-year money is $828.81.

The process continues each year. After a number of years, each year's remaining money will be entirely absorbed or rolled over into later year's new money classes.

The amount of interest that the insurer actually credits to any policy depends on the timing and size of premium payments. If policyowners make large premium payments in years when the new-money rate is high and no premium payments in years when new-money rates are low, cash values will grow more rapidly (relative to total premium contributions). However, even if policyowners make no premium payments in years when new-money rates are low, the amount the insurer credits to cash values will reflect the low new-money rates because the specified percentage of each prior year's money is always rolled over to the new-money rate of the current year.

With either the weighted-average portfolio method or the modified portfolio method, the rate insurers credit to cash values will be more responsive to changes in new-money rates if the new-money percentage or the rollover percentage is higher. If market rates currently are low by historical standards and one expects market rates to increase, one should look for companies with high new-market or rollover percentages. Conversely, if market rates currently are high by historical standards and one expects them to fall, one should look for companies that use lower new-money or rollover percentages.

- *Direct recognition* – Some companies use the direct-recognition method to determine the rate they credit to the portion of the cash value that is secured by policy loans. Companies that use this method typically credit interest on the portion of the cash value that secures policy loans at the minimum guaranteed rate or 2 percentage points lower than the policy loan rate, whichever is higher.

- *Persistency bonus* – Some companies also pay periodic bonuses for persistency, that is, to reward long-term policyowners. Companies may pay these bonuses either as retrospective increases in the general interest rate or as lump-sum additions to the policy cash value. However, one should view projected persistency bonuses that are not guaranteed with caution. Bonuses that are not guaranteed may, in some cases, merely be a way for insurers to make illustrated values appear higher, without any requirement that the company actually pay the bonuses as illustrated.

Death Benefit Options

Most UL policies offer two death benefit patterns, called option A and option B, or option I and option II and many, if not most, now offer an option C, or option III.

- *Option A* – This option, which is similar to a traditional whole life policy, offers a fixed (level) death benefit. As cash values grow larger, the net amount at risk (or pure insurance) is reduced to keep the total death benefit constant (unless the cash value grows to an amount where the death benefit must be increased to avoid classification as a modified endowment contract).

- *Option B* – This option operates in a manner similar to the death benefit one would receive from a traditional whole life policy with a term insurance rider that is equal to the current cash value. Under option B, the death benefit at any time is equal to a specified level of pure insurance, plus the policy's cash value at the time of death. Therefore, the death benefit increases as the cash value grows.

- Option C – This option provides a Return of Premium (ROP) feature that increases the

death benefit by the cumulative premiums. Some ROP options also provide for an interest factor that will increase the cumulative premiums by a specified interest rate. This option has become more popular as a result of premium financing and the need to maintain a level death benefit for the insured net of the amount that is owed back to a lender.

USING A UNIVERSAL LIFE LEDGER STATEMENT

The principal source of information regarding a new policy is the policy illustration or ledger. Figure 18.1 shows an annotated UL policy illustration. Each of the numbers in the ledger corresponds to the following notes:[1]

1. Universal life is the type of insurance.

2. The premium is $2,001.

3. The initial death benefit of $100,000 is increased each and every year by the cash value amount of the policy. This is referred to as universal life option B or option II.

4. Insurability status – e.g., nonsmoker or smoker (would be standard), or rated (extra charge because of a higher risk for medical or occupational reasons). The preferred risk for this company means nonsmoker, non-rated. It is the company's best insurability classification.

5. Gender and issue age – male, age forty-five.

6. A premium of $2,001 is paid each year for twenty years. Starting in year twenty-one the premium is 0.

7. The initial face amount of life insurance payable to the named beneficiary is $100,000.

8. The premium is to be paid annually (once a year).

9. This is an end-of-the-year ledger statement.

10. A yearly premium of $2,001 is paid once a year each and every year for the first twenty years.

Figure 18.1

UNIVERSAL LIFE									

1 UNIVERSAL LIFE

Premiums: First Year: $2,001.00 2

Increasing Death benefit Option 3

Classification: Preferred 4

Insurance Age: 45 Sex: Male 5

Thereafter: Varying 6

Initial Face Amount: $100,000 7

Payment Mode: Annual 8

9 End of Year	Age	10 Yearly Premium	11 Annual Withdrawal	12 Guaranteed Interest of 4.5%			13 Assumed Interest of 8.00%		
				Cash Value	Net Cash Value	Death Benefit	Cash Value	Net Cash Value	Death Benefit
1	46	$2,001.00	$0	$ 1,749	$ 809	$101,749	$ 1,749	$ 809	$101,749
2	47	2,001.00	0	3,198	2,362	103,198	3,615	2,779	103,615
3	48	2,001.00	0	4,658	3,927	104,658	5,606	4,874	105,606
4	49	2,001.00	0	6,124	5,497	106,124	7,731	7,104	107,731
5	50	2,001.00	0	7,589	7,067	107,589	9,999	9,476	109,999
6	51	2,001.00	0	9,047	8,629	109,047	12,416	11,998	112,416
7	52	2,001.00	0	10,490	10,177	110,490	14,994	14,681	114,994
8	53	2,001.00	0	11,911	11,702	111,911	17,744	17,536	117,744
9	54	2,001.00	0	13,301	13,196	113,301	20,678	20,574	120,678
10	55	2,001.00	0	14,650	14,650	114,650	23,810	23,810	123,810
11	56	2,001.00	0	15,948	15,948	115,948	27,155	27,155	127,155
12	57	2,001.00	0	17,180	17,180	117,180	30,724	30,724	130,724
13	58	2,001.00	0	18,332	18,332	118,332	34,533	34,533	134,533
14	59	2,001.00	0	19,386	19,386	119,386	38,596	38,596	138,596
15	60	2,001.00	0	20,326	20,326 ·	120,326	42,925	42,925	142,925
16	61	2,001.00	0	21,129	21,129	121,129	47,538	47,538	147,538
17	62	2,001.00	0	21,773	21,773	121,773	52,444	52,444	152,444
18	63	2,001.00	0	22,235	22,235	122,235	57,658	57,658	157,658
19	64	2,001.00	0	22,486	22,486	122,486	63,189	63,189	163,189
20	65	2,001.00	0	22,495	22,495	122,495	69,052	69,052	169,052
21	66	0	0	20,262	20,262	120,262	73,226	73,226	173,226
22	67	0	0	17,621	17,621	117,621	77,590	77,590	177,590
23	68	0	0	14,522	14,522	114,522	82,149	82,149	182,149
24	69	0	0	10,909	10,909	110,909	86,907	86,907	186,907
25	70	0	0	6,730	6,730	106,730	91,866	91,866	191,866
26	71	0	0	1,931	1,931	101,931	97,027	97,027	197,027
27	72	0	0	*******	*******	*******	102,393	102,393	202,393
28	73	0	0				107,962	107,962	207,962
14 29	74	0	0				113,730	113,730	213,730
30	75	0	0				119,691	119,691	219,691

Figure 18.1 (cont'd)

9 End of Year	Age	10 Yearly Premium	11 Annual Withdrawal	12 Guaranteed Interest of 4.5%			13 Assumed Interest of 8.00%		
				Cash Value	Net Cash Value	Death Benefit	Cash Value	Net Cash Value	Death Benefit
31	76	0	0				125,835	125,835	225,835
32	77	0	0				132,128	132,128	232,128
33	78	0	0				138,495	138,495	238,495
34	79	0	0				144,836	144,836	244,836
35	80	0	0				150,981	150,981	250,981
36	81	0	0				156,756	156,756	256,756
37	82	0	0				162,020	162,020	262,020
38	83	0	0				166,526	166,526	266,526
39	84	0	0				170,032	170,032	270,032
40	85	0	0				172,170	172,170	272,170

Assumed interest rates are for illustrative purposes only; actual rates may be more or less than those shown.

UNIVERSAL LIFE

Plan Summary Page 15

Based on the Current Interest Rate

End of Year	(1) Total Premiums	(2) Total Withdrawals	(3) Net Cash Value	(4) Difference (1) - [(2) + (3)]	(5) Cash Value	(6) Death Benefit
5	$10,005	$0	$ 9,593	$ 411	$10,116	$110,116
10	20,010	0	24,450	4,440-	24,450	124,450
15	30,015	0	45,445	15,430-	45,445	145,445
20	40,020	0	76,137	36,117-	76,137	176,137
Age 65	40,020	0	76,137	36,117-	76,137	176,137

Interest-adjusted Indexes Based on a 5.00% Interest Rate for Basic Policy Only **16**

	Guaranteed Interest of 4.5%		Current Interest of 8.5%		Assumed Interest of 8.00%	
	10 Years	20 Years	10 Years	20 Years	10 Years	20 Years
Surrender Cost	$ 8.39	$12.18	$ 1.38	$ 1.58-	$ 1.82	$ .60
Net Payment	18.84	18.01	18.41	16.46	18.44	16.60

Figure 18.1 (cont'd)

FLEXIBLE PREMIUM ADJUSTABLE LIFE
Explanatory Notes Page **17**

The current rate is 8.50% for the first 10 years and 9.10% thereafter. **18**

Each premium is credited with interest at the current rate of the company. The rate for the policy reflects the weighted average of the rate on each premium. A portion of the cash value is reinvested at the end of each year at the then-current rate. **19**

The interest rates shown are effective annual rates. Interest is credited after deduction of expense and cost of insurance charges. **20**

A policy loan balance may not be credited with the full current interest rate, but the rate applied will not be less than the greater of 4.5% and 2% less than the policy loan interest rate. **21**

The net cash value equals the cash value minus any policy loan balance minus any surrender charge. **22**

Actual amounts may differ from those shown due to changes in: current interest rate, cost of insurance rate, face amount, timing or amount of premiums, or death benefit option. **23**

It is unlikely that dividends will be paid on this policy. Dividends, if any, will be small and paid only in later policy years. **24**

This illustration incorporates the company's interpretation of the Tax Reform Act of 1984 as it pertains to the definition of life insurance in general and universal life in particular. The company will comply with any IRS regulations issued regarding its interpretation of the definition of life insurance. **25**

The "Current" column uses current mortality costs and current interest rate, which are not guaranteed beyond the first year. **26**

The "Guaranteed" column uses the current mortality costs for the first year and the current interest rate guaranteed for the initial premium. Thereafter, this column uses the guaranteed minimum interest rate and guaranteed maximum mortality costs. **27**

28 A fixed policy loan interest rate of 8% applied against the net cash value.

---

11. The amount withdrawn from the cash value as a living benefit. For this ledger statement, there are no withdrawals.

12. Guaranteed interest of 4.5 percent column. This is the minimum percentage rate at which the insurance company will accumulate the reserve. Under this column are cash value, net cash value, and death benefit. The cash value is the amount of reserve earning interest. It is not, however, available to borrow against nor is it the amount received if the policy is surrendered. The net cash value is the amount of money in any given year that is available to borrow against and is the amount of money payable if the policy is surrendered. It is also the amount that must appear on the balance sheet when necessary. The death benefit is based on the current interest rate of 8.5 percent for the first year only. Thereafter, the guaranteed minimum rate of 4.5 percent applies. The current mortality charges are for the first year only. Thereafter, the maximum mortality charges can be imposed. Under these assumptions, if no further premiums are paid, the insurance will lapse at age seventy-two. For assumption purposes, the guaranteed section is the worst possible scenario.

13. Assumed interest rate of 8 percent column (the current interest rate is 8.5 percent for the first ten years and 9.1 percent thereafter) is 50 basis points (0.50 percent) for the first ten years and 110 basis points (1.1 percent) *less* than the current rate. Cash value is predicated on an 8 percent interest assumption. This is also true for the net cash value and the death benefit.

14. Life expectancy of a forty-five-year-old male is twenty-nine years, or age seventy-four.

15. Summary page indicates values based on the current interest rate, not the assumed rate. The assumed rate of 8 percent is less than the current rate (i.e., 8.5 percent for the first ten years and 9.1 percent thereafter).

16. Interest adjusted index: guaranteed interest rate, current interest rate, and assumed rate. (See Chapter 4, "How to Determine the Right Policy.")

17. Explanatory notes page.

18. Statement about the current interest rate at the time the ledger statement was printed.

19. Investment strategy of the insurance company.

20. Statement about how interest is credited.

21. Borrowed money does not earn the current interest rate of 8.5 percent. It will earn either 4.5 percent or 2 percent less than the current rate, whichever is greater.

22. The net cash value and the cash value are different up to year ten. Prior to year ten, the cash value is less than the net cash value because of a rear-end load. There are penalties if the policy is surrendered prior to the end of year ten.

23. Variables due to changes in interest rates, mortality charges, how premiums are paid, or changes in the death benefit option (e.g., going from option II to option I).

24. Dividend statement.

25. Insurance company statement that the ledger statement conforms to the Tax Reform Act of 1984 and meets the various tests (i.e., the net single premium, cash value accumulation, and corridor tests, as well as the guideline on annual premium for all policies issued on or after December 31, 1984).

26. Current column not used for this ledger statement. Guaranteed and assumed columns are used.

27. Guaranteed interest rate column statement.

28. Fixed contractual loan interest rate on loans against the reserve (net cash value) is 8 percent.

What Ledger Statements Do Not Tell

You should be told either verbally or in writing the following additional information:

- The investment strategy employed by the life insurance company is a modified portfolio rate, using a percentage rollover concept with investments having a maturity date of six to eight years. Percentage rollover means that X percent of previously invested money plus interest earned on the reserve (the cash value) is rolled over each and every year into a new money rate.

- The ratio of current mortality charges as used in the ledger statement to the maximum charges that can be imposed should be revealed. For this ledger statement, the ratio of current charges to maximum charges for sequential years is as follows. The charges are shown on an annual basis (the actual mortality charges are deducted monthly) per $1,000 of insurance at risk.

Year	Age	Current	Maximum	Ratio
1	45	2.80	5.35	52%
5	50	3.72	7.60	49
10	55	5.37	11.91	45
15	60	7.69	18.62	41
20	65	11.93	29.11	41

- This reveals that there is ample margin for the insurance company to increase its mortality charges to protect itself against unduly high rates of mortality (such as among AIDS sufferers), changes in current tax law that govern how life insurance companies pay taxes, and just about any other area that may increase the cost of doing business.

- This particular universal life product has been priced by the insurance company to make a profit or a contribution to surplus, essentially through the investment spread.

- If necessary, the insurance company by contract can and will decrease the current interest rate to as low as 4.5 percent and increase the mortality charges to their maximum—if the cost of doing business so dictates.

- The rate of return expressed in terms of compound interest should be given either on the ledger statement or by the life insurance agent. Ideally, it should be provided for each year.

- The rate of return upon death for this policy for sequential years is as follows:

Year	Rate of Return
1	4,984.91%
5	94.28
10	31.93
20	12.37
29 (life expectancy)	8.38

- Once the rate of return upon death is known, then it can be determined what would have to be earned before taxes in other financial services products such as mutual funds, certificates of deposit, real estate, or commodities to duplicate the tax-exempt rate of return provided by life insurance. (For this purpose, it is assumed that the death benefit is considered life insurance proceeds and as such not subject to federal or state income taxes.) The before-tax rate of return is determined by dividing the life insurance rate of return by the marginal tax bracket subtracted from 100 percent (for 15 percent, the factor is 0.85; for 25 percent, 0.75; for 28 percent, 0.72; for 33 percent, 0.67; and for 35 percent, 0.65). The result is shown in Figure 18.2.

- The rate of return upon surrender should also be provided. When the rate of return upon surrender is positive, it means that taxes are due. Taxes are due on the difference between

the cash surrender value and the premiums paid. The result before taxes is as follows:

Year	Rate of Return
1	−59.57%
5	−1.81
10	3.14
20	4.95
29 (life expectancy)	5.27

- The rate of return upon surrender even before taxes never equals the interest assumption of 8 percent.

- The ledger statement should be the official ledger statement produced by the computer service of the life insurance company. It should be bug-free.

TAX IMPLICATIONS

The income tax rules for UL policies that do not run afoul of the Modified Endowment Contract (MEC) rules are the same as for other types of life insurance policies. Beneficiaries receive death benefits that, usually, are free of any federal income tax. UL policies also are subject to the same estate, gift, and generation-skipping transfer taxation rules as all other types of life insurance policies.

Also, the income tax rules for living benefits paid from UL policies are the same as living benefits paid from other types of life insurance policies. Generally, the cost-recovery rule governs the taxation of these living benefits. The cost-recovery rule, which is sometimes called the First-In First-Out (FIFO) rule, treats amounts received as nontaxable recovery of the policyowner's investment in the contract. Only after policyowners fully recover their investment in the contract are additional amounts that they receive treated as taxable interest or gain in the policy. Included in this category of living benefits are policy dividends, lump-sum cash settlements of cash surrender values, cash withdrawals, and amounts received on partial surrender. Policyowners include these amounts in gross income only to the extent they exceed the investment in the contract (as reduced by any prior excludable distributions received from the contract). In other words, the income tax rules generally treat nonannuity distributions during life first, as a return of the policyowner's investment in the contract—and only after the owner has recovered

Figure 18.2

BEFORE-TAX RATE OF RETURN					
Year	15% taxpayer	25% taxpayer	28% taxpayer	33% taxpayer	35% taxpayer
1	5,864.60%	6,646.55%	6,923.49%	7,440.16%	7,669.09%
5	110.92	125.71	130.94	140.72	145.05
10	37.56	42.57	44.35	47.66	49.12
20	14.55	16.49	17.18	18.46	19.03
29 (life expectancy)	9.86	11.17	11.64	12.51	12.89

the entire investment in the contract—then as taxable interest or gain.

Exception to the Cost Recovery Rule

An important exception to the general cost-recovery rule applies for withdrawals within the first fifteen years after the policy issue date that are coupled with reductions in death benefits. Because insurers generally reduce death benefits in an amount equal to any withdrawal of cash values, policyowner withdrawals frequently may trigger a tax on all or part of these withdrawals to the extent of gain in the policy.

The rules tax such withdrawals in whole or in part as ordinary income to the extent that they are forced out of the policy as a result of the reduction in the death benefits. The taxable amount depends on when the owner makes the withdrawal:

- *Within first five years* – If the withdrawal takes place within the first five years after policy issue, a very stringent and complex set of tests applies.[2] Potentially, a larger portion, or perhaps all, of any withdrawal within the first five years will be taxable if there is gain in the policy.

- *Fifth to fifteenth years* – For withdrawals between the end of the fifth year and the end of the fifteenth year from the issue date, a mathematical test applies. Essentially, the rules tax the policyowner on an income-first basis to the extent the cash value before the withdrawal exceeds the maximum allowable cash value under the cash value corridor test for the reduced death benefit after the withdrawal.[3] Frequently, in these cases, only a portion or even no part of the withdrawal will be taxable.

Changing from option B (increasing death benefit) or from option C (return of premium) to option A (level death benefit) will trigger a test to see whether any amount must be forced out of the policy. In general, option B and option C contracts allow for greater cash accumulations within the policy than option A contracts. Consequently, if a policy with option B and option C has close to the maximum permitted cash value, a switch to option A generally will trigger a taxable distribution. (See Chapters 22 through 29 for a complete discussion of the taxation of life insurance.)

Caveat: Potential Taxation under the Modified Endowment Contract Rules

The flexibility inherent in UL policies with respect to changes in premiums and death benefits raises the possibility that the policy could become a modified endowment contract (MEC).[4] The penalty for classification as a MEC relates to distributions. If a policy is classified as a MEC, distributions under the contract are taxed under the interest-first rule rather than the cost recovery rule. In addition, to the extent taxable, these distributions are subject to a 10 percent penalty if they occur before the policyowner reaches age 59½, dies, or becomes disabled. So MEC categorization of a UL contract means both faster taxation of investment gains and a possible penalty tax for early receipt of that growth.

Distributions under the contract include nonannuity living benefits (as described above), policy loans, loans secured by the policy, loans used to pay premiums, and dividends taken in cash. Distributions under the contract generally do *not* include dividends used to pay premiums, dividends used to purchase paid-up additions, dividends used to purchase one year term insurance, or the surrender of paid-up additions to pay premiums.

Changes in premiums or death benefits may inadvertently cause a UL policy to run afoul of the MEC rules in basically three ways:

1. An increase in premium payments during the first seven contract years may push the cumulative premiums above the amount permitted under the seven-pay test.[5]

2. A reduction in the death benefit during the first seven contract years triggers a recomputation of the seven-pay test. The seven-pay test is applied retroactively as of the original issue date as if the policy had been issued at the reduced death benefit.

3. A material increase of the death benefit at any time triggers a new seven-pay test which is applied prospectively as of the date of the material change.

When issued, most UL policy illustrations show the maximum amount (the seven-pay guideline annual premium limit) that the policyowner may pay within the first seven years without having the policy classified as a MEC. If policyowners inadvertently exceed that maximum, they can avoid MEC status if insurers return excess premiums to the policyowner with interest within sixty days after the end of the contract year in which the excess occurs. The interest will be subject to taxation.[6]

In general, a reduction in death benefit within the first seven contract years that is caused by and equal in amount to a withdrawal is less likely to cause the policy to fail the recomputed seven-pay test than a death benefit reduction without a withdrawal. However, a policy will fail the seven-pay test if in any year the cumulative premiums paid to that year exceed the sum of the seven-pay guideline annual premiums to that year.

Example. Assume the guideline annual premium is $10,000 based on the original death benefit. The policyowner pays $9,000 each year for the first six years. In year seven, the policyowner withdraws $36,000, with a corresponding decrease in the death benefit. The recomputed guideline premium is $8,000. The policy now fails the seven-pay test and is a MEC because cumulative premiums paid in just the first year, $9,000, (and through year six as well) exceed

the sum of the recomputed guideline annual premiums of $8,000.

Any reduction in death benefits attributable to the nonpayment of premiums due under the contract will not trigger a recomputation of the seven-pay test if the benefits are reinstated within ninety days after being reduced.[7]

A change from option B (face amount plus cash value) or option C (face amount plus return of premium) to option A (face amount) appears to be a decrease that triggers the look-back rule and a retroactive reapplication of the seven-pay test. In general, one would not expect the switch in options to result in a lower seven-pay limit unless the face amount of insurance was also reduced to less than the face amount at the time of issue. Therefore, switching from option B or C to option A should not, in general, cause the policy to be reclassified as a MEC.

The term "material" change is not defined in the statute. However, the statute states that it "includes any increase in death benefit under the contract,"[8] but *not* increases attributable to dividends (for paid-up additions), interest credited to the policy's cash surrender value, increases necessary to maintain the corridor between the death benefit and the cash surrender value required by the definition of life insurance,[9] or cost-of-living adjustments. Whether changing from option A to option B constitutes a material change in death benefit is unclear. Other increases in death benefits that require evidence of insurability will be considered material changes that invoke a new seven-pay test. See Chapter 22, "Modified Endowment Contracts" for more information.

ALTERNATIVES

Insurers and policyowners can configure a UL policy's premium payments and death benefits to resemble virtually any type of life insurance policy, from annually-renewable term to single premium whole life. Consequently, any other type of policy that meets a policyowner's needs is a suitable and, perhaps, preferable alternative if the policyowner does not need the UL's flexibility. However, a number of other types of policies or strategies offer some of the features of UL and not others, if policyowners desire only certain features.

1. *Current-Assumption Whole Life (CAWL)* – Sometimes called interest-sensitive whole life, CAWL

is essentially UL without the adjustability features. CAWL, similar to UL, uses current interest rates in determining additions to cash values. However, similar to traditional ordinary whole life and in contrast with UL, CAWL generally offers the policyowner little flexibility with respect to changing premium payments or death benefits.

2. *Adjustable Life (AL)* – AL combines elements of traditional, fixed premium ordinary life insurance and the ability, within limits, to alter the policy plan, premium payments, and the face amount. Essentially, one can view AL as UL without the current-assumption feature.

3. *Variable Life (VL) and Variable Universal Life (VUL)* – If a VL policyowner selects a portfolio of investments within the policy that is similar to the general investment portfolio of the insurance company (mostly long-term bonds and mortgages), they can expect investment performance and cash value accumulations to be similar to those with UL.

4. *Flexible Premium Deferred Annuity (FPDA) combined with term insurance* – A combination of a FPDA with level term can generate cash value accumulations and death benefit levels similar to UL under option B or C. A FPDA combined with a decreasing term policy is similar to UL under option A. The FPDA, however, has less favorable tax treatment for withdrawals and loans than a UL policy.

5. *Section 1035 exchanges* – The exchange provisions under Internal Revenue Code section 1035 allow certain types of exchanges from one policy type to another without adverse tax consequences. Clearly, these exchange provisions provide nowhere near the flexibility or convenience that a UL policy does to change premium levels or death benefits. However, the existence of these exchange provisions means that other types of policies are not quite as inflexible as they might otherwise seem.

WHERE CAN I FIND OUT MORE?

The following references include authoritative discussions of various types of life insurance including universal life insurance:

1. T. Steuer, *Questions and Answers on Life Insurance: The Life Insurance Toolbook* (Thousand Oaks, CA: Life Insurance Sage Press, 2010).

2. B. Baldwin, *New Life Insurance Investment Advisor: Achieving Financial Security for You and Your Family Through Today's Insurance Products*, 2nd ed. (Hightstown, NJ: McGraw-Hill Trade, 2001).

3. J. Belth, *Life Insurance: A Consumer's Handbook*, 2nd ed. (Bloomington, IN: Indiana University Press, 1985).

4. K. Black, Jr. and H. Skipper, Jr., *Life Insurance*, 13th ed. (Old Tappan, NJ: Prentice Hall Inc., 1999).

5. E. Graves, Editor, *McGill's Life Insurance*, 7th ed. (Bryn Mawr, PA: The American College, 2010).

The following references are useful guides for policy and company rating information:

1. *Best Insurance Reports* (Oldwick, NJ: A. M. Best Company, published annually).

2. *Best's Review – Life/Health Edition* (Oldwick, NJ: A. M. Best Company, published monthly).

CHAPTER ENDNOTES

1. This illustration is adapted from William D. Brownlie's treatise, *The Life Insurance Buyer's Guide*, McGraw-Hill Publishing Company, 1989.

2. I.R.C. §§7702(f)(7)(B), 7702(f)(7)(C).

3. I.R.C. §§7702(f)(7)(B), 7702(f)(7)(D). The cash value corridor test is discussed in Chapter 24, "Taxation of Benefits."

4. In cases where there are extreme reductions in the death benefit or very large premium payments, it is even possible for a policy to fail the tests for life insurance under I.R.C. §7702 with much more disastrous tax consequences. See the discussion of the definition of life insurance in Chapter 24, "Taxation of Benefits."

5. I.R.C. §7702A(a)(1)(B). Classification as a MEC occurs in the year when the seven-pay test is first violated and for each year thereafter. See Chapter 22, "Modified Endowment Contracts," for a more complete discussion of the seven-pay test.

6. I.R.C. §7702A(e)(1).

7. I.R.C. §7702A(c)(2)(B).

8. I.R.C. §7702A(c)(3).

9. I.R.C. §7702. See chapter 24 "Taxation of Benefits."

VARIABLE AND VARIABLE UNIVERSAL LIFE

CHAPTER 19

INTRODUCTION

Variable Life

Variable Life (VL) insurance combines traditional whole life insurance with mutual fund type investments. Basically, it is a whole life policy where the policyowner may direct the investment of cash values among a variety of different investments. VL has a guaranteed minimum face amount and a level premium like traditional whole life insurance, but it differs in three respects:

1. *The policyowner's funds are placed in separate accounts that are distinct and separate from the company's general investment fund.* Insurers place policyowner premiums, less an expense or sales load and a mortality charge, into a separate investment account. The policyowner may choose to invest premiums and cash values among several mutual-fund type alternatives, typically including, at a minimum, stock funds, bond funds, and money market funds. Many companies that market VL offer a broader array of investment options such as foreign stock funds, bond funds, GNMA funds, real estate funds, zero-coupon bond funds, and specialized funds such as small capitalization stock funds, market-index funds, and funds that focus on specific sectors of the economy or industries (medical, high tech, gold, leisure, utilities, etc.). Some companies offer a managed fund option where the company's investment manager assumes the responsibility for allocating investments among the various alternative funds. Some VL policies also offer a guaranteed interest option similar to the declared interest rate on universal life policies. Policyowners typically may switch or rebalance their investments among the funds one or more times per year.

2. *The insurer does not guaranteed a minimum cash value.* The cash value at any point in time is based on the market value of the assets in the separate account. VL policyowners bear *all* the investment risk associated with the policy.

3. *The death benefit is variable.* The face value may increase or decrease but not below the guaranteed minimum (based on a formula that relates the investment performance of the separate account to the face value). Companies use two methods to establish the relationship between the investment performance and the face amount. Under what is called the corridor percentage approach, the insurer periodically adjusts the death benefit so that it is at least equal to a specified percentage of the cash value, as required by current tax law.[1] The mandated corridor percentage is 250 percent until the insured reaches age forty or so and then gradually declines to 100 percent by age ninety-five, typically.

Example. Assume the cash value is $40,000 at the beginning of the period and $50,000 at the end of the period. The insured is sixty years old. The initial death benefit is $52,000 and the corridor percentage factor is 130 percent. At the end of the period, the death benefit will be $65,000, or 130 percent of $50,000.

Under what is called the net single premium approach insurers adjust the death benefit so that it matches the amount of insurance that the policyowner could purchase with a single premium equal to the cash value, assuming guaranteed mortality rates and a low rate of return, typically 4 percent. Although both methods are equally valid, most policyowners find the corridor percentage method easier to understand.

Example. Assume the net single premium factor in the example above is 0.65374. That is, it takes $0.65374 to buy $1 of insurance for life. At the end of the period, the death benefit will be $50,000/0.65374, or $76,483.

VL has most of the usual features of traditional level premium life insurance including guaranteed maximum mortality charges, nonforfeiture values, a policy loan provision, a reinstatement period, and settlement options.

Also, VL policies may be participating or nonparticipating. In contrast to traditional par policies, dividends paid on par VL policies depend only on possible mortality and expense savings and include no element of excess investment earnings. Excess investment earnings, less an asset management fee, are reflected directly in the value of the separate account.

Similar to other traditional forms of insurance, policyowners may add various options or riders including, particularly, waiver of premium, guaranteed purchase or insurability, and accidental death benefits, as well as others. (See Chapter 6; "Special Policy Provisions and Riders," for further discussion of options and riders.)

Insurers that market VL often offer a number of initial premium payment plans including single premium, limited pay (for a specified number of years or until a specified age), and lifetime pay plans.

Variable Universal Life

Variable Universal Life (VUL), which also is called flexible premium variable life or universal life II, is a combination of universal life and variable life. VUL offers policyowners the flexibility of universal life (UL) with respect to premium payments and death benefits. Specifically, VUL owners can:

1. determine the timing and amount of premium payments (within limits);

2. skip a premium payment if the cash value is sufficient to cover the mortality and expense charges;

3. adjust the amount of the death benefit in response to inflation or changing needs (subject, generally, to policy minimums and, with respect to increases, evidence of insurability requirements);

4. withdraw money without creating a policy loan and without an interest charge if there is sufficient cash value to cover mortality and expense charges; and

5. choose between two death benefit options similar to options A (or I) and B (or II) for UL policies. Under option A, the death benefit remains level, similar to a traditional policy. Under option B, the death benefit is equal to a level pure insurance amount plus the cash value.

The death benefit of a VUL policy is not variable in the same sense as the death benefit of a VL policy. Under option B, the death benefit will vary directly, not indirectly by formula, with changes in the cash value. Under option A, the death benefit is level. However, the death benefit of VUL policies is flexible or adjustable, within limits and subject to insurability requirements, at the discretion of the policyowner.

VUL policyowners receive periodic reports that explicitly show mortality and expense charges and changes in the investment value of their accounts.

Because variable life products are considered securities, the insurer (or insurer's agent) must give the prospective purchasers a prospectus. The prospectus contains the identity and nature of the insurer's business, the use to which the insurer will put the premiums, financial information on the insurer, and the investment characteristics of the product, as well as the policy's expenses, fees, loads, and policyowner rights. In addition, the agent must be properly licensed to sell security products.

WHEN IS THE USE OF THIS DEVICE INDICATED?

Variable life products are most suitable for those individuals who want control over their cash values and need or desire increasing life insurance protection. They should have a basic understanding of investments and believe they are capable of making good investment decisions. They must be willing to bear the entire risk of their investments because the insurance company does not guarantee the cash values of VL products. If the policyowner expects the need for death protection to grow, VL death benefit levels will increase with favorable investment experience on the underlying assets. However, policyowners have no assurance that this growth will be consistent. Policyowners face a risk that the market value of the underlying assets and, therefore, the death benefit level, will be depressed when the insured dies.

VUL offers greater certainty of death benefit levels than VL as long as policyowners continue to pay premiums at the level necessary to maintain the death benefit. Under option B, death benefit levels are more certain to increase. VUL also permits the policyowner to increase the face amount of coverage with evidence of insurability.

Given the risks and uncertainties associated with both cash values and death benefit levels, some people may find variable life products an attractive supplement to an existing life insurance plan that assures a minimum required base level of coverage. Generally, VL and VUL are less suitable as the means of providing the minimum basic level of coverage.

VL and, more particularly, VUL are especially suitable for many business insurance needs where flexibility and growth of cash values and death benefits are necessary or attractive features. Businesses can use these policies to provide potentially higher tax-deferred cash value accumulations in nonqualified deferred compensation plans than traditional policies or UL. With successful investment of cash values, the death benefit levels of variable products are more likely than those of traditional products to keep pace with increases in the values of closely-held business interests when a variable product funds a buy-sell agreement. Businesses may also find VL and VUL equally attractive for key person insurance and other business applications or in insured pension plans.

Advantages

1. Policyowners have control over how premiums and cash values are invested. They generally may allocate their investments as desired among a variety of mutual fund-type investment accounts.

2. Insurers permit switches or transfers between funds at least once and usually more times per year, usually with no charge.

3. Switches or transfers between funds are tax-free.

4. Cash values of VL and VUL policies are more secure in the event of insurer insolvency than cash values of other types of policies. Assets backing VL and VUL policies are in separate, segregated accounts from the general investment portfolio of the insurer. Also, insurers base cash values on the market value of the assets in the separate accounts. Therefore, cash values are readily available in the event of insurer insolvency. In contrast because insurers do not adjust cash values in other types of policies to the market value of the assets in the insurer's general portfolio, in the event of insolvency, the general portfolio may not have sufficient assets to cover cash values.

5. Earnings on the assets underlying the policy cash values accumulate tax-free or tax deferred, depending, respectively, on whether the policy pays distributions of gains as death benefits or as lifetime benefits as a result of cash value withdrawals or payments under a nonforfeiture option.

6. VL provides some measure of automatic increases in death benefits that may keep pace with inflation. Death benefits of VL policies are tied to changes in the underlying value of the assets backing the policy. Because the rate of return assumed when setting the guaranteed minimum death benefit is relatively low, death benefits generally should trend upward and provide some measure of inflation protection.

7. A VUL policyowner has wide discretion or flexibility in selecting the timing and amount of premium payments. Provided that there is enough cash value to cover mortality and other account charges, the policyowner may even skip premium payments. In contrast with other types of policies, skipping premiums does not result in the creation of policy loans.

8. VUL permits the policyowner to change the level of death benefits. Insurance companies permit decreases in the death benefit at virtually any time. However, policyowners who reduce death benefits within the first seven years of issue may face adverse tax consequences under the modified endowment contract (MEC) rules. Insurers

generally permit increases in face amount, subject to evidence of insurability. Increases in the death benefit also may subject the policy to a new test period under the MEC rules. (See the following discussion under "Tax Implications".)

9. VUL policies are transparent. Annual reports break out and report each of the policy elements separately. This unbundling allows the policyowner to specifically identify and track premiums, death benefits, interest credits, mortality charges, expenses, and cash values and to check projections against actual performance over time.

10. Most VUL policies offer three death benefit patterns, two original patterns called "Option A" (or I) and "Option B" (or II), as well as a more recent pattern called "Option C" (or III).

   Option A, similar to a traditional whole life policy, offers a fixed or level death benefit. As cash values grow larger, the net amount at risk, the pure insurance, is reduced to keep the total death benefit constant (unless the cash value grows to an amount where the insurer must increase death benefit to avoid classification as a MEC).

   Option B operates in a manner similar to the death benefit one would receive from a traditional whole life policy with a term insurance rider equal to the current cash value. Under option B, the death benefit at any time is equal to a specified level of pure insurance plus the policy's cash value at the time of death. Therefore, the death benefit increases as the cash value grows.

   Option C provides a Return of Premium (ROP) feature that increases the death benefit by the cumulative premiums. Some ROP options also provide for an interest factor that will increase the cumulative premiums by a specified interest rate. This option has become more popular as a result of premium financing and the need to maintain a level death benefit for the insured net of the amount that is owed to a lender.

11. Some companies offer cost of living riders to VUL Option A policies that, without evidence of insurability, automatically increase the policy death benefit periodically by the increase in the CPI. The increasing death benefit associated with option B generally makes the need for a cost of living rider under this option moot.

12. In contrast with most traditional whole life policies, many VUL policies use back-end loads rather than front-end loads to recover the initial policy expenses. Consequently, most or all of the policyowner's initial premiums go into cash values subject, of course, to regular annual expense and mortality charges. Therefore, cash values tend to build up more quickly than with traditional whole life policies.

13. Policyowners can borrow policy cash values at a low net cost. Although policyowners must pay interest on policy loans, the insurer credits the cash value backing the loan with an interest rate that is usually slightly lower than that paid by the policyowner on the loan. Consequently, the actual net borrowing rate is less than the stated policy loan rate.

14. In most VUL policies, policyowners may withdraw a substantial portion of their cash value without surrendering the policy. However, if policyowners withdraw money, the insurer often reduces the pure life insurance portion of the death benefit by the amount of the withdrawal. In addition, withdrawals may be subject to income tax. (See the following discussion under "Tax Implications".)

15. Life insurance proceeds are not part of the probate estate unless the estate is named as the beneficiary of the policy. Therefore, the policyowner can have the proceeds paid to the beneficiary without the expense, delay, or uncertainty caused by administration of the estate.

Disadvantages

1. The policyowner bears all investment risk. VUL policies provide no minimum schedule of cash values as with UL or traditional whole life policies. Instead, cash values are equal to the market value of the policy assets in the separate accounts.

2. VL death benefits depend on the investment performance of the assets underlying the policy. If market values are down when the insured dies, the policy may pay a lower death benefit than anticipated. However, the death benefit cannot fall below the guaranteed minimum benefit.

3. If the investment performance of a VUL policy is poor, to maintain the face amount of coverage the policy may require the policyowner to pay additional premiums.

4. VUL policyowners must accept all responsibility for premium payments. The disadvantage here is that policyowners can too easily allow their policies to lapse. The policy has no forced savings feature, because it does not require the policyowner to make premium payments as long as the cash value is sufficient to carry the policy. To reduce the likelihood of lapse, most companies bill policyowners for a target premium set by the policyowner.

5. VL and VUL policyowners bear some mortality and expense risk because these policies are "current assumption policies with respect to mortality and expenses. VL and VUL only guarantee that mortality charges and expense rates will not exceed certain maximums. In contrast, traditional participating whole life policies guarantee mortality and expense charges. Consequently, policyowners bear more of the risk of adverse trends in mortality or expenses than if they owned traditional whole life policies. However, if the trend of mortality costs and expenses improves, policyowners may participate in the improvement through lower charges.

6. Lifetime distributions or withdrawals of cash values are subject to income tax to the extent attributable to gain in the policy.

7. Realized capital gains on the underlying assets when taking withdrawals or surrendering the policy are taxed as ordinary income. In contrast, capital gains recognized on sales of similar mutual fund shares were treated as capital gains. In addition, under current tax law, taxpayers may use capital gains to offset other capital losses if the gains are from a mutual fund but not if they are from a life insurance policy. (In future years, ordinary and capital gains tax rates will probably change. However, that some kind of differential in the ordinary and capital gains tax rates will remain is highly likely. Also, the portions of distributions of cash values of life insurance that are attributable to capital appreciation of the underlying assets are highly likely to continue to be taxed at ordinary income tax rates, rather than lower capital gains tax rates.)

8. Surrender of the policy within the first five to ten years may result in considerable loss because surrender values reflect the insurance company's recovery of sales commissions and initial policy expenses. In addition, most VUL policies levy surrender charges rather than up-front fees or loads. These surrender charges generally decline each year the owner continues to hold the policy. Typically, insurers assess no explicit charges if the owner surrenders the policy after about seven to ten years.

9. The flexibility with respect to premium payments and death benefits in VUL permits policyowners to change the policy in such a way that, inadvertently, it may become a modified endowment contract with adverse tax consequences.

10. Expense loadings generally are greater than with other types of policies.

POLICY FEATURES

The VL contract works like this:

1. Premiums (less an investment expense and/or sales load, state premium tax, and a mortality charge) are paid into separate investment accounts.

2. The policyowner selects among several separate accounts. These include mutual-fund type alternatives such as stock funds, bond funds, and money market funds to invest the remaining premium.

3. Policyowners may typically switch or rebalance their investments among the funds one or more times per year. The insurer may or may not charge a fee for each such movement of cash.

The single most important distinction between variable life and traditional whole life is in the investment flexibility and the consequent shifting of the investment risk from the insurer (with classic whole life) to the policyowner (with variable life). In the variable life contract the policyowner's funds are segregated, since they are placed in accounts that are distinct and separate from the company's general investment fund.

Determining the Death Benefit

In a very general sense VL contracts provide two death distinct benefits. The first provides for a minimum payment and is guaranteed. The second death benefit is only paid if the actual investment return on the separate account exceeds the assumed rate of return. The insurer uses excess interest credits to buy additional blocks of insurance under this second death benefit.[2]

Technically, the face value may increase or decrease based on a formula that relates the investment performance of the separate account to the face value. Companies use two methods to establish the relationship between the investment performance and the face amount. Under what is called the corridor percentage approach, insurers adjust the death benefit periodically so that it is at least equal to a specified percentage of the cash value, as required by current tax law.[3] The mandated corridor percentage is 250 percent until the insured reaches age forty and then gradually declines to 100 percent by age ninety-five.

Insurers adjust the death benefit under what is called the net single premium approach so that it matches the amount of insurance that policyowners could purchase with a single premium equal to the cash value, assuming guaranteed mortality rates and a low rate of return, typically 4 percent.

Although both methods are equally valid, most policyowners find the corridor percentage method easier to understand.

As mentioned above, the insurer provides a floor that protects the beneficiary of a variable life contract. The death benefit cannot fall below a guaranteed minimum, the initial face amount of the policy. If the return on the selected portfolio, called a separate account, is greater than the rate of interest assumed at the inception of the contract, the actual death benefit may increase beyond the policy's scheduled face amount.

Legal Protections for Policyowners

Unlike the traditional whole life policy, in the variable contract insurers do not guarantee minimum cash values. The cash value at any point in time is based on the market value of the assets in the separate account the policyowner has chosen. VL policyowners bear *all* the investment risk associated with policy. So cash values can grow well beyond the assumed rate or not at all. There can even be negative growth. That is to say that it is possible in a variable life contract for the policyowner to lose the entire amount in the selected portfolio.

Otherwise, the insurer provides the VL policyowner with most of the usual features of traditional level premium life insurance including guaranteed maximum mortality charges, nonforfeiture values, a reinstatement period, and settlement options.

Options or riders available under VL contracts include waiver of premium, guaranteed purchase or insurability, accidental death benefits, and disability income, as well as others commonly available with other types of policies.

Dividends

Insurers issue VL policies in both participating and nonparticipating forms. But insurers base dividends paid on par VL policies solely on favorable mortality and loading experience and include no element of excess investment earnings. The insurers reflect excess investment earnings, less an asset management fee, in the value of the separate account.

Policy Loans

Insurers allow loans from VL contracts. But policy loan provisions are not, however, the same as in the traditional insurance policy. This is because a loan equal to the full cash value could leave the insurer with less than complete security for the debt if the value of the underlying portfolio dropped after the insurer made the loan. For this reason, most insurers limit loans on VL products to about 75 percent of the policy's cash values (compared with about 92 percent on traditional contracts). If a policyowner takes a loan, the insurer will credit the loan with a lower rate than the full portfolio investment rate, usually a percent specified in the policy.

Comparing VL, VUL, and UL Policies

A VUL prospectus generally discloses more about expense charges than is disclosed in a UL policy illustration and contract. VUL has higher expenses resulting from the need to prepare prospectuses, to register with the SEC, and to provide investment flexibility. These additional costs are offset somewhat by lower profit requirements on VUL, where the investment risk is assumed by the policyowner.

Front-end sales loads, premium tax loads, and administrative charges on VUL and UL do not differ materially. Surrender charges on VUL policies are generally lower than those on UL to enable the VUL to comply with SEC limits on sales loads. Investment expenses are higher on VUL because the fee paid to the investment manager is usually higher than the typical investment expense for a UL policy. Profit margins are slightly less for VUL than for UL.

Figure 19.1 compares and contrasts the key features of universal, variable, and variable universal life. As the table shows, variable universal life combines most of the advantages of universal and variable life. Figure 19.2 shows how VUL and UL compare from an investor's perspective.

TAX IMPLICATIONS

VL products that do not violate the modified endowment contract rules are taxed in the same manner as other types of life insurance policies. Death benefits usually are paid free of any federal income tax. Variable life insurance policies are subject to the same income, estate, gift, and generation-skipping transfer taxation rules as all other types of life insurance policies.

Figure 19.1

KEY FEATURES OF UNIVERSAL, VARIABLE, AND VARIABLE UNIVERSAL LIFE			
Feature	**UL**	**VL**	**VUL**
Death benefit guaranteed while the policy is in force	Yes	Yes	Yes
Premium amounts are flexible	Yes	No	Yes
Policyowner chooses how premiums are invested	No	Yes	Yes
Policyowner may vary frequency or amount of premiums paid	Yes	No	Yes
Policyowner may use cash values to pay monthly deductions	Yes	No	Yes
Policyowner may increase or decrease death benefit	Yes	No	Yes
Death benefit options A and B available	Yes	No	Yes
Cash values fluctuate depending on performance of underlying investment	No*	Yes	Yes
Guaranteed minimum interest rate on cash values	Yes	No	No
Partial withdrawals from cash value allowed	Yes	No	Yes
Cash value grows on tax deferred basis	Yes	Yes	Yes
Annual statements detailing monthly deductions and cash value growth	Yes	No	Yes
Considered a security	No	Yes	Yes

* The current interest credited to cash values of UL policies fluctuates with the performance of the insurer's general portfolio, but cash values, once accumulated, do not fluctuate in value with fluctuations in the market value of the assets in the general portfolio.

Figure 19.2

VUL COMPARED WITH UL FROM THE INVESTOR'S PERSPECTIVE		
Characteristic	**Universal Life**	**Variable Universal Life**
Investment Control	Generally intermediate maturity fixed income assets. Control is with the insurance company.	Choice of investment vehicle (equities, fixed income) left to policyowner.
Asset Security	Assets are part of general account and, as such, are chargeable with all liabilities arising out of the general account. Liabilities also are part of the general account and therefore are backed by all the assets of the general account.	Separate account assets are not chargeable with liabilities arising out of any other business the insurer may conduct. Separate account cash value liabilities are backed by separate account assets only. Separate account death benefits in excess of the cash value are backed by the assets in the general account.
Market Value of Assets	Principal is guaranteed and cash value is not marked to market. Interest guarantee is at 4% to 5%. Credits once earned are not forfeitable.	Assets are marked to market daily, thus creating volatility. No cash value guarantees.
Variations in Charges		
Mortality Charges	Charges are subject to modification up to guaranteed maximum, now generally the 1980 CSO table.	Charges are subject to modification up to guaranteed maximum, now generally the 1980 CSO table.
Expense Charges	Current and guaranteed expense loads sometimes identical.	Current and guaranteed expense loads sometimes identical.
Investment Return	Generally, all earnings above a guaranteed rate of 4% - 5% are declared at the insurer's discretion.	The return on the assets in the fund net of expenses is the policy's investment return. Therefore, while greater investment risk is present on VUL for the policyowner, the risk is entirely with the performance of the fund and not controlled by the insurer's declarations.

The tax rules for living benefits from VL products also are the same as for living benefits from other types of life insurance policies. The cost-recovery rules of Internal Revenue Code Section 72 govern the taxation of annuity-type distributions. These rules state that policyowners recover their investments in their contracts (generally, total premiums paid less prior nontaxable distributions) ratably over their expected payout periods.

Interest paid on or credited to living benefits held by the insurer under an agreement to pay interest is taxable immediately in full. The cost-recovery rule generally applies for the taxation of all other types of living benefits. The cost-recovery rule, which is some-times called the First-In First-Out (FIFO) rule, treats amounts received first as a nontaxable recovery of the policyowner's investment in the contract. Only after policyowners fully recover their investment are additional amounts they receive treated as taxable interest or gain in their policies. Included in this category of living benefits are policy dividends, lump-sum cash settlements of cash surrender values, cash withdrawals, and amounts received on partial surrender. Policyowners include such amounts in gross income only to the extent such amounts exceed the investment in the contract (as reduced by any prior excludable distributions owners receive from their contracts). In other words, nonannuity distributions during life generally are first treated as a return of the policyowner's investment in the contract and then as taxable interest or gain.

Exception to the Cost-recovery Rule

The general cost-recovery rule may not apply for withdrawals within the first fifteen years after the policy issue date that are coupled with reductions in death benefits. Because insurers generally reduce death benefits in an amount equal to any withdrawal of cash values, policyowner withdrawals frequently may trigger a tax on all or part of these withdrawals to the extent of gain in the policy.

The rules tax such withdrawals in whole or in part as ordinary income to the extent that they are forced out of the policy as a result of the reduction in the death benefits. The taxable amount depends on when the owner makes the withdrawal:

- *Within first five years* – If the withdrawal takes place within the first five years after policy issue, a very stringent and complex set of tests applies.[4] Potentially, a larger portion, or perhaps all, of any withdrawal within the first five years will be taxable if there is gain in the policy.

- *Fifth to fifteenth years* – For withdrawals between the end of the fifth year and the end of the fifteenth year from the issue date, a mathematical test applies. Essentially, the rules tax the policyowner on an income-first basis to the extent the cash value before the withdrawal exceeds the maximum allowable cash value under the cash value corridor test for the reduced death benefit after the withdrawal.[5] Frequently, in these cases only a portion or even no part of the withdrawal will be taxable.

Changing from option B (increasing death benefit) or from option C (return of premium) to option A (level death benefit) will trigger a test to see whether any amount must be forced out of the policy. In general, option B and option C contracts allow for greater cash accumulations within the policy than option A contracts. Consequently, if a policy with option B or option C has close to the maximum permitted cash value under that option, a switch to option A generally will trigger a taxable distribution. (See Chapters 22 through 29 for a complete discussion of the taxation of life insurance.)

Caveat: Potential Taxation under the MEC Rules

The flexibility inherent in VUL policies with respect to changes in premiums and death benefits raises the possibility that the policy could become a modified endowment contract (MEC).[6] The penalty for classification as a MEC relates to distributions. If a policy is classified as a MEC, distributions under the contract are taxed under the interest-first rule rather than the cost-recovery rule. In addition, to the extent taxable, these distributions are subject to a 10 percent penalty if they occur before the policyowner reaches age 59½, dies, or becomes disabled. So MEC categorization of a VUL contract means both faster taxation of investment gains and a possible penalty tax for early receipt of that growth.

Distributions under the contract include nonannuity living benefits (as described above), policy loans, loans secured by the policy, loans used to pay premiums, and dividends taken in cash. Distributions under the contract do *not* include dividends used to pay premiums, dividends used to purchase paid-up additions, dividends used to purchase one year term insurance, or the surrender of paid-up additions to pay premiums.

Changes in premiums or death benefits may inadvertently cause a VUL policy to run afoul of the MEC rules in basically three ways:

1. An increase in premium payments during the first seven contract years may push the cumulative premiums above the amount permitted under the seven-pay test.[7]

2. A reduction in the death benefit during the first seven contract years triggers a recomputation of the seven-pay test. The seven-pay test is applied retroactively as of the original issue date as if the policy had been issued at the reduced death benefit.

3. A material increase of the death benefit at any time triggers a new seven-pay test which is applied prospectively as of the date of the material change.

When issued, most VUL policy illustrations show the maximum amount (the seven-pay guideline annual premium limit) that the policyowner may pay within the first seven years without having the policy classified as a MEC. If policyowners inadvertently exceed that maximum, they can avoid MEC status if insurers return excess premiums to the policyowners with interest within sixty days after the end of the contract year in which the excess occurs. The interest will be subject to taxation.[8]

In general, a reduction in death benefit within the first seven contract years caused by and equal in amount to a withdrawal is less likely to cause the policy to fail the recomputed seven-pay test than a death benefit reduction without a withdrawal. However, a policy will fail the seven-pay test if, in any year, the cumulative premiums paid to that year exceed the sum of the seven-pay guideline annual premiums to that year.

Example. Assume the guideline annual premium is $10,000 based on the original death benefit. The policyowner pays $9,000 each year for the first six years. In year seven, the policyowner withdraws $36,000, with a corresponding decrease in the death benefit. The recomputed guideline premium is $8,000. The policy now fails the seven-pay test and is a MEC because cumulative premiums paid in just the first year, $9,000, (and through year six as well) exceed the sum of the recomputed guideline annual premiums of $8,000.

Any reduction in death benefits attributable to the nonpayment of premiums due under the contract will not trigger a recomputation of the seven-pay test if the benefits are reinstated within ninety days after being reduced.[9]

A change from option B (face amount plus cash value) or option C (face amount plus return of premium) to option A (face amount) appears to be a decrease that triggers the look-back rule and a retroactive reapplication of the seven-pay test. In general, one would not expect the switch in options to result in a lower seven-pay limit unless the insurer also reduced the face amount of insurance to less than the face amount at the time of issue. Therefore, switching from options B or C to option A should not, in general, cause the policy to be reclassified as a MEC.

The term material change is not defined in the statute. However, the statute states that it "includes any increase in future benefits under the contract,"[10] but *not* increases attributable to dividends (for paid-up additions), increases in the policy's cash surrender value attributable to the investment performance of assets underlying the policy, increases necessary to maintain the corridor between the death benefit and the cash surrender value required by the definition of life insurance,[11] or cost of living adjustments.

Clearly, increases in death benefits attributable to cash value increases from favorable investment performance will not trigger testing under the material change rules. Whether changing from option A to options B or C constitutes a material change in death benefit is unclear. Other increases in death benefits requiring evidence of insurability will be considered material changes that invoke a new seven-pay test. See Chapter 22, "Modified Endowment Policies," for more information.

Taxation of Capital Gains on the Underlying Assets

Capital appreciation on the assets underlying a VL or VUL policy loses its character as capital gain. To the extent taxable, withdrawals or surrenders are taxed at ordinary income tax rates. The maximum federal tax table rate on ordinary income is (in 2015) 39.6 percent, but effective tax rates can be even higher due to the phaseout of personal exemptions and itemized deductions as well as the 3.8 percent Net investment Income tax (NIIT). In contrast, capital appreciation recognized on the sale of similar mutual fund investments is treated as capital gains. The maximum federal tax rate on long-term capital gains is 15 percent. In addition, taxpayers may use capital gains to offset capital losses.

Taxation of Transfers between Investment Funds

Transfers or switches between one fund and another offered by an insurer under a VL or VUL policy are tax-free. In contrast, similar switches between funds in a family of mutual funds are treated as taxable sales and repurchases. However, in recent years, legislation has been proposed to tax transfers or switches between one fund and another under a VL or VUL life policy or annuity in a manner similar to switches between funds in a mutual fund family. Although these proposals have never survived legislative debate, the possibility clearly exists that such proposals could be enacted in the future.

ALTERNATIVES

VL is the insurance industry's answer to the "buy-term-and-invest-the-difference" strategy. It provides investment options similar to those available from mutual funds, but wrapped within the insurance policy. The loadings and expense charges in the VL policy typically exceed the combined loadings and expense charges of a buy-term-and-invest-in-a-mutual-fund strategy. However, investment earnings within the policy are tax deferred and beneficiaries receive death proceeds tax-free. In contrast, mutual fund dividends and realized capital gains are taxable when received or recognized. For long-term insurance/investment needs, the benefit of a VL policy's tax deferred accumulation will typically overcome the cost of the higher loadings and fees.

A policyowner can configure a VUL policy's premium payments and death benefits to resemble virtually any type of life insurance policy, from annually renewable term life to single premium whole life. As a practical matter, insurers issue most VUL policies with target premiums at least equal to a lifetime payment plan of insurance. Consequently, any other type of policy that meets a policyowner's needs may be a suitable and, perhaps, preferable, alternative if the policyowner does not desire the VUL's premium and death benefit flexibility or the policyowner does not wish to bear all the investment risk. However, a number of other types of policies or strategies offer some of the features of VUL and not others, if policyowners only desire certain features.

1. *Traditional universal life* – UL offers the same premium and death benefit flexibility as VUL, but it also provides a minimum cash value guarantee. If the insurer's general portfolio has the risk and return characteristics desired by the policyowner, UL may be a better alternative than VUL. Policy loadings and expenses generally are lower on UL policies than on VUL policies.

2. *Adjustable Life (AL)* – AL combines elements of traditional, fixed premium ordinary life insurance and the ability, within limits, to alter the policy plan, premium payments, and the face amount. Policyowners may view AL as VUL without the investment options.

3. *Flexible Premium Variable Annuity (FPVA) combined with term insurance* – A combination of a FPVA with level term can generate cash value accumulations and death benefit levels similar to VUL under option B. A FPVA combined with a decreasing term policy is similar to VUL under option A. The FPVA, however, has less favorable tax treatment for withdrawals and loans than a VUL policy.

WHERE AND HOW DO I GET IT?

Many life insurance companies, including some of the largest, are marketing variable life products. Most of the major stock brokerage firms also market variable life products. Agents who sell variable life products must be properly licensed to sell security products.

FEES AND ACQUISITION COSTS

Fees and charges on variable products tend to be somewhat higher than on traditional products because of the additional expenses of registering the contracts with the Securities and Exchange Commission and the additional administration, record keeping, and reporting responsibilities associated with the products. In contrast with traditional life products, the securities laws require extensive disclosure of fees and charges in the offering prospectus. VL and VUL policies have two broad classes of fees—charges to the policy and charges to the cash value account. Because of differences in the way insurers handle premiums and face amounts in VL and VUL policies, some of these fees and charges are treated differently in each type of policy.

Charges to VL Policies

Charges to VL policies include sales loads, a one-time policy fee, annual administration charges, a state premium tax charge, a risk charge and, in some cases, switching fees.

Most companies levy sales loads (principally to pay commissions) in the first year of not more than 30 percent of the premium. The percentage generally is lower on higher-premium limited-pay policies than on lifetime pay policies. The sales load on premiums in the subsequent years typically grades down from a maximum of 10 percent in the second year to 7.5 percent or lower in later years. In general, SEC rules prohibit aggregate fees and charges from exceeding a reasonable amount in relation to the services provided and the risks assumed.

Policy fees generally range from $3 to $10 per $1,000 of guaranteed face amount. Annual administrative charges typically range from $5 to $70, often with a higher charge in the first year and lower charges in subsequent years. The premium tax charge varies by state but is usually about 2 to 2½ percent of each premium. Risk charges, which the companies assess to compensate for the risk that the insured may die when the death benefits are below the guaranteed amount, often are specified as a percentage of the premium, ranging from 1 to 3 percent. Alternatively, some companies compute the risk charge as a dollar amount per $1,000 of guaranteed face amount with charges generally ranging from $0.50 to $1.50 per thousand of face amount. Most companies permit one or more switches or transfers of money among the various accounts each year without fees. Insurers generally permit additional switches but the company usually charges from $5 to $30 for this service.

Charges to the VL Cash Value Accounts

Charges to the cash value account include the cost of insurance (mortality charges), mortality and risk expense, and investment management fees and expenses.

Mortality charges are based on the company's current mortality rate as applied to the net amount at risk (the difference between the death benefit and the cash value). Current mortality rates will vary depending on the company's experience but the companies guarantee they will not exceed certain maximums at each age as specified in the contract. The mortality and risk expense charge is taken against each account within a policy for the risk that the insureds as a group will live for a shorter period of time than estimated and the risk that the administrative expenses will be greater than estimated. This charge usually ranges from 0.1 to 0.9 percent of the assets in the account. Management fees and expenses vary by the type of fund and the investment activity within the fund and are similar to those fees and expenses associated with mutual funds. For instance, money market funds, bond funds, and stock index funds have lower management fees and expenses than general stock funds, which also have lower fees and expenses than real estate funds and foreign stock and bond funds. Management fees typically range from 0.25 to 2 percent of the assets in the fund. Expenses, expressed as a percent of assets in the fund, similarly range from about 0.25 to 2 percent.

Charges to VUL Policies

Policy and account charges on VUL policies are similar to those on VL policies with the exception of the sales loads. Similar to regular universal life, VUL policies charge front-end and/or back-end loads or

surrender charges to recoup commissions paid to the selling agent and the expense of issuing the policy. Most companies levy a surrender charge of up to 25 percent if policyowners withdraw money in the first year. The surrender charge generally declines in later years. Surrender charges often start declining yearly after about the fifth policy year or sooner and reach zero in from ten to twenty years. As a result of competition in the industry, the trend has been towards starting the phaseout of surrender charges sooner and more quickly.

SELECTING THE BEST OF ITS TYPE

The key factors in choosing the best VL or VUL policy are the policy loadings and expenses, the suitability and variety of the investment options, and the relative performance of the company's alternative investment accounts. The prospectus must list and explain the various loadings and charges. However, because there is a great deal of variability in these loadings and expenses, it is difficult to determine which policy provides the lowest effective package of fees over the long term. The best procedure is to ask for policy illustrations with equal face amount and rate of return assumptions and to compare future cash value accumulations. This is not without its problems, however, because the companies may have different current mortality assumptions and may or may not be assuming future improvements in their mortality experience.

Some companies offer a broader array of investment options than others. All else being equal, potential policyowners should prefer the company with the broadest array of offerings.

Potential policyowners can evaluate relative performance of various investment accounts in much the same manner as one would evaluate mutual funds. The prospectus provides historical information about total returns, expense ratios, and turnover rates. In addition, it must describe the investment management fees. One should compare similar types of funds offered by each company to control for risk. For example, only compare long-term bond funds with long-term bond funds or diversified stock funds with diversified stock funds. A sophisticated analysis would compare risk-adjusted returns, but that can be a daunting task for less knowledgeable investors.[12]

All else being equal, look for companies offering funds with the lowest management fees, the lowest turnover rates, the lowest investment expense ratios, and the highest total returns (or best risk-adjusted return).

USING A VARIABLE LIFE LEDGER STATEMENT

The principal source of information regarding a new policy is the policy illustration or ledger. Figure 19.3 shows an annotated policy illustration with the following commentary.[13]

1. Initial death benefit is $100,000; plan of life insurance is variable life.

2. Gender and issue age–male, age forty-five.

3. $2,394 is the annual premium.

4. Projected dividends are determined by mortality and expense factors used to purchase variable benefit paid-up life insurance. The projected dividends are small (e.g., at the beginning of the second year—$490; at the beginning of the fifth year—$592; at the beginning of the tenth year—$652; and at the beginning of the twentieth year—$453).

5. End-of-year ledger statement. This means the initial death benefit of $100,000 is assumed to be paid at the beginning of the year. Subsequent death benefit, depending upon the interest assumption (e.g., 0 percent, 6 percent, and 12 percent), is assumed to be paid at the end of the year. Cash values (the assumed values of the separate investment account–0 percent, 6 percent, and 12 percent) are calculated as of the end of the year.

6. Out-of-pocket cash payment is $2,394 each year, paid on an annual basis.

7. 5 percent interest assumption column. The value of $2,394 compounded at 5 percent if not used to purchase life insurance.

8. Death benefit increase because of the projected dividends purchasing additional paid-up life insurance. In the absence of dividends, the death benefit would not increase because the separate investment account must produce a rate of return in excess of 4 percent in order for the death benefit to increase.

9. Death benefit increases due to the projected dividends purchasing additional paid-up life insurance and the 6 percent interest assumption.

10. Death benefit increases due to projected dividends purchasing additional paid-up life insurance and 12 percent interest assumption.

11. This column has a value even at 0 percent interest assumption because not all of the premiums paid were required to meet the insurance company's expenses.

12. The projected value of the separate investment account (cash value) based on a net investment return (after expenses and deductions) of 6 percent.

13. The projected value of the separate investment account (cash value) based on a net investment return (after expenses and deductions) of 12 percent.

14. Annual premium for $100,000 variable life is $2,394. The monthly premium by automatic deduction from checking account is $211.10.

15. The underwriting requirements (medical, social, and economic) of the insurance company must be met, in order for the insurance to be issued.

16. Insurability status – e.g., nonsmoker or smoker, or rated (extra charge because of being a higher risk for medical or occupational reasons). Select for this company means nonsmoker, nonrated. It is the company's best insurability classification.

17. Statement about dividends, assumed investment returns (e.g., 6 percent and 12 percent) and loan interest of 8 percent. In addition, there is a statement pertaining to the prospectus which clearly indicates that variable life is considered a security and as such must be registered with the Securities and Exchange Commission (SEC).

What Ledger Statements Do Not Tell

You should be told either verbally or in writing the following additional information:

- The separate investment account, which is analogous to the reserve (cash value) of

Figure 19.3

LEDGER STATEMENT FOR VARIABLE LIFE

$100,000 Variable Whole Life Plan 1
For Age 45 Male 2
Annual Premium $2,394 3

			4 Dividends Used to Purchase Paid-up Additions					
5	6	7	8	9	10	11	12	13
			Death Benefit*Assumed Investment Returns			Cash Value*Assumed Investment Returns		
End of Year	Annual Premium	Premiums Accumulated at 5%	0%	6%	12%	0%	6%	12%
1	$2,394	$ 2,514	$101,367	$101,391	$101,532	$ 1,103	$ 1,154	$ 1,205
2	2,394	5,153	102,707	103,880	103,510	3,145	3,372	3,606
3	2,394	7,924	104,024	104,471	105,962	5,164	5,700	6,268
4	2,394	10,834	105,304	106,157	108,904	7,156	8,137	9,216
5	2,394	13,890	106,549	197,941	112,382	9,201	10,776	12,572
6	2,394	17,098	107,749	109,818	116,420	11,214	13,536	16,286
7	2,394	20,467	108,910	111,797	121,060	13,190	16,422	20,395
8	2,394	24,004	110,023	113,872	126,335	15,126	19,434	24,935
9	2,394	27,717	111,088	116,046	132,287	17,013	22,573	29,949
10	2,394	31,617	112,107	118,327	138,968	18,853	25,845	35,485
11	2,394	35,712	113,068	120,705	146,416	20,634	29,248	41,591
12	2,394	40,011	113,961	123,176	154,678	22,351	32,782	48,320
13	2,394	44,525	114,772	125,729	163,796	23,999	36,451	55,733
14	2,394	49,265	115,490	128,357	173,818	25,570	40,255	63,896
15	2,394	54,242	116,104	131,052	184,800	27,055	44,192	72,874
16	2,394	59,468	116,604	133,808	196,801	28,444	48,262	82,743
17	2,394	64,955	116,984	136,624	209,890	39,727	52,460	93,580
18	2,394	70,716	117,238	139,502	224,146	30,891	56,784	105,469
19	2,394	76,766	117,359	142,443	239,654	31,923	61,230	118,496
20	2,394	83,118	117,334	145,442	256,496	32,806	65,790	132,756
60@	2,394	54,242	116,104	131,052	184,800	27,055	44,192	72,874
65@	2,394	83,118	117,334	145,442	256,496	32,806	65,790	132,756
75@	2,394	167,007	112,535	180,166	527,026	34,997	118,565	74,646

14   Insurance Premiums   Annual   Mo. ISA

                                          2,394.00   211.10

Subject to Underwriting Limits 15
Select 16

17   *Dividends based on current scaled 1988 issue. Not an estimate or guarantee of future results. Hypothetical investment results are illustrations only and should not be deemed representative of past or future investment results. Results illustrated assume no loans. 8% loan provision. The illustration must be preceded or accompanied by a current prospectus.

traditional whole life, graded premium life, interest sensitive, and universal life, is made up of four divisions: (1) stock; (2) bond; (3) money market; and (4) master portfolio. The master portion typically consists of common stock, other equity securities, bonds, and money market instruments. Inquire about what percentage of your net premium can go into each. In addition, find out how often you can change from one to the other.

- Note whether the various expenses and deductions are contractually guaranteed not to increase. For this company, variable life policy charges to the policy are: sales loads, policy fees, annual administration charges, state premium tax, and risk charge. Charges to the separate investment account are: cost of insurance (mortality charges), mortality and risk expense, and management fees and expenses. Ask for a total disclosure of each.

- The rate of return expressed in terms of compound interest should be given either on the ledger statement or by the life insurance agent. Ideally, it should be provided for each year.

- The rate of return upon death for this policy for sequential years is as follows:

Year	Rate of return
1	4,141.10%
5	86.94
10	30.81
20	14.25

- The above rates are based on a 12 percent interest assumption death benefit.

- The rate of return upon death can be used when comparing various variable life policies among respected companies. (It can also be used for any life insurance policy.) Consider the following example:

Rate of return upon death in year 20	Cost per $1,000 of life insurance per year for 20 years
14.25%	$ 9.34
14.23	9.36
13.25	10.59
13.00	10.93

- How were these numbers determined? $1,000 is the future value (death benefit) to be paid, twenty years is the time. Interest is known (14.25 percent, 14.23 percent, 13.25 percent, 13 percent). You then solve for payment—how much must be spent each year to accumulate $1,000 in twenty years at the various interest rates?

- Once the rate of return upon death is known, then it can be determined what would have to be earned before taxes in other financial services products such as mutual funds, certificates of deposit, real estate, or commodities to duplicate the tax-exempt rate of return provided by life insurance. (For this purpose, it is assumed that the death benefit is considered life insurance proceeds and as such not subject to federal or state income taxes.) The before-tax rate of return is determined by dividing the life insurance rate of return by the marginal tax bracket subtracted from 100 percent (for 15 percent, the factor is 0.85; for 25 percent, 0.75; for 28 percent, 0.72; for 33 percent, 0.67; and for 35 percent, 0.65). The result is shown in Figure 19.4.

- The rate of return upon surrender should also be provided. When the rate of return upon

Figure 19.4

Year	15% taxpayer	25% taxpayer	28% taxpayer	33% taxpayer	35% taxpayer
1	4,871.88%	5,521.47%	5,751.53%	6,180.75%	6,370.92%
5	102.28	115.92	120.75	129.76	133.75
10	36.25	41.08	42.79	45.99	47.40
20	16.76	19.00	19.79	21.27	21.92

surrender is positive, it means that taxes are due. Taxes are due on the difference between the cash surrender value and the premiums paid. The result before taxes is as follows:

Year	Rate of return
1	−49.67%
5	1.64
10	7.05
20	8.95

- The above rates of return are based on a 12 percent interest assumption separate investment account performance. The rate of return upon surrender even before taxes never equals the separate investment account investment performance of 12 percent.

- The Premiums Accumulated at 5 percent column on the ledger statement replaces the Interest Adjusted Index. This is what your money would be worth at 5 percent net after taxes if not used to purchase life insurance. In order to net 5 percent after taxes, the before-tax rates of return in the following tax brackets are:

15% taxpayer	25% taxpayer	28% taxpayer	33% taxpayer	35% taxpayer
5.88%	6.67%	6.94%	7.46%	7.69%

- The ledger statement should be the official ledger statement produced by the computer service of the life insurance company. It should be bug-free.

The Prospectus

Because the SEC considers variable life products to be securities, insurers must give prospective purchasers a prospectus. It contains: the identity and nature of the insurer's business; the use to which the insurer will put the premiums; financial information on the insurer; the investment characteristics of the product, expenses, fees, and loads; and the rights of the policyowner. In addition, the securities laws require agents to pass exams and to be properly licensed to sell securities, including VL and VUL.

WHERE CAN I FIND OUT MORE?

Readers may find the following references useful:

1. Lawrence J. Rybka, "A Case for Variable Life," *The Journal of the American Society of CLU & ChFC* (May, 1997).

2. Ben G. Baldwin, "Understanding and Managing VUL," *The Journal of the American Society of CLU & ChFC* (September, 1996).

3. Gary Snouffer, *Variable Life Essentials* (Cincinnati, OH: The National Underwriter Company, 1998).

4. Carl E. Anderson and James B. Ross, *Modern Mutual Fund Families & Variable Life: Tools for Investment Growth and Tax Benefits* (Homewood, IL: Dow Jones-Irwin, 1988).

FREQUENTLY ASKED QUESTIONS

Question – Life insurance pundits sometimes describe VL and VUL as life insurance wrapped around a mutual fund investment and as a better alternative than a buy-term-and-invest-the-difference strategy. How does the investment performance of the funds offered by life insurance companies compare with the performance of mutual funds?

Answer – Numerous studies have measured the investment performance of mutual funds, but far fewer studies have assessed the performance of other institutional investors, such as the separate accounts of life insurance companies. However, one study examined the attractiveness of the stock portfolios of life insurance companies as an alternative investment to mutual funds.[14] Using testing methods similar to those used to evaluate mutual funds, the study concluded that on the basis of risk-adjusted investment performance alone, both life insurance and mutual fund portfolios yield similar returns. However, as life insurance contracts offer the opportunity for individual investors to defer taxes, these investment vehicles offer an edge over mutual funds when investors consider after-tax investment performance.

Question – What investments other than the normal stock, bond, and money market separate accounts are available?

Answer – For the more aggressive or knowledgeable investor, some companies now offer GNMA funds, real estate funds, and zero coupon bond funds. Some specialized funds such as small capitalization stock funds, market index funds, and funds that focus on specific sectors of the economy or industries (i.e., medical, high tech, gold, leisure, and utilities) are also available. In recent years, Exchange-Traded Funds (ETFs) based on broad stock indexes and others ETFs based on industry sectors, and even less-broadly-diversify portfolios have become popular with investors.

Some companies offer a managed fund option where the company's investment manager assumes the responsibility for apportioning investments among the various alternative funds. Some VL policies also offer a guaranteed interest option similar to the declared interest rate on universal life policies. Recently, some insurance companies have offered investments in hedge funds for policyowners who meet certain income and net worth requirements. Hedge funds are investment companies that are generally unregulated by the SEC; hedge funds may use high risk techniques, such as borrowing and short selling, to make higher returns for their investors.

One of the more popular trends in recent years has been the target age funds that are portfolios designed and managed to have asset allocations appropriate to various investment horizons ranging from five to thirty, or more, years.

CHAPTER ENDNOTES

1. I.R.C. §7702(d).

2. Black and Skipper, *Life Insurance*, 12th ed. (Englewood Cliffs, NJ: Prentice-Hall, 1994), pp. 114-115.

3. I.R.C. §7702(d).

4. I.R.C. §§7702(f)(7)(B), 7702(f)(7)(C).

5. I.R.C. §§7702(f)(7)(B), 7702(f)(7)(D). The cash value corridor test is discussed in Chapter 24.

6. In cases where there are extreme reductions in the death benefit or very large premium payments, it is even possible for a policy to fail the tests for life insurance under I.R.C. §7702 with much more disastrous tax consequences. See the discussion of the definition of life insurance in Chapter 24.

7. I.R.C. §7702A(a)(1)(B). Classification as a MEC occurs in the year when seven-pay test is first violated and for each year thereafter. See Chapter 22 for a more complete discussion of the seven-pay test.

8. I.R.C. §7702A(e)(1).

9. I.R.C. §7702A(c)(2)(B).

10. I.R.C. §7702A(c)(3).

11. I.R.C. §7702. See Chapter 24.

12. An excellent book on this subject is *Modern Mutual Fund Families & Variable Life: Tools for Investment Growth and Tax Benefits*, by Carl E. Anderson and James B. Ross (Homewood, IL: Dow Jones-Irwin, 1988).

13. This illustration is adapted from William D. Brownlie and Jeffery L. Seglin's treatise, *The Life Insurance Buyer's Guide* (new York, NY: McGraw-Hill Publishing Company, 1989).

14. Robert T. Kleiman and Anandi P. Sahu, "Life Insurance Companies as Investment Managers: New Implications for Consumers," *Financial Services Review: The Journal of Individual Financial Management*, Vol. 1, No. 1, 1991.

INDEXED UNIVERSAL LIFE

CHAPTER 20

INTRODUCTION

Indexed Universal Life (IUL) is a pseudo-hybrid of regular (or fixed) Universal Life (UL) and Variable Universal Life (VUL). Like regular UL, it is a flexible premium, current assumption, adjustable death benefit type of cash value permanent life insurance with a guaranteed minimum interest crediting rate. Like VUL, the amount the insurer credits to the cash accumulation account is tied to an equity index such as the S&P 500 or the Nasdaq 100. Most IUL policies allow policyowners to allocate their cash value amounts between a fixed account and one or more equity index accounts. Thus, insurers have designed IUL to give policyowners the opportunity to participate in the gains when market indexes turn up while being protected from market downturns. Although the amount credited to the cash value account is based upon one or more equity indexes, the cash value account is NOT directly invested in the stock market. This is why IUL is called a pseudo-hybrid in that it somewhat mimics, but does not actually duplicate, the cash value account methods of VUL policies.

WHEN IS THE USE OF THIS DEVICE INDICATED?

Potential policyowners may consider IUL for any life insurance need. Initially, the insurer and policyowner may configure an IUL policy's death benefit and target premium level to resemble virtually any type of life insurance policy from annually renewable term insurance to single premium whole life. However, both because of policy costs and because equity-type investments generally are more suitable for middle- to longer-term investment horizons, IUL generally is best suited for longer-term coverage needs. For short-term

needs (less than five to ten years), a nonrenewable term policy generally will be more cost effective.

1. Some sort of UL, including IUL for those people looking for some of the upside potential of equities in their cash values while being protected on the downside, is indicated whenever policyowners desire the ultimate in flexibility in life insurance. Policyowners whose circumstances change can later reconfigure the policy by changing their premium payments and/or the death benefit.

2. UL has been extremely popular in the family market and IUL is now not far behind in popularity. For example, young parents with growing families and modest incomes can acquire IUL policies that they initially configure with low premiums and high death benefits resembling traditional renewable term policies. As the parents' incomes grow, they can increase premiums to build tax-sheltered cash within the policy. At later times when they need cash, such as to pay for a child's education, they can reduce premium payments or stop them altogether and use the cash values to help pay the school expenses. After a time, they can increase premiums once again to build cash values. Similarly, if the amount of death protection that they need changes, they may decrease or increase the death benefit. However, increases in death benefits usually will require evidence of insurability.

3. IUL also has become extremely popular in the business market where flexibility often is essential and the higher investment earning potential is very attractive. IUL is beginning to

surpass UL as the preferred vehicle in all sorts of business applications including split dollar plans, funding for nonqualified deferred compensation plans, key person insurance, funding vehicles for buy-sell agreements, and even in insured qualified retirement plans.

Advantages

Policyowners of indexed universal life enjoy virtually all the advantages they would enjoy if they owned regular universal life policies including (among others associated with all life insurance in general):

- the flexibility to vary premiums and change face amounts;

- the transparency and unbundling of the policy elements allowing them to easily track and compare insurance company projections of these elements and actual performance over time;

- the availability of all three death benefit pattern options;

- access to the whole panoply of riders and special policy provisions;

- use of back-end loads (surrender charges) that phase out over time rather than the front-end loads typical of other types of policies;

- the availability of policy loans from cash values at low or (in periods of high equity index returns) even negative net cost; and

- a guaranteed minimum interest crediting rate.

The unique advantage of IUL, however, is that it allows policyowners to earn potentially higher returns tied to the performance of equity indexes, similar to VUL policies, while retaining the safety afforded by the insurer's guaranteed minimum interest crediting rate, similar to regular UL policies. This advantage has several dimensions:

1. *The safety of no negative returns*. Clients burned in recent years by declining values in the equity, bond, and real estate markets now understand the value of a guarantee that their annual returns will never be negative. That guarantee

is precisely what IUL provides. If the index used by the product (or selected by the policyowner) declines over the period measured, the client is completely protected from that risk. The contract's cash value will never decline due to declining values in the reference index.

2. *The insurer absorbs the investment risk*. The insurance company provides interest credits to the IUL policy by investing in bonds and index options (or options on index futures). Suppose some experts expect bond defaults this year to be several times historical averages or that the counterparty to the index options defaults, like Lehman Brothers did to many insurers. How would such events affect the amounts credited to an IUL policy's cash values? The answer is that the insurer bears the entire investment risk and protects its policyowners from this risk.

3. *The possibility of high positive returns*. Safe alternatives with low investment risk currently are earning very low yields. Many are at historical lows, making them unattractive to many savers. Even if and when interest yields on safe alternatives rise, the probabilities are that returns on higher-risk equities generally will be higher. With IUL, if the index performs well over the period measured, the amount the insurer will credit on the cash values tied to the index should be quite attractive. Some IUL policies even include interest-crediting formulas that compare multiple indices and more heavily weight those that are performing better.

4. *The ability to create tax-free cash flows*. Many other vehicles investors can use to save create taxation. IRAs and 401(k)s, for example, delay but do not eliminate taxation. IUL, in contrast, can create a totally tax-free cash flow. Through the use of policy loans, policyowners can completely avoid federal, state, and local income taxes, as well as the alternative minimum tax on the cash flow. And IUL, like all life insurance policies, provide a tax-free death benefit. This tax-free feature makes the IUL policies more attractive than other alternatives, even if those alternatives may create a somewhat higher pretax return.

5. *An ability to take advantage of the design of certain insurance products*. Studies show that the interest crediting on most IUL policies is higher than

the interest crediting on most index annuity products. Why? Because insurers have a second source of profit on index universal life—the spread between the insurers' mortality charges versus the expected mortality of the people they insure. In some cases, the insurers are generating much if not all of their profits from the mortality spread. Therefore, customers who buy IUL policies and minimize the insurance coverage relative to the premium they pay get a better deal. From one perspective, this means that the many policyowners who will maximize their insurance coverage relative to the premiums they pay essentially will be subsidizing these customers' who maximize their coverage relative to the premiums they pay.

6. *Life-long insurance without paying for a lifetime.* One perhaps unexpected bonus for clients who use IUL to save for retirement is that once the clients stop paying premiums and start taking cash flows as policy loans, the insurance coverage does not end. In fact, clients often can continue to be insured for the rest of their lives without ever having to pay additional money into the contracts.

Disadvantages

Policyowners of index universal life bear virtually all the disadvantages they would bear if they owned regular universal life policies. Many of these disadvantages stem from or are natural consequences of the advantages IUL offers. Disadvantages include (among others associated with all life insurance in general):

- The flexibility associated with premium payments can be a disadvantage because policyowners can too easily allow their policies to lapse. There is no forced savings feature, because IUL policies do not require premium payments as long as the cash value is sufficient to carry the policy. To reduce the likelihood of lapse, most companies have a voluntary provision where the policyowner agrees to let the insurer "bill" the policyowner for a target premium set by the policyowner. (As is discussed in Chapter 21 "No-Lapse Universal Life", the insurance market has evolved and many insurers now offer UL policies with provisions and guarantees which are designed to ensure that cash values do not fall below levels necessary to keep the policies in force (i.e., do not lapse as a result of paying inadequate premiums).

- In traditional participating whole life policies, insurers guarantee the mortality and expense charges. In contrast, IUL policies only guarantee that mortality charges and expense rates will not exceed certain maximums. Consequently, policyowners bear more risk of adverse trends in mortality or expenses than if they owned traditional whole life policies. The converse is also true. If the trend of mortality costs and expenses improves, IUL policyowners may participate in the improvement through lower charges.

- Some IUL policies, similar to many traditional whole life policies, use what is called the direct recognition method to determine the amounts the insurer will credit to cash values subject to policy loans. Under this method, insurers credit the current rate to only that portion of the cash value not used to secure a loan. Insurers credit amounts backing loans with the minimum guaranteed rate or a rate usually 1 to 2 percentage points lower than the loan rate. Insurers most commonly use the direct recognition method in policies that have fixed loan rates. Typically, policies with variable loan rates, and some others with fixed loan rates, do not employ the direct recognition method and instead credit current rates on the entire cash value without regard to loans.

- Surrender of the policy within the first fifteen years may result in considerable loss because surrender values reflect the insurance company's recovery of sales commissions and initial policy expenses. In addition, most IUL policies now assess surrender charges rather than up-front fees or loads. These surrender charges generally decline each year the owner holds the policy. Typically, after about seven to fifteen years insurers assess no explicit charges if the owner surrenders the policy.

- The flexibility with respect to premium payments and death benefits permits policyowners to change the policy in such a way that the policy inadvertently may become a Modified Endowment Contract (MEC) with adverse tax consequences. However, insurers always test all proposed changes to policies and will inform the policyowner if the proposed changes will trigger MEC treatment and adverse tax consequences.

As described previously in the "ADVANTAGES" section of this chapter, the unique advantage of IUL is that it allows policyowners to earn potentially higher returns tied to the performance of equity indexes, similar to VUL policies, while retaining the safety afforded by the insurer's guaranteed minimum interest crediting rate, similar to regular UL policies. This advantage is real, but like all real-world advantages, it has several negative aspects:

1. *Potential bond-like returns over time.* IUL provides for an index-linked interest credit at the end of each crediting period with the guarantee that the interest credit can never go below the guaranteed minimum crediting rate. This is a very attractive feature. But remember that carriers invest the majority of their IUL premiums in bonds. This means that clients can expect—over a long period of time—for the average return on their IUL policies to be weighted towards the same range as bond returns, or slightly more, but less than the returns one might expect on the underlying equity indexes upon which the insurers base their crediting rates. To clients who strongly believe that stock returns will soundly beat bond returns over time, this is a disadvantage of IUL. Such clients might find variable Universal Life Policies (VUL) a better fit for their needs.

2. *The ability of insurers to change elements of their interest crediting formulas.* In most IUL policies, the insurers provide interest crediting formulas that have a cap, participation, or spread rates that the insurers can change from time to time. The insurers do this simply because it is unaffordable for the insurers to provide strong long-term guarantees on their index-related interest crediting formulas. For the policyowners, this means that insurers can change a formula that the policyowners find attractive for the first interest crediting period to one that is less attractive in later interest crediting periods.

3. *Illustrations are unreliable.* Insurers often sell IUL as a retirement savings vehicle through the use of an illustration showing premiums for a period of years, followed by a series of

policy loans over the retirement period. These illustrations frequently show projected values for twenty years, forty years, or even more years in the future. However, the assumption that will underlie the future index return formula may differ greatly from the assumptions used in creating the illustration. Plus, as mentioned above, the insurers have the ability to change the mortality charges and certain elements of the interest crediting formula over time. All of these items conspire to render long-term illustrations unreliable.

4. *Policy lapse can trigger adverse tax consequences.* Ideally, using IUL to save for retirement means this for the client: paying a premium for a limited period of time, then receiving tax-free policy loans over time that greatly exceed the premiums paid, and, ultimately, paying off the accumulated policy loan at death by a tax-free death benefit. This can all work beautifully, unless the accumulated loans cause the policy to lapse. In that unfortunate case, the sum of the cash taken out of the policy less the premiums that policyowner originally paid, are taxable to the policyowner. The amount of tax policyowners may have to pay can be substantial and, typically, the policyowners have already used up all or most of the cash that they borrowed from the policy. Some insurers provide coverage provisions (no-lapse provisions) to prevent this from happening, but some leave the responsibility to monitor this up to the policyowner.

TAX IMPLICATIONS

The income tax rules for IUL policies are virtually identical to the tax rules for UL policies which are essentially the same as the tax rules for other types of life insurance policies. Beneficiaries receive death benefits that usually are free of any federal, state, and local income tax. IUL policies also are subject to the same estate, gift, and generation-skipping transfer taxation rules as all other types of life insurance policies.

Also, the income tax rules for living benefits paid from IUL policies are the same as living benefits paid from other types of life insurance policies. Generally, the cost-recovery rule governs the taxation of these living benefits. The cost-recovery rule, which is sometimes called the First-In First-Out (FIFO) rule, treats amounts received as nontaxable recovery of the policyowner's investment in the contract. Only after policyowners fully recover their investment in the contract are additional amounts that they receive treated as taxable interest or gain in the policy. Included in this category of living benefits are policy dividends, lump-sum cash settlements of cash surrender values, cash withdrawals, and amounts received on partial surrender. Policyowners include these amounts in gross income only to the extent they exceed the investment in the contract (as reduced by any prior excludable distributions received from the contract). In other words, the income tax rules generally treat nonannuity distributions during life, first, as a return of the policyowner's investment in the contract and then—only after the owner has recovered the entire investment in the contract—as taxable interest or gain.

Being that the equity-indexed interest crediting method is the distinguishing feature of IUL, most policyowners are looking to enhanced cash value accumulations as compared with cash-value accumulations in other types of policies that use conventional interest-crediting methods. Consequently, the exceptions to the cost-recovery tax rule for payments of living benefits under IUL policies and the tax risks associated with IUL policies being classified as modified endowment contracts are especially important tax considerations.

Chapter 18 "Universal Life", covers exceptions to the cost recovery tax rule for living benefits and the risks and tax consequences of a policy being treated as a MEC for tax purposes for those readers who want to view an in-depth discussion of these topics.

ALTERNATIVES

Insurers and policyowners can configure an IUL policy's premium payments and death benefits to resemble virtually any type of life insurance policy, from annually-renewable term to single premium whole life. Consequently, any other type of policy that meets a policyowner's needs is a suitable, and perhaps preferable alternative if the policyowner does not need the IUL's flexibility or equity indexing feature. However, a number of other types of policies or strategies offer some of the features of UL and not others, if policyowners desire only certain features.

1. *Current-Assumption Whole Life (CAWL)* – Sometimes called interest-sensitive whole life, CAWL is essentially IUL without the adjustability features or equity-indexed interest crediting rate. However, similar to IUL's equity-indexed interest crediting formula, CAWL uses current interest rates in determining additions to cash values. However, similar to traditional ordinary whole life and in contrast with IUL, CAWL generally offers the policyowner little flexibility with respect to changing premium payments or death benefits.

2. *Adjustable Life (AL)* – AL combines elements of traditional, fixed-premium ordinary life insurance and the ability—within limits—to alter the policy plan, premium payments, and the face amount. Essentially, one can view AL as IUL without the current assumption and equity-indexed interest crediting features.

3. *Variable Life (VL) and Variable Universal Life (VUL)* – If VL and VUL policyowners select a portfolio of investments within their policies that are similar to the equity index used in an IUL equity-indexed interest crediting formula, they can expect investment performance and cash value accumulations to be at least as great as, and generally greater than, that for the IUL policy when equity markets are up. However, because IUL policies have guaranteed minimum interest crediting rates while typically VL and VUL policies do not, in down markets the IUL generally will outperform the VL and VUL. Over the long-term VL and VUL should outperform IUL, but one has no assurance of that, which is part of what makes IUL an attractive insurance alternative to many people.

4. *Flexible Premium Deferred Index Annuity (FPDIA) combined with term insurance* – FPDIA is the annuity analog of IUL. It is a pseudo-hybrid of a Flexible-Premium Deferred Annuity and a Flexible-Premium Deferred Variable Annuity (FPDVA). A combination of a FPDIA with level term can generate cash value accumulations and death benefit levels similar to IUL under option B or C. A FPDIA combined with a decreasing-term policy is similar to IUL under option A. The FPDIA, however, has less favorable tax treatment for withdrawals and loans than an IUL policy.

5. *Section 1035 exchanges* – The exchange provisions under Internal Revenue Code section 1035 allow certain types of exchanges from one policy type to another without adverse tax

consequences. Clearly, these exchange provisions provide nowhere near the flexibility or convenience that an IUL policy does to change premium levels or death benefits. However, the existence of these exchange provisions means that other types of policies are not quite as inflexible as they might otherwise seem.

WHERE AND HOW DO I GET IT?

There are about 2,000 life insurance companies actively marketing coverage in the United States. Many, if not most of these companies offer IUL policies, and the number is growing every year. In addition to commercial insurance companies, some fraternal organizations, savings banks, professional associations, membership organizations, and stock brokerage houses offer IUL policies. A person can purchase a policy through one of many agents that represent a licensed insurance company.

Most companies have minimum death benefit requirements, ranging from $25,000 to $100,000, depending on age and policy form.

FEES AND ACQUISITION COSTS

Some IUL policies charge front-end loads, but most charge back-end loads or surrender charges to recoup commissions paid to the selling agent and the expense of issuing the policy. In other words, most insurers credit the policyowners' entire premium to the cash value and—if they later surrender the policy—assess a surrender charge that generally declines with longer durations. Surrender charges often start declining yearly after about the fifth policy year or sooner and reach zero in seven to fifteen years. As a result of competition in the industry the trend has been towards starting the phase out of surrender charges sooner and more quickly.

Policyowners can determine the surrender charge by explicitly looking at the policy illustration or ledger statement. This statement shows both a cash value figure and a net cash value figure for each policy year. The cash value is the amount on which the insurer bases interest credits. The net cash value is the amount that the company would pay if the owner surrendered the policy. The difference is the surrender charge.

Commissions paid to agents depend on the size and timing of premium payments and how the insurer/

policyowner initially configures the policy. Commissions typically range from 20 to 55 percent (or higher) of the first-year premium for premium amounts up to the target level premium. The target level premium generally is the level annual premium the policyowner would have to pay if the policy was configured as a level premium whole life policy. The commission on the portion of any premium payment that is in excess of the target level premium is lower; often about 3 percent to 8 percent. Commissions on subsequent premiums are usually lower. Total initial and renewal commissions usually equal about one year's target level premium if the original plan of insurance remains the same.

Insurers may recoup policy issue expenses and commissions in a number of ways including a flat policy assessment charge, a percentage of premium charge, a fee based on each $1,000 of face amount, or some combination of each. The trend has been towards lower policy assessment charges and level percentage of premium charges. Many insurers now charge about $25 to $50 per year plus 2.5 percent to 20 percent of each premium. The percentage of premium charge generally is lower for higher premium, higher death benefit policies than for lower premium, lower death benefit policies.

SELECTING THE BEST OF ITS TYPE

Selecting the best cash value life insurance policy is a difficult task involving a number of complicated concepts. (See Chapter 4 "How to Determine the Right Policy", for a further discussion of the basic principles.) However, because the amount insurers credit to cash values on IUL policies is a critical element of the overall cost of the protection, one primary area of focus should be how the company determines the amount it credits to cash values.

The amount insurers credit to cash values each year depends on four factors:

1. The expenses insurers charge against the policy

2. The mortality charges insurers assess against the policy

3. The net investment yield earned by the insurers on their portfolio of investments

4. The method insurers use to allocate interest to various blocks of policies

The cash value at the end of any given year is equal to the cash value from the end of the prior year plus premiums (or less withdrawals) paid during the year less expense and mortality charges and plus interest credited. The annual report usually will explicitly show the expense and mortality charges and the interest credits each year.

Expense Charges

As described previously, two elements usually comprise the expense charge; a fixed annual fee plus a percentage of premiums paid. The company may or may not reveal these fees in its original policy illustration. However, even if it does, the company usually makes no guarantee that they will not change the expense charges. Actual expense charges may increase or decrease in future years.

Mortality Charges

Every IUL policy explicitly states the maximum mortality rates it will charge for all ages and guarantees that mortality rates will not exceed those maximums. Many companies now use the 2001 Commissioner's Standard Mortality (CSO) table as the basis for their contractually guaranteed maximum rates, but some companies still use the older 1980 CSO mortality table for their new policies. In addition, all policies issued before 2002 used the 1980 CSO mortality table or, possibly, the 1958 CSO mortality table. All three tables are very conservative—that is, they assume mortality rates that are considerably higher than what is actually expected—but the 1980 CSO table and, even more so, the 1958 CSO table are considerably more conservative than the 2001 CSO table. Virtually every company currently charges less than the stated maximums, but those using the more conservative 1980 or 1958 CSO tables have more room to increase mortality charges in future years if their mortality experience is poor.

Although annual statements explicitly show actual mortality charges, many policy illustrations do not. In fact, some illustrations assume very low or no mortality charges, which tend to show projected cash values that are overstated relative to what policyowners can actually expect. Other illustrations include mortality charges based on rates the company is assessing currently, but they also may assume that mortality experience will improve in future years. If the mortality improvements do not materialize as anticipated, actual cash values are unlikely to match the projected cash values.

Net Investment Yield on Investment Portfolio

Over the long run, insurance companies cannot credit more interest to policy cash values than they earn on their general investment portfolios. To assess a company's long-run interest crediting ability, one should evaluate the insurer's current portfolio and its investment philosophy.

As a general rule, insurance companies invest their portfolios predominantly in long-term corporate and government bonds and mortgages. However, there are differences in the proportions invested in each type of asset and in the quality, duration, yields, and risk. In the past, overly aggressive investments in high yield and high risk junk bonds and developmental mortgage loans pushed some companies to insolvency. Therefore, one's objective should be to select companies with investment portfolios and investment philosophies that show a reasonable and acceptable combination of risk and return. What is reasonable and acceptable, of course, depends on the level of risk and the certainty of return desired by the policyowner.

Companies offering IUL policies typically do not actually invest directly in the stocks in the equity indexes they use in their equity-index interest crediting formulas. Rather, they invest the majority of policyowners' net premiums in the conventional assortment of long-term corporate and government bonds and mortgages. They take the remainder of the net premiums and buy options on the equity indexes (or on futures contracts on the equity indexes) they use in their interest-crediting formulas.

Chapter 3 "How to Determine the Right Company", discusses procedures for evaluating the investment portfolios of insurance companies.

Interest-Crediting Methods

Just as with UL—when the policyowner pays IUL premiums—a portion pays for the pure insurance cost based on the age and rating of the insured. Another portion pays for various fees and expenses, including amounts for any riders or special provisions attached to the policy; the rest goes into the cash value. What happens next—in general terms—is that, unlike whole life and regular UL, IUL uses an equity-index interest crediting formula allowing the interest credited to the cash value account to fluctuate in relation to one or more stock market indexes of financial performance such as the S&P's 500 or the Nasdaq 100.

Equity Indexes

The equity indexes that insurers use for their interest crediting formulas are *price* indexes, not *total return* indexes. Price indexes do not include dividends, interest, or other investment income investors would earn if they purchased a mutual fund tracking one of the major indexes, such as the S&P 500. To get index returns comparable to a mutual fund investing in the S&P 500 in an IUL policy, the equity index would have to be the S&P 550 Total Return Index, not the S&P 500 Index. Therefore, the rates of return on the indexes used in IUL policies generally will be lower than the rates of return policyowners would earn if they actually bought the stocks in the index (or an efficient mutual fund or ETF tracking the index).

There is no reason, in theory, that companies could not use other indexes of financial assets, such as various bond indexes, REIT indexes, commodity indexes, or precious-metals indexes, etc., in their interest crediting formulas. However, the authors are unaware of any companies currently offering IUL policies using any of these other types of nonequity indexes.

Three other factors, in addition to the performance of one or more equity indexes, enter into the interest crediting formula: *a guaranteed minimum crediting rate, a cap rate,* and *a participation rate.* IUL policies usually allow insurers to change these key parameters annually, at the discretion of the insurance company.

1. *Guaranteed minimum crediting rate.* The guaranteed minimum crediting rate is the minimum rate insurers will apply to cash value balances if the rate determined by their interest crediting formula is less than the guaranteed minimum rate. For most policies, this minimum rate is 0 percent, but some policies have minimum rates of 1 to 2 percent, annual (or about one-twelfth of this rate when the interest crediting formula uses the monthly point-to-point method). This guaranteed minimum rate prevents the interest crediting formula from computing a rate that would reduce principal value in the cash value account.

2. *Cap rate.* The cap rate is an upper limit on the equity index rate that the interest crediting rate formula will use to determine the amount the insurer will credit to cash values. For instance if the cap is 8 percent, insurers will ignore any gains in the indexes over 8 percent when they compute the amounts to credit to cash values.

3. *Participation rate.* Insurance companies also control interest crediting through participation rates. For example, if a policy earns 8 percent in any given year, uses an annual point-to-point crediting method, and has a 100 percent participation rate, the interest crediting formula will use the full 8 percent rate in determining amounts the insurer credits to policy cash values. However, if the participation rate is only 60 percent, the interest used in the interest crediting formula will be only 4.8 percent (8 percent × 60 percent). If the participation rate is 140 percent, interest crediting formula would use an 11.2 percent rate to determine the amounts credited to cash values. Participation rates typically vary from between 60 and 150 percent. Also, insurers can adjust the participation rates either up or down, making future cash value growth predictions difficult. A low participation rate on a policy is an obvious sign of a reduced interest crediting potential.

Equity-Index Interest Crediting Formula

The amount that insurers credit to IUL policy cash values depends on four factors:

- the **G**ain rate on the selected equity index for the relevant period: **G%**

- the **C**ap rate, if applicable: **C%**

- the guaranteed **M**inimum rate, if applicable: **M%**

- the **P**articipation rate: **P%**

The cash value crediting rate (**CV%**) is determined using the following formula:

$$\mathbf{CV\%} = \text{Max}(\mathbf{M\%}, \text{Min}(\mathbf{G\%}, \mathbf{C\%})) \times \mathbf{P\%}$$

Example. Assume **G% = 10%, C% = 7%, M% = 0%,** and **P% = 80%**

$$\mathbf{CV\%} = \text{Max}(\mathbf{0\%}, \text{Min}(\mathbf{10\%}, \mathbf{7\%})) \times \mathbf{80\%}$$

CV% = Max(0%, 7%) × 80%

CV% = 7% × 80% = <u>5.6%</u>

The insurer would credit cash values with 5.6% interest.

Interest Crediting Strategies

Insurers determine the rate of return to enter into their interest crediting formulas in their IUL policies using a variety of crediting strategies. The most common are the *point-to-point* (or "ratchet") method—calculated either annually or monthly—and the *monthly averaging* method.

1. *Point-to-point crediting methods.* Both of the point-to-point crediting strategies begin the crediting cycle with a marker at the beginning of the contract, and track the movement of the underlying stock index(es) to the next point. For *annual point-to-point*, the insurer tracks the index for one year; for *monthly point-to-point*, one month. The difference from the first point to the second point represents the percent of interest that enters the policy's interest crediting formula.

2. *Monthly averaging method.* Under monthly averaging, insurers track monthly index changes and then average them over twelve months. This annualized average rate then enters the annual interest crediting rate formula to determine the amounts insurers will credit to cash values at the end of the year.

Example. Using the annual strategy, if the index rose 5 percent over the course of a year, 5 percent would serve as a starting point in the interest crediting formula determining the amount the insurer will credit to policy cash values. Under the monthly strategy, if the index rose 1 percent in a month, the interest crediting formula would use 1 percent in the calculation of the amount of interest to add to cash values.

Problems with averaging strategies. The problem with the interest crediting strategies is that they are usually hard for policyowners to understand. Additionally, one never knows in advance which crediting strategy will produce the best outcome for a policyowner over the course of the next twelve months. Also, many policies make the policyowners commit to a crediting strategy for relatively long-term periods, such as five-year segments. This means that if a particular crediting strategy does not perform as the policyowners had hoped, the policyowners cannot move the money that they already have allocated to that crediting strategy until the end of the five-year segment.

WHERE CAN I FIND OUT MORE?

The following references include authoritative discussions of various types of life insurance including universal life insurance:

1. B. Anderson, *Anderson on Life Insurance* (Waltham, MA: Little, Brown and Company, 1991).

2. B. Baldwin, *New Life Insurance Investment Advisor: Achieving Financial Security for You and Your Family Through Today's Insurance Products*, 2nd ed. (Hightstown, NJ: McGraw-Hill Trade, 2001).

3. J. Belth, *Life Insurance: A Consumer's Handbook*, 2nd ed. (Bloomington, IN: Indiana University Press, 1985).

4. K. Black, Jr. and H. Skipper, Jr., *Life Insurance*, 13th ed. (Old Tappan, NJ: Prentice Hall Inc., 1999).

5. E. Graves, Editor, *McGill's Life Insurance*, 7th ed. (Bryn Mawr, PA: The American College, 2010).

The following references are useful guides for policy and company rating information:

1. *Best Insurance Reports* (Oldwick, NJ: A. M. Best Company, published annually).

2. *Best's Review – Life/Health Edition* (Oldwick, NJ: A. M. Best Company, published monthly).

FREQUENTLY ASKED QUESTIONS

Question – Is the CSO 2001 table mentioned in "Mortality Charges" above the most recently available mortality table?

Answer – Yes, though a new mortality table is expected to be adopted soon. In 2014 the Society of Actuaries (SOA) introduced updated mortality tables RP-2014 and MP-2014, its first updated tables since 2000.[1] Those tables came under some criticism for overstating potential longevity, and the SOA has revised them several times since then.[2] None of the new SOA mortality tables has been officially adopted by the IRS.

However, the IRS is required, under the Pension Protection Act, to update its mortality tables every ten years, and the last update came in 2008 with the adoption of the CS 2001 table. Recently the IRs did adopt new static mortality tables for use in defined benefit plans, and in that Notice it announced its intention to adopt new base mortality rates and projection factors with new regulations that would apply beginning in 2018.[3] Given the statutory deadline and the announced intent to have new a table adopted by the beginning of 2018, one would expect new a new regulation to be proposed fairly soon.

CHAPTER ENDNOTES

1. SOA, "RP-2014 Mortality Tables Report," (Revised November 2014), available online at: https://www.soa.org/Files/Research/Exp-Study/research-2014-rp-report.pdf.

2. Nick Thornton, "New mortality tables may reduce pension liabilities for some sponsors," *BenefitsPro* (October 22, 2016).

3. IRS Notice 2016-50, "Updated Static Mortality Tables for Defined Benefit Pension Plans for 2017".

GUARANTEED NO-LAPSE UNIVERSAL LIFE

CHAPTER 21

INTRODUCTION

Briefly, Guaranteed No-Lapse Universal Life (GNLUL or just NLUL), also called guaranteed universal life, Secondary Guarantee Universal Life (SGUL), universal life with secondary guarantees, or other variations thereon, is a variant of the regular universal life design. The no-lapse feature is a secondary guarantee promising owners that their policies will remain in force and pay death benefits so long as they continue to meet the secondary guarantee requirements (essentially, to pay required minimum premiums on a timely basis). The policy may make the secondary guarantee either as a provision within the policy or as a rider attached to the policy.

In a nutshell, the principal objective of NLUL policies is to provide policyowners with a guaranteed death benefit (for a specified period up to the lifetime of the insured) for the lowest possible guaranteed premium level. In essence, therefore, the insurance industry has designed NLUL to serve as an extended-period, low-cost, level-premium, fixed-death-benefit TERM insurance policy. Like regular term policies (and unlike most regular UL policies), the focus is on providing the maximum guaranteed death benefits for the lowest premium cost; NLUL develops relatively little or no cash value. Unlike regular term insurance policies, which insurers typically do not issue for terms exceeding thirty years and which they usually will not issue for such terms on insureds over age fifty, insurers will issue NLUL virtually at any age of the insured and will permit guaranteed coverage to continue until the death of the insured, even if the insured's life expectancy exceeds thirty years.

As with all such promises in life insurance (and in life), the secondary guarantees come with corresponding costs and tradeoffs, as discussed in more detail in subsequent sections of this chapter.

Although insurance companies have built their NLUL policies upon the regular UL design platform, the critical point readers should grasp is that NLUL and UL are very different animals. NLUL policies have distinctly different objectives and more specialized applications, offer quite different levels of flexibility and unique characteristics, and use different internal valuation methodologies than regular UL policies with which readers may be more familiar. These issues and features are addressed further in later sections of this chapter.

HOW DOES IT WORK?

Secondary Guarantee

The reason the guarantee feature is called a "secondary guarantee" is that it provides an additional guarantee above and beyond the primary guarantees that are part of all regular UL policies. The primary guarantees apply with respect to the maximum expense and mortality charges that the insurer can debit and the minimum interest rate that the insurer must credit to policy cash values. Regular UL policies will lapse if premium payments are insufficient to cover policy charges and the cash-value account balance is inadequate to cover the premium shortfalls. Regular UL policyowners, ultimately, will have to pay higher premiums to maintain the same face amount of coverage if actual expense, mortality, and interest rate experience is not as favorable as the insurers had assumed when setting target premiums.

In contrast, secondary guarantee no-lapse policies will remain in force and the death benefits will remain level, even if the cash-value accounts fall to zero as long as the policyowners have paid the specified required premiums in a timely fashion. If policyowners continue to timely pay at least the minimum specified premiums for as long as required under the policy design, the secondary guarantee will remain in force, regardless of the cash-value balance.

NLUL policies and the secondary guarantees have changed over time as a result of evolving market conditions, insurance company experience, and changing reserving requirements. As a result, NLUL policies come in different "flavors" depending upon when they were issued, the reserving regulations that apply to them, their market niche, and insurance company design and marketing ingenuity. In order to better understand current NLUL policies and their appropriate uses, prospective insureds and their advisers need to know something about the history of how the product has evolved.

Evolving Product

The insurance industry created the No-Lapse Universal Life (NLUL) version of UL in the mid-1990's in response to UL policyholder concerns. In the 1990s, many policyowners discovered that the planned premiums for their UL policies were insufficient to keep their policies in force for life because the insurers had set the target premiums based on overly optimistic assumptions, such as the continuation of high credited interest rates. In response to consumer dissatisfaction with premium uncertainty, insurance companies began to add no-lapse guarantees to universal life policies. These guarantees supplemented the primary guarantees of the policies, so they were called secondary guarantees.

With the original types of secondary guarantees, owners could rest assured that their policies would remain in force, their death benefits would not decline, and their premiums would not increase for a specified period, such as ten years. Over time, on newly-offered policies, insurance companies gradually extended the period over which the secondary guarantees could be applied until it included the entire life of the insured. Universal life policies with no-lapse guarantees stay in force as long as their no-lapse guarantees are in effect, even if the policies do not have enough money (in the cash value accounts) to cover the nonguaranteed monthly charges. Although insurers will issue NLUL policies with time-limited or shorter-term guarantee periods, most NLUL policies currently sold have the guarantee period extend for the life of the insured.

From an economic or financial standpoint, the premiums required by the secondary guarantee are always less than the premiums required by the primary guarantees (that is, less than the premiums the insurer could require if it had adverse expense, mortality, and interest experience and charged the guaranteed maximum expenses and mortality rates, and credited the minimum interest rate). After all, the principal purpose of the secondary guarantee is to provide a lower guaranteed cost to policyowners while maintaining the face amount of coverage. However, the premiums insurers require for policies with the secondary guarantee may be higher or lower than the premiums they require for otherwise comparable regular UL policies without the secondary guarantee; the premium levels depend on the pricing of each contract and on future interest rates, mortality experience, and expenses.

Since the advent of the no-lapse concept, three main NLUL product designs have arisen in the marketplace: stipulated-premium, shadow-account, and hybrid designs. Variations are possible, so these descriptions may not fully describe all policies. However, the differences are important because they typically involve different costs and tradeoffs for policyowners.

Stipulated-Premium Designs

This is the simplest and oldest design and the one, typically, with the least flexibility from the policyowner's perspective. The policy stays in force if the actual premiums paid, accumulated at a specified interest rate, are at least equal to the stipulated no-lapse premiums accumulated at the same interest rate. Insurers usually do the no-lapse test calculation each month. In most cases, policyowners have the flexibility to pay more than the no-lapse premium each month, and this flexibility creates opportunities to reduce the effective cost of the policy. However, many of these policies charge a high load on excess premiums, as much as 75 percent of the excess, so policyowners really have little incentive to pay more than the stipulated amount. On the other hand, generally policyowners may not skip premium payments or pay less than the stipulated amount unless they have previously paid sufficient premiums in excess of the stipulated amounts (after the surcharge loads) so that the policy still passes the no-lapse test calculation. In some policies, failure to pay premiums exactly when due could void or shorten the no-lapse guarantee, even if the policyowner ultimately pays the premium within the policy grace period. Many other policies do not void or shorten the guarantee if the policyowner makes a catch-up premium payment (with interest and, sometimes, penalty) during the usual thirty-day grace period.

Shadow-Account Designs

The introduction of the shadow-account designs produced a more complex secondary guarantee design. This design has no stipulated premium, per se, but instead the secondary guarantee remains in effect and, thus, the policy remains in force as long as the shadow fund is greater than or equal to zero, even if the policy cash-value account is zero or negative. The shadow account itself is purely a bookkeeping reference value that insurers use solely for the purpose of determining if the no-lapse guarantee remains in effect. The nominal cash in the shadow account is not available to the policyholder.

In contrast with other regular UL policies, shadow-account design NLUL policies have three sets of specified values for determining various policy values: the primary guarantee values and the current (nonguaranteed) values, similar to regular UL policies, and the no-lapse (secondary guarantee) values. The primary guarantee values are the maximum expense loads, maximum mortality charges, and minimum interest crediting rates the insurer can apply in determining cash-value accumulations. The current (nonguaranteed) values are the actual expense loads, mortality charges, and interest crediting rates the insurer applies in determining actual cash-value accumulations. The current values change over time based upon the company's mortality, expense, and interest rate experience, but almost always are more favorable than the guaranteed values. The no-lapse (secondary guarantee) values are those values the insurer uses to compute the shadow-account cash values for the purpose of testing whether premiums are (or have been) sufficient to keep the secondary guarantee in force.

Specifically, the shadow account is similar to the cash-value accumulation account of nonguaranteed UL policies, but the insurer determines the shadow-account value using a different set of more favorable mortality and expense charges and interest credits than it uses for the actual cash-value account. The current no-lapse values insurers use for the NLUL shadow accounts usually are similar to, but more favorable than, the current values they use for their regular UL cash-value accounts. However, the current values that insurers typically use for the NLUL cash-value accounts include loads for the secondary guarantee and, therefore, are less favorable than the current values they use for the cash values of their nonguaranteed UL policies. As a result, NLUL policies generally will accumulate much less in the cash-value accounts than otherwise similar regular nonguaranteed UL policies. Technically, of course, these cash values are policyowner assets. In regular UL polices,

policyowners generally may borrow against or make partial withdrawals of cash values with considerable ease without affecting any guarantees under the policy. Despite cash values being the policyowner's asset, by design, most NLUL policies will void or shorten the no-lapse guarantee if policyowners choose to borrow against or withdraw any cash values from the policy.

In contrast with the original stipulated-premium design policies, most shadow-account design policies do give policyowners somewhat broader flexibility with respect to premium payments. Similar to some of the stipulated-premium design policies, many of the shadow-account design policies will permit policyowners to make catch-up premium payments to preserve the no-lapse guarantee in the event they miss premium payments or pay them late and the shadow account falls below zero. Many, if not most, shadow-account design NLUL policies also charge an excess premium load, similar to the stipulated-premium design policies.

Hybrid Designs

Hybrid designs have a dual test for satisfying the no-lapse provision. During an initial period, such as ten years, the insurer uses a minimum-premium test similar to that used in policies with stipulated-premium designs. This assures insurers that they will receive sufficient premium payments in the early years to cover their considerable up-front costs of putting the policies on the books. After that initial period, the insurer applies a shadow-account test. By making policies subject to the dual tests for maintaining the no-lapse guarantee, hybrid designs sometimes can provide policyowners with more premium flexibility than the other designs, and this can create cost-saving opportunities.

Multifund Shadow-Account Designs

Finally, the most recent step in NLUL product evolution involves the broadening of the shadow-fund design concept to include multifund shadow-account designs with multiple sets of shadow-fund charges. The multiple sets of cost of insurance charges, credited interest rates, various policy loads, and other company-specific or industry-wide pricing factors that apply to the shadow-fund account are different from the cost of insurance charges, credited interest rates, and policy loads that apply to the policy cash-value account. Because the insurers can set the shadow-account charges, loads, and interest rates to any chosen level when they design the product, the companies effectively can control the desired level of the shadow accounts. Usually, the shadow-fund account has much lower levels of cost of insurance charges than cost of insurance charges that apply to the policy cash-value account.

Regulation, Pricing, and Design Uncertainty

As the previous discussion indicates, prospective buyers and their advisers are faced with a myriad of designs that are difficult to compare and to understand.

Furthermore, shadow-account designs are inherently complex and especially difficult to explain to the consuming public. The complexity has arisen primarily as a result of a natural tension between insurance regulators and insurance companies. The regulators are responsible for setting statutory cash reserve requirements, assuring that insurance companies remain solvent. They typically argue for higher reserve requirements. For each change in the regulations that would tend to increase required reserves, the insurance companies and their actuaries have an incentive to come up with ever more unusual product designs that may somewhat circumvent the regulations and allow them to use lower reserves. From the insurers' perspective, lower reserves lead to a lower cost of capital, lower premiums, and therefore a more competitive product which better serves consumer needs. From the regulators' perspective, these lower reserves may be insufficient to protect consumers from potential insolvencies. This has been a back-and-forth battle between regulators and insurers for the past decade.

In fact, as a result of several newly-issued sets of reserve calculation regulations, brought on by the continuing development and evolution of the no-lapse secondary guarantee UL policies and market considerations, insurance companies have begun to take a somewhat broader and less formulaic perspective with respect to the methods they use for their reserve and pricing calculations. As described above, many insurers are now using multiple shadow accounts that involve multiple sets of a wider spectrum of different insurance cost and risk components. These principle factors include considerations beyond the traditional (mortality, expense, and interest rate) factors. They include such factors as lapse rates, and other quantifiable risk factors based on both industry and company-specific experience that the companies feel can help them to more finely tune their pricing and reserve calculations so as

to maintain a competitive market balance between the risk and the cost of the insurance for consumers.

As a result of the uncertainties in reserve requirements going forward and insurer fears that reserve regulations might adversely affect the profitability of the NLUL market, NLUL policy sales declined in recent years, despite the product's popularity. Although sales of no-lapse UL policies have decreased 3 percent (by annualized premiums) since the second quarter of 2010, the guarantee is still quite popular, with no-lapse policies taking 45 percent of UL market share in 2011. However, many companies are leaving the market or cutting back on sales. For example, Sun Life exited the market in 2010. NLUL has fallen from 97 percent of its life business in 2007 to about 32 percent in late 2011.

Regulatory Rescue?

The National Association of Insurance Commissioners (NAIC) is a national organization made up of all the state insurance commissioners who are responsible for oversight and regulation of the insurance industries within their states. One of its principal objectives is to set reserve standards that will assure the financial solvency of insurance companies, individually, and the industry as a whole. The NAIC generally takes the lead in promulgating uniform regulatory legislation within the states.

Recognizing the popularity of the low-cost secondary guarantee products to the insurance-consuming market, on the one hand, and the need for adequate reserves which could squeeze carriers' profit margins, on the other, the NAIC, in 2011 and 2012, began to take constructive steps to resolve the differences between regulators and insurance companies on the conflicting issues arising with respect to secondary guarantee policies. The NAIC initiated a movement to develop a new regulatory approach employing a more comprehensive Principle-Based Reserving (PBR) system. The specifics are still far from complete, but the NAIC has outlined the basic elements of this approach as follows:

- Identifies all identifiable, quantifiable and material risks, not just mortality and interest rate risk

- Utilizes risk analysis and risk management techniques to quantify risks

- Permits the use of company experience to establish assumptions for risk that the company can influence (e.g., mortality through underwriting)

- Uses assumptions that must be consistent with a company-wide risk assessment process

- Assumptions change as experience changes[1]

As of early 2016 the NAIC surpassed its goal with forty-six states having adopted laws implementing PBR.[2] Because it has been adopted by at least forty-two jurisdictions which constitute a 75 percent "supermajority" of U.S.-based life insurance premiums, it has now become operational.[3] Such efforts should go far to remove many of the uncertainties for regulators, insurance providers, and most importantly, the insurance-consuming public surrounding the future design, features, costs, and applications of no-lapse (secondary guarantee) universal life policies. There is, beyond any doubt, an important market segment to be served by such products; a resolution of conflicting issues and further clarity surrounding these products is welcomed and necessary.

WHEN IS THE USE OF THIS DEVICE INDICATED?

Among all policy types, NLUL can provide policyowners with the lowest guaranteed premium for a given guaranteed death benefit for an extended period of time. Therefore, the use of NLUL policies would be indicated for clients:

1. whose foremost goal is to obtain liquidity at death while optimizing the death benefit relative to premiums paid and who, therefore, have less interest in or need for cash values for lifetime income purposes;

2. interested in eliminating performance risk such as those policyowners whose current policies have underperformed due to market volatility or due to reduced interest or dividend crediting rates;

3. planning to use irrevocable life insurance trusts to pass wealth to heirs and desiring a policy with the lowest lifetime premium so as to minimize potential gift taxes; and

4. who primarily want liquidity to pay estate taxes.

Given the costs and tradeoffs involved with secondary guarantees, NLUL generally would be *less* suitable for clients:

1. who wish to insure shorter-term protection needs where traditional term policies for the needed term generally will be less expensive than NLUL policies;

2. looking to have their death benefit levels rise in future years to keep pace with inflation or anticipated increases in liquidity needs at death as a result of a growing estate;

3. unwilling to give up the greater upside cash value and death benefit potential and the more flexible premium-paying options inherent in regular UL policies for the secondary guarantee;

4. who are younger and whose lifetime protection needs, retirement income needs, and estate objectives are not well defined or known and, thus, who probably should retain greater flexibility in their life insurance planning;

5. whose incomes are variable and who are uncertain whether they can commit to paying the periodic premiums required to maintain the secondary guarantee;

6. wishing to preserve their rights to borrow from the cash values of the policy or to make partial withdraws without the limitations and penalties typical of policies with secondary guarantees; and

7. who wish to use their insurance policy cash values as a source for additional retirement income in the event they live longer than expected or otherwise need the cash values for health-related expenses or other unanticipated needs.

Advantages

The secondary guarantee of NLUL policies promises policyowners that if they play by the rules and maintain timely specified premium payment levels, their policies will maintain at least a level death benefit without ever requiring an increase in premiums for the insured's lifetime, even if the cash value account balance falls to zero or below. However, this promise comes with considerable tradeoffs in costs, other risks, and flexibility.

- There are several advantages from a design standpoint for the company and the insured as well. Companies are able to offer these guarantees for several reasons, including the following:

  - The no-lapse guarantee is a death benefit and premium-level guarantee only and does not affect the cash value guarantee which permits the insurer to set the premiums lower than for policies without the no-lapse guarantee.

  - The various criteria required to maintain the no-lapse guarantee help to ensure premium persistency, which enables better pricing.

  - Because of the more predictable cash flows, no-lapse guarantee products can support longer-term investment strategies that can boost the underlying asset yields and reduce required premiums.

Disadvantages

1. *Lack of Flexibility.* Any changes to NLUL policies such as loans, partial withdrawals, changes in the death benefit, changes in scheduled premiums, and adding riders may terminate the guarantee or reduce its duration. In most cases, policyowners may make additional payments to place the guarantee back into effect, but this will result in increased out-of-pocket costs.

2. *Limited Cash Values.* Cash values may seem to be relatively unimportant for those who are only interested in a policy's ultimate death benefit. But, circumstances can change, making cash values and living benefits more important. If a policy builds little or no cash value, the policyholder has no future ability to switch policies to a more competitive one without losing most of the initial investment or to use portions of the cash value for living benefits during the insured's lifetime. Essentially, the purchase decision literally becomes a point of no return. Policy pricing a NLUL policy that is already competitive in a low interest rate period might fall even lower if higher interest rates over

a sustained period prompt a further reduction in premiums. Those policyowners who buy at one premium price would be hard-pressed to make a switch to a lower-priced product several years later, even if their health permits. The high policy surrender charges and limited cash values would effectively lock them into their existing policies and make them forfeit most of their past investment of premiums if they attempted a policy exchange.

Especially if the insured lives a significantly long time, owner might desire to pass along some of a policy's value during the insured's lifetime. If a policy is owned in trust, for example, the grantor/owner can distribute portions of the cash value from traditional cash value policies to trust beneficiaries so they do not have to wait until the end of an insured's long life to obtain some of a policy's benefits. Most of the guaranteed death benefit universal life policies are expected to have little or no cash value in them at the life expectancy of the insured or beyond. This flexible use of a policy's living benefits is not an option where no such benefits exist.

3. *Opportunity Cost.* The secondary guarantees feature fix death benefits and pricing, but very limited cash value accumulation potential. Although nonguaranteed policies have some risk that premiums will rise or death benefits decline—or at worst—the policies lapse, studies show that the choice of guaranteed policy may well sacrifice a significant upside potential return from the best nonguaranteed policies structured in the most efficient way. The best nonguaranteed policies in most scenarios will produce much higher returns for most insureds who live long lives. If the policyowner's goal is to maximize returns from an investment of insurance premiums assuming a relatively long life, the most competitive nonguaranteed policies will most likely be the better as well as the safer choice.

4. *Conflict of Interest between Insurers and Policyowners.* One of the more troubling issues for the authors involves the role of lapse-supported pricing in the design of NLUL policies. The financial risks to insurers if owners retain policies in larger numbers than insurers have projected place the companies in a conflict of interest with their policyowners. A potential financial problem thus takes on an ethical dimension. This actuarial practice allocates profits and losses from policies in such a way that the profitability of a product for the company depends on a high level of policy lapses. The company and the

minority of remaining policyowners gain because the departing policyowners are denied a fair return on the net premiums they have paid. The unfairness of lapse-supported pricing is extreme where the payments of the relatively high premiums required for permanent insurance yield little or nothing in the way of cash value for those who drop their policies. Worse, this policy design pits the company's financial interest in maximizing the number of policyholders dropping or losing their coverage and forfeiting all or most of their premium investment against their customers' interest in obtaining a reasonable return on those premiums.

5. *Regulatory Uncertainty and Insurer Insolvency Risk.* As was discussed above, the regulatory environment surrounding NLUL policy pricing and reserving currently is in flux, although the NAIC is taking steps to resolve the issues. However, for the time being, the unanswered questions regarding the adequacy of reserves and the risk of insolvencies, on the one hand, and the possibility of setting reserve requirements too high and making the pricing of NLUL policies uncompetitive, on the other, is confusing the markets and making it extremely difficult to properly evaluate cost/benefit relationships of these policies compared to the more traditional whole life and universal life policy designs.

TAX IMPLICATIONS

The income tax rules for NLUL policies are virtually identical to the tax rules for UL policies, which are essentially the same as the tax rules for other types of life insurance policies. Beneficiaries receive death benefits that, usually, are free of any federal, state, and local income tax. NLUL policies also are subject to the same estate, gift, and generation-skipping transfer taxation rules as all other types of life insurance policies.

Although, the income tax rules for living benefits paid from NLUL policies are the same as for living benefits paid from other types of life insurance policies, their generally limited cash value accumulations make this a relatively moot point. In cases where policyowners do surrender NLUL policies with some cash value or are able to withdraw some cash value from NLUL policies, the general cost-recovery rule governs the taxation of these living benefits. The cost-recovery rule, which is sometimes called the First-In First-Out (FIFO) rule, treats amounts received as nontaxable recovery of the policyowner's investment in the contract. Only

after policyowners fully recover their investment in the contract are additional amounts that they receive treated as taxable interest or gain in the policy. Included in this category of living benefits potentially payable from NLUL policies are lump-sum cash settlements of cash surrender values, cash withdrawals, and amounts received on partial surrender. Policyowners include these amounts in gross income only to the extent they exceed their investment in the contract (as reduced by any prior excludable distributions received from the contract). In other words, generally the income tax rules treat nonannuity distributions during life, first, as a return of the policyowner's investment in the contract and then, only after the owner has recovered the entire investment in the contract, as taxable interest or gain.

Being that the secondary guarantee is the distinguishing feature of NLUL and that NLUL policies generally accumulate little if any cash values, most NLUL policyowners should be seeking guaranteed death benefits at low premium cost rather than enhanced cash-value accumulations and increasing death benefits as is often the case when purchasing regular UL policies. Consequently, the exceptions to the cost-recovery tax rule for payments of living benefits and the tax risks associated with being classified as modified endowment contracts are nearly irrelevant tax considerations for NLUL policyowners.

ALTERNATIVES

Term insurance offers lower guaranteed premiums, but even with thirty-year level-term plans, coverage usually ceases before the term of the insured's life expectancy. Insurers generally will not issue thirty-year level-term policies after age fifty, so term policies generally cannot provide the lifetime guarantees of NLUL.

Whole life offers lifetime guaranteed premiums, but with the added expense of high guaranteed cash value. Whole life premiums can be one-and-a-half to two-and-one-half times that of a NLUL premium. Blending whole life with term can reduce the premium outlay, but only by sacrificing the death benefit or premium guarantee. In many cases, if investment performance meets expectations, the whole life/term combination can significantly outperform a NLUL policy. But what if investment performance is poor, as in the recent past decade?

Insurers and policyowners can configure regular UL policies' premium payments and death benefits to resemble virtually any type of life insurance policy, from annually-renewable term to single-premium whole life. The major problem is that it is virtually impossible to design a cost-effective level-premium term-for-life UL policy without some kind of secondary guarantee. Without a secondary guarantee, policyowners would be exposed to the risk of having to pay exorbitant and unaffordable premiums at advanced ages (when they likely are least able to afford it) to keep their policies in force in the event actual investment performance and actual values for other factors used in setting the target premiums do not quite meet expectations.

WHERE AND HOW DO I GET IT?

There are about 2,000 life insurance companies actively marketing coverage in the United States. Many of these companies offer NLUL policies, but the number has leveled off or declined in recent years as a result of insurer uncertainties regarding required reserves and the potential profitability of this segment of the insurance marketplace. The NAIC is moving to resolve these uncertainties regarding required reserves in a way that will permit insurers to cost-effectively serve that portion of the market desiring such guarantees at a reasonable premium cost. A person can purchase a policy through one of many agents that represent a licensed insurance company.

FEES AND ACQUISITION COSTS

Insurers may recoup policy issue expenses and commissions in a number of ways including a flat policy assessment charge, a percentage of premium charge, a fee based on each $1,000 of face amount, as well as back-end loads or surrender charges, or some combination of each. Premium loads vary, but can be as high as 30 percent or more on all premiums, and even up to 75 percent on excess premiums (above target or stipulated premium levels). Surrender charges often start declining yearly after about the fifth policy year or sooner but typically do not reach zero for fifteen to twenty years.

Commissions typically range from a low of 20 to 55 percent up to 99 percent, or even higher in some cases, of the first-year premium for amounts up to the target level premium or stipulated premium amount. The commission on the portion of any premium payment that is in excess of the target level premium generally is much lower, often only about 3 percent, but sometimes slightly more. Renewal commissions on subsequent premiums usually are lower, about

5 percent, and typically terminate after a specified period, such as fifteen to twenty years.

SELECTING THE BEST OF ITS TYPE

Even considering the risks, the relative inflexibility, and the potential missed up-side opportunity with NLUL, some consumers will find the low-priced guarantee desirable. Those who proceed to shop for this product should carefully follow these guidelines and consider independent and objective assistance in doing so:

- Check the policy language and determine the consequence of a missed premium payment and the means of determining whether a policy premium has been paid on time. Generally, agents do not discuss or understand these points and, whether intentionally or not, give incorrect or misleading reassurance. Policy terms in these areas often are not well defined and, in some cases, seem designed to cause the high level of policy lapses insurers require for these policies to be profitable.

- Review the insurer's financial ratings and trends in ratings, especially from those rating agencies that have taken the lead in this area and most carefully weighed and publicly discussed the potential impact of the guaranteed death benefit universal life product on an insurance company's future financial condition.

- Fully explore the market and compare policy costs and benefits. Guaranteed death benefit policies' death benefits can vary by 15 to 30 percent or more for the same premium outlay. The more highly-rated companies generally have the lower-cost alternatives.

- Look for lower commissions and surrender charges. Most NLUL policies pay high commissions to selling agents. For example, both the Moody's and Fitch reports show typical first-year commissions equal to 99 percent of the premium and annual renewal commissions of 5 percent of the premium. However, some policies have lower commissions, with surrender charges lasting only five years, instead of the more common fifteen- to twenty-year period. This difference not only may result in a higher death benefit, but the relatively much greater cash value build-up provides policyowners with the flexibility to consider a policy exchange in future years if increasing interest rates result in a lower premium for an equivalent death benefit in a new policy.

- Consider the possible savings from a step-rated or increasing premium NLUL policy. A policy that starts with a comparatively lower premium that increases in later years may, in some cases, offer a significant savings over a level-premium design. Of course, this would be the case especially if the insureds die early and avoid the much higher-level annual premium cost of the later policy years. That particular scenario generally is not the most desirable plan or probable outcome, but in some cases the benefit might also result even if the insureds live a long time. Purchasers or their advisers need to evaluate such cost comparisons on a case-by-case basis. Part of the savings results from a reduced agent's commission, because insurers pay commissions based on the initial lower premium.

WHERE CAN I FIND OUT MORE?

The following references include authoritative discussions of various types of life insurance including universal life insurance:

1. B. Anderson, *Anderson on Life Insurance* (Waltham, MA: Little, Brown and Company, 1991).

2. B. Baldwin, *New Life Insurance Investment Advisor: Achieving Financial Security for You and Your Family Through Today's Insurance Products*, 2nd ed. (Hightstown, NJ: McGraw-Hill Trade, 2001).

3. J. Belth, *Life Insurance: A Consumer's Handbook*, 2nd ed. (Bloomington, IN: Indiana University Press, 1985).

4. K. Black, Jr. and H. Skipper, Jr., *Life Insurance*, 13th ed. (Old Tappan, NJ: Prentice Hall Inc., 1999).

5. E. Graves, Editor, *McGill's Life Insurance*, 7th ed. (Bryn Mawr, PA: The American College, 2010).

The following references are useful guides for policy and company rating information:

1. *Best Insurance Reports* (Oldwick, NJ: A. M. Best Company, published annually).

2. *Best's Review – Life/Health Edition* (Oldwick, NJ: A. M. Best Company, published monthly).

CHAPTER ENDNOTES

1. American Council of Life Insurers, "Principle-Based Reserving: An Introduction for Lawyers and Other Non-Actuaries," slides from 2008 ALCI Annual Conference, available at: www.acli.com/Events/Documents/1226fc0f961a49959341879a0cef4213Tues102108IntroductiontoPrinciplesBasedReservingfo.pdf.

2. NAIC, "Key Issue: the national Systme of State Regulation and Principle–Based Reserving" (revised Dec. 8, 2016), available at: http://www.naic.org/cipr_topics/principle_based_reserving_pbr.htm.

3. American Council of Life Insurers, "Principle-Based Reserves: Overview" (2014), available at: www.acli.com/Issues/Principle-Based%20Reserves/Pages/76.aspx.

MODIFIED ENDOWMENT CONTRACTS

CHAPTER 22

INTRODUCTION

To counteract what was perceived as an abusive use of single-premium, limited-pay, and universal life policies as short-term, tax-sheltered cash accumulation or savings vehicle, Congress passed legislation modifying Internal Revenue Code section 7702, which provides the tax law definition of a life insurance contract. Code section 7702A, which was drafted to correct the perceived abuses, defines a new class of insurance contracts called Modified Endowment Contracts (MEC).[1]

The basic difference between MECs and other life insurance contracts is the federal income tax treatment of amounts received during the insured's life. Certain distributions under the contract that are not generally subject to tax when received from other life insurance contracts are subject to income tax and, in some cases, a 10 percent penalty when received from MECs.

In other respects, MECs are treated and taxed under the same rules applying to other life insurance contracts that are not MECs. Basically, compared with policies that are not classified as MECs, MECs have detrimental tax consequences for some living benefits but the tax treatment of cash accumulations within the policy and death benefits is no different than other policies.

What is a MEC? A MEC is a policy that meets the section 7702A definition of life insurance and is funded more rapidly than a paid-up policy based on seven statutorily-defined level annual premiums. (See Chapter 24 for more information on section 7702A.)

The basic rules:

1. Policies entered into before June 21, 1988, are grandfathered from the MEC rules unless the policies undergo a material change.

2. All policies entered into after June 20, 1988, and any policy, whenever issued, that undergoes a material change must be tested under the MEC classification rules.

3. Once a policy is classified as a MEC, it remains a MEC. A MEC will not change its MEC status if it is changed, adjusted, or reconfigured as a policy that would otherwise not be classified as a MEC.

4. A policy received in exchange for a MEC is also a MEC, even if the policy that is received would otherwise not be classified as a MEC.

MEC TAX TREATMENT

The tax treatment of certain amounts received from MECs prior to death—called distributions under the contract—is generally the same as the tax treatment afforded to annuity distributions. To the extent of gain in the policy, distributions are taxed on an income-first basis. In other words the first distributions out of the contract are not considered a tax free return of the policyowner's cost but rather the investment earnings on the contract. Those earnings are deemed to be withdrawn, and therefore become taxable, before the policyowner can recover his or her tax free basis. So, only after all income or gain in the policy has been received are additional amounts treated as nontaxable return of the policyowner's cost basis or investment in the contract.

In addition to the tax on distributions under the contract, a second tax is imposed in certain cases. This second tax is a 10 percent penalty tax. It is imposed on amounts received that are included in gross income.[2]

This 10 percent penalty tax does not apply to any distribution:

1. made on or after a taxpayer attains age 59½ years of age;

2. attributable to a taxpayer's becoming disabled; or

3. that is part of a series of substantially equal periodic payments made for the life (or life expectancy) of the taxpayer or for the joint lives (or life expectancies) of the taxpayer and beneficiary.[3]

Note that the exceptions to the 10 percent penalty tax focus on the taxpayer, rather than the insured. Where the taxpayer (generally the policyowner) is a non-natural person, such as a business or a nongrantor irrevocable trust, there may be no exceptions to the 10 percent penalty tax. This is due to the fact that a non-natural person doesn't have an age, can't become disabled, and doesn't have a life or life expectancy over which substantially equal periodic payments can be made. Thus, making a life insurance contract a MEC when the owner will be a non-natural person should be avoided if there is any possibility that distributions may need to be taken from the policy during the life of the insured. However, if the non-natural owner is tax-exempt, the 10 percent penalty is likely not an issue.

Generally, gain in the contract is determined by subtracting adjusted premiums paid from policy cash values. Adjusted premiums are total premiums paid (excluding premiums paid for supplementary benefits such as waiver of premium and accidental death benefit features) less any dividends received in cash or credited against premiums and less the nontaxable portion of any previous withdrawals. Cash value is computed without regard to surrender charges and so, for this purpose, is really the policy's reserve or account value. Therefore, gain may exist and result in taxation of a distribution even though a policyowner cannot actually access it. Also, in some cases a full surrender could yield less tax than a partial withdrawal.

Amounts received that are treated as income-first distributions under the contract include:[4]

- policy loans (to pay premiums as well as for all other purposes);

- loans secured by the contract;

- interest accrued on a policy loan;

- withdrawals;

- cash dividends; and

- dividends retained by the insurer as principal or interest on a policy loan.

Amounts received that are not treated as income-first distributions under the contract include:[5]

- dividends retained by the insurer to pay premiums or other consideration for the contract;

- dividends used to purchase paid-up additions, term insurance, or other qualified additional benefits; and

- surrender of paid-up additions to pay premiums. (However, it should be noted that the status of surrendering paid-up additions to pay premiums is uncertain. Most commentators feel they are not income-first distributions under the contract, but the issue has not yet been completely settled.)

Using a MEC contract as collateral is a tax trap that can also cause a taxable distribution of any gain in the contract to the extent of the collateral assignment. This is due to the fact that pledges or assignments of any portion of the contract are treated as distributions.[6] Situations where this tax trap can arise include using a MEC contract in a split dollar, loan, or premium financing arrangement. Note that the absence of gain in the contract at the time of the collateral assignment doesn't necessarily mean that there is no tax issue. Although there does not appear to be any IRS guidance, it is the authors' opinion that once gain begins to accrue in the contract, if the assignment is still in place, then such gain may become taxable each year until the assignment is removed.

MEC tax treatment applies to amounts received during the contract year in which a policy effectively becomes a MEC as well as to amounts received in any subsequent contract year. It also applies to any distributions in the two years before the policy fails the seven-pay test.[7]

Example. Kathy purchased a life insurance contract on January 1, 2015. As of January 1,

2017, her basis in the policy is $100,000. The contract has a cash value of $140,000. The policy is a MEC. She borrows $50,000 from the policy's cash value on her fiftieth birthday. Kathy's taxable gain from the loan is $40,000 ($140,000 cash value – $100,000 basis in the policy). If Kathy is in the 25 percent income tax bracket, she must pay income tax of $10,000 and a 10 percent penalty on the taxable amount ($4,000), leaving her with a total tax bill of $14,000 from the policy loan. Note that all amounts included in Kathy's gross income as a result of taking a loan from the policy will be added to her basis in the policy for purposes of determining future taxable amounts. Therefore Kathy's basis in the policy after taking the loan will be $140,000 ($100,000 original basis plus $40,000 taxable portion of loan). The $10,000 nontaxable portion does not affect Kathy's basis in the contract because the transaction is a loan and not a withdrawal.

MODIFIED ENDOWMENT CONTRACT DEFINED

A MEC is a life insurance contract that meets the requirements of Code section 7702 and:

1. was entered into on or after June 20, 1988, and fails to meet the seven-pay test; or

2. is received in exchange for a MEC.[8]

A policy that originally satisfies the seven-pay test in its first seven contract years may nonetheless become a MEC if it undergoes certain material changes, which are described below. Policies that undergo material changes are subjected to a new seven-pay test.

The Seven-Pay Test

The test for MEC status is called the seven-pay test. The seven-pay test must be applied in basically three situations:

1. To initially test policies entered into after June 20, 1988.

2. To retest policies entered into after June 20, 1988 if death benefits are reduced within the first seven contract years.

3. To test or retest *any* policy, even those entered into before June 21, 1988, when there is a material change in future benefits.

Policies Entered into after June 20, 1988

A contract fails to meet the seven-pay test if the accumulated amount paid under the contract at any time during the first seven contract years exceeds the sum of the net level premiums that would have been paid on or before such time if the contract provided for paid-up future benefits after the payment of seven level annual premiums.[9] Generally, amount paid is defined as the premiums paid under the contract reduced by any distributions but not including amounts includable in gross income. For purposes of this test, the death benefit for the first contract year is deemed to be provided until the maturity date without regard to any scheduled reduction after the first seven contract years. However, certain limited scheduled increases in death benefits may be taken into account.[10]

Example. If the annual net level premium for a $100,000 seven-pay policy is $4,500, then any $100,000 policy for the same insured on which aggregate premiums exceed $4,500 during the first year, $9,000 during the first two policy years, $13,500 during the first three policy years, $18,000 during the first four policy years, $22,500 during the first five policy years, $27,000 during the first six policy years, or $31,500 during the first seven years of the policy will be considered a modified endowment contract.

The seven-pay test does not require that a policy provide for seven level annual premiums to be paid over seven years. Rather, the test limits the cumulative amount that may be paid for each of the first seven years. Premiums may not be paid in advance in an amount that violates the annual premium limit. However, it is possible to make up for premiums paid in prior years that were less than the maximum amount permitted.

If the aggregate premiums paid during the first seven years are less than aggregate premiums that would have been paid on a level annual-premium basis using the net level premium amount ($4,500 a year in the example) for a seven-pay policy (for the same insured), the policy will not be a modified endowment contract and will receive the same tax treatment previously applicable to all policies.

Definition of Net Level Premium

The definition of a net level premium under these new rules is based on the guideline level premium concept under section 7702. The net level premium is not the same as the actual premium payable under the contract. It is also not the same as what many life insurance agents refer to as a net premium. "Net level premium" is a technical term of art that refers to an artificially constructed net level premium that is computed using mandated interest, mortality, and expense assumptions.[11] Therefore, it is possible that even policies that require seven level annual premiums will not pass the seven-pay test in some cases because the artificial net level premium (as calculated under the regulations) will be less than the actual premium. In other words, if the net level premium is less than the actual premium payable, the payment of the actual premium due will cause the policy to fail the seven-pay test.

Actuarial studies show that the seven-pay test is generally quite generous in the amount of permitted premiums. For nonsmoker universal life policies under option A, the net level premium limits under the seven-pay test are higher than the guideline annual premium limits under section 7702 at all ages and for either sex. Under option B, the crossover age where the seven-pay test limits are more restrictive than the section 7702 limits is in the mid-fifties for male nonsmokers and early fifties for male smokers. For females, it is in the mid-sixties for nonsmokers and slightly earlier for smokers.[12] All term insurance policies and virtually all guaranteed premium whole life policies without paid-up additions premium riders will meet the seven-pay test.

Riders to policies are considered part of the base insurance policy for purposes of the seven-pay test. Since the cost of such riders will be included in the calculation of the seven-pay test, a term rider may help a policy avoid classification as a MEC. Examples of such riders would be guaranteed insurability, family term, accidental death or disability, disability waiver, or other allowed benefits.

Contracts with Death Benefits under $10,000

There is a variation on the application of the net level premium amount in the seven-pay test that applies to policies under $10,000 in face amount. For such policies, $75 a year can be added to the seven-pay-test premium.[13] The $75 additional allowance permits some small seven-pay policies to pass the seven-pay test that otherwise might not. The smaller the policy is, the more likely it is that the actual premium will be less than the net level premium plus $75. The full $75 can be used for any amount of coverage between $1,000 and $10,000, resulting in a maximum allowable additional expense loading of $7.50 per $1,000 of coverage on a $10,000 policy.

Congress anticipated the added attractiveness of this small policy expense allowance and its potential abuses. Therefore the statute requires that all policies issued by the same insurer for the same policyowner be treated as one policy for purposes of determining that the face amount does not exceed $10,000.[14] This prevents policyowners from purchasing a large number of small policies to take advantage of the allowable expense loading. Note that the statute does not require that policies from different insurers be aggregated for this purpose. This may present a planning opportunity for taxpayers purchasing several small policies from different insurance companies.

Refund of Excess Premiums

If the insurer returns premiums paid in excess of the net level annual premium limit plus the interest on the excess premiums within a sixty-day grace period of the end of the contract year in which the excess occurs, the contract will not fail the seven-pay test. The returned amount will reduce the sum of premiums paid under the contract during such contract year for purposes of the seven-pay test. Interest paid will be includable in the gross income of the recipient.[15]

BENEFIT REDUCTIONS WITHIN THE FIRST SEVEN CONTRACT YEARS

For Single Insured

For contracts insuring a single insured, if death benefits are reduced within the seven-year testing period, there is a look-back requirement. The seven-pay test must be reapplied as if the contract originally had been issued for the reduced benefit amount.[16]

Example. Assume the guideline annual premium is $10,000 based on the original death benefit. The policyowner pays $9,000 each year for the first six years. In year seven, the policyowner withdraws $36,000, with a corresponding decrease in the death benefit. The recomputed guideline premium is $8,000. The policy now fails the seven-pay test and is a MEC since cumulative premiums paid in just the first year, $9,000, (and through year six as well) exceed the sum of the recomputed guideline annual premiums of $8,000. The $36,000 withdrawal will be subject to tax to the extent of gain in the policy. If the policyowner is under age 59½, a 10 percent penalty will also be imposed on the taxable portion of the distribution.

The seven-year rule for benefit reductions for contracts insuring a single insured appears to apply only during the first seven contract years unless there is a material change. Therefore, absent a material change, a benefit reduction after the first seven years has no effect. A benefit reduction itself is not a material change. However, a material change may restart the seven-year look-back period for benefit reductions because a material change is treated like a new policy issuance. Apparently, benefit reductions within the first seven years after a material change will require a recomputation of the seven-pay test back to the date of the material change rather than the policy's original issue date, even if the periods overlap.

For Joint Life or Second-To-Die Contracts

A death benefit reduction at any time, not just during the first seven contract years, for a joint life, survivorship life, or second-to-die contract results in section 7702A retesting.[17] The seven-pay test must be reapplied as if the second-to-die contract originally had been issued for the reduced death benefit amount.

Distributions Affected

If a policy fails the seven-pay test as a result of the look-back rule, certain distributions are treated as potentially taxable distributions from a MEC. These distributions include all future distributions, distributions in the contract year the policy is treated as failing the seven-pay test, and prior distributions taken in anticipation of failure of the test. The statute authorizes the IRS to promulgate regulations defining what distributions are taken in anticipation of failure of the test, but

it specifically states that any distribution made within two years before the failure will be treated as made in anticipation of such failure.[18]

Reductions of Benefits Attributable to Nonpayment of Premiums

Any benefit reductions attributable to the nonpayment of premiums due are not taken into account if the benefits are reinstated within ninety days after being reduced.[19] This rule applies to a nonforfeiture option of reduced paid-up insurance within the first seven contract years. In other words, if a policy that is put on reduced paid-up status fails the seven-pay test as a result of the look-back rule, the failure may be reversed if the policy is reinstated to its original death benefit within ninety days. Alternatively, failure of the test could probably be avoided by electing the extended term option rather than the reduced paid-up option. The policy could also be surrendered without adverse consequences since the complete surrender of a life insurance policy during the policy's first seven years is generally not considered to cause the policy to be treated as a MEC.

MATERIAL CHANGE RULES

Policies entered into prior to June 21, 1988, and policies entered into on or after that date with low enough premiums to avoid being classified as MECs are generally treated the same as life insurance policies have been treated in the past. This means there will generally be no income tax applicable to withdrawals until the policyowner's cost basis has been recovered (tax free). This is the cost-recovery rule or First-In-First-Out (FIFO) treatment long associated with life insurance policy taxation.[20] Distributions or withdrawals that are subject to tax are not subject to the additional 10 percent penalty unless the policy is reclassified as a MEC.

However, a grandfathered policy or a policy that originally passed the seven-pay test when it was issued can become a MEC if there is a material change in the policy. A material change, in itself, does not cause a policy to become a MEC. A material change only subjects the policy to the seven-pay test. It is reclassified as a MEC only if it fails the test. For example, a single-premium life insurance policy acquired before June 21, 1988 is not a MEC. However, if there is a material change in the policy, it is subjected to the seven-pay test, which it would probably fail. It would then be a MEC.

Similarly, an elective increase in the death benefit (requiring evidence of insurability) of a universal life policy that was acquired before June 21, 1988 would also subject the policy to testing. However, depending on the timing and level of premium payments and the cash value in the policy, the policy after the change, in many cases, would pass the test. The policy would continue to be treated under the normal rules for life insurance contracts.

Changes That Are Not Material

What constitutes a material change under the law? What is not a material change is somewhat clearer than what is a material change, so the changes that are specifically excluded from consideration as material changes are addressed first. The statute provides the following specific exceptions to the material change rules:[21]

1. cost-of-living increases in death benefits based on a broad-based index (such as the consumer price index) if the increase is funded ratably over the remaining life of the contract;

2. increases in death benefits due to the premiums paid for the policy to support the first seven contract years' level of benefits; and

3. death benefit increases inherent in the policy design due to the crediting of interest or other earnings.

Exception (1) would be met by the standard cost-of-living rider where there is a level step-up of future annual premium charges for cost-of-living increases in death benefits. Exception (2) appears to exempt any increase in death benefits necessary to keep the required relationship between the death benefit and the policy guideline cash value or guideline premiums as specified in section 7702 from being classified as a material change. Exception (3) appears to exempt the increasing death benefits of an option II universal life policy or a variable life policy from being classified as a material change.

Also, certain changes will not be treated as material which, by inference, adds the following exceptions to the material change rules:[22]

1. increases in death benefits, without limit, on policies which, as of June 21, 1988, required at least seven level annual premium payments

and under which the policyowner continues to make at least seven level annual premium payments; and

2. increases in death benefits (or the purchase of an additional qualified benefit after June 21, 1988) if the policyowner had a unilateral right under the contract to obtain such increase or addition without evidence of insurability.

The first exception means that level premium whole life policies entered into before June 21, 1988, are permanently grandfathered from the material change rules as related to increases in death benefits (but other material changes, such as an exchange, would make them subject to seven-pay testing). Universal life or other flexible-premium policies are, presumably, not included since they do not require the payment of level premiums. The second exception appears to be a grace amount or safe harbor for death benefit increases that the policyowner had a contractual right to obtain without evidence of insurability such as might be provided by guaranteed insurability riders.

Material Change Defined

The statute says "the term 'material change' includes any increase in the death benefit under the contract or any increase in, or addition of, a qualified additional benefit under the contract."[23]

Material Increases in Death Benefits

Any increase in death benefits under a policy (excluding the exceptions mentioned above) will be treated as a material change if:

1. before June 21, 1988, the policyowner did not have a unilateral right under the contract to obtain such increase or addition without providing evidence of insurability;[24] or

2. the policyowner has a unilateral right under the contract to obtain increases or additions without evidence of insurability but such increases exceed the death benefit under the contract in effect on October 20, 1988, by more than $150,000.[25]

Basically, any increases in benefits that require evidence of insurability and even contractually-guaranteed increases that do not require evidence but that cumulatively exceed the amount in (2) will be treated as material changes. Shifting a universal life policy from death benefit option I to option II would be a material change since the election usually requires evidence of insurability.

On the other hand, increases without evidence of insurability may not be considered material. Examples of such could be safe contractual rights include increases pursuant to guaranteed insurability riders, guarantee issue offers, scheduled option II face amount increases, and section 7702 cash value corridor increases. Death benefit increases for grandfathered policies due to premium payments, reserve earnings, cash value corridor, and/or regular option II increases should not cause loss of grandfathering, even if over $150,000, because they are covered by the necessary premium exception to the material change rules.

Other Material Changes

The following other types of changes are also considered material:

1. term life insurance conversions to permanent forms of coverage;[26] and

2. exchanges of one policy for another, whether or not tax free under Code section 1035.[27]

It is uncertain whether changes in contract mortality charges or interest rate guarantees are material changes.

Seven-Pay Test as Applied to Material Changes

A material change in a contract's benefits (or other terms) that was not reflected in any previous determination under the seven-pay test requires seven-pay testing. Apparently, a material change may take place anytime during the policy's existence. When a material change occurs, the contract is treated as if it were a new contract entered into on the date when the change takes effect. The seven-pay test, as described above, is applied as of the date of the material change, not the issue date of the policy. In addition, the seven-pay test is adjusted by a rollover rule that takes account of the contract's existing cash surrender value at the date of change.[28]

The procedure is as follows:

1. Determine the seven-pay premium (based on the insured's then attained age) for each of the next seven contract years after the material change.

2. Multiply (a) the cash surrender value as of the date of the material change (determined without regard to any increase in the cash surrender value that is attributable to the amount of premium that is not necessary) by (b) a specified fraction. The fraction is the ratio of:

   i. the seven-pay premium for the future benefits under the contract after the change to;

   ii. the net single premium for such benefits computed using the same assumptions used in determining the seven-pay premium.

3. Subtract the product of the multiplication in step (2) from the amount determined in step (1).

The remainder is the adjusted seven-pay premium used to test actual premiums paid in each of the next seven contract years.

The adjusted seven-pay premium so determined could be negative if the cash value is large enough. This should not automatically make the contract a MEC. However, payment of additional premiums in the next seven years might make the policy a MEC.

CHAPTER ENDNOTES

1. The Technical and Miscellaneous Revenue Act of 1988 (TAMRA '88), P. L. 100-647. TAMRA '88 §5011 amended I.R.C. §7702. TAMRA '88 Section 5012(c) created. I.R.C. §7702A which defines a modified endowment contract.

2. I.R.C. §72(v).

3. I.R.C. §72(v).

4. I.R.C. §72(e); H.R. Conference Rep. No. 100-1104, (TAMRA '88) *reprinted in* 1988-3 CB 592. There is an exception under I.R.C. §72(e)(10)(B) for loans made solely to cover burial expenses if the policy's maximum death benefit does not exceed $25,000.

5. H.R. Conference Rep. No. 100-1104, (TAMRA '88) *reprinted in* 1988-3 CB 592.

6. I.R.C. §72(e)(10)(A)(i), which references and incorporates the rule applicable to pledges or assignments of annuities in I.R.C. Section 72(e)(4)(A)(ii).

7. I.R.C. §7702A(d).

8. I.R.C. §7702A.

9. I.R.C. §7702A(b).

10. I.R.C. §7702A(c)(1)(B) with reference to I.R.C. §7702(e)(2)(A) allows that "… an increase in the death benefit which is provided in the contract may be taken into account but only to the extent necessary to prevent a decrease in the excess of the death benefit over the cash surrender value of the contract". This provision is essentially provided to accommodate option II of universal life policies where the death benefit is the cash value plus a level pure insurance amount.

11. I.R.C. §7702A(c)(1)(B).

12. *Estate & Business Planning Technical Release*, Report No. 23, November 1988, State Mutual Companies, 440 Lincoln Street, Worcester, Massachusetts 01605.

13. I.R.C. §7702A(c)(4).

14. I.R.C. §7702A(c)(4).

15. I.R.C. §7702A(e)(1). The rate of interest is an open issue. The consensus is that the interest rate should be that which was credited to premiums while in the policy. Administrative expenses and losses, such as commissions that are not recoverable, should be able to be factored into the ultimate interest amount paid. The net refund would then equal the excess premium plus the inside buildup thereon less the cost of the refund.

16. I.R.C. §7702A(c)(2)(A).

17. I.R.C. §7702A(c)(6).

18. I.R.C. §7702A(d).

19. I.R.C. §7702A(c)(2)(B).

20. It is important to remember that withdrawals from policies associated with a reduction in policy benefits during the first fifteen policy years are currently subject to a limited income-first or LIFO-type federal income taxation. The MEC rules have been imposed *in addition to* the existing rules that were imposed by the Tax Reform Act of 1986. However, the 1986 rules do not apply to policy loans. The MEC rules *do* apply to loans as well as to withdrawals. Therefore a policy withdrawal can result in income tax liability even if the policy is not a MEC. However, the 10 percent penalty tax does not apply unless the policy is a MEC.

21. I.R.C. §§7702A(c)(3)(B)(i), 7702A(c)(3)(B)(ii).

22. TAMRA '88, P.L. 100-647, §5012(e).

23. I.R.C. §7702A(c)(3)(B).

24. TAMRA '88, P.L. 100-647, §5012(e)(3).

25. TAMRA '88, P.L. 100-647, §5012(e)(2).

26. TAMRA '88, P.L. 100-647, §5012(e)(3).

27. H.R. Conf. Rep. No. 100-1104, (TAMRA '88) *reprinted in* 1988-3 CB 596; Priv. Ltr. Rul. 9044022.

28. I.R.C. §§7702A(c)(3)(A)(i), 7702A(c)(3)(A)(ii).

SECTION 1035 EXCHANGES

CHAPTER 23

INTRODUCTION

Insurance programs must be flexible enough to change as an insured's financial status, family responsibilities, and business needs change. Furthermore, as new types of policies are developed, ethical agents will seek, when appropriate, to match the product to the problem. If a new product solves the problem in a more cost effective manner than the old product, a client should be apprised of the opportunity and should be given the chance to exchange the old policy for the new. This is particularly important if the insurer that sold the existing contract is financially unstable. Federal income tax law facilitates certain exchanges by providing that in some instances they may be made without the immediate recognition of gain. Although such transactions are sometimes referred to as section 1035 tax-free exchanges the gain at the time of the transaction is deferred rather than forgiven.

Factors indicating that a Code section 1035 exchange should be considered include the following:

1. A client feels that a higher rate of return can be realized with a new policy.

2. A client is concerned that the present insurer may become insolvent or that its investment experience will not warrant the dividends projected and that a more stable insurer can be obtained through a policy exchange or that diversification of insurance carriers will increase safety or return.

3. The client's current policy is subject to a substantial loan, the interest paid on the policy is nondeductible, costs are increasing, and the client needs to continue coverage.

4. The client would like to change from an individual to a group product.[1]

5. The death benefit under a new product will exceed the death benefit under the old product.[2]

6. The client would like to change an ordinary life policy into a single premium policy to eliminate the premium paying burden, obtain a higher rate of return on the underlying cash values, and obtain a higher death benefit.

7. A newly-developed type of policy (perhaps one with a more flexible premium structure or with a more adjustable death benefit) is more suitable to the client's needs, circumstances, or investment philosophy than the policy presently owned. For instance, a client may want to exchange an ordinary life contract for a universal, variable, or interest sensitive policy.[3]

8. Premium rates on the new policy are lower due to such factors as improved mortality tables, a nonsmoking discount, a volume discount for several policies aggregated into one,[4] or other factors.[5]

BASIC INCOME TAX IMPLICATIONS OF AN EXCHANGE

The Internal Revenue Code provides generally that all income, from whatever source derived, is reportable by the recipient.[6] So if an existing life insurance policy or annuity is surrendered, the gain, i.e., the excess of the amount received over the policyowner's basis, is taxable at ordinary rates.[7] Gain can therefore be thought of generally as the excess of amounts distributed under the policy over the amounts paid in. For example, assume a client surrenders a policy after paying $100,000 in premiums. If the client receives $130,000, the $30,000 excess over basis would be considered an ordinary income gain and would be immediately reportable. This same result (absent a proper exchange under Code section 1035) will occur even if the client immediately uses the proceeds to purchase a new insurance policy that is far more appropriate for his needs, purposes, and for the satisfaction of his goals than the old policy.

But mere appreciation in property does not result in taxation. There must be a disposition of the property, typically a sale or exchange, before that gain becomes taxable. Sometimes, when there is ostensibly a disposition but in reality the taxpayer has merely changed the form of investment without in fact "closing the books on the original purchase," the Internal Revenue Code will acknowledge that the gain, even though technically realized, should not have to be recognized (i.e., reported as taxable).

Section 1035 of the Internal Revenue Code is such a provision. It allows the tax that would otherwise be imposed on a lump sum disposition of certain life insurance policies and annuities to be postponed. Specifically, the law provides that no gain (or loss) is recognized on the exchange of:

1. a life insurance contract for another life insurance contract[8] (one that the face amount or death benefit is not ordinarily payable in full during the insured's life);[9]

2. a life insurance contract for an endowment contract (one that depends in part on the life expectancy of the insured but which may be payable in full in a single payment during the insured's lifetime);[10]

3. an ordinary life insurance contract for an annuity (one payable during the life of the annuitant only in installments);[11]

4. an endowment contract for another endowment contract that provides for regular payments beginning at a date not later than the date payments would have begun under the contract exchanged;[12]

5. an endowment contract for an annuity contract; or[13]

6. an annuity contract for an annuity contract.[14]

Although the above implies that only a single annuity can be exchanged for another single annuity, the IRS has provided guidance indicating that a single annuity can be exchanged for two annuities (i.e., a split 1035 exchange), regardless of whether the issuing insurance companies are the same.[15] In addition, it has been held that transferring a portion of an existing annuity into a new annuity constitutes a valid 1035 exchange.[16] Although no such guidance exists for split 1035 exchanges of life insurance policies, some carriers have extrapolated the annuity guidance and will permit such exchanges.

For exchanges that occur after 2009, a life insurance contract can be exchanged for a qualified long-term care insurance contract, an endowment contract can be exchanged for a qualified long-term care insurance contract, an annuity contract can be exchanged for a qualified long-term care insurance contract, and a qualified long-term care insurance contract can be exchanged for another qualified long-term care insurance contract.[17] Also, an annuity or life insurance contract without a long-term care rider can be exchanged for an annuity or life insurance contract with such a rider.[18] There is, of course, a cost for the privilege of postponing the reporting of the gain. When any of the above tax-deferred exchanges occur, the new contract received takes the basis of the policy exchanged for it. The new policy's basis will be the cost basis of the old policy plus any premiums paid after the exchange minus any excludable dividends received after the exchange. In other words, as noted above, the tax on the gain is delayed rather than forgiven. For this reason, section 1035 exchanges are referred to in this chapter as tax-deferred rather than tax-free.

Although losses are not deductible, it is possible that Code section 1035 can be used to the client's advantage when a policy is in a loss position.

Example. X has paid $10,000 a year for ten years into a whole life contract and therefore has a $100,000 basis. Assume the policy cash value at that time is only $80,000. He exchanges the old policy for a new policy.

Because of the carryover of basis rules, X's entire $100,000 basis carries over into the new policy he receives in a section 1035 exchange. So if he later begins to draw money out of the new contract, the first $100,000 he draws out is considered income tax free return of cost. Had X surrendered his contract and then purchased a new contract with the $80,000, his new basis would be only $80,000 rather than $100,000, a $20,000 difference in tax free recoveries.

Can this concept be carried further by combining a term conversion with a section 1035 exchange? For instance, assume Y had paid $10,000 a year for term insurance for ten years and at the end of that time the policy had no cash value. He decides to convert the term to whole life. Simultaneous with a conversion of the term to whole life insurance, the insured requested a section 1035 exchange of the whole life to a "new" contract.

There would be no gain, of course, nor a deductible loss. But would the section 1035 carryover of basis requirement mean the $100,000 of premiums he had paid for term insurance could be added to whatever additional amount he paid to convert the term to whole life? If so, he significantly boosts the amount that can later be withdrawn during lifetime as an income tax free recovery of basis. If this simultaneous conversion/exchange technique works, a client can recover in tax savings a great deal of the otherwise wasted outlay for term insurance. The answer is uncertain at this point.

Partially Tax-Deferred Exchanges

Tax law does not cause a section 1035 exchange to crash merely because the client receives cash or some other property to boot which is not of like-kind in addition to the new policy or annuity. But if cash or any in kind payment of value such as a life insurance contract in return for an annuity is received as part of the exchange, gain must be currently recognized to the extent of such boot (i.e., cash or in kind property.[19]) Cash includes repayment of any outstanding loans at surrender. In other words, if a taxpayer sells or exchanges property subject to a debt, relief from that debt is treated in the same manner as if cash were received by the seller.

Where the transaction is largely tax-deferred but involves some boot such as cash, additional property, or the extinction of debt, gain is equal to the amount realized by the client less the client's basis.

Where boot (other than cash or the payoff of debt) is received, the client's basis must be split proportionately

between the tax-deferred contract received in the exchange and the taxable in kind boot (i.e., the taxable asset).[20] For instance, if the client exchanges one annuity with a basis of $10,000 for another annuity worth $10,000 but to boot receives a small life insurance contract worth $2,000 from the new insurer, the value of the life insurance policy would be currently taxable. The client's $10,000 basis for both the annuity and the new policy would be apportioned according to their value ($10,000/$12,000 of the $10,000 basis going to the new annuity and $2,000/$12,000 of the $10,000 basis going to the life insurance policy). To the extent the life insurance policy is taxable, that amount should be added to its basis.

Taxable Exchanges

The policy behind Code section 1035 is not to allow a tax-free exchange but rather to defer the tax on any gain. Therefore, Code section 1035 will not apply if the exchange: (a) increases the possibility of eliminating the tax by extending the period of life insurance protection; or (b) by providing life insurance protection where none previously existed.[21] For this reason, in the opinion of the authors, a section 1035 exchange of term insurance for whole life will be viewed by the IRS as an attempt to do just that—extend the period of life insurance protection. Although nothing in the Code or regulations specifically denies the taxpayer the right to make such an exchange under Code section 1035, it is likely the IRS will make this claim anyway.

Any gain inherent in a contract must be reported by the client in any transaction that does not fully meet Code section 1035 rules. Therefore, if an endowment or annuity contract is exchanged for a life contract, any gain will be currently reportable. This is because if either an endowment or annuity contract matures, the proceeds would be taxable. If a contract owner could exchange either policy for one that provides income tax free death benefits by holding on to the policy until death, the owner could avoid tax on the gain forever.

For this same reason, an endowment contract may not be exchanged tax free for a life insurance contract. While an endowment contract will pay tax-exempt death benefits only if the insured dies before the endowment maturity, a life insurance policy (unless it is surrendered) will assuredly pay tax-exempt death benefits. Any gain on this type of exchange is fully taxable since to allow a deferral would defeat the intent of the law.[22] Similarly, an exchange of an endowment policy is not protected under Code section 1035 for another endowment policy with a later maturity date since the extended date increases the chances of the insured's dying prior to maturity and the proceeds being paid income tax free.

How much is taxable if the exchange does not meet Code section 1035 requirements? The gain is the value of the new policy plus the cash (or in kind property), if any, received minus the net premium cost of the old policy (gross premiums less excludable dividends).

The value of the new policy depends on its premium paying status. If the policy is a single premium or a paid-up policy, it is valued at its replacement cost, the single premium a person of the same sex and age as the insured would pay for a similar policy from the same company.[23] The value of a premium paying policy is the policy's interpolated terminal reserve plus any unearned premium.[24]

Issues under Code Sections 7702 and 7702A

Life insurance contracts that are considered Modified Endowment Contracts (MEC) receive less favorable income tax treatment than those that are not so classified.

First, any lifetime distribution from a MEC is includable in the income of the recipient to the extent of the built-in gain in the contract at the time the distribution occurs. Distribution is defined broadly to include all loans and partial surrenders and even dividends. Only dividends retained by the insurer to pay premiums or purchase paid-up additions are excluded from the definition of distributions. Second, a 10 percent penalty tax is imposed on the amount of a distribution, unless the distribution is due to the death or disability of the policyowner or is made after the policyowner is 59½ or is paid over the life expectancy of the taxpayer or the joint life expectancies of the taxpayer and the beneficiary. (See Chapter 22 for more on MECs.)

Therefore, MECs are more expensive contracts from a tax standpoint and should be avoided if possible.[25] So to the extent possible, planners should not taint a non-MEC contract through a policy exchange.

What is the tax implication if a MEC is exchanged for a new contract? If a contract is issued in exchange for a MEC, the new contract is also considered a MEC. The

exchange does not change the policy's characterization or remove the taint.[26]

What are the implications of exchanging a non-MEC policy for a new contract? Since policies issued prior to June 21, 1988, are not subject to the MEC seven-pay test, if such a protected policy is exchanged for a new policy the question is whether the new policy loses its grandfathered status? The answer seems to be yes. For purposes of the seven-pay test, the IRS appears to have taken the position that a life insurance contract received in a section 1035 exchange in which the old policy was issued prior to June 21, 1988, should be treated as if it were a new contract issued on the date of the exchange. This means the new policy would be fully subject to the seven-pay test. Grandfathering would be lost.[27] However, the exchanged policy generally should not be a MEC if no new premiums are paid. New premiums may cause the new policy to fail the seven-pay test.

MECHANICS OF THE EXCHANGE

If a client were to sell property to one person and use the proceeds from the sale to purchase new property from a second party, the first transaction would be considered a sale rather than an exchange. The IRS will follow this same reasoning even if the client intended from the beginning to use the proceeds from the first transaction to purchase the second asset. How does this reasoning apply when the asset is a life insurance policy?

Take, for example, Gary who owns a life insurance policy on his life with a current cash value of $90,000. He has paid a total of $60,000 in premiums but has received back a total of $20,000 in dividends. If he were to surrender the policy, his realized gain would be $50,000 calculated as follows. He receives $90,000. His basis is $40,000 ($60,000 paid in less $20,000 recovered income tax free). So his realized gain is $50,000, the $90,000 received less the $40,000 basis. But if he had exchanged this policy for a new one under Code section 1035, no tax would be payable in the current year. His basis would be the same $40,000 as the basis he had in the original policy increased by any premiums he pays subsequent to the exchange.

For this reason, when a client owns a policy issued by one company, rather than cash it in and use the proceeds to purchase another company's product, the client should, if possible, assign his present contract to the new insurer in return for the new contract.

At times, planners are tempted to avoid this classic approach and use what seem to be less complicated and time consuming methods. In most of these, the policyholder first cashes in the old contract, obtains the policy surrender value and then either pays it over to the new insurer or directs the insurer of the old policy to pay the proceeds directly to the new insurer. Under either approach, the old policy is never transferred to the new insurer. Will the IRS be kind to this type of transfer and call it an exchange or will it insist the transaction is first a sale followed by a purchase of a new contract? Some authorities say no.[28]

There is an exception to this approach for Tax Deferred Annuities (TDA). A significant difference between TDAs and other types of policies is that the Internal Revenue Code itself requires a tax deferred annuity to be nontransferable. Thus, an employee is barred from assigning such a contract in exchange for one more financially advantageous or otherwise more appropriate for the employee's needs and is, in effect, locked in. The IRS has provided that the holder of a TDA may make a direct transfer of the funds in the annuity between two insurers if the transferred funds continue to be subject to distribution requirements at least as strict as those that applied under the old contract.[29]

Although each company may have its own procedure, in general the mechanics are as follows:

1. An absolute assignment and exchange agreement form should be signed by the client transferring all rights to the old policy to the insurer that will issue the new policy. The legal name of the insurer should be used. The client's social security number or taxpayer ID number should accompany or be included in these forms.

2. An unsigned copy of the old company's surrender form (to be signed by an officer of the company that will surrender the old policy and issue the new policy) should accompany the assignment of the policyowner's interest.

3. The original policy is attached to the above forms.

4. A new policy is issued before the company issuing the new policy surrenders the old policy. This procedure ensures that the insured is covered by at least one policy during the transaction. If the old policy was surrendered before the new one was issued, and the insured died during the exchange process, there would be no coverage.

5. If the requested exchange is not a valid life to life, endowment, or annuity exchange or if the issuance of the new policy is declined (or issued "rated" or issued at a premium or under terms other than as applied for), the insured should be notified immediately by the insurer.

6. If the new policy is issued, the old policy is then surrendered. The insured should then receive a letter from the insurer stating the section 1035 cost basis of the new policy and the amount of any boot reportable as income.

Form 1099R (Total Distributions From Profit-Sharing, Retirement Plans, Individual Retirement Arrangements, Insurance Contracts, etc.) is sent by the insurer to the IRS showing basis and distribution as well as the taxable amount for each policy surrendered by the insurer in a section 1035 exchange. If a policy surrendered as part of a section 1035 exchange had no loan at the time of surrender, no entry will be made in the taxable income box.

Planners should be aware of the pros and cons of the inside versus the outside procedure in the exchange of policies. The major advantage of the inside approach is safety and reliability of tax result. Although there appears to be nothing in the Internal Revenue Code or regulations as to how a section 1035 exchange must be structured, the IRS appears to be comfortable with this procedure. The disadvantage is that the insurer who issued the old contract may take an undue amount of time to process the new company's request for surrender proceeds. Both normal time delay and a healthy resistance to a loss of business and an attempt to buy time to conserve the business may result in an inordinate amount of aggravation and uncertainty.

The outside procedure involves a surrender of the old contract by the client. The cash proceeds are used immediately to purchase a new contract from the new insurer. The advantage of the outside approach is that it is faster and simpler than the inside technique. But it is almost certain to result in a claim by the IRS that the policyholder had actual or constructive receipt of the proceeds and should therefore be taxed on the gain.

Exchanges Involving Loans

As mentioned above, if all the policyowner receives is the new policy, generally no gain will be realized if all the Code section 1035 requirements are met. But even if all the Code section 1035 requirements are met, if the policyowner receives the new policy and cash to boot, the cash will be taxable to the extent of any gain.[30] So where any of the surrender proceeds from the old policy are paid in cash to the policyholder, that amount will be taxable to the extent of gain.

Extinction of indebtedness is boot. Surrender proceeds include payment of any outstanding loans on the old policy at surrender. That is, if a loan on the old contract is paid off pursuant to the exchange, the retirement or assumption of that liability is treated as boot.[31] Why? It would be very easy to avoid tax on a life insurance policy surrender if there were no such rule.

Example. Z had paid $80,000 in premiums for a life insurance policy on his life. The policy cash values total $100,000 so the policy has a built-in gain of $20,000. Were there no boot rule applying on the extinction of debt, Z could first borrow $99,000 and then make a tax deferred section 1035 exchange, and when the old policy was surrendered by the new insurer and the net equity of $1,000 paid to Z, only $1,000 (the cash boot received by Z) would be taxable.

Because extinction of indebtedness is boot, if there is a policy loan on the old policy, the exchange agreement should provide that the loan (including any accrued loan interest) is outstanding and that the new carrier will assume the liability on the loan and the new policy will serve as security for that loan. In other words, to the extent the old debt is not carried over to the new policy, the policyowner will be subjected to current income tax. On the other hand, to the extent the property received in the exchange is substantially a continuation of the old investment, no income is recognized. So when there is indebtedness against the old policy, if possible, it should be exchanged for a new policy subject to the same amount of debt. The transaction will not result in a current tax.[32]

This favorable result will apply even if one policy is exchanged for another subject to the same indebtedness and the client was planning to make withdrawals or partial surrenders from the policy to reduce the debt.[33] It should be noted that taking withdrawals or partial surrenders to reduce a policy loan in close proximity (before or after) to the exchange may be considered a step transaction (the withdrawal and exchange are treated as a single event), resulting in the loan extinguishment being treated as boot.[34] Thus, it is generally wise to avoid using withdrawals or surrenders to repay a policy within a year of the exchange. An alternative is for the client to use other cash assets or borrow money from a bank or from other life insurance policies to pay off the debt. That way, there will be no loan outstanding and the problem is eliminated. The payment increases the cash values of the new policy so that after the exchange, the client can borrow the same amount out.

What about exchanges of minimum deposit plans? What pitfalls apply here? Since an income tax deduction for consumer loan interest is no longer available, nonbusiness policyholders who have systematically minimum deposited (taken out maximum loans to pay premiums) and maintained a low after-tax outlay through deductible interest payments can no longer deduct interest outlays. To many, this disallowance of the interest deduction made the cost of continuing the policy (depending on the size of the outstanding loan) prohibitive. Of course, the client could continue to borrow more money from the policy but eventually substantial payments would be required to keep the policy in force. If the policy lapses, the lapse may be considered a taxable event.

Some companies have created policy loan rollovers, cash value riders that facilitate a section 1035 exchange as an alternative to a continuation of borrowing, a lapse of the old policy, or the surrender of the old policy followed by a purchase of a new policy. In essence, the existing loan is rolled into the new policy. It appears that a loan transferred from the old policy to the new policy does not amount to a taxable distribution (boot). The client's basis in the old policy is carried over intact into the new policy and there is no taxable boot (because the loan is not canceled).[35]

How should exchanges of trade or business-owned insurance be handled? A trade or business can take an income tax deduction for interest incurred on a life insurance policy loan. With respect to policies purchased on or before June 21, 1986, there is no limitation as to the amount of the deduction. That liberal rule no longer applies to policies purchased after June 20, 1986; interest deductions are either denied or severely limited.[36] (See the discussion in Chapter 24 under Policy Loan Interest.)

A grandfathering provision continues the unlimited deduction for interest payable on a life insurance policy loan incurred by a trade or business for policies issued before this date. The question is, will the grandfathering be lost if the policy is now exchanged? The answer is both yes and no. The new policy will probably be treated as just that, a new policy, if it is issued by a new insurer. However, if the new policy received in exchange is issued by the original insurer, the grandfathering protection may continue.

Exchanges Involving Qualified Pension or Profit Sharing Plans

If a qualified pension or profit sharing plan owned a life insurance policy and exchanged it for one of the permissible types, it could qualify under Code section 1035 for a tax-deferred exchange. But as a tax exempt entity,[37] it does not need to qualify under the Code section 1035 safe harbor.

However, another and much more serious problem is possible with respect to a seemingly innocuous exchange. Specifically, if a qualified plan exchanges a whole life policy for a universal life product, it might violate the rule requiring that a qualified plan must exist primarily to provide retirement benefits to participants and that life insurance, while permissible, must be incidental.[38] The problem is that if certain percentages are exceeded (49.9 percent of total aggregate contributions to the plan for ordinary life and 25 percent for all other than ordinary life), the plan may be disqualified.

Some industry experts believe that universal life products should be considered other than ordinary life products. This is a dangerous situation since, as mentioned above, what appears to be a routine exchange could result in a disqualification of the entire plan.

FATAL FLAW CHECKLIST

The following is a checklist of the major tax traps incurred in section 1035 exchanges:

1. *Failure to meet same insured requirement* – The tax deferred nature of a section 1035 exchange presumes that both the old and the new contract are on the life of the same insured.[39] In the case of an exchange of annuity contracts, the contracts exchanged must be payable to the same person or persons.[40]

    A taxable event will occur if the policies are on the lives of different insureds. For instance, a wife cannot exchange a policy on her life for a similar policy on the life of her husband. It is permissible, however, for the exchange to involve the policies of two different insurance companies. (There is no rule that requires the insurer of the new contract received in the exchange to be the same as the insurer of the old contract.)

    A Change of Insureds Provision (also called Substitution of Insureds Option or Business Exchange Rider) allows a business to purchase a policy on one individual (typically a key employee or shareholder) but if that person leaves the firm, the firm has the option to substitute another key employee as the insured under the policy. The provision is advantageous because it does not require the policyowner business to incur new costs but the insurer does usually require medical evidence of the new person's insurability.

    But the exercise of a change of insured option is a taxable event because it does not meet the same insured requirement.[41] Instead, when a new individual becomes insured under the old policy, a taxable event has occurred because the IRS treats the transaction as a surrender of the old contract. It's as if the policy on the terminating executive had been canceled.

    The employer is liable for the difference between the policy's cash surrender value and the amount of premium the employer paid. Such riders will continue to be highly useful despite this unfavorable taxation since it takes the form of an option that can be used only when it is deemed appropriate by the client's advisers and the tax costs are minimal.

    It is the opinion of the authors that the same insured logic would prevent a tax deferral when a single life is exchanged in return for a joint life contract or vice versa. The essence of a life insurance contract is the life that is insured under it. Therefore, when a contract goes from one life to two or two lives to one, the same insured test could not be met.

    It is permissible, however, to exchange two contracts for one—as long as they are all on the same life. For example, suppose an individual wants to exchange a nonparticipating flexible premium life insurance policy with an adjustable death benefit, issued by company A, and a similar contract issued by company B solely for a nonparticipating flexible premium variable deferred annuity contract issued by company C. The IRS has held that Code section 1035 allows for situations other than only a one for one exchange. The IRS pointed out in a private letter ruling that Code section 1031 (which deals with real estate exchanges) allows exchanges of more than one property for one property and also that, unless the specific words or context indicates to the contrary, words stated in the singular can be construed in the plural.[42]

2. *Poor timing* – Another fatal flaw is where there has been something other than an exchange of insurance contracts. The discussion above regarding the mechanics of the exchange implies that a major key to success is the timing and manner in which the transaction occurs; "neatness counts" in avoiding litigation. It is preferable (if not essential) that the existing contract be assigned to the insurer that will issue the new contract in exchange. This evidences that the transaction was in kind rather than in cash. Unfortunately, it is not always easy to discern between an exchange and a surrender and purchase.

If the IRS takes an extremely conservative (harsh) view, it would hold that Code section 1035(a) would not apply if a new life insurance policy has been issued prior to the surrender of the old policy.[43] But as a practical matter, it would be foolish to surrender an in-force policy before obtaining new coverage. To blindly require the surrender of the old before the issuance of the new policy is a form over substance mentality that would seem to defeat the Congressional purpose of Code section 1035: to allow a taxpayer to defer the reporting of income if he has merely substituted one policy for another without truly reducing the built-in gain in the policy to his possession. Perhaps the key to success is to keep the interval between the issuance of the new policy and the surrender of the old policy as short as is mechanically feasible.

3. *Failure to give up the old policy in exchange for the new contract* – For there to be an exchange, the old policy must be relinquished by the

policyholder. Where the taxpayer borrows on the old policy and sends the loan check from the old policy to the new insurer as a premium payment for the new policy (either with the old insurer or a new insurer), since the old policy is still in force (even though subject to the loan) Code section 1035 should not be available.

Closely akin to this problem is the failure to physically obtain the new policy in exchange for the old. For instance, suppose the IRS can show that the new policy was put in force through the payment of new premiums rather than from cash received from the surrender of the old policy. The IRS could argue that the new contract of insurance was not received in exchange for the old policy but rather in exchange for the first premium which was paid from an outside source. This would seem to be a red flag against company assignment forms which indicate that the first premium is to be paid with funds other than those received from the old contract and with the amount received upon the surrender of the old contract being applied to future premiums.

A partial exchange of contracts will be allowed in the proper circumstances. For example, in one case, the Tax Court held that a woman's exchange of only a portion of one annuity contract for an annuity contract issued by another company was a nontaxable exchange. When the court looked at the regulations promulgated under Code section 1035, it noted that in order for an exchange to qualify for nonrecognition treatment, it is required only that the contracts be of the same type, e.g., an annuity for an annuity and that the obligee under the two contracts be the same person. The regulations do not state any other requirements. The court noted that for deferral to be allowed, the only requirements are that: (a) the contracts be of the same type; and (b) that the obligee(s) be the same person(s). Here, the contract owner was in the same economic position after the exchange as she was prior to the transaction. The same funds are invested in annuity contracts and none of the money was reduced to the taxpayer's possession. So the exchange remained nontaxable even though partial.[44]

4. *Exchanges of unexchangeable* – Government policies are technically owned by the government.

Since they cannot be assigned, they cannot be exchanged and therefore cannot be protected under Code section 1035.

5. *Failure to carry over policy loans* – as discussed earlier, the extinguished loan can result in taxable "boot" to the extent of gain in the policy.

ALTERNATIVES

There is an alternative to almost every tool or technique in life insurance planning, each with its attendant advantages and disadvantages. Keep in mind that 1035 exchanges have a number of disadvantages that should be carefully considered, such as:

- possible surrender penalties on the old contract;

- a new surrender charge period on the new contract; and

- new incontestable and suicide periods on the new contract.

As an alternative to a 1035 exchange, planners should consider the judicious use of cash dividend options or reduced paid-up insurance. Cash dividends can be used to purchase new insurance coverage. Placing an old policy on reduced paid-up or extended term makes it possible to free up significant premiums that can then be used to purchase new coverage without surrendering existing contracts or facing the uncertainty inherent in an unsettled area. In addition, an internal 1035 exchange with the same life insurance carrier may be a better option for the client.

CHAPTER ENDNOTES

1. See Priv. Ltr. Rul. 9017062. There, the IRS sanctioned the exchange of two individual life insurance policies for two participating interests in a Group Universal Life Insurance Policy (GULP). The ruling noted that at no time did the insured have the chance to elect to receive cash or any other type of property in exchange for his individual policies.

2. Generally, there seems to be no requirement that the contracts have the same face amount. Care should be taken to assure that overall the new contract is not significantly more valuable than the old one, so as to permit an argument that the difference should be taxable to the policyholder. See I.R.C. §1035(d)(1), I.R.C. §1031(b).

3. See Manno and Nolan, "Internal Revenue Code Section 1035 and the Other Side of Exchange Programs," *Journal of the American Society of CLU & ChFC*, November 1985, p. 66.

4. There is no logical reason for the IRS to prohibit the exchange of multiple policies and there does not appear to be a prohibition. However, some commentators argue that the use of the term "exchange" implies a one-for-one transaction. But see Letter Ruling 9708016 discussed below.

5. See Mercer, "The Life Insurance Revolution: New Reasons for Using Section 1035 Exchanges," *Estates, Gifts, & Trusts Journal* 65 (March 14, 1991) and the follow-up entitled "Section 1035 Life Insurance Exchanges: Case Study" published in the May 9, 1991 issue of the *Estates, Gifts, & Trusts Journal* on page 112.

6. I.R.C. §61.

7. I.R.C. §72(e); Treas. Reg. §1.72-11(d). Taxable sales or exchanges of policies do not qualify for capital gain or loss treatment. See *W. Stanley Barrett v. Comm.*, 42 TC 993 (1964), *aff'd* 348 F.2d 916 (1st Cir. 1965).

8. The definition of life insurance is fairly broad and it appears to make no difference if the contracts exchanged are different varieties such as variable or universal or are whole life and limited pay. (See Rev. Rul. 68-235, 1968-1 CB 360.) Also, changes from individual to group do not seem to pose a problem. See Priv. Ltr. Rul. 9017062.

    At this point, it is not clear as to the direction the IRS would take on an exchange of term coverage into some form of permanent coverage such as ordinary or universal life. It is the authors' opinion that the IRS will claim that this is an attempt to artificially extend the tax free nature of the contract and will claim that such exchanges should not be afforded Section 1035 protection. However, the authors also feel this position is not justified by the Code itself.

9. I.R.C. §1035(b)(3).

10. I.R.C. §1035(b)(1).

11. I.R.C. §1035(b)(2). Revenue Ruling, 68-235, 1968-1 CB 360, and Revenue Ruling, 72-358, 1972-2 CB 473, state that the exchange of a life insurance policy, endowment contract, or fixed annuity contract for a variable annuity contract with the same company or a different company qualifies as a tax-deferred exchange under IRC Section 1035(a).

12. I.R.C. §1035(a)(2).

13. I.R.C. §1035(a)(2).

14. I.R.C. §1035(a)(3).

15. Priv. Ltr. Rul. 199937042.

16. *Conway v. Comm'r.*, 111 TC 350 (1998).

17. The Pension Protection Act of 2006 amended I.R.C. §1035(a) to allow these exchanges after 2009.

18. I.R.C. §1035(b)(2), I.R.C. §105(b)(3).

19. In TAM 8905004 the taxpayer purchased an annuity from an insurance company. Later, through a series of transactions, the taxpayer received both an annuity contract and a life insurance contract in exchange. The IRS held that the transaction was governed by the step transaction doctrine. The IRS therefore recharacterized the transaction as an exchange of annuity contracts with the taxpayer receiving boot in the form of a life insurance contract. The taxpayer was therefore charged with income to the extent of the fair market value of the life insurance contract he received.

20. Treas. Reg. §1.1031(b)-1(c).

21. See Treas. Reg. §1.1035-1.

22. It is thought by some that the exchange is fully taxable even if the new policy is issued as of the old policy's original issue date

and pursuant to a plan exchange option. See Lynch, "Exchanges of Insurance Policies Under Internal Revenue Code Section 1035: The Myths and the Realities," *Journal of the American Society of CLU & ChFC*, October, 1983, p. 32.

23. *Charles Cutler Parsons v. Comm.*, 16 TC 256 (1951); *W. Stanley Barrett v. Comm.*, 348 F.2d 916 (1st. Cir. 1965) *aff'd* 42 TC 993; Rev. Rul. 54-264 1954-2 CB 57; Reg. §25.2512-6(a), Example 3.

24. Rev. Rul. 59-195, 1959-1 CB 18; Treas. Reg. §25.2512-6(a), Example 4.

25. See Friedman, "Section 1035 Exchanges and Modified Endowment Contracts", *Journal of the American Society of CLU & ChFC*, July 1989, p. 62 for an excellent discussion of this topic.

26. I.R.C. §7702A(a)(2).

27. Priv. Ltr. Rul. 9044022. See H.R. Conf. Rep. No. 100-1104, (TAMRA '88) *reprinted in* 1988-3 CB 596.

28. See Rev. Rul. 72-358, 1972-2 CB 473, Priv. Ltr. Ruls. 8344029, 8343010, 8501012, 8526038, 8741052, 9233054. Compare Priv. Ltr. Ruls. 8310033, 8515063. See Lynch, "Exchanges of Insurance Policies Under Internal Revenue Code Section 1035: The Myths and the Realities", *Journal of the American Society of CLU & ChFC*, October 1983, p. 32.

29. Rev. Rul. 90-24, 1990-1 CB 97.

30. I.R.C. §1035(d)(1), 1031(b), 1031(c).

31. See Treas. Reg. §1.1031(b)-1(c).

32. Priv. Ltr. Ruls. 8604033, 8816015.

33. Priv. Ltr. Rul. 8816015.

34. See, e.g., Priv. Ltr. Rul. 9141025.

35. Priv. Ltr. Rul. 8604033.

36. I.R.C. §264(a)(4).

37. I.R.C. §401.

38. Treas. Reg. §1.401-1(b)(1)(ii).

39. Treas. Reg. §1.1035-1.

40. Treas. Reg. §1.1035-1. In the authors' opinion, this suggests that in an exchange of an annuity for another annuity the obligee (or obligees) under the contracts must be the same. If an old annuity contract has no contingent annuitant, it cannot safely be exchanged for one in which there is a contingent annuitant. It is good practice to make sure that in each exchange situation that the parties (and their rights) are identical both before and after the transaction.

41. Rev. Rul. 90-109, 1990-2 CB 191. Note that this ruling does not appear to imply that I.R.C. §7702 grandfathering is lost by exercise of the option.

42. I.R.C. §1035(b); Rev. Rul. 85-159, 1985-1 CB 29; Priv. Ltr. Rul. 9708016; Priv. Ltr. Rul. 9644016.

43. For instance, See Priv. Ltr. Rul. 8810010. However, Rev. Rul. 2002-75, 2002-2 CB 812 allowed Section 1035 treatment when an annuity contract was consolidated with another pre-existing annuity contract.

44. *Conway v. Comm'r.*, 111 TC No. 20 (1998). The IRS has also ruled on the proper way to allocate investment in the contract when one annuity is split up into two annuities. Rev. Rul. 2003-76, 2003-33 IRB 355. The IRS has also said that it is considering issuing regulations to prevent abuse when one annuity is split into two annuities using Section 1035. Notice 2003-51, 2003-33 IRB 361.

LIFE INSURANCE INCOME TAXATION AND PLANNING OPPORTUNITIES

CHAPTER 24

INTRODUCTION

Bottom line planning requires that a client focus only on the financial security he (or his beneficiaries) will have below the line. This forces a concentration on the impact of taxes and other reasons for slippage in retaining and transferring income and wealth. If the planner and client cannot identify where losses will occur, they cannot take the proper steps to avoid, reduce, or compensate for those outflows. The consequential result of not understanding the forces that erode income and wealth and taking the proper action is obvious.

This chapter will cover two areas with respect to life insurance:

1. Taxation of benefits during the insured's lifetime

2. Taxation of benefits at the insured's death

Because of their particular importance to planners, the subjects of estate, gift, and generation-skipping taxation, section 1035 exchanges, and transfers for value all are covered in separate chapters.

No deduction is allowed for premiums paid on any life insurance policy when the taxpayer is directly or indirectly a beneficiary under the policy. In fact, with the exception of an employer's deduction for premiums to pay group term life insurance, there is no situation where life insurance premiums, per se, are directly deductible. There are, of course, situations such as a donor's charitable gifts of money to pay premiums and an employer's bonus or compensation to an employee that takes the form of life insurance premiums. But in each of these cases, the deduction, to be allowed, must meet charitable or ordinary and necessary business expense tests and in neither case is the deduction allowed because the gift or payment is life insurance.[1]

TAXATION DURING THE INSURED'S LIFETIME

Life Insurance Defined

All currently issued contracts[2] must contain elements of both risk shifting and risk distribution in order to be considered life insurance and be taxed for federal purposes according to the rules that follow.[3] Currently issued contracts must also meet Code section 7702 requirements of either a cash value accumulation test or fall within a cash value corridor and meet certain guideline premium requirements.[4] These tests are incredibly complex and require actuarial determinations beyond the practical ability of most practitioners. It is wise, therefore, in the case of a large policy to obtain a written assurance from the home office of the insurer that the contract will, in fact, meet the current definition of life insurance in all respects and will continue to do so.

If a contract meets the definition of life insurance, the year by year increase in cash surrender value will not be subject to current income taxation. If the contract is not considered life insurance, each year the policyowner will be taxed on the annual increase in the policy's value.

Cash Value Increases

As noted above, as the cash value in a policy grows each year, the owner of the policy is not currently taxed on the increase.[5] No current income tax is payable no matter how large the internal build up may be.

Dividends

Dividends are considered the result of favorable insurer experience in mortality, income, and loading that make possible a return of a policyowner's outlay and are usually income tax free. Until total dividends received exceed the policyowner's cost, whether or not the policy is paid up, these distributions are income tax free regardless of whether received in the form of cash, used to purchase paid-up additions, one year term insurance, or left to accumulate at interest. But any interest earned under this last alternative will be taxable in the year it is earned.[6]

Once dividends, together with any other nontaxable distributions, exceed the premiums paid by the policyowner, the excess is taxable each year at ordinary income rates.[7] In other words, once a policyowner has recovered his investment in the contract (generally total premiums less any tax-free distributions received), dividends as well as any other distributions are taxable as ordinary income.

Election to Make Policy Paid-Up

A policyowner can elect to make an existing contract paid-up by applying cash values to purchase a single premium permanent plan of the same type as the existing plan but with a lowered death benefit. Since the cash values are never either actually or constructively received by the policyowner at that time, no gain must be recognized and the transaction results in no income taxation. However, if an outstanding loan is reduced during this transaction, the policyowner may incur some taxation.

National Service Life Insurance

No gain realized during the policyowner's lifetime from government life insurance is subject to income tax. The income enjoyed at the surrender or maturity of such a policy or any paid-up additional insurance is completely free of income tax.[8] Dividends paid from these policies are exempt.[9] Furthermore, interest on dividends is also income tax free.[10]

Policy Withdrawals

A withdrawal is the partial surrender of a policy. A policyowner will not have taxable income until withdrawals (including previous withdrawals and other tax-free distributions from the policy such as dividends) made from the cash reserves of a flexible premium (i.e., universal or adjustable life) policy exceed the policyowner's cost (accumulated premiums). Until the policyowner has recovered his aggregate premium cost, he will generally be allowed to receive withdrawals tax free under what is known as the cost-recovery first rule.

But, this income tax liability is accelerated if a cash distribution occurs within fifteen years of the policy's issue and that distribution is coupled with a reduction in the policy's contractual death benefits. A withdrawal within fifteen years of policy issuance coupled with a drop in death benefits triggers income. Subject to a statutory ceiling, all the income growth in the cash surrender value is deemed to have been received by the policyowner.[11] Once the fifteen-year period expires, no immediate taxation will occur upon a withdrawal.

This fifteen-year rule does not apply to policies issued prior to 1985, or to policy loans. Loans are not treated as distributions and do not reduce policy death benefits.

A notable exception to the cost-recovery rule applies to life insurance contracts classified as Modified Endowment Contracts (MECs) which are covered in more detail in Chapter 22. Generally, distributions from MECs are taxed under the interest-first rule which provides that the first distributions out of the contract are deemed to be taxable interest.

Surrender, Redemption or Maturity of a Policy

Gain, in the form of ordinary income,[12] is realized in many surrender, redemption, or maturity situations. These include:

1. *Lump sum cash-in* – The excess of the amount received by a policyholder in the complete redemption or surrender of a policy) over the policyowner's investment in the contract (i.e., cost) is taxable as ordinary income.[13] The policyowner determines the amount of lump sum payable and then subtracts from it the cost of the contract.

   A lump sum generally includes the cash value of paid-up additions, dividend accumulations, termination dividend, and unrepaid policy loans. Any interest previously paid on policy dividends that has already been taxed reduces taxable amount of the lump sum.

Generally, cost means net premiums (gross premiums less the total of tax-free dividends received by the policyowner). Any dividends paid by the insurer that were accumulated at interest or used to purchase paid-up additional insurance must be included in the lump sum amount as part of the policyowner's cost.

2. *Policy maturity* – Older cash value life insurance policies are typically set to mature at age 95 or 100. This means that if the insured is still alive at that age, the policy matures and the cash value is paid to the policy owner in lieu of the death benefit. The amount received would be taxed as discussed above instead of being received as a tax-free death benefit. Due to longer life expectancies, many life insurance carriers have added policy maturity extension riders to their older policies to prevent them from maturing at age 95 or 100 and thus causing adverse tax consequences to the policy owner. Newer products avoid the problem by maturing at much older ages, such as age 120.

3. *Interest only option* – If the lifetime proceeds are left intact with the insurer to earn interest, that interest is taxable each year as received or credited.[14] The gain on the proceeds is taxable immediately (assuming it can be withdrawn by the policyowner) even if the "interest only" election is made prior to surrender or maturity.

A policyowner's investment in the contract is defined as the total premiums (or other consideration) paid less the total amount of nontaxable distributions (i.e., dividends, unrepaid loans, and tax free withdrawals) received.[15] Figure 24.1 details what exactly is included in investment in the contract.

Annuity Taxation

An annuity is a systematic liquidation of principal and interest over a fixed or contingent period of time.[19] Thus, the term annuity includes payments for a fixed period or payments of a fixed amount in addition to payments lasting for one or more lives. Payments of interest only will not qualify for annuity taxation because there is no liquidation of principal.[20]

Amounts received as an annuity are taxed under special rules that allow the annuitant to exclude from tax a fixed (return of cost) portion of each payment from gross income each year and require the payment of income tax at ordinary rates on the balance of each payment. Stated in another manner, a fixed portion of each payment received can be excluded from income as a return of capital while the balance of each payment is reportable as taxable income. See Chapter 8, Annuities for a complete discussion of these taxation rules.

Deductibility of Premium Payments

No deduction is allowed for the premiums paid on a personally owned life insurance policy, regardless of who is the premium payer or who is the policyowner. Such outlays are considered a nondeductible personal expense.[21] This rule applies even where the owner of the policy is someone other than the insured.

Business policyowners generally fare no better. No deduction is allowed for premiums paid on any life insurance policy if the taxpayer is directly or indirectly a beneficiary under the policy.[22] This "all or nothing"[23] prohibition blocks the deduction of premiums even if they would otherwise be deductible as ordinary and necessary business expenses.[24]

Deductibility of Policy Loan Interest

Depending on the disbursements of the loan to specific expenditures, the IRS will classify interest incurred

Figure 24.1

INVESTMENT IN THE CONTRACT	
Includes:	Does not include:
• Dividends used to purchase paid-up additions (actually, the cash values in paid-up additions are part of the amount realized by the policyowner and, thus, do not reduce his investment in the contract). • The economic benefit reportable income from the term insurance portion benefit received under a qualified retirement plan.[16]	• Premiums for disability income • Premiums for accidental death benefits • Premiums for waiver of premium[17] • Interest paid on policy loans[18]

on a loan as: (1) trade or business interest; (2) investment or passive activity interest; or (3) personal interest.[25]

1. *Trade or business situations* – Contracts purchased before June 21, 1986 are not subject to any limit on deductibility of interest.[26] Severe limitations on interest deductions apply in all other policy loan situations making it almost impossible to obtain an interest deduction.

   After 1996 legislation, the general rule of nondeductibility for policy loan interest on company owned policies does not apply to policy loan interest paid on policies insuring a key person up to $50,000 of indebtedness. A key person is an officer or 20 percent owner of the taxpayer. The number of persons who may be treated as a key person is limited to the greater of: (1) five persons; or (2) the lesser of 5 percent of the total officers and employees or twenty individuals. Generally, this rule of nondeductibility is applicable to interest paid or accrued after October 13, 1995, but there are several transitional provisions.[27]

   Additionally, the Internal Revenue Code imposes an interest rate cap for interest paid or accrued after December 31, 1995. Interest in excess of that which would have been paid had the applicable rate of interest been used cannot be deducted. The applicable rate of interest is that rate described in Moody's Corporate Bond Yield Average—Monthly Average Corporates as published by Moody's Investors Service. The Code also specifies a manner in which to determine the applicable rate of interest for pre-1996 contracts.[28]

   After 1997, the rule concerning the deduction of policy loan interest states that no deduction shall be allowed for "… any interest paid or accrued on any indebtedness with respect to 1 or more life insurance policies owned by the taxpayer covering the life of any individual."[29]

   Although the exception from the general disallowance rule for policies on key employees and the interest rate caps put in place by 1996 legislation remain unchanged, 1997 legislation added a new provision[30] which generally provides that no deduction will be allowed for the part of the taxpayer's interest expense that is "allocable to unborrowed policy cash values." This portion that is "allocable to unborrowed policy cash values" is an amount that bears the same ratio to the interest expense as the taxpayer's average unborrowed policy cash values of life insurance policies and annuity and endowment contracts issued after June 8, 1997 bears to the sum of: (1) in the case of assets that are life policies or annuity or endowment contracts, the average unborrowed policy cash values; and (2) in the case of assets of the taxpayer that do not fall into this category, the average adjusted bases of such assets.

   Unborrowed policy cash value is defined as the excess of the cash surrender value of a policy or contract (determined without regard to surrender charges) over the amount of the loan with respect to the policy or contract.

   Finally, there is an exception to the general rule of nondeductibility of interest expense allocable to unborrowed policy cash values. The exception applies to policies and contracts owned by entities if the policy covers only one individual who, at the time first covered by the policy, is: (1) a 20 percent owner of the entity; or (2) an individual who is an officer, director or employee of the trade or business. A policy or contract will not fail to come within this exception simply because it covers both the owner and the owner's spouse. Apparently, spouses of officers, directors, or employees who are not also 20 percent owners cannot be covered and still have the policy or contract qualify for this exception.

2. *Investment or passive activity situations* – In the authors' opinion, where the policyowner can document that the proceeds of a policy loan were used to purchase an investment or expended on a passive activity, the interest should be considered investment interest or passive activity interest. For instance, if a policy loan was used to help the policyowner purchase land to be used for development, the loan interest should be deductible subject to investment interest limitations.[31]

3. *Personal situations* – In personal situations, the rule is simple and absolute. Interest on a policy loan is not deductible if it is neither trade or business nor investment interest.[32]

Single Premium Contracts

Even if a deduction is otherwise allowable, no deduction is allowed for interest paid or accrued on indebtedness incurred to purchase or continue in effect a single premium life insurance contract.[33] The term single premium is defined broadly. Essentially it is a policy on which substantially all the premiums are paid within four years of the date the policy was purchased or a policy on which an amount is deposited with the insurer for the payment of a substantial number of premiums.[34]

The interest deduction prohibition applies to existing as well as to newly-issued policies. If an existing policy which falls into the definition of single premium is pledged as collateral for a loan, it is likely that interest on that loan will not be deductible.[35]

Financing the Policy through Policy Loans

Generally, even if a deduction is otherwise allowable, when premium payments are financed through policy loans, no deduction is allowed for interest payments.[36] There are four exceptions to this general rule:

1. *Four-out-of-seven premiums paid without borrowing (the "four-out-of-seven" rule)* – As its name implies, if no part of four of the first seven years' annual premium, measured after the date of issue (or after the last substantial increase in premiums if later) are paid through a loan, the interest deduction will be allowed (if otherwise deductible).[37] Stated in the reverse manner, if more than three premiums are borrowed during the first seven policy years (or during the first seven years after the last substantial increase in premiums), even if the interest would otherwise be deductible, it may not be deducted. Once the four-out-of-seven test is failed, not only are prior interest deductions lost but all future deductions are barred as well.

   Repayment of the loans during or after the seven-year period will not wash the taint. Once the four-out-of-seven rule is violated by the payment of more than three premiums by loans, interest can never qualify for a deduction.[38] Nor can the taint be removed by a gift or even a sale of the policy. The new owner carries over both payments by loan and payments by debt from the prior owner. So if the old owner borrowed two years' premiums, the new owner can borrow only one more without jeopardizing the

interest deduction. Conversely, if the old owner had paid four premiums without borrowing, the new owner can borrow all of the next three years' premiums. The bottom line is that a new seven-year period does not begin merely because of a change of ownership.[39]

If the seven-year rule is met during the first seven years, there is no limit to the amount that can be borrowed in subsequent years (assuming no substantial increase[40]) in premiums. This means the policyowner could borrow the policy's entire cash value for any purpose whatsoever every year starting in the eighth policy year. Assuming the interest was otherwise deductible, it would not be barred by the tax prohibition regarding financing of premiums through loans.

Most experts feel that the IRS would not bar interest deductions on loans from universal life contracts merely because there is no specified premium that must be paid during each of the first seven years. Some say that the safest course of action is for the policyowner to pay four out of the first seven of the lowest premiums necessary to sustain the policy. Others say that no borrowing is permissible in a universal life policy.

2. *The $100 exception* – Even if there is found to be a systematic plan of borrowing to pay premiums, the interest deduction will not be disallowed if the interest does not exceed $100 for the policyowner's taxable year. This is an "all or nothing" exception. The entire deduction, not merely the excess, will be disallowed if the interest incurred in a year is more than $100.[41] So, for most business-owned policies, this exception is a minor one.

3. *The unforeseen events exception* – A deduction is not disallowed even if there is a loan and even if that loan is used to pay premiums if the reason for the systematic plan of borrowing was either that: (a) there was an unforeseen substantial increase in the policyowner's financial liability; or (b) the policyowner suffered an unforeseen substantial loss in income.

   The interest deduction will be disallowed if the economic shock was foreseeable at the time the policy was purchased.[42] For instance, college education or retirement expenses are both foreseeable events. On the other hand, a layoff or firing is not.

4. *Trade or business exception* – An otherwise allowable interest deduction will not be disallowed if the loan was incurred in connection with the taxpayer's trade or business. But this requires that the policyowner prove that the amounts borrowed against the life insurance contract were actually used for business purposes. Business purposes, however, do not include outlays for key employee, buy-sell coverage, split dollar agreements, or retirement plans. Thus, the policyowner must be able to document (perhaps by a tracing of cash flows showing how the funds were used) not only indebtedness, but also a business purpose other than the purchase of cash value life insurance.[43] The IRS will look at all the facts and circumstances of each case. If it finds that other business loans increase annually by the same amount as the premiums on a new policy, it will probably disallow the interest deduction. But probably the interest deduction on regular business loans (for instance indebtedness to purchase new equipment) will not be disallowed merely because the business used money in a year to buy life insurance instead of paying off or paying down the loan.

Interest Paid on Conversion of a Term Policy

Where a term policy is converted into a permanent contract, in some cases that conversion is made on an original age basis. This means the new contract is issued as though the policy were originally permanent coverage. The advantage is that premiums will be much lower than if the new policy were issued on an attained age basis. But to restore the insurer to where it would have been had the policy really been issued at the insured's original age, the policyowner must pay back premiums plus interest (the difference between the premiums that have actually been paid on the term policy and the premiums that would have been paid on the permanent policy had it been issued instead of the term contract plus interest on that difference at a specified annual rate). This interest is not deductible.[44]

Policy Loan to Purchase Tax Exempt Securities

No deduction is allowed for interest on a loan incurred or continued to purchase or carry tax exempt securities. If the loan is taken out to finance the purchase of any type of tax exempt asset, an interest deduction is barred. On the other hand, if the deduction is otherwise

allowable, it will not be blocked merely because the policyowner also held tax exempt securities.[45]

Timing of Interest Deduction

In those rare cases where policy loan interest is allowable as a deduction, the timing of the deduction becomes important. Some of the basic rules concerning the timing of the interest deduction and the party who can take it:

- Accrual basis policyowners take the deduction in the year interest—accrues even if payment of the interest has not been made in that year.[46]

- Cash basis policyowners take the deduction only in the year that the interest is paid.[47]

- Only the policyowner may take a deduction and only if the policyholder has paid the interest. A father, for example, cannot pay and deduct interest on a policy owned by his son nor can a shareholder pay and deduct interest on a policy owned by his corporation.[48] But interest otherwise deductible will not be disallowed if the loan (including interest) reduces the benefit paid at an insured's death. The IRS will treat the situation as though interest were paid at the time of the insured's death.[49]

- An assignee cannot deduct interest that accrued before the policy was transferred to him.[50]

Taxation of Policyowner or Insured in Business Situations

If the employer is directly or indirectly a beneficiary of the insurance contract, then the insured-employee is not taxed on the corporation's payment of policy premiums.[51]

The policyowner may be subject to income tax in a number of situations. These include:

1. where an insured's employer pays premiums on a policy owned by employee (or employee's third party assignee) and proceeds are paid to employee's named beneficiary or estate;[52]

2. where the proceeds of a policy owned by the corporation are payable to the personal beneficiary or estate of an employee;[53]

Where a corporate owned policy will be used to fund a stock redemption agreement in which the corporation will use the proceeds to buy back its own stock, premiums the corporation pays will not be taxed to any shareholder.

Where a policy to fund a buy-sell agreement is personally owned by a shareholder and the shareholder has named a personal beneficiary or designated his or her estate as recipient of policy proceeds, premium payments by the corporation may be considered a distribution of dividends.[54]

Likewise, where a policy on one person's life (e.g., another shareholder) is owned by a coshareholder (for instance to fund a buy-sell agreement), premium payments made by the corporation will be considered dividends or compensation paid on a shareholder-employee's behalf.[55]

Employer-owned Contracts

For life insurance contracts entered into after August 17, 2006, certain requirements must be met for the death proceeds of an employer-owned life insurance contract to be received income-tax free. One set of requirements is that before an employer-owned life insurance contract is issued, the employer must meet certain notice and consent requirements. The insured employee must be notified in writing that the employer intends to insure the employee's life, and the maximum face amount the employee's life could be insured for at the time the contract is issued. The notice must also state that the policy owner will be the beneficiary of the death proceeds of the policy. The insured must also give written consent to be the insured under the contract and consent to coverage continuing after the insured terminates employment.[56]

Another set of requirements regards the insured's status with the employer. The insured must have either been an employee at any time during the twelve-month period before his death, or, at the time the contract was issued, a director or highly compensated employee.[57]

Alternatively, the death proceeds of employer-owned life insurance will not be included in the employer's income (assuming the notice and consent requirements are met) if the amount is paid to a member of the insured's family (defined as a sibling, spouse, ancestor, or lineal descendent), any individual who is the designated beneficiary of the insured under the contract (other than the policy owner), a trust that benefits a member of the family or designated beneficiary, or the estate of the insured. If the death proceeds are used to purchase an equity interest from a family member, beneficiary, trust, or estate, the proceeds will not be included in the employer's income.[58]

An employer-owned life insurance contract is defined as a life insurance contract owned by a person or entity engaged in a trade or business and that person or entity (or certain related persons) is a beneficiary under the contract, and the contract covers the life of an insured who is an employee when the contract is issued.[59]

Taxation of Policyowner in Creditor Situation

If a creditor receives life insurance proceeds as payment of the debt, the IRS may claim that the proceeds should not be considered tax-free life insurance proceeds.[60] For instance, in a collateral assignment (nonsplit dollar) case where a creditor must prove the existence and amount of debt in order to collect the proceeds, proceeds are received because of the indebtedness rather than because of the insured's death. Of course, the creditor could still receive the proceeds income tax free as a recovery of basis (the sum of any unpaid debt and premiums paid but not deducted) except to the extent the creditor already enjoyed a bad debt deduction.[61]

Taxation of Policyowner in Alimony Situations

Where the insured pays premiums on a life insurance policy pursuant to a divorce or separation agreement signed after 1984, payments are taxable as alimony to the noninsured spouse owner.[62]

Taxation of Advance Premium Deposits

A discount is allowed to a policyowner who pays premiums more than one year before they fall due. The IRS taxes the interest increment earned on those prepaid premiums.[63]

This makes the fund, set aside by the policyowner and placed in the insurer's hands, taxable before it is applied to pay premiums. Each year, as the interest on the remaining discounted fund is applied toward the payment of a new year's premium (or when it becomes available to be withdrawn by the policyowner without substantial restrictions or limitations); it is considered constructively received and therefore taxable. If the interest cannot be taken by the policyowner, it becomes taxable each year when it is applied toward the payment of the next due annual premium. If the policyowner cashes in a policy or it matures, the policyowner can lower taxable gain by any advance premiums paid and any interest increments that were already taxed. In other words, the policyowner can include in his basis the sum of discounted premiums plus interest upon which he paid tax.

Taxation of Accelerated Death Benefits

Amounts received under a life insurance contract on the life of a terminally ill insured will be treated as an amount paid by reason of the death of the insured and are therefore not includable in the insured's gross income.

Amounts paid on behalf of a chronically ill individual are subject to the same limitations applying to long-term care benefits. They are treated as tax-free amounts paid by reason of the death of the insured as long as they don't exceed the greater of the actual costs incurred for qualified long-term care services provided for the insured or the $330 per day limitation in effect for 2015 (as indexed for inflation).[64]

There are several special rules that apply to chronically ill insureds. Generally, the favorable tax treatment outlined above will not apply to any payment received for any period unless such payment is for costs incurred by the payee (who has not been compensated by insurance or otherwise) for qualified long-term care services provided to the insured for the period (note that with an indemnity type of chronic illness rider, as opposed to a reimbursement rider, the benefits may be used for any purpose). Additionally, the terms of the contract under which such payments are made must comply with the requirements of Code section 7702B plus several other requirements.

Terminally ill is defined as an illness or physical condition that can reasonably be expected to result in death within twenty-four months following certification by a doctor. A chronically ill individual is a person who is not terminally ill and who has been certified by a physician as being unable to perform, without substantial assistance, at least two activities of daily living for at least ninety days or a person with a similar level of disability. Further, a person may be considered chronically ill if he requires substantial supervision to protect himself from threats to his health and safety due to severe cognitive impairment and this condition has been certified by a health care practitioner within the previous twelve months.

There is one exception to this general rule of non-includability for accelerated death benefits. The rules outlined above do not apply to any amount paid to any taxpayer other than the insured if the taxpayer has an insurable interest in the life of the insured because the insured is a director, officer or employee of the taxpayer or if the insured is financially interested in any trade or business of the taxpayer.[65]

Sale of a Life Insurance Policy

Prior to 2009 the general rule was that gain on the sale of a life insurance contract was taxable as ordinary income.[66] Gain was determined as if the contract had been surrendered by the policyowner. So the excess of the sales proceeds over the net premium cost (premiums paid less tax free dividends received) was taxable.

In 2009 the IRS issued guidance providing that the sale of a life insurance policy may produce both ordinary income and capital gains taxes. The amount of taxable income is the difference between the sale proceeds and the policyholder's adjusted basis in the policy (aggregate premium payments minus cost of insurance charges). The portion of taxable income that will be considered ordinary income is the difference between the cash surrender value and the aggregate premiums (i.e., the taxable amount for an ordinary cash surrender). The portion of taxable income that will be considered capital gains is the difference between the sale price of the policy and the adjusted basis in the policy minus any amounts subject to ordinary income tax.[67]

The facts of 2009 guidance involved a sale to an unrelated third party who had no insurable interest in the life of the insured (i.e., an investor or life settlement company). It is unclear whether the 2009 guidance would apply to a sale involving a related third party or a party that has an insurable interest in the life of the insured. In the authors' opinion such a sale would be governed by the pre-2009 rules applicable to the sale of life insurance policy.

Generally, if a life insurance policy is sold for less than its basis, no loss deduction is allowed since most courts have characterized the portion of the policyowner's premium going toward pure insurance protection as a current expense rather than an investment. The balance of the premium is directed toward policy reserves so to the extent that policy reserves and cash value are the same, no loss has been incurred.[68]

If the policy is sold at less than its fair market value, the difference in this bargain sale may be taxable income to the buyer in certain situations. For instance, if a business sells a key employee policy to the insured employee, the excess of the policy's fair market value over the price paid will be taxed to the buyer as additional compensation.

Suppose a corporation pays an annual premium today and then tomorrow sells a policy on an employee's life to her in return for an amount equal to its cash value. The difference between the value received and the amount paid is treated as a bonus to the employee. Since the policy's value will often exceed the cash surrender value, even a sale of a policy for its cash value on the last day of a policy year may result in taxable income to the employee.

These same rules apply where an employee or shareholder sells a policy to a corporation; ordinary income is realized by the seller to the extent that the value of the policy exceeds net premium cost.[69]

Corporate Distribution of a Policy

In some situations, life insurance policies have been used by a corporation to pay for the purchase of stock or other assets. For instance, assume a corporation buys back its own stock or purchases land and in return pays for the purchase by distributing a life insurance policy on the life of the selling shareholder or landowner. Here, the transaction is considered an exchange of the policy for stock (or land). The seller of the stock would realize gain equal to the excess of: (1) the value of the policy over; (2) the seller's basis in the stock (or land). That gain would be capital gain if the parties can prove that the policy was given in exchange for the property the corporation receives.

A more common scenario is that a business may distribute a policy on the life of an employee or shareholder. If this property transfer occurs in connection with the performance of services (i.e., a Section 83 transfer), then the value of the policy for distribution purposes is its Fair Market Value (FMV). IRS guidance provides that the safe harbor fair market value for life insurance is the greater of Interpolated Terminal Reserve (ITR) or PERC (premiums plus earnings minus reasonable charges—essentially the cash value without regard to surrender charges).[70] For more information, please refer to Chapter 26, "Life Insurance Valuation".

If the transferee is a shareholder of a C corporation, then the FMV of the policy transferred may constitute a taxable dividend.[71] If the transferee is an owner of a pass-through entity (partnership, limited liability company (LLC) or S corporation), then the FMV value of the policy will serve to reduce the owner's outside basis first. With LLC or partnerships, any excess FMV reduces the basis of the policy transferred. With S corporations, any excess FMV is taxed as capital gain. If the transferee is a nonowner employee, then the FMV of the policy will constitute taxable compensation (and the basis of the policy going forward will be the FMV of the policy at the time of the transfer plus any additional premiums paid into the policy).

From the business' perspective, the transfer may also have income tax consequences. With S and C corporations, any gain in the policy at the time of transfer is taxable to the corporation. If the transfer constitutes taxable compensation to the transferee, then the corporation will receive a deduction that likely more than offsets its taxable income. With LLCs and partnerships, a transfer to an owner is disregarded for income tax purposes and no gain is triggered at the time of the transfer. However, if the transfer is to a nonowner employee, then gain should be triggered, but an offsetting deduction for the full FMV of the policy should be available.

TAXATION AT AND AFTER THE INSURED'S DEATH

Implications of Meeting Definition

Essentially, what is defined as life insurance under income tax law will be treated as life insurance under the rest of federal tax law. If a contract meets the definition of life insurance, death benefits will be (generally[72]) exempt from income tax.[73] So, for instance, a death benefit that is not considered taxable as ordinary income will not be included in the calculations for the Net Investment Income tax (NIIT).[74]

Proceeds Payable at Insured's Death

Generally, the recipient of life insurance proceeds payable at the insured's death will receive those proceeds income tax free.[75] This favorable tax treatment applies even if the proceeds are paid to the insured's estate or to a corporation, partnership, trust, LLC, or other entity rather than to one or more individual(s). Proceeds are also income tax free regardless of whether paid in a lump sum or in installments, although any interest earned is taxable. Death benefits paid from term riders or paid-up additional insurance are likewise income tax free as are payments from an accidental death (double indemnity) rider and group term life insurance. The exclusion is applicable regardless of who owned the policy or who paid premiums.

Proceeds Payable at a Date Later than Death

There are many times when life insurance policy proceeds are paid at a time later than the insured's death. Where that delay results in the payment of interest (as it almost always does), regardless of the reason for the delay, interest is taxed to the recipient at ordinary rates.[76] So no matter what the cause or who made the decision to postpone payment of the proceeds (the insured, the beneficiaries, or the insured's estate), interest is taxable at ordinary income tax rates.

Payments Taken in Installments

A beneficiary can choose to settle the debt owed by the insurer at the death of an insured in several forms other than a lump sum. The most common are the selection of payments for life (a life income option) and payments for a specified period of time (term certain). In either event, the amount of proceeds is systematically liquidated over the appropriate period of time. Part of each payment will be considered tax free and part will be taxable, in much the same way that annuity payments are taxed.[77]

The tax free portion is called the "amount held by the insurer." This is the total amount that may be recovered by the beneficiary income tax free. This consists of the face amount of the policy, supplementary insurance, and accumulated dividends if applied to increase guaranteed payments. When computing the ratio that follows, the value of a guarantee must be subtracted from the amount held by the insurer.

Taxable interest is determined through a subtractive method. First, calculate the principal (tax free) portion of each payment. Second, subtract that result from the payment. The difference is the taxable interest. The amount of each payment's income tax free principal portion is found by the following process:[78]

1. Compute the amount held by the insurer.

2. Determine the number of years in the payment period.[79]

3. Divide the step one answer by the step two answer.

Life Income Option Elected

This tax free amount remains tax free regardless of how long the beneficiary lives. So even if the beneficiary outlives the life expectancy assumed in step two, these amounts remain income tax free. But anything in excess of the tax free principal calculated under this formula is taxable interest.[80]

Assume the beneficiary elected to take payments for life but agreed to take smaller amounts in return for the insurer's guarantee that if the beneficiary should die before receiving a specified amount of guaranteed payments, the balance would be paid to a secondary beneficiary. The secondary beneficiary would be allowed to receive the balance of the payment guaranteed by the insurer income tax free.[81]

Example. Assume a beneficiary is entitled to receive $80,000 but instead of a lump sum chooses to take $5,000 a year for life with the guarantee that regardless of when he dies, payments will continue until at least that amount has been paid out. Assume that the commuted value of the refund guarantee by the insurer is $15,000. This would lower the amount held by the insurer to $65,000 ($80,000 – $15,000). If the beneficiary has a thirty-year life expectancy, the excludable amount would be about $2,167 ($65,000 ÷ 30). This would leave about $2,833 of each $5,000 payment ($5,000 – $2,167) taxable at ordinary income rates. If the beneficiary died before receiving the full $80,000, the balance of that guaranteed amount would be received tax free by the secondary beneficiary.

Fixed Period Option Elected

A beneficiary can choose to take the insurance proceeds in installments over a number of years. The total amount of proceeds—plus interest—is paid pro-rata over the fixed period. The same three step procedure used above to determine nontaxable and taxable amounts in the case of a life income option is used here. The number of installment payments to be made in the fixed period is the number of years in the payment period.

Fixed Amount Option Elected

Here, the beneficiary selects an amount to be paid to him each month (or year). The length of time over which the lump sum will be paid depends on the size of the proceeds and the amount selected to be paid. Once again, the three-step procedure used above applies. In this case the amount held by the insurer is divided by the number of payments the insurer will guarantee based on the fixed amount selected. The number of payments is that number which, using the insurer's guaranteed interest rate is required to exhaust both principal and the guaranteed interest specified by the insurer. But if excess interest increases the number of payments, all additional payments made by the insurer after the guaranteed number of payments are fully taxable since the exclusion ratio no longer applies.

If the primary beneficiary dies before the end of the guaranteed payment period, the same amount of prorated principal can be excluded from gross income by the secondary beneficiary.[82]

Interest Only Option Elected

If the beneficiary chooses to leave the proceeds with the insurer and takes only interest, that interest is fully taxable but the proceeds are income tax free.[83] The result is the same even if the insured elected the interest only option. Generally, interest is taxable as soon as it is credited to the policy even if it is not in fact taken out by the beneficiary.[84]

Exception for Government Life Insurance

None of the interest element payable under a life income or installment settlement option is subject to income tax if the proceeds are payable under government life insurance.[85]

Exception to the General Transfer for Value Rule

Where a policy or an interest in a policy is transferred in return for any type of valuable consideration in money or money's worth, the proceeds, except to the extent of the dollar value of that consideration and any premiums paid after the transfer by the new policyowner, lose their income tax free status. This extremely important rule is the subject of Chapter 25.

Exception for Proceeds Considered Compensation or Dividends

Often, the insured is an employee and/or a shareholder-employee of a corporation. Here, payment of the policy proceeds may be considered payment of compensation (deductible by the corporation and taxable as ordinary income in full to the recipient) or as the payment of a dividend (nondeductible by the corporation and taxable, at generally capital gain rates, to the extent of the corporation's earnings and profits to the recipient). The exact result will depend to a great extent upon facts, circumstances, and the existence or nonexistence of documentation of those facts and circumstances:

1. If the insured employee never reported income from the corporation's payment of premiums on a policy owned by the employee or a third party and it was discovered after his death by the IRS, the tax on the corporate-paid premiums plus interest and penalties would be payable by the employee's estate but the proceeds should remain income tax free. The income tax liability to the estate would be the same whether the payment was considered compensation or a dividend but if the payment was made on behalf of a shareholder-employee with respect to his stock, the premium payments would be considered nondeductible dividends.[86]

2. If the corporation owns and is beneficiary of the policy and pays all premiums, the proceeds will be received by the corporation income tax free (except to the extent of any corporate AMT). However, if it then pays out those proceeds for any reason to an employee (for instance in payment of the corporation's obligation under a nonqualified deferred compensation agreement), the payments would lose their life insurance status and be treated as taxable compensation.[87]

3. If the corporation owns the policy and pays all premiums but the proceeds are payable to an employee or employee-shareholder's beneficiary, payments would be considered compensation in the case of a common law employee or dividends in the case of a shareholder employee.[88]

In summary, where income is not reported during lifetime, at an insured's death where the corporation paid premiums on a policy payable to the insured employee's personal beneficiary or estate, the IRS will first argue that the proceeds are dividends (where the insured was a shareholder-employee) or compensation (where the insured held no stock). Failing that argument, the IRS will argue that the estate must pay income tax on the income that should have been reported during lifetime year after year. The IRS will likely assess interest and penalties on the unpaid tax as well.

The best solution is to name the corporation as owner and beneficiary of any insurance for which it pays premiums or to report corporate payments as bonuses year after year as the corporation pays premiums on a personally owned contract.

Exception for Policy Owned by Qualified Retirement Plan

A portion of the proceeds equal to the cash surrender value of the policy immediately before the insured's death will be taxable as ordinary income when death benefits are paid from a qualified annuity plan or employee benefit trust at the death of the insured. The net amount at risk (pure insurance) portion of the proceeds is income tax free (assuming that the plan participant has been annually income taxed on the reportable economic benefit cost of the net amount at risk).[89]

CHAPTER ENDNOTES

1. *Edward E. Thorpe and Co. v. Comm'r.*, T.C. Memo. 1998-115 [1998 RIA TC Memo ¶98,115], Tax Ct. Dkt. No. 23900-95; I.R.C. §264(a)(1).

2. No statutory definition must be met by a policy issued prior to January 1, 1985 assuming the policy is not a flexible premium contract. I.R.C. §7702(j) exempts certain plans or arrangements provided by churches to their employees or their beneficiaries from the requirement that the arrangement must meet the local law definition of life insurance.

3. See *Helvering v. LeGierse*, 312 U.S. 531 (1941). State law requirements must also be met. I.R.C. §7702(a).

4. I.R.C. §7702(a).

5. See *Theodore H. Cohen v. Comm'r.*, 39 TC 1055 (1963), acq. 1964-1 CB 4; *Abram Nesbitt II v. Comm'r.*, 43 TC 629 (1965).

6. As soon as there are no restrictions on a policyowner's right to receive the interest, under the doctrine of constructive receipt, it becomes taxable whether or not actually taken. Treas. Reg. §1.451-2; *Theodore H. Cohen v. Comm'r.*, 39 TC 1055 (1963), acq. 1964-1 CB 4.

7. I.R.C. §72(e)(5); Treas. Reg. §1.72-11(b)(1).

8. 38 U.S.C. §5301(a); Rev. Rul. 72-604, 1972-2 CB 35.

9. Rev. Rul. 71-306, 1971-2 CB 76.

10. Rev. Rul. 91-14, 1991-1 CB 18.

11. I.R.C. §§7702(f)(7)(A), 7702(f)(7)(B). This rule applies only to policies issued after 1984.

12. Capital gain is not available upon the surrender or maturity of a life insurance contract. See *Avery v. Comm'r.*, 111 F.2nd 19 (9th Cir. 1940); *Ralph Perkins v. Comm'r.*, 41 BTA 1225 (1940); *Blum v. Higgins*, 150 F.2nd 471 (2nd Cir. 1945).

13. I.R.C. §72(e); Treas. Reg. §1.72-11(d).

14. I.R.C. §72(j); Treas. Reg. §1.72-14(a).

15. I.R.C. §72(c)(1); Treas. Reg. §1.72-6(a)(1).

16. Treas. Reg. §1.72-16(b).

17. Rev. Rul. 55-349, 1955-1 CB 232.

18. *Chapin v. McGowan*, 271 F.2d 856 (2nd Cir. 1959).

19. Treas. Reg. §1.72-1(b).

20. Rev. Rul. 75-255, 1975-2 CB 22.

21. I.R.C. §262; Treas. Reg. §1.262-1(b)(1).

22. I.R.C. §264(a)(1).

23. Even if the premium payer may only receive a small part of the proceeds, if IRC Section 264(a)(1) applies, none of the premium is deductible. Rev. Rul. 66-203, 1966-2 CB 104.

24. Treas. Reg. §1.264-1(a).

25. Temp. Treas. Reg. §1.163-8T(a)(4).

26. See I.R.C. §264(a)(4).

27. I.R.C. §264; Health Insurance Portability and Accountability Act of 1996, §501.

28. I.R.C. §264(e).

29. I.R.C. §264(a)(4).

30. This provision is applicable to contracts issued after June 8, 1997. Taxpayer Relief Act of 1997, §1084; I.R.C. §264(a); I.R.C. §264(f).

31. Not all authorities agree. See Brody, Weinberg, Jansen, Asmar, and Kahn, *Federal Income Taxation of Life Insurance*, The American Bar Association, Real Property, Probate, and Trust Law Section, p. 50.

32. I.R.C. §163(h)(1).

33. I.R.C. §264(a)(2). This denial of deductibility applies for contracts purchased after March 1, 1954.

34. I.R.C. §264(c). See *Frederick Dudderar v. Comm'r.*, 44 TC 632 (1965), acq. 1966-2 CB 4; *Campbell v. Cen-Tex Inc.*, 377 F.2d 688 (5th Cir. 1967).

35. See Rev. Rul. 79-41, 1979-1 CB 124.

36. I.R.C. §264(a)(3). The Internal Revenue Service is attacking Corporate-Owned Life Insurance (COLI) interest deductions. Technical Advice Memorandum (TAM) 199901005 and Letter Ruling 9812005 are both situations where the IRS held that a

corporation's deductions for interest claimed under COLI should be disallowed. The IRS stated in the 1999 TAM that the corporation did not really make policy loans to pay premiums but merely arranged for the appearance of cash transfers that flowed in both directions. The IRS looked behind the form the parties created to the substance: The facts indicated that a significant portion of amounts the corporation paid and classified as premiums were returned by the insurer concurrently with their payment. The result was a circular cash flow. So, the IRS treated the interest payments as amounts paid to support an interdependent and circular structure of charges and credits designed to increase the corporation's tax deductions while simultaneously increasing amounts credited to the COLI policies' tax deferred cash values rather than as interest payments for the use or forbearance of money. The IRS has also been successful in litigation regarding COLI interest deductions. See *American Electric Power Co. v. U.S.*, 2003-1 USTC ¶50,416 (6th Cir. 2003); IRS v. CM Holdings, Inc., 2002-2 USTC ¶50,596 (3rd Cir. 2002).

37. I.R.C. §264(d)(1); Treas. Reg. §1.264-4(d)(1).

38. Rev. Rul. 72-609, 1972-2 CB 199.

39. For more information on this tack on of previous history, see Rev. Rul. 71-309, 1971-2 CB 168.

40. Neither the Code nor the regulations provide guidance as to what will be considered a substantial increase in premiums. But in the opinion of the authors, only net premiums will be considered.

41. Treas. Reg. §1.264-4(d)(2).

42. Treas. Reg. §1.264-4(d)(3).

43. Treas. Reg. §1.264-4(d)(4). *American Body and Equipment Co. v. U.S.*, 511 F.2nd 647 (5th Cir. 1975).

44. See *Samuel J. Johnson*, TC Memo 1943; *J.I. Fleischer*, TC Memo 1943. The interest is not deductible mainly because it is not payable on indebtedness but rather as part of the cost of the permanent contract.

45. See *Levitt v. U.S.*, 517 F.2nd 1339 (8th Cir. 1975).

46. *M.G. Corlett v. Comm'r.*, TC Memo 1946-046.

47. I.R.C. §163(a). See *Keith v. Comm'r.*, 139 F.2nd 596 (2nd Cir. 1944); *Nina Cornelia Prime, Exec. v. Comm'r.*, 39 BTA 487 (1939).

48. *J. Simpson Dean v. Comm'r.*, 35 TC 1083 (1961).

49. *Estate of Pat E. Hooks*, 22 TC 502 (1954), acq. 1955-1 CB 5.

50. *Agnes I. Fox*, 43 BTA 895 (1941).

51. *Casale v. Comm'r.*, 247 F.2nd 440 (2nd Cir. 1957); Rev. Rul. 59-184, 1959-1 CB 65.

52. *Yuengling v. Comm'r.* 69 F.2nd 971 (3rd Cir. 1934); Treas. Reg. §1.61-2(d)(2)(ii)(a). Only net premiums are includable in the employee's income when policy dividends are used to reduce premium payments. *Nelson H. Sturgis, Jr. v. Comm'r.*, TC Memo (1951).

53. Treas. Reg. §1.61-2(d)(2)(ii). *Comm'r. v. Bonwit*, 87 F.2nd 764 (2nd Cir. 1937). See *Ruth C. Rodebaugh v. Comm'r.*, TC Memo 1974-36, aff'd 75-2 USTC ¶9526 (6th Cir. 1975).

54. *Thomas E. Brock, Jr. v. Comm'r.*, TC Memo 1982-335. See also Rev. Rul. 79-50, 1979-1 CB 138 where a split dollar plan was held to result in dividend payments to a nonemployee stockholder.

55. Rev. Rul. 59-184, 1959-1 CB 65.

56. I.R.C. §101(j)(4).

57. I.R.C. §101(j)(2)(A).

58. I.R.C. §101(j)(2)(B).

59. I.R.C. §101(j)(3)(A).

60. Treas. Reg. §1.101-1(b)(4).

61. *St. Louis Refrigerating & Cold Storage Company v. U.S.*, 162 F.2nd 394 (8th Cir. 1947); *T.O. McCamant v. Comm'r.*, 32 TC 824 (1959).

62. Temp. Treas. Reg. §1.71-1T, A-6.

63. Rev. Rul. 65-199, 1965-2 CB 20; Rev. Rul. 66-120, 1966-1 CB 214.

64. I.R.C. §7702B(d)(2).

65. I.R.C. §101(g)(5).

66. See *Century Wood Preserving Co. v. Comm'r.*, 69 F.2nd 967 (3rd Cir. 1934); *London Shoe Co.*, 80 F.2nd 230 (2nd Cir. 1935).

67. Rev. Rul. 2009-13.

68. *Gallun v. Comm'r.*, 327 F.2nd 809 (7th Cir. 1964).

69. *George W. Parsons v. Comm'r.*, 54 TC 54 (1970).

70. Rev. Proc. 2005-25.

71. See *Peter J. Wilkin v. Comm'r.*, TC Memo 1969-130; *Charles J. Thornley v. Comm'r.*, 41 TC 145 (1963).

72. If a contract issued after 1984 does not meet the definition of life insurance under I.R.C. §7702, only the pure insurance (excess of death benefit over net surrender value) portion will be income tax free. I.R.C. §7702(g)(2).

73. I.R.C. §101.

74. I.R.C. §1411(c)(1)(A).

75. I.R.C. §101(a)(1).

76. I.R.C. §101(c).

77. I.R.C. §101(d)(1); Treas. Reg. §1.101-4(a)(1)(i).

78. Treas. Reg. §1.101-7 provides that life expectancy (the number of years in the payment period in the case of life income option) is found by using IRS Table V (one life) and VI (two lives).

79. An exclusion of up to $1,000 of interest is allowed to the surviving spouse of an insured who died prior to October 23, 1986. I.R.C. §101(d)(1)(B) prior to repeal by TRA '86, §1001(a).

80. Treas. Reg. §1.101-4(d) provides that in the case of a joint and survivor option, the amount held by the insurer is divided by the life expectancy of the beneficiaries as a group in computing the annually excludable amount. This tax free amount can be excluded as long as any survivor lives.

81. Treas. Reg. §1.101-4(a).

82. See Treas. Reg. §1.101-4(g), Example 7.

83. Taxability applies to both guaranteed and excess interest. I.R.C. §101(c).

84. Treas. Regs. §§1.61-7, 1.451-2. If the beneficiary has no contractual right to make a withdrawal of either principal or interest for a given period of time, interest is not taxable until that date. At that time, whatever interest has gone untaxed becomes immediately taxable. Treas. Reg. §1.101-4(g), Example 1. As soon as the beneficiary can take principal, the interest earned by that principal becomes taxable even if contractually the beneficiary cannot actually take it. Rev. Rul. 68-586, 1968-2 CB 195. See also *Rubye R. Strauss v. Comm'r.*, 21 TC 104 (1953).

85. 38 U.S.C. §5301(a).

86. See *Estate of J.E. Horne v. Comm'r.*, 65 TC 1020 (1975), acq. in result, 1980-1 CB 1.

87. *Essenfeld v. Comm'r.*, 311 F.2nd 208 (2nd Cir. 1962).

88. *Golden v. Comm'r.*, 113 F.2nd 590 (3rd Cir. 1940). See also Rev. Rul. 61-134, 1961-2 CB 250; *Ducros v. Comm'r.*, 272 F.2nd 49 (6th Cir. 1959).

89. I.R.C. §72(m)(3)(C); Treas. Reg. §1.72-16(c)(4).

THE TRANSFER FOR VALUE RULE

CHAPTER 25

INTRODUCTION

The utility of life insurance diminishes in direct proportion to any tax burden it must bear. Any planner dealing with life insurance must therefore obtain a strong working knowledge of the transfer for value rule—a tax trap that can cause all or a major portion of the death proceeds to become subject to ordinary income taxes.

For this reason, this entire chapter is devoted to the transfer for value rule.[1]

This chapter will:

1. define and explain the rule;

2. list its exceptions; and

3. analyze common factual situations in:

    a) personal planning;

    b) buy-sell planning; and

    c) employee benefit planning.

Planners should suspect a potential problem in any transfer where a policy, or any interest in a policy, is transferred for any type of valuable consideration. To fail to identify this tax trap could be the most expensive mistake a practitioner can make.

WHAT IS IT?

The transfer for value rule, contained in Code section 101(a)(2), provides:

In the case of a transfer for a valuable consideration, by assignment or otherwise, of a life insurance contract or any interest therein, the amount excluded from gross income by [the beneficiary of death proceeds under a life insurance contract] shall not exceed an amount equal to the sum of the actual value of such consideration and the premiums and other amounts subsequently paid by the transferee.

If transfers of a life insurance policy fall within the transfer for value rule, the result is a harsh penalty: with the exceptions listed below, transferees for value of life insurance policies are taxable at ordinary income rates on receipt of the policy proceeds less the sum of amounts paid by them to acquire the policy plus later premiums and other amounts. The term "other amounts" includes any interest paid or accrued by the transferee on indebtedness with respect to a contract, but only if the interest is not allowable as a deduction under Code section 264(a)(4).[2]

The questions the planner must ask are:

1. Is there a transfer?

2. Will the transferee pay any type of consideration for that transfer?

If the answer to both questions is yes, the results are likely to be harsh. For example, if a $1,000,000 term life insurance policy on an insured's life is transferred from the insured to his or her son for $10,000, there is a transfer of an insurance contract for valuable consideration. If the transferee, the son, then pays four $5,000 premiums before the insured's death, the amount excludable from the owner's gross income for amounts received under the policy will be limited to the value of the consideration paid for the policy ($10,000) plus the four $5,000 premiums paid after the transfer ($20,000), a total of $30,000. This means $970,000 ($1,000,000 less $30,000) would be subject to ordinary income tax! So instead of receiving $1,000,000 net, the son could owe a federal income tax of over $300,000 and net less than $700,000!

Planners should be aware of the following points:

1. It does not matter whether the policy is term or permanent insurance.

2. The transfer for value rule applies to every type of life insurance contract and encompasses group as well as individually purchased coverage.

3. The method by which the policy is transferred is irrelevant for purposes of this rule.

4. The transfer for value rule can apply even if ownership of a policy has not been transferred. A mere shift in an interest in the contract may be sufficient to trigger the rule. A transfer for value can occur from an absolute assignment of all the transferor's rights, a transfer of some lesser degree of policy rights, or a different type of transfer.

5. For the rule to apply there must be both a transfer of a policy or an interest in a policy and valuable consideration paid for that transfer to the transferor.

The Requirement of Transfer

The Internal Revenue Code does not define the term "transfer for valuable consideration," but the regulations provide that a transfer for valuable consideration occurs whenever any absolute transfer for value of a right to receive all or any part of the proceeds of a life insurance policy takes place. This includes, as mentioned above, the creation for value of an enforceable right to receive all or part of the proceeds of a policy, but excludes any pledge or mere assignment of a policy as collateral security.[3]

The pledge or assignment of a policy (or an interest in a policy) as collateral security is not a transfer. A pledgee or assignee receiving the pledge or assignment of a policy as collateral for a loan will be able to recover proceeds income tax free (but as a repayment of capital, rather than as the proceeds of a life insurance policy).

The IRS defines the phrase transfer for valuable consideration broadly. The term encompasses any absolute transfer—for value—of a right to receive all or any part of a life insurance policy, including the creation for value of an enforceable contractual right to receive all or any part of the proceeds. If the insured in the above example had merely named his or her son as the policy beneficiary (for valuable consideration), that alone would constitute a transfer for purposes of the rule.

Planners should remember that any shifting of a beneficial interest in a policy is sufficient to trigger the transfer for value rule. No physical transfer of the policy or the policy's ownership is necessary, nor must every interest in the policy be transferred for the trap to be set.

The Requirement of Consideration

It is impossible to fall within the trap unless there is a transfer of a policy or an interest in a policy. It is also clear that even if there is a transfer, the transfer for value trap will not be triggered if there is no consideration given for that transfer.

Even if there is a nominal promise by the transferee to pay value and even if the policy assignment says, "for one dollar," the proceeds will be tax-free if in fact no consideration is ever paid, regardless of the formal recitation of consideration in the assignment form furnished by the insurer. Of course, the better and recommended practice is to show that a gift and only a gift is intended. To be safe, the assignment form should state that the transfer is solely "for love and affection.

If, in exchange for any kind of valuable consideration, a policy beneficiary of all or any portion of the proceeds is named or changed, there will be a transfer for value. This rule applies even if:

• there is no assignment of the policy;

• the policy has no cash surrender value at the time of the transfer; and

• the policy is term insurance, so that it never has and never will have any cash value.

Even though the transfer is found to be for a valuable consideration and none of the exceptions to the transfer for value rule apply, if the consideration paid for the transfer plus any amounts paid subsequent to the transfer by the transferee equal or exceed the policy proceeds, the entire amount of the proceeds will be excludable from gross income. But it will be rare that the transferee will pay a sum equal to the proceeds for the policy.

It is not necessary that cash change hands for the trap to be set. Any consideration sufficient to support an enforceable contract right will be sufficient. For example, in the leading case in the buy-sell area, the mutuality of shareholders' agreements to purchase each other's stock in the event of death and relieve the business from the burden of paying premiums was held to be enough consideration for invoking the rule.[4]

Planners should therefore always inquire—whenever there is a transfer of either a policy or an interest in a policy—whether the transferring party will receive anything of any value in exchange for the transfer. A quid pro quo ("I'll do this for you if you do this for me") type transaction is consideration just as surely as if $1,000,000 changes hands. The quid pro quo does not have to be in writing, nor does it have to be explicitly stated by the parties. If it is logical to assume that the transfer of a policy or an interest in a policy would not have been made absent some consideration and that action or inaction was in fact taken, the IRS will presume that valuable consideration did pass to the transferor.

EXCEPTIONS TO THE RULE

It is essential that planners understand why the rule exists: Congress wanted to discourage speculation in human life through insurance via the sale of policies to those who do not have an insurable interest in the life of the insured (essentially, a stronger preference for the continued life of the insured than for receipt of the insurance proceeds).[5] The parties specified below as exempt from the transfer for value rule are those who are likely to have an insurable interest.

But it is equally important for practitioners to note that the mere fact that the beneficiary should or does have an insurable interest in the life of the insured is not sufficient. Even some parties who clearly have an insurable interest are not included in the exempt categories described below. For instance, the following individuals are not exempt from the rule:

- the policyholder's children;

- the policyholder's parents; and

- the policyholder's co-shareholders.

Furthermore, even if the beneficiary can show that there is no risk or intent of speculation on the death of the insured and the only violation is a technical one, proceeds will be taxable under the transfer for value rule.

Do not try to use logic as a working guideline to this rule. Read the Internal Revenue Code and the Treasury regulations. Again, suspect a problem whenever there is:

- a transfer of a policy or any interest in a policy; and

- any type of valuable consideration is (or could be) given in return for that transfer.

The safe course is to consider every transfer as suspect until scrupulously examined. As noted below, even what appears to be an outright gift of life insurance may incorporate a fatal element of consideration in certain circumstances.

Five safe-harbor exceptions may shelter a transfer from the transfer for value rule penalty—even if there is a transfer for valuable consideration.

These five safe harbors consist of the following:

1. the transferor's basis (in whole or in part) exception;

2. the transfer to the insured exception;

3. the transfer to a partner of the insured exception;

4. the transfer to a partnership in which the insured is a partner exception; and

5. the transfer to a corporation in which the insured is a shareholder or officer exception.

Exception 1: The Transferor's Basis

Code section 101(a)(2)(A) provides that the transfer for value rule does not apply if the transferee's basis for determining gain or loss upon a subsequent sale of a policy or an interest in a policy is determined in whole or in part by reference to the transferor's basis. In a nutshell this means that if the basis in the contract is carried over from the transferor to the recipient the death proceeds will remain income tax free.

The rule above states that the beneficiary will receive tax free proceeds if basis is determined in whole or in part by reference to the transferor's basis. There are two common examples of the in whole portion of this exception. One is the case of outright gifts of policies that generally take the form of an absolute assignment of a policy for love and affection. Here, no consideration of any kind changes hands. The transferor merely gives the policy to the transferee.

Example. Assume an insured sells his son a $100,000 policy on his life for $100 when the policy's gift tax value is $1,000. The son's basis for determining gain or loss upon a subsequent sale will be the father's basis (the net premiums he has paid) with an adjustment for any gift taxes the father may pay on the transfer. Here, the son's basis is determined in part by his father's basis. Even though there is a sale by the father of a policy worth $1,000 in return for $100 cash paid by the son, to the extent of the $900 balance ($1,000 value less $100 consideration paid) there is a gift from the father to the son. Tax law requires that the son carry over the father's basis (cost) for the portion of the transfer that was a gift. The proceeds are income tax free at the father's death because the tests of the transferor's basis exception are met.

The other common example of a clear carryover basis situation is when a policy is transferred from one business to another in a tax-free corporate reorganization.

So where the transferee's basis is determined by carrying over the donor's basis (with an adjustment for any gift taxes paid), the proceeds will be income tax free even if there is a transfer and even if it is made in return for valuable consideration.

Planners must be wary of the seeming simplicity of this exception. Many think that as long as the transfer is characterized by the taxpayer as a gift or part gift-part sale, the proceeds will be exempt from the transfer for value rule. This is a very dangerous and misleading presumption.

The problem is based on the technical way the basis laws work. In some cases, the transferee's basis is determined in whole or in part by reference to the transferor's basis (and therefore the transfer for value rule is avoided due to this first exception).

In other cases, the transferee's basis is not determined by reference to the transferor's basis even though at least part of the transfer constitutes a gift and is considered so by the parties. Instead, basis is determined by the amount deemed paid by the transferee for the property.[6] This falls outside the protective safe harbor.

In the example above where an insured sells his son a $100,000 policy for $100 when the policy's gift tax value is $1,000, there is clearly a $900 gift and the son will determine his basis at least in part by carrying over his father's basis (plus any gift tax payable). (The son can then add to his basis the $100 he paid, plus any premiums he pays after the transfer.) The entire proceeds will be received income tax free because the son's lifetime basis in the policy is determined at least in part by referring back to the basis of the policy in his father's hands.

Now let's look at the result where the son's basis may be determined by what he pays. Remember, the part gift-part sale protective rule only applies when it results in a carryover of all or a portion of the transferor's basis.

The problem is that the transferee is considered to pay not only what he actually pays for the policy, but also any amount the transferee is deemed to pay by relieving the transferor of the obligation to pay a policy loan.

Here is where the trap lies: If the policy loan (and any cash or other property received in the exchange) is *greater* than the transferor's basis, the transferee takes as his basis the higher of: (1) the amount the buyer actually pays for the policy *plus* the amount he is deemed to pay by reason of relieving the transferor of the obligation to repay the loan, or: (2) the transferor's basis. Any gift tax payable is then added to the contract's basis.[7] So in this situation, the transfer is treated as if the transferee-buyer acquires the policy in a sale and not a gift!

Example. Assume a client has a $28,000 basis in a policy that he gives to his son. The basis is due to premiums he paid net of any dividends. At the time he gives the policy to his son, it is subject to a policy loan of $25,000. The client's basis is $3,000 greater than the loan. At the date of the gift, the replacement value of the policy is $30,000. In this situation there will be no transfer for value problem. The father is deemed to "sell" his son $25,000 worth of policy (the amount of the loan debt he is relieved of) for consideration in that amount. The father is deemed to make a gift of $5,000 (the difference between the policy's $30,000 value at the time of the transfer and its sale portion of $25,000). The son takes the policy at least partially with reference to his father's basis. So the proceeds will be received income tax free.

Now assume the same facts as above except the father's basis is only $22,000 rather than $28,000. The $25,000 loan against the policy exceeds the $22,000 basis by $3,000. If the father sells the policy for its loan amount rather than gives it to his son, the father will realize a $3,000 gain. Under this circumstance, the son's basis is determined solely by the $25,000 amount he is deemed to have paid his father (i.e., the debt he is considered to have relieved his father of and assumed in the transaction). For purposes of computing the son's basis, the father's basis is irrelevant. Unfortunately, this means the son's receipt of the proceeds will be subject to the transfer for value rule because the son does not determine his basis in whole or in part by reference to the transferor's (his father's) basis. He determines it solely on the amount paid for the policy. There is a transfer of a policy, for valuable consideration received, with none of the exceptions met, and therefore the entire proceeds are subject to ordinary income tax.

———————

Under the transferor's basis exception, it is generally safe to transfer life insurance to the insured's spouse or ex-spouse (if the transfer is incident to a divorce).[8] Why is such a transfer safe even if cash changes hands? Code section 1041 treats interspousal transfers as nontaxable events, so in the case where one spouse transfers a life insurance contract to another spouse, the consequences are:

1. No gain is recognized by either party for income tax purposes even if the policy is received in exchange for a surrender of marital rights.

2. The transferee spouse (or ex-spouse) takes as her basis the transferor's basis and therefore falls within the transferor's basis exception.

Under the transferor's basis exception, the transferee stands in the shoes of the transferor. This means that a transfer of a policy to a transferor's basis category of transferee carries over and retains the same tax treatment of the policy that it had in the hands of the transferor. In other words, if the proceeds were exempt before the transfer, they remain exempt after the transfer.

The opposite is also true. If the proceeds of a policy were subject to tax under the transfer for value rule before the present transfer, they continue to be tainted. A transfer to a transferor's basis transferee is not enough to eliminate the taint. Where the last owner's basis is determined in whole or part by reference to the prior owner's basis, the income tax exclusion is limited to the sum of:

*   the amount which the transferor could have excluded had no transfer taken place; plus

*   any premiums and other amounts paid by the final transferee.

———————

Example 1. Assume that an insured purchases a $500,000 policy on his own life and gives it to his daughter, who later sells it to the insured's son. Here, the son must report the entire $500,000 (less the amount he pays for the policy and any premiums he later pays) as ordinary income when his father dies. Although the transfer from father to daughter is protected because of the daughter's carryover of the father's basis, that protection does not extend to the sale from her to the insured's son.

———————

Example 2. Assume an insured gives the policy on his life to his daughter, who later gives it to her own daughter. Here, the granddaughter's basis is determined by a carryover of her mother's basis which, in turn, is carried over from (and therefore determined by reference to) the insured's basis. The proceeds will be income tax free.

———————

Example 3. Assume a transfer of a policy from a corporation to X, a co-shareholder of Y, the insured. X pays the corporation an amount equal to the policy's value at the time of transfer. Assume further that X, the new policyowner, then transfers the policy on his co-shareholder's life to W, X's wife, for love and affection. Although a transfer of a policy on X's life to W, his wife, would be protected (because of the "in whole or in part" exception), the transfer of the policy on Y's life was tainted even before X transferred it. The subsequent transfer to W from X does not cleanse the taint.

———————

There is a solution. Make the next-to-last transfer to one of the four protected parties (the insured, a partner of the insured, a partnership in which the insured is a partner, or a corporation in which the insured is a shareholder or officer). At that point, the transfer for value taint is washed away.[9] Proceeds will be income tax free if that party then makes an untainted gift.

Exception 2: Transfers to the Insured

Code section 101(a)(2)(B) provides that the transfer for value rule will not apply to transfers to the insured, to a partner of the insured, to a partnership in which the insured is a partner, or to a corporation in which the insured is a shareholder or officer. These protected party exceptions are obviously the safest of all the exceptions because they require the least verification and are easy to implement.

Of all of these protected party safe harbors, the most certain is the insured. The clearest, safest, most positive way to avoid the transfer for value rule is to be sure that the last transfer for valuable consideration is to the insured. No matter how little or how much money or other consideration is paid by the insured to obtain the policy, once the insured becomes the transferee, all prior transfer for value taint is eliminated and the proceeds regain (or retain) their income tax free status.

Since the transfer for value rule is an income tax provision, any transfer that is treated as made to the insured for income tax purposes should qualify for the transfer to the insured exception. Thus, a transfer to a trust for which the insured is treated as the income tax payer (e.g., an intentionally defective grantor trust) should qualify for the exception.[10]

Exception 3: Transfers to a Partner of the Insured

If the transfer is to someone who is the insured's partner in a legitimate partnership, proceeds will be income tax free even if the transfer is for valuable consideration. The same is true for a transfer to a co-member of a Limited Liability Company (LLC), as long as the LLC is taxed as a partnership.

Assume two individuals are partners in a real estate development partnership and each partner owns a policy on his own life. Each partner purchases the policy on the other's life. There is a transfer for value because there is a transfer of a policy for valuable consideration. However, because the transfer is to a partner of the insured, the proceeds will be received income tax free.

It appears that the only requirement under this safe harbor is that the transferee partner must own a legitimate (no matter how small) share of an operating or investment partnership.[11] Even though the life insurance policy is in no way connected with the partnership or its operation, as long as the recipient partner is a partner of the insured (presumably at the date of receipt of the policy or the interest in the policy), the insurance proceeds should be income tax free.

Exception 4: Transfers to a Partnership in Which the Insured is a Partner

This exception, like the one above, has become quite popular in recent years because of its planning flexibility.[12] It requires only that the policy be transferred to a partnership in which the insured is a partner (or to an LLC taxed as a partnership in which the insured is a member).

Example. Assume two individuals are partners in a real estate development partnership, and each partner owns a policy on his own life. Each partner sells the policy on his life to the partnership. Based on these facts there is a transfer for value, but it is exempt from the transfer for value rule because it is made to the insured's partnership.

Practitioners often ask if a client can establish a partnership in name only to avoid the sting of the transfer for value rule. The IRS has approved a transfer of a policy to a partnership established specifically to receive and hold policies insuring the lives of its partners.[13] However, a safer and suggested course is to transfer the policy to a partnership (or LLC electing taxation as a partnership) established for independent business or investment purposes.[14]

Exception 5: Transfers to a Corporation in Which the Insured is a Shareholder or Officer

Under this safe harbor, the transfer for value rule does not apply to a transfer to a corporation if the insured is either: (1) an officer; or (2) a shareholder in the corporation (presumably on the date the policy is transferred).

Example. Assume an individually owned policy is transferred to the insured's corporate employer to be used as key employee coverage or to fund a stock redemption buy-sell agreement. The insured at the time of the transfer is the treasurer of the company and owns 30 percent of the company's stock. Thus, the transfer for value rule does not apply because the insured is both an officer (treasurer) and a shareholder.

Beware: This exemption does not protect transfers to persons who are merely:

- co-shareholders of the insured;

- key employees (no matter how important); or

- directors who are neither officers nor shareholders.

Summary of Safe Harbors

Transfers to the following persons are protected:

- Anyone whose basis is determined by reference to transferor's basis

- The insured

- The spouse of insured

- The ex-spouse of insured, if the transfer is pursuant to a divorce or separation agreement

- A partner of the insured

- A partnership in which insured is a partner

- A corporation in which insured is a shareholder or officer

Transfers to any of the following are not protected and may set the transfer for value trap:

- A co-stockholder of insured

- A purchaser who takes the policy subject to a loan in excess of the transferor's basis

- Any other person or entity not listed above

TYPICAL PERSONAL LIFE INSURANCE PLANNING PROBLEMS

Transfers of life insurance policies between family members other than spouses are a quicksand pit for clients and their planners.

Assume an insured purchases a policy on his life from his corporate employer. He then immediately names his wife as beneficiary. She collects the policy proceeds upon the insured's death. The proceeds should be exempt because the transfer is to a proper party, the insured.

Not so easy to recognize are the much more deadly part gift-part sale situations discussed above which are usually triggered by policy loans. If a transferred policy is subject to a policy loan, the amount of that loan is treated as an amount paid for the policy. In most cases the insured's basis (net premiums paid) exceeds the amount of the loan. Therefore, the transferee's basis is determined by reference to the transferor's and there will be no problem.

But where the amount of the policy loan exceeds the transferor's basis, two adverse results are likely:

1. To the extent the loan exceeds the transferor's net cost; ordinary income is realized just as if the policy is sold to the transferee for a payment in the amount of the loan.

2. The transferee's basis is determined, neither in whole nor in part by reference to the transferor's basis but by the sale price—the amount of the loan. The result? The transferor's basis exception is not applicable.

There is a solution to the policy loan tax trap: Limit the amount of any proposed loan to some level that is clearly less than the transferor's basis. Then there will be no taxable sale and the transferee's basis will clearly be determined by reference to the transferor's basis.

TRANSFER FOR VALUE PROBLEMS IN BUY-SELL PLANNING

In planning for corporate or partnership buy-sell agreements funded with life insurance, as in any of the other "high risk areas discussed below, it is essential to examine (and suspect) any transfer of a life insurance policy funding the buy-sell arrangement.[15]

Here is a checklist of potential transfer for value traps in the buy-sell planning area.

The Uninsurable Shareholder Trap

An uninsurable shareholder sells her individually owned insurance to a co-shareholder to help fund a cross-purchase agreement. The transaction clearly falls within the transfer for value rule—as do the following two transfers.

The Switch from Stock Redemption to Cross-Purchase Trap

A corporation sells a policy to a co-shareholder of the insured because the company wants to switch from a stock redemption plan to a cross-purchase agreement and sells its corporate-owned policies on the lives of its shareholders to their co-shareholders.

The Gift of Policies by Corporation Double Trouble Trap

Two shareholders want to change an insured stock redemption agreement to a cross-purchase plan. But instead of selling the policies, they intend merely to have the corporation give each shareholder the policy on the life of the insured.

Although the shareholders may call this transaction a gift to each other, the IRS is not likely to accept this transaction as a gift (and will probably challenge the distribution from the corporation as a dividend or as compensation).

The Purchase by Insured Followed by Gift Trap

Two shareholders want to change an insured stock redemption agreement to a cross-purchase plan. They intend to avoid the transfer for value rule by a purchase of the policy from the corporation by the insured followed by a gift of the policy from the insured to the other shareholder.

They will probably not succeed. The IRS will doubtlessly argue that the double transfer is really one directly from the corporation. Failing that argument, the IRS will claim the reciprocity—I'll give you the policy on my life if you give me the policy on yours—constitutes consideration for the transfers.

The Sale by Estate Trap

Assume there are three shareholders, X, Y, and Z. The buy-sell agreement is set up on a cross-purchase basis so that each owns policies on the other shareholders' lives. If X dies, the policy X owned on Y is sold by X's estate to Z. The policy X owned on Z is sold by X's estate to Y.

The proposed transactions will trigger the trap because Y and Z, as mere co-shareholders, are not protected parties. There are several possible indirect solutions to this problem:

1. Both policies can be sold to the corporation. A sale of a policy to a corporation in which the insured is an officer or shareholder is a safe transfer. The corporation can then establish a stock redemption or Code section 303 partial stock redemption plan that meshes with the existing cross-purchase agreement. The result would be a hybrid plan, because the survivors, Y and Z in the example above, would still own policies on each other's lives. Of course, they can also transfer those policies to the corporation and use a stock redemption agreement.

2. The decedent's estate can surrender each policy for cash or can keep the policies in force, or place the policies on extended term or make the policies paid up for a lower face amount.

3. The survivors can purchase the policies on their own lives and continue them as personal insurance.

The Sale by a Trust Trap

A trust's sale of an interest in a life insurance policy to trust beneficiaries other than the insured can trigger the trap. For example, suppose a couple creates an irrevocable life insurance trust and places cash inside the trust for the trust to purchase and pay premiums for a second-to-die life insurance policy on their lives. At some later date, the couple decides to discontinue contributions. Since the trust does not have sufficient funds to keep the insurance in force, the couple's children decide to purchase the policy and pay premiums.

There would be a transfer of a policy and it would be for valuable consideration.

In many of these situations, the solution is to make the buyers partners with the insured prior to the transaction. It is essential in these situations that the partnership be created and actively managed for reasons other than to merely to shield the transaction from the transfer for value rule. Be sure the entity is recognized as a partnership under state law. Also be sure that the partnership files federal income tax returns. It is also important to show that the parties intend to continue operating as a partnership at least through and including the year in which the purchase of the life insurance policy is consummated. Overall, create evidence that the firm is a legitimate operating entity.[16]

The Trusteed Cross-Purchase Trap

Assume a cross-purchase buy-sell agreement is established and a trust is created to facilitate the transaction and assure an orderly transfer of the corporate stock (i.e., a trusteed cross-purchase arrangement). A corporate-owned life insurance policy on each shareholder's life is then transferred to the trustee who is to collect the proceeds and pay them to shareholder's estate.

The buy-sell agreement requires the insured's co-shareholders to pay premiums on the policy. At the insured's death, the trustee will collect the proceeds (on behalf of the surviving shareholders) and, in exchange for the stock held by the insured stockholder, pay the estate the appropriate amount of cash.

There is a transfer of a life insurance policy. But is there valuable consideration? If so, what is it and when is it paid? At least one court has held under these facts that the agreement of the co-shareholders to relieve the business of the burden of making premium payments and to buy the insured's stock at his death with the policy proceeds was sufficient consideration to give rise to a transfer for value—even though no cash was paid for the policies.[17]

In another example, assume six shareholders, all related, would like to establish a buy-sell agreement. But they are concerned about the bookkeeping and costs of the thirty policies needed to insure each shareholder individually.[18] Their attorney suggests that they form a trust, contribute cash to the trust to pay the premiums, have the trust buy one policy on each shareholder's life, and use the proceeds to buy the stock for the surviving

shareholders. When a shareholder dies, his interest in the policies on the lives of the surviving shareholders disappears (according to the contract).

In the authors' opinion, trouble awaits those who fund a cross-purchase buy-sell in a trust which provides that, at the death of one shareholder, the interest he had in the policies on the lives of the others terminates (vanishes into thin air) and magically the survivors end up with an interest (through the trust) in the remaining policies on the other survivors lives. This "one trust-one policy on each shareholder's life" cross-purchase technique (unless the shareholders are also partners) is almost certain to attract litigation with the IRS.

Why? Upon the first death, there will be no physical transfer, and legal title to the policies on the lives of the survivors will not change. The trust will still be the legal owner of the policies. But the beneficial interest in the decedent's share of the policies on his co-shareholders' lives will shift to them. Each survivor will gain a beneficial interest he did not have before on the life or lives of his co-shareholders. Furthermore, on each subsequent death, there will be an additional transfer of equitable ownership to the surviving co-shareholders.

Where is the valuable consideration? No policyowner would allow the beneficial interest in a policy he or she owned on another shareholder's life to pass to the other shareholders unless each of the other shareholders did the same. That reciprocity would be consideration enough for the IRS.

The Group Funded Cross-Purchase Buy-Sell Tax Trap

Abe and Sadie are unrelated shareholders. Each is insured for $100,000 under a corporate-owned group term life contract paid for by the corporation. They name each other as beneficiaries of their respective group term life coverage in order to fund the buy-sell with (from the corporation's perspective) tax deductible dollars. Each agrees to accept the proceeds of the other's group term life insurance as payment for his share of the business.

There is clearly a transfer of an interest in a policy and, although no cash is paid in return for the policies and even though the coverage is pure term insurance, there is the requisite valuable consideration, which is reciprocity. Abe would not have named Sadie as his beneficiary without her agreement to do the same.

The Endorsement Type Split-Dollar Tax Trap

Ted and Carol want to set up a cross-purchase buy-sell agreement. Neither has the after-tax cash to pay premiums. Their corporation sets up a split-dollar arrangement to assist them in funding the buy-sell. The corporation will purchase a policy on the life of each shareholder. At the death of either insured, the corporation will recover its outlay first. Any death benefit in excess of the corporation's interest (i.e., its cumulative outlay) will be payable to the insured's co-shareholder. The net proceeds of the policy on Ted's life will be paid to Carol and the net proceeds of the policy on Carol's life will be paid to Ted.

In the authors' opinion, when the corporation as policyowner names each insured's co-shareholder as beneficiary of part of the proceeds, there is a transfer of part of the corporation's interest in the policy, a portion of the death proceeds. In reality the corporation shifts the beneficial right to the death proceeds from itself to each insured's co-shareholder in consideration of the insured's continuing services as an employee. Thus, there is a transfer of an interest in a policy from the corporation to the co-shareholder of the insured employee (i.e., the corporation allows the insured to name the policy beneficiary) in return for the valuable consideration of the employee's services.

A further argument the IRS could make is that—to the extent each shareholder recognizes income (economic benefits)—it is as if the corporation purchases term insurance on his behalf. Normally, such a transaction would not be a problem because the term insurance purchased is usually on the insured's life and, if it is transferred to someone other than the insured, it is typically done without consideration. In a cross-purchase endorsement split-dollar, however, the employer owns each policy at inception. The policy insures the life of a co-shareholder of the person to whom the company endorses (shifts an interest in) a portion of the policy proceeds. This is clearly a transfer of an interest in a policy and the reciprocity, the fact that each shareholder tacitly allows the other to do so, provides the requisite consideration.

Avoiding the transfer is the answer to the problem. Instead of using the endorsement method in which the corporation is the original owner of the policy, the collateral assignment method eliminates any need to transfer an interest in the policy. Under the collateral assignment method, each shareholder purchases a policy on the life of his or her co-shareholder and owns it from the beginning. He or she then collaterally assigns it to

the corporation (a protected party) as security for the loan. Because there is no transfer of a policy or an interest in a policy (except to a protected party), the transfer for value rule will not apply.

The Perhaps not so Safe Gift Tax Trap

Assume a father gives a policy on his life to his son and the father pays the gift tax. After the gift of the policy, the father and son enter into a cross-purchase agreement for the purchase of the father's stock in a corporation at the father's death. The father dies and the son, in fact, uses the policy proceeds to purchase the father's stock.

Does the son take the insurance income tax free? At first glance, the answer seems to be yes: the father intends the transfer of the policy to be a gift to his son (even though the father enters into a buy-sell agreement) and even files a gift tax return on the transaction and pays a gift tax.

But wise practitioners will ask some additional questions.[19] These include:

1. Do the transfer of the policy and the execution of the agreement occur contemporaneously?

2. How far apart do the two transactions occur? In other words, are the two events apart of the same transaction? If so, the IRS can argue that the son pays a price (kept the policy in force) as part of his agreement to buy the father's stock.

3. Is there further evidence (such as continued gifts from the father) that establishes an intent to make the life insurance transfer a gift rather than part of a business transaction?

4. Is there an explicit agreement between the parties that the son will use the insurance proceeds to buy the father's stock at his death?

The IRS may try to prove that, although the transaction is cast as a gift, it is really part of a larger arrangement in which the transfer of the policy was bargained for by the son. Could it then be argued that even if the son's agreement constitutes some consideration for the transfer of the policy, so long as the son's basis is—at least in part—determined by reference to his father's basis, the proceeds retain their income tax free status? In the authors' opinion this technique is dangerous unless the facts are exactly right.

TRANSFER FOR VALUE PROBLEMS IN EMPLOYEE BENEFIT PLANNING

There are a number of situations in which clients can fall into the transfer for value trap in the employee benefit planning area. One is where there is a transfer of life insurance policies to the trustee of a qualified retirement plan. The transfer may take place as a part of the corporate employer's contribution to the plan on behalf of the participant or as a part of a participant's voluntary contribution to the plan.

In most cases the client will succeed if the transaction is properly structured and the following no significant change of ownership rationale is employed.

1. Assume an agreement between an employee, his employer, and a trust that provides for the employer to purchase an existing life insurance policy from the employee for its cash value. The employer proposes to transfer the policy to the trust as a part of the employer's required annual contribution to the trust. The trustee will pay the premiums on the policy. At the employee's death the trustee will pay the insurance proceeds to his designee. Assume the proceeds are in fact paid to the plan trustee, who turns them over to the insured's designee.

    There is no transfer for value problem here because there is no significant change in beneficial ownership. The proceeds retain their income tax free status because, in essence, there is no transfer and therefore the transfer for value rule cannot apply.

2. Assume a successor corporation's retirement plan buys life insurance contracts from a predecessor employer's Keogh plan. Here, the purchase of the insurance by the new trustee from the old trustee for the policy's cash value at the date of purchase should not be a transfer for value because no significant change in the beneficial interest of the contract occurs.

3. Assume an employee-participant personally owns a life insurance contract with a cash value. The employee-participant wants to transfer that policy (as a voluntary employee contribution) to a profit sharing trust of which she is a participant. Under the plan terms, the proceeds continue to be payable to the employee's

beneficiary and the policy's cash surrender value is payable to the participant upon her retirement or other termination of employment.

Because the proceeds are payable to the employee's designated beneficiary upon her death and the cash surrender value is payable to the participant upon her retirement or other termination of employment, there is no significant change in the policy's beneficial ownership. Therefore, the IRS should conclude that there is no transfer for value.

4. Assume a corporation establishes an irrevocable rabbi trust with a third party trustee. Assets in the rabbi trust remain subject to creditors of the corporation if it becomes insolvent or bankrupt. Participants receive only an unsecured right to the assets in the trust. The employer transfers certain life insurance contracts to the trust. The employer or the trust will pay the premiums and the trust will become the nominal owner and beneficiary of the contracts upon their transfer to the trust.

    Is there a transfer of a policy or an interest in a policy by the corporation? Here, the proceeds should be excludable from income tax of the trust and of the employer because there is never the requisite transfer. The trust should be viewed not as a trust but as an agency or alter ego of the employer. There is no change in equitable ownership of the policies, so the death benefits of the policies will retain their income tax free status.

Split-dollar life insurance arrangements are tricky and, as noted above, are potential transfer for value problem areas.

1. Assume the insured's wife owns a policy on his life. She then collaterally assigns the policy to the insured's solely-owned corporation to fund a split-dollar arrangement. Thereafter, the wife transfers her interest in the policy, subject to the corporation's rights under the split-dollar arrangement, to the insured.

    The insured and the corporation propose to enter into a new split-dollar agreement. The insured intends to assign his interest in the policy to his wife. She will then name herself as beneficiary of the proceeds in excess of the amount due the corporation under the split-dollar plan.

Is there a problem with this arrangement? The transfer of rights in the policy to the corporation qualify for the proper party exemption provided for transfers to a corporation in which the insured is either an officer or shareholder. So any amounts received under the policy upon the death of the insured should be entirely income tax exempt. The transfer of any rights in the policy to the insured should be similarly exempt. The final transfer, a gratuitous transfer of the insured's policy rights to his wife, should also be exempt because she takes as her basis in the contract an amount determined in whole or part by reference to the insured's basis.

2. Assume an insured owns all of the stock of a professional corporation. The firm owns a $1,000,000 life insurance policy on the shareholder's life. The insured purchases the policy from the corporation in exchange for its cash value. The insured then gives the policy to his wife. The wife sets up a split-dollar arrangement with the insured's corporation and collaterally assigns the policy to the corporation.

Here, the beneficiary should collect the proceeds free of income tax because the first transfer from the corporation to the insured is a transfer to the insured and the second transfer is one in which the transferee's basis is determined in whole or in part by reference to the transferor's.

3. Assume a corporation owns several policies on the life of its shareholder, M. The corporation sells the policies on M's life to an irrevocable trust established for his spouse and children. The trust is a partner of the insured and his son in a business venture and has been so for almost twenty years.

Here, the IRS will probably hold that because the trust is the insured's business partner, the proceeds will be income tax free as long as the partnership itself has an independent business or investment reason for existence separate and apart from meeting the transfer for value exception.

SUMMARY

1. Suspect a transfer for value problem in every transfer of an existing policy—or any shift of an interest in a policy.

2. Whenever possible, make transfers only to protected parties (those excepted from the rule).

3. Do not transfer a policy with a loan in excess of the policyowner's basis. Reduce the loan below the transferor's basis or do not make the transfer.

4. Eliminate prior tainted transfers by making a further transfer to a protected party. If the insured is in good health (likely to live more than three years), consider a transfer to the insured followed by a gift.

CHAPTER ENDNOTES

1. For more information, see Brody and Leimberg, "The Not So Tender Trap – The Transfer for Value Rule," *Journal of the American Society of CLU & ChFC* (May 1984), p. 32, and Commito, "Transfer for Value Rulings Offer Planning Opportunities," *Journal of the American Society of CLU & ChFC* (Nov. 1991), p. 38.

2. This provision applies to contracts issued after June 8, 1997. TRA '97, Sec. 1084(d); I.R.C. §101(a)(2).

3. Treas. Reg. §1.101-1(b)(4).

4. *Monroe v. Patterson*, 197 F. Supp. 146 (N.D. Ala. 1961).

5. "Insurable interest" is a term covered in more detail in Chapter 5 of this text.

6. See "Rearranging the Ownership of Life Insurance, The Part Gift, Part Sale Exception to the Transfer for Value Rule," *Keeping Current*, Vol. 12, Number 1 (December 1981), and "Careless Financial Planning By Violating the Transfer for Value Rule Can Transform Tax-Free Life Insurance Proceeds into Taxable Income," *Trusts and Estates* (January, 1989), p. 56.

7. Treas. Reg. §1.1015-4.

   "Perhaps it could be argued that even if the indebtedness is greater than the transferor's basis, the transferee's basis is still determined in part by the transferor's basis because the computation required by Treas. Reg. §1.1015-4 to determine the transferee's basis involves reference to the transferor's basis. Nevertheless, until the matter is resolved, it may be advisable to either avoid the transfer of a policy where the indebtedness exceeds the transferor's basis or to reduce the indebtedness below the transferor's basis prior to the transfer." 111-4th T.M. *Estates, Gifts, and Trusts Portfolio*, p. A-40.

8. A transfer of property between spouses is considered a gift, with the transferee taking the basis of the transferor. I.R.C. §1041(b). A transfer is "incident to a divorce" if the transfer occurs within one year after the date the marriage ends or is related to the cessation of the marriage. I.R.C. §1041(c). A transfer is generally treated as related to the cessation of the marriage if it is pursuant to a divorce or separation instrument and the transfer occurs not more than six years after the date on which the marriage

ends. Temp. Treas. Reg. §1.1041-1T(A-7). This protection does not extend to nonresident alien spouses. I.R.C. §1041(d). I.R.C. §1041 applies to transfers of property after July 18, 1984, or after December 31, 1983, if both spouses so elect.

9.   Where the transfer is made to one of the proper party individuals or entities described in I.R.C. §101(a)(2)(B), the entire amount of the proceeds will be excludable from the transferee's gross income. Treas. Reg. §1.101-1(b)(3).

10. See for example Rev. Rul. 2007-13.

11. The size of that share can be relatively small. The IRS has approved a transfer of a life insurance policy to a partner owning a 1 percent interest in a partnership in which the insured was a partner. Let. Rul. 9045004.

12. See for example, Let. Ruls. 9725009, 9725008, and 9725007.

13. Let. Rul. 9309021. Note that the Service will not issue rulings concerning whether or not the exception applies where substantially all of a partnership's assets consist of life insurance policies on the lives of its members. Rev. Proc. 2007-3, 2007-1 IRB 108.

14. See *Swanson v. Comm.*, 518 F.2d 59 (8th Cir. 1975).

     See Let. Rul. 9843024 for an example of how a sale of a life insurance policy from an irrevocable trust to a limited partnership in which the insured is a partner fell within a safe harbor to the transfer for value rule. Here, a Family Limited Partnership (FLP) was formed to acquire, hold, invest in, manage, trade, sell, or otherwise deal with real and personal, tangible and intangible property—expressly including life insurance. The partnership indicated that it wanted partnership rather than corporate income tax treatment. The previously established irrevocable life insurance trust created by the insured (who is also the general partner of the FLP) proposed to sell its interest in the insurance on the insured's life to the FLP. Each policy will be sold for an amount equal to the fair market value of the policies, i.e., their interpolated terminal reserve plus any unearned premium on the date of the sale. Here, the partnership held substantial assets in addition to the insurance.

This ruling contained a number of warnings that should be considered by planners before relying on the "transfer to a partnership in which the insured is a partner" safe harbor exception. Specifically, the IRS refused to express an opinion on whether the insured partner reduces his interest in the FLP. Likewise, the IRS was noncommittal regarding the FLP's federal tax classification as a partnership if it disposes of all assets other than life insurance. As the authors have noted in the past, it appears that the "check-the-box" regulations may not be a total and absolute solution to transfer for value problems—at least not at this point. This means a partnership that owns only life insurance and has no purpose other than to hold that life insurance and thus escape the orbit of the transfer for value rule might be something other than a partnership for purposes of the exception to the rule. The solution is simple and one the authors have been advocating since the first edition of this book: Don't rely upon a partnership to fall within a transfer-for-value safe harbor unless the insured has some real and meaningful partnership interest and unless you can show the entity is doing something more than just holding assets, particularly if the only assets consist of life insurance contracts that require nothing more than the payment of premiums.

15. Let. Rul. 9727024. See "Cross-Purchase Life Policies Did Not Result in Transfers for Value," *Journal of Taxation* (October, 1997), pg. 250.

16. Let. Rul. 199903020.

17. *Monroe v. Patterson*, 197 F. Supp. 146 (N.D. Ala. 1961).

18. The number of policies needed in a cross-purchase grows every time the business grows and the formula in the agreement calls for a revaluation. That number is N × (N-1) where N is the number of shareholders. With six shareholders, thirty policies are needed–every time the company is revalued.

19. "Questions and Answers on Estate Planning and Administration," *Trusts and Estates* (November, 1985), p. 47.

LIFE INSURANCE VALUATION[1]

CHAPTER 26

INTRODUCTION

Life insurance must be valued for various reasons in a variety of income, gift, estate tax, and nontax situations. Although one would think that the value of life insurance is simply its cash surrender value, in many situations this is not the case. When it comes to actually valuing this asset[2]—because of new product designs, new reserving rules, different methodologies used by life insurance companies, different IRS rules for estate, gift and income tax purposes, and other factors—there can be a great deal of uncertainty raising the potential for dispute and litigation. In order to best serve your clients, it is important that you have a basic understanding of how to value life insurance in the following situations.

1. When determining a person's net worth, generally the value can easily be determined by simply contacting the insurance company and requesting the policy's current cash surrender value.

2. When a policy is being gifted to a trust or heirs.

3. When a policy is being gifted to a charity.

4. When the policy owner has predeceased the insured and the policy is being valued for purposes of completing the deceased owner's estate tax return.

5. When a policy is being distributed by an employer to an employee.

6. When a policy is being distributed or purchased from a qualified retirement plan.

7. Where a policy is being sold by one party to another.

VALUATION FOR ESTATE AND GIFT TAX PURPOSES

For estate and gift tax purposes the Internal Revenue Service (IRS) has provided specific guidance as to the value of a life insurance policy. Treasury Regulations sections 20.2031-1 and 25.2512-1 provide that the value of a life insurance policy, just like any other type of property, is its Fair Market Value (FMV). This is the price at which the property would change hands between a willing buyer and a willing seller; neither party being under any compulsion to buy or to sell, and both having reasonable knowledge of relevant facts. The FMV is determined by reference to all the facts and circumstances relating to the transfer.[3]

Until the last decade or so, there was no organized market for life insurance policies. In most cases a policy owner had no choice other than to surrender the policy back to the life insurance company that issued it. The advent of the secondary market (i.e., life settlement market) has created an opportunity for policy owners to sell their policies to third party investors for an amount significantly greater than the cash surrender value. However, the secondary market is generally limited to the purchase of policies on older, unhealthy insureds, larger policies, and single life policies. Therefore, younger, healthier insureds may still have to look to the insurance company as the only market for their life insurance policies. To date, the IRS has neither insisted on nor opined on whether or not prices in the settlement market must (or can) be considered in the determination of valuation for tax purposes. It is the opinion of the authors that the secondary market value is the very essence of FMV (i.e., willing buyer, willing seller), and thus should be determinative of FMV in the limited situations where there is documentation showing it is higher than the value reported by an insurer.

Due to the fact that in the past there were no organized market forces available to determine the FMV of a life insurance policy (and there still isn't one for most insureds), the IRS issued regulations in the early 1960's to provide guidance as to what constitutes the fair market value of a life insurance policy for estate and gift tax purposes.

In Treasury Regulations sections 20.2031-8 and 25.2512-6 the IRS indicated that the value of a life insurance policy is based on the cost of a hypothetical comparable contract.

1. For newly issued policies (contracts transferred immediately after purchase or those within their first year), FMV is the cost of the policy (i.e., the gross premiums paid by the transferor).[4] Note: This rule may apply to policies which are transferred within a year of a section 1035 exchange (see discussion in first Frequently Asked Question at the end of this chapter).

2. For policies which are single premium (one in which one premium, paid on the date the policy is issued, funds the contract completely for the life of the insured) or paid-up (one in which no further premiums remain to be paid), the value is the single premium which the issuing company would charge currently for a comparable contract of the same amount on the life of a person the insured's age at the time of the transfer.[5]

3. For policies that have been in force for some time and that have continuing premiums, FMV can be approximated by using Interpolated Terminal Reserve (ITR) plus unearned premiums. (Note: This method may not be used if such approximation is not reasonably close to the full value (e.g., the insured is terminally ill).

Interpolated Terminal Reserve (ITR)

ITR is a key concept when it comes to valuing life insurance. An insurance company must set aside a reserve each year to meet its contractual obligations to the policy owner. The terminal (year-end) reserve typically will be greater than the policy's cash value in the early years of the contract. When a taxable event occurs at any time other than the policy's anniversary date, the reserve on the date of the event must be interpolated, i.e. extrapolated by using both the last policy anniversary date reserve and the reserve on the next anniversary date.

Example. Assuming the policy had been in force for some time, if the reserve as of the last anniversary date is $15,000 and the reserve for the next anniversary date is $20,000 and a gift of the policy is made exactly six months after the last anniversary, then the interpolated terminal reserve would be $17,500 (half of the $5,000 increase in reserves, $2,500, is added to the $15,000 last anniversary reserve).

The computational process is:

Step 1: State the policy's terminal reserve at the end of the next policy year.

Step 2: State the policy's terminal reserve at the end of the prior policy year.

Step 3: The difference between the Step 1 and Step 2 result is the increase in the terminal reserve for a full year. If the valuation date occurs, say four months (one-third of a year) after the anniversary date of the policy, one-third of the increase would be added to the prior year's (Step 2) terminal reserve to estimate (interpolate) the terminal reserve on the date of the taxable event. Any unearned premium as of the date of the taxable event would be added to this amount.

To compute the unearned premium:

Step 1: State the premium paid from the anniversary date of the policy to the date of the taxable event (e.g. gift).

Step 2: Multiply the premium actually paid by the remaining percentage of the year (e.g. in the example above, assuming an annual premium was paid, multiply the premium by two-thirds).

If there is a loan outstanding on the valuation date, that amount would be subtracted.[6] In other words the value of the policy can be reduced by the amount of any loans against the contract.

When the ITR guidance was originally issued by the IRS back in the early sixties, the two most prominent types of life insurance products were Annual Renewable Term (ART) and Whole Life.

ART provides death benefit protection for one-year only and does not have a reserve value because the policy matures at the end of each policy year. Therefore, the value of ART is simply the unearned premium for the remainder of the policy year. Unearned premium is premium which has been paid to the insurer but on the valuation date has not been earned by the insurance company.

Whole Life provides permanent protection and an insurance company is legally required to maintain reserves on its balance sheet with respect to its unmatured obligations (i.e., expected future death benefit claims). With Whole Life, the terminal reserve value (i.e., value of the reserves for a particular policy at the end of the policy year) is known in advance. Thus, it is possible to interpolate the terminal reserve value of the policy to reflect a valuation prior to the end of the policy year. For instance, if the transaction date occurred exactly one quarter of the year after a policy's anniversary date, the terminal reserves of the year preceding and the year following the taxable event would be interpolated to reflect that timing.

Applying ITR to a New Generation of Life Insurance Products

Since the IRS originally issued the ITR guidance back in the early sixties, the insurance industry has developed numerous new product types, including but not limited to: Universal Life (UL); Variable Life; Variable Universal Life (VUL); Indexed Universal Life (IUL); Guaranteed No-Lapse Universal Life (NLGUL); and five-, ten-, fifteen-, twenty-, and thirty-year level term (unlike ART products, insurance companies have to set aside reserves for level term products). As is discussed below, it is difficult to apply the outdated ITR guidance to this new generation of products.

All of these newer products have a reserve value associated with them. However, unlike the case with Whole Life, with the new product types, the terminal reserve value is not known or published ahead of time. It isn't known until the end of the policy year. Therefore, that makes it impossible to follow the dictates of the regulations to interpolate the terminal reserve value prior to the end of the policy year.

In addition, back when the ITR guidance was originally issued there was only really one type of reserve value. Today there are several different types of reserve values, including:

1. *Tax Reserve* (Tax) – this is the reserve value used in the determination of an insurance company's federal income tax.

2. *Statutory Reserve* (Stat) – this is the reserve value reported in an insurance company's statutory financial statement filed with the state insurance departments. The primary difference between this and the tax reserve is the interest rate used. In a low interest rate environment, there may be very little practical difference between the Tax and Stat reserves.

3. *AG 38 Reserve* (can be either Tax or Stat) – this is the reserve value used for a UL policy with a no lapse secondary guarantee (i.e., a NLGUL). The AG ("Actuarial Guideline" per the NAIC) 38 reserve is generally greater than the basic Tax or Stat reserve used for current assumption products that do not provide long-term death benefit guarantees.

4. *Deficiency Reserve* – For policies with secondary guarantees (e.g., a NLGUL), in some cases the calculation of Minimum Reserves is required. Deficiency Reserves are the excess of the Minimum Reserves over the AG 38 Basic Reserves. The AG 38 reserve including the deficiency reserve will be greater than the AG 38 reserve not including the deficiency reserve.

The question that insurance companies face is: Which of these reserves should be used for purposes of calculating ITR? For universal life products without long-term death benefit guarantees, are they supposed to use the Tax or Stat reserve? For universal life products with long-term death benefit guarantees, are they supposed to use the Tax or Stat basic AG 38 reserve? More importantly, are they supposed to include the deficiency reserve, if any? The reserve used can make a big difference in the ITR value that the insurance company reports for the policy.

Due to the fact that the IRS has not updated the ITR guidance to reflect the newer generation of products or the fact that there are now several possible reserve values for a policy, insurance companies individually have reached different conclusions on how to apply the ITR guidance. This has resulted in companies having different methodologies for calculating ITR. What this means is that the value for a similarly situated life insurance policy from one company to another may be dramatically different.

A few insurance companies, due to the ambiguity involved, have chosen to use alternate methodologies that aren't even based on any type of policy reserve. For example, a few insurance companies simply report the cash surrender value or the cash accumulation value as the ITR value of a policy. A few others use what is known as the California Method,[7] whereby they take the average of the cash surrender value and the cash accumulation value and report that as the ITR value.

Avoiding the Three-year Rule

Code Section 2035 provides that if a policy (that would have been includible in the insured's estate pursuant to Code Section 2042) is transferred and the insured dies within three years, then the entire death benefit is pulled back into the insured's taxable estate. However, an exception exists if the transfer is a bona fide sale for adequate and full consideration. In order to avoid the adverse consequences of the three year rule, an insured will oftentimes sell his policy to an Irrevocable Life Insurance Trust (ILIT) or adult child for adequate and full consideration.

Unfortunately, the IRS has provided no formal guidance as to what constitutes adequate and full consideration for this purpose. If the value that the policy is sold for is not sufficient, the IRS could assert that there is a gift component and a part gift/part sale results. In addition, it would appear that at least a portion, if not all, of the death benefit would be pulled back into the insured's estate pursuant to Code Section 2035.

In Private Letter Ruling 9413045, which has no precedential value, the IRS indicated that ITR would constitute adequate and full consideration. Of course, knowing what we know about the uncertainty surrounding ITR, one wonders if the IRS will retain this position in the future.

Reporting the Value of Life Insurance for Estate & Gift Tax Purposes

For situations involving the transfer of a life insurance policy for estate and gift tax purposes, the value of the policy must generally be reported on IRS Form 706 (estate tax return) or 709 (gift tax return). The instructions for Forms 706 and 709 stipulate that if the value

of a life insurance policy is being reported, then an IRS Form 712 (Life Insurance Statement) should be attached for each policy.

Form 712 comports with the IRS guidance on life insurance valuation and requires that certain values be reported on the form, such as ITR and gross premiums paid. This form is filled out by the insurance company and requires that an officer of the company certify that the information listed is "true and correct".

VALUATION FOR INCOME TAX PURPOSES

In the case of certain income tax situations, the IRS has provided more recent guidance regarding the value of a life insurance policy. In 2005, primarily in reaction to certain perceived valuation abuses occurring with fully insured defined benefit plans (section 412(e)(3) plans, formerly known as section 412(i) plans), the IRS issued Revenue Procedure 2005-25.[8] This revenue procedure applies for purposes of determining the value of life insurance distributed from a qualified plan, determining the value of life insurance distributed by an employer to an employee in conjunction with the performance of services, and determining the cost of permanent benefits provided under a group life plan.

The revenue procedure indicates that the general rule for income tax purposes for which the revenue procedure applies is that the value of life insurance is its FMV. Conceptually, this is no different than the guidance provided for estate and gift tax purposes. However, the revenue procedure provides a safe harbor value that does differ from the estate and gift tax rules. The safe harbor value is the greater of ITR or Premiums plus Earnings less Reasonable Charges (PERC). PERC is a newly created formula for determining the value of a policy in the above situations.

It should be noted that there are actually two different PERC formulas. With respect to a distribution of a life insurance policy from a qualified plan, the PERC formula can take into account an average surrender factor of as much as 30 percent. With respect to the distribution of a policy from an employer to an employee or when determining the cost of permanent benefits for a group life plan, an average surrender factor is not permitted as part of the PERC formula.

As a result of the creation of the PERC formula, it may appear that this revenue procedure provides more clarity when it comes to the valuation of a life insurance policy for income tax purposes. However, this is not necessarily the case. With ITR being a component of the safe harbor value, there will still be considerable uncertainly as insurance companies continue to struggle with how to calculate ITR for products other than whole life.

VALUATION FOR SALE PURPOSES

There are a variety of techniques for valuing life insurance for sale purposes. The appropriateness of each technique depends on the type of sale being contemplated.

- *Sale to an unrelated third party* – the value should generally be whatever the parties agree it is. That is the very essence of fair market value (assuming a willing buyer and willing seller, neither being under any compulsion to buy or to sell, and both having reasonable knowledge of relevant facts).

- *Sale to a related third party* (e.g., the insured's child) – if the IRS determines that the sale price is not adequate, then it could be determined to be a part gift/part sale, and gift issues may arise. In this situation the safest course of action is to use the ITR value as the purchase price.

- *Sale from an employer to an employee* (or a qualified plan to a plan participant, or to a trust on behalf of the plan participant) – Revenue Procedure 2005-25 should be determinative of the minimum value needed to avoid adverse income tax consequences (i.e., greater of ITR or PERC should be used as the value).

- *Sale by a trustee* – Sometimes an insured has created an Irrevocable Life Insurance Trust (ILIT), the terms of which are no longer satisfactory. In this situation a common strategy is for the insured to create a new ILIT with more acceptable terms and have the trustee of the old ILIT sell the life insurance policy owned by it to the new ILIT. Since the insured has to seed the new ILIT with a gift, the insured quite likely wants to keep the purchase price as low as possible.

In this case the goals of the old ILIT trustee may conflict with the goals of the insured. The trustee owes a fiduciary duty to the beneficiaries of the trust, and pursuant to such duty should seek to sell the policy for its fair market value. To do otherwise could constitute a breach of fiduciary duty. The question here is, "What constitutes its fair market value?" Can the trustee sell the policy for its cash surrender value? What about for its ITR value? Does the trustee have an obligation to see if there is a secondary market for the policy, and if so, use that value?

There are no clear answers here. The value used will likely depend upon the specific facts involved. Just be aware of the potential conflict that exists and the fact that the trustee has some potential fiduciary liability issues. If the risks of a valuation dispute are great, such as where the new ILIT is being established to exclude a beneficiary of the old ILIT, you may want to suggest that your client use the most conservative value available (which may involve seeing if there is a secondary market value). A sign-off by adult beneficiaries of the selling trust might also be considered.

FREQUENTLY ASKED QUESTIONS

Question – If a client who owns a policy is considering gifting the policy and also exchanging the policy for a better performing policy, is it better for gift valuation purposes to gift the policy first or do the 1035 exchange first?

Answer – There is no clear answer to this question and the client should seek guidance from his or her tax and legal advisor. The key issue is whether the policy received in the 1035 exchange constitutes a new policy for purposes of applying the IRS guidance, or is considered a continuation of the old policy.

If the client's tax and legal advisor decides it should be treated as a new policy, then the FMV of the newly exchanged policy, assuming it is transferred within a year of the exchange, should be the cost of the newly exchanged policy (i.e., gross premiums paid, which is the cash surrender value transferred from the old policy plus any additional premium paid into the new policy). In this situation it would likely be more advantageous from a gift tax valuation standpoint to complete the 1035 exchange first and then gift the newly exchanged policy. This is because the value of the newly exchanged policy (gross premium paid into the new policy) may be lower than the value of the old policy (ITR).

However, if the client's tax and legal advisor determines that the newly exchanged policy is a continuation of the old policy for valuation purposes and that ITR applies, then the answer generally depends upon the type of product into which the client is exchanging. In general, a lower ITR value may be achieved by doing the 1035 exchange first and then gifting the newly exchanged policy. However, the ITR values for products with no-lapse guarantees are generally going to be higher than the ITR values for nonguaranteed products; and in some cases will be substantially higher. Therefore, if the 1035 exchange is from a nonguaranteed product into a no-lapse guaranteed product, it may be beneficial for the client to make the gift first and base the gift on the ITR value of the old product.

Question – Is unearned premium the appropriate value to use with all term products?

Answer – Although the value of an ART product is unearned premium, level term products generally have an ITR value and thus, the value of level term products will generally be higher than the unearned premium.

Question – How is a life insurance policy that is being gifted to a charity valued?

Answer – The amount of the deduction for a charitable gift of a life insurance policy is generally the lower of: (a) the FMV of the policy; or (b) the donor's cost basis. Therefore, where the FMV at the date of the gift is greater than the net premiums the client has paid, the deduction will be limited to the client's net premiums.

FMV is generally determined the same as discussed earlier in this chapter for gifts of life insurance in general. However, if the FMV of the policy is greater than $5000, then a qualified appraisal must be obtained pursuant to Code section 170(f)(11)(E). Neither the donor, the insurance agent, nor the insurer who issued the policy can perform this appraisal.

Question – What are the options if the client is unhappy with the gift or estate tax value of a life insurance policy reported by a life insurance carrier on IRS Form 712?

Answer – It is unlikely that you are going to get the insurance company to change their figure, since they have to certify that the information is true and correct and are likely reluctant to change their methodology for one policy holder out of concern of discriminating against all policy holders (this doesn't mean you shouldn't try to do so). Since Forms 706 and 709 indicate that the Form 712 should be attached, the best course of action would be to attach the insurance company value and attach an explanation which states why it is not reflective of the FMV. If you don't attach the Form 712, you may be red flagging the client for an IRS inquiry. Regardless of what you decide to do with the Form 712, if you do decide to use another value, the instructions to Form 712 indicate that you must provide a full explanation as to how the value was determined.

Question – What are some best practice considerations for obtaining a fair and reasonable value of a life insurance policy for a client?

Answer – The following best practice tips may be helpful:

- When you request the value of a policy from an insurance company, be specific about what value you're looking for (e.g., is it the value for gift, income or some other purpose). Also, if you are requesting the PERC value, be specific about which PERC value you need (i.e., with or without the average surrender factor).

- Start out by informally requesting the value from the insurance company. For example, instead of asking the carrier to send you a Form 712, have some idea what the ITR value on the 712 will be before they send it to you. This might make it easier for you to argue for and obtain an alternative value before the insurance company has formally issued the Form 712.

- Ask the insurance company how they calculated the value that they have informally provided you. Knowing their methodology can put you in a better position to determine if the value you've been provided is reasonable.

- Negotiate the value with the insurance company, if possible. Most insurance companies probably won't be willing to change the number they put on the Form 712, but some companies may be willing to do so due to the ambiguities involved. It certainly doesn't hurt to ask.

• If all else fails and your client is still unhappy with the value of the policy reported by the insurance company, be prepared to consider another approach, such as obtaining an independent appraisal that can be used to support the explanation provided on the tax return.

CHAPTER ENDNOTES

1. A significant amount of the content of this chapter is derived from the following article: K. Buck and S. Leimberg, "Life Insurance Valuation: What Advisors Need to Know," 37 *Estate Planning* 17 (May 2010).

2. S. Leimberg, "Policies for Valuation of Life Insurance," 139 *Trusts & Estates* 46 (March 2000).

3. For instance, when an insured is in imminent danger of dying on the transaction date (say within twelve months of death), the IRS is likely to argue that the impossibility of valuing the insurance makes the use of the standard interpolated terminal reserve plus unearned premium an inappropriate method of valuing the contract. Treas. Reg. §25.2512-1 imply that the IRS will use all relevant facts and circumstances and probably value such an irreplaceable policy at a price closer to the death benefit. "The value rises in inverse ratio to the length of the insured's life expectancy." *Estate of Prichard v. Comm'r.*, 4 T.C. 204, 1944; *U.S. v. Ryerson*, 312 U..S. 260, 1941; Treas. Reg. §2512-1; 54 Harvard L. Rev. 895; Priv. Ltr. Rul. 9413045. It is likely in such situations that the IRS will claim the value of such a contract approaches the death benefit payable. Probably, the IRS will require that the policy be valued by ascertaining (based on the federal midterm rate as a discount rate) the present value of the right to receive the death benefit on the valuation date)—although at some point it is likely the IRS will resort to use of the secondary market (i.e., life settlement market) for such valuations.

4. Treas. Reg. §25-2512-6(a), example 1.

5. Treas. Reg. §25.2512-6(a), example 3.

6. See IRS Form 712, Part II.

7. The California Department of Insurance apparently created the California Method in order to assist smaller insurers that didn't have sophisticated systems in place to calculate their statutory reserves for universal life products. This method permits life insurance companies to calculate statutory reserves for a product simply by taking the mean of the cash surrender value and the cash accumulation value. Some carriers adopted this methodology for purposes of calculating ITR, and although it appears to be on the decline, it remains a methodology used by a small numbers of carriers for ITR reporting purposes for certain products types.

8. S. Leimberg and C. Ratner, "Valuation of Life Insurance: Rev. Proc. 2005-25 Provides New Guidance," *Estate Planning*, August 2005, Vol. 32, No. 8, Pg. 1, 13; "Valuation Gaming with Life Insurance Policies: Don't Bet on It," 110 Tax Notes 627 (Feb. 2006).

ESTATE TAXATION OF LIFE INSURANCE

CHAPTER 27

INTRODUCTION

Any one of seven reasons can cause life insurance to be includable in a decedent's gross estate. (Note that in some cases inclusion will result in the lifetime value being includable and in other situations the policy proceeds will be included). Planners should always consider the impact of state death taxation, which sometimes parallels federal estate tax law but often diverges significantly.

1. *Section 2033 Inclusion.* The value of life insurance owned by the decedent on the life of another will be includable in the decedent's estate if the decedent dies first.

2. *Section 2035 Inclusion.* Life insurance proceeds will be includable in the insured's estate if the insured held an incident of ownership (i.e., any significant ownership right) within three years of death, even if at the date of death the insured didn't own the policy or any policy rights.

3. *Sections 2036, 2037, 2038 Inclusion.* Policy proceeds will be includable in the insured's estate if the insured transferred the policy to another party but retained a lifetime right to:

   a. enjoy the legal rights to the policy;

   b. have the policy revert back to him or his estate under certain conditions; or

   c. alter, amend, revoke, or terminate the policy.

4. *Section 2042 Inclusion.* If (a) the policy proceeds were paid to (or for the benefit of) the insured's estate or (b) the insured owned at the date of

his death an incident of ownership in the policy, the proceeds will be includable in the insured's gross estate.

5. *Section 2039 Inclusion.* When a life insurance policy is used as part of the financing of an employee benefit, proceeds may be includable as an annuity.

6. *Section 2041 Inclusion.* If the insured elected a settlement option for a beneficiary and also gave that person a general power of appointment over the policy proceeds, the proceeds will be includable in the beneficiary's gross estate.

7. *Section 2044 Inclusion.* Life insurance proceeds may be includable in the estate of a beneficiary who was the insured's spouse and who had received the proceeds as a qualifying income interest for life under QTIP rules.

This chapter will first briefly focus on the definition of life insurance for federal estate tax purposes and then examine in detail the most common reasons for estate tax inclusion of life insurance, Code sections 2033, 2035, and 2042.

WHAT IS IT?

Life insurance is a very broadly defined term for estate tax purposes. In its simplest definition, it is a contract under which the insurer agrees to pay a specified death benefit to a specified beneficiary at the death of the insured. The term encompasses life insurance of every description, as long as there is both: (a) risk shifting; and (b) risk sharing in the event of the policyowner's loss through the insured's death.

So accidental death benefits under a health insurance policy, payments under a fraternal society's lodge system, accidental death payments, group insurance, paid up additions, or other payments under a policy rider at the insured's death would all be considered life insurance for purposes of federal estate tax inclusion.

The element of risk must be present at the time of the insured's death for the proceeds of the contract to be includable as life insurance in the insured's gross estate. Furthermore, to be considered life insurance for estate tax purposes, the death benefit must:

1. be payable unconditionally; and

2. have no effect on other legal liabilities or rights in connection with the insured's death.

The issue arises most often in accident situations with respect to payments under automobile or air travel policies. For example, suppose a contract between an insurance company and the owner of an airplane provided that a specified payment would be made to the estate of any individual killed in an accident while flying in the owner's plane. If the contract further required that the passenger's estate would have to sign a release of all claims for damages against the owner or his estate in order to collect, that condition would affect other rights of the deceased. The contract would therefore not be considered life insurance.

Where there is no element of risk, the payment is not (at least for estate tax purposes) considered life insurance. It may, however, be subject to inclusion in the gross estate under one or more tax law provisions (for example, as an annuity).

INSURANCE OWNED ON THE LIFE OF ANOTHER (SECTION 2033)

There are many situations in which one party purchases life insurance on the life of one or more other individuals. For instance, a business partner may purchase insurance on the lives of each of her three partners. Assume she dies before the three insureds do. The policies she owned on their lives would be includable in her estate (to the extent of the value of the policy as of the date of the insured's death) as property in which the decedent had an interest. Likewise, a son may purchase insurance on the life of a parent. If the

son predeceases the parent, the value of the unmatured policy will be in the son's estate.

Estate Tax Value

The estate tax value of third party owned, unmatured policies includable in the estate of someone other than the insured is generally the replacement cost of the policy. Replacement cost is ascertained using the same rules governing valuation of policies for gift tax purposes (the date of death is substituted for the date of the gift in valuing the policy). In most cases, this approximates the sum of: (a) the cash surrender value of the policy (technically, the interpolated terminal reserve of the policy is the amount includable and in early policy years this can significantly exceed the cash surrender value); plus (b) the unearned premium (any premium the insured paid but that was not earned by the insurer as of the date of the policyowner's death). For more information, please refer to Chapter 26: Life Insurance Valuation.

Common Disaster

Although the IRS has tried to include the entire proceeds in the insured's estate when the insured and the policy owner were killed in a common disaster, after a number of Circuit Court reversals, the IRS gave up. It now holds, in cases in which the presumption of the Uniform Simultaneous Death Act applies (i.e., that the insured survived the beneficiary), that the policy's interpolated terminal reserve is the appropriate measure of inclusion rather than the death benefit. If, however, the presumed order of deaths is reversed (i.e., the presumption is that the beneficiary survived the insured), simultaneous deaths of the insured and the policyowner will cause the death proceeds to be includable in the policyowner's estate.

Excludable Growth

No inclusion is required for the increase in the value of a policy from the date of the policyowner's death to the valuation date resulting from the estate paying premiums or earning interest on a policy insuring a third party. So, if at the date of death a client owned a $1,000,000 policy insuring the life of a business associate and the interpolated terminal reserve (reflecting income earned by the policy reserve invested with the insurer during the period from the date of death) increased $2,000 from the owner's death to the valuation date, that increment would be excluded from the policyowner's gross estate.

Alternate Valuation Date Trap

Planners should beware of this situation: A decedent owns a life insurance policy insuring the life of a third party (such as a spouse or business associate). Within six months of the deceased policyowner's death, the insured dies. If the policyowner-decedent's executor uses the alternate valuation date to value assets in the estate, the increase in value caused by the insured's death, and not merely the interpolated terminal reserve plus any unearned premium, will be includable.

This alternate valuation date trap is especially dangerous with respect to last-to-die (also called second-to-die) life insurance in which a policy pays proceeds only when the second insured dies. When the first insured dies, the policy must be included as an asset in the estate of the decedent[1] at its replacement value, which is essentially the interpolated terminal reserve plus any unearned premium. But if the decedent's executor elects the alternate date and the second insured has died between the first spouse's death and the alternate valuation date six months later, the entire proceeds will be includable in the first spouse's estate. The executor of the later dying spouse must include the entire amount of the proceeds again in that spouse's estate because of the incidents of ownership rules described below.[2]

Beneficiary Who Predeceases Insured

Typically, a primary beneficiary's rights to policy proceeds expire with his death. So, if the named beneficiary dies before the insured and no rights pass to the beneficiary's heirs, nothing will be in the beneficiary's estate. This assumes the beneficiary had no other rights in the policy and all rights in the proceeds terminated (as they usually do) upon predeceasing the insured. Note that state law determines the existence and extent of such ownership rights or interest in proceeds.

INCIDENT OF OWNERSHIP WITHIN THREE YEARS OF DEATH (SECTION 2035)

Code section 2035 is entitled "Adjustments for certain gifts made within three years of decedent's death." The statute states that transfers in certain situations will be brought back into the gross estate for estate tax purposes if the decedent held at death an interest which would have been included under one or more of the following sections:

- Section 2036 (transfers with retained life estate)

- Section 2037 (transfers taking effect at death)

- Section 2038 (revocable transfers)

- Section 2042 (proceeds of life insurance)

Inclusion is also mandated if the property would have been included under one of those four Code sections but the decedent gave up fatal rights within three years of death.[3]

Section 2042 inclusion will be discussed in detail below. For purposes of section 2035, it is sufficient to understand that section 2042 requires inclusion if either:

1. policy proceeds are payable to or for the benefit of the insured's estate; or

2. the insured, at the time of death, held one or more incidents of ownership (i.e., valuable property rights) in the contract.

Adequate Consideration Rule

However, section 2035 specifically excludes from estate tax inclusion a sale of property made for an adequate and full consideration in money or money's worth.[4] So, if life insurance is sold for adequate and full consideration in money or money's worth, it should not be included in the insured's gross estate under section 2035 in any event.

It would appear at first glance that all problems under section 2035 could easily be avoided by selling the policy rather than giving it away. Planners should proceed with caution because of:

1. the "transfer for value" rule discussed in Chapter 25; and

2. the problems inherent in a situation in which the IRS finds the consideration inadequate.

"Adequate" is often (but not always) measured (by the IRS) relative to what would have been included in the estate had no transfer been made rather than the value of what was transferred. However, no one in the real world would pay, even on the life of a terminally ill insured, the full face amount because such a payment would ignore the cost of the time value of money. Some discount should be taken for the fact that some time (that proceeds could have been earning money) will pass before the proceeds are actually paid. Nevertheless, the courts have generally supported the IRS's interpretation of how adequate consideration is measured. Absent extenuating circumstances such as a terminal illness, the IRS has indicated that the Interpolated Terminal Reserve (ITR) value constitutes adequate and full consideration for purposes of section 2035.[5]

Example. Your client was a doctor who knows he was dying of cancer. So, rather than give the policy on his life away, he sells them to his wife in return for her check in an amount equal to the policy's cash value. The IRS would claim that in the light of the actual circumstances, the policies were near to maturity and therefore worth much more than the cash values. It would include the difference between actual worth under the circumstances and the amount paid by the doctor's wife in the client's estate on the grounds that he had not, in fact, received adequate and full consideration.

Premiums Not Brought Back

Does the language of the Internal Revenue Code encompass a bring-back of cash the donor intended the donee to use for paying premiums on life insurance? In other words, does the mere payment of premiums within three years of death cause the death proceeds of a policy to be brought back into the estate? It is clear now that it does not.

Gifts of Policies within Three Years of Death

A gift of a life insurance policy or a release or transfer of any of the incidents of ownership in a life insurance policy by the insured within three years of the insured's death will result in inclusion under section 2035 regardless of the insured's motive for the transfer.

Note that section 2035 applies only to transfers of policies (or transfers or releases of incidents of ownership) by the insured. There will be no inclusion under section 2035 if someone else transfers a policy on the life of the insured within three years of the insured's death or within three years of the owner's death. (Section 2042 pertains only to proceeds of insurance on the decedent's life. A policy owned by a third party on the decedent's life would be includable, if at all, under Code section 2033. But section 2035 pulls back the proceeds only if it would have been includable in the insured's gross estate under Code sections 2036, 2037, 2038, or 2042.)

Example. If a daughter owned a policy on the life of her eighty-five-year-old father and the daughter made a gift of the policy to her niece, no inclusion under section 2035 would be required even if the father died within three years of the daughter's transfer to the niece.

In the case of second to die policies, the three year period is measured back from the death of the surviving insured since inclusion under section 2035 is conditioned on a section 2042 inclusion (but for the policy transfer). Since the only inclusion possible at the first death was under section 2033, section 2035 does not begin to apply until the second death. For example, if a client and her husband purchase a second to die policy and assign it to an irrevocable trust for their children, there will be no section 2035 inclusion unless both spouses have died within three years of the gift to the trust.

Gifts of Policies beyond the Three-year Period

What if an insured pays premiums within three years of his or her death but the policy itself was purchased more than three years prior to the insured's death by a third party and the insured never had an incident of ownership? What if the insured pays premiums within three years of death and the policy was purchased by the insured but he or she transferred it to a third party more than three years prior to death? The answer to both questions is the same: there should be no inclusion since no section 2042 rights were transferred within three years of death and none of the other sections (2036, 2037, or 2038) apply.

Payment of Premiums by Third Party Owner

What if the donee of the policy pays some or all of the premiums on the policy? According to several cases and regulations, if the donee rather than the insured pays premiums after the policy is received, even if the transfer from the insured occurred within three years of death, only a portion of the policy proceeds would be includable in the insured's estate. The inclusion ratio is:

$$\frac{\text{Premiums Paid by Donor}}{\text{Total Premiums Paid}}$$

Example. Assume a client purchases a $1,000,000 policy on his or her life. Premiums are $25,000 payable semiannually. One year after purchasing the policy and paying $50,000 in premiums, she or he transfers the policy to his or her thirty-eight-year-old son who pays—out of his own personal funds—the next four semi-annual premiums of $25,000 each. If the insured client died at that point, the client would have paid $50,000 out of the total of $150,000 (i.e., one-third of all premiums). Therefore, one-third of the $1,000,000 death benefit ($333,333) would be includable in his or her estate.

The "Beamed Transfer" Theory

Why has section 2035 caused such a multiplicity of court cases? The answer lies in the less than clear manner in which section 2035 was previously written and in this common fact pattern: A third party such as a spouse, child, or irrevocable trust purchases a life insurance policy on the life of a client but pays premiums with funds provided by the insured. In this scenario, the insured typically (but not always) has initiated the insurance purchase. The insured dies within three years of the issuance of the policy.

In the past, the IRS has argued that if the insured significantly participated in the procurement of a policy on his or her own life, that action, together with the transfer of amounts to pay premiums on the policy, was equivalent to purchase and transfer of the policy by the insured to the third party. This has been called the "beamed transfer" theory. After a number of losses in court, the IRS has announced that it will no longer pursue this theory.

For those preferring to play it safe, the odds of avoiding the issue generally increase if:

- the insured never owns the policy (it should be owned from inception by a third party);

- an adult beneficiary or independent trustee takes all the actions to purchase the policy on the life of the insured and place the policy into effect;

- the trustee, if a trust is used, is authorized but not required, to purchase insurance on the life of anyone on whose life the trust's beneficiaries have an insurable interest;

- the trust specifically prohibits the insured from obtaining any rights in any policy the trust may ever hold on the insured's life;

- the trust permits, but does not require, the trustee to pay premiums;

- the insured gives the trustee enough money to pay premiums for more than one year;

- the cash gift to the trust (or adult policyowner) is given outright with no strings attached;

- the gift is made well in advance of the date on which premiums are due;

- the facts indicate that the trustee or adult policyowner is not acting mechanically as the insured's agent but is in fact making an independent decision to purchase the insurance without direction from the insured;

- the document (in the case of a trust) contains as few references as possible to life insurance and is not titled "Irrevocable Life Insurance Trust"; and

- the actual policyowner could, for at least the first three years, pay premiums from a source other than from gifts from the insured and if necessary borrow from another relative or bank.

Exchange of Contracts within Three Years of Death

What is the impact of an exchange of policies within three years of death? For instance, say the client transfers a policy on his life to an irrevocable trust or adult child. More than three years later, the trustee exchanges that policy with the insurer for a new one on the insured's life. Assume the client is not in any way involved in the replacement except for a written acknowledgement that the trustee's statements were correct. If the insured dies within three years of the exchange (i.e., the acquisition of the new policy), will the proceeds of the new policy be includable in the client's gross estate?

The answer is, "no." The exchange of policies by an irrevocable trust should not be treated as a transfer within three years of death if the original transfer occurred more than three years before death and the decedent possesses no interest in the policy at the date of the exchange. The key to success in policy exchanges is: (a) be sure the facts don't indicate that the trustee's actions can be imputed to directions from the insured; and (b) be sure the facts indicate that there was no transfer from the insured.

Group Term Life

An employee can successfully transfer all incidents of ownership in group term life coverage if:

1. the master contract or state law gives the employee a conversion privilege; and

2. both state law and the master contract allow assignment of all the covered employee's rights including the right to convert the contract to permanent coverage at termination of employment.

An assignment of the policy must transfer all of the insured's interest in the group coverage including any right to convert the protection to permanent coverage. (These general rules are covered in more detail under the section 2042 discussion.)

In the context of the "Transfers within Three Years of Death" statute, it is clear that the transfer by the insured of group term life insurance to another within three years of the insured's death will result in federal estate tax inclusion under section 2035. It is also certain that a transfer (within the scope of section 2035) takes place when—at the inception of coverage—someone other than the insured employee is named as owner of the group term coverage.

Can the transfer of group term life ever escape the three year limit? The problem is that, by definition,

group term life is typically annually renewable. Each year's premium automatically renews the coverage. If the IRS took the position that each payment created new coverage, it would be impossible to escape the three year limit.

Fortunately, the IRS has stated that the mere payment of the renewal premium does not create a new agreement. It merely continues the old agreement and therefore, with respect to an employee who has absolutely assigned his coverage, renewal is not a new transfer of insurance coverage for purposes of section 2035. This favorable position is contingent on two conditions: first, no additional evidence of insurability can be required of the insureds in the group; second, there can be no variation or break in the coverage.

One issue that often comes up pertains to a change in insurers. Assume, for example, that a corporate client finds the rates of one carrier more favorable than those of the current insurer and decides to switch. Each employee receives a new piece of paper with the name of a new insurer. Assume a client had transferred his coverage to his daughter more than three years ago. Does that transaction constitute new coverage and therefore start the three year clock ticking all over again? The answer depends on how much real change (if any) occurred from the covered employee's perspective.

In all probability, the clock will not start to tick again and the IRS will consider the three year period begun when the assignment of the first policy was executed if "the new arrangement is identical in all relevant aspects to the previous arrangement." So if the client dies more than three years after the first assignment, according to this ruling, there will be no inclusion of the group term life even if he dies within three years of the second assignment.

Practitioners should view this seemingly favorable viewpoint with caution, however, because of its unusual condition: a new arrangement must be identical in all relevant respects to the previous arrangement. In one favorable ruling, the employee did not use the company's standard assignment form. Instead, his attorney drew a form assigning not only all his rights in the original group coverage but also any right he might have in any future group term coverage. Although this technique of assigning present and future rights would seem to be a solution to the change in carriers issue, it creates a potential practical trap; if the employee assigns all present and future coverage to his current wife, for example, how will he feel if he later becomes divorced and his then ex-wife reaps the benefits of every increase he enjoys in group coverage, with him paying ever increasing Table I costs as well as possible gift taxes on the annual gifts?

Obviously, if the insured under a group contract is notified by the employer and the new carrier that any prior assignments are void because of the change of carriers and will not be recognized by a new insurer, the section 2035 clock will tick anew when the new coverage begins. No protection would be afforded by the standard assignment of coverage form in this type of situation. The insured would have to make a new absolute assignment of his coverage and outlive the three year period beginning at the date of the new assignment.

Clients with substantial amounts of group term coverage who wish to remove that insurance from their estates should therefore consider an absolute assignment to a trust or named beneficiary and make the transfer as quickly as possible. A new assignment should be made every time an employer changes group carriers.

Corporate Owned Life Insurance

Section 2042 treats a shareholder who owns more than 50 percent of a corporation's stock as if he owned life insurance actually owned by the corporation. This provision applies only to the extent insurance owned by the corporation is payable to or for the benefit of a party other than the corporation or its creditor. If the corporation holds the policy insuring the controlling shareholder at such shareholder's death, the proceeds would be includable in his estate under section 2042.

If the corporation transfers the policy to a third party within three years of the insured's death, for purposes of section 2035, the insured would be deemed to have made a fatal transfer and inclusion of the proceeds would be the result.

_____

Example. Suppose a client owned 80 percent of·the stock of a closely held corporation. The business owned a $1,000,000 life insurance policy on the client's life but the proceeds were payable to the client's children. Upon learning that Code section 2042 would require inclusion of the proceeds in the client's gross estate, the client's corporation immediately transfers ownership of the policy to the client's children but the client

dies within several months of the transfer. The IRS would argue that the corporation's transfer of the incidents of ownership was really an indirect transfer by the insured and since the transfer occurred within three years of the insured's death, section 2035 applies.

_____

Can a client who is a controlling shareholder avoid the 2035 problem by transferring just enough stock so that he no longer meets the more than 50 percent test and then have the corporation transfer the life insurance? The IRS has answered these questions by stating that a transfer of a majority shareholder's stock within three years of death could itself trigger taxation under section 2035. A gift of a controlling interest in the stock of the corporation is considered a release of the incidents of ownership in the corporate owned policy on the insured's life that in turn is deemed to constitute a transfer of the policy by the insured. The IRS would make this argument even if the insured owned no stock in the corporation at death, because its argument rests on the constructive transfer within three years of the insured's death rather than on the insured's control of a corporation that owns insurance on his life when he dies.

_____

Example. A corporation owns a $1,000,000 policy on the life of a client who owns 80 percent of the voting stock of the corporation. The client is deemed to own the policy on her life that is actually owned by the corporation (to the extent that it was payable to someone other than the corporation or its creditors). Assume further that the proceeds are payable to the client's son. Two years ago, the company transferred the policy to the son who became owner as well as beneficiary. The client has contracted terminal cancer and has only days to live. She makes an immediate gift of 20 percent of her voting stock to her daughter who runs the business. Two days later, the client dies. The IRS would argue that by giving up control of her corporation, the client made a transfer of incidents of ownership in the life insurance and thereby made a transfer within three years of death and the $1,000,000 of proceeds are included in her estate. On the other hand, a sale of the stock for a price based on all the assets and liabilities of the corporation, i.e., for fair market value, is much more likely to be successful.[6]

_____

Community Property Issues in Section 2035 Situations

Community property laws, if applicable, add another layer of complexity to the already difficult section 2035 issues. These laws may work for or against the taxpayer, as the two examples below illustrate.

Example 1. Assume a client lives and works in a community property state. The client's employer applies for a policy on the life of the client but all the facts, including the policy itself, indicate that the client's husband is the policy owner. Even if the client does not control the employer corporation, the IRS would argue that there was a constructive transfer of the insurance by the decedent to her husband. If the client died within three years of that constructive transfer, the IRS would include half the proceeds in her estate because the policy payments by the corporation would be deemed as compensation to the client and under community property law, only one half of that money would be hers to transfer.

Example 2. Assume a policy was issued in which the insured's wife was named owner and beneficiary and the first premium was paid from the couple's community property checking account. Say the insured dies two months after the policy was issued. The use of community funds to pay the premium would be considered tantamount to a transfer by the insured of his interest in community funds that, in turn, would constitute a transfer of the policy itself. The IRS would include a percentage of the proceeds equal to the insured's community property portion of the premium multiplied by the insurance proceeds.

Techniques for Success

To obtain the highest probability of success, be sure the insured never possesses an incident of ownership. This technique will work in most cases where a policy is about to be issued.

But suppose a client transferred a policy to a trust more than three years ago and therefore has already outlived the statutory three-year period. Assume a new insurer is willing to assume the obligations of the old insurer and issue a new policy to the trust with more favorable terms. Even if the insured died within three years of the issuance of the new policy, no inclusion would be required if the facts indicate that the exchange occurred strictly between the independent trustee and the insurance company. Note that from the date of the original transfer the insured never held an incident of ownership. Clearly, no incident was held at the date of the exchange and therefore none could have been released or transferred by the insured. If this technique is used, it is important that the trustee be independent and act as trustee rather than as the insured's agent. The insured should not be involved in the transaction in any way except to sign as insured.

A sale of an existing policy may avoid the three year rule but result in the unfortunate income tax consequences discussed in Chapter 25 with regard to the transfer for value rule. Even if the transfer for value problem is not an issue, the IRS could argue that the amount paid for the policy was not a full and fair payment (especially if the insured was ill at the time of the transfer). But if the insured is healthy, the problem may be cured by transferring the policy to a spouse for full and adequate consideration (from the spouse's funds) and at some later date from the spouse to a trust for the couple's children or other mutually acceptable beneficiary (selected independently by the noninsured spouse). The transfer from the spouse to the trust would not be within the reach of Code section 2035.

PROCEEDS PAYABLE TO THE INSURED'S ESTATE (SECTION 2042(1))

Insurance Payable Directly to Estate

Regardless of who purchased the policy, owned the incidents of ownership, or paid premiums, if the proceeds are payable directly to the insured's estate (executor or administrator), they are includable for federal estate tax purposes. The entire value of the proceeds must be included.

Insurance Payable Indirectly to Estate

Regardless of who purchased the policy, owned incidents of ownership, or paid premiums, if the proceeds are for whatever reason payable for the benefit of the estate, they are includable for federal estate tax purposes.

Insurance proceeds would be considered payable for the benefit of the estate if used to pay:

- federal estate tax;

- state death taxes;

- income or gift or any other taxes; or

- debts or other charges against the estate.

Inclusion of insurance proceeds payable for the benefit of the estate but not payable directly to the estate (executor or administrator) is conditioned on the following two tests.

First, the beneficiary to whom the proceeds are payable must be legally obligated to use the insurance money for one or more of the purposes described in the list of examples above. If there is no legal obligation for the beneficiary to use the money to meet the type of estate obligation described above, there should be no inclusion. So, for example, the mere power or authority to use insurance proceeds to satisfy debts of the insured will not cause inclusion since such a right does not amount to a legal obligation.

This makes the wording in a classic irrevocable life insurance trust crucial; if the trustee is given discretion to use or not use proceeds to purchase assets from the decedent's estate, the proceeds should not be includable. A loan from the trust to the estate, or even the purchase of assets by the trust from the estate, will not cause inclusion. But if the trustee is directed to pay the insured's estate taxes, debts, or administrative costs to the extent directed by the estate's executor, the proceeds required to pay those expenses will be includable to the extent so used.

Second, there must also be actual use of the insurance money to pay taxes or other claims against the estate. To the extent the trustee has the legal right to use the proceeds to pay taxes or other expenses but life insurance policy proceeds are not in fact used to pay off such claims, they will not be includable.

Insurance Payable to Beneficiary Barred from Collecting

What if the named beneficiary is barred by state law from collecting the policy proceeds? For example, what if the beneficiary murdered the insured in a state which

provides that where a beneficiary takes the life of the insured and is convicted of a felony in the offense, the killer forfeits his beneficial interest in the insurance and the forfeited interest passes by law to the insured's other heirs at law unless otherwise disposed of by the insured.

Where state law diverts the proceeds to heirs of the insured's estate, the proceeds are treated for federal tax law purposes as if they had passed into the insured's estate first and were then paid out to the insured's heirs (even if the named beneficiary is convicted of voluntary manslaughter of the insured rather than murder). Thus, if a husband first insured and then murdered his wife and later killed himself, the murdered wife would be deemed to have the equitable right to dictate disposition of the proceeds even though she never owned the policy. The proceeds would probably be distributed according to the terms of the wife's will (as though her murderer had died first) and, for tax purposes, the IRS would tax the money in her estate as if it were paid to her estate's administrators.

Insurance Payable to Executor or Testamentary Trustee Payable to Others under Governing Instrument

The implications of state law must be examined: There are a number of cases which hold that insurance should be considered payable to the ultimate beneficiary rather than to the estate even though the instrument itself appears to make the proceeds payable to the estate or its executor. This is particularly true where state law allows insurance on a parent's life to pass free from the claims against the estate even if payable to the insured's estate. In such cases, federal law honors state law and treats the insurance as if it had been paid directly to the ultimate beneficiary.

Even more common is the case where insurance is payable to the trustee under a trust established in a will. Insurance payable to a testamentary trustee for the benefit of a named beneficiary other than the insured's estate will be treated as if received by the named beneficiaries rather than by the estate and will therefore be estate tax free (unless the insured held an incident of ownership in the policy).

But does the term "executor" mean anyone who happens to be an executor of the estate or does it mean only the person receiving the proceeds specifically as the estate's representative? If the proceeds are received in the new owner's individual capacity as beneficiary and not as the representative of the estate, proceeds are not deemed payable to or for the benefit of the estate. The test is whether or not the recipient is bound to the legal duty of then distributing the money according to the terms of the insured's will or state intestacy laws. If the recipient is so bound, then inclusion is mandated.

INSURANCE RECEIVABLE BY BENEFICIARIES OTHER THAN INSURED'S ESTATE (SECTION 2042(2))

If, at the insured's death, any incidents of ownership in a policy on his life were held by the insured, (regardless of the monetary value of the incident retained, whether exercisable alone or only in conjunction with another, or how the interest was acquired), the proceeds are includable in the insured's gross estate.

The physical ability of the insured to exercise the ownership right is immaterial; the IRS and the courts generally look to the insured's legal right to exercise ownership. Mere possession of the incident and not its exercise is all that is necessary for inclusion, but the insured must in fact hold legal right to exercise the power in question.

Amount Includable

If section 2042(2) applies, the entire amount receivable by beneficiaries (other than the estate) is includable in the insured's gross estate. It is important to note that any incident of ownership will trigger inclusion; an insured does not have to possess all of the incidents of ownership nor does the incident of ownership have to be of great value to be fatal.

Incidents of Ownership Defined

Think of an incident of ownership as the right of the insured (or his estate) to one or more economic benefit from the policy. Such a benefit may take the form of the right to:

- cancel the policy;
- assign the policy;
- surrender the policy;
- obtain a policy loan;

- change the beneficiary;
- pledge the policy for a loan;
- change contingent beneficiaries;
- change beneficiaries' share of proceeds;[7]
- require consent before change of beneficiary; or
- require consent before assignment of the policy.

Whether or not other rights will or will not be considered an incident of ownership is not always clear cut. Some of the more frequently litigated issues (and the typical results) have been:

1. the mere possession of the right to alter the time and manner of payment of the proceeds to a beneficiary (with no right to change the beneficiary or alter in any way the total amount of proceeds payable to that party)[8] (includable);

2. the right to require consent to the designation of a beneficiary who does not have an insurable interest in the life of the insured (includable);

3. the right to receive dividends on a mutual policy[9] (not includable);

4. the right to change the beneficiary of a policy held in trust[10] (includable);

5. the right to change the terms of a trust that holds a policy[11] (includable);

6. the right to exercise ownership rights only in conjunction with another (includable);

7. the naming by a third party owner as beneficiary "the person named by my husband (the insured) as the beneficiary of his will" (not includable);

8. the inability of the insured to exercise a retained power (includable);

9. the absence of intention on the part of the insured to retain an incident of ownership[12] (includable);

10. instructions to the insurance agent/and or insurer to divest the insured of any incident[13] (not includable);

11. the right to designate or make a change of beneficiary on a policy on the insured's life owned by the insured's employer even though the insured's employer retains the right to amend or cancel the policies without the insured's consent (includable);

12. the right to terminate a spouse's interest in a policy by divorcing her[14] (not includable);

13. the right to obtain cash values of a policy irrevocably assigned for the benefit of the insured's children to a trust (includable);

14. the right to cancel insurance payable to a trust providing income for life to the insured (including income from the proceeds of surrendered policies) (includable);

15. the right to cancel a no-fault auto insurance policy that provided survivors' loss benefits (not includable);

16. the right to purchase the policy from its owner[15] (generally includable);

17. the right to convert from term to whole life or from whole life to limited pay (includable);

18. the right to substitute policies of equal value for those held by a trust (not includable);

19. the right of one partner under a cross purchase buy-sell to veto another partner's right to borrow, surrender, or change beneficiaries (not includable);

20. the insured's right to alter, amend, or revoke a trust that is named as the beneficiary of a policy on the insured's life (not includable);

21. the right to select settlement options[16] (includable);

22. loans made by the insured to an irrevocable life insurance trust to fund the premiums on a trust-owned life insurance contract were not considered incidents of ownership;[17]

23. the continuing power to determine the compensation of a trustee of an irrevocable life insurance trust was not considered the retention of an interest in the trust by the grantor

and, therefore, did not cause federal estate tax inclusion of the trust's assets;[18] and

24. the insured-grantor's right to remove a trustee for cause will not cause inclusion.[19]

Attribution of Ownership

In some cases, the IRS will attribute an entity's actual ownership of a life insurance policy to an owner of the entity. For instance, if a partnership owns a policy on the life of one of its partners, to the extent that policy is payable to a party other than the partnership or its creditors (for example to a partner's grandson), the insured partner will be deemed to hold an incident of ownership in the policy.

Because the partnership's actual incident of ownership is deemed constructively owned by the insured partner, it will be includable in his estate. There is no minimum partnership interest required for this result to occur. On the other hand, as long as the policy proceeds are payable to or for the benefit of the partnership, its incidents of ownership will not be attributed to its partners.

A partnership's ability to surrender or cancel its group term coverage will not be attributed to its partners. So, if a partner transfers (more than three years prior to his death) all of the incidents of ownership he holds in group term coverage, he will not be considered to constructively hold incidents of ownership through the partnership's ability to cancel the group term coverage.

When a corporation holds incidents of ownership in a life insurance policy, its ownership rights may be attributed to the insured. Here, the rule for corporations is slightly more formalized than is the case for a partnership: if (at death) the insured owns more than 50 percent of the total combined voting power of all classes of the corporation's shares entitled to vote, he is deemed to own incidents actually owned by the corporation to the extent proceeds are payable to anyone other than the corporation or its creditors.

Example. Assume a client owns 80 percent of a corporation that owns an insurance policy on his life. If the policy is payable to the corporation (or its creditor), the client will be deemed to hold no incident of ownership in the policy.

But if the proceeds of the corporate owned policy are payable to the client's daughter, then the policy actually owned by the corporation will be deemed to be owned by the client and includable in his estate. (The payment of the proceeds may also be considered a constructive dividend or compensation to the shareholder, followed by a gift from the shareholder to his daughter.)

If, however the proceeds were payable to a bank to which the client's corporation owed money and the proceeds were accepted in payment of that debt, to that extent the corporation's incidents of ownership would not be attributed to the client. Naturally, the payoff of the debt would have the effect of increasing the value of the corporation's stock.

———

There are at least two reasons why the difference (inclusion of proceeds in insured's estate as insurance versus inclusion of stock with higher value) is important. First, treating insurance proceeds as a corporate asset may result in a smaller increase than a dollar for dollar inclusion of insurance proceeds and only the decedent's proportionate share would be includable. For instance, if the decedent only owns 80 percent of the corporation, at worst 80 percent and not 100 percent of the proceeds would be includable. In many cases, since the net asset value of a corporation is not the predominant factor in valuing a going concern, there might not be a dollar for dollar increase in corporate value when insurance proceeds are payable to the corporation.

Second, inclusion of life insurance in the insured's estate as life insurance makes qualification for a section 303 stock redemption or a section 6166 installment payment of estate tax more difficult.

If corporate owned policy proceeds are used to redeem stock from a shareholder's estate, will the proceeds be considered payable to or for the benefit of the estate (and therefore includable separately as life insurance) or will the IRS treat the proceeds as payable to the corporation? The answer is that, in a classic stock redemption or section 303 stock purchase, there will be no attribution of ownership even though indirectly the proceeds enhance the estate's liquidity and make stock held by the estate marketable. But if the decedent was a controlling shareholder of the corporation owning the policy and the proceeds are payable to a second corporate beneficiary to redeem its stock (or for general corporate purposes), the IRS would probably claim that

the proceeds are not payable to or for the benefit of the (first) corporation and therefore should be included.

A corporation's ability to cancel group term life insurance coverage is not considered an incident of ownership held by its shareholder. Therefore, there should be no attribution, even in the case of a controlling stockholder.

Community Property Issues

When life insurance is purchased by community property domiciliaries, federal law usually recognizes it as being owned one half by the wife and one half by the husband. The result is that, where the insured spouse dies first, only half the proceeds are includable in his gross estate, regardless of who the beneficiary is.

———

Example. If a client and his wife live in a community property state and purchase a $1,000,000 life insurance policy on the client's life, only $500,000 will be in the client's estate because the client never owned incidents of ownership over more than one half of the policy. This one half rule applies even if all the proceeds are payable to the insured's estate.

———

State community property law determines the extent to which the insured had incidents of ownership in a policy. For example, incidents of ownership do not apply merely because state law gives one spouse the right to manage a community owned policy and thus has the legal power to surrender the contract.

Likewise, regardless of whose name is listed on the policy application as owner, absent strong proof to the contrary, each spouse holds one half of all incidents of ownership. So generally, life insurance acquired by spouses in a community property state is presumed to be community property even if the title is held in only one spouse's name. However, the parties can establish, through clear and convincing evidence that they intended to hold the property in some form other than all as community.

It is also possible that life insurance will be deemed to have been purchased partially with community property funds and partially with separate property funds. A common example is where the policy itself was purchased prior to marriage or before the couple moved to a community property state. Then, if premiums are paid from community funds, the proceeds have been generated by a mixture of separate and community premiums.

In Texas, Louisiana, New Mexico, and Arizona, the concept of inception of title is used to classify the proceeds; insurance proceeds on a policy purchased prior to the couple's marriage or move to a community property state remains as it was at inception, separate property, even though community funds were used to pay some premiums. Under state law, the proceeds would therefore be the insured's separate property, but the surviving spouse would have a right to be reimbursed for half of the community funds used to pay premiums. That, of course, would be the measure of federal estate tax inclusion; the entire proceeds would be includable less the one half of the community funds that were used to pay premiums.

California and Washington use a concept called the premium tracing rule; each spouse is deemed to own his share of the policy proportionate to his share of the premium contribution. Therefore, only the portion that belonged to the insured would be includable.

An unintended and unexpected gift tax trap may await the unwary; if the client names neither his estate nor his spouse as beneficiary of the proceeds, the IRS could argue that the uninsured spouse made a gift to the beneficiary when the proceeds are paid. The gift becomes complete upon the insured's death and the amount of the gift is one half the amount of the insurance proceeds.

Where the noninsured spouse dies first and the insurance is community property, half the value of the unmatured policy is includable in that spouse's gross estate. Then, if the insured spouse receives the policy under the noninsured spouse's will, the entire proceeds will be includable in his estate.

More Than 5 Percent Test

In some situations, a client has made a conditional transfer, i.e., a gift of a policy coupled with a "but if… back to me" string. If certain events did (or did not) occur, the policy would revert (i.e., come back) to the donor insured (or his estate).

Such a reversionary interest in a policy held by the insured or the insured's estate will be considered an incident of ownership under section 2042 if the actuarial value of that interest exceeds 5 percent of the value of the policy (measured immediately prior to the insured's death). This reversionary interest must be just that, a right retained by the insured (either in the policy provisions or by some other instrument or operation of law) when the insured transferred the policy. The mere possibility that a policy could return to the insured as a bequest by will at the donee's death or through the intestacy of the donee (or through the right of the insured to elect against a spouse's will) is not considered a reversionary interest and will therefore not cause inclusion.

Even if a reversionary interest exists, it must be actuarially (according to current monthly government discount rates) be worth more than 5 percent of the value of the policy as measured immediately before the insured's death. So, if someone else had an interest that lowered the value of the insured's interest, the value of the other person's interest could prevent estate tax inclusion in the insured's estate.

Example. Suppose a client gave a policy on his life to his son and retained the right to regain the policy if the son died before the insured. Suppose, in the same transfer, the donor insured gave the son the unfettered right to surrender the policy for cash at any time. The son's power to completely eliminate the insured's right to regain the policy would reduce the value of the father's interest to zero.

As a practical matter, if the donee of a policy is the owner and has all rights normally associated with ownership except the right to name a successor owner (the reversionary right held by the insured), the value of the insured's reversionary right would be well below the more than 5 percent threshold. If the donee had the right to revoke the insured's successive ownership designation in addition to the ability to surrender the contract, the value of the insured's reversionary interest should approach zero.

Reversionary Interest and Death of Third Party Owner

What is the result where a third party owner of a policy on the insured's life dies before the insured does and the policy passes back to the insured? Here, state law must be examined very carefully. The results may be surprising. For example, suppose a client's wife purchased a $1,000,000 policy on the client's life. Assume the wife is killed in an automobile accident in which the client dies one hour later. As the beneficiary of his wife's will, the client becomes (if only for an hour) the owner of the insurance proceeds that are actually paid to the specified contingent beneficiaries.

Did the client have incidents of ownership? The answer will depend on state law. If title and legal right and possession of personal property pass to the estate's executor and that party is someone other than the client, the client would not have legal power to exercise incidents of ownership in the insurance. Therefore, nothing would be includable in his estate under section 2042. But if he was the personal representative (executor) of the estate, as well as heir, he would have incidents of ownership since he would have immediate legal rights over the insurance. The same result would occur if the insured were named as contingent owner of the policy. Were he merely personal representative but not an heir of the wife's estate, there would be no inclusion because there would be no personally exercisable incidents of ownership.

Insured as Trustee

Often, insureds have served as a trustee of a trust which held insurance on their lives. Unfortunately, such an arrangement has often led to expensive litigation and often federal estate tax inclusion of policy proceeds on these grounds: the trust owned the policy, the trustee controlled the trust, the insured was trustee, and therefore the insured is deemed to have held incidents of ownership in a policy on his life actually held by the trust. Of course, this argument conveniently overlooks the most basic premise of trust law: a fiduciary is barred from using such funds for personal benefit absent express provision in the governing instrument (assuming the fiduciary is not also a beneficiary).

Although it would appear a sound argument therefore, that incidents held purely and solely in a fiduciary capacity cannot be used except to benefit a trust's heirs (and therefore should not be included in the decedent's estate as insurance), the IRS doesn't see it that way. Fortunately, the courts don't always agree with the IRS. The result is a confusing and dangerous mix of cases and rulings that vary in result depending more on domicile than on facts.

Two types of situations may trigger the problem: The most common is where the client creates a trust and transfers life insurance to it and insists on being named trustee. But the problem can also occur where the policy on the insured is owned by a third party (such as the insured's spouse) and, at that third party's death, the policy passes to a trust over which the insured is trustee.

The following will summarize the section 2042(2) issues with respect to life insurance trusts where the IRS will act aggressively against the deceased taxpayer's estate:

- If the decedent (acting alone or in conjunction with others) had the power as trustee to change the time or manner of enjoyment, even if the decedent had no beneficial interest in the trust, the IRS will treat him as having held an incident of ownership in a policy on his own life held in a trust if he was trustee.

- If the decedent transferred the policy to the trust or paid premiums, the IRS will treat him as having held an incident of ownership in a policy on his own life held in a trust if he was trustee.

- If the decedent could have exercised his powers as trustee for his own benefit, regardless of how those powers were acquired and regardless of whether or not the decedent transferred property to the trust, the IRS will treat him as having held an incident of ownership in a policy on his own life held in a trust if he was trustee.

The following will summarize the section 2042(2) issues with respect to life insurance trusts where the IRS will not claim the deceased taxpayer held incidents of ownership:

- if the decedent held powers only in a fiduciary capacity and could not exercise those powers for his personal benefit;

- if he did not transfer the policy or any of the premiums or other consideration for purchasing or maintaining the policy from personal assets; and

- if the return of powers to the decedent was not part of a prearranged plan.

The following will summarize the section 2042(2) issues with respect to life insurance trusts where the courts in some jurisdictions are likely to agree with the IRS that the deceased taxpayer had held incidents of ownership:

- According to the Fifth Circuit,[20] a decedent has incidents of ownership in a policy on his life held in trust if the decedent is trustee, even if incidents of ownership are possessed only in a fiduciary capacity and the insured made no transfer of the policy to the trust.

The following will summarize the section 2042(2) issues with respect to life insurance trusts where the courts in some jurisdictions are likely to agree with the IRS that the deceased taxpayer had held incidents of ownership:

- According to the Second,[21] Sixth,[22] and Eighth Circuits,[23] a decedent does not have incidents of ownership in a policy on his life held in trust if the decedent transfers policies on his life to a trust, even though the decedent is named trustee, as long as he cannot exercise his fiduciary powers for his own benefit.

What is certain is that this confusion and danger can be avoided by naming someone other than the insured as the trustee of a trust that has or could have insurance on his life. As a next best alternative, planners should consider the following provisions:

1. Specifically forbid an insured serving as trustee from taking any action with respect to a policy on his life held by a trust over which the insured is trustee or co-trustee.[24]

2. If a nongrantor insured is a beneficiary of a trust, make sure that the insured does not possess any incidents of ownership in the life insurance policy.

3. Specify that the insured, as trustee, cannot use trust income or assets to satisfy his or her legal obligation to support his or her children.

4. Place assets in the trust to generate sufficient income to pay premiums.

5. Follow the terms of the trust closely and avoid conflict fact patterns which indicate that the insured acting as trustee can use trust property for personal gain.

Insured as Fiduciary Other than Trustee

When the insured becomes the executor or administrator of an estate or the custodian of a minor or otherwise legally incompetent person's assets, there is a strong possibility that an incident of ownership problem may arise if the estate or custodial account holds a policy on the insured's life.

Example. Assume a wife purchased a policy on her husband's life but the wife predeceased her husband. The policy would be considered personal property in her estate. Assume the wife's will left the entire estate to the husband, if living, otherwise to the couple's children.

When the insured becomes the administrator or executor of an estate and is also a beneficiary of the estate, as is the case in this example, it is highly likely that should the insured die, even before distribution of the policy, the IRS will claim he had incidents of ownership in a policy on his life held by the estate. It would argue that, as executor, the insured could exercise powers over the insurance for his own benefit.

Inclusion is clear where the husband was the sole beneficiary of the estate. But what if the estate was split in thirds between the insured husband and the couple's two children? What if the wife's estate was payable entirely to the three children?

In the authors' opinion, these two later situations do not meet the three tests the IRS itself set out:

1. the insured must have transferred the policy or provided consideration for purchasing or maintaining it from the insured's personal assets;

2. the rights and powers the insured obtained were part of a prearranged plan involving the participation of the insured; and

3. the insured can personally benefit from the powers held as fiduciary.

Even if the first and third tests were met (i.e., if the insured paid premiums from personal funds to keep the policy on his life in force and personally could benefit from the arrangement), it would be difficult for the IRS to argue that the wife and the husband colluded and she died first so that he could obtain control without inclusion of the policy in his estate.

Many states' version of the Uniform Gifts to Minors Act (UGMA) or Uniform Transfers to Minors Act (UTMA) allows a custodian for a child to purchase and/or maintain life insurance. It is clear that, if a client transfers life insurance on his life to a custodial account for his child and names himself as the custodian, assets in the account will be includable in his estate if he died before the minor child reaches the age where the custodial funds must be paid out under state law. If life insurance is one of the custodial account's assets, it will be included in the insured-custodian's estate. Likewise, if the client becomes successor custodian and then dies, the value of the property transferred will be includable in the client's estate.

There are situations in which an individual gives another person a power of attorney over assets in order to care for and protect the individual. Assume a client's mother owned a life insurance policy on the client's life. To protect herself against incompetency, the mother gave her son a general durable power of attorney with wide boilerplate provisions. Would the power given to the son amount to an incident of ownership in the policy on his life?

There appears to be no cases or rulings directly on point. If the insured could exercise power over the life insurance as holder of the power, at the very least, the IRS could engage his estate in costly litigation. The authors conclude that the best course of action is to provide in the power of attorney that the holder of the power is barred from exercising any right whatsoever with respect to a policy of life insurance on his life.

Split Dollar Insurance

In the classic split dollar arrangement in which a corporation makes an outlay equal to the annual increase in policy cash values and a selected employee pays the balance of the premium, if any, the insured is given the power to name and change the beneficiary of the portion of the proceeds not going to the corporation (usually an amount at least equal to its cumulative outlay). That ability to name and change the beneficiary is an incident of ownership and will cause inclusion of the proceeds.

The right to name the beneficiary of proceeds in excess of the cash value (or in the case of reverse split dollar, the right to name the beneficiary of the policy's

cash value) would seem to be sufficient to warrant inclusion of the entire proceeds. All the proceeds would be includable even if the insured possessed only one incident of ownership and even though a portion of the proceeds were payable to someone other than the insured's beneficiaries.

Example. Assume a client owned 40 percent of the stock of a company that provided $1,000,000 of life insurance on his life. The corporation paid an amount equal to each year's increase in cash values and the client paid the balance of the premium. At the client's death, the proceeds were to be paid to the corporation in an amount up to its total outlay and any balance would be paid to the client's daughter. Assuming the client doesn't assign the policy to his daughter more than three years prior to his death, the entire proceeds would be included in his estate.

However, a claims against the estate deduction might be allowed for proceeds paid to the corporation (or other party receiving a portion of the proceeds in return for having paid a portion of the premiums). This claim against the estate deduction should apply whenever:

1. the insured owned 50 percent or less of the corporation (i.e., was not a controlling shareholder);

2. there was a bona fide written agreement as to the reimbursement arrangement; and

3. the agreement was entered into initially for full and adequate consideration as part of a business transaction. This implies that the client's estate may not be allowed an estate tax deduction where the client merely names a family trust as beneficiary.

A much more difficult problem is faced when an individual controls (owns more than 50 percent of the combined voting stock in) a closely held corporation. In that case, to the extent proceeds of a corporate owned policy are payable to or for the benefit of a party other than the corporation, such proceeds are includable as insurance in the insured's estate (because the insured is deemed to possess incidents of ownership).

As the law stands today, it appears that the only way to remove a split dollar life insurance policy from the gross estate of a controlling shareholder is to insulate all incidents of ownership from the corporation (because once the corporation owns any incident, including the right to borrow against the cash surrender value, that incident is attributed to its controlling shareholder).

But how is it possible to set up a split dollar plan with the corporation advancing the bulk of the premium and yet not providing security for the corporation's outlays? One answer lies in the problem itself; there is only a problem if the shareholder is controlling (i.e., owns more than 50 percent of the vote). By definition, therefore, that person should be able to persuade the corporation to forgo the customary protection or right to borrow against the policy's cash value or veto a loan against or surrender of the policy. This can generally be accomplished by having the corporation receive only a restricted collateral interest in the policy. This means that the corporation only has the right to receive back its interest in the event of the death of the insured or the termination of the split dollar arrangement (it should not have the unilateral right to terminate). Thus, it would have no incidents of ownership via the collateral assignment that could be deemed to be possessed by the insured.

If the policy is owned by a third party, such as a trust for the client's children (or if adult children own the policy), from inception or the policy is assigned to an irrevocable trust (or to adult children) more than three years prior to the client's death, the insured would hold no incidents of ownership either personally or through the corporation (since the corporation would have no rights whatsoever except the right to receive that portion of the proceeds equal to its premium outlay).

If the insured owned more than 50 percent of the corporation which is splitting the premium and proceed dollars, it is appropriate (but not certain at this point) that since the amount payable to the corporation will already be included in the insured's gross estate due to the impact it will have increasing corporate value, those proceeds should not again be includable separately as insurance.

Although most split dollar arrangements are between corporations and employees, there are many agreements to split premiums, cash values, and death proceeds of life insurance that are made between individuals. Such an arrangement is often called private split dollar. A father in law, for example, may protect his daughter and grandchildren by entering into a split dollar agreement with his son in law. The father would help the son in law obtain more insurance at a lower cost than might otherwise be possible.

If the insured is given or retains any incident of ownership in the policy, the proceeds will be includable in his estate. Suppose a parent, for instance, sets up a trust for his children and the trust purchases a life insurance policy on the father's life. To help the trustee pay premiums (and to lower gift tax costs), the father advances amounts equal to the annual increase in the policy's cash surrender value. The trustee must pay the balance of each year's premium. The father retains the right to recover an amount equal to his cumulative outlays or to borrow against the policy for up to that amount. That retained right will cause inclusion of the proceeds in his estate.[25] However, if the insured only has a restricted collateral interest in the policy as discussed above, then estate inclusion will not be an issue.

INCLUSION OF LIFE INSURANCE IN RETIREMENT PLANS (SECTION 2039)

At one time, Code section 2039(c) provided an unlimited exclusion for the amount distributed at a participant's death from a qualified retirement plan to the extent attributable to employer contributions. That exclusion has been eliminated.

Subject to certain transition (grandfathering) rules, a decedent's executor must include in the gross estate the value of any payment "receivable by any beneficiary by reason of surviving the decedent under any form of contract or agreement…(other than as insurance under policies on the life of the decedent)," if certain other conditions are met. So section 2039 will not cause the inclusion of the proceeds of a life insurance policy on a plan participant's life. Does this mean the proceeds are estate tax free? The answer is "yes," only if inclusion is not warranted under any other IRC section.

The Subtrust Concept

Some authorities have suggested that it is still possible to avoid federal estate taxation on life insurance proceeds paid as part of a distribution from a qualified retirement plan through a subtrust concept. One configuration of the technique works like this:

1. The insured employee makes an irrevocable beneficiary designation that divests him of the right to change the beneficiary of plan proceeds.

2. The qualified plan is amended to provide that the policy will not be distributed to the insured

at retirement. This amendment is made to eliminate an IRS argument that the insured retained a reversionary interest in the policy.

3. The plan is amended to give the insured a right to purchase the policy for its full value at retirement.

4. To insulate an insured who is also a trustee of the plan from an incidents of ownership attack by the IRS, a special trust (subtrust) is created. Policies on the life of the insured-trustee are placed into the subtrust. The insured is given no control over the subtrust and cannot remove its independent trustee.

Will this subtrust concept work? The answer appears to be a resounding NO! In an unpublished Technical Advice Memorandum, the IRS has indicated that a life insurance subtrust may disqualify the pension plan. Though this TAM was not published, the taxpayer to whom it was issued sent a copy of it to Steve Leimberg who published it in his *Employee Benefits and Retirement Planning Email Newsletter*—Archive Message #385 (September 19, 2006).

Alternative to the Subtrust Concept

It is possible and sometimes desirable to remove life insurance from a qualified plan. Advantages of life insurance outside of a qualified plan include:

• the ability to invest in more assets producing otherwise currently taxable income and have the income on such assets grow income tax free;

• the ability to exclude life insurance purchased outside the plan from federal estate taxes and be assured that, if arranged properly, exclusion is a very high probability if not a certainty.

The easiest way to remove life insurance from a qualified plan is for the trustee to allow the policy to lapse and for new insurance to be purchased outside the plan (preferably by adult beneficiaries or a trust for the intended recipient of the proceeds). A sale by the retirement plan of the policy to the insured is another possibility. This is a more appealing choice where the insured is in ill health, the policy in question is beyond the incontestable period, or, for whatever other reason, the client does not want the original policy to lapse.

A sale to the insured or to the policy's beneficiary is permissible under an exception to the prohibited transaction rules.[26] In most cases, the preferred course of action is to have the insured (or an intentionally defective grantor trust created by the insured) purchase the policy to nullify the danger under the transfer for value rule (see Chapter 25). It is extremely important to document evidence that:

1. the contract would have been surrendered by the plan even if the sale had not taken place; and

2. the plan was placed financially in the same position it would have been in had it surrendered the contract and made a distribution of the amount the plan owed to the insured participant.

There are disadvantages of the sale to the insured technique. First, the insured does not receive credit for the income tax paid on the costs of life insurance protection. In other words, the plan participant cannot count as part of his basis the taxes paid for the term insurance protection he received year after year.

A second possible disadvantage is that the purchase by the insured does not solve the estate tax inclusion problem. That can only be accomplished if the insured then divests himself of all incidents of ownership and lives for more than three years after the transfer.

A third potential problem lies with valuation issues; if the insured is terminally ill or in exceptionally poor health, the amount necessary to purchase the policy may be significantly more than the greater of the Interpolated Terminal Reserve (ITR) or Premiums plus Earnings less Reasonable Charges (PERC) value that the IRS indicates must be used as the fair market value when life insurance is distributed or sold by a qualified plan.[27]

ESTATE TAX MARITAL DEDUCTION (SECTION 2056)

An unlimited deduction is allowed for property includable in the gross estate that passes in a qualifying manner to the surviving spouse of the decedent. The surviving spouse must be a U.S. citizen or the property must pass to a Qualified Domestic Trust (QDOT) for the benefit of the surviving spouse. No deduction is allowed, however, for certain nondeductible terminable interests, in general, interests which may terminate or fail to vest upon the lapse of time or upon the occurrence or nonoccurrence of a specified event or contingency.

A spouse's interest in life insurance proceeds is terminable and would be nondeductible if:

1. there is any possibility that her interest will terminate upon the occurrence or nonoccurrence of a contingency or event;

2. some other person or persons will receive the property as a result of the termination; and

3. that other person or persons will receive the property interest without paying consideration in money or money's worth.

If all three tests are met, the interest will not qualify for the marital deduction.

Form of Payment

Generally, proceeds will qualify for the federal estate tax marital deduction if they are paid in the form of a:

- lump sum;

- life annuity ending at spouse's death;

- life annuity with principal remaining paid to spouse's estate;

- payment to spouse (interest only or installments) and principal remaining paid to specified beneficiary coupled with surviving spouse given general power of appointment over principal;

- payment to spouse of interest only, with remaining principal qualifying under QTIP rules; and

- outright payment under insured's will;

- outright payment under state intestacy laws;

- payment of proceeds to trust which itself qualifies for marital deduction.

Lump Sum or Life Annuity to Spouse

Life insurance will qualify for the federal estate tax marital deduction if payable in a lump sum to the decedent-insured's surviving (U.S. citizen) spouse. Since the spouse will receive the entire interest in the proceeds rather than a nondeductible terminable interest, the marital deduction will be allowed even if the insured names secondary or other contingent beneficiaries in the event the noninsured spouse does not survive the insured. The marital deduction will also be allowed if the surviving spouse chooses to receive proceeds under a settlement option (life annuity) rather than take a lump sum, as long as the choice is hers.

Life Annuity to Spouse, Balance to Spouse's Estate

A marital deduction will be allowed if the insured or the surviving spouse selects a settlement option with the insurer giving the surviving spouse income from the proceeds for her life with the balance of the proceeds going to her estate. This follows the principle that a nondeductible terminable interest is one in which someone other than the surviving spouse might take her interest with no consideration upon the occurrence or nonoccurrence of a specified event. Since no one other than the spouse will take an interest (payment to the spouse's estate is equated to payment to the spouse), the interest is not a nondeductible interest. Therefore, a life annuity to the spouse with no refund or no period certain guarantee would qualify for the marital deduction. Likewise, a life annuity to the spouse coupled with a period certain guarantee (for example, a guarantee that at least fifteen years' payments will be made) with the balance of any payments going to the spouse's estate will qualify.

Income to Spouse, Power of Appointment

As another exception to the nondeductible terminable interests rule, the interest can be payable to the spouse and then to some other beneficiary and still qualify, if the surviving spouse is given a general power of appointment over the proceeds and certain other requirements are met.

There are five conditions that must be met:

1. *All income to spouse rule*: There must be an agreement with the insurer that the proceeds (or a specified portion of the proceeds) will be paid in installments to the surviving spouse, or that the surviving spouse will receive all the income and no one else will receive installment or interest for as long as such spouse lives.

2. *Annually or more frequently rule*: The installments or interest payable solely to the surviving spouse must be payable annually or more

frequently. Payments must begin no later than thirteen months after the insured's death. As long as payment can begin within thirteen months after the decedent's death, and the only person with any choice in that decision is the surviving spouse, the thirteen month test is met even if, in fact, no payment is elected for more than thirteen months. This condition is satisfied even if the insurance contract requires the surviving spouse to provide proof of death before the first payment is made.

3. *Power to appoint rule*: The surviving spouse must have the general power to appoint all or a specific portion of the amounts held by the insurer to either herself, her estate, her creditors, or the creditors of her estate. The power will be considered general if the surviving spouse can revoke the contingent beneficiaries the insured had named and substitute her estate. Likewise, if she can require the trustee to pay her principal for her own use, she will be deemed to have a general power.

4. *Alone and in all events rule*: The power to make appointments of principal must be exercisable by the surviving spouse without the need to consult or obtain anyone else's consent. This requirement will not fail merely because the insurer places administrative restrictions on withdrawal rights. For example, the requirement that the beneficiary give formal written notice, or that some reasonable time interval must be allowed between partial exercises of the surviving spouse's powers, will not be considered to thwart the spouse's right to withdraw in all events. The power can be exercised either by will or by an instrument during the spouse's lifetime, but must be an unconditional right exercisable without limitations.

5. *No power except to provide for spouse rule*: The amounts payable under the arrangement with the insurer cannot be subject to a power of appointment in anyone's hands other than the surviving spouse, except for a power in the hands of another to appoint some or all of the insurance proceeds to the surviving spouse.

QTIP Rules

Another exception to the nondeductible terminable interests rule is Qualified Terminable Interest Property

(QTIP). Under this exception, income only payments to the spouse with payments to a beneficiary following the termination of her interest can qualify for a marital deduction even if the surviving spouse is given no general power of appointment.

QTIP rules require that the proceeds pass from the decedent, that the surviving spouse be given a qualifying income interest for life, and that the original decedent's executor make an irrevocable election on the federal estate tax return to have the marital deduction apply. Any principal left at the time the surviving spouse dies will be includable in her estate.

Payment under Insured's Will or Intestacy Laws

In some instances, life insurance is payable to an insured's estate. Most often, this occurs where the insured has neglected to name a specific beneficiary or contingent beneficiary or where the beneficiary named has predeceased the insured and the insured died before naming a new beneficiary.[28] But even such payments can qualify for the marital deduction if assets in the estate pass outright by will to the surviving (U.S. citizen) spouse.[29] Likewise, if the insured's life insurance is payable to his estate and he dies intestate, the proceeds will qualify for the federal estate tax marital deduction even though passing under state inheritance tax laws to the surviving spouse rather than by will or through specific direction in the policy itself.

Payment to Estate Trust or Marital Deduction Trust

Payment of life insurance proceeds directly to a trust which otherwise qualifies for a marital deduction will qualify the proceeds for the marital deduction. Therefore, payments to an estate trust (income may be paid out to the spouse or may be accumulated at the trustee's discretion, but principal remaining at the surviving spouse's death is payable to her estate) or power of appointment trust (the surviving spouse receives all income annually or more frequently and has the general power to appoint principal to herself or her estate) will qualify for a marital deduction.

Time Delay Clause

To qualify for the marital deduction, property must pass to a surviving spouse. If the beneficiary spouse does not survive the insured, the marital deduction is not allowed. In some situations, the beneficiary spouse may survive the insured spouse and yet the proceeds will not pass to the surviving spouse and so the marital deduction is lost. Planners must therefore make sure when using a time delay clause or common disaster provision that—if the marital deduction is important—its requirements are met.

A time delay clause is a provision that can be inserted in an insurance company's beneficiary form which provides that payment will be made to the surviving spouse of the insured, but only if such spouse is living at the end of a given period of time, typically thirty or sixty days[30] after the death of the insured. If the surviving spouse does not survive the time delay clause period, the proceeds are paid to contingent beneficiaries. Such a clause is designed to assure that the proceeds don't fall into the hands of a surviving spouse's relatives or to avoid a needless probate in the surviving spouse's estate (and perhaps needless state death taxes) if she doesn't survive the specified period of time.

The problem with a time delay clause is that probate costs and state inheritance taxes may be saved at the expense of much higher federal estate taxes; the marital deduction is denied if the surviving spouse dies before the end of the specified time period, since the proceeds will not pass to her. For instance, if a client provides in his life insurance beneficiary designation that his wife must survive him by thirty days in order to receive the proceeds of his $1,000,000 policy and she dies eighteen days after he does, the money will not be paid to her or to her estate and will pass to the secondary beneficiary. The marital deduction will be lost.

Will a marital deduction be allowed even if the surviving spouse does survive the time delay period? The problem is that a time delay clause creates a condition which may terminate the surviving spouse's interest and result in property passing to someone other than the surviving spouse's estate and no consideration would be paid to her or her estate for the transfer. In other words, a time delay clause is a classic nondeductible terminable interest.

Fortunately, however, there is a specific statutory provision that enables the marital deduction to be obtained even if a time delay clause is used.[31] There are two requirements:

1. The delay period cannot exceed six months.

2. The spouse must actually survive whatever period is specified.

If both requirements are met, the marital deduction will be allowed. On the other hand, if under the clause there is any possibility that the surviving spouse may have to survive longer than six months to receive the proceeds, no matter how remote that possibility is, the marital deduction will be disallowed. The deduction will be disallowed even if the spouse does survive the specified period and the proceeds in fact pass to her.

A good example of such a fatal clause is one that paid the proceeds to the insured's wife "if she were living at the time the insurer received proof of the decedent's death." Proof of death was provided to the insurer within six months and payment of the proceeds was made to the widow. However, the IRS ruled that the marital deduction would not be allowed because proof of death might not have been made within the requisite six-month period.

A time delay clause must be carefully considered because it can result in a lose-lose situation: if the spouse lives longer than the minimum time, the clause is inoperative. If the spouse outlives the insured but does not survive the specified period, the marital deduction is forfeited. Selection by the insured of a settlement option that qualifies for the marital deduction or payment of proceeds to a trust qualifying for the marital deduction may be a better choice.

Common Disaster Clause

A common disaster clause provides a presumption as to the order of death. If both the insured and the beneficiary die in the same accident, the insured will be deemed to have survived the beneficiary. In other words, a common disaster clause is triggered, not by an arbitrarily specified length of time the survivor must live, but rather by whether or not the beneficiary died in a common accident with the insured. No matter by how long the beneficiary survives the insured, if the beneficiary subsequently dies as the result of the accident which killed the insured, the proceeds will pass to the contingent beneficiary (or the insured's estate) and will therefore not qualify for the marital deduction.

A common disaster clause therefore would appear to cause a loss of the marital deduction; there is always a possibility that the surviving spouse's interest may terminate. The marital deduction will be lost if at the final audit of the estate tax return "there is still a possibility that the surviving spouse may be deprived of the property interest by operation of the common disaster provision as given effect by the local law."

But under a special exception to the normal rules disqualifying terminable interests, the deduction will be allowed if in fact the noninsured spouse does survive and receives the proceeds. Planners should not count on this occurrence if the federal estate tax marital deduction is important.

Uniform Simultaneous Death Act (USDA)

Almost all the states have adopted the USDA. This law provides that if the insured and the beneficiary die at so nearly the same time that the order of their deaths cannot be ascertained, there is a legal presumption that the beneficiary died first. This, of course, would cause the loss of the marital deduction with respect to the proceeds. Note that the cause of death is irrelevant. In fact, the insured and the beneficiary can be at the opposite ends of the earth; if they die about the same time and the facts don't clearly indicate who died first, the presumption is that the beneficiary died first and therefore no marital deduction would be allowed.

In smaller estates, where federal estate taxes are not a major issue, this presumption would be favorable, since it would eliminate an unnecessary probate (and perhaps state taxation) of the proceeds in the beneficiary's estate. In a larger estate, the USDA could be a disaster.

Fortunately, a client can reverse the presumption of order of deaths merely by stating that desire in the insurance policy application or in a separate beneficiary agreement. This so called reverse simultaneous death clause nullifies the effects of a statutory presumption that the noninsured died first. Specifically, a reverse simultaneous death clause would state that if it cannot be determined who died first, the beneficiary will be deemed to have survived. Such a clause will be recognized by the IRS. Of course, if the facts show that the beneficiary did die first, a reverse simultaneous death clause will be worthless and the marital deduction will be lost.

ESTATE TAX CHARITABLE DEDUCTION (SECTION 2055)

An unlimited charitable deduction is allowed for the net amount of life insurance proceeds included in the insured's estate if they are then paid to a qualified charity. If the proceeds are reduced by a policy loan, only the net amount includable in the estate and payable to the charity will qualify for the charitable deduction.

If the policyowner is not the insured but dies first, a charitable deduction will be allowed if the unmatured policy passes to a qualified charity. The inclusion and value of the deduction will be measured by the same rules governing a lifetime gift to a charity. In most cases, the deduction will be measured by the sum of the interpolated terminal reserve plus the unearned premium (as of the date of the policyowner's death).

APPORTIONMENT RULES: WHO PAYS THE ESTATE TAX ON INSURANCE PROCEEDS?

This is an extremely important issue that is often overlooked or that falls between the cracks of an otherwise good estate plan.

As a general rule, to collect the federal estate tax, the IRS can follow life insurance proceeds as far as it can trace them. Any person who receives includable property is personally liable to the IRS for a deficiency in the estate tax. Each life insurance beneficiary is liable for that deficit, up to the full amount of the proceeds payable to him that were included in the insured's gross estate, regardless of a direction in the will exonerating the beneficiary from payment of the tax or a direction that the tax be paid from the probate estate. The IRS can follow any person who received life insurance proceeds and collect its tax from other property even if the proceeds themselves have been spent. If the proceeds have been spent, the government's lien extends to any property bought by or for the beneficiary with the proceeds.

Ordinarily, this tracking is not necessary because the executor, who is primarily liable, usually pays estate taxes out of probate funds. But what happens when significant nonprobate assets such as life insurance generate a tax but the proceeds are not payable to the executor to pay that tax?

Executor's Right to Recover

The Internal Revenue Code specifically authorizes an executor to recover from named beneficiaries of life insurance proceeds on the decedent's life a proportionate share of the taxes. The executor cannot claim reimbursement or contribution until after the executor pays the tax. Each beneficiary must (absent direction otherwise under the decedent's will or local law) reimburse the executor for his proportionate share of the federal estate tax. The IRS technically can't go against an insurance company for the tax regardless of how the proceeds are payable. But the executor may be able to reach the insurance proceeds held by the insurer to the extent the executor is entitled to contribution from the insurance beneficiary.

In the apportionment formula, total tax paid is multiplied by:

$$\frac{\text{Proceeds included in estate \& received by beneficiary}}{\text{Taxable estate}}$$

Example. Assume a client died and a $5,000,000 policy on his life was paid in equal shares to his two children. Assume further that the insurance was equal to about one half the client's taxable estate (total taxable estate was $10,000,000) and that the total estate tax was $1,750,000. The insurance in this simplified example would have generated ½ of the $1,750,000 estate tax (assuming a $5 million estate tax exemption), $875,000. Each child received ½ of the $5,000,000 proceeds, so each would be liable for about $437,500, one-fourth of the estate tax.

Marital Share Exception

If life insurance proceeds were paid to the insured's surviving spouse in a manner qualifying for the estate tax marital deduction, the rule is different. There, the executor can require reimbursement by the beneficiaries only for the tax attributable to the excess of proceeds over the aggregate amount of marital deductions.[32] So, if the entire amount of proceeds payable to the surviving spouse qualified for the marital deduction, the spouse would have no duty to contribute toward the payment of the federal estate tax.

If only a portion of the proceeds paid to the surviving spouse qualified for the marital deduction, then the surviving spouse would be liable to reimburse the executor for the proportionate share of tax on the balance. For instance, if $200,000 of life insurance was payable to a spouse but only $120,000 qualified for the marital deduction, the executor would be entitled to reimbursement on the $80,000 taxable difference. If the total taxable estate were $250,000, then $80,000/$250,000 would be multiplied by the total tax payable to ascertain the spouse's required contribution.

Apportionment Provisions by Client

Clients can engineer a different result through a combination of state law and careful will planning. For instance, if the will directs how the tax burden is to be apportioned, those directions will generally be followed by both state and federal authorities (to the extent tax collection is not jeopardized). For example, if the client's will provides that "my son and daughter shall pay all death taxes," they would end up paying even the estate tax on life insurance payable to other beneficiaries. This can obviously lead to unintended results and emphasizes the importance of co-ordination between the attorney drafting the client's will and the client's life insurance agent.

Use of Disclaimers

A disclaimer is an unqualified refusal to accept property (such as assets left under a will or trust or life insurance proceeds). Can a disclaimer avoid a potential tax disaster? For example, assume a client's will provides that all estate taxes will be paid out of the residue (what's left after specific gifts) of the probate estate. The client's spouse was the beneficiary of the residue (which would qualify for an estate tax marital deduction.) The client's son was the beneficiary of a $10,000,000 policy on the client's life (which obviously would generate a very sizable federal estate tax). The client died. The son received $10,000,000 of insurance proceeds and the mother received a notice from the estate's executor that the tax on that money had to come out of her share of the estate (thus dramatically increasing the federal estate tax). To increase the size of the marital deduction and therefore decrease the amount of the estate tax, the client's son disclaims his right to have his mother pay the federal estate tax on the insurance he received.

Will the son be successful? The answer is "Yes," if the right steps are taken at the right time. A bequest is a direction to the executor to pay someone a part of the probate estate's assets. A common form of bequest is the forgiveness of a debt owed the testator. If, under state law, the decedent's allocation of estate taxes to the wife in the example above is from the son's perspective a valuable property interest tantamount to forgiving a debt, it may be disclaimed.

No Exception for Charity

Suppose a client named a charity as beneficiary of a large life insurance policy. Assuming the charity was qualified, the payment of the insurance, no matter how large, would not generate any federal estate tax. Yet, absent specific provision in a state law apportionment statute or in the decedent's will, the charity may have to bear (to the extent of the insurance it received) a portion or all of the federal estate tax on assets paid to other beneficiaries.

This doesn't seem to mesh with the rules exonerating a surviving spouse from a reimbursement obligation; to the extent life insurance payable to a surviving spouse qualifies for a marital deduction, it is exempted from the reimbursement obligation under federal law. Yet federal law provides no comparable protection for proceeds payable to charities.[33]

If the charity's share of life insurance proceeds is reduced by the reimbursement requirement then the decedent's charitable deduction will be decreased. This in turn increases the decedent's estate tax burden, which increases the charity's burden, which... results in complex calculations.

Planning in Advance

Estate tax apportionment of life insurance should be arranged deliberately and carefully while the client is alive and his wishes can be known. The place to do this planning is in the client's will or revocable trust so that estate taxes and other expenses are shouldered by the parties the client wishes to carry them. It is important to be sure that in the attempt to lower the tax burden to its minimum legal level, the planning team does not lose sight as to what is necessary to uncover and effectuate the intended dispositive plan of the client.

CHAPTER ENDNOTES

1. I.R.C. §2033.
2. I.R.C. §2042(2).
3. I.R.C. §2035(a).
4. I.R.C. §2035(d).
5. Priv. Ltr. Rul. 9413045.
6. FSA 1998-328.
7. If not includable under section 2042, then under section 2038(a)(1) as a transfer with a retained right to alter, amend, revoke, or terminate a gift. section 2036(a) may also apply since the insured retains the power to select who will possess or enjoy the income from the property transferred.
8. The IRS holds that it is an incident of ownership and will include proceeds under that argument in all states except in Pennsylvania, Delaware, New Jersey, and the Virgin Islands.
9. Typically, this right has been held to be merely a reduction in premium cost, rather than an incident of ownership. However, the right to take dividend accumulations or surrender dividend additions for their cash value would be considered an incident of ownership.
10. An insured will have an incident of ownership if he can change the policy's beneficiary, even if he has no right to change the terms of the trust which itself holds the policy and even if the insured has no beneficial interest in the trust.
11. If the insured can change the terms of a trust (either alone or in conjunction with another), he will be deemed to have an incident of ownership in a policy held by the trust even though he holds no rights under the policy.
12. The existence of an incident of ownership is a fact ascertainable only under state law. Of course, where the insured intended never to possess an incident of ownership but an agent's mistake resulted in one, an exception (appropriately called the agent's mistake exception) may be made by the courts (after much legal expense and aggravation).
13. An insured will not be considered to have held incidents of ownership where the insured requested that the beneficiary be the owner and hold all incidents of ownership but by mistake the policy read otherwise. Likewise, if the insurance agent without authority and contrary to the instructions of a third party applicant fills in the application and names the insured as owner, no inclusion will be required.

    The issue is one of policy facts versus intent facts where the terms of the policy as to ownership conflict with the apparent intention of the insured. State law is determinate and usually it looks to the terms of the policy, although sometimes courts will apply principles of equity and contract law in concluding that the insured held none of the incidents of ownership.

    An insured would not be considered to hold incidents of ownership, even though he was named as owner, if his corporation carried the policies on its books as key man coverage and paid all the premiums and the other facts corroborate that the insured merely acted as the corporation's agent and that the designation of the insured as owner was an error.

14. A decedent will not be considered to have an incident of ownership in a policy merely by virtue of a trust provision that would terminate his wife's interest in the event of a divorce. The act of divorcing one's spouse is an act of independent significance and the termination of the spouse's interest would be an incidental consequence of that act.

15. This problem is especially important when dealing with key employee coverage and with insurance used to fund a buy-sell. It is the authors' opinion that a right to purchase existing life insurance in return for the then fair market value of the coverage should not be considered an incident of ownership. But the IRS continues to claim that the right to purchase an existing life insurance contract is an incident of ownership when that right is created in an employment or business ownership context even though, on almost identical facts, the Tax Court has reached the opposite result. For instance, the power to veto the cancellation of a policy by purchasing it at its fair market value was held not to be an incident of ownership.

    Practitioners can feel most safe when the insured's right to purchase is based on the occurrence of a prior event of independent significance. For instance, if the insured's right to purchase the insurance on his life was predicated on the corporation's prior purchase of his stock in the event of disability or other

16. The retention of the right to select settlement options is viewed by the IRS as a right to alter the timing of the payment of the proceeds, which is considered an incident of ownership.

17. Priv. Ltr. Rul. 9809032. Here, the trustees of the irrevocable trust borrowed amounts from the insured's revocable trust which they then used to pay premiums on the policies the irrevocable trust held on the insured-grantor's life. These loans were fully documented with notes, five of which were outstanding when the insured died. The IRS properly held that the identity of the premium payor is irrelevant in determining whether a decedent retained any incidents of ownership in the policy for estate tax purposes.

18. Priv. Ltr. Rul. 9809032. Conceivably, this power could provide the insured with the ability to encourage the trustees to resign by controlling the trustee's compensation. But according to the IRS, the grantor's right in this instance did not amount to a retention to affect the beneficial enjoyment of the trust property, since the grantor did not have the power to appoint a successor trustee.

19. Priv. Ltr. Rul. 9832039.

20. The Fifth Circuit includes Louisiana, Mississippi, and Texas. The Fifth Circuit may even be more difficult to live or die with than the IRS itself.

21. The Second Circuit includes New York, Vermont, and Connecticut.

termination of employment, that act, being: (a) contingent; (b) dependent on the occurrence of events which did not occur; and (c) beyond the control of the insured, should eliminate the incident of ownership problem.

22. The Sixth Circuit includes Michigan, Ohio, Kentucky, and Tenn.

23. Arkansas, Mo., Iowa, Minn., Neb., S.Dak., N. Dak.

24. The issue can occur in any fiduciary relationship. Planners must therefore be wary in fiduciary situations other than trusts.

25. Actually, the portion of the proceeds paid to the father's estate in repayment of the father's outlays would be included under Code section 2042(1). The balance of the proceeds, even though payable to the children's trust, would be included in the father's estate under section 2042(2). Note also, that the parent is making annual gifts of the economic benefit to the trust's beneficiaries.

26. See Prohibited Transaction Exemption 77-8 and PTE 92-5.

27. Rev. Proc. 2005-25.

28. Some authorities have suggested that naming the estate as beneficiary of a modest amount of life insurance to satisfy creditors and pay death taxes and other estate settlement costs may be appropriate. In the authors' opinion, there are few situations that suggest that a client's estate be named as beneficiary of life insurance. There is almost always a more suitable designation than an insured's estate.

29. I.R.C. §§2056(a), 2056(d).

30. The insurer can't settle its obligation to the beneficiary until the end of whatever period of time has been specified. As a practical matter, this suggests that the time delay be kept to no more than sixty days, and in most cases thirty days.

31. I.R.C. §2056(b)(3).

32. I.R.C. §2206.

33. I.R.C. §2206.

GIFT TAXATION OF LIFE INSURANCE

CHAPTER 28

INTRODUCTION

Planners must be constantly aware of the gift tax implications of transactions involving life insurance. Gifts of life insurance, as opposed to gifts of income-producing property, are favored vehicles for many reasons. These include:

1. A gift of life insurance may increase the donor's spendable income since, after the gift, the donee often pays the premiums and the donor then can spend, invest, or give away the money that otherwise would have been paid in life insurance premiums. Conversely, a gift of income-producing property will deprive the donor of the net after tax income from that property.

2. The donee is less inclined to surrender a policy for its cash value than to dispose of income-producing property. This increases the probability that the policy, and therefore the proceeds, will be available to the beneficiaries. The likelihood of achieving the client's objectives (enhancement of the beneficiary's financial security or creation of a source of liquidity for the client's estate) will be met.

3. The gift tax cost of the transfer, when the gift is life insurance, is relatively low since essentially only the replacement value, rather than the face amount, is subject to gift tax. When income-producing property is given, the entire fair market value is subject to gift tax. In other words, for the same gift tax cost a much larger amount can be excluded from a client's gross estate. For example, a ten-year-old whole life policy that will generate $1,000,000 of death benefit could be removed from a client's estate at the cost of a relatively low gift tax based on the policy's value at the date of the gift.

4. There is no gain for income tax purposes when a life insurance policy matures at death, even if that policy was obtained by gift. If any other type of property is given away, the recipient takes as his basis the donor's basis (with certain adjustments). In other words, the donor's basis is carried over from the donor to the recipient. Thus, no step up from the donor's basis is allowed to the donee on a gift except for perhaps a portion of any gift tax paid on the transfer. So, a gift of property other than life insurance results in a carryover basis and, upon a later sale by the donee, the entire gain inherent in the property must be recognized.

5. The client's personal financial security is diminished only by the transferred cash value and even this potential problem can be minimized by a carefully measured pretransfer loan.[1]

6. A gift of life insurance may be a way to assure children of a first marriage of financial security and a share of their parent's wealth in the event of a second marriage.

7. Assume a client has a large estate and wants to provide children with an amount greater than the unified credit equivalent during the lifetime of his spouse. The client is going to leave all but the unified credit equivalent to his spouse, but doesn't want his children to have to wait until the surviving parent dies to receive their inheritance. A gift of life insurance from the client to the children more than three years

before the client's death would help assure the achievement of the multiple goals.

FOUR QUESTIONS FOR CONSIDERATION

As is the case with any other gift tax analysis, when life insurance is the subject of a transfer, the planner must ask four questions:

1. Was there a gift, a gratuitous transfer for less than adequate and full consideration?

2. Was the gift completed?

3. What is the value of the gift?

4. Is there an exclusion (such as the annual exclusion) or a deduction (such as the marital or charitable deduction) that can reduce or eliminate the taxable gift or a credit (such as the lifetime exemption) that can reduce or eliminate the tax on the gift?

To qualify a transfer of a life insurance policy for the gift tax marital deduction, the assignment to the insured's spouse must be: (a) outright; or (b) consist of the transfer of a life interest coupled with a general power of appointment vested in the spouse; or (c) meet qualified terminable interest property (QTIP) rules.

Typically, a gift of a life insurance policy to charity will qualify for the charitable deduction and therefore no gift tax will be payable regardless of the size of the policy or its value.

However, the gift tax charitable deduction is allowed only if the client assigns his entire interest (or an undivided portion of the donor's entire interest). Thus, if a client gives a charity the right to the death benefit but keeps the policy cash values or gives the charity the right to policy cash values and retains the right to name the beneficiary of the death benefit, no gift tax (or income tax) deduction would be allowed.

A further tax trap pertains to insurable interest. If the law in the state of the donor's domicile doesn't recognize that the charity has an insurable interest in the donor's life, the IRS may argue that the insured's estate may have rights in the policy or its proceeds. This in turn could thwart both the income tax deduction and the gift tax deduction since the donor's gift

to charity would be considered a transfer of a partial interest rather than a gift of the donor's entire interest. A lack of insurable interest may also result in the disallowance of a charitable gift tax deduction for future premium payments made by the client to charity after the transfer of an existing policy or purchase by the charity of a new one.[2]

Typically, most gift tax problems with respect to life insurance arise where a client makes a gratuitous transfer of a policy. But several other situations can also trigger gift tax problems. The first is the case where a policy on one person's life is owned by a second person and payable to a third.[3] Another scenario that triggers gift tax is where one party pays premiums on behalf of another. Each of these and other gift tax generating types of transactions will be covered in detail in the following section.

OUTRIGHT GIFTS OF POLICIES

An outright gift of a life insurance policy is a time tested technique for accomplishing a number of estate planning objectives including, but not limited to, saving federal and state death taxes and protecting proceeds from the claims of the original policyowner's creditors. The primary advantage of an outright gift of a life insurance policy is incredible leverage; the gift tax value of the lifetime transfer is considerably less than the death proceeds removed from the client's estate. If the future value of the gift tax (if any) actually payable currently is exceeded by the future value of the estate tax saved, the gift is advantageous.

Example. Assume a client is in a 40 percent federal estate tax bracket. Assume further that the client owns a $1,000,000 life insurance policy on his own life with a gift tax value of $200,000. If the client does nothing, $400,000 (40 percent of $1,000,000) will be lost in federal estate taxes. But if the client makes a gift of the policy and survives the gift by more than three years, none of the proceeds will be in the client's estate.[4]

Of course, if the lifetime value of the policy is large enough, there will be (assuming the transfer does not qualify for the gift tax annual exclusion or the client has used up the allowable gift tax exemption) federal gift tax payable currently on the transfer. In the example above, the gift tax is 50 percent of the $200,000 value of the policy at the time it was transferred. Assuming a long-term growth rate of 8 percent or less over a twenty-year life expectancy, the tradeoff of paying a small tax today to save a much larger tax in the future makes sense. If any current gift tax is payable, the future value of this gift tax must be calculated and compared against the potential estate tax savings to measure the true advantage of a gift of the policy.

When is a gift of a life insurance policy a completed gift? In other words, at what point does the taxable gift occur? The IRS has held that the relinquishment of every right that would normally cause a life insurance policy to be included in the insured or in the policyowner's estate would mark the completion of a gift of the contract. So as long as the insured held any incident of ownership that would cause the policy proceeds to be included in his estate or as long as a client owned a policy on the life of another, no gift is yet made. A completed gift occurs at the moment every interest the insured and/or policyowner held is surrendered or otherwise assigned. So the insured must give up the right to the policy's cash value, to borrow on the contract, pledge it as collateral, name, change or veto a change of beneficiary, and every other right of any significant value. Until then, no completed gift occurs.

What is the effect of a reversionary interest on whether or not a completed gift of a policy has been made? Will the possibility of a reversion back to the donor of a life insurance policy render the gift incomplete? For example, the insured makes an absolute assignment of life insurance on his life to his wife. Assume the wife then names the insured's estate as beneficiary in the event the insured dies before the new policyowner (the wife) dies. There is a possibility that the proceeds would revert back to the insured. But that possibility is not enough to prevent the gift from being considered complete and therefore taxable. However, a possibility of reverter may allow a reduction in the value of the taxable gift assuming recognized actuarial standards can be applied to measure the value of the reversion.

When a gift of a life insurance policy is made or an individual is named as beneficiary, the new owner's (or beneficiary's) right to receive the policy's proceeds is conditioned on surviving the insured. This does not, however, affect the completeness of the gift. It merely affects the valuation.

Of course, if the trust to which a life insurance policy is transferred is revocable, so is the gift and therefore no completed gift has been made.

But what if the policy is given to an irrevocable trust? Is there a gift (and, if so, will it qualify for and be sheltered by the annual exclusion)? Both the transfer of a policy to such a trust and the payment of premiums subsequent to the transfer will be considered completed gifts subject to the gift tax. Absent special provisions, no annual exclusion would be allowable in either case because the typical irrevocable trust, by design, limits the time or manner in which the beneficiaries of the trust enjoy the property (including any life insurance policy transferred to the trust).

Assume, for example, a father transferred life insurance on his own life to a trust he created for his daughter's benefit. The trust provides that upon the father's death, policy proceeds are to be invested and the income paid to the daughter for the rest of her life. The daughter does not have the immediate, unfettered, and ascertainable right to use, possess, and enjoy that income or any other right inherent in the life insurance policy until after the death of her father. Since the donee daughter's interest does not take effect until sometime in the future (i.e., at her father's death), the donor father will not be allowed an annual exclusion for either his gift of the policy or for future premiums he pays to keep it in force.

Do the results differ if the policy in question is group term insurance? Will a gift of a group term policy be considered a gift of a present interest? The answer depends again upon the terms and conditions of the irrevocable trust rather than upon the type of insurance involved. The gift of a life insurance policy will not be considered a future interest or will fail to qualify for the annual exclusion merely because it is a term insurance policy.

A gift tax annual exclusion would be allowed, for example, if the rights to a $50,000 group term contract together with cash were contributed to the trust. The annual exclusion could be obtained through a trust provision which allows the beneficiary the noncumulative right to withdraw a specified amount each year and provides that any asset in the trust, including life insurance coverage, could be used to satisfy that demand right. Furthermore, since the coverage itself should qualify for the annual exclusion as a present interest, so should subsequent premium payments on the group coverage.

Assume that the terms of a trust provide that immediately upon the death of the insured covered under a group term contract, the trust's only beneficiary is to receive the entire policy proceeds as soon as they are received by the trust. As soon as the proceeds are transferred and the deemed gift occurs, the beneficiary has the immediate, unfettered, and ascertainable right to use, possess, and enjoy the money. So an annual exclusion should be allowed for the value of the coverage at the moment of transfer. Gifts deemed to be made by the employee insured each time the employer made an actual premium payment on the group term should be considered gifts of a present interest and qualify for the annual exclusion.

Would the result have been the same had the terms of the trust required the trustee to hold and invest policy proceeds and pay only the income to the trust's beneficiary? The answer is that such a gift (each actual payment by the employer and deemed payment by the insured employee) would be considered a gift of a future interest and would therefore not qualify for the annual exclusion.

Particular care must be used when a life insurance policy is contributed to a Section 2503(c) trust, an irrevocable trust for a minor beneficiary. Gifts of a life insurance policy to a Section 2503(c) trust for a minor will typically qualify for the annual exclusion if:

1. policy values can be used for the minor's benefit; and

2. the policy will pass to the minor at age twenty-one (or, if the minor dies prior to that date, the policy will pass to the beneficiary named in his will or to the person(s) appointed by the minor during lifetime or by will).

Premiums paid on the policy by the trust's grantor should also qualify for the annual exclusion.

Planners should also note the following points about life insurance and the gift tax:

- Gifts to minors can qualify for the annual exclusion even if the child has no legal right to exercise ownership privileges under the policy and even if no guardian has been appointed.

- Generally, gifts of life insurance to minors in states that have adopted the Uniform Gifts to Minors Act (UGMA) or Uniform Transfers to Minors Act UTMA (UTMA) will qualify for the gift tax annual exclusion. (There may be some question of qualification, however, if the state statute departs from one of these

two Uniform Acts and allows custodianship to extend beyond the donee's twenty-first birthday.)

- Clients making gifts of large policies should consider splitting the contract into two or more smaller policies (assuming the life insurance carrier so permits) and transferring one policy in one year and the other(s) in other years so that all gifts fall within annual exclusion limits. (This technique may slightly increase the total premium cost and administrative burden.) Alternatively, a loan could be taken against the policy to reduce the gift tax value (but not in excess of the policy basis, as the "transferee's basis is determined by reference to the transferor's basis" exception to the transfer for value rule would not apply to this part gift/part sale). The loan could then be repaid gradually over the next few years using the gift tax annual exclusion.

- An outright gift of a life insurance policy from one spouse to another will qualify for the gift tax marital deduction and eliminate any gift tax on intraspousal transfers.

THREE PARTY SITUATIONS

Planners should red flag every situation where one party owns a life insurance policy on the life of another and the proceeds are payable to a third party (commonly known as the "Goodman Triangle" as a result of a well-known court case[5]). Sometimes, in business cases, the situation results in income tax problems, while in other situations it causes serious and unexpected gift tax problems. Indirect, but nevertheless taxable, gifts can occur where one party (e.g., a wife) owns a policy on the life of a second party (e.g., a husband) and makes the proceeds payable to a third party (e.g., the couple's children).

Example. Charlee Sterling purchases a $1,000,000 policy on the life of her husband Rob and names their son Max as beneficiary.

At the death of the husband, the wife is deemed to have made a gift to her son in the amount of the $1,000,000 policy proceeds. The reason for this harsh result is this: Generally when a policy-owner-client names a beneficiary (other than the client's estate) as beneficiary, the client is technically making a gift to that party. The reason no gift tax is imposed at that moment, in most cases, is because that gift remains incomplete until the policyowner no longer has the right to change that beneficiary designation. Retention of a power to revoke a gift renders the gift incomplete and therefore not taxable until the power is released or lapses.

Conversely, if the policyowner makes the policy beneficiary designation irrevocable, at that moment, a completed gift has been made. From that point on, every time a premium is paid, a further gift is made. Worse yet, since the gift is contingent upon the insured's death, it would be considered a future interest gift and therefore will not qualify for the annual exclusion.

When there is a three party situation, the gift becomes irrevocable when the insured dies. The gift that the policyowner makes when a third party is designated as beneficiary changes from uncompleted to completed at the insured's death. Thus, a taxable event occurs in that instant. The amount of the gift is the entire amount of proceeds paid to someone other than the policyowner. So, in the example above, the wife Charlee is deemed to be making a gift of $1,000,000 to her son Max at the moment of her husband's death.

The following common examples of the gift tax version of the three party situation will serve both as a warning and a review for planners:

Example 1. A wife owns a policy on her husband's life. She names her children as beneficiaries. When the husband dies, she is deemed to have made a gift to the children in the amount of the entire policy proceeds.

Example 2. A wife purchases a policy on her husband's life. She revocably names a trust she previously established as beneficiary of the proceeds. The trust provides that income from trust assets is to be paid to her husband for life, but upon his death principal is to be split in equal shares between the couple's children. A simultaneous death provision states that if the couple dies simultaneously, the wife would be presumed to have survived her husband. If the husband dies first or the couple does in fact die simultaneously, the wife will be deemed to have made a gift of the proceeds to her children.

Had the trust been irrevocable, the annual premiums rather than the proceeds would have been the measure of the gifts.

Example 3. A husband creates a revocable living trust. Under the terms of the trust, income was payable to his wife for life. At her death, any principal in the trust was to pass to the couple's children. The wife purchases a life insurance policy on her husband's life and names the revocable trust established by her husband as beneficiary. Upon the husband's death, the wife is deemed to have made a completed gift to her children equal to the entire proceeds less the present value of her right to a life income from the trust. If the wife had named the trust as irrevocable beneficiary, a completed gift would have been made at that time, but it would have been significantly less than the value of the proceeds.

The solution to all of the three party problems is relatively simple: Where one party will purchase a policy on the life of another from an insurer, name the purchaser as both policy owner and beneficiary.

PAYMENT OF PREMIUMS ON BEHALF OF ANOTHER

Payment by a client of one or more premiums would be considered a gift if the policy itself was owned by another person or party. The amount of the gift is the full premium paid. A reduction in the amount of the taxable gift would be allowed for the actuarial value of any interest in the policy's benefits retained by the donor.

For example, if a father paid premiums on a policy owned by his daughter, he is making gifts to her each time he pays a premium. Of course, where the parties are husband and wife, the gift may qualify for the unlimited marital deduction and no adverse gift tax implications will result.

Likewise, if a client makes cash transfers to an irrevocable trust for enabling the trustee to pay premiums on one or more policies owned by the trust (or if the client makes payments directly to the insurance company), each premium payment would constitute a gift to the beneficiaries of the trust.

If a client funds an irrevocable trust by transferring income producing property to the trust to pay premiums, the fair market value of that property (in addition to the value of any policy transferred to the trust) would be subject to gift tax. But as soon as the income producing property is owned by the trust, income it produces is not deemed to be an additional gift—even if the client is considered the owner of trust income for income tax purposes.

Premiums paid by one of several beneficiaries of an irrevocable life insurance trust will be considered gifts to the other beneficiaries to the extent the payor's payments cover their share of the premiums. Intent to make a gift is irrelevant. The IRS would determine the value of the gifts by subtracting the actuarial value of the share retained by the premium paying beneficiary from the total premiums paid.

Usually, the donor of the gift will be the party making the actual premium payments. However, if an individual assigns group term coverage to a beneficiary or to a trust on behalf of one or more beneficiaries, group term premiums subsequently paid by the individual's employer will be deemed to be gifts from the employee to the beneficiary or to the beneficiaries of the trust. If the group insurance plan is nondiscriminatory (or if the client is not a key employee) the amount of each gift is found under Table I rates. If the employee chooses not to use the Table I rates, or the plan is found to be discriminatory (and the client is a key employee), the gift will be the actual cost of insurance on that employee. In any case, the gift would be based on the full face amount of the insurance and not merely the amount in excess of the first $50,000 of coverage.

There are many hidden gift situations. For instance, split dollar life insurance (an arrangement under which different parties share costs and benefits of a life insurance policy, see Chapter 41) often involves gift tax implications. For instance, assume a client has assigned his cash value interest in a policy in a split dollar arrangement to an irrevocable trust for his daughter. The client is making a gift of the policy, just as if he had made a gift of a previously purchased premium paying policy. So, the interpolated terminal reserve plus any unearned premium less amounts, if any, repayable to the employer would be the value of the gift.

Obviously, if, after the transfer of his interest in the policy to the trust, the client also pays premiums (including premiums paid by an employer), either directly to the insurer or as cash contributions to the trust, further gifts are made. The treatment of the split dollar arrangement depends on whether the client is the owner of the policy. Even if the trust is named as the policy owner, the client may be treated as the owner if the only economic benefit provided to the trust is the value of current life insurance protection.

If the client (or employer) is treated as owner of the policy, the employee client is deemed to have received premiums paid by the employer and then made a gratuitous transfer. What is the value of such annually recurring gifts? It appears that the value of those transfers would be measured by the same amount the employee reports each year as income.

If the trust is treated as the owner, the client (or employer) makes premium payments, and the client (or employer) is entitled to recover premiums, the client (or employer) is treated as making a loan to the trust. The client is treated as making a gift of interest on the loan to the trust. If there is no right to repayment, the entire value of the premium would be treated as a gift.

GIFT THROUGH SETTLEMENT OPTION

Assume a client died and the proceeds were payable to his surviving spouse in a manner which provided that she would receive only the income on the proceeds with the balance going to the couple's children at the client's death. Coupled to the widow's right to income for life was a general power of appointment that gave her the right to draw down unlimited amounts of principal at any time. To the extent she failed to exercise that right, she would be making gifts to her children, the remainder persons.

Since the children's right is neither immediate nor certain, it would be a future interest gift and, therefore, would not qualify for the gift tax annual exclusion. Under a de minimis rule, a gift would be made only to the extent that the amount subject of a right to withdrawal exceeded the greater of $5,000 or 5 percent of the principal held by the insurance company. The total value of the gift would be measured by the actuarial value of the children's interest.

HOW IS THE GIFT VALUED?

When a policy is transferred from one party to another, to the extent the transferor receives less than full and adequate consideration, the transfer is a gift. In other words, the difference between the value of the policy and the amount received in exchange for it is a gift.

Usually, this gift is taxed at its replacement value, the hypothetical amount it would cost to replace the contract with an identical contract issued by the same insurer on an insured of the same age and insurance rating. To simplify the procedure (since seldom, if ever, are identical contracts ever found in real life), several rules have been established.

Generally, most gift transactions break down into one of these three types:

1. Gift of an established policy in premium paying status

2. Gift of a paid up or single premium policy

3. Gift of a policy just purchased

Life insurance companies will provide a statement of the gift tax value of any one of the three types of policies described above.[6]

If the transaction involves a policy on which further premiums are payable, the value of the policy is the sum of: (a) the interpolated terminal reserve; plus (b) the value of any unearned premiums less the amount of any outstanding loan.[7] Interpolated terminal reserve is essentially the reserve held by the insurer to meet its claims under the policy, but adjusted from the contract's anniversary to the date of the gift. The unearned premium is the value of the unearned portion of the last premium payment made to the insurer prior to the gift.

IRS regulations give the example of a gift made four months after the last premium due date of an ordinary life policy. The policy itself is nine years and four months old at the date of the gift.

To compute the value of the gift (in this example):

State the terminal reserve at the end of
 the (10th) year .... ($14,601)

State the terminal reserve at the end of
 the (9th) year .... ($12,965)

The difference is annual increase in
 terminal reserve .... ($ 1,636)

If the gift was made X/12s (4/12) of a
 year after the premium due date, than
 Y/12 (1/3) of annual reserve is .... ($ 545)

State the terminal reserve at premium
 payment date .... ($12,965)

Sum of beg of yr terminal reserve &
 increase in reserve .... ($13,510)

Unearned premium (8/12ths) of ($2,811)
 annual premium .... ($ 1,874)

Gift value = (a) reserve at gift +
 (b) unearned premium .... ($15,384)

If the transaction involves a previously purchased single premium or paid up policy, its gift tax value is the single premium the insurer would charge at the time of the gift for a comparable contract of equal face value on the life of a person the insured's age at the time of the gift.[8]

If the transaction involves a new policy purchased by one person or party on behalf of another, or if a new policy is transferred as a gift immediately after its purchase, the gross premium paid to the date of the transfer is the gift. Planners should advise clients to minimize the gift tax implications of a transfer by:

1. making gifts as close to the premium paying date as possible so as to minimize any unearned premiums; and

2. borrow on the policy up to but not more than the client's basis.[9]

If the subject of the gift is group term life insurance, the IRS in a questionable but favorable ruling stated that there was no taxable gift because the policy had no ascertainable value.[10] Note, however, that in that ruling the coverage was assigned one day before a monthly premium was due. Stated differently, the IRS probably reasoned that the benefit of the prior month's premium payment had essentially expired. Thus, the value may, in fact, have been quite low but clearly had some value.

If the insured is an impaired risk or has become uninsurable by the date of the gift, the value of the policy for gift tax purposes may be increased. Likewise, if the insured is terminally ill or otherwise uninsurable at the time of the gift, it is likely the IRS would argue that the policy could be expected to mature shortly and, therefore, the replacement value should more closely approximate the face amount. Since these same valuation principles should apply for purposes of the income tax charitable deduction, the gift of a policy to a charity by a dying individual should result in a value that approaches the face amount of the policy.

For more information, please refer to Chapter 26: Life Insurance Valuation.

COLLECTION OF GIFT TAX

A donee of any of the types of gifts described above is liable for the full gift tax to the extent it is not collected from the donor. The donee's liability is not limited to the cash value of the policy.

CHAPTER ENDNOTES

1. The authors suggest that the loan be somewhat less than the client's net cost. Otherwise, the client will be deemed to have received an amount equal to the loan in a constructive sale. The difference between the sales proceeds (i.e., the loan) and the client's basis would be immediately taxable at ordinary income tax rates.

2. For a detailed discussion of the marital and the charitable deduction, see *The Tools & Techniques of Estate Planning, 18th Edition*.

3. Alternatively, adverse income tax treatment can be triggered. For instance, if a corporation owns a policy on the life of an employee but makes it payable to a party other than the corporation or a corporate creditor, payment of the death proceeds could be considered a dividend.

4. Both the policy and any gift tax paid on the policy will be included in the gross estate if death occurs within three years of the transfer. I.R.C. §2035.

5. *Goodman v. Comm'r.*, 156 F.2d 218 (2nd Cir. 1946).

6. Request IRS form 712.

7. See IRS form 712, Part II.

8. What if the cash value of the policy given away is significantly larger than the replacement cost of a similar policy? If a twenty-year-old single premium life policy had a replacement cost well below the actual policy's cash value, would the replacement contract be comparable? Absent information as to what a truly comparable contract would cost, the policy's value should be found by reference to its interpolated terminal reserve.

9. A loan in excess of basis would result in an income tax gain upon transfer of the policy.

10. In the authors' opinion, this conclusion is at best risky to rely on since no matter how little value the right to death proceeds on a given employee might be it will always have some value. Secondly, it is actuarially always possible to assign a value to life insurance even if it is term coverage; especially if it is level term coverage, as such coverage has a reserve value.

LIFE INSURANCE AND THE GENERATION-SKIPPING TRANSFER TAX

CHAPTER 29

INTRODUCTION

The GST Tax in a Nutshell

A Generation-Skipping Transfer (GST) tax is levied, in addition to any gift or estate taxes that apply to the transfer, on the value of life insurance (and/or any other property) transferred during lifetime or at death without adequate consideration to a transferee who is in (or who is assigned by statutory law to) a generation that is at least two generations below the transferor's generation (such a transferee is called a skip person).[1] For example, the GST tax will be imposed when an exceptionally large life insurance policy (and/or other asset) is payable to (or for the benefit of) a client's grandchild.

The GST tax does not apply to transfers to nonskip persons, such as the client's child, brother, or sister or to anyone in a generation higher than the transferor's generation (e.g., a gift made by a grandchild to a grandparent). Likewise, a transfer to a trust for a nonskip person would not be subject to the GST tax. On the other hand, if all the beneficiaries of a trust are skip persons, a transfer to a trust for such people would be considered a transfer to a skip person; and, as discussed later, certain transfers from trusts to skip persons are subject to the GST tax.

The GST tax is broadly applied to life insurance transfers. It can be imposed regardless of whether proceeds are paid outright, in a lump sum, under settlement options, or in trust.[2] The GST tax may also be imposed upon a transfer of a large policy with substantial cash values to a trust during the insured's lifetime. The value upon which the tax will be based is the same as the value of the policy or the proceeds for gift or estate tax purposes.

In general, when life insurance (or other property) is transferred to a trust that has one or more skip persons as beneficiaries, the GST tax is imposed when distributions are made from the trust to those skip persons or when the interests of any nonskip persons terminate. For instance, if life insurance proceeds were left to a trust that provided income to the client's son for life and then paid the income and principal to the client's grandchildren, the tax would be imposed when the nonskip person (son) died.

The GST tax may be levied in addition to any applicable federal estate or gift tax and is imposed as a flat tax at the highest federal estate tax level, 40 percent (in 2017).[3] Note that the GST tax rate applies regardless of the taxpayer's actual estate or gift tax bracket.

Fortunately, through careful planning it is possible to shelter all or a portion of even a very large transfer to a skip person through the use of one or both of two devices, the annual exclusion and the GST tax exemption.

GST Tax Annual Exclusion

Certain direct gifts that qualify for the $14,000 (as indexed in 2017) gift tax annual exclusion (or the unlimited exclusion allowed for direct payment of tuition or medical expenses) may also qualify for an annual exclusion that can be applied against the GST tax.[4] This means an outright transfer of a policy or of premium dollars to a skip person will be subject to the GST tax only to the extent the value of the gift exceeds the $14,000 ($28,000 if gifts are split between spouses in 2017) annual exclusion limit. So the easiest and most certain way to take advantage of the GST tax annual exclusion is for the client to make gifts of cash each year of up to $14,000 to a skip person, who then leverages the gift by purchasing life insurance on the life of the client and/or the client's spouse.

_____

Example. Suppose a wealthy client, who has made large gifts and used up his gift and GST tax exemptions in prior years, gives a grand-daughter a $2,000,000 policy on his life in 2017. At the time of the gift, the policy has a gift tax replacement value of $200,000. The gift would qualify for the gift tax annual exclusion and also qualify for the GST tax annual exclusion. So there would be no gift tax imposed on the first $14,000 ($28,000 if the client were married and split the gift) of value. Likewise, there would be no GST tax imposed on the same amount.

_____

Only direct skips (outright transfers to skip persons or transfers to trusts that have only skip persons as beneficiaries and meet certain other criterion) can qualify for this GST tax annual exclusion. So, if the transfer is to a trust, it can still qualify for the GST tax annual exclusion but only if:

1. all trust beneficiaries are skip persons;

2. no distributions could ever be made to nonskip persons; and

3. each skip person's share is held in an account separate from the others or there are separate trusts for each.[5]

Such entities are often called vested or subtrust trusts since the trust can benefit only one beneficiary and, at that person's death, assets in the trust must be included in the vested beneficiary's estate. Planners should note that the typical life insurance trust will not qualify.

Even if the transfer otherwise qualifies for the gift tax annual exclusion, if a trust benefits beneficiaries other than skip persons, it will not qualify for the GST tax annual exclusion. For example, assume the same facts as above, but the gift is made to a trust for the benefit of the client's son (a nonskip person) for life and then granddaughter. Even if the granddaughter is given a valid Crummey power and $14,000 of the gift to her qualifies for the gift tax annual exclusion from gift taxes, it will not qualify for the GST tax annual exclusion.

To leverage the annual exclusion, an irrevocable life insurance trust receiving the client's money could purchase life insurance on his life using the entire contribution as the policy premium. During the client's lifetime, neither federal gift tax nor GST tax would be imposed on the cash used as premiums. At the client's death, there would be neither federal estate tax nor GST tax imposed on the policy proceeds.

Either split dollar or the use of survivorship type contracts (or both techniques) can be used to pack the trust and squeeze in as much GST tax free life insurance as possible to maximize the leverage of the nontaxable gift technique. The trust can purchase insurance on the life of any person on whom the beneficiaries have an insurable interest, including parents as well as grandparents. Insuring a younger/healthier life than the beneficiary's grandparent would further the packing possibilities (at the cost of a potentially longer wait for the proceeds). But such sophisticated planning requires extremely careful drafting and the use of highly competent counsel in order to achieve all of its tax and personal objectives.

Another way to compound the advantage of the annual exclusion is to have the transferor's spouse make an identical gift or to have the transferor split the gift with his spouse.

Disadvantages to Using the GST Annual Exclusion

There are downsides to qualifying for the GST tax annual exclusion:

1. If the beneficiary dies before the client-grantor, the cash values of the policies in the trust will be included in the beneficiary's estate. Of course, if the beneficiary survives the insured and then dies, the proceeds shielded from the GST tax may still generate significant federal estate tax in the beneficiary's estate. However, the estate tax at a lower generational level may not be a significant disadvantage where the older generation possesses substantially greater wealth than the lower generation.

2. Many Crummey power techniques, such as the hanging power, will not qualify for the GST tax annual exclusion, since there can be no indirect skip (i.e., the trust beneficiaries must include only skip persons). If nonskip persons, such as the client's children, are beneficiaries of the trust, this GST tax exclusion is denied. So, where there are several generations of beneficiaries and some are nonskip persons, the

nontaxable gift exclusion is not available, and the client should use the GST tax exemption described below.

3. This exclusion requires undue dispositive rigidity. In other words, this exclusion, though appealing, will only work where the client is willing to set up a separate trust or allocate separate shares for each beneficiary and therefore precludes the flexibility inherent where a trustee is given discretion to spray principal or sprinkle income within a family unit. As a practical matter, few transfers will qualify for the GST tax annual exclusion and few clients will use the exclusion, even if they could qualify, because of these inflexible and impractical rules.[6] Most clients must therefore place all or most of their planning efforts on the next level of defensive measures.

4. The trust can't provide financial security for the intervening skipped generation, since the client's contributions to the trust must pass directly to the skip person.

GST Tax Exemption

Over and above any allowable annual exclusion from the GST tax, each transferor is allowed to make a total of $5,430,000 (in 2015, as adjusted for inflation) of generation-skipping transfers and pay no tax.[7] This exemption can be used during lifetime or at death.[8] If a married client makes a generation-skipping transfer during lifetime, gift splitting (similar to the way gift tax split-gifts works) is allowable.[9] This enables a doubling of the $5,490,000 exemption to as much as $10,900,000 (in 2017) even though the transfer was made only by one spouse.

How the GST Tax is Triggered

Three situations can trigger a GST tax: (1) a direct skip; (2) a taxable termination; and (3) a taxable distribution.

Direct Skip

A direct skip could occur when a client writes a check payable to a skip person, gives property outright during lifetime, leaves property by will directly to a skip person, or names a skip person as a direct beneficiary of a life insurance policy.[10] Therefore, if a client assigns an existing life insurance policy on his life to a grandchild, that gift would constitute a generation-skipping transfer. Assuming the entire transfer is taxable, the GST tax would be imposed on an amount equal to the policy's interpolated terminal reserve plus any unearned premium (less any gift tax payable on the transfer). Likewise, if a client died and the $1,000,000 proceeds of a policy on the father's life were paid to the grandson and the full $1,000,000 was taxable, a 40 percent (in 2017) tax would be imposed (after reducing the $1,000,000 by the estate tax also payable on the transfer, see the following).

Taxable Termination

A taxable termination occurs when there are no more nonskip persons ahead of the skip person. In essence, the client's generation-skipping transfer to the skip person is deemed to occur at the moment nothing stands between the skip person and the transferred cash or other asset. Assume, for example, that a client creates a life insurance trust that provides, "Income from this trust is to be paid to my three children for life. At the death of the last survivor, principal is to be distributed to my six grandchildren." When the last nonskip person's (children's) interest terminates (in this example, by death), the property in the trust is subjected to the GST tax.

Taxable Distribution

A taxable distribution occurs when either income or principal is distributed from a trust to a skip person.[11] Such a distribution can occur while nonskip beneficiaries are still alive. For example, suppose a client created a life insurance trust that directed the trustee (during the lifetime of the client's three children) to pay income and principal to the client's three children and to the client's six grandchildren. The payments made by the trustee to grandchildren while the children were still alive would be considered a taxable distribution. Again, the taxable event occurs at the moment nothing stands between the skip person and the property transferred by the client.

Computing the Taxable Amount

The taxable amount is computed differently depending upon the type of taxable transfer involved.

Direct Skips

In a direct skip, the amount subject to the GST tax (i.e., the taxable amount) is generally equal to the value of the transfer reduced first by the estate tax imposed on it.[12]

Example 1. A client dies in 2017 and a $4,000,000 policy is payable directly to his grandson. Assume the property would bear the estate tax and the GST tax. Assuming the client's estate was large and pushed the proceeds into the 40 percent federal estate tax bracket, the estate tax would be $1,600,000. The 40 percent GST tax (in 2017) would be imposed, not on $4,000,000, but on the $2,400,000 left after the federal estate tax ($4,000,000 proceeds less $1,600,000 federal estate tax imposed on the proceeds). The GST tax would be $685,715 $[(($2,400,000 \times 0.40) \div (1 + 0.40))$ where transfer bears GST tax]. In total, the federal taxes levied would amount to $2,285,715 ($1,600,000 + $685,715)! The grandson receives a net transfer of $1,714,285 ($4,000,000 − $2,285,715).

Example 2. Assume, instead, that other property would bear the estate tax and the GST tax and that only $1,925,926 of the proceeds would be payable to the grandson. At a 40 percent federal estate tax bracket, the estate tax on $4,000,000 would be $1,600,000. The 40 percent GST tax would be imposed on $1,714,285 (there is no reduction for estate tax since the transfer to the grandson does not bear the estate tax). The GST tax would be $685,715 ($1,714,285 × 0.40). In total, the federal taxes levied would amount to $2,285,715 ($1,600,000 + $685,715)!

Thus, different methods are used to determine the GST tax depending on whether or not the GST bears the estate tax and the GST tax. However, as can be seen, the amount of the total tax ($2,285,715) on the direct skip is the same for the same net transfer ($1,714,285).

Of course, transfers to grandchildren made during the client's lifetime will also be subjected to the GST tax.

Example. Suppose a wealthy client who has made many large taxable gifts in prior years gives his granddaughter a policy on his life in 2017. Assume it is a policy with a face value of $4,000,000 and a replacement value of $400,000.

The GST tax would be imposed on $400,000 at a 40 percent rate (in 2015). The GST tax would be $160,000 (0.40 × $400,000). For gift tax purposes, the $400,000 gift is increased by the amount of the GST tax imposed on the transferor to $560,000 ($400,000 + $160,000). The gift tax on the gift (assuming the transfer is taxed at a 40 percent federal gift tax bracket in 2017) would be $224,000 ($560,000 × 0.40). Federal taxes would therefore total $384,000 ($160,000 + $224,000).

Taxable Terminations

In a taxable termination, the amount on which the tax is computed is the value of the property to which the termination pertains.

Example. Assume a client dies and $4,000,000 in policy proceeds are paid to a trust providing income to the client's son for life. At the son's death, the entire amount in the trust is to be paid to the client's grandson. Assuming the client's estate was large and pushed the proceeds into the 40 percent federal estate tax bracket in 2017, the estate tax would be $1,600,000 ($4,000,000 × 0.40). Assume this estate tax is paid by the trust and reduces the net proceeds in the trust to $2,400,000. In addition, when the son's interest terminates on his death (in 2017), that taxable termination generates a GST tax equal to 40 percent (in 2017) of the assets paid to the client's grandchild (ignoring for illustrative purposes the GST tax exemption). Assuming no growth or loss in the funds, the tax on the $2,400,000 termination would be $960,000 (0.40 × $2,400,000). The total federal tax on the $4,000,000 proceeds would be $2,560,000 ($1,600,000 + $960,000).

Taxable Distributions

In a taxable distribution, the amount upon which the tax is computed is the value of the property the transferee receives.[13]

Example. A client dies in 2017 and $4,000,000 in policy proceeds are payable to a trust providing that the trustee can sprinkle income or spray principal to either the client's son or grandson or both. The federal estate tax on the $4,000,000 (assuming the client's estate was large and pushed the $4,000,000 into a 40 percent bracket - in 2017) would be $1,600,000. Assume this estate tax is paid by the trust and reduces the net proceeds in the trust to $2,400,000. Also, assume the trustee immediately distributes the entire $2,400,000 to the client's grandson. In addition, a $960,000 GST tax would be payable (0.40 × $2,400,000); a total federal tax of $2,560,000 ($1,600,000 + $960,000)!

Inclusion Ratio

Technically, the amount of a generation-skipping transfer that is subject to the GST tax is found through an inclusion ratio. The formula is:

$$1 - [\text{AMOUNT OF EXEMPTION} \div \text{TOTAL VALUE OF GIFT (or BEQUEST)}]$$

If a transfer to a trust, for example, has an inclusion ratio of zero, no future distributions or terminations from that trust will generally ever be subjected to the GST tax. However, if a trust beneficiary were to be treated as a transferor because property in the trust is included in his estate or the person is treated as making a taxable gift, a new inclusion ratio based upon the new transferor's GST tax exemption may be required.

Example. If in 2017 the value of the gift was $1,500,000 and there were no exemptions or exclusions available,[14] all of it would be subject to the GST tax. If the client had only $120,000 of his $5,120,000 per grantor exemption remaining (in 2015), the inclusion ratio would be 0.977 [1 – ($120,000 ÷ $5,120,000)]. Almost 98 percent of the transfer would be subject to the GST tax. If the value of the gift was $5,120,000 and the amount of the exemption was also $5,120,000, the inclusion ratio would be 0. This would mean, not only that none of the transfer is taxable at the time it is made,[15] but also that the transfer (indeed, whatever it grows to by the date it is actually distributed to the skip person) will generally never be subjected to the GST tax.

This inclusion ratio concept has enormous leverage implications with respect to contributions of cash to irrevocable life insurance trusts. Assuming the annual

exclusion is not sufficient or is for some reason not available to shield a transfer from the GST tax, clients should consider allocating a portion of the GST tax exemption to any transfer involving life insurance. The reason is that, once the exemption shields a gift of life insurance premiums or a gift of a life insurance policy, the proceeds generated by those protected premiums or policy will not be subjected to the GST tax when paid out. Applying the exclusion against the discounted future dollars represented by the premiums can save a client's estate literally millions of dollars.

Example. Assume an irrevocable trust for a client's grandchildren purchased a $20,000,000 policy on his life. If his premium outlay is $100,000 a year for ten years and he allocates $100,000 of his GST tax exclusion against each year's premium payments, the inclusion ratio would be zero [1 - ($100,000 ÷ $100,000)]. None of the $20,000,000 proceeds would ever be subjected to the GST tax.[16] Had the client not allocated the exemption to protect the premiums from inclusion, the proceeds would have been subjected to the GST tax and the client's personal representative would be able to exclude only $5,120,000 (assuming death in 2017) of the $20,000,000, a difference in tax of $5,952,000 (0.40 × $14,880,000)!

In the example, the client retained a zero inclusion ratio each year and guaranteed total exclusion of the policy proceeds by using a policy that became paid up before the transfers to the trust exhausted the GST tax exemption. The use of limited payment life insurance is essential in this regard. Had the premium payment period continued beyond the protection of the GST tax exemption, the inclusion ratio would have grown year by year with more and more of the proceeds becoming subject to the GST tax each year.

REVERSE QTIP ELECTION

It is currently possible to obtain a marital deduction for property that is not left outright to a spouse. In fact it is possible to specify that the principal of a client's estate must pass to his children or some selected party other than the surviving spouse and still obtain the marital deduction. The vehicle for such planning is called a QTIP trust, a trust that holds qualifying terminable interest property. Through a QTIP trust, a client can provide income for life to a spouse but at that spouse's death the client can be sure it will pass to the person or persons he has selected.

There is a cost to this flexibility and tax deferral; whatever assets remain in the QTIP trust at the surviving spouse's death must be included in the surviving spouse's estate just as if the surviving spouse had transferred the property. The problem is (aside from the obvious estate tax and liquidity problem) that this same fiction applies for GST tax purposes. The surviving spouse is treated as if she was the transferor of property, which was really transferred by her husband. This might cause a portion or all of her husband's GST tax exemption to be wasted.

Example. A client, David Jones, died in 2010 leaving $4,000,000 of life insurance. Assume for simplicity that this was his entire estate. David had previously made gifts using $500,000 of his unified credit equivalent. $1,500,000 passed into a Credit Equivalent Bypass Trust (CEBT) for his five children and their five children. The balance of the proceeds ($2,500,000) was paid into a QTIP trust for his wife (who is assumed to die in 2017). So no federal estate tax was payable on any of his $4,000,000 estate. But absent a reverse QTIP election, David's wife is deemed to be the transferor of $2,500,000 and so none of David's GST tax exemption can be applied against the assets in the QTIP trust.

With a reverse QTIP election, the first spouse to die (David) will be treated as the transferor of both trusts and therefore his GST tax exemption can be allocated to both trusts. David's executor would allocate $1,500,000 of his $2,000,000 GST tax exemption (in 2007) to the CEBT and entirely eliminate the GST tax on this portion of his estate. The remaining $500,000 could then be applied against the $2,500,000 remaining portion. Of course, only $500,000/$2,500,000 of the future value of that trust would be protected against the GST tax. The surviving spouse could not use her $5,490,000 exemption (in 2017) against the GST tax since she was not the transferor (because of the reverse QTIP election).

Perhaps a better course of action to fully utilize both spouse's GST tax exemptions would be to split the QTIP trust into two trusts, one by formula equal to the amount of the GST tax

exemption left after funding the CEBT ($500,000 in this example) and the other equal to the remaining estate ($2,000,000 in this example). The predeceased spouse's estate would make a reverse QTIP election and wipe out the GST tax in the first trust. The surviving spouse could then apply her $5,490,000 exemption (in 2017) to this second trust since she would be treated as its creator. In this way, all trusts have been fully sheltered from GST tax. This splitting of trusts for the purpose of making a reverse QTIP election must be made before the due date of the estate tax return of the first spouse to die.

GST TAX AND IRREVOCABLE LIFE INSURANCE TRUSTS

Almost all individuals who establish irrevocable life insurance trusts are wealthy individuals. Many of these are super wealthy and are attempting to transfer many millions of dollars of assets downstream, not only to their children, but also to their grandchildren. A classic arrangement is for a client to place assets (including life insurance) into a trust and direct that income is to be paid to the client's spouse for life and then to the client's children for life and when they died, principal would be distributed to the client's grandchildren. The trust might give the client's children limited access to and control over some or all of the principal.

A trust such as this might last for several generations and, absent any GST tax, the IRS would receive no tax when the children died. This is the reason Congress imposed a generation-skipping transfer tax—so that even if a trust or a transfer skips an outright distribution (or vesting of rights) to the next generation down, a tax is nevertheless imposed on that skip at the time of the skip.

Transfers from irrevocable life insurance trusts are potentially subject to the GST tax. Where distributions from an irrevocable trust will be made to a client's grandchild or other skip person, a planner must consider potential GST tax problems. Unfortunately, transfers to the typical irrevocable life insurance trust will not qualify for the GST tax annual exclusion because such a trust usually gives a trustee sprinkle and spray powers to distribute income and principal among, not only grandchildren, but also children and the spouse of the client-transferor. Mere Crummey powers will not be enough to save the GST tax annual exclusion since, as mentioned previously, the trust must have only one beneficiary and must terminate in favor of that beneficiary to qualify for the GST tax annual exclusion.

Three ways to utilize the GST tax exemption with an irrevocable life insurance trust include:

1. Use it immediately! Allocate the exemption (a) to the gift of the policy itself and any remaining exemption to (b) one or more of the premium payments.

2. Wait until the client dies: Save the GST tax exemption and use it then against the much larger death benefit.

3. Wait until the client dies: Use the GST tax exemption to shelter transfers of other estate assets.

From a leveraging standpoint, the preferred choice is, obviously, the first of these three. In most cases, if there is any chance that the assets in the trust will be subjected to the GST tax, the client should consider immediately allocating a portion of his GST tax exemption to protect each transfer (and what it grows to) from the GST tax. The allocation is generally made by an election on the gift tax return for the year in which a transfer is made.[17]

It is the timely and creative use of the GST tax exemption—coupled with life insurance—that is the key to maximizing the exemption. This combination of exemption and life insurance provides the single most effective and pragmatic solution to the GST tax problem. It is the technique that super wealthy clients with multimillions will use most to make an irrevocable trust into a dynasty trust and, thereby, keep great wealth within a family.

Example 1. Suppose a client and the client's spouse wanted to set up a trust that would last for the lives of their children, grandchildren, and great grandchildren, but wanted to avoid the confiscatory GST tax. They could set up an irrevocable trust. The trustee could purchase $15,000,000 of survivorship life insurance on their lives. Assume the clients pay ten annual $200,000 premiums and, as each premium is paid, they allocate $200,000 of their combined GST tax exemptions to the payments.

The results? Since the GST tax exemption protects not only the money contributed to the trust but also whatever that money generates, none of the $15,000,000 should be subject to GST taxes at either spouse's death. Nor should the GST tax be imposed when later generations terminate. Assuming the $15,000,000 in assets grow at the rate of 5 percent per year and are held intact for the nearly one hundred years the trust is projected to last, over $1 billion dollars would ultimately be distributed to the client's great grandchildren!

By insulating a relatively small amount of premiums (say up to $100,000 a year for ten years), an incredibly large amount of insurance proceeds can be protected forever.

Example 2. Suppose a client establishes an irrevocable trust and the trustee applies for and becomes the owner and beneficiary of a $10,000,000 policy on the client's life. Each year, the client pays an annual premium that is shielded by a portion of the GST tax exemption. It is projected that $100,000 a year for ten years is required before premiums are suspended and the $10,000,000 policy is paid up. Assume the trust provides that the client's son is to receive income for life at the client's death and at the son's death, principal in the trust is to be distributed to the client's four children in equal shares if all are living. If a child dies, his share is to go in equal shares (per stirpes) to that child's child or children (the client's grandchildren).

If the client dies, predeceased by a child with three children, a transfer subject to the generation-skipping transfer tax has occurred. But since the inclusion ratio has always been zero, that is, since each transfer of premiums was covered by the GST tax exemption, none of the $10,000,000 will be subject to the GST tax. Alternatively, had the client not taken the trouble to allocate the GST tax exemption as each premium was paid, it could have been used at his death in 2007. But at that time, it could only have protected $2,000,000 of the total $10,000,000! The remaining $8,000,000 would have been subjected to a 45 percent tax! Careful planning and timely allocation of the GST tax exemption is worth about $3,600,000 in tax savings in this example.

Because of the incredible leverage that life insurance makes possible (by sheltering a relatively small amount of premiums, a disproportionately larger amount of proceeds can be protected), a client should almost always allocate the GST tax exemption against each premium, year by year. This forever protects the proceeds, regardless of how large they are. In a nutshell, by sheltering a million dollars of premiums, tens of millions of dollars of life insurance are freed from the GST tax because of the "once exempt, always exempt" character of the GST tax exclusion.

There are, of course, costs to using the exclusion to shelter premium payments:

1. The GST tax exemption is not available to avoid the tax on other transfers to skip persons.

2. Because the client will be required to file annual tax returns to make this allocation, the client will have to pay an advisor a relatively small fee for this mostly administrative task.[18]

3. There is an opportunity cost. If, for some reason, the transfers from the trust are not considered generation-skipping, the allocation of the GST tax exemption to the trust may result in its being wasted. If it's not likely that the trust will make such distributions, clients may want to save the GST tax exemption for a taxable transfer. This "save it for a rainy day" approach is not for the super wealthy who, almost inevitably, will have to face the GST tax problem in order to preserve great family wealth.

CHAPTER ENDNOTES

1. I.R.C. §2613.
2. I.R.C. §2663(3) gives the IRS authority to issue regulations that might provide that the beneficiary of an insurance policy be required to pay any GST tax.
3. I.R.C. §2641.
4. I.R.C. §2642(c).
5. This separate share rule applies to trusts established before April 1, 1988 if the client transfers assets (such as policies or cash for premium payments) after March 31, 1988. A possible solution is to have any life insurance policies in such a trust be made paid up. A new trust could then be created which meets the three requirements described above.

    As a substitute for the use of the annual exclusion against the GST tax, in more modest estates where the client is not willing or able to meet the three requirements above, consider the use of the GST tax exemption.

6. A married client will usually want to provide his surviving spouse, in addition to the Crummey withdrawal power necessary to obtain the gift tax annual exclusion for a gift to the trust, a lifetime income interest after the grantor's death. This would violate both the second and third requirements above.

    Most clients with more than one child or grandchild provide multiple Crummey withdrawal powers and beneficial interests to the grantor's several children (if for no other reason than to multiply the annual exclusions and reduce the gift tax cost of the transfer). This also violates at least two of the three rules above.

    Few clients would want large amounts of cash and/or other investments to be paid to the estate of a grandchild with no direction as to the eventual beneficiary. So few clients will sacrifice this control to gain GST tax savings.

7. I.R.C. §2631.
8. If the gift is made during lifetime, the client takes the GST tax exemption on his gift tax return. If the gift is made at death, the exemption is taken by the decedent's executor or administrator on the federal estate tax return. The exemption can be taken partially during lifetime and partially at death. But if no allocation is made, the exemption is generally deemed to have been allocated to lifetime direct skips in the order of their occurrence. I.R.C. §2632(a). Once made, the GST tax exemption allocation is irrevocable. I.R.C. §2631(b).
9. I.R.C. §2652(a)(2).
10. I.R.C. §2612(c).
11. I.R.C. §2612(b).
12. I.R.C. §2623.
13. I.R.C. §2621.
14. As noted below, the annual exclusion can be used as an offset in the calculation of the inclusion ratio only with respect to direct skips.
15. I.R.C. §2631.
16. The client should be given no interest that would cause the policy or other trust property to be included in his estate. Care should be taken with regard to the client's spouse; no interest should be given to the spouse that would cause the property to be included in her estate had she been the grantor. The reason for this later precaution is that if the proceeds would have been included in her estate had she been the grantor, and the proceeds are received before her death, the GST tax exemption must be allocated against the proceeds rather than merely the policy premiums. The benefit of the GST tax exemption would be diluted and much more of the proceeds will become subject to the GST tax.
17. The election is not automatic. A client should generally take affirmative steps to secure the allocation's protection. It should be made on a timely filed gift tax return, which is typically due on April 15th of the year following the transfer.
18. Gift tax returns should generally be filed for most gifts to irrevocable life insurance trusts–even if the gifts are within the gift tax annual exclusion, they may be subject to the GST tax. Filing would allow the client to allocate a portion of his GST tax exemption to the annual gifts and thereby insure that the trust will be subject to neither current GST tax on the premiums nor GST tax on the policy proceeds.

VIATICAL AND LIFE SETTLEMENTS

CHAPTER 30

INTRODUCTION

Historically, policy owners of permanent insurance had very limited options when they no longer needed their coverage or needed funds due to financial difficulties. Their only market was the life insurance carriers, through which they could either take distributions from their cash value or surrender the policy. With respect to term life insurance, the only option was to surrender the policy and receive back any unearned premium. Today, however, policy owners have many more options. A significant reason for this is the development of a secondary market in which life insurance policies can be sold to viatical and life settlements companies. Another reason, discussed primarily in Chapter 6, is the creation of terminal illness, chronic illness, critical illness, long-term care, and other policy riders which enable the policy owner to accelerate the policy death benefits. This Chapter will focus primarily on viatical and life settlements.

Viatical and life settlements are similar in that they both involve the sale, by the policy owner, of his or her life insurance policy to a third party (typically a viatical or life settlement company) in exchange for a lump-sum cash payment. Once the buyer has purchased the policy, it then takes over the premium payments and collects the death benefit when the insured passes away.

What makes viatical and life settlements different is the life expectancy of the insured to whom the policy is being sold.

- With a *viatical settlement*,[1] the insured (the *viator*) typically has a life expectancy of less than two years due to a life-threatening disease or terminal illness. However, some viatical settlement companies will purchase policies from insureds with life expectancies of up to five years. The policy owner receives a one-time payment that usually ranges from 50 percent to as much as 90 percent of the policy's face value. Generally, the shorter the insured's life expectancy, the greater, the purchase price will be. It should be noted that viatical settlements gained popularity in the late 1980s and early 1990s as a result of the AIDS epidemic and the need of terminally ill insureds to obtain funds for health care purposes.

- *Life settlements*, on the other hand, are available for insureds with longer life expectancies (generally up to fifteen years, although from a practical standpoint it may be difficult to receive an offer that exceeds the cash value for life expectancies greater than eleven years or so). Unlike viatical settlements, the insureds generally are not terminally or chronically ill. Due to the longer life expectancy of the insured, payments for life settlements are typically substantially lower than for viatical settlements—the average life settlement value is around 20 percent of the policy face value.[2] Life settlements gained popularity in the 2000s, primarily in the older age market for seniors who no longer had a need for continued life insurance coverage.

WHEN IS THE USE OF THESE DEVICES INDICATED?

Viatical Settlements

The emotional stress of dealing with one's own impending death due to a terminal or serious chronic illness is further compounded by the customary increase in medical bills and the additional costs of special care in conjunction with a likely reduction in earning capacity. A viatical settlement may make sense for an insured in this situation if:

- the policy owner is in need of cash to pay medical or other expenses of the insured; and

- other options to meet those needs are not available or are not as attractive (see "Frequently Asked Questions" below for a discussion of alternatives to a viatical settlement).

Life Settlements

A life settlement typically isn't entered into because the insured's death is impending, but rather because the needs of the policy owner or insured have changed. A life settlement may be indicated when:

- the policy owner or insured no longer needs the life insurance coverage;

  - personal needs coverage is no longer needed because the children are grown up and are financially independent;

  - buy-sell coverage is no longer needed because the buy-sell arrangement has been terminated;

  - key person coverage is no longer needed because the insured is no longer employed by the business;

  - estate tax liquidity coverage is no longer needed because changes in estate tax laws or the size of the insured's estate now exempt the estate from estate taxes;

- the policy owner can no longer afford the premiums and wishes to be relieved from the payment of further premiums;

- the policy owner desires to receive a lump-sum payment of cash in exchange for the policy that can be used for any purpose; and

- other options to eliminate the coverage, eliminate the premium obligations, or obtain

liquidity are not available or are not as attractive (see "Frequently Asked Questions" below for a discussion of alternatives to a life settlement).

ADVANTAGES

Viatical Settlements

The principal advantage is that terminally ill or severely chronically ill insureds can receive advanced payments on policy death benefits potentially free of income tax. If the insured is terminally ill, he can use the proceeds for virtually any purpose desired. For example, insureds may desire to use the proceeds to:

- cover out-of-pocket medical expenses;

- finance alternative treatments not covered by existing medical insurance;

- purchase a new car or finance a dream vacation before he or she cannot enjoy such things;

- personally distribute cash to loved ones;

- maintain his or her dignity by not dying destitute; and/or

- pay off loans.

Life Settlements

Although insureds entering into a life settlement enjoy many of the same advantages as viatical settlements with respect to the use of the lump-sum proceeds from the sale (although they generally don't enjoy the same tax advantages as is discussed in "Tax Implications" later), some additional advantages include:

- a greater amount of proceeds may be received than if the policy had been surrendered;

- relief from premium payments for coverage they no longer need or desire; and

- proceeds can be used to purchase potentially more coverage than would be available via a 1035 exchange (or in situations where a 1035 isn't available, such as going from single life to second-to-die coverage).

DISADVANTAGES

Unless otherwise noted below, viatical and life settlements share many of the same disadvantages:

- *Reduced total payout for dependent spouse and children* – once the policy is sold, it will no longer pay a tax-free death benefit to the insured's surviving spouse and children. Thus, the primary disadvantage of a viatical or life settlement is that the surviving spouse and children are deprived of the death proceeds and instead only have whatever lump-sum sale proceeds remain unspent at the insured's death. This may make a viatical or life settlement inappropriate in situations where there are not sufficient other assets to provide for the surviving spouse and children. In addition, with a life settlement the total payment may be even more reduced because of the fact that a portion of the life settlement proceeds may be income taxable (see discussion in "Tax Implications" later).

- *May impact eligibility for governmental assistance programs* – the receipt of the lump-sum sale proceeds from a viatical or life settlement could jeopardize the eligibility of an insured who is receiving benefits from a needs based governmental assistance program.

- *May expose life insurance proceeds to creditors* – when life insurance death proceeds are paid to a designated beneficiary, most states exempt them from the claims of the insured/ deceased's creditors. Once these proceeds are paid to a living insured, however, the insured's creditors may be able to reach them, unless state law has extended creditor protection to viatical or life settlements.

- *Settlement offers can vary considerably* – unless the policy owner does a good job of comparison shopping, he or she may not receive a fair amount for the policy.

- *Not all policies qualify* – for both viatical and life settlements the policies generally must be at least two years old (i.e., beyond the incontestable and suicide periods).

- *Very few insureds generally qualify* – viatical settlements are only available to those with terminal or seriously chronic illnesses. Although there are many people who would benefit from selling their unneeded policies for more cash than they could receive from surrendering the policies, in practice, life settlements are generally only available for those age seventy or older (i.e., those with life expectancies not exceeding eleven to fifteen years). The percentage of life settlement offers that exceed the existing cash value is relatively low in comparison to the number of policies shopped for a life settlement.

- *No control over the ultimate owner of the policy* – once the policy is sold as part of a viatical or life settlement, the insured has no control over who ultimately owns the policy and who would benefit from the insured's death.

- *Reduces overall life insurance capacity and ability to obtain new coverage* – life insurance capacity is the maximum amount of coverage that the insurance industry is willing to issue to a specific insured. A policy that is sold to a life settlement company remains in force and counts against the total amount of coverage that the insured financially qualifies for. If the insured's needs later change and the insured desires to obtain new coverage, he or she may find that there is little to no insurance capacity left and they will be unable to get new life insurance.

TAX IMPLICATIONS

To the Seller

As a general rule, anytime a life insurance policy is sold to an unrelated third-party investor, the proceeds are taxed according to guidance issued by the IRS in 2009.[3] This guidance will generally govern the taxation of life settlement proceeds. However, as is discussed later in this section, a couple of major exclusions apply that may exempt part or all of the proceeds from taxation, and these exclusions will typically apply to the proceeds of viatical settlements. The 2009 IRS guidance indicates that the sale of a life insurance policy may produce both ordinary income and capital gains taxes. The total amount of taxable income is the difference between the sale proceeds and the policyholder's adjusted basis in the policy.

- *Ordinary income portion* – the difference between the cash surrender value and the cumulative premiums paid (i.e., the gain in the policy at the time of the sale).

- *Capital gain portion* – the difference between the sale price of the policy and the adjusted basis in the policy minus any amounts subject to ordinary income tax. Note that the adjusted basis is aggregate premiums paid by the seller minus the cost of insurance charges. So unlike policy surrenders, where the basis is equal to the cumulative premiums paid, for sales to unrelated third parties where the proceeds are not covered by the terminal or chronic illness exclusions, the cumulative premiums must be reduced by the cumulative cost of insurance to arrive at the adjusted basis.

Example – If a policyholder sells a $500,000 life insurance policy with a cash surrender value of $78,000 to an unrelated third party for $150,000 and has paid premiums totaling $64,000 with insurance charges of $10,000, then he or she must recognize ordinary income in the amount of $14,000 ($78,000 – $64,000, which equals the gain in the policy) and capital gain in the amount of $82,000 [$150,000 – ($64,000 – $10,000) – $14,000].

As mentioned above, there are two major exclusions which may override the general rule and exempt some or all of the living proceeds from life insurance from taxation. These exclusions were contained in The Health Insurance Portability and Accountability Act of 1996 (HIPAA 96)[4], which added IRC Section 101(g).[5] Specifically, the insured in a viatical or life settlement transaction must either be a *terminally ill individual* or a *chronically ill individual* in order for amounts received to be potentially tax-free.

- *Terminally ill individual* – A person is deemed to be terminally ill if he has been certified by a physician as having an illness or physical condition that reasonably can be expected to result in death within twenty-four months of the date of certification.[6] If the terminal illness exclusion applies, it applies to the entire amount of the living proceeds paid (i.e., there is no upper limit on the amount that can be excluded) and there is no restriction on the use of the proceeds by the recipient.

Most viatical settlements will qualify for this exclusion, with the exception of viatical settlements for insureds with a life expectancy of greater than two years (who may qualify for the chronic illness exception discussed below). The terminal illness exclusion should not be applicable to life settlements, as they are for insureds with life expectancies typically much longer than two years.

Once the insured obtains the certification based upon the doctor's reasonable medical opinion, the reality of what later happens does not matter. In other words, the statute does not contain a look-back rule.[7] If the insured actually lives months, years, or decades longer than expected, the viatical settlement proceeds continue to be excluded from income.

- *Chronically ill individual* – A person qualifies as chronically ill if he has been certified within the previous twelve months by a licensed health care practitioner as meeting one of three criteria: (1) he is unable to perform without substantial assistance at least two activities of daily living (bathing, dressing, eating, transferring, continence, or toileting) for at least ninety days due to a loss of functional capacity; (2) he has a level of disability similar to the level of disability described in clause (1); or (3) he requires substantial supervision to protect him from threats to health and safety due to severe cognitive impairment. People who are terminally ill are not included within the class of people who qualify as chronically ill.[8] This exclusion may apply to viatical settlements that don't qualify for the terminal illness exclusion, and in some situations may apply to life settlements where the insured qualifies as chronically ill. However, unlike the terminal illness exclusion, the amount excluded from income pursuant to this exclusion may be limited.

In order to qualify for the income exclusion, payments to chronically ill individuals must be reimbursements for the costs of qualified long-term care services provided for the insured that are not compensated for by insurance or otherwise.[9] Qualified long-term care services include "... necessary diagnostic, preventive, therapeutic, curing, treating, mitigating, and rehabilitative services, and maintenance or personal care services which: (A) are required by a chronically ill individual; and (B) are provided pursuant to a plan of care prescribed by a licensed health care practitioner."[10]

In other words, unlike terminally ill insureds, chronically ill individuals do not have the discretion to use viatical or life settlement proceeds in whatever manner they desire. Despite the limitation to long-term care costs, the Internal Revenue Code protects periodic payments by providing that a payment will not fail to qualify "... by reason of being made on a per diem or other periodic basis without regard to the expenses incurred during the period to which the payment relates."[11] The amount of periodic payments that may be excluded is subject to a dollar limit that is adjusted annually. In 2012, the per diem limitation amount is $310 ($113,150 per year).

Also, to qualify for the favorable tax treatment, the viatical or life settlement contract may not "... pay or reimburse expenses incurred for services or items to the extent that such expenses are reimbursable under the title XVIII of the Social Security Act [Medicare] or would be so reimbursable but for the application of a deductible or coinsurance amount."[12]

Finally, the chronic illness income tax exclusion does not apply to amounts paid to any taxpayer other than the insured in certain circumstances. If the payee has an insurable interest in the insured's life because the insured is a director, officer or employee of the payee, or because the insured is financially interested in any trade or business carried on by the payee, the exclusion does not apply.[13]

Viatical settlements must comply with additional requirements for the proceeds of the sale or assignment in order to be excluded from income tax. First, the payments must be made by a viatical settlement provider. To qualify as a viatical settlement provider, the purchaser must be "... regularly engaged in the trade or business of purchasing, or taking assignments of, life insurance contracts on the lives of insureds..."[14] who are terminally or chronically ill.

Second, the provider must either be licensed to provide viatical settlements under the laws of the state in which the insured resides, or if the insured's state does not require licensing of viatical settlement providers, the provider must meet the requirements specified in the Internal Revenue Code. With regard to terminally ill individuals, the viatical settlement provider must meet the requirement of: (1) Sections 8 and 9 of the Viatical Settlements Model Act prepared by the National Association of Insurance Commissioners; and (2) the Model Regulations of the National Association of Insurance Commissioners relating to standards for evaluation of reasonable payments in determining amounts paid by the viatical settlement provider in connection with the purchase or assignment of life insurance contracts.[15]

With respect to chronically ill insureds, the provider must meet requirements similar to those contained in Sections 8 and 9 of the Viatical Settlements Model Act along with the standards of the National Association of Insurance Commissioners, if any exist at the time of the settlement, for evaluating the reasonableness of the amounts paid by the provider in connection with viatical settlements for chronically ill individuals.[16]

To the Buyer

Guidance issued by the IRS in 2009[17] clarifies that when a third party that has no insurable interest in the life of the insured (e.g., a viatical or life settlement company) purchases a policy from the insured, the transfer-for-value rule causes the purchaser to have ordinary income equal to the amount by which the death benefit proceeds exceed the amount that the purchaser paid to purchase the policy plus any premiums paid by the purchaser to the carrier subsequent to the purchase.

The transfer for value rule, contained in IRC Section 101(a)(2), provides:

> In the case of a transfer for a valuable consideration, by assignment or otherwise, of a life insurance contract or any interest therein, the amount excluded from gross income ... shall not exceed an amount equal to the sum of the actual value of such consideration and the premiums and other amounts, subsequently paid by the transferee.

Since viatical and life settlement providers make their profit in the transaction on the difference between what they pay and what they receive, the taxation of the differential requires them to pay less for the policies than they would otherwise pay if the death benefits were received tax free.

ALTERNATIVES TO VIATICAL AND LIFE SETTLEMENTS

It is important for insurance planners to do all they can to protect their clients who may be contemplating entering into a viatical or life settlement. First, however, there needs to be a decision about whether or not the policy needs to be sold and whether any of the below alternatives might be in the client's best interest.[18]

1. *Withdraw or borrow cash values –*

    Permanent type policies such as whole life, variable life, universal life, etc., build up cash values over the years. The owner of the policy is usually able to withdraw or borrow from the cash value. Withdrawals reduce the face amount at the time of the withdrawal. Policy loans, because they can technically be repaid prior to death, are subtracted from the face amount of the policy upon the insured's death before payment is made to the named beneficiary.

    The advantages of taking withdrawals or borrowing from the policy are: (1) the policy will still pay the remaining face amount at death to the beneficiary named by the policyowner (in other words, the policyowner does not have to settle for less than the full amount of insurance); (2) withdrawals (up to policy basis) and loans are generally received income-tax free (assuming the policy is not a Modified Endowment Contract), similar to the policy death benefit. Contrast this with the fact that life settlement proceeds may be partially taxable.

    The major disadvantage is that the amount one can withdraw or borrow generally will be considerably less than the amount a terminally ill policyowner could get in a viatical settlement, and may be less than what can be received in a life settlement. Thus, if the owner needs more cash than is available from policy withdrawals or loans, then a viatical or life settlement should be considered.

2. *Surrender the policy –*

    Policies with cash value buildup can be surrendered to the insurance company. However, this would generally not be desirable, since the face amount of the policy is usually much higher than the surrender value. In addition, amounts received in excess of the policyowner's basis (paid in premiums less dividends received less amounts previously withdrawn, if any) are subject to income tax. The policyowner would almost always be better off withdrawing or borrowing against the policy or entering into a viatical or life settlement.

3. *Borrow funds from a third party –*

    As an alternative to a viatical settlement, other friends, family members, the beneficiary of the policy, or possibly a bank may be willing to lend money to the person who is terminally ill and then receive repayment from the insurance proceeds within a relatively short period of time (i.e., within a couple of years). Although insurance companies and institutional lenders generally will not lend money in excess of the cash value in the policy, friends and family may be willing to do so.

    Depending on how the loan is secured, lenders run some risk in lending money to the policyowner. For example, if the policyowner issues an unsecured note, the lender runs the risk that other claimants against the policyowner's estate may have a higher priority and there may be insufficient assets to repay the note. Consequently, the note should be secured with specific collateral.

    However, if the policy itself or any interest in the policy (e.g., the cash value or the death benefit) is assigned to the lender as collateral, it may trigger the transfer for value rule with potentially adverse tax consequences for the lender.[19] The best opportunities involve transactions with parties who qualify under one of the exceptions to the transfer for value rule: partners of the insured, partnerships of the insured, or a corporation in which the insured is a shareholder or officer.

    Given that the time frame for repayment from the death proceeds in the case of a life settlement may be ten or more years, borrowing from friends and family may not be as feasible an alternative for life settlements.

4. *Convert or exchange existing coverage into paid up coverage –*

    If the main impetus behind the desire to settle the policy is the inability to pay additional premiums due to financial hardship—but there is a desire to maintain some coverage in effect—then it may make sense to reduce the death benefit of the existing policy and suspend further premiums or 1035 exchange the current policy for a paid-up policy with a smaller face amount.

5. *Exercise accelerated death benefit or other policy riders (if any) –*

Two common types of accelerated death benefit riders are terminal illness and chronic illness riders, which permit part or all of the life insurance death benefit to be accelerated in the event the insured suffers a terminal[20] or chronic illness[21]. The advantage of exercising these riders as opposed to doing a viatical or life settlement is that the policy beneficiaries may potentially still receive a death benefit at the insured's death, albeit reduced by the amount of the accelerated death benefit advance(s) previously paid to the policyowner. In addition, as a general rule a terminal illness rider will provide a higher payout than a viatical settlement, but typically impose a great number of restrictions on medical conditions.

If the insured needs funds to pay medical costs, other riders to consider exercising as an alternative to a viatical or life settlement, assuming the policy has one of them, may include critical illness, long-term care, and disability income riders. Note that benefit payment under these riders may reduce the policy death benefit.

- *Critical illness rider* – a lump sum is paid if the insured is diagnosed with one of the critical illnesses specified in the rider, such as cancer, heart attack, stroke, kidney failure and others.

- *Long-term care rider* – provides reimbursements for nursing home care or home health care costs of the insured.

- *Disability income rider* – pays a regular income from the insurance company if the insured becomes totally disabled and can't work.

For more information regarding accelerated death benefit riders, see Chapter 6: Special Policy Provisions and Riders.

FREQUENTLY ASKED QUESTIONS

Question – What factors will determine the amount of a viatical or life settlement?

Answer – The following factors will affect the amount of settlement received:

1. *The insured's life expectancy* – The shorter the period until the insured is expected to die, the more the settlement company will pay.

2. *The period in which the company can contest the existence of a valid contract must have passed* – The incontestable period, as well as the suicide provision (typically two years), generally must have expired. This period may begin again for policies that have been reinstated after a lapse for nonpayment of premium.

3. *Company's financial rating* – The company that issued the policy must have a high financial rating.

4. *The amount of the premiums* – The premium level is important, since the buyer of the policy must continue making the payments for the remainder of the insured's lifetime.

5. *The size of the policy* – Most settlement companies have upper and lower limits. For example, for viatical settlements a top limit of $1,000,000 scaling down to a minimum of $50,000 is typical. For life settlements the death benefit must generally be at least $250,000, and some providers will only consider policies of $1 million or more.

6. *The current prime interest rate* – The prime rate is important, since the buyer will compare the settlement agreement to other types of investments.

7. *Time of payment* – The time between applying for the settlement and having the cash is generally three to eight weeks (but can be as long as six months). However, this will depend on how quickly the medical information, life expectancy reports, beneficiary release forms, etc. are in the hands of the settlement company.

Question – What other considerations are involved in deciding whether or not to enter into a viatical or life settlement?

Answer – Planners and those insureds who are considering viatical and life settlements should also consider the following:

1. *Confidentiality and beneficiaries* – Most companies stress the confidential nature of the transaction

but they require the named beneficiary to release any possible claim to the proceeds. If the insured does not want the beneficiary to know of the sale, he or she may change beneficiaries just prior to completing the settlement. If the estate is named as beneficiary, the insured (owner) would be the only one who would need to sign the release forms. However, if death occurred after the time the beneficiary was changed, but before the settlement was completed, the insurance proceeds would be paid to the estate and would, therefore, be subject to probate administration.

2. *Group insurance* – Group insurance policies may be eligible to be sold in viatical and life settlements, but they generally must be portable. If a group insurance policy is sold this will usually require that one's employer is notified.

3. *Resale of policies* – Confidentiality may be lost if the policy is sold by the settlement company in the secondary market to individual investors, since a new investor would want to know the health status and life expectancy of the insured.

4. *Escrow accounts* – An escrow account is generally used to make certain that the payment of the agreed upon amount is made to the insured shortly after the insurance company notifies the escrow company that the ownership of the policy has been transferred.

5. *Shop and negotiate* – Several settlement companies should be investigated in order to negotiate the best offer.

Question – What types of life insurance policies are typically sold in the secondary market?

Answer – Single life policies are generally much more attractive to viatical and life settlement providers. A viatical settlement of a survivorship policy is unlikely due to the fact that both insured's would have to be terminally ill or have very short life expectancies. The life settlement market for survivorship policies isn't much better, because the settlement companies have to wait until the death of the second insured to collect the death proceeds. Both insureds would need to have life expectancies not exceeding eleven to fifteen years.

As for product types, Universal Life (UL) policies are generally more attractive to settlement companies, especially in the case of life settlements. This is because the settlement companies have flexibility to reduce premiums to just cover the annual cost of insurance charges or pay some other minimum premium amount, flexibility to take cash value out of the policy and invest it in a different manner, and flexibility to reduce the face amount if needed. This includes Variable Universal Life (VUL). However, as discussed below, special rules apply when a VUL policy is settled.

Term insurance and group term insurance can also frequently be settled. However, certain factors make them more attractive to settlement companies; such as conversion features which enable them to be converted to a flexible premium cash value product.

Whole life policies, especially in the case of life settlements, may be less attractive to settlement companies because they tend to be less flexible when it comes to premium flexibility, ability to pull out cash values, and the ability to adjust the death benefit. In addition, since these products are generally designed to endow at maturity (e.g., age 100), they tend to have higher cash values. This makes it less likely that the settlement offer will exceed the surrender value.

Question – What special rules apply when a variable life or variable universal life policy is settled?

Answer – Since a variable life insurance product is treated as a security, the settlement of a variable life insurance policy is subject to Financial Industry Regulatory Authority (FINRA) best practices standards that apply to broker-dealers and registered representatives.[22] The five primary areas of concern that FINRA identified for its members engaging in settlements of variable life policies include: (1) suitability; (2) due diligence; (3) best execution; (4) training and supervision; and (5) compensation. As a result of these standards, most broker-dealers have developed suitability and due diligence questionnaires, disclosure forms, and standardized the amount of acceptable compensation for variable life insurance settlements. In addition, a principal of the broker-dealer will generally review each variable life settlement transaction to ensure that it is suitable for the client.

Question – Can a life settlement followed by the purchase of a new policy with the settlement proceeds qualify as a 1035 exchange?

Answer – It has been suggested that if the settlement proceeds are never in the hands of the policy owner and the proceeds are sent by the settlement company (via an escrow agent) directly to a life insurance carrier to be used to purchase a new life insurance policy, then a 1035 exchange treatment applies. It is the authors' opinion that this would not qualify as a valid 1035 exchange, due to the fact that there is a sale in the middle of the exchange transaction.

Question – Can a viatical settlement be used as a means of getting a life insurance policy out of one's estate for estate tax purposes?

Answer – For the individual who will not live more than three years, a transfer of an existing policy to an irrevocable trust or a third person will be ineffective to avoid inclusion of the policy in the gross estate at death. For example, an individual who owns a $500,000 life insurance policy on his life and whose estate is in the 55 percent estate tax bracket will only pass on $225,000 to the beneficiaries of the policy (.55 × $500,000 = $275,000; $500,000 – $275,000 = $225,000).

A sale of the policy avoids the three-year rule because the viatication is a sale for fair market value in money or money's worth. This could provide additional value to the insured's family and reduce estate taxes because the conversion into cash converts the intangible asset into cash that can be given to family members in the form of tax-free annual exclusion gifts, spent down by the individual, or a combination of the two.

For example, the same individual who owns a $500,000 policy on his life will leave his beneficiaries only $225,000 if he dies owning the policy. Instead, the individual sells the policy and receives $350,000 (70 percent of the face amount). The individual can make annual exclusion gifts of the $350,000 to his four children, their spouses, and ten grandchildren over his remaining assumed life expectancy of two years. Under the viatical settlement, the individual has transferred $350,000 to his family tax-free, providing them an additional $125,000 ($350,000 - $225,000). (In addition, the estate can pass the after-estate tax value of the premiums not spent in maintaining the policy as well as the after-income-and-estate tax on the earnings on the declining balance of the $350,000 viatical proceeds over his remaining life.)

Getting a life insurance policy out of the insured's estate can sometimes save the estate administration costs of having to file an estate tax return.

Question – Can an owner of a policy who is not the insured enter into a viatical or life settlement?

Answer – Yes. Only the policy owner can viaticate or settle an insurance policy. However, if the policy owner is not the insured, the cooperation of the insured will be required in order to do so.

CHAPTER ENDNOTES

1. The term "viatical settlement" originated from the Latin "viaticum" which means provision for a journey.

2. See Conning Research & Consulting's 2011 study on life settlements – "Life Settlements: An Asset Class Resets."

3. *Rev. Rul.* 2009-13.

4. Health Insurance Portability and Accountability Act of 1996 (HIPAA 96), P.L. 104-191.

5. IRC Sec. 101(g). This provision applies to payments made after December 31, 1996. For a discussion of this exclusion, see generally Gary J. Gasper, "Viatical Settlements-Cashing Out Life Insurance," *Probate & Property*, March/April 1997, p. 20.

6. IRC Sec. 101(g)(4)(A).

7. Gary J. Gasper, "Viatical Settlements-Cashing Out Life Insurance," *Probate & Property*, March/April 1997, p. 21.

8. IRC Secs. 101(g)(4)(B), 7702B(c)(2)(A).

9. IRC Sec. 101(g)(3)(A)(i).

10. IRC Secs. 101(g)(4)(C), 7702B(c)(1).

11. IRC Sec. 101(g)(3)(C).

12. IRC Secs. 101(g)(3)(A)(ii)(I), 7702B(b)(1)(B).

13. IRC Sec. 101(g)(5).

14. IRC Sec. 101(g)(2)(B)(i).

15. IRC Sec. 101(g)(2)(B)(ii).

16. IRC Sec. 101(g)(2)(B)(iii).

17. *Rev. Rul.* 2009-14.

18. See Hal Stucker, "Viatical Settlement: What's a Good Fit," *National Underwriter*, Life and Health/Financial Services edition, February 1, 1999.

19. See "Tax Implications" above and Chapter 25 for further discussion of the implications of the transfer for value rule.

20. A terminally ill individual is one "who has been certified by a physician as having an illness or physical condition which can reasonably be expected to result in death in 24 months or less after the date of the certification." IRC Sec. 101(g)(4)(A).

21. A chronically ill individual is one who has been certified by a licensed health care practitioner as being either unable to perform at least two (2) Activities of Daily Living (ADLs) for a period of at least ninety days or requiring substantial supervision due to a severe cognitive impairment. IRC Sec. 7702B(c)(2).

22. NASD Notice 06-38 (August 2006). "The purpose of this Notice is to remind firms and associated persons that life settlements involving variable insurance policies are securities transactions, and firms and associated persons involved in such transactions are subject to applicable NASD rules."

BUY-SELL AGREEMENTS

CHAPTER 31

INTRODUCTION

A buy-sell agreement is a legal contract restricting the right to dispose of a business interest to specified parties according to specified terms. Typically, this arrangement requires a sale of the business interest, at a formula-determined price, upon one or more of the following triggering events:

- Death

- Disability

- Retirement

- Withdrawal from the business at some earlier time

- In some cases upon attachment of the owner's property by creditors or in a divorce

These triggering events will vary depending on the needs, desires, and circumstances of the parties.

WHEN IS USE OF THIS TECHNIQUE INDICATED?

1. When it is essential or desirable to create a market for a business interest upon the death, long-term disability, retirement, divorce, or bankruptcy of an owner.

2. When a shareholder is unwilling or unable to continue running a business with the family of a deceased co-stockholder or someone outside the business.

3. When the continuation of a business at an owner's death involves a high amount of financial risk and it is desirable or necessary to convert the business into cash at that time. For example, if the client's estate is large and will not qualify for the estate tax marital deduction, a means to turn the business interest into cash at a fair price must be found so that taxes can be paid.

4. When a highly-paid owner-employee dies, his or her salary often dies too. Proceeds from the buy-sell help replace this salary.

5. When federal or state law make it imperative that the closeness of a close corporation be maintained. For example, too many shareholders or the wrong type of shareholder could result in an involuntary termination of S corporation status. Likewise, in most states, nonprofessionals may not be stockholders in a professional corporation. In at least one state, if no buy-back occurs within thirteen months of a shareholder's death, the attorney general of the state could remove the corporation's charter, a potentially disastrous result.

Advantages

There are a number of advantages to using a buy-sell agreement. Some of these include the following:

1. Life insurance funding has a relatively low cost, is simple to explain and implement, and will not adversely affect the working capital or credit position of the business.

2. Life insurance is the only means of guaranteeing that death—one event that creates the need for cash—also creates the cash to satisfy that need.

445

3. Survivors of the deceased shareholder are freed from financial dependence on a business that has just lost a key individual.

4. Survivors of the deceased shareholder are assured of a fair (and hopefully sufficient) amount of both capital and income.

5. The insurance proceeds are paid quickly after the insured's death, making it easy to close the sale in a timely fashion.

6. If a cash value life insurance policy is used, the cash value can be used as a tax-deferred sinking fund for a lifetime buy-out, which is generally more likely to occur than a buy-out at death. Keep in mind that if the owners were planning on using term insurance to fund the buy-out at death, they are already paying the mortality cost, so the additional premium needed for a cash value policy generally goes towards building cash value.

7. If the life insurance policy has a chronic illness rider, the death benefit can be accelerated and used to buy-out a chronically ill owner.

8. If life insurance is used to fund an entity purchase arrangement for a partnership, Limited Liability Company (LLC), or S corporation, upon the death of an insured owner the receipt of the tax-free death proceeds causes a basis increase (the lack of a basis increase is generally a major disadvantage of an entity purchase arrangement). It is possible to have the entire basis increase allocated solely to the remaining owners—with S corporations this is accomplished by making an election to terminate the tax year and causing the death proceeds to be received in the next tax year; with partnerships and LLCs this is accomplished by including a provision in the operating agreement allocated the basis to the surviving owners.

Disadvantages

There are, of course, costs associated with a life insurance funded buy-sell. Some of these costs include the following:

1. Premiums must be paid with after-tax dollars.

2. Uninsurable shareholders present a problem. Planners should note, however, that very few individuals are refused insurance because of age or physical health. Most insurers will agree to cover almost any age (up to the mid-seventies) and will insure illnesses by adding a rating, which is a charge that equates the total premium to the appropriate level of additional risk the insurer is assuming.

3. With a stock redemption plan, the corporation needs only one policy on each shareholder's life. But in the case of a cross purchase plan, especially one that involves more than three shareholders, where each shareholder owns a policy on each other shareholder's life, the number of policies (and therefore the administrative complexity, cost, and potential for error) multiplies each time new insurance is added because of an increase in the valuation of a stock interest.

To ascertain the number of policies needed where a cross purchase agreement is used, multiply the number of shareholders by that same number less one. In other words, the formula for determining the number of policies is $N \times (N - 1)$ with N being the number of shareholders. So if there were four shareholders, twelve new policies would be needed each time the business interest was revalued.

WHAT ARE THE REQUIREMENTS?

Buy-sell agreements are used to accomplish many important estate planning objectives, the four most important of which are:

1. To create a market for a shareholder's stock which in turn reduces or eliminates the liquidity problems created by the ownership of closely-held stock and helps the owner harvest the fruit of his or her labor.

2. To help establish the value of the stock of a closely-held enterprise for both federal and state death tax purposes and between the parties and their heirs.

3. To prevent the sale or other transfer of stock or other equity interests beyond the current owners and therefore maintain the closeness of the closely-held business. Remaining shareholders are assured that they are protected against

inactive and potentially dissident shareholders who often cause conflict over management policies such as the size of dividends relative to salaries or risks the corporation should take for growth.

4. To preserve the tax status of an S corporation or the professional status of a professional corporation.

However, this technique comes with several important requirements, outlined below.

Restraints on Transferability of Stock

Restraints on the transferability of stock must be placed in the charter of the corporation. Absent these provisions, a disposition of stock may be effective to transfer the shares even if that gift or sale violates the buy-sell agreement. Even though the parties may successfully sue the person who breaches the buy-sell contract, the damages received will probably be in the form of cash rather than a restoration of the status quo, certainly an inadequate remedy.

Furthermore, absent a legend (warning of the existence of the buy-sell agreement) on the stock certificates, restrictions based solely on the buy-sell itself may be considered personal to the parties to the agreement. Subsequent shareholders may not have either the prohibitions or protections of the buy-sell agreement.

Stock Certificates Must be Marked with a Legend

Stock certificates in the corporation must be marked with a legend. This is a note which clearly states that the stock is subject to restrictions and specifies where those restrictions can be found. Generally, unless the stock certificate states there is a restriction on the transferability, that restriction will not be effective against a transferee. State law will determine the degree of detail necessary. The buy-sell should itself require that each stock certificate be marked with this legend.

Written Agreement

A written document between the parties to the agreement should be drawn up and properly executed. This legal agreement should:

1. state the business purpose to be served for the agreement;

2. refer to the events which will trigger a buy-out;

3. provide a formula for determining the price at which shares are to be exchanged;

4. explain how and when the purchased stock is to be delivered;

5. list any restrictions on lifetime transfers;

6. state any exceptions to the general terms (for instance, to allow a gift or sale to immediate family members);

7. explain how funding is to be arranged with specific reference to life insurance (a schedule of policies should be appended to the agreement or listed within it);

8. specifically provide for the purchase of additional insurance as the value of the stock increases;

9. state how funding of any sales price in excess of insurance proceeds is to be made including interest on the unpaid balance;

10. explain what is to happen in the event of bankruptcy, receivership, or dissolution of the corporation, the purchase or disposal during lifetime or death of all the stock of a shareholder, or termination of the agreement by a voluntary action of the parties; and

11. state the applicable jurisdiction under whose laws the document is to be construed.

HOW IT IS DONE

Buy-sell agreements can take a number of forms based on the tax and other objectives and circumstances of the parties to the contract:

1. *Stock redemption* – In this type of buy-sell arrangement, the business itself purchases the shareholder's interest upon the triggering event, preferably according to a formula-determined price. With respect to any insurance, the corporation should be the applicant, owner,

beneficiary, and premium payer. This arrangement is sometimes called an entity purchase.

2. *Cross purchase* – In this type of arrangement, the remaining business owners buy the business interest upon the triggering event, preferably under a formula-determined price. With respect to any insurance, the shareholders should be the applicants, owners, beneficiaries, and premium payers. This arrangement is sometimes called a criss cross.

3. *Wait and see* – This highly flexible approach allows planners to defer the decision regarding the eventual purchaser until a triggering event occurs. It is appropriate when the corporation or surviving shareholders may not have sufficient funds to purchase a decedent shareholder's stock alone, when the client's advisers seek more flexibility in light of rapidly-changing tax laws and client circumstances, or when the client's advisers seek an escape hatch to avoid adverse income tax consequences. Mechanically, the wait and see buy-sell works as follows:

   a. The corporation is given a first option to purchase any or all of the exiting shareholder's stock. At this stage, the wait and see buy-sell takes the form of a stock redemption plan. To the extent that option is not exercised within a designated period, the parties enter Stage B.

   b. At this stage, the remaining shareholders are given an option to purchase the stock. Here, the arrangement is similar to a cross purchase plan.

   c. Any stock remaining at the expiration of the second option must be purchased by the corporation. In this final stage, the purchase takes the form of a stock redemption.

   The order of the three stages is important. If the parties were reversed and the corporation were to purchase shares under option (b), relieving shareholders of an obligation to purchase stock under option (c), the IRS would classify the payment by the corporation as a constructive dividend.

   The insurance policies that fund the wait and see can be arranged in a number of ways.

The corporation could purchase a policy on the life of each shareholder and use the proceeds to finance its purchase of stock from a decedent-shareholder's estate, to effect a Section 303 partial stock redemption, or to loan the proceeds to the surviving shareholders in order that they might purchase the decedent's shares under option (b). The shareholders could purchase the insurance as under a cross purchase plan and, if they choose not to purchase the decedent's shares themselves, loan the proceeds to the corporation or make additional capital contributions to the corporation, thus increasing their basis in their own stock. Finally, a third party, such as an irrevocable trust, could purchase the insurance as a means of keeping the proceeds out of the decedent's estate.

4. *Third party buy-out (a.k.a., a unilateral or one-way buy-out)* – A third party agrees contractually to purchase the business interest upon a triggering event.

––––––––––

Example. Joe and Paul, two brothers, have operated a highly successful auto repair and parts business. Joe runs the day-to-day operation of the business and makes the long-run hiring and firing decisions. Paul, the younger brother, is the super salesman who "makes things happen."

Joe knows that either brother would have a difficult time continuing to run the business at its present level if the other brother died (or became permanently disabled). Furthermore, both brothers know their stock is worth in excess of $3 million and will therefore generate considerable federal estate tax when added to their other assets. Both brothers realize their families are dependent on their annual salaries of $300,000 a year, salaries which would stop at their deaths.

Joe and Paul have their attorney draft a "wait and see" buy-sell agreement which provides that if either brother dies, either the corporation or the surviving shareholder will purchase the stock of the decedent and in return pay the estate the full fair market value of the stock in cash.

To finance the purchase upon either brother's death, each brother purchases a life insurance policy on the life of the other. To help them with the premiums, the corporation can agree to pay

each brother a sufficient bonus so that, after taxes, each will net an amount large enough to pay policy premiums. (See Chapter 40, "Section 162 Plans.") Alternatively, the corporation might enter into a split dollar agreement with the brothers to help them pay the premiums. (See Chapter 41, "Split Dollar Life Insurance.")

The decedent's family will no longer be tied to the economic success of the business, will not need to bother the surviving brother, and will not be able to interfere in the operation of the business. The surviving brother will have no debt to his late brother's family and will enjoy 100 percent of the financial rewards for his increased burdens.

TAX IMPLICATIONS

1. Premiums used to fund a buy-sell agreement are not deductible regardless of who (the corporation, shareholders, or a third party) owns the policy.[1] Planners should therefore consider the comparative tax brackets involved in deciding whether to use the stock redemption or cross purchase approaches to funding a buy-sell agreement.

If the corporation is in a higher income tax bracket than the shareholders, it may be wise to make tax-deductible salary payments or bonuses to the shareholders and have them buy and own the insurance on a cross purchase basis. If the corporation is the lower bracket, it may make more sense (other things being equal) to use a stock redemption plan.

2. Death proceeds will be received income-tax free regardless of who (the corporation, shareholders, or a third party) owns the policy.[2] However, this favorable general rule is modified where the amount of life insurance is large, the business has substantial revenue, and the proceeds are payable to certain C corporations. Life insurance proceeds received by a C corporation may generate an Alternative Minimum Tax (AMT) liability of up to 15 percent of the amount of the proceeds. (See the discussion of the AMT in Chapter 35, "Key Employee Life Insurance.")

The corporate AMT is not a problem where the policy proceeds are received by an S corporation,

a partnership, or the individual coshareholders or partners of the insured. Thus, there is no AMT concern with a cross purchase type agreement.

3. The general rule that life insurance proceeds are income-tax free may not apply where there has been a transfer for valuable consideration. If a life insurance policy or an interest in a policy is transferred for valuable consideration, proceeds exceeding the consideration paid plus any premiums paid after the transfer may be subject to income tax at ordinary rates. (See Chapter 25, "The Transfer for Value Rule.")

4. For life insurance contracts entered into after August 17, 2006, certain requirements must be met for the death proceeds of an employer-owned life insurance contract to be received income-tax free. One set of requirements is that before an employer-owned life insurance contract is issued the employer must meet certain notice and consent requirements. The insured employee must be notified in writing, at the time the contract is issued, that the employer intends to insure the employee's life, and the maximum face amount the employee's life could be insured for. The notice must also state that the policy owner will be the beneficiary of the death proceeds of the policy. The insured must also give written consent to be the insured under the contract and consent to coverage continuing after the insured terminates employment.[3] For more on the requirements of employer-owned life insurance, see Chapter 24, "Taxation of Benefits."

5. The payment of premiums by a corporation that is the beneficiary of a policy on the life of a shareholder will not be taxed to the shareholder as either a constructive dividend or as salary.[4]

But if the corporation pays premiums for a policy owned by one shareholder on the life of another, that payment is likely to be considered a distribution of dividends to the policyowner-shareholder.[5] Likewise, if a corporation pays premiums on the life of an insured employee and the proceeds are payable to the estate or personal beneficiary of the employee, the premiums will be includable in the employee's income.[6]

6. Typically, there will be no accumulated earnings tax problem where cash values accumulate in policies used in funding a stock redemption. Amounts accumulated to fund life insurance for

stock redemptions are considered to satisfy a reasonable business need and, thus, are not subject to the accumulated earnings penalty tax.[7] But planners should take care to document the business purposes (as contrasted with shareholder) served by the accumulation. The accumulated earnings tax is not a problem when life insurance is owned on a cross purchase basis because no corporate funds are involved.

7. Where shareholders own insurance on the life or lives of other shareholders (a cross purchase plan), at the death of one shareholder, the policy or policies owned by the other shareholders on his life will not be includable in his estate.[8] But the cash values (plus premiums paid but unearned on the date of his death) of the policies the decedent owned on the surviving shareholders' lives will be included in his estate.[9]

There should be no estate tax inclusion of the life insurance proceeds if the corporation (in the case of a stock redemption) is the owner and beneficiary of the policies.[10] However, planners should check the terms of the buy-sell agreement to determine the degree to which policy proceeds are excluded from the price paid to the deceased shareholder's estate. This is a major decision in drafting a buy-sell plan: if the value of insurance proceeds received under a stock redemption plan is ignored, it can be argued that the surviving shareholders receive a windfall at the expense of the decedent shareholder's family.

Perhaps the best solution is for the purchase price to include the cash values (but not the death benefits) of the policies on the lives of all shareholders. This is appropriate because the cash values represent a corporate asset to which the insured shareholder had indirectly contributed.

8. There appear to be two sets of tests for determining whether the formula price for the stock set forth in a buy-sell agreement will fix the value of the stock for estate tax purposes. The first applies where the buy-sell is between parties other than the "natural objects of the others' bounty". The second, more difficult set of tests, applies when the buyer and seller are either family members or the natural objects of each other's bounty.

When the buyer and seller are not the natural objects of the others' bounty, courts will generally accept the formula price as the value of stock for estate tax purposes if the sales price in the buy-sell agreement meets the following requirements:[11]

a) The estate must be obligated to sell the stock at a shareholder's death.

b) The price must be fixed by the terms of the agreement or the agreement must contain a formula or method for determining the price.

c) The agreement must prohibit the owner from selling the stock during lifetime without first offering it to the other party or parties at a price that does not exceed the death time price.

d) The price must be fair at the time the agreement is entered into.

When the buyer and seller are natural objects of the others' bounty, courts will generally accept the formula price as the value of stock for estate tax purposes only if the sales price in the buy-sell agreement meets the requirements above and, in addition:[12]

a) the document must represent a bona fide business agreement;

b) the agreement must not be a device to transfer the stock to the family or other natural objects of the transferor's bounty for less than full and adequate consideration in money or money's worth; and

c) the agreement's terms must be comparable to terms that similar businesses would agree to in a similar arm's length transaction.

As a practical matter, these rules imply that the buy-sell price must be determined by formula, the formula must be based on currently accepted valuation techniques, and the formula price must approximate the fair market value of the business interest at the date of the triggering event. Further, the formula must be generally recognized as suitable to valuing the type of business involved; at the time the buy-sell is signed, it must be the result of good faith arm's length bargaining.

If all of the requirements above are met, the price at which a deceased stockholder's shares must be sold under a buy-sell agreement will bind the IRS and the courts as the estate tax value of the stock.

9. No taxable gift occurs upon the execution of a buy-sell agreement. Likewise, sales required under the agreement should not be taxable gifts because adequate consideration is given to all parties through their mutual promises, and because the agreement and sales are transactions in the ordinary course of business.

10. A buy-sell agreement will not usually fix the gift tax value of stock because most agreements either prohibit gifts without the written consent of the other shareholders or permit gifts only after the shareholder first offers to sell the shares to the other shareholders.[13] But, in the authors' opinion, a well drafted buy-sell agreement (i.e., one which meets the requirements for binding the IRS to the value set where the parties are the natural objects of the others' bounty) should be considered highly relevant and will probably succeed in establishing a gift tax value.

11. The nonexcercise of a favorable purchase right under a buy-sell may have gift tax implications. It is possible that the IRS could argue that the waiver of an option to buy stock under a buy-sell agreement is, itself, a taxable gift to the extent the holder of the right to buy chooses not to require the sale and a family member benefits by this inaction.

Cross Purchase Agreements

When a cross purchase form of buy-sell is used, upon a sale triggering event (such as death, long-term disability, or retirement), the seller is required to sell shares to the other shareholders at the price and conditions set in the agreement. Any gain on the sale is a capital gain (regardless of the character of the corporation's underlying assets).[14]

If the seller is the shareholder's estate, and the stock is sold shortly after the shareholder's death, there is usually little or no gain realized by the estate. This is because the estate's income tax basis is the federal estate tax (fair market) value of the stock on the date of death.[15] If the buy-sell meets the Chapter 15 requirements discussed under Tax Implications, the formula price should peg the stock's estate tax value and no gain should be realized.

A cross purchase is advantageous from the perspective of the purchasing shareholders. They increase the income tax basis in their total stock interests by the price they pay for the stock bought under the agreement (even if tax-free life insurance proceeds provided the cash for the purchase). So if a surviving shareholder decides at some later date to sell his interest, because of the increase in basis, his gain on the sale will be lower.

Example. If a shareholder paid $500,000 to the estate of a deceased co-shareholder, the stock he just purchased would now have a $500,000 basis. If that stock was later sold by the surviving shareholder for $700,000, only the $200,000 gain would be taxable. Contrast this with a stock redemption where the survivor gets no increase in basis no matter how much the corporation pays for the deceased shareholder's stock.

Stock Redemptions

As discussed below, a stock redemption has several potential disadvantages when used with a C corporation. However, it should be noted that these disadvantages can be eliminated or mitigated when used with a pass-through entity, such as a partnership, Limited Liability Company (LLC), or S corporation.

Tax Disadvantages:

1. *Lack of step up in basis* – when the business interest of a departing or deceased owner is purchased by the business, the pro rata interest of the remaining owners is increased. However, their basis in the business remains the same. This means that if they later sell their interest in the business during their lifetime, there may be adverse capital gain consequences. This is especially the case with C corporations.

   In the case of an entity purchase arrangement involving a pass-through entity that is funded with life insurance, the remaining owners will receive a basis increase to the extent of the receipt of the tax-free death proceeds by the business. This basis increase can be fully allocated to the surviving owners by putting such a provision in the partnership or LLC operating agreement, or in the case of a S corporation, by electing to terminate the tax year and causing the death proceeds to be received in the next tax year.[16] If it is a lifetime buy-out of an owner, then no death proceeds are paid to the entity and there is no basis increase. Thus, lifetime entity purchase buy-outs result in a lack of step up in basis to the remaining owners of pass-through entities.

2.   *Alternative Minimum Tax (AMT)* – the receipt of the income tax-free life insurance death proceeds by the business may trigger the AMT. This should only be an issue for C corporations. It should not be an issue for entity purchase arrangement involving pass-through entities, as pass-through entities are not subject to a separate AMT (the individual AMT may apply to the owners).

3.   *Dividend treatment of sales proceeds* – For entity purchase arrangements involving C corporations, the IRS may treat the redemption price amount as a dividend to the shareholder selling the stock. Once again, this should not be an issue for entity purchase arrangements involving pass-through entities (with the possible exception of an S corporation that was formerly a C corporation). Unless the transaction meets certain tests, a corporate distribution in redemption of its stock is classified and taxed as a dividend.[17] That means every cent paid to the seller (not just the gain) is taxable in full, generally at capital gains rates, to the extent of the shareholder's share of corporate current and accumulated earnings and profits. No credit or offset is allowed for the selling shareholder's basis, no matter how large it may have been or how that basis was obtained.[18] The result when the redemption occurs during lifetime may not be so dramatic but in comparison to the typically favorable tax implications when the sale occurs after a shareholder's death, dividend treatment is a tax misfortune.

Example. Assume the following:

1. The client's stock is to be purchased at his death for $1,000,000 ($1,000 per share for 1,000 shares).

2. The buy-sell meets Chapter 15 tests and the price paid by the corporation will also be recognized by the IRS as the estate tax value of the stock.

3. The corporation has accumulated earnings and profits far in excess of the distribution.

At the client's death, if the redemption is taxed under sale or exchange rules, the estate realizes $1,000,000, its income tax basis is $1,000,000, and it recognizes no gain because the amount it has realized does not exceed its basis. So the tax is zero.

But if the redemption is taxed as a dividend, the estate realizes $1,000,000 of ordinary income and its basis does not reduce that income. State and federal taxes would likely exceed $150,000.

Safe Harbor

Code section 302 provides that a redemption will be treated as a sale or exchange if the redemption meets any of the three following tests:

1.   The redemption is not equivalent to a dividend.

2.   The redemption is substantially disproportionate with respect to the shareholder (the shareholder's interest in the corporation after the redemption is less than 80 percent of his or her interest before the redemption, and the shareholder's interest after the redemption is less than 50 percent of the total combined voting power of all shares).

3.   The redemption completely terminates the shareholder's interest in the corporation.

Planners cannot rely on the first test because it is one that can be determined only after the fact. And, as with much of the tax law, neither the substantially disproportionate nor the complete termination test is as easily met as it would appear when there are certain relationships between the seller and other parties who own (or who are deemed to own) stock.

Meeting either of these tests when the corporation is family-owned is extremely difficult because of the attribution (constructive ownership) rules of Code section 318. In a nutshell, stock is owned constructively by (treated as if owned by) the seller if it is actually owned by certain family members or entities in which the shareholder holds an interest.

So in the typical family-owned business in which all stock is held by parents and their children, the sale of stock back to the corporation—even if it is all the stock the seller actually owns—may be neither substantially disproportionate nor a complete termination of the selling shareholder's interest because the seller is deemed to own stock actually owned by others.

———————

Example. Assume the following:

1. Out of 1,000 shares outstanding, the client and his wife each own 250 shares of their family corporation's stock.

2. The client's son and daughter each own 250 shares.

3. At the death of a shareholder, the buy-sell agreement requires the corporation to purchase all the shares the decedent owned from his estate.

4. The purchase price is $1,000 a share.

5. The client dies and leaves his entire estate to his wife.

6. His executor receives the 250 shares at the client's death and under the agreement sells the stock to the corporation which pays the estate $250,000 in return.

The $250,000 payment the corporation makes to the executor in return for the stock is treated as a dividend rather than a sale or exchange. Why? Because the estate is deemed to own—both before and after the transaction—100 percent of the corporation's stock.

Under the attribution rules, the client's widow is deemed to own the 500 shares of stock actually owned by her two children. Of course, the widow also actually owns her own 250 shares. The client's estate is deemed to own the stock owned by its beneficiary, the client's widow. So, due to the attribution rules, before the redemption the estate is deemed to own 100 percent (1,000) of the 1,000 outstanding shares of the corporation. After the redemption, the estate

is still deemed to own 100 percent of the 750 shares still outstanding.

———————

There is a limited way to break this link between family members called a "waiver of family attribution."[19] The selling shareholder can waive (cut the string on) the family attribution rules and treat the transaction as a substantially disproportionate or complete termination of interest—but only if all three of the following additional requirements are met:

1. During ten years prior to the redemption, the selling shareholder must not have transferred any stock to or received any stock from someone from whom the stock would have been attributed to the seller (unless the seller can prove that the transfer did not have avoiding federal income taxes as one of its principal purposes).

2. Immediately after the redemption, the seller must have no interest in the corporation (other than as a creditor), including interests as an employee, officer, or director.

3. The seller must agree not to acquire any interest in the corporation (other than as a creditor) during the next ten years and to notify the IRS if a prohibited interest is acquired during this period.

Sale or Exchange by the Selling Shareholder

This last resort safe harbor is known as "Section 303 redemption." It applies only if the sale of stock occurs after a shareholder's death and thus will not protect the seller in a lifetime redemption. In general terms, to qualify for a Section 303 redemption and its protection against dividend treatment, the stock owned by the deceased shareholder must have comprised a substantial portion of his or her estate.

More specifically, Code section 303 allows sale or exchange treatment on the redemption of closely-held stock to the extent of the estate's federal and state death taxes, administrative expenses, funeral expenses and generation-skipping transfer taxes.

To qualify for this favorable treatment, the stock owned by the decedent must comprise more than 35 percent of the adjusted gross estate (defined as the decedent's gross estate less deductible losses and expenses).

Stock can be redeemed under the umbrella of section 303 only to the extent it generates an estate tax. So in many clients' estates, because of the unlimited marital deduction and the unified credit, the amount of stock that can be redeemed is minimal. Further limiting the usefulness of section 303 is the requirement that it applies only to the extent that the redeemed shareholder's interest is reduced directly (or through a binding obligation to contribute to the tax) by any payment of estate taxes or expenses. This makes it impossible for the trustee of the client's marital trust to safely sell stock back to the corporation under section 303 because such trusts specifically forbid the payment of taxes.

USING LIFE INSURANCE IN A BUY-SELL AGREEMENT

It is highly recommended that if at all possible the buy-sell be fully funded from inception. This is because the value of a business interest (and therefore the need for cash to buy that interest) increases because of the real value increases in the interest itself as well as because of inflationary growth. For instance, a business interest worth $500,000 today enjoying a 6 percent real growth and a 4 percent inflationary growth will be worth almost $1,300,000 just ten years from now and over $3,000,000 in twenty years.

Another reason full funding is imperative is that at the death of one owner, the value of the survivor's stock increases significantly. When there are three or more owners, this entails the purchase of more insurance at future dates.

To help meet future needs, it is strongly suggested that life insurance used to fund a buy-sell be purchased using dividends to buy paid up additions (blocks of additional permanent insurance purchased with no commissions or acquisition cost) and/or one year term insurance (pure term insurance with no commissions or acquisition cost). Alternatively, if universal life insurance is used, then option B (increasing death benefit) can be used to help meet future death benefit needs as the value of the business increases over time).

Split Dollar Arrangement

The split dollar technique is explained in detail in Chapter 41. Essentially, the corporation pays all or the bulk of the premium necessary to finance the insurance

that one shareholder buys on the life of another. To secure the repayment of its outlays, the corporation requires the policyowner to collaterally assign his interest to the firm. Under regulations issued in September 2003, the split dollar arrangement must either be a nonequity arrangement that falls within the economic benefit regime (the business is generally entitled to receive back the greater of its premium outlay or the policy cash value) or a loan arrangement that falls within the loan regime (the business is entitled to receive back its premium outlay only). For nonequity split dollar arrangements, the policyowner will either pay or be taxed on the economic benefit cost of the death benefit protection. For loan arrangements, the policyowner must pay or be taxed on market interest rates on the loans. If the policyowner pays or is taxed on less than market interest rates, the split dollar arrangement will be subject to the below market loan rules, which are discussed in detail in Chapter 41.

Transfer for Value Problems

A transfer for value problem can exist when a deceased shareholder's executor or administrator sells policies on the lives of the surviving stockholders. (See Chapter 25, "The Transfer for Value Rule.") There is both a transfer of a policy and consideration paid for the transfer—the two crucial elements required for the transfer for value rule to be invoked at the death of the insured.

Possible solutions include:

1. The estate can sell the policies it owns on the lives of surviving shareholders to the corporation, which can then establish a stock redemption plan, Section 303 partial redemption, or a wait and see buy-sell agreement that integrates properly with the existing cross purchase agreement.

2. The estate can surrender each policy to the insurer for cash. Surviving shareholders can then purchase additional life insurance on each other's life (assuming they are insurable). Premiums will be higher because the insureds will be older than when the surrendered policies were purchased. Poor health of the survivors or risk-taking avocations may result in rated premiums.

3. The survivors can purchase the policies on their own lives from the decedent shareholder's executor and continue them as personal

insurance. The proceeds will be received by the insured's beneficiaries income-tax free because a transfer of a policy to the insured is one of the exceptions to the transfer for value rule.

4. Perhaps the safest approach, if the circumstances are appropriate, is for a partnership consisting of the surviving partners to purchase the policies.

Using Group Term Insurance

The potential for a transfer for value problem exists where group term life insurance is used to fund a cross purchase agreement.

Example. Marcy S and Marsha R are two shareholder executives of the S&R Corporation. Each is covered for $500,000 under their company's group term life plan. Marcy S names Marsha R as her beneficiary and Marsha R names Marcy S as her beneficiary. Although no money changes hands between the two and even though the policies are term insurance, there is a transfer for valuable consideration. Their reciprocal promises to name each other as beneficiary provides the requisite valuable consideration. At the death of either, proceeds will be subject to ordinary income taxation.

Alternatives to Using Life Insurance

There are three ways other than life insurance to fund a buy-sell: (1) cash; (2) installment payments; and (3) borrowing. Each option presents its own considerations.

Cash

If the buy-out is to depend on cash:

1. How much will be needed?

2. Will after-tax dollars be kept on hand to finance the purchase?

3. Will a higher rate of return have to be sacrificed in order to have adequate cash on hand?

Installment Payments

If the buy-out is to depend on installment payments from the buyer to the seller:

1. Can the decedent-shareholder's family afford to leave large sums of money at the risk of the business?

2. Where will the deceased shareholder's family obtain cash to pay taxes, debts, and other immediate estate settlement costs?

3. What rate of interest will the decedent's family need to charge on the unpaid balance?

4. Will the interest paid by the buyer be deductible?

5. What will the total cost of payments be in terms of sales necessary to generate the cash to pay both principal and interest?

Borrowing

If the buy-out is to depend on borrowing from a bank or other third party:

1. Will the firm or the surviving shareholders be able to borrow money after the death or long-term disability of a shareholder-employee?

2. What rate of interest will be required on the unpaid balance—and will that interest be deductible?

3. How seriously will the cash drain affect corporate and personal reserves?

In most cases careful consideration of these factors will lead to the conclusion that life insurance is the best option for setting up a buy-sell arrangement.

FREQUENTLY ASKED QUESTIONS

Question – What should be done with existing life insurance where a corporation changes from a stock redemption to a cross purchase agreement?

Answer – In the case of a corporation that switches to a cross purchase from a stock redemption (perhaps to avoid or minimize the impact of any corporate AMT), planners should consider leaving currently owned corporate insurance on a reduced paid up basis (the cash values in the policies pay future premiums but the death benefit is reduced) and using that corporate coverage as key employee insurance. Parties to the agreement can then purchase new coverage without fear of violating the transfer for value rule. See Chapter 25 for further discussion of this rule.

Question – Can a trustee be used to solve the "multiple policy problem" when funding a cross purchase buy-sell?

Answer – Planners should beware of an often mentioned solution to the multiple policy problem in a cross purchase arrangement: the use of a trustee. It has been suggested that if the shareholders in a cross purchase agreement give cash to a trustee who will purchase insurance on each shareholder's life on behalf of the others, only one policy is necessary on each shareholder's life.

While this statement is correct, when the first shareholder dies, his estate still owns an interest in the policies he owned on the other shareholders' lives. When that interest is transferred to the other shareholders (regardless of the form of the transfer) who have beneficial interests in the trust, the surviving shareholders now have a right to insurance proceeds they did not have before. This could easily trigger an adverse income tax consequence under the transfer for value rule, as discussed in Chapter 25.

An alternative strategy is to use a partnership to own the insurance for the cross-purchase arrangement. Upon the death of an insured partner, the death proceeds can be distributed to the remaining partners who can use the proceeds to purchase the business interest of the deceased owner. Since all the owners are partners, transfer for value should not be an issue (however, it is suggested that the partnership owning the life insurance should have a valid business purpose).

Question – Is there a simplified way to explain Chapter 15's Code section 2703 and its implications to my clients?

Answer – Yes. In a nutshell, neither the IRS nor the courts will be bound for estate tax purposes to the price established in a buy-sell agreement unless the seller would in fact sell the interest to a totally independent nonfamily member for that price and that party (assuming reasonable knowledge of the relevant facts) would reasonably and without coercion pay that price.

Buy-sell agreements among related parties must now use an appraisal or a reasonable formula. Fixed prices set in buy-sells will probably not be accepted by the IRS or the courts as determinative of estate tax value no matter how reasonable when drafted.

Planners should review all buy-sell arrangements for compliance with the latest estate freeze rules and safe harbor requirements for buy-sell agreements. Many of these agreements should be revised to provide a more realistic price.

WHERE CAN I FIND OUT MORE?

The following references include authoritative discussions of how buy-sell agreements can be used:

1. Joseph B. Darby, *The Practical Guide to Mergers, Acquisitions and Business Sales* (National Underwriter 2017).

2. Stephan R. Leimberg et al. *The Tools and Techniques of Estate Planning*, 18th Ed. (National Underwriter 2017).

CHAPTER ENDNOTES

1.   I.R.C. §§264(a)(1), 265(a)(1).
2.   I.R.C. §101(a).
3.   I.R.C. §101(j).
4.   *Casale v. Comm'r.*, 247 F.2d 440 (2d Cir., 1957); Rev. Rul. 59-184, 1959-1 CB 65.
5.   *Doran v. Comm'r.*, 246 F.2d 934 (9th Cir. 1957); Rev. Rul. 59-184, 1959-1 CB 65.
6.   Treas. Reg. §1.61-2(d)(2).
7.   *Mountain State Steel Foundries, Inc. v. Comm'r.*, 284 F.2d 737 (4th Cir. 1960); *Oman Constr. Co. v. Comm'r.*, TC Memo 1965-325. But see also *John B. Lambert & Assoc. v. U.S.*, 76-1 USTC ¶9466 (Ct. Cl. 1976).
8.   I.R.C. §2042.
9.   I.R.C. §2033.
10. I.R.C. §2042.

11. *May v. McGowan*, 194 F.2d 396 (2nd Cir. 1952); *Comm'r. v. Child's Est.*, 147 F.2d 368 (3rd Cir 1945); *Comm'r. v. Bensel*, 100 F.2d 639 (3rd Cir. 1938); *Est. of Seltzer v. Comm'r.*, TC Memo 1985-519.

12. I.R.C. §2703.

13. *Est. of James v. Comm'r.*, 148 F.2d 236 (2nd Cir. 1945); *Kline v. Comm'r.*, 130 F.2d 742 (3rd Cir. 1942).

14. I.R.C. §1221.

15. I.R.C. §1014.

16. I.R.C. §1377(a)(2).

17. I.R.C. §301(a).

18. I.R.C. §316(a).

19. I.R.C. §302(c)(2).

CHARITABLE USES OF LIFE INSURANCE

CHAPTER 32

INTRODUCTION

A transfer of cash or other property to certain charitable, religious, scientific, educational, or other organizations may result in favorable income, gift, and estate tax results for the donor.[1] Income taxes can be reduced and estate taxes can be saved. More importantly, a gift to charity serves to reward the donor in significant psychological and moral ways. Charitable giving is one of the most important of all estate and financial planning considerations.

Life insurance is an important vehicle for accomplishing these tax and nontax objectives. It is used in one of two ways:

1. as a direct means of benefiting the charity; or

2. as a way to allow the donor to give other assets during lifetime or at death to charity without denying or reducing the financial security of his family. It may even serve as a form of wealth enhancement.

Wealth Replacement Strategies

Life insurance used as a wealth replacement tool enables a client to meet both charitable and personal objectives by assuring an immediate and certain gift to charity while also assuring his family that they will receive as much, if not more, than they would have received had no gift been made to charity. Since a qualified charity can sell assets contributed to it without an income tax liability on any gain, a client who lacks liquid assets can make a charitable gift of illiquid assets, while still affording the charity a source of cash through the sale of the assets.

Consider this technique as a way of enabling a business owner to harvest the fruits of a lifetime of labor without the penalty and loss of heavy income tax on any gain. Compare, for instance, the retirement income derived, net after taxes, from the sale of a family business with the income derived if the business is donated to a charitable remainder trust. The trustee of the trust could sell the business and pay the donor client an income for life or a term of years with 100 percent of the sales proceeds since the trust would pay no income tax on any appreciation inherent in the gift. Likewise, consider this technique as a way to enable a highly successful investor to convert taxable gain on an investment portfolio into retirement income without the income tax slippage inevitable upon a direct sale.

There are many ways the wealth replacement technique can be employed. One way is to create a charitable remainder trust funded with highly appreciated property that generates a low income yield. The client receives an annuity from the trust (a fixed annuity if the remainder trust is an annuity trust, or a variable annuity if the trust is a unitrust), with the remaining principal going to the qualified charity upon termination of the trust.[2] The advantages of this technique are:

1. The present value of the charity's right to receive the property when the noncharitable beneficiary's interest ends is currently deductible by the client.

2. Even if the property contributed to the trust has built-in gain, no tax on that appreciation is imposed on the client.

3. If, and when, the trustee sells the property, neither the client nor the trust must report any capital gains. However, part of the noncharitable

beneficiary's distributions from the trust may be treated as a distribution of capital gain and taxed at the time of distribution.

4. In many cases the client's income from the donated property will be significantly increased because the trustee will have been able to sell the property (at no tax to the trust) and use the net proceeds to invest in higher yielding securities. Had the client sold the property, his net investable amount would have been reduced by the tax on the gain. So, the tax savings as well as the higher return from the new investment enhance the yield from the trust.

A portion of the cash generated by both the client's immediate income tax deduction and from the increased return from the property can be given to the client's intended heirs. The heirs can choose to use that money to purchase insurance on the life of the client (and/or the client's spouse) so that, at the client's death, the wealth passing to charity through the trust is replaced. Note that replacement requires only the net amount that the intended heirs would have received had the client retained the asset, and had that property been subjected to state and federal death taxes and other transfer costs.

Using Life Insurance for Charitable Purposes

Life insurance can be used both during the client's lifetime and at death to make meaningful gifts to charity. Some of the strategies used to provide direct gifts of life insurance to charity include:

- Donation of existing insurance policies on the life of a client to a qualified charity.

- Purchase and donation to a charity of new insurance on the life of the client, the client's spouse, or both.

- Disposition by will of a policy on another's life to a charity. The value of the policy at the policy owner's death will be includable in his estate, but an equal and offsetting deduction will be allowed for the gift to the charity by will.

- Contribution of cash directly to a charity, which in turn uses that cash to purchase a new (or existing) policy on the life of the donor (or other supporter).

- Naming the charity revocable or irrevocable beneficiary of one or more life insurance contracts (individual or group).

- Contribution of an asset other than life insurance in order to generate an income tax deduction, which in turn can save the client money otherwise payable in tax. This tax savings can then be gifted to the client's children or other beneficiary (or to an irrevocable trust for their benefit) who could use that cash to purchase life insurance on the client's life, or on the life of the client's spouse. The charity receives an immediate and certain gift and the client's beneficiary receives what he would have received (or, in many cases, even more) after taxes had there been no charitable gift. This use of life insurance is often called wealth replacement.

WHEN IS THE USE OF THIS TECHNIQUE INDICATED?

1. When the client would like to benefit one or more charities for reasons other than tax savings.

2. When the client would like to benefit himself and/or his family through tax savings and create more income and capital at the same time a charity is benefited.

3. When a client would like to achieve the first and second objectives and is willing to incur expense to accomplish both. Planners and clients should both be aware that tax advantages do not mean a charitable gift is without cost. Charitable tax incentives may reduce the overall cost of the gift, and the achievement of noncharitable financial security goals may be facilitated through charitable giving techniques. But charitable giving should be considered as a planning tool only if the client has genuine charitable motives and has examined more direct alternatives for the accomplishment of noncharitable objectives.

Advantages

1. The death benefit of a life insurance contract owned by or payable to a charity is a guaranteed, self-completing gift; as long as the insurance is maintained in force by the payment of premiums

the charity is assured of the gift. If the client lives, cash values can be used as soon as they are available by the charity for an emergency or opportunity. These cash values will grow constantly year after year. If the client becomes disabled, the policy will remain in full force through the Waiver of Premium feature. This guarantees the ultimate death benefit to the charity, as well as the same cash values and dividend buildup that would have been earned had the client not become disabled. Even if the client were to die after only one premium payment, the charity is assured of the full intended gift. This distinguishes life insurance from other intended gifts through which the charity may or may not be the beneficiary, or may or may not receive what has been promised. So, the life insurance gift to the charity provides an immediate certainty rather than a mere expectation.

2. The life insurance gift is fixed in value and is not subject to the risks and price variations of the securities or real estate markets.

3. A client who might not otherwise be able to afford a significant gift can magnify the utility of a given number of dollars by leveraging them through life insurance. Through a relatively small fixed and budgetable annual cost (the premium), a significant benefit can be provided for the charity of the client's choice. Furthermore, premiums can be spread out over the client's lifetime, making the payment of the gift less burdensome.

4. Life insurance makes it possible to create a sizable gift without impairing or diluting a family's control over its other investments. Other assets earmarked for the client's family can be kept intact. The charity is benefited while the family's financial security is maintained and, perhaps, enhanced.

5. Life insurance is a cost effective means of making large charitable gifts. Life insurance is transferred free of probate, administrative fees, delays, or any other transfer costs. It is not subject to the claims of present or former spouses, or creditors. The charity, therefore, receives 100 percent of the money and is more certain of that receipt. This prompt and certain payment should be compared with the payment of a gift to the same charity by will.

6. A gift to charity through life insurance can be completely confidential. Conversely, if publicity is desired, it can be arranged very effectively; amplified gift can lead to public recognition. For instance, a charitable organization could establish a Millionaires Club consisting of individuals who donated a policy amounting to $1,000,000 or more.

7. Because of the contractual nature of the life insurance contract, large gifts to charity are seldom subjected to attack by disgruntled heirs.

Disadvantages

1. Life insurance requires the payment of a stream of dollars in the form of premiums. Fortunately, if unrestricted cash is given to a charity, which then uses those dollars to pay premiums on a policy insuring the donor (or some other individual), the client will receive a current income tax deduction.

2. Life insurance is typically a gift that will not benefit the charity until some future date. This is particularly true if the policy has not been assigned to or purchased and owned by the charity. Life insurance is not, therefore, the indicated means of providing for a charity that is desperate for cash to meet current operating expenses. (However, any charity that seeks to grow must eventually think of its long-term needs, and the use of life insurance in an effective planned giving program will help to insure the long-term financial stability of the organization.)

WHAT ARE THE REQUIREMENTS?

1. The gift of the policy or other property must be made to a qualified charity such as a nonprofit school or hospital, a church or synagogue, or a local or civic organization such as the Boy Scouts or Girl Scouts of America. Qualified means that the charity meets three conditions:

    (a) the organization is operated exclusively for religious, charitable, scientific, literary, or educational purposes, or to foster national or international amateur sports competition, or to prevent cruelty to children or animals;

    (b) no part of the earnings of the organization can be used to benefit any private shareholder or similar individual; and

    (c) the organization cannot be one disqualified for tax exemption because it attempts to influence legislation or participates in, publishes, or distributes statements for, or intervenes in, any political campaign on behalf of any candidate seeking public office.

2. The gift of the policy or other property must be made before the end of the taxable year, even if the client is an accrual basis taxpayer. (Corporations reporting income on the accrual basis are subject to a less stringent standard.[3])

3. The gift must be of the donor's entire interest; generally, no deduction will be allowed for a gift of a partial interest (unless strict and narrow rules are met). So in most cases where a policy will be co-owned, or the death proceeds, cash values, or dividends will be split between noncharitable and charitable beneficiaries, no deduction will be allowed.[4]

4. Records must be kept, preferably in the form of canceled checks payable to the charity and/or a receipt from the charity showing the date, amount, and identity of the donor and donee.

5. The gift must exceed any benefit the client receives from the charity. If the client receives a benefit from the charity in conjunction with his gift, the deduction will be limited to the excess of the amount donated over the value of the benefit received from the charity.

Insurable Interest

Assume your client purchases a policy on her life and donates it to a charity in a state in which the charity has no insurable interest in the client's life. The IRS could argue that under state law the decedent's estate (and therefore her heirs) could claim the policy proceeds in spite of the charity's ownership because the charity has no insurable interest. The IRS could then argue that the client's ostensible transfer of all her rights really gave the charity less than her entire interest in the policy. The IRS would state that even though the donor clearly thought she gave all the interest she actually had, because her estate could claim an interest in the proceeds, she was actually in control of the proceeds. The IRS would then seek to disallow income, gift, and estate tax deductions and include the proceeds in the insured's estate, which would be the worst of all possible tax consequences.[5]

Practitioners must carefully read the precise wording of applicable state law. Under New York law, for example, a charity has an insurable interest only if the insured is the policy purchaser and transferor.[6] The statute does not appear to apply to a transfer where one spouse purchases a contract on the other spouse's life and then assigns it to the charity, nor where the charity itself is the purchaser. Other states (Georgia, for example) provide that any institution that meets the Internal Revenue Code definition of a qualified charity has an insurable interest in the life of any donor.

Life insurance carriers generally look not only at whether an insurable interest exists, but also examine the extent of the insurable interest as part of their financial underwriting. For example, they may examine the donor's history of giving to the charity and limit the amount of death benefit to what it would take to replace that amount.

Substantiation Rules

Substantiation rules set out the requirements that a donor must meet in order to document the value of the charitable gift. Failure to meet these requirements will result in the deduction for the charitable contribution being disallowed by the IRS. A gift of a life insurance policy is considered a noncash gift, and the substantiation requirements vary based on the value of the gift.

Less than $250

The donor should obtain a receipt from the charitable organization showing:

1. the name of the charitable organization;

2. the date and location of the charitable contribution; and

3. a reasonably detailed description of the property.

Additional records must also be kept as detailed in IRS Publication 526.

Between $250 and $500

The charity provides the donor with a contemporaneous *written acknowledgement* of the contribution showing the same information listed above. The same additional records must also be kept.

Between $500 and $5,000

The requirements for noncash gifts of greater than $250 are met, more detailed additional records are kept, and the donor must complete Section A of IRS Form 8283, which provides:

- the charity's name and address;

- a description of property;

- how and when the donor acquired the property;

- basis;

- fair market value;

- method by which the property was valued.

More than $5,000

The requirements for noncash gifts of greater than $5,000 must be met and a "qualified appraisal" is required. Under Code section 170(f)(11)(E) neither the donor nor the insurance agent (or insurer who issued the policy) can perform this appraisal. Section B of IRS Form 8283 must be completed. A qualified appraisal must include the following information:

- A description of the property in sufficient detail to determine that the property appraised is in fact the property transferred to charity

- The date of the contribution

- The valuation date

- Information about the qualified appraiser, including qualifications and relationship to the donor

- The appraised fair market value of the property

- The methodologies used in determining the valuation

Like closely held stock, charitable gifts of life insurance will generally be subject to the deduction limitations for gifts of ordinary income property. Obtaining a qualified appraisal for a life insurance policy can be difficult since neither the issuing insurance company nor the donor's agent would be allowed to perform the appraisal. It is likely that the IRS would accept an appraisal by another insurance agent, CLU, ChFC, or insurance analyst.

The value of a life insurance policy for charitable deduction purposes is its replacement cost. The manner in which replacement cost is determined depends on the nature of the policy. If the policy is a single-premium or paid-up policy, then the value of the policy is the amount the company would charge for a single premium contract of the same amount on the life of the insured as of the date of the gift.[7]

If the policy requires additional premiums, the value is the interpolated terminal reserve, increased by unused premiums and accumulated dividends, less outstanding loans against the policy.[8] If the policy is newly issued, the value of the policy is the premium paid to bring the policy into force.[9]

A donor should never transfer a life insurance policy that is subject to a loan because such a transfer may result in application of the bargain sale rules and could trigger immediate partial taxation upon the transfer of the policy. Note also, that donors contributing life insurance policies with any loan—no matter how small—will be barred from ever deducting either the value of the policy itself or subsequent premiums.

HOW IT IS DONE

Life insurance creates an instant expanded estate, and in many cases the proceeds can be transferred free of estate tax. If arranged properly, all parties could end up with a greater economic benefit than if life insurance were not used. Below is a more detailed explanation of some of the strategies used to provide for charity through indirect uses of life insurance:

1. A charity can be named as the annual recipient of any dividends received from life insurance. As dividends are paid to the charity, the client receives a current income tax deduction.

2. Dividends from an existing policy can be used to purchase a new policy. The client can name the charity as the owner and beneficiary of the new policy. An income tax deduction is allowed for the premiums paid by the client.

3. A charity can be named as contingent (backup) beneficiary or final beneficiary under a life insurance policy protecting dependents of a

client. Should a primary beneficiary predecease the client, the charity will receive the proceeds, assuming the client does not have the opportunity or desire to change the beneficiary. Because the policy itself is never transferred to charity the proceeds are subject to estate tax. However, the proceeds will qualify for the unlimited federal estate tax charitable deduction and will offset the estate tax liability.

4. A charity can be named as the beneficiary of a currently owned or a newly acquired life insurance policy. Although this strategy will not yield a current income tax deduction and the proceeds will be included in the client's gross estate, it will result in a federal estate tax deduction for the full amount of the proceeds payable to charity, regardless of how large the policy.

5. An absolute assignment (gift) of a currently owned life insurance policy can be made to a charity. Alternatively, a new life insurance policy can be purchased and immediately transferred to the charity. Either strategy will yield a current income tax deduction.

6. Group term life insurance can be used to meet charitable objectives. By naming a charity as the (revocable) beneficiary of group term life insurance for coverage over $50,000, a client can make a significant gift to charity while avoiding any income tax on the economic benefit.

Example. A sixty-six-year-old executive with an average top tax bracket of 40 percent who had $1,050,000 of coverage would save $6,096 each year, 40 percent of the $15,240 annual Table I cost (the amount reportable as income). The advantage of this technique was significantly enhanced by the introduction of higher group term rates for individuals over age sixty-five who receive group term insurance. So the client saves income taxes every year the charity is named as beneficiary. In a later year if the client changes his mind, he can change the beneficiary designation and name a new charity or even a personal beneficiary. Note that the charity must be the sole beneficiary for the entire tax year.

7. Property can be donated directly to a charity and life insurance can be used to replace the wealth that might otherwise have been received by the client's children.

Example. Your client, a widow in a 40 percent combined state and federal income tax bracket, contributes property worth $100,000 to a tax-exempt charitable entity such as Temple University. Assuming the client is entitled to a deduction on the full value of the gift, the $40,000 that she otherwise would have paid in income taxes is instead still available to her. She can choose to give the tax savings from the charitable gift to her child or grandchild who can, in turn, purchase and maintain insurance on her life.

Assume the amount of the insurance is at least enough to make up for the property the heirs would have received had no gift been made to charity. Life insurance takes the place of the net after-tax (and other cost) assets the heirs would have received had no planning been accomplished and had no gift to charity been made. In some cases the heirs will be able to take the tax savings realized by the client and purchase insurance to cover the value of the assets they would have received (after federal and state death taxes) had no gift been made. Here, life insurance is used to provide wealth replacement. Alternatively, they could purchase enough insurance to receive what they would have been left by the client had there been no estate tax on the property that was given to charity. In this case, life insurance provides wealth enhancement.

Gifts to a Charity vs. Gifts "For the Use of" a Charity

The mechanics of a gift of life insurance to a charity can determine how much is deductible by a client in a given year. Gifts of life insurance are more valuable when they are made directly to rather than for the use of a charity. For instance, if a client pays premiums to the insurance company on a policy owned by a charity on his life, it is true that he is indirectly helping the charity, but this form of payment of the premiums is deductible as a gift for the use of the charity and the deduction in a given year, maximum, will thus be limited to only 30 percent of the client's adjusted gross income.

If the client makes a direct cash gift to the charity, the gift will certainly be deductible up to 50 percent of his adjusted gross income (assuming the gift is to a public charity).[10] Direct cash gifts to charity in the form of checks also make it easier for the client to substantiate:

- the fact of the gift;

- the identity of the charitable donee;

- the timing of the gift; and

- that the donee did in fact receive the gift.

Direct gifts are therefore less likely to cause an audit or generate litigation, and are the recommended way to secure a deduction for gifts to be used to pay premiums.

Policies Subject to Loans

A gift of a life insurance policy subject to a loan may, in certain circumstances, cause significant tax problems including: (1) generating taxable income to the donor under the bargain sale rules; (2) generating taxable income to the charity under rules relating to charitable unrelated business taxable income; and (3) imposing excise tax penalties under the charitable prohibited transaction rules.

Bargain Sale Problem

When encumbered property is contributed to a charity, the donor is treated as if he cashed in the policy, received an amount equal to the loan; as reportable income, and made a gift of the difference.[11] Technically, bargain sale rules apply and treat the contribution as two separate transactions: (a) the client is treated as if he sold part of the policy to the charity with the charity paying him an amount equal to the loan; and (b) the client is then treated as if he made a gift of the net value of the policy to the charity.

Unrelated Business Taxable Income (UBTI) Problem

All tax-exempt organizations, including charities, are treated as if they are taxable to the extent they receive UBTI. Essentially, UBTI is income received by the tax-exempt organization or entity that is unrelated to its tax-exempt purpose.[12] However, the definition of UBTI also includes debt-financed income. This is income generated through borrowing on a charity owned asset to finance the purchase of another income-producing asset.[13] If a charity borrows against the cash values of a life insurance policy in order to buy income-producing assets, the IRS may classify the income produced by the new investment as debt-financed income. The income produced by the new investment may be considered unrelated business taxable income and taxed to the charity at corporate tax rates.

For instance, assume a private foundation owned and was the beneficiary of life insurance policies with cash values in excess of $2,000,000. Assume further that the foundation borrows against the cash surrender at about 5 percent and finds a way to invest the borrowed funds in marketable government securities yielding more than 10 percent. The IRS, in such a situation, would argue that the income from the newly purchased marketable securities was passive income generated from debt-financed property and, thus, UBTI.

The solution is simple: charities should borrow against the cash surrender values of life insurance policies only for cash needs of the charity, and not to invest in other income-producing assets. For instance, there should be no problem if the charity in the example above borrowed $2,000,000 from policies it owned in financing the purchase of a new building to provide care for disabled children.

With the advent of interest sensitive, variable, and universal life contracts, borrowing from a life insurance policy by a charity to achieve current rates of return is no longer necessary. Most importantly, life insurance owned on many lives by a charity can serve as a money pump to deliver millions of dollars to an important charity.

Prohibited Transaction Problem

This problem relates only to transfers of encumbered policies to private foundations (organizations that receive a significant part of their support from one or more specific sources, rather than from the general public). Gifts to private foundations are subject to harsh and complex prohibited transaction rules intended to prevent the abuse of their tax-exempt status by related parties.

These abuses include:

1. self-dealing between the entity and certain disqualified persons (including the donor);[14]

465

2. holding more control of a closely held corporation or unincorporated business than a Code specified maximum;[15] and

3. the purchase and maintenance of investments that jeopardize the exempt purpose of the charity (so-called jeopardy investments).[16] (Unfortunately, many of these same rules may also apply to transactions between related parties and charitable lead trusts or charitable remainder trusts.)

Certain gifts to a private foundation of life insurance subject to a policy loan have been held to violate the prohibitions against self-dealing and jeopardy investments. Prohibitions against self-dealing, particularly where the client who sets up the foundation gains an unfair advantage from his dealing with the trust at taxpayers' (federal treasury) expense, can result in severe tax consequences. Any lending of money from the foundation to the donor, and most sales or exchanges of property as well as transfers of mortgaged property, could trigger a self-dealing excise tax penalty.

Where does a life insurance policy subject to a loan fit into this set of rules? Assume the client gives a life insurance policy on his life to a private foundation. Assume further that the policy was subject to a loan. The client, as a donor, would be considered a disqualified person by the IRS. This means he is prohibited from engaging in certain related-party transactions with the foundation. According to the IRS, a private foundation commits a prohibited act of self-dealing if it takes an asset subject to a mortgage or similar lien that a disqualified person placed on the property within the ten-year period ending on the date of the transfer. So in the example, the IRS could treat the policy loan as a mortgage or similar lien for purposes of applying the excise tax on acts of self-dealing in private foundations. The IRS might characterize the client's relief from the loan by the foundation as an act of self-dealing and impose prohibited transaction penalty taxes.

Generally, the problems described in this question will rarely occur when competent counsel is present and the policy in question is financially sound. Note also that it is not life insurance, per se, which causes the problem, but rather the acceptance and payment by the foundation or trust of the donor's debt and obligation to pay interest and principal on the policy loan. If there is no policy loan and the insurer is financially sound, there should be no problem with life insurance.

TAX IMPLICATIONS

Income Tax

A current income tax deduction is allowed for the transfer of a cash value life insurance policy to a qualified charity. The client will save an amount equal to the value of the deductible gift multiplied by the client's effective tax bracket. For example, a $10,000 gift by a client in a 40 percent combined federal and state income tax bracket will yield a $4,000 tax savings. This means the cost of the gift is lowered to the amount contributed less the tax savings. In this example, the gift cost $6,000 ($10,000 – $4,000).

The deduction for a charitable gift of a life insurance policy is subject to the same limitations as other charitable gifts.[17] One such limitation relates to the amount of a current deduction allowed based on a percentage of the donor's adjusted gross income in that year.[18]

A second limitation is that to be deductible the gift must be total and absolute. An outright gift of all of the incidents of ownership and all rights and benefits in a life insurance policy will be deductible up to the allowable percentage of the donor's income. A gift of less than the client's entire interest in a life insurance policy (or any other asset) will be deductible only if it constitutes one of the following interests:[19]

- A remainder interest in a qualified charitable remainder unitrust or annuity trust

- A remainder interest in a pooled income fund

- A charitable gift annuity

- A remainder interest in a personal residence or farm

- A qualified conservation easement

- An undivided portion of the taxpayer's entire interest in property

- A guaranteed annuity interest or unitrust interest in a charitable lead trust

In other words, a client can usually deduct the value (as defined below) of a life insurance policy given to charity (or to an irrevocable charitable trust). Furthermore, after a complete and irrevocable gift of the policy, the client can deduct any premiums paid after the transfer of the policy to the charity (or to an irrevocable charitable trust).[20] However, no deduction will be allowed for any portion of the gift unless the client donates to the charity either his entire interest or an undivided portion of his entire interest in the policy. A gift of an undivided portion of a policy would include a fraction or percentage of each and every substantial right in the policy. Alternatively, a deduction for a gift of a partial interest in property will be permitted if the partial interest is the client's entire interest in the property.[21]

A gift of the cash value will be considered a transfer of less than the client's entire interest regardless of whether the client: (a) retains a continuing right to name some other party as the recipient of the net amount at risk (i.e., the pure death benefit); or (b) irrevocably designated the recipient of the death benefit before making the gift of the cash value to charity.[22]

If a client creates a split-dollar plan with a qualified charity, under which he contributes to the charity the policy's cash surrender value but designates a noncharitable beneficiary as owner of the death benefit, the IRS will not allow an income tax deduction.[23]

Some flexibility is allowed where the client retains a very limited right that cannot be used for the client's personal benefit. For instance, it appears a client can make a gift of a life insurance policy and reserve the right, exercisable only in conjunction with the donee charity, to add another qualified charity as beneficiary, change the portion of the proceeds one or more qualified charities will receive, or even shift all of the proceeds to another qualified charity. Technically, the IRS has reasoned in such situations that even though the donor shares with the charitable owner of the insurance policy the right to designate other qualified charitable recipients, the donor has still made a charitable gift of any rights he held in the policy and, therefore, the gift is not considered a gift of a partial interest.[24]

Merely naming a charity as the beneficiary of a life insurance policy will not result in an income tax deduction, even if the designation is irrevocable. This follows the rule discussed above that the charity must be given the client's entire interest in the policy. If the charity is named only as beneficiary, regardless of whether that designation is revocable or irrevocable, the policy proceeds will be includable in the client's gross estate. But when the death benefit is paid to the charity, the client's estate will be allowed an offsetting charitable deduction.

There is an important exception to this all or nothing rule: an employee who names a charity as the beneficiary of the total death benefit (or at least the entire amount in excess of the first $50,000) under a group term life insurance policy on his life for the entire tax year can exclude from income the value of the otherwise taxable coverage attributable to the charitable portion of the proceeds.[25] This charitable technique can shield considerable amounts from income tax; yet, the client can retain the flexibility to change his mind the following year and name a personal beneficiary. The cost of this exclusion from income taxation is that the term coverage will remain in the client's estate and, unless actually paid at death to the designated charity, will generate federal estate tax.

Amount of Deduction

When all incidents of ownership in an existing life insurance policy are donated to charity, the transfer is treated as a gift of ordinary income property in the year it is assigned absolutely to the charity. This means the donor must reduce his contribution amount by the gain that would have been realized had he cashed in the policy or sold it.[26] The policy owner will be entitled to a current income tax deduction.

The amount of the deduction for a charitable gift of a life insurance policy is generally the lower of: (a) the fair market value of the policy; or (b) the donor's cost basis.[27] Stated another way, where the policy's value at the date of the gift is greater than the net premiums the client has paid, the deduction will be limited to the client's net premiums so in most cases, the donor's deduction will be limited to basis.

Fair market value is dependent on the replacement cost of the policy. This depends on which of the following is involved:

1. *Newly Issued Policy* – Typically, the deduction for a policy transferred immediately after its issue or within its first year is based on the net (gross premium less dividends, if any) premium payments made by the date of the transfer.

2. *Premium Paying Policy* – The deduction value is for the sum of the interpolated terminal reserve plus any unearned premium at the date of the gift. The term "unearned premium" is defined as the unexpired payment to the insurer between the date of the gift and the premium due date after the gift. Dividends accrued to the date of the gift are also added. Any loans against the policy are subtracted.

3. *Paid-up or Single Premium Policy* – The deduction is based on the single premium the same insurer would charge for a policy of the same amount at the insured's attained age.[28]

If the insured is in impaired health, it could be argued (by both the taxpayer in charitable giving cases and the IRS in noncharitable situations) that adverse health increases the value of the gift to charity. This argument is logical since impaired health to some extent must affect life expectancy. To this point, however, there are no rulings, nor is there a formal IRS position on the subject.

Deductions for Payment of Premiums

Premiums are generally deductible on policies contributed to or owned by charity. Once a policy is donated to or purchased on the donor's life by the charity, subsequent premiums are deductible if: (a) paid in cash to the charity; or (b) paid directly to the insurer. Cash payments made directly to a qualified charity will qualify for a current deduction of up to 50 percent of the donor's adjusted gross income. The current deduction for premium payments made to the insurer (but for the use of charity) may be limited to 30 percent of the donor's adjusted gross income. The charity could, of course, use other money to pay premiums if the client decided to discontinue contributions.

It makes no difference whether premiums are paid all at once (such as in a single premium policy) or over just a few years (such as in a suspended premium arrangement). The deduction will, nevertheless, be allowed in the year the donor parts with dominion and control over the cash. Note that if the client merely collaterally assigns the policy to the charity as security for a note, premiums he pays on the policy will not be deductible. This makes sense because the charity is not the absolute owner of the policy and the policy could easily end up in the client's hands if he pays off the note.

Gifts of Annuities

A charitable gift of an annuity issued after April 22, 1987, whether the gift occurs in the year of maturity or before it matures, will result in the immediate recognition of gain. When the donor gives the contract to charity, it is treated for income tax purposes as if he surrendered it. Reportable gain is equal to the excess of: (a) the cash surrender value at the time of the gift; over (b) the client's investment in the contract. But in return, since the client must currently recognize the gain as ordinary income, that amount becomes part of the client's basis and so the entire value of the annuity given to charity is fully deductible.[29]

AMT Implications

The AMT is a tax designed to assure that individuals who pay little or no regular income tax, because they have taken advantage of certain exclusion, deduction, and credit obtaining techniques called "preferences," will pay at least this minimum tax. Ironically, many of these preferences are in reality tax incentives designed to encourage taxpayers to take certain risks or make certain investments or contributions that are deemed to be in the public interest. So, on the one hand, Congress encourages the action and, on the other hand, it seeks to discourage the same pattern of behavior by diminishing the tax benefits for the same action.

For tax years beginning before 1993, the major preference item in terms of charitable giving was a contribution of appreciated property. Specifically, the unrealized gain inherent in a gift of long-term capital gain property was considered a preference item for purposes of the AMT. However, for taxable years beginning after 1992, a charitable contribution of appreciated property is no longer treated as a tax preference. As a result, if a taxpayer makes a gift to charity of long-term capital gain property that is real property, intangible property, or tangible personal property, the use of which is related to the donee's tax-exempt purpose, the taxpayer is allowed to claim a deduction for both regular tax and AMT purposes in the amount of the property's fair market value (subject to applicable percentage limitations).[30]

Since life insurance is an ordinary income type asset and a donation of life insurance is not considered a preference item, and since the receipt of insurance proceeds will not be taxable in any way to the charity, it does not present AMT problems in and of itself.

Gift Tax Implications

Regardless of the size of the gift of life insurance, no federal gift taxes are payable on transfers to qualified charities, but there is an important qualification, especially where life insurance policies are involved. A gift tax charitable deduction is allowed without limit for an outright transfer of a new or existing life insurance contract but, except in certain defined situations, any deduction will be denied if the transfer is of less than an entire interest in the policy.[31]

For instance, your client would not be allowed a gift tax charitable deduction for a gift of a split-dollar policy between an individual and a charity. In such situations, the insured's gift of the right to the cash surrender value of the policy is a gift of a partial interest, less than the donor's entire interest in the property and, consequently, does not meet one of the exceptions that will qualify the gift for a charitable deduction. Note that this disallowance cannot be avoided by having the client make an irrevocable designation of a personal beneficiary before making the gift to the charity.

In addition, if a policy is donated to a charity in a state where the charity has no insurable interest in the insured's life, and the lack of such an interest is deemed to give the insured's estate some rights to control the ultimate disposition of the proceeds, the IRS will disallow the deduction on the grounds that the insured retained an incident of ownership.[32] It would seem that if the charity was the original policy purchaser, even where statutory law gives the insured's estate some right over the ultimate disposition of the proceeds, it could not be said that the insured retained some right since he never had it. But smart planners will avoid the issue and check state law to be sure that insurable interest in the life of the insured is not a problem.

Estate Tax Implications

If a client holds any incident of ownership in the policy at death, regardless of whether the charity owns the policy or whether a charity has been irrevocably named as the beneficiary of the proceeds, the entire amount of the payment made by the insurer at the insured's death will be subject to federal estate tax in the insured's gross estate.[33] (See Chapter 27 for a discussion of what constitutes an incident of ownership.)

If a client assigns all incidents of ownership in a life insurance contract to a charity, and survives for more than three years after the transfer, the policy should be excludable from the donor's estate for federal estate tax purposes.

Gifts of life insurance made at death to a qualified charity (as well as those made prior to death to charity that for some reason were brought back into the client's gross estate) are includable in a client's estate, but will receive a federal estate tax charitable deduction. This deduction is unlimited. The policy proceeds could amount to millions

of dollars or more and, regardless of how large, could be left to a qualified charity and the estate tax charitable deduction would eliminate the federal estate tax the proceeds would otherwise have generated.[34]

However, even though the estate tax on the insurance paid to charity may be entirely eliminated, there may be a cost. The inclusion of the life insurance may adversely affect the estate's ability to qualify for the benefits of: Section 303 partial stock redemptions; Code section 6166 (installment payments of estate tax); and (before 2004) Code Section 2057 deduction for Qualified family-Owned Business Interest, (QFOBI).

Once again, however, there is an important qualification. As is the case with both the income and gift tax laws, for estate tax purposes the deduction will be disallowed if the entire interest in property is not transferred to the charity. This is due to the fact that if the insured has not given up each and every incident of ownership he owns, he continues to hold a property interest in the policy. This is sufficient to cause estate tax inclusion of the entire proceeds no matter how seemingly small that incident is.

Tax Implications for the Charity

No tax is paid by the charity upon receipt of either a lifetime gift of a life insurance policy or a bequest of a policy at death. Likewise, the payment of premiums by a charity on a policy it owns and is the beneficiary of will not generate a gift tax to the original donor of the policy.

Income earned by a charity on assets it owns generally will not be subject to income tax. But as noted below, if a charity borrows policy cash values to finance the purchase of income producing investments, the income produced by these investments may be considered unrelated business taxable income and result in a tax to the otherwise tax-exempt charity.[35]

WEALTH ENHANCEMENT TRUSTS

Some professionals refer to the combination of life insurance and a charitable remainder trust as a "Wealth Enhancement Trust." Through a combination of charitable trust planning and life insurance replacement of wealth, beneficiaries may receive more wealth than if no charitable gift were made. This is sometimes referred to as wealth enhancement rather than mere wealth replacement.

Charitable remainder trusts are generally exempt from income taxes. This enables a client to convert highly appreciated property such as stock, real estate, or even a business interest into income-producing assets without the amount of capital being used to produce income being reduced by any capital gains taxes. Thus, the entire value of the property, undiminished by federal or state taxes, is available for investment. The increased income produced (over that which would have been produced had the contributed asset been sold and the after-tax proceeds reinvested) can then be used to pay for wealth replacement life insurance.

Example. Suppose a client is a sixty-year-old widow with five children. Assume she is in the 40 percent combined state and federal income tax bracket and in a 45 percent estate tax bracket. One of her assets is a $1,000,000 parcel of undeveloped land she bought for $100,000 many years ago. She wants to perpetuate the memory of her late father. However, she needs additional income for retirement and wants to be sure her children, one of whom is handicapped, have sufficient financial security at her death.

If she does nothing, the client's five children will receive only $550,000 of her $1,000,000 parcel of land. Federal death taxes alone will consume the other $450,000 of the asset. Under this scenario, the charity will receive nothing. Alternatively, the client could transfer the land to a Charitable Remainder Annuity Trust or Unitrust (a CRAT or CRUT). Assume she retains an annuity or unitrust interest for life with an annual percentage payout of 5.3 percent. In the case of a CRAT, she will receive a fixed annuity of $53,000 per year (0.053 × $1,000,000) for life. In the case of a CRUT, she will be paid $53,000 in the first year and a future annuity of 5.3 percent of the value of the trust funds as revalued at the beginning of each year, with payments continuing for as long as she lives.

Assume that the most favorable Section 7520 rate allowable is 5.0 percent.[36] If she sets up a CRAT, she will receive a $370,620 income tax charitable deduction. See Figure 32.1. If she sets

Figure 32.1

CHARITABLE REMAINDER ANNUITY TRUST
(One Life – Table 90CM)

Transfer to Trust:	$1,000,000	Annuity Payment:	$53,000
Age:	60	Frequency of Payments:	Annual
Payments:	End of Period	Section 7520 Interest Rate:	5.0%
Check Possibility Charity Will Not Receive Interest			
Annuity Factor Exhaustion:	18.8679	Years to Exhaust Trust:	59
Mortality L(119):	0	Mortality L(60):	85537
Possibility:	0.0%	5% or Less Possibility Test Passed	
Check Exhaustion of Trust Fund			
Ann. Factor (50 years, 5.0%):	18.2559	Adj. Factor (Annual, 5.0%):	1.0000
Annuity Test Value:	$967,563	Special Factors:	Not Required
Valuation			
Ann. Factor (Age 60, 5.0%):	11.8751	Adj. Factor (Annual, 5.0%):	1.0000
Annuity Value:	$629,380	Charitable Contribution:	$370,620

Source: Trust Calculator (part of *The Ultimate Trust Resource*, a National Underwriter Company publication).

Figure 32.2

CHARITABLE REMAINDER UNITRUST (One Life – Table 90CM)			
Transfer to Trust:	$1,000,000	Unitrust Payout Rate:	5.3%
Age:	60	Frequency of Payments:	Annual
Months Until First Payment:	0	Section 7520 Interest Rate:	5.0%
Adjusted Payout Rate Factor (Annual, 0 months, 5.0%):			1.000000
Adjusted Payout Rate [5.3% × 1.000000]:			5.300%
One Life Unitrust Remainder Factor (Age 60, 5.2%):			.37761
One Life Unitrust Remainder Factor (Age 60, 5.4%):			.36542
Difference [.37761 – .36542]:			01219
Interpolation Adjustment (5.300%):			00609
Unitrust Remainder Factor [.37761 – .00609]:			.37152
Charitable Contribution [$1,000,000 × .37152]:			$371,520
Unitrust Value [$1,000,000 – $371,520]:			$628,480
Source: Trust Calculator (part of *The Ultimate Trust Resource*, a National Underwriter Company publication).			

up a CRUT, she will receive a $371,520 deduction. See Figure 32.2.

The charitable gift to the CRAT would result in an income tax savings of $148,248 (0.40 × $370,620). This is about 14.8 percent of the transfer to trust ($148,248 ÷ $1,000,000). The charitable gift to a CRUT would result in an income tax savings of $148,608 (0.40 × $371,520). This is about 14.9 percent of the transfer to trust ($148,608 ÷ $1,000,000).

Note that the client's return in either case is based on the entire value of the capital contributed to the charitable trust ($1,000,000), rather than what it would have been if she sold the land for $1,000,000, paid income taxes of $135,000 [15 percent capital gain tax rate on the $900,000 ($1,000,000 amount realized – $100,000 basis)] of gain on the land], and invested the $865,000 ($1,000,000 sales proceeds – $135,000 tax) difference. The result can be a significantly higher return.

The client then transfers: (a) income tax deduction generated savings[37]: and/or (b) a portion of the income retained from the charitable remainder trust as a gift to one or more individuals. They, in turn, could use that money to purchase insurance on her life to replace the wealth transferred to the charitable trust and enhance the net after-tax wealth they would have received.

The major advantage is that the client receives an immediate income tax deduction for the present value of what the charity will someday receive. The tax savings is then given to a personal beneficiary who purchases life insurance on the life of the client, the client's spouse, or the survivor of the two, in order to replace the wealth provided to charity. Because the insurance is not in the client's estate, it is not subject to state and federal death taxes and is exempt from the claims of the client's creditors.

Payouts from a CRAT or CRUT

The annual payout to the noncharitable beneficiary must be at least 5 percent and not exceed 50 percent of:

1. the initial fair market value of the property contributed to the trust (in the case of a charitable remainder annuity trust); or

2. the net fair market value of the trust's assets determined at least annually (in the case of a charitable remainder unitrust).

In addition, the value of the remainder interest in a charitable remainder trust must be a least 10 percent of the value of assets contributed in the trust. In the case of a CRAT, the value of the remainder interest must be at least 10 percent of the initial fair market value of all property placed in the trust; in the case of a CRUT, the 10 percent requirement applies to each contribution of property to the trust. The value of the remainder interest in either event is calculated using the Section 7520 interest rate, which is published monthly by the IRS.

In the event that an additional contribution is made to an existing CRUT that does not meet the 10 percent remainder interest requirement, it will not cause the trust to cease being treated as a CRUT, but it will be treated as a transfer to a separate trust that is not a CRUT.[38]

Using a Last-to-die Policy in Conjunction with a Joint-and-survivor Charitable Remainder Trust

In many cases the client will be married and will wish to provide financial security beyond his death for his surviving spouse's life. Here, planners should consider a joint and survivor charitable remainder trust that provides an annuity or unitrust amount to the client and his spouse for life. After the death of one spouse, the annuity or unitrust amount will continue to be paid to the surviving spouse. Upon the death of the surviving spouse, the trust assets will then be paid to the charity. Because of the federal estate tax marital deduction, at the first spouse's death, there should be no federal estate tax imposed on the present value of the annuity that continues for the surviving spouse's life. Using the same annuity trust and unitrust examples as presented above, and assuming the client is sixty years old and has a fifty-eight-year-old spouse, the calculations would be as shown in Figure 32.3 for a CRAT and Figure 32.4 for a CRUT.

Note that the charitable deduction for the remainder interest is reduced when the value of the noncharitable payout is increased by making payouts for two lives, rather than just for one life. In the case of a CRAT, the deduction is reduced from $370,620 (one life) to $240,266 (two lives). In the case of a CRUT, the deduction is reduced from $371,520 (one life) to $247,450 (two lives).

Since the client's federal estate tax liability on assets not in the charitable remainder trust will not be triggered until the second spouse's death, insurance placement can be more flexible. A policy can be purchased on the client's life, his spouse's life, or a last-to-die policy can be purchased on the lives of the couple since it will not be until the proceeds are payable under this latter policy that estate taxes will be due and the income from the charitable remainder trust will stop.

FREQUENTLY ASKED QUESTIONS

Question – How can life insurance combined with gifts of stock to charity help a client keep a family business in the family?

Answer – Life insurance can be used creatively to combine business continuity objectives and charitable goals in a number of ways. For instance, suppose your client wants to benefit charity, provide liquidity for her own estate, and guarantee that no one but her son can obtain the stock. One possible solution is for her to transfer stock to the charity directly. She could make a gift to her son of the income tax savings that the donation of stock generates. He could use those tax savings to purchase insurance on his mother's life and enter into a buy-sell agreement to assure him that at her death he will have the money to buy her out. At some time in the future, the corporation could purchase the stock from the charity after an arm's-length valuation. This provides the charity with cash and returns the stock to the corporation.

Question – Suppose a client has a very large estate and believes that if he gives his children too much when he dies, he will limit their personal growth incentives. Also, he is charitably inclined. If he leaves his entire estate to his children, his charitable objectives will not have been met and estate taxes will consume a large portion of his estate. He also knows that if he leaves his entire estate to charity, his children will have no financial security. How can life insurance be used to solve this problem?

Figure 32.3

CHARITABLE REMAINDER ANNUITY TRUST (Two Lives – Table 90CM)			
Transfer to Trust:	$1,000,000	Annuity Payment:	$53,000
First Age:	60	Second Age:	58
Frequency of Payments:	Annual	Payments:	End of Period
Section 7520 Interest Rate:	5.0%		
Check Possibility Charity Will Not Receive Interest			
Annuity Factor Exhaustion:	18.8679	Years to Exhaust Trust:	59
Mortality L(119):	0	Mortality L(60):	85537
Mortality L(117):	0	Mortality L(58):	87397
Possibility:	0.0%	5% Possibility Test Passed	
Check Exhaustion of Trust Fund			
Ann. Factor (52 years, 5.0%):	18.4181	Adj. Factor (Annual, 5.0%):	1.0000
Annuity Test Value:	$976,159	Special Factors:	Not Required
Valuation			
Ann. Factor (60, 58, 5.0%):	14.3346	Adj. Factor (Annual, 5.0%):	1.0000
Annuity Value:	$759,734	Charitable Contribution:	$240,266

Source: Trust Calculator (part of *The Ultimate Trust Resource*, a National Underwriter Company publication).

Answer – Life insurance can serve as a partial wealth replacement vehicle to accomplish many or even all the client's planning goals. Suppose, for example, that the client is in his middle fifties and is extremely wealthy, but has a spouse with a relatively small estate. He would like to leave most of his estate to a charity, but would also like to provide his wife with income for life and to provide each of his four children with roughly $1,000,000 after taxes to help them build their own fortunes.

Here's one way the client can accomplish his objectives using life insurance:

- **Step 1:** The client and his spouse can make cash gifts to each of their four children. This money is used by each child to purchase $1 million policy either on the client's life, his spouse's life, on the survivor of the two, or a combination of these. The children own and are beneficiaries of the insurance, none of which will be in the client's estate, and none of which is subject to the claims of the client's (or his spouse's) creditors.

- **Step 2:** Simultaneous with the large cash gifts, the client establishes a testamentary charitable remainder trust which provides that at the client's death prior to his wife, she will receive all the income from the trust for as long as she lives. At her death, all the assets in the trust will pass to her alma mater. The entire estate remaining at the client's death passes into this trust, which entirely eliminates the federal estate tax at his death and provides his wife with significant income for as long as she lives. This technique provides a substantial benefit to the charity as well.

The wealth replacement concept is supported by two factors. First, the four children purchase life insurance for pennies on the dollar. Second,

Figure 32.4

CHARITABLE REMAINDER UNITRUST			
(Two Lives – Table 90CM)			
Transfer to Trust:	$1,000,000	Unitrust Payout Rate:	5.3%
First Age:	60	Second Age:	58
Frequency of Payments:	Annual	Months Until First Payment:	0
Section 7520 Interest Rate:	5.0%		
Adjusted Payout Rate Factor (Annual, 0 months, 5.0%):			1.000000
Adjusted Payout Rate [5.3% × 1.000000]:			5.300%
Two Life Unitrust Remainder Factor (Age 60, Age 58, 5.2%):			.25364
Two Life Unitrust Remainder Factor (Age 60, Age 58, 5.4%):			.24125
Difference [.25364 – .24125]:			01239
Interpolation Adjustment (5.300%):			00619
Unitrust Remainder Factor [.25364 – .00619]:			.24745
Charitable Contribution [$1,000,000 × .24745]:			$247,450
Unitrust Value [$1,000,000 – $247,450]:			$752,550

Source: Trust Calculator (part of *The Ultimate Trust Resource*, a National Underwriter Company publication).

some or all of the premiums are financed by money that otherwise would have been paid in taxes or by income that would not have been enjoyed by the client had he done nothing. In the case of a testamentary charitable gift such as the one in the example directly above, the income of the client's spouse is enhanced by income earned on money that otherwise would have been paid in death taxes.

Question – Is it appropriate to contribute a life insurance policy to a Charitable Remainder Annuity Trust (CRAT) or a Charitable Remainder Unitrust (CRUT) rather than directly to a charity?

Answer – In the opinion of the authors, generally, neither a CRAT nor a CRUT should be the transferee of a life insurance policy. One reason that a client should not contribute life insurance to such a trust is that both trusts are required to make steady payouts of annuities to the client (and/or some other party in

many cases). Adding life insurance to the trust will further drain the trust's cash flow and leave less money for the required annuity payouts.

It is clear that a charitable remainder trust can be named recipient of a life insurance policy's proceeds if the trust is a unitrust created during either the client's lifetime or under the client's will. But because charitable remainder annuity trust rules do not allow contributions after the date the trust is originally created and funded, a CRAT cannot be named as recipient of life insurance proceeds.

Question – What is charitable split dollar (and charitable reverse split dollar)?[39]

Answer – In both of these arrangements, donors use a charity as a conduit to purchase large amounts of life insurance on a tax-deductible basis. The plans mimicked a similar corporate split dollar technique and while the strategy may or may not have worked under insurance law, it violated several aspects of charity law, in particular private benefit rules.

The IRS effectively shut down this technique with IRS Notice 99-36, and Congress imposed harsh penalties for becoming involved in such plans by enacting legislation in December, 1999 that makes it clear that no deduction is (or was) allowed for the donation of a personal benefit contract.[40] Current law defines a "personal benefit contract" as "any life insurance, annuity, or endowment contract if any direct or indirect beneficiary under such contract is the transferor, any member of the transferor's family, or any other person (other than [certain charitable organizations]) designated by the transferor." Charities that continue to pay premiums on personal benefit contracts must report all payments made after February 8, 1999 to the IRS on Form 8870 and must pay a 100 percent excise tax on all premiums paid after December 17, 1999.

Because the legislation that was passed in December 1999 made it clear that charitable split dollar and charitable reverse split dollar never did give rise to an income tax deduction, it is possible that some of the charities involved will face legal suits and may even lose their tax-exempt status as a result of their participation in promoting or agreeing to implement these programs.

Question – What is "financed" charitable life insurance?[41]

Answer – This is a technique that is also growing in popularity in the noncharitable marketplace. To summarize, the charity takes out a loan from a bank to pay premiums on a pool of insurance contracts. The death benefits, or in some cases other assets of the charity, are used as collateral for the cumulative loan. This planning is problematic in several ways. Depending on the circumstances, it may trigger unrelated business taxable income, and if the policy does not perform as well as projected, the underlying contract could lapse and the charity would be forced to repay a substantial cumulative loan plus interest with nothing to show in return. Such planning should be considered highly speculative and be scrutinized carefully by legal counsel.

Practitioners are cautioned to carefully evaluate the actual performance of the policies and the economic viability of the overall strategies. The more money borrowed, the greater the risk the client is taking and the higher the cost—because the ultimate loan balance must be paid either out-of-pocket during the insured's lifetime or from death proceeds. If the intent is to pay the loan off at death, then sufficient additional death proceeds must be purchased to satisfy the obligation and still have enough proceeds to accomplish the objective of the insurance. If premium financing is used to support a large life insurance contract, it is suggested that advisors borrow as little as possible, keep the duration of the loan relatively short, consider worst case scenarios, and develop an "exit strategy" before implementing the plan. Constant monitoring of policy performance and disclosure of the cost and risk to the client are essential.[42]

Question – What are Investor Owned Life Insurance (IOLI), Charity Owned Life Insurance (CHOLI), Foundation Owned Life Insurance (FOLI), and Stranger Owned Life Insurance (SOLI)?

Answer – "In the context of charitable planning, these are all variations of the same plan. In Investor Owned Life Insurance (IOLI), a group of policies are established on the lives of the charity's wealthier donors. The charity (or a trust controlled by the charity) purchases the policies and pays the premiums, sometimes using a financing or bond program arranged for by the plan promoter, for a minimum of two years. At the end of that period, the charity sells the policies to an investor or investor group. Since the investors could not otherwise purchase these policies directly, the charity effectively is renting out their insurable interest to benefit this investor group.

Many of these plans vary in how they are established—the source of the premiums, the arrangement for the charity to keep or sell the policies at the end of the contestability period, and so on—but in the long run, the result will be the same. The Senate Finance Committee has proposed a 100 percent excise tax on all costs involved in these transactions, and while this legislation has not yet passed into law, restrictive legislation in some form is almost certainly to be passed in the near future.

To gather information to better form this future legislation, the Pension Protection Act of 2006 imposed a two-year reporting requirement on all charities that have entered into arrangements where life insurance interests are in anyway split between the charity and private investors. Furthermore, the Treasury Department has been charged with assembling a report to Congress detailing whether these plans are suitable for a charity's tax exempt purpose."[43]

CHAPTER ENDNOTES

1. See Stephan R. Leimberg, *Tools & Techniques of Charitable Planning* (The National Underwriter Company, 3rd Ed. 2014), Ch. 2.; Stephan R. Leimberg, *Tools & Techniques of Estate Planning* (The National Underwriter Company, 18th ed. 2017), Ch. 34.

2. See Stephan R. Leimberg, *Tools & Techniques of Estate Planning* (The National Underwriter Company, 18th ed. 2017), Ch. 35.

3. A corporate charitable contribution paid on or before March 15 will be treated as paid in the prior taxable year if the corporation's board authorizes the contribution in that prior year and makes an appropriate election. I.R.C. §170(a)(2).

4. I.R.C. §170(f)(10); Tax Relief Extension Act of 1999 (P.L. 106-170); Notice 99-36, 1999-1 CB 1284. See also *Addis v. Comm'r.*, No. 02-73628 (9th Cir. 2004), *aff'g.*, 118 TC 528 (2002), and *Weiner v. Comm'r.*, TC Memo 2002-153 (involving deductions taken in 1997 and 1998—before the enactment of I.R.C. §170(f)(10) on December 17, 1999—and denying the charitable income tax deduction on the basis of failure to meet the substantiation requirements of I.R.C. §170(f)(3)).

5. See Let. Rul. 9110016 for a description of the adverse tax consequences associated with such gifts in states where charities do not have an insurable interest in donors' lives. Letter Ruling 9110016 was revoked by Let. Rul. 9147040 after legislation was passed granting charities insurable interests by the state in which the gift occurred.

6. Note that some states are currently considering modifying their insurable interest statues to permit charities to assign their insurable interest to outside investors. For more information, see the testimony of JJ McNab, CFP, CLU, QFP, before the Senate Finance Committee in the hearing, "Charity Oversight & Reform: Keeping Bad Things from Happening to Good Charities," held on June 22, 2004, at: finance.senate.gov/hearings/testimony/2004test/062204jmtest.pdf.

7. *U.S. v. Ryerson*, 312 U.S. 260 (1941); Treas. Reg. §25.2512-6(a), Ex. (3).

8. Treas. Reg. §25.2512-6(a); Rev. Rul. 59-195, 1959-1 CB 18.

9. *Powers v. Comm'r.*, 312 U.S. 259 (1941).

10. I.R.C. §170(b)(1). There are cases that seem to imply that even payments made directly to the insurer on the charity's behalf will qualify for the larger current deduction. The authors suggest the more conservative and certain approach of the donor writing a check to the charity, and the charity writing its check to the insurer. This approach makes an IRS audit less likely, especially if the amount of the check is rounded upward (e.g., an $1,895 premium is rounded to $2,000), and makes compliance with an IRS audit a much easier process.

11. See Treas. Reg. §1.1011-2(a)(3).

12. See I.R.C. §§511, 512.

13. See I.R.C. §514.

14. See I.R.C. §4941.

15. See I.R.C. §4943.

16. See I.R.C. §4944.

17. See I.R.C. §170.

18. I.R.C. §170(b). The amount of charitable contributions that can be deducted for federal income tax purposes in a given year is limited by the Code. Technically, there exist percentage limitations of 30 percent and 50 percent of the donor's "contribution base", essentially adjusted gross income without considering loss carrybacks. The 50 percent limit is reserved for cash type gifts to hospitals, schools, mosques, synagogues, and churches, and other publicly supported charities. Most gifts of property to public charities as well as contributions "for the use of" charity are subject to a 30 percent limit. A 20 percent limitation is imposed where the contribution consists of appreciated capital gain property donated to private foundations.

19. I.R.C. §§170(f)(2), 170(f)(3).

20. See *Eppa Hunton IV v. Comm'r.*, 1 TC 821 (1943); *Behrend v. Comm'r.*, 23 BTA 1037 (1931).

21. Treas. Regs. §§1.170A-7(a)(2)(i); 1.170A-7(b)(1).

22. Rev. Rul. 76-143, 1976-1 CB 63.

23. I.R.C. §170(f)(10); Tax Relief Extension Act of 1999 (P.L. 106-170); Notice 99-36, 1999-1 CB 1284. See also *Addis v. Comm'r.*, No. 02-73628 (9th Cir. 2004), *aff'g.*, 118 TC 528 (2002), and *Weiner v. Comm'r.*, TC Memo 2002-153 (involving deductions taken in 1997 and 1998—before the enactment of I.R.C. §170(f)(10) on December 17, 1999—and denying the charitable income tax deduction on the basis of failure to meet the substantiation requirements of I.R.C. §170(f)(3)).

24. See Let. Rul. 8030043.

25. I.R.C. §79(b)(2)(B).

26. I.R.C. §170(e)(1)(A).

27. See *Behrend v. Comm'r.*, 23 BTA 1037 (1931); *Tuttle v. U.S.*, 305 F. Supp. 484 (1969), *rev'd on other grounds*, 436 F.2d 69 (2nd. Cir. 1970).

28. See Treas. Reg. §25.2512-6.

29. See Treas. Reg. §1.170A-4(a).

30. See, generally, I.R.C. §57(a)(6).

31. I.R.C. §§2522(a), 2522(c).

32. See Let. Rul. 9110016, which was revoked by Let. Rul. 9147040 because of a retroactive change in the statutory law of the taxpayer's state of residence.

33. I.R.C. §2042.

34. I.R.C. §2055.

35. See I.R.C. §511(a).

36. In the case of charitable deductions, the client can choose either the current month's I.R.C. §7520 rate, or look back to either of the two prior months' rates and select the most favorable of the three. By waiting until the date the I.R.C. §7520 rate is announced by the IRS (usually between the 18th and 21st of the month), the client can determine which of four months' rates is most favorable. The I.R.C. §7520 interest rate is published at www.taxfactsonline.com as it becomes available.

37. An income and gift tax charitable deduction is allowed for the present value (measured actuarially) of the charity's right to someday receive what remains in the trust (i.e., the donor is given an immediate deduction for the value of the charity's remainder interest in the trust). That present value is computed using the monthly varying federal discount rates under I.R.C. §7520.

38. I.R.C. §664(d). More extensive information on charitable trusts can be found in Stephan R. Leimberg, *Tools & Techniques of Charitable Planning* (The National Underwriter Company, 2001).

39. Adapted from Stephan R. Leimberg, *Tools & Techniques of Charitable Planning* (The National Underwriter Company, 2001), p. 114.

40. I.R.C. §170(f)(10); Tax Relief Extension Act of 1999 (P.L. 106-170); Notice 99-36, 1999-1 CB 1284. See also *Addis v. Comm'r.*, No. 02-73628 (9th Cir. 2004), *aff'g.*, 118 TC 528 (2002), and *Weiner v. Comm'r.*, TC Memo 2002-153 (involving deductions taken in 1997 and 1998—before the enactment of I.R.C. §170(f)(10) on December 17, 1999—and denying the charitable income tax deduction on the basis of failure to meet the substantiation requirements of I.R.C. §170(f)(3)). For commentary on charitable split dollar, see www.leimbergservices.com.

41. Adapted from Stephan R. Leimberg, *Tools & Techniques of Charitable Planning* (The National Underwriter Company, 2001), pp. 114 - 115.

42. For more information, see Lawrence L. Bell, "Charities and Insurance: The Next Big Thing," Steve Leimberg's Estate Planning Newsletter No. 671) at: htpp://www.leimbergservices.com; Michel Nelson, "Insurance Interest Under Siege, Steve Leimberg's Estate Planning Newsletter No. 670 at: http://www.leimbergservices.com; Stephan Leimberg and Albert Gibbons, "TOLI, COLI, BOLI, and Insurable Interests—an Interview with Michel Nelson, *Estate* Planning (July 2001), p. 333; Stephan Leimberg and Albert Gibbons, "Premium Financing: The Last Choice—Not the First Choice," *Estate Planning* (January 2001), p. 35. See also the testimony of JJ McNab, CFP, CLU, QFP, before the Senate Finance Committee in the hearing, "Charity Oversight & Reform: Keeping Bad Things from Happening to Good Charities," held on June 22, 2004, at: finance.senate.gov/hearings/testimony/2004test/062204jmtest.pdf.

43. From Stephan R. Leimberg, *Tools & Techniques of Charitable Planning*, Chapter 13, Charitable Uses of Life Insurance, (The National Underwriter Company, 2nd edition to be released 2007). See also Leimberg, Stephan. "Stranger Owned Life Insurance (SOLI): Killing the Goose that Lays Golden Eggs," *Estate Planning*, January 2005.

DEATH BENEFIT ONLY (DBO) PLAN

CHAPTER 33

INTRODUCTION

A DBO plan (sometimes called a survivors' income benefit plan) is an executive benefit promising payments from the employer to the survivors of an eligible employee at the employee's death. As its name implies, a DBO plan provides only death benefits and promises no payments to the employee during his lifetime. In essence, the DBO plan is a form of deferred compensation plan, which does not provide any retirement benefit for the covered employee and defers payments until the employee dies. Payment of DBO benefits is typically conditioned upon: (a) the survival of the employee by an employer-designated beneficiary; and (b) the employee's continued employment with the employer until the time of his death.

Although a DBO plan typically provides only pre-retirement death benefits, in the authors' opinion it should be possible to structure a plan to provide both pre- and postretirement death benefits or to just provide postretirement death benefits to select retirees. A postretirement plan may be an attractive alternative to using an endorsement split dollar arrangement to provide death benefits to retirees, due to the escalating Reportable Economic Benefit (REB) costs associated with split dollar arrangements. Although the death benefit paid pursuant to a DBO plan would be income taxable, this may be preferable to the escalating income tax consequences of the REB. It should be noted, however, that a postretirement DBO plan would run a higher risk of estate inclusion of the death benefits—if the primary employer-designated beneficiary is not alive at the insured's death, then the plan would likely pay the death benefits to the insured's estate as a default beneficiary. The remainder of the discussion in this chapter will focus on more typical preretirement DBO plans.

The key goals of a DBO are to provide a significant (and often estate tax free) death benefit, generate substantial amounts of income and/or capital to an employee's family, and help recruit, retain, and reward employees while acting as a counterbalance to the limitations upon highly compensated employees found in qualified retirement plans.

Although payments can take the form of a lump sum, in most cases, benefits will be payable in monthly installments over a fixed period of time (such as five years) or as a lifetime annuity. The death benefit can be a set, predetermined amount, a multiple of the participant's final salary, or a multiple of the covered employee's final average compensation (an average of the covered employee's three final years of compensation is common).

WHEN IS THE USE OF THIS TECHNIQUE INDICATED?

1. When the employer client seeks an employee benefit to recruit, retain, reward, and counterbalance the limitations upon key employees found in qualified retirement plans.

2. When the employer client wants an employee benefit that is simple, cost effective, and free from administrative burdens. Cost effective, in this sense, means the employer pays nothing if the plan does not achieve its goals and pays a minimal amount if the plan is successful. No payments are required under a DBO program if the employee leaves the employer, for any reason, before his death—all benefits are forfeited. This is a strong incentive for an employee to remain with the employer. The employee also becomes aware of the fact that

the after-tax personal cost of a death benefit (such as $100,000 per year for ten years) is significant, even if term insurance is used. This enhances the employee's appreciation of the employer, increases employee loyalty and makes it less likely that an employee will leave the employer. Additionally, should an employee leave, the employer may still maintain the life insurance on the employee's life and retain 100 percent of the proceeds (net of premium costs), since there would be no obligation to make payments to the employee's survivor. The net (after any AMT) proceeds would be a direct positive addition to corporate surplus.

3. When the employer wants to pick and choose who will be covered, under what terms and conditions, and at what amounts.

4. When the employer wants a supplement to a qualified retirement plan.

5. When a shareholder-employee wishes to utilize his corporation to provide personal financial security.

6. When a means is sought to supplement payments under a buy-sell agreement. Instead of increasing the valuation of stock to the highest level reasonable minds might agree to, this difference could be made up outside the buy-sell through the DBO plan. This technique might be particularly useful in a large professional corporation.

7. When an employer would like to provide liquidity and income security for a younger employee's surviving family if the employee were to die while employed, and then, if the employee should survive until retirement, convert the DBO plan to a nonqualified deferred compensation plan in order to provide retirement security. If the employee dies while working, but before retirement, payments will be made from the DBO plan. After the employee reaches age sixty-five (or whatever retirement age is selected), payments can be made from a deferred compensation plan established voluntarily by the employer shortly before the employee's retirement and financed fully or partially with assets (typically policy cash values) that otherwise would have been used in the DBO Plan.

8. When a client is over age fifty, is currently providing protection for his family under a split dollar arrangement, and would like to avoid rapidly rising costs of the taxable insurance protection element. Conversion of the split dollar arrangement to a DBO plan provides a way to continue the security without the income tax (but changes tax-free income to taxable income at death).

9. When a client has a large estate subject to federal estate tax, is in a high income tax bracket, has no need for additional retirement income, but wants to provide additional income or estate liquidity for survivors.

10. Where the group term life insurance plan is adequate for rank and file employees but is not sufficient (or is becoming overly expensive in large amounts) for top executives or other key individuals. It is often possible to provide DBO coverage of equivalent value at comparable cost to the employer and reduced cost to the executive.

11. Where an employer is truly and deeply concerned with the well being of the families of company employees but does not want death benefits diverted to someone other than a survivor of a deceased employee. Especially, because widows between the ages of fifty and sixty-five have a particularly difficult time finding employment and are less likely to remarry, and because many executives have children in college, graduate, or professional school about that same time, covering key employees in this same age range can be particularly important.

Advantages

1. Under current law, if the covered employee is a shareholder who owns 50 percent or less of the stock of the corporation, payments under the DBO plan will be excludable from the covered employee's gross estate. This avoidance of federal estate tax is particularly valuable to individuals whose estates, for one reason or another, will not qualify for a marital deduction.

2. Large amounts of continuing income can be provided through a business to the beneficiary of a key employee. This significant financial assistance is available to employees without regard to whether they are shareholders.

3. During the employee's lifetime, since the employee has no current right to payments or

to the life insurance financing the employer's obligation under the plan, the employee is not taxable on premium payments. Compare this with the taxable income reportable under large amounts of group term life insurance (Table I costs), split dollar life insurance (cost of the pure death benefit), or life insurance maintained inside a qualified retirement plan (cost of the pure death benefit).

4. Employers can pick and choose who will be covered under a DBO plan, the terms of that coverage, and the level of benefit payments to be provided to recipients. There are no government (state or federal) mandated limits. This makes the DBO plan an ideal way to help solve the employer's problem of attracting, retaining, and rewarding employees, as well as counterbalancing the limitations upon highly compensated employees found in qualified retirement plans, without the costs of extending such benefits to the entire work force.

5. When payments are made by the employer, income is taxed at the brackets of the beneficiaries, which are likely to be lower than the covered employee's tax bracket.

6. An employer can leverage payouts with income tax deductions. So if tax rates increase the amount that can be paid out increases. Conversely, if the employer decides to keep payouts level, the corporation will often receive enough, even after all promised payouts are made, to realize not only a return of all outlays, but, in some cases, net a profit that can serve to offset the cost of the use of money expended for premiums.

Disadvantages

1. The entire payment by the corporation to the beneficiary under a DBO plan is subject to ordinary income tax.

2. No deduction is allowed to the employer until the benefit is paid, and the beneficiary must include payments received in income. Even if the employer sets funds aside in advance to meet promised payments (almost always through the purchase of a life insurance contract), the employer's deduction is deferred until benefits are paid. (But, of course, the total deductions are almost certain to significantly exceed the outlays).

3. To avoid federal estate tax inclusion of payments, the employee can be given no right to name or veto the naming of the beneficiary of death benefit payments. Avoiding federal estate tax requires careful plan design, which, to some degree, limits flexibility in plan design for controlling (i.e., greater than 50 percent) shareholder-employees.

4. A plan covering a large and broad group of employees may have to comply with Employee Retirement Income Security Act (ERISA) provisions for vesting, funding, reporting, and disclosure.

   But, in most cases, a DBO plan will be unfunded and limited to a select group of management or highly compensated employees, and will therefore be exempt from virtually all provisions of ERISA, with the exception of a simple, one page notification of the existence of the plan, which must be filed with the Department of Labor.

5. Premiums on life insurance used to finance a DBO plan must be paid with after-tax dollars.

6. Formal funding of a DBO plan through a trust, escrow account, or other means by which money, mutual funds, life insurance, or any other asset is placed beyond the claims of the employer's creditors can trigger constructive receipt of the funds, may cause estate tax inclusion, and will probably result in ERISA reporting, disclosure, and funding requirement implications.

   If the employer's obligation under a plan of deferred compensation is represented by an unsecured promise, the participants are general creditors of the employer and their claim (or the claims of their heirs) is subordinated to the claims of the employer's secured creditors, and their interests are nontransferable, there should be no reportable income under either the constructive receipt or economic benefit doctrines. Beneficiaries are therefore dependent upon the financial ability and willingness of the employer to make payments as promised.

WHAT ARE THE REQUIREMENTS?

The employer installs a nonvoluntary DBO plan by a written contract between the employer and the selected employee stating the terms of the contract.

The employee should have no choice with respect to whether to elect coverage.

The agreement should specify:

1. the amount of the benefit, or the formula upon which the benefit is based;

2. the employee (or employees) covered by the plan;

3. the class of beneficiaries entitled to the benefit;

4. the terms upon which the benefit can be forfeited; and

5. collection procedures.

There is no IRS or Department of Labor guidance or requirement with respect to the formula for determining how much survivors will be paid—the amount is entirely up to the employer. Most will want to keep the formula simple. A common formula uses multiples of $10,000 (such as $30,000, $40,000, $50,000 per year) and combines that with a specified number of years ranging from two to fifteen. An alternative is to make payments based upon either a percentage of the employee's final salary or an average of the top three or five years of salary prior to death. Some use the same formula as is used in the firm's qualified pension or profit sharing plan.

It is suggested that, instead of specifying the name of the employee's spouse and children, the contract should be drafted to state that benefits are payable to "the covered employee's surviving spouse, if living, otherwise the children of the covered employee, in equal shares." (Some plans also provide benefits to parents of covered employees). No benefit should be payable if the employee is not survived by an eligible beneficiary.

A corporate resolution by the company's board of directors should be adopted in writing well in advance of the time payments are to be made (and preferably before the contract with the employee is signed). Note that:

1. no amounts are set aside beyond the claims of the corporation's creditors in a trust, escrow account, or annuity to meet the employer's obligation (since benefits are unfunded, survivors are general unsecured creditors of the employer); and

2. the obligation of the corporation to make payments is contingent upon both: (a) the employee's continued employment with the employer as of his date of death; and (b) survival of a beneficiary from among the employer specified eligible class.

Life insurance is almost always used to finance the employer's obligation under a DBO. Although, in most cases, a form of whole life insurance is used, term coverage could be used to minimize employer outlays, if coverage will cease under the DBO contract by age sixty or sixty-five. Life insurance guarantees that adequate amounts will be available to make promised payments, even if the eligible employee dies immediately after being insured (in fact, the employer may want to wait until the employee's insurability is assured and actual coverage is in force before executing the DBO contract).

This life insurance should not be mentioned in the contract with the employee. A linking of the life insurance with the promised benefits could cause unnecessary estate tax inclusion, income taxation on premium payments, and Department of Labor intrusion.

Under a separate corporate resolution, the board of directors should authorize the purchase of the life insurance as key employee insurance.

HOW IT IS DONE – AN EXAMPLE

A client, Red Leitz, is an employee of Traffic Jammers, Inc. He enters into an agreement with the corporation. The contract provides, in part:

> In consideration of Red Leitz's past service and continued performance of services, Traffic Jammers, Inc. will pay a death benefit of $100,000 per year for a continuous period of ten years in equal annual installments to Red's spouse, if living, otherwise to Red's children.

To finance its obligation under the plan, Traffic Jammers purchases a $1,000,000 policy on Red's life. The corporation names itself owner and beneficiary of the life insurance. At Red's death, the corporation receives the proceeds, owes no AMT, and decides to invest the amount received, net of the cost of premiums, in tax-free municipal bonds. Assume the bonds yield $80,000 annually. Each year for ten years, Traffic Jammers sends

Red's widow or children a check for $100,000. The recipient declares that amount as income.

Since Traffic Jammers is in a combined federal and state tax bracket of 40 percent, the cost to pay $100,000 per year (classified as a continuation of salary) is $60,000 per year ($100,000 – $40,000 deduction). That amounts to $600,000 over 10 years ($60,000 × 10).

The business receives $80,000 each year from the tax-free bonds. It pays out, after tax deduction, $60,000. So each year, Traffic Jammers has received $20,000 more than it needs to meet its obligation. If Traffic Jammers invests the $20,000 each year at 8 percent for ten years, it will grow to $289,731. The corporation also has the tax free municipal bonds. Most importantly, the DBO plan has helped to place "golden handcuffs" on a key executive.

TAX IMPLICATIONS

1. No income tax is payable by the covered employee on the premiums that the employer pays for key-person insurance, which is used to finance the employer's obligation under a DBO plan. To obtain this result, the promises made by an employer under a DBO plan should not be, and should not appear to be, dependent upon and funded directly by an insurance policy. The facts should indicate that if and when a liability to make payments occurs, the employer is always directly responsible for those payments and has not, at any time, shifted that obligation to an insurer.[1]

2. Premiums on the policy, of which the corporation is both the owner and beneficiary, are not deductible.[2]

3. Except for any Alternative Minimum Tax (AMT), proceeds of the key-person life insurance policy used to finance the employer's obligation under the plan are received income tax free.[3] (AMT is discussed in more detail in the Frequently Asked Questions section of this chapter.)

   As a conservative rule of thumb, planners should figure that when more than $1,000,000 of insurance is involved, the corporate AMT will result in a slippage of approximately 15 percent of the face value of the life insurance payable to the corporation. An additional amount of insurance should therefore be purchased in order to assure receipt of

the net amount required (or desired). Because the additional insurance may itself generate additional AMT, the formula used to calculate the appropriate coverage is:

$$\text{Net proceeds desired} \div (1 - .15)$$

For instance, if $1,000,000 is the target amount, the employer should purchase $1,176,471 ($1,000,000 ÷ .85). A more simple way to arrive at the approximate amount is to merely multiply the target amount by 118 percent. In this example the result would be $1,180,000 ($1,000,000 × 1.18).

There is an important small corporation exemption that is discussed in detail in the Frequently Asked Questions section of this chapter.

4. Corporate earnings and profits are decreased by the amount of premium payments, but increased by the sum of: (a) cash surrender value increases; and (b) the excess of death proceeds over cash values in the year received.

5. Cash values should not, per se, trigger an accumulated earnings tax.

6. Benefits paid by a corporation to the employee's beneficiary are taxable in full as ordinary income to the beneficiary, just as if the payments were a continuation of the deceased employee's salary. Even though the employer generally receives the insurance proceeds income tax free, that characterization is lost once the employer pays out the promised continued salary to the beneficiary. So whether the DBO payments are made for a period of years or in the form of a lump sum, payments are taxable to the beneficiary at ordinary income tax rates.

   Death benefit payments are considered income in respect of a decedent (IRD, also known as "Section 691 income"). No stepped-up basis is allowed for IRD.[4] However, the beneficiary is allowed to take an income tax deduction for any federal estate taxes paid on that income.[5] In other words, to prevent the beneficiary from paying a tax on a tax (i.e., income taxation on the portion of the death benefit depleted by estate tax), an income tax deduction is allowed on estate taxes paid.

7. When benefits are paid, they are deductible as deferred salary by the employer corporation, to

the extent that amounts represent reasonable compensation (in amount and duration) for the services actually rendered by the deceased employee. In addition, the plan must serve a valid business purpose. One article has suggested that if an employer purchases key employee life insurance to recover a portion of the costs associated with the plan, payments made by the employer to the beneficiary would not be deductible, on the grounds that no deduction is allowed for a business expense which is reimbursed by insurance or otherwise.[6] But this reasoning appears flawed because there is no nexus between the life insurance and the employer expenses, a connection essential to operation of Code section 265(a)(1), which would then block the deduction.

As a practical matter, the issue of nondeductibility seldom arises except when: (a) the decedent was a controlling or major shareholder employee; (b) the beneficiary is a stockholder; (c) there was no written agreement to pay the benefit prior to the employee's death; or (d) the facts indicate a lack of arm's length bargaining. In such cases, the IRS may attempt to disallow the corporation's deduction and treat payments as a dividend, rather than as a form of deferred compensation. Careful documentation of the bargaining process and of the employer's need to recruit, retain, or reward a true key employee will minimize the chance for an IRS success.

8. Payments from the corporation to the beneficiaries of the covered employee may be excludable from the employee's gross estate. For instance, if the payment is purely and truly voluntary on the part of the business and is not made under a contract or plan, it should be excludable from the employee's estate because, at death, the covered employee never had a right subject to transfer. But even if the DBO payments are made under a formal and binding contract or plan, estate tax exclusion is possible. To assure estate tax exclusion:

a. Give the employer (rather than the covered employee) sole discretion as to the class of beneficiary to receive the death proceeds (preferably by stating a class of beneficiary such as "the employee's spouse, if living, otherwise the employee's children in equal shares"). No rights over the life insurance policy used to finance the employer's obligation should be given to the employee. If the agreement gives the employee the right to name, change, or veto an employer change of beneficiary, payments will be includable in the employee's estate. The employee's estate should not be named as beneficiary.

b. Give the employee no lifetime postretirement benefit or plan (other than a qualified pension or profit sharing plan). Be sure that the DBO plan provides only death benefits and provides no postretirement lifetime payments to the employee. (Keep in mind that the IRS can also link lifetime payments under other plans to the DBO plan and consider the two as a single plan, even if they are separate plans. So estate tax inclusion cannot be avoided by providing death benefits under the DBO and lifetime postretirement payments under a separate plan.) (See Frequently Asked Questions below for more details.)

c. Give the employee (and the employee's estate) no right to dispose of the payments, should one or more specified beneficiaries die. If the employee is found to hold a reversionary interest (one which could revert back to his estate) and that interest has an actuarial value exceeding 5 percent of the benefit, the IRS will include the payments in his estate.

d. The employee should be given no right to alter, amend, revoke, or terminate the agreement or change its terms. If the employee had any of these rights (either alone or in conjunction with any other person), the IRS would require inclusion. This inclusion by virtue of the employee's right to make changes to the agreement spurs a number of issues. For instance:

1) Will the mere possibility of exerting influence upon an employer to make changes to the agreement cause inclusion? What if the covered employee were an officer, director, or shareholder? Can the employee, by terminating employment, terminate the plan? To each of these questions, the courts have held that no inclusion was required.

2) Will a controlling (more than 50 percent) shareholder, merely by virtue of such control, have the power to unilaterally make a change to the agreement that would cause

estate tax inclusion? It is likely that the IRS will attack any situation where the covered individual owns more than a 50 percent interest, although, in the authors' opinion, the fiduciary responsibility one owner owes to another, regardless of the size of the other's interest, negates the ability to make unilateral decisions that affect others. (See Frequently Asked Questions section for more details.)

If there is estate tax inclusion and the DBO benefit is paid in a lump sum, the entire lump sum will be taxable. If there is estate tax inclusion and benefits are payable in installments, the present value of payments to be made at the covered employee's death would be includable in his gross estate. For instance, assuming a 5 percent federal discount rate, payments of $100,000 per year for ten years would have a commuted (present) value of about $772,170 ($100,000 × 7.7217).[7]

Payments under a DBO plan, if paid to a surviving spouse outright or to the estate of a surviving spouse or to a general power of appointment or QTIP trust, could qualify for the federal estate tax marital deduction. This would eliminate the federal estate tax at the death of the first spouse.

Planners should note, however, that if payments are subject to contingencies, such as a reduction or cessation of payments upon remarriage, there will be both positive and negative results. A contingency typically reduces the value of the amount includable in the decedent employee's estate. But that same contingency could also cause a forfeiture of the estate tax marital deduction. If the contract provides that after the surviving spouse's interest ends, payments will be made to another beneficiary (other than the surviving spouse's estate), the spouse's interest is terminable (i.e., one which may end or fail upon the lapse of time or on the occurrence or failure to occur of some contingency). Annuities are, by definition, a systematic liquidation of principal and interest over a period of time, and are therefore terminable interests.[8] Since payments to the employee's beneficiary take the form of an annuity from the employer for a given term of time, DBO payments that pass to someone other than the surviving spouse at the employee's death (or for any other reason) are terminable interests.

Some terminable interests are still deductible for federal estate tax purposes. For instance, if payments were for the shorter of ten years or the life of the employee's surviving spouse, the interest would be deductible. Furthermore, a Qualified Terminable Interest Property (QTIP) election could obtain an estate tax deduction for what might otherwise be a nondeductible interest.[9]

9. The IRS will no longer claim that the payment of the death benefit at the employee's death constituted a completed gift at the time of death.[10]

10. Death benefits paid to beneficiaries are not considered wages subject to income tax withholding.

11. If a DBO plan covers only a single employee (as opposed to a class or classes of employees), then, for FICA purposes, only the benefits paid to the beneficiaries in the calendar year of the employee's death will be subject to FICA taxes.[11] Benefits paid after that calendar year should escape FICA taxes.[12] If an entire class or classes of employees are covered under a DBO plan, benefits paid to beneficiaries should be totally exempt from FICA taxes.[13]

ERISA IMPLICATIONS

A DBO plan is considered to be an employee welfare benefit plan subject to the requirements of Title I of ERISA. Fortunately, most DBO plans are exempt from ERISA's participation, vesting, and funding requirements. Reporting and disclosure is streamlined if the DBO plan is limited to a select group of management or highly compensated employees (generally, less than 5 percent of total employees should be participants). So, in most cases, no annual ERISA filings need be made with the Department of Labor.

In order to successfully avoid ERISA's funding requirements:

1. Counsel should state in the contract between the employer and employee that employees have no right to any instrument that will be used to finance the employer's potential obligations under the DBO plan.

2. The employer should maintain any life insurance as part of its general unrestricted assets (the employer should be the owner and beneficiary of the insurance). No financing vehicle,

especially life insurance, should be tied to the DBO plan in any way. Life insurance should not be mentioned as a financing vehicle in the plan, nor should the phrase "fund" or "informally fund" be used in discussing the use of life insurance in any documents (such as corporate resolutions or SEC annual report disclosure statements) related to the DBO plan.

3. Only a select group of management and highly compensated employees should be covered under a DBO plan.

FREQUENTLY ASKED QUESTIONS

Question – How should the corporate resolution authorizing the plan and the purchase of supporting life insurance be phrased?

Answer – Part of the corporate resolution might read as follows:

RESOLVED: In order to insure itself against all financial losses and other economic detriment that the Corporation would incur in the event of a preretirement death of [name of key executive], the vice president of the Corporation is authorized to enter into a contract of [description of type of policy] life insurance with the [name of insurer] life insurance company for coverage in the amount of [$] insuring the following person(s).

Question – How is the amount of insurance necessary to finance a DBO plan determined?

Answer – Most DBO plans promise to make payments over a number of years (e.g., $100,000 per year for ten years, if death occurs prior to age sixty-five). Assume a plan promised a $10,000 annual death benefit for ten years to the surviving spouse of a key executive, otherwise to the executive's children. Assume the employer corporation is expected to be in a 40 percent (or higher) combined state and federal income tax bracket at the time payments are made. After its $4,000 deduction for each payment, the net cost would be only $6,000 per payment. So it could purchase a $60,000 policy on the employee's life, and even if it earned no interest on the unpaid balance, it would have sufficient funds to make the promised annual payments. Actually, when interest earnings are

factored in, the policy death benefit could even be less than $60,000.

The corporation would own and be the beneficiary of the policy and pay all premiums. Note that the $60,000 of life insurance would be received by the employer-corporation income tax free (and, in this example, because of the relatively low amount of insurance, would probably not be subject to any AMT). However, in the case of a larger life insurance policy, planners should multiply the target amount that the employer firm needs to net by 118 percent, in order to find the proper level of insurance to purchase (assuming a worst case scenario and a large corporation). For example, if the company needed to net $60,000 in a worst case situation, it should purchase $70,800 ($60,000 × 1.18) worth of insurance coverage.

If the benefit is to be paid to the beneficiary over a period of years, rather than in a lump sum, the amount of life insurance needed by the corporation is further reduced. This is because the corporation can invest the life insurance proceeds received at the date of the employee's death. Since it will pay those funds over a number of years, it can continue to invest any balance and use the net after-tax interest income to help fund the benefit payments. The use of a calculator or software package with discounting tables will quickly show the low cost of providing a large benefit when the employer can use both tax leveraging and the time value of money. Alternatively, the employer could obtain the full amount of insurance needed and use interest earnings as a cost recovery vehicle to reimburse itself for premium outlays. For instance, in the example above, by purchasing $100,000 of coverage, rather than $60,000 or $70,800, the corporation would have much more than necessary to make the promised payments. The excess could serve as an economic shock absorber and a way to return to the corporation a significant portion of its premium outlays.

Question – How could Code section 2033 be used by the IRS to require inclusion of the DBO plan payments, and how can this result be avoided?

Answer – Code section 2033 requires that property in which the decedent has an interest at the time of death be included in his estate. Inclusion is required to the extent of the decedent's interest. The courts have uniformly held that under a properly structured DBO plan, the decedent has completely and irrevocably transferred any interest he may have had to the named recipient and thus, at the time of death, has no interest under Code section 2033.

The key to avoiding inclusion under Section 2033 is to avoid giving the employee (and the employee's estate) any vesting or reversion rights. Language specifically stating that neither the employee nor his estate has any interest or rights in the payments to be made to the beneficiary after the employee's death should be included in the plan documents, as well as a statement that under no circumstances will payments be made to the decedent's executor.

Question – How could Code section 2036 be used by the IRS to require inclusion of the DBO payments, and how can this result be avoided?

Answer – Section 2036 applies to transfers with a retained life estate and requires that gratuitous transfers, in which the decedent retained the right to the income or property from the gift or the right to say who will possess or enjoy that property or its income, be included in the decedent's estate. Courts have held that the beneficiary's right to receive a death benefit can be considered an indirect gratuitous lifetime transfer by the covered employee. So if the employee is given and retains the right to name or change the beneficiary of the DBO plan benefit, the IRS could argue that the employee has retained a Section 2036 right. The solution is to state in the DBO plan or agreement that the employee has no right to name or change the beneficiary and that the right to do so vests solely in the employer.

The mere possibility that the employee could negotiate a new contract with the employer or terminate the plan by terminating employment is not considered a retention of Section 2036 powers. Close family relationships or stock holdings are not, in and of themselves, enough to be considered a Section 2036 retained power. However, DBO plan payments could be included in the estate of a controlling shareholder.

Question – How could Code section 2037 be used by the IRS to require inclusion of the DBO payments, and how can this result be avoided?

Answer – Section 2037 requires inclusion in the decedent's gross estate only if there is a reversion

(i.e., the property given away comes back), either to the decedent or to the decedent's estate and the actuarial value of that reversion right is greater than 5 percent of the value of the property in question. For instance, if the attorney who drafted the agreement did not specify a contingent beneficiary, then, should the first named beneficiary predecease the covered employee, there could be a Section 2037 inclusion.

For example, if the death benefit is payable to the employee's child, but the child did not survive the employee, payments would revert to the deceased employee's legal representative (in other words, the employee's estate). If the relative ages of the parties were such that the potential payment to the employee's estate (the value of the reversionary interest) was worth more than 5 percent, the death benefit payable by the corporation would be includable in his taxable estate. So, naming the covered employee's executor or making the benefit payable to the employee's revocable living trust (or testamentary trust) would result in inclusion.[14] If an employer agrees to pay benefits either to the surviving spouse or to the employee's estate, this may create a reversionary interest that, if valued in excess of 5 percent of the estate, will result in inclusion of the present value of the benefit.

The solution to the potential section 2037 problem is for the employer to create several levels of beneficiaries, in order to provide for the contingency of one or more beneficiaries predeceasing the covered employee. For example, the DBO contract might provide words to the effect that payments were to be made "to the employee's surviving spouse, if living, otherwise to the employee's surviving children in equal shares, or to the survivor of them, but if no such children survive the employee, then all liability under this agreement ceases." Clearly, the estate of the employee should not be named contingent beneficiary.

Question – How could Code section 2038 be used by the IRS to require inclusion of the DBO payments in the employee's estate, and how can this result be avoided?

Answer – Section 2038 provides that if a gratuitous transfer is made coupled with the retention of the right to alter, amend, revoke, or terminate the gift, the value of the property interest given away is brought back into the donor's estate. So, if the covered employee is given any right to change the amounts or terms of the coverage under the plan or the identity of the beneficiaries, inclusion will result under Section 2038. The clearest example of this is where the contract gives the employee a continuing right during employment to change the beneficiary of the death benefit under the DBO plan. Likewise, if a revocable trust established by the employee is named as beneficiary, payments will be included in the beneficiary's estate since, by definition, the employee reserved the right to alter, amend, revoke, and terminate the revocable trust and can therefore change the identity of the DBO plan's beneficiaries.

One solution is to make the designation of the beneficiary irrevocable. But that would involve gift tax implications and loss of control (and create the implication that the employee had the right to make changes up until that time). The preferred solution is for the employer to state in the agreement that the employer reserves total, sole, and unlimited right to name or change the beneficiary. The agreement should specifically provide that the employee has absolutely no power to "alter, amend, revoke, or terminate" the plan or the identity of beneficiaries under the plan in any way, either alone or in conjunction with any other party. It is important not to make the mistake of drafting the DBO contract to provide that the employee can, with the mutual consent of his employer, modify the beneficiary's rights. If such an express power to modify or change the beneficiary's rights should exceed those rights allowable under applicable state law, estate inclusion will result. This adverse impact occurs even though the employer's consent is required to change the DBO beneficiary.

Code section 2038 poses a more insidious problem: the more than 50 percent shareholder. Specifically, the question posed is, "Does an individual who owns the controlling voting power in a corporation have, as the mere result of that power over corporate actions, the right to alter, amend, revoke, or terminate the DBO agreement or change the designation of its beneficiary?" In a private letter ruling, payments under a DBO plan escaped estate tax inclusion, even though the decedent owned 85 percent of the corporation's voting stock. The IRS held that the deceased owner's fiduciary duty and responsibility to the other shareholder (his wife) was enough to prevent his control from resulting in inclusion.[15] However, in facts almost

indistinguishable from those in the letter ruling, the IRS successfully argued that if the employee-decedent controlled the corporation, the DBO payments would be includable.[16] This same case seems to confirm that a properly drafted DBO plan covering employees of a publicly held corporation or of a noncontrolling (50 percent or less) shareholder should not be subject to either estate or gift taxation. The outcome where the covered shareholder owns 51 percent or more is uncertain.

Question – How could Code section 2039 be used by the IRS to require inclusion of the DBO payments, and how can this result be avoided?

Answer – Section 2039 deals with annuities and other payments. The annuity or other payment requirement is satisfied if one or more payments are made over any period of time, regardless of whether those payments are equal or unequal, conditional or unconditional, periodic or sporadic, fixed, or variable. Essentially, it requires estate tax inclusion of amounts received at an individual's death under any form of contract or agreement that provides **both** an annuity or similar payment during lifetime **and** a death benefit.

A pure DBO plan, as its name implies, provides only death benefits and no payments while the employee lives. So standing alone, the properly drafted pure DBO plan should not require inclusion under section 2039.

Where postdeath and lifetime postretirement benefits exist in a single plan (or the IRS treats two separate plans that provide such benefits to the same employee as one plan), Section 2039 will require estate tax inclusion of the death benefit. Payments would be treated as though received by the survivor from a joint and survivor annuity (which, in essence, they would be). In such a case, the lump sum paid to the beneficiary or the present value of the stream of payments would be subject to estate tax.

For example, suppose a client has the right to $60,000 per year for ten years after retirement in one plan. In an entirely separate agreement, executed five years later, the client's employer promises to pay $100,000 per year for ten years to the client's children. The present value of the children's rights to the stream of income will be includable in the client's estate.

Just what sort of postretirement lifetime payments will be linked to death benefit payments under section 2039? Does the mere acceptance of wages constitute postretirement lifetime payments? The answer is no.[17] What if an employee signs an agreement with his former employer to serve as a consultant for life? Will this be considered an annuity? Again, the answer is negative. Assuming payments are made for services actually rendered after retirement, those salary payments will not be linked to payments under the DBO plan.[18] Likewise, if substantial services are necessary to receive payments, such amounts will be considered salary, rather than retirement benefits. Benefits payable under a short-term sickness and accident income plan or wages paid for a period of illness or other temporary incapacities, after which the employee is expected to return to work, are considered compensation.[19]

On the other hand, if the agreement calls for payments to be made to the employee after he becomes too incapacitated to perform services, or requires only nominal services after the employee reaches a certain age, payments will be treated as postretirement benefits. Also, payments made if an employee becomes totally incapacitated before retirement are considered an annuity or other payment. Benefits payable under a long-term disability plan that, in essence, assumes that the employee will never return to work and retires the employee on disability payments are not considered compensation, and will be treated as postretirement payments. Linked constructively with a DBO plan, the result will be inclusion of the annuity under section 2039.

Note that for linkage to be made, the employee must be receiving (or have the right to receive at the date of death) an annuity or other payment for life (or for a stipulated term that does not end before the employee's death). For inclusion to be warranted, payments must continue to a survivor as they do in a normal joint and survivor annuity. For instance, if payments were being made to the disabled employee and the employee died before exhausting the fund, and the remaining payments were made to the next class of beneficiary, the long-term disability plan would be coupled with payments under a DBO plan.

Another key issue in determining whether a deceased employee had the right under the plan to any postretirement lifetime payments is, "What is meant by a plan?" The answer is that all rights and benefits that the employee had by virtue of employment (except those under qualified retirement plans) are considered part of one contract or plan in determining whether section 2039 applies. So it is not possible to avoid inclusion by providing death benefit payments under one contract and lifetime retirement benefits under another.

What is meant by the term contract? The term is applied broadly and includes not only contracts enforceable under state law but also payments made under an agreement, understanding, or plan. For example, a corporate resolution may constitute such an understanding.[20]

Question – How could Code section 2041 be used by the IRS to require inclusion of the DBO payments, and how can this result be avoided?

Answer – Code section 2041 is concerned with general powers of appointment—the ability to determine who is to receive someone else's property. If a decedent has a general power (i.e., the unlimited ability to reduce property to the possession of himself, his creditors, his estate, or the creditors of his estate), the entire amount subject to that power will be included in the decedent's estate.

Suppose the death benefit was payable to a trust, over which the decedent retained or was given a general power of appointment. If the payments from a DBO plan are made to that trust, they will be includable under Code section 2041.

Question – How could Code section 2042 be used by the IRS to require inclusion of the DBO payments, and how can this result be avoided?

Answer – Code section 2042 requires inclusion where the insured decedent held any significant incident of ownership over the policy or (even where no incident of ownership was held at death or given up within three years of death by the insured) where the proceeds are paid to or for the benefit of the insured's estate. Where life insurance is used as the financing mechanism for the employer to meet its potential obligations under the DBO plan, the IRS would probably claim inclusion under Code section 2042 where the employee either owns the policy or is given any right of substance with respect to the policy. For example, if the employee is given veto rights over a change of beneficiary, the IRS would likely argue that this is an incident of ownership, causing inclusion.

It is possible that the IRS would also claim inclusion where the DBO plan or some other employment related agreement gave the covered employee the right to prevent the cancellation of the policy, by providing that the employee could purchase the policy from the corporation. Of course, there would be no inclusion merely because the corporation could voluntarily choose to sell a life insurance policy to a terminating employee for its fair market value.

The safest course of action is for the corporation to name itself owner and beneficiary of the policy and to give the insured employee no rights whatsoever with respect to the policy or its values. The policy should be carried on the company's books as key employee coverage and should not be mentioned in the DBO agreement with the employee.

Question – Why shouldn't DBO payments always be made voluntarily on the employer's part in order to avoid estate tax inclusion?

Answer – It is true that if the death benefit payments are not made under a contract or plan and are completely voluntary on the employer's part, there should be no inclusion in the covered employee's estate for federal estate tax purposes. Such voluntary payments are not includable in the employee's estate, because neither the employee nor the employee's beneficiary ever possessed the right to compel the employer to pay the benefit and the employee made no transfer of property or an interest in property.

But a plan that is completely voluntary on the employer's part fails to achieve the "golden handcuffs" effect that is the goal of many employers (i.e., the employee who is not sure of a benefit is given no incentive to come to a business or stay with the business). Such an employee does not feel rewarded by the firm for his efforts in a way that builds loyalty toward the employer. From the employee's viewpoint, a benefit provided at the whim of the employer provides neither peace of mind nor financial security. The mere possibility of such a benefit does not free up other dollars that the employee has discretion to use during lifetime.

Question – What happens to the interest of an employee (or his beneficiary) if the employer goes bankrupt?

Answer – Both the covered employee and his beneficiaries have only the status of an unsecured creditor. A living employee typically has no rights under a DBO plan, since there are no obligations that become fixed until and unless the employee dies while working for the employer. Beneficiaries, as unsecured creditors, have no priority claim to any employer assets, including life insurance used by the employer to finance potential obligations.[21] The likelihood is that beneficiaries would take a pro rata share of the assets that remain (if any) after any secured creditors and priority unsecured claimants have been satisfied.

Question – How does the corporate exemption from the AMT work?

Answer – Certain small corporations will qualify for an exemption from the AMT.[22] In order to initially qualify for the exemption, the corporation's average annual gross receipts for its first three-year period must not exceed $5 million. Thereafter, in order to continue to qualify for the exemption, the corporation's average annual gross receipts must not exceed $7.5 million in subsequent three-year periods. For a corporation that has not been in existence for three full years, its years of existence are substituted for the three-year period (with annualization of any short taxable year). A corporation will generally be exempt from the AMT in its first year of existence. Once a business fails to meet the gross receipts test, it cannot qualify as a small corporation in any later year. If a corporation fails to maintain its small corporation status, it loses the exemption from the AMT.

CHAPTER ENDNOTES

1. Compare *Casale v. Comm.*, 247 F.2d 440 (2nd Cir. 1957) with *Goldsmith v. U.S.*, 586 F.2d 810 (Ct. Cl. 1978).

2. I.R.C. §264(a)(1).

3. I.R.C. §101(a).

4. I.R.C. §1014(c).

5. I.R.C. §691(b).

6. See Roberts, "Tax Traps in Tax-Leveraged Employee Death Benefit Plans; Analysis and Planning," 59 J. Tax. 324 (1983). For a somewhat different analysis, see Swirnoff, "Interplay of Deductions for Non-qualified Compensation and Employee Life Insurance," 62 J. Tax. 130 (1985).

7. See *The Tools & Techniques of Estate Planning, 17th Edition* for information on the computation of annuity, life estate, and remainder values and the AFMR. The rates, which vary from month to month, are published monthly in a revenue ruling.

8.   I.R.C. §2056(b).

9.   For more information on the marital deduction, see Chapter 27.

10. *Est. of DiMarco v. Comm.*, 87 TC 653 (1986), acq. in result, 1990-2 CB 1.

11. I.R.C. §§3121(a)(14), 3121(a)(13)(B).

12. I.R.C. §3121(a)(14).

13. I.R.C. §3121(a)(13)(B).

14. See *Est. of Fried v. Comm.*, 445 F.2d 979 (2nd Cir. 1971).

15. Let. Rul. 8701003.

16. *Est. of Levin v. Comm.*, 90 TC 723 (1988).

17. See *Est. of Fusz v. Comm.*, 46 TC 214 (1966), acq. 1967-2 CB 2, which held that "other payment" means postemployment benefits paid or payable to the decedent during his lifetime. Fusz was an employee who signed an employment contract that provided: (a) monthly salary payments to him; and (b) monthly payments after his death to his surviving spouse. Section 2039 was held to be inapplicable because the only postemployment promise that was made to Fusz was to pay a salary for services rendered.

18. Planners should caution clients that merely stating that a payment is salary will not be sufficient to have it treated as such. For instance, if the IRS can show that services actually (or to be rendered) were not worth the agreed upon payments, or that (in view of close family ties or voting control) it was never intended that services be performed in return for the promised payments, the IRS will treat such payments as a retirement arrangement. See *Kramer v. U.S.*, 406 F.2d 1363 (Ct. Cl. 1969), where the IRS used this very argument (but was unsuccessful only because it failed to prove the services to be rendered were nominal or pro forma).

19. Planners must make a distinction between a wage continuation plan, which presumes that the employee will return to work, and a disability plan, which presumes that the employee will not (i.e., benefits are payable only if the disability is expected to be total and permanent and the employee is retired on disability). If the employee is never expected to render additional services to the employer after payments begin, benefits are considered an annuity or other payment within the scope of Section 2039. See *Est. of Schelberg v. Comm.*, 79-2 USTC ¶13,321 (2d Cir. 1979).

20. In *Neely v. U.S.*, 613 F. 2d 802 (Ct. Cl. 1980), the court held that it was immaterial whether the widow could enforce payment, since she held (individually or as her husband's executrix) 70 percent of the voting stock of the company after her husband's death.

21. See 11 U.S.C.A. §§724(b), 726(a), 726(b).

22. I.R.C. §55(e).

IRREVOCABLE LIFE INSURANCE TRUSTS

CHAPTER 34

INTRODUCTION

Life insurance is an almost magic tool in estate planning. But because its utility is diminished in direct proportion to the taxes imposed on it and the security it provides becomes elusive, often it makes sense for highly successful clients to give it away. Gifts of life insurance offer special planning opportunities not available with other assets.

These include:

1. Life insurance proceeds can be removed from a client's estate at a relatively low gift tax cost. Compare this with most other property, which has the same value for gift tax purposes as it does for estate tax calculations.

2. A gift of other assets may result in a loss of a stepped up basis to the client's heirs.[1] But a gift of life insurance does not result in such a loss in income tax savings; there is generally no income tax payable on the proceeds and the loss of a step-up in basis is no concern.

3. Psychologically, life insurance is an easier gift for a client to part with than most other assets since it is not income producing and is generally thought of as a post death security vehicle for others.[2]

There are a number of advantages and disadvantages, as well as important details, to consider when helping clients understand the use of irrevocable life insurance trusts in the planning process. These include:

1. advantages of ownership of life Insurance by third party;

2. disadvantages of third party ownership of life insurance;

3. why make a gift of life insurance to an irrevocable life insurance trust;

4. disadvantages to ownership of life insurance by an irrevocable trust;

5. irrevocable trust – what it is and how it works;

6. mechanics;

7. selection of a trustee;

8. reducing or eliminating gift taxes on policy transfers and premium payments through Crummey powers;

9. gift, estate, and income tax problems related to Crummey powers;

10. reducing or eliminating gift taxes on premium payments through methods other than Crummey powers;

11. what the attorney should consider in drafting;

12. how to avoid the transfers within three years of death rule;

13. structuring the trust for "what ifs";

14. allocation of the federal estate tax;

15. income tax implications;

16. how to handle last to die (survivorship) insurance in an irrevocable trust;

17. how to handle group term life insurance in an irrevocable trust;

18. community property issues.

ADVANTAGES OF OWNERSHIP OF LIFE INSURANCE BY THIRD PARTY

The benefits of shifting ownership of life insurance to save estate taxes are most easily and certainly obtainable if a party who has an insurable interest in the insured's life purchases the policy and pays all the premiums and is the beneficiary of the proceeds when the insured dies. That party should be someone other than the insured or the insured's estate. Since the proceeds are not paid to or for the benefit of the estate of the insured and because the insured owned no incidents of ownership over the policy and because there was no transfer of the policy within three years of death, there will be no estate tax inclusion.

The second best alternative is to transfer existing policies by gift to the insured's spouse or some other trusted person or, the most preferable method when the combined estates exceed the unified credit exemption equivalent, transfer the policies to an irrevocable life insurance trust. Removing the proceeds from the insured's gross estate in this manner not only lowers the overall tax burden but also provides a means of creating estate liquidity (cash to pay the decedent's debts, taxes and other expenses of estate administration). The recipient of the policy proceeds can make fully secured interest bearing loans to the estate's executor or purchase assets from the estate. This gives the estate cash and helps assure that desired assets remain within the family unit.

Liquidity could be provided by the direct purchase of life insurance by the grantor. However, the incredible advantage of third party ownership of life insurance is that it provides liquidity for the estate without causing inclusion of the life insurance proceeds in the client's estate (or, where the insurance is owned by a third party such as the insured's child or an irrevocable life insurance trust, without causing inclusion in the estate of the client's spouse).

If the policy is originally owned or transferred to the insured's spouse who is also the premium payor and beneficiary, the estate tax will be delayed until the death of the surviving spouse. Assuming the insured's spouse survives the insured, this means that money that otherwise would have been paid in federal estate taxes can instead be used to provide support for the spouse and children. To the extent used by the surviving spouse, those proceeds will never be subject to federal estate tax.

If the policy is originally owned or transferred to the insured's children, then no estate tax is imposed until the next generation and even then only to the extent the children have not used the money.

DISADVANTAGES OF THIRD PARTY OWNERSHIP OF LIFE INSURANCE

Planners must not let the advantages to third party ownership totally obscure the potential risks or costs. These disadvantages generally fall into two categories.

First, the client must give up direct control over the policy through a complete and permanent transfer to avoid the federal estate tax. An absolute assignment or total change of ownership must be made if a presently existing policy is to be removed from the client's estate. This means the client must forgo the right to name or change the policy beneficiary, veto a change, borrow against the cash values of the policy, and give up every other meaningful and significant incident of ownership.

Many events, unpredictable at the time third party ownership is arranged, can drastically change the way or the parties the client would prefer to own coverage on his life. For instance, the insured's marriage could become unstable, the insured may no longer get along with the children who are the owners of a policy on the insured's life, or the insured's spouse or other owner could predecease the insured. The insured may remarry. Tax laws can change. During this time, the insured may become highly rated due to health problems or even become uninsurable or insurable only at prohibitive cost. Business reverses or opportunities may suggest a need for insurance cash values, which are unavailable if the policy is no longer owned by the insured.

ADVANTAGES TO OWNERSHIP OF LIFE INSURANCE BY AN IRREVOCABLE TRUST

Incredible federal estate and state death tax savings are possible though an irrevocable trust which has as one of its assets a life insurance policy on the life of the grantor. For the highly successful individual, no means exists under current law to transfer large amounts of wealth and provide financial security that are as certain or as dramatic as the irrevocable life insurance trust.

Reasons for the popularity of this estate planning tool include almost all of the advantages listed for implementing revocable trusts and these important additional reasons:

1. Federal estate taxes on millions of otherwise taxable dollars can be avoided, not only when the client dies, but also when the client's spouse dies. Leveraging life insurance through tax savings in this manner means death taxes bypass both spouses' estates and the amount effectively passing to heirs is substantially increased.

2. State death taxes can be saved in the same manner as federal estate taxes. This advantage becomes particularly important in states that provide limited exemptions for life insurance proceeds and those that have high rates on transfers at death to persons other than spouses.

3. In most cases, relatively little (and in many cases, no) gift tax is required to create and simultaneously shelter high amounts of life insurance from transfer taxes. At a relatively low gift tax cost (because the gift tax value of life insurance transferred to the trust is valued at its much lower lifetime value, in most cases the interpolated terminal reserve plus any unearned premiums on the date of the gift) the many times larger amount of the policy proceeds is removed from the client's estate. This leverage is impossible to find with any other estate transfer tool or technique under current law.

4. There will be no probate expenses, delays, or uncertainties with respect to the transfer of assets in an irrevocable life insurance trust. Had the surviving spouse owned the coverage on her husband's life, proceeds she didn't exhaust during her life would be subject to both federal and state death taxes and probate costs.

5. By making loans to the client's estate or purchasing assets from the estate, the trustee can use trust assets at the client's death to help provide estate liquidity, prevent a forced sale of a family business, valuable real estate, or a securities portfolio, and keep treasured property in the family. Furthermore, because the life insurance used to make that loan or purchase is not included in either spouse's taxable estate, the irrevocable life insurance trust provides estate liquidity without increasing the liquidity problem. Had some other third party policy ownership arrangement been used, it is possible that such a person, depending on the terms of the insured's will or that person's relationship with the other beneficiaries, may be unwilling to make loans to the estate or purchase assets from the estate with the proceeds.

6. Significant income and capital can be provided for, or on behalf of, the surviving spouse without causing inclusion of the life insurance proceeds or other trust assets in the surviving spouse's estate.

7. The irrevocability of the trust generally translates into protection from the claims of creditors.

8. Trusts that are irrevocable generally provide protection from a surviving spouse's rights of dower, courtesy, or right of election under state law.

9. A gift of an insurance policy to a life insurance trust gives the insured more control over the ultimate disposition of both the policy and its proceeds than would an outright policy gift. In other words, when an irrevocable trust is the owner of life insurance on the client's life, the client controls the ultimate disposition of the policy after the surviving spouse's death through provisions in the trust. It also resolves the problem of what happens to the policy if the third party owner predeceases the insured. An individual donee policyowner can give or bequeath the policy to third persons, frustrating the insured's planned use of the proceeds. The use of a trust provides greater assurance that the proceeds will be used for the grantor's intended purpose. For instance, if a client transfers a policy to a potential beneficiary, such as a child, and that party predeceases the client, it is possible that the policy would revert back to the client and end up being taxed in the client's estate. The use of an irrevocable trust can prevent this result. The irrevocable trust also reduces the potential that a policy owned by a spouse on the other spouse's life

will inadvertently lapse upon the death of the owner prior to the insured.

10. Sprinkle and spray powers (i.e., giving the independent trustee discretion to sprinkle income and spray capital among the trust's beneficiaries in the manner that best meets the client's dispositive objectives and the beneficiaries' needs and minimizes the income taxes of the family unit) are highly advantageous. Most importantly, the trustee can deny payments, when appropriate, on a more objective basis and with less potential for family conflict than if a family member received the insurance proceeds and then attempted to provide family security.

11. When compared to the use of settlement options (an often overlooked alternative to trusts in small estates), the trust offers greater flexibility and, in some cases, an opportunity for increased capital and income. A trust can provide for payments according to the beneficiaries' needs and circumstances by giving the trustee sprinkle and spray powers and by giving beneficiaries limited powers of appointment. This is particularly important where a primary function of the trust is to fund a large security reserve for beneficiaries who are inexperienced, minor, or disabled. The trustee can be authorized to invest aggressively to maximize income and growth (but in comparing trusts to settlement options, planners should also consider the increased risk).

12. Generation-Skipping Transfer (GST) tax problems can be reduced or eliminated by judicious use of GST tax annual exclusions and the GST tax exemption. Significant leverage can be obtained through the use of life insurance inside the trust.

13. Wealth replacement is another advantage to the use of irrevocable life insurance trusts. A client may want to make a tax deductible gift to a charity during lifetime or at death, yet replace the net after estate tax wealth his heirs would have received had no charitable gift been made. This goal can be accomplished through gifts to an irrevocable trust followed by a purchase by the trustee of life insurance on the client's life in an amount sufficient to replace the (after estate tax) value of the donated land, stock, or other gift made to charity.

14. Clients who establish GRITs, GRATs, or GRUTs[3] or charitable lead trusts and who die during the initial term of the trust will have all or a large portion of the trust's assets included in their estates. If the client survives that term, nothing will be included in the client's gross estate and great wealth can be shifted at a gift tax discount. Clients can insure the estate tax savings by making annual gifts to a trustee who uses the money to purchase insurance on the client's life equal to the potential estate tax savings.

15. An often overlooked advantage of an irrevocable life insurance trust is that through the leverage of life insurance and the flexibility of the trust vehicle, even a person of modest means can be assured that adequate financial security and the achievement of important and costly economic goals such as the education of children or grandchildren can be met.

16. An irrevocable trust provides all the above advantages, in addition to the classic uses for trusts in general:[4] professional management, protection from creditors, postponement of receipt of inheritance, and avoidance of guardianship for minors or other incompetents.

DISADVANTAGES TO OWNERSHIP OF LIFE INSURANCE BY AN IRREVOCABLE TRUST

Loss of Control and Flexibility

When transferring ownership of life insurance to an irrevocable trust, the client must give up:

a) the income produced by any income producing trust assets if the trust has been funded;

b) the use and enjoyment of any property including the life insurance cash values held by the trust or use of the cash values as collateral;

c) the right to name, add, subtract, or change the size or terms of a beneficiary's interest;

d) the right to regain assets (including life insurance) placed into the trust; and

e) the ability to alter, amend, revoke, or terminate the trust.

The psychological cost of losing this control and flexibility should not be underestimated. Many clients should not set up such trusts, in spite of the tremendous potential death tax savings, because of the offsetting lifetime loss of peace of mind and flexibility. Clients who are relatively young will be faced with a long lifetime of rapidly changing personal and financial circumstances.

Planners must make clients aware of the problems inherent in the event the client's objectives, client's or beneficiary's circumstances, or tax laws change. The client may decide at some future date that he does not like the payout provisions and would like them to be longer (or shorter) or provide more (or less) to a given beneficiary. Counsel may find the powers in the trust instrument are tainted in such a manner that trust assets will be included in the client's estate. The client may have failed to name enough backup trustees or there may be a personality conflict between the client and the trustee.

Clients must also be made to understand that there is a certain level of paperwork and record keeping that cannot be safely ignored. "Responsibilities of this nature can seem unduly complex and frustrating to the client, who, unless he has been forewarned, may well become unhappy with his attorney for placing him in the situation in the first place."[5]

Costs

There are up front and continuing cash costs involved with an irrevocable life insurance trust. Obviously, there are legal fees for preparing the trust agreement. These costs range from over $1,000 to more than $10,000 depending on the nature and extent of the client's assets and the part the irrevocable trust plays in the overall planning process.

Accounting costs must also be considered. As long as the trust is unfunded, no annual income tax returns will be required because the trust will have no income. But records must be kept and an accounting should still be made to trust beneficiaries and the trust must have a Taxpayer Identification Number (TIP).

Professional trustees, such as banks operating as trust companies, often charge an acceptance fee and all charge a fee for management and investment services. Although these fees are typically nominal during the insured's lifetime (when the trust has little or no assets and the trustee has few responsibilities other than safeguarding the trust document), they can be significant when the trust is swelled with policy proceeds and other assets poured over into the trust at the death of the insured.

There may be a termination fee if the trust is terminated before the insurance policies have matured and the trustee has had the opportunity to recover set up costs.

Loss of Contributions

Yet another consideration is the potential loss of the donor's contributions out the back door of the trust. Irrevocable life insurance trusts usually require special provisions (Crummey powers) that enable the client's gifts to the trust to qualify for the gift tax annual exclusion. By definition, these Crummey powers are withdrawal powers. They give the powerholder the legal right to demand specified amounts at given times. If the demand powers are not real, they will not eliminate gift taxes. Yet, if they are real powers, there is always a possibility that money which could and should have been used to pay life insurance premiums will instead be drained off by the power holding beneficiaries. There are techniques and devices to persuade the beneficiary not to exercise this right. But the IRS has been vigorous in attempts to disallow the gift tax annual exclusion in just such situations.

To the extent the annual exclusion cannot shield the premium outlays, the client will first have to use up his unified credit and then pay gift taxes on each transfer.

"Escape Hatches"

Although there are potential solutions to problems confronted when dealing with an irrevocable trust, there is no free lunch. Tax savings and additional flexibility comes with a cost. Escape hatches are less than perfect. Yet, in weighing these disadvantages, planners should consider:

- The client can discontinue premium payments, let the policy inside the trust lapse (or use policy cash values to purchase extended term insurance for a limited time or a lower amount of paid up insurance for the insured's life) and start over with a new trust with new terms and new insurance (assuming insurability at affordable rates).

- Even an irrevocable trust can be revoked by court action assuming the written consent of all (including guardians for minor) beneficiaries. A trust can be revoked, in whole or in part, in many states assuming all persons beneficially interested (i.e., who have a vested interest) agree to the revocation in writing and file a notarized copy of the request for revocation in the appropriate county clerk's office. The mere state statutory power enabling such a revocation would not be enough to require inclusion of irrevocable trusts in the estates of such persons. However, when the trust terminates, the property may end up back in the client's estate if there is no specific provision in the trust paying over the assets to beneficiaries named in the event of a premature termination by revocation. The client must then create a new irrevocable trust or make a further disposition of trust assets to remove them from his gross estate.

Planners should keep in mind that revocation is not automatic and is usually granted only as an escape hatch from unforeseen events occurring subsequent to the creation of a trust. If beneficiaries are below the state age of majority, it will be necessary to have guardians ad litem appointed since the minors cannot consent to the termination or amendment.

- One common objection to the creation of an irrevocable life insurance trust is the loss of the use of life insurance cash values. When a cash value policy is placed in or purchased by an irrevocable trust, the client normally does lose all control over the policy values. The trustee, acting in a fiduciary capacity, is the only party that can utilize those values. But, by giving the trustee the authority to make distributions to the beneficiaries during the grantor's lifetime, the cash value and/or dividends of the policy can be used during the lifetime of the insured client. In other words, it is possible to draft an irrevocable life insurance trust in such a way that distributions could be made to beneficiaries before the client's death (including a spousal beneficiary).

- The client could purchase the policies from the trust at their fair market value. This gives the trust a relatively small amount of cash but returns the insurance (transfer for value tax free) back to the client, who can then create a new trust with new terms and contribute the old policies into that new trust. If the policy held extensive cash values, the out of pocket cost of the purchase could be reduced by stripping out all or a portion of the cash values prior to the transfer. Of course, the purchase cannot be guaranteed by requiring such a sale in the trust agreement. A call on trust assets would result in estate tax inclusion. The legal right to purchase a policy would clearly be an incident of ownership.

- A special power of appointment could be inserted from inception into the irrevocable life insurance trust. That power would give the insured's spouse, an adult child, or someone else the insured implicitly trusts the ability to appoint (direct ownership of) trust property to herself or her children (or anyone else other than back to the insured-grantor, his estate, his creditors, or the creditors of his estate). The authors suggest that the trust bar the holder of the power from using it to pay for any item that could be considered in satisfaction of either spouse's legal obligation of support. This special power should cause no inclusion in the estate of the holder and, unless the policy is in fact transferred back to the insured-grantor, it should not attract estate tax in his estate. A contingent limited powerholder should also be named.

The disadvantage of this technique is, if the parties divorce or the holder dies before the grantor-insured, the ability to remove trust assets and appoint them in a direction consistent with the client's desires is eliminated. Obviously, if there is marital discord at the time of planning, the spouse should not be considered as the holder of this power.

- Name the grantor's spouse as initial holder of the power to appoint trust assets but provide if: (a) the spouse dies first; (b) the spouse is no longer married to the grantor; or (c) for any reason the spouse no longer has the legal or mental capacity to exercise the power, the limited power would automatically pass to the individual named as contingent holder.

- It is possible to name as beneficiary "my wife if I am legally married at the time of my death, otherwise." This designation will eliminate payment to an ex-spouse without causing inclusion of the policy proceeds or any other trust property in the insured's estate.[6] In other words, a client's attorney could question the client exhaustively and attempt to anticipate, in drafting the trust document, every possible circumstance in which the client might want to change the terms. It is clear, for example, that an irrevocable life insurance trust can now safely provide that "Upon a legal separation or divorce, any and all interest my wife, Sadie may have in this trust shall cease."

- Consider a provision giving the independent trustee sole discretion to terminate the trust in the event that the trust can no longer meet its intended objectives due to unforeseen circumstances. In other words, the trustee (assuming the trustee is a party other than the insured or a beneficiary) can be given a discretionary power to collapse the trust and assign the life insurance or distribute assets to the trust's beneficiaries, if the trust should become unworkable because of a tax or other legal change or if funds are no longer available to pay premiums. The trustee may also be given the power to distribute trust assets, including life insurance policies and the right to benefits under group term life, in kind.

  The drawbacks here are: (a) the assets in the trust go to the trust's beneficiaries, perhaps prematurely; and (b) the trustee may be reluctant to exercise this power unless all beneficiaries will sign an agreement that the action is proper and in conformance with the trustee's fiduciary responsibilities to all beneficiaries.

- The trustee (assuming the trustee is a party other than the insured or a beneficiary) can be given a power to sprinkle or spray income and principal among a class of persons and thus add additional flexibility to the dispositive terms of the trust without adverse tax consequences.

- The trust could provide that, if the grantor died within three years of transferring life insurance held within the trust or if, for any reason, life insurance owned by the trust was includable in the grantor's estate, the proceeds would be paid to the insured-grantor's executor. That way, the proceeds could be channeled to the insured's surviving spouse and qualify for the marital deduction. In fact,

the trust could contain a marital clause so that if the client doesn't want the trust to end upon his death or doesn't want the proceeds paid to his probate estate, the tax savings objectives can be accomplished within the trust itself.

- The noninsured spouse could create a split dollar arrangement (see Chapter 41) with the trust in which such spouse retains access to policy cash values. This would indirectly give the insured spouse access to policy values without risking estate tax inclusion of the proceeds. The drawback here is the possibility of spousal estrangement.

WHAT IT IS AND HOW IT WORKS

There are two basic ways an irrevocable trust becomes a life insurance trust. The first way is when a client makes an absolute assignment of one or more life insurance policies to the trust. The obvious disadvantage to this method is the potential for estate tax inclusion under the transfers within three years of death rule of Code section 2035 (purchase of the policy by the trust for fair and adequate consideration can avoid the three-year rule, but creates potential transfer for value issues). Alternatively, under the preferred approach, the trust is established, cash contributions are made by the grantor to the trust, and then the trustee uses cash or income from funds provided by the grantor or others to purchase new insurance on the life of the grantor. Preferably, the trustee should initiate the purchase of life insurance, own from inception all the incidents of ownership in the policy, be the premium payor, and be named as beneficiary.

An irrevocable life insurance trust may either be funded or unfunded. In the most general sense, the term funding means that assets other than life insurance policies have been placed into the trust. In the narrower and commonly used sense, when applied to irrevocable life insurance trusts, funding means the placement of income producing assets into the trust. These assets typically are placed inside the trust in order to produce sufficient income to pay the insurance premiums. If the trust is funded, the trust agreement should specify:

1. what should happen if the income of the trust is insufficient to pay the entire premium; and

2. what should happen if trust income is more than sufficient and there is an excess of income.

Usually, the trust will provide that if trust income will not be sufficient to pay the entire premium, the trustee is responsible for notifying the grantor (or beneficiary or other interested party) of the shortfall. The trust should specifically authorize the trustee to borrow on the policy to keep it in force or to place the policy on extended term or purchase paid up whole life coverage if the grantor fails to pay the balance of the premium.

Most irrevocable trusts are unfunded and contain only life insurance policies. The insured typically pays premiums on policies held by an unfunded life insurance trust, by either making direct payments to the insurer or by the preferred method, annual gifts to the trustee in amounts large enough for the trustee to pay the premiums and have enough cash left over to cover any incidental trust expenses. Here, the trustee typically assumes no obligation to keep the life insurance in force or even the responsibility to notify the client that premiums are due or overdue.

The major tax objectives of many irrevocable life insurance trusts are to: (1) make the maximum amount of income and capital available to the surviving spouse and increase both her personal financial security and that of those she loves and feels responsibility toward; and (2) avoid inclusion of the proceeds in both spouses' estates.

To accomplish these goals, the draftsperson of the trust inserts certain provisions that:

1. allow the trustee (and only the trustee) discretion to sprinkle income or spray capital to the spouse and the grantor-insured's children; and/or

2. give the surviving spouse "all of the income for life and as much principal as necessary for her Health, Education, Maintenance, and Support" (HEMS); and

3. state "when she dies, my surviving spouse can appoint the remainder of the trust assets among our then living children."

Most irrevocable life insurance trusts are designed to do more than provide food, clothing, and shelter for the grantor's survivors. A major goal of such trusts is to keep assets, such as a family business or real estate, in the family by avoiding the forced (and often fire) sale that results from a lack of liquidity. Properly arranged, an irrevocable trust does just that; provides liquidity for the insured grantor's estate without increasing the estate tax burden.

These twin goals, estate liquidity and exclusion of the life insurance that provides that liquidity, must be carefully planned. If the provisions of a life insurance trust required the trustee to pay to the insured's estate any cash needed to pay debts, expenses, and taxes, such an instruction would result in federal estate tax inclusion of all amounts that could be so expended (as amounts receivable by the executor). This would cause a loss of the estate tax savings objective. However, the IRS has provided guidance that giving the trustee the "discretion" to use proceeds of life insurance to pay federal estate taxes will not cause inclusion of the life insurance proceeds pursuant to Code section 2042.[7] Presumably, if the trustee were actually to use some of the death proceeds to pay estate taxes, this portion would likely be includible in the estate as an "amount receivable by the executor,"[8] which makes this a less than attractive option except in extenuating circumstances.

The solution is simple. A provision is placed into the trust document authorizing, but not directing, the trustee to:

1. lend money to the estate at an interest rate equal to or in reasonable excess of the current bank lending rate in the area; or

2. purchase assets at their fair market value from the estate of the insured and the estate of his spouse.

Such loans and/or purchases will (to the extent of the life insurance relative to the taxes and other expenses) solve or reduce the decedent's estate's liquidity problem while keeping purchased estate assets within the family unit. If the draftsperson has been careful to frame the wording of the trust in the form of a permission rather than as a command, neither loans by the trust nor purchases from the estate should cause the insurance proceeds to be included in the insured's gross estate. Neither should be interpreted as falling within the scope of the statute dealing with the inclusion of life insurance proceeds.

Furthermore, the estate should realize little or no gain on the sale, because appreciated assets in the estate receive a stepped up basis equal to the estate tax value of each piece of property. Best of all, when the trustee pays the executor cash for an appreciated asset, the trustee then takes that asset with a basis that is stepped up to its purchase value. The trustee (or the trust's beneficiaries if the assets are distributed) can then invest the assets, or sell them with relative income tax impunity and diversify their portfolio to achieve higher safety, liquidity, growth, or income.

These clauses must be carefully inserted into an irrevocable life insurance trust so as to accomplish a delicate balancing act. On the one hand, they are designed to enhance the trust's flexibility and usefulness as a means of providing managed financial security for the surviving spouse. Yet, on the other hand, they must not give the surviving spouse powers broad enough to be considered a general power of appointment (i.e., a virtually unlimited right to say who receives the proceeds), since such a power would cause the policy proceeds to be included in the surviving spouse's gross estate. The three standard clauses above are designed to accomplish these two important objectives.

Mechanics

A policy should be placed into the trust as follows:

1. An attorney drafts and the client signs the irrevocable trust document.

2. The trustee then applies for the policy on the insured's life, under a provision in the document allowing the trustee to purchase a policy and/or pay premiums on a policy insuring the life of the grantor.

Of course, that is the ideal arrangement and, with a lawyer who is expert in estate planning and who has a modern well-automated office, the appropriate speed, accuracy, and efficiency, is possible. But it will not always work so smoothly. More often, the insured wants to put a policy in force immediately, but the trust will not be established until a future date. Here, several alternatives are available.

Under Plan A

Putting a plan into place under Plan A works like this:

1. The client could apply for the policy as policyowner.

2. After the trust is created, the client could transfer ownership of the policy to the trust by an absolute assignment or ownership form "for love and affection." (Note that if a beneficiary transfers a policy to the trust, he will

be considered a grantor of the trust. So, for example, in a community property state, rather than having the insured grantor's spouse transfer an existing policy on his life directly to the trust, the insured should purchase the policy on his life from his wife and then transfer it—in a time-separated and independent step—to the trust by gift.) A copy of the executed trust is sent to the insurance company together with the absolute assignment form.

3. In a nonprepaid case, an informal application could be submitted to the insurer for an informal opinion as to whether the policy will be issued on a select, standard, or rated basis. Once the policy's issue status is known, plans can be made to establish the trust, and then the trust formally applies for the policy.

Under Plan B

A second alternative, Plan B, works like this:

1. The client applies for term life insurance.

2. When the trust is established, the trustee applies for new permanent life insurance coverage. (Some form of permanent protection is almost always indicated as the sole, or the bulk of the, insurance coverage when a major objective of the irrevocable trust is to provide estate liquidity, since a term contract may expire before the client dies and the need for liquidity begins). Once the permanent coverage is issued, the term policy can be lapsed. Some companies treat the two transactions as a policy conversion.

Under Plan C

Often called the substitute application, Plan C works like this:

1. The applicant, owner, and policy date of a recently issued policy (less than a year old) are changed to coincide with the effective date of the trust. At this point, the policy may appear to have been originally purchased by the trustee. Under this substitute application procedure, a short term premium is charged to pay for coverage from the date of the original application to the new policy date. A variant of this is to

use an informal life insurance application. This allows the underwriting of the policy to take place while the trust is being created. Once the trust is created, then the informal application is cancelled and a new application is completed by the trustee of the trust.

Planners should note that the IRS could claim in Plan A, B, and C that a constructive transfer of a policy occurred and so, if death results within three years of that transfer, inclusion may result. Whenever possible, therefore, the trust should be in existence prior to the purchase of the life insurance and the trustee should apply for and own the policy from inception. A copy of the signed trust document accompanies the policy application and the trustee signs as owner-applicant and the insured signs only as proposed insured.

What about the case where a client wants to transfer existing policies to an irrevocable trust? Existing policies may be transferred to the trust through an absolute (and gratuitous) assignment of ownership from the insured to the trust or through a change of ownership form obtained from each insurer. Again, the client must survive the three year period commencing on the date of the transfer or ownership change in order for the proceeds to be excludable from his gross estate.

It is important that the client transfers all ownership rights to the trustee, not only to divest himself of incidents of ownership and avoid the transfers within three years of death rule, but also to avoid a conflict between the terms of the trust instrument and the terms of the policies. A list and description of all the policies transferred to the irrevocable trust should be attached to the trust document. Included in the description should be the following information:

1. policy number;

2. name of insurer; and

3. face amount of coverage.

There are alternatives to these fairly standard ways to set up an irrevocable trust. For instance, someone other than the insured can establish the trust and one or more persons other than the insured could fund the trust. If some third party sets up the trust and funds it, some or all of the income and estate tax traps common under the classic arrangement can be avoided. For instance, once grandparents set up and fund a trust, the trustee could split the premium

dollars with the son or daughter of the clients and insure the son or daughter for the benefit of grand-children. Arranged this way, it can be shown that the insured never held any incidents of ownership and the proceeds should be excludable from the insured's estate as well as the estate of the insured's spouse.

SELECTION OF A TRUSTEE

A trustee of an irrevocable life insurance trust must review the trust document for efficacy in meeting both tax and dispositive objectives, set up a trust account, purchase the life insurance, receive premiums from the grantor, notify beneficiaries holding demand powers of their rights each year, and pay premiums to the insurance company. Clients, even though charged only a hundred dollars or so each year for this service, often do not perceive the value they are receiving as worth the cost.

For this and other reasons (such as control), many clients will want to be the trustee themselves or name their spouses as trustees. Both choices are contraindicated because of potential adverse estate tax ramifications and both choices would limit the flexibility that should be built into an irrevocable life insurance trust.

1. *Grantor-insured as trustee* – If the grantor-insured is named as trustee, the IRS could argue that even as trustee and in spite of a trustee's definitional fiduciary obligations, the insured has retained an incident of ownership that causes the insurance proceeds to be includable in his estate. For instance, if the insured is named as trustee, it is likely the IRS will argue that the policy proceeds should be included in the insured-trustee's estate, even if he holds no interest in the trust as a beneficiary, because of the control (incidents of ownership) he as trustee holds over trust property (the life insurance).[9] Furthermore, the discretionary and administrative powers of a trustee, if retained by the insured-grantor, could be held to be rights over the trust's assets that cause estate tax inclusion. An independent trustee, one who is not a beneficiary and who is not legally subservient to the grantor is the preferable choice for a trustee.

2. *Spouse of insured-grantor as trustee* – Could the problem be solved and intrafamily control be maintained by naming the insured's spouse

as trustee? There are no attribution rules that impute the trustee's incidents of ownership to the insured grantor merely because the two happen to be married. So, it is possible for the insured's spouse to be the trustee of an irrevocable life insurance trust, assuming such spouse hasn't made transfers of property into the trust and thereby become a co-grantor.

Naming the insured's spouse as trustee may not be a bad choice during the insured's lifetime while there are no assets in the trust other than the life insurance policy and the duties of the trustee are practically nonexistent. Then, when the insured dies, the spouse can automatically be removed as trustee and a corporate fiduciary inserted (or added to the surviving spouse who would be prohibited from making the types of decisions which would cause inclusion of the proceeds in her estate). But if the insured's spouse is given a general power of appointment over the policy in the trust document, the proceeds will be in her estate.[10]

Here are some guidelines for safely naming a spouse as trustee:

- name at least one other (preferably independent) individual or corporate fiduciary as co-trustee;

- specifically exclude the surviving spouse from all potential exercises of incidents of ownership in the policy(ies) held by the trust insuring her life;

- allow distributions to the surviving spouse from the irrevocable life insurance trust only if and when the principal of the marital trust is exhausted;

- forbid any distributions to individuals that would relieve or discharge the spouse from a state legal support obligation (such as the providing of food, clothing, or shelter, or in some states education);

- limit the surviving spouse to a special power of appointment over trust assets, but specifically exclude from this power the right to dispose of life insurance on her own life; and

- exclude the surviving spouse as trustee from making any decisions involving the distribution of principal or income to herself as a beneficiary except those limited by a

health, education, maintenance, and support ascertainable standard.

The authors' opinion is that the advantages of naming the spouse as trustee are outweighed by the potential tax traps and drafting difficulties. At the least, if a spouse is named, another individual should be named as a co-trustee with the trust wording noted above.

One of the more important issues in a country where there is great geographic mobility (not only of beneficiaries, but also of trust administration personnel) is the question of changing trustees. Can the trust safely provide for replacement of trustees if the beneficiaries move or, for any reason, decide they want a new trustee?

It is clear that the grantor should not be given the power to remove the trustee and become the successor trustee. Even if the grantor never exercises that removal power and even if the removal power is subject to a condition or contingency, such as the trustee's death, resignation, or malfeasance, which has not yet occurred, the mere existence of the right will cause the inclusion of the trust's assets in the grantor's estate.

The IRS claims that a grantor should be considered to hold those powers over a trust that are in fact held by an independent trustee if the grantor has the power to remove the trustee, even if the replacement trustee is legally independent. It is the opinion of the authors that the IRS position is wrong because it imputes to a grantor powers that he can never hold personally. It ignores entirely the independence and fiduciary obligations of the trustee.

As a practical matter, many authorities approach the selection of a trustee by considering the existence of the trust during two time periods: (1) Who should be the trustee during the insured's lifetime? and (2) Who should be the trustee thereafter?

During the insured's lifetime, the trustee must be a person who will cooperate with the grantor and the grantor's family. This criterion may include the attorney, accountant, trusted friend, or adult child of the grantor. Generally, the time commitment (and therefore the trustee's compensation) is minimal during this stage of trusteeship.

But after the grantor's death, the trustee's role changes drastically. At this point, the trustee must invest, safeguard, and manage the insurance proceeds and other funds that may have poured over from the client's estate into the trust. Those assets must now be administered over a long period of time and countless difficult decisions may be required.

So, in many cases, an individual is selected for the predeath period, while a corporate trustee (with or without individual co-trustees) takes over the burdensome task of trust administration after the death of the grantor. Certainly, a bank or other professional trustee should be named in the trust instrument as a contingent trustee in case the individuals named cannot, or become unwilling or unable to serve.

A corporate trustee during this second phase of the irrevocable trust's existence avoids all of the potential tax traps, provides continuity of investment, management, and record keeping, and relieves the client's family and other advisors of a myriad of bothersome and time consuming details. Since the trust may remain in existence for several generations, this continuity can be extremely important. A collateral (but not insignificant) advantage to the use of a corporate fiduciary is that the bank or trust company usually will have highly competent counsel to provide a second opinion and review the trust document and its provisions.

REDUCING OR ELIMINATING GIFT TAXES ON POLICY TRANSFERS AND PREMIUM PAYMENTS THROUGH CRUMMEY POWERS

When a client transfers a life insurance policy to an irrevocable trust, a gift is made subject to the gift tax. The tax, if any, payable on that transfer depends on the fair market value of the policy, the availability of the annual exclusion, and the availability of the lifetime exemption. If the annual exclusion is available, then up to $14,000 (in 2017, as indexed for inflation) of the value of the gift is shielded if the client is unmarried and up to $28,000 (in 2017, as indexed for inflation) if the client is married and the spouse consents to split the gift so that each is treated as making a gift of one half of the policy.[11] The value of the transfer in excess of that amount would be taxable to the extent not protected by the client's remaining lifetime exemption. If the annual exclusion is not available, the entire value of the contract on the date of the gift would be a taxable transfer to the extent not protected by the lifetime exemption.[12]

The gift tax valuation rules can be summarized as follows (see Chapter 26: Life Insurance Valuation for more information):

Policy Transferred	Gift Tax Value
New policy transferred immediately after issue	Cost (net premiums paid)
Existing policy – no further premiums due	In case of a paid up or single premium policy, cost of replacement
Policy in "premium paying" stage	"Interpolated terminal reserve" plus any unearned premiums paid on the date of death less any policy loans
Group term life insurance	At the client's option, the actual cost or Table I cost
Policy is about to mature on the date of transfer (for instance, client is within a few weeks of death due to cancer)	IRS may value the policy at or near its face amount.

To minimize gift tax exposure upon the contribution of a policy to an irrevocable trust, a client may want to borrow a portion of the cash values out of the policy before making the gift. This reduces the initial gift tax value of the policy itself. However, caution should be used when utilizing this strategy as it may create an inadvertent violation of the transfer for value rule—see Chapter 25: Transfer for Value for more information. Because the trust assumes the loan, it is treated as if it paid an amount equal to the transferred loan for the policy. This creates a part sale/part gift. If the loan amount exceeds the transferor's basis in the policy, then the "transferee's basis is determined by reference to the transferor's basis" exception to the transfer for value rule will not apply, and another exception to the transfer for value rule will be needed. Therefore, as a general rule, avoid taking a policy loan in excess of the policy basis before making the gift.

When more than one large policy is to be transferred to the trust, they can be transferred over a period of years to fully utilize the annual exclusion and yet stay within the "five-or-five" maximum limitations. Alternatively, one large policy could be split into several smaller ones and staggered gifts could be made to the trust.

Payment of premiums by the client following a transfer of a policy to an irrevocable trust is an additional gift, regardless of whether the client makes the payment directly to the insurer or makes a cash contribution to the trustee who then pays the premium.

If someone other than the person who created the trust pays the premiums, there is a potential gift tax problem if that additional grantor is not a beneficiary of the trust. For instance, the aunt of a beneficiary makes contributions to a trust set up by her brother for her niece. Each premium the aunt pays is a gift to the niece.

If a beneficiary of the trust pays premiums to keep the insurance in force and protect his interest, the portion of the premium equal to the payor's share of the trust would not be considered a gift but the portion of the premium that enriches the other beneficiaries would be treated as a gift from the payor to the others.

Example. Suppose the client cannot or will not make further contributions and the policy on his life held by the trust is about to lapse. To the extent the beneficiary's contribution will be returned in the form of insurance coverage the beneficiary will receive, he has made a (nontaxable) gift to himself. But to the extent the money paid exceeds his share, the difference would be considered a gift to the other beneficiaries. So if three brothers were three equal beneficiaries of a trust and the oldest gave $12,000 to the trustee who in turn used it to pay a $12,000 premium, he would be deemed to have made a $9,000 (two-thirds of $12,000) gift to his siblings.

This gift tax liability is imposed even if there was no donative intent by the premium paying brother. Should the grantor not have the funds (or the will) to pay the premiums, one solution is for the trustee to have the insurer divide the policy up into separate policies for each beneficiary and ask each to contribute his share of the premiums. That way, in the event of a lapse, only the beneficiaries who did not pay premiums will suffer.

In general, since gift tax rates are identical to estate tax rates, in the long run a client would be trading dollars if he incurred gift tax in the attempt to save estate tax. Actually, because gift tax must be paid currently while estate tax can be put off until death, each dollar of gift tax, in essence, costs (time value of money wise) more than each dollar of estate tax. At the least, psychologically, each dollar of gift tax hurts more. Of course, there is no current gift tax cost to the extent gifts are covered by the annual exclusion or lifetime exemption.

The high financial and psychological cost of gift tax on taxable gifts is why planners must use every effort to accomplish the estate tax saving goals of an irrevocable life insurance trust at the least possible gift tax cost (and if possible without using up all or any of the client's available estate and gift tax exemptions).

The major tool for getting the most estate tax savings at the least gift tax cost is the gift tax annual exclusion. As the following calculation shows, a long term systematic use of the annual exclusion, even without life insurance leveraging, can result in amazing federal estate tax savings.

Donor's Age	40
Donor's Life Expectancy	42.5 Years
Annual Exclusion	$14,000 (in 2017)
Split Gifts	Yes
Number of Donees	5
Annual Gifts ($14,000 × 2 × 5)	$140,000
Donor's Projected Estate Tax Bracket	40% (in 2017)

No Growth

Total Amount of Gifts ($140,000 × 43)	$6,020,000
Potential Estate Tax Savings (40%)	$2,408,000

With Growth

Annual After-Tax Return on Gifts	4%
Value of Gifts at Life Expectancy	$15,975,265
Potential Estate Tax Savings (40%)	$6,386,106

If the beneficiaries, either inside or outside a trust, used the annual gifts (each of the five donees were given $28,000, a total of $140,000 a year of gifts in the above example) to purchase life insurance on the life of the client, the estate tax leverage in the illustration above could be multiplied many times over.

However, the annual exclusion is available only for gifts of a present interest. Present interest is defined for gifts of life insurance under the same rules as it is for other gratuitous transfers. Essentially, to be considered a present, as opposed to a future, interest, the donee must receive the immediate, unfettered, and ascertainable right to use, possess, or enjoy the transferred property. No annual exclusion will be allowed if the beneficiary's right to take can possibly be threatened or delayed for even one minute. For instance, if the trustee has the discretion to invade trust corpus for the benefit of non-Crummey beneficiaries, even if that discretionary right is never actually used, the gift tax annual exclusion is not available for the transfer.

If a client gave his intended beneficiary an outright gift of a life insurance policy, the transfer would qualify for the gift tax annual exclusion (unless the gift of the policy was made to two or more people, in which case it would be a gift of a future interest since a joint owner could not withdraw his or her interest without the consent of the other joint owner(s)). The mere fact that the policy will not pay off until the death of the insured at some distant and uncertain date in the future does not cause the transfer to be considered a future interest since the recipient has the immediate, unfettered, and ascertainable right to use, possess, and enjoy all of the incidents of ownership in the contract.

But a gift of an insurance policy to a trust designed, almost by definition, to delay the timing and control the beneficiary's use, possession, and enjoyment of its assets will be a gift of a future interest. Absent a special trust provision creating a present interest in one or more of the trust's beneficiaries, each time a client made a contribution to a trust, enabling the trustee to pay life insurance premiums, the client would have to use up more of his unified credit to avoid gift taxes or actually pay gift taxes.

The solution to the problem of the beneficiary's inability to immediately use, possess, and enjoy the client's contribution is to create a window through which the beneficiary could reach to take all or a portion of that annual contribution or alternatively use the policy. This window is what practitioners call the Crummey power which is named after the successful taxpayer[13] who was able to obtain a gift tax annual exclusion because of his beneficiaries' rights to make a demand of the trustee even though:

1. each beneficiary was a minor and obviously could not exercise the demand power without the appointment of a legal guardian;

2. no guardian was ever, in fact appointed on behalf of the children;

3. the demand power was never actually exercised by either the children or by a guardian on their behalf and none of the children had received any payment from the trust fund; and

4. the power had a limited duration of only thirteen days (the demand was to be made by the end of the year in which the transfer was made from the gift the donor made that year but most transfers were made about the middle of December).

The key to recognition of this window as an effective gift tax exclusion device is therefore not the actual enjoyment of the right by holders of the Crummey power but rather the reasonable and realistic legal right to enjoy. The trust must therefore specify that each trust beneficiary to whom a Crummey power is to be granted is given an absolute but noncumulative right to withdraw a specified amount from the client's annual contribution. The client may wish to limit this noncumulative right to the lowest of: (1) the amount of the annual exclusion per donor/donee per year; (2) the amount actually contributed; or (3) the greater of $5,000 or 5 percent of the value of the trust's assets at the time of the withdrawal (see below).

Although the IRS has accepted the Crummey power as a means of creating a present interest and has even privately approved the use of Crummey powers to satisfy the present interest requirement with respect to gifts of life insurance policies in trust, it continues to disallow the annual exclusion unless both the letter of the law and good intent are shown by the taxpayer.

When a grantor sets up the Crummey power window through which a beneficiary can reach in and make a withdrawal, the grantor is attempting to qualify each year's transfer to the trust for the gift tax annual exclusion. But the grantor does not want to make the window opening so large and keep it open so long that the beneficiary will actually reach in and take the contribution. If the beneficiary does exercise the right to withdraw, the money will not be available to pay premiums on the life insurance that is meant to provide estate liquidity and provide financial security for the trust's beneficiaries. (It would not be wise to provide for a shutting of the window in the event a holder does take a given year's contribution, since that would be evidence that the power was a sham.)

But the client could maintain some control by providing in the trust agreement that each year's contributions to the trust would be earmarked to specific donees. That way, if a powerholder actually took money in the prior year, the client could decide not to make a contribution subject to that beneficiary's withdrawal right. In other words, the trust could provide that each powerholder had a right to withdraw funds from the trust only if specific contributions were designated as subject to that beneficiary's right of withdrawal. The trust could also provide that if a beneficiary is subject to a bankruptcy proceeding, the right of withdrawal lapses. This would prevent the bankruptcy trustee from exercising the withdrawal right.

The open window (demand period) must be allowed to remain open long enough to give the beneficiary a meaningful interest in the property given to the trust. In other words, the beneficiary must know of his right to make a withdrawal and have a realistic and reasonable opportunity to actually exercise that right. So the trustee should keep sufficient funds in the trust during the open window period so that a demand can be realistically and immediately satisfied. If a client contributed money to the trust but the trustee paid the premiums for trust owned life insurance the very same day, the IRS could argue that, in reality, the Crummey powerholder never had a chance to make a withdrawal. So if the demand period is too short, the IRS will argue that the power was a sham and disallow the exclusion.

Trustees should notify all demand powerholders of the right to make withdrawals. In the case of minor beneficiaries, notification should be made to the person who can legally exercise the demand power on the minor's behalf, typically the minor's parent or legal guardian. This notice should take the form of a return receipt requested letter informing the beneficiaries that gifts to the trust can be expected on specified dates (coincident with premium payment dates). The letter should inform them of their demand rights, and promise supplementary information if gifts are not made according to this schedule or if additional gifts are made. An alternative is to request that the beneficiary acknowledge receipt of each year's notice by initialing a copy and returning it to the client or trustee. The safer course would be to provide notice to the powerholder of each contribution with respect to which a withdrawal power is available.

What if no guardian has been appointed for a minor beneficiary? The IRS position is liberal:

"If there is no impediment under the trust or local law to the appointment of a guardian and the minor donee has a right to demand distribution, the

transfer is a gift of a present interest that qualifies for the annual exclusion."[14]

There is no specific number of days during which a demand power can be exercised which assures that a demand power will create a present interest. The number of days within which the beneficiary can exercise the power is measured by both the terms of the trust and the date of the gift. The bottom line is that the trust agreement should give the beneficiary adequate time to realistically make a demand and exercise the right to enjoy the contribution the insured-client has made to the trust.

It is essential that the beneficiary or guardian for the beneficiary to whom the Crummey power is granted be given proper and timely written notice of the right to make a withdrawal. Regardless of the form of the gift, a withdrawal power will not be considered a present interest unless the beneficiary is aware of its existence. In the authors' opinion, thirty days from the date of the notice seems to be the shortest reasonable period. So if the beneficiary's power to make a withdrawal lapses at the end of the year, contributions should be made to the trust before December 1.

On the other hand, if the window is held open too long, there may be adverse tax implications to the Crummey powerholder. So if the beneficiary were to die while the window was open, the assets subject to that power to withdraw would be included in his estate.[15] By limiting the duration of the opening to one month each year, if the beneficiary dies during any other month of the year (during which he had no power to make a withdrawal), there should be no estate tax inclusion.

If the window is opened too high, i.e., if the "five-or-five" power were not included in the withdrawal limitations, the value of any unexercised demand right existing at the beneficiary's death would be included in his estate. This is because the absolute power to make a withdrawal is technically a general power of appointment, an unlimited right to direct the disposition of the property subject to the power to anyone, including the powerholder, his estate, his creditors, or the creditors of his estate. The mere possession of such a general power is enough to require estate tax inclusion.[16] So if a beneficiary had the right to take an unlimited amount from the trust, the entire value of the trust's principal would be included in his estate.

Furthermore, each year that the beneficiary allowed the right to make a withdrawal lapse, the IRS would claim that by not taking what could have been taken;

the beneficiary is making a gift to the trust's remainder person. Allowing a general power to lapse or expire is treated for gift and estate tax purposes as a release (i.e., as if the powerholder made an actual transfer of the property subject to the power). For instance, if the client's wife is to receive income for life and then trust assets are to pass to the client's children, to the extent the client's wife does nothing and allows this year's Crummey power to lapse, she is in essence making a gift to her son of what she could have withdrawn. That would trigger both gift taxes and gift tax filing requirements since the gift would not pass to the son immediately and would therefore be a future interest gift that by definition could not qualify for the annual exclusion. Worse yet, the wife retains for life the income from the gift she is deemed to have made. This is a classic gift with a retained life estate that requires inclusion in the wife's estate of the date of death value of the entire property producing the income.

Here's where the "five-or-five" provision comes in. Under a de minimis rule, the gift/estate tax problem of the powerholder who doesn't exercise the power is avoided to the extent the lapse of the power each year does not exceed the greater of $5,000 or 5 percent of the value of the trust's assets at the time of the lapse. In other words, the lapse of a Crummey power is considered a release (taxable gift) only to the extent that the value of the property in question exceeds the greater of $5,000 or 5 percent of the total value of the assets out of which the exercise of the lapsed power could have been satisfied. This is the reason why the familiar "five-or-five" limitation is built into the wording of most irrevocable life insurance trusts.

Planners should note, however, that it may pay—in certain cases—to use a higher withdrawal limit where it is expected the Crummey powerholder will never have a significant estate or gift tax problem and the major objective is to shield the client's premium payments on a large policy from gift tax.

Many clients, who have discovered the irrevocable life insurance trust's advantages, place sizable policies in such trusts. The large premiums that are generated by those policies quickly exceed the per donee annual exclusion limit. For this reason, clients want to multiply the annual exclusions available by giving many beneficiaries a Crummey withdrawal power.

A trust may grant demand powers to several individuals and therefore multiply the number of available gift tax annual exclusions, which in turn allows the grantor to make larger gifts in the form of policy assignments and/or premium payments without gift tax. It's also good planning for the trust to provide for contingent powerholders, so that if a spouse or child who holds a power dies, another person would take over and the present interest exclusion could be maintained. But there are limitations on the grantor's ability to use multiple Crummey demand powers in this fashion:

First, each beneficiary's interest must be ascertainable at the moment the client's annual contribution is made to the trust. Proper apportionment of demand rights is necessary. If the donee's exact present interest can't be immediately ascertained, no annual exclusion will be allowed since it would be impossible to determine whether the client should be credited with the full amount of the exclusion or some lesser amount. The trick is, therefore, to either: (a) make the number of eventual donees immediately ascertainable at the time of each gift to the trust, or (b) assure that the interest of each Crummey powerholder be immediately capable of valuation.

If a trust does not have sufficient principal to satisfy all of the Crummey demand powers given to its beneficiaries, the IRS could argue that none of the interests are capable of valuation and the gift was one of a future interest since no beneficiary's right can be ascertained on the date of the gift. The solution is for the trust to provide that if any year's contribution is insufficient to meet all the possible Crummey demands, then the contribution must be distributed on a pro rata basis among the powerholders. The trust should further require that if any donee receives an amount greater than his pro rata share of the trust corpus, that donee must immediately reimburse the trustee for the excess amount in the event there are insufficient assets satisfying the potential demands made by other powerholders.

Second, it remains the IRS' position that a demand holder must have a significant, beneficial interest in the trust. The IRS believes that the critical test is whether the grantors ever expect that a particular demand power will be exercised. Because remote beneficiaries have little or no reason not to exercise their demand rights, the IRS views the failure of remote beneficiaries to exercise their demand rights as evidence that some understanding exists between them and the grantors. According to the IRS, this is fatal to the annual exclusion.

However, it has been the authors' opinion that it should be immaterial that the donor does not want particular demand powers to be exercised. The statute requires only that the donees are appraised of their rights and legally can exercise those powers. The Tax Court agrees with the authors. It clearly stated in several cases that the sole criteria for allowing an annual exclusion is the existence in the donee's hands of the immediate, unfettered, and ascertainable right to use, possess, and enjoy the subject of the gift on the date the power is issued. The Tax Court expressly rejected the IRS's contention that "evil intent"—even when manifested by a family discussion about how funds transferred to the trust would be used by the trustee—taints the transfer and makes it a future interest. The only relevant test is: "Does the donee have the legal right to make a demand for payment?" and "Is the trustee legally obligated to comply with a demand from a Crummey power-holder?"

Having stated both the authors' and the Tax Court's opinion, the authors continue to suggest that notices in fact be made in writing on a timely basis. Further, family discussions as to what might or might not happen to the fortunes of a powerholder who made a withdrawal should be avoided. Counsel should insert wording into the agreement to the effect that "Trustee shall promptly comply with every demand for payment under the above withdrawal power."[17]

Another solution may be to give all demand powerholders at least a discretionary right to current distributions from a life insurance trust, despite the fact that no such distributions are likely.

Not all authorities agree on how gifts to the irrevocable life insurance trust should be structured or how best to word the trust so that an annual exclusion will be allowed, regardless of what type of gift is made to the trust or how large that gift is.

When a trust is unfunded, the client's contribution may be in the form of: (a) direct payment of the insurance premiums to the insurance company by the insured-grantor; or (b) indirect payments by grantor to a trust, either by check or through his employer (for example, as payments toward group insurance or split dollar premiums). In such cases, the Crummey provisions of the trust should authorize beneficiaries to demand both direct and indirect gifts to the trust, ensuring that indirect gifts qualify for the annual exclusion.

Where the trust is unfunded, there are only two sources from which the demand right can be satisfied: (1) the cash contributions made by the grantor to the trustee in order to pay premiums (but if the premium payments go directly into the policy, due to surrender charges and other policy fees, the amount available to satisfy a demand may be considerably less than the full premium payment); and (2) the life insurance policy itself.

An annual exclusion should be allowed even if the trust holds only term insurance or permanent life insurance that has little to no cash value on the date contributed. However, the trust must give the trustee the authority to make payments in cash or in kind. This ability to satisfy the demand by distributing a fractional interest in individual life insurance policies or group term insurance should enable the grantor to obtain the annual exclusion in exactly the same way that an outright gift of a fractional interest in an insurance policy would qualify.

Conservative planners may protect the insured-grantor's gift tax annual exclusion even further by funding the trust with some assets other than life insurance policies. If the trust has an amount of cash or other liquid assets equal to the annual premiums (the required amount of annual exclusion), the trustee could always distribute that cash to satisfy a beneficiary's demand.

The recommended course of action in most cases is for the insured grantor to give the trustee a cash sum each year that the trustee could hold for the duration of the demand period. Only after the expiration of the demand period would the trustee use this contribution to pay the premiums. This requires that the client grantor make premium payments well ahead of their scheduled due date to avoid a policy lapse.

One conceptually simple alternative approach is for the client to make direct gifts of cash to the trust's adult beneficiaries who then make contributions back to the trust. The amount given to each beneficiary should equal his proportionate share of the trust. Since the gifts are both direct and outright, the client should obtain an annual exclusion gift for each transfer. Then, when the children contribute the gifts back to the trust, they should not be deemed to be making gifts since each should be contributing only his share and that should be going only to his portion of the trust.

This technique may prove more difficult, however, in real life because of the administrative difficulties and the fact that beneficiaries may not co-operate. This technique should pose few problems during the life of the grantor or the grantor's spouse, but may result in a portion of the trust being included in the beneficiary's estate under Code section 2036(a). This may not be a major problem if the beneficiary does not have a very large estate or is young and likely to exhaust the trust funds.

There are two major reasons why a client may wish to give a spouse Crummey powers:

1. The client may be worried that children or other donees will exercise their demand powers and thus defeat the purpose of the trust by depriving the trustee of funds from which to pay premiums.

2. The client may want to increase the number of available annual exclusions.

In most cases, there is no good reason to deny the client's spouse a demand power, but it should be limited to an annual amount not exceeding the greater of: (a) $5,000; or (b) 5 percent of the trust fund. To allow a greater right of withdrawal would invite IRS inclusion of the policy proceeds in the spouse's estate. If the grantor's spouse has the requisite beneficial interest in the trust, the IRS could argue that the lapse of the spouse's demand power (i.e., the spouse's failure to exercise the withdrawal right on her own behalf) is equivalent to the release of a general power of appointment.

Under Code section 2041(a)(2), a decedent's gross estate includes the value of property subject to a general power of appointment that was released or exercised before the decedent's death, if the result of the release or exercise is the creation of a retained interest described in Code sections 2035, 2036, 2037, or 2038. If the spouse is also an income beneficiary, therefore, this would create estate tax inclusion.[18]

One technique that will not work is the use of reciprocal demand powers. For instance, suppose a client and his brother both want to shelter very large life insurance premiums from gift tax, so both simultaneously create irrevocable life insurance trusts in order to increase the number of available gift tax annual exclusions. Assume, further, that each brother gives his own children and his brother a Crummey power. The reciprocal powers the brothers gave each other will be ignored for purposes of the gift tax annual exclusion. Furthermore, the trusts will be included in each brother's estate as a transfer with a retained life estate under section 2036.

GIFT, ESTATE, AND INCOME TAX PROBLEMS RELATED TO CRUMMEY POWERS

Unexpected gift tax problems can arise in certain situations upon the lapse (nonexercise) of a Crummey power. In most cases, this problem will not occur or, if it does, it will be minor. But planners should be aware of it in cases where the value of a life insurance policy or subsequent premiums are large.

Specifically, the problem most frequently arises where premium outlays will exceed the greater of $5,000 a year or 5 percent of the trust's assets in the year of the grantor's contribution. The trap is set when the client, in an attempt to create a larger window through which the beneficiary can make withdrawals in order to take full advantage of the annual exclusion (including the annual exclusion of the client's spouse where the client is married and splits the gift), opens that window too much. This may reduce the grantor's gift tax problems, but increase those of the beneficiary.

Why might opening the window too much create a gift (and possibly estate) tax problem for the beneficiary? The problem stems from the fact that another term for an absolute demand or withdrawal or Crummey power is a general power of appointment (a power the beneficiary has to appoint trust funds to the beneficiary himself). By allowing that general power to lapse, the beneficiary who could have taken the cash, but didn't, is making a taxable gift to anyone who has interests in the trust that are enlarged by the lapse.

Unfortunately, those donees will not receive their gifts immediately. That makes such gifts future interests and, therefore, the gifts are ineligible for the gift tax annual exclusion. This means the Crummey beneficiary who permits the withdrawal power to lapse would (absent the "five-or-five" de minimis rule) be required to file annual gift tax returns (no matter how small the gift) and may have to use part of his lifetime exemption or pay a gift tax.

In many cases, as a practical matter, the annual right of withdrawal for each Crummey powerholder will be limited to $5,000 each year. That presents a major problem in the large premium situation, i.e., those where the premium significantly exceeds the amount sheltered under the normal Crummey limits. A client who sets up a trust with four Crummey powerholders can safely contribute only $20,000 ($5,000 × 4 beneficiaries) a year before running into gift tax problems. Yet if the premium were $60,000 a year, the $40,000 annual difference would soon exhaust the client's unified credit.

There are ways in which the irrevocable trust can be designed to avoid or minimize this problem, described below.

Limited Pay and Suspended Premium Types of Life Insurance

Limited pay life insurance can be useful. For instance, a ten-pay life contract would be complete in ten years. The amount saved in estate taxes would be considerable compared to the relatively small gift taxes paid during the ten year period.

Suspended premium insurance is a variation on the first theme. However, while premiums may be projected to suspend at some point, they may not actually do so.

Increase the Number of Legitimate Powerholders

The use of multiple powerholders must be coupled inversely with the client's desire not to have to litigate with the IRS and his fear that such powerholders will exercise their rights. There is no question that success with multiple powerholders requires giving them all legitimate and realistic rights to exercise their powers. There must be no implied or express agreement that they will not exercise their rights.

The problem can't be solved by creating multiple trusts with multiple demand rights for the same beneficiary. Multiple demand powers held by the same beneficiary over the same or different trusts are aggregated to determine if the grantor has exceeded the $5,000 portion of the "five-or-five" limitation.[19]

Add Testamentary Control

Here, the powerholder is given testamentary (by will only) control as a means of preventing a taxable gift when the power lapses. There are two different ways to utilize this approach, a general testamentary power of appointment and a special testamentary power of appointment.

Under the general testamentary power technique, each beneficiary is given a general ("name anyone you want to receive it") testamentary power of appointment over his share of the trust. So each beneficiary can choose who will receive that share of the trust if he doesn't live to get it. But that right to direct who will receive it can be exercised only at death and only by a specific written provision in his will referring to the general power in the trust. The trust will provide that if the beneficiary doesn't properly exercise the power, the property will pass to the other beneficiaries in the trust. So if the beneficiary dies without diverting the property to someone other than the client-named remainder person in his will, not only will the property go to the party the client desired but it will pass at the time and in the manner desired.

Using this technique, a client can make gifts equal to the full annual exclusion amount and couple those gifts with equal withdrawal rights. So with five donees, the client could give up to $70,000 per year (in 2017, as indexed for inflation) rather than just $25,000. If the powerholder didn't exercise the right to take the $14,000 in a given year, the lapse would not be considered a completed gift (i.e., it wouldn't be subject to the gift tax) because the powerholder can, at any time, name someone other than the client-specified remainder person as the recipient of the property subject to the power.

There are, of course, costs and downsides to the general power of appointment approach: First, whether or not the powerholder chooses to allow the power to lapse without use, property subject to the power will be in his estate because the power is general.[20] Second, this powerholder controlled ability to shift property rights equates, by definition, to a loss of control by the client.

The second variation on the testamentary Crummey power technique is to grant each beneficiary only a limited (special) power of appointment. Assume the trust provides separate shares for each beneficiary and, if the beneficiary dies, his share will pass to whomever he provides by will within a client-specified class such as the powerholder's siblings (i.e., the beneficiary is given a special testamentary power of appointment to choose who will take the property if he does not exercise the Crummey power, but the powerholder's choices are limited to parties or classes of individuals selected by the client-grantor). The class of limited takers can, in fact, be quite broad and include anyone other than the powerholder, his estate, his creditors, or the creditors of his estate.

Here again, the trust provides that, if the beneficiary fails to make a withdrawal within the specified time frame, his right to make an immediate withdrawal ends. The window closes. But the cash or other assets he could have taken are earmarked for his exclusive benefit. This avoids the gift tax problem since the cash subject to the power does not pass to anyone else until the beneficiary's death. The lapse of the withdrawal power is therefore not a completed taxable transfer. The powerholder could, at any moment until death, name some new beneficiary or change the size of the interest going to the client-named beneficiaries. Of course, since the cash he could have taken is held in his name, there is an estate tax implication: The proportionate share of the principal of the trust attributable to the lapsed withdrawal powers will be includable in the Crummey holder's estate if the beneficiary dies before the trust ends.[21]

There are, of course, costs and downsides to the limited testamentary power of appointment approach: First, whether or not the powerholder chooses to allow the power to lapse without use, some portion of the property subject to the power will be in his estate if the powerholder dies before the trust ends. So, like the general testamentary power technique, the limited power in someone else's hands in a separate trust means the client can't fully use generation-skipping exclusions to shift wealth without the generation-skipping transfer tax. Second, this powerholder controlled ability to shift property rights equates, by definition, to a loss of control by the client. The Crummey holder has actual dispositive rights that may or may not mesh with the trust grantor's dispositive objectives.

Use a Hanging Power

Some authorities claim that this alternative gives the client the best of all worlds by avoiding the gift tax problem upon the lapse of the power and allows full use of the maximum annual exclusion without creating estate tax or control problems. Is it possible to make maximum annual exclusion gifts and yet avoid inclusion of any portion of the lapsed power in the beneficiary's estate while retaining control in the grantor-client?

The hanging power works like this: The holder is allowed to make a withdrawal each year equal to his share of the client's contribution up to the maximum allowable annual exclusion ($14,000 in 2017). The right to that aliquot share is cumulative. So, to the extent no withdrawal (or less than the holder's share is withdrawn) is made in a given year, the balance hangs over and can be used in a following year. Specifically,

each year, assuming the power is not used, the right to take the greater of $5,000 or 5 percent of the trust's principal lapses. But the right to take any amount over that amount continues. It carries over or hangs over to future years.

So if the client contributed $10,000 to the trust and there was only one powerholder, the right to take $5,000 would lapse in the first year but the right to withdraw the remaining $5,000 would continue. In later years, the right to take the first $5,000 (or 5 percent of trust corpus if greater) continues to lapse while a pot builds up of the excess amounts. By the second year, if no withdrawals were made, $10,000 worth of contributions would have lapsed but $10,000 worth of excess contributions ($5,000 from the first year and $5,000 from the second year) are now available as credits against future years. This pot of credits builds up until the client stops or slows down contributions. Figure 34.1 illustrates this concept. Note that, in the example, premiums are assumed to be suspended along with the need to make additional gifts to the trust after 2003. Also, the hanging power was extinguished in 2010.

The hanging power concept assumes that the major premium payments will be made in the early years and then suspend, while at a certain point the beneficiary's right to make withdrawals (and therefore estate and gift tax liability) will be extinguished.

If the beneficiary dies while money is in the pot (i.e., while amounts remain available at the beneficiary's demand), whatever is subject to that general power is includable in the powerholder's estate. Once there is no longer any amount which can be taken, nothing should be includable. Note that in the early years of the policy the amount lapsing is $5000. However, as the cash value of the policy grows and once it exceeds $100,000, then the 5 percent amount kicks in, helping to extinguish the pot sooner and mitigate the risk of inclusion in a beneficiary's estate.

The nontax problem here is one of control; while there are funds that can be taken, the client's dispositive objectives are at risk. The hanging powerholder can legitimately and realistically take a sizable sum. So beneficiaries could frustrate the client's intent by making withdrawals of large amounts. (Of course, minors could only exercise this right through the unlikely course of action of having a guardian appointed to exercise the right.) This should serve as a warning. Clients should be cautioned to carefully select powerholders mature enough to understand the client's objectives and the

Figure 34.1

		HANGING POWERS			
YEAR	**GIFT**	**CORPUS**	**POWER**	**LAPSE**	**CARRYOVER**
1997	$10,000	$10,000	$10,000	$5,000	$5,000
1998	10,000	20,000	15,000	5,000	10,000
1999	10,000	30,000	20,000	5,000	15,000
2000	10,000	40,000	25,000	5,000	20,000
2001	10,000	50,000	30,000	5,000	25,000
2002	11,000	61,000	36,000	5,000	31,000
2003	5,000	66,000	36,000	5,000	31,000
2004	0	66,000	31,000	5,000	26,000
2005	0	66,000	26,000	5,000	21,000
2006	0	66,000	21,000	5,000	16,000
2007	0	66,000	16,000	5,000	11,000
2008	0	66,000	11,000	5,000	6,000
2009	0	66,000	6,000	5,000	1,000
2010	0	66,000	1,000	1,000	0

potential consequences of their actions. Remember, also, that the client can always choose not to make future gifts to a beneficiary.

Yet a further problem is the IRS position on hanging powers. The IRS has equated a hanging power with the following language to a mere tax savings clause that is adverse to public policy and should be disregarded; an invalid subsequent condition that discourages enforcement of federal gift tax provisions.

The clause that triggered the negative IRS response to hanging powers read: "If upon the termination of any power of withdrawal, the person holding the power will be deemed to have made a taxable gift for federal gift tax purposes, then such power of withdrawal will not lapse but will continue to exist with respect to the amount that would have been a taxable gift and will terminate as soon as such termination will not result in a taxable gift."

Many experts feel that the IRS is wrong in its position but suggest that a modification of the hanging power language will counter the IRS argument. They suggest avoiding any reference to the term taxable gifts or to a recharacterization of a gift as an incomplete gift if the IRS finds such a gift. The drafting attorney should clearly delineate the lapse formula including the timing and amount so that it can be shown that all the

withdrawal rights could have been determined at the moment granted and the powerholder didn't have to wait until a tax audit or court determination to ascertain his rights to take trust property.

It is suggested that the client contribute the full $14,000 (up to $28,000 per married couple, annual exclusion amounts as indexed for 2017) and give each powerholder the right to withdraw an amount equal to the "five-or-five" limits. This right will lapse each year thirty days after each year's contribution has been made and that same amount will lapse each further year. This way, all gifts made by the powerholder are safe gifts in that they fall within the protected "five-or-five" limits. If there are excess gifts, the amount of the excess can't exceed $21,000 ($28,000 maximum annual exclusion limit in 2017 for a married couple less $5,000 protected amount). Even after twenty years of premiums, this would be within the estate tax exemption limits. This relatively small use of the exemption would be a good investment since it would be leveraged many times over by the shifting of wealth through the use of estate tax-free life insurance.

Single Beneficiary Trusts

Providing separate trusts or separate trust shares may be the simplest way to overcome the "five-or-five" limits if the client is willing to give up flexibility and risk several disadvantages; the trustee will not be able to make discretionary trust distributions to persons other than the beneficiary since there will be only one beneficiary (or one trust with separate "sole benefit" shares for each beneficiary). Furthermore, all the income and principal must be payable to the estate of the beneficiary if he dies before the trust pays out all its principal and each beneficiary must be given a testamentary general power of appointment over his trust share. When a Crummey power lapses, no gift is made to someone else since there are no other beneficiaries. Since the lapse results in a transfer only to the sole beneficiary's estate, there is no taxable gift. So a married parent splitting gifts and who has four children can fund a trust with separate shares for each of her four children, a total of $112,000 in 2017.

In addition to the loss of flexibility, other disadvantages include:

a.   the trust's assets can't be sprinkled or sprayed to the person who needs or deserves it the most or who is in the lowest tax bracket, since there is only one beneficiary;

b.   the property will pass as if owned by the beneficiary rather than the client, possibly to a person and in a manner that would be objectionable to the client;

c.   the property will be includable in the beneficiary's estate, for tax, probate, and creditor purposes; and

d.   the property may be distributed (due to the untimely death of the beneficiary) prior to the date expected by the client.

Grant Withdrawal Rights to Secondary/Contingent Beneficiaries

This was the strategy used in the now well-known *Cristofani* case.[22] Here, grandchildren who were contingent beneficiaries were given withdrawal rights in addition to those provided to the client's children who were the primary beneficiaries of the trust. These grandchildren were entitled to principal and income only to the extent the prior level of beneficiaries (their parents) hadn't exhausted trust assets.

The IRS found that this level of powerholders had, as beneficiaries, such a remote chance of actually receiving

assets from the trust that there must have been some implied understanding between them and the grantor client that they would not make a withdrawal; why else would they not have exercised their power and taken some of the assets in the trust?

But the Tax Court disagreed with the IRS and focused on the central issue: Did the powerholders (no matter what level or how remote their chance of taking a share of the trust as a beneficiary) have the absolute legal right to make an unfettered withdrawal of property from the trust? The authors suggest, in spite of the court's favorable conclusion, that conservative practitioners will limit Crummey rights to beneficiaries who have a realistic chance to receive something from the trust as beneficiaries rather than merely as powerholders.

Even this tack has its downsides and costs. The most obvious is that the IRS is right in one sense; with nothing to lose, what will stop a remote beneficiary from making a withdrawal? Aside from that, the right to make a withdrawal does carry estate tax inclusion if the powerholder dies while the window is open. Likewise, the lapse of a power will be considered a future interest gift and so there may be gift tax consequences.

REDUCING OR ELIMINATING GIFT TAXES ON PREMIUM PAYMENTS THROUGH METHODS OTHER THAN CRUMMEY POWERS

Split-gifts

A split-gift is yet another way to increase the number of gift tax annual exclusions and unified credits available for each gift to a Crummey trust. A gift can be split by having the nondonor spouse agree to be treated as if he had made one-half of the gifts made by the donor spouse.[23]

The election for a split-gift is made on the gift tax return for the year in which the gift is made. The gift tax return must be filed on or before April 15 of the following year.[24] But the amount or existence of the beneficiary's right to make a withdrawal should not be dependent in any way on the donor's spouse's agreement to split gifts. The reason is that this would make the beneficiary's power contingent on an event that will not yet have occurred by the date of the gift.

The trust should specifically empower the grantor with the right to expand the beneficiary's demand power with respect to future gifts by stating at the time of the gift that it is to be treated for demand purposes as if it had been made equally by the donor and his spouse.

Split-gifts can therefore increase the annual exclusion to $28,000 as indexed ($14,000 per spouse in 2017) per donee. But giving a powerholder the right to withdraw this amount sets up a tax trap in the powerholder's estate; if the right to demand that much is allowed to lapse, the excess over the "five-or-five" maximum will be considered a gift to the remainder person subject to gift tax. That gift, coupled with the retention of a lifetime interest, will cause inclusion of a portion of the trust in the powerholder's estate. Of course, if the beneficiary lives until the trust ends, a great deal of the trust may be in his estate anyway.

Permanent Withdrawal Rights

An additional way to increase the window is to make the withdrawal rights permanent. However, the powerholders' rights do not lapse and therefore grow each year. The advantage is that a larger premium can be paid and sheltered by the gift tax annual exclusion. The disadvantage is that as the value of the property that can be taken grows, so does the beneficiary's temptation to make a withdrawal. Another downside is the growing estate tax liability in the beneficiary's estate. But, in the right circumstances (for instance if there are many beneficiaries, all of whom can avoid the temptation to make a withdrawal, and all of whom are likely to survive the grantor), this solution may prove quite advantageous.

All Out Maximum Transfers

This method is simple. The client makes a first gift equal to $280,000 (doubled to $560,000 if the client's spouse will be splitting gifts and is not an income or principal beneficiary). The bulk of such a gift (i.e., the excess over $14,000 or $28,000, in the case of split-gifts, in 2017) will not qualify for the annual exclusion, so the client must use his lifetime exemption to avoid a current gift tax liability.

But, once at least $280,000 of assets are in the trust, the greater of $5,000 or 5 percent of the trust's corpus is $14,000 ($28,000 if $560,000 is placed into the trust). So, from this point on, the client can make gift tax free

gifts of the maximum annual exclusion amount. Even if the beneficiary doesn't exercise his withdrawal rights, no taxable gift occurs because the entire contribution is shielded by the de minimis greater of $5,000 or 5 percent of trust principal rule. A married client with four children could therefore give each child $100,000 ($400,000 total) which would mean $28,000 (in 2017) would qualify for the annual exclusion and $72,000 of the client's lifetime exemption would be exhausted per child (a total of $288,000). In all of the following years, the client could give up to $28,000 per child ($112,000 total) and there would be no taxable gifts per donee.

The all out maximum transfers technique is simple, easy to implement, and avoids naming an estate as beneficiary, the drafting of Crummey powers, or the uncertainty inherent in some of the more exotic and untested methods of balancing between the client's tax and dispositive objectives.

The two downsides of the technique are equally obvious: First, the client must have a large amount of cash or other easily liquidated assets that he can afford financially and psychologically to permanently part with. Second, the client must be willing to use all or a large portion of his remaining unified credit.

WHAT THE ATTORNEY SHOULD CONSIDER IN DRAFTING

Although life insurance agents and financial planners do not draft documents, an understanding of certain drafting tools and techniques is helpful, if for no other reason than, to provide a back-up and a second pair of eyes for the attorney.

An irrevocable life insurance trust should generally contain one or more of the following provisions:

1. The right of the Crummey power beneficiaries to make withdrawals extends to contributions to the trust from all sources. This makes it possible for the gifts of persons other than the grantor to qualify for the annual exclusion. It should also extend to both direct and indirect gifts, so that direct premium payments by the grantor (or by an employer) to the insurance company will qualify for the annual exclusion.

2. The amount subject to the Crummey power should be limited to the smallest amount that will protect the client's annual contributions.

This will reduce or eliminate the gift tax payable and the gift tax return that must be filed by the Crummey powerholder (and the potential federal estate tax payable) if the holder's power extends beyond the de minimis $5,000 or 5 percent protected amount and he lets that excess right of withdrawal lapse.

3. Require the trustee to give return receipt requested notice of any additions to principal and keep the right of withdrawal open for at least thirty days. This gives the beneficiary ample opportunity to realistically exercise his withdrawal rights.

4. Require that the beneficiary exercise the withdrawal right within a period of time well within the policy's grace period for payment. This assures that the trustee will have adequate time either to pay the premiums or to notify the grantor or others that the premiums must be paid from a source outside of the trust.

5. Require that the beneficiary exercise withdrawal rights in writing.

6. Allow any power given to a minor (or otherwise incompetent) beneficiary to be exercised on his behalf by a guardian. It is important to document that the legal right of the minor could, in fact, be exercised on his behalf. But provide that only the named individual or his guardian (or, if incompetent, his conservator) can exercise the power. That way, if the powerholder is declared bankrupt, his trustee cannot make withdrawals.

7. Give the trustee the ability to satisfy a demand in-kind (e.g., with a fractional interest in the life insurance policy death benefit) in the event there is not sufficient cash or cash value in the trust.

8. Terminate the power of withdrawal upon the insured's death (except in the case where the trust may hold a survivorship policy, in which case the demand power should continue until the surviving spouse insured dies).

9. Name back up powerholders so that, if a primary Crummey powerholder dies, the annual exclusion is not lost.

10. Have the grantor irrevocably renounce all rights in any policies or other assets in the trust.

11. Be sure the noninsured spouse pays no premiums and contributes no premiums, policies, or any other assets to the trust. If the noninsured spouse pays premiums, she may be considered a co-grantor of the trust. If she is also an income beneficiary of the trust, all or a portion of the proceeds purchased with her contributions may be includable in her estate.

12. The trustee should be given a duty to collect proceeds and indemnification for costs involved in a suit if required. Authority should be given to settle any such suit.

13. Give the trustee the right, if the insurer allows, to take one or more policy death benefits under the settlement options provided by the insurer.

14. In community property states, the grantor should indicate that any insurance contributed to the trust was the separate property of the grantor. If possible, premiums should be paid by the grantor with separate property funds.

15. Consider including flexible provisions in the trust (see "Structuring the Trust for 'What Ifs'" later) to help address the current uncertain estate tax environment and overcome potential client concerns regarding creating an irrevocable trust.

Among the "Do Nots" often suggested in setting up these trusts are:

1. Do not require that the trustee purchase life insurance or apply contributions to the trust to be used to buy life insurance or pay life insurance premiums.

2. Do not name the trust the "Lotta Doe Life Insurance Trust," especially, if it is important to document that the trustee acted independently in the purchase of life insurance rather than as the client's agent and at the client's direction.

3. Do not allow the client to sign the policy application as applicant or owner (unless an informal application is being used to get underwriting started as a prelude to the actual application being completed once the trust is in existence). The client should sign only in the place where it says, "Insured."

4. Do not allow the trustee to merely endorse the client's contribution to the trust each year and send them directly to the insurance company. It is important that the trustee reduce those funds to possession by cashing each check in a separate checking account in the trust's name and writing a check drawn against the trust's account to the insurance company.

Structuring the Trust for "What Ifs"

In real life it is not always possible to structure the transactions as described above in the preferred approach. For instance, the client may have purchased a policy years before discovering the federal estate tax inclusion problem. It may be transferred into the trust too late to escape federal estate tax inclusion, or some other unforeseen problem may cause the proceeds to be included in the client's estate.

There is an escape or failsafe (or bail-out) contingency provision that can be placed into a trust where the irrevocable trust is to be the recipient of a pre-existing policy. This escape provision can require the trustee to hold any insurance proceeds that are included for any reason in the grantor's gross estate, and to pay them out in a manner that qualifies the proceeds for the estate tax marital deduction, either a general power of appointment or Qualified Terminable Interest Property (QTIP) deduction. So, if the proceeds are for any reason includable in the insured's gross estate, this escape clause will eliminate the tax if the insured is, in fact, survived by a U.S. citizen spouse.

Such failsafe trust clauses are extremely important for most insurance trusts created by married grantors, but must be drafted with considerable care. The reason is that tax law requires that the surviving spouse receive property outright, or in a manner tantamount to outright, to qualify for the marital deduction. Conversely, most life insurance trusts usually limit the powers given to the surviving spouse in order to avoid inclusion in the surviving spouse's estate, rather than to qualify for the estate tax marital deduction. This eliminates the use of QTIP planning because the QTIP marital deduction is allowed only at the cost of estate tax inclusion of the trust's assets in the surviving spouse's estate. So, the drafting attorney must walk the tightrope between estate tax exclusion of the life insurance proceeds, if at all possible, and the obtaining of the marital deduction, if all else fails.

The clause could obtain the marital deduction by providing for:

1. outright payment of included insurance proceeds to the surviving spouse;

2. an income interest to the surviving spouse coupled with a general power of appointment; or

3. payment of the proceeds to a trust the surviving spouse can revoke at will.

Another reason to structure a trust for "What Ifs" has to do with uncertainty regarding the future of the estate tax and the reluctance of some clients to make gifts to irrevocable trusts in light of this uncertainty. In essence, they may be afraid of giving up control before it is absolutely necessary to do so. Or they may be afraid of running out of money. Regardless of what the reason is, there are provisions that can be incorporated into an irrevocable trust (commonly referred to as a flexible ILIT) to make it more flexible and help mitigate client fears. These include:

*   If the clients are married, make one spouse a beneficiary of the trust and one spouse the grantor of the trust. This would potentially enable the trustee to make distributions to the spousal beneficiary in the event of a financial need. If control is paramount, the spousal beneficiary can also be made the trustee (except in situations where the spousal beneficiary is also an insured under a policy owned by the trust). However, if the spousal beneficiary is also the trustee, his or her ability to make distributions to himself or herself must be limited by ascertainable standards (Health, Education, Maintenance, and Support (HEMS)).

    Any distributions made to the spousal beneficiary could indirectly benefit the grantor spouse via the unlimited marital deduction. Of course, the grantor spouse loses this indirect access should the spousal beneficiary die first or there is a divorce. This risk can be addressed by drafting the trust to benefit the person to whom the grantor is currently married, as opposed to naming that person. In the event that there is a subsequent remarriage by the grantor, the new spouse would then step in and become the lifetime beneficiary of the trust.

- For maximum flexibility in conjunction with the use of a spousal beneficiary, use an independent trustee and give the trustee the absolute discretion to make distributions to the spousal beneficiary for any reason, to the exclusion of any other trust beneficiaries (i.e., nonpro rata distributions). This way, distributions would not be limited to HEMS. If the estate tax were to be repealed in the future, it may be possible for the trustee to exercise his or her absolute discretion to distribute the entire assets of the trust to the spousal beneficiary, thus effectively unwinding the trust. However, any trustee considering doing so should carefully consider his or her fiduciary duty to act in the best interest of all trust beneficiaries.

- Include a loan provision in the trust that gives the trustee the discretion to make arm's length loans to the grantor. The terms of the loan must reflect an arm's length transaction, so the grantor should provide security or collateral for the loan and the trust must charge an interest rate at least equal to the Applicable Federal Rate (AFR). Note that if the loan is still outstanding at the grantor's death, it should constitute a debt against the estate and reduce the grantor's taxable estate.

ALLOCATION OF THE FEDERAL ESTATE TAX

Life insurance proceeds, if includable in the insured's gross estate, will generate federal estate taxes if the insured is not survived by a spouse and/or does not wish to leave the insurance proceeds in a manner that will qualify for the estate tax marital deduction. Who will pay this tax? Should it be paid by the beneficiaries out of the proceeds or by the heirs of the probate estate? Should it be apportioned between them? The answer, of course, should only be given by the client.

The problem can, and should, be addressed by the planner drafting the client's will and irrevocable trust. The insured decedent's executor or administrator has the legal right to recover from the beneficiary of the insurance proceeds any estate taxes attributable to the inclusion of those proceeds in the insured's taxable estate. On the other hand, if the proceeds were not taxable (for example because they passed outright to the insured's surviving spouse or to a charity), the beneficiary has no liability for their payment.[25] The

Internal Revenue Code allows the insured to specify, by an allocation clause in his will, who will bear the burden of any estate tax.

INCOME TAX IMPLICATIONS

Typically, an irrevocable life insurance trust will not be funded. Since it holds no income producing assets, generally no income tax problems are created.

In general, if an irrevocable life insurance trust is funded, income it generates is taxed to the trust since it is a separate entity. To the extent income is paid to the trust's beneficiaries, it is taxed to them rather than to the trust.

However, if the trust is treated as a grantor trust, the income earned by the trust will be taxed to the grantor and any deductions, gains, losses, or credits realized by the trust can be used by the grantor.

The following will cause the trust to be considered a grantor trust:

1. Retention by the client or the client's spouse of a reversionary interest (right to receive property back or determine its disposition) in the income or the principal of any portion of a trust, but only if the actuarial value of the retained reversionary interest is greater than 5 percent of the value of the income or principal that may revert.[26]

2. Retention of the power by the client or the client's spouse to control the beneficial enjoyment of the income or principal of the trust.[27]

3. Retention of certain administrative powers by the client or the client's spouse. These powers include:[28]

   a) power to purchase, deal with, or dispose of the income or principal of a trust for less than adequate and full consideration;

   b) power to borrow from income or principal without adequate interest or security (an exception is made where a trust authorizes such loans under a general lending power by a trustee who is not the grantor);

   c) if a related or subordinate trustee lends income or principal to the client and the loan is made without adequate collateral or a reasonable rate of interest (and the loan is not repaid before the beginning of the next tax year); or

    d)   if someone other than the trustee can vote corporate stock held by the trust, or has the power to control the investment of stock or securities held by the trust, or has the power to reacquire the principal of the trust by substituting property of equal value.

4.   Retention of the power by the client or any non-adverse party (including the client's spouse) to revoke the trust.[29]

5.   If the income of the trust is, or in the discretion of the client or a nonadverse party, *may be*:[30]

- distributed to the client or his spouse;

- held or accumulated for future distribution to the client or his spouse;

- used to pay premiums on a policy insuring the life of the client or his spouse (since there is little or no income in the typical irrevocable life insurance trust, this should not be a problem); or

- used to discharge a legal obligation of the client or his spouse.

A trustee, beneficiary, or some party other than the grantor-client can be taxed on the income of a funded irrevocable trust if that person has the power to vest (obtain without conditions or risk of forfeiture) the income or principal of all or a portion of the trust in himself.[31]

When a trust beneficiary allows a Crummey power to lapse, there may be income tax consequences. Unfortunately, the income tax consequences of the lapse of the Crummey withdrawal right are far from certain.

HOW TO HANDLE LAST TO DIE (SURVIVORSHIP) INSURANCE IN AN IRREVOCABLE TRUST

Last-to-die (or second to die) policies (see Chapter 16) pay at the second death, regardless of which insured dies first. These survivorship contracts are often used in estate planning with irrevocable trusts for the following reasons:

1.   The payment pattern of last to die policies often tracks with the estate's need for cash; by paying proceeds only after the survivor of the insureds (typically, a husband and wife) has died, the event which creates the need for the greatest amount of federal estate tax creates the cash to solve that liquidity problem. But planners should note that, even with married couples who will eliminate all or much of the federal estate tax at the first death through the marital deduction, not all of the demand for cash is delayed until the second death. In fact, a distressing amount of money is needed to pay off debts, expenses, and state death taxes at the first death. Also, a surviving spouse can, and often will, survive for decades and need hundreds of thousands of dollars to provide food, clothing, and shelter, as well as education for herself and the couple's children.

2.   Last to die policies require a lower outlay than if the same amount of coverage were obtained on the older of the two insureds, since: (a) the premium will in many cases be paid for a longer period of time; and/or (b) the insurer will have the use of policy dollars for longer periods of time. (The probability of two people dying in the early years of a contract is much less than the probability of one of those persons dying during such period.)

From a planner's perspective, last-to-die policies placed in an irrevocable trust present potential problems not raised with regular policies because, for tax purposes, both spouses are insureds under a last-to-die policy. Here are some guidelines:

- If either insured spouse is a grantor of the trust, do not name a grantor spouse a life beneficiary of the trust. If a grantor is given the right to the income of the trust for life, the proceeds will be includable in that spouse's estate as a retained life interest.[32] However, it is possible to name a nongrantor insured spouse as a beneficiary of the trust. Merely being both an insured and a beneficiary of the trust should not cause estate inclusion in that spouse's estate, as the insured spousal beneficiary would not have the requisite incidents of ownership to cause estate inclusion pursuant to Code section 2042.

- As a general rule, do not name either insured spouse as the trustee of a trust holding a last-to-die policy. Since both spouses are insured, if the spouse who serves as trustee dies second, it is likely the IRS will include the proceeds in the spouse's estate under an argument that "As trustee, the insured held incidents of ownership." Should the insured trustee discover the problem and resign as trustee during the three years prior to death, the proceeds will nevertheless be included in his estate as a transfer within three years of death.[33]

  Even if the trustee spouse dies first, the consequences could be severe. The fair market value of the policy at that time (usually, interpolated terminal reserve plus unearned premium on the date of death) is included in his gross estate, since that best reflects the estate tax value of the policy. This may be quite a large amount and can aggravate the first decedent's liquidity problem, since it creates a cash need but the policy's reserve cannot be used to provide cash to satisfy that need.

  It may be possible to have a nongrantor spouse who is both an insured and a trust beneficiary serve as trustee as long as a special trustee is used to hold the incidents of ownership on the policies insuring the spousal beneficiary's life. This may be desired in situations where more flexibility is desired, as discussed in the previous "What Ifs" section.

- How does the three-year rule of Code section 2035 operate where a survivorship policy is owned by an irrevocable trust (or other third party)? Only if: (a) both spouses die within the three year period following the transfer of a second to die policy to an irrevocable trust; and (b) the transferor spouse is the second to die, will the life insurance proceeds be includable under the three year rule. If both spouses died within three years of the transfer but the transferor spouse died first, the policy would have been included, if at all, under section 2033, as an interest one person held in a policy on another person's life. That section does not apply, however, unless an interest was held at death—which it was not. Furthermore, section 2035 applies only if, within three years of the transfer, section 2042 (incidents of ownership) would have applied had there been no transfer.

Planners should note that there are many situations in which survivorship policies are not indicated (or should be used in conjunction with first to die contracts). These include:

- estates where the client wants to pass significant wealth to someone other than a surviving spouse;

- estates where there is no surviving spouse;

- estates where the surviving spouse is not a U.S. citizen and the qualified domestic trust (QDOT) is contra indicated; and

- estates where the need to provide funds to maintain the survivors' standard of living will require significant capital.

HOW TO HANDLE GROUP TERM LIFE INSURANCE IN AN IRREVOCABLE TRUST

Group insurance is an ideal type of life insurance to transfer to an irrevocable trust for many reasons:

- A transfer of group term life to an irrevocable life insurance trust makes significant estate tax savings possible at minimal gift tax cost.

- There is a considerable psychological advantage to the use of group term life with an irrevocable trust; since the premiums are paid for by the insured's employer, the employee feels the cost is low since little of current value is given up.

- In the case of an insured who also controls or influences the employee benefit decisions of the corporation, since the employer controls the ability to cancel the master contract—indirectly at least—the employee can terminate the coverage inside of the trust by suggesting that the employer purchase coverage from a new carrier. (However, this control will not be deemed an incident of ownership.) For practical purposes, however, an employee who wishes to remove group insurance from his estate will usually assign all rights in replacement policies, as well as in the original policy (see below).

Virtually all states specifically allow the absolute assignment of group term life insurance. This creates an opportunity to remove huge amounts of insurance from both the estate of the insured employee and the estate of his spouse through a transfer to an irrevocable life insurance trust.

But there are special problems inherent where group term life insurance is contributed to or owned by the irrevocable trust.

Assignability

The insured must divest himself of all incidents of ownership through an absolute assignment. The insurance company's form should be examined to be sure it transfers all the insured's rights with respect to the coverage. Be sure to obtain an endorsed copy of the form from the insurance company as evidence that the transfer has, in fact, been officially made. If the date or the existence of the transfer becomes an issue, that endorsed copy will prove that the insurer recognized the change of ownership.

Obviously, the terms of the master contract between the employer and the insurer should allow the assignment. But if there is a prohibition, the master policy should be amended at the employer's request and documentation retained by the firm's counsel. State law must also permit the assignment. As mentioned above, almost all states currently allow an insured under group term coverage to make an absolute assignment of all rights.

Assuming both the terms of the policy and state law permit a client to assign interests in group term coverage to an irrevocable trust (or other third party), the transfer should be effective to avoid federal estate tax. Furthermore, the payment of each premium by the employer is not considered to start a new three year period for purposes of Code section 2035 estate tax inclusion.

Planners must beware, however, of events beyond some employee-clients' control (e.g., a change by the employer of the group insurance carrier). An assignment with one company typically doesn't apply to the new coverage with the new insurer.

At first glance, the solution seems obvious; transfer all rights, not only in the current coverage, but also to any future coverage. Assuming the new coverage was purchased without the employee's direction, was necessitated by the change in the master contract, and was identical in all relevant aspects to the old plan, the IRS will recognize the anticipatory assignment, at least in

removing the proceeds from the insured's estate. This implies that if the amount or terms of coverage was significantly different, the IRS might not consider itself bound to honor the assignment.

More importantly, what havoc might such an anticipatory assignment play on a client who, after having assigned away all future group term coverage, is divorced from his spouse? Not only must the client report Table I costs[34] (regardless of who owns the contract) as income and report an amount equal to the Table I costs as gifts, but every time his salary is increased, assuming group coverage is a function of salary, the ex-wife is potentially enriched at the client's current expense.

Obtaining the Annual Exclusion

Attainment of the annual exclusion is not certain. Although there is no official requirement that the exact property contributed to a trust each year be the property subject to the power, in the opinion of the authors, if the beneficiary can't get what the grantor puts in, the IRS may someday argue that the withdrawal power is ineffective and the gift tax exclusion should be denied. In the case of an irrevocable trust—where there are no assets except group term life coverage contributed to the trust—the employee-insured-grantor is making only a constructive transfer of premium dollars; premiums are in fact actually paid directly to the insurer by the employee-insured-grantor's employer. The employee is deemed to have made a gift to the trust for gift tax purposes. The authors feel it is essential that, in such cases, the initial and annual rights of the beneficiary to make withdrawals be satisfiable by any property held by the trust including, but not limited to, group term coverage.

When a client is covered by a large amount of group term insurance, premiums can be substantial. Absent an annual exclusion, the annual gift the client is deemed to make every time his employer pays a premium on coverage absolutely assigned to an irrevocable trust could be costly. For instance, a sixty-one-year-old executive covered by $1,000,000 of taxable group term coverage would be deemed to transfer about $7,920 each year to the donees of his trust. A sixty-five-year-old with the same coverage would be considered to be making gifts of $15,240 each year. See Chapter 11 regarding Table I and the cost of group term life insurance.

As mentioned above, a purely tax oriented solution for obtaining the annual exclusion would be to give the donee the right to take the coverage out of the trust and/

or give the donee the right to an immediate distribution of the insurance proceeds at the moment of an insured-employee's death. But if this right is exercised, it would defeat some of the tax and personal objectives the client had when establishing the trust. If the beneficiary in fact exercises the power and takes the coverage during the client's lifetime, the client has lost all control. Until the master contract is changed to a new carrier or dropped by the employer, the Crummey powerholder (or the person who buys the coverage from him) owns the insurance on the client's life. If the beneficiary has the right to take the proceeds at the moment of the client's death, again, the dispositive and limiting objectives of the client are defeated.

To avoid these problems, consider giving the beneficiaries, in addition to the normal Crummey withdrawal right, the right to require the trustee to sell any group term coverage on the insured employee and pay them their share of the sales proceeds. To prevent the policy from ending up in the wrong hands should they in fact exercise this right, the trust would provide that the trustee could sell it only to the insured. The sale price would be an amount exactly equal to the premium paid that year by the employer on the employee's behalf. In essence, this would give the beneficiaries a withdrawal power operative on the amount of the constructive gift made by the employee client; as soon as the employer pays the premium, the beneficiaries can demand the equivalent of that amount from the trust. The grantor must buy if the trustee exercises his put, but the grantor has no right to compel a sale.

Group Term Life Insurance and Community Property Issues

Planners in community property states (see below) must remember that one-half of the compensation and, therefore, the assets purchased with or because of that portion of the employee's compensation are considered the property of the nonworking spouse. A retained life estate is held by the nonworking spouse with respect to that one-half. Some authorities have suggested that the nonworking spouse should assign his one-half of the future premium payments made by the employer to the working spouse or have the working spouse reimburse the nonworking spouse from separate property.

COMMUNITY PROPERTY ISSUES

There are currently ten states subject to community property or marital property (Alaska, Arizona,

California, Idaho, Louisiana, Nevada, New Mexico, Texas and Washington are community property; Wisconsin is a quasi-community property state). Life insurance obtained by one or both of the spouses during the marriage while domiciled in any of these states is typically community property. Essentially, this means each spouse, from inception, is the owner of one half of the policy.

This community property treatment can have adverse estate tax consequences. The noninsured spouse's interest in the community's property may be included in her estate. By extension, if community funds are used to pay premiums and the policy purchased with those premiums becomes community property, a noninsured nongrantor has made a gift of her interest. Coupled with the life income so often given to spouses by an insured grantor, the surviving spouse may have made a constructive gift followed by lifetime retention of income. This is a classic estate tax inclusion-type tax trap.[35]

The inclusion may be somewhat ameliorated by claiming a consideration offset for the actuarial value of the survivor's life income interest. In other words, it may be possible to argue that the amount of the includable proceeds should be reduced by the consideration paid (i.e., the noninsured spouse gave up a remainder interest in his community share of the proceeds in return for a life income interest in the other share of the proceeds). But to avoid inclusion altogether:

1. do not give a grantor spouse a life income in the trust;

2. convert the insurance, prior to its transfer to the trust, to separate property of the insured; and

3. ensure that future premiums are paid using only separate property of the insured grantor spouse.

Some attorneys suggest that the couple deliberately classify the life insurance as the separate property of the insured spouse. The reason for this is to make it possible for that spouse to transfer it to the irrevocable trust. Mechanically, in some states this is accomplished with a waiver by the noninsured spouse of his rights. In other community property states, married persons may—by agreement or transfer and with or without consideration—change or transmute the character of their community property to separate property of either spouse. To be effective, a transmutation agreement must be in writing. Alternatively, the noninsured spouse's rights can be sold to the insured spouse (in return for a payment from noncommunity funds) or transferred by gift. Once the life insurance policy has become separate property of the insured, the insured then (some time later) can transfer the insurance to the trust.

A similar problem arises with respect to the imputed (Table I) income from large amounts of group-term life insurance and Table 2001 income from noncontributory split dollar plans. In both cases, the imputed income is treated as community property, which is then deemed to be transferred (by the employee receiving that income) to the trust. This deemed transfer will result in the non-insured spouse being treated as a grantor. The solution is to make sure neither spouse is an income beneficiary of the trust.

CHAPTER ENDNOTES

1. For instance, if a client gave away a home that cost $200,000 and was worth $2,000,000 on the date of the gift and remained the same until the donor's death, the donees' basis would be only $200,000 (plus an adjustment for gift taxes paid). If it is later sold by the donees for $2,000,000, the gain would be $1,800,000 ($2,000,000 amount realized minus $200,000 basis). Had the home been kept until death, its basis would have been stepped up to its date of death value, $2,000,000.

2. Donors concerned with a loss of the policy's cash values can borrow before the transfer, but should note two things: First, a loan in excess of basis can trigger reportable gain to the donor and, perhaps, set the transfer for value tax trap for the purchaser. (See Chapter 25 regarding the transfer for value rule.)

    Second, a client who borrows on a life insurance contract should note that, in most cases, there will be no income tax deduction for interest on policy loans.

3. See *The Tools & Techniques of Estate Planning, 18th Edition* for information on these trusts.

4. See Chapter 35 "Key Employee Life Insurance" regarding revocable trusts.

5. Skerik, 38th Annual N.Y.U. Institute, ¶35.05[6].

6. Planners are urged to check state law to determine whether it is possible to name "my spouse" as opposed to a specific individual as the holder of a special power.

7. Priv. Ltr. Rul. 200147039.

8. I.R.C. §2042(1).

9. Treas. Reg. §20.2042-(1)(c)(4) provides that:

    "A decedent is considered to have an incident of ownership in an insurance policy on his life in trust if, under the terms of the policy, the decedent (either alone or in conjunction with another person or persons) has the power (as trustee or otherwise) to change the beneficial ownership in the policy or its proceeds, or the time or manner of enjoyment thereof, even though the decedent has no beneficial interest."

    Some authorities say the potential for this problem is reduced or eliminated by Revenue Ruling 84-179, 1984-2 CB 195, which holds that a decedent will not be deemed to possess incidents of ownership held in a fiduciary capacity if:

    (1) the insured's powers over the trust are not exercisable for his personal benefit;

    (2) the insured did not transfer the policy, nor did any consideration for purchasing or maintaining it come to the trust from the insured's personal assets; and

    (3) the trust powers held by the insured were not part of a prearranged plan.

    So, if the insured did not provide the consideration (premium payments) and can't use trust assets for his own benefits, it appears that the grantor insured could safely be the trustee.

    But it would be impossible for an insured who creates a life insurance trust to meet the last two tests, since it is usually the insured who is both the grantor and the party who dictates the terms of the trust. It is, therefore, likely that the IRS will claim that any insured grantor personally holds incidents of ownership held by him as trustee (regardless of a claim that the powers held by the client are limited due to his fiduciary duty to the beneficiaries of the trust and even though he can't personally benefit from the trust in any way).

    The solution to the cautious practitioner is obvious: Do not allow the insured to serve as trustee of a trust that holds life insurance on his life.

    Where the trust was created by someone other than the insured, if the insured is to also be the trustee, these precautions should reduce the potential for estate tax inclusion:

    (1) Do not give the insured any beneficial interest in the trust.

    (2) Preclude trust distributions to anyone (such as the insured's children) to the extent those payments are in satisfaction of a legal obligation of support under state law.

    (3) Provide a source of premium payments (e.g., fund the trust with income producing assets) other than the insured (in order to support an argument that the insured did not furnish consideration for maintaining the policies).

10. I.R.C. §2041.

11. I.R.C. §2513.

12. I.R.C. §2503(b), 2502.

13. *Crummey v. Comm'r.*, 397 F2d 82 (9th Cir. 1968).

14. Rev. Rul. 73-405, 1973-2 CB 321.

15. I.R.C. §2041.

16. I.R.C. §2041.

17. *Est. of Holland v. Comm'r.*, TC Memo 1997-302; *Est. of Kohlsaat v. Comm'r.*, TC Memo 1997-212.

18. This problem does not exist, however, if the spouse's interest in the trust (apart from the demand power) is merely a right to principal and income at the discretion of an independent trustee or is limited to an ascertainable standard, such as the right to make withdrawals for health, education, maintenance, or support (HEMS).

19. I.R.C. §2514, according to the IRS, refers to the lapse of powers during a calendar year. So, the IRS position is that a beneficiary's demand powers must be aggregated to decide whether their lapse exceeded the permissible five-or-five limit.

20. I.R.C. §2041.

21. Technically, the amount includable is the sum of the products obtained by multiplying the value of the trust share (using the federal estate tax value) by the following fraction:

Amount of each lapse in excess of the

$$\frac{\text{greater of \$5,000 or 5\% of trust corpus}}{\text{Value of the trust share at the date of lapse}}$$

There is a maximum inclusion amount: The includable amount can't exceed the federal estate tax value of the assets from which the power could have been satisfied.

22. 94 TC 74 (1991).

23. I.R.C. §2513.

24. I.R.C. §§6019, 6075.

25. I.R.C. §2206.

26. I.R.C. §673. Note that if the interest is held by the grantor, it will probably result in the inclusion of trust assets in the grantor's estate. However, if the interest is held by the grantor's spouse, it will not result in estate tax inclusion even if the income is taxed to the spouse.

27. I.R.C. §674. This will also cause estate tax inclusion of the policy proceeds if the power is held by the grantor, but not if it is held solely by the grantor's spouse.

28. I.R.C. §675.

29. I.R.C. §676. This would also cause estate tax inclusion.

30. I.R.C. §677(a).

31. I.R.C. §678(a).

32. I.R.C. §2036

33. I.R.C. §2035.

34. Technically, the value of a gift of an interest in group term coverage is the lower of the actual cost or the Table I cost. If the group coverage discriminates in favor of certain key employees, the actual cost of coverage will determine the gift. The value of the gift includes the actual cost or Table I cost (as appropriate) of the full amount of coverage (including the first $50,000 of coverage).

35. I.R.C. §2036.

KEY EMPLOYEE LIFE INSURANCE

CHAPTER 35

INTRODUCTION

Key employee life insurance is a life insurance policy owned by and payable to a business that insures the life or lives of employees (or outsiders) whose death(s) would cause a significant economic loss to the business, upon whose skills, talents, experience, or business or personal contacts the business is dependent, and who would be difficult to replace.[1]

WHEN IS THE USE OF THIS TECHNIQUE INDICATED?

1. When the profits or the financial soundness of a client's business would be threatened or when a client's business will have a difficult period of adjustment following the death of a key employee such as a leading salesperson or an employee instrumental in the development of new products.

2. When the success of a business is dependent upon the unique skills and abilities of one or more key employees and the business' creditors insist that its indebtedness must be collateralized through the purchase of key employee life insurance.

3. When a business desires to fund one or more obligations of the business at the death of a group of key employees (for example, the funding of large health and retirement benefits).

4. When business owners have been required by creditors to co-sign or guarantee that if the corporation defaults, they will personally be responsible for paying off the debt. Key employee insurance will protect those individuals and their estates.

5. Publicly held businesses quite often use key employee coverage to assure shareholders that the price of stock will not plummet nor will dividends fall with the death of a president or other senior executive.

6. Where the nature of the business involves the rendition of personal services (e.g., legal, medical, or other licensed professionals), the death of a key person can cause a drop in business income.

7. Where the psychological impact of the unexpected death of a key employee may be accompanied by disproportionately large costs involved in meeting the time table for work-in-progress, pending negotiations, and incomplete projects. There are almost always significant costs of searching for, finding, and hiring a successor. Key employee coverage can reimburse the business for these costs.

8. Although it is rare that the death of a key person creates a void which cannot competently be filled given enough time, there are cases (especially in closely held businesses) in which key individuals are the business. At the death (or long term disability) of such a driving force, the business will often fail entirely. Key employee coverage can protect the financial interests of investors.

9. Key employee coverage is particularly indicated in a closely-held business where profits are often dependent on the ability, initiative, judgment, or "rainmaking" ability of a single individual or small group of persons.

WHAT ARE THE REQUIREMENTS?

Key employee insurance should be owned by and payable to the corporation, which should also pay the premiums. As will be noted below under the discussion of taxation, adverse consequences are likely when the proceeds of an employer-owned policy are paid to a party other than the corporation or its creditors.

A corporate resolution should be entered into the corporate minutes stressing that the coverage has been purchased to indemnify the business for potential loss at the death of a key person and to serve any other corporate purpose. The resolution of the board of directors might stress the loss in words similar to the following:

> "The death or permanent disability of Jo-Ann Egly, Senior Vice President, would result in the loss of her unique fishing experience, special management abilities, dealer contacts, and understanding of the sports fishing industry and its economic direction."

HOW IT IS DONE – AN EXAMPLE

Steve and Bob form a computer software company called "L and L." At first, the firm has only one product, but after a number of years it has created several financial and estate planning programs and markets client-oriented brochures as well.

Steve is the creative and marketing genius but has little patience for the day-to-day details required in the actual operation of the business nor does Steve have the business background to handle the bookkeeping and accounting for the firm—and wouldn't want to even if he could. Bob on the other hand is brilliant at methodically organizing every detail of the production and distribution process and manages to maximize the profit-making potential of the firm's strong cash flow. Bob, however, does not have the marketing expertise, contacts, or technical skill of his co-shareholder.

Neither individual could, on his own, physically accomplish what both men do. Nor could either in any profitable degree match the skills of the other. At the death or long term disability of either, the remaining shareholder of L and L would suffer an incredible economic loss and would be faced with the costly burden of trying to replace the lost associate and paying for the mistakes and lost business incurred during that aggravating process.

L and L's board of directors, in recognition of these costs, signs a corporate resolution that provides authorization for the purchase of key employee life insurance coverage on both men's lives. The corporation will be the applicant, owner, premium payor, and beneficiary of the coverage. At either person's death, the insurance proceeds will be received by the corporation and can be used for any of the corporation's needs.

TAX IMPLICATIONS

1. Premiums paid by the corporation are not tax deductible.[2]

2. Generally, policy proceeds are free of federal income taxes.[3]

3. Where a key employee policy—or an interest in a key employee policy—has been transferred for any type of valuable consideration, proceeds may lose their income tax free status. (See Chapter 25, "The Transfer for Value Rule," for more information.) Fortunately, even if there has been a transfer for value, there are exceptions which, if met, will enable the policy proceeds to maintain their income tax free status. These exemptions allow transfers to the following transferees: (1) the insured; (2) the insured's partner; (3) a partnership in which the insured is a partner; or (4) a corporation in which the insured is a shareholder or officer.[4]

   It should be noted that transfers *to* co-shareholders of the insured are *not* among the protected transfers. Also, transfers *to* a corporation in which the insured is merely a director but is not an officer or shareholder are *not* among the protected transfers.

   The transfer for value tax trap is so deadly (both in complexity and potential expense to all parties) that no transfers of life insurance policies should be made without careful review of the transfer for value rules by competent legal counsel.

4. In spite of the general rule that life insurance proceeds will generally be received income tax free, life insurance death benefits received by a large C corporation will generate adjusted current earnings and profits for purposes of computing the corporation's Alternative Minimum Tax (AMT) liability. In a nutshell, this means that about 75 percent of the death proceeds in excess of the cash value received by a large corporation at the date of the insured's death will be treated as an adjustment for AMT purposes.

   Therefore, roughly 75 percent of the total proceeds may be subject to a 20 percent surtax in a worst case scenario. This is essentially equivalent to a 15 percent tax (20 percent × 75 percent) on 100 percent of the proceeds.[5] So, in a worst case situation, about $150,000 will be lost out of a $1,000,000 death benefit.

To compensate for a worst possible case AMT loss, multiply the target or net amount needed by 118 percent to arrive at the necessary amount of insurance. For instance, if the corporation predicted a loss or cash need of $1,000,000 at the death of its president, it should purchase $1,180,000 of life insurance on the president's life.

No AMT is imposed on a small corporation. A corporation qualifies as a small corporation for purposes of the small business exemption from the AMT if its average gross receipts for all three-tax-year periods (starting in tax years beginning after 1993) were $7.5 million or less. The $7.5 million threshold amount is reduced to $5 million for the corporation's first three-year period (or part of that period) beginning after December 31, 1993.[6]

5.   For life insurance contracts entered into after August 17, 2006, certain requirements must be met for the death proceeds of an employer-owned life insurance contract to be received income-tax free. One set of requirements is that before an employer-owned life insurance contract is issued the employer must meet certain notice and consent requirements. The insured employee must be notified in writing, at the time the contract is issued, that the employer intends to insure the employee's life, and the maximum face amount the employee's life could be insured for. The notice must also state that the policy owner will be the beneficiary of the death proceeds of the policy. The insured must also give written consent to be the insured under the contract and consent to coverage continuing after the insured terminates employment.[7] For more on the requirements of employer-owned life insurance, see Chapter 24, "Taxation of Benefits."

6.   A corporation's Earnings and Profits (E&P) will be increased to the extent that the death proceeds exceed: (a) total premiums in the case of term insurance; or (b) corporate owned cash values in the case of permanent coverage. This is important because the amount and character of income distributed from a corporation to its shareholders is determined in large part by reference to the firm's E&P.[8]

Also, C corporations are subject to the accumulated earnings tax—a 15 percent surtax on unreasonable accumulations of earnings and profits.[9] The accumulated earnings tax may be imposed on a corporation that has E&P in excess of the reasonable needs of the business. A corporation is allowed to accumulate up to a safe harbor amount of $250,000 ($150,000 for certain personal service corporations).

During the lifetime of the insured, the internal build-up of cash values should not trigger an accumulated earnings tax problem. Many courts have agreed that an accumulation of earnings is appropriate to pay for insurance (or to self insure) as a means of protecting the business against such contingencies as unsettled business conditions and the loss of a key employee. Generally, therefore, the cash values inside of permanent coverage should not create a problem under the accumulated earnings tax.[10]

A corporation typically acquires a key person life insurance policy to assure adequate working capital after a key employee's death. To the extent key employee death proceeds are used up in ordinary business operations, they should not cause an accumulated earnings tax problem.

7.   Premiums paid by the corporation will not be taxable to the insured employee as long as that person is given no current rights in either the policy or its values.[11]

If the proceeds are payable to the employee's estate or personal beneficiary, the result changes. In that case, premiums will *likely* be taxable to the employee where the policy is owned by the corporation[12] and the premiums will be taxable to the employee where the policy is owned by the employee.[13]

8.   Generally, interest paid on loans secured by a key employee life insurance policy is not deductible unless one or more of the following exceptions are met:[14]

a.   *Four out of seven exception* – At least four of the first seven annual premiums are paid without recourse to policy loans.

b.   *$100 a year exception* – If the interest does not exceed $100 for any taxable year, the interest deduction will not be disallowed even if there is a systematic plan of borrowing.

c.   *Unforeseen event exception* – If the debt was incurred because of an unforeseen substantial loss of income or substantial increase in obligations, the deduction will not be disallowed even though the policy loan was used to pay premiums.

d. *Trade or business exception* – If the debt is incurred in connection with the client's trade or business, the interest deduction will not be summarily disallowed. Generally, amounts to finance key employee coverage will not be considered to fall within this exception and in any event interest deductions for company-owned life insurance are severely restricted. See Chapter 24, "Taxation of Benefits".

Generally, with respect to contracts issued after June 8, 1997, no interest deduction is allowed for any interest paid or accrued with respect to a policy loan on a contract owned by a business. Almost all exceptions making an interest deduction possible on newly issued policies have been eliminated and the IRS is currently attacking interest deductions on many older contracts on the grounds that in reality the taxpayer did not meet at least one of the four tests above.[15]

Obviously, corporations in a relatively low tax bracket will have little interest in systematic borrowing in any event.

9. If the insured key employee holds no equity interest in the business, at his or her death, there should be no estate tax inclusion due to the payment of the key employee life insurance proceeds.[16]

10. The death proceeds of a corporate-owned life insurance policy on the life of a sole or controlling (one who owns more than 50 percent of the voting stock) shareholder will not be included separately as life insurance in the insured's gross estate to the extent that the proceeds are paid to—or for the benefit of—the corporation.[17]

Instead, the life insurance paid to the corporation (or to its creditors) is considered together with all other nonoperating assets in the valuation process. That cash which includes what was policy proceeds is therefore part of the weighing that occurs in the determination of corporate net worth, prospective earning power, and dividend earning capacity.

11. To the extent the proceeds of a corporate owned life insurance policy on the life of a controlling shareholder are payable to a party other than the corporation or its creditors, those proceeds will be includable separately from the valuation of the business—as life insurance—in the insured shareholder's estate.

12. When a corporation owns a policy on the life of a noncontrolling (50 percent or less) shareholder, the proceeds when paid to the corporation at the insured's death impact the value of the business. The life insurance paid to the corporation or its creditors is added together with all other nonoperating assets in the valuation process. That cash is therefore part of the weighing that occurs in the determination of corporate net worth, prospective earning power, and dividend earning capacity.

13. Proceeds payable to or for the benefit of a partnership that owns a policy on the life of a partner are not included separately as life insurance in the gross estate of the key partner. The partnership rather than its partners is considered owner of the policy and its incidents of ownership. Of course, the proceeds increase the value of the insured partner's proportionate interest in the partnership for estate tax purposes.[18]

14. If proceeds of a partnership owned policy are payable to someone other than the partnership (or its creditors), they will be included separately as life insurance proceeds in the gross estate of an insured partner since the insured is deemed to hold incidents of ownership actually possessed by the partnership. The proceeds will be fully includable in the insured partner's estate (even if the insured is a minority partner).[19] Contrast this with the requirement of control (more than 50 percent of the voting power) required in the case of corporate-owned life insurance.

15. When an employee retires, quits, or is fired, a business owning insurance on his or her life may choose to sell it to the employee. If a key employee policy is sold to the insured at retirement or other termination of employment, even though it is a transfer and is for valuable consideration, since it is to the insured, it falls within an exception to the transfer for value rule.[20] The value of the policy for sale or transfer purposes is its fair market value, which is generally the greater of its interpolated terminal reserve (ITR) or PERC (premiums plus earnings less reasonable charges) value. For more information see Chapter 26: Life Insurance Valuation. Planners

should beware of transfers of key employee coverage by the business to others and check to be sure such assignments fall within one or more of the exceptions to the transfer for value rule.

16. Consideration should be given to the income tax implications when a business transfers a key employee policy to the insured who is an employee or owner:

   a. If the business transfers the policy to a non-owner employee, the employee will realize taxable income equal to the difference between the Fair Market Value (FMV) of the policy and the amount paid by the employee.[21] If a C corporation transfers a key employee policy to an owner, the IRS could classify the difference between the FMV and the amount paid by the owner as a dividend rather than as compensation. If an S corporation transfers a key employee policy to an owner, the difference between FMV and the amount paid by the owner will reduce the owner's basis in the corporation (but not below zero) and the excess above basis will be subject to capital gains taxation. If a partnership or Limited Liability Company (LLC) taxed as a partnership transfers a key employee policy to an owner, the difference between FMV and the amount paid by the owner will reduce the owner's (outside) basis in the business (but not below zero) and the excess above outside basis will reduce the basis of the policy being transferred.[22]

   b. If the nonowner employee pays nothing for the policy, the entire fair market value is taxable to the employee as ordinary income.[23]

   c. If the amount paid by the nonowner employee exceeds the business' net premium cost or the FMV of the policy distributed to the nonowner employee exceeds the business' net premium cost, the business will realize taxable income equal to that excess. However, the business may receive an offsetting deduction to the extent that the FMV of the policy transferred to the nonowner employee exceeds the amount paid by the employee.

   d. The tax consequences to the business of transferring a policy to an owner depends upon the business entity type. If the business is a C corporation or S corporation and the amount paid by the owner exceeds the corporation's net premium cost, or the FMV of the policy distributed to the owner exceeds the corporation's net premium cost, the corporation will realize taxable income equal to that excess. If the business is a partnership or LLC (taxed as a partnership) and the amount paid by the owner exceeds the corporation's net premium cost, or the FMV of the policy distributed to the owner exceeds the corporation's net premium cost, there will be no income tax consequences to the business, as transfers of property by a partnership or LLC to an owner are disregarded for income tax purposes.[24]

17. A key employee sometimes sells a policy on his life to the corporation that will use it as key employee coverage. This transaction not only has the practical disadvantage of reducing personal coverage that may be needed but also has a number of serious adverse tax implications:

   a. If the insured is neither an officer nor shareholder of the company, the transfer for value rule is triggered. (See Chapter 25, "The Transfer for Value Rule.")

   b. Taxable gain (ordinary income) will be realized by the seller to the extent that the amount paid by the corporation exceeds his net premium cost.[25]

   c. If the insured sells the policy to the corporation for less than his net premium cost, he will not be able to claim a deductible loss.

FREQUENTLY ASKED QUESTIONS

Question – What are the advantages of key employee life insurance?

Answer – There are a number of advantages of key employee life insurance. These include:

   1. The value of the business owners' investment (and the ongoing credit of the business itself) is stabilized and maximized immediately by the existence of key employee life insurance coverage. During the insured's lifetime, policy cash values are carried as a corporate asset and can easily, quickly, and inexpensively be made available to the corporation for a business

emergency or opportunity. At death, the infusion of large amounts of cash will serve as a shock absorber to cushion the impact of the key employee's loss.

2. From the time the first premium is paid, the business and its creditors have the assurance of instant capital at the death of a key employee. In this sense key employee coverage can serve both as a form of commercial loan protection as well as collateral for securing future commercial loans. Many banks and other lending institutions will refuse to make large loans to closely-held corporations unless life insurance in appropriate amounts can be obtained on pivotal personnel in the business.

3. A business receiving life insurance at the death of an employee is not restricted as to the manner in which that cash can be utilized. Key employee proceeds can be used for many purposes including finding a qualified replacement for the deceased key employee, paying for the training of the replacement, replacing lost profits, protecting the firm's credit rating, providing benefits under one or more employee benefit plans, and financing a buy-out of one or more deceased or disabled business owners.

Question – What are the disadvantages or costs of key employee coverage?

Answer – Key employee life insurance has disadvantages and costs which include:

1. Instant, discounted capital provided by business-owned life insurance comes at a cost. Premiums must be paid with after-tax dollars. Also, the corporation must pay an opportunity cost: it cannot use money allocated to premiums for any other corporate purpose.

2. To the extent that the corporate AMT applies, the utility of key employee coverage is diminished.

Question – Is there a way around the nondeductibility of insurance premiums for key employee life coverage?

Answer – As a practical matter, the answer is no. This limitation extends to both term and permanent coverage. As a general rule, a client will not be allowed an income tax deduction for the payment of key employee life insurance premiums.

Question – How much insurance should be purchased by a business on its key employee?

Answer – A common method of calculating the economic effect of the loss of a key employee is the discount approach. This technique applies a percentage discount to the fair market value of the business. The discount approach requires an appropriate discount factor. Some authorities believe that if the business will survive the loss of the key employee and, in time, will hire a competent replacement, an appropriate discount factor is 15 to 20 percent. But if the business will fail at the death of a specified key person, or will be placed in jeopardy from the loss of the key employee, an appropriate discount factor is from 20 to 45 percent. The officers of the company and the firm's accounting and legal advisors, however, should determine the exact discount factor.

Consider the following questions when determining the discount factor:

1. How long will it take the replacement to become as efficient and productive as the lost key employee was?

2. How much will it cost to locate, situate, and train a replacement, and will the new employee want a higher salary?

3. Is the replacement likely to make costly mistakes during the training period?

4. Will the loss of the employee result in a loss of clientele?

5. What percent of the firm's current net profits are attributable to the key employee?

While there are other methods of calculating the value of a key employee's contribution to a corporation, the discount approach illustrated below, courtesy of NumberCruncher™ Software, is a quick and effective method that sidesteps many of the difficulties posed by alternative methods.

KEY EMPLOYEE VALUATION

Fair Market Value of Business with Key Employee: $750,000

Discount Percent	Value without Key Employee	Value of Key Employee
17.000%	$622,500	$127,500
18.000%	$615,000	$135,000
19.000%	$607,500	$142,500
20.000%	$600,000	$150,000
21.000%	$592,500	$157,500
22.000%	$585,000	$165,000
23.000%	$577,500	$172,500

Computation Courtesy: *NumberCruncher™ Software*

Keep in mind that regardless of what approach is used to calculate the value of a key employee, a life insurance carrier will limit a business' insurable interest to the loss which the business would sustain in the event of the death of the employee. For financial underwriting purposes, the amount of death benefit that a life insurance carrier will issue is usually evaluated based on multiples of compensation for the number of years needed to replace the person and recover the losses. Generally, a maximum death benefit of five to ten times the key employee's compensation is permitted.

Question – Should the insurance under a key employee policy be term or permanent?

Answer – As in every business planning problem, the product must match the problem. If the need is for a short period of time, term insurance is indicated. Likewise, if the firm has a cash flow problem or is a recent start-up business, term coverage is generally indicated.

But in most cases the value of the truly key employee to a business increases over time. Therefore, the need is long-term. Often, key employee coverage will be converted to solve a long-term need such as funding a buy-sell agreement with an indeterminate time span or to finance the employer's obligation under a nonqualified deferred compensation plan. Thus, the preferred coverage is almost always some form of permanent insurance.

Question – How does a business account for key employee life insurance coverage?

Answer – Accounting for key employee life insurance depends on the type of policy. Term insurance

premium payments represent a pure current expense. Such costs should be charged against income rather than retained earnings.

Insurance premiums paid on a permanent (cash value) type of policy are bifurcated. To the extent a premium payment generates an increase in the policy's cash value, a charge should be made to an asset account. To the extent the premium paid exceeds the increase in the policy's cash value, a charge should be made to expense.

The firm's balance sheet should show policy cash values as a non-current asset. When an insured dies, the gain upon the receipt of the insurance payment is typically reflected as a special entry for nonrecurring amounts on the Annual Statement of Operations. Alternatively, a corporation's gain on the receipt of death proceeds may be carried directly to the Retained Earnings Account.

It is the opinion of the authors that the method of accounting described above is antiquated and does not reflect the economic reality of the transactions over time considering the present products and riders available to businesses in the late 1990s and early twenty-first century.

An alternative method of accounting, called the ratable charge method, seems to provide a more realistic approach and has been used by a number of accounting firms even though it is not officially accepted. In essence, under the ratable charge method total premiums to be paid over a predetermined period (such as for ten years or to age fifty-five) are determined on the assumption that the insured is likely to live and will continue to remain an employee of the business that long. The guaranteed cash surrender value at the end of the selected period is then subtracted from the total premiums to be paid. The result is a net cost which is then amortized (ratably) as a level annual charge over the premium paying period.

This prime assumption upon which the ratable charge method relies becomes more likely if the policy in question contains what is often called a policy exchange rider, which is an option the client's firm has to continue the policy on another life if the insured employee should decide to leave the firm. In other words the company could substitute a new key employee for the one no longer employed. (In most cases the rider allows the exchange with no additional costs to the client's company.) The existence of an exchange rider would seem to offer an answer to the criticism that if the policy is discontinued prior to the end of the selected premium payment period, the ratable charge method would result in a large write-off of an unamortized deferred charge.

Question – Is there an income tax problem where a policy on the life of a controlling shareholder is payable to someone other than the corporation or its creditor?

Answer – Yes. There is a potential adverse tax consequence in this situation. If a policy death benefit that otherwise could (and should) have been paid to the corporation is, in fact, paid to the beneficiary of a shareholder, in the opinion of the authors, the IRS is almost certain to argue that the entire amount was constructively paid to that shareholder and is taxable as a dividend. If this argument should fail, the IRS is likely to claim the entire proceeds should be taxed to the recipient as compensation. Should that argument be deflected, the IRS could also argue that premiums for any open tax years should have been charged to the insured as dividends or at least as compensation.[26]

Question – What are the tax implications where a corporation attaches a disability income rider to a key person life insurance policy?

Answer – If the disability income policy is payable to the policyowner corporation, the premium payments for the disability portion as well as the life insurance portion will be nondeductible.[27] Income, when paid to the corporation upon the disability of the insured key employee, is income-tax free to the corporation.[28] Upon the payout to the disabled key employee, assuming the amount and terms of the payout are reasonable, the corporation should be able to deduct the payments as ordinary and necessary business expenses. Upon receipt by the key employee, the payments would be considered salary rather than proceeds from a disability income policy and therefore subject to ordinary income tax.

If the employee is named directly as payee of the disability income generated from the rider on a policy owned by the corporation, the taxation will probably be as follows:

1. Premiums paid by the corporation for the disability coverage should be deductible by the business as an ordinary and necessary business expense.

2. The key employee should not have to report as income premiums paid by the corporation on the disability coverage.

3. Income, when payable to the disabled key employee, would be treated as salary and subject to ordinary income tax when and as received.

Question – Does a business have an insurable interest in a key employee?

Answer – Insurable interest is essentially the expectation of a financial benefit from the continued life of the proposed insured. The question in basic terms is, "Does the business expect to benefit financially from its relationship with the proposed insured?" Generally, a business has an insurable interest in the life of a key employee if the continued success of the business depends upon the special skills and talents of the key employee, and the policy is purchased to protect the business against loss in the event of the key employee's death. The insurable interest is not unlimited though—it is limited to the loss which the business would sustain in the event of the death of the key employee (generally the maximum death benefit is five to ten times the key employee's compensation).

Generally, if a business has insurable interest in an individual when the policy is purchased, the issue is not again raised when the insured dies. However, the definition of insurable interest and its requirements is determined by state law. Practitioners must look to the law of the proposed insured's domicile to determine if the business does in fact have an insurable interest. If there is no insurable interest, the IRS might claim that the proceeds are not paid by reason of the insured's death but instead are paid from a wagering contract and therefore are taxable at ordinary income rates.[29]

Question – What is a policy exchange rider and how is it used in key employee insurance?

Answer – A policy exchange rider (often called a substituted insured rider or exchange of insureds option) provides that at the termination of the insured's employment, a new key employee can be substituted as the insured under the original policy (assuming the new person can provide evidence of insurability). Of course, appropriate adjustments in premium, cash value, or face value are made to the policy reflecting differences in age or insurability between the original insured and the new insured. Typically, there is no additional charge by the insurer at the time the new insured is substituted nor are commissions paid to the agent at that time. For these reasons, the corporate owner of the key employee coverage saves both underwriting and commission costs and receives an actuarially equivalent policy on the life of the new key employee.

Unfortunately, to be protected by Internal Revenue Code section 1035, an exchange must be on the life of the *same* insured. So the substitution of one insured for another under a policy exchange rider on a corporate-owned key employee life insurance contract will be taxed as if the corporation sold the first policy and used the proceeds to purchase the new contract. The corporation will have to report gain at ordinary income rates on the difference between the fair market value of the policy at the time of the exchange and the net premiums it had paid to that date.[30]

Question – If an S corporation or other type of pass-through entity purchases a policy on the life of a key employee, are the tax implications different from those of a C corporation?

Answer – In an S corporation, partnership, or limited liability company (LLC) taxed as a partnership, the income of the business flows through directly to its owners. Generally, when a policy's proceeds are paid to the business as death proceeds, they are received income-tax free, and each owner's pro rata share of the proceeds flows through income-tax free. The basis of each owner's interest in the business is increased by his or her share of the tax-free proceeds.[31]

Question – Can a federally regulated bank purchase a life insurance policy on the life of a key employee?

Answer – A national bank may purchase key employee life insurance for the benefit of the bank if the bank has an insurable interest in the key employee's life.[32] According to the Office of the Comptroller of the Currency (OCC), key employee life insurance on the lives of executives and directors of banks is an appropriate investment when purchased as a funding mechanism for nonqualified deferred compensation plans. The OCC held that it was appropriate for banks to purchase the insurance to meet the bank's contractual obligations of payments upon early, normal, or late retirement as well as to families of covered employees at their deaths. It also held that life insurance could be properly held by a federal bank to serve as an actuarial cost recovery vehicle.[33]

CHAPTER ENDNOTES

1. Once, this was called key man insurance. Note that the term has no relationship to key employee as it is used for top-heavy pension and profit sharing rules.

2. I.R.C. §264(a).

3. I.R.C. §101(a); Treas. Reg. §1.101-1(a).

4. I.R.C. §101(a)(2).

5. I.R.C. §§55-59. There is a flat 20 percent tax imposed on the company's Alternative Minimum Taxable Income (AMTI), after subtracting out a $40,000 exemption. The exemption starts to phase out beginning at an AMTI of $150,000, and is completely phased out at an AMTI of $310,000. Life insurance proceeds are added to a corporation's earnings and profits, becoming part of an adjustment added to a corporation's ordinary taxable income to determine its AMTI and, therefore, its potential alternative minimum tax liability.

6. I.R.C. §55(e).

7. I.R.C. §101(j).

8. Rev. Rul. 54-230, 1954-1 CB 114.

9. I.R.C. §§531-537.

10. *Vuono-Lione, Inc. v. Comm.*, TC Memo 1965-96; *Harry A. Koch Co. v. Vinal*, 228 F. Supp. 782 (D. Neb. 1964); see also *Emeloid Co. v. Comm.*, 189 F.2d 230 (3rd Cir. 1951); *Bradford-Robinson Printing Co. v. Comm.*, 1 AFTR 2d 1278 (D. Colo. 1957).

11. *Casale v. Comm.*, 247 F.2d 440 (2d Cir. 1957); Rev. Rul. 59-184, 1959-1 CB 65.

12. Treas. Reg. §1.61-2(d)(2)(ii)(a); *Comm. v. Bonwit*, 87 F.2d 764 (2nd Cir. 1937).

13. Treas. Reg. §1.61-2(d)(2); *Canaday v. Guitteau*, 86 F.2d 303 (6th Cir. 1936); *Yuengling v. Comm.*, 69 F.2d 971 (3rd Cir. 1934); *Lee v. U.S.*, 219 F. Supp. 225 (W.D. S.C. 1963); *Jameson v. Comm.*, TC Memo 1942.

14. I.R.C. §264(d).

15. See *IRS v. CM Holdings, Inc.*, 2002-2 USTC ¶50,596 (3d Cir. 2002); TAM 199901005; TAM 9812005.

16. I.R.C. §2042.

17. Treas. Reg. §20.2042-1(c)(6).

18. I.R.C. §2033.

19. I.R.C. §2042(2); Rev. Rul. 83-147, 1983-2 CB 158.

20. See Chapter 25, "The Transfer for Value Rule."

21. I.R.C. §83; Treas. Reg. §1.83-3(e).

22. I.R.C. §731.

23. *Parsons v. Comm.*, 54 TC 54 (1970); *Thornley v. Comm.*, 41 TC 145 (1963).

24. I.R.C. §732(b).

25. *Gallun v. Comm.*, 327 F.2d 809 (7th Cir. 1964).

26. *Golden v. Comm.*, 113 F.2d 590 (3rd Cir. 1940). But see *Ducros v. Comm.*, 272 F.2d 49 (6th Cir. 1959); Rev. Rul. 61-134, 1961-2 CB 250.

27. I.R.C. §265(a)(1).

28. I.R.C. §104(a)(3).

29. *Atlantic Oil Co. v. Patterson*, 331 F.2d 516 (5th Cir. 1964); see also *U.S. v. Supplee-Biddle Hardware Co.*, 265 U.S. 189 (1924).

30. Rev. Rul. 90-109, 1990-2 CB 191.

31. I.R.C. §§1366(a)(1)(A), 1367(a)(1)(A).

32. Letter by John H. Noonan, Director, Commercial Activities, Administrator of National Banks, Comptroller of the Currency, October 28, 1986. See also Interpretive Ruling 7.7115, "Insuring Lives of Bank Officers."

33. OCC Interpretive Letter No. 848 and OCC Bulletin 96-51 (which supersedes a 1983 Letter to the contrary).

LIFE INSURANCE IN QUALIFIED PLANS

CHAPTER 36

INTRODUCTION

Life insurance can often be purchased under favorable terms and conditions through a qualified pension or profit sharing plan.[1] The insurance is purchased and owned by the plan, using employer contributions to the plan as a source of funds.

WHEN IS THE USE OF THIS TECHNIQUE INDICATED?

1. When a substantial number of employees covered under a qualified plan have an otherwise unmet life insurance need, either for family protection or estate liquidity.

2. When there are gaps and limitations in other company plans providing death benefits, such as group term life insurance plans, nonqualified deferred compensation plans, and split dollar plans. Planners should consider using life insurance in a qualified plan to fill those gaps or supplement those plans.

3. When a qualified plan for a closely held business or professional corporation is overfunded or close to the full funding limitation for regular trusteed plans, the addition of an incidental life insurance benefit, or a change to fully insured (Section 412(e)(3)—formerly 412(i)) funding, may permit future deductible contributions at a higher rate than before.

4. When life insurance would be attractive to plan participants as an additional option for investing their plan accounts. This technique is most often used in a profit sharing or 401(k) plan but can be used in other types of defined contribution plans as well.

5. When an employer wants an extremely secure funding vehicle for a plan, with guarantees as to future plan costs and benefits.

6. Life insurance in a plan can provide funds to pay estate taxes, if any, thereby enhancing the ability of plan proceeds to provide financial security for the participant's survivors.

Advantages[2]

1. The premium is deductible by the employer as part of its annual contribution on behalf of covered employees.

2. Life insurance products in a qualified plan can provide employees with retirement benefits at more favorable terms than would be available through individually purchased products.

   a. *Lower premiums and higher dividends* – In many cases, the economies of scale and efficiency of operation combined with a lower lapse rate make life insurance sold through a qualified plan highly cost effective for the insurer. This administrative savings can be passed through to the plan in the form of lower premiums and/or higher dividends than would otherwise be payable (even on individual products).

   b. *Locking in present mortality standards* – Upon retirement, the employee's balance in the plan can be converted into an annuity for life at rates guaranteed today. When life insurance with a built in conversion to an annuity feature is acquired long before retirement, the employee may achieve more favorable guaranteed rates than might be offered in the future. The reason is that yearly payouts from life annuities may decrease as insurance companies adjust their mortality tables to account for longer life spans. But through life insurance purchased now, there is a rate guarantee that the annuity purchase rate will not increase in spite of longer life expectancies. Locking in at current rates may increase ultimate retirement income.

   c. *No sales fees or other costs to purchase annuities –* Unlike the case of a noninsured plan where the trustee must eventually sell trust assets (and incur attendant costs) and then purchase annuities to provide lifetime benefits (and incur yet another round of costs), when there is insurance in the plan, no extra fee or commission is paid for the purchase of lifetime annuities for retirees if done through the life insurance contract.

3. Assuming that the insured plan participant is annually taxed on the Reportable Economic Benefit (REB) cost, the pure insurance portion of a qualified plan death benefit (i.e., the death proceeds less any policy cash values) is not subject to regular income tax. In other words the tax is not imposed on death benefits in excess of the cash surrender value immediately before the employee's death. This makes it, dollar for dollar, a more effective means of transferring wealth than any other type of plan asset.

4. A fully insured plan (Section 412(e)(3)) holding only life insurance policies and annuity contracts and meeting certain other requirements) is tax privileged. Fully insured plans generally are not subject to the Internal Revenue Code's minimum funding standards[3] and:

   a. are exempt from costly actuarial certification requirement—reducing the administrative overhead and complexity of a defined benefit plan; and

   b. generate a higher initial level of deductible plan contributions than a regular trusteed plan.

The Pension Protection Act of 2006 moved the provisions for fully insured plans from Section 412(i) to 412(e)(3) with no substantive changes.

Note that although they are known as fully insured plans, they still must meet the incidental death benefit rules which limit the amount of life insurance that can be owned inside a qualified retirement plan.

5. Some life insurance companies provide low cost installation and administrative services for plans using their investment products. This also reduces the employer's cost for the retirement plan.

6. In comparison to group term life insurance costs, life insurance within a qualified plan may be less expensive to the employee. This is because the employee can report the lower of the Table 2001 costs (see Figure 36.1; formerly P.S. 58 costs were used) or the insurance company's rate (which in almost every case will be significantly lower than the reportable Table 2001 cost). That reportable amount can be lower than the reportable income under Table I for the same amount of group term insurance.

7. From the employer's perspective, life insurance within the qualified plan may be less expensive than comparable group term insurance because the employer in a qualified plan saves the conversion cost of group insurance. In a large group insurance plan of 1,000 employees, the group conversion charge may range from $60 to $100 per thousand. Overall, this could result in a significant charge against dividends.

8. Greater amounts of life insurance can be provided to owner-employees through creative pension formulas than through group term plans. This is because there is more plan design flexibility in pension law than with respect to group term life law.

9. Substandard risks can obtain insurance that might otherwise not be available on an individual basis. The additional diversification and spreading of risk available in a retirement plan often enables an insurer to accept a risk that would be turned down on an individual basis. This guaranteed issue leverage can be quite important where the owner-employee is the individual who is considered a higher than standard risk.

10. Even if the life insurance company is not willing to issue life insurance on a guaranteed issue basis (generally starting at five or more insured lives), any ratings that must be paid are part of the employer's

contribution to the plan and, thus, income tax deductible to the employer. If the additional rating is significant, the fact that the employer can deduct it may be extremely important.

11. Substandard ratings costs are not taxed to the insured employee. Not only is the employer paying the premium (through the plan) but the employer is also paying for any rating. Yet, in reporting taxable income, the employee reports the lower of Table 2001 (formerly P.S. 58) costs or the insurer's standard term rates—no matter how high the actual rating paid by the plan.

12. Life insurance in the plan transfers the death benefit risk to the insurer. This satisfies the moral obligation of the employer toward the family of the insured and will often provide significantly more dollars than if only the fund deposited to the employee's account were distributed at death.

13. In defined contribution plans, employees may elect to purchase insurance on the lives of certain relatives and even unrelated persons in whom they have an insurable interest. Within the statutory limits, the employee can buy as much as he wants to buy of the type of coverage he wants.[4] This makes creative planning and "matching the product to the problem" more likely. For instance, a plan participant can purchase insurance on a business partner and use the proceeds to fund a buy-sell agreement.

14. Life insurance within a defined benefit plan may create a larger deduction, even in plans that are maxed out. Furthermore, it is possible to maintain a large death benefit in a defined benefit plan even if a participant's salary drops. For instance, if the plan's benefit formula is based on the employee's three highest consecutive years, the funding is based on those years even if currently the employee is earning significantly less. So the death benefit remains the same. Compare this with group coverage where the benefit drops if salary drops. In addition, life insurance within a defined benefit plan does not adversely impact the participant's retirement income, as the plan will pay the same specified retirement benefit regardless of whether the plan holds life insurance. Compare this with life insurance inside of a defined contribution plan, where the life insurance costs soak up some of the retirement assets that would otherwise be available at retirement.

15. A qualified plan may be used to incubate (some say season) a policy. In other words, the acquisition costs—the high upfront costs in the early years of the policy when outlays are not reduced by dividends—can be supported by the pension plan at the cost of reporting the economic benefit of the term insurance. Assuming the covered employee then purchases the policy from the plan for its full value after—say eight years—the employee may be receiving a policy with a lower premium than if he waited eight years and bought it on his own. If he has invested the money that he otherwise would have paid in premiums over those eight years, there may be enough to purchase the policy from the pension plan. However, the policy must be purchased for its Fair Market Value (FMV), which is generally the greater of the interpolated terminal reserve or Premiums plus Earnings less Reasonable Charges PERC (PERC) value—for more information see Chapter 26 "Life Insurance Valuation". In some cases, especially if the policy is guaranteed no lapse universal life, the FMV may substantially exceed the cumulative premiums paid. Once the policy has been purchased from the plan, at that time the dividends or cash value may be considerable and may even be enough to suspend the premiums.

16. At termination of employment for any reason or upon retirement, an employee can generally obtain an individual life insurance contract at original issue age rates. This makes coverage highly portable. It is also highly inexpensive in comparison to the conversion of group term insurance at the employee's then attained age. A policy rolled out to the insured can often be kept in force with little or no outlay at retirement.

17. It is often possible in a defined benefit plan to pay out both a benefit of one hundred times and the auxiliary fund to the beneficiary of an older owner-employee participant.

Disadvantages[5]

1. The plan participant must be annually taxed on the Reportable Economic Benefit (REB) cost of the net amount at portion of the death benefit. This cost becomes more expensive as the insured ages. However, if the policy is distributed to the participant, the cumulative REB constitutes basis and that amount is deducted from the FMV to determine the amount of

taxable income.[6] In addition, upon the death of the insured participant, the taxable cash value portion of the policy that is paid out as a retirement benefit can be reduced by the cumulative REB cost.[7]

2. Some life insurance policies may provide a rate of return on their cash values which, as compared with alternative plan investments, may be relatively low. However, rates of return should be compared on investments of similar risk.

3. Policy expenses and commissions on life insurance products may be greater than for comparable investments.

4. Upon the death of the insured, income is recognized by the beneficiary in an amount equal to the cash value portion of the policy immediately before the insured's death. This taxable amount may be lowered by the sum of any Table 2001 costs reported by the employee (formerly P.S. 58 costs were used). But this should be compared with the receipt of the entire proceeds income tax free when the policy is purchased outside a qualified plan with after-tax dollars.

5. Some authorities believe that since life insurance outside a qualified plan can definitely be kept from the insured's estate while life insurance within a qualified plan from the insured's estate is includible in the estate, it makes sense from an estate tax viewpoint to purchase life insurance outside a qualified plan (assuming the insured is healthy and insurable at standard rates). However, if estate inclusion is an issue, another solution is to purchase the insurance in the plan and then later have the insurance purchased from the plan for its FMV by the insured's Irrevocable Life Insurance Trust (ILIT). Such a purchase would not be considered a prohibited transaction.[8] It would also avoid the three-year estate inclusion rule, which does not apply to any bona fide sale for an adequate and full consideration in money or money's worth.[9] Transfer for value may be an issue, but this can generally be avoided by making the ILIT a partner of the insured or making the ILIT an intentionally defective grantor trust with respect to the insured.[10]

HOW IT IS DONE

Example. Your client is the sole shareholder and president of a cash-rich, highly profitable closely held corporation that employs ten other individuals. The business has set up a qualified pension and a qualified profit sharing plan. The client is highly rated for insurance purposes and his attorney has suggested he increase his estate liquidity by purchasing at least $1,000,000 of additional life insurance. Although your client has a salary of $400,000 a year from the business, his standard of living is exceptionally high and he has six children, all in Ivy League colleges or graduate schools which leaves him with little spendable income.

Instead of purchasing the high premium life insurance with personal, after-tax dollars (of which he has little), he has both the pension and profit sharing plan amended to allow the purchase of life insurance on the lives of plan participants. The trustees then purchase life insurance on his life equal to the maximum amount allowable under current pension law and the client's irrevocable trust set up for his wife and children purchases the balance of the $1,000,000 his attorney suggested.

TAX IMPLICATIONS

1. Employer contributions to a qualified plan, including amounts used to purchase life insurance, are generally deductible. The amount of life insurance purchased must fall within incidental limits.

The incidental test – A qualified retirement plan must be primarily just that—a plan providing retirement benefits. But it may also provide for the payment of death benefits—through insurance or otherwise—as long as those benefits are incidental. Life insurance can be used to provide an incidental death benefit to participants in a qualified retirement plan, either a defined contribution or defined benefit plan. The IRS considers any nonretirement benefit in a qualified plan to be incidental so long as the cost of that benefit is less than 25 percent of the total cost of the plan. Stated as a fraction, this would be as follows:

Cost of providing current life and health insurance

Cost of providing all current and deferred benefits under the plan

The ratio must be less than 25 percent. Since this standard by itself is difficult to apply, the IRS has developed two practical tests for life insurance in a qualified plan.

If the amount of insurance meets either of the following tests, it is considered incidental:

a. *100 to 1 test* – The participant's insured death benefit must be no more than one hundred times the expected monthly normal retirement age benefit,[11] or

b. *Less than… test* – The aggregate premiums paid over the life of the plan for any insured death benefit must at all times be less than the following percentages of the overall cost to provide plan benefits for that participant:

ordinary life[12]	50%
term insurance	25%
universal life	25%
variable life[13]	50%

Traditionally, defined contribution plans such as profit sharing plans have used the percentage limits in determining how much insurance to provide. Defined benefit plans have typically used the one hundred times limit. However, any type of plan can use either limit.

A profit sharing plan may be subject to slightly different rules. It may provide for the distribution of funds accumulated in the plan after a fixed number of years (as few as two).[14] If the plan provides that life insurance can only be purchased with funds that have been on deposit for the specified period, there is no statutory limit as to how much can be used to purchase life insurance.[15]

2. Some qualified retirement plans allow participants to supplement employer contributions with their own after-tax contributions. These after-tax contributions can be used to purchase life insurance without limit. Also, tax-exempt plan earnings can be used to purchase life insurance without regard to the incidental limitations discussed above. Note, however, that if amounts attributable to Voluntary Deductible Contributions (VDECs) under prior law, including net earnings allocable to them, are used to purchase life insurance, such amounts are treated as distributed to the employee in the year so applied.[16]

3. In the case of life insurance purchased by a profit sharing plan on the life of a key individual who generated significant profits to the employer, the incidental test above should not apply to the extent the policy was payable to the profit sharing plan and shared with all plan participants as an economic shock absorber, (i.e., as a key employee policy for the plan).

4. The economic value of pure life insurance coverage on a participant's life is taxed annually to the participant at the lower of: (a) the IRS Table 2001 cost (see Figure 36.1 for Table 2001, which replaced the former P.S. 58 rates); or (b) the life insurance company's actual rates for individual one-year term policies available to all standard risks made known to all purchasers of term insurance from that company and is regularly sold.[17] Any amount actually contributed to the plan by the participant is subtracted from this taxable amount if the plan provides for employee after-tax contributions to be applied to the purchase of life insurance.[18] For a policy insuring more than one life, the IRS says that appropriate adjustments should be made to the premium rates that are used to determine a participant's income.[19]

5. The income taxation of an insured death benefit received by a plan participant's beneficiary is as follows:

a. The pure insurance (also called net amount at risk) element of an insured plan death benefit (i.e., the death benefit less any cash value) is income tax free to a participant's beneficiary (as long as the participant is annually taxed on the reportable economic benefit cost).[20]

b. The total of all Table 2001 costs (formerly P.S. 58 costs were used) paid by the participant can be recovered tax free from the plan death benefit (if it is paid from the same insurance contracts that gave rise to the costs).[21]

c. The sum of all nondeductible contributions toward the plan made by the employee in a contributory plan is tax free to the participant's beneficiary.[22]

d. Any loans made by the plan and taxed to the employee are recovered tax free by the beneficiary.

Figure 36.1

TABLE 2001					
One Year Term Premiums for $1,000 of Life Insurance Protection – One Life					
Age	**Premium**	**Age**	**Premium**	**Age**	**Premium**
0	$0.70	34	$0.98	67	$15.20
1	0.41	35	0.99	68	16.92
2	0.27	36	1.01	69	18.70
3	0.19	37	1.04	70	20.62
4	0.13	38	1.06	71	22.72
5	0.13	39	1.07	72	25.07
6	0.14	40	1.10	73	27.57
7	0.15	41	1.13	74	30.18
8	0.16	42	1.20	75	33.05
9	0.16	43	1.29	76	36.33
10	0.16	44	1.40	77	40.17
11	0.19	45	1.53	78	44.33
12	0.24	46	1.67	79	49.23
13	0.28	47	1.83	80	54.56
14	0.33	48	1.98	81	60.51
15	0.38	49	2.13	82	66.74
16	0.52	50	2.30	83	73.07
17	0.57	51	2.52	84	80.35
18	0.59	52	2.81	85	88.76
19	0.61	53	3.20	86	99.16
20	0.62	54	3.65	87	110.40
21	0.62	55	4.15	88	121.85
22	0.64	56	4.68	89	133.40
23	0.66	57	5.20	90	144.30
24	0.68	58	5.66	91	155.80
25	0.71	59	6.06	92	168.75
26	0.73	60	6.51	93	186.44
27	0.76	61	7.11	94	206.70
28	0.80	62	7.96	95	228.35
29	0.83	63	9.08	96	250.01
30	0.87	64	10.41	97	265.09
31	0.90	65	11.90	98	270.11
32	0.93	66	13.51	99	281.05
33	0.96				

e. Any employer contributions to the plan that for some reason were taxed to the employee are tax free to the beneficiary.

f. The remainder of the distribution is taxed as a qualified plan distribution. This taxable portion of the distribution may be subject to the limited availability of ten-year averaging if the plan participant was over 59½ at death.[23] (ten-year averaging is available only to plan participants born before 1936.)

6. Under regulations issued in 2005, the value of a life insurance contract sold or otherwise distributed from a plan is the contract's fair market value at the time of the sale or distribution. Fair market value includes the policy cash value and all other rights under the contract (including any supplemental agreements, and whether or not the rights are guaranteed).[24] The IRS has also issued safe harbor guidance for determining the fair market value of a life insurance contract.[25] The safe harbor provides that a contract's fair market value may be the greater of:

a. the interpolated terminal reserve and any unearned premiums, plus a pro rata portion of a reasonable estimate of dividends expected to be paid for that policy year; or

b. the sum of the premiums paid and earnings under the contract minus reasonable mortality charges and distributions from the contract (the so-called PERC amount).

For more information, see Chapter 26 "Life Insurance Valuation".

7. Qualified plan death benefits are, in general, included in a decedent's estate for federal estate tax purposes. However, some authorities (not including the authors) believe it may be possible to exclude the insured portion of the death benefit if the decedent had no incidents of ownership in the policy. This subtrust planning technique is discussed further in the following Frequently Asked Questions section.

TRANSFERRING EXISTING POLICIES

Transferring into a Qualified Plan

Life insurance owned by a business or plan participant can (with care) be transferred by contribution or sale into a qualified retirement plan. This will generally make premiums deductible and relieve the corporation or participant from the burden of paying those premiums.

Before any such transfer, planners should consider:

- *The insurance needs of the transferor* – Perhaps the corporation that needs key employee coverage or the individual whose family needs coverage should not be assigning current coverage but should instead be encouraging the retirement plan to purchase additional coverage.

- *Prohibited transaction rules* – Ensure that the contribution of a life insurance policy to a plan by an employer or by the individual participant satisfies the prohibited transaction exemption.[26]

- *The taxation of life insurance proceeds from a qualified plan* – Payments made from the plan to the employee's beneficiary will not be totally income tax free (as they would have been had no transfer been made). Only the pure life insurance (i.e., the net amount at risk) will continue to be treated as life insurance. In other words, once an existing policy is transferred to the retirement plan, only the excess of the death benefit over the policy's cash value at the time of the participant's death will retain its income tax free status when paid out.[27]

Removal from a Qualified Plan

There are several reasons that a planner may consider removing life insurance from a qualified retirement plan. These include the following:

1. Fund assets can be invested more profitably in an alternative manner.

2. It is more likely that the assets can be safely excluded from the participant's estate.

A life insurance policy may be distributed from a plan to: (a) the insured (who must also be a plan participant); or (b) a relative of the insured participant (who is also a beneficiary under the policy).[28] In addition, it may be distributed or sold to a trust established by or for the benefit of the insured participant or a relative of the plan participant.[29]

The tactics to remove a policy from a qualified plan will depend on whether the policy is term or permanent life.

If the policy is a *term* policy, the intended third party owner (e.g., the participant's irrevocable trust or child) should purchase a new term contract. Once it is in force, allow the term policy inside the retirement plan to lapse. (Of course, this assumes the participant is insurable at standard rates. If the participant is insurable only at a high rating or is uninsurable, use the procedure for whole life.)

If the policy is a *permanent* policy, sell the policy to the insured or the insured's trust. However, note that under 2005 guidance, the value of the policy coming out of the plan is determined under special rules. See item 6 under "What are the Tax Implications?" If sold to the insured, the insured can then make a gift (i.e., a transfer of the policy for love and affection) to the third party who is meant to be the eventual owner and beneficiary. However, this two-step process will result in estate inclusion of the policy is the insured does not survive for three years.[30] Alternatively, if the sale is made directly to the insured's irrevocable trust, the three-year rule can be avoided.[31] However, in order to avoid the deadly impact (proceeds lose income tax free status) of the transfer for value rule,[32] the trust will need to be a partner of the insured or be an intentionally defective grantor trust with respect to the insured.[33]

FREQUENTLY ASKED QUESTIONS

Question – Can life insurance be used in a Keogh (HR-10) plan?

Answer – A Keogh plan is a qualified plan covering a proprietor or one or more partners of an unincorporated business. Life insurance can be used to provide a death benefit for regular employees covered under the plan, and the rules discussed in this chapter apply. Life insurance can also be provided under the plan for a proprietor or partners. However, slightly less favorable rules apply.[34] For example, amounts contributed to the plan for the purchase of life insurance for a self-employed person are not deductible,[35] nor can such amounts be recovered tax free from benefits received under the policy.[36]

Question – Can life insurance be used in a Section 403(b) tax deferred annuity plan?

Answer – Life insurance can be provided as an incidental benefit under a tax deferred annuity plan.[37] It is provided on much the same basis as in a qualified profit sharing plan and subject to the same limits. Covered employees will have Table 2001 (formerly P.S. 58) costs to report as taxable income, as in a regular qualified plan.

Question – Can universal life insurance be used to provide an insured death benefit under a qualified plan?

Answer – Universal life and similar products may be used. However, even though universal life has an investment element like that in a whole life policy, the IRS has taken the view that the incidental limits are applied as in the case of term insurance –that is, the aggregate premiums paid must be less than 25 percent of aggregate plan contributions for the participant. While this is clearly incorrect (since a portion of a universal life premium represents a savings or investment element), neither the IRS nor the courts have yet offered relief from this 25 percent limitation.

Question – Can a participant in a qualified plan have the plan purchase life insurance on the life of a spouse or a business partner?

Answer – Yes. Some of the applications of this technique are: (1) the purchase of life insurance on a co-shareholder to help fund a buy-sell agreement; or (2) to provide for a beneficiary and avoid estate taxes on the death of the employee-participant. Second-to-die insurance is sometimes used for this latter purpose.

These third-party insurance techniques are primarily used in qualified profit sharing or stock bonus plans because of the need for an earmarked or directed investment account, as well as rulings prohibiting pension plans from providing third-party insurance.[38]

Question – Can a qualified plan trustee borrow against the cash value of life insurance policies held in the plan?

Answer – Yes, but borrowing by the plan creates unrelated business taxable income from any reinvestment of the loan proceeds. For example, if the loan proceeds are reinvested in certificates of deposit, the plan must pay tax on interest income from those certificates.[39]

Question – Why is life insurance in defined benefit plans particularly advantageous?

Answer – Life insurance is particularly advantageous in defined benefit plans because it *adds* to the limit on deductible contributions. This add-on feature allows greater tax deferred funding of the plan. A defined benefit plan can be funded to provide the maximum tax-deductible contribution for retirement benefits for each participant. The cost for life insurance can then be added to this amount and deducted.

By comparison, in a defined contribution plan, the costs of the life insurance must be part of the contributions to each participant's account. Using life insurance does not increase the Code section 415 annual additions limit for participants' accounts in defined contribution plans. That limit is the lesser of: (a) 100 percent of compensation; or (b) $55,000 (in 2017, as indexed) whether or not life insurance is provided.[40]

Question – How can life insurance help to solve the problem of excessive taxation when a large distribution from a qualified plan is made upon the death of the participant to the participant's grandchild?

Answer – Rather than accept the imposition of three different taxes[41] (i.e., estate tax, generation-skipping transfer tax, and income tax at the beneficiary's rate), the participant should consider leveraging the qualified plan account to provide tax-free benefits for future generations. This can be accomplished by establishing an irrevocable trust to be the applicant-owner-beneficiary of insurance on the participant's life and taking early distributions[42] from the qualified plan to pay the annual premiums.

If the above plan was not undertaken and all three taxes applied, the participant's grandchild would likely receive less than 20 cents on the dollar. By withdrawing substantial sums and purchasing life insurance through an irrevocable trust, the grandchild would likely receive twice that amount (the net proceeds payable from the plan plus the tax free proceeds from the life insurance on the participant's life). If the participant were married, a survivorship life policy could be purchased by the trust that would pay off upon the death of the second to die. In such a case, much more insurance could be purchased with the same annual premium and the heirs could net as much as two or three times what they otherwise would have received.

Question – How can an employer cut turnover costs involved where life insurance is purchased on covered employees?

Answer – Turnover costs involved in buying cash value insurance policies can be minimized by having a longer waiting period for insurance than the plan's waiting period for entry. In the interim period, the death benefit for participants not covered by cash value policies can be provided by term insurance. In the past, many plans did not provide insurance for employees who were beyond a specified cutoff age. Under current age discrimination requirements, this probably is no longer allowed.

Question – Can insurance coverage be conditioned on the taking of a medical examination?

Answer – Yes. Insurance coverage can be conditioned on taking a medical exam if this does not result in discrimination in favor of highly compensated employees. For employees who do not pass the medical exam, insurance is typically limited to the amount, if any, that can be purchased for them using the amount of premium dollars that would be available if they were insurable. For example, if the plan's insurance formula provides insurance of one hundred times the monthly benefit for standard risks (i.e., those employees who pass the medical exam), the insurance provided for a medically rated employee might be only fifty times the monthly benefit, since a fifty-times benefit for that employee would cost as much to provide as a one-hundred-times benefit for a standard risk.

Question – Does the Department of Labor (DOL) have a problem with permanent life insurance in pension plans?

Answer – The DOL has alleged that it is a breach of fiduciary duty to fund death benefits in qualified pension plans with permanent life insurance.[43] Their suggestion is that permanent insurance is too expensive to fund such death benefits and that less expensive term should be used. Planners should note, however, that in each of the cases where the DOL alleged a breach of fiduciary duties under the Employee Retirement Income Security Act (ERISA), the plans were very large, yet the policies purchased were individual contracts with relatively high loadings and commission structures.

In the authors' opinion, had the plans used low load group vehicles rather than individual contracts the DOL would not have objected nor would the courts have supported the DOL. The plan trustees, insurance agents, and insurer did not match the product with the problem. The issue also gives fair warning to life underwriters not to serve as plan fiduciaries if a conflict of interest attack is to be avoided.

Question – Under the concept of pension maximizing, how can life insurance be used for retirement planning as an alternative to the joint and survivor annuity?

Answer – If an individual participates in a qualified defined benefit plan or other pension plan maintained by his employer or business, the participant's spouse is generally entitled to a survivor annuity under the plan. Under most of these provisions, if the plan participant dies before the spouse, the plan pays the spouse an annuity (at least) equal to 50 percent or more of the joint annuity paid (or payable) during the participant's life.[44] This spousal benefit is a right guaranteed under federal law. However, the spouse generally has the option under the plan of waiving the right to the spousal benefit; the result of waiving this benefit is that the participant receives a larger monthly benefit during the participant's lifetime. Under a technique referred to as pension maximizing, it may be better in a few cases to provide security for the spouse using life insurance on the participant's life. The spouse can then waive the survivor annuity, and the extra monthly income received during the participant's lifetime can help to recover, in part or fully, the cost of the life insurance. This concept, along with its caveats, is fully explained in Chapter 38.

Question – What is the subtrust concept and does it work?

Answer – Some authorities have suggested that it is possible to avoid federal estate taxation on life insurance proceeds paid as part of a distribution from a qualified retirement plan through a subtrust concept.[45] One variation of this technique works like this:

- Step 1: The insured-participant makes an irrevocable beneficiary designation that divests him of the right to change the beneficiary of plan proceeds.

- Step 2: The qualified plan is amended to provide that the policy will not be distributed to the insured at retirement. This amendment is made to eliminate an IRS argument that the insured retained a reversionary interest in the policy.

- Step 3: The plan is amended to give the insured a right to purchase the policy for its full value at retirement.

- Step 4: To insulate an insured who is also a trustee of the plan from an incidents of ownership attack by the IRS, a special trust (subtrust) is created. Policies on the life of the insured-trustee are placed into the subtrust. The insured is given no control over the subtrust and cannot remove its independent trustee.

Will this subtrust concept work? The answer appears to be a resounding NO! In an unpublished Technical Advice Memorandum, the IRS has indicated that a life insurance subtrust may disqualify the pension plan. Though this TAM was not published, the taxpayer to whom it was issued sent a copy of it to Steve Leimberg who published it in his *Employee Benefits and Retirement Planning Email Newsletter* - Archive Message #385 (September 19, 2006).

Alternative to the subtrust concept – It is possible and sometimes desirable to remove life insurance from a qualified plan. The easiest way is for the trustee to allow the policy to lapse and for new insurance to be purchased outside the plan (preferably by adult beneficiaries or a trust for the intended recipient of the proceeds). A sale by the retirement plan of the policy to the insured or the insured's irrevocable trust is another possibility where the insured is in ill health, the policy in question is beyond the incontestable period, or for whatever other reason the participant does not want the original policy to lapse (see previous discussion).

Question – Can second-to-die insurance be used inside a qualified pension plan?

Answer – Many authorities seem to believe it should not. In a 1997 bulletin reporting on the American Society of Pension Actuaries Conference that year, the AALU reported that the IRS may question the acceptability of the acquisition by a qualified pension plan of a second to die contract—presumably on the lives of an employee participant and that person's spouse. The Bureau of National Affairs (BNA), a private tax reporting service has reported that "Employers considering second-to-die life insurance contracts inside defined benefit or money purchase plans would be well advised to reconsider."[46]

Question – Can springing value life insurance be safely used in qualified retirement plans?

Answer – Regulations issued in 2005 regarding the value of life insurance contracts in qualified plans generally put an end to the usefulness of springing cash value life insurance contracts in qualified retirement plans. For details, see item 6 previously mentioned, under "What are the Tax Implications?"

CHAPTER ENDNOTES

1. For information on qualified plan rules, see S. Leimberg and J. McFadden, *The Tools and Techniques of Employee Benefit and Retirement Planning*, 15th Ed. (Cincinnati, OH: The National Underwriter Company, 2017). See also, H. Zaritsky and S. Leimberg, *Tax Planning with Life Insurance* (RIA Group, 1999).

2. For an excellent summary of over forty such reasons, see Deppe, "Life Insurance in Qualified Retirement Plans," *The First Annual Henry A. Deppe Lecture* (Bryn Mawr, PA: The American College, 1990). See also, Zaritsky and Leimberg, note 1 above.

3. I.R.C. §§412(i), 412(h), prior to amendment by PPA 2006. The Pension Protection Act of 2006 moved the provisions of Section 412(i) to 412(e)(3) and the provisions of Section 412(h) to 412(e)(2) with no substantive changes. The advantages of fully insured plans described in this chapter assume that the plan operates within the requirements of the Code and satisfies the guidelines set forth in the following 2004 guidance: REG-126967-03, 2004-10 IRB 566; Rev. Proc. 2004-16, 2004-10 IRB 559; Rev. Rul. 2004-20, 2004-10 IRB 546, and Rev. Rul. 2004-21, 2004-10 IRB 544.

4. Where an individually allocated account exists, the participant may be able to decide whether or not to use employer dollars to pay premiums. For example, a young individual with family obligations can elect to have anything less than 50 percent of the employer profit sharing allocations paid as premiums on a low premium policy. An older participant with no family may direct that lesser amounts be used to purchase life insurance. Still others may choose to have none of the contributions directed toward life insurance.

5. In deciding whether to place needed life insurance inside or outside a qualified plan, the following steps should be taken: list the alternatives available, state the advantages and disadvantages of each, and assign a ranking of importance to each advantage and disadvantage. The final decision should be based on a quantitative assessment of economic value and psychological gains and costs.

6. Treas. Reg. §1.72-16(b)(4).

7. Treas. Reg. §1.72-16(b)(4); -16(c)(3), example 1.

8. On September 3, 2002, the Department of Labor amended Prohibited Transaction Exemption 92-6 to permit the sale of insurance contracts and annuities owned by a retirement plan to a trust established by or for the benefit of the insured participant or a relative (as defined in PTE 92-6) of the plan participant. 67 Fed. Reg. 56, 314.

9. I.R.C. §2035(d).

10. See for example Rev. Rul. 2007-13.

11. Stated more completely, the incidental test is automatically satisfied if the death benefit will not be more than the amount of death benefit that would be payable if all plan benefits were funded through retirement income endowment policies that have a death benefit of $1,000, or the reserve, if greater, for each $10 per month of life annuity the policy guarantees at retirement age. See, e.g., Rev. Rul. 60-83, 1960-1 CB 157; Rev. Rul. 61-121, 1961-2 CB 65. So if a participant covered under a defined benefit pension earns $48,000 a year and the plan will pay $2,000 a month at normal retirement age, the pension can purchase up to $200,000 of life insurance. Technically, the 100 to 1 ratio test is not a Code imposed limitation, but a safe harbor.

12. Certain types of whole life insurance with decreasing coverage generally will be treated as term insurance by the Service. In that case, the amount of employer contribution allocated to purchase insurance must be less than 25 percent. See, e.g., Rev. Rul. 76-353, 1976-2 CB 112.

13. See Let. Rul. 9014068.

14. A profit sharing plan may also provide for the distribution of plan assets at the attainment of a specified age or upon the prior occurrence of an illness, death, termination of employment, or even a layoff. Treas. Reg. §1.401-1(b)(1)(ii).

15. See Rev. Rul. 61-164, 1961-2 CB 99; Rev. Rul. 66-143, 1966-1 CB 79.

16. I.R.C. §72(o)(3)(B).

17. I.R.C. §72(m)(3)(B); Treas. Reg. §1.72-16(b); Notice 2002-8, 2002-1 CB 398.

18. Rev. Rul. 68-390, 1968-2 CB 175.

19. Notice 2002-8, 2002-1 CB 398.

20. Treas. Reg. §1.72-16(c)(4). This portion will be taxed as ordinary income if the employee failed to report the Table 2001 costs.

21. Treas. Reg. §1.72-16(b)(4).

22. See Treas. Reg. §1.402(a)-1(a)(5).

23. If the decedent participated in the plan before 1987, there are also some favorable grandfather provisions that may apply. See Leimberg and McFadden, note 1 above, at p. 223-224.

24. Treas. Reg. §1.402(a)-1(a)(1).

25. Rev. Proc. 2005-25, 2005-17 IRB 962.

26. PTE 92-5, 57 Fed. Reg. 5019.

27. I.R.C. §72(m)(3)(C).

28. Ordinarily, a sale of any asset—including life insurance—by the retirement plan to a participant would be considered a prohibited transaction. See I.R.C. §4975(c)(1)(A); ERISA Sec. 406(a)(1)(A). However, PTE 92-6, 57 Fed. Reg. 5189, permits the sale of a life insurance contract by the plan to: (a) the insured; (b) the insured's relative who is a beneficiary under the contract; (c) an employer whose employees are covered under the plan; or (d) to another employee benefit plan if: (1) the contract would, but for the sale, be surrendered by the plan; (2) the amount received, in exchange for the policy, by the plan is at least equal to the amount necessary to put the plan in the same cash position it would have

been had it retained the contract, surrendered it, and made any distribution owing to the participant; (3) the sale does not discriminate in form or operation in favor of plan participants who are officers, shareholders, or highly compensated employees; and (4) with respect to sales of the policy to anyone other than the insured, the participant is informed of the proposed sale, is given an option to purchase the policy before the plan can sell it to anyone else, and consents in writing to the sale.

29. See footnote 8.

30. I.R.C. §2035.

31. I.R.C. §2035(d).

32. For information on the transfer for value rule, see Chapter 25.

33. See footnote 10 and related text.

34. For a discussion of these rules, see Leimberg and McFadden, note 1 above, at p. 73.

35. I.R.C. §404(e).

36. Treas. Reg. §1.72-16(b)(4).

37. Treas. Reg. §1.403(b)-6(g).

38. See Leimberg and McFadden, note 1 above, Chapters 15 and 18.

39. See, e.g., *Sisken Memorial Foundation, Inc. v. U.S.*, 790 F.2d 480 (6th Cir. 1986), *aff'g* 603 F.Supp. 91 (E.D. Tenn. 1984).

40. See I.R.C. §415(c), Notice 2006-98, 2006-46 IRB 906.

41. For decedents dying prior to 1997, there was also a 15 percent excess accumulations tax imposed on excess plan assets at the death of the participant. See I.R.C. §4980A, repealed by TRA '97, Sec. 1073.

42. Income taxes and, possibly, the 10 percent early withdrawal penalty would apply. See I.R.C. §72(t).

43. See, e.g., *Washington Report* (AALU 1992), Nos. 92-88, 92-80, 92-46, 92-22.

44. I.R.C. §417(b).

45. See Eliasberg, "IRS Opens the Way Toward Favorable Estate and Income Tax Treatment of Plan Distributions," 10 *Estate Planning* 208, July 1983; "Here's How to Exclude Insurance in the Pension Plan from the Taxable Estate," *Life Association News*, August 1985, p. 179. See also Fair, "The Qualified Plan as an Estate Planning Tool," The Guardian Life Insurance Company of America.

46. AALU Bulletin No. 97-99; BNA Pensions and Benefits Daily, November 6 1997.

NONQUALIFIED DEFERRED COMPENSATION

CHAPTER 37

INTRODUCTION

Deferred compensation is a contractual arrangement between the employer and employee in which the employer generally makes an unsecured promise to pay benefits in a future tax year in exchange for services rendered currently. Nonqualified plans can also be set up for outside directors and other independent contractors. In general, the same tax rules that apply in employer-employee plans apply to plans that cover independent contractors.[1] One distinction with respect to plans covering only independent contractors is that ERISA does not apply.

A nonqualified deferred compensation plan is a deferred compensation plan that does *not* meet the tax and labor law requirements applicable to qualified plans.[2]

There are two major types of nonqualified deferred compensation plans:

1. *in addition plans*, (also called "salary continuation" or "Supplemental Executive Retirement Plans"—SERPs); and

2. *elective plans*, also called "salary reduction" or "salary deferral" plans.

"In addition" nonqualified deferred compensation plans are used to provide retirement benefits to a select group of executives (or other key employees), or to provide that select group with supplemental benefits *over and above* those provided by the employer's qualified plan. This is a nonelective form of deferred compensation; the employer provides it in addition to the key employee's salary and other compensation.

Elective nonqualified deferred compensation plans are those under which a select group of key employees voluntarily choose to defer a portion of their future salary (or bonus) as a means of tax deferred savings.

WHEN IS THE USE OF THIS TECHNIQUE INDICATED?

A nonqualified deferred compensation plan should be considered by planners using the same critical overlay and analysis as is appropriate with any other life insurance planning tool. There are no clear cut right or wrong answers, and there are no "no cost" solutions. The best course of action is to evaluate each of the viable alternative tools or techniques (such as Section 162 plans, split dollar life insurance, etc.) based upon the following criteria:

- What is the relative *tax* efficiency based upon current and probable future tax rates?

- What is the probability of achieving the employer's objectives? In other words, what is the cost efficiency?

- How important is an upfront income tax deduction to the employer?

- Does the employer desire a lot of control (i.e., "golden handcuffs") over the participating key employees?

- What security does the tool provide against employer insolvency?

- Does the plan provide security in the event of management or ownership changes?

- Can the employer keep or obtain the use of plan funds for an emergency or opportunity?

- How easy is it to implement, explain, and maintain the plan?

A nonqualified deferred compensation plan is indicated in the following situations:

1. When an employer has had enough of the qualified plan blues: increasing costs, decreasing employer discretion and control, and too many limitations on the benefits that may be provided to highly paid and owner-employees. In short, a nonqualified plan should be considered when an employer wants to decrease or eliminate the costs associated with a qualified plan.

2. When an employer would like to provide a retirement and/or death benefit to one or more key employees, but does not want the prohibitive cost or aggravation of a qualified plan or does not want to cover all the employees that must be covered under a qualified plan.

3. When an employer wants to provide *additional* benefits to an executive who is already receiving the maximum benefits or contributions under the employer's qualified plan. Supplemental benefits provided to key individuals under a nonqualified plan provide an excellent means of overcoming the limits placed upon a qualified plan by Code section 415.

4. When an employer wants certain key employees to have tax deferred compensation in different *amounts* or under different *terms* or different *conditions* from that provided to other employees.

5. When an employer seeks to establish an automatic and relatively painless investment program that uses *corporate* tax deductions to *leverage* the employee's future benefits. Because amounts paid by the corporation are generally deductible when paid, employer tax savings can considerably boost the amount payable to the key employee. For instance, suppose the employer is in a 40 percent combined federal and state bracket when benefits are paid. To pay benefits of $100,000 per year costs only

$60,000, because a 40 percent deduction of the $100,000 distribution yields a $40,000 tax saving.

6. When an employer is seeking a tool to recruit, retain, retire, and reward key personnel without the limitations of a qualified plan.[3] Because nonqualified deferred compensation plans work in closely held corporations, smaller firms can use them as a replacement for (or to compete against) the equity-based compensation packages, such as company stock or stock options that an employee of a publicly held company would expect to receive.

A nonqualified deferred compensation plan is generally not indicated when it is not likely that the business will survive the death, disability, or retirement of its key employees.

ADVANTAGES

Flexibility

There is much more *flexibility* in nonqualified deferred compensation plan design than in qualified plan design. For instance, an employer can pick and choose who will be covered, the levels of coverage (subject to the reasonable compensation limits on deductibility), and the terms and conditions of coverage. Also, an employer can provide that plan benefits attributable to employer contributions will be forfeited *entirely* according to *any* vesting schedule or upon any reasonable contingency. For instance, an employer can cut off all benefits attributable to employer contributions if the employee terminates prior to a specified age or if the employee goes to work for a competitor. This means a nonqualified deferred compensation plan can be highly effective with respect to both costs and taxes.

Restrictions can be placed in the plan that will enable the employer to either: (a) achieve its business goals; or (b) recoup its funds, so that either the plan accomplishes what it was intended to accomplish or the employer gets its money back.

Nonqualified plans can escape (completely or in large part) a variety of government requirements imposed upon qualified plans, such as reporting and disclosure requirements, participation and vesting requirements, and fiduciary responsibility requirements.[4]

Tax Deferral

In general, covered employees are not taxed on benefits under nonqualified plans until they actually receive a distribution. Dollars growing over the deferral period currently grow tax free and, therefore, typically grow beyond the level that the employee would have realized, had the employee invested the after-tax dollars.

Employers using properly arranged nonqualified deferred compensation plans financed with life insurance are not currently taxed on the earnings, because tax on the inside buildup of cash surrender values is deferred until distribution. Note that business owned annuities do not enjoy this same tax deferred growth.[5]

The employer's deduction generally may be based upon benefits paid out of the plan, rather than upon contributions paid into the plan (this does not apply to a funded nonqualified deferred compensation plan). Consequently, the employer's deduction may be based upon an amount that is much larger than its original investment. So, if the employer's tax rates *do* increase between the date when the contributions are made to the plan and the payment of benefits, the value of the employer's deduction—and therefore its leverage—also increases.

Tax Leverage

The employee and employer may also take advantage of additional tax leverage. At the time when the payout period begins, the employer takes the cash it has and pays it out as tax deductible salary. Because of the employer's deduction, it can pay a larger amount to the employee. For example, if an employer is in a combined 40 percent state and federal bracket and is obligated to pay out $10,000 a year, the after-deduction cost is only $6,000. But the employer could choose to incur a cost of $10,000 a year—and in fact pay out $16,667 [$16,667 − (0.40 × $16,667) = $10,000].

The formula in the agreement between the employer and the covered employee could provide that the corporation would pay out a given percentage of earmarked cash funds on hand each year,

multiplied by a fraction reflecting the employer's tax bracket that year.

DISADVANTAGES

Income Deferral

The employer's income tax deduction is ordinarily deferred until the year in which income is taxable to the covered employee. This may be as many as twenty or more years from the time when the employer begins financing the obligation (for example, by paying premiums on a life insurance policy). However, if cash flow is a problem, the employer can reduce the contribution to the amount equal to the net, postdeduction contribution cost that the employer would have incurred, had an immediate deduction been available. For example, if the employer is in a 40 percent bracket (federal and state), and a deduction were allowed immediately, a contribution of $10,000 would result in a $4,000 deduction and an after-deduction cost of $6,000. So, in this example, a solution to cash flow problems might be to contribute only $6,000 each year.

Uncertainty

From the employee's perspective, the right to assets in a nonqualified plan is ordinarily less than bulletproof. The executive is relying mainly on the employer's unsecured promise to pay.

To prevent current taxation of the employee, the plan is technically unfunded (i.e., no money or other assets are placed beyond the claims of the employer's other creditors). In essence, even if the employer has been regularly paying life insurance premiums to finance its obligation under the agreement, the employee relies not on the life insurance policy, but rather on the naked (albeit contractual) promise of the employer to pay the designated benefits.

Other than that contractual promise, the employee has no assurance of being paid. When the time for payments comes, the employer may not be willing to make promised payments, or may not have enough money to make them. Furthermore, if there is a corporate takeover, future management may not keep the prior management's promises, or at least not without a long, expensive, grueling lawsuit. The bottom line is that a nonqualified deferred compensation plan is generally not as secure as a qualified plan, from the retiring employee's perspective.

The current solution of choice to this lack of security is the rabbi trust (so called because the first such trust was established to provide post-retirement security for a rabbi). A rabbi trust is generally an irrevocable trust that holds the assets of the plan apart from the employer, but not apart from the employer's creditors. The employer gives up the use of plan investments and cannot reclaim those plan assets until all plan obligations have been met. Trust assets are dedicated solely to providing benefits to the employees covered under the plan, with one major exception: if the employer becomes insolvent or bankrupt, the assets become available to the general creditors of the employer, so that covered employees are compelled to line up with all other general creditors of the employer.

In short, the rabbi trust will protect employees against the employer's change of heart, and against change of management, but not against the employer's insolvency.

AMT Implications

Life insurance payable to a large corporation may be subject to the Alternative Minimum Tax (AMT) at the corporate level. This means that the employer must purchase enough insurance so that, even after any possible AMT, there will be enough cash to meet obligations under the plan. Although the AMT will be, at most, about 15 percent of the death benefit (and in most cases far less), it is suggested that the employer obtain about 18 percent more life insurance than the amount needed to meet cash flow demands under the plan. Any excess proceeds can be used as key employee coverage to cushion the financial shock of the loss of the key employee.

Certain small corporations will qualify for an exemption from the AMT.[6] In order to initially qualify for the exemption, the corporation's average annual gross receipts for its first three-year period must not exceed $5 million. Thereafter, in order to continue to qualify for the exemption, the corporation's average annual gross receipts must not exceed $7.5 million in subsequent three-year periods. For a corporation that has not been in existence for three full years, its years of existence are substituted for the three-year period (with annualization of any short taxable year). A corporation will generally be exempt from the AMT in its first year

of existence. Once a business fails to meet the gross receipts test, it cannot qualify as a small corporation in any later year. If a corporation fails to maintain its small corporation status, it loses the exemption from the AMT.

Example. Assume that a calendar-year corporation started its business on January 1, 2013. The corporation will generally be exempt from the AMT in 2013. It will be exempt in 2014 if its gross receipts in 2013 do not exceed $5 million. It will continue to be exempt in 2015 if its average receipts for 2013 and 2014 do not exceed $7.5 million.

Lack of Confidentiality

Required accounting disclosure reduces confidentiality.[7] A complete discussion of accounting for deferred compensation is beyond the scope of this book, and plan sponsors should consult an accounting professional for advice regarding accounting for deferred compensation. However, in general nonqualified plans entail obligations that must be reflected on the employer's books and may therefore be subject to scrutiny under certain circumstances. This is compared to many forms of qualified plans in which the employer is free of any accounting responsibilities once a contribution has been made to a third-party plan provider.

Limited Availability

Not all employers can or should take advantage of these plans. Pass-through entities such as an S corporation, a partnership, Limited Liability Company (LLC), or a sole proprietorship generally cannot effectively utilize a nonqualified plan for owner employees (with the possible exception of minority owners), so that the use of such a plan is generally limited to a C corporation if the intent is to include an owner employee. Thus, the use of these plans with pass-through entities is limited to a select group of nonowner key employees.

Nonprofit corporations and governmental organizations can use these plans, but they are subject to special, highly restrictive rules under Code section 457. Second, there should be a high probability that the corporation will be fiscally sound long enough to be around when the promised payments are to be made. A nonqualified plan is of no use to either the employer or the covered employee if the business is no longer in existence when the distribution date arrives.

WHAT ARE THE REQUIREMENTS?

Cash value life insurance is an attractive vehicle for financing an employer's obligations under a nonqualified deferred compensation plan. There are essentially six steps necessary to implement a nonqualified deferred compensation plan financed by a company-owned life insurance policy.

1. The employer adopts a corporate resolution authorizing an agreement between the corporation and the employee (or independent contractor) to be covered, promising to make specified benefit payments upon the occurrence of certain triggering events, (e.g., retirement, death and, in some cases, disability) in return for the continuing services of the employee. The resolution usually will note the importance of the employee to the firm and the recruitment, retention, retirement, or reward benefits to be gained by implementing the plan.

2. A second and separate corporate resolution is adopted, authorizing the purchase of life insurance to indemnify the employer for the significant expenses it is likely to incur and the loss it is likely to realize at the death before retirement of the covered employee (or independent contractor).[8]

3. The appropriate amount of life insurance is purchased by and made payable to the employer. The employer is the owner, and no interest in the policy is given to the employee. The policy remains on the employer's books as a corporate asset, subject to the claims of the employer's creditors.

4. The employer's attorney drafts a nonqualified deferred compensation agreement, to be signed by an authorized officer of the employer and the covered employee. The plan should not mention how the employer will meet its obligations. In particular, when life insurance is

used, the plan should contain no reference to or incorporation of the life insurance.[9]

5. A rabbi trust may also be established to hold the life insurance.[10]

ERISA Requirements

ERISA's requirements can be quite burdensome.[11] However, a properly designed unfunded top hat nonqualified deferred compensation plan can escape all or most of the requirements applicable to qualified plans.

- A plan is considered unfunded as long as the contributions are not held in trust for the exclusive benefit of paying out benefits, as is the case for qualified plans. The assets that are accumulated must be subject to the claims of the business' creditors. This does not prevent the employer from informally accumulating assets for the purpose of paying benefits, such as purchasing mutual funds, corporate owned life insurance, or any other accumulation vehicle, as long as such assets are subject to the claims of the business' creditors.

- A top hat plan is a plan that is limited to a select group of management or highly compensated employees. There is no clear definition of management, select group, or highly compensated. As a general rule of thumb, a plan should limit participation to a small group of highly paid executives, relative to the employee population—not to exceed 10 to 15 percent of the employees of an organization. To qualify as highly compensated, their compensation should also be in the top 10 to 15 percent of overall employee compensation. In addition, a participant should have definitive management responsibilities and duties to be considered as management.

For example, an unfunded excess benefit plan is freed from satisfying all of ERISA's reporting, disclosure, participation, vesting, funding, fiduciary responsibility, administrative enforcement and plan termination insurance requirements.[12] Also, if a plan is an unfunded top hat plan, it will be exempt from ERISA's participation, vesting, funding, fiduciary responsibility, and plan termination insurance requirements.[13] However, such a plan will be subject to streamlined reporting and disclosure requirements, recordkeeping requirements and at least some of ERISA's administration and enforcement requirements (including the requirement that a claims procedure be established).[14]

The streamlined reporting and disclosure rules require that a short statement be filed with the Secretary of Labor. A one-page ERISA notice should be completed and filed with the Department of Labor. The statement must include:

- the name and address of the employer;

- the employer's tax identification number;

- a declaration that the employer maintains a plan (or plans) primarily for the purposes of providing deferred compensation to a select group of management or highly compensated employees;

- a statement of the number of such plans maintained and the number of employees participating in each such plan.[15]

The streamlined reporting and disclosure rules also require that plan documents be provided to the Secretary of Labor upon request.[16]

HOW IT IS DONE

The attorney drafting the nonqualified deferred compensation plan must first identify who is in control of the decision-making process—the employer or the employee. The employer has three main objectives:

- Attracting new employees

- Retaining highly productive key employees

- Providing incentives for superior performance

Employer Objectives

If the attorney's mission is to maximize *employer* objectives, the plan should contain a vesting (forfeitability) schedule or other forfeiture of benefits provision desired by the employer. For example, many employer-controlled plans remain unvested for a number of years and then have only graduated vesting. ERISA's vesting requirements do not apply to a properly designed nonqualified deferred compensation plan. Planners, particularly the attorneys who draft nonqualified plans, should keep in mind that, regardless of whether an employee's benefits are subject to forfeiture, the plan must never give the employee any right in the assets that the employer may have purchased to meet its obligations under the plan. Even if plan benefits are fully vested, there should be no adverse income tax implications to the covered employee, as long as: (1) the employer's promise to pay benefits is unsecured; and (2) the agreement is signed before the employee earns the income.

The individual drafting a nonqualified deferred compensation plan should consider the following:

1. Confining eligibility to certain key executives or technical or sales personnel

2. Making plan eligibility either part of a predetermined company policy or adopting the plan for specific individuals as the need arises

3. Including performance incentives (e.g., basing benefits or contributions on salary increases, profits, sales goals, the value of employer stock, or upon the satisfactory achievement of specified objectives)

4. Including clauses that trigger a forfeiture of benefits for termination of employment or for undesirable conduct

5. Delaying vesting

6. Establishing a two-tier interest rate on participant deferrals or employer contributions toward financing the benefit of a given employee (e.g., the plan could credit dollars at a lower rate of return if the employee retired or terminated employment prior to a given date, and at a higher rate if the employee stayed and met other employer conditions)

7. Paying benefits only upon the same terms and conditions as in the employer's qualified plan

Employee Objectives

Where an employee is the more powerful force in the bargaining process, his objectives are typically the following:

- Additional forms of compensation, the income tax on which is deferred as long as possible, so that money otherwise paid in taxes may continue to work for the employee for many years (this compounding of dollars otherwise paid in taxes is a major benefit of a nonqualified deferred compensation plan)

- Benefit certainty

- Immediate vesting of all benefits, without forfeiture provisions

If the mission of the attorney who is drafting the nonqualified deferred compensation plan is meeting the *employee's* objectives, he should consider the following drafting points:

1. The inclusion of performance incentives (e.g., basing benefits or contributions on salary increases, profits, sales goals, the value of employer stock, or upon the satisfactory achievement of specified objectives)

2. The elimination of any clauses that trigger a forfeiture of benefits for termination of employment or for undesirable conduct

3. Immediate 100 percent vesting

In addition, where the employee has a strong influence, planners should consider requiring the plan to pay benefits in the event of disability. Typically, such benefits should begin immediately upon disability. In addition, the definition of disability should be less stringent than the normal total and permanent disability required for Social Security payments. Possible disputes about disability status can be minimized by shifting the determination of disability to an insurance company or a physician chosen jointly by the employer and the employee.

Example. The Uncanny Corporation promises Jo-Ann Egly, a key executive, that, in return for her continued services until age sixty, she will receive (in addition to her normal salary and other fringe and qualified pension or profit sharing benefits) $100,000 a year for ten years, beginning at her retirement. Should she die prior to retirement, her children will be paid that amount, beginning at her death.

Like almost all nonqualified deferred compensation plans, the Uncanny Corporation's plan provides both lifetime retirement and at death payments. If the covered employee retires, the employer pays the promised annual payments from corporate surplus. The employer holds the life insurance policy until the employee's death, thus realizing income tax free proceeds that will help the employer's business recover its costs, and in some cases, may even result in a net gain—even after figuring the time value of the employer's premium dollars. Insurance agents refer to this as cost recovery deferred compensation.

TYPES OF PLANS

There are two types of plans that have significantly different design and drafting philosophies: *salary continuation plans* and *salary reduction plans.*

Salary Continuation Plan

A *salary continuation* plan is a type of nonelective nonqualified deferred compensation plan that provides a benefit payable in the future. A salary continuation plan is a fringe benefit provided by an employer with employer dollars in addition to other benefits and therefore requires *no* reduction in the covered employee's salary. For example, the contract might provide:

"At retirement, disability, or death, the XYZ Corporation will pay you or your designated beneficiary $100,000 a year for ten years."

The salary continuation plan is often used when an employer wants to provide something *in place of* or *in addition to* a qualified plan.

The salary continuation plan is usually a defined benefit type of plan. Plan benefits are often measured as a percentage of compensation. For instance, the employee will receive payments based upon average earnings over his final three years of service for the employer. Benefits may also be based upon years of service, so that the longer the employee has worked for the employer, the higher the benefit. Another possibility is that benefits may be based upon the achievement of specified goals.

A salary continuation plan can also be a defined contribution plan. Here the employer makes defined contributions to the plan (e.g., $10,000 each year that the participant remains employed with the employer) without reducing the participant's salary, and the contributions are credited with interest. The actual retirement benefit depends upon the participant's plan balance at retirement.

SERP Plans

A Supplemental Employee Retirement Plan (SERP) is a plan for a selected group of executives. A SERP generally provides extra retirement benefits for key personnel. An excess benefit plan is a special kind of supplemental plan. It is a creature of ERISA, and is a plan maintained by an employer solely for the purpose of providing benefits for certain employees in excess of the limitation on contributions and benefits imposed by Code section 415.[17] An excess benefit plan can restore parity between the percentage of preretirement pay provided to highly paid employees at retirement and the percentage of preretirement pay provided to rank and file employees at retirement.

Salary Reduction Plans

A *salary reduction* plan is a true elective deferral of a specified amount of employee compensation.

Salary reduction plans typically utilize a defined contribution type of formula. An amount is added to the participant's account each year (funded with employee deferrals). That amount may be an actual accumulation of funds, or simply a bookkeeping account.

If the account is only a bookkeeping account, the employer will often guarantee a specified minimum rate of return on the money credited. The rate of return may be based upon some index beyond the employer's control—such as Moody's Bond Index. Alternatively, the rate of return may be tied to the value of the employer's stock.

Contributions are generally a specified percentage of the employee's compensation each year or can be designed to meet a target retirement benefit similar to a target benefit qualified retirement plan.

TAX IMPLICATIONS

In a properly drafted plan (one which avoids constructive receipt, the economic benefit doctrine, and Code section 83, and is compliant with Code section 409A—see below), the employee will not be taxed until benefits are actually received, at which time he reports the benefits as ordinary income.

Amounts received from the plan by beneficiaries are taxable as received at ordinary rates, with one exception: to the extent that the inclusion of the benefit results in federal estate tax upon the covered employee's estate, an income tax deduction may be allowed to recipients under Code section 691 (for income in respect of a decedent). No income averaging is available to either the employee or the employee's survivors.

Payments made to the employee (or his beneficiary) from a nonqualified plan—either directly by the employer or through a trust established to hold the financing vehicles for the plan—are deductible by the employer in the year that benefits are includable in the employee's (or beneficiary's) income, to the extent that they meet the ordinary, necessary, and reasonable tests applied to all compensation.[18]

Contributions to a plan that is primarily for the benefit of shareholders are not deductible (and may be treated as dividends).[19] This emphasizes the importance of documenting the business purpose for the plan in a corporate resolution.

Funding the Plan

The internal buildup of value inside a life insurance contract is currently income tax deferred. By contrast, to the extent that the employer finances its obligation under the contract with mutual funds, stocks, bonds, or other assets producing taxable income, that taxable income is reportable—as earned—by the employer, at the employer's tax rate. This is another reason why life insurance is so often the principal (or an important auxiliary) financing vehicle.

When assets are held inside a rabbi trust designed to hold the financing mechanism, the tax consequences are essentially the same as when the assets are held directly by the employer. If properly drafted, the trust will be considered an employer grantor trust for income tax purposes. This means all trust income, deductions, and tax credits are treated as if earned by or allowable to the employer for tax purposes.

FICA and FUTA

Amounts deferred under a nonqualified plan are considered to be wages for Federal Unemployment

Tax (FUTA) purposes and subject to Social Security tax when:

1. the services are performed; or

2. when the employee no longer has a substantial risk of forfeiture, whichever is later.[20]

However, because federal unemployment tax is imposed only on the first $7,000 of wages for the calendar year, an employee's nonforfeitable interest in a nonqualified plan should not create any FUTA tax liability.

It appears that outside directors who defer receipt of their fees for services performed must include their fees in net earnings for self-employment for Social Security tax purposes when the deferred fees are actually or constructively received.[21]

Where an employee is fully vested in his benefit under a nonqualified deferred compensation plan, Social Security taxes apply immediately to deferred amounts—up to the applicable wage base ceilings. However, because most participants in nonqualified plans will earn more than the Social Security taxable wage base ($127,200 as indexed in 2017), a participant would pay little or no Social Security tax on such deferred benefits.

Estate Tax Consequences

The present value of any death benefit (or, if the payment is made in a lump sum, that lump sum amount) payable to a beneficiary is includable in a deceased employee's estate. The discount rate for computing the present value of the stream of income payments is the Section 7520 interest rate (basically 120 percent of Applicable Federal Midterm Rate or AFMR) and varies monthly.

Keep in mind that inclusion of this asset in the gross estate is moot if the annuity is payable solely to the surviving spouse, since it will qualify for the federal estate tax marital deduction. But planners should remember that if payments are contingent, or if they continue beyond the surviving spouse's death (as is usual in the case of payments for a fixed number of years), then, absent a timely and proper Qualified Terminable Interest Property (QTIP) election by the deceased employee's executor, there will be no marital deduction.

GSTT Consequences

Subject to the annual exclusion deduction[22] and the $5,490,000 Generation Skipping Transfer Tax (GSTT) exemption (as indexed for inflation in 2017),[23] if nonqualified deferred compensation payments are made by a corporation to someone classified as being two or more generations below the employee (for example, the client's grandchild), GSTT will be imposed. Gift tax implications depend upon whether the employee retains the right to change the designation of the beneficiary. Assuming that the employee retains the right to change the beneficiary designation (typically by notifying the employer in writing), and that the prior beneficiary's consent is not required to make such a change, there is no completed gift to the new beneficiary for gift tax purposes. So most nonqualified deferred compensation plans will not have any gift tax implications.

But, at the time when the employee makes an irrevocable assignment of the right to receive payments from the plan, the gift of the employee's property interest in the plan will be complete and gift tax will be imposed.[24] No annual gift tax exclusion would be allowed, because such a gift would be of a future interest as the beneficiary does not have the immediate, unfettered, and ascertainable right to use, possess, and enjoy the payments.

Section 409A Requirements

Added by the American Jobs Creation Act of 2004, Code Section 409A imposes special requirements for participants making elections to defer compensation. Participants now must generally make deferral elections prior to the end of the preceding taxable year. In the first year in which a participant becomes eligible to participate in a plan, however, the participant may make an election within thirty days after the date of eligibility, but only with respect to services to be performed subsequent to the election. In the case of any performance-based compensation covering a period of at least twelve months, a participant must make an election no later than six months before the end of the covered period.[25]

Distribution Provisions

Distribution provisions must also comply with the rules of Code section 409A. Under these rules, plan distributions may not be made (without penalty) earlier than one of the following events:[26]

1. *Separation from service* – If the employee is a key employee of a publicly-traded company, as defined under the top-heavy rules of Code section 416(i), a distribution upon separation from service may not begin until six months after separation.

2. *Disability* – Disability is defined as either the strict Social Security definition of total and permanent disability, or, under certain conditions, disability under an accident and health plan covering employees of the employer.

3. *Death* of the employee.

4. *A time specified under the plan* – Payment upon occurrence of an event, such as the employee's son's graduation from high school, is not considered payment at a specified time.

5. *A change in ownership or control*, as defined in regulations.[27]

6. *Occurrence of an unforeseeable emergency* – The distribution may not exceed the amount necessary for the emergency plus taxes on the distribution. Section 409A(a)(2)(B)(I) spells out the definition of "unforeseeable emergency":

   a. a severe financial hardship to the participant resulting from an illness or accident of the participant, spouse, or dependent;

   b. loss of the participant's property due to casualty; or

   c. other similar extraordinary and unforeseeable circumstances beyond the participant's control.

This change resulted from a view in the Congress and the Treasury Department that prior restrictions on distributions for nonqualified plans were not stringent enough to justify the deferral of taxes on the amounts in question. For example, under prior law, many plans allowed employees to withdraw amounts without restriction except for a haircut provision, under which a small penalty (such as 6 percent) was imposed on the amount withdrawn, or the participant was restricted

from deferring subsequent compensation for a period such as six months. These haircut provisions will no longer be allowed.

Loss of the Haircut Provision

The loss of haircut provisions is arguably the most negative feature of section 409A from the employee's standpoint. A haircut provision was an important safeguard: if the employee felt that financial or other conditions within the company might threaten the deferred compensation benefit within the near future, the employee could get his money out under the plan's haircut withdrawal provision. In effect, Congress views the use of this type of safeguard as an abuse, regardless of whether the employee is a high-level executive capable of actually manipulating the situation or just a mid-level executive trying to preserve his retirement funds in a failing or hostile corporate environment.

Accelerated Payments

Section 409A(a)(3) also penalizes "acceleration of the time or schedule of any payment under the plan." The rule is generally not violated if the benefit acceleration doesn't change the timing of income inclusion. For example, the plan could provide a choice between a lump sum and a fully (immediately) taxable annuity contract. Regulations define certain other circumstances under which a plan may permit the acceleration of payments:[28]

1. An accelerated distribution may be permitted if it is not elective and is beyond the control of the employee, such as a distribution to comply with a court-ordered divorce settlement or a Federal conflict-of-interest requirement.[29] For example, if federal authorities required a government official to cash out his deferred compensation contract with a company currently doing business with the government rather than allowing it to continue in effect throughout his term of office, creating a scandalous impression of bias and corruption, this would not violate section 409A(a)(3).

2. A Section 457(f) plan (a plan for executives of governmental or nonprofit organizations) may allow a payout to provide for taxes due on a vesting event.

3. Payments may be accelerated in order to pay employment taxes (FICA and FUTA) and the income tax withholding resulting from this acceleration. This relief provision is required because in an unfunded plan, FICA and FUTA taxes are payable upon vesting of the amounts involved, while income taxes may not be due until a much later year (the year of receipt or constructive receipt).

4. Payments may be accelerated to terminate a participant's interest in a plan under certain circumstances:

    a. after separation from service where the payment is not greater than $10,000;

    b. where all arrangements of the same type are terminated;

    c. in the twelve months following a change in control event; or

    d. upon a corporate dissolution or bankruptcy.

5. Payments may be accelerated to terminate a deferral election following an unforeseeable emergency (see definition above).

The purpose of the nonacceleration rule is to prevent executives from taking money out of a failing corporation when they see financial trouble approaching for the corporation. This is the type of practice involved in the Enron and similar corporate scandals of the last several years, and Congress has decided to try to prevent such practices with IRC Section 409A. The rules, however, limit design flexibility in many situations where abusive practices are not likely.

Penalties

Code section 409A includes substantial penalties for failing to meet its requirements when deferring compensation. Any violation of the deferral or distribution requirements results in retroactive constructive receipt, with the deferred compensation being taxable to the participant as of the time of the intended deferral. In addition to the normal income tax on the compensation, the participant must pay an additional 20 percent tax, as well as interest at a rate 1 percent higher than the normal underpayment rate.[30]

CONSTRUCTIVE RECEIPT DOCTRINE

Under the constructive receipt doctrine, an amount becomes currently taxable to a cash basis taxpayer, even before it is actually received, if it is *credited* to the employee's account, *set aside*, or *otherwise made available* to the employee.[31]

Once income is unconditionally subject to the taxpayer's demand, that income must be reported, even if the taxpayer has *not* chosen to reduce that income to his possession.

Amounts due from the employer will be includable in the income of an employee who is a cash basis taxpayer as soon as:

1. the money is available to him;

2. the employer is able and ready to pay;

3. the employee's right to payment is unrestricted; and

4. the failure to receive the money results from the exercise of the employee's own choice.[32]

Since the major advantage of a nonqualified deferred compensation plan to an employee is the deferral of tax (which deferral is analogous to an interest free loan from the government), it is essential that the plan avoid constructive receipt.

There is no constructive receipt if the employee's control over receipt is subject to a *substantial limitation or restriction*.[33] Perhaps the easiest way to avoid constructive receipt is to design the plan so that:

1. the compensation is deferred before it is earned;

2. the employer's promise to pay benefits is completely unsecured; and

3. ultimate payment of the benefits is conditioned upon the passage of time or the occurrence of an event beyond the employee's control.

Such actions will avoid constructive receipt even though the benefits are completely nonforfeitable.[34]

The problem of constructive receipt (keeping the time and manner of payment outside the employee's control) extends beyond the asset buildup period. Plan provisions must also assure that the employee is not taxed on more than is actually received during the distribution period.

Example. Assume that a plan provides for a distribution of benefits over ten years in equal annual installments, starting at age sixty-five. If the employee could elect, at any time during the distribution period, to accelerate the balance of payments, then the constructive receipt doctrine would require an immediate inclusion in income of the entire amount that the employee could elect to receive. Alternatively, assume that a plan provides for a ten-year distribution period, but allows the employee to elect, during the distribution period, to spread the ten annual payments over fifteen years. Even if the employee chose the fifteen-year option, he would still be taxed as if plan assets were received over the original ten-year period.

Employee Elections

If the covered employee's election to reduce his salary is made before rendering services for which compensation is deferred then—in order to avoid constructive receipt—all that is necessary is that there be a substantial limitation or restriction on the employee's ability to reach plan assets. But, according to the IRS, in order to defer compensation *after* services have been performed, the plan must provide *substantial risk of forfeiture* provisions, a much more severe standard than a mere substantial limitation or restriction.[35]

Many attorneys believe that an election regarding the mode of payment can safely be made without constructive receipt as long as it is made *before* any amount is actually *payable*.[36] However, the IRS refuses to rule favorably on a nonqualified plan that allows elections *after* the beginning of the period of *service* in which the compensation is earned–unless substantial forfeiture provisions are in effect.[37] Therefore, most plans require that participants must choose the time and manner in which benefits will be paid *before* the deferred amount is *earned*.

It is possible to build a great deal of flexibility into a salary reduction arrangement without triggering the constructive receipt doctrine, by permitting prospective

adjustments to be made to the percentage of compensation to be deferred in future years on an annual basis.[38]

Substantial Risk of Forfeiture

A substantial risk of forfeiture exists where rights in transferred property are conditioned directly or indirectly upon the performance (or nonperformance) of substantial services. For instance, if property must be returned to the employer should total earnings not increase in a given period of time, the property is subject to a substantial risk of forfeiture.[39]

A common misperception is that a nonqualified deferred compensation plan requires a substantial risk of forfeiture. As discussed above, this is not generally true. What is required is a substantial limitation on the employee's ability to reach the plan assets. A substantial risk of forfeiture is generally only required for 457(f) plans for tax-exempt employers. A substantial risk of forfeiture, however, is frequently included in plans for taxable employers that involve employer contributions as a way of tying the participant to the employer (i.e., golden handcuffs).

When is a risk substantial? The answer will always depend upon the facts and circumstances of each case.[40] Planners must be sure that there is a clear line of demarcation between a mere contractual right to receive compensation in the future—which is safe from the application of the economic benefit theory—and a right that is secured and is not subject to a substantial risk of forfeiture.

Controlling Shareholders and Constructive Receipt

The IRS will not issue a private ruling with respect to the tax treatment of a controlling shareholder-employee's participation in a nonqualified deferred compensation plan.[41] The IRS seems to be concerned, in part, that a controlling shareholder, by virtue of his control, has the power to modify the terms of a deferral agreement at any time, and to access deferred amounts at will, and is therefore necessarily in constructive receipt of deferred amounts (i.e., there is no substantial limitation on the ability of the controlling shareholder to access plan assets).[42]

It is the authors' opinion that if the plan is properly drafted and designed, a controlling shareholder-employee should be able to participate and be taxed (or escape current taxation) in the same manner as a nonshareholder employee.[43]

Steps to thwart an attack on a plan in which a controlling shareholder is a participant include the following:

1. Separate the financing of the employer's obligation from the plan itself. For example, if a life insurance policy is to be used, do not match the policy benefit with the promises made. When the vehicle used to finance benefits is identical to and directly keyed into the benefits promised under the plan, the IRS may deny favorable tax treatment.[44] If the life insurance is maintained by the employer as key employee coverage and is kept totally separate from the agreement, there should be no constructive receipt or economic benefit issues.

2. If possible, include at least one highly compensated person who is not a shareholder-employee in the plan. The participation of a nonshareholder-employee greatly enhances the argument that the plan is for corporate, rather than shareholder, purposes, and will serve to justify a corporate income tax deduction when benefits are to be paid. Do not create a plan for the sole benefit of a controlling shareholder.

3. Create a full documentation of the corporate advantage to be gained and the business purpose to be served by the plan in corporate minutes and in the agreement itself. Use wording that indicates that other successful competitive companies are providing similar supplemental compensation in their benefit programs. Incorporate wording from trade journals evidencing that such plans are commonly used in the employer's industry or profession as a form of compensation for the recruitment, retention, retirement, and reward of key employees.

4. Consider using a rabbi trust. A rabbi trust can serve as a device that creates a substantial restriction or limitation upon the ability of even a controlling (however defined) shareholder to reach deferred amounts until the occurrence of specific events. Under state law, the independent trustee has the fiduciary responsibility to deny access to anyone until the covered person has satisfied the plan's triggering criterion (for example, disability, death, or attainment of a specified retirement age). Thus, the rabbi trust

should negate any raw power that a controlling shareholder may have to reach benefits.

5. Establish an independent compensation review committee with the power to deny benefits to participants who do not meet plan criteria. Have the committee actually meet and review the operation of the plan and police its provisions.

6. Do not provide a plan for shareholder-employees with terms and benefits more generous than would be provided to nonshareholder-employees. Provide that contributions or benefits on behalf of shareholder-employees cannot be proportionately greater than those provided to key employees who are not shareholders. In other words, base the plan benefit formula upon a reasonable and uniform percentage of salary.

FINANCING VEHICLES

The use of the term "finance" is a reminder that the distinction between financing and funding is an important one. There is a way to finance the employer's obligations without the tax and ERISA problems associated with a funded plan: keep assets in the fund *accessible* to the employer and its creditors and provide no explicit security to the employee beyond that provided to other creditors of the employer. Note that, although for many purposes, the definitions of unfunded and funded are the same for both tax and ERISA purposes, in some important situations those definitions will differ.

The term financing implies that, regardless of the investment vehicle used, no money or other asset is placed beyond the reach of the employer or its creditors. Conversely, the term funded has adverse implications under both tax and ERISA law. A plan is funded if the employer has placed money or property credited to the employee's account in an irrevocable trust or otherwise placed restrictions upon the access to the fund by the employer and its creditors.

There are a number of problems presented by a funded plan.

First, once a plan is considered funded, the value of the employee's interest in the fund will become taxable to the employee as soon as his interest in the fund is substantially vested.[45] With funded salary reduction plans, this is almost always immediately. In other words, an employee could be taxed on benefits years before actually receiving any payments from the fund.

Second, funded plans may be subject to burdensome ERISA requirements, including the vesting and fiduciary requirements imposed on qualified plans.[46]

Thus, the question is, "How can an employee's security in his benefit be increased without triggering the adverse implications of a funded plan?" The easiest solution is an earmarked reserve account maintained by the employer. This means that the employer sets up an account invested in assets of various types. There is no trust—assets in the account are, at all times, fully accessible to both the employer and its creditors.

The employer could set up an actual reserve account with limited employee investment direction. Under such an arrangement, the employee is given the right to select the investments in the account. That right of direction must be limited to a choice of broad types of investment. If the employee is permitted to choose specific investments, the IRS could argue that the employee had constructive receipt of investment funds.[47] So the employee should be given the right to choose between equities, bonds, a family of mutual funds, etc.

The employer typically purchases, pays premiums on, and is the beneficiary of life insurance. Proceeds can be used to provide a death benefit if the employee dies in the early years of the plan. Employees should not be taxable on the current economic benefit of this type of security, because the insurance is strictly an employer asset.[48]

Three methods are commonly used to help an employer meet its obligations under a nonqualified plan: (1) pay-as-you-go; (2) alternative investments; and (3) corporate-owned life insurance.

Pay-as-you-go

Pay-as-you go is, by definition, an obligation for the employer to use the working capital of its business (or draw on its line of credit) every time a payment is due. This approach is simple and postpones the cash outflow as long as possible. The employer accrues a liability on its balance sheet under the category of deferred compensation. Some employers feel that this method makes sense as long as the employer itself can earn more after-tax return by reinvesting the money in its business than could be earned through an alternative investment.

This opportunity cost of capital decision-making tool is another way of saying that the employer expects to finance plan obligations through the future growth of its business. The problem with this thinking is that if expectations are not met, the necessary cash will not be there when needed. The obligation is then shifted to the future management of the business, and may fall due at the worst possible time (in terms of cash flow). It puts the financial security of the covered employees at the risk of the business. It must also be considered that future management may not be willing to make promised payments—even if able to.

Alternative Investments

Alternate investments are, of course, those investments other than life insurance that can be used to finance the employer's obligation. These should be long term conservative investments, such as mutual funds, that are highly liquid.

Corporate-Owned Life Insurance (COLI)

Corporate-Owned Life Insurance (COLI) is the preferred financing vehicle for most publicly-held and almost all closely-held businesses. Although there is no one type of contract that is best for nonqualified deferred compensation plans, most planners, after examining plan goals and other factors, tend to favor plans with high premium payment and investment flexibility and low mortality and expense costs. Permanent, rather than term, coverage is indicated where the plan contemplates use of some or all of policy values to finance retirement benefits.

Permanent life insurance is an attractive informal financing vehicle for many reasons, including:

- the cash value acts as a tax-deferred sinking fund to pay benefits (this is important for smaller employers that may not be able to pay benefits from business cash flow);

- costs can almost always be recovered from the death benefit—including the after-tax cost of the use of corporate dollars;

- a competitive internal rate of return, as compared with alternative investments;

- the ability to offer a pre-retirement death benefit, with no risk to corporate cash flow.

Generally, formally funding a nonqualified deferred compensation plan will result in current income taxation to the employee and will result in the imposition of onerous ERISA rules. Fortunately, a properly designed nonqualified deferred compensation plan will not be considered funded for tax or ERISA purposes merely because it is financed with life insurance.[49]

It is important that the plan document not specifically reference the life insurance or any other asset that is being used to informally finance the plan benefits. To do so could be considered to give a plan participant an exclusive right to the asset. If the intent is to pay a benefit equal to the life insurance cash value at retirement, then a hypothetical account should be used in the plan document which may use the performance of the life insurance policy as a benchmark for purposes of crediting and debiting the hypothetical account value. The amount of life insurance purchased should be a function of:

1.   the plan benefits promised;

2.   the Alternative Minimum Tax (AMT), if any, expected to be applied to the proceeds;

3.   the expected tax leveraging; and

4.   the employer's goals with respect to the financial implications of the plan to its business.

The most generous plan, from the employee's viewpoint, is one in which all plan assets are leveraged with the employer's tax deduction to produce the maximum benefit. This is, of course, the least favorable to the employer and will result in the highest life insurance cost, since none of the proceeds are used to defray any of the employer's: (1) premium outlay; (2) after-deduction cost of benefits; or (3) the time value of money during either the premium paying or benefit paying period.

Cost Recovery Plans

It is, of course, appealing to the employer to be able to accomplish all of its recruitment, retention, retirement, and reward objectives without the limitations upon benefits for the highly compensated and owner-employees in a qualified plan. In addition, the employer can pay out all promised benefits to a covered employee and then recover some or all of the costs involved in the plan. These goals can all be accomplished through the purchase of corporate-owned life insurance.

Cost recovery nonqualified plans can be thought of as having at least three levels.[50]

1.   Recovery of the net premiums paid, plus the after-deduction cost of the deferred salary paid to the employee or survivors, plus the cost of the use of money on the net premiums or the deferred benefits. This is the highest level of cost recovery and will therefore require the most life insurance to accomplish.

2.   Recovery of the net premiums paid, plus the after-deduction cost of the deferred salary paid to the employee or survivors. This is the middle level of cost recovery and will require less life insurance.

3.   Recovery of only the net insurance premium outlay or the after-deduction cost of the deferred salary paid to the employee or survivors. This is the lowest level of cost recovery and will require the least amount of life insurance.

Ensuring Plan Security through Guarantees

Security is an important goal for many reasons. Security of promised benefits is endangered by the possibility that the employer will be: (1) unwilling to pay benefits as they come due (either because of a change of heart or a change of management); or (2) unable to pay benefits as they come due.

Surety Bonds

A surety bond is a contractual agreement by a bonding insurance company to pay the promised benefits in the event that the employer is unable or unwilling to make payments. If the employee purchases a surety bond and pays all premiums personally, and if the insurer requires some form of collateralization agreement with the employer, then, in the authors' opinion, the plan may be considered secured.[51] As a practical matter, few companies will issue such bonds; they are expensive, and so limited that they are of little interest to most covered employees.

Indemnification Insurance

The IRS has indicated that an employee can buy indemnification insurance to protect his deferred benefits without causing immediate taxation. The result is the same even if the employer reimburses the employee for the premium payments, as long as the employer has no other involvement in the arrangement. The employee's premium payments must be treated as nondeductible personal expenses, and any premium reimbursements must be included in the employee's income.[52] The consequences of such an arrangement under ERISA are not clear.

Third-party Guarantees

A shareholder of the employer corporation can personally guarantee payment under a nonqualified deferred compensation plan *without* causing the employee to be taxed. A third party guarantee is merely a promise to pay, and, although it may broaden a participant's protection, it should not require the inclusion of the primary obligation amount in currently taxable income.[53] For example, where a parent corporation guaranteed payments under a subsidiary's contract with an executive, the IRS held that the guarantees would not cause the plan to be funded.[54] But if the employer's obligation is backed by a letter of credit from the employer or by a surety bond obtained by the employer, the promise may be considered to be secured, and thus cause current taxation.

Under a third party guarantee, the employer obtains a guarantee from a third party to pay the employee if the employer defaults. This guarantor may be a shareholder, a related corporation, or a bank (through a letter of credit). There is precedent for a favorable IRS position on third party guarantees.[55] Unfortunately, too much *employer* involvement may cause the IRS to claim that the plan is formally funded for tax purposes. A better course of action is to have the employee, independent of the employer, obtain a third party guarantee.

Ensuring Plan Security with Trusts

One partial answer to the desire for more security is the rabbi trust. Rabbi trusts enhance employee security with minimal threat to the income tax advantages of the nonqualified deferred compensation plan. While there is some uncertainty in the area, the use of a rabbi trust (at least in the context of a nonqualified plan that is maintained for a select group of management

or highly compensated employees or that is an excess benefit plan) should not cause the plan to be funded for ERISA purposes.[56]

A rabbi trust holds the assets of the plan apart from the corporation, but *not* apart from its creditors. The rabbi trust is generally an irrevocable trust that holds assets that will be used, wholly or partially, to satisfy the employer's obligation. The employer gives up the use of plan investments, so that those assets are dedicated solely to the employees covered under the plan, with one major exception: if the employer becomes bankrupt or insolvent, the assets become available to the general creditors of the employer. This means that covered employees must essentially line up with the employer's other general creditors.

Factors that would indicate the use of a rabbi trust include:

1. a fear that the management or ownership of the business is likely to change before all benefits will be paid;

2. a fear that hostile new management might renege on the employer's contractual obligations to its key employees; and

3. a perceived probability that if litigation were necessary, a win by key employees would come at a prohibitive cost.

The three costs of a rabbi trust (aside from the legal costs of creating the rabbi trust and the accounting costs of maintaining it) include:

1. the employer loses the use of plan assets (i.e., they are not available for a corporate emergency or opportunity);

2. the rate of return on plan assets in the trust may be less than what could have been earned had the money been invested in the employer's business;

3. a rabbi trust does not provide any protection against the ultimate risk of employer insolvency.

A deferred annuity is probably an unsuitable investment for a rabbi trust, because increases in income inside the annuity would be currently taxable to the employer as grantor of the rabbi trust. Tax-advantaged investments, such as municipal bonds, preferred stocks, life insurance or a combination of these, are likely to be a better choice.

Securing or distributing deferred compensation upon the employer's falling net worth or other financial events unacceptably secures the payment of the promised benefits.[57] This includes hybrid rabbi/secular trust arrangements that distribute assets from nominal rabbi trusts to secular trusts on the occurrence of triggering events indicating the employer's financial difficulty. Under any such arrangement, otherwise deferred compensation is immediately taxable and subject to a 20 percent additional tax. Interest on the underpayment of taxes is due at the normal underpayment rate plus 1 percent.[58]

Setting aside assets in an offshore trust to directly or indirectly fund deferred compensation also unacceptably secures the payment of the promised benefits.[59] Under any such arrangement, the otherwise deferred compensation is immediately taxable and subject to a 20 percent additional tax. Interest on the underpayment of taxes is due at the normal underpayment rate plus 1 percent.[60]

Drafting Requirements

Like a deferred compensation plan itself, any related rabbi trusts must comply with requirements under Code section 409A, which prohibits securing or distributing deferred compensation upon the employer's falling net worth or other financial events. This includes hybrid rabbi/secular trust arrangements that distribute assets from nominal rabbi trusts to secular trusts on the occurrence of triggering events indicating the employer's financial difficulty. Setting aside assets in an offshore rabbi trust to directly or indirectly fund deferred compensation also unacceptably secures the payment of the promised benefits.

Under any such prohibited arrangements, otherwise deferred compensation is immediately taxable and subject to a 20 percent additional tax. Interest on the underpayment of taxes is due at the normal underpayment rate plus 1 percent.

Prior to Code Section 409A, the IRS released a model rabbi trust instrument intended to serve as a safe harbor for employers adopting rabbi trusts and to expedite the processing of requests for advance rulings on these arrangements. The IRS will no longer issue advance

rulings on unfunded deferred compensation arrangements that use a trust other than the model trust, except in rare and unusual circumstances.[61]

Prior to Section 409A, the rabbi trust documents that previously received favorable rulings from the IRS generally were irrevocable and:

1. required that plan assets be deferred until the participant's termination of employment;[62]

2. precluded investment in employer stock;[63]

3. made the assets available to all general creditors of the corporation should the employer become bankrupt or insolvent under state law (i.e., do not give the covered employee greater rights to trust assets than creditors have under state law);

4. included a requirement that the employer (specifically, the CEO and the Board of Directors) must notify the trustee if the employer becomes insolvent or subject to bankruptcy proceedings;

5. provided that if the employer notifies the trustee of its bankruptcy, the trustee must suspend all payments to covered employees, hold all assets for the benefit of creditors, and provide that no further assets can be distributed to the covered employees until allowed by a bankruptcy court; and

6. did *not* provide an insolvency trigger, that is, a provision that triggers immediate payments to covered employees from the trust should the employer become insolvent or experience a drop in net worth below a specified level. The IRS viewed this type of provision as giving the employee greater rights to the assets than other corporate creditors, so that tax benefits are lost. (This is now explicit in Section 409A.)

Drafters might also consider provisions which:

1. Provide that investment authority will automatically shift to the trustee of the rabbi trust in the event of an unfriendly takeover, thus preventing the new management from making investments in illiquid employer-leased real estate or other employer-related ventures.

2. Include some type of acceleration provision that enables an employer, upon a change in tax law or an IRS audit with an unfavorable result that makes rabbi trust money taxable to participants, to immediately distribute trust assets. If neither the plan nor the trust has such a provision, the employee may incur a current tax, but have no cash with which to pay it.

3. Preclude the addition of new beneficiaries in the event of an unfriendly takeover and restrict the ability to make amendments. This avoids dilution of assets or the insertion of unfavorable provisions, and prevents new management from adding plan amendments that adversely affect already accrued plan benefits.

4. Make it clear that liability for promised benefits is joint and several between the trust and the employer. If plan liability is shifted completely to the trust, then aside from the obvious problems that arise if trust assets are insufficient, ERISA problems may also be triggered.

5. Do not condition the trustee's ability to pay benefits upon instructions from the employer.

6. Set up separate trusts if employees of both a parent and a subsidiary corporation are to be covered by salary continuation plans. This helps to keep creditors of an insolvent corporation from reaching assets that should go to employees of a financially sound related corporation.

7. Make the trust irrevocable, but specify a written procedure as to how the trustee and the employer can amend the trust with the consent of trust beneficiaries.

8. Provide that the trust will not terminate until all benefits promised under the nonqualified plan have been paid, and that any remaining trust assets will be returned to the employer at that time.

Creative tax planners have improved the classic rabbi trust with a number of clever drafting concepts, including:

- *The carry-on rabbi trust* – In addition to paying out deferred retirement benefits, a rabbi trust may hold funds for the purpose of continuing the same approximate level of life insurance, hospitalization, and major medical insurance that the employee enjoyed just prior to retirement.[64] This type of rabbi trust can be used to carry on an executive's postretirement insurance needs.

- *The double duty rabbi trust* – A single rabbi trust can be used to fund the assets of multiple deferred compensation plans.[65]

Secular Trusts

A secular trust is an alternative to a rabbi trust. It is generally an *irrevocable* trust designed to address the two major drawbacks of both the traditional naked promise by the employer to pay benefits and the rabbi trust: neither the employer's naked contractual promise nor the rabbi trust provides any protection against the employer's insolvency nor results in an up-front income tax deduction.

How does the secular trust give the employee protection against employer insolvency, and, at the same time, provide the employer with an immediate income tax deduction? The answer lies in the way that the secular trust is designed. First, the employer's creditors *cannot* reach assets placed in a secular trust. Second, as soon as funds are put into a secular trust, the employee is generally immediately taxed. As soon as the employee is taxed on funds placed in a secular trust, the employer can take an immediate income tax deduction.[66]

The purported advantages of the secular trust over the nonqualified deferred compensation plan (with or without a rabbi trust) include the following:

1. It is less expensive to create and maintain.

2. It can result in tax savings, since the contributions may generate an employer's deduction taken at a higher tax bracket than the bracket in which the contributions are taxed to the employee.

But there are potential problems involved with a secular trust, including:

1. Covered employees will generally be taxed each year on income that they have not received, so that they may not have the cash on hand to pay the taxes. This means that the employer may have to make additional cash payments,

in order to enable the employee to pay the required tax.

2. A secular trust may create double taxation, (i.e., both the trust and the highly compensated employees may be taxed each year on the trust's earnings).[67]

3. A secular trust is considered to be funded for ERISA purposes. As a result, a secular trust may have to satisfy a wide array of ERISA requirements, including reporting and disclosure, participation and vesting, funding, and fiduciary responsibility requirements.

FREQUENTLY ASKED QUESTIONS

Question – Where does life insurance fit in a nonqualified deferred compensation plan?

Answer – Life insurance is the tool of preference to finance an employer's promises under a nonqualified plan. Typically, the employer purchases a life insurance policy on the life of each covered employee. The employer owns each policy and names itself the beneficiary. The employee is given no rights in the policy and no right to name or change the beneficiary of the policy. In essence, the policy is held as a key employee contract (see Chapter 35), and will be subject to the same tax rules applicable to all such policies. In order to avoid both tax and ERISA problems, the agreement between the employer and the employee should not mention the life insurance.

Question – How have recent changes in pension law affected nonqualified deferred compensation?

Answer – The trend of tax law in the qualified retirement plan area is one of increasing costs, increasing limitation on the amount of benefits that may be provided to highly paid and owner-employees, and decreasing employer discretion and control.

Planners should point out that each of the following points pertaining to changes in the qualified retirement plan area makes nonqualified plans an appealing alternative.

First, regardless of how much the retiree was earning prior to retirement, the amount that can be

paid to that person from a defined benefit pension plan is severely restricted. As of 2012, the maximum yearly benefit that can be distributed from a defined benefit plan is only $200,000 (indexed for inflation), or, if lower, 100 percent of the participant's average three years' compensation.[68] Furthermore, a reduction must be made if the plan under which the payments will be made contains a pre-age sixty-five normal retirement age, or if the plan participant has fewer than ten years of service.[69]

Second, as of 2012, the ceiling on the annual additions that can be added by an employer to the account of a plan participant in a qualified defined contribution (e.g., money purchase) plan—regardless of how much he or she is earning—is only $50,000 (indexed for inflation), or, if less, 25 percent of compensation.[70]

Third, all qualified retirement plans are limited with respect to the maximum compensation that can be used in computing either benefits or contributions. As of 2012, the maximum compensation that can be considered in computing a plan's permissible benefit distribution or annual additional contribution for an individual is the first $250,000 (indexed for inflation) of his annual compensation.[71]

The result of these rules is a severe restriction upon the benefits that may be provided to the highly paid and owners of the business—the people who work the hardest and add the most to the profits of the employer. Consequently, these same individuals will receive the least of all employees as a percentage of average pay before retirement. For example, an executive earning $500,000 a year who is covered under a 10 percent money purchase plan is credited with not 10 percent of $500,000, but only 10 percent of $250,000 (in 2012). He receives no credit for the other $250,000 of salary earned—even though he's taxed on all $500,000!

Fourth, participants in most qualified plans must become fully vested twice as quickly as was required under pension law just a few years ago. While this means fewer forfeitures from an employee viewpoint, benefit costs have increased significantly from an employer's perspective.

Fifth, tougher nondiscrimination rules place additional restraints on an employer's discretion with respect to who can be excluded from plan participation. This not only increases costs, but also reduces the employer's ability to direct cash flow to those who make the greatest contribution to it.

Sixth, Social Security integration rules (now referred to by the IRS as permitted disparity) have been changed to further favor rank and file employees, which further adds to employer costs.

Question – What is the economic benefit theory?

Answer – Under the economic benefit theory, an employee is currently taxable whenever he receives something of value that is the equivalent of cash.[72] In other words, if a compensation arrangement provides a current economic benefit to an employee, the employee must include the value of the benefit in income, even if there is no current right to receive cash or other property. The employee need only receive the *equivalent of cash*—something with a current, real, and measurable value—from his employer. As soon as such an event occurs, even if the employee cannot currently take possession of either the asset or the income it produces, he is taxable on the value of the benefit.

Question – How may Code section 83 cause the covered employee to be taxable on compensation even before it is actually received?

Answer – Code section 83 provides that the person who performed the services must include in income the amount by which the fair market value of property transferred in connection with the performance of such services exceeds the amount paid for such property. That amount is includable in the first taxable year in which the property becomes transferable or is no longer subject to a substantial risk of forfeiture.

The use of a rabbi trust will not cause the covered employee to be taxed under section 83.[73] The claims of participants and their beneficiaries to funds held in a rabbi trust are unsecured and the funds held in the rabbi trust can be reached by the employer's creditors. Because a rabbi trust does not cause the employer's promise to be other than unfunded and unsecured, the IRS has repeatedly held that the adoption of a nonqualified deferred compensation plan and the creation of a related rabbi trust do not result in a transfer of property in connection with the performance of services.[74]

In the case of a life insurance policy, the plan should give no interest in the policy to the employee. The policy should remain on the employer's books as a corporate asset (i.e., subject to the claims of the employer's creditors) and the employer should be the sole applicant, owner, and premium payor. All of the favorable income and estate tax rulings in this area involve plans in which the employer owns the sole interest in the policy. Some authorities feel that the ability to defer taxation might, therefore, be threatened if the plan contemplates the use of split dollar contracts as an asset reserve.

Question – Is there a certain size or financial strength of the employer beyond which a naked promise is nevertheless viewed as secured?

Answer – Size of the employer makes no difference. A plan is not considered funded, even if a corporate employer as large as Microsoft makes a contractual promise to make payments in the future–as long as that promise is neither negotiable nor assignable. Such a promise is considered incapable of valuation and therefore not currently taxable because— regardless of the size or financial condition of the employer—the promise is subject to the hazards of economic and business conditions. There should be no taxation of the employee unless and until funds are placed beyond the reach of the employer or its creditors and the employee no longer runs a substantial risk of forfeiture.

The solution is to give an employee no greater rights than those of a general creditor. The earmarking of assets by the employer in order to meet its obligations under the plan will not cause the employee to be taxable. Even if cash or other property has been physically transferred to an irrevocable trust, the economic benefit theory will not apply, so long as the employee's rights to that asset remain subject to a substantial risk of forfeiture.

Question – Does it make sense in today's changing tax and economic environment to voluntarily defer compensation?

Answer – Many attorneys and accountants have asked just this question. In most cases, the answer is a very emphatic "YES!"

Here are some of the factors to consider:

1. Corporate tax rates may go up. When tax rates go down, the value of a corporate

level tax deduction and the leverage it can produce when benefits are paid out is reduced. However, when rates go up, so does the employer's leverage. Higher tax brackets at distribution mean more benefits can be paid with the same post-deduction outlay, or that the same payments can be paid out at a lower net corporate cost.

2. A reduction in tax rates reduces the value of tax deferral to participating employees. However, when rates go up, so does the value of deferring next year's bonus.

3. The value of tax deferral is lower at a 36 percent bracket than at a 50 percent bracket. But as personal rates rise, so does the value of a deferral. From the employee's standpoint, deferral is advantageous even if rates rise to 40 percent (or even 45 percent), provided that the deferral period is long enough.

4. In a few situations, the employee may be better off taking the money, paying tax on it and investing on his own rather than risking being a general creditor of the employer for many years. But few employees would, year after year, invest the after-tax difference. If they did, *and* if they never touched the investment, *and* if it never suffered a capital loss, *and* if it always earned a specified after tax rate of interest, then they might be better off.

5. The mathematics of the deferral issue show that the benefit of deferral varies according to three factors: (a) the tax rate when the funds are distributed (if rates increase, the value of the interest-free loan from the government is offset by the amount of the increased tax that must be paid); (b) the length of the deferral; and (c) the interest rate that the deferred funds earn.[75] At what point will the deferral of current taxation offset the increase in tax rates? Under almost any scenario, a key employee is better off deferring compensation, assuming that tax rates will increase, if the deferral period exceeds six years and the interest rate is 6 percent or greater.[76]

6. When top corporate rates drop, the employer's cost of deferral can still be significant. In fact, the cost of deferral to the corporate employer can actually be greater than the value of deferral to the employee.

On the other hand, the employer can use the money it has on hand but is not paying out. It can put the earmarked investments to work at the corporation's earnings level, both during the accumulation period and during the distribution period. It could earn a rate of return sufficient not only to put the employee in a better position than he would have been had he taken current salary and invested it, but it can also retain a portion of the earnings to offset the cost of deferral.

With a salary continuation plan, the corporate client can set up the plan so that the employer maintains control and achieves its business purpose, or else it gets its money back. And, unlike the current payment of a salary, earmarked funds can be available for a corporate emergency or opportunity.

Question – How are benefits paid under a nonqualified deferred compensation plan?

Answer – At retirement, benefits are generally paid either in a lump sum, or more often, in a series of annual payments. For instance, payments for a fixed number of years (for example, ten years) are common, as are life annuities and survivor annuities.

Question – Can nonqualified deferred compensation plans be used by a partnership or Limited Liability Company (LLC) taxed as a partnership?

Answer – A partnership or LLC, for tax purposes, is essentially a conduit through which the income and deductions of the business flow directly to the owners. Income tax is imposed on each individual owner's distributive share of the business' income at the tax rate payable by each owner as an individual. The key point to note is that income tax is imposed whether or not that share is, in fact, distributed by the business to the owner.[77]

The general taxation of partnerships or LLCs results in the absence of the tax deferral for owners, which is a major reason for the deferral of compensation. To summarize:

1. No deduction is allowed to the partnership or LLC for any premiums paid on life insurance used to finance the nonqualified deferred compensation plan (the partnership or LLC is the beneficiary of the policy, and therefore, deductions are not allowed under Code section 264(a)).

2. Amounts used to pay premiums remain part of the taxable income of the partnership or LLC, since they cannot be deducted by the partnership or LLC. This means that amounts used to pay premiums will be currently taxable to the owners. Each owner will pay, at his or her personal tax rate, tax on those amounts divided between the owners according to his or her distributive share.[78] As a result, a deferred compensation plan makes little sense for owners, with the possible exception of minority owners (employer contributions used to fund the plan may exceed what the minority owners would otherwise be entitled to receive via their distributive share, and the tax brunt is born primarily by the majority owners). However, a deferred compensation plan may make sense for nonowner key employees of a partnership or LLC.

3. Because the character of items of income is carried through from the partnership or LLC to its owners, when tax free life insurance proceeds are received by the partnership or LLC,[79] it remains income tax free to the owners.

4. A reduction in basis must be made by each owner for the amount of the (undistributed) premiums paid. Total premiums paid each year are allocated to each owner according to his or her distributive share.[80]

5. Each owner's adjusted basis is increased when the partnership or LLC tax conduit distributes those life insurance proceeds.[81]

Question – Can an S corporation use a nonqualified deferred compensation plan?

Answer – Like a partnership or LLC taxed as a partnership, an S corporation passes through directly and immediately all the income, losses, and deductions of the firm to its owners. This means that on a per-share, per-day basis, each shareholder of an S corporation is taxed on the income of the business. So, as is the case with partnerships or LLCs, the ability of a shareholder in an S corporation to defer tax liability on income is lost (but only if the shareholder in question owns more than 5 percent of the corporation's stock).[82] However, a deferred compensation plan may make sense for nonowner key employees of an S corporation.

Question – Can a tax-exempt organization implement a nonqualified deferred compensation plan?

Answer – Yes. However, nonqualified deferred compensation plans of tax-exempt organizations are subject to special rules per Code section 457(f). This Code section stipulates that ineligible deferred compensation plan benefits are included in gross income in the first taxable year in which there is no "substantial risk of forfeiture" of the rights to such compensation. Thus, these plans are subject to more onerous requirements than plans of for profit employers, in which benefits aren't currently taxed as long as they are subject to a substantial limitation on the employee's ability to reach the plan assets.

Why are plans of tax-exempt organizations subject to more onerous rules? Because they are tax exempt, there is no disincentive for them to limit the amount of compensation that a participant can defer (i.e., the loss of the upfront tax deduction is meaningless to a tax-exempt employer). Thus, there would be nothing stopping a participant from deferring 100 percent or his or her compensation. Realizing this, Congress implemented special rules for tax-exempt organizations by creating Code section 457(f).

From a practical standpoint, the requirement of a substantial risk of forfeiture (in addition to a substantial limitation on the right to access the benefits) for tax-exempt plans has the following consequences:

1. Salary deferral plans are rarely implemented, because few employees desire to put their own money at risk of being forfeited.

2. Plan benefits are generally not vested until retirement. Vesting them earlier causes immediate income tax consequences at the time of vesting (i.e., the lapse of the

substantial risk of forfeiture), regardless if the benefits have actually been paid out.

3. Plans benefits are generally paid out lump-sum at retirement. This is due to the fact that at retirement the substantial risk of forfeiture lapses, resulting in the benefits being subject to income taxation. Therefore, it generally makes sense from the participant's perspective to pay out the benefits lump-sum. Note that if the benefits will be paid out over a period of years, the present value of the periodic payments will be taxable in the year of retirement.

One final comment regarding nonqualified deferred compensation plans of tax-exempt organizations deserves mention. The use of life insurance to finance the plan benefits loses one of its main advantages because of the fact that the employer is tax-exempt—namely; using permanent life insurance (which grows tax-deferred) as an alternative asset to avoid taxation of the investment income if the employer were to instead accumulate taxable assets for the purpose of paying plan benefits. However, the other benefits of using life insurance, such as cost recovery and the ability to provide a pre-retirement death benefit, still apply.

Question – Are there securities regulation issues with respect to nonqualified deferred compensation plans?

Answer – The answer is uncertain. At a meeting of the Securities and Exchange Commission (SEC), an SEC spokesperson stated that the SEC considered all nonqualified deferred compensation plans (with certain exceptions noted below) to be register able and indicated that the SEC would be issuing a formal statement on its position. As of the date of this printing, that statement has not been issued. It is possible that the SEC may require the registration of nonqualified deferred compensation plans as securities, but only if the plan involves employee contributions and the employees are motivated by investment rather than tax deferral. If the employees making the contributions have investment motives (i.e., the plan involves investments in underlying securities whose return is credited to the employee), registration appears to be required. On the other hand, if employees are making contributions because of tax deferral motives (i.e., primarily to save income taxes), no registration with the SEC is

necessary. In other words, an investment motivated nonqualified deferred compensation plan will be considered to be a security, while a nonqualified deferred compensation plan motivated by tax deferral need not be registered, because the plan will not be considered to be a security. In making its decision, the SEC will look at all the facts and circumstances. In the authors' opinion, most businesses which establish nonqualified deferred compensation plans for twenty or fewer key executives will probably qualify under one of the three safe harbor exemptions noted below, but plans covering a very large number of individuals or exceptionally large amounts of money may have to register. Certainly, no employer can ignore the issue and all should obtain competent legal advice on the registration issue.

The key registration exemptions that would apply to most small corporation plans are for intrastate exemptions (securities offered and sold only to persons resident within a single state), small offerings, and nonpublic offerings. Regulation D, Rules 505 and 506 are safe harbors which define the latter two exemptions, as follows:

1. Offers and sales of securities with a total offering price of $5,000,000 or less, in which there are no more than thirty-five purchasers and which meet certain other rules will be protected from registration requirements.

2. Offers and sales of securities which do not involve more than thirty-five purchasers are protected from registration requirements (regardless of the dollar amount of the offering) if every purchaser who is not considered an accredited investor is considered capable of evaluating the merits and risks of the prospective investment.[83]

Question – What is the impact of a nonqualified deferred compensation plan on the benefits payable under a qualified pension or profit sharing plan?

Answer – There is authority that might allow[84] and authority that might disallow[85] the inclusion of amounts deferred under a nonqualified deferred compensation plan in computing the amount that can be contributed to a qualified retirement plan on behalf of an employee.[86] In the authors' opinion, the IRS is most likely to argue that qualified retirement plan benefits discriminate in favor of the highly compensated where the qualified retirement plan takes into consideration amounts deferred under a nonqualified deferred compensation plan.[87]

Question – How does the Medicare surtax affect beneficiaries of nonqualified plans?

Answer – Because benefits are considered wages when they are distributed, they will generally be considered as earned income and may be subject to the Medicare surtax at the time of distribution, depending on the recipient's other tax attributes.

Question – Can life insurance be used as a financing mechanism with respect to nonqualified deferred compensation plans for bank executives and directors?

Answer – Yes. The Office of the Comptroller of the Currency (OCC) has stated that life insurance purchased on the lives of executives and directors of banks is an appropriate investment when purchased as a funding mechanism for nonqualified deferred compensation plans. The OCC has held in an opinion letter that there were two legitimate justifications for banks to purchase insurance in this context. The first legitimate justification is to meet the bank's contractual obligation to make payments upon early, normal, or late retirement, as well as to families of covered employees at their deaths. The second legitimate justification is to serve as an actuarial cost recovery vehicle. In the opinion of the authors, the bank should own and name itself total beneficiary of the insurance. We feel it is essential for the parties to document (prior to the purchase of the life insurance) that the bank's obligation to make payments under the nonqualified deferred compensation plan would have existed with or without the presence of the insurance, and that the insurance was purchased to reduce or eliminate that previously existing liability.[88]

CHAPTER ENDNOTES

1. See e.g., I.R.C. §404(d); Rev. Rul. 71-419, 1971-2 CB 220; Rev. Rul. 60-31, 1960- 1 CB 174, Case 3. However, the IRS will not issue a private letter ruling with respect to the treatment of an independent contractor in an unfunded deferred compensation plans unless the independent contract is identified. Rev. Proc. 2004-3, §3.01(37), 2004-1 IRB 114.

2. For excellent coverage of the overall topic of nonqualified deferred compensation plans, see S. Leimberg and J. McFadden, *The Tools & Techniques of Employee Benefit and Retirement Planning*, 15th. (The National Underwriter Company, 2017); "A Fresh Look At Deferring Compensation: The Nonqualified Plan Alternative," *Pension Plan Guide No. 715* (Commerce Clearing House);.

3. See "Meeting and Beating the 5R Problem," an employee benefit marketing brochure available from Leimberg & LeClair, Inc.

4. See, e.g., ERISA §§4(b)(5), 104(a)(2)(A), 201(2), 301(a)(3), 401(a)(1); Labor Reg. §2520.104-23.

5. I.R.C. §72(u), which provides that annuities owned by non-natural persons are not treated as tax-deferred.

6. I.R.C. §55(e).

7. See FASB Statement No. 106 (December 1990).

8. See the example in Chapter 35, in the section entitled, "How It Is Done–An Example."

9. See *Dependahl v. Falstaff Brewing Corp.*, 653 F.2d 1208 (8th Cir. 1981); *Goldsmith v. U.S.*, 586 F.2d 810, 78-2 USTC ¶9804 (Ct. Cl. 1978); *Frost v. Comm'r.*, 52 TC 89 (1969).

10. Sample documents for nonqualified deferred compensation plans can be found in H. Zaritsky and S. Leimberg, *Tax Planning with Life Insurance*, 2d ed. (Warren, Gorham, Lamont, 1999), as well as in L. Richey and L. Brody, *Comprehensive Deferred Compensation*, 3d ed. (The National Underwriter Company, 1997).

11. Title I of ERISA imposes reporting and disclosure, participation and vesting, funding, fiduciary responsibility and other requirements on deferred compensation plans. Title IV of ERISA establishes plan termination insurance requirements.

12. ERISA §§4(b)(5), 4021(b)(8).

13. ERISA §§201(2), 301(a)(1), 401(a)(1), 4021(b)(6).

14. See Labor Reg. §1.2520.104-23; ERISA §§107, 503.

15. Labor Reg. §1.2520.104-23(b)(1).

16. Labor Reg. §1.2520.104-23(b)(2). Electronic filing is now required.

17. ERISA §3(36).

18. See I.R.C. §404(a).

19. Treas. Reg. §1.404(a)-1(b).

20. I.R.C. §§3306(r)(2), 3121(v)(2). See TD 8814, 1999-9 IRB 4 and TD 8815, 1999-99 IRB 31.

21. See I.R.C. §1402(a).

22. I.R.C. §2642(e).

23. I.R.C. §2631.

24. Rev. Rul. 70-514, 1970-2 CB 198.

25. I.R.C. §409A(a)(4)(B); Treas. Reg. §1.409A-2.

26. I.R.C. §409A(a)(2)(A); Treas. Reg. §1.409A-3.

27. Treas. Reg. §1.409A-3(g)(5).

28. Treas. Reg. §1.409A-2(h).

29. More specifically, to comply with a domestic relations order under IRC Section 414(p)(1)(B) or a certificate of divestiture under IRC Section 1043(b)(2).

30. I.R.C. §409A(a)(1)(i), (a)(1)(B).

31. See I.R.C. §451(a); Treas. Reg. §1.451-2(a). See generally Rev. Rul. 60-31, 1960-1 CB 174.

32. See *Gullett v. Comm'r.*, 31 BTA 1067 (1935).

33. Treas. Reg. §1.451-2(a).

34. See Rev. Rul. 60-31, 1960-1 CB 174, as modified by Rev. Rul. 64-279, 1964-2 CB 121 and Rev. Rul. 70-435, 1970-2 CB 100. The IRS will not issue an advanced ruling concerning the tax consequences of an unfunded arrangement if the arrangement fails to meet the guidelines set out in Rev. Proc. 99-3, §3.01(30), 1999-1 IRB 103, at 107; Rev. Proc. 71-19, 1971-1 CB 698, as amplified by Rev. Proc. 92-65, 1992-2 CB 428.

35. See Rev. Proc. 71-19, 1971-1 CB 698. The Tax Court has been more lenient with elections to defer compensation after commencement of the earnings period. See, e.g., *Martin v. Comm'r.*, 96 TC 814 (1991); *Oates v. Comm'r.*, 18 TC 570 (1952), aff'd 207 F.2d 711 (7th Cir. 1953), *acq.*; *Veit v. Comm'r.*, 8 TCM 919 (1949); *Veit v. Comm'r.*, 8 TC 809 (1947), *acq.*

36. There is some authority to support this belief. See, e.g., *Martin v. Comm'r.*, 96 TC 814 (1991); *Oates v. Comm'r.*, 18 TC 570 (1952), aff'd 207 F.2d 711 (7th Cir. 1953), *acq.*; *Veit v. Comm'r.*, 8 TCM 919 (1949); *Veit v. Comm'r.*, 8 TC 809 (1947), *acq.*

37. Rev. Proc. 71-19, 1971-1 CB 698.

38. See Let. Rul. 8607029.

39. Treas. Regs. §§1.83-3(c)(1), 1.83-3(c)(2).

40. Treas. Reg. §1.83-3(c)(1).

41. See Rev. Proc. 99-3, §3.01(29), 1999-1 IRB 103, at 108.

42. See TAM 8828004.

43. See, e.g., *Commerce Union Bank v. U.S.*, 76-2 USTC ¶13,157 (M.D. Tenn. 1976); *First Trust Company of St. Paul v. U.S.*, 321 F.Supp. 1025 (D. Minn. 1970); and Rev. Rul. 77-139, 1977-1 CB 278 which support the proposition that a controlling shareholder's power to terminate a qualified pension plan does not cause the constructive receipt of the plan benefits for estate tax purposes. See also, *Moline Properties, Inc. v. Comm'r.*, 319 U.S. 436 (1943); *Casale v. Comm'r.*, 247 F.2d 440 (2nd Cir. 1957); and Rev. Rul. 59-184 which support the proposition that a corporation carrying on a valid business activity that is not a sham is a valid entity separate from its controlling shareholder.

44. See *Goldsmith v. U.S.*, 78-1 USTC ¶9312 (Ct.Cl. Tr. Div. 1978), *adopted by full court w/out appeal*, 586 F.2d 810 (Ct. Cl. 1978). But see Let. Ruls. 8103089, 7940017. For a number of convincing arguments as to why *Goldsmith* should not be followed by the courts, see Richey and Brody, note 5 above, at p. 20.

45. See I.R.C. §§402(b), 83; Treas. Reg. §1.83-1(a)(1).

46. See, e.g., ERISA §§201, 301(a), 401(a).

47. See Let. Ruls. 9815039, 9805030.

48. But see *Goldsmith v. U.S.*, 78-1 USTC ¶9312 (Ct. Cl. Tr. Div. 1978), *adopted by full court w/out appeal*, 586 F.2d 810 (Ct. Cl. 1978) (employee taxable on economic benefit of insurance protection).

49. See, e.g., Rev. Rul. 72-25, 1972-1 CB 127; Rev. Rul. 60-31, 1960-1 CB 174; DOL Advisory Opinion 81-11A. Compare *Dependahl v. Falstaff Brewing Corp.*, 491 F. Supp. 1188 (E.D. Mo. 1980), *aff'd in part*, 653 F.2d 1208 (8th Cir. 1981), *cert. denied*, 454 U.S. 968 (1981) and 454 U.S. 1084 (1981) (death benefit only plan financed with life insurance considered a funded plan) with *Belka v. Rowe Furniture Corp.*, 571 F. Supp. 1249 (D. Md. 1983) (nonqualified deferred compensation plan provided retirement and death benefit and financed with life insurance considered an unfunded plan) and *Belsky v. First National Life Insurance Company*, 818 F.2d 661 (8th Cir. 1987) (nonqualified deferred compensation plan providing retirement and disability benefits and financed with life insurance considered an unfunded plan).

50. See Richey and Brody, note 5 above, p. 11.

51. But see Let. Rul. 8406012 (purchase by employer of surety bond does not by itself cause inclusion of deferred amounts before receipt). The IRS did not really understand that, in the typical situation, the employer must apply for the bond and consent to the employee's ownership. In reality it is the employer that stands behind the bond, and, for this reason, the authors believe the position of the IRS in the private letter ruling should not be relied upon.

52. Unnumbered letter ruling, dated August 2, 1993, *reprinted in* 20 Pens. Ben, Rep. (BNA) 1802 (1993).

53. See *Berry v. U.S.*, 593 F.Supp. 80, 85 (M.D.N.C., 1984), *aff'd* 760 F.2d 85 (4th Cir. 1985).

54. See Let. Rul. 8741078.

55. See, e.g., *Robinson v. Comm'r.*, 44 TC 20 (1965), (guarantees of boxer's deferred pre-fight payments by major owner of corporate fight promoter and by parent corporation of fight promoter did not cause the boxer to be other than an unsecured creditor) *acq.* 1970-2 CB xxi; Let. Rul. 8741078 (parent's guarantee of subsidaries, deferred compensation obligations did not cause plan to be funded); Let. Rul. 7742098 (guarantees of corporation's deferred compensation obligations did not affect effectiveness of deferred compensation agreement). See also notes 42 and 43, above, and accompanying text.

56. See, e.g., DOL Advisory Opinions 92-13A, 91-16A, 90-14A, and 89-22A.

57. See Rev. Proc. 92-64.

58. Ibid.

59. Ibid.

60. Ibid.

61. See Rev. Proc. 92-64, 1992-2 CB 422.

62. But see, e.g., Let. Rul. 9041053 (benefits payable after four, or fewer, years of employment).

63. For some time the IRS has refused to rule on rabbi trusts holding employer stock. This position seems to be changing, and the IRS apparently will now rule on the use of employer stock in a rabbi trust.

64. See Let. Rul. 8736045.

65. In Let. Rul. 8834041, the plans were sponsored by an employer and its subsidiary.

66. See e.g., Let. Ruls. 9212024, 9212019, 9207010, 9206009.

67. See e.g., Let. Ruls. 9207010, 9206009.

68. I.R.C. §415(b).

69. See I.R.C. §415(b)(2)(c).

70. I.R.C. §415(c).

71. I.R.C. §401(a)(17).

72. See, e.g., *Sproull v. Comm'r.*, 16 TC 244 (1951), *aff'd.* 194 F.2d 541 (6th Cir. 1952); *Goldsmith v. U.S.*, 78-1 USTC ¶9312 (Ct. Cl. Tr. Div. 1978), *adopted by full court w/out appeal*, 586 F.2d 810 (Ct. Cl. 1978).

73. See, e.g., Let. Rul. 9214035.

74. Under Treas. Reg. §1.83-3(e), an unfunded and unsecured promise to pay money or property is not property within the meaning of §83.

75. For an excellent in-depth discussion of the mathematics of deferral, see Doyle, "Employing Tax Leverage In a Time of Tax Uncertainty," in S. Leimberg, et al., *Financial Services Professional's Guide to The State of the Art* (The American College, 2nd ed., 1990).

76. See Tacchino, "Nonqualified Retirement Planning" in S. Leimberg, et al., *Financial Services Professional's Guide to The State of the Art* (The American College, 2nd ed., 1990).

77. Treas. Reg. §1.702-1(a).

78. I.R.C. §702. A partner's capital interest in the partnership generally determines his or her distributive share.

79. I.R.C. §101(a); Treas. Reg. §1.101-1(a).

80. I.R.C. §705(a)(2)(B); Treas. Reg. §1.705-1(a)(3)(ii).

81. I.R.C. §705(a)(1)(B); Treas. Reg. §1.705-1(a)(3)(ii). This Section provides that each partner's share of all undistributed amounts of income are included in basis adjustments.

82. I.R.C. §1366.

83. AALU Bulletins No. 97-106, 97-97, 97-82, 97-51, 95-104, and 95-46; Securities Act of 1933; *SEC v. Howey*, 328 US 293 (1946).

84. Rev. Rul. 69-296, 1969-1 CB 127 (contributions made under I.R.C. §403(b) annuity arrangement are compensation and can be considered in establishing contributions to a qualified money purchase pension plan).

85. Rev. Rul. 80-359, 1980-2 CB 137 (contributions to nonqualified plan may be used in computing benefits under qualified plan if such use does not result in discrimination against rank and file).

86. See Morrison and Hack, "Nonqualified Deferred Compensation Plans Can Reward Key Employees While Postponing Taxes," *Taxation for Lawyers*, March-April 1983, p. 291.

87. A private letter ruling is therefore suggested. See also, Treas. Regs. §§1.414(s)-1(c), 1.415-2(d)(3).

88. OCC Interpretive Letter No. 848 and OCC Bulletin 96-51 (which supersedes a 1983 Letter to the contrary). See also AALU Bulletin No. 99-5.

PENSION MAXIMIZATION

CHAPTER 38

INTRODUCTION

A life insurance strategy called pension maximization or, sometimes pension enhancement may provide a more attractive overall benefit package for married couples than the normal Joint and Survivor (J&S) annuity option from a qualified plan. The concept is simple. Rather than electing to receive the normal (normal default) J&S annuity from a pension plan, the retiring participant, with the consent of his or her spouse, selects the higher benefit payable under the Single Life (SL) annuity option. The couple then purchases life insurance on the participant to assure the financial security of the spouse in the event the participant dies first and pension benefits cease. The difference between the pension benefit payable under the SL annuity and the lower joint benefit payable under the J&S annuity is available to pay premiums on the insurance.

A fundamental but often misperceived concept is that a J&S annuity is itself a type of insurance. Whenever a couple selects some form of J&S annuity, rather than the SL annuity, they are essentially buying insurance to assure survivor benefits for the spouse. The premiums they pay for this protection are equal to the difference between the benefit payable under the SL annuity and the joint benefit payable under the J&S annuity. For example, if the pension would pay $3,000 a month under the SL annuity option, but only $2,550 under the normal joint and 50 percent survivor annuity option, the couple is effectively paying a $450 monthly premium to insure that the spouse will be paid $1,275 per month (50 percent of the $2,550 joint benefit) in the event the plan participant dies first.

WHEN IS THE USE OF THIS TECHNIQUE INDICATED?

1. When the participant and spouse wish or need to have more flexible survivor benefit options than those provided by a qualified plan's joint and survivor option.

2. When the participant's spouse is in poor health. In this case a qualified plan's joint and survivor option may be an inefficient and expensive means to provide survivor benefits in the unlikely event the participant predeceases the spouse. The cost for the amount of insurance needed to provide income for the spouse who is in poor health for his or her remaining life in the event the participant predeceases the spouse "may" be less than the cost of the survivor benefit from the qualified plan.

3. When the participant's spouse has income and asset resources, such as his or her own retirement benefits, that can provide some of the spouse's required income needs if the participant predeceases the spouse. In this case, the cost of purchasing only so much life insurance on the participant as is necessary to supplement the spouse's other retirement income can be less expensive than the cost of the qualified plan's survivor benefit.

4. When the participant already has life insurance in place on his or her life that can provide the bulk of the surviving spouse's retirement income needs in the event the participant predeceases the spouse.

5. A pension maximization strategy is more likely to be feasible if the participant is a female. Pension

benefits are computed based upon unisex mortality factors. Most life insurance policies are priced according to sex-based mortality factors. Since women still tend to live longer than men, the relative cost of survivor benefits acquired through insurance will generally be less than the cost of those same benefits acquired from a qualified plan.

Advantages

The principal advantage of a pension maximization strategy is planning flexibility as compared with the J&S annuity survivor benefit from a qualified plan.

The insurance feature of the J&S annuity has several unattractive elements. First, with this type of insurance the plan participant will generally have to continue paying the monthly premium (receive the lower J&S benefit payments rather than the higher SL benefit) even if the spouse dies first and the survivorship insurance is no longer necessary. Unless the plan has a pop-up feature, where benefits payable to the participant jump or pop-up to the SL annuity amount in the event the spouse predeceases the participant, the participant will continue to receive the lower J&S benefit after the spouse's death. Typically, all else being equal, the joint benefit paid on J&S annuities with a pop-up feature is less than the joint benefit paid on normal J&S annuities. Either way, the couple must pay for the survivorship benefit by receiving lower joint benefits; it's just a matter of timing when the premiums are due.

A second unattractive element of the insurance feature of the J&S annuity is its lack of flexibility. Essentially the only option or choice a couple has with respect to the pension's survivor benefit is to select the survivor benefit ratio, that is, the percentage of the joint benefit that will be payable to the spouse in the event the participant dies first. The default ratio is 50 percent, but most plans will permit the couple to elect ratios of 66 ⅔ percent, 75 percent, or 100 percent. Of course, as the survivor benefit ratio goes up, the joint benefit typically goes down, effectively increasing the premium for the survivorship benefit.

Furthermore, a pensioner generally has no rights to: (1) accelerate benefit payments if the need arises; (2) choose an alternative or substitute beneficiary if the spouse predeceases the participant; or (3) wait to select what type of benefit payout pattern will be paid to the surviving spouse if the participant dies first.

In contrast, the pension maximization plan is often attractive because a life insurance policy on the participant offers considerably more planning flexibility than the implicit insurance within the pension's J&S annuity.

If the spouse dies first, the participant has several alternatives as to what to do with the life insurance policy.

First, he may continue to pay premiums, keep the insurance in force and name a new beneficiary, perhaps a child, grandchild, or even a favorite charity.

Second, he can suspend premium payments and effectively increase spendable retirement income. This is essentially a home-made equivalent to the pop-up feature described above.

However, the participant still has several additional options with respect to the insurance coverage that are not available under the J&S annuity. If the policy has cash value, the participant may elect to keep the policy in force under either the reduced-face-amount fully-paid-up whole-life option or the full-face-amount term-life option. Alternatively, if life insurance is no longer needed or desired, he or she may surrender the policy and take cash value as a lump sum or under one of the many nonforfeiture (essentially annuity) options all life insurance policies must offer.

A life insurance policy also provides more flexibility than the J&S annuity with respect to the options available to the surviving spouse. Where the J&S annuity provides only one option—a life annuity for the spouse at some pre-specified proportion of the joint benefit—the life insurance provides many options as to how the proceeds may be distributed to the surviving spouse.

Although a couple may initially anticipate that a life annuity will be the best way to distribute the life insurance proceeds to the surviving spouse, circumstances may change. For example, if the spouse is not in good health, some form of higher-benefit, limited and guaranteed term annuity may be more suitable than a life annuity.

Alternatively, the couple may take a wait and see approach by setting up a trust to receive the life insurance proceeds. The trustee may be given discretion as to how to distribute the funds to best insure the surviving spouse's financial security. In such cases, payments could be accelerated to meet special needs, such as large medical expenses. Such flexibility is virtually never available under the pension's J&S annuity benefit.

Finally, a life insurance policy provides more flexibility to handle special or changing needs while both the participant and spouse are alive. For example, if the health of either partner begins to fail, they may borrow cash values from the policy to help pay medical expenses. If the policy has a chronic illness or long-term care rider, they may be able to accelerate the death benefit or have access to a pool of benefits to help meet chronic illness and long-term care expenses. No such acceleration provision is generally available from the J&S pension option.

Disadvantages

The life insurance option has its costs and risks. By far the biggest risk with the pension maximization plan is that the life insurance premiums will not be paid and the insurance will not be in force if the insured plan participant dies first. Since there is no J&S benefit being paid due to the election to take the single life benefit instead, this potentially leaves the surviving spouse without sufficient income with which to live. In order to mitigate the risks associated with pension maximization, the following should be considered:

1. Buy enough death benefit on the plan participant sufficient at the insured's death to purchase an after-tax life only immediate annuity payout for the surviving spouse to replace the same after-tax income as the foregone J&S pension benefit.

2. In determining how much death benefit to purchase, assume the worst case scenario, which is that the plan participant dies the day after retiring. The reason for this is that the cost to purchase a life only immediate annuity for a sixty-five year old surviving spouse would be considerably more than to purchase one for a seventy-five or eighty-five year old surviving spouse. If the life insurance contract is flexible enough, it may be possible to periodically reduce the death benefit over time in order to make the life insurance premium less costly.

3. To minimize the risk that the life insurance death benefit will not be in force when needed, use conservative products and assumptions. Ideally, the death benefit should be guaranteed for the insured's life (or at least to the insured's age 100).

4. Have the plan participant purchase the life insurance well before reaching retirement age. A pension maximization plan that is implemented some years before retirement will generally cost less than one that is implemented later. In general, the premium cost for an adequate amount of life insurance in a pension maximization plan that is implemented entirely when your client reaches retirement will be greater than the differential between the single and joint life annuity payouts from your client's pension. Whether the additional features and flexibility of the life insurance are worth the additional cost while the couple both live depends on what they want their plan to accomplish.

5. Pension maximization should be employed only by those couples who are financially disciplined enough to see the plan through. Often, if the plan is implemented early enough, this risk can be reduced or eliminated altogether by paying enough up-front to entirely fund the life insurance policy at or soon after retirement.

6. Ideally, pension maximization should generally only be employed by those couples who have sufficient other assets, so that the surviving spouse could tap those assets for retirement income in the event that the life insurance policy were to lapse prior to the insured's death.

WHAT ARE THE REQUIREMENTS?

The principal requirement involved in implementing a pension maximization strategy is compliance with the requirements of the Retirement Equity Act of 1984 (REA) for spousal benefits.

The law mandates that a spouse's interest in the participant's qualified retirement benefits must be protected and specifies that certain benefits must be paid to the spouse if the participant predeceases the spouse either before or after retirement. If these mandated benefits are not those desired by the participant and spouse, they may elect alternative forms of benefits or designate a beneficiary other than the spouse, but only by following strict compliance rules.[1]

Required (Default) Spousal Benefits

Unless expressly waived by both spouses in accordance with strict rules, qualified plans must generally automatically provide certain benefits for the participant's spouse. The first required benefit is a *Qualified Preretirement Survivor Annuity (QPSA)*. The QPSA is the automatic default benefit for the surviving spouse of a participant who dies before retirement, unless the participant and spouse have made a proper election otherwise. The second required benefit is a *Qualified Joint and Survivor Annuity (QJSA)*. The QJSA is the automatic default benefit for the participant and spouse at retirement, unless they have made a proper election otherwise.

Annuity Starting Date

The annuity starting date is a key date for purposes of determining whether benefits are payable as a QPSA, a QJSA, or another selected optional form of benefit payable under the plan. A participant who is alive on the annuity starting date must have benefits payable as a QJSA, unless the participant and the spouse have made a qualifying election otherwise. The surviving spouse of a participant who dies before the annuity starting date must receive a QPSA, unless once again, both the participant and the spouse made a qualifying election to waive the QPSA or to receive some other form of benefit in the event of the participant's death before the annuity starting date. The annuity starting date is also important for tax purposes, since amounts received as an annuity (periodic payments) and amounts not received as an annuity (nonperiodic payments) are subject to differing tax rules.

As a general rule, the annuity starting date is the first day of the first period for which an amount is paid as an annuity or in any other form as a retirement benefit to the participant under the plan.[2] In other words, it is the date at which payments are to commence to the participant under the QJSA or an alternative payout schedule, if properly elected with spousal consent. For most participants this date is the normal retirement age. However, for participants who retire early, it is the earliest date when benefit payments may begin for early retirement or the first date when benefits are payable after retirement, if later. For participants who continue to work beyond normal retirement age, the annuity starting date is generally the date when benefit payments are to begin under the plan once the participant retires.

REA Requirements Apply Generally to All Qualified Pension Plans

Plans that must meet the requirement include defined benefit, money purchase, target benefit, and cash balance plans. They also apply to benefits payable to a participant under a contract purchased by the plan and paid by a third party.[3]

Under a defined benefit plan, the survivor annuity requirements apply only to benefits in which the participant was vested immediately before death. They do not apply to benefits in which the participant's beneficiary becomes entitled by reason of the participant's death, or to proceeds of a life insurance contract, to the extent those proceeds exceed the present value of the participant's nonforfeitable benefits that existed immediately before death.[4]

The survivor annuity requirements also apply to nonforfeitable benefits payable under any defined contribution plan that is subject to the minimum funding standards of Code section 412 (money purchase pension plans but not profit sharing or stock bonus plans), including the proceeds of insurance contracts.[5] The rules also apply to profit sharing and stock bonus plans unless the plans meet the exception described below.

Exception for Profit Sharing, Stock Bonus Plans, and ESOPs

Profit sharing and stock bonus plans and ESOPs must conform unless *all* the following requirements are met:

- each participant's vested benefit is payable on death to the surviving spouse, or, if there is no spouse, to a designated beneficiary (a spouse may consent to payments to a designated beneficiary);[6]

- the participant has *not* elected to receive benefits in the form of a life annuity; and [7]

- the qualified plan is not the recipient of a direct plan-to-plan transfer of benefits from a defined benefit, money purchase, target benefit, or cash balance pension plan. (If it is the recipient of a direct plan-to-plan transfer, then the general rules apply to the transferred benefit).[8]

In addition, the benefit must be available to the surviving spouse within a reasonable time after the participant's death. Access within a ninety-day period following the participant's death is considered reasonable.[9] The benefit payable to the surviving spouse must also be adjusted for gains or losses occurring after the participant's death in accordance with plan rules governing the adjustment of account balances for other distributions.[10]

If these requirements are met, a participant does not need the spouse's consent to elect to take living benefits in some form other than a joint-and-survivor annuity. Permitted non-joint-and-survivor annuity distribution options would include:

- term-certain annuities;

- discretionary (nonannuity) installments; and

- lump sum distributions.

Exception for Certain Benefits

Benefits are not required to be paid in the form of QPSA or QJSA if, at the time of death or distribution, the participant was vested only in employee contributions and the participant died, or distributions commenced, before October 22, 1986.[11] Also, if the present value of the participant's nonforfeitable benefit is $5,000 or less, a distribution may occur (usually a lump sum) without satisfying the spousal consent requirements for distributions other than the QPSA or QJSA.[12]

The REA requirements do not apply to IRAs.

Qualified Preretirement Survivor Annuity (QPSA)

The QPSA is essentially a property right of the spouse created by law. The survivor benefit payable under the QPSA is an immediate annuity for the life of the participant's surviving spouse equal to the amount that would have been paid under the QJSA if the participant had either retired on the day before death or separated from service on the date of death and survived to the plan's earliest retirement age, then retired with an immediate joint and survivor annuity. If, before the participant's annuity starting date, the participant elects a form of joint-and-survivor annuity that satisfies the requirements for a QJSA and then dies before the participant's annuity starting date, the form of benefit elected is the QJSA, and the QPSA payable to the surviving spouse must be based on that form.[13]

Under a defined benefit plan, the plan must permit the surviving spouse to elect to receive payments under a QPSA no later than the month in which the participant would have reached the earliest retirement age. The plan may permit the surviving spouse to elect to begin receiving payments under the QPSA within a

reasonable time after the participant's death (generally within ninety days), even if this date is before the plan's earliest retirement age.[14] If the surviving spouse elects to begin receiving payments before the earliest retirement date, the plan may actuarially adjust the value of the benefits to reflect the earlier distribution date.

The participant may elect an alternate form of benefit, if so offered by the plan, but only with spousal consent. Typically, considerable attention is paid to the form of benefit that will be paid at retirement and who should be named as beneficiary, but the form of benefit that will be paid and who should be named as the beneficiary in the event of the participant's death before retirement is often overlooked. It is important to coordinate elections regarding the QPSA with those anticipated regarding the QJSA. If, for example, the spouse has adequate pension benefits in the spouse's own right or other sources of retirement income, the participant may wish to name a child, parent, charity, or other person as the beneficiary of the retirement benefits. If this is desirable for retirement benefits, it is presumably also desirable for preretirement benefits. These objectives will be thwarted in the event of the participant's premature death unless the participant takes positive action to specify his intentions.

The participant may select a benefit other than the preretirement survivor annuity at any time after age thirty-five and can also change this election at any time before retirement. Generally, electing out of the preretirement survivor annuity entirely will increase the benefit payable at retirement, unless the plan specifically subsidizes the retirement benefit. The younger the participant is at the time the participant elects out, the greater, generally, will be the increase in the benefit payable at retirement.

Qualified Joint and Survivor Annuity (QJSA)

The spouse's survivor benefit under the plan's default QJSA may be not less than 50 percent and not more than 100 percent of the joint benefit. For a married couple, the QJSA must be at least as valuable as any other optional form of benefit payable under the plan at the same time. Therefore, if a plan has two joint-and-survivor annuity options that would satisfy the requirements for a QJSA (e.g., a joint-and-50 percent survivor annuity and a joint-and-75 percent survivor annuity), but one has a greater actuarial value than the other (e.g., the joint and survivor annuity with

75 percent survivor benefit), the more valuable joint-and-survivor annuity is the QJSA.

If the plan offers two joint and survivor annuities that are actuarially equivalent, the plan must specify which is the QJSA. However, the participant may elect the other equivalent joint and survivor annuity without spousal consent. The participant may elect an alternate form of benefit, if so offered by the plan, but only with spousal consent.

An election to waive the normal form of joint and survivor benefit must be made ninety days before the annuity starting date (the date on which benefit payments begin).[15] Notice of the election period must be provided to participants along with an explanation of the consequences of the election within a reasonable period of time before the annuity starting date, at least ninety days before the annuity starting date.

Spousal Consent[16]

In general, any waiver of QJSA or QPSA benefits or election of an alternative benefit option will not be effective unless:

- the participant's spouse consents in writing to a change in either the QPSA or QJSA benefit;

- the election designates a beneficiary who may not be changed without spousal consent (unless the spouse expressly permits designation by the participant without further spousal consent);

- the election designates a form of benefit, which may not be changed without spousal consent;

- the consent acknowledges the effect of such election on benefit rights; and

- the consent is witnessed by a plan representative or a notary public.[17]

HOW IT IS DONE – AN EXAMPLE

The amount of insurance necessary to match the survivor benefits of the pension's J&S annuity can be estimated using the following present value of annuity due formula:[18]

$$InsAmt = SurBen \bullet (1 - T) \bullet \frac{1 - (1 + r^*)^{-N}}{r^*} \bullet (1 + r^*)$$

The terms of the formula are defined as follows:

$InsAmt$ = Amount of insurance needed

$SurBen$ = Initial annual survivor benefit from pension's J&S annuity plus the dollar value of any other benefits, such as medical benefits, tied to continuation of pension payouts)

T = Assumed tax rate applicable to pension benefit (combined federal, state, and local tax rate)

N = Assumed number of years surviving spouse lives beyond participant's death

r^* = Assumed after-tax inflation-adjusted rate of return on insurance proceeds
= $(r - I) \div (1 + I)$

r = Assumed aftertax investment rate of return on insurance proceeds

I = Inflation or Cost-Of-Living Adjustment (COLA, if any) for J&S survivor pension

The values for the assumptions should be conservative. This means the value for the assumed tax rate, T, should be at the high end of reasonable expectations. The assumed after-tax investment rate, r, should generally be at the low end of expectations. The COLA adjustment, I, (if any) should be at the high end of reasonable expectations (however, the COLA variable realistically should be less than r).

The appropriate assumption for N is a conservatively long estimate of the spouse's life expectancy.[19] This differs from the commonly-held wisdom that the appropriate assumption for N is a period considerably longer than the spouse's life expectancy in order to assure funds are not depleted in the event the spouse survives beyond his or her life expectancy. For example, one rule-of-thumb is to extend the period to 1 times the spouse's life expectancy at the date of the participant's retirement. However, this is overly conservative. The objective of the formula is to estimate the amount of insurance proceeds that would be necessary to reproduce the no-refund single-life survivor annuity that would otherwise be payable to the spouse under the pension plan's J&S annuity. The amount necessary to purchase (or receive as a life insurance settlement option) a no-refund single-life annuity can be estimated by using a conservatively long value for life expectancy together with conservative values for the other assumed variables. If an even longer period is used, the insurance need so calculated will be enough to provide not only a life annuity, but also a refund if the spouse dies before the end of the specified term. This overestimates the value of the spouse's survivor benefit from the pension plan.

The appropriate assumption for N depends initially not only on the spouse's age but also the spouse's health at the time the participant retires. If the spouse is in poor health with an expected life span that is shorter than normal for his or her age, the computation of the required insurance amount should use a value less than normal life expectancy.

For example, assume the spouse is age sixty when the participant retires. Assume also the survivor benefit under the pension's normal J&S annuity initially would be $24,000 (SurBen) per year, but the pension benefits are indexed for inflation, capped at a maximum of 4 percent per year. Assume a 5.5 percent after-tax return (r), a combined tax rate of 31 percent (T), a maximum COLA of 4 percent (L), and a life expectancy of 24.2 (N) years [the Table V value for age sixty].

$$r* = (r - I) \div (1 + I)$$

$$r* = (.055 - .04) \div (1 + .04)$$

$$r* = .01442$$

$$InsAmt = SurBen \bullet (1 - T) \bullet \frac{1 - (1 + r*)^{-N}}{r*} \bullet (1 + r*)$$

$$InsAmt = \$24,000 \bullet (1 - .31) \bullet \frac{1 - (1 + .01442)^{-24.2}}{.01442}$$

$$\bullet (1 + .01442)$$

$$InsAmt = \$341,115$$

Based on the formula, the initial amount of required insurance would be $341,115. If the couple both survive for ten years, the spouse's age would be seventy, life expectancy declines to sixteen years, and the required amount of insurance falls to $238,497. At the spouse's age eighty-five, life expectancy is 6.9 years and the required insurance amount is $109,581. The amount of insurance required to finance the spouse's survivor benefit will generally decline each year that the participant and the spouse both survive. Figure 38.1 shows insurance requirements at various ages for three different assumed COLA rates.

TAX IMPLICATIONS

1. Survivor benefit distributions from a qualified plan and from a life insurance settlement option share some tax features, but differ in at least one important respect. In either case, income taxation

Figure 38.1

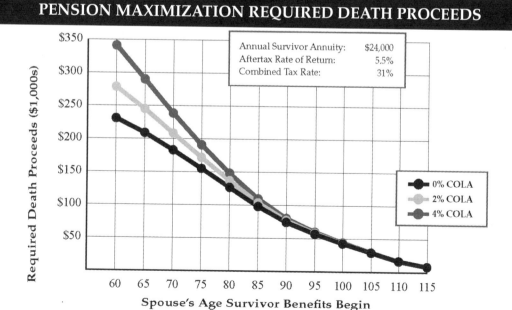

PENSION MAXIMIZATION REQUIRED DEATH PROCEEDS

Annual Survivor Annuity:	$24,000
Aftertax Rate of Return:	5.5%
Combined Tax Rate:	31%

Required Death Proceeds ($1,000s)

Spouse's Age Survivor Benefits Begin

- 0% COLA
- 2% COLA
- 4% COLA

TAX IMPLICATIONS

on investment earnings is deferred until distributions are received. However, the distributions from a qualified plan will generally be subject to tax in their entirety, unless the participant acquired some nontaxable basis in the plan (for example, through nondeductible contributions, Table 2001 costs (formerly P.S. 58 costs) for insurance, or for loans that were treated as distributions and then repaid).

Life insurance death proceeds are generally paid free of income tax. Consequently, if the death benefits are essentially used to purchase the equivalent of the qualified plan's survivor annuity under the settlement options, the survivor-annuitant will have a sizeable basis in the annuity. This basis will be recovered in a pro-rata fashion under the rules of Code section 72, leaving only a portion of each payment subject to income tax.

Therefore, in determining the amount of insurance required so as to match the survivor benefit payable from a J&S annuity from the plan, planners have to consider the difference in the taxation of the benefits. Much less insurance is necessary to match the after-tax survivor payments from the qualified plan than to match the before-tax payments from the plan.

2. Similarly, planners must recognize that the amount which will be available to pay premiums on life insurance if the participant elects a SL annuity rather than a J&S annuity must be adjusted for taxes. The participant will only have the after-tax difference available to pay premiums.

3. The value of the survivor benefit from a qualified plan J&S annuity will be included in the taxable estate of the participant. If the spouse is named as the beneficiary, it qualifies for the marital exclusion. However, if anyone other than the spouse is named as beneficiary, no exclusion applies.

If the participant retains any incidents of ownership in the life insurance policy, the death proceeds will be included in the estate. Similar to the survivor benefits from a qualified plan, if the spouse is named as beneficiary, the proceeds will qualify for the marital exclusion. If anyone else is named as beneficiary, the proceeds will be subject to estate tax.

However, if the participant creates an irrevocable life insurance trust, the death proceeds can escape inclusion in the estate. Often, even when the spouse is intended to be the primary beneficiary,

an irrevocable life insurance trust can provide planning flexibility that is unavailable with the survivor benefit from a J&S annuity. For instance, the irrevocable life insurance trust can be arranged to handle contingencies, such as the possibility that the spouse will predecease the participant, by naming contingent beneficiaries. Such planning options are generally unavailable with a J&S annuity survivor benefit from a qualified plan.

FREQUENTLY ASKED QUESTIONS

Question – How does one determine if a pension maximization strategy is feasible?

Answer – A pension maximization plan is not for everyone. The pension maximization plan is clearly advantageous if the extra pension benefit payable under the SL annuity option (as compared with the joint benefit payable under the standard J&S annuity option) is large enough to pay the premiums for a sufficient amount of life insurance. But this is not always, or even usually, the case. This is especially true when you factor in the considerations discussed in the "Disadvantages" section earlier in this chapter.

The survivor benefits payable from a retirement plan are determined using actuarial methods and factors similar to those used to determine life insurance benefits. Assuming for argument's sake that all the assumptions used in the calculation of benefits for each alternative are identical, it is clear that the cost of the life insurance in the pension maximization plan would have to be greater than the cost (the difference in the payout under the single life or J&S annuity) of the insurance feature of the J&S annuity from the plan. As was described above, the pension maximization plan offers greater flexibility and more attractive features than the J&S annuity option, but this flexibility and these features must cost something.

The real question is whether the advantages and flexibility of the pension maximization plan warrant the additional cost. The monthly pension benefit payable under the SL annuity option will typically range from 10 percent to 25 percent greater than the normal joint benefit payable under the J&S annuity. Among the factors affecting this differential is the difference in the spouses' ages, the participant's age at retirement, and the selected survivor benefit payable under the J&S option. The differential will be larger if the survivor is paid 100 percent rather than only 50 percent of the joint benefit. Additional factors have an effect as well, such as whether or not the pension plan subsidizes one option at the expense of the others. Although each of the pension payout options is usually roughly equivalent on an actuarial basis, it is not uncommon for the underlying actuarial assumptions to favor one option over the others. Most often the normal joint and 50 percent survivor benefit annuity is the actuarially-favored option.

If the participant is insurable, a carefully designed pension maximizing plan can put the surviving spouse in a better position than just relying on the pension plan's survivor benefit and also provide the couple with a more attractive overall package of flexible options. Given the greater flexibility and the many advantages, a pension maximization plan may even be a desirable choice if the insurance premiums somewhat exceed the pension payout differential. But a bad design, or failure to follow through with the plan, can jeopardize the spouse's financial security in old age.

Question – What key points should planners keep in mind as they consider the pension maximization alternative for a client?

Answer – First, the spouse has rights to survivor benefits from the pension plan unless he or she expressly waives those rights in writing.

The normal form of pension benefit for married couples is a J&S annuity with a survivor benefit ranging from 50 percent to 100 percent of the joint benefit. In addition, a spouse is entitled to a preretirement survivorship benefit if the plan participant should die before normal retirement age. This preretirement survivorship benefit is essentially the same as the survivorship benefit the spouse would have received under the normal J&S annuity if the plan participant had retired or terminated service on the day of death. If a couple wishes to elect any other form of benefit, such as the SL annuity, the spouse must give informed and written consent (witnessed by a notary public or plan administrator) waiving his or her rights to the survivor benefit under the normal J&S annuity. In general, a spouse should never waive his or her rights to survivorship benefits without guarantees

that he or she will receive comparable nonforfeitable benefits in some other way. These benefits are typically assured by an insurance policy on the participant's life. The spouse or a trust set up for the benefit of the spouse should be the owner and named beneficiary of the policy.

Second, be sure you know what benefits the pension will pay under the SL annuity and the J&S annuity options.

The pension administrator must give a Summary Plan Description (SPD) to every plan participant. The SPD should describe all the options and participant rights under the plan. If necessary, the plan documents themselves can be reviewed to clarify the participant's and the spouse's rights. In addition, no later than within ninety days of retirement, the plan administrator must present retirees with a statement describing their options under the plan. Since it is advisable to begin planning sooner than ninety days before retirement, the participant may ask the plan administrator to estimate monthly benefits under various options before the ninety-day period. The key factor is the relative difference between the single life and joint life payouts.

The differential between the SL and J&S annuities may be affected by whether the spouse is permitted to waive his rights to preretirement survivorship benefits and, if permitted, when he so elects. Typically, if the spouse waives rights to a preretirement survivor annuity, the value of the postretirement J&S or SL annuity benefits are correspondingly increased. Therefore, it is often best to implement the pension maximization plan before retirement, especially if the plan permits the spouse to waive preretirement survivor benefits as well as postretirement survivor benefits. The sooner the election to waive preretirement survivor benefits is made, the larger, generally, will be the upward adjustment of the postretirement benefits. Once again, a spouse should generally not waive his rights to preretirement survivorship benefits until adequate insurance has been secured on the life of the plan participant.

Third, be sure to fully account for all of the benefits associated with the pension plan.

Some pension plans include specific Cost-Of-Living Adjustments (COLAs) or have a policy of making occasional ad hoc inflation adjustments to pension benefits. If the pension plan includes these adjustments, the couple's pension maximization plan will need a greater amount of insurance to provide benefits comparable to those offered by the inflation-adjusted pension.

In addition, employer-provided postretirement medical benefits are sometimes tied to participation in the pension plan. In such plans, if the couple selects a J&S annuity, the company continues to pay certain medical benefits for both the participant and the spouse for as long as either one lives. However, if a couple selects the SL annuity from the pension plan, the spouse's medical benefits would typically cease upon the participant's death. Before proceeding with a pension maximization plan, check with the employer's benefits counselor to see how postretirement medical benefits, if any, will be handled.

Fourth, a pension maximization plan is more likely to be a feasible alternative if some life insurance is already in force on the life of the participant before retirement. Often, the reasons for keeping life insurance in force change over time. For example, many people purchase life insurance to protect dependent children or to help finance their children's educations if the primary breadwinner dies. However, as the parents approach retirement age and the children leave the nest, these needs may diminish. Life insurance that was originally acquired for these kinds of purposes may then be used to help finance a pension maximization program. In such cases, the additional insurance required to fund the pension maximization program and its premium cost may be relatively low or zero.

Fifth, a pension maximization program is more likely to be feasible if insurance is acquired before retirement.

Keep in mind, the premium cost for insurance increases with the age of issue. The sooner an insurance program is implemented, the lower the average cost of coverage. Premiums must also be paid sooner, so there is an opportunity cost for setting up the program earlier rather than later. However, if a couple has legitimate life insurance needs before retirement, the purchase of life insurance with the anticipation of funding a pension maximization program at retirement becomes much more feasible.

One very important retirement reason for purchasing life insurance before retirement is to supplement the spouse's preretirement survivorship benefits from the pension plan.

Typically, pension benefits and correspondingly, the spouse's survivorship benefits, will increase with the length of participation in the pension plan. If a participant dies before normal retirement age, contributions to the plan or benefit accruals for his or her account will be smaller than if the participant had survived to normal retirement age. Consequently, the spouse's survivorship benefits generally will be less than if the participant had survived to normal retirement age. However, the spouse's needs will actually be greater, since he will be younger and have a longer life expectancy than his life expectancy at the participant's normal retirement age. This deficiency can be corrected through the use of life insurance. If the participant survives to retirement age, at least a portion of the insurance needed for a pension maximization program will already be in place and have been partially or completely funded.

Sixth, a pension maximization strategy is more likely to be feasible if the participant is a female.

Despite some narrowing in the difference in longevity between men and women, women still exhibit longer life expectancies than men, on average. This enhances the feasibility of a pension maximization plan in two ways. First, private insurance uses sex-based mortality tables that are more favorable for females. Therefore, for a female the premium cost for life insurance purchased outside a pension plan will generally be less than that for a male, all else being equal. Second, since males of all relevant ages, on average, survive for a shorter period of years than females of the same age, less insurance is required to provide the same expected total survivor benefits until death for a male than for a female.

Seventh, a pension maximization strategy is more likely to be feasible if the participant's spouse is not in good health.

A J&S annuity is generally a poor "insurance" choice if the participant's spouse is less healthy than average for a person of his or her age. The greater the likelihood the spouse will not live as long as average for his or her age, the less insurance the pension maximization plan requires to assure a sufficient survivor benefit. For example, assume a participant-husband is in normal health, but the beneficiary-wife has advanced heart disease and is expected to survive, say, at most ten years. In this case the amount of insurance needed to provide survivor benefits for ten years in the event the husband predeceases the wife is considerably less than the amount needed for the normal duration of life for a healthy woman at normal retirement age.

Question – What information will be needed to analyze whether a pension maximization strategy should be implemented?

Answer – The types of information required are presented in the following checklist:

- a determination of what survivor elections are available from the pension plan, including joint and full survivor, joint and two-thirds, etc.;

- a comparison of the monthly dollar amount payable from the pension plan under the preferred joint and survivor option and under the single life option;

- analysis of the current plan, including whether it provides cost-of-living increases and whether it requires a survivor election in order to maintain medical benefits if the participant predeceases the spouse;

- an assessment of the spouse's health;

- an assessment of the participant's health and insurability or rating classification;

- standard information for insurance policies, including name, sex, date of birth, smoker/nonsmoker, physicals, etc.; and

- generally, as Figure 38.1 demonstrates, the amount of insurance required declines as

the couple ages, so some form of declining coverage, such as some combination of level premium whole life and decreasing term or universal life should be considered.

CHAPTER ENDNOTES

1. Retirement Equity Act of 1984 (REA). The REA added Section 417 to the Code and made amendments to IRC §401(a). Technical and other corrections were made to REA by the Tax Reform Act of 1986. Additional guidance is provided in regulations issued under IRC §§401(a)(20), 411, and 417. See Treas. Regs. §§1.401(a)-20, 1.411(a)-11.

2. Treas. Reg. §1.401(a)-20, Q&A-10(b)(1).

3. Treas. Regs. §§1.401(a)-20, Q&A-1, 1.401(a)-20, Q&A-2.

4. Treas. Regs. §§1.401(a)-20, Q&A-3(a), 1.401(a)-20, Q&A-12(b).

5. Treas. Regs. §§1.401(a)-20, Q&A-3(a) and Q&A-12(b).

6. I.R.C. §401(a)(11)(B)(iii)(1).

7. I.R.C. §401(a)(11)(B)(iii)(2).

8. Treas. Reg. §1.401(a)-20, Q&A-3(a)(3).

9. Treas. Reg. §1.401(a)-20, Q&A-3(b)(1).

10. Treas. Reg. §1.401(a)-20, Q&A-3(b)(2).

11. Treas. Reg. §1.401(a)-20, Q&A-8(c).

12. Treas. Reg. §1.401(a)-20, Q&A-8(d).

13. Treas. Reg. §1.401(a)-20, Q&A-18.

14. Treas. Reg. §1.401(a)-20, Q&A-22.

15. Treas. Reg. §1.401(a)-20, Q&A-10(a).

16. I.R.C. §417(a)(1).

17. I.R.C. §417(a)(2); Notice 97-10, 1997-1 CB 370.

18. To use a financial calculator in computing the *InsAmt* value, first set the calculator to payments at the beginning of each period (annuity due). Next, put the value of r^* into the interest rate register (usually designated r or I), the value of N into the years or periods register (usually designate n), the value of *SurBen* $(1-T)$ into the payment register (usually designated *Pmt*), the value of 0 (zero) into the future value register (usually designated *FV*), and then *compute* the present value (usually designated *PV*), which is the estimated insurance need, *InsAmt*.

19. Table V – Ordinary Life Annuities – Expected Return Multiples, as provided in Treas. Reg. §1.72-9, is a useful source of conservative unisex life expectancy values. Table V is reproduced in Chapter 2.

REVOCABLE LIFE INSURANCE TRUSTS

CHAPTER 39

INTRODUCTION

As one estate planning authority has stated:

> "As an estate planning tool, life insurance has no peer. The benefits of life insurance as an estate planning tool can be increased through careful planning for the disposition of the life insurance itself. The personal life insurance trust is the premiere vehicle for achieving maximum flexibility in utilizing the death proceeds of life insurance to accomplish the decedent's personal and tax goals."[1]

This chapter should be read together with Chapter 34 on irrevocable life insurance trusts. Together, they will provide an excellent overview of how life insurance as a pivotal estate planning tool can be leveraged through another key tool, the trust.

WHAT IS A TRUST?

Picture in your mind a box.[2] Let's call that fictional box a trust. Into that box you can put cash, stocks, bonds, mutual funds, the deed to your home, or even life insurance. You can put almost any asset into the box. When you do put property into the box, you are funding the trust (although some authorities restrict the definition of the term funding to the transfer of income producing assets into the trust). Funding (in the sense of adding income producing assets to a life insurance trust) is usually for the purpose of providing a source for premium payments where the trust will actually own and hold one or more policies.

State law determines the existence or nonexistence of a trust. In fact, a trust does not technically come into existence until the trust is at least nominally funded (often with little more than a small U.S. Savings Bond). Some states allow a trust to be considered funded merely by naming it the beneficiary of life insurance proceeds. Almost any type of asset can be placed into the trust. Assets typically found in trusts include cash, stocks, bonds, mutual funds, the deed to real estate, and life insurance. Additional assets can be placed into a trust even after it is initially funded. For example, a small government bond may form the initial funding of a trust but then later the same trust can be named as beneficiary of a life insurance policy, a pension plan, an IRA, or HR-10.

A trust is therefore a legal relationship that enables one party (a trustee) to hold money or other property (the trust principal or res or corpus) transferred to the trust by a second party (the grantor, settlor, or trustor) for the benefit of one or more third parties (the beneficiaries) according to the terms and conditions of a legal document (the trust agreement). In other words, a trust is a means by which a property owner may separate the burdens of property ownership from the benefits of property ownership to whatever degree, upon whatever terms, for whatever period (within reasonable limits imposed by law), and for the benefit of whomever he pleases.[3]

Again, the key to understanding a trust is that for investment, management, and administration purposes the trustee holds full legal title to the property in the trust. But that trustee (or trustees, since there can be more than one) must use or distribute the property and the income it produces solely for and to the beneficiaries (or class of beneficiaries) selected by the grantor and named in the trust.

Should the trust fail (perhaps because the trust is declared invalid for technical reasons), the beneficiary holds the proceeds under what is called a "resulting trust." This is a fictitious trust created by law to prevent unjust enrichment. Usually, the proceeds held in such a resulting trust are eventually paid to or for the benefit of the would-be grantor's estate. However, if the trust is poorly drafted and there is not sufficient evidence to show that the presumptive grantor intended to create a trust, the beneficiary takes total and absolute title to the proceeds.[4]

Living Trust Defined

A trust set up during the lifetime of the client is called an intervivos (living) trust. That trust can hold assets (including life insurance contracts) placed into the trust by its creator during his lifetime. It could also provide for the acceptance of additional assets at its creator's death. His will could "pour over" assets from the estate into the previously established trust. This is the Life Insurance Trust–Pour Over Will (LITPOW) combination that has been used as an effective estate planning tool for generations.

WHAT IS A REVOCABLE LIFE INSURANCE TRUST?

A revocable trust, as its name implies, is a trust established during a client's lifetime that can be revoked by the client. The client who sets up a revocable trust specifically reserves the right, at any time (until specifically making the trust irrevocable or until death, at which time it becomes irrevocable), to alter or amend its terms or terminate the trust and recover its assets. In most states, a trust is irrevocable unless the trust document specifically provides otherwise. Also, a revocable trust is generally irrevocable while the grantor is incompetent.

If the revocable trust, through its trustee, is designated as the beneficiary (or as both the owner and beneficiary) of one or more insurance policies on the life of the trust's grantor, the trust is a revocable life insurance trust. The policy owner names the trust as beneficiary of the policy proceeds and the trustee is directed in the trust agreement to hold those proceeds for the beneficiaries of the trust to be distributed in the time and manner specified in the trust document.

When a revocable life insurance trust is created, the policy owner typically reserves all of the ownership rights in the policies and, unless the trust is funded with income producing assets, the policyowner will continue to be responsible to pay all premiums. If the trust is funded with income producing property, the trustee usually will be required to use the income from those assets to keep the insurance in force.

Actually, life insurance policies are seldom transferred to a revocable trust. Although the mere designation of a trust as the beneficiary of life insurance is sufficient in most states to create the trust, most cautious authorities suggest some other cash or other asset be placed into the trust as well to thwart an argument in a jurisdiction that may not clearly accept such a designation as adequate.

Note that a formal trust document should always be created since the mere designation of trustee as policy beneficiary will not, per se, establish a trust. Absent sufficient evidence to prove that a trust was intended, the policy proceeds will be paid outright (probably to the insured's estate if no other beneficiary was named). But if it can be shown that a trust was intended, even if the trust should fail for technical reasons, a resulting trust (a fictitious trust created by law to uphold the creator's wishes) occurs and the proceeds are held for the beneficiary.[5]

A revocable trust can be named as a contingent beneficiary of policy proceeds so that if the primary or even backup beneficiary died before the insured, there would be a receptacle for the money. For instance, a parent might name the other parent as primary beneficiary but provide in the insurance application that "If my spouse predeceases me, proceeds are to be paid to Thomas Trustworthy, trustee of the living trust I have established."

There is one good reason to transfer ownership of life insurance policies to a revocable trust and have the trustee name the trust as beneficiary: if the grantor becomes incapacitated, the trustee can if necessary, borrow the cash value of the policies to keep them in force.

WHY SHOULD A CLIENT SET UP A TRUST?

There are many reasons why a client may want to make a gift in trust as opposed to outright. There are, of course, tax savings goals but, typically, these cannot be accomplished through revocable life insurance trusts.[6] Generally speaking, revocable life insurance trusts save neither income nor estate taxes. So it is the people oriented objectives of revocable trusts that provide the greatest incentive for their creation.

These can be categorized into the following broad terms of income and wealth:

1. Management

2. Conservation

3. Distribution

More specifically, clients set up revocable trusts during their lifetime (intervivos revocable trusts) to accomplish the following objectives:

1. *Postpone ownership during incapacity or inability of the beneficiary* – Quite often a client will feel that the beneficiary is unwilling or unable to invest, manage, or handle the responsibility of an outright gift. Gifts to minors, for example, would fall into this category. But a trust should also be considered for persons who are legally adults but who lack the emotional or intellectual training, experience, physical capacity, or willingness to handle either large sums of money or assets which require constant and high level decision making ability. So a trust is often used to postpone full ownership until the donees are in a position to handle the income and the property itself properly.

2. *Maintain control over a beneficiary* – Some clients are reluctant to place all the ownership rights in the hands of a donee. They utilize trusts as the solution to the ambivalent position of wanting to institute a gift program but fear the possible results of an outright no strings attached transfer that lessens the donee's dependence on them.

3. *Avoid fragmentation of property* – A further impetus for the use of a trust is where the proposed gift property does not lend itself to fragmentation, but the client wants to spread beneficial ownership among a number of people. For example, a large life insurance policy and the proceeds generated by it at the insured's death are often better held by a single trustee than jointly by several individuals.

4. *Retention of control over assets* – A revocable life insurance trust, which the client can alter, amend, revoke, or terminate at will, should be considered where conservation of assets and particular dispositive plans are important. In other words, if retention of lifetime control is essential to the client, such as where the client wants to limit the class of beneficiaries (e.g., no in-laws) or where the client wants to prevent the beneficiary from disposing of the property to persons outside the family, a trust provides a vehicle for a client to make a gift with minimal loss of lifetime control. At the same time, the client builds in flexibility to meet future contingencies and attain personal objectives.

5. *Unifying receptacle for other assets* – Because a trust can be named as recipient of almost any type of asset and because such property can be placed into trust at any time (and because parties other than the party who originally established the trust can make contributions of cash or property), a revocable trust makes an ideal vehicle for later contributions to "pour-over" into it. This unification of assets is particularly important if the client owns many different types of assets or owns property in more than one state. Bringing the assets together may save administrative costs and avoid multiple probates where property is owned in more than one state.

6. *Avoidance of publicity* – The terms of a trust are not public knowledge. Therefore, the amount placed into trust, the terms of the transfers, and the identity of the income and ultimate recipients does not become public knowledge. Privacy is particularly important where there are (or there is the potential for) intra-family conflicts. Since there are no requirements that nonbeneficiary family members must be notified of the nature or extent of trust assets or the details of the dispositive plan of a revocable trust, the potential for family disputes is low. This is particularly important where the client wants to disinherit a particular family member or name a friend who is not a family member as a beneficiary.

7. *Opportunity for a trial run* – Setting up a trust during the client's lifetime affords an opportunity of seeing how well the trustee manages the property placed into the trust and how well the beneficiaries handle the income or other rights given to them. It also familiarizes the

trustee with the client's assets, family, plans, and relationship of each to the others. If the client doesn't like what he sees, changes can be made.

8. *Selection of a favorable forum* – A revocable trust allows the client to select a state where the laws are most favorable to accomplishing his dispositive and administrative objectives. It is not necessary to use the laws of the client's domicile when creating a revocable living trust. To accomplish this objective, the trust should specify the state law that is to govern it. In some cases, it may be necessary to have trust proceeds paid to a trustee in the selected state. Planners must, however, take care not to set up a multiple domicile issue when setting up a trust outside the state of the grantor's domicile.

Cases where it may pay to shop for more favorable state law include (as well as where it may pay to use a trust rather than dispose of property by will) where the other (nondomiciliary) state has a more favorable (from the client's viewpoint) law regarding:

a. *The rule against perpetuities* – This would allow the trust to continue longer than might be permitted otherwise.

b. *Elective share (surviving spouse's rights to a statutory share of a deceased spouse's estate)* – For instance, in Florida, if property is placed into a revocable living trust, the surviving spouse has no right to it, since the elective share is defined as a percentage of the probate estate.

c. *Will contests* – If the client anticipates an attack on the will, a revocable trust should be considered. One reason is that the trustees can use assets to defend the trust against a challenger. On the other hand, in a will contest, until the validity of the will is determined, neither side has access to estate funds and each must personally bear the costs of litigation. Furthermore, the criterion for proper execution of a trust may be more lenient and, therefore, more easily defended than the requirements for a valid will.

d. *Creditor's rights* – However, if the transfer is made to the trust in avoidance of existing or anticipated claims of creditors, it may be voidable.

e. *Charitable bequests* – Some states contain charitable rules, called "mortmain" statutes that nullify or otherwise limit gifts to charities if made within a specified period prior to death. The use of a revocable living trust may avoid this rule in some states.

f. *Restrictions on qualification to serve as executor* – Careful selection of applicable state law may allow a party to serve who might not be qualified under the law in the client's state of domicile.

9. *Equalize risk and potential* – A living trust can be a great equalizer for both downside risk and upside potential. For instance, if a parent owned several parcels of land of equal value or used life insurance proceeds to purchase several parcels of land, he could make outright gifts of Parcel A to his daughter and Parcel B to his son. However, the children may be treated unequally since one property could drop in value while the other could rise. Alternatively, both properties could rise or fall at different rates. Placing both properties in trust could equalize the risks and potential rewards between the children. Investment results of life insurance proceeds invested in a pool by the trustee could be shared equally by the beneficiaries.

10. *Provide for ownership flexibility during beneficiaries' minority* – Major decisions and actions cannot be taken if property is placed directly in a minor's hands, but can be taken if the same property is placed in trust for the minor. This generally makes it possible to sell, exchange, or mortgage a minor's property without the expensive, inflexible, and troublesome process of appointment of a guardian.

11. *Assure dispositive objectives* – An outright gift to a beneficiary will often return to the child's parents or go to the child's spouse or someone other than to whom the client would want it to go. This may defeat many of the client's nontax objectives. A revocable trust would provide an assurance that the client's dispositive objectives could not be easily defeated.

12. *Provide for the helpless* – Physically, mentally, emotionally, and legally incompetent beneficiaries can be financially provided for through a revocable trust.

13. *Relieve the overburdened* – Even beneficiaries who are competent adults can be both protected against their own indiscretions and relieved of the burdens of investment, management, and record keeping.

14. *Back-up for the healthy* – A funded revocable trust can provide for the grantor in the event he is incapacitated and avoids the expensive, complex, aggravating, and embarrassing court process necessary to declare a person legally incompetent. A revocable trust, coupled with a durable power of attorney, can provide the basis for a contingency plan to deal with a client's inability to handle his own financial affairs.

15. *Multistate administration can be avoided through the use of a revocable trust* – For instance; many clients will own property in more than one state. Ancillary administration (i.e., estate administration by a state other than the client's domicile state) is both expensive and aggravating. The client can unify the process and, in many cases, significantly cut down administration costs by placing title to out of state assets in a single revocable trust.

16. *Reduce the risk of a successful challenge* – Once an intervivos (during lifetime) trust is created, its ability to perform the task for which it was designed is more certain than a will. This is at least one reason to establish an intervivos trust, rather than a testamentary trust (one established under the grantor's will). Particularly, when one or more provisions of the client's will are controversial or likely to stir up a family dispute, a will is likely to be challenged or a surviving spouse may elect against (i.e., exercise a statutory right to take a share of the estate regardless of the terms of) the will. A trust is much less likely to be broken than a will based on the lack of capacity of the grantor or upon a claim of fraud or distress. Furthermore, the trustee can use trust assets to defend against a party who disagrees with the terms of the will.

ADVANTAGES

Among the advantages of a revocable life insurance trust, in addition to or as a consequence of making a revocable trust beneficiary of life insurance proceeds, are the following:

1. If a revocable trust is named as the beneficiary of all of a client's life insurance, a simple amendment to the trust can instantly achieve a redistribution of the proceeds of dozens of policies. This should save the client considerable time and aggravation, compared to filling out a multiplicity of forms from numerous insurance companies.

2. Life insurance proceeds payable to a revocable trust are immediately available for the trustee's disposition. Conversely, insurance proceeds payable to a testamentary trust will not be available to the beneficiaries until the will has been admitted to probate and the trustee has accepted the trust. In some cases, there may be a delay of several years between admission of the will to probate and acceptance and final funding of the trust.

3. The transfer of a life insurance policy to the trust, the designation of the trustee as the beneficiary, and even the distribution of the proceeds to the trustee can generally be structured as tax-free transactions.

4. Use of a trust makes the disposition of a policy easier where the beneficiary predeceases the insured. Compare this with an outright gift of the policy to a beneficiary who then dies before the insured. If a trust is used, it can continue to hold the policy after the predeceasing beneficiary's death and eventually transfer it to another party and in the way the insured client intended.

5. Probate is avoided with respect to a policy held by or payable to a revocable trust that continues after the beneficiary's death. Compare this with an outright gift of a policy to a beneficiary who then dies. If the intended individual beneficiary dies either prior to or after the insured, the policy or its proceeds are likely to be subjected to the costs, delays, and uncertainties of probate. Under the revocable trust document, interim distributions to the client's surviving spouse

and/or children can be made without waiting for court approval.

Use of a revocable life insurance trust assures continuation of the privacy of life insurance since there is no publicity and the amount of proceeds and other assets in the trust, as well as the terms of the trust, are not open to public scrutiny as are the reports and accounts filed with the probate court. Use of a revocable living trust as the receptacle for life insurance continues the exemption of proceeds from some states' death tax.

6. To some limited extent (varying widely from state to state),[7] life insurance proceeds payable to a revocable trust may be insulated from the claims of the grantor's creditors and the claims of the grantor's surviving spouse through an attack on the will or election against the will.

7. Using a trust continues the privacy afforded through life insurance. Confidentiality of who receives the proceeds and how much they receive is generally maintained for a longer period of time than if the proceeds were paid outright.

8. All the client's assets (such as life insurance, pension plan, IRA, and personal property) can be "poured over" into a revocable living trust. The trust serves as a unifying receptacle for the collection of assets from a variety of sources and makes it easier to coordinate life insurance with other sources of financial security.

9. Compared to the use of settlement options, a trust provides significantly greater flexibility in terms of the trustee's ability to sprinkle income or spray capital when and as needed by the beneficiaries.

10. Compared to the use of settlement options, a trust makes it possible for the beneficiary to receive greater income and appreciation of capital. (Of course, both advantages entail greater risk.)

DISADVANTAGES

There is no tool or technique that is without cost and totally risk free. Trusts, even revocable trusts, are no exception. There are costs, paperwork, and other potential problems. These include:

1. *Legal and accounting fees* – Legal fees to draft a trust may range from $500 to $5,000 or more depending on the degree of complexity in the trust, the expertise and reputation of the attorney, the prevailing legal fees in the area, and issues collateral to the creation of the trust that must be resolved. Compare these costs to buying an insurance policy and selecting a settlement option. In cases where the amount of insurance concerned is modest, a policy settlement option to provide for the management of insurance proceeds for the insured-grantor's family may prove to be a more cost efficient and objective effective mechanism than a revocable life insurance trust.

Once a revocable trust is funded, filing of income tax returns may be required even though the trust may be treated as a grantor trust. IRS Form 1041, the Fiduciary Income Tax Return, is used to show the trust's income, deductions, and credits which must be reported by the grantor for taxable years beginning before the grantor's death. If the same person is both the grantor and the trustee (or co-trustee) or if one or both spouses are grantors and one or both spouses are trustees or co-trustees, Form 1041 is not required. If the trust has no income (as it typically would not, as long as its only significant asset was the potential receipt of life insurance proceeds), no income tax returns need be filed. At the insured's death, as long as the trust continues in existence, income earned from insurance proceeds payable to the trust must be reported on returns filed by the trust.

2. *Trustee's commissions* – Although typically nominal when a trust is still unfunded, trustees' fees may run as high each year as 1.5 to 2 percent of trust assets and therefore must be considered. The younger the client is, the longer the trust will run and the higher the overall fees.

3. *Hidden obstacles* – There are also hidden obstacles, such as the problem where a bank that holds a mortgage on property refuses to allow the mortgage to be carried over to the trust because a lender might have difficulty selling the mortgage on the secondary market. Will the client's property and casualty company insure

cars and homes owned by a trust? (Consider the question of who has the right to drive trust owned cars?)

Perhaps the biggest hidden obstacle is the time and trouble it takes to continually assign assets to the trust. Special forms must be completed at banks and brokerage houses and new deeds must be prepared (entailing conveyance costs) and recorded (and in some cases transfer taxes must be paid) to transfer real estate to a revocable trust. Even if the client takes the time to transfer title to all his assets to the trust at its creation, after a number of years the client will often forget or not go to the trouble of titling new assets such as a car or personal effects in the name of the trust. Yet if such items are not transferred to the trust, the benefits of probate avoidance and property management and dispositive control for which the revocable trust is formed are unobtainable.

4. *Estate taxes* – Since by definition, the trust is revocable, insurance proceeds paid to the trust will be includable in the insured-grantor's gross estate for federal estate, and generation-skipping transfer tax purposes. Of course, this may not be a disadvantage if the estate is less than the federal estate tax exemption amount.

5. *Panacea syndrome* – Many promoters of the revocable trust imply that somehow this tool is—by itself—a magic pill that can be purchased generically and once swallowed will solve all problems. "Buy my book, rip out the form, sign your name, and all your problems are solved." Not only is this incorrect; it is dangerous. Why? Because it deprives the estate owner of the advice of true estate planning professionals. It blocks questions about other problems the client may not know he has and eliminates the potential to use other tools and techniques, either as alternatives or complementary devices to the revocable trust.

ROLE OF THE TRUST DOCUMENT

Sometimes called a "trust indenture" or "trust agreement," this document sets forth the agreement between the parties (and serves as evidence for the other parties

in interest in every trust agreement, the federal and state taxing authorities) and spells out:

1. how assets are to be managed;

2. who will receive income and capital from the trust;

3. how the trust income and capital is to be paid out; and

4. when (date or beneficiary's age) or under what circumstances (birth, death, marriage, etc.) the income and capital is to be paid to each beneficiary.

Where a trust is to be the beneficiary of life insurance or is to hold one or more policies, specific wording should be provided in the trust document to enable the trustee to accept the proceeds and hold the policies. Even more important, if the trustee is to purchase life insurance on the grantor's life or the lives of others, or is to pay premiums on one or more such policies, it is necessary that the terms of the trust specifically authorize such action. Many states do not permit the investment of trust assets in life insurance unless authorized by the terms of the trust or under provisions of the state's trust laws.[8]

WHAT IS THE JOB OF THE TRUSTEE?

The trustee is responsible for safeguarding and investing the assets in the trust and making payment as directed (or if given discretion, as appropriate under the guidance provided in the trust) to the named beneficiaries. This responsibility may run for as short as a few years or for generations.

Any natural person with the legal capacity to take and hold title to property and deal with it or any corporation authorized by its charter or articles of incorporation to act as trustee and which meets relevant state law requirements can be named as trustee. Unincorporated associations or partnerships cannot be trustees since they are not separate legal entities.

Although legally, there is no limit to the number of trustees, most clients select one, two (often a corporate trustee and an individual), or three (to avoid a voting tie). In some states, individuals and nonbank corporations serve as professional trustees. When more than one party is named, each is a co-trustee and all make decisions (and bear responsibility for mistakes) jointly. The authors recommend that at least two backup trustees be named in every trust in case the one can't continue to act or refuses to serve.

A trustee's job can be a dangerous one depending on the funding of the trust. Life insurance is a relatively clean and safe asset to make payable to or have owned by the trust. But consider real estate, perhaps an apartment house, manufacturing business, or gas station placed into the trust to provide income and avoid probate. Consider the liability of the trustee for fines, cleanup costs, and damage to the environment if hazardous waste is found on the property, even if the hazard was created long before the trust and without the knowledge of the trustee.

WHO CAN BE THE BENEFICIARIES OF A TRUST?

Beneficiaries of a trust receive income from trust assets and/or principal at the ages and under the terms specified in the trust document. They can (and often do) include the person who established the trust. The first people to receive distributions are called primary beneficiaries. The class of beneficiaries who receive what remains when a trust terminates are called remainderpersons.

Although beneficiaries do not have to be identified by name, or even all exist at the date the trust is created, they must be an identifiable and definite class or group and must be in existence within the period measured by the appropriate state's rule against perpetuities. This makes it possible for a trust to be created for the children of the grantor even though all the members of that class of beneficiaries (the grantor's children) may not be in existence at the moment the trust is created, since the grantor is presumed capable of having more children. As long as the class is limited and definite and all its members must be in existence within the period of the rule against perpetuities, the trust will be valid.

The rule against perpetuities is a state law restriction designed to limit the period during which a trust can withhold property or its income from outright ownership. The operation of the rule will vary from state to state, but typically provides that a restriction will fail if it ties up property longer than a length of time equal to "lives in being" plus twenty-one years. In other words, the right to outright ownership of property must "vest" (can't be indefinitely restricted) within a given time frame.[9]

The Uniform Statutory Rule Against Perpetuities, which has now been adopted by a number of states, takes a slightly different approach. Rather than invalidating property interests at inception, this law adopts a flat period of ninety years from the creation of the interest (rather than a period measured by lives in being at the creation of the interest) and waits to see if the rule is violated before invalidating the interest.

SELECTION OF A TRUSTEE

When selecting a trustee, the major attributes to consider are the trustee's willingness to serve and at what cost; the trustee's experience with trust, financial, business, accounting, and tax matters; the trustee's temperament and relationship with the beneficiaries; and the tax effects of serving as trustee.

There are important tax considerations that go into the selection of a trustee. The grantor must consider whether a particular family member or related person can serve as trustee without creating unanticipated and adverse income, gift, or estate tax consequences.

During the grantor's lifetime, the trustee of an unfunded revocable life insurance trust has a relatively simple task. If the trust is merely the policy beneficiary, the trustee has virtually no responsibilities, not even to ascertain if premiums are paid or the policy is in danger of lapsing. If the trust is the policy owner and beneficiary, the trustee will have to use the trust funds and contributions by the grantor or others to pay the policy premiums. At the insured's death, the trustee must file the death claim, assuming the insured's executor hasn't already done so.

It is permissible and often the case, that the person who establishes the trust names himself as the trustee while the only asset in the trust is the right to receive policy proceeds. But in such cases, there must be at least one other individual named as beneficiary of the trust. The reason for this is an ancient trust rule known as the "doctrine of merger." In a nutshell, this rule requires that the trustee and the beneficiary of the trust not be identical. Otherwise, the same party would hold both legal and equitable title; an event that nullifies the existence of the trust. If the sole trustee is the sole beneficiary, the trust is dissolved.

It is sometimes suggested that a trust should never have the following:[10]

- One of two or more beneficiaries as sole trustee

- One of two or more trustees as sole beneficiary

- Beneficiaries who are the same persons as the trustees

Many expert planners suggest that someone other than the grantor be named as trustee because of the difficulty of accomplishing a smooth succession if the grantor becomes incapacitated. If the trustee is a corporate trustee, on the other hand, management of trust assets can continue without interruption even if the grantor becomes physically or mentally incapacitated. A potential compromise is for the grantor to be co-trustee. In any event, provision should be made for at least two or three successor trustees to take over administration of the trust in the event the current trustee, for whatever reason, cannot or will not continue to serve.

ESTATE TAX IMPLICATIONS

There are a number of estate tax related issues that must be considered with respect to revocable life insurance trusts. One concerns inclusion of trust assets. A second relates to the taxation of proceeds from policies owned by a third party but payable to the revocable trust. A third concerns the mechanism through which policy proceeds payable to a revocable trust can be used to provide estate liquidity.

1. *General estate tax inclusion issues* – Picture the box that represents a trust. Now imagine that the client retains a string on that box, enabling him to pull back the assets in the box at any time or use the income from the assets in the box for any purpose. Precisely because the client retains until death that right to alter, amend, revoke, and terminate the revocable trust, all the assets in such a trust will be included in the client's estate. The provision encompassing such transfers is IRC Section 2038 which deals with lifetime gratuitous transfers in which the transferor retains the right to alter, amend, revoke, or terminate the gift. So revocable trusts—contrary to what is sometimes conveyed to the public—provide absolutely no shelter from the federal estate tax. Policy proceeds and any other assets in the trust at the client-grantor's death are estate tax includable. However, this may not be an issue for most people, as the federal estate tax exemption became $5 million effective as of January 1, 2013 and is indexed annually for inflation.

2. *Third party owner issues* – Can the IRS include a life insurance policy in an insured-decedent's estate merely because the policy names a revocable trust established by the decedent as beneficiary? The IRS has (unsuccessfully) argued that by virtue of his power to appoint (i.e., direct the disposition of) trust property, the grantor of a revocable trust had to include in his estate a policy on his life purchased and owned by his spouse. In other words, through the ability to change the trust and its beneficiaries, the husband had the indirect ability to change the beneficiary of the life insurance. But the court held that unless the property over which one holds a power was in existence prior to the decedent's death, there is nothing to tax. In this case, the insured-decedent had a mere expectancy.[11]

   But there are other traps for the unwary. For instance, the IRS will argue that even though the proceeds may not be estate tax includable under these facts, when the insured's death occurs, the surviving spouse (who was the policy owner) is deemed to have made a gift to the other beneficiaries. For instance, if the trust set up by the deceased insured provided income to the surviving spouse for life with the remainder passing at her death to her children, the IRS would claim that, at the moment the insured died, a gift equal to the present value of the children's remainder interest was made by the wife. Worse yet, since the surviving spouse is deemed to have made a gift (the remainder interest) but retained a lifetime income from the gift, the IRS would claim that the entire amount in the trust at the time of her death should be included in her estate.[12]

3. *Providing estate liquidity* – The trust document should provide that assets in the trust at the decedent-insured's death can (or even must) be used to: (a) pay the expenses, administrative costs, and taxes of the estate; and (b) of the surviving spouse's estate if other funds are not available. But planners should note that if the surviving spouse is the trustee or has the power

to appoint the trustee, the IRS could argue that the proceeds should be included in the surviving spouse's estate to the extent those proceeds could be used if the trustee is required (or even authorized) to pay the surviving spouse's debts, administrative expenses, or taxes.

Of course, the revocable life insurance trust—although not technically an estate tax planning vehicle—can save estate taxes and thereby enhance relative liquidity by including provisions that create a combination of a Credit Shelter Trust (a.k.a., Bypass Trust) and a marital trust upon the death of the grantor. The revocable trust would allocate a portion of the grantor's estate into the Credit Shelter Trust so that an amount equal to the federal estate tax exemption (equal to $5,490,000 in 2017, as indexed for inflation) would pass to it without federal estate tax, and the balance of the assets passing into the trust would pass to the surviving spouse in a manner qualifying for the marital deduction. It should be noted that the need for the use of a Credit Shelter Trust for individuals dying after 2012 is substantially diminished due to the combination of a high federal estate tax exemption and enactment of portability rules which enable a married couple to use any remaining federal estate exemption at the second death that was unused at the first death. For more information, see Chapter 27: Estate Taxation of Life Insurance.

GIFT TAX IMPLICATIONS

There are only a few gift tax considerations with respect to revocable trusts. But they can be significant:

- *No gift until the client gives up power to revoke* – A direct gift of an asset from a client to a revocable trust will not cause any gift tax, because the client has never parted with dominion and control of the assets placed into the trust. This rule applies up until the moment when the client gives up the right to alter, amend, revoke, or terminate the trust. If the trust becomes irrevocable for any reason during the client's lifetime—at that moment, since the client can no longer control the use, possession, or enjoyment of the property transferred into the trust—the client has made a gift.

Note that gift tax implications are based on the value of trust assets as of the date the grantor parts with dominion and control. For example, assume a client creates a revocable life insurance trust and retains the power to revoke the trust anytime until the youngest beneficiary reaches age twenty-one. At that date, the client loses all dominion and control over the trust's assets and the gift becomes complete. Gift taxes will be based on the value of the assets in the trust at that time.

- *Third party payment of premiums is a gift* – If someone other than the grantor of the trust pays premiums while the trust is revocable, the IRS will treat such payments as gifts directly to the grantor even if the payor is a possible beneficiary of the trust or heir to the grantor.

- *Gift when policy owned by other than insured is paid to third party* – Whenever an insurance policy is owned by one party on the life of a second party and is payable to a third party, there is almost always a potentially serious and adverse tax consequence. For instance, suppose a revocable trust is set up by a client's wife for the benefit of her children. Suppose she contributed to that revocable trust a $1,000,000 policy on the life of her husband. The IRS will argue that, at the husband's death, the wife (who as owner, both before and after the transfer to the revocable trust) could have been the beneficiary of the proceeds. When instead, policy proceeds are paid to the trust (i.e., to her children), the wife is making a $1,000,000 (indirect but nevertheless taxable) gift to her children. Since she could have revoked the gift at any time, the gift from the mother to the children did not become complete at the moment of the husband's death. However, the gift does become complete when the trust becomes irrevocable (or the trust is included in her estate if the power to revoke is retained until death). Furthermore, the value of the gift includes proceeds, which are generally worth substantially more than the value of the policy or premiums when transferred to the trust.

INCOME TAX IMPLICATIONS

For most income tax purposes, there is no significant impact when assets are transferred to a revocable living trust. The client must report trust income, losses, deductions, and credits as though they were personally incurred. No fiduciary income tax return need be filed if the client who establishes the trust is also the trustee. (This suggests that the grantor of a revocable trust should be the trustee or co-trustee). This tax theory that the revocable trust is the income tax alter ego of the grantor is known collectively as the grantor trust rules. But if the grantor is not the sole or co-trustee, the trust must obtain a separate ID number and file information Form 1041.

Usually, the holding period of the client is tacked on to the holding period of the trust for purposes of determining capital gain and loss when an asset transferred to a revocable trust is sold. But, if for any reason (such as the death or permanent incapacity of the grantor), the trust becomes irrevocable, a new holding period begins. That period starts on the day the trust becomes irrevocable. Planners should also note that if the trust becomes irrevocable during the grantor's lifetime, and then the grantor dies, the basis of the assets in the trust may not receive a step up.[13]

The ability to treat the grantor and the trust synonymously for most income tax purposes means that it is generally safe to transfer installment obligations,[14] a principal residence,[15] a partnership interest,[16] or a U.S. savings bond[17] to a revocable living trust.

There are, however, some important exceptions to the rule that generally transfers of assets to or from a revocable trust have no adverse income tax implications. There are several assets that, if transferred to a revocable trust, will not have the expected tax neutral effect and instead result in adverse consequences.[18] These assets include:

1. *S corporation stock problem* – The problem here is particularly dangerous since it occurs, not during the client's lifetime, but rather, after his death. If the revocable trust does not meet S corporation requirements under Code section 1361 (essentially requiring all income to be distributed currently to one beneficiary or that the trust be taxed at the highest income tax rate), the S election may be inadvertently terminated. S corporation stock can be owned by a revocable trust until the trust becomes (for whatever reason) irrevocable. So if the trust becomes irrevocable (for instance at the grantor's death), S corporation stock must generally be transferred out of the trust within two years.

2. *Professional corporation stock problem* – Most states allow only professionals to hold the stock of a professional corporation. This may not include a revocable trust.

3. *Section 1244 stock problem* – Ordinary, rather than capital loss, is allowed when stock in a small business corporation (defined in Code section 1244) is sold at less than its basis. But this favorable treatment does not apply if the seller is either an estate or trust. For favorable tax treatment, the seller must be an individual. So the loss on a sale by a revocable living trust of closely held stock would be a capital rather than an ordinary loss.

4. *Incentive stock option problem* – An Incentive Stock Option (ISO) is a right to purchase stock issued to corporate employees and contain certain statutory tax advantages.[19] The ISO must be granted to a specific employee and must be expressly nontransferable as long as the employee lives. But if the options are held by a revocable trust, the tax advantages will be denied. The transfer to a revocable trust may be considered a taxable disposition.

5. *IRAs, retirement plans, and annuities* – Although revocable trusts are often the beneficiary or contingent beneficiaries of IRAs and qualified retirement plans, some authorities caution that it may not be possible to roll benefits over tax free (as would be the case if the client's spouse were the recipient).

There may also be problems when trust assets are distributed to beneficiaries. One such potential problem concerns the loss disallowance rules. Losses may be disallowed when assets are distributed to beneficiaries after the grantor's death to fund a pecuniary (specific dollar amount) bequest.[20] Furthermore, the rental loss deduction allowed for losses incurred of up to $25,000 a year can be used to offset other income of an estate (provided the decedent actively participated in the property's management), but no such deduction is permitted to a trust.

CREDITOR IMPLICATIONS

It is a delusion to think that a client protects himself or his beneficiaries from creditors by placing assets in a revocable trust. The avoidance of probate does not equate to the avoidance of creditors. Creditors clearly have access to the assets in a revocable life insurance trust until and unless the client dies or for some other reason the trust becomes irrevocable. All states currently allow creditors access to any asset the client can revoke or liberally amend. Furthermore, where creditors of an estate generally have a very short period of time to press their claims (four to six months in many jurisdictions), creditors of a trust have no such abbreviated deadline and can file suits even years after the grantor's death as long as the time is within the statute of limitations (as long as six or seven years in some states).

COORDINATING THE REVOCABLE TRUST WITH THE OVERALL ESTATE PLAN

No tool or technique, no matter how useful, should be employed in a vacuum. For this reason, the revocable life insurance trust must be meshed with the overall estate plan. Therefore, the planner must consider the following when suggesting the use of a revocable trust (no matter how it is to be funded).[21]

Importance of a Will

A will is necessary in almost every estate plan for many reasons:

- Few clients will take the time or trouble to place all their assets into a revocable trust no matter what real or even perceived advantages there are.

- No matter how careful and diligent a client may have been about assigning assets to a revocable trust, there will almost always be some asset, such as a car, household items, or jewelry, that will unintentionally be missed and that will pass through intestacy absent a valid will. There may be some assets, such as the proceeds from a lawsuit arising out of the wrongful death of the client that would be impossible for the client himself to assign to the trust. But if the will is coupled with a revocable trust, such assets can be poured over from the probate estate to the trust and unified with other estate assets. (Note that the trust should be in existence before the execution of the will since, in some states, a provision

in a will referring to a trust created after the signing of the will is not recognized).

- There are certain objectives that can only be accomplished by will. For instance, a client can't appoint guardians of the person for his children in a trust, but a will can provide for both guardians and backups.

Importance of a Durable Power of Attorney

A power of attorney is a relatively simple and inexpensive legal document by which a client gives a spouse, child, other relative, or trusted friend (technically called the attorney-in-fact) the legal right to act on behalf of the client and in his place with respect to specified financial matters. The power of attorney can be drawn as broadly or as narrowly as desired.

The power of attorney should generally be durable. This means the power given to the agent is not affected by the client's subsequent disability or incapacity. (Each state has slightly different magic words that make a power durable).

A well drafted power may negate the need to petition a court to have a guardian or conservator appointed for handling assets during the client's lifetime that have not already been placed into the revocable trust. In the case of a revocable life insurance trust where the trust has been formed but the only asset in the trust is the trust's right to receive life insurance proceeds, the coordination of the durable power with the trust is essential to protect the client. This planning is essential, not only if the client is suffering from a physical disability or illness that could lead to permanent or long term incapacity, but also by healthy clients who would like to assure continuity of asset management if for any reason they can't handle their own affairs for a period of time. If the power is broad enough, the attorney-in-fact could transfer assets into the previously established revocable trust.[22]

CHAPTER ENDNOTES

1. Simmons, 210-2nd T.M., Personal Life Insurance Trusts.
2. From Leimberg, "Trust Me: A Nutshell Primer on Trusts," (Financial Data Center).
3. *National Underwriter Advanced Markets*, §21, Part A (http://nationalunderwriteradvancedmarkets.com).

4. *National Underwriter Advanced Markets*, §21, Part B (http://nationalunderwriteradvancedmarkets.com).

5. *National Underwriter Advanced Markets*, §21, Part B (http://nationalunderwriteradvancedmarkets.com).

6. Tax savings goals can often be accomplished with irrevocable life insurance trusts. See Chapter 34 on Irrevocable Trusts.

7. See the *National Underwriter Advance Markets* (The National Underwriter Company) for a summary of state laws in this area.

8. A list of statutes of the various states that permit fiduciaries to invest in life insurance can be found on *National Underwriter Advance Markets; nationalunderwriteradvancedmarkets.com* (The National Underwriter Company).

9. For a discussion of the rule against perpetuities, see *National Underwriter Advanced Markets, §21, Part B (nationalunderwriteradvancedmarkets.com)*.

10. *National Underwriter Advanced Markets*, §21, Part B (http://nationalunderwriteradvancedmarkets.com).

11. *Est. of Margrave v. Comm.*, 45 AFTR 2d ¶148,393 (8th Cir. 1980); Rev. Rul. 81-166, 1981-1 CB 477.

12. I.R.C. §2036(a).

13. See I.R.C. §1014(b), 2511.

14. Were the trust considered a separate income tax entity, the transfer of a client's right to receive installment sales payments to the trust would be considered a taxable disposition of the obligation. That would trigger an immediate acceleration of the entire deferred gain.

15. Here, the client will not want to jeopardize the ability to exclude up to $250,000 ($500,000 in the case of certain married couples) of gain from the sale of a personal residence. Since the revocable trust and the grantor are considered for income tax purposes as the same entity, the holding period for the personal residence by the trust and the grantor can be added together making it more likely that the client can qualify for the exclusion for gain from a principal residence. But if the client is not considered the owner of the entire trust, the IRS may deny the exclusion for gain. Planners should also note that some states (such as Florida) will not honor a homestead exemption if the deed is registered in the name of a revocable trust.

16. One of the most important estate planning post-death elections is the one that allows a step-up in basis of the underlying assets of a partnership upon the death of the partner. This I.R.C. §754 election will not be lost through a transfer of a partnership interest to a revocable trust.

17. The holder of a Series E, EE, H, or HH bond need not worry that a transfer to a revocable trust will trigger an acceleration of income. All interest income will be reportable by the client when the trust cashes in the bonds or they mature.

18. See Gassman, Robinson, and Conetta, "Living Trust Checklist," *The Practical Lawyer*, Fall 1991, Pg. 89. Planners should also note that there are tax problems when the assets used to fund a living trust are generating passive activity losses.

19. For additional information on ISOs, see *The Tools & Techniques of Employee Benefit and Retirement Planning*, 15th Edition.

20. I.R.C. §267.

21. See Hira, "Revocable Trusts: Appealing But Beware," *Journal of Accountancy*, October 1991, Pg. 91.

22. For more on powers of attorney, see *The Tools & Techniques of Estate Planning*, 18th Edition.

SECTION 162 PLANS

CHAPTER 40

INTRODUCTION

Often called an Executive Bonus plan, a Section 162 plan involves the purchase of a life insurance policy on the life of one or more employer-chosen employees. The employer pays premiums on the policy but charges the employee with a bonus in an amount equal to that payment.[1]

The employee (or the third party such as an irrevocable trust designated by the employee) purchases and owns the policy and names the beneficiary. The policyowner has all rights in the policy. The corporation never has any right to any part of the policy cash values, dividends, or death benefits and at no time does the corporation own any incident of ownership in the policy.

The arrangement is called a Section 162 plan because the corporation will take an income tax deduction under Internal Revenue Code section 162 for the amount of the bonus charged to the covered employee.[2] In some cases the corporation will pay premiums directly to the insurer while in other situations the corporation will actually pay the money to the employee or a trust for the payment to the insurer.

Usually, the bonus paid by the employer is the same as the premium on the selected policy but in some cases, to increase retirement and death benefits, employees will choose to add their own after-tax contributions to increase the premium amount.

WHEN IS THE USE OF THIS TECHNIQUE INDICATED?

1. As an alternative for split dollar coverage.

2. When the business is in a relatively high income tax bracket and wants to provide fringe benefits to selected key employees.

3. When an employer would like to carve out large amounts of coverage under the group term life insurance plan and provide individual coverage to specified key employees.

4. When an employer seeks a replacement for, or a supplement to, a qualified pension or profit-sharing plan.

Advantages

There are a number of reasons a Section 162 Plan is a favored executive perquisite. These include:

1. The plan provides valuable life insurance for key employees at little or no out-of-pocket cost. This results in less of an after-tax outlay for personal financial security.

2. The corporation has a great deal of freedom with respect to: (a) who will be covered; (b) the amount of insurance offered to each selected individual; and (c) the terms and conditions of eligibility.[3] In addition, the employer has considerable flexibility, depending on the product type, regarding how much premium to pay. For example, if cost is an issue for an employer, it could pay the charges only for a permanent universal life product, which essentially provides the employee with just a term insurance equivalent unless the employee decides to pay in additional premium.

3. The terms of a Section 162 plan are completely confidential. No one other than covered employees need to be informed about the plan nor does any covered employee need to be given information concerning the terms of benefits provided to other plan participants.

4. It is the authors' opinion that if the Section 162 plan covers only one or two employees who are shareholder or senior management employees, there should be no Department of Labor requirements for the employer to meet.[4] Even if a number of common law employees are covered and the plan is considered an employee welfare benefit plan under the Employee Retirement Income Security Act ERISA (ERISA) and the employer has stated an intention to create a plan, requirements are minimal.[5]

5. A Section 162 plan can be terminated by an employer at any time for any reason without justification to the IRS or Department of Labor. No penalty is attached to a plan termination as is the case when a qualified plan is terminated.

6. Almost no employee benefit plan is as easy or as inexpensive as a Section 162 plan to implement and maintain. The authors suggest that in the agreement with the employer the employee request in writing (as a convenience) that the employer pay the bonus directly to the insurance company.

7. Section 162 plans are appreciated because they provide real benefits for employees, who know the benefits cannot be forfeited. For example, the employer corporation cannot take all or any part of what the employee owns away or even place policy values at risk of corporate financial problems, nor can the employer corporation's creditors reach the policy or its cash values because the employee (or a third party on the employee's behalf) owns the policy from inception and holds all rights to policy cash values and death proceeds.

8. Another factor that increases the employer appreciation of covered employees is the portability of the policy. The life insurance policy and all its benefits remain the employee's sole property. Termination of employment has no adverse impact on any of these values.

9. Present or future management can decide to discontinue premium payments but the employee will not lose anything he or she presently has if the business is sold or there is a corporate takeover.

10. Premium payments under a Section 162 plan may self-complete if the selected employee becomes sick or suffers an accident, assuming the policy has a disability waiver of premium or waiver of charges rider. If the covered employee is permanently and totally disabled, all premium payments will be taken over by the insurer and the policy's death benefits and cash values continue to grow as before.

11. Because the employee is the sole owner of the life insurance contract, its cash values (which accumulate income tax free) can be turned into supplemental retirement income at the employee's choice or be used for a child's college education or a variety of other cash needs.

Disadvantages

There are several major problems or drawbacks to the Section 162 plan. These are:

1. Once each premium is paid, the employer generally no longer has any control over either the employee or the policy through the plan. The employee can literally "take the money and run." This can, however, be somewhat controlled using a "Controlled Executive Bonus arrangement" discussed in the Frequently Asked Questions section later in this chapter.

2. The employer has no access to policy cash values for an emergency or business opportunity (let alone to use to supplement normal cash flow or ease a temporary shortage of cash).

3. None of the employer's outlay for the cost of a Section 162 plan will ever be recovered by the employer. Compare this with a split dollar plan, which allows recovery of the employer's costs.

WHAT ARE THE REQUIREMENTS?

Assuming that the plan covers only one or two stockholder or top management executives, installation of a Section 162 plan is quite simple. There should be a corporate resolution by the company's board of directors adopted in writing before the agreement with the employee is signed. The resolution should specify the corporate objectives to be met and the general terms of the Section 162 plan.

A separate contract with the employee should state that the corporation is making a special benefit available to the employee in return for his or her past and continued services and will provide that benefit as a bonus over and above all other compensation. The agreement should retain for the employer the right to terminate the plan at any time and for any reason. The agreement should also list the amount of the death benefit, the type of policy to be purchased, and the terms upon which the employee will cease to be eligible for the benefit.

HOW IT IS DONE – AN EXAMPLE

Your client, Red Waggon, is an employee of Drywells Fargo, Inc. He enters into an agreement with his corporation that provides, in part:

In consideration of Red Waggon's past service and continued performance of services, Drywells Fargo, Inc. will pay him an annual bonus equal to the amount of premium payable on the $300,000 whole life policy from the ABC Life Insurance Company. Drywells Fargo, Inc. will also pay an additional bonus in the amount of any income tax payable by Red Waggon on the first bonus (but not to exceed the tax payable assuming a 40 percent combined federal and state bracket).

Red's wife purchases a $300,000 policy on Red's life and names herself as beneficiary. Although the Fargo company's payment of premiums is considered income to Red and an indirect gift from him to his wife, because of the gift tax marital deduction there will be no gift tax liability. The policy will also be outside of Red's estate for federal estate tax purposes and not accessible by Red's creditors.

TAX IMPLICATIONS

The tax implications of a Section 162 plan include the following:

1. Payments made as a bonus to an employee, whether made directly by the employer to the insurer, or from the employer to the employee and then from the employee to the insurer, are currently deductible by the employer[6] even if the employer derives an indirect benefit such as the enhanced morale or increased efficiency of the employee.[7]

2. The entire bonus (premium) is reportable as income by the insured.[8]

3. If the employer pays premiums directly to the insurance company, the payments will probably be considered a noncash fringe benefit for withholding purposes. Thus, the premiums should be added to regular cash wages paid during the year and the appropriate withholding adjustment made. In other words, employer payments of premiums are subject to both Social Security (FICA) tax and Federal Unemployment Tax (FUTA).

4. Since the employee has already paid tax on the full cost of the policy, he or she has a cost basis equal to the sum of all premiums paid by the employer. This basis, or investment in the contract, can be used to offset income tax as amounts are withdrawn or when the policy is surrendered.

FREQUENTLY ASKED QUESTIONS

Question – What is a controlled executive bonus arrangement?

Answer – A controlled executive bonus arrangement, also known as a restrictive or golden executive bonus arrangement, generally prohibits the insured employee from accessing the policy cash values without the consent of the employer. Thus, with a standard controlled executive bonus arrangement the employer has some very limited control over the policy, although it can't recover its outlay in the event the insured employee terminates employment. This is generally accomplished by filing a restrictive endorsement with the insurance carrier which prohibits the insured employee from accessing the policy cash values or surrendering the policy without the written consent of the employer. This limited element of control should not be sufficient to cause the employer to lose its up-front income tax deduction, since the policy is not subject at any time to a risk of forfeiture.

There is a more aggressive variant of controlled executive bonus which does allow the employer to be repaid its premiums in the event the insured employee terminates employment. This is generally accomplished via a separate employment agreement which requires the insured employee to repay any bonuses if the employee terminates employment for any reason prior to being vested in the bonuses. It is the authors' opinion that since the policy appears to be subject to a substantial risk of forfeiture, no up-front income tax deduction should be available to the employer for its premium bonuses (and the employee also does not incur up-front taxable income). Instead, the tax consequences associated with this type of arrangement should not occur until such time as the insured employee is vested.

Question – What is a double bonus?

Answer – Some employers pay not only an amount sufficient to pay premiums but also the tax on the bonus. This second bonus to pay the tax on the first payment is often called a double bonus.

To compute the amount that the employer must pay the employee so that he or she will net an amount sufficient to pay both the premium and the tax on it, divide the premium by one minus the employee's combined income tax bracket. For instance, suppose the covered employee is in a combined federal and state income tax bracket of 30 percent and the premium is $10,000. The employer must bonus out $14,285.71 for the employee to net $10,000 after tax. [$10,000 divided by one minus .30 (.70) equals $14,285.71. Thus, $14,285.71 multiplied by .70 equals $10,000.]

Question – Can a Section 162 Plan be used with business owners in addition to key employees?

Answer – The use of an executive bonus arrangement with C corporation owners is entirely appropriate and can allow them to use business dollars to pay the premiums for personally owned life insurance. However, the use of such arrangements with owners of pass-through entities may not be appropriate, except in situations where it is used to reallocate pass-through income to minority owners in assisting them to purchase personally owned life insurance.

Its use with partners of partnerships and members of Limited Liability Companies (LLCs) that are taxed as partnerships is generally tax neutral, so there is generally no advantage (aside from reallocating income to minority owners) to using such an arrangement as opposed to having an owner utilize his or her distributive share of pass-through income

to pay premiums. Its use with S corporation owners can actually cause adverse tax consequences. This is because S corporation owners do not have to pay payroll taxes on their distributive share of pass-through (K-1) income. Thus, paying a bonus to an S corporation owner can unnecessarily cause him or her to incur payroll taxes that would not have been incurred if the owner had simply used pass-through income to pay the premiums for the personally owned life insurance.

Question – What type of life insurance policy is typically used to fund a Section 162 plan?

Answer – Any permanent or even term coverage can be used in a Section 162 Plan although almost always some form of permanent insurance is indicated to pay-up the policy by the time the insured reaches retirement age. Consider a policy on which cash dividends, the surrender of paid-up additional insurance, or there is sufficient cash value that the employee can withdraw or borrow that can be used offset the employee's tax on the premiums paid by the employer.

CHAPTER ENDNOTES

1. See Christensen, "Several Methods Have Been Devised Which Allow Companies to Provide Life Insurance Benefits as an Executive Prerequisite [sic]," p. 83, *Trust and Estates* (February 1988).

2. I.R.C. §162(a)(1).

3. Neither the IRS nor the DOL impose rules in this area. The employer can select each desired plan provision with little concern as to antidiscrimination requirements.

4. Assuming the employer merely pays a cash bonus to selected employees who then use that extra money to pay life insurance premiums, no plan should come into existence merely because of this action. Likewise, if the employer pays the insurer directly as an administrative convenience for those covered employees who want to take advantage of that offer, there probably would still be no plan. But at a certain point, as yet undefined by case law or ruling, employer involvement will become so great that the DOL could argue that a plan exists.

5. If a plan is found to exist by the Department of Labor, the plan would have to be in writing, a summary plan description would have to be provided to covered employees, plan documents would have to be furnished to participants upon request, and some party would have to be named as a plan fiduciary with specified fiduciary obligations. Written documents would have to spell out how the plan will meet its obligations and specify the terms of payment and the claims procedure.

6. No deduction will be allowed unless premiums paid on behalf of the key employee are considered, together with all other compensation paid on the employee's behalf, to be reasonable. Treas. Reg. §1.162-9. Since this problem generally arises only

where the employee in question is also a shareholder, if the total amount is more than what is considered reasonable, the excess may be taxed as a dividend rather than as compensation. This would mean the corporation's deduction would be disallowed. For this reason, the business objective(s) to be met by a Section 162 plan should be detailed in a corporate resolution authorizing the arrangement.

7. Treas. Reg. §1.264-1(b). See also Treas. Reg. §1.162-9; Rev. Rul. 58-90, 1958-1 CB 88; *Brown Agency, Inc. v. Comm.*, 21 BTA 1111 (1931), Acq. 1931 CB 10; *Berizzi Brothers Co. v. Comm.*, 16 BTA 1307 (1929), Acq. 1931 CB 6; *Peerless Pacific Co. v. Comm.*, 10 BTA 103 (1928), Acq. 1931 CB 55.

8. I.R.C. §61(a).

SPLIT-DOLLAR LIFE INSURANCE

CHAPTER 41

INTRODUCTION

Split-dollar insurance is a benefit that has been provided to executives for almost forty years and plays an integral role in financial and estate planning. Split-dollar insurance is not a kind of insurance like whole life or term. A split-dollar life insurance plan is a contractual arrangement under which the costs and benefits of life insurance are shared between two parties (oftentimes an employer and employee). The agreement will provide how the parties will share the premium payments and the benefits if the policy either matures in a death benefit or is surrendered for cash. The policy is a normal policy of permanent life insurance, but the two parties to the agreement execute a separate split-dollar contract.

WHEN IS THE USE OF THIS TECHNIQUE INDICATED?

1. When an employer wants to provide a key employee or shareholder employee with a valuable benefit at a relatively low long-term cost. In fact, in certain situations the employer's only real cost (aside from the drafting of the documents) is the after-tax cost of the use of its money. In other words, the employer pays for a split-dollar plan by giving up only the after-tax income the employer's portion would have earned had it been invested by the employer.

2. When an employer seeks an employee benefit that is highly flexible and avoids the aggravation involved in most other benefit plans, yet yields a high return in terms of employee appreciation. The employer can decide who will be covered and the terms and benefit levels each covered employee will receive. The plan can be designed so that the employer can modify or terminate it to meet changing circumstances.

3. When a corporation wants to facilitate a cross purchase of its stock. Two or more shareholders can purchase policies on each others' lives and have the corporation pay all or most of the premiums. Each policy owner will pay a portion of premium equal to the pure insurance cost (a.k.a., the Reportable Economic Benefit (REB) cost) for the insurance owned on the other shareholder's life based on the age of the insured shareholder (not the age of the policyowner-shareholder) (see "Tax Implications," later). Alternatively, the corporation can pay the entire premium and the policy owners will be taxed on the REB cost. At the death of the insured, the policy owner will receive the death proceeds and use that cash to buy stock from the decedent shareholder's estate.

4. When a business owner needs estate liquidity and would like to tap business dollars to amass the available cash for his or her estate.

5. Whenever one party (such as a senior family member) is able and willing to help another party (such as a junior family member) subsidize the cost of providing financial security through life insurance. This type of arrangement is commonly known as private split-dollar.

6. Whenever an insured desires to have life insurance owned outside the estate (e.g., in a trust) for the purpose of providing estate liquidity and wants to minimize the gift tax consequences of paying the premium payments (i.e., the gift is limited to only the REB cost rather than the entire premium). This is also a type of private split-dollar arrangement.

7. When an income tax free benefit is desired as an alternative to the taxable death benefit of a

nonqualified deferred compensation plan. The use of a split-dollar arrangement to provide a tax-free preretirement death benefit in conjunction with a nonqualified deferred compensation plan to provide taxable retirement benefits is often referred to as the "Dynamic Duo."

8. When there is a significant income tax bracket differential between the employer and the employee. When the employer is in a lower tax bracket than the employee, the employer can pay the same premium with fewer taxable dollars than the employee. For example, suppose the premium is $10,000 a year. To an employer in a combined federal and state bracket of 30 percent, it costs only $14,286 to pay the premium. To an employee in a 40 percent combined bracket, it costs $16,667. (If the employer is in a significantly higher tax bracket than the employee, a Section 162 executive bonus may be appropriate. See Chapter 40, "Section 162 Plans.")

9. When the client is in impaired health or for some other reason must pay a rating on a life insurance policy. The insured employee generally reports the economic benefit received just as a standard risk insured would have to. Ironically, this is advantageous because the reportable income is based on standard rates no matter how much higher than normal the premium may be.

Advantages

1. A split-dollar arrangement is an extremely cost effective tool that helps an employer to recruit, retain, and reward key employees.

   a. The major cost of the plan is the after-tax opportunity cost of the use of the employer's outlay.

   b. The employer will, in most cases, recover the entire amount advanced upon the employee's death (from the policy's death proceeds) or termination of the insured's employment (from the policy's cash value).

2. An employer can pick and choose who will be covered, the amounts of coverage, and the terms of the coverage, and vary these elements from employee to employee.

3. There are virtually no ERISA reporting and disclosure requirements for split-dollar plans because

these plans are typically provided only to a select group of top-level employees.

4. In most types of split-dollar plans, the employer's outlay is fully secured at all times.

5. Split-dollar provides a way to guarantee the employee's insurability. For example, the employer could voluntarily sell the employee the insurance if the employee's health deteriorates in the future.

Disadvantages

1. Premium outlays are required by the parties to put and keep the insurance in force.

2. Premiums are not tax deductible at any time by either party to a split-dollar arrangement.

3. The Reportable Economic Benefit (REB) cost must be properly accounted for each year that the split-dollar arrangement is in effect. REB costs rise appreciably as the insured's age increases and may become prohibitive in later years.

4. Due to the increasing REB costs, a rollout strategy is generally required. The implementation of a rollout strategy can greatly increase the cost and sophistication of the planning involved.

TYPES OF SPLIT-DOLLAR PLANS

Classic split-dollar—which is the original version of split-dollar—involves the splitting of a policy between a business and a participating key employee. The business annually contributes the amount of premium equal to the increase in the Cash-Surrender Value (CSV), while the participant pays the remainder of the premium. The business will receive the CSV at the earlier of the termination of the plan or the participant's death. The participant holds the right to designate the beneficiary of the policy. Note, although the employee generally must pay a substantial part of the first premium, after the first year the employee's share of the premium decreases rapidly, and, in some cases, it even becomes zero after a relatively few years. The employee, thus, gets valuable insurance protection (decreasing each year, but still substantial for a long time) with a relatively small outlay for premiums in the early years and at little or no cost to the employee in later years.

Although all of the initial tax authority on split-dollar involves the classic arrangement, it is rarely seen in practice. During the last several decades the types of split-dollar arrangements used generally fall into two categories: collateral assignment arrangements and endorsement arrangements. As discussed later, these two types have several variations.

Collateral Assignment Split-Dollar

Collateral assignment split-dollar involves one party paying a portion of the premium for a policy and as a result receiving a collateral interest in the policy cash value and death benefit (the collateral assignee). The other party owns the life insurance policy (the policy owner) and is entitled to receive any cash value and death benefit not collaterally assigned to the collateral assignee. Depending on the amount of the premium paid by the collateral assignee, the arrangement can be either contributory or noncontributory:

- *Noncontributory* – the collateral assignee pays the entire premium and the policy owner is annually taxed on the REB cost for the portion of the death benefit he or she is entitled to receive.

- *Contributory* – the policy owner pays a portion of the premium at least equal to the REB cost for the portion of the death benefit he or she is entitled to receive (note that unlike classic split-dollar, the policy owner's share of the premium increases over time), and the collateral assignee pays the remainder of the premium. As a result of paying a portion of the premium equal to the REB cost, the policy owner avoids being annually taxed on this amount. Note that as a result of the Final Split-Dollar Regulations (discussed later), any amount paid by the policy owner may have to be treated as taxable income by the collateral assignee.

As discussed below, there are two types of collateral assignment split-dollar arrangements—equity split-dollar and nonequity split-dollar.

Equity Split-Dollar

Equity split-dollar has created all of the controversy[1] (starting with a ruling in 1996) in the tax treatment of split-dollar life insurance. At the time of the insured's death or when the plan terminates, the collateral assignee is repaid the *lesser of* the policy's Cash Surrender Value (CSV) or the aggregate amount of its premiums (note that another variant of equity split-dollar repays the collateral assignee its cumulative premiums paid, rather than the lesser of the CSV or its cumulative premiums paid). The policy owner receives the excess of the total amount distributed from the policy over the collateral assignee's share of the benefits. Since the collateral assignee will at most have an interest in the CSV equal to the cumulative premiums paid, any gain in the policy inures to the benefit of the policy owner. This gain, also known as equity, is what gives equity split-dollar its name.

The tax controversy involves the income-tax treatment of the policy owner's equity component of the CSV, given that the amount of premium it paid, if any, generally only covered the cost of the death protection it was receiving. In other words, the gain is primarily, if not entirely, attributable to the premiums paid by the collateral assignee. Due to the fact that the collateral assignee is only receiving its cumulative premiums paid back, their claim in an equity split-dollar arrangement is similar to the nature of an interest free loan. So much so, in fact, that the IRS has provided guidance in the Final Split-Dollar Regulations (discussed later), providing that such arrangements can only be done as loan arrangements going forward. Therefore, it is no longer possible to enter into a new equity split dollar arrangement.

Nonequity Split-Dollar

With nonequity split-dollar, at the time of the insured's death or when the plan terminates, the collateral assignee is entitled to receive back the *greater of* the policy's cash value or its cumulative premiums paid (note that another variant of nonequity split-dollar repays the collateral assignee just the cash value, rather than the greater of the cash value or its cumulative premiums paid). As a result, the policy owner has no interest in the cash value and is provided with a death benefit only. The entire cash value, including any equity, belongs to the collateral assignee. As a result, there is no tax controversy with nonequity split-dollar and it was unaffected by the IRS guidance that makes it impossible to enter into new equity split-dollar arrangements. Nonequity split-dollar remains a viable planning technique.

Endorsement Split-Dollar

Endorsement split dollar involves the policy owner (generally an employer) paying most or all of the premiums and endorsing a portion of the death benefit to the insured (generally an employee), who is permitted to name a personal beneficiary. The policy owner will thus own the entire cash value, and the insured is provided with a death benefit only. Endorsement split-dollar, therefore, achieves similar results as nonequity collateral assignment split dollar, but the ownership of the policy is different. The insured's portion of the death benefit is typically equal to the net amount at risk (the difference between the total death benefit and the cash value). However, in the authors' opinion it may be possible for the employer to endorse the entire death benefit, as long as the employee is annually taxed on the REB cost for the entire endorsed death benefit. Note that similar to collateral assignment split-dollar, endorsement split-dollar can be either contributory or noncontributory with respect to the insured's portion of the premium payments.

Reverse Split-Dollar

Reverse split-dollar is a variant of endorsement split-dollar where the roles of the parties to the arrangement are reversed. If the parties are an employer and employer (which is typically the case), the employee would own the policy and endorse a portion of the death benefit to the employer. Reverse split-dollar is almost always contributory, as the employer, in turn, pays a portion of the premium equal to the REB cost. However, the rates used by the employer were generally based on the P.S. 58 tables, which were very outdated and were very expensive rates. In addition, the employer, instead of paying an increasing REB rate, will pay a levelized premium that results from adding up the P.S. 58 costs for a term of years and dividing that amount by the number of years involved. The employer is essentially overpaying in the early years and underpaying in the later years. The gist of reverse split-dollar is that the combination of using higher REB rates and levelizing the employer's premiums enables money to be moved tax-free from the business to the employee (generally the business owner).

Notice 2002-592 is believed to have ended the viability of reverse split-dollar. In Notice 2002-59, the IRS stated that one party cannot use inappropriately high current term insurance rates (i.e., REB rates), prepayment of premiums, or other techniques to confer policy benefits other than current life insurance protection on another party. The IRS also indicated that a party participating in a split-dollar life insurance arrangement may use the premium rates in Table 2001 or the insurer's lower published premium rates only for the purpose of valuing current life insurance protection for Federal tax purposes when, and to the extent, such protection is conferred as an economic benefit by one party on another party, determined without regard to consideration or premiums paid by such other party. Thus, if one party has any right to current life insurance protection, neither the premium rates in Table 2001 nor the insurer's lower published premium rates may be relied upon to value such party's current life insurance protection for the purpose of establishing the value of any policy benefits to which another party may be entitled.

WHAT ARE THE REQUIREMENTS?

Assuming that the arrangement is between an employer and employee, there are no nondiscrimination rules that must be met, nor is IRS approval required prior to or after a plan's installation. Split-dollar can be established for as many employees as an employer desires. No notice must be given to any employee who is not covered. (Securities and Exchange Commission rules require publicly held corporations to disclose split dollar plans on the lives of members of the executive group, as noted in the following section.)

Section 409A Requirements

Code section 409A provides a strict set of rules that affects any employer-sponsored plan that provides for the deferral of compensation, and potentially impacts certain equity split-dollar arrangements.[3] Whether it is employer contributions or executive deferrals of salary, if an arrangement meets the definition of deferred compensation under section 409A and that arrangement contains amounts that were earned or vested after December 31, 2004, that plan must meet section 409A's requirements. The key features of section 409A are the limitations on distributions from NQDC plans and the standardization of deferral elections.

In Notice 2007-34 the IRS took the position that the equity in employer-sponsored equity split-dollar arrangements constitutes deferred compensation. Therefore, these arrangements are subject to section 409A and must comply with its requirements. If an employer-sponsored equity split-dollar arrangement is not in compliance, then any post-2004 equity is currently taxable, there is a 20 percent penalty, and interest at the underpayment rate (plus 1 percent) applies.

The position taken by the IRS in Notice 2007-34 that the equity constitutes deferred compensation makes it very difficult for parties to employer-sponsored equity split-dollar arrangements to rely on the no inference language in Notice 2002-8 and take the position that the equity is not taxable upon a lifetime termination of the split-dollar arrangement.

HOW IT IS DONE

Employers install a split-dollar plan by:

1. Selecting the appropriate permanent product to match the employee's needs and risk tolerance.

2. Selecting the type of split-dollar arrangement to be used (a collateral assignment, endorsement, or loan arrangement, as defined later) and drafting an agreement governing the terms and conditions between the parties. The agreement should answer the following questions:

   a. What will each party receive upon given events such as the insured's death?

   b. What are the respective rights and obligations of each party upon early and normal termination of employment by the employee?

   c. Who may terminate the plan and under what terms or conditions?

   d. Does the insured have the right to purchase the policy upon plan termination or upon termination of employment? If so, for what amount?

   e. How and under what circumstances may the plan be amended?

   The agreement is strictly between the employer and the insured employee. The insurance company will respect its terms but is not privy to its terms or conditions. The Employee Retirement Income Security Act of 1974 (ERISA) may impose certain requirements with regard

to the naming of a fiduciary, funding policy, claims procedure, and statement of the covered employee's rights under the plan.

3. Determining what (death benefit, premiums, cash values, and dividends) will be split and among what parties.

4. Drafting a corporate resolution authorizing the purchase of the life insurance and stating the business reasons and advantages to be gained by the action.

5. Completing beneficiary designations and filing the appropriate documents with the insurance company.

Example. Herb Hindes is the president, chief operating officer, and owner of 48 percent of the stock of Pin Wheels Inc., a manufacturer of children's toys. The remaining 52 percent of the corporation is owned equally by two unrelated individuals. Herb's attorney recently confirmed that his federal and state death taxes and other estate settlement costs would approximate $2,000,000. Because the business comprises almost all of Herb's net worth, a sale of the business to pay taxes would be inevitable absent some outside source of cash. Yet all the parties feared that such a sale would precipitate a break-up of the business, the loss of jobs, a forced sale turning into a fire sale of the stock at pennies on the dollar, and the end of Herb's dream of keeping the business he founded in his family.

A section 303 partial stock redemption and a section 6166 estate tax deferral were investigated, but when the numbers were run—factoring in the corporate alternative minimum tax—all of the parties felt that an alternative solution should be considered. That alternative was to have Herb's daughters, Dianne and Laura, purchase insurance on Herb's life. At his death, the cash from the insurance could be used to purchase the stock from his estate. That would give the estate cash to pay taxes and other expenses and assure the children that no outsider could obtain the stock and that no other single shareholder could gain control of the business.

Dianne and Laura will be the original owners of the insurance, but cannot afford to pay the full premiums. To help them, Pin Wheels enter into a nonequity collateral assignment split dollar arrangement with them, with the company paying the bulk of the premiums and the daughters paying a portion of the premium equal to the REB cost (i.e., it is a contributory arrangement). None of the insurance will be includible in Herb's or his wife's taxable estate. At Herb's death, Pin Wheels will recover every cent it advanced so its only cost will be the after-tax income its share of the premiums would have earned.

Rollout Strategies

A split-dollar or loan arrangement may terminate during the insured's lifetime or upon the insured's death. The REB cost, however, increases as the insured gets older, and loan interest cost increases as the amount of loan principal increases. From an income and/or gift tax perspective, the parties should ideally terminate a split-dollar or loan arrangement before the value of the REB or loan interest cost becomes too expensive or exceeds the actual premium cost. If the parties knew that the insured(s) would die before the REB or loan interest cost exceeded the actual premium, they might not need to plan for an exit or rollout of the arrangement. However, the actual life expectancy of the insured is almost never known. Therefore, prudence dictates that a rollout strategy be strongly considered when the split-dollar or loan arrangement is entered into.

A rollout of a collateral assignment split-dollar or loan arrangement requires that the policy owner repay the collateral assignee's interest in the policy. Without proper advanced planning, however, the policy owner may not have enough assets to repay the collateral assignee and still maintain the insurance coverage in force after the rollout. This is especially true if the policy owner is an irrevocable trust that has no assets other than the life insurance policy.

The following are some common rollout strategies:

- *Rollout via employer bonus* – if a collateral assignment split-dollar or loan arrangement is employer-sponsored, the employer can make a bonus that can be used to repay the employer's collateral interest. With an endorsement split-dollar arrangement the employer can terminate the arrangement and bonus out the life insurance policy.

- *Rollout via a Supplemental Executive Retirement Plan (SERP)* – similar to a bonus rollout, this strategy may prove useful for employer-sponsored split-dollar or loan arrangements. Unlike a bonus, there is actually an agreement in place for the employer to pay a lump-sum deferred compensation benefit that can be used to repay the employer's split-dollar or loan arrangement interest or purchase a policy from the employer after an endorsement split-dollar arrangement is terminated.

- *Rollout via forgiveness of the Collateral Assignee's interest* – for both employer-sponsored and private collateral assignment split-dollar and loan arrangements, the collateral assignee can choose to simply forgive its collateral interest.

- *Rollout via policy values* – if the goal is to maintain the coverage after the rollout, then this strategy will not work with nonequity collateral assignment split-dollar arrangements, as the entire cash value is owed back. It may be viable with equity split-dollar and loan arrangements, assuming there is sufficient equity in the policy to maintain the coverage until the insured's death. However, note that rolling out of an equity arrangement during the insured's lifetime may cause the equity to become taxable for income and/or gift tax purposes.

- *Rollout via a sinking fund* – for split-dollar or loan arrangements involving an Irrevocable Life Insurance Trust (ILIT), annual exclusion gifts can be made to the ILIT over a period of years for the purpose of creating a sinking fund that can be used by the trustee to repay the collateral assignee.

- *Rollout via a Grantor Retained Annuity or UniTrust (GRAT or GRUT)* – this is another strategy that can be used with split-dollar or loan arrangements involving an ILIT as a gift tax efficient way to get funds into the ILIT that can be used to repay the collateral assignee. The GRAT/GRUT is typically created around the same time that the split-dollar or loan arrangement is entered into, and the ILIT is named as the remainder beneficiary of the GRAT.

- *Rollout via a Charitable Lead Annuity or Unitrust (CLAT or CLUT)* – similar to a rollout via

GRAT/GRUT, this is another gift tax efficient way to get funds into an ILIT that can be used to rollout of a split-dollar or loan arrangement. The ILIT is named as the remainder beneficiary of the CLAT/CLUT.

- *Rollout via an installment sale to an Intentionally Defective Grantor Trust (IDIT sale)* – this is yet another gift tax efficient way to get assets into an ILIT that can be used to repay the Collateral Assignee under a split-dollar or loan arrangement. The ILIT is made intentionally defective for income tax purposes and assets are sold to the ILIT in exchange for a note. Once the note is repaid, any excess assets in the ILIT can be used to repay the collateral assignee.

TAX IMPLICATIONS

The tax treatment of a split-dollar arrangement depends on when the arrangement is first entered into. Generally, for split-dollar arrangements entered into after September 17, 2003, the taxation of the arrangement is governed by the Final Split-Dollar Regulations that were issued in 2003. Split-dollar arrangements entered into before September 18, 2003, are generally governed by revenue rulings and other guidance issued by the IRS between 1964 and the issuance of the final regulations.

Treatment under Final Split-Dollar Regulations

For split-dollar arrangements entered into or materially modified after September 17, 2003, the tax treatment will be under one of two mutually exclusive regimes: the economic benefit regime—the arrangement will be treated as the life insurance policy owner providing economic benefits to the non-owner, or the loan regime—the arrangement will be treated as the non-owner making loans to the owner.[4] According to the final regulations, a split-dollar arrangement is one between a policy owner and a nonowner where:

- Either party pays all or part of the premiums, with at least one paying party entitled to recover the premiums. Recovery is secured by the policy proceeds.

- The arrangement is in connection with the performance of services, the employer or service recipient pays all or part of the premiums and the employee or service provider has the right to name the beneficiary or has an interest in the policy cash value.

- The arrangement is between a corporation and a shareholder, the corporation pays all or part of the premiums and the shareholder has the right to designate the beneficiary or has a share in the policy cash value.

Economic Benefit Regime Treatment

If the split dollar arrangement is not treated as a loan, the contract's owner is treated as providing economic benefits to the non-owner. Economic benefit treatment will generally occur in either a nonequity collateral assignment arrangement or an endorsement arrangement. The person named on the policy as the owner is generally considered the owner of the policy.

A non-owner is generally any person (other than the owner) having an interest in the policy (except for a life insurance company acting only as the issuer of the policy).[5] However, a special rule regarding who is treated as the owner applies to certain arrangements:

1. an employer or service recipient is treated as the owner of a life insurance contract under a split-dollar life insurance arrangement entered into in connection with the performance of services if, at all times, the only economic benefit provided under the arrangement is current life insurance protection (i.e., the employer is treated as the owner of a nonequity collateral assignment arrangement involving an employee); and

2. a donor is treated as the owner of a life insurance contract under a split-dollar life insurance arrangement that is entered into between a donor and a donee (for example, a life insurance trust) if, at all times, the only economic benefit that will be provided under the arrangement is current life insurance protection (i.e., the premium payer is treated as the owner of a private nonequity collateral assignment arrangement).

The non-owner (and the owner for gift and employment tax purposes) must take into account the full value of the economic benefits provided to the non-owner by the owner, reduced by any consideration paid by the non-owner. Depending on the relationship between the owner and the non-owner, the economic benefits may consist of compensation income, a dividend, a gift, or some other transfer under the tax code.

The value of the economic benefits is equal to:

1.   the cost of life insurance protection provided to the non-owner;

2.   the amount of cash value the non-owner has current access to (to the extent that amounts were not taken into account in previous years); and

3.   the value of other benefits provided to the non-owner.

The cost of life insurance protection will be determined by a life insurance premium factor put out by the IRS.[6] Presumably, Table 2001 will be used until the IRS issues another table (See Figure 41.1).[7]

Under the economic benefit regime, the non-owner will not receive any investment in the contract with respect to a life insurance policy subject to a split dollar arrangement. Thus, the arrangement provides death benefits only to the non-owner. Premiums paid by the owner will be included in the owner's investment in the contract. Also, any amount the non-owner pays toward a policy will be included in the income of the *owner* and increase the *owner's* investment in the contract (i.e., contributory arrangements have income tax consequences to the deemed owner of the contract).[8]

Death benefits paid to a beneficiary (other than the owner of the policy) by reason of the death of an insured will be excluded from income to the extent that the amount of the death benefit is allocable to current life insurance protection provided to the non-owner, the cost of which was paid by the non-owner or the benefit of which the non-owner took into account for income tax purposes.[9]

Upon the transfer of the policy to a non-owner, the non-owner is considered to receive generally the cash value of the policy and the value of all other rights in the policy, minus any amounts paid for the policy and any benefits that were previously included in the non-owner's income. However, amounts that were previously included in income due to the value of current life insurance protection provided to the non-owner may not be used to reduce the amount the non-owner

is considered to receive upon roll-out. Thus, the taxation on the value of current life insurance protection will not provide the non-owner with any basis in the policy, while taxation for a previous increase in cash value will add basis for the non-owner.[10]

Loan Regime Treatment

If the arrangement is not an economic benefit arrangement, that is if the owner is not the premium payer, then it is a split-dollar loan arrangement. A split-dollar loan will be found in the following four situations:[11]

1.   where an owner and non-owner are treated, respectively, as borrower and lender;

2.   premium payments are made directly or indirectly by the non-owner (lender);

3.   it appears to be a loan under Federal tax law or a reasonable person would expect repayment in full; and

4.   repayment is secured by the policy's death benefit or cash value or both.

If the split-dollar arrangement is treated as a loan, the owner is considered the borrower, and the non-owner is considered the lender.[12] For example, in a split-dollar loan arrangement between an employer and employee, the lender would be employer and the borrower the employee. If the split-dollar loan is a below market loan, then interest will be imputed at the Applicable Federal Rate (AFR), with the owner and the non-owner of the policy considered to transfer imputed amounts to each other.[13] Each payment under the split-dollar arrangement will be treated as a separate loan.

The employer is considered to transfer the imputed interest to the employee. This amount is considered taxable compensation, and generally will be deductible to the employer (however, no deduction will be allowed in a corporation-shareholder arrangement). The employee is then treated as paying the imputed interest back to the employer, which will be taxable income to the employer. This imputed interest payment by the employee will generally be considered personal interest and therefore not deductible.

The calculation of the amount of imputed interest differs depending on the type of below market loan involved. A below market loan is either a demand loan or a term loan. A demand loan is a loan that is payable in full upon the demand of the lender. A split-dollar demand loan is tested each calendar year for sufficient interest. The AFR rate used for demand loans is the blended annual rate. All other below market loans are term loans. (A term loan is where repayment is fixed at some point in the future).[14] A split-dollar term loan is tested on the date the loan is made for sufficient interest. The AFR rate for term loans depends upon the length of the term loan:

- the short-term rate is used for loans that mature in three years or less;

- the mid-term rate is used for loans that mature in more than three years, but not more than nine years;

- the long-term rate is used for loans that mature in more than nine years.

Generally, a split-dollar term loan will cause more interest to be imputed in the early years of the arrangement, with the amount of imputed interest decreasing each year. In a split-dollar demand loan, the imputed interest will be smaller in the early years of the arrangement, but will increase each year the arrangement is in place.

Effective Date of Regulations

These regulations apply to split-dollar arrangements entered into after September 17, 2003, and arrangements entered into on or before September 17, 2003, that are materially modified after September 17, 2003.[15] The final regulations provide a non-exclusive list of changes that will not be considered material modifications. This list includes:

1. a change solely in premium payment method (for example, from monthly to quarterly);

2. a change solely of beneficiary, unless the beneficiary is a party to the arrangement;

3. a change solely in the interest rate payable on a policy loan;

4. a change solely necessary to preserve the status of the life insurance contract under Code section 7702;

5. a change solely to the ministerial provisions of the life insurance contract (such as a change in the address to send premiums); and

6. a change made solely under the terms of the split dollar agreement (other than the life insurance contract) if the change:

   a. is dictated by the arrangement;

   b. is nondiscretionary to the parties; and

   c. was made under a binding commitment in effect on or before September 17, 2003.[16]

Notably, an exchange of policies under Code section 1035 is not on the list of nonmaterial modifications, even though the authors are aware that comments were submitted to the IRS prior to the issuance of the final split-dollar regulations requesting that 1035 exchanges not be considered a material modification.

The final regulations also contain rules on when a split-dollar arrangement is considered to be entered into. A split-dollar arrangement is entered into on the *latest* of the following dates:

1. the date the life insurance contract is issued;

2. the effective date of the life insurance contract under the arrangement;

3. the date the first premium on the life insurance contract is paid;

4. the date the parties to the arrangement enter into an agreement with regard to the policy; or

5. the date on which the arrangement satisfies the definition of a split-dollar life insurance arrangement.[17]

Excluded Transactions

The only arrangements excluded from the definition of split-dollar are group term life insurance plans under Code section 79 (other than those providing permanent protection to the employee), the purchase of life insurance between the policy owner and the life insurance company issuing the policy, and key person insurance where the corporation owns all of the rights in the policy. In addition, any plan under which there is no expectation of reimbursing the party advancing the premiums is not a split-dollar plan. In such situations, the premium payments will be treated as taxable income, a dividend, or a gift, depending on the relationship between the parties.

Split-Dollar Prior to Regulations

Split-dollar arrangements that were entered into before September 18, 2003, are governed by various rulings and other guidance that have been issued by the IRS between 1964 and the issuance of final regulations on split-dollar arrangements in 2003. This guidance includes Notice 2002-8,[18] which provides transition rules for arrangements not subject to the split-dollar regulations and is primarily focused on equity collateral assignment arrangements. However, no inference is to be drawn from Notice 2002-8, or the proposed or final regulations regarding the appropriate tax treatment of split-dollar arrangements entered into before September 18, 2003.

Value of Economic Benefit

For collateral assignment and endorsement split-dollar arrangements, the party receiving the death benefit protection is taxed on the value of the Reportable Economic Benefit (REB) he or she receives from participating in the split-dollar arrangement (unless he or she pays a portion of the premium at least equal to this amount).[19] The REB cost may be calculated by using government premium rates. For many years, P.S. 58 rates were used to calculate the value of the protection.[20] However, the IRS revoked the use of P.S. 58 rates and provided new Table 2001 rates. P.S. 58 rates may generally be used prior to 2002; Table 2001 rates may generally be used starting in 2001. Notice 2002-8 does provide for some grandfathering of P.S. 58 rates. For split-dollar arrangements entered into before January 28, 2002, in which a contractual agreement between an employer and employee provides that P.S. 58 rates will be used to determine the value of current life insurance protection provided to the employee (or the employee and one or more additional persons), the employer and employee may continue to use P.S. 58 rates.

If the insurer publishes rates for individual, initial issue, one-year term policies (available to all standard risks), and these rates are lower than the P.S. 58 or Table 2001 rates (as applicable), these insurer rates may be substituted.[21] Only standard rates may be substituted,

not preferred rates (e.g., those offered to nonsmoking individuals).[22] The substituted rate must be a rate charged for initial issue insurance and must be available to all standard risks.[23]

For arrangements entered into before September 18, 2003, taxpayers may use the insurer's lower published premium rates that are available to all standard risks for initial issue one-year term insurance. However, for arrangements entered into after January 28, 2002, and before September 18, 2003, for periods after December 31, 2003, an insurer's rates may not be used unless: (1) the insurer generally makes the availability of the rates known to those who apply for term insurance coverage from the insurer; and (2) the insurer regularly sells term insurance at those rates to individuals who apply for term insurance coverage through the insurer's normal distribution channels.[24]

These more stringent requirements for an insurer's alternative term rates were contained in Notice 2002-8. In the authors' opinion it will be very difficult for an insurer's alternative term rates to meet the regularly sold requirement. This is due to the fact that in order to make these rates less expensive than the currently available government table rates (i.e., the Table 2001 rates), insurer's typically make their one-year term products noncommissionable and nonrenewable. This begs the question of how they can be regularly sold if few producers are interested in selling them (because they won't be paid a commission) and few insureds are interested in buying them (because they have to undergo medical underwriting each year to requalify). For split-dollar arrangements entered into after January 28, 2002 (or materially modified after that date), before using an insurer's alternative term rates to calculate the REB cost, it is strongly suggested that an inquiry be made as to how many of the one-year term policies the insurer has actually sold so that the client's tax advisor can determine whether such rates qualify as regularly sold.

There are no rulings on the amount of economic benefit to be included when the employee has not had a full year's benefit under a policy (e.g., the policy was purchased on September 1 for a calendar year employee). It would seem that the IRS would accept any reasonable attempt at allocating the cost in such a year. Also, there has been no formal guidance from the IRS as to which rates should be used to measure the economic benefit resulting from a split-dollar arrangement using a policy which insures more than one life. The IRS has said that taxpayers should make appropriate adjustments to

Figure 41.1

INTERIM TABLE 2001 ONE-YEAR TERM PREMIUMS FOR $1,000 OF LIFE INSURANCE PROTECTION					
Attained Age	§79 Extended and Interpolated Annual Rates	Attained Age	§79 Extended and Interpolated Annual Rates	Attained Age	§79 Extended and Interpolated Annual Rates
0	$ 0.70	34	$ 0.98	67	$ 15.20
1	$ 0.41	35	$ 0.99	68	$ 16.92
2	$ 0.27	36	$ 1.01	69	$ 18.70
3	$ 0.19	37	$ 1.04	70	$ 20.62
4	$ 0.13	38	$ 1.06	71	$ 22.72
5	$ 0.13	39	$ 1.07	72	$ 25.07
6	$ 0.14	40	$ 1.10	73	$ 27.57
7	$ 0.15	41	$ 1.13	74	$ 30.18
8	$ 0.16	42	$ 1.20	75	$ 33.05
9	$ 0.16	43	$ 1.29	76	$ 36.33
10	$ 0.16	44	$ 1.40	77	$ 40.17
11	$ 0.19	45	$ 1.53	78	$ 44.33
12	$ 0.24	46	$ 1.67	79	$ 49.23
13	$ 0.28	47	$ 1.83	80	$ 54.56
14	$ 0.33	48	$ 1.98	81	$ 60.51
15	$ 0.38	49	$ 2.13	82	$ 66.74
16	$ 0.52	50	$ 2.30	83	$ 73.07
17	$ 0.57	51	$ 2.52	84	$ 80.35
18	$ 0.59	52	$ 2.81	85	$ 88.76
19	$ 0.61	53	$ 3.20	86	$ 99.16
20	$ 0.62	54	$ 3.65	87	$ 110.40
21	$ 0.62	55	$ 4.15	88	$ 121.85
22	$ 0.64	56	$ 4.68	89	$ 133.40
23	$ 0.66	57	$ 5.20	90	$ 144.30
24	$ 0.68	58	$ 5.66	91	$ 155.80
25	$ 0.71	59	$ 6.06	92	$ 168.75
26	$ 0.73	60	$ 6.51	93	$ 186.44
27	$ 0.76	61	$ 7.11	94	$ 206.70
28	$ 0.80	62	$ 7.96	95	$ 228.35
29	$ 0.83	63	$ 9.08	96	$ 250.01
30	$ 0.87	64	$ 10.41	97	$ 265.09
31	$ 0.90	65	$ 11.90	98	$ 270.11
32	$ 0.93	66	$ 13.51	99	$ 281.05
33	$ 0.96				

premium rates if life insurance protection covers more than one life.[25] Where the policy death benefit is payable at the second death, it is generally believed that following the first death, the Table 2001 or P.S. 58 rates for single lives should be used to measure the survivor's economic benefit.

The REB cost, regardless of whether the government's table rates or an insurer's alternative term rates are used, get more expensive as the insured gets older, and may become prohibitively expensive once the insured lives past age seventy. Although the REB cost for second-to-die arrangements may be very inexpensive while both insureds are alive, even at older ages, upon the first death single life rates apply and the REB cost can skyrocket. As a result of the increasing REB cost, split-dollar arrangements tend to be good short- and mid-term plans, but not particularly attractive long-term plans. For this reason, an exit or rollout strategy is generally recommended prior to the point where the REB costs become too expensive from and income and/or gift tax standpoint (see discussion of rollout strategies in the Frequently Asked Questions below).

Private Split-Dollar Plans

The use of private split-dollar life insurance has grown substantially as a result of favorable rulings.[26] It appears that private *nonequity* collateral assignment split-dollar remains viable (as well a private loan arrangements), but the issues in the new Regulations related to the income-tax compensation measures (discussed above) should be applicable to the gift-tax treatment of private *equity* collateral assignment split-dollar. Thus, agreements entered into before January 28, 2002 would be unchanged. In fact, existing agreements using the P.S. 58 table rates could potentially be enhanced by switching to the Table 2001 rates. One advantage of private split-dollar is the smaller gift-tax cost associated with the transfer of the premium for the pure term insurance protection. The Table 2001 rates would create a lower gift-tax cost for entering into a split-dollar agreement with the insured's irrevocable life insurance trust. In fact, survivorship (second-to-die) coverage would result in an extremely low Table 2001 rate.

Estate and Gift Tax Issues

Many split-dollar arrangements were entered into with the goal of avoiding inclusion of the proceeds in the insured's gross estate while at the same time limiting the gift tax consequences of the premium payments to just the REB cost. Under this type of arrangement, the insured's Irrevocable Life Insurance Trust (ILIT) is the policy owner and a collateral-assignment agreement is formed with the insured's employer (or the insured, in the case of private split-dollar). If it is an employer pay all (i.e., a noncontributory arrangement), the REB cost is taxable to the employee under the economic-benefit theory. In addition, the REB cost is also treated as gifts by the employee to the trust. Plans entered into prior to January 28, 2002 are grandfathered with respect to the measure of the economic benefit. However, plans entered into after that date would be subject to treatment under Table 2001 rates and the new restrictions with respect to the insurer's standard term rates. This should not be a significant problem since lower economic-benefit rates result in a smaller income- and gift-tax cost. Again, pre-January 28, 2002 plans using P.S. 58 rates may consider the benefits of shifting to Table 2001 rates.

Loan arrangements (i.e., Loan Regime Split-Dollar) can also be used to accomplish the same estate planning goals. With a loan arrangement that involves an employer and the employee's ILIT, assuming that the employer pays the entire premium and isn't paid the loan interest by the trust, the loan interest would be income taxable to the employee and would also be treated as a gift from the employee to the ILIT. In the case of a private loan arrangement, there should be no income tax consequences, but the loan interest if imputed would be treated as a gift.

Some critical issues are presented for the split-dollar and loan arrangements entered into with an insured's ILIT:

- First, with equity split-dollar agreements if there is a lifetime rollout the equity may create not just adverse income tax issues, but also adverse gift tax issues.

- Second, with both equity and non-equity collateral assignment split-dollar and loan arrangements that involve the insured's employer or the insured having a collateral interest in the policy to secure the premium payer's interest in the policy, such collateral interest can cause estate inclusion of the policy in the insured's estate. In order to avoid this, a restricted collateral assignment should be used whenever the insured is a controlling owner of the employer or is directly the collateral assignee pursuant to a private split-dollar arrangement. A restricted collateral assignment avoids the collateral assignee having incidents of ownership in the policy by limiting the rights of the collateral assignee to being repaid its interest in the event the arrangement is terminated or upon the death of the insured(s). Thus, the collateral assignee would have no right to access the policy cash value.

- Third, demand loan arrangements should be avoided where the arrangement is between the insured or a business controlled by the insured and the insured's ILIT. Using a demand loan in either of these situations could cause inclusion of the policy in the insured's estate. This is due to the fact that the right to call the loan could be considered tantamount to the right to force a withdrawal or loan from the policy, which would constitute an incident of ownership in the policy.

Use of Whole Life Dividends

Generally, dividends paid under participating life insurance contracts are income-tax free because they are considered a return of the policy owner's capital due to favorable mortality, interest, and loading experience.

But in a split-dollar arrangement, dividends paid to the insured more closely resemble a transfer of capital from the employer to the employee and may be added to any other taxable economic benefit provided by the policy. Generally, the results are as follows:

- If the employee receives the policy dividend in cash, the employee must report ordinary income in that amount and the employer will receive no deduction.

- If the dividend is paid in cash to the employer, the employee has no taxable income and the employer has no taxable income (until amounts received tax-free from the contract exceed the employer's premiums).

- If the dividend is used to reduce the employee's share of the premiums, the employee will have taxable income and the employer will receive no deduction.

- If the dividend is used to reduce the employer's share of the premiums, the employee will have no taxable income and the employer will have no taxable income.

- If the dividend is left on deposit at interest for the employee's account, both the dividend and the interest on it are taxable income to the employee. The employer receives no deduction.

- If the dividend is left on deposit at interest in the employer's account, the employee has no taxable income. The dividend is a nontaxable return of capital but any interest is taxable to the employer.

- If the employee owns and controls any paid-up additions (i.e., both the cash value and death benefits), the dividend is taxable to the employee and no deduction is allowable to the employer.

- Where the employer owns and controls the cash value of any paid-up additions but any death benefit in excess of the cash value is controlled by the employee, the employee is charged with the cost of insurance protection from the net amount at risk in the dividends. The employer receives no deduction.

- If the dividend is used to purchase one-year term insurance under the so-called fifth dividend option and the death benefit is payable to the employee, the full amount of the dividend is taxable as ordinary income to the employee. The employer receives no deduction.

- If the dividend is used to purchase one-year term insurance under the so-called fifth dividend option and the death benefit is payable to the employer, the employee receives no taxable income and the employer receives no deduction.

FREQUENTLY ASKED QUESTIONS

Question – What are the grandfathering provisions for equity split-dollar plans entered into prior to September 18, 2003?

Answer – The answer depends on when the parties entered into the equity split-dollar arrangement. If an employer and employee entered into an equity split-dollar plan before January 28, 2002, and the plan was terminated on or before December 31, 2003 by the employee repaying the employer's premium advances (i.e., a rollout), any then existing policy equity was not subject to tax. That provision was a big opportunity for employees in mature plans with a substantial equity buildup to roll out of the plan with no tax on the excess equity, but for more immature plans with little or no equity buildup this provision provided no real benefit. If the immature plan were terminated by December 31, 2003, the employee would be faced with the prospect of paying the full amount of future premiums with after-tax dollars (or finding some other source for future premium payments), and those same amounts would also be subject to gift taxation if the policy were owned by an ILIT.

As an alternative to terminating an immature equity split-dollar plan entered into prior to January 28, 2002 (i.e., one without substantial equity buildup), the parties to the plan could agree to switch to a loan regime prior to January 1, 2004. Converting to a loan before January 1, 2004 avoided taxation to the employee of policy equity existing both at the time of the switch and at a later rollout. This loan safe harbor required that the beginning loan balance include all pre-2004 employer premium payments as of the beginning of the taxable year in which the switch occurs (although interest need not retroactively accrue on these prior employer payments), and that subsequent employer premium payments be treated as additional loans. This is the safe harbor that was most frequently used by immature old split-dollar plans and the technique has come to be called switch-dollar.

Note, not all old plans needed to be rolled out or switched to a loan by December 31, 2003 to enjoy the benefits of taxation under the loan regime. Old plans that did not have equity by December 31, 2003 can delay the switch to a loan until just before the plan accrues equity in a future year (i.e., the cross-over point) without causing adverse tax consequences. The reason for delaying the switch to a loan and continuing in split-dollar is to preserve the use of favorable REB rates for as long as possible instead of having to use loan interest rates. This delayed switch is another facet of the switch-dollar technique.

Question – Are there any income tax consequences to the employer or the policy beneficiary in an endorsement plan when the death benefit is paid?

Answer – The amount, if any, received by the employer in excess of its aggregate premiums appears not to be taxable to the employer pursuant to the Code section 101(a) death benefit exclusion.

In contrast, the death benefit proceeds (despite Code Section 101(a)) are excluded from the beneficiary's gross income only to a certain extent. The amount excluded is that portion of the current life insurance protection provided to the nonowner to the extent the cost for such protection (REB) was paid by the nonowner or the value of such protection was taxed to the nonowner as an economic benefit. Therefore, the entire employee death benefit would be taxed to the beneficiary if the employee never contributed or paid tax on the REB cost.

Question – What are the consequences for a loan arrangement if an adequate interest rate is charged?

Answer – If adequate interest (based on the Applicable Federal Rate or AFR) is charged on a loan, then Code section 7872 generally does not apply (i.e., the loan is not a below market loan). As a result, especially when interest rates are low, some planners suggest that the best course of action may be to arrange the transaction as a term loan that states adequate interest so that the loan interest rates can be locked in for a period of time. Because adequate interest is stated, it can be paid annually, or even accrued until the end of the term, instead of being treated as transferred upon creation of the loan. However, if an employer directly or indirectly pays the interest to the employee (e.g., through bonus compensation), the stated interest is disregarded, and the loan is treated as a below-market loan under section 7872.

Question – Is there basis in the policy for the REB cost?

Answer – The Final Split-Dollar Regulations state that the non-owner does not receive any investment in the contract, or basis, for the payment of the reportable economic benefit into the policy.[27] So for split-dollar arrangements that are subject to the final regulations, there is no basis for the REB cost regardless of whether it is paid or the insured is taxed on this amount. For split-dollar arrangements that are not subject to the final regulations, however, the answer is unclear. Dicta in a recent Tax Court case suggests that the REB cost does create basis.[28]

Question – What life insurance rates are mandated for split-dollar arrangements involving survivorship life insurance?

Answer – Table 2001 only provides individual—not survivorship—term rates, and Notice 2002-8 leaves it up to taxpayers to figure out survivorship rates based on the Table 2001 individual rates. It is anticipated that for new plans, the IRS will provide survivorship life insurance premium factors in addition to individual premium factors and will permit all of these new rates to be used to measure the term costs in plans entered into prior to September 17, 2003 as well as in new plans.

The authors calculated the survivorship term rates based on Table 2001 factors and found that they are actually lower than one insurer's existing alternative survivorship term rates up to the age where a husband and wife are both seventy. Thereafter, the rates cross over so that the insurer's alternative survivorship rates are lower than the survivorship rates based on Table 2001 factors. In addition, the survivorship rates based on Table 2001 factors will always be lower than the U.S. 38 rates commonly used in survivorship plans before the new regulations because the U.S. 38 rates are based on the higher P.S. 58 rate table. The favorable conclusion is that, in many if not most cases, survivorship split dollar plans will be able to use more favorable survivorship rates than the survivorship rates previously used in those plans.

Question – Is an economic benefit crawl out a viable rollout strategy?

Answer – An economic benefit crawl out is simply a contributory collateral assignment split dollar arrangement in which the REB payments made by the policy owner are considered to reduce the collateral assignee's interest. In the authors' opinion this strategy is unlikely to pass IRS muster. When the policy owner pays the REB cost each year, it is paying for that year's death benefit protection that is being provided. To also use the REB payment to reduce the collateral assignee's interest would appear to constitute double dipping. It would be akin to paying interest on a loan and claiming that the interest payment also reduces the outstanding loan balance.

Question – What is switch-dollar?

Answer –It is a hybrid plan that starts as non-equity collateral assignment split-dollar and then switches to a loan at some point. The switch may occur at the point where the cash value of the policy exactly equals the premiums paid, or when the REB costs start to get expensive in relation to the loan interest costs. By proceeding in this manner, the insured

can take advantage of low REB rates for as long as possible, assuming they are lower than loan interest costs.

Question – How are split-dollar plans affected by Sarbanes-Oxley Act, which prohibits a public company, either directly or indirectly, from providing any type of credit to any director or executive officer?

Answer – Since the Sarbanes-Oxley Act's interpretation and administration is within the jurisdiction of the Securities and Exchange Commission, the final split-dollar regulations do not address this issue. Most experts seem to think that collateral assignment split-dollar plans and split-dollar loan arrangement would fall under this Act. It is unlikely that the Act would apply to endorsement type split-dollar arrangements because the employer owns the policy under this arrangement and there is no loan of any premiums—the employee only pays for and is entitled to an interest in the death benefit under such an arrangement. As of the date of this writing, the SEC has expressed no opinion on the application of the Act to split-dollar arrangements.

Therefore, until the SEC provides further guidance, directors and executive officers of public companies should be very wary about paying any new premiums after July 30, 2002 pursuant to a collateral assignment split-dollar or loan arrangement (keeping existing collateral assignment or loan arrangements in place may be okay as long as there are no further extensions of credit, but additional premiums should be paid via a bonus arrangement instead). The plans may be beyond the reach of the Act if the plans can be considered as a binding commitment entered into prior to the Act's effective date and are grandfathered under the Act. The consequences of violating the Act can be severe—up to and including the imposition of fines and criminal penalties. However, remember that Sarbanes-Oxley applies only to senior executives of public companies and not to closely-held companies. Closely-held companies are probably the largest market for split-dollar plans.

CHAPTER ENDNOTES

1. TAM 9604001. This technical advice memorandum questions the tax treatment of equity split-dollar–the first time the IRS had done so. This received so much attention from the insurance industry, it became known as the "infamous TAM." In this private ruling, the IRS indicated that the buildup in the CSV

accruing to the employee is taxable as ordinary income. To say the least, the IRS received a significant amount of commentary from the insurance industry and even the American Bar Association. Notice 2001-10, 2001-1 CB 459, discussed below, is the first official reaction of the IRS as a result of this commentary.

2. 2002-2 CB 481,

3. For more information, see Ratner, Brody, and Mancini, "A New Split-Dollar Imperative," *Trusts and Estates* (March 2008).

4. Treas. Reg. §1.61-22(b)(3).

5. Treas. Reg. §1.61-22(c).

6. Treas. Reg. §1.61-22(d).

7. See Notice 2002-8, 2002-1 CB 398.

8. Treas. Reg. §1.61-22(f).

9. Treas. Reg. §1.61-22(f)(3).

10. Treas. Reg. §1.61-22(g).

11. Treas. Reg. §1.7872-15(a)(2)(i).

12. Treas. Reg. §1.7872-15(a)(2).

13. See I.R.C. §7872.

14. I.R.C. §7872(f).

15. Treas. Reg. §§1.61-22(j), 1.7872-15(n).

16. Treas. Reg. §1.61-22(j)(2).

17. Treas. Reg. §1.61-22(j)(1)(ii).

18. 2002-1 CB 398.

19. See Rev. Rul. 64-328, 1964-2 CB 11.

20. See Rev. Rul. 55-747, 1955-2 CB 228.

21. See Rev. Rul. 66-110, 1966-1 CB 12.

22. Priv. Ltr. Rul. 8547006.

23. Rev. Rul. 67-154, 1967-1 CB 11.

24. Notice 2002-8, 2002-2 CB 398.

25. Notice 2002-8, 2002-2 CB 398.

26. Rev. Rul. 81-198, 1981-2 CB 188; Rev. Rul. 78-420, 1978-2 CB 67.

27. Treas. Reg. §1.61-22(f)(2i).

28. *Neff v. Comm'r*, T.C. Memo. 2012-244 (2012) (footnote 9).

CURRENT TRENDS IN LIFE INSURANCE PLANNING

CHAPTER 42

INTRODUCTION

As any good planner knows, planners must stay on top of current trends in planning in order for their practice to thrive and to remain relevant to clients. The purpose of this chapter is to help planners to stay current by highlighting some of the significant developments that have taken place since the publication of the 5th edition of Tools and Techniques of Life Insurance in 2012 and to discuss their impact on the use of life insurance in planning.

Two such developments were the enactment of The American Taxpayer Relief Act of 2012 (ATRA)[1] (effective at the beginning of 2013) and the United States Supreme Court's ruling in 2013 that a key component of The Defense of Marriage Act (DOMA)[2] was unconstitutional. Below is a discussion of life insurance planning trends created by the rise of ATRA and the demise of DOMA.

PLANNING TRENDS RELATING TO THE RISE OF ATRA

ATRA's Impact on Estate Planning

For over twenty years, from 1987 through 2003, the federal estate and gift exemption remained relatively unchanged (gradually increasing from $600,000 to $1,000,000) and the federal estate tax rate was at least 50 percent. Thus, during this time period the federal estate tax was likely one of the top estate planning concerns for wealthier individuals and couples worth more than $1 million. Using life insurance to provide liquidity for the payment of estate taxes was commonplace and formed the backbone of any professional's practice that incorporated the use of life insurance.

No area of planning was more impacted by ATRA than estate planning. As a result of ATRA, beginning in 2013, the federal estate, gift and generation-skipping tax (GST) exemption was "permanently" set at $5 million per person ($10 million for a married couple), subject to annual adjustments for inflation effective for tax years beginning after 2011 (as of the date of the date of publication of this edition in 2017, the inflation adjusted exemption was $5,490,000). In addition, the estate, gift and GST tax rate was set at a flat rate of 40 percent. Finally, another key provision of ATRA made permanent the portability of the estate tax exemption amount between spouses. This enables any exemption amount unused at the death of the first spouse to be used at the death of the second spouse.[3]

As a result of these changes, it is estimated that less than 1 percent of taxpayers in the United States now have a federal estate tax problem. Thus, ATRA has fundamentally changed many planners' approach to estate planning and the use of life insurance in estate planning. Planners who focused on primarily on the consequences of the federal estate tax needed to adapt their estate planning practices in order to survive. This brings us to our first planning trend arising from ATRA—professionals whose practices focus on the federal estate tax exempt masses (i.e., the other 99 percent of taxpayers) have, out of necessity, become more holistic in their approach to estate planning.

These planners have come to the realization that estate planning is much more than minimizing federal estate taxes and providing liquidity to pay any federal estate taxes. It is the process of preserving wealth and arranging for how to pass on wealth efficiently upon the client's death according to his or her goals and desires. With the recent changes in ATRA, important priorities now include:

- providing for a surviving spouse;

- providing for the orderly transition of a business;

- ensuring that nonbusiness heirs are treated fairly;

- minimizing acrimony in blended families when there are children from former relationships;

- ensuring that outstanding debts are paid off at death;

- providing for special needs children;

- carrying out the charitable goals of the client;

- preserving wealth against the costs of long-term care;

- paying for state death taxes and estate administration and funeral expenses;

- providing a legacy for future generations.

Going beyond estate tax reduction and estate tax liquidity planning involves conducting more in-depth fact finding. It also involves asking some difficult questions, including:

- How do you intend to balance providing for your spouse/partner versus providing for your children?

- When you die, what is the potential for conflict among family members?

- Who do you want to end up with your business and how to you want to treat other family members?

Adapting one's estate planning practice to address the impact of ATRA on estate planning is critical to remaining successful in this planning arena. However, not all the consequences of ATRA on estate planning were negative and certain planners have been able to thrive by focusing on a few estate planning opportunities that resulted from ATRA.

1. *ATRA created an estate planning boom in the ultra high net worth market* – planners fortunate enough to have access to clients that fall into

the top 1 percent of taxpayers have actually benefitted from ATRA. One reason is that ATRA provided estate tax certainty for the ultra-wealthy. With the federal estate, gift and GST exemptions set so high, many no longer realistically believe that the federal estate tax will be permanently repealed. Therefore, the ultra-wealthy are now willing to move forward with their estate planning after years of being in limbo. Another benefit of ATRA is that the ultra wealthy have more to work with in the form of higher exemptions, which enhances their ability to do sophisticated planning (such as dynasty trusts).

2. *ATRA simplified other types of planning for everyone else* – lower net worth individuals and couples may be more likely to engage in certain life insurance planning strategies now that they do not have to worry about the adverse estate tax consequences. For example, purchasing life insurance inside of a qualified plan may be more attractive now that they don't have to get involved in the complexity of creating an irrevocable trust and having the trust purchase the insurance out of the qualified plan. The same is true with using an overfunded cash value life insurance policy to accumulate funds for supplemental retirement income.

3. *ATRA created policy review opportunities for trust owned life insurance* – numerous life insurance trusts were funded with life insurance back when a much larger percentage of the population thought they had a federal estate tax liability. Many of these policies need to be reviewed to ensure they still meet the needs of the clients. These policy reviews may create opportunities to exchange some policies for lower paid up death benefit policies, for better performing policies, or for deferred annuities. Alternatively, there may be the opportunity for a life settlement for policies that are no longer needed for estate tax liquidity purposes.

ATRA's Impact on Income Tax and Business Planning

ATRA also had far reaching consequences for higher-earning taxpayers by enacting several income tax increases. For individual taxpayers with an Adjusted Gross Income (AGI) of more than $400,000 and joint income tax filers making more than $450,000,[4] the top individual income tax rate was increased from 35 to 39.6 percent and the top capital gains rate was increased from 15 to 20 percent. In addition, for individual taxpayers with an AGI of more than $250,000 and joint income tax filers making more than $300,000,[5] ATRA causes a potential phase out of the personal exemption and up to 80 percent of itemized deductions.

As with ATRA's estate and gift tax changes discussed earlier, these four tax increases were effective as of the beginning of 2013. As if that wasn't bad enough for higher earning taxpayers, at the same time several minor tax increases enacted as part of the Patient Protection and Affordable Care Act of 2010[6] became effective. These tax increases included a 3.8 percent Medicare surtax on net investment income and a 0.9 percent Medicare payroll tax surcharge on earned income, which impacted individual taxpayers with a modified AGI of more than $200,000 and joint income tax filers making more than $250,000.

The result of these six income tax increases all coming into play at the same time led to the second planning trend arising from ATRA—many planners revised their practices to focus less on estate planning and more on income tax and business planning. So what ATRA took away from estate planning it partially gave back in the form of income tax and business planning opportunities.

Many higher earning business owners are paying considerably more in income taxes than they were before the enactment of ATRA. These business owners are likely to be open to exploring strategies that can help them reduce their taxable business income, assuming that such strategies otherwise meet a need that they have. Thus, one opportunity enhanced by ATRA is the use of various tax deductible strategies that can be implemented by businesses. Life insurance may or may not play a role in connection with these tax deductible strategies, which include:

1. *Qualified retirement plans (particularly defined benefit plans)* – contributions made to qualified plans on behalf of the business owners are fully deductible. However, qualified retirement plans are subject to nondiscrimination rules, so there can be considerable employee expense involved with a qualified plan. The key is to use them in selective situations where they can provide more of the benefits to the owners of a business. (See Chapter 36 for more details.) For business owners looking for larger deductions, defined benefit plans can potentially provide deductions of $200,000 - $300,000 or more for business owners with less than fifteen years before retirement. Including life insurance in a defined benefit plan can potentially increase the deductible contribution.

2. *Section 419(e) post-retirement medical benefit plans* – businesses that desire to provide post-retirement medical benefits can establish a 419(e) plan and fully deduct contributions to the plan. Similar to qualified retirement plans, 419(e) postretirement medical benefit plans are subject to nondiscrimination rules, so there can be considerable employee expense involved. As a result, if the goal is to primarily benefit a business owner, they will generally be selectively used only in small businesses that have relatively few non-owner employees.

3. *Captive insurance companies* – a captive insurance company is a licensed insurance company that is created for the express purpose of writing property and casualty (P&C) insurance for a specific business or group of businesses. For a business owner with a company or companies (the "parent company") in need of additional P&C coverage to supplement existing commercial coverage, forming a captive may be a way to obtain this coverage in a tax-favored manner. Any premiums paid by the parent company to the captive are fully deductible, and premiums can often be $500,000 - $1,000,000 or more.

4. *Permanent Benefit Section 79 Plans* – a Permanent Benefit Section 79 Plan is a benefit plan designed to provide permanent benefits that are in addition to the group term life insurance coverage available through Code section 79. Under such an arrangement participating employees can typically choose between three options: (a) $50,000 of group term insurance, (b) supplemental term insurance in excess of $50,000 (typically some multiple of compensation), or (c) permanent benefits provided by individually owned cash value life insurance. Premiums paid by the employer for any of the three options are fully tax deductible by the business. A Section 79 Plan is on the only way to directly deduct life insurance premiums.

Another business planning opportunity enhanced by ATRA is the use of voluntary deferral plans with higher compensated non-owner executives of businesses. To the extent that these executives desire to reduce their taxable compensation (potentially below the income limit for the top federal income tax bracket), their employer can implement a voluntary deferral plan, which is a type of non-qualified deferred compensation plan. Participants in the plan can then choose to defer a portion of their salary and bonuses, thus reducing their exposure to income taxes in the current tax year. Any deferrals made into the plan will typically be paid out at a later date, often at retirement, when the executives will hopefully be in a lower tax bracket.

PLANNING TRENDS RELATING TO THE DEMISE OF DOMA

As states began to legalize same-sex marriage in the early part of the twenty-first century, an inevitable conflict arose with the federal Defense of Marriage Act (DOMA), which broadly prohibited the federal government from recognizing the legality of same-sex marriage even when such marriages were permissible under state law. The legal requirements of marriage has always been governed by state law, and DOMA created circumstances in which same-sex couples saw their marriages recognized by some states and ignored by other states and the federal government. This lead to tremendous practical difficulties with things like filing tax returns. Same–sex couples would often have to prepare multiple versions of their returns for the various jurisdictions in which they had tax reporting obligations, filing as married couple in some states and filing as single in other states and on their federal returns. It also complicated insurance planning.

DOMA was overturned by the United States Supreme court in 2013.[7] While this decision allowed federal recognition of same-sex marriages, the situation in the various states is still unclear. A number of states have allowed same-sex marriages through state court decisions or legislative enactments, and there is currently extensive litigation about the legality of same-sex marriage pending. These recent changes and continued uncertainty have given rise to several important insurance planning issues.

1. *Insurable interest* – Recall from Chapter 5 that insurable interest between two individuals is most easily demonstrated by marriage. While there are other ways to achieve an insurable interest, they are complicated and may require circumstances that do not apply to all couples. Same-sex couples should review the current state of the law for their particular states to see if there have been changes in the legal recognition of their marriage which may give rise to additional planning opportunities that were not present just a few years ago.

2. *Second-to-die insurance* – This is another area in which the legal recognition of a marriage is important and may give rise to significant estate planning opportunities. These can include buy-sell agreements and use of second-to-die insurance through an ILIT to provide estate liquidity. Again, clients who may not have previously qualified for this type of insurance because their marriages were not legally recognized may now have additional options if those marriages become recognized due to litigation or changes in state law.

3. *Qualified plan benefits* – A same-sex couple who may not have been recognized as married couple may have been unable to take advantage of various survivorship benefits that are available through qualified retirement plans. These types of benefits are available in both defined contribution and defined benefit plans, so if the couple has recently had their marriage legally recognized, they may be able to utilize newly-available survivorship benefits from a qualified retirement plan. Utilization of these new benefits may in turn change their life insurance needs.

While the litigation currently pending regarding same-sex marriage is far from complete, same-sex couples have already seen significant changes that may affect their life insurance planning requirements. Planner would do well to stay apprised of the latest developments in this area, particularly as they apply to jurisdictions in which their clients live, work, and own property.

CHAPTER ENDNOTES

1. Pub.L. 112–240, H.R. 8, 126 Stat. 2313, enacted January 2, 2013.

2. Pub.L. 104–199, 110 Stat. 2419, enacted September 21, 1996. DOMA is a United States federal law that allows states to refuse to recognize same-sex marriages granted under the laws of other states. Section 3 of the Act was ruled unconstitutional in 2013.

3. An election to elect portability must be made on the Form 706 estate tax return of the first spouse to die.

4. These income thresholds are indexed for inflation.

5. These income thresholds are indexed for inflation.

6. Pub. L. 111-148, H.R. 3590, enacted March 23, 2010 (commonly called the Affordable Care Act).

7. *U.S. v. Windsor*, 1333 S.Ct. 2675 (2013).

TAX TABLES

INCOME TAX

TAXABLE YEARS BEGINNING IN 2017

STANDARD DEDUCTION:

Married, filing jointly	$12,700
Married, filing separately	6,350
Head of Household	9,350
Single	6,350
PERSONAL EXEMPTION:	$4,050

SCHEDULE X
SINGLE INDIVIDUALS

Taxable Income			Tax on Lower Amount	Tax Rate on Excess
$ -0-	to	$ 9,325	$ -0-	10%
9,325	to	37,950	932.50	15%
37,950	to	91,900	5,226.25	25%
91,900	to	191,650	18,713.75	28%
191,650	to	416,700	46,643.75	33%
416,700	to	418,400	120,910.25	35%
418,400	to	......	121,505.25	39.6%

SCHEDULE Y-1 – JOINT RETURNS
AND SURVIVING SPOUSES

Taxable Income			Tax on Lower Amount	Tax Rate on Excess
$ -0-	to	$ 18,650	$ -0-	10%
18,650	to	75,900	1,865.00	15%
75,900	to	153,100	101,452.50	25%
153,100	to	223,050	29,752.50	28%
223,050	to	416,700	52,222.50	33%
416,700	to	470,700	112,728.00	35%
470,700	to	......	131,628.00	39.6%

SCHEDULE Y-2
MARRIED FILING SEPARATELY

Taxable Income			Tax on Lower Amount	Tax Rate on Excess
$ -0-	to	$ 9,325	$ -0-	10%
9,325	to	37,950	932.50	15%
37,950	to	76,550	5,226.25	25%
76,550	to	116,675	14,876.25	28%
116,675	to	208,350	26,111.25	33%
208,350	to	235,350	56,364.00	35%
235,350		......	65,814.00	39.6%

SCHEDULE Z
HEAD OF HOUSEHOLD

Taxable Income			Tax on Lower Amount	Tax Rate on Excess
$ -0-	to	$ 13,150	$ -0-	10%
13,350	to	50,800	1,335.00	15%
50,200	to	131,200	6,952.50	25%
129,600	to	212,500	27,052.50	28%
209,850	to	416,700	49,816.50	33%
411,500	to	444,550	117,202.50	35%
439,000	to	......	126,950.00	39.6%

INCOME TAX (CONTINUED)

ESTATES AND TRUSTS

Taxable Income			Tax on Lower Amount	Tax Rate on Excess
$ -0-	to	$ 2,500	$ -0-	15%
2,550	to	6,000	382.50	25%
6,000	to	9,150	1,245.00	28%
9,150	to	12,500	2,127.00	33%
12,500	to	......	3,232.50	39.6%

CORPORATIONS†

Taxable Income			Tax on Lower Amount	Tax Rate on Excess
$ -0-	to	$ 50,000	$ -0-	15%
50,000	to	75,000	7,500	25%
75,000	to	100,000	13,750	34%
100,000	to	335,000	22,250	39%
335,000	to	10,000,000	113,900	34%
10,000,000	to	15,000,000	3,400,000	35%
15,000,000	to	18,333,333	5,150,000	38%
18,333,333	to	......	6,416,667	35%

†Personal Service Corporations are taxed at a flat rate of 35%.

GIFT AND ESTATE TAX

2013-2017 Gift and Estate Tax Table

Taxable Gift/Estate		Tax on	Rate on
From	To	Col. 1	Excess
$ 0	$ 10,000	$ 0	18%
10,001	20,000	1,800	20%
20,001	40,000	3,800	22%
40,001	60,000	8,200	24%
60,001	80,000	13,000	26%
80,001	100,000	18,200	28%
100,001	150,000	23,800	30%
150,001	250,000	38,800	32%
250,001	500,000	70,800	34%
500,001	750,000	155,800	37%
750,000	1,000,000	248,300	39%
1,000,000		345,800	40%

IRC Secs. 2001(c), 2502(a), 2210, as amended by EGTRRA 2001 and ATRA.

2010 ESTATE AND GIFT TAX TABLE

Taxable Gift/Estate From	To	Tax on Col. 1	Rate on Excess
$ 0	$10,000	$ 0	18%
10,001	20,000	1,800	20%
20,001	40,000	3,800	22%
40,001	60,000	8,200	24%
60,001	80,000	13,000	26%
80,001	100,000	18,200	28%
100,001	150,000	23,800	30%
150,001	250,000	38,800	32%
250,001	500,000	70,800	34%
500,001	....	155,800	35%

2011-2012 Gift and Estate Tax Table

Taxable Gift/Estate From	To	Tax on Col. 1	Rate on Excess
$ 0	$ 10,000	$ 0	18%
10,001	20,000	1,800	20%
20,001	40,000	3,800	22%
40,001	60,000	8,200	24%
60,001	80,000	13,000	26%
80,001	100,000	18,200	28%
100,001	150,000	23,800	30%
150,001	250,000	38,800	32%
250,001	500,000	70,800	34%
500,001	750,000	155,800	35%

IRC Secs. 2001(c), 2502(a), 2210, as amended by EGTRRA 2001.

UNIFIED CREDIT

Estate Tax Unified Credit

Year	Exclusion Equivalent	Unified Credit
2000-2001	$675,000	$220,550
2002-2003	$1,000,000	$345,800
2004-2005	$1,500,000	$555,800
2006-2008	$2,000,000	$780,800
2009	$3,500,000	$1,455,800
2010	$5,000,000	$1,730,800
2011	$5,000,000	$1,730,800
2012	$5,120,000	$1,772,800
2013	$5,250,000	$2,045,800
2014	$5,340,000	$2,081,800
2015	$5,430,000	$2,113,800
2016	$5,450,000	$2,121,800
2017	$5,490,000	$2,141,800

IRC Sec. 2010(c), as amended by EGTRRA 2001 and ATRA. Rev. Proc. 2013-35

Gift Tax Unified Credit

Year	Exclusion Equivalent	Unified Credit
1977 (1-1 to 6-30)	$30,000	$6,000
1977 (7-1 to 12-31)	120,667	30,000
1978	134,000	34,000
1979	147,333	38,000
1980	161,563	42,500
1981	175,625	47,000
1982	225,000	62,800
1983	275,000	79,300
1984	325,000	96,300
1985	400,000	121,800
1986	500,000	155,800
1987-1997	600,000	192,800
1998	625,000	202,050
1999	650,000	211,300
2000-2001	675,000	220,550
2002-2009	1,000,000	345,800
2010	$5,000,000	$1,730,800
2011	$5,000,000	$1,730,800
2012	$5,120,000	$1,772,800
2013	$5,250,000	$2,045,800
2014	$5,340,000	$2,081,800
2015	$5,430,000	$2,113,800
2016	$5,450,000	2,121,800
2017	$5,490,000	2,141,800

IRC Secs. 2505(a), 2010(c), as amended by EGTRRA 2001 and ATRA. Rev. Proc. 2013-35

ACCOUNTING FOR LIFE INSURANCE

INTRODUCTION

Selecting the appropriate risk management and funding strategies in business planning ordinarily requires at least some input from other advisors to the client. Attorneys are integrally involved in drafting agreements and explaining the legal ramifications of transactions. Accountants provide insight into the effects that specific solutions will have for tax as well as financial reporting purposes. The client will best be served when all the client's advisors work as a team and are able to communicate.[1]

In order to minimize any communication problems due to technical terms or a misunderstanding regarding the impact of a specific solution on a specific financial statement, it is useful to review accounting fundamentals and language. Costly or incorrect policies, adverse tax consequences, or an adverse impact on the company's financial statement that is used to obtain corporate loans can each cause the client great distress and possibly cause the client to seek professional guidance elsewhere.

Financial reporting and income tax reporting are two separate and distinct methodologies. Companies will often keep two sets of books to meet the different requirements. The Internal Revenue Code determines tax reporting, the regulations issued by the Internal Revenue Service, the outcome of judicial cases, and various informative rulings and releases. Financial reporting must meet the standards of Generally Accepted Accounting Principles (GAAP), which are a body of rules and interpretations to ensure that financial reporting is transparent and consistent from one organization to another.

The rules and interpretations currently embody statements from the Accounting Principles Board (APB) and the body, which replaced it, the Financial Accounting Standards Board (FASB). The American Institute of Certified Public Accountants develops issues through its Emerging Issues Task Force (EITF) and makes recommendations to the FASB. The FASB issues informative releases that may come in the form of Accounting Opinions, Accounting Interpretations, and Technical Bulletins. This appendix will focus on accounting for financial statement purposes.

FINANCIAL REPORTING

A complete set of financial statements includes:

1. an accountant's report (also called a cover letter) indicating the level of assurance provided by the accountants and any departures from Generally Accepted Accounting Principles (GAAP);

2. an income statement;

3. a balance sheet;

4. a statement of changes in stockholders' equity;

5. a statement of cash flows; and

6. notes to the financial statements.

Additional supplementary information may be provided, for which the accountants may (or may not) provide any assurance.

Accountant's report – The accountant's report is the best place to begin reading the financial statements. It will explain whether the accountants have compiled, reviewed, or audited the financial statements.

- A compilation is an engagement in which the accountant presents the client's information in the appropriate financial statement format without expressing any assurance as to whether the numbers provided by the client are correct.

- A review ordinarily includes analytical review, inquiries of management, and other procedures designed to give limited assurance as to whether the statements are prepared in accordance with GAAP.

- An audit includes an understanding of internal controls and assessment of risk that will lead to auditing procedures designed to provide the highest degree of assurance that the statements are prepared in conformity with GAAP. Accountant's reports for audits are of four types: unqualified, qualified, no opinion, and disclaimer.

Other important information in the accountant's report includes any departures from GAAP and will explain the accountant's position, if any, regarding the effect of the departure on the financial statements. It will indicate any omission, such as the notes to the financial statements or perhaps the statement of cash flows. It may also indicate if there is a concern or uncertainty as to whether the company will continue operating. This concern or uncertainty is expressed as a going concern issue.

The amount of detail to include in the financial statements is always a consideration. While it is desirable to present a simple, summarized statement so that an investor/reader can readily discover the important facts, it is also desirable to fully disclose the results of all activities. Generally, it is expected that the financial statements will provide more than a synoptic report.

Income statement – The income statement shows the current period's income and expense activities since the prior period's financial statements. It may be on an interim (or part-year basis) or a full year basis. It is ordinarily broken down into operating activities and nonoperating activities so that the user may segregate recurring and unusual (referred to as extraordinary) activities from typical day-to-day operations. It provides the income and loss information for the activity. The following is an example of a moderately detailed income statement:

INCOME STATEMENT

For the Year Ended December 31, xxxx

Gross Sales Revenue	$1,000,000
Less: Sales Discounts, Returns and Allowances	$ 10,000
Net Sales Revenue	$ 990,000
Less: Cost of Goods Sold	$ 490,000
Beginning Inventory	$ 125,000
Plus: Purchases (less Discounts)	$ 573,000
Freight & Transportation-in	$ 42,000
Total Inventory Available for Sale	$ 740,000
Less: Ending Inventory	$ 250,000
Cost of Goods Sold	$ 490,000
Gross Profit on Sales	$ 500,000
Less: Operating Expenses	
Selling Expenses	$ 200,000
Administrative Expenses	$ 100,000
Income from Operations	$ 200,000
Other Revenue & Gains	
Dividend & Rental Income	$ 20,000
Other Expenses & Losses	
Interest Paid on Bonds & Notes	$ 10,000
Income before taxes	$ 210,000
Less: Income taxes	30,000
Income before extraordinary item	$ 180,000
Less: Loss from extraordinary item	100,000
Net Income	$ 80,000
Earnings per Common Share	$ 0.80

Balance sheet – The balance sheet is a snapshot of the company's financial condition at the end of business activity on a given day. It will ordinarily include the company's assets, liabilities, and the owners' or shareholders' equity. Basically, the balance sheet shows what the company owns. Assets are shown at historical cost (defined later). The balance sheet also shows what is owed on those assets. It shows in report form the fundamental accounting equation:

$$ASSETS = LIABILITIES + EQUITY$$

This means that what the business has–less what it owes–leaves the owners' equity (what they own). This principle can be easily understood in terms of a simple personal asset like a residence. Because of the "=" sign, one side of the equation *must* equal the other side for the equation to balance. This, of course, is the derivation of the term balance sheet.

As mentioned above, most of the information included in the balance sheet is stated at historical cost, the price originally paid by the business for the asset.

The theory of historical cost has a number of weaknesses, but remains the standard.

There are a number of exceptions to the historical cost rule. Among these are:

- Obsolescent inventory

- A loss on marketable securities such as stocks or an impairment of fixed assets

- Fixed assets, such as real estate or equipment, which are shown at original cost less an allowance for depreciation (which is used to reflect the accounting expression of the recovery of the cost of an asset over its useful life).[2]

The key point to understand is that balance sheet figures are not necessarily intended to represent the current fair market or net realizable values of the assets (and often are quite different from those figures). The balance sheet is based on the going concern concept which assumes that the business will remain in existence rather than be liquidated. The following is an example of a synoptic balance sheet:

BALANCE SHEET

As of December 31, xxxx

ASSETS

Current Assets

Cash and cash equivalents	$ 40,000
Accounts Receivable-trade	100,000
Inventories	50,000
Prepaid Expenses	10,000
Total current assets	$200,000
Long-Term Investments	
Property, Plant and Equipment, Less: Depreciation	300,000
Other Asset-Cash Surrender Value of Insurance	10,000
Intangible Assets - Goodwill	50,000
Total Assets	$560,000

LIABILITIES AND
STOCKHOLDERS' EQUITY

Current Liabilities:

Accounts payable	$ 25,000
Notes & Accrued Interest Payable	0
Accrued salaries, wages	0
Deposits Received from customers	0
Total current liabilities	$ 25,000

Long-term Debt	75,000
Deferred Income Taxes	10,000
Total Liabilities	$160,000

Stockholders' Equity

Common Stock (100,000 shares @ $1.00 par/sh	100,000
Preferred Stock	0
Retained Earnings	$300,000
Total stockholders' equity	$400,000

Total Liabilities and Stockholders' Equity	$560,000

Statement of changes – The statement of changes in stockholders' equity reflects all activity occurring to equity accounts during the financial statement period. This activity is usually related to the issuance or repurchase of the company's stock. The following is an example of a simplified statement of changes:

STATEMENT OF CHANGES IN STOCKHOLDERS' EQUITY

For the Year Ended December 31, xxxx

	Common Stock	Retained Earnings	Total Stockholders' Equity
Balance as of January 1, xxxx	$100,000	$250,000	$350,000
Net Income		70,000	70,000
Dividends		(20,000)	(20,000)
Balance as of December 31, xxxx	$100,000	$300,000	$400,000

Statement of cash flows – The statement of cash flows shows changes in the cash element (in terms of sources and uses of cash) and cash flows of the company that took place during the financial statement period. It is particularly relevant to the planner in determining whether sufficient cash flow is available to meet the needs of the business and fund other objectives such as life insurance premiums, nonqualified deferred compensation contributions, or contributions to employee benefit or retirement plans. The following is an example of a simplified statement of cash flows:

STATEMENT OF CASH FLOWS
For the Year Ended December 31, xxxx

Cash Flows Provided from (Used by) Operating Activities	
Income from continuing operations	$170,000
Adjustments to reconcile income from continuing operations to net cash provided from continuing operations	10,000
Depreciation and amortization	10,000
Changes in assets and liabilities:	
Accounts receivable-trade	1,000
Inventories	(2,200)
Accounts payable	1,000
Other assets and liabilities	250
Net cash provided from Operating Activities	$180,050
Cash Flows Provided from (Used by) Investing Activities Capital additions	$(120,000)
Net Cash (Used by) Investing Activities	$(120,000)
Repayment of long-term debt	$(10,000)
Cash dividends paid	(20,000)
Net Cash (Used by) Financing Activities	$(30,000)
Increase (Decrease) in Cash and Cash Equivalents	$ 30,050
Cash and Cash Equivalents as of January 1, xxxx	9,950
Cash and Cash Equivalents as of December 31, xxxx	$ 40,000
Interest Paid (Continuing Operations)	$ 7,500
Income Taxes Paid (Continuing Operations)	$ 30,000

Notes to the financial statement – The notes to the financial statement will ordinarily contain vast amounts of useful information including, but not limited to:

- the accounting methods utilized;

- leases and terms;

- loans and loan repayment terms;

- detailed fixed asset information;

- related party transactions;

- income taxes; and

- information regarding subsequent events that occurred after the financial statement closing but before the financial statement release.

INTERNATIONAL STANDARDS

As insurers have become larger and rely increasingly on reinsurance contracts offered by multination insurers, they have also started experience tension between international regulatory systems. In the United States, insurers are primarily regulated at the state level for their insurance operations and at the federal level for their corporate, accounting, and taxation issues. Currently, the U.S. GAAP accounting standards are required only for publicly traded companies under federal securities law. The standards are consolidated in the Accounting Codification Standards (ACS).

Multinational insurers face potential conflicts between regulatory schemes in the United States and Europe. While the SEC and IRS follow GAAP, European insurers are regulated by the Basel III accord.[3] Basel III is a voluntary (though widely adopted) set of rules governing financial institutions, and it utilizes the internationally-recognized International Financial Reporting Standards (IFRS) rather than GAAP. Since first becoming a mandatory requirement in European Union countries in 2005, IFRS has become the financial accounting standard in more than one hundred countries. Financial professionals working with public companies need to be aware of these changes as they come into existence.

Regulatory authorities are on track to make the International Financial Reporting Standards (IFRS) a requirement for all publicly traded companies in the U.S., Canada, and Mexico over the next few years. For public companies in these countries, the transition to IFRS will be the most significant regulatory change in many years and one with potential to directly impact overall competitive position.

With regard to private companies (nonpublicly traded), U.S. GAAP standards have been applied to private companies planning to go public, since they would eventually be required to comply with the standards.

There is an organized effort in the accounting industry to implement a separate private company GAAP. Although the direction seems to be to take the current GAAP and simply modify it for private companies, over time it seems that a separate set of standards is needed for the private company, especially since U.S. GAAP is becoming increasingly more "internationalized". This separate set of standards would help make them compatible with foreign public companies. This proposal to create a separate GAAP for private companies is an important project, since it will bear on the accounting procedures that private companies would be using to account for all purposes, but including all their executive benefit plans, like nonqualified deferred compensation and stock options.

Basel III also contains its own set of regulations that cover reserve requirements and risk management. Insurers that do business both domestically and internationally are currently developing plans to accommodate both the IFRS and GAAP reporting.[4]

The rest of this Appendix will focus on GAAP accounting standards, however practitioners should be aware of the increasing importance of IFRS in the insurance field.

ACCOUNTING BASICS

Business accounting systems ordinarily use what is commonly referred to as double-entry accounting. Double entry accounting is based on a notion similar to that put forth by Sir Isaac Newton in his third law of motion: "For every action, there is an equal and opposite reaction." These actions are given the names debit and credit in accounting. And just as Newton's Laws of Motion carried no particular connotation of good or bad, debits and credits are generally interpreted in a similarly neutral manner.

Once the professional is able to put aside the good and bad connotation of debits and credits, the mind is free to comprehend how the accounting system functions.

Staying in general terms and referring to the balance sheet equation:

$$ASSETS = LIABILITIES + EQUITY$$

Another general truth is that for every debit there must be a credit and vice-versa:

$$DEBITS = CREDITS$$

So, for every debit entry, there must be an equal and opposite credit entry. There must always be a balancing of the books.

One final general rule necessary to understand the environment is the bridge across the first two equations:

Certain accounts generally carry debit balances while other accounts (equal and opposite but not good or bad) generally carry credit balances.

Here are some general rules of thumb:

- Assets generally have debit balances. Therefore, liabilities and equity accounts must have credit balances.

- Expense and loss accounts ordinarily have debit balances. Revenue and gain accounts must therefore ordinarily have credit balances.

DEBIT BALANCE ACCOUNTS	CREDIT BALANCE ACCOUNTS
Assets	Liabilities
Expenses	Stockholder Equity
Losses	Revenue
	Gains

Specific transactions, commonly referred to as journal entries, may adjust a debit or credit type account. The key to understanding what impact the transaction has on a specific account is to note what accounts ordinarily have debit and credit balances. Some specific examples may serve to clarify the rules:

Debit (Dr.) Cash 100
Credit (Cr.) Sales 100

The above would be a journal entry to reflect a sale for cash. The debit to cash, a debit balance account in the balance sheet, would serve to *increase* the debit balance, or show *more* cash. The credit to sales in the income statement, a credit balance account, would serve to *increase* the credit balance, or show *more* sales.

(Dr.) Insurance Expense	50	
(Cr.) Cash		50

The above entry is an example of a debit and a credit that both affect debit balance accounts. The debit entry to "insurance expense" in the income statement serves to increase the debit balance or increase insurance expense. The credit entry to "cash" in the balance sheet, a debit balance account, serves to reduce the debit balance in the cash account. This is logical because the balance in the cash account is reduced when the expense is paid.

This background is necessary to understand accounting for life insurance. The basic rules are:

1. Cash surrender values will generally be assets of the company if the company owns the policy and is the beneficiary.

2. Cash values will carry debit balances on the balance sheet.

3. The current insurance expense will also carry a debit balance on the income statement.

4. Any income from the policy, including a death benefit, or any increase in the cash surrender value in excess of the premium paid in the current period will be a credit entry to an income (credit) account.

The debit/credit rules and effects on each type of account are illustrated in the following diagram. Study it to understand the fundamentals.

ASSETS = LIABILITIES + STOCKHOLDER EQUITY

ACCOUNTING RULES SPECIFICALLY AFFECTING LIFE INSURANCE

The most common forms of life insurance that companies carry on their officers and stockholders are term and permanent insurance (including limited pay, ordinary whole life, universal, or variable universal life). Term insurance generally has no cash surrender value and thus represents only a pure insurance expense. Permanent insurance may have a cash surrender value and a loan value in addition to the insurance expense.

If the insured officers or their heirs are the beneficiaries of the policy, the premiums paid by the company represent compensation expense (or possibly a dividend) rather than insurance expense and represent income to the officer insured. In this case, the cash surrender value may not be an asset of the corporation. (If the company is both owner and beneficiary of the policy, then the policy may be an asset of the company.)

Here are some accounting guidelines for life insurance:

1. Unearned premiums (prepaid insurance) are classified as part of "working capital,"[5] but cash surrender values are not.[6]

2. "Loans accompanied by pledge of life insurance policies should be classified as current liabilities when, by their terms or by intent, they are to be repaid within twelve months."[7] (So short-term loans that are based on the policy as collateral should be shown as current liabilities.)

3. When a loan on a life insurance policy is obtained from the insurance company with the intent that it will not be paid but will be liquidated by deduction from the proceeds of the policy upon maturity or cancellation, the obligation should be excluded from current liabilities. (So loans that are not intended to be repaid in the short-term, such as loans that will be satisfied at the time of the maturity of the policy, should not be treated as short-term liabilities, which means that those loans do not reduce working capital).

								Common Retained					
Assets	=	Liabilities	+	Stock	+	Earnings	−	Dividends	+	Revenues	−	Expenses	
Dr. | Cr.		Dr. | Cr.		Dr. | Cr.		Dr. | Cr.		Dr. | Cr.		Dr. | Cr.		Dr. | Cr.	
+ | −		− | +		− | +		− | +		+ | −		− | +		+ | −	

4. If a company takes out policy loans from the insurance company on life insurance policies that it owns and if there is no intention to repay the loan during the ensuing operating cycle of the business, such loan may be excluded from current liabilities.[8]

5. The amount of the loan should be shown to reduce the cash surrender value, with disclosure of the amount so offset.[9]

6. Where a corporation maintains life insurance policies on its principal stockholders to fund the purchase of stock in the event of a stockholder's death, the footnote disclosure should first show the cash surrender value on the balance sheet[10] and then indicate disclosure of any commitments.

Example. The company is the owner and beneficiary of key employee life insurance policies carried on the lives of X, Y, and Z bearing face value amounts of $500,000, $500,000 and $450,000 respectively. No loans are outstanding against the policies, but there is no restriction in the policies regarding loans. These life insurance contracts are accompanied by mandatory stock purchase agreements to the amount of the proceeds of the life insurance. In the event of the insured's death, the 'fair market value' of the stock will, by previous action, be established by the A Appraisal Company. The insured's estate will be obligated to sell, and the company will be obligated to purchase the insured's stock up to the appraisal value of the stock or the proceeds of insurance, whichever is the lesser. The purpose is to protect the company against an abrupt change in ownership or management.

So the original position taken by the accounting profession was that the cash surrender value, less any policy loans, which were intended to be satisfied by set-off, should be shown as a noncurrent asset. Also, the portion of the insurance premium shown as an expense would be the difference between the premium payment and the increase in cash surrender value.

Examples of Accounting Journal Entries

If Corporation X pays an insurance premium of $4,800 on a $100,000 policy that covers its president and the policy's cash surrender value increases from $20,000 to $22,000, the proper journal entry would be:

Life Insurance Expense (Dr.)	2,800
Cash Surrender Value of Insurance (Dr.)	2,000
Cash (Cr.)	4,800

If the insured officer died half-way through the most recent period of coverage for which the $4,800 premium was made, the following entry would be made (assuming cash surrender value of $21,000 and refund of a pro rata share of the premium paid):

Cash	102,400
Cash Surrender Value of Insurance	21,000
Life Insurance Expense	2,400
Gain on Life Insurance Coverage	79,000

The gain on life insurance coverage is not generally reported as an extraordinary item because it is considered to be an ordinary business transaction.

Alternative Methods

This line of thinking came under attack a number of times and for a number of reasons. During the late 1960's and throughout the 1970's, new methods for expensing the insurance cost were offered to try to cure what was perceived as a significant flaw. This flaw is best highlighted by way of an example:[11]

TABLE 1
$100,000 LIFE PAID-UP AT AGE 65

Year	Annual Premium	Cash Value Increase	Total Premiums	Total Cash Value
1	$7,767	$1,344	$ 7,767	$ 1,344
2	7,767	6,119	15,534	7,463
3	7,767	6,308	23,301	13,771
4	7,767	6,514	31,068	20,285
5	7,767	6,741	38,835	27,026
6	7,767	6,991	46,602	34,017
7	7,767	7,272	54,369	41,289
8	7,767	7,589	62,136	48,878
9	7,767	7,951	69,903	56,829
10	7,767	8,365	77,670	65,194

Note: Maximum premium deposits	$77,670
Guaranteed cash value at age 65	65,194
Aggregate net cost	$12,476

Which would provide the following charges against income:

Year	Annual	Cumulative
1	$6,423	$ 6,423
2	1,648	8,071
3	1,459	9,530
4	1,253	10,783
5	1,026	11,809
6	776	12,585
7	495	13,080
8	178	13,258
9	184 Cr.	13,074
10	598 Cr.	12,476

The example clearly shows that the charge to income is significantly higher in the early years, particularly year 1, and yet the benefit provided in each year is the same. One solution that has been proposed is called the "Ratable Charge Method." This method amortizes, or expenses the true cost of the insurance coverage in a straight line (i.e., ratably in equal increments) over the period of coverage. In the example this would mean that the $12,476 cost would have been expensed over the ten years at the rate of $1,247.60 per year.

This solution was based on the premise that a company buys a policy to cover a fixed period of time and the net costs should be recognized evenly over that period of time. A variation of the ratable charge method adjusts the charge against income by taking into account the time value of the money involved.

One method follows the treatment of policies on the books of the life insurance company. The flaw with a small company using the same accounting as a life insurer is that the actuarial assumptions appropriate when a large group of policies is involved breaks down when the employer company holds just one or only a relatively few policies. Yet another accounting method charges an amount against earnings measured by the pure insurance portion of the payment (similar to the term insurance costs, such as P.S. 58 or Table 2001, used by the IRS).

It is important to understand that these alternative methods do *not* fall within the realm of Generally Accepted Accounting Principles (GAAP). This means that although they may provide a more desirable (and perhaps realistic) result in the early policy years than would be available under GAAP, the use of any of these alternatives would require a cover letter explaining the

deviation and could prevent the accountant from providing an unqualified opinion (the equivalent of an A).

On November 14, 1985 the Financial Accounting Standards Board issued FASB Technical Bulletin No. 85-4, Accounting for Purchases of Life Insurance.[12] This Bulletin stated the FASB's position (effective for insurance policies acquired after November 14, 1985). The Technical Bulletin clearly stated in response to the question of how an entity should account for an investment in insurance:

- "The amount that could be realized under the insurance contract as of the date of the statement of financial position should be reported as an asset."

- "The change in cash surrender or contract value during the period is an adjustment of premiums paid in determining the expense or income to be recognized under the contract for the period."

The Technical Bulletin was intended to apply to "all entities that purchase life insurance in which the entity is either the owner or the beneficiary of the contract, without regard to the funding objective of the purchase. Such purchases would typically include those intended to meet loan covenants or to fund deferred compensation agreements, buy-sell agreements, or post-employment death benefits."

The Technical Bulletin recognized that an insurance contract is significantly different from most investments and that payment may take a number of different forms. It concluded that the:

"...pattern of premium payments is a decision that does not alter the underlying nature of the insurance contract. ... A portion of the premium [is for the] mortality risk and provides for recovery of the insurers contract acquisition, initiation, and maintenance costs. Another portion of the premium contributes to the accumulation of cash values. ... The relative amounts of premium payment credited to various contract attributes change over time as the age of the insured party increases and as earnings are credited to previously established contract values."

Respondents to this proposed technical bulletin argued that the primary objective of a life insurance contract is investment. Some argued that the company acquiring the policy is, in many cases, economically or contractually committed to maintaining the contract in force. Both positions concluded that different values should be assigned than the settlement or cash surrender values because of the significant factors.

But both arguments were flatly rejected. The FASB found no compelling justification for departure from the contractually agreed upon settlement values between the buyer and seller (company and insurer) and stated that the arguments either had to do with future events, in which case it would be inappropriate to address them now, or that they just did not change the measurement of the agreed upon settlement values.

The FASB also rejected the argument that a business exchange rider made the accounting for life insurance incorrect. The FASB noted that:

"Such a provision does not affect the realization of future benefits under the insurance contract, nor does it change the traditional underwriting decisions involved in insuring a new life. Instead, the provision only reduces the cost of obtaining those benefits by allowing a new employee to be insured without the costs that are typically associated with obtaining a new policy."

FASB 96, Accounting for Income Taxes, indicates that the temporary difference for the excess of cash surrender value of life insurance over premiums paid is an example of the type of transaction that must be analyzed to determine the deferred income tax consequences. Conservatism requires that the deferred tax computation take into account any taxable income that would be recognized if a policy were surrendered.

To offset the negative impact on earnings created by a business-owned life insurance contract in the early years, many companies have designed contracts especially for business use, without surrender charges so that the first-year cash value can equal or exceed the first year premium. Other companies offer riders that allow the owner to pay an extra premium to eliminate the surrender charge. For larger face amounts, private placement contracts are often used to alleviate the issues.

Journal Entries for a Deferred Compensation Plan

Typically, the frequent occasion for concern over the accounting rules for life insurance is in the use of life insurance to finance an executive nonqualified deferred compensation plan. In the basic arrangement, the executive(s) elect(s) to forgo receipt of a portion of their compensation (salary and/or bonus) until a later date, usually retirement or a specified time in the future. While a comprehensive discussion of executive compensation planning techniques is not appropriate in this discussion, the reader is urged to refer to the several books written by Louis R. Richey and others focused on Code section 409A and its application.[13]

The sample entries for a typical plan would be similar to those below based on the accounting procedures of the particular corporate plan sponsor for a multiple participant plan.

TECHNICAL ACCOUNTING UPDATE FOR NONQUALIFIED PLANS

With the implementation of the Accounting Standards Codification (ASC) project to integrate all sources of U.S. GAAP standards, and the subsequent project to integrate U.S. GAAP (as codified in ASC) with the international standards (IFRS), there has been some confusion about the accounting authority for nonqualified pension style deferred compensation plans.

Most nonqualified pension plan practitioners know that the primary sources of accounting treatment authority in FAS 87 and 106 have found their way into ASC 715, entitled "Compensation-Retirement Benefits", and FAS 109 (as to the future income tax deduction) into ASC 74, entitled "Income Taxes".

There was some difficulty, initially locating some more rarified authority, for instance, like the accounting for the use of company stock in funding a nonqualified deferred compensation plan. This accounting issue was originally treated in ETIF 97-14. That guidance has now been incorporated into ASC 710, entitled "Compensation-General". Incidentally, ASC 710 is also the location for old APB 12, which was one of the important original sources for accounting for nonqualified arrangements that were treated as individual contracts rather than as a "plan". Section 710 applies only to arrangements that are to be treated as "individual contracts", so this would appear to apply to the situation of company stock used as funding with a nonqualified pension type plan.

DESCRIPTION BENEFIT ENTRIES	ACCOUNT NAME	DEBIT	CREDIT
To accrue compensation expense incurred, but not paid	Compensation Expense	300,000	
	Deferred Compensation Liability		300,000
To accrue interest expense incurred on deferred compensation	Compensation Expense	24,000	
	Deferred Compensation Liability		24,000
To record deferred tax benefit on compensation	Deferred Tax Benefit	90,000	
	Income Tax Expense		90,000
To Record Payment of Deferred Compensation	Deferred Compensation Liability	324,000	
	Cash		324,000
To Record Reduction in Taxes Paid as a Result of the Payment of Deferred Compensation	Cash	90,000	
	Deferred Tax Benefit		90,000
NET FINANCING ENTRIES			
To Record the Insurance Premium Paid	Increase in Cash Value	300,000	
	Cash		300,000
To Record Increase in Cash Value	Insurance Cash Value	309,000	
	Increase in Cash Value		309,000
To Record the Death Benefit Proceeds(Not actually recorded until the death of a plan participant)	Cash	100,000	
	Gain on Death Benefit		70,000
	Insurance Cash Value		30,000

SUMMARY

Generally Accepted Accounting Principles (GAAP) continues to recognize conservatively only the cash surrender value method of accounting for life insurance policies.[14] Any other method will be deemed to be a departure from GAAP if based on future possible events and assumptions applicable to unamortized deferred charges and should be discussed with the company's accountants.

Policy loans may, under certain circumstances, be set off against the cash surrender value rather than be reported as a liability on the balance sheet. The general reporting rules apply whether the policy is funding a buy-sell, a nonqualified deferred compensation plan,[15] or just protecting the interests of the business like a key employee policy.

Accounting for key employee life insurance depends on the type of policy:

- *Term insurance* – Premium payments represent a pure current expense. Such costs should be charged against income rather than retained earnings.

- *Permanent (cash value)* – Premium payments are bifurcated. To the extent a premium payment generates an increase in the policy's cash value, a charge should be made to an asset account. To the extent the premium paid exceeds the increase in the policy's cash value, a charge should be made to expense.

- *Cash values* – The firm's balance sheet should show policy cash values as a noncurrent asset.

- *Death proceeds* – When an insured dies, the gain upon the receipt of the insurance payment is typically reflected as a "special entry for nonrecurring amounts" on the Annual Statement of Operations. Alternatively, the gain on receipt by a corporation of death proceeds may be carried directly to the business's Retained Earnings Account since it is in effect adjusting prior years' activities.

WHERE CAN I FIND OUT MORE?

1. *Accounting Standards – Original Pronouncements Issued Through June 1973* (Financial Accounting Standards Board), Chapters 2 and 3.

2. *AICPA Technical Practice Aids – As of June 1, 1989* (AICPA), p. 1391.

3. *Accounting Standards – Original Pronouncements July 1973-June 1, 1987* (Financial Accounting Standards Board), pp. 1441-1443.

4. Louis Richey, Richard Baier, and Lawrence Brody, *The Nonqualified Deferred Compensation Advisor*, 4th ed. (Cincinnati, OH: The National Underwriter Company, 2006).

5. Stephan R. Leimberg and John McFadden, *The Tools and Techniques of Employee Benefit and Retirement Planning*, 12th ed. (Cincinnati, OH: The National Underwriter Company, 2012).

ENDNOTES

1. This appendix was originally written expressly for *The Tools & Techniques of Life Insurance Planning* by Barton Francis, CPA, CFP, of Ernst and Young, and edited by the authors. We express appreciation David Parsons, CPA/PFS, CLU, ChFC®, CFP® for his significant assistance in revising this material.

2. This is not intended to be a clear and complete explanation of depreciation, but rather a familiarization with the concept that a piece of equipment, such as a business car, will benefit a number of accounting periods and the original cost or the reduction in value should not be charged against the income statement of one period. The depreciation allowance attempts to expense the vehicle over the periods that it is used to match the annual expense of its use against operating activities.

3. For an overview of the Basel III accord, see "International regulatory framework for banks (Basel III)," Bank for International Settlements (BIS) at: http://www.bis.org/bcbs/basel3.htm.

4. See "International Financial Reporting for Insurers," Society of Actuaries, IFRS Seminar (Aug. 20, 2103) available at: https://www.soa.org/files/pd/2013/ifrs/2013-hk-ifrs-30-horbatt.pdf.

5. According to ARB (Accounting Research Bulletin) 43, the balance sheet is "…the connecting link between successive income statements." Working capital is defined as "…the excess of current assets over current liabilities, the relatively liquid portion of total enterprise capital which constitutes a margin or buffer for meeting obligations within the ordinary operating cycle of the business." It identifies current assets as specifically including "prepaid expenses such as insurance."

6. According to ARB 43, "This concept of the nature of current assets contemplates the exclusion from that classification of such resources as: (a) cash and claims to cash which are restricted as to withdrawal or use for other than current operations, are designated for expenditure in the acquisition or construction of noncurrent assets, or are segregated for the liquidation of long-term debts; …(d) cash surrender values of life insurance policies…"

7. Footnote to ARB 43. The pledging of life insurance policies does not affect the classification of the asset any more than does the pledging of receivables, inventories, real estate, or other assets as collateral for a short-term loan.

8. Technical Practice Aids – Section 2240, Paragraph 7-1 of Accounting Principles Board Opinion No. 10 states: "It is a general principle of accounting that the offsetting of assets and liabilities in the balance sheet is improper except where a right of setoff exists." See also AICPA Technical Practice Aids Section 2240.

9. This is appropriate since the owner of a policy normally has the right to offset the loan against the proceeds received on maturity or cancellation of the policy.

10. A question was raised as to whether showing the cash surrender value as an asset was misleading if the company never intended to use the cash surrender value in operating. The response was: "If the enterprise retains all valuable contract rights incident to ownership of the life insurance policy, then it is mandatory from the standpoint of full accountability to reflect the asset status of the cash surrender value of the policy. Not to reflect the cash surrender value would be tantamount to creating a hidden reserve which would be contrary to generally accepted accounting principles."

11. See Gatewood, "Accounting for Business Life Insurance: The Ratable Charge Method," *CLU Journal*, July, 1967, p. 11; Tolan, "An Accrual Basis Alternative to Cash Basis Accounting for Corporate Life Insurance," *CLU Journal*, July, 1967, p. 60; Hodges, "Accounting for Corporate Owned Life Insurance," *CLU Journal*, January, 1978, p. 44, and Chapter 6 (Accounting for Deferred Compensation) in L. Richey and L. Brody, *Comprehensive Deferred Compensation*, 3rd ed. (Cincinnati, OH: The National Underwriter Company, 1997).

12. The Technical Bulletin included information regarding the thinking behind continuing to account for policies using the cash surrender value method and explained the thinking behind the rejection of other methods. The Technical Bulletin was released in response to the AICPA's Accounting Standards Executive Committee (AcSEC) concern that a number of different methods would be utilized in practice if GAAP was not clarified.

13. Richey & Baird, *The Nonqualified Plan Advisor: Covered and Exempt Retirement Plans under Section 409A*, 4th ed. (The National Underwriter Co., 2006). Berglund & Richey, *Section 409A: The 100 Most Frequently Asked Questions*, (ALI-ABA, 2011).

14. The authors' opinion is that the GAAP method of accounting described above is antiquated and does not reflect the economic reality of the transactions over time considering the present

products and riders available to businesses in the early twenty-first century.

The alternative "ratable charge" method seems to provide a more realistic approach and has been used by a number of accounting firms even though it is not officially accepted. (See the unofficial statement of the Accountancy Principles Board in the *Journal of Accountancy*, November, 1970.)

In essence, under the ratable charge method total premiums to be paid over a predetermined period (such as for 10 years or to age fifty-five) are determined on the assumption that the insured is likely to live and will continue to remain an employee of the business that long. The guaranteed cash surrender value at the end of the selected period is then subtracted from the total premiums to be paid. The result is a net cost which is then amortized (ratably) as a level annual charge over the premium paying period.

This prime assumption upon which the ratable charge method relies becomes more likely if the policy in question contains what is often called a policy exchange rider, an option the client's firm has to continue the policy on another life if the insured employee should decide to leave the firm. In other words the company could substitute a new key employee for the one no longer employed (in most cases the rider allows the exchange with no additional costs to the client's company). The existence of an exchange rider would seem to offer an answer to the criticism that if the policy is discontinued prior to the end of the selected premium payment period, the ratable charge method would result in a large write-off of an unamortized deferred charge.

15. FASB 106 should be reviewed where life insurance policies are funding vehicles for nonqualified deferred compensation plans. This release affects the accounting for these plans and may directly impact the timing of the recognition of the liability for postretirement benefits, while having no direct impact on the accounting for the underlying insurance product.

GLOSSARY[1]

absolute assignment: A transfer of a policy through which the policyowner shifts full and absolute control and all policy rights to the assignee. See also: assignment; collateral assignment.

absolute ownership: All legal rights and control of the incidents of ownership (e.g., selection of beneficiaries, settlement options, etc.) in a policy, without limitation, qualification, or restriction, are held by the policyowner.

accelerated option: Accumulated dividends and cash value are used to pay-up a life insurance policy sooner than scheduled.

accidental death benefit: An optional provision that provides an additional payment for loss of life due to an accident that was the direct cause of death. If the additional amount equals the face amount of the policy, this provision is frequently called a "double indemnity" provision. Some companies issue "ADB" in multiples of two or three times the face amount. See also: double indemnity.

account: The individual cash-value investment funds in a variable life insurance product. Also the cash-value accumulation account of universal or current-assumption policies.

accumulated dividends: Dividends left with the insurer to accumulate at interest. These dividends are generally income tax free but the interest is taxable as earned.

actuarial assumptions: An insurer, in establishing premium rates, scheduling policy cash values, and projecting future dividends must make certain estimates. The most important assumptions are based on probabilities of death using large numbers of insureds (so called mortality assumptions) and assumptions about interest and capital gains as well as sales commissions and other expenses.

actuarial cost: Projected cost as ascertained through assumptions and reduced to present values.

actuarial equivalent: Mathematically equivalent from an actuarial cost standpoint. For any type of life insurance policy or annuity issued by an insurer there are (theoretically at least) actuarial equivalent (i.e., mathematically equal) policies or annuities with different features or terms. For example, for any particular level-premium whole life policy with a given premium level there is some (higher) level of premium that will make a 10-pay life policy its actuarial equivalent.

actuarial present value: The present worth of an amount or stream of payments receivable in the future, where each future amount is discounted at an assumed rate of interest and adjusted for the probability that it will in fact be received.

actuary: A professional highly educated in a number of fields such as mathematics, statistics, and accounting. An actuary must have superior knowledge as to the underlying principles of life insurance and their mirror image, annuities. Actuaries are responsible for creating new life insurance products and their pricing, value, and profit structures.

additional death benefit: See also: accidental death benefit; double indemnity.

additional premium: The amount of gross premium in excess of the recommended or "target premium" for the policy in universal and variable universal life policies.

additional provisions: Each life insurance contract contains "insuring" and "benefit" provisions as well as "uniform" provisions that define and limit coverage. Additional (general) provisions are often inserted into a contract to add to the protections, options, or flexibility of the policyowner.

adhesion: There is no true bargaining or "meeting of the minds" in a life insurance contract. Bluntly, a policyowner can "take it or leave it" but may not bargain for specific terms or conditions. In other words, the party who buys life insurance must adhere to an established, pre-existing standard contract and its terms. The law provides special protection to one forced to accept a contract of adhesion and, other things being equal, will interpret the terms of such a document in favor of the policyowner rather than the insurer.

adjustable death benefit: Certain life insurance products allow the policyowner to increase or decrease the face amount (within limits and often only with evidence of insurability). For instance, universal and adjustable life policyowners can increase or decrease the amount of death benefit payable by adjusting the level of their premium payments.

adjustable life insurance: Many of the most attractive features of both term and whole life are contained in this highly flexible type of coverage. Premiums, death benefits, duration of coverage, and cash value levels can all be adjusted (both upward and downward within limits) by the policyowner to meet changing needs and circumstances.

adjustable premium: Term applicable to policies where the company has the contractual right to modify or change premium payments under certain specified conditions or to policies where the policyowner has the right to change scheduled premiums in universal or adjustable life.

adjusted gross estate: The adjusted gross estate is the gross estate less debts, funeral costs, and administrative expenses. This adjusted gross estate is the starting point for the balance of the federal estate tax computation and serves planners as a rough approximation of the before-death tax amount of assets that heirs might receive.

adjusted taxable gifts: Sum of taxable portion of post-1976 gifts other than those for any reason included in a deceased's gross estate.

administrator: The person or persons appointed by the probate (also called Surrogates' or Orphans') court to settle the estate of a person who died without a valid will. See also: executor.

admitted assets: In regulating insurers, a state insurance department will carefully examine and document as existing so called "admitted assets," i.e., all the assets of the insurer countable in ascertaining the insurer's financial soundness under state law. Such assets generally include all funds, securities, property, equipment, rights of action, or resources of any kind owned by the company or held in trust for others.

advanced life underwriter: This term refers to the agent marketing products and services where a sophisticated knowledge of law and high degree of creativity is required. Estate and financial planning, retirement planning, business insurance, and employee benefit planning are good examples of the fields in which an advanced life underwriter will work.

advance premium: Any premiums paid before their due date.

adverse selection: The tendency of people who are less than standard insurance risks to seek or continue insurance to a greater extent than other individuals. This so called "selection against the insurer" is a form of stacking the deck and is also found in the tendency of policyowners to take advantage of favorable options in insurance contracts.

AG 38 reserve: this is the reserve value used for a UL policy with a no lapse secondary guarantee.

age: The age in years of an applicant, insured, or beneficiary. Some companies use the age at the last birthday. Other companies use the age at the nearest birthday (last or next).

age at issue: The age of an insured at the time coverage goes into effect. Some insurers define issue age as the age at the insured's last birthday. In others, it is defined as the insured's age at the nearest birthday.

age limits: Minimum or maximum age limits for the insuring of new applicants or for the renewal of policies.

agency: The legal relationship empowering one party to act on behalf of another in dealing with third parties. (A life insurance agent does not generally have the authority to bind the insurance company.) The term agency is also defined as a sales office under the direction of either a general agent or a branch manager. A third definition of the term "agency" is an office operated by an independent agent who has an agent's contract with at least one insurer.

agent: A person who solicits insurance or aids in the placing of risks, delivery of policies, or collection of premiums on behalf of an insurer. Typically, a person placing products for a specific insurer is considered the insurer's agent rather than an agent of the policyowner.

agent of record: Typically, the agent who takes the initial policy application and who is entitled to any and all commissions on the issued insurance contract is considered the agent of record. If an insurer assigns an agent to service its "orphans" (policyowners who no longer have a servicing agent), the newly assigned agent will become the agent of record. Many times an agent will obtain a written authority from a current or prospective policyowner to be the sole party with the right to investigate and negotiate life insurance contracts. If any other agent does sell insurance to the client, the agent of record usually receives a percentage of the commission earned on the new policy. In this later case, the agent of record legally represents the interests of the client.

aggregate mortality table: A mortality table where the mortality rates at any age are based on all insurance in force at that age, without reference to the duration of insurance. See also: select mortality table and ultimate mortality table.

aleatory contract: Where a contract between two parties depends upon an uncertain event and where one party may pay a very small amount and receive a very large amount upon the occurrence or nonoccurrence of the specified event, it is called an aleatory contract. Life insurance is such a contract.

alternate valuation date: Typically, for federal estate tax purposes, assets are valued as of the date of a decedent's death. However, the estate's personal representative (executor or administrator) may elect to value all property in the estate as of its value six months from the date of death. If property is sold between the date of death and the date six months after death, that date becomes the alternate valuation date.

amount at risk: The pure insurance element of a life insurance policy. The net amount at risk is equal to the difference between the face value of a policy and its accrued cash value at a given time. The net amount at risk decreases as the cash value increases each year. If the cash value becomes the face value, the policy is said to mature or endow.

annual premium: The premium amount required on an annual basis under the contractual requirements of a policy to keep a traditional level premium whole life or term policy in force.

annuity: A systematic liquidation of principal and interest over a specified period. An annuity can be measured by a fixed duration (e.g., 20 years) or by the lifetime of one or more persons. A second definition for the term is the contract providing such an arrangement. An annuity can be commercial (e.g., such as the annuity an individual can purchase from an insurer) or private (e.g., a son can promise to pay his father an income for life that the father can never outlive but that ends at the father's death).

annuity, cash refund: See: cash refund annuity.

annuity certain: An annuity that pays a specified amount for a definite and specified period of time, such as five or ten years, with remaining payments going to a designated beneficiary if the annuitant dies before the end of the specified period.

annuity certain, life: An annuity payable for a specified minimum number of periods or, if longer, for as long as the annuitant lives; a combination of an annuity certain and a life annuity.

annuity, deferred: See: deferred annuity.

annuity due: An annuity under which payments will be made at the beginning, rather than at the end, of each period (i.e., monthly, quarterly, yearly, et al.) For contrast, see: immediate annuity.

annuity, flexible premium: See: flexible premium annuity.

annuity, installment deferred: See: installment deferred annuity.

annuity, installment refund: See: installment refund annuity.

annuity, joint and survivor: See: joint and survivor annuity.

annuity, joint life: See: joint life annuity.

annuity, life: See: life annuity.

annuity, private: See: private annuity.

annuity, refund: See: refund annuity.

annuity, single-premium deferred: See: single-premium deferred annuity.

annuity, temporary: See: temporary annuity.

annuity, variable: See: variable annuity.

anti-rebate laws: State laws that prohibit an agent or company from giving part of the premium, or any other valuable consideration, back to the insured as an inducement to purchase life insurance.

applicant: The person(s) or party(ies) applying for and signing the written application for a contract of life insurance either on his or her own life or that of another.

application: A written form provided by an insurer typically completed by the insurer's agent and its medical examiner (in most cases) on the basis of information on the physical condition, occupation, and avocation of the proposed insured. The policy application is signed by the applicant (typically, but not always, the insured) and becomes a legal part of the insurance contract. The application is the major source of information for the insurer in deciding whether or not or on what terms and conditions a contract should be issued.

assign: To transfer a right or risk.

assignee: The person or party who receives a transferred right or risk when a life insurance policy is assigned.

assignment: The shift of rights and benefits of a life insurance contract from a policyowner to an assignee.

assumed interest rate: The rate of interest used by an insurance company to calculate its reserves.

attained age: Most insurers base premium rates on the age an insured has attained as of the application for insurance or its issue date, i.e., the age an insured has reached on a specific date. Generally, this is the age of the proposed insured based on his or her nearest (or, in some cases, last) birthday.

automatic premium loan provision: An option that will allow the insurer to automatically borrow money from a policy's cash value to pay any premium in default at the end of the grace period in order to keep a policy from lapsing.

aviation exclusion: A contract provision that excludes from coverage deaths due to airline accidents unless the insured was a passenger on a regularly scheduled commercial airline.

back-end load: A load is a charge against policy values for business expenses of the insurer in issuing the contract. These charges can be imposed at the inception of the contract (i.e., a "front-end" load) or at the termination of the contractual relationship (i.e., a "back-end" load). In the case of most variable, universal, and current-assumption life insurance products, the load is imposed when the policy is surrendered. Back-end loads typically decrease each year and disappear completely after the number of years specified in the contract.

banding: Banding refers to the recovery of ongoing administrative and handling costs. Insurers generally "band" premiums by policy size. This is a "cheaper by the dozen" concept in which larger policies are charged a more favorable rate than smaller policies. In other words a $1,000,000 policy will be charged significantly less per year than ten $100,000 policies for ongoing administrative and handling costs. Fewer policies are less expensive than more policies of the same aggregate amount. This is one reason why buy-sell policies may be purchased on a stock redemption rather than cross-purchase basis.

beneficiary: The recipient of life insurance proceeds at the death of the insured is the policy's beneficiary. A primary beneficiary is first in line to receive that money. A secondary beneficiary is entitled to payment only if no primary beneficiary is alive when the insured dies. Final beneficiaries are those entitled to proceeds if no primary or secondary beneficiaries are alive at the death of the insured. These "backup" beneficiaries are often called "alternate" or "contingent" beneficiaries, since their claims are contingent on the deaths of everyone in the higher class of primary beneficiaries.

binding receipt: The receipt for payment of the first premium. This assures the applicant that if he or she dies before receiving the policy, the company will pay the death proceeds if the policy is in fact issued (or would have been issued) as applied for had death not intervened.

broker: A broker differs from an agent since the broker legally represents the customer rather than the insurer. Brokers may purchase policies on behalf of their clients though almost any insurer.

brokerage agency: A life insurance general agency servicing business of agents other than full-time (career) agents of the company represented by the agency.

broker-agent: A business entity licensed and registered with the Securities and Exchange Commission (SEC) with the legal right to offer securities products to the public. An agent selling variable life products and related securities (such as mutual funds) must be registered with a broker-dealer.

business insurance: Coverage concerned primarily with the protection of an insured's business against the economic loss incurred at the death or disability of a key executives and/or other key employees. Business insurance is also designed to stabilize and maximize the value of a business by assuring a practical plan for business owners to be bought out and receive fair value for their interests at the death of one or more of the owners.

buy-sell agreement: An agreement in which either the business or the surviving owners (or both) will purchase the shares owned by a deceased or retiring shareholder at a value or formula previously agreed upon by the parties and stipulated in the agreement.

capital conservation method: When an individual's needs for insurance are ascertained, there are two choices for determining how much income a given amount of capital will produce. One method assumes only income will be used so as to protect (conserve) capital. The capital conservation method, therefore, assumes only the earnings on principal (not the principal itself) will be used to satisfy those needs. The other approach is to annuitize capital (i.e., break down capital and pay out both income and capital to meet needs). This will generally result in a lower amount of capital needed (but at the expense of less future security and inheritance for others). See also: capital need analysis.

capitalization of policy loans: The process of increasing the policy loan in order to "pay" unpaid loan interest.

capital needs analysis: Capital needs analysis (CNA) is an appraisal of needs system popularized by supersalesman Tom Wolf. A client's financial needs are met though the economic value and income-producing capabilities of current and future assets.

capital stock insurance company: An insurance company owned by its stockholders (similar to the ownership of IBM by its shareholders). This form of corporate ownership should be contrasted with a mutual insurance company that is owned by its policyowners and operated solely for their benefit. See also: mutual company.

capital utilization method: A life insurance "needs computation" method based on the assumption that both the earnings and principal will be used up over the period during which the income will be needed. This method should be compared and contrasted with the capital conservation method of needs analysis.

captive insurance company: A licensed insurance company that is created for the express purpose of writing property and casualty insurance for a specific business or group of businesses.

cash accumulation policy: A contract that builds significant cash value or equity. Such policies include whole life policies, endowment policies, universal life, and the various variable life products.

cash refund annuity: A cash refund annuity pays a lump-sum cash benefit to a beneficiary if the annuitant dies before a recovery of premiums paid. The lump-sum cash benefit is equal to the difference between the total amount paid by the purchaser over the total annuity payments received before the annuitant's death.

cash surrender value: Cash surrender value is the amount available to the policyowner when a life insurance policy is surrendered. It is also the amount upon which a policy loan is based. In the first 8 to 10 years after a policy is issued, the cash value is typically the insurer's reserve to meet future liabilities reduced by a surrender charge that enables the insurer to recover expenses incurred in setting up the policy. If a policy is surrendered in later years, the cash surrender value usually equals or closely approximates the reserve value of the policy.

change of beneficiary provision: A provision that gives a policyowner the right to change the beneficiary at any time he or she chooses (unless an irrevocable beneficiary designation has been made).

classified risk: Most insureds are classified as "standard" risks. Those who are less likely to die (based on their health) than the standard risk may qualify for "preferred risk" classification, while those who are more likely to die than standard risks their age are called "substandard" risks and pay premiums accordingly. See also: substandard risk.

clause: A specific provision of a life insurance contract (or rider attached to it) dealing with a particular subject in that policy.

collateral assignee: The person or party to whom a collateral assignment is made.

collateral assignment: When a life insurance contract is transferred to an individual or other party as security for a debt, this usually temporary assignment does not transfer all policy rights. Under a collateral assignment, the creditor is entitled to be reimbursed only to the extent "his interest may appear," i.e., policy proceeds will be payable only for the amount owed by the policyowner at that time. Any death benefit in excess of the debt owed by the policyowner to the creditor is paid to the policy's beneficiary. For comparison, see: absolute assignment.

collateral assignment plan: A collateral assignment plan is a variation in a split dollar life insurance arrangement in which the insured initially applies for and owns the policy and names the beneficiary but collaterally assigns the policy to the payor of the bulk of the premiums as security for that party's outlays.

collateral loan: A loan guaranteed by the pledge of the life insurance contract as collateral.

commission: The percentage of the premium paid to an insurance agent or broker by the insurer as compensation.

commissioner: Also called superintendent in some states, a commissioner of insurance is the head of a state insurance department who supervises the insurance business in the state and administers insurance laws.

commissioners standard ordinary mortality table (CSO): A standard mortality table approved by the National Association of Insurance Commissioners and used in life insurance rate calculations.

commissions, graded: This is the typical life insurance commission arrangement in which larger commissions are paid to the agent or broker during the first policy year than in renewal years.

commissions, level: This is a commission arrangement in which an agent is paid commissions of equal amounts over several years and is favored in ultra large cases in order to spread out the taxable commissions and thereby reduce taxes paid on the commissions.

commutation rights: The right of the beneficiary to receive – in one lump sum – the value of the remaining stream of future payments under a settlement option selected by the insured of a life insurance policy.

commute: To compute and pay – as of a given date – the lump-sum actuarial equivalent to a series of future payments that would be due under a life insurance contract.

commuted value: The present (i.e., discounted) actuarial value of a series of installments payable at fixed future dates. The commuted value is ascertained on the basis of an assumed rate of interest and mortality factors (if payments are contingent on the life or lives of one or more individuals).

compound interest: Interest earned on interest.

concealment: Intentional failure of the insured to disclose a material fact to the insurance company at the time application is made.

conditional assignment: An assignment made solely for the purpose of securing a debt. A conditional assignment is typically automatically terminated when the obligation is repaid. See also: assignment.

conditional premium receipt: This is the receipt given to a policy applicant if all or part of the premium is paid at the time of application. This receipt does not provide absolute interim insurance until the company acts on the application. It provides that the insurer will assume the risk of the death or a change in the health of the insured after the date of the application if it later approves the application or, more frequently, if the insured meets with the company's rules of insurability for the plan applied for as of the date of the application. See also: interim term insurance.

consideration: Consideration is an essential element of a binding contract. In a life insurance contract, the policyowner's consideration is the first premium payment and the application; the insurance company's consideration is the promise(s) contained in the contract. Future premiums are not consideration but rather a condition precedent to the insurer's obligation.

contestable clause: Sometimes called the incontestable clause. The provision in the insurance contract that states the time (called the contestable period) the insurer has to contest and the grounds under which the policy may be contested or voided by the insurer. By law, the maximum contestable period is two years, but many policies limit the period to one year.

contingent beneficiary: A contingent beneficiary is one who will receive death proceeds if the principal beneficiary predeceases the insured.

contract of insurance: A legally binding agreement in which an insurer agrees to pay a death benefit upon the death of the insured in return for the consideration of the policyowner's payment of an initial premium and the policy application. Once the insurer issues the contract, the policyowner pays premiums as a condition which precedes the insurer's duty to pay the death benefit upon the demise of the insured. This legally enforceable agreement comprises more than just the policy. The application and any attached supplements, riders, or endorsements form the entire contract.

contract rates: Life insurance settlement option rates (i.e., the guaranteed rates at which the policyowner's dollars can be converted into one or more forms of annuity payouts) are listed in the policy. In fact, the insurer may allow the purchase to be made at current rates if those are more favorable to the policyowner but because of increased longevity trends, guaranteed (contract) rates are often more favorable than current rates.

conversion: One type of life insurance contract can be exchanged for a different type assuming the contract is "convertible." For instance, term insurance can be converted to whole life or some other form of permanent insurance. Conversion occurs under a group policy when an insured individual applies for an individual policy without evidence of insurability within a stipulated period of time before the group insurance coverage terminates.

conversion, attained age: The premiums for the converted policy are based on the insured's age attained at time of conversion.

conversion, original age: Premiums for the converted policy are based on the insured's original age at issue. The policyowner must pay the difference in premiums, plus interest, for the time the policy has been in force.

convertible: A provision giving the policyowner the right to exchange the policy for another without evidence of insurability.

convertible term insurance: A term contract that may be converted to a permanent form of insurance without a medical examination, if conversion is made within a limited period as specified in the contract. The premium is usually based on the attained age of the insured at the time of conversion.

cost of insurance: In the case of a split dollar arrangement or life insurance in a qualified plan, the value of the pure insurance protection in any year is the difference between the face amount of the policy and its cash value multiplied by a life insurance premium factor provided by the IRS (currently Table 2001; formerly P.S. 58 rates) or, (in certain cases) if lower, the insurer's rates for individual one-year term policies available to all standard risks (initial issue insurance).

cost of living adjustment (COLA): A rider available with some policies that provides for automatic, periodic increases in benefits based on increases in the consumer price index (CPI) or other index of inflation.

credit life insurance: A policy issued on the life of a borrower with the creditor named as beneficiary to cover the repayment of a loan in the event the borrower dies before the loan has been repaid. Usually written using monthly decreasing term based on a relatively small, decreasing balance installment loan.

cross purchase: A buy-sell arrangement that provides that in the event of one owner's death, the surviving shareholders or partners are bound to purchase, and the estate of the deceased is bound to sell, the deceased's interest in the business. A cross-purchase agreement is often funded with life insurance policies owned by each owner on the life or lives of all other owners.

crummey power: A provision in a trust that gives a beneficiary a limited period of time to demand all or a portion of a gift be made to the trust for the purpose of converting what would otherwise be a future interest gift (not qualifying for the annual gift tax exclusion) into a present interest gift (that does qualify for the annual gift tax exclusion).

current-assumption policy: Current-assumption policies reflect the insurer's current interest, mortality, and expense experience directly in cash value credits and charges rather than indirectly through dividends. As a result, actual cash values accumulations are uncertain, although there is a minimum cash value guarantee. The most prevalent type of current-assumption policy is universal life, although it is also sold in fixed-premium modes. Although inaccurate, the term "interest-sensitive" is sometimes used synonymously with "current-assumption." Current-assumption is actually a broader concept implying direct sensitivity not only to current interest rates but also to mortality and expense experience. Although traditional participating whole life policies may reflect the company's current performance with respect to investment, mortality, and expenses through its declared dividends, these policies are not classified as current-assumption policies.

current interest rate: This is the interest rate credited to current-assumption and universal life products (versus the fixed rate of traditional life insurance policies).

current value: The fair market value of a security or other property at the present time.

date of maturity: The date upon which a life insurance policy endows if the insured is still living.

date of policy: The date appearing on the front page of an insurance policy indicating when the policy went into effect.

death benefit: The amount stated in the policy as payable upon the death of the insured.

death claim: When the insured dies, this is the form that must be signed by the policy beneficiary and, along with the death certificate, sent to the insurer to provide proof of the date the insured died and to establish the beneficiary's right to the policy's proceeds.

deficiency reserve: For policies with secondary guarantees, in some cases the calculation of minimum reserves is required. Deficiency reserves are the excess of the minimum reserves over the AG 38 basic reserves. The AG38 reserve including the deficiency reserve will be greater than the AG 38 reserve not including the deficiency reserve.

declared interest rate: In a universal life policy (or in the general account of a variable universal life or interest-sensitive whole life policy), cash values earn a minimum interest rate. However, they will actually be credited with a current rate of return that may be substantially higher. This rate is declared by the insurance company and may be periodically changed.

decreasing term insurance: If the face value of term insurance decreases over time in scheduled increments until the policy expires, the insurance is a form of decreasing term. Typically in such policies, the premium remains level.

default: If a policyowner fails to make a premium payment by a policy's final due date or by the end of its grace period, the policy is in default and will lapse.

deferred annuity: A series of payments that are not begun until the lapse of a specified period of time or until the annuitant reaches a specific age.

delivery of policy: Delivery is, in general and nonlegal terms, the presentation of the policy to the policyowner. Actual delivery is legally determined by the intent of the parties and, therefore, does not necessarily require that the policy physically change hands. For instance, a conditional binding receipt (or, at times, verbal acknowledgement) may constitute delivery.

dependency period: In computing life insurance needs, the years when children are dependent upon parents, usually until the youngest is 18 years old, is called the dependency period.

deposit term life insurance: Deposit term is a form of temporary coverage, normally sold for ten-year terms, with the first-year premium more than twice the amount of the annual premiums paid for the remaining years. This higher first-year premium is called a deposit. If the insured dies, double the deposit is added to the death benefit; if the insured lives, double the deposit is returned at the end of the term. The insured forfeits the deposit and receives no refund if the policy lapses. A form of tontine, most states now severely restrict or totally prohibit this type of policy.

disability premium waiver insurance: This is an important option or rider in a life insurance policy that provides that if an insured becomes totally disabled for six months or longer, no further premiums will be due and the policy will be continued in full force until death or recovery occurs. Upon recovery, the policyowner does not have to repay premium payments made by the insurer on behalf of the policyowner during the disability period.

dividend: When a policy participates in the favorable investment, mortality, and expense experience of the insurer (so called "par" policies), the policyowner receives "dividends" as a refund of an "overcharge" in premiums. For tax and other purposes, these dividends are considered a return of capital rather than a profit payment.

dividend additions: Participating policies provide that their dividends may be used as single premiums to purchase paid-up insurance at the insured's attained age as additions to the amount of insurance specified on the face of the contract. These additions are purchased at net rates (no commissions or other charges) to the policyowner. See also: paid-up additions.

dividend class: All policyowners are grouped into categories in which members who bought the same type of contract at the same age are classed. This classification method allows precise determination of how much premium should be returned to each class as a dividend.

dividend deposits: Cash dividends and interest arising from the policy left on deposit with the company under the terms of the dividend option.

dividend, extra: A dividend that is paid in addition to any regular, periodic dividends. See also: dividend.

dividend options: The different ways in which the insured, under a participating policy, may elect to receive dividends. The dividend options generally include receiving payments in cash, applying them to reduce premiums, purchasing additional paid-up insurance, having them held by the insurer to earn interest for the policyowner, or purchasing additional term insurance.

divisible surplus: The amount of the company's surplus earnings available for distribution among the policyowners in the form of dividends.

double indemnity: A clause in a life insurance contract providing for a double benefit if death occurs under certain circumstances. The most common circumstances that would result in a double benefit is an accidental death.

earned premium: The amount of premium that would compensate the insurance company for its loss experience, expenses, and profit year to date.

economic benefit: The economic benefit is, in a split-dollar or other employer-provided insurance plan, the amount that the insured employee or party must report currently as income.

emergency fund: When calculating the amount of life insurance needed, the amount figured into the client's needs that should be kept on hand by survivors as a fund for emergencies (similar to the reserve all clients should hold for an emergency such as an accidents or an unexpected but potentially profitable business opportunity). The increasing loan value of a life insurance policy also constitutes, and is often referred to as, an emergency fund for the insured during lifetime.

endorsement: A written modification to an insurance policy, usually written on the printed policy page. An endorsement may also be in the form of a rider. No endorsement is valid unless signed by an executive officer of the company and attached to and made a part of the policy. See also: rider.

endow: A life insurance policy is said to endow when its cash value equals the face amount. The policyowner then receives, in cash, the face amount.

endowment: A life insurance contract that provides for the payment of the face amount at the end of a fixed period, or at a specified age of the insured, or at the death of the insured before the end of the stated period.

evidence of insurability: A statement or proof of a person's physical condition, occupation, etc., affecting the acceptance of the applicant for insurance.

exceptions provision: An insurance policy provision that limits the insurance company's liability by excluding coverage for certain losses, such as death in an aviation accident other than on a regularly scheduled commercial airline.

excess initial expenses: An insurer's first-year expenses that exceed first-year expense loading. These are generally a result of higher first-year commission rates and the expense of selection and issue.

excess interest: The positive difference between the rate of interest an insurer guarantees to pay on proceeds left under settlement options and the higher interest actually paid. A second meaning of the term is the difference between the guaranteed rate of return on cash value and the higher, current rate in universal life and other interest-sensitive policies.

exclusion clause: A policy provision that excludes certain risks from coverage, such as aviation, war, or pre-existing conditions. See also: exceptions provision.

exclusion ratio: A fraction used to determine the amount of annual annuity income exempt from federal income tax. The fraction is generally found by dividing the policyowner's investment in the annuity contract by the expected return.

executor: A person appointed in a person's will to carry out the terms of the will. See also: administrator.

expense charge: In variable, universal life, and other current-assumption policies, all costs are individually deducted and accounted for within the policies. These expense charges are fixed amounts or percentages deducted from gross premiums paid and cash value, as specified in the policy.

expense loading: The amount added to the premium during the rate-making process to cover the expenses of maintaining the business, commissions, administration, and overhead.

experience: The loss record of a type of insurance written. This record is used in adjusting premium rates and predicting future losses.

experience modification: The adjustment of premiums as a result of the application of experience rating; usually expressed as a percentage.

extended term option: A nonforfeiture option that provides that the net cash surrender value of a policy may be used as a net single premium at the attained age of the insured to purchase term insurance at the face amount of the original policy for as long a period as possible.

extra dividend: A dividend that is paid in addition to regular, periodic dividends.

extra premium: The amount charged in addition to the regular premium to cover an extra hazard, special or substandard risk.

extra protection benefit: An insurance policy provision that provides an extra amount of insurance payable if death occurs during the term of the provision.

face amount: The amount payable in the event of death, as stated on the front page of the policy. The face amount may be decreased by loans or increased by additional benefits payable under specified conditions, or as stated in a rider.

fair market value (FMV): The price at which the property would change hands between a willing buyer and a willing seller, neither being under any compulsion to buy or to sell, and both having reasonable knowledge of relevant facts.

family income policy: A life insurance policy that combines whole life and decreasing term to provide income protection against the premature death of the family breadwinner. If the insured dies within a specified period, the family will receive a stated amount of income from date of death until the end of the period. The face amount of the policy is then paid to the family. For comparison, see: family maintenance policy.

family income rider: Similar to a family income policy except that the decreasing term coverage is written as a rider to a whole life policy rather than as combination of both coverages.

family maintenance policy: A life insurance policy combining level term and whole life to provide income protection against the premature death of the family breadwinner. If the insured dies within a specified period (say, 20 years) the family will receive a stated monthly amount from the date of death to 20 years in the future. The face amount of the policy is then paid to the family. For comparison, see: family income policy.

family policy: A policy that combines whole life and convertible term to provide insurance on each family member in units of coverage. Each unit generally consists of $5,000 of whole life on the wage earner, $1,250 of convertible term on the spouse and $1,000 of convertible term on each child.

family rider: An optional policy supplement attached to the insurance policy issued to the head of a family and insuring other members of the family, generally the spouse and children.

fifth dividend option: Because this option is usually listed after four other possibilities, it is often called the "fifth dividend" option. If selected, each year the insurer will use the prior year's dividend to purchase (at no commission or expense charge) one-year term insurance up to specified limits (usually no more than the policy's cash value) with the balance applied toward one or more of the other options. The fifth dividend option is useful to maintain level or increasing protection, to keep coverage high even if a policy loan has been taken out, or where the parties are involved in a split dollar arrangement.

final expenses: Costs incurred during a last illness, funeral and burial costs, debts, probate expenses, death taxes and any other taxes or obligations that must be paid in order to settle the estate of a decedent.

financed insurance: The payment of insurance premiums, in whole or in part, with funds obtained by systematic borrowing, usually from the cash value of the contract.

first-year premium: Insurance premiums that are due during the first policy year, regardless of whether they are paid annually, semiannually, quarterly, monthly, or weekly. Premiums due after the first year are known as renewal premiums.

fixed-amount settlement option: A life insurance policy beneficiary can request that proceeds be paid in regular installments of a fixed dollar amount. The number of payment periods is determined by the policy's face amount, the amount of each payment, and the interest earned. For contrast, see: fixed-period settlement option.

fixed annuity: An annuity that provides fixed payments during the annuity period. For contrast, see: variable annuity.

fixed-period settlement option: A life insurance settlement option in which the number of payments is set by the payee, with the amount of each payment determined by the amount of proceeds. For contrast, see: fixed-amount settlement option.

flexible premium annuity: An annuity that allows the owner of the contract to vary premium payments (within limits) from year to year.

flexible premium variable life: See: variable universal life.

fraternal insurance: Life or health insurance protection provided by fraternal benefit societies. Before purchasing fraternal insurance, an individual must become a member of the organization.

fraud: An act of deceit; misrepresentation of a material fact made knowingly, with the intention of having another person rely on that fact and consequently suffer a financial hardship.

free-look provision: A provision in life insurance policies that gives the policyowner a stated amount of time (usually ten days) to review a new policy. It can be returned within this time for a 100% refund of premiums paid, but cancellation of coverage is effective from date of issue.

front-end load: A contract is front-end loaded when certain of the insurer's expenses are deducted from the gross premium before the remaining net premium goes into the cash value account.

full disclosure: The requirement that prospective purchasers of variable and universal life products be fully informed of the charges and costs and provided with all important information about their policies. Also includes the requirement that they are given a current prospectus and that no statements or guarantees are made by the agent regarding cash values or interest rates.

fully insured plan: Pension plans that are funded entirely through individual insurance contracts issued on the lives of participants. The insurance company products provide any pre-retirement death benefits and the entire retirement benefit for the employee.

general account: Traditionally, the term describing a company's overall investment portfolio. More recently, it also refers to the separate investment funds upon which the declared rate of return in a universal life policy is based. Also, with variable and variable universal life policies, one of the investment account options that earns a declared rate of return.

grace period: Most life insurance contracts provide that premiums may be paid at any time within a period of generally 30 or 31 days following the premium due date, during which time the policy remains in full force. If death occurs during the grace period, the insurer will pay the face amount less the amount of the earned but unpaid premium (and any outstanding loan). Generally, an insurer will not charge interest on overdue premiums if they are paid before the end of the grace period.

graded death benefits: A life insurance policy provision that provides for death benefits that, in the early years of the contract, are less than the face amount of the policy, but that increase with the passage of time.

graded premium life insurance: To make life insurance premiums more affordable (and therefore marketable), some insurers sell a form of modified life insurance that starts with relatively low premiums that increase slowly each year. After a period of years, the premium remains level. The death benefit remains level throughout the term of coverage.

gross premium: This is the premium paid by the policyowner. More technically, the gross premium is the net premium, plus the expense of operation less the interest factor. For contrast, see: net premium.

group life insurance: A form of life insurance covering a group of persons generally having some common interest or activity, such as employees of the same company or members of the same union or association. Most group insurance is issued using yearly renewable term, without requiring medical examinations.

group ordinary life insurance: Level premium ordinary life insurance issued on a group basis.

guaranteed cash value: The guaranteed amount available to the insured on surrender of a policy according to a table of guaranteed values scaled to the number of years in which the policy is in force. In a universal or variable policy, there is no guaranteed cash value.

guaranteed cost: This is another term for nonparticipating (non par) insurance. Guaranteed cost can also be defined as the maximum costs that can be deducted from cash value under the terms of the policy in universal or variable universal life contracts.

guaranteed insurability rider: A rider, now offered on most life insurance policies, that gives the policyowner the right to purchase additional insurance at specified future times without evidence of insurability. Rates are generally based on attained age at the time of purchase.

guaranteed interest rate: The minimum annual rate of interest used in calculating policy reserves from year to year, or annual increases in dividend accumulations, or the interest factor in proceeds held under a settlement option, or the amount payable under the interest income option, etc. This term also refers to the minimum rate credited to cash value in interest-sensitive policies.

guaranteed purchase option: See: guaranteed insurability rider.

human life value: One method of determining how much insurance a person should own is to measure his or her "human life" value, an estimate of the present value of a person's remaining economic worth. In general terms, this projects future net after-tax salary and other earnings, reduces them by future expenses, and then discounts these future net values at interest to determine a lump-sum present value.

immediate annuity: An annuity contract that pays the annuity at the *end* of each period of payment. The interval may be monthly, quarterly, semiannually, or annually.

incidents of ownership: The right to exercise any of the privileges in the insurance policy (e.g., change the beneficiary, withdraw cash values, make loans on the policy, etc.). Any retention of an incident of ownership will cause federal estate tax inclusion of policy proceeds.

incontestable clause: See: contestable clause.

increasing term insurance: Term life insurance coverage that increases in face value each year (or certain period) from the date of policy issue to the date of expiration. For contrast, see: decreasing term insurance and level term insurance.

indexed universal life insurance (annuities): these policies have all the traditional features of regular universal life policies except that, similar to variable universal life, the interest crediting method is based upon the performance of one or more indexes, typically of stocks, such as the S&P 500, the Russell 2000, and other large and small, foreign and domestic, value and growth stock indexes. In contrast with variable universal life, these policies still give policyowners a minimum crediting rate guarantee assuring that they will not lose money in periods when the underlying index values fall. Thus, policyowners can enjoy the upside potential of stock investments when stock values rise, but be protected from losses when stock values fall. Insurance companies offer a similar indexed interest crediting rate design feature with their indexed annuities.

indeterminate premium: Refers to policies where the actual premium charged may be lower than the guaranteed premium stated in the policy. Policies with indeterminate premiums generally make reference to the *guaranteed* (or maximum) premium that can be charged, and the *current* (or lower) premium, based on the current and projected mortality and/or investment experience.

individual life insurance: Life insurance contract that covers only one insured, but that may sometimes cover several people, such as the members of a family, through the use of riders. The term "individual" is often used to distinguish this type of life insurance from group life insurance.

industrial life insurance: Often called debit or home service insurance, life insurance issued on individual lives from birth to age 70 in small amounts. Weekly or monthly premiums are collected at the individual's home by a home service agent. Usually, no medical examination is required.

initial death benefit: In flexible feature life insurance policies, the original face value of the policy; the specified amount.

initial premium: The first premium, generally payable with the application or upon delivery of the policy.

initial reserve: The reserve amount determined at the beginning of the policy year. It equals the preceding year's ending reserve, plus the annual net premium.

installment deferred annuity: An annuity in which the annuitant pays into the annuity fund over a period of time, after which (usually starting immediately) annuity payments begin coming back to the annuitant and continue for life.

installment premiums: Premiums paid over time rather than as a single premium.

installment refund annuity: A life annuity that will continue to make payments to a stipulated beneficiary after the death of the annuitant until the total payments equal the consideration paid to the insurer. For contrast see: cash refund annuity.

installment settlement: A series of periodic payments of proceeds instead of payment in a lump-sum. Any of the income settlement options in a policy. A policy clause allowing the beneficiary to choose to receive proceeds in installments.

insurability: The term insurability encompasses all conditions pertaining to an individual that affect his or her health, susceptibility to injury, as well as life expectancy and other factors considered by the insurer in its underwriting and rating process. If the risk is too high, the insurance company will refuse coverage.

insurable interest: A person who has a reasonable expectation of benefiting from the continuance of another person's life or of suffering a loss at his or her death is said to have an insurable interest in that life.

insurance reserves: The present value of future claims minus the present value of future premiums. Reserves are balance sheet accounts set up by insurers to reflect actual and potential liabilities under outstanding insurance contracts.

insured: The individual or group covered by the contract of insurance.

intentionally defective grantor trust: a trust drafted with an intentional flaw that runs "afoul" of the rules contained in sections 671 through 679 of the internal revenue code with the result that the grantor of the trust is taxed on all trust income, as income tax laws will not recognize that assets have been transferred away from the trust grantor.

interest-adjusted cost method: A method of comparing costs of similar policies by using an index that takes into account the time value of money due at different times through interest adjustments to the annual premiums, dividends, and cash value increases at an assumed interest rate.

interest factor: One of three factors taken into consideration by an insurance company when calculating premium rates. This is an estimate of the overall average interest that will be earned by the insurer on invested premium payments over a long period of time.

interest-only option: A settlement option under which all or part of the proceeds of a policy are left with the insurance company for a definite period at a guaranteed minimum rate of interest. Interest may be paid (usually subject to certain minimums) annually, semiannually, quarterly, or monthly – or, in some cases, may be added to the proceeds left with the insurer.

interest-sensitive whole life: A traditional whole life policy with fixed premiums and traditional nonforfeiture values where interest is credited directly to the cash value at current rates. Often used somewhat erroneously to refer to current-assumption policies. Generally loads, mortality costs, and interest credits are separately stated. The cash value of the policy is the greater of this fund less surrender charges, and the guaranteed cash values.

interim term insurance: Term life insurance issued to an applicant during the period between submission of the application and the time the insurance company either issues a permanent insurance policy or rejects the application. See also: conditional premium receipt.

interpolated terminal reserve: A reserve fund that an insurance company uses to cover its liability in a particular policy. It is used in determining the value of certain life insurance policies for gift tax purposes.

investment account: A separately managed cash value investment fund (usually similar to a mutual fund) into which variable and variable universal life insurance policyowners allocate the premiums and cash value. Policies generally have several of these accounts, each with its own investment objective and degree of risk.

investment portfolio: A list detailing the securities owned by a person, business, or mutual fund. Most insurance companies carry a broadly varied investment portfolio. Also refers to the equity-based accounts in variable and other interest-sensitive products.

investment year method of dividend calculation: Any dividend calculation method that recognizes differences in earned interest rates depending upon the year in which the investment is made. For contrast, see: portfolio method of dividend calculation.

issue: A term applying to the insurer's approving and forwarding new policies to the agent for delivery to applicants.

issue limit: The maximum amount of coverage a company is willing to extend on a given risk.

joint and survivor annuity: A life annuity payable over the lives of two or more annuitants that continues to make payments until the death of the last surviving annuitant.

joint and x-percent survivor annuity: An annuity that pays an income to two individuals. The specified percentage of the joint income continues to the survivor for life if the principal annuitant dies first. If the secondary annuitant dies first, the unreduced joint benefit continues to the principal annuitant for life. In its second-death form, X percent of the joint income is paid to the survivor regardless of which individual dies first. Common percentages are 100% (full), 75% (three-fourths), 66% (two-thirds), or 50% (one-half).

joint and survivorship option: A contract option that permits policy proceeds to be paid out as a joint and survivor annuity.

joint control: A life insurance policy provision that states that a person, persons, or organization other than the insured, usually the beneficiary, has a joint right with the insured to the exercise of the rights, powers, benefits, privileges, and options of the policy.

joint insurance: A life insurance contract covering two or more lives that pays death proceeds and terminates at the first death among the insured lives. Often used to fund cross purchase buy-sell agreements among more than two partners or shareholders.

joint life annuity: A life annuity payable to two or more annuitants that continues payments until one of the two annuitants dies.

jumbo risk: An insurance contract with exceptionally high limits, such as $250,000 or more.

juvenile insurance: Life insurance policies written on the lives of minors within specified age limits, generally with the parents or grandparents as the policyowners and premium payors.

key employee (sometimes called key executive or key man) insurance: Provides cash to absorb the financial loss caused by the death or disability of a vital individual in a business.

lapse: Termination of an insurance policy because of nonpayment of premiums or, in the case of variable and universal life policies, the depletion of cash value below that amount needed to keep the policy in force.

last to die insurance: A life insurance contract on two or more persons that pays proceeds only upon the death of the last insured. Also called second-to-die insurance, last survivor insurance, or survivorship life.

level premium: A life insurance premium that remains fixed through the life of a policy. It must be large enough so that in early years the insurer will develop a surplus large enough so that in later years – together with interest and future premiums – there will be enough to pay all death claims.

level term insurance: Term life coverage on which the face value remains the same from the date the policy is issued to the date the policy expires. For contrast, see: decreasing term insurance; increasing term insurance.

life annuity: An annuity contract that pays only until the annuitant dies. Payments cease at that time even if the amount paid by the insurer does not equal the total premiums paid by the annuity owner.

life expectancy: The average remaining term of life for a number of persons of a given age, according to probability statistics of a mortality table.

life income option: One of the settlement options under which the proceeds of a life insurance or annuity policy may be applied to buy an annuity payable to the beneficiary for life.

life income with period certain option: A life insurance proceeds settlement option that will pay at least a minimum specified number of periodic installments in a guaranteed amount whether the named beneficiary lives or dies.

life paid-up at age ( ): A form of limited payment life insurance that provides protection for the whole of life, with premium payments stopping at the indicated age. For example, if a 45-year old bought a life paid-up at age 65 policy, premiums would be payable for 20 years and coverage would continue for the insured's life.

life settlements: This involves the sale, by the policy owner, of his or her life insurance policy to a third party (typically a life settlement company) in exchange for a lump-sum cash payment. Life settlements are generally available for insureds with life expectancies not exceeding fifteen years.

limited-payment (limited-pay) policy: A life insurance policy that provides for payment of the premium for a period of years less than the period of protection provided under the contract.

loading charge: The additional charge for overhead costs added to the net premium. This charge is required by actuarial tables to cover mortality and interest factors.

loan: Money loaned at interest by the insurance company to a policyowner on the security of the cash value of his or her policy. See also: automatic premium loan provision; loan value.

loan value: A specified amount that can be borrowed from the insurance company by the policyowner, using the cash value of the policy as collateral.

lump sum: Payment of the entire proceeds of a life insurance policy at one time. This is the method of settlement provided by most policies, unless an alternate settlement is elected by the policyowner before the insured's death or thereafter by the beneficiary before receiving the payment.

mature: The time when a policy becomes payable. A whole life policy matures upon the death of the insured or when its cash value equals its face amount (usually at age 100).

medical information bureau (MIB): This is an entity that collects and stores medical data on life and health insurance applicants. The information is exchanged among member insurance companies. Its purpose is to guard against fraud and concealment by helping insurers discover pertinent yet undisclosed health facts.

minimum deposit policy: A cash value life insurance policy having a first-year loan value that is available for borrowing immediately upon payment of the first-year premium. These types of contract are much less popular since Congress disallowed the deduction for personal interest.

minimum premium: A minimum premium is the smallest amount of premium the insurer requires to be paid in the first year of a universal life contract.

minor beneficiary: A beneficiary who is under the state's legal age of majority and, thus, not considered competent to make certain financial transactions on his or her own. A legal guardian must be appointed to accept death benefits on behalf of a minor beneficiary.

misrepresentation: A false statement as to a past or present material fact made in an application for insurance intended to induce an insurance company to issue a policy it would not otherwise issue, or to rate the policy more favorably than it otherwise would have, or to issue the policy with a larger face amount than it otherwise would have.

misstatement of age: Giving the wrong age for oneself in an application for insurance or for a beneficiary who is to receive benefits on a basis involving a life contingency. Also, a provision in most life policies setting forth the action to be taken if a misstatement of age is discovered after policy issue.

mode of payment: The frequency with which premiums are paid (e.g., annually, semiannually, etc.)

modified life: Whole life insurance with reduced premiums payable during the first few years (usually three to five) that are only slightly higher than the rate for term insurance. Thereafter, the annual premiums are higher than that for a comparable whole life policy.

moral risk: Moral condition as reviewed by a study of habits, environment, mode of living, and general reputation that an underwriter must take into consideration in determining whether an applicant for insurance is a standard insurable risk. This information is usually obtained from inspection reports.

mortality factor: One of the basic factors needed to calculate basic premium rates. It utilizes mortality tables in attempting to determine the average number of deaths at each specific age that will occur each year.

mortality risk: The risk of death. The risk carried by a life insurance company and sometimes called the pure insurance risk. The degree of risk is the difference between the policy reserve (usually equal to the cash value of a permanent life policy) and the face amount of the policy.

mortality table: A table of the mortality experience of groups of individuals categorized by age and sex that is used to estimate how long a male or female of a given age is expected to live. Some tables are required to be unisex, i.e., those used for actuarial calculations involving qualified pension plans. The mortality table is the primary starting point for calculating the risk factor, which in turn determines the gross premium rate.

multiple life policy: A life insurance policy taken out on the lives of three to five persons, with benefits payable upon the death of each person, except, generally, the last one to survive. Also called a last-to-die policy, its most popular use is to fund buy-sell agreements.

mutual company: A life insurance company that has no capital stock or stockholders. Rather, it is owned by its policyowners and managed by a board of directors chosen by the policyowners. Any earnings in addition to those necessary for the operation of the company and contingency reserves are returned to the policyowners in the form of policy dividends. For contrast, see: stock company.

national association of insurance commissioners (NAIC): An association of state insurance commissioners attempting to solve insurance regulatory problems, create uniform legislation and regulations, and promote life insurance company solvency and responsibility.

net amount at risk: The difference between the face amount of an insurance contract and the policy's cash value.

net cost: A term ordinarily referring to the actual cost of insurance to a policyowner in a mutual company after the policy dividends are deducted from the premiums deposited. Since there are no dividends on nonparticipating policies, the net cost of these policies is equal to the total premiums paid. In determining the true net cost (sometimes called net ledger cost) of a life insurance policy over a period of years, allowance should also be made for the cash surrender value at the end of the given period. See also: net premium.

net level premium: The pure annualized level mortality cost of a life insurance policy from age of entry to maturity date. It is determined by dividing the net single premium for the policy by the present value of an annuity due for the premium-paying period.

net premium: This term has several meanings, depending on context: (1) premium paid minus agent's commission; (2) the original premium minus any returned premium; (3) the net charge for insurance cost only minus expenses or contingencies; or (4) a participating premium minus dividends paid or anticipated.

new money interest rate: See: investment year method of dividend calculation.

nonassignable contract or policy: A policy that the owner cannot legally assign to a third party.

nonconvertible term insurance: A term policy that may not be converted to a permanent policy.

nonforfeiture values: Those values or benefits in a life insurance policy that by law the policyowner does not forfeit, even if he or she chooses to discontinue payment of premiums. It usually includes cash value, loan value, paid-up insurance value, and extended term insurance value.

nonmedical insurance: Life insurance issued on a regular basis without requiring the applicant to submit to a medical examination. The insurer relies on the applicant's own answers to questions regarding his or her physical condition, and on personal references or inspection reports to decide whether to issue the policy.

nonparticipating life insurance: So called "non-par" life insurance does not pay policy dividends. The policyowner is not in any way an owner and therefore is not entitled to share in any divisible surplus of the company. Any profits from the excess of the premium over the costs of insurance accrue to the nonpar company's stockholders, which is fair since they would be the ones to absorb any losses. For contrast, see: participating insurance.

nonrenewable contract: An agreement or policy written for a specific period and purpose and that does not contain an option to be renewed for successive terms. For contrast, see: renewable and convertible term.

nontransferable: A contract in which the benefits or any of its value cannot be sold, assigned, discounted, or pledged as collateral for a loan or as security for the performance of an obligation or for any other purpose, to any person other than the insurance company.

offer and acceptance: An offer is made by the life insurance policy applicant when he or she signs the application, submits to a physical examination, and pays the first premium. That offer is accepted by the insurer when the policy is issued and delivered. Sometimes the offer will be deemed to be made by the insurer and acceptance will be by the applicant in the form of a premium payment on the offered contract.

optional benefit: An additional benefit offered by the company, which may be included in a policy at the applicant's request, usually for an additional premium.

Waiver of premium, accidental death benefit, and cost-of-living riders are examples of optional benefits.

optional paid-up insurance: One of the guaranteed nonforfeiture options in a policy where the cash value of the policy is used to buy a single premium paid-up insurance at the attained age.

ordinary life: Also referred to as straight life and whole life insurance. These three synonymous terms refer to the type of life insurance policy that continues during the whole of the insured's life, generally with level premiums payable each year until death or until age 100 when the policy endows if the insured is still living.

override: An override is the commission paid to a general agent or manager in addition to the commission paid the agent or broker who sells the policy.

ownership provision: A provision stating who the owner is when the owner is someone other than the insured.

paid-up additions: A dividend option that allows the policyowner to use policy dividends to purchase paid-up additional insurance on a net single premium basis at the insured's attained age.

paid-up policy: A policy on which the policyowner has completed payments, but that has not yet matured. This may be (1) reduced paid-up insurance provided under the nonforfeiture provision, (2) a limited payment policy under which all premiums have been paid, or (3) a policy on which accumulated dividends have been applied to pay the net single premium required to pay up the difference between the policy's reduced paid-up insurance and its face amount.

partial withdrawals (surrenders): The policyowner's right in universal and variable universal life insurance policies to receive a portion of the accumulated cash value without a policy loan and without terminating the policy. Some insurers also permit surrenders of paid-up additions from traditional participating policies without terminating the underlying policy. Partial withdrawals may incur a surrender charge and/or a processing fee.

participating insurance: An insurance policy, usually issued by mutual companies, that shares a portion of the surplus of the company with policyowners through dividends. The dividends represent the difference between the premiums charged and the actual costs (i.e., claims, expenses, earnings, etc.) experienced during the period for which the premiums were charged. For contrast, see: nonparticipating life insurance.

payor: The person who pays the premiums on a policy. Also, the applicant for a policy insuring the life of a juvenile.

perc value: PERC, which stands for Premiums plus Earnings les Reasonable Charges, is a newly created formula for determining the income tax value of a policy. There are two difference PERC formulas. With respect to a distribution of a life insurance policy from a qualified plan, the PERC formula can take into account an average surrender factor of as much as thirty percent. With respect to the distribution of a policy from an employer to an employee or when determining the cost of permanent benefits for a group life plan, an average surrender factor is not permitted as part of the PERC formula.

permanent insurance: Any form of life insurance in which the insured has the guaranteed right to keep the policy in force as long as he or she pays the premium. Also refers to any life insurance policy that builds cash value. For contrast, see: term insurance.

persistency: Perhaps the most important objective test of a good insurance agent, persistency is a measure of the number of policies sold that "stay on the books." This "staying quality" is an indication that the policyowners were satisfied with their contracts, were not oversold, and have found the means and the desire to keep the policies in force over a long period of time. A low persistency (i.e., a high percentage of policies that have lapsed) is an indication that products were not matched with clients' problems or abilities to pay or that clients did not understand (or were allowed to forget) the importance of the coverage.

pledge: The placing of policy cash values as collateral for a loan.

policy: The basic written contract between the insurer and the policyowner. The policy together with the application and all endorsements and attached papers, constitutes the entire contract of insurance. See also: contract of insurance.

policy anniversary: The anniversary of the date of issue of a policy, as shown in the policy schedule.

policy change provision: A life insurance provision stating that the policyowner has the right to change his or her coverage from a term policy to a permanent, cash value policy, such as whole life, without providing evidence of insurability. To protect the company against adverse selection, evidence of insurability is usually required to change coverage from a permanent policy to a term plan.

policy date: The date on which coverage becomes effective, as shown in the policy.

policy fee: A small annual charge (sometimes a one-time charge) to the policyowner, in addition to the premium, to cover the costs of policy administration (premium collection and tax payments).

policyholder: The person or organization having rightful possession of a policy, irrespective of ownership rights or life insured. See also: policyowner.

policy loan: A loan to the policyowner by the insurer with the cash value of the policy assigned as the only security for the loan.

policy maturity date: The date at which a policy matures if the insured is still alive at that age. At the policy maturity date the cash value is paid to the policy owner in lieu of the death benefit.

policyowner: The person who has ownership rights in an insurance policy and who may or may not be the insured. See also: policyholder.

policy period: The length of time during which the policy contract provides protection. Also called policy term.

policy proceeds: The amount payable in a single sum (if so elected) to the beneficiary or policyowner under a policy at death, surrender, or maturity. Policy proceeds generally may be applied under the policy's settlement options to provide income rather than a single lump sum.

portfolio method of dividend calculation: The method whereby dividends are calculated based on the average interest rate earned on total portfolio of investments. For contrast, see: investment year method of dividend calculation.

preferred risk: A person whose physical condition, occupation, mode of living, and other characteristics (including the size of policy to be purchased) indicate an above-average life expectancy and, therefore, who qualifies for a premium rate that is more favorable than that offered to standard risks. For contrast, see: standard risk.

preferred risk policies: Policies warranting a lower premium charge on the basis of rigid underwriting criteria that indicate better-than-average mortality risk. Certain classes of insureds may be favorably selected, such as business or professional people, for example, where the mortality experience is expected to be better than average. Typically, such policies are of larger than normal size.

preliminary term insurance: Term insurance attached to a newly issued permanent life insurance policy extending term coverage for a preliminary period of one to 11 months, until the permanent insurance becomes effective. The purpose of preliminary term insurance is to provide full life insurance protection immediately, but to delay the start of the larger permanent insurance premium and the policy anniversary to a later date.

premium: The periodic payment required to keep a specific insurance policy in force.

premium loan: Payment of the premium by taking a loan against the cash value of a policy. Frequently referred to as an automatic premium loan, a provision found in many life policies. See also: automatic premium loan provision.

premium mode: The frequency with which premium payments are made, as selected by the policyowner. Typical premium modes are annual, semiannual, quarterly, or monthly (or weekly in industrial insurance).

premium payment period: The number of years during which premiums are payable. For example, a 10-pay life policy has a 10-year premium payment period.

premium refund: A life insurance provision or rider that is a form of increasing term insurance. The beneficiary receives an amount equal to the premiums paid to date in addition to the face amount if death occurs during a stipulated period.

premium return: A return of premium may occur as a result of cancellation, rate adjustment, or calculation that an advance premium is in excess of actual premium.

primary beneficiary: The beneficiary specifically designated by the insured as the first in priority to receive policy proceeds.

private annuity: Annuity issued by an individual or organization other than an insurer or other company regularly engaged in annuity sales.

proceeds: The net amount of money payable by the insurance company at the death of an insured or at the maturity of a policy.

prohibited provisions: Life insurance policy provisions that are not allowed in the contract under state law, such as a provision eliminating the insured's right to sue the insurance company.

protection: A term synonymous with the term "coverage" that denotes the amount of insurance provided by the policy.

pure endowment: A theoretical contract that provides for payment only if a specific person survives to a certain date and not in event of that person's prior death. It contains no insurance elements and can be viewed mathematically as the actuarial opposite of a term contract, which provides for payment only in event the insured person dies within the term period specified.

ratable charge method: A method of accounting for policy cash values, policy loans and premiums. This method calls for amortization of the *cost of life insurance* on a straight-line basis over the policy life.

rated: A rated policy is one issued on a substandard risk with higher than standard premiums.

rating: The premium classification given to a person who applies for life insurance. The term is usually used when an applicant is designated as a substandard risk. A higher premium reflects the increased risk.

rebating: Generally, the return of part of the agent's commission to the policy purchaser but it also includes any form of inducement, favor, or advantage to the purchaser of a policy that is not available to all under the standard policy terms. Rebating is prohibited by law in most states. Both the agent and the person accepting the rebate can be punished by fine or imprisonment, and in most states the agent is subject to revocation of license.

reduced paid-up option: A nonforfeiture option that permits the insured to have the cash surrender value of his or her policy used to purchase a paid-up policy for, generally, a reduced amount of insurance.

re-entry term: Renewable term insurance that will charge lower new-issue term premiums if the insured periodically provides suitable evidence of insurability.

refund annuity: An annuity that will make payments after the death of the annuitant to a designated beneficiary, either as a lump-sum or in installments, until the total amount paid equals the total premiums paid for the annuity.

reinstatement provision: A policy provision defining a policyowner's right to reinstate a lapsed policy within a reasonable time after lapse, as well as the conditions necessary for reinstatement such as evidence of insurability and payment of back premiums and interest. The right is usually forfeited once a policy has been surrendered for its cash value.

renewable and convertible term: Term life insurance offering the policyowner both the option to renew the coverage at the end of the term period and the option (within the term period) to convert it to a permanent form of insurance.

renewal: Continuance of coverage under an insurance policy beyond its original term. Also, the payment of premiums after the first year of a policy or the agent's commissions on such second and subsequent years' premiums.

renewal commission: The commission paid or credited to an agent after the first policy year for premiums received by the company on business written by the agent.

renewal premium: Any premium due after the first policy year.

reportable economic benefit cost (REB): The term cost of life insurance death benefit protection that is provided to a participant in a split dollar arrangement or a qualified plan.

representations: Statements made by an applicant on the application that the applicant attests are substantially true to the best of his or her knowledge and belief, but which are not warranted as exact in every detail, as compared to warranties. See also: warranties and representations.

required provisions: Certain provisions must be included under state law in an insurance policy. Such provisions include the incontestability clause, misstatement-of-age clause, a provision for a grace period, as well as others mandated by state insurance laws.

reserve: The funds held by the company for all policies which, together with future premiums and interest earnings, are sufficient to meet all future claims.

reserve basis: The mortality and interest rate assumptions used in the computation of premiums and necessary reserves.

retirement income policy: A type of limited-pay life insurance contract designed to build cash values with the principal objective of funding a desired level of guaranteed monthly income for life, beginning at a certain age, usually 65. Unlike annuities, they also provide a death benefit.

retroactive conversion: Conversion of a term life insurance policy to a permanent policy with premiums determined as if the permanent policy were issued at the insured's original issue age rather than at the insured's attained age at the time of conversion. It usually requires payment of back premiums and interest from the original date of issue.

return of premium rider: A type of increasing term rider that will pay an amount equal to the sum of all premiums paid to date if the insured dies within a specified term, such as within the first 20 years after policy issue.

return premium policy: A life insurance policy that pays a death benefit equal to the face amount upon maturity plus all or a portion of the premiums paid.

rider: An attachment to a life insurance policy that modifies the policy by expanding or restricting benefits or excluding certain conditions of coverage.

risk factor: One of the three principal factors entering gross premium calculations. It is the estimated mortality costs of a group of policies, based on the mortality tables for life insurance. The factors insurers consider when estimating the chance of loss are age, sex, physical impairments, medical history, habits, occupation, and finances. See also: gross premium.

scheduled premium: The recommended or ideal premium in variable and universal life policies.

secondary guarantee universal life: Insurers include secondary guarantees in some universal life policies to produce a policy with a guaranteed death benefit for a specified period of time, or even for life, with the lowest possible premiums. These policies are designed for people whose principal objective is to assure a given level of death benefit for a specified period of time, or for life, without the risk that they later may have to pay higher, and unaffordable, premiums to maintain the desired death benefit level. Thus, they are typically most suitable for policyowners who need an assured level of death benefit for estate liquidity purposes and who are unlikely to need lifetime benefits, because the cost of the guarantee comes in the form of much lower cash surrender values over the life of the policy or guarantee period as compared to universal life policies without the guarantee.

section 79 plan: Merely a group-term life insurance plan but so called because of the favorable taxation under Internal Revenue Code section 79. The employee must report as gross income only the economic benefit (i.e., the Table I cost) of insurance over $50,000. When properly arranged, the cost of the premiums is also fully deductible by the employer.

section 162 plan: A plan that involves the purchase of a life insurance policy on the life of one or more employer-chosen employees. The employer pays premiums on the policy but charges the employee with a bonus in an amount equal to that payment. The employee (or the third party such as an irrevocable trust designated by the employee) purchases and owns the policy and names the beneficiary. The policyowner has all rights in the policy. The corporation never has any right to any part of the policy cash values, dividends, or death benefits and at no time does the corporation own any incident of ownership in the policy.

section 419(e) medical benefit plan: A post-retirement medical benefits plan that businesses can establish to cover retiree medical expenses.

select mortality table: A mortality table showing better-than-average mortality rates in the initial years after issue as a result of the insurer's ability to screen out bad risks through its underwriting process.

separate account: An investment account that is segregated from the general investment portfolio of the insurer. Required by law for assets backing variable products.

settlement: A term that is synonymous with the payment of a claim. It implies that both the policyowner and the insurance company are satisfied with the amount and the method of payment.

settlement dividend: A special or extra dividend payable at the time of termination of a policy by death, surrender, or maturity. Also called a terminal dividend.

settlement options: The various methods by which policy proceeds may be paid to the beneficiary. The options include: (1) a lump-sum cash payment; (2) leaving proceeds with the insurer at interest; (3) installment payments for a fixed period; (4) installment payments for life; and (5) installment payments of a fixed income as long as proceeds and interest will last.

single-premium deferred annuity: Annuity purchased with one premium, well in advance of the time the income period is to begin.

single-premium policy: A policy that is paid-up with one premium.

spendthrift provision: A policy provision to shelter policy proceeds, to the extent permitted by law, from the claims of creditors of any beneficiary or contingent beneficiary or to any legal process against any beneficiary or contingent beneficiary.

split-dollar insurance: An arrangement between two parties (often employer and employee) where there is a sharing or splitting of premiums, cash values, dividends, and/or death benefits.

standard policy: A policy issued with standard provisions and at standard rates; not rated or with special restrictions.

standard risk: A person who meets the insurer's underwriting criteria for standard policies. For contrast, see: rated; substandard risk.

statutory reserve: This is the reserve value reported in an insurance company's statutory financial statement filed with the state insurance department. The primary difference between this and the tax reserve is the interest rate used. In a low interest rate environment, there may be very little practical difference between the tax and the statutory reserves.

stock company: A company that is owned and controlled by stockholders rather than policyowners. See also: mutual company.

straight life policy: See: ordinary life. For contrast, see: limited-payment policy.

straight term: A basic form of term life insurance, written for a specific number of years, having a level premium and automatically terminating at the end of the period.

substandard insurance: Life insurance issued at premium rates higher than standard, to applicants who are rated or substandard risks. For contrast, see: standard policy.

substandard risk: A person whose mortality risk is greater than average for his or her age. Substandard rating factors include various medical conditions such as diabetes, hypertension, and heart ailments; high risk occupations such as airline pilots, race car drivers, miners, and high-altitude construction workers; high risk avocations or hobbies such as scuba diving or sky diving; detrimental habits or addictions such as smoking, a history of drug use or alcohol abuse; and possible moral turpitude as evidenced by excessive gambling, criminal convictions, and bankruptcy. Substandard risks, if covered at all, are usually charged additional premium.

suicide provision: Life insurance policies include a provision that if the insured commits suicide within a specified period, usually one or two years after date of issue, the company is not liable to pay the face amount of coverage. Generally, liability is limited to a return of premiums paid.

supplemental term insurance: A supplemental agreement or rider available in some policies, providing for the payment of an additional specified sum in event the insured dies during the given term period. In general, any coverage purchased in addition to ongoing, base plans.

surplus account: The difference between a company's assets and liabilities. Net surplus includes contingency reserves and unassigned funds, while gross surplus also includes surplus assigned for distribution as dividends.

surrender: The policyowner's return of a policy to the insurance company in exchange for the policy's cash surrender value or other equivalent nonforfeiture values. See also: nonforfeiture values.

surrender charge: In a variable or universal life policy, a special charge that is levied on the available cash value to reimburse the insurer for the unrecovered costs of issuing the policy.

surrender dividend: See: terminal dividend.

surrendered policy: A life insurance policy that has been returned to the insurance company and terminated, generally under the nonforfeiture provisions of the policy after surrender values have become available.

suspension point: In some cash value policy illustrations the projected point in time that premium payments will be suspended and, based on the premium amount, current policy charges, and assumed rate of return, no further premiums are anticipated to be needed.

suspended premium: A feature in some cash value policy illustrations whereby the premium, based on current policy charges and assumed rate of return, is projected to end after a specified period of time and no further premiums are anticipated to be needed.

target premium: The suggested or recommended annual premium for a universal life policy that will maintain the plan of insurance if the actual interest, mortality, and expense experience matches the underlying assumptions used to compute the premium.

tax reserve: This is the reserve value used in the determination of an insurance company's federal income tax.

temporary level extra premiums: A type of rating most frequently used with physical impairments where the risk is considered to be a temporary nature.

temporary annuity: A life annuity that terminates at the earlier of the end of a stipulated period or the death of the annuitant.

term contract or policy: See: term insurance.

terminal dividend: Dividends that may be payable upon termination of a policy at death, maturity, or surrender for its cash value, usually after the policy has been in force for at least a specified number of years.

termination: Refers to a policy's becoming of no effect. No more premiums are payable on the policy after termination, and it no longer has any value. Termination can occur in a number of ways, including failure to pay premiums as required or surrendering the policy for its cash value.

term insurance: Life insurance protection that expires after a specified term without any residual value if the insured survives the stated period. The protection period may be as short as 30 days (as in temporary insurance agreements) or as long as 20 years or more. For contrast, see: whole life insurance.

term insurance rider: A form providing term life insurance that is attached to a permanent life insurance policy, with the purpose of increasing the total amount of protection during the term period.

term of policy: The period for which a policy is in force. This is to the end of the term period for term insurance, the maturity date for endowments, and to the insured's death (or, usually, age 100) for whole life policies.

term to age ( ): A form of long-term life insurance continuing to the designated age of the policyowner. If the insured survives the term, there is no residual value as would be the case with a cash-value policy that endows if the insured survives the term of coverage.

third party ownership: an arrangement in which the life insurance policy is owned by an entity other than the insured or the beneficiary. This technique is often used in ILITs where the trust is the third party.

tontine: A type of insurance policy whereby a group of policyowners share various advantages on such terms that upon the death or default of any policyowner in the group, his or her advantages are distributed among the remaining policyowners on the expiration of an agreed period. See with respect to: deposit term.

traditional net cost comparison method: A method of determining policy cost over a stipulated period by adding a policy's premiums and subtracting dividends and the cash value at the end of the stipulated period.

traditional product: A life insurance product with fixed premiums, death benefit, and cash value growth. For contrast, see: universal life; variable life.

ultimate mortality table: A mortality table based on average life insurance experience after the period when the benefit of favorable "selection" attributable to the insurer's underwriting process has worn off.

unbundled fees: Refers to the legal requirement that variable, universal, and other current-assumption life insurance policy costs and deductions be clearly stated and explained.

underwriter: Technically, the person who writes his or her name under an insurance agreement, accepting all or part of the risk. Often refers to the home office employee who reviews the facts about the risk, accepts or declines the risk, and assigns the rate – the home office underwriter. Also, used in reference to the agent offering the insurance, since the agent does exercise underwriting discretion in selecting the risks (prospects) he or she contacts.

unearned premium: The portion of the premium applicable to the unexpired or unused part of the period for which the premium has been charged. Thus, in the case of an annual premium, at the end of the third month of the premium period, three-fourths of the premium is unearned.

uniform policy provision: A provision that is required by state statute to be in all insurance contracts of a given type; generally taken from or patterned after the model provisions provided by the National Association of Insurance Commissioners (NAIC).

uniform simultaneous death act: This law states that, when an insured and beneficiary die at the same time, or when they die together and it cannot be determined who died first, it is presumed that the insured survived the beneficiary. The insurance company then pays the proceeds to the next beneficiary in line, the secondary or contingent beneficiary, or to the insured's estate if the policyowner has not named a secondary beneficiary.

unilateral contract: A contract in which only one party pledges anything. A life insurance is a unilateral contract since only the insurance company can be sued for breach of contract.

universal life: A flexible-premium, current-assumption, adjustable-death-benefit policy. Similar to traditional policies, universal life pays a death benefit and accumulates cash value. Unlike traditional products, universal life completely separates the protection element from the accumulation element of the policy.

variable annuity: An annuity that invests the contract holder's funds in security-type investments and that does not guarantee the level of payments. Instead, payments may fluctuate up and down in relation to the earnings and market value of the assets in a separate account. Thus, the investment risk is assumed by the contract holder.

variable annuity accumulation unit: A unit similar to a share in a mutual fund that represents a share of a contract owner's ownership in the separate account backing the contract during the years prior to the annuity starting date. The value of the unit fluctuates in relation to changes in the market prices of the separate variable annuity portfolio securities owned by the insurance company and with investment income earned on these securities.

variable death benefit: A death benefit option in most variable life policies. The death benefit varies based on a formula relating the cash value to the death benefit. The death benefit is also variable in variable universal life policies under option B (or II) which pays a pure level death benefit plus the cash value at the time of the insured's death.

variable life insurance: Life insurance that provides a guaranteed minimum death benefit, but the actual benefit paid may be more, depending on the fluctuating market value of investments in the separate account backing the contract at the time of the insured's death. The cash surrender value generally fluctuates with the market value of the investment portfolio.

variable universal life: The generic name for a flexible-premium universal life insurance policy, distinguished by a flexible premium and separate cash value investment accounts.

viatical settlement: This settlement involves the sale, by the policy owner, of his or her life insurance policy to a third party (typically a viatical settlement company) in exchange for a lump-sum cash payment. The insured (viator) typically has a life expectancy of less than two years due to a life-threatening disease or terminal illness.

waiver of premium provision: See: disability premium waiver insurance.

waiver of premium with disability income rider: A life insurance rider that not only waives the premiums but also pays a specified monthly income if the insured becomes totally and permanently disabled.

war clause: A clause in an insurance contract limiting the insurance company's liability for specified loss caused by war.

warranties and representations: Almost every state provides that all statements made by a life insurance policy applicant, whether in the application blank or to the medical examiner, are considered, in the absence of fraud, to be representations and not warranties. The distinction is crucial since a warranty must be literally true. Even a small breach of warranty, even if by error, could be sufficient to render the policy void, whether the matter warranted is material or not and whether or not it had contributed to the loss. See also: representations.

whole life insurance: A form of life insurance offering protection for the whole of life, proceeds being payable at death. Premiums may be paid under a continuous premium arrangement or on a limited payment basis for virtually any desired period of years (e.g., 1, 10, 20, 30, or to ages 60 or 65). See also: ordinary life.

yearly renewable term insurance: A 1-year term insurance contract that may be renewed each year at, generally, successively higher premiums corresponding to the insured's attained age with no evidence of insurability. The right of renewal may extend to ten years or more or to an age such as 60 or 65. See: renewable and convertible term.

ENDNOTES

1. The authors highly recommend Ingrisano and Ingrisano, *The Insurance Dictionary*, 3rd ed. (Longman Financial Services Publishing). Their text, which was extremely useful in the creation of this glossary, contains an extensive and highly practical list of almost every technical term commonly used in life insurance parlance and should be considered essential for the life insurance professional.

INDEX

D

E

F

G

H

I